The Stage Year Book

Editor

L. Carson

Alpha Editions

This edition published in 2020

ISBN : 9789354038372

Design and Setting By
Alpha Editions
www.alphaedis.com
email - alphaedis@gmail.com

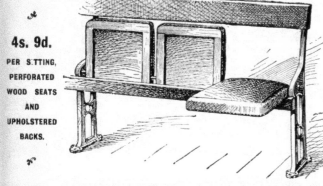

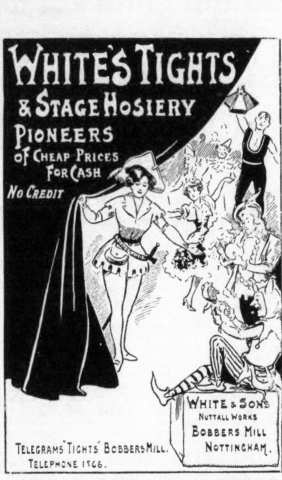

THE WALLAW PICTURE CO.'S

(Under the direction of WALTER LAWSON).

ENGLAND'S GREATEST BIOSCOPEST.

The

A C M E

of

Life-Motion

Picture

Entertain-

ments.

No. 1 Company.
Standing: Mr. J. HINDMARSH HOWORTH, Mr. EMIL ADAMS.
Sitting: Mr. WOODHOP, Miss GERTIE GRAY, Mr. WALTER LAWSON.

THE WALLAW PICTURES SPELL SUCCESS

And Managers and Proprietors of Halls should send list of vacant dates to

Headquarters, Co-operative Offices, Stanley, Durham.

2

DRAMATIC CARDS.

ALFRED LESTER.
'Phone.
1272, North.

MISS AMY ST. JOHN.
Address,
10, Milton Chambers, Cheyne Walk, S.W.

Always a Comedian.
SHAUN GLENVILLE.
Permanent Address, "Thistledown," Tooting, London, S.W.

"Briefly and without Preamble."
GEOFFREY CHATE.
The Aristocratic Light Comedian.   All coms., 7, Woodville, Gravesend.

"Confido Conquiesco."
MR. EDWARD AVINAL.
Heavy Lead.   Business Management.   C/o "The Stage."

J. TELLY DILLSEN.
Comedian.
Puts Comedy into Character and Character into Comedy.   Perm. Add., 75, Lodge Lane, Liverpool.

MR. GORDON ROBEY.
Juveniles or Gentlemanly Heavies.
Permanent Address, Oakham, Dudley.

MISS ANNIE MEGSON.
Soubrettes or Special Comedy Parts.
Permanent Address, Oakham, Dudley.

HAMILTON DEANE.
Address, c/o Sturt House, Paignton, South Devon.

MISS CISSIE CLEVELAND.
Principal Comedienne (Sing and Dance). Versatile.
Perm. address: 60, Longden Road, Crowcroft Park, Longsight, Manchester.

MISS IDA FANE.
Heavies, Char., Com., Aris., O.W., Broken English and French Parts.
C/o A. Carter, 226, Southwark Bridge Road, S.E.

CHRIS A. OLGAR.
Lead.   On Tour.
Permanent Address, Prince of Wales' Hotel, Longton, Staffs.

MISS ELEANOR GILBART.
Character, Comedy, and Aristocratic Old Women. Quick studies a speciality.
Address: 5, Archibald Road, Tufnell Park, N., or A. A.

THE ROYAL ACADEMY OF MUSIC,

TENTERDEN STREET, HANOVER SQUARE.

INSTITUTED, 1822.   INCORPORATED BY ROYAL CHARTER, 1830.

Patron — HIS MOST GRACIOUS MAJESTY THE KING.

President—H.R.H. THE DUKE OF CONNAUGHT AND STRATHEARN, K.G.
Principal—SIR ALEXANDER CAMPBELL MACKENZIE, Mus.D., LL.D., D.C L., F.R.A.M.

THE ROYAL ACADEMY OF MUSIC offers to students of both sexes (whether amateur or professional) a thorough training in all branches of music under the most able and distinguished Professors. In addition to receiving individual lessons in the various branches of the Curriculum, students have the advantage of attending the Orchestral, Choral, and Chamber Music Classes, and the weekly lectures on music and musicians. Evidence of their progress is given at the Fortnightly and Public Concerts and by periodical Operatic and Dramatic Performances.

There are three Terms in the Academic year—viz., the Michaelmas Term, from Michaelmas to Christmas; the Lent Term, from early in January to Easter; and the Midsummer Term, from early in May until the end of July.

The Fee for the ordinary curriculum is 11 Guineas per Term.

A large number of Scholarships and Prizes are founded and are competed for periodically.

Students who show special merit and ability receive the distinction of being elected by the Directors Associates of the Institution, and are thereby entitled to the use after their names of the initials A.R.A.M. Students who distinguish themselves in the musical profession after quitting the Institution may be elected by the Directors Fellows of the Royal Academy of Music, and are thereupon entitled to the use after their names of the initials F.R.A.M.

Subscribers have the privilege of attending the Lectures and Public Concerts and of introducing friends in proportion to the amount of their subscriptions.

An examination of persons trained independently of the Academy is held twice a year—viz., during the Summer and Christmas vacations—successful candidates at which are elected Licentiates of the Academy, and are thereupon entitled to the use after their names of the initials L.R.A.M.

An examination of persons engaged in the Training of Children's Voices is held annually in September and during the Christmas vacation and a certificate is granted to successful candidates.

Prospectus, entry form, and all further information may be obtained on application.

F. W. RENAUT, *Secretary.*

THE STAGE
YEAR
BOOK

WITH WHICH IS INCLUDED

THE STAGE PROVINCIAL GUIDE

1909

EDITED BY L. CARSON

LONDON:

CARSON & COMERFORD, LTD.

16, YORK STREET, COVENT GARDEN.

CONTENTS.

PAGE.

"Across the Atlantic," by W. H. Denny 27
"Actor's Art, The," by J. Fisher White 33
Actors' Association 45
Actors' Benevolent Fund 61
Actors' Church Union 81
Actors' Day 32
Actors' Orphanage Fund 66
Actors' Union 62
Actresses' Franchise League 232
American Stage, The 82
    ,,   ,,   Alphabetical List of Plays 233
    ,,   ,,   Fires in Theatres 245
    ,,   ,,   New Theatres Opened 245
    ,,   ,,   Obituary 240
    ,,   ,,   Organisations 86

"Back to Romance," by L. H. Jacobsen 24
Baddeley Cake, The 11
Books of the Year 49
British Empire Shakespeare Society 59

Censorship 20
"Character and the Actor," by J. Martin Harvey 12
Chinese Stage, The 68
Circuits 232
Clubs 70
Command Performances 48
Copyright Play Protection Association 76

Dinners, Banquets, etc. 224
Doggett's Coat and Badge 7
Dramatic Critics' Society, The 50
"Dramatic Dream, A," by Mostyn T. Pigott 10
"Dramatic Year, The," by J. T. Grein 5

Fires and Accidents in Theatres and Halls 231
Foreign Seasons in London 67

Gallery First Nighters' Club 80
General Meetings of Societies, Funds, etc. 224
"Germany, The Theatrical Year in," by F. E. Washburn Freund 102
German Music Hall War, The 74
German Plays, Alphabetical List 250
German Theatres, Alphabetical List 461
German Music Halls, Alphabetical List 465

	PAGE.
Incorporated Stage Society, The.,	131
International Copyright Convention	226
Irving Memorial, The	55
Lectures and Addresses	223
Legal Cases	252
Legal Cases (Index to same)	320
London Guide, The, Theatres	210
,, ,, The, Music Halls, with Barring	213
,, ,, The, Other Halls Possessing Licenses..	217
Miscellaneous Events	225
" Musical Year, The," by B. W. Findon	21
New Theatres and Music Halls Opened	222
Obituary	208
Opera Seasons at Covent Garden..	222
" Our Guild," by Fanny Brough	55
Paris, The Dramatic Year	92
Paris Orphelinat des Arts	99
Paris Plays of the Year	246
Passing of the Imperial, The	58
Play Actors, The	64
Plays of the Year (Full cast)	139
,, ,, ,, (Alphabetical List, London)	190
,, ,, ,, (Alphabetical List, Provincial)	193
,, ,, ,, (Principal Revivals)	195
" Portraits and Pictures "	8
Provincial Guide, The	326
Recitals and Concerts	199
Rehearsal Club, The	69
" Rogues and Vagabonds," by B. Weller	39
Royalty at the Play	46
Royal General Theatrical Fund	119
Russian Stage, The, by Baroness Bila and Percy Burton	131
Scene Shifting by Electricity	56
Shakespeare Memorial, The	60
Sketches of the Year	196
Society of Authors, The	31
" Spanish Stage, The," by Leonard Williams	120
Staff Organisations	136
" Stage and the Arts in Germany," by F. E. Washburn Freund	112
Theatrical Ladies' Guild	52
Theatrical Managers' Association..	65
Theatres Alliance, The	135
Touring Managers' Association	61
Variety Organisations	77
" Variety Stage, The," by W. H. Clemart	71
West End Theatre Managers' Association	65

INDEX TO ILLUSTRATIONS.

ART SUPPLEMENTS.

Sir John Hare, by Sir John Everett Millais .. .. .. *facing page* 6
"Faust." Poster by Charles A. Buchel .. .. .. ,, ,, 8
Mr. Martin Harvey. Poster by Charles A. Buchel .. •• ,, ,, 14
Miss Ellen Terry, by W. Graham Robertson .. .. .. ,, ,, 20
Miss Ethel Irving, by F. Howard Michael .. .. .. ,, ,, 24
Miss Fanny Brough, by Joliffe Walker.. .. .. .. ,, ,, 28
Mme. Sarah Bernhardt, by W. Graham Robertson .. .. ,, ,, 36
Mr. Edward Compton, by Hermann Herkomer .. .. ,, ,, 44
Mr. E. S. Willard, by Louis Kronberg .. .. ,, ,, 64
Miss Marie Lloyd .. .. ,, ,, 71

SUCCESSES OF THE YEAR.

"What Every Woman Knows," "Her Father," "The Flag Lieutenant,"
"The Merry Widow " .. .. *pages* 26-27
"The Thief," "The Passing of the Third Floor Back," "Idols," "Diana
of Dobson's " .. .. *pages* 32-33
"Jack Straw," "The Marriages of Mayfair," "Mrs. Dot," "Lady
Frederick " .. .. *pages* 38-39
"Havana," "A White Man," "Butterflies," "The Lyons Mail" ,, 48-49
"Pete" .. .. *facing page* 50

TOURING COMPANIES.

"Diana of Dobson's" (S.), "My Mimosa Maid" .. .. .. *pages* 60-61
"Miss A. E. F. Horniman's, "Diana of Dobson's" (N.), "When Knights
Were Bold " .. .. *page* 62

THE VARIETY STAGE.

Mr. Joe O'Gorman and Mr. Joe Elvin .. .. *pages* 74-75
Mr. W. H. Clemart and Mr. Wal Pink.. .. .. .. ,, 76-77
Mr. Harry Lauder and Mr. R. A. Roberts .. .. .. ,, 78-79

THE ACTORS' ORPHANAGE FUND.

Views of the Homes at Croydon.. .. .. , 66-67

THE THEATRICAL LADIES' GUILD.

Mrs. C. L. Carson .. .. *page* 52
Views of the Offices, etc. .. .. *pages* 52-54-55

THE CHINESE STAGE.

Open-air Theatre in Chefoo ; Chun Kwei Theatre, Shanghai ; Tai Kwei
Theatre, Shanghai .. .. *page* 68

THE FRENCH STAGE.

Mlles. Delza, Roggers, Cassive, Cécile-Sorel .. .. i. .. *pages* 92-93
Mlles. Lifraud, Cassiny, Gabrielle Robinne, de Mornand .. .. ,, 94-95
Mlles. Renée Desprey, Renver, Nelly Martyl, Arlette Dorgère .. ,, 96-97

THE GERMAN STAGE.

Meta Illing, Ida Wüst 102-103
Albert Heine, Alexander de Moissi .. .. ,, 104-105
Dr. K. Hagemann's Scenery for "Hamlet" .. .. .. ,, 112-113
Hebbel Theatre in Berlin (four views) 114-115-116
Gartnerplatz Theatre, Munich .. .. ,, 117
Münchner Künstlertheater and the Weimarer Hoftheater .. .. ,, 118-119

THE RUSSIAN STAGE.

Mme. Mitschurina, Mme. Portschinskaja, M. Glagolin, Lydia Yavorskaja.
Mme. Rostschina-Insarova, V. Dalmatoff .. .. .. *pages* 132-133
The Alexandra Theatre, St. Petersburg .. .. .. *page* 134
Rafael and Robert Adelheim .. .. ,, 135

THE SPANISH STAGE.

Jose Echegaray, Santiago Rusiñol, Jacinto Benavente, the Brothers 125-126
Quintero .. .. *pages* 124-125
Maria Guerrero, Rosario Pino, Enrique Boras, Fernando Diaz de Mendoza,
Benito Pérez Galdos .. .. *pages* 126-127
Scene-shifting by Electricity .. .. *page* 56

THE DRAMATIC YEAR 1908.

By J. T. GREIN.

A LMOST on the eve of its close, the year 1908 has left its mark on the history of our modern stage. It is difficult to predict what the Afternoon Theatre is going to do for our Drama, but since it is governed by three men of the calibre of Mr. Beerbohm Tree, Mr. Frederick Whelen, and Mr. Henry Dana, a triumvirate as well harmonised as could possibly be imagined, it is no exaggeration to speak of great expectations. If 1908 had given us nothing but a new enterprise, over the portals of which is chiselled "Let all be welcome," it would have redeemed itself from the commonplace. The production of *Hannele* reflects credit on the courage and on the artistic sense of the new management—on their courage, because it is well known that certain people look askance at Hauptmann's plays ; on their artistic sense, because with due consideration of difference of temperament between English and Germans, the performance was one of quality. The other irregular theatres, such as The Play Actors, the now defunct Pioneers, the New Productions Club of Miss Mouillot, and especially the Stage Society, have given signs of health and activity, and many new names have swelled the ranks of our dramatists.

BERNARD SHAW.

Bernard Shaw's play, or I should rather say his conversation, *Marriage*, formed the farewell of Messrs. Vedrenne and Barker's memorable era of *matinées*. Although this latest work of our most original dramatist has many of the qualities of its predecessors, the peculiar weaknesses of Shaw are glaringly manifest in it. His loquacity is literally torrential in this play; and since Mr. Shaw is not an idle talker, but whatever he says is charged with thought, now deep, now whimsical, it cannot be gainsaid that from time to time the hearer's mind is taxed to over-straining. Moreover, since the play is formless, and the characters vacillate between reality and caricature, it is timely to ask whether the pursuance of this artistic policy will not interfere with the vitality of the Shawesque drama. Already in Germany, where Shaw is a greater prophet than in his own country, serious critics have raised a protest against the form and the tendency of *The Doctor's Dilemma*, and some have predicted that if he continues to neglect the drama for the exuberance of his verbal fluency his plays will be forgotten as rapidly as they have become fashionable. Earlier, and again under the auspices of Vedrenne and Barker, *Cæsar and Cleopatra*, Mr. Shaw's obvious effort to run the gauntlet with Shakespeare met with lukewarm appreciation. Delightful as the play is to read, it tended to confirm that as a dramatist, in the accepted sense of the word, the old master remains superior to the new.

REPRESENTATIVE AUTHORS.

Having dealt with Mr. Shaw separately, since he stands on a different plane from the other playwrights, I now come to the activity of those whose names have been for many years household words in stageland. First and foremost among them **Mr.** A. W. Pinero scored a *succès d'estime* with *The Thunderbolt*, a work of wonderful craftsmanship, replete with such caustic types as Mr. Pinero knows how to create, yet not quite satisfactory nor very sympathetic by the nature of its story. The main theme of *The Thunderbolt* is an inherit-ance, therefore a question of money, and it is peculiar to observe that when-ever money is the basis of a drama in England the **public** are loth to warm up to it. Mr. Jones, after a period of reverse, has once more given signs of vitality in *Dolly Reforming Herself*. The old craftsman shows in it that he has lost none of his cunning; and, although the comedy is neither very witty nor throughout amusing, it contains a scene dealing with woman's weakness for dress which will appeal intensely to the fair sex, and thereby impel the other to visit the theatre. Mr. R. C. Carton for once has gone astray into the realm of melodrama, where he does not seem to feel at home. His adaptation from J. C. Snaith's novel, "Lady Barbarity," was, artistically, at any rate, a failure. Mr. Haddon Chambers, who, like Mr. Jones, had to redeem some checks, made a triumphant re-entry with *Sir Anthony*, a comedy of the lightest texture, yet dealing with much humour and considerable power of observation with the amenities of suburban life.

An Individual and a Unique Play.

But of all the older dramatists none has made so distinct a mark as Mr. J. M. Barrie in *What Every Woman Knows*. Mr. Barrie's humour is as individual as that of our grand old Gilbert, some of whose Savoy operas have been revived during the year with considerable success. If anyone would endeavour to explain, let alone to imitate, the humour of Mr. Barrie, he would find himself nonplussed, for Barrie knows how to blend the ideal, the romantic, and the realistic in a manner which is indescribable, yet appealing to all sorts and conditions of men. He is, *par excellence*, the narrator of fairy tales for grown-up folk. That Mr. Barrie's play owes some of its triumphant vogue to the exquisite acting of Miss Hilda Trevelyan and Mr. Gerald Du Maurier does not discount its value; on the contrary, it proves that Mr. Barrie gauges the power of actors as well as the nature of the public. Another work of a peculiar nature, and one which is practically unique on the modern English stage, because it introduces the supernatural with reverence and delicacy of feeling, is *The Passing of the Third Floor Back*, by Mr. Jerome K. Jerome, which brought new fame and fortune to its producer, Mr. Forbes Robertson. If Mr. Jerome's work had to be judged as a play pure and simple it would be open to many objections, but the sympathetic vein which runs through it, and the cleverness with which Mr. Jerome brings his familiar humour to bear, enfranchise the play from conventional scrutiny.

Lighter Works.

As specimens of undisciplined humour, coupled with ingenuity and efficiency of technique, Mr. Roy Horniman's two comedies—*The Education of Elizabeth* and *Bellamy the Magnificent*—should here be mentioned. But far superior to the work of this disciple of Oscar Wilde is Mr. W. S. Maugham's tetralogy of comedies which held their sway during the year in four leading London theatres. These plays were *Lady Frederick*, *Jack Straw*, *Mrs. Dot*, and *The Explorer*, baggage of the lightest, one and all, but vastly amusing, and introducing French methods without resorting to the naughtiness of the boulevards. When one considers that Mr. W. S. Maugham has written in the past such powerful books as "Liza of Lambeth" and "Mrs. Craddock," and such an intensely human play as *A Man of Honour*, there is no saying to what heights he may fly if he is not tempted to render his art subservient to the box-office.

Considerations for the Untried.

At the little Kingsway, which, under the guidance of Miss Lena Ashwell, and with the valuable assistance of a singularly competent reader, Mr. Knoblauch, the exploration of fresh fields and pastures new continues gaily. Miss Cicely Hamilton's *Diana of Dobson's* is evidence of the dramatic instinct of one of our leading suffragists. *The Sway-Boat*, by Mr. Wilfrid Coleby, dealt in an interesting manner with a phase of the marriage problem, and in *Grit* Mr. Hermann Chilton manifested that it is possible to be an astute man of business as well as a promising dramatist, and that the theme which Georges Ohnet handled in *Le Maître de Forges* is by no means worn out.

Mr. Sutro.

At the St. James's Mr. Alfred Sutro gave *The Builder of Bridges*, not a symbolical play, as the title might lead to believe, but a comedy carefully worked on the precepts of Victorien Sardou, he who recently went home, and was for many years the spiritual father of English playwriting. *The Builder of Bridges*,

SIR JOHN HARE.
From the picture by the late Sir John Everett Millais, P.R.A.
By permission of Sir John Hare.

from the stage point of view, is by no means one of Mr. Sutro's best plays; but, having had the privilege of reading it after production, I can testify that the quality of his dialogue entitles it to be voted superior when compared with the style of average English society drama.

TRAGEDY AND HIS MAJESTY'S.

Of tragedy we have had but two examples—*Lanval*, by T. E. Ellis, which was stately if somewhat heavy, and *Don Quixote*, by G. E. Morrison and R. P. Stewart, which is the best of the many versions of the famous novel which have come under my notice. For to call *Faust*, such as it was adapted from Goethe by Comyns Carr and Stephen Phillips and produced at His Majesty's, a tragedy, would be idle flattery and hardly be reverential to one of the greatest dramas the world possesses. Other plays produced at His Majesty's were a rather charming adaptation of W. J. Locke's *Beloved Vagabond*, which, at least in one act, preserved the delightful flavour of the book; and an adaptation of *The Mystery of Edwin Drood*, by Comyns Carr, which goes a long way to confirm that Dickens's stories do not make good drama. A signal personal success was scored by Mr. Tree in his revival of *The Merchant of Venice*. If his conception of Shylock did not win universal approval, it was appreciated by those who are familiar with the characteristics of the Chosen People.

OTHER PLAYS.

The Playhouse, after some vicissitudes, produced a stirring picture of naval life, by Messrs. Trevor and Major Drury, entitled *The Flag Lieutenant*, which has some value, since it is the first time in the present century that dramatists have made an effort to depict fairly realistically our most potent factor of national defence. At the Criterion one of the youngest and most successful of our playwrights, Mr. Hubert Henry Davies, produced a graceful and airy piece of badinage—*Lady Epping's Lawsuit*—which contained a fanciful and somewhat mordant skit on the manners of some legal luminaries.

In 1908 the new vogue of melodrama, which was heralded in the preceding year by the great success of the Lyceum under popular management at popular prices, has become strongly accentuated. During the month of October no fewer than six theatres were devoted to the romantic school. Most of the revivals were concerned with melodrama of ripe age, yet, skilfully adapted, they proved as acceptable to modern audiences as to the public of the second half of the nineteenth century, before the advent of the realistic school. Another salient feature of the year 1908 was the comparative paucity of adaptations from foreign plays—a happy sign this, since those who preside over our theatres have at length learned to understand that the intelligence of our public is capable of assimilating foreign work in faithful translation. With a complimentary reference to the promising work proffered by such interesting novices as Mr. John Masefield, whose *Nan* was a forcible picture of life in England in the times of our forefathers, Mr. Arnold Bennett, who, in *Cupid and Commonsense*, depicted a corner of rural England, and to Mr. F. D. Bone, who has more than once evinced dramatic instinct and knowledge of the Army from within, I may fitly say of 1908 in valediction that it was a year of fair harvest and great progress.

DOGGETT'S COAT AND BADGE.

This race was rowed on Monday, July 27, between London Bridge and Chelsea. For the origin of this competition it is necessary to go back so far as 1715, when the then famous comedian, Thomas Doggett, presented the livery and badge to be competed for by six "young watermen." Doggett left enough money to provide for the coat and badge annually. The Fishmongers' Company, who took over the trust from the Admiralty, have seen that the event is in no way allowed to languish, or to diminish in interest among the watermen, for whose benefit it was started, for they have themselves provided an annual prize of £10 10s., in addition to which there is Sir William Jolliffe's prize of £7 3s. 4d. The race in 1908 was won by James Graham in 29 min. 22 secs., G. P. Jeffries coming in second.

PORTRAITS AND PICTURES.

OF the various reproductions of pictures and photographs included in this year's edition of THE STAGE YEAR BOOK, one of more than usual interest is that of Sir John Hare, by the late Sir John Everett Millais. Sir John, through whom the King, in creating a Knight, has again recognised the claims of the art of acting, is now bringing to a close a long and honourable service in the cause of the drama. A farewell season in such old-tried favourite plays as *The Gay Lord Quex* and *A Pair of Spectacles* has been one of the theatrical events of the past year in London. Sir John has also taken a round of certain provincial houses and said his adieux. A good-bye to other towns and possibly another season in London are contemplated by the popular actor before he finally leaves the boards which his art has adorned for so many years.

The portrait reproduced is a favourite one with Sir John, for with it are bound up some of his happiest memories of an intimate association with the great painter. It was Millais, always an admirer and keen critic of the drama, who requested Sir John, then plain Mr. Hare, to sit for the picture, and until it was completed he laughingly refused to allow the subject to view it. Some twenty sittings were given, and Sir John recalls how, when, pardonably inquisitive as to the progress of the portrait, he occasionally attempted to view it, Millais would turn its face to the wall and say. "Run away, boy," and push the actor playfully out of the room. When the picture was completed, however, Millais presented it to the actor, who has it now in his house.

MISS ELLEN TERRY AND MME. SARAH BERNHARDT.

To Miss Ellen Terry, perhaps, belongs the distinction of having sat for more portraits than any other actress connected with the British stage. The picture with which the public are the more familiar is that of Mr. J. S. Sargent, R.A., as Lady Macbeth, which was reproduced in the YEAR BOOK last year. This picture, under the terms of Sir Henry Irving's will, is now the property of the nation at the National Gallery of British Art. The portrait of Miss Terry by Mr. W. Graham Robertson is chosen for reproduction as being to an extent topical, for by a happy shuffling of the dramatic cards Miss Terry at the time of writing is playing a principal part, in Mr. Robertson's fanciful children's play *Pinkie and the Fairies* at His Majesty's. Mr. Robertson, whose sitters from stageland, in addition to Miss Terry and Mme. Sarah Bernhardt, have included Miss Ada Rehan, Mrs. Patrick Campbell, Miss Julia Neilson, the late Miss Nellie Farren, and others, is also well known as a writer for the youngsters. The first work of his, illustrated by himself, was "A Masque of May Morning," and this was followed by "Gold, Frankincense, and Myrrh, and Pageants for a Baby Girl," with twelve designs in colours by the author. He is likewise responsible for the text and drawings of "A Year of Songs for a Baby in a Garden" and "The Baby's Day Book for a Woman of Four," which was published in the early part of 1908.

Mr. Robertson's portrait of Miss Terry was painted in 1891 in his studio, and is in his possession now. A study for the head in this picture is reproduced in Miss Terry's "Story of My Life." Mr. Robertson, who has painted two portraits of Miss Terry, regards her as a most helpful sitter, as, "besides great appreciation," he says, "she has a very thorough technical knowledge of painting."

The other picture, one of Mme. Sarah Bernhardt, was commenced by Mr. Robertson in the same year, being painted, for the most part, from studies made in Mme. Bernhardt's studios in Paris, where she posed for the artist many times. It was finished from a final sitting in Mr. Robertson's London studio in 1893. It represents Mme. Bernhardt as Adrienne Lecouvreur, in the second act, when she appears in the costume of Roxane. This picture also remains in the possession of the artist.

"FAUST" AT HIS MAJESTY'S.

One of the most striking and imaginative posters of the year, by Mr. Charles Buchel.
Produced by J. Miles & Co., Ltd., of Wardour Street.
By permission of Mr. Beerbohm Tree.

Miss Fanny Brough as Peg Woffington.

The picture of Miss Fanny Brough as Peg Woffington is the work of a young artist, Mr. Joliffe Walker, who at the time of writing is abroad painting. It was painted a few years ago, when Miss Brough was touring *Peg Woffington*, a performance of temperamental charm and artistic power, which it was London playgoers' loss not to witness. The costume in which she is represented was designed by Mr. Percy Anderson, as were the costumes of her company. The picture is in the possession of the Rev. Talfourd Major, and to his kindness in placing at our disposal the negative of a photograph taken by himself we are indebted for the reproduction.

Other Portraits.

With the portrait of Miss Ethel Irving as Lady Frederick many playgoers are familiar, as it has done duty as a souvenir of that clever play. *Lady Frederick* is one of Mr. Somerset Maugham's most successful plays, and since it was produced at the Court, under the management of Mr. Otho Stuart, it has stood the extreme test of four removals. Temporary homes for the play were during the year found at the Criterion, the Garrick, the New, and the Haymarket. Of Miss Ethel Irving's impersonation of the title-*rôle* it is not necessary now to speak in any detail; it brought her to a position to which her abilities have justly entitled her. The picture is the work of Mr. E. Howard Michael.

Mr. E. S. Willard's season at the St. James's a few years ago, when he produced in London *The Cardinal*, will readily be called to mind. Mr. Louis Kronberg commenced a picture of Mr. Willard in the name-part, but for various reasons the finishing of the painting was not completed at the time. Only just recently Mr. Kronberg put the last touches to his work, which remains in his studio in Kensington, where we were enabled to have it photographed.

Posters and "London Successes."

Of the three *facsimile* reproductions of posters chosen as being among the most original and striking of those in use during the year, London readers, perhaps, are better acquainted with Mr. Buchel's imaginative illustration of *Faust*, which, in the autumn of 1908, was liberally displayed on the London hoardings. Mr. Martin Harvey, who has played a season at the Adelphi, during which he received a "command" to play before the King, has used Mr. Buchel's poster, illustrating *The Breed of the Treshams*, mainly in the provinces, and for provincial playgoers has been reserved the artistic reproduction of Mr. Edward Compton as David Garrick, from the painting by Hermann Herkomer.

Scenes from some of the most successful plays of the year serve as a pictorial record, the endeavour being to present to the reader the more dramatic moments in the various pieces, as in *The Thief* at the St. James's, or, where this was found impossible, the scenes in which most of the characters are on the stage, as in *Pete* at the Lyceum and *The Flag Lieutenant* at the Playhouse.

The variety stage is represented by photographs of some of its most prominent members, and of those who are associated with its organised and charitable bodies.

Foreign Photographs.

An endeavour has been made in the other photographs in the book to bring before our readers the "live" stages of other countries. New ideas in the architectural and structural lines, suggested reforms in theatres for safety exits, and artistic departures in scenic display in the German theatres have been collected in a pictorial form. The Paris stage has been dealt with by a series of photographs of actresses who, during the past year, have met with success in various parts—success which brought some suddenly to the front in the dramatic ranks and increased the popularity of others. The Spanish theatre, of which little is heard in England, has been liberally illustrated with portraits of its leading dramatists and players; while Russian drama, as represented by St. Petersburg, has also its illustrations.

The Eastern drama, of course, bears little relation in its form to ours, so the few illustrations of Chinese theatres serve, perhaps, interest born only of curiosity. Photography is not highly developed in China; possibly the atmosphere is not congenial to the chemicals. In any case, one reason why these pictures have not all the distinctive attributes of the most up-to-date London or Paris studio lies in the fact that our photographer, after waiting for a month for the rain to leave off, decided to do the best he could on a wet and muggy day. The mail would not wait for him, so he could wait no longer for the weather.

3

A DRAMATIC DREAM.

By MOSTYN T. PIGOTT.

It was possibly the Clicquot
    Which I shared with an *amico*,
Though at such things I am hardly a beginner,
    Or it may have been the *sorbet*,
    Or the sole that hailed from Torbay,
Or the coffee I partook of after dinner;
    Or it may have been the beauty
    Of the music full and fruity
That was batonised by Bexhill's erudite Mayor,
    But, whatever the causation,
    It is past all disputation
That I had that night an interesting nightmare.
    It began in calm composure,
    For at Ascot the Enclosure
Was alive with England's silliest and smartest,
    And the blending of the bandstand
    With the paddock and the grand stand
Would have fascinated any scenic artist.
    But I soon learnt that a lady,
    With her antecedents shady,
And enveloped in the filmiest of wrappers,
    Had got fast within her clutches
    The young daughter of a Duchess
Just betrothed to someone who was in the Sappers.
    But the harassed Lady Bridget,
    Who was in a state of fidget,
Hadn't up to then confided in her mother,
    For a very comic person,
    A small caddie named Macpherson,
Was on oath to save her somehow or another.
    Then a curtain quickly lifted.
    And I found the scene had shifted
To a houseboat on the river bank at Marlow,
    And I saw an obvious villain
    Make a fierce attempt to kill an
Old attorney he had met at Monte Carlo.
    And my blood sank down to zero
    Till a more than obvious hero,
Who was seeking how to find a *via media*,
    Stopped the contemplated murder
    By the hurling of a girder
And some volumes of the *Times* Encyclopædia.
    Then a company of Cossacks
    Came cavorting down the Trossachs
(Very neatly represented by a back-cloth),
    And an ancient U.P. minister,
    Of an aspect somewhat sinister,
Made a few remarks on ashes and on sackcloth.
    Then came Suffragettes by dozens,
    All accompanied by cousins,
Who recounted to the heroine's great-uncle

How the Limerick regalia
Had been pillaged *inter alia*
Of the celebrated Cullinane carbuncle.
So a Scotland Yard detective,
Just arrived in time from Bective,
From his pocket drew a magisterial warrant,
And he spoilt the hero's grand cuffs
With a pair of clanking handcuffs,
While his mother's tears came gushing in a torrent.
Next I found myself transported
To a place where they distorted
Patent truths in fairly fluent Esperanto,
And they all seemed to be hoping
The old Duchess was eloping,
For they'd heard that she was packing her portmanteau;
But there supervened a duel
All about the stolen jewel,
In the course of which the heroine was wounded,
And they handed to the villain
A book published by Macmillan,
And advised him to skedaddle, which he soon did.
The adventuress in blue gauze,
Wearing pearls and other gew-gaws,
Then put in a claim for all the Duke's possessions,
But Macpherson cracked three wheezes,
And said, " If your Lordship pleases,"
Which drew from her the most cringing of confessions.
Then came rushing in the lover,
Who announced that Mr. Glover
Had been re-elected *nem. con.* to the Mayorship;
And they all, 'mid cheering hearty,
Formed themselves into a party,
And went sailing off to Bexhill in an airship.
Thus the whole embroglio ended
With a picture truly splendid,
Though the moral wasn't absolutely certain,
And I found myself belauding
And ecstatically applauding
All the characters who came before the curtain.
Whilst I felt my spirits rising,
I considered it surprising
That my figure was enveloped in pyjamas,
Till at last I fully woke up
And vociferously spoke up
In a voice that could be heard in the Bahamas,
" I have found my true vocation!
" It must be collaboration
" With friend Raleigh in Old Drury's Autumn Dramas! "

THE BADDELEY CAKE.

The time-honoured custom of cutting the Baddeley Cake at Drury Lane on Twelfth Night still remains in force, though the occasion is not now made the excuse for a social function, as was the case when the late Sir Augustus Harris directed the fortunes of Drury Lane. The practice was the outcome of a bequest on the part of Richard Baddeley, a comedian at the theatre, who, by his will, left the sum of £100 to the Drury Lane Fund, to be invested in Consols, in order to provide cake and punch for the members of the Drury Lane company to partake of on Twelfth Night of every year. The first recorded occasion of this having taken place was in 1796, and the custom has been continued without a break every year since. In 1908 Twelfth Night fell on a Monday. Mr. Harry Nicholls, the Master of the Drury Lane Fund, performed the ceremony for the fourth year in succession.

CHARACTER AND THE ACTOR.*

BY J. MARTIN HARVEY.

THE consideration of "Character and the Actor" is as fascinating as the width of the subject is appalling. Pondering upon the matter I become aware that the consideration embraces "Character and Art," and on that road where is one to stop? And yet, that I may present my reflections in order, I must first consider the nature of the art of acting. I take it for granted that acting is an art. I know this has been disputed; never, I think, by a great thinker or of a great actor. I know of no definition of art which is not essentially the definition of great acting. It would be as useless to deny that in much acting there is little art, as there is little art in much painting and sculpture.

IMITATION V. REPRESENTATION.

Some have been found, it is true, to speak of the art of acting as a sham—Mr. Augustine Birrell, for instance. Well, the words "sham" and "imitation" are synonymous, and Mr. Birrell, in his essay on actors, in choosing the word "sham" is doing so purposely to belittle an art, in describing which Shakespeare has, with profound sympathy and understanding, chosen the word "imitation." And I will venture to say that in no way is the character of a man more surely indicated than by his choice of words. All art is imitation—a representation of nature, or, if Mr. Birrell still prefers the expression, all art is a sham. What has the great French sculptor, Rodin, said?

"People tell me I create, that is not true. God alone creates, man but reveals. My one effort is to 're-present' what I find in God's creation—above all in the form of man, which is the highest, most perfect of architectural constructions."

If Rodin thinks thus highly of the representations of man's body, what does he think, I wonder, of the representations of man's soul, the province of the actor? Let us seek for a definition of this art of acting from one whose opinion is incontrovertible, from one who lived his life among them, inspired them to their loftiest efforts, the greatest human understanding this world has known—let us seek of Shakespeare himself.

A LUMINOUS DEFINITION.

We shall find it—the most luminous definition of the art of acting—in Hamlet's second soliloquy. He says :—

> "Is it not monstrous that this player here,
> But in a fiction, in a dream of passion
> Could force his soul so to his own conceit
> That from her working all his visage wanned."

Then comes a description of the effect of the actor's art upon the vehicles of his expression :—

> "Tears in his eyes, Distraction in 's aspect."

And so on.

I doubt whether a more subtle, or a more accurate description of the actor's mental and psychical process at the moment of exercising his art will ever be expressed.

How it is possible that an actor can "force his soul so to his own conceit," that tears will spring to his eyes, that, in other words, his physical functions will operate involuntarily, and that his whole function will suit with forms to his

---

* Mr. Harvey delivered his lecture on "Character and the Actor" to the Ethnological Society, of which he is a Vice-President, at the Royal Society of Arts on January 3.

conceit, may be even now something of a mystery. But though Shakespeare was not concerned for the moment with this question, he seems almost to have anticipated what may be the reason for the curious mental condition of the actor when imitating Humanity.

AN EXPLANATION.

May I venture to suggest that an explanation of this psychical process may be found in the discoveries of psychic research? The fact that "man is the microcosm of the universe" seems to have received additional proof by the evidence of recent researches in hypnotic suggestion. It seems more and more clear that man is composed of many egos, if I may use the expression, and as in hypnotic suggestion the subject will answer in keeping with an identity of which in its normal condition it is unconscious, so in the exercise of his art by an actor, one of the innumerable egos of which he is composed will live before us, in the person of the artist who has called up one of these separate identities.

This is the explanation, it seems to me, of the creative element in the actor, this is what Shakespeare calls the "conceit," viz., the conception, what can be born, and to what he realised the actor could force his soul.

This, it seems to me, is what, at its noblest and highest, is called inspiration. This is what Garrick speaks of when he says :—

"I pronounce that the greatest strokes of genius have been unknown to the actor himself till circumstances and the warmth of the scene have sprung the mine, as much to his own surprise as to that of the audience."

Sir Henry Irving, I think, has said that an actor, in the exercise of his art, is calling upon a certain quality of mind, and I would venture to go further and to suggest that the actor is myriad-minded, and that the greater number of egos he can express, and the more completely he can express the complex nature of each of these egos, the greater actor he is.

"'Tis in ourselves that we are thus or thus."

SELF-IDENTIFICATION WITH A PART.

The dramatist would seem to possess the same capacity for self-identification with other beings, and in this light Shakespeare is the greatest of all artists, because he could express an almost infinite number of egos and so completely that the man Shakespeare himself can only be found by inference.

When a great actor performs a part, he *is* the man he represents : it is not a question of pretence, of assumption, of sham, of mimicry, it is one of his many egos, one of his own creatures, which is speaking. I say "creatures," for Shakespeare allows to the actor the power to create.

"Is it not monstrous that this player . . . . could force his soul so to his own conceit."

Now observe another point in his definition, strikingly precise. "Force his soul" —not his *mind*—his *soul*. His mind is not forced, that is calm, alert, critical, intent upon the expression of his soul, intent upon the means he is using, upon his audience, upon the effect he is making, watching his creature, curbing him at times, noting the inflexions of his voice, storing up knowledge of technique. He has given birth to a creature and he watches him live. "His whole function suiting with forms to his conceit." That is Shakespeare's definition of the art of acting, and in the light of this brilliant illumination upon the subject we may disregard the poor little glimmer of Mr. Augustine Birrell's pronouncement, when he says, "The art of acting is the art of mimicry, or the representation of feigned emotions called up by sham situations." Such a little flicker of light upon the subject as this is only sufficient to make Mr. Birrell's own right honourable darkness visible.

PHYSICAL ADVANTAGES.

Those who had the privilege of hearing Mr. Walkley's address on "Some Aspects of the Modern Stage" will call to mind that he referred to the actor as "something less than a man"—whatever such a nebulous description as that may mean—and found that there was "something unmanly in the actor's making capital out of his physical advantages." That Mr. Birrell should betray strange ignorance on a question of dramatic art is not surprising, but that Mr. Walkley, who nightly sits in judgment upon plays and actors, should plumb a lower depth of Philistinism even than Mr. Birrell, gives one furiously to think. During what "brain-storm" did

Mr. Walkley utter this nonsense? What physical advantages did they possess which made such unmanly creatures of Kean, of Garrick, of Robson, of Burbage, of Betterton, of Dillon? If physical advantage enter into the question at all, and the great French actor, Le Kain, does not even mention this as a requisite for the actor, the eminence which these men attained is a direct proof that physical advantages are not the actor's capital, for they triumphed in spite of the fact that they possessed none. The veriest tyro of theatrical history knows that most of the great men and great women have succeeded on the stage, in spite of their lack of physical advantages. But if they had possessed physical advantages why would it have been unmanly to use them? If this infantile argument held good, the " heavenly choir " of an Adelina Patti would be a subject for scorn, and the thunders of Demosthenes himself would have been unmanly, because he used the physical advantage of the voice which God had given him.

Such arguments as those of Mr. Walkley and Mr. Birrell would not justify the time spent on their serious consideration were it not for this danger, that the unthinking may accept such statements seriously, coming from men who may conceivably carry some authority.

The wisdom and the wide tolerance of the generation we have the good fortune to live in have made it superfluous to defend either actors or their art. But occasionally, I take it, an actor is justified in trying to explain something of the mysteries of his art, lest the " dicta " of such gentlemen as I have referred to come to be accepted by the unreflecting. If we cannot think for ourselves let us at least adopt the conclusions of great original thinkers, and on the subject of the art of acting let us adopt the conclusions of the chief thinker of the world rather than those of the Chief Secretary for Ireland. In a word, let us accept Shakespeare's definition of the art of acting and proceed.

Now, what of the actor himself? Can we speak of the actor himself? Which of these innumerable egos are we to speak of? We see the characters which Shakespeare has created, but where is the man Shakespeare himself? You will find him in his work, in his artistic selection, in the theme of his tragedies, in the motive of his comedies. In a word, you will find the man in his art. And there, too, you will find the actor. You will find the man behind the actor in the guiding intelligence, the critical faculty, the artistic point of view, and that aspect of his own personal character which he brings to bear on his interpretations.

Do Interpretations Affect the Actor's Character?

Now an actor is called upon, or his own idiosyncrasy impels him, to interpret a variety of beings, noble and ignoble. Do these interpretations affect the actor's character? That depends, it seems to me, upon the strength of his own personal character.

Is his character tarnished by the exhibition of the ignoble, the unworthy? Not necessarily, not even, I think, frequently.

Let us look for a moment at the worst period of the Restoration. It is astonishing that through this morass of immorality any human being could walk unblemished; yet several examples of private worth at once spring forward among the interpreters of that incredibly corrupt drama which the morals of the period brought forth— Betterton, Mistress Bracegirdle, Mistress Saunderson, who later became Mistress Betterton.

Says Mr. Clark Russell in his " Representative Actors " :—

" It is almost impossible to believe that any woman could have been found to pronounce publicly some of the language that is to be read in the plays of Dryden and Wycherly. Yet among the actresses in these and even worse dramas the reputations of some have been handed down to us as unimpeachable. Such was Mistress Betterton, such was Mistress Bracegirdle. Later on, when the licensing of plays came in vogue, a fine was levied upon any actor or actress giving utterance to an immoral sentence. Among the first who were mulcted for this offence were Betterton and Mistress Bracegirdle."

Betterton! for fifty-one years the pride of the English theatre, a man who " off the stage was," says an article in the *Cornhill Magazine* of 1862, "exemplary in his bearing, true to every duty, as good a country gentleman on his farm in Berkshire as he was perfect actor in town." The venerable representative of all that was most honourable in the drama of his day, fined for giving voice to the immorality of a play of Dryden's, yet whose private worth was so little affected

CHAS A· BUCHEL
1905

thereby, that Addison could say, that the name of "Betterton ought to be recorded with the same respect as Roscius among the Romans," and whose bones were laid to rest by a grateful country in the Abbey at Westminster.

Mistress Betterton! the mouthpiece of the indecencies of Nat Lee and Congreve, yet of whom Colley Cibber could write :—

"She was the faithful companion of her husband and his fellow-labourer for five-and-forty years, and was a woman of unblemished and sober life."

Mistress Bracegirdle! that "Diana of the stage," as Dr. Doran calls her, and of whom he gives us this delightful thumbnail sketch. Says he :—

"Before Mistress Bracegirdle, Congreve and Lord Lovelace, at the head of a troop of bodkined fops, worshipped in vain. The noblest of the troop, and it reckoned the Dukes of Devonshire and Dorset, and the Earl of Halifax, were wont at the coffee-house and over a bottle, to extol the Gibraltar-like virtue, if I may so speak, of this incomparable woman. 'Come,' said Halifax, 'you are always praising the virtue, why don't you reward the lady who will not sell it? I propose a subscription, and there are 200 guineas, *pour encourager les autres.*' Four times that amount was raised, and with it the nobles, with their swords in their hands, waited on Mistress Bracegirdle, who accepted their testimonial, as it was intended, in honour of her virtue. I will only add that had Mistress Bracegirdle been rewarded for her *charity*, the recompense would have been at least as appropriate. For it *is* true of her that when the poor saw her they blessed her, and, we may add, she richly merited their well-earned benedictions."

Thus Dr. Doran. And so little was the private character of this lady injured by uttering the gross indecencies of the Restoration Drama that Dibdin declares her name was always mentioned with "great respect, both on account of her public merit and her private virtues."

Of the rank and file of the Restoration actors and actresses we naturally know less than of the conspicuous and representative examples I have mentioned, but it is obvious that in spite of the degrading material in which they worked, their characters might emerge spotless. How was this possible? I venture to suggest that either the ego which spoke in these interpretations was constantly controlled by the superior strength of their own personal character, or that the dramatis personæ of the Restoration Drama had no capacity to receive the breath of life which an actor can bestow upon them—that therefore the ego was not called upon to live, and that those mere puppets of an hour required nothing more than the voice and gesture of an actor to give them that slight semblance of reality which was necessary. For we must remember that the fame of Betterton rests, not on such puppets as the Belvilles, the Dorimants, and the Lovemores, but on Hamlet, Lear, and Macbeth.

To gather some illustrations nearer home, we are all aware that at a comparatively early stage in his career Sir Henry Irving possessed almost a monopoly for the representation of villains, such as the amiable Mr. E. S. Willard also acquired a decade or so later. Can it be contended that the daily interpretation of passions which disgrace humanity, affected the moral fibre of either of these gentlemen? Surely not. I think we may safely conclude that the character of the actor or the actress is not necessarily degraded by the interpretation or voicing of what is unworthy.

And what of the other side of the question? Does the constant illustration of all that is noble, tolerant, charitable, and high-minded help to refine and to elevate the character of the illustrator? I think it does. In support of this opinion we have the overwhelming evidence of Sir Henry Irving, who said that he never performed the part of Becket without feeling a better man after it. It seems to me that we must return to the same conclusion. It is the character of the man behind the actor which is the determining factor. A man of intrinsic or acquired high-mindedness and honesty can come scatheless through work which may be degrading, and may add to his own beauty of character by contact with what is noble.

Development of Character with that of the Art of Acting.

I am aware that to many enlightened minds it would appear superfluous to assert this, but I would ask any such to consider that there may still be found those who, from love of advertisement, from motives of envy and jealousy, or from ignorance and Philistinism, will deliberately misrepresent the influence upon the actor of the exercise of his art.

It is with this consideration in view that I would bring to your remembrance one of the most remarkable instances of the steady development of character side by side with the steady prosecution of the art of acting. I refer to Shakespeare himself. It does not seem to have been widely realised, until Mr. Sidney Lee pointed it out, that Shakespeare "remained a prominent member of the actors' profession till near the end of his life." Of the parts he played we have only scanty knowledge, though we have reason to believe they were important. I cannot do better than quote Mr. Sidney Lee's words :—

> "That Shakespeare chafed under some of the conditions of the actors' calling is commonly inferred from the 'Sonnets.' There he reproaches himself with becoming ' a motley to the view,' and chides fortune for having provided for his livelihood nothing better than 'public means that public manners breed,' whence his name received a brand. If such self-pity is to be literally interpreted it only reflected an evanescent mood. His interest in all that touched the efficiency of his profession was permanently active. His highest ambitions lay, it is true, elsewhere than in acting, and at an early period of his theatrical career he undertook, with triumphant success, the labours of a playwright. But he pursued the profession of an actor loyally and interruptedly until he resigned all connection with the theatres within a few years of his death."

SHAKESPEARE'S KNOWLEDGE OF ACTORS.

And to digress, perhaps, a little, we may say : " How well he knew them ! " Their faults, their weaknesses, their powers of imagination, their humour, their complex and difficult art. Is there one word of scorn for his calling—with the exception of this one passage Mr. Sidney Lee quotes from the sonnets ?—that, too, written when a young man—and the meaning of which is still disputed. One word of scorn for his fellow-members of that calling, through whose medium his creatures were to be reanimated with the gift of " form and moving "? Not one, I think. Shakespeare's references to his fellow-actors are always made with the tenderness and charity of true knowledge and actual experience. And yet how he must have suffered at their hands. The members of the Globe Theatre Company were not all Burbages, Alleynes, or Hemminges. What pigmies must his creatures sometimes have appeared in flesh and blood, beside his own sublime imagination ! What inevitable heart-burnings must there have been among his company, as each fresh play was cast. What was said when the author, himself a fellow-player, was announced to appear as the Ghost in *Hamlet* ? In spite of it all, how deeply he must have been beloved by his associates, when Hemminge and Condell, his fellow-actors, seven years after his death, brought together his precious manuscripts for publication ; not for pecuniary gain, scarcely, it would seem, with a full understanding of the genius of the poet, but in the enthusiasm of their love for their dead comrade. What is the uppermost thought in their minds? What are the words of their dedication? " To keepe the memory of so worthy a Friend and Fellow alive, as was our Shakespeare." Nor did Shakespeare, in his will, forget his old comrades in art. " To each of his ' fellows ' John Hemminge, Richard Burbage, and Henry Condell, he leaves twenty-six shillings and eightpence with which to buy memorial rings."

This apparent digression, it seems to me, proves much. Here was the greatest creative artist that ever lived, not only maturing his stupendous powers as a dramatist, living in beloved and loving comradeship with his fellow-actors, " pursuing," as Mr. Sidney Lee says, " the profession of an actor loyally and uninterruptedly," but, at the same time, developing his own character.

Says Professor Dowden, in his subtle and fascinating work, " Shakespeare : His Mind and Art " :—

> " It is clearly ascertainable from his plays and poems that Shakespeare's will grew with advancing age, beyond measure, calmer, and more strong."

In other words, Shakespeare was gaining that " captaincy of the soul " which the dramatic critic of the " Times " has affirmed is what a man must necessarily lose in the exercise of an actor's calling.

Is there any reason why the " captaincy of the soul " may be lost in the practice of the actor's art? None, because the man is an artist. None, because the work of his life is the imitation of humanity.

SHAKESPEARE, THE ACTOR.

Here I think I might leave this portion of my reflections. Reflections sketchy and immature, I greatly fear. I would call them suggestions rather than conclusions. Suggestions which may lead, perhaps, other and more capable students to enlarge upon, and may I venture to propose a subject to Shakespearean scholars—a subject hitherto almost disregarded, viz., "Shakespeare, the actor?" It seems curious that this side of Shakespeare's life should not have invited more consideration and research. Might I venture to hope that Mr. Sidney Lee, who has touched upon the subject in his delightful biography, will some day greatly enlarge our knowledge of this side of Shakespeare's life; all important, it seems to me, when we consider the fact that the practice of his profession as an actor must have absorbed by far the greater portion of his days, and that his character and outlook upon life were developing in the midst of daily devotion to this calling.

EFFECT OF CHARACTER ON ACTING.

And now I would dwell for a little upon the question—To what extent is acting affected by character?

I am not sure that such poor reflections as I will try to express do not equally apply to character and all art. I find myself continually seeking illustrations from the arts of painting, sculpture, and dramatic literature. The conviction I would like to impart is that character is of greater importance than art. It is more important to the world at large. I feel it is more important even to the artist himself.

It seems to me a right instinct which urges people to seek for the man behind the artist. Is the instinct which urges people to accept charily the artist who works alone for art's sake, also right? Perhaps it is.

At the moment when man began to express himself through a piece of work, art began, and in recognising a work of art we recognise the mind and character of the man who wrought it. And that mind and character is never stationary. It is either developing or deteriorating. I might venture the suggestion that at the moment that art is practised solely for the sake of art, decadence has set in; decadence of character, and hence, it seems to me, of art. There seems a subtle truth in Eleonora Dusé's words, when she says :—

> "If the sight of the blue skies fills you with joy, if a blade of grass spring-ing up in the fields has power to move you, rejoice, for your soul is alive; and then aspire to learn that other truth—that the least of what you receive can be divided. To help—to continually help and share—that is the sum of all knowledge, that is the meaning of art."

Now, the artist who practises art for art's sake does not share with humanity. He is apt to keep his point of view and his sense of beauty to himself, or to share it only with a few equally exclusive fellow-artists.

"The Herd," as humanity at large is so often referred to by these elect, are scorned, and it seems to me that the really great artists love humanity and do not scorn it.

THE OLD BOHEMIANISM.

A similar companionship was that old Bohemianism which, in addition to being a comradeship in artistic endeavour, was largely a protest against, and a defiance of, the realities of daily life. Such defiance one may be excused for taking to be an indication of some weakness in the character. I think he is a stronger man who can admit the claims of fact while practising the imitation of nature or humanity, than he who dodges a dun in an ecstatic disregard of his duties as a simple citizen.

The most incorrigible Bohemian, the most precious and exclusive in the Brother-hood of the Elect, might well reflect, perhaps, that while Shakespeare was project-ing the greatest tragedies in literature, he was also suing Philip Rogers, at Strat-ford-on-Avon, for £1 9s. 10d., due to him for malt supplied.

I would again return to Professor Dowden's reference to the development of Shakespeare's mind and art in comparison with that of his early contemporaries, Marlowe and Greene. Calling our attention to the reckless Bohemianism of the last-named ill-balanced but brilliant dramatic artists, he says :—

> "It must have appeared to Shakespeare (who well understood honest frolic) a poor affair, a flimsy kind of idealism—this reckless knocking of a man's head

against the solid laws of the universe. The protest against fact, against our subjections to law made by such men as Marlowe and Greene, was a vulgar and superficial protest."

What was the end of the Bohemian Marlowe? An ignominious death in a tavern brawl. That of the greater artist, who had won the captaincy of his soul, through that noble development of his mind and art "which was based on a resolute fidelity to the facts of life," an honoured retirement upon his estate at Stratford-on-Avon.

CULTIVATION OF CHARACTER.

And I will venture to say that the cultivation of the character is of more consequence to the actor than to any other artist.

The loss of character is the loss of self-discipline, and the actor's self-discipline is more tried than in any other art. The poet is his retreat, the sculptor and the artist in the quiet of their studios, know nothing of the difficulties of performing their work amidst the distractions of that busy hive of activity, the modern theatre. The irritability, which is a necessary condition of an actor's nervous system, renders him doubly susceptible to the loss of his self-restraint. The applause of an audience night after night tests his sense of proportion, and makes it trebly difficult, but trebly important, that he should discipline his emotions and control his highly-wrought nervous organisation.

That "Imitation of Humanity," which Shakespeare describes as the actor's art, is a constant assault upon a due recognition of the "solid laws of the universe." The imitation of humanity may so easily become confused with the facts of humanity that he may lose that sanity of mind without which his character cannot develop. In the light of his cherished imitation of Macbeth the butcher's bill may easily become a prosaic and negligible quantity. The power to imitate humanity—that art which Voltaire has described as the most difficult of all arts—must be balanced with a knowledge and an understanding of the facts of actual daily life. Without this balance the character deteriorates, and thus, slowly, but certainly, the deterioration is visible in his work, and the end is reached in bitterness and blind conflict with those very imperturbable *facts* which he has ignored or defied.

The artist's fate is in his own hands. There is nothing in the imitation of humanity or nature which brings inevitable deterioration.

PREPARATORY DISCIPLINE.

Betterton went further, and thought a strict preparatory discipline of the character before adopting the stage as a profession was essential. For, he says, "there is no manner of doubt but that the lives and characters of those persons, who are the vehicles, as I may call them, of these instructions must contribute very much to the impression the fable and moral will make. For to hear virtue, religion, honour, recommended by a sinner, an atheist, or a rake, makes them a jest to many people, who would hear the same done with awe by persons of known reputation in those particulars."

Such preparation of his mental state, as this of Betterton's, when he was to come the interpreter of a great character, is not unusual. It is not, I hope, unbecoming in me to speak of a very remarkable instance of such mental, I may almost say spiritual, preparation.

A CONTRAST.

When Sir Henry Irving played Hamlet he deliberately lived the life almost of an anchorite. So solemn a charge he held his interpretation, so essential did he consider the fine poise of his spirit while being the medium of so great a creation, that throughout the run of the Shakespearean tragedy at the Lyceum he purposely refrained from indulging in any social distractions, or allowing his mental equilibrium to be disturbed from a sweet serenity and a continual self-restraint.

Here is a picture on the reverse side. An actor was to make his appearance in a *rôle* of not less importance than Hamlet. The night came, the theatre was only half-filled, and many of the critics were so little interested that their seats were empty or occupied only during a portion of the evening. The actor's pride was wounded, the empty seats galled him, a taint of irritability and defiance grew through his representation, he lost his self-restraint, and he failed. Not, I take it, that he did not understand his creature, but a lower side of his own nature gradually obtruded itself, and stained the fine qualities of the noble creature he was representing.

LIMITATIONS OF THE CHARACTERLESS.

To those artists who have not realised the necessity of developing their own character, in order that it may speak through their work, how inexplicable, how heart-breaking it must be, when they find that the practice of their art has carried them to a certain point and never further. In spite of perfect technique, great intelligence, long experience, physical endowment, their audiences are unmoved; while another artist, with these qualifications possessed only to a limited extent, will enter profoundly into their affections—and why? For ever and ever, it seems to me, the same reason. This one possesses already, or has achieved by the development of character, sympathy, and love of humanity, while to the other humanity has been an object of scorn.

It is the character of the actor which is speaking in his interpretations. As Dusé has said :—

"The artist-actor gives the best of himself—through his interpretations he unveils his inner soul."

May I paraphrase the dictum once pronounced by a dramatic author on the essentials of play-writing? He said there were three. First, construction; second, construction; third, construction! Then I would say of the essentials for the building up of an actor that they are character, character, character!

Yes, it seems to me that it is a right instinct which urges us to seek the man in his work. According to our discovery do we place him in our hearts and affections, or in our intelligence, and no one can doubt that it was the heart and the affection of the nation which spoke, when it demanded that Sir Henry Irving should be laid to rest in the Abbey at Westminster.

I know, of course, that many actors of genius, possessed, too, of great qualities of heart, do not repose in Westminster Abbey—that their end was obscure, unhonoured. Why? Because the unthinking world has sometimes spoken slightingly of a life devoted to art? Never! Because of the medium in which they worked? Never! But because in the sad instances I have in my mind, for reasons into which it were only painful to inquire, they had step by step lost that "captaincy of the soul," by vices acquired or of the blood which finally left them "lagging superfluous." Because, in a word, their characters had deteriorated.

IMITATION OF HUMANITY.

The train of thought which this consideration opens up covers too vast a field for me to pursue, I only touch upon it to enforce my conviction that the actor in imitating humanity is largely dominated by one of his many egos, and that he, in turn, must acquire the force of character to keep in subjection the worst or ignoble traits of these egos. Let us follow the advice of old Crome to his son : "My boy, paint what you see, but if it is only a pigsty, dignify it." And as we hang the picture of the pigsty on our walls and look at it with ever fresh delight, let us remember that the work of art gives us joy because we see the character of the man behind the art, who has purposely selected the beautiful side of his subject and disregarded the base.

The power of an actor of well-disciplined character over his audience is immense ; that power, as Sir Theodore Martin has said, is " divine in its origin."

May I quote another eloquent passage from the same brilliant and rarely endowed critic :—

"The power of his genius, which has been reflected to him in the palpable emotion or ringing plaudits of his audience, has opened up to them a world of poetry and emotion, which, but for him, they would never have known. His ' so potent art ' has awakened them to a knowledge of their own hearts, ' shown them noble lights in their own soul.' It has lifted them for a time above the commonplace of their daily life ; it has widened the sphere of their sympathies, flashed light upon the conceptions of the greatest poets which has made them living realities, and, in doing this, it has communicated impulses which may exercise a lasting influence for good on the lives of thousands. Not in vain has he lived, who owes such success to having wrought with a pure aim to turn to the highest account the special gift of genius."

A TRIBUTE TO SIR HENRY IRVING.

If ever there was an actor to whom these eloquent words could apply it is to my great master, Sir Henry Irving. Never, perhaps, was there an actor whose character, one felt instinctively, was more highly and nobly developed through his art.

I was for fifteen years under him, and was never nearer to him, in one sense, than the veriest boy in the gallery of his theatre. There was something enigmatical, mysterious, and baffling about him. But it was because, through his art, I was unconsciously brought face to face with his soul, his great, enduring, steadfast soul, that I adored him. It was for the same reason that the boy in the gallery adored him, that the English people adored him, and it is for his steadfast soul, rather than his rare accomplishments, that his name will be imperishable.

If our Saviour has sometimes puzzled us because, during His ministry on this earth, He said nothing about art, we may be sure that it was not because He ignored the supreme importance of art in our daily life; but because His first care was for the character, and He must have known that, if the character is noble, noble art will follow.

CENSORSHIP.

At the Home Office on February 25 Mr. Herbert Gladstone, who was accompanied by Mr. Herbert Samuel, M.P. (Under-Secretary), and Mr. Cuninghame and Mr. C. E. Troup (Under-Secretaries), received a deputation of playwrights and authors, headed by Mr. J. M. Barrie, who claimed that the licensing of plays should be abolished. Seventy-one gentlemen signed the protest against the Censorship of plays which led to the deputation. "The office of Censor," they said, "was instituted for political, and not for the so-called moral ends to which it is perverted, and is an office autocratic in procedure, opposed to the spirit of the Constitution, contrary to common justice and to common sense."

The deputation included Sir William S. Gilbert, Mr. A. W. Pinero, Mrs. Henry de la Pasture, Mrs. M. L. Woods, Professor Gilbert Murray, Messrs. Henry James, Comyns Carr, St. John Hankin, John Pollock, Laurence Housman, George Bancroft, Maurice Hewlett, W. H. Hudson, Cecil Raleigh, Granville Barker, W. J. Locke, Ernest Rhys, Alfred Sutro, Cosmo Gordon Lennox, and Frederick Fenn.

Mr. A. W. Pinero, Mr. J. M. Barrie, and Sir W. S. Gilbert were the speakers.

Mr. Pinero, in the course of his speech, said :—" While dramatists are ready for the abolition of the Censorship, we admit the possibility that the public mind—habituated to the fallacious notion that the Censorship affords some guarantee for the morals of the stage—may not be yet quite ripe for the granting of the freedom we ask for. Should this prove to be the case, we recognise as reasonable men that Parliament may not feel justified for the present in granting us a full measure of relief. The support received from the Press, however, shows us that the public mind is at least alive to the worst of the evils of which we complain, and that, even assuming the necessity for a Censorship, there is no necessity and no defence for its secrecy and irresponsibility. These are the characteristics of the office which we feel to be absolutely intolerable. This injustice would be obviated by the institution of a court of appeal, and, should entire freedom prove unattainable for the moment, we should be willing to accept such a court as a transitional expedient.

Sir W. S. Gilbert more clearly outlined the proposal.

The suggestion was, he said, that the office of the Censor of Plays should have the status of a Court of First Instance, from which there should be an appeal to arbitrators constituted under the Act, and consisting of three gentlemen, one to be appointed by the author, one by the Lord Chamberlain, and the third to be selected either by the first two or by the Lord Chancellor. With a view to preventing appeals on insignificant and trivial matters, he suggested that the fees payable to these gentlemen should be ten guineas each, and that the cost should be paid by the appellant or the respondent, as the arbitrators might direct.

Mr. Gladstone gave the deputation a sympathetic hearing, and promised to put their views before the Prime Minister.

On December 17 a Bill was introduced in the House of Commons by Mr. Robert Harwood. The objects of the Bill were to abolish the powers of the Lord Chamberlain in respect of stage plays, and to transfer to the local authority the powers of the Lord Chamberlain in respect of the licensing of theatres in London. The Bill was backed by Mr. A. E. W. Mason, Mr. T. P. O'Connor, and Mr. Ramsay Macdonald.

MISS ELLEN TERRY.
From the picture by W. Graham Robertson
By permission of the Artist.

THE MUSICAL YEAR.

BY B. W. FINDON.

A GLANCE at the lengthy list of concerts that have been given during the present year in the metropolis ought to be sufficient in itself to disabuse the mind of the intelligent foreigner of the old-time belief that we are not a musical nation. But our musical energies are not consumed by concerts alone; we have our seasons of opera, and there are those musical celebrations in the chief cities of the provinces that draw largely on London for their artistic support. Then such towns as Manchester, Liverpool, and Glasgow—to name only three—have their big orchestral and choral associations, and there is scarcely a county town or cathedral city that is not a sphere of musical influence.

ACTIVITY IN OPERA.

At one time grand opera was considered the monopoly of the rich and a mere appendage to society. But of recent years there has been a great change in this direction. The middle classes are beginning to show a decided leaning towards this form of relaxation from the cares and worries of the strenuous life of the period. An important factor in achieving this desirable consummation is undoubtedly the wide-spreading influence which Wagner has gained in recent years in this country. So manifest was this to the directors of the Covent Garden Opera Syndicate that at the beginning of the year they had the courage to announce a series of performances of *The Nibelung's Ring* in the vernacular, and with native artists as the representatives of the leading characters. It was an enterprise that owed much to the advocacy of Dr. Hans Richter, and to his ability as musical chief. Without the magic of his name, it is possible that the public would not have responded as they did, and that it answered the expectations of its promoters may be safely assumed, inasmuch as a similar series will be given in January, 1909. That English speaking artists were equal to the exacting demands of the great tetralogy was fully demonstrated, and, among others, it brought to the front a young tenor, Mr. Walter Hyde, who was only known previously as a pleasing singer in the domain of musical comedy.

THE SUMMER SEASON.

Society assembled in full force on the opening night of the grand season at Covent Garden, for it was to be the social *début* of an artist who had captured "the town" during the Italian season, which was given in the early part of the preceding winter. Then it was that Madame Tetrazzini, an unknown singer, came, saw, and conquered. To the bulk of the regular subscribers, however, she was known only by hearsay, and consequently there was a natural desire to see if she would maintain her reputation when brought into competition with the famous "stars" who were so well known to the habitués of Covent Garden. It was felt there would be a keen fight for superiority between her and Mme. Melba, and the merits of the two artists were freely discussed. It reminded one of the Titanic struggles between singers in the old days, and the result was much the same. Each *diva* had her ardent and enthusiastic supporters, and each side found beauties in the one which were denied the other.

So far as the list of operas went there was nothing in the way of absolute novelty. For Mme. Tetrazzini's sake there was a revival of Bizet's little known *Les Pêcheurs de Perles*, and, curiosity having been satisfied, the work dropped out of the repertory. A word of recognition is due to the excellent performance of Gluck's *Armide*, and among the other notable events of the season was the gala performance given in honour of M. Fallières, the President of the French Republic. In this, the Italian and Australian prime donne were brought into vivid contrast, the one appearing in the first act of the above-named opera of Bizet's, and the other in the Garden Scene in *Faust*. Mention must be made of the brilliant operatic *matinée* organised by Mme. Melba to commemorate her twentieth anniversary at Covent Garden ; the regular continuity of her appearance, however, will be broken in the coming year, as she is engaged on an extensive tour in Australia and America, which will last until 1910. Mr. Walter Hyde and Mr. John McCormack, a young Irish tenor, repeated their success of the autumn season, and an excellent feature in the policy of the present management is the encouragement given to English singers, who now take their place side by side with the best vocalists of the Continent. Once more our King and Queen gave consistent support to the opera by their presence, and it is largely due to their powerful influence that there is such keen competition for the pit and grand tier boxes.

MOODY-MANNERS AND THE CARL ROSA.

Those of us who are advocates of a National Opera naturally take a sympathetic interest in the work accomplished by such notable provincial companies as those of the Carl Rosa and the Moody-Manners. The record of the former is one of the brightest landmarks in our operatic history since the days of the Pyne and Harrison combination. Although it has undergone many vicissitudes since the death of its founder, the Carl Rosa is still doing good work in the provinces, and its merit is put to the test by occasional seasons at Covent Garden. We must not forget that to its initiative in recent years we owe the English production of *Hänsel and Gretel*, and many other works have been produced and revived which bear eloquent testimony to its enterprise and devotion to art.

Mr. Charles Manners and his talented wife, Mme. Fanny Moody, have certainly made more commotion of recent days in the musical world than their older-established rivals. With an energy and an enthusiasm which entitle him to unqualified praise, Mr. Manners has pushed the cause of Opera in English in season and out of season. Year after year he boldly plunges into metropolitan waters, and at the Lyric theatre makes court to our musical amateurs in the holiday month of August, when all good citizens are supposed to be amid green pastures or idling their days on the golden sands of popular seaside resorts. But I am not sufficiently optimistic to believe that Mr. Manners, with all his good intentions and with all his incessant labour, does much to advance the cause of National Opera, and though the admirable series of performances he gives in Shaftesbury Avenue have an artistic value far in excess of the moderate prices charged for admission, they do not convey to the people at large that Opera sung in English is an indispensable requisite of our national life.

CONCERTS AND CONCERT GIVERS.

Of recent years an evil has crept into the concert world which bids fair to wax even more serious as time advances. I refer to the increasing number of concert agents who establish themselves with the hope of trading on the weakness and foibles of those who think they have only to be heard for their talent to be universally recognised. Let readers glance through the list of vocal and instrumental recitals which is published in another page in this Annual, and picture to themselves the disappointed hopes and shattered illusions they represent. Money has been lavished on the student's education, oftentimes by those ill able to afford it, and the final effort is made to give the young artist that publicity which may eventually result in the anticipated pecuniary reward and its attendant fame. In the vast proportion of cases the reward resolves itself into the applause of friends, a few cold, critical, notices, and then—silence. What becomes of the *débutantes* the outside world neither knows nor cares. The public will pay its money only for the best, and that it frequently ignores in favour of some sensational executant. Even such violinists as Ysaye and Kreisler have to fight hard to maintain their positions ; while the difficulties of the pianists are enhanced by the general accomplishment of the majority who have mastered nearly all there is to master in the way of technique, but lack the saving grace of that indefinable quantity described as temperament.

Of the many young pianists who owe their training entirely to English teachers, the one who has come forward most prominently during the past year is Miss Myra Hess, a young lady still in her 'teens, and of whom we may expect really great things in the future. Vladimir de Pachmann still remains supreme as an exponent of Chopin, and his recitals are invariably well attended, and that the personal popularity of Paderewski remains unimpaired was instanced by the crowded state of Queen's Hall when he gave his one and only recital of the year.

Many excellent singers have also courted notice, a few of whom have added to their artistic success by capturing the attention of musical amateurs, but the year has produced no concert singer who gives any likelihood of achieving high rank in the profession. Chamber music has not been neglected, but there is not the eagerness to hear this delightful form of music there was in the old days of the Popular Concerts. Among the combinations, however, which deserve a passing word of mention is the London Trio, composed of Mme. Amina Goodwin, and Messrs. Simonetti and Whitehouse. The generous encouragement given by Mr. E. Palmer to musical art in founding the Patrons' Fund has not succeeded in unearthing any creative genius of first rank, although it has brought forward a number of young composers of undoubted ability.

THE REIGN OF THE ORCHESTRA.

The greatest advance in public taste is shown in the domain of orchestral concerts, which mainly through the exertions of Mr. H. J. Wood and Mr. Robert Newman, have now firmly established themselves in the good graces of the public. The Promenade Concerts are a case in point. From the middle of August to the middle of October the Queen's Hall nightly draws large audiences, and it is a wonderful sight to see the floor of the hall packed close by those who think it no fatigue to stand for two hours listening to the classical works of the great tone masters of this and preceding generations. The Queen's Hall Orchestra has achieved a remarkable reputation, and its fame is as widespread as that of the old Crystal Palace organisation what time the late Sir August Manns was in his prime. The Saturday Symphony Concerts, under the direction of Mr. Wood, have a large and increasing clientèle, and better music one could not wish to hear.

Another organisation which has made its mark in the metropolis is the London Symphony Orchestra, which, under the magnificent direction of Dr. Richter and Herr Arthur Nikisch, stands second to none in the estimation of the public. Its bi-weekly Monday night concerts invariably attract crowded audiences. In the same field there has recently appeared Mr. Thomas Beecham, who has formed what is known as the New Symphony Orchestra, and his energy and enthusiasm are producing excellent results. It was with the assistance of this orchestra that Miss E. M. Smyth gave a concert performance of her opera *The Wreckers*, a work which had been twice accepted abroad, but regretfully refused by the Covent Garden Syndicate on the plea that new works did not pay. It proved to have many merits, but as an opera it cannot be judged when separated from its natural environment.

A work of a dramatic character, and the subject of a unique experiment, was the poem of "Apollo and the Seaman," the music to which was by Mr. Joseph Holbrooke. In a darkened hall, and by means of the magic lantern, the words of the poem were shown on a screen as the music progressed; but the effect was by no means encouraging, and the precedent is not likely to be followed.

The sensation of the year in the sphere of orchestral music was the production at Manchester on December 3 of Sir Edward Elgar's Symphony. This work was received with an enthusiasm and an amount of critical approbation which seem to indicate that Elgar has contributed a permanent masterpiece to the literature of English music. Time, however, is the surest critic on works of this description, and I hope that he will endorse the contemporary verdict.

Before leaving this branch of art a tribute must be paid to the admirable series of Sunday Orchestral Concerts which are given at the Albert and Queen's Halls, which do much to make pleasurable and interesting the dulness of our winter Sunday afternoons. The venerable Philharmonic Society continues its career of uninterrupted prosperity under the direction of Dr. Cowen and other conductors.

PROVINCIAL FESTIVALS.

The abundance of first-class music in London has done not a little to weaken metropolitan interest in the Triennial Festivals which are held in certain of our provincial and cathedral cities. At one time they practically embraced the whole music of the autumn, but now they form but a factor in the autumnal musical life of the country. This year there were festival celebrations at Gloucester, Bristol, Norwich, and Sheffield, at which all the leading native artists found engagements, but the novelties were few and of no great importance. The Festivals, however, more than fulfilled their purpose in proving that English supremacy in the art of chorus singing is in no danger of being superseded.

In the limited space at my command it was impossible to do more than give a comprehensive backward glance at the music of the year, and my aim has been to trace broadly the progress that has been made and the general state of musical art in this country, rather than weary the reader with multitudinous details. For these he must have recourse to the categories of official commentators.

BACK TO ROMANCE.

By L. H. JACOBSEN.

IS the whirligig of Time indeed bringing round its revenges, and is the great, many-headed, and many-throated monster, alike so beloved and feared, the British Public, again taking heartily to the enjoyment of good, honest, straight-forward, romantic drama and melodrama, as a change, at any rate, from the varied delights of music-hall entertainments and animated picture shows? We put the question interrogatively, for there are both pros. and cons. to be considered. In the West End, at least, we have had important revivals of well-known plays with Mr. Lewis Waller, Mr. H. B. Irving, and Mr. Martin Harvey in the leading parts; and something more than popular appreciation of the acting of Mr. Waller and Mr. Harvey, in *The Duke's Motto* and *The Corsican Brothers* has been shown by their appearances at the Command Performances at Windsor Castle, given in honour of the King and Queen of Sweden. Royal favour, as has often been pointed out, counts for a great deal with theatrical enterprises; and that inveterate playgoer, both in London and in Paris, King Edward, may be held to be as good a judge as "the man in the street," whose opinions are thrust before us in or out of season, or as the supercilious persons who air their own impressions in type and columns of all sizes. We hold no brief for or against Ibsen, Problem Plays, the Naturalistic Drama, or any other Advanced forms of theatrical entertainment; but still we may be allowed to regard as healthy and commendable any such tendency as has been noted at the outset. Mr. Arthur Bourchier, Mr. Martin Harvey, Miss Gertrude Kingston, Mr. Henry Arthur Jones, and others have lately been holding forth concerning the past, present, and future of the British Drama, and we feel inclined to take as our text some sentences of Mr. Bourchier in the speech he delivered in September before the members of the Liverpool Stage Club. His words were, "It is still that spirit of irreverence and flippant ignorance which has wrecked many a good enterprise at the outset. The sneer of the man of fashion in the stalls is echoed by the titter of the boy up aloft, and a good scene and a fine piece of interpretation go for nothing."

WHY LAUGH AT THE HERO?

It is not twenty years since there started the trick (fashion is too dignified a term for it) of poking fun at the once-admired gallant mien and bold speeches of the typical Stage Hero such as Charles Fechter, Henry Neville, and William Terriss used to represent before audiences that did not try to find matter for mirth in stirring deeds of valour of which nobody need have been ashamed. Perhaps the dramatists may have partly contributed to this by beginning to set forth wretched, mean-spirited creatures in lieu of heroes; but still the trend of feeling has been obvious, and we have latterly commented upon, and tried to combat, a growing desire on the part of some eminent actors to play romantic parts in a serio-comic or even farcical vein—to portray "the Hero *pour rire*," that is to say. We might have been disposed to regard this as a mere modernism had we not by chance lighted upon some phrases in the late Joseph Knight's valuable volume of Theatrical Notes, in which that lamented critic said, "To Mr. Neville's growing inclination to play such *rôles*, partly chivalrous, partly comic, in the romantic drama as have been associated with the fame of M. Mélingue, may be ascribed his production at the Olympic (February, 1876) of a version of *The Gascon*." Now, no one ever approached more nearly to the *beau idéal* of the valiant champion of virtue in distress than did Henry Neville, and we accept Mr. Knight's statement with deference, yet with a shade of doubt. Certainly Mr. Neville did not play Lord Clancarty in Tom Taylor's drama in the light and airy manner adopted by Mr. Waller in a recent revival at the Lyric, nor can we remember any such farcical business as was to be witnessed in the same popular player's assumptions in *Brigadier Gérard* or *Miss Elizabeth's Prisoner*, for example, or in the later performances given by Mr. George Alexander

MISS ETHEL IRVING.

As Lady Frederick, from the picture by F. Howard Michael.

By permission of Miss Irving.

as the King-personating Rassendyll in *The Prisoner of Zenda*, a play in which Mr. H. B. Irving made an early success as the bold and insolent Rupert of Hentzau. To make love whilst dragging a chair about is one of the rather humiliating experiences to which Mr. Waller has been condemned.

THE RETURN TO CHIVALRY.

Fortunately, Mr. Waller has lately been enjoying a happier fate in the *rôle* of that spirited, dashing hero of "I am here" renown, Henri de Lagardere, in *The Duke's Motto*, as revised by Justin Huntly McCarthy. In this new edition of Paul Féval Mr. Waller had no comic business except for a moment or two, "with the baby on his knee," and the result was a bold, vigorous, emphatic, fervent performance, quite in the proper key of romantic drama. Moving for the moment to the contiguous compartment of melodrama, we have not witnessed for years a more affecting and pathetic stage presentment of the good man struggling in the meshes of destiny, with a cunning scoundrel as wielder of the net, than that of Joseph Lesurques given by Mr. H. B. Irving in *The Lyons Mail*, his performance of this portion of the famous dual *rôle* being thought by many, in spite of some cheap gibes by an Impressionist writer, to surpass in its gentle dignity and astounded innocence the work here done by his illustrious father. This is the sort of acting that we want nowadays in romantic drama, neither namby-pamby, finicking, kid-glove stuff, nor bombastic, ultra-heroic spouting and artificial posing. The Real Hero, presented as a living man, and not as a conventional puppet of the hack-playwright, will appeal as forcibly as ever to the average playgoer. It was because Mr. Fred Terry had to play a milk-and-water hero, placed ignominiously in the stocks and threatened with the whip, that his Matt Compton was unable to gain for *Matt of Merrymount* a tithe of the favour long bestowed upon the popular *The Scarlet Pimpernel*, thanks largely to his own performance of Sir Percy Blakeney. The authors of *The Scarlet Pimpernel*, we may note, have recently supplied Mr. Reginald Dance with an effective highwayman romance in *Beau Brocade*. We shall, ere these lines appear, see how Mr. Terry fares here in that new semi-historical drama of the Massacre of St. Bartholomew days, *Henry of Navarre*, from the practised pen of William Devereux, who did similar work for Mr. Waller with *Robin Hood*. Mr. Terry should give a picturesque embodiment of the bold Béarnais (referred to only in Meyerbeer's opera *The Huguenots*). Performances have already been given in Greater London of another play written round a Henry of history, *Henry of Lancaster*, in which have appeared Miss Ellen Terry and her husband, Mr. James Carew, the latter as Shakespeare's Richmond, who afterwards became Henry VII. One could hardly take seriously the rather absurd incidents of that "comedy of the Middle Ages," *The Two Pins*, and hence Mr. Oscar Asche and Miss Lily Brayton, though well suited enough with parts, failed to convince or to gain success with it in Town, though less critical audiences, we believe, have taken to the piece pretty kindly. There was no lack of earnestness shown in the playing associated with *The Three Musketeers* "boom" of a few years back, and it is largely on account of his imaginative gifts and romantic fervour of style that Mr. Martin Harvey has been drawing crowded audiences to the Adelphi with his latest revival of *The Corsican Brothers*. Besides his well-contrasted expositions of those closely linked twins, Louis and Fabien Dei Franchi, Mr. Harvey has just been showing the effect of this combination of the earnestness and the romantic (a point upon which too much stress cannot be laid) as the temporarily dethroned King Konrad of Polavia, in *The Conspiracy*.

RURITANIANS ALL.

This brings us on to an important and generally-to-be-commended modern development in the genre of romantic drama. It was Anthony Hope (with the aid of the late Edward Rose) that started upon a new path with *The Prisoner of Zenda* and its sequel, *Rupert of Hentzau*. Since the early nineties many novelists (Allen Upward and Sir William Magnay, for instance) and several dramatists (with Walter Howard and C. Watson Mill at the head) have dealt with imaginary realms, either small German Kingdoms or Principalities or States somewhere in the troubled regions of the Balkans; but, whatever their locale may have been styled, it has always been Ruritania and Strelsau all over again. To Walter Howard and the present spirited and energetic management of the Lyceum due credit must be given for the introduction of honest, wholesome, picturesque, not too extravagant or improbable, romantic drama to audiences that might otherwise have been content to batten upon commonplace blood-and-thunder stuff or machine-made pieces with the sen-

4

sation and not the play as the thing. Mr. Walter Howard had won popularity as a dramatist in the provinces and in the suburbs before his plays reached Central London; and more recently, in the last couple of years, how many thousands of susceptible theatregoers have not taken interest, at the Lyceum, in the Earl of Strathmere and Lionel, Prince Ulric of Ravensburg, and Princess Iris, in *Her Love Against the World*, in Paul Valmar, Crown Prince Leopold, and another Princess, of the House of Von Strelsburg, in *The Midnight Wedding*, and in those three ably differentiated brothers, Princes Olaf, Hildred, and Michael of Sylvania, and Princess Monica of Illyria, in *The Prince and the Beggar Maid*. On the same day in April another prolific playwright, Mr. C. Watson Mill, who is somewhat too fond of presenting gruesome horrors, had brought out two dramas of his, with similar titles, *The Love of the Princess* and *For Love and the King*, the former dealing with Prince Conrad Ramona of Uldersburg, Princess Idalia, and King Josef of Ilarnia, and the latter with the Obrenovic and Dragomir families, of Sylvonia (Servia, presumably), a couple more Princesses, and Jarval, an English soldier of fortune. Other writers have been engaged in cutting out pieces on much the same pattern, the glowing colours of which we prefer, at any rate, to the tawdry checks of inferior melodrama. Thus, from Mrs. F. G. Kimberley (Miss Lottie Addison) has come *The Power of the King*, with its wicked Crown Prince Oscar, Lady Anastasia, Catpain Rupert Landgrave, and the King of Vallombrosa, a country that ought to have Miltonic associations. Another experienced dramatist, Mr. E. Hill-Mitchelson, has given us King Vladimir and Prince Bora, in *Who Is She?* The King of Ravonia figures in *Send Her Victorious*, by Herbert Skardon, and among other dramas of the same class may be mentioned *The Woman Who Gambles*, *A Fight for a Throne*, and Arthur Shirley's *A Queen Without a Crown*.

SUGGESTED REVIVALS.

With Romance thus again in favour, there seems no reason why other dramas popular in the much-decried Mid-Victorian epoch should not be revived, with judicious alterations and modernising, of course, if such be deemed necessary. There has been talk, for instance, of a new Stephen Phillips version of Victor Hugo's *Le Roi s'Amuse*, known also through Tom Taylor's adaptation *The Fool's Revenge*, and through the libretto of *Rigoletto*. Then there is *Belphegor*, which Wilson Barrett played under the title of *The Acrobat*, early in the days of the New Olympic. Again, one might think of Watts Phillips's *The Dead Heart*, which Mr. Walter Pollock revised for Irving; and there are still acting possibilities in Lovell's *The Wife's Secret*. These are only *obiter dicta*, but certainly there might be some chance of profit from a reproduction of *The Marble Heart*, in which, at the Adelphi, in May, 1854, Leigh Murray (John Hare's first instructor) made the success of his life as Raphael Duchâtelet, the young sculptor lured from his work by the blandishments of Mlle. Marco, a callous woman of the world, against whose marble heart his own is broken. In this adaptation by Charles Selby of Barrière and Theboust's drama, *Les Filles de Marbre*, Murray and Mme. Céleste had a fine scene in the fourth act, and a dual *rôle* was played by Benjamin Webster. Other instances might be adduced, but the foregoing will be sufficient to show that there are some effective romantic dramas to be routed out from the lumber-room of the fifties and sixties, in the case of the inventive fount of Walter Howard and his colleagues running dry. Such pieces, if played in the proper manner, as we have been endeavouring to point out, would prove more edifying at any rate than some of the nauseating "slices from life" or dramas of the gutter, the Morgue, and the dissecting table, which have been thrust under the noses or down the throats of revolted and revolting playgoers. In such a Renascence of Romance, which need not conflict either with Shakespeare reverently staged or with the Drama of Ideas, leading parts might quite well be played by Mr. Lewis Waller, Mr. Martin Harvey, Mr. H. B. Irving, Mr. Henry Ainley, Mr. Matheson Lang, and other actors who have brains as well as imagination. Thus the white flag of conquering and blameless chivalry might once more be hoisted, as symbol not of cowardly surrender but of the irresistible onset of the Real Hero.

"WHAT EVERY WOMAN KNOWS" AT THE DUKE OF YORK'S.

Mr. Hume, Mr. Eugene Mayeur, Mr. Edmund Gwenn, Mr. Sidney Valentine, Mr. Gerald du Maurier, and Miss Hilda Trevelyan.

Dove St. Studios.

"HER FATHER" AT THE HAYMARKET.

Miss HENRIETTA WATSON, Miss MARIE LÖHR, and Mr. ARTHUR BOURCHIER.

"THE FLAG LIEUTENANT" AT THE PLAYHOUSE.

The Fourth Act: The Flag Lieutenant reading the list of Birthday Honours.

Reading from left to right: Mr. Lewis Broughton, Miss Winifred Emery, Mr. Clarence Blakiston, Mr. C. Aubrey Smith, Mr. W. Percyval, Mr. Cyril Maude, Miss Rosalie Toller, Mr. Arthur Holmes-Gore, Miss Lilian Braithwaite, Mr. Robert Averell, Mr. Eric Mathers, and Miss Mabel Lander.

(Foulsham & Banfield.

"THE MERRY WIDOW" AT DALY'S.

Mr. George Graves.   Mr. Robert Evett.   Miss Lily Elsie,   Mr. Joseph Coyne.

ACROSS THE ATLANTIC.

SOME ADVICE TO ACTORS ABOUT TO VISIT AMERICA.

BY W. H. DENNY.

IN view of the great number of members of the theatrical profession and others who are continually leaving these shores for the United States, an article dealing with the matter will, perhaps, prove acceptable to those who, for the first time at least, contemplate making the trip, though naturally the space allotted in the present volume will merely admit of treating only the fringe of the subject. With this in mind, it may be imagined that brevity and conciseness form rather the aim than an ornate style and a diffuse method.

REGISTRATION OF CONTRACT.

To jump at once into the matter, the first thing to be considered is the question of the contract, and with whom the contract should be made. It is most important to bear in mind that contracts made in England have no legal standing in America unless they be registered at the United States Consulate in St. Helen's Place, Bishopsgate, where for a small fee they may be registered, recorded, and made valid wherever the American flag flies. With regard to with whom the contracts should be made, that is, perhaps, a more difficult matter, for in the States, as here, theatrical business is very much of a lottery; and there are many who, if the money comes in, pay salary, and if it does not, don't pay.

Such managers as Charles Frohman, David Belasco, Klaw and Erlanger, Henry B. Harris, Harrison Grey Fiske, the Shuberts, James K. Hackett, Henry W. Savage, the Lieblers (George Tyler), Charles B. Dillingham, William A. Brady, and others are as safe as the Bank of England; but in all cases where the name of the manager is not well known it is just as well to make inquiries, for once in America it is a deuce of a long swim back.

The Vaudeville managers, too, are mostly reliable. The bulk of the business is done through the United Booking Offices in St. James Building, Broadway, where the bookings of Keith and Proctor and Percy Williams are carried through; and William Morris, on Broadway and Thirty-ninth Street, who has also an office in Bedford Street, Strand. At these offices the Vaudeville arrangements are gilt-edged.

HIGHER TERMS AND EXPENSES.

It must be remembered that the terms in vogue in the States are greater than those in this country, but at the same time the work is heavier, and the travelling expenses are much larger. In the theatres the salary covers, as a rule, all *matinées*. The item of sleepers on the train, which the artist pays himself, is quite a heavy one, particularly on one-night stands, when the expenses are all round much increased. Out West, too, and down South, Sunday performances are given, sometimes two a day; so it will be easily seen that the money must necessarily be more, to repay the wear and tear. In Vaudeville particularly it means "two a day" for the seven days, and no "let up," while in some of the stock companies out West fourteen performances a week are the custom.

Take it to heart, and underline it heavily, that the one aim of every soul in the business portion of the drama in America is to make money as fast as possible, and every other consideration is rendered subservient to that idea.

BAGGAGE TROUBLES.

When you have made the contract, the next proceeding is the booking of the passage. Usually it is booked for you, though to comply with the law dealing with contracts it is always understood that the actor pays his own passage, and it is as well to remember that one is supposed to have not less than fifty dollars, or ten pounds, to land with, otherwise you run the risk of being sent back.

From the office of the steamship company you are sailing with you get labels, which you affix to your baggage. That which you require on the passage has been specially labelled to that effect. It is then put in your state-room. The rest is put down the hold.

It will also be necessary to obtain labels with your initial on to put on the baggage, since on arrival it is taken to the Customs shed, where baggage is ranged alphabetically under the initial letter. If your baggage has no initial, it will cost you much time and bother to find it. A good plan is to have the initial painted in some particular way, and in certain colours, so that you may recognise it at once, for it is marvellous how one trunk looks like another when they are piled up together. As a suggestion I may mention in my own case I have a large red D on a white disk. In order to get your baggage on board with the least possible trouble, it may be added that Messrs. Carter Paterson, for a comparatively small charge, collect baggage from the house and deliver it at the ship's side. This will be found to save an enormous amount of worry and trouble, and possibly expense in the way of tips for porters, etc. Provided your luggage has been properly labelled, you will find no further care necessary, for the stewards of the ship take each parcel intended for your state-room and place it there, and there you will find it.

One most important thing to bear in mind is the liability to lose things from pilfering, even among the passengers. Unless your valuables, in the way of jewellery and trinkets, are placed safely under lock and key, you will have cause to remember the voyage. Furs, valuable rugs, indeed anything which may be turned into cash at the port of arrival, are liable to disappear. This disappearance is most apt to occur during the bustle and confusion of landing, when, as a rule, the passenger is completely off guard. Bundles of wraps, etc., have an unhappy knack of disappearing on these occasions.

On Board.

As regards what is necessary for the passage, that will depend to a great extent on the habits and tastes of the voyager, but it will be well at all times to remember that the less you can do with the better. It will be desirable, however, no matter what time of the year you travel, to take a good overcoat, for during the summer the northerly course is steered, and when the Arctic current is reached that article of clothing will be found most welcome. A travelling rug, too, is desirable for use on deck. A deck chair is not necessary, since this may be hired on board at a charge of one dollar (4s. 2d.), or in English money 5s.

It is not always necessary to dress for dinner, as on the P. and O. boats; but many do it from sheer custom, though it is a bit of a fag, at least for professional people, who as a rule have as much of changes of dress to satisfy anybody. A liberal supply of collar studs will be found useful, as they have an awkward knack of passing out of ken, and on these occasions a stud in hand is worth a dozen at home. Besides these few things, the usual articles one takes on tour will be sufficient.

Tips.

Tips are a rather important item. They present a difficulty to many people. The general rule for a first cabin passenger is to give the state-room steward and saloon steward ten shillings each, the bath-room steward five shillings, the boots half-a-crown, the smoke-room steward in proportion to the services he renders you, but as a rule less than the state and saloon stewards; and there is a usual whip-round for the deck steward of perhaps a shilling, as a recompense for attending to the deck games, which are a feature of an Atlantic trip. The second-class passengers usually give about half these amounts.

With regard to ladies requiring the attentions of the stewardess, the amount of the tip depends upon the services rendered, for it often happens that the fair voyager is unable to put in an appearance at the table, when the stewardess has to bring each meal to the state-room, and the frequency of this service has to be taken into account when the farewell is said. While on this subject it is as well to take into consideration the matter of that dreadful malaise, sea-sickness. Some people must always suffer from it, but the worst effects may be minimised by going into training before sailing, avoiding rich foods, for it is akin to biliousness, and if the liver be put in good condition it will go far to prevent any violent symptoms. I have frequently cured cases with a ten-grain dose of bromide of potassium, but any nerve

MISS FANNY BROUGH,

As Peg Woffington, from the picture by Joliffe Walker. Now in possession of the
Rev. Talfourd Major.
By permission of Miss Brough and the Rev. Talfourd Major.

sedative will be useful. It will be just as well to remember, however, that these nerve sedatives are extremely lowering, indeed dangerous, if taken to any extent, and bromides should be used most sparingly.

Perhaps the very worst thing to take is alcohol in any form, particularly brandy, except a few drops added to a spoonful of iced beef tea—not the greasy beef tea made on board, but made from the usual extracts, Bovril for choice. It must be remembered also that the beef tea must be taken in teaspoonfuls at intervals, for what has to be avoided is to give the stomach, which is in an irritated condition, much to do. It is advisable to lie as flat as possible, without a pillow, and to give with the motion of the vessel. Above all it should be borne in mind that on deck is the best place to combat this insidious enemy. Nothing is so conducive to a continuance of the complaint as the close atmosphere below.

ENTERTAINMENTS ON BOARD.

One of the items of the voyage is the entertainment, which usually takes place the night before the arrival, and it is then that the wisdom of those who can sing in putting a song or two in their cabin trunk is evident. The proceeds are given to the various charitable institutions.

One thing to be most careful about is card playing, for sharpers travel on nearly every boat, on the look-out for dupes, and long practice has made them most plausible and seductive in their manner of approaching a victim. They are, as a rule, quite well known to the officers on board ship, but, beyond the usual notice cautioning the passengers regarding this evil, little can be done. I have known, however, in flagrant cases stringent action on the part of the captain.

SANDY HOOK AND CUSTOMS.

On the arrival at Sandy Hook the medical and Customs officers come on board, and then the fun begins. A medical inspection takes place, which, however, is not so minute among the saloon passengers as in the second class.

This done, you are handed over to the tender mercies of the Customs and immigration officers, and various forms have to be filled up with particulars which need not be recapitulated here, for the forms are handed round and instructions given regarding the filling of them up. It is necessary, however, to remember the information given at the beginning of this article regarding the amount of money in your possession and whether you paid your passage yourself.

As regards what may be taken into the United States free from a foreign country, the position in life of the immigrant is taken into consideration. The personal effects of a saloon passenger would naturally be of a more extensive and expensive description than, say, those of a steerage passenger; but it may be taken for granted that clothing and effects for the personal use of the individual arriving are admitted without question, but in every case the articles should bear evidence of wear, except, of course, gloves and such items of a like nature which are intended to last during your stay in the country.

Members of the dramatic and musical profession were allowed great latitude in this respect formerly, but the generosity of the Customs officials has been so abused that instead of having their baggage hastily examined as before on the arrival pier, the latest regulation is for them to be taken to the Appraiser's Office (John Wanamaker), who, however, shows every consideration to the artists. The uncouth and brutal manner of many of the Continental officials is not met with. In all my experience I have not known a single instance of incivility on the part of the Customs officers on arrival at the piers at New York. Indeed, the deputies, Messrs. Bishop and Matt Coneys, seem to take a pleasure in rendering the task of examination as little irksome as possible. The new regulations necessarily absorb more time, but I rather imagine that they are only temporary, and that before very long a reversion will be made to the original method.

On landing the first thing to do is to see that all your baggage is placed under the proper initial. This is when you will find the benefit of the distinctive mark on your trunks, for there will be no rushing backwards and forwards to discover a missing piece of luggage. When you have all in readiness you take your place in the line before the desk of the Chief Customs Inspector and await your turn. You give your name and receive a ticket, and, armed with this, you are put in charge of an inspector, who will overhaul your stuff and mark it for removal. Outside the barrier you give your luggage to the express man to forward to any address you may have. Should you, however, not have an address ready, it may be left at the

Customs for twenty-four hours free, but after that period rather heavy storage fees are charged.

THROUGH THE CUSTOMS.

When you have got through the Customs examination, it will be necessary to see about your baggage being sent to the place decided upon as your residence while in New York. For cartage a charge of forty cents (1s. 8d.) is made for each article, large or small, and in view of this it is advisable to have as few packages as possible. Don't buy expensive trunks in England. They will be smashed to smithereens on the first trip. Procure the usual theatrical trunks in use in the States, which defy an elephant's attempt at destruction.

An important thing to remember is the high charges made for cabs in the cities, nothing, as a rule, being under one dollar. There is a movement on foot to reduce these prices, and certain cab companies have a charge for a certain distance of fifty cents. The omnipresence of the street car, subways, and elevated railways renders one practically independent of cabs.

COINAGE.

The coinage will be rather difficult to understand, owing to its extreme simplicity. Except for the smallest amounts, in New York at least, and the Eastern States, paper money is used, but out West and down South silver and gold are more generally used.

The smallest coin is the cent, equal to our halfpenny; the next is the five-cent piece, usually termed a nickel, being made of that metal. It is equal to twopence halfpenny. This is, perhaps, the coin most used in the States, owing to the fact that the car rides are almost invariably that amount. Then comes the ten-cent piece, or dime, so called because it is the tenth part of a dollar. It is equal to our fivepence. Then comes the twenty-five-cent piece, or quarter as it is termed, since it is the fourth of a dollar, and is generally looked upon as the equivalent of the shilling, though in reality it is one cent or a halfpenny more. Then comes the fifty-cent piece, or half. This is considered the equivalent of the two-shilling-piece, though it contains one penny or two cents more. The dollar is mentioned elsewhere, but it may be borne in mind that very few silver dollars are in circulation except in the districts already referred to.

LIVING.

It is most advisable to inquire of one of the passengers a likely hotel where you may pass the first night until you are able to make arrangements for your permanent stay if you remain in New York long. In the event of a long stay it is usually most economical and advantageous to take a room, if by yourself, in a private house in the neighbourhood of West Fifty-first Street, where a very nice room, with hot and cold running water and the use of a bath, may be obtained for five dollars (one pound) and upwards. Hotels are more expensive. If more than one, say a wife and "encumbrances," a furnished flat may be obtained at a very reasonable rate. The desirability of living in this style arises from the fact that the commissariat department in boarding-houses and hotels in the United States does not quite agree with the insular ideas of the Britisher, and for a time at least, until you have become acclimatised to the stomach-trying food in vogue in America, it will be as well to cater for yourself. If care be taken in the respect of living this way, the expenses in the States are not so appalling; indeed, three pounds per week make a very liberal allowance. But, of course, you must not expect to live at the Waldorf-Astoria for this amount. For the individual who values his health, it may be just as well to mention that the various seductive compounds under the cocktail denomination are most destructive. The careful man, who desires to live well and comfortably, will never take a drink of any sort in a saloon, but will go to the best wine and spirit stores, where the best stuff is sold, Macy's for choice, and pay a good price and get a warranted article.

REMITTING MONEY HOME.

When you have settled down, and are earning a salary, it is necessary to know as to the best means of remitting money home. In New York this may be accomplished through the American Express Company at their offices near Thirty-ninth Street, on Broadway.

In order to understand the remitting of money at the least possible cost, it will be necessary to understand the coinage with regard to the relative value of the two countries. The cent is the equivalent of one halfpenny, and one hundred cents, or one hundred halfpennies, make one dollar, or four shillings and twopence. Now, there are four hundred and eighty halfpennies in one pound, so that four hundred and eighty cents, or four dollars and eighty cents, represent the normal value of the English sovereign. It may, however, be understood that the bankers are not going to send the money without a consideration, and that is represented by the rate of exchange, which fluctuates with the demand. Sometimes it goes up to as much as four hundred and ninety-five or six, though this is heavy. I have bought as low as four hundred and eighty-three. These figures mean that for each pound sent home at the highest rate mentioned the cost is eightpence, and at the lowest three-halfpence. It may be easily understood that in cases of large amounts it is greatly to one's advantage to get a low rate. At the post-office, in addition to a fixed rate, they charge for the order.

The banks have a "flat" rate of 4.88, and some even 4.90, but the American Express, for all amounts over ten pounds, will give market rate, or perhaps a slight shade above it. If the rate of exchange is watched a large amount may be saved. As a matter of fact, I find the officials most obliging and willing to give me information regarding the tendency of the market.

For use on the voyage one should buy a few dollars at one of the numerous money-changers in London, providing you can get them within a reasonable relation to 4.80. On board their arithmetic is of the simplest description. Five dollars go to the pound, a loss of tenpence on the home journey. On the outward journey sixpence is accepted as the equivalent of the dime, or ten cents, otherwise fivepence.

CONCLUDING ADVICE.

I think that this is about all the information I can get into the space, so I will conclude by giving a little advice which may prove of great assistance. While in the States remember that you "cannot expect a' the comforts of the Saut mairket when ye gang visiting your Hielan' kinsfolk," and that because you have not been used to them, the habits of the people you are amongst are not necessarily incorrect, no matter how objectionable they may be to you. Remember you are in the way of being a guest there, and take matters as they come. The universal worship of the dollar may be distasteful to the average English mind, but you will find the usual mix-up of bad and good. Above all, put out of your mind that the American actor is "up against" the English professional; nothing is farther from the truth. From a long experience I have always found the greatest courtesy and hospitality at the hands of the American, both professional and private. Indeed, most of the incivility and brusqueness has been forthcoming from English actors who have been in America for a little time, and have been successful. Underline in your mind that if you don't care for the country or the people, there is nothing to compel you to remain. So don't kick when you are scooping in the dollars from Uncle Sam. If you feel hurt, jump on the steamer and go home.

SOCIETY OF AUTHORS (INCORPORATED).

Dramatic authors stand in the position of having no society of their own to look after their interests exclusively. During the year 1908 several meetings of dramatists were held, under the chairmanship of Mr. A. W. Pinero, when the question of establishing such a society was under consideration. Eventually, however, in December, it was decided not to disturb the existing arrangement by which dramatists are represented in the Society of Authors through the medium of a Sub-Committee. The Society of Authors has a Council of more than sixty, and a Committee of Management consisting of:—Mr. Douglas Freshfield (Chairman), Mrs. E. Nesbit Bland, Mr. J. W. Comyns Carr, the Hon. Mrs. Alfred Felkin (Ellen Thorneycroft Fowler), Mr. Maurice Hewlett, Mr. Sidney Lee, Mr. Arthur Rackham, Mr. G. Bernard Shaw, Sir Squire Sprigge, Mr. Francis Storr, and Mr. Sidney Webb. The Dramatic Sub-Committee is constituted by the following:—Mr. Henry Arthur Jones (Chairman), Mr. William Archer, Mrs. E. Nesbit Bland, Mr. H. Granville Barker, Mr. J. W. Comyns Carr, Mr. Jerome K. Jerome, Mr. W. J. Locke, Mr. W. Somerset Maugham, Capt. Robert Marshall, Mr. Paul Rubens, and Mr. G. Bernard Shaw. Copyright Sub-Committee:—Mr. Harold Hardy, Mr. Anthony Hope Hawkins, Mr. E. J. MacGillivray, Sir Gilbert Parker, M.P., Sir Charles Villiers Stanford, Mus. Doc., and Mr. J. H. Yoxall, M.P. Secretary:—Mr. G. Herbert Thring. Offices:—39, Old Queen Street, Storey's Gate, S.W.

ACTORS' DAY.

THE initiation of Actors' Day took place on Thursday, October 18, 1906. The Organising Committee appointed by the Council of the Actors' Association were Messrs. Acton Bond, A. E. Drinkwater, Norman McKinnel, Cecil Raleigh, and Brandon Thomas. The Trustees were Sir George Lewis, Sir Squire Bancroft, and Mr. George R. Sims. The idea was thus set out :—

That in every Theatre in the United Kingdom, on one night in every year, actors should combine to make provision for their Funds and Charities. That the date shall be the third Thursday in October. Actors and Actresses, wherever acting, are asked to give their services for this one night without salary. Authors are invited to allow their plays to be acted for this one night without fee. Managers are invited, for this one night, to give their total receipts.

The result of the collection was not made known until January 10, 1907, when at a meeting held in the St. James's, with Sir Squire Bancroft in the chair, the report of the Organising Committee disclosed that, though before the appointed day the Committee had 2,214 promises of support, only about 867 of this number actually gave to the Fund, the amount received being £1,469 2s. 1d. The appointment of an Advisory Board was confirmed at this meeting, and it was left with the Board to draw up a scheme for the distribution of the money collected.

After some proposals were made to the Actors' Benevolent Fund, which the Committee of that body refused to entertain, the Advisory Board eventually handed over £622 14s. 7d. to the Benevolent Fund, £40 to the Actors' Orphanage Fund, and £40 to the Theatrical Ladies' Guild.

The annual meeting in 1903 was held on Thursday, March 19, on the stage at the Kingsway, with Mr. Laurence Irving in the chair, when it was stated that the subscribers numbered 331 and had subscribed £363 15s. 6d. As the subscribers had been supplied with forms on which they could indicate the objects to which they wished their money to be devoted, it was found that up to that date the wishes of the contributors were as follows :—That £41 15s. be given to the Actors' Benevolent Fund, £22 4s. 9d. to the Actors' Orphanage Fund, and £22 19s. 9d. be given to the Theatrical Ladies' Guild.

This meeting had the satisfying quality of producing a definite outline of the object of the Fund. What Mr. Irving described as a " contradiction that had hitherto hampered their actions at every turn," the clause that suggested the Actors' Day was to " benefit existing charities," had, it was stated, been eliminated. Actors' Day was to stand on the basis of a thrift society, to be worked on the principle of mutual relief, so that only those who contributed should have power to draw on it or participate in any of the benefits it might offer. " We must freely admit," said Mr. Irving, " that the contradiction crept into the drafting of the first announcement of Actors' Day. The contradiction was that actors were invited to relinquish a night's salary (1) in order to benefit existing theatrical charities, (2) in order to establish a fund to which contributors could appeal, not as a charity, but as a right." " These two aims," added Mr. Irving, " were incompatible."

The balance-sheet to the end of September, 1908, was published in December. It showed that during the year September, 1907, to September, 1908, £320 had been contributed towards the Actors' Day Fund. £31 4s. had been spent in grants and loans (less amount repaid), and £167 9s. 10d. on rent, office fittings, advertisements ; printing, postage, etc. At the end of September the Fund had a balance of £841 7s. 3d. in hand. At the end of December the contributions received on account of the 1908 Actors' Day, which fell on October 15, were £258 14s. 7d.

The Advisory Board stands as follows :—

Chairman, Mr. Sydney Valentine.   Deputy Chairman, Mr. Henry Ainley.

Mr. Blake Adams,	Mr. Burton Cooke,	Mr. Walter Maxwell,
Mr. George Alexander,	Mr. Alfred Denville,	Mr. W. H. Rotherham,
Mr. Allan Aynesworth,	Mr. Kenneth Douglas,	Mr. H. A. Saintsbury,
Mr. Cecil Barth,	Miss Vane Featherston,	Mr. E. Lyall Swete,
Mr. A. E. Bishop,	Mr. J. Forbes-Robertson,	Mr. Brandon Thomas,
Mr. Arthur Bourchier,	Mr. C. T. H. Helmsley,	Mr. H. Beerbohm Tree,
Miss Fanny Brough,	Mr. Laurence Irving,	Miss Beatrice Wilson.
Mr. C. Hayden Coffin,		

Hon. secretary, Mr. A. E. Drinkwater, Dudley House, 37, Southampton Street, London, W.C.

"THE THIEF" AT THE ST. JAMES'S.

Mrs. Irene Vanbrugh and Mr. George Alexander

SUCCESSES OF THE YEAR. VI.

Foulsham & Banfield

"THE PASSING OF THE THIRD FLOOR BACK" AT THE ST. JAMES'S.

(Later Transferred to Terry's.)

MISS GERTRUDE ELLIOTT, MR. WILFRED FORSTER, MISS ALICE CRAWFORD, MR. ERNEST HENDRIE, MR. FORBES ROBERTSON, MISS KATE CARLYON,
MISS KATE BISHOP, MR. IAN ROBERTSON, MISS HALDEE WRIGHT. MR. EDWARD SASS and MISS AGNES THOMAS.

"IDOLS" AT THE GARRICK.

Miss Fanny Brough (in the box), Mr. Herbert Waring (at table), Mr. Howard Sterne (the Judge), Mr. Charles Brookfield, Mr. C. W. Somerset (leading Counsels), Mr. Allan Aynesworth (in the dock).

SUCCESSES OF THE YEAR VIII.

"DIANA OF DOBSON'S" AT THE KINGSWAY.

Dover Street Studios.

The Third Act. Mr. Dennis Eadie, Miss Gertrude Scott, Miss Lena Ashwell, Mr. C. M. Hallard, and Miss Frances Ivor.

"THE ACTOR'S ART."*

By J. FISHER WHITE.

IN most respects I feel but poorly equipped for the task I have undertaken. I am neither philosopher, metaphysician, nor dialectician. "I only speak right on: I tell you that which you yourselves do know." In other words, what I write is the outcome of personal experience, rather than of abstract study—is what I feel, rather than what I know.

WHAT THE ACTOR'S ART MEANS TO THE ACTOR.

I propose to speak of the Actor's Art from the inside point of view; to give you my own experience of what the actor's art means to the actor. The very title of this article begs the question, often disputed, whether acting may or may not justly be dignified by the name of art. I am not going to enter into any discussion on this point. It belongs more to the "outside" aspect of the actor's activity, and is to be considered in estimating the position of this activity in the body politic. For my own part, I am content to accept Tolstoi's definition of Art, and then to leave it to reasonable minds to say whether acting is art. This is the definition, "Art is a human activity, consisting in this, that one man consciously, by means of certain external signs, hands on to others feelings he has lived through, and that other people are infected by these feelings, and also experience them." Accepting this definition, I dismiss the question, and take it for granted henceforth in this paper that acting is art. Indeed, perhaps no other of the arts so completely fulfils the conditions of this definition as does the actor's art.

THE TRAINING OF THE ACTOR.

Our subject naturally divides itself into the two main departments of training and practice. though, of course. there is no hard and fast line of division between them; and, indeed, it is very doubtful whether it can ever be said that the actor's training has ceased. Few, at least, would venture to say that they had nothing more to learn. We are familiar with the old dictum that it "takes ten years to make an actor." Some gallant gentlemen—or could it be some sarcastic Suffragette—has added, "and five years to make an actress."

To deal first, then, with the training of the actor. I am not one of those who advocate an early specialised training. I would suggest that the actor and actress should have the ordinary general schooling of the average boy and girl, without any specialisation whatever with a view to their subsequent career.

THE ATHLETIC INSTINCT.

Let the boys be proficient in all athletic exercises and games. How useful to them afterwards in heroic *rôles* to have the instinct of the athlete in the carriage of spear or sword, or in the mimic struggle or fight! Let the girls, too, acquire firmness of muscle and steadiness of nerve in the gymnasium or the field, even perhaps to the extent of playing that ungainliest of games, hockey. One is told to admire the technical proficiency of the Japanese actors of the old national drama, whose training begins at the age of five years or thereabout. But, after all, this old drama of Japan is a pure convention, involving an elaborate specialised mechanism, and may be compared more properly with violin playing, or with pantomime, or acrobatics, or with certain trades, where certain muscles have to execute movements of such speed or complexity, that great skill cannot be acquired unless these muscles be early moulded into a particular habit of activity. The ordinary athletic training of the

---

* Mr. Fisher White read a paper on the above subject before the Playgoers' Club at the Hotel Cecil on October 18. He has revised and extended it for the purpose of this article.

average boy or girl may possibly produce some excessive development of certain muscles, resulting in the physical condition generally known as being "muscle-bound." But this condition is not an essential result of athleticism; it arises from faulty athletics, and may, as we shall see presently, be cured by subsequent specialised physical training. At any rate, I am sure it is better for the actor to have acquired the athletic instinct, even at the expense of some subsequent pains to unbind or loosen some of his muscles.

MIND TRAINING.

And what of the early training of the mind of the actor or actress? Does some learned "opposer" murmur that the mind of the actor is of no account? Well, there is something in that argument, as we shall see later on, for it is more essential for the actor to feel than to think. Nevertheless, the culture of the mind is important. A treasury of knowledge at once stimulates and renders more effective the faculty of observation, which is perhaps of greater value to the actor than to any other member of the community, unless it be to a member of the Criminal Investigation Department of Scotland Yard. There is, as I have often thought, not a little similarity between the calling of the actor and that of the detective. But that is by the way. Mind training, therefore, which succeeds in imparting an acute faculty of observation, and a restless spirit of inquiry, is as good for the future actor and actress as for the Astronomer Royal or the latest aeroplanist.

PRELIMINARY EXPERIENCE OF THE PRACTICAL.

Our budding stage-aspirant has now left school, in the ordinary acceptance of the term. Should he or she at once proceed to the specialised training which I, for one, deem necessary to the practice of the actor's art? I think not. I would have him or her enjoy some short experience of commerce, or law, or medicine, or journalism, or what not; of some phase of life which is practical rather than emotional. Such an experience will prove useful in the business side of the actor's calling, though that does not concern my present argument. It will aid the actor's art by enlarging his knowledge of men, and of the motives which influence them; by teaching him the "perspective" of life, and its relative values; by giving him a sense of proportion. For though imagination plays the chief part in the art of the actor, yet experience fills a position nearly as important. My contention is supported, though not proved, by the fact that most of our eminent actors have followed for a time other callings before turning to the exclusive cult of Thespis. And I know one actor, not by any means eminent, who had never even been inside a theatre till he had passed the age of twenty years.

SPECIALISED TRAINING.

And now we come to the period in the actor's or actress's career when he or she must seek specialised training in the technique of the art. Let me not be misunderstood. An actor, like a poet, is born, not made. But the poet must know the rules of versification, as the painter must know the rules of perspective and the values of colours. So are there rules of the stage, which the actor must learn, and I maintain it is better for him to learn them systematically, than to pick them up haphazard in the course of painful experience. But the actor in one respect compares more closely with the musician than with either poet or painter: he can express himself only through the medium of a mechanical instrument. In the actor's case this instrument is his own body. It follows, then, that his chief concern must be to obtain an instrument which will express with completeness all that he may feel. In other words, the chief aim of his specialised training will be to acquire physical adaptability.

PHYSICAL ADAPTABILITY.

By physical adaptability I intend to convey a state of development in which the voice, the face, and the whole body of the actor shall be so pliable, so responsive, that they will instantly and instinctively adopt the tones, or the facial expressions, or the attitudes and movements of the character conceived, "his whole function suiting with forms to his conceit." The process should be automatic. The actor conceives old age, for example, and instinctively the tones of his voice, the expression of his face, and the movements of his limbs take upon themselves respectively the attributes of old age. There should be no painful mimicry of an individual, no laborious drilling of the face and limbs before a mirror, and registering of the drill upon the brain. But the actor's whole physique should, in the practice of his art, lose all personal idiosyncrasies. The idiosyncrasies he exhibits should be those of the character he represents. In fact, as I have said, the body of the actor may very aptly be compared to a musical instrument. It must be in tune, but passive, ready to be played on. Imagine the annoyance of the skilled pianist whose instrument should strike, independently of his fingers, one insistent note throughout every varying piece he played! And yet how often this phenomenon occurs upon our stage, apparently without annoyance either to the actor or to his auditor! But I have digressed, and am trespassing upon the province of the "practice" of the actor's art. "*Revenons à nos moutons.*"

I have said that the attainment of complete physical adaptability should be the chief aim of the specialised training of the would-be actor or actress. Let me quote Tolstoi once more:—"To evoke in oneself a feeling one has once experienced, and, having evoked it in oneself, then, by means of movements, lines, colours, sounds, or forms expressed in words, so to transmit that feeling that others may experience the same feeling—this is the activity of Art."

PHYSICAL ADAPTABILITY IMPLIES CONTROL.

Applying this statement to the art of acting, it is obvious that the more responsive or adaptable the body of the actor, the more readily and accurately will he be able to transmit his feeling so that others shall experience the same feeling. And physical adaptability implies control. The body of the actor—the instrument which he uses to transmit his feelings to others—should be passively ready to move at his will, and only as his will dictates; it should not have predilections towards one habit of movement more than to another. One may illustrate the point by a comparison between the actor's will and a hypnotist. Only when the subject has rendered his or her mind passive, can the hypnotist make a suggestion to do or think any given thing; only then, in the language of the science, does he gain control. The subject who will not surrender his will to the hypnotist; who is not passive, but insists on thinking for himself; who, in a word, "resists," is no subject for hypnotic treatment at all. It is exactly the same with the actor's will and the actor's body, by which I mean his whole physique. There must be no "resistance" in the actor's body, whether of nervous or muscular tension, or of habit, to the suggestion of his will. And how complete control of the body, which does not resist, obviates fatigue! And that which obviates fatigue gives power. To turn for a moment to a practical illustration. It is the voice which is obviously the most important, and at the same time the most delicate, portion of the actor's body, of the instrument by means of which he expresses himself. And what is the main factor in producing the voice? The breath. The actor should have, then—it seems almost too obvious to mention—lungs which are under his complete control, which adapt themselves at once to the requirements of his vocal activity. And it should be the same, of course, with the rest of his vocal organ. There must be no tension of nerve or muscle that is involuntary. The vocal apparatus must have no will of its own. It must be simply passive, adaptable, responsive, only contracting for a definite purpose, and at the will of its operator. Very little then would be heard of throat trouble, loss of voice, and other frequent ailments—haunting bugbears—of the actor's life. There would be less liability to fatigue, and more power in execution, with less effort.

EFFORT AS AGAINST POWER.

I am quite aware that, in some classes of the community, at least, *effort* stands for power. They like to see the mechanism working, and then they know they have their money's worth. A great friend of mine, an actor who has now attained a position of considerable eminence, will forgive me for telling a story which he has often told with charming humour against himself. You will understand that the incident I am about to relate happened many years ago, when he was yet an infant in the practice of his art. He was playing in Barnsley—a delectable resort in Yorkshire—and lodged under the roof of a sympathetic miner. One day his landlord come into the sitting-room and said, "I went to theatre last night to see thee. I think thou'rt finest actor we've had in Barnsley since Charley Melville. Why, the veins in thy neck stood out as thick as my thumbs!"

METHOD OF TRAINING.

Well, having tried to show how important for our young friends, the incipient actor and actress, is the attainment of physical adapability, which is to be the chief aim of their specialised training, it is now time to say one word about the method of training to be adopted. The method is simple, like every good thing in art. As we have seen, our young friend has been through his or her ordinary schooling, followed by a short period of experience in the world of commerce, or what not. If a boy, he may, and probably has, acquired some undue development of certain muscles, owing to the faults of an athletic training which falls short of perfection; and this has resulted in his being, perhaps, what is called "muscle-bound," in his having a cramping tension of the limbs. If a girl, she will probably have less of this muscular tension, but will suffer, on the other hand, from nervous tension more than does the boy.

Relaxation of the Body.

The first thing then is to "loosen up" both boy and girl. To induce a relaxation of the body, of the voice, facial muscles, and limbs, in order that they may have no idiosyncratic habits of activity, which might possibly be at variance with the activity of any particular character that our young friend may be called upon to impersonate. And it is not so easy as it sounds to induce this state of relaxation. The stress of our modern civilisation—with which, by the way, the actor should have nothing to do!—causes us all to "hold on" to ourselves, as it were. We must have, then, exercises for our young stage aspirants, in the patient practice of which they shall attain the capability of relaxing all muscular and nervous tension at will. Don't mistake my meaning. I would not for a moment wish to convey the idea that actors and actresses should be "floppers." What I mean is that they should be able at any moment to "switch off" the tension. It is not a continued state of relaxation that I advocate, but a capability of relaxation at any moment.

Power Through Repose.

And, indeed, far from producing "floppiness," this capability will produce greater activity. It is quite natural. It is the old principle of the conservation of energy. It is "power through repose." And this capability to relax should include the whole physique—the voice, the face, the body and limbs. Then, when our young friend has acquired this capability of relaxing, he or she must have other reconstructive exercises designed to train the various muscles to move in such a way that they may produce the maximum of effect with the minimum of effort. Remember the actor's body is the instrument of his art, and his body is liable to fatigue; his training, therefore, must aim at postponing the coming of fatigue as long as possible. But, not only that, these exercises must aim at producing flexibility, pliability, responsiveness, alertness; the capability of carrying out with speed and efficiency the orders of the brain, and of expressing with fidelity and completeness the feelings of the soul.

Voice Must be Trained.

For instance, the voice must be trained for resonance, for attack, for flexibility. What nonsense to say that this, the most important, as I said just now, and the most delicate part of the actor's instrumental equipment, should not be trained! One has heard it said that voice-production ruins spontaneity; that it "kills acting." If acting consists in having a voice of some peculiar quality which happens to suit some particular character, or class of characters, then this might be true. But I venture to think that the real actor's voice—perhaps I should say the ideal actor's voice—should be capable of suiting any part. And then the body and limbs, too, must be exercised for pliability and for responsiveness. In this age of mind even our bodies have become mentalised, as it were. Our carriage, our walk, and our gestures have lost the grace of the less-civilised man. Witness the movements, for instance, of a Zulu or other African savage of the best type. There is a litheness, a smoothness, a succession and co-ordination, which we, as a rule, entirely lack.

The Actor should be to some extent Elemental.

Now the actor must be to some extent elemental. When he has to portray a character in modern civilised life, he must adopt the characteristics of the modern man as he would those of an old man, or a lunatic, or any other individual outside the normal. Hence, our student must practise exercises which will train his muscles to move in proper succession, that is to say, to move in such a way that one may see the passage of the impulse from the nerve centres in the brain to each muscle in succession; the muscle nearest to the brain moving first, and so on till the extremity is reached by the impulse. Patient practice induces a habit, and

MME. SARAH BERNHARDT.

As Adrienne Lecouvreur, from the picture by W. Graham Robertson.

By permission of the Artist.

habit obliterates thought. Thus, properly practised, there is no fear of the student becoming mechanical in his movements. The study of voice-production, or any method of physical training, only becomes valuable when the student is able to forget that he has learnt it. Let it not be thought that I am implying that gesture can be taught. No fallacy was ever more pernicious; and woe betide the unfortunate student who allows himself to be imposed upon in this respect. It is, as I say, the habit which should be acquired; and that is second nature.

PERSONALITY AND A CRIPPLING CUSTOM.

I often think with sorrow that it is due to a lack of physical adaptability in us actors, that the most pernicious custom now prevails upon our stage of casting for each part in a play only the actor whose own personality nearest approaches that of the character to be portrayed. Owing to this crippling custom the actor, in play after play, merely reproduces himself. It is not acting; it is pot-boiling. The actor thus compares with the painter who, having once painted a picture containing a presentable hippopotamus, and sold it, puts a hippopotamus into every picture he paints henceforth.

FROM TRAINING TO PRACTICE.

And now our would-be actor and actress, having learnt something of the technicalities of their art, emerge from the student state into that of the professor, and pass from the period of training to that of practice. Now, and only now, do they discover—or do other people discover for them, a less pleasant alternative—whether or not they are artists, whether or not they can act. There is no school and no system of training, no matter how good, that can justly claim to teach acting, to turn out actors and actresses. As I said before, an actor is born, not made. Well, the first consideration for our young people is, of course, to obtain an engagement. Not an easy thing to do, by any means.

SCHOOLS AND REPERTORY THEATRES.

In this connection it is much to be desired that every school of dramatic art should have working in conjunction with it a repertory theatre, into which the finished students (I use the word "finished" in a temporal sense!) might be drafted, and put through their paces. Those who had the gift of acting would get the chance of being seen by people whose business it is to find actors and actresses; and those who had not the gift would be "weeded out," with less heart-burning, perhaps, than in the commercial theatre, and with less damage to the sensibility of the public.

REPERTORY COMPANIES.

In default of such a theatre, I would advise our young friends to make every endeavour to enter a repertory company. Here they will have many parts to study, and but few rehearsals, and here the stage manager will not have time to give them too much attention. They will be thrown upon their own resources; they will have to "work out their own salvation." The public may suffer at first, but they will be the gainers in the long run! I can conceive of nothing worse for the young man or woman starting upon a stage career than to obtain a part in a company which is going to play in the provinces a piece produced in London. The part is a small one, as a rule—though, perhaps, not as small as it ought to be—and the young person is painfully drilled by the stage manager to imitate, word for word, gesture for gesture, even glance for glance, the actor or actress who played the part in the London production. Is there any art in this? Is there any acting? Rather, is the system not wholly pernicious from beginning to end?

OLD STOCK DAYS AND SCOPE FOR ORIGINALITY.

It is a pity for our young actors and actresses of to-day that the old stock companies have vanished. There, indeed, if one may believe the tales that are told, were beginners given opportunity to "find themselves." In the old days it meant very often, of course, that they acquired bad mannerisms, which no one had the grace, or the time, to correct; but, at least, there was left some scope for originality—without which where is Art? With proper training beforehand, such as I have tried to sketch out for you—training which would have given them a knowledge of the why and the wherefore of things in their art—there could, I feel sure, be nothing better for young people starting the dramatic life than a long stock season.

Be Sincere.

And now, having started our young friends in the practice of their art, let me make one earnest appeal to them. I would say to them : Be sincere. Be faithful to your own feeling, and strive to express that feeling. Be true to your conception of a character. Do not be swayed by any consideration as to whether your conception will please, will be attractive. If you are an artist, and know your art, your feeling will ring true, and will arouse similar feeling in your audience.

The Feeling is the Thing.

The feeling is the thing. People have asked the question, "Masks or Faces?" There is no doubt about it. "Faces have it" every time! Of course, the actor feels. To examine the question more scientifically. The same nerve-centres— "sensori-motor arcs" physiologists call them, I believe—are excited when the actor expresses an emotion (or a feeling) in the practice of his art as are excited when in ordinary life he experiences that emotion or feeling. In the latter case the stimulus comes through the senses; in the former through the imagination. Why (apart altogether from acting), the feeling of physical pain can be experienced as vividly through the imagination as through sensation. Does it alter the case that with the actor the stimulus comes from within himself, and not through one or more of his five senses? And, moreover, the movements expressive of the feeling are the same in acting as in real life. Let me quote an instance in proof of this. Many years ago an actor was playing one Marrall in *A New Way to Pay Old Debts,* by Philip Massinger. Marrall is a pettifogging attorney, the tool of Sir Giles Overreach in his villainous practices. But Sir Giles gives him "more kicks than halfpence," and Marrall hates, while he fears, his master. Opportunity occurs to obtain revenge. He engrosses an important deed in ink that will fade completely away. That deed is afterwards called for by Sir Giles as proof of some act of spoliation. Marrall produces it—a mere blank parchment. He is now under the protection of the man whom Sir Giles would have robbed. The fury of triumphant revenge for long-endured oppression comes upon him ; and Marrall, from a safe distance, turns upon Sir Giles with a torrent of abuse. On the first night on which the actor I speak of played this scene his sub-conscious mind registered the fact that he was jumping off the floor both feet at once. This phenomenon came as a complete surprise to him. So far from having conceived this gesture when studying the part, it was not till afterwards that he discovered—I think in Darwin's "Expression of the Emotions"—that this gesture is characteristic of extreme anger among monkeys, apes, and primitive man! Does not this go to prove that the anger this actor was then expressing in his capacity of actor was the same feeling as that he might have expressed in similar circumstances in ordinary life, had he been an elemental person like Master Marrall? But this is not by any means an isolated instance even in this actor's experience, and I suppose there is no actor to whom something similar has not occurred. Therefore I am bold to say once more, "Of course, the actor feels." And woe be to the actor who would save himself the pain and the exertion of feeling by mechanically imitating himself, by consciously reproducing merely the outward signs of feeling he has once felt! This is insincerity.

Be Simple.

Then be sincere; "add but the other grace," Be simple. Don't embroider; don't over-elaborate. Let the idiosyncrasies of your impersonation grow out of your conception of the character, be suggested by your feeling. Do not take a peculiarity or a mannerism mechanically practised and graft it on to the outside of your character, just because you think it will be effective. That is not art. And when you abandon truth for popularity, sincerity for attractiveness, and simplicity for elaboration, you cease to be an artist, and become merely a showman.

Conclusion.

Let me, in conclusion, proclaim my conviction that to him who follows it, not for ambition solely, nor for filthy lucre, but with a single-hearted purpose to become as perfect in his art as lies within his power—to him, I am convinced, the actor's art brings such consolation as few other forms of human activity can bring. Perhaps it is fitting that the actor should with his art infect his fellow-beings more potently than any other artist ; because his work is of all the most fleeting, and perishes with himself.

"JACK STRAW" AT THE VAUDEVILLE.

Seated: Mrs. Harry Clift, Miss Van Tuyll, &c., &c., Mrs. Max Hecht, Mrs. Charles Bewrey, Mrs. Pool Facer, &c., Miss Van Tuyll. *Standing:* Mrs. Detail Webb, and Mrs. Roorje Webb, &c.

SUCCESSES OF THE YEAR X.

"THE MARRIAGES OF MAYFAIR" AT DRURY LANE. ["Daily Mirror" Studio.

Deerminster Chase. Third scene in the first act.

"MRS. DOT" AT THE COMEDY.

Miss Marie Illington, Mr. Kenneth Douglas, Mr. Fred Kerr, Miss Marie Tempest, Mr. Graham Browne, Mr. Robert Ross, and Miss Iris Hawkins.

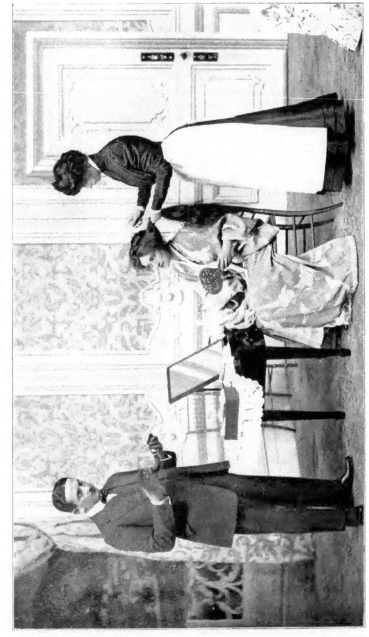

Dover Street Studios.

"LADY FREDERICK."

The Dressing Room Scene. MR. GRAHAM BROWNE, MISS ETHEL IRVING, and MISS ISA PELLY.

"ROGUES AND VAGABONDS."

AN EXPLANATORY NOTE.

BY BERNARD WELLER.

T HE position of actors before the law is, historically, a long, vague, and complicated one. It is the more so because it has to be considered in conjunction with a non-statutory control of the stage, prevailing up to 1737. To deal with it in much detail is not possible in a short article. It appears to be a position that has hitherto been very sparingly examined. There has been plenty of picturesque writing about the stage of the past, but it has been mostly biographical, mostly of actors in their individual capacities. The legal status of actors is another matter altogether ; and the sundry scattered enactments that cover it—enactments, as far as I have been able to trace them, from the remnant of an Act of Edward III. to 6 and 7 Vict., c. 68—do not seem to have invited much attention. There is a lingering notion in the popular mind that by an old Act—a dead letter, but figuring on the Statute-book—actors are still rogues and vagabonds. Many know better than that, of course, but these latter have little or no idea when, if ever, in the eyes of the law actors were rogues and vagabonds ; to what extent actors were rogues and vagabonds—whether the whole body or certain sections of it—or when and how actors ceased to be rogues and vagabonds.

Even authorities on statute law appear to go badly astray on the subject. Take, for example, a deliverance by the late Lord Russell of Killowen when Lord Chief Justice. Speaking at an annual dinner of the Royal General Theatrical Fund some years ago, Lord Russell said :—"Are you aware, gentlemen play-actors, that until the year 1825 you were one and all vagabonds by Act of Parliament?" The only authority that his lordship gave for this statement was the statute passed in the fourteenth year of the reign of Elizabeth, a portion of which he paraphrased thus :—"All fencers, bearwards, common players of interludes, and minstrels (not belonging to any baron of the realm or person of greater degree), wandering abroad without license of two justices at the least, are liable to be grievously whipped, and burned through the gristle of the ear with a hot iron of the compass of about an inch." Now this statement is erroneous and misleading ; and it is plainly absurd to quote in connection with it a statutory passage in open contradiction to the assertion that up to 1825 actors "one and all" were vagabonds by Act of Parliament. The Elizabethan Act that matters is the one passed in the thirty-ninth year of the reign. But the importance of 39 Eliz., c. 4—usually the statute solely referred to —is also much overrated. For one thing, this Act was repealed by 13 Ann., c. 26. But, more than that, it is not to the Elizabethan Act, which exempted all players acting under authority, that we must go for the severest form of legislation against actors. This statute did not condemn all actors as rogues and vagabonds ; whereas, it is to be feared, other enactments did.

" PLAYERS OF INTERLUDES."

In the early statutes and indeed up to the Act of 1737 the term used is "common players of interludes." In practice, there can be no doubt a distinction was observed between actors authorised in one form or another and wandering players of interludes. But interludes represented, roughly speaking, the first forms of secular drama following the mysteries and the moralities ; and the term, once having taken its place on the Statute-book, was repeated in successive Acts. The Elizabethan Acts exempted players of interludes acting under authority, using this term as covering all actors and all forms of play. That is to say, players of interludes were relieved from the provisions of the Acts in certain circumstances—(1) under 14 Eliz., c. 5, if belonging to a baron of the realm or personage of greater degree, or (2) if licensed by two justices; and under 39 Eliz., c. 4, only if in the service of a baron or higher personage. It seems a right construction therefore to say that actors of all classes of stage play were comprehended in the term players of interludes. The players were not, as individuals, continuously authorised in the foregoing ways; and when not so authorised they necessarily fell, in following their calling, within the meaning of these Vagrant Acts.

ENACTMENTS, ETC., PRIOR TO ELIZABETH.

Taking the history of the subject somewhat farther back, in 1378 a petition was presented to Richard II. quaintly praying him " to prohibit some unexpert people from presenting the history of the Old Testament, to the great prejudice of the said clergy, who have been at great expense in order to represent it publicly at Christmas." Earlier yet, in the reign of Edward III., an Act was passed ordaining that "a company of vagrants who have made masquerades be whipped out of London for representing scandalous things." 4 Henry IV., c. 27 (1402), makes mention of " certain wasters, master-rimours, minstrels, and other vagabonds infesting the land of Wales," and prohibits all such making " commoiths or gatherings upon the people there." 1 Ed. VI., c. 3 (1547), ordained that any able-bodied man or woman " loitering or idle-wandering by the highway side, or in streets, towns, or villages, not applying themselves to some honest and allowed art, science, service, or labour," could be taken and kept as a slave, and punished by beating, chaining, branding, and putting to death. How far acting was an allowed art at this period is very doubtful. In the reign of Henry VIII. various Vagrant Acts were passed, particularly 22 Henry VIII., c. 12, and 27 Henry VIII., c. 25. Herein amongst other dreadful penalties for vagrancy is that of being stripped naked and whipped at the coat-tail through the market-town. In another Act, 34 and 35 Henry VIII., c. 1, not vagrant, but dealing with the promotion of " true religion "—it imposes death " by burning at the stake for heresy—the realm is to be purged and cleansed of pestiferous and noisome ballads, plays, rhymes, songs." However, there is a provision to this effect :— " Provided always and be it enacted that it shall be lawful to all and every person to set forth songs, plays, and interludes, so always the said songs, plays, and interludes meddle not with interpretations of Scripture contrary to the doctrine set forth by the King's Majesty."

About this time, it should be noted, Henry instituted the dramatic censorship still surviving in the Lord Chamberlain. In 1544 Sir Thomas Carden was appointed " Magister jocorum revellorum et mascorum." It was then, and continued to be for many years, an authority without legislative sanction. The Magister had under his control the actors attached to the Royal household. During the next reign—Edward VI.—a Royal proclamation was issued, and in this proclamation a certain measure of authority was given to the Privy Council. The proclamation—which distinguished between " the King's players and the common players of interludes and plays "—temporarily forbade, in the name of the Privy Council, the performance of any stage play, on the ground that the plays then enacted did tend " to sedition and contemprying of sundry good orders and laws, whereupon are grown and daily are like to grow and ensure much disquiet, division, tumults, and uproars of this realm." Mary called the Star Chamber to the re-inforcement of the Privy Council and the Master of the Revels. In 1556 Lord Rich is informed that " order was given in the Star Chamber openly to the justices of the peace of every shire, this last term, that they should suffer no players, whatsoever the matter was, to play, especially this summer, which order his Lordship is willed to observe and to cause them that shall enterprise the contrary to be punished."

POLITICAL CONSIDERATIONS.

So far, very briefly, the early enactments and proclamations. It is obvious from them, especially to anyone who has made any researches into the subject, that Church and State looked askance at the stage. Even in its humble beginnings, Church and State scented heresy and sedition, realising the power of popular appeal that lay with the players—those " abstract and brief chronicles of the time," as Shakespeare, with a knowledge of the circumstances, called them. The injustice to the stage under the law undoubtedly sprang from political considerations. The poorer players were, as far as possible, reduced to vagabondage and persecuted under the Vagrant Acts. The remainder secured a limited recognition, a grudging and selfish recognition. They had, however, no real security under the law in their calling. Their plays were mutilated and disallowed; their performances were arbitrarily interfered with and summarily stopped; and they, in their own persons, were fined and thrown into prison. They were at the mercy of Court rule. This rule was unconstitutional, but it prevailed; and the reign of Elizabeth saw it supplemented by various measures of control—sometimes conflicting with that of the Court—on the part of the City. By an Act of Common Council in 1574 the Corporation sought to exercise the widest powers, harassing the players by all sorts of restrictions, and even prohibiting all plays in London. This particular prohibition brought the Corporation into conflict with the Privy Council. Later—in 1589—the Star Chamber instituted a triune censorship, representing the Crown, the Church, and the City. The alleged ground for this action was that the players handled "matters of Divinity and State without judgment or decorum." In 1596, through the Lord Mayor, the City "banished" the players for the time being. In 1600 the Privy Council restricted the number of playhouses to two—a very serious matter, seeing that at this time the playhouses in London were numerous. In *Biographia Dramatica* it is said that between the years 1570 and 1629 no fewer than seventeen playhouses were built. All this persecution of the more or less authorised players was beside the law. Perhaps most unconstitutional of all was the extraordinary patent granted by the Crown to one Tylney as Master of the Revels. Tylney was empowered to impress into service "all and every player or players, with their playmakers," and all necessary mechanics, and if they disobeyed his behests to put them in prison and keep them there at his pleasure—"any act, statute, ordinance, or provision heretofore had or made to the contrary hereof in any wise notwithstanding." In short, the players, where they did not suffer under the Vagrant Acts, had against them the arbitrary and illegal dictations of the Privy Council, the Star Chamber, the Master of the Revels, and the City of London.

The Elizabethan Acts.

Coming now to the Elizabethan statutes, the one referred to by Lord Russell— 14 Eliz., c. 5, was followed twenty-five years later by 39 Eliz., c. 4. which superseded it. 39 Eliz., c. 4, has, as has been noted, this difference from the preceding Act, that the proviso as to licensing by the justices disappears. This alteration must have fallen hardly on players not in the service of the Crown or the nobles. The amended section, as far as it relates to players, runs :—" All persons that be or utter themselves to be . . . fencers, bearwards, common players of interludes and minstrels wandering abroad, other than players of interludes belonging to any baron of this realm or any other person of greater degree, to be authorised to play under the hand and seal of such baron or personage . . . shall be taken, adjudged, and deemed rogues and vagabonds and sturdy beggars . . . and shall suffer such pain and punishment as by this Act is in that behalf appointed . . . be stripped naked from the middle upwards, and shall be openly whipped until his or her body be bloody . . . and shall be forthwith sent from parish to parish the next straight way to the parish where he or she was born or last dwelt by the space of one year." The poor wretch carries with him an official statement of his punishment, and if he does not reach his place of settlement within the time stipulated in this document his pace is to be quickened by scourging town by town on the way.

Acts of James I.

These statutes—1 Jac. I., c. 7, and 7 Jac. I., c. 4—are yet more drastic. The former puts the players farther—if not completely, in point of legal enactment— under the Vagrant Acts. 1 Jac. I., c. 7, says that no license by any nobleman shall exempt players. There being "divers doubts and questions for a plain declaration, be it declared and enacted that from henceforth no authority to be given or made by any baron of this realm or other honourable personage of greater degree unto any other person or persons shall be available to free and discharge the said persons or any of them from the pains and punishment in the said statute mentioned [39 Eliz., c. 4]." Thus the exemption previously enjoyed—in twofold form under the first Elizabethan Act named and in restricted form under the second—goes completely. It may be said that the regular actors were not common players of interludes. On the other hand, the Elizabethan Acts speak of the companies in the nobles' employ as the players of interludes. If this term did not sufficiently describe the companies, it would have been easy to use another. Perhaps "wandering abroad " is a saving clause to a certain extent. 7 Jac. 1., c. 4, amongst other things, gives the local authorities power to apprehend by warrant rogues and vagabonds for a general privy search twice a year.

LICENSES TO PLAYERS.

Yet the Court of James I. was not illiberal; and plays, interludes, and masques were in much favour at it. The King and Queen and courtiers frequently performed in the masques. Shakespeare was the great head of a brilliant group of poets, actors, and dramatists. In the same year as the Act denying to players the exemption enjoyed under the last Elizabethan Act, the King granted a license to Shakespeare and others, under the privy seal, in terms that form a curious commentary, in this respect, on that Act. "Know ye," ran the license, "that we have licensed and authorised these our servants, Lawrence Fletcher, William Shakespeare, Richard Burbage, and the rest of their associates freely to use and exercise the art and faculty of playing comedies, tragedies, histories, interludes, morals, pastorals, stage plays, and such-like other . . . within our realm and dominions." This list of plays, by the way, much suggests Polonius's. Further, James tells his subjects to allow the players "such former courtesies as hath been given to men of their place and quality . . . and also what further favour you shall show them we shall take kindly at your hands." A Royal license, granted by Elizabeth to Burbage and others about a quarter of a century earlier, also speaks of "the art and faculty" of playing. The license enjoins all justices and mayors to permit and suffer without hindrance or molestation the five servants of the Earl of Leicester to play comedies, tragedies, interludes, etc., "as well for the recreation of our loving subjects as for our own solace and pleasure when we shall think good to see them." The license applied "within and without all cities and boroughs throughout our realm of England." But no plays were to be performed until allowed by the Master of the Revels. The fact of these licenses certainly implies serious disabilities generally, but the phraseology is far from suggesting the statutory position of players of interludes.

THE ROUNDHEAD INTERDICTION.

No substantial change in the law appears to have taken place until the Revolution. Sir Henry Herbert was Master of Revels during the reign of Charles I., an able, if not impeccable holder of the office. His was a control of considerable latitude, except on the grounds of supposed profane matter or of alleged dangerous political matter. On the latter grounds, plays of Middleton, Massinger, and others were disallowed or suppressed. At the time of the first plague all shows and plays were stopped by order of the Lord Chamberlain; while, when the plague was over it was the King who withdrew the prohibition.

At the end of the first civil war, in 1646, came for the players their darkest hour. The Ordinance of the Lords and Commons for the total suppression of the stage was passed on February 11, 1647. Herein "it is ordered and ordained by the Lords and Commons in this present Parliament assembled that all stage players and players of interludes and common players are hereby declared to be and are and shall be taken to be rogues and vagabonds, and punishable within the statutes of the thirty-ninth year of the reign of Queen Elizabeth, and the seventh year of the reign of King James, and liable unto pains and penalties therein contained, and proceeded against according to the said statutes, whether they be wanderers or no, and notwithstanding any license whatsoever from the King or any person or persons to that purpose." Further, the justices and other authorities were required to pull down all play-houses within their respective jurisdictions, and to apprehend any person convicted of acting, who were to be whipped publicly and otherwise dealt with. Attendance at plays and shows by the public was also made an offence.

Prior to this Ordinance there had been considerable interference with the affairs of the stage under the rapid spread of Puritanism. The stage of the time was not in too cleanly a state, nor were its surroundings good. As much—not to say more—was admitted in that humiliating petition, "The Actors' Remonstrance and Complaint." The fact that most of the players capable of bearing arms joined the Royal cause naturally inflamed the Puritan temper towards the stage. Yet the stage was simply what the Court and the public had made it. The wonder is that the stage, never with any right independence of its own, always restricted, seldom free from persecution in one form or another, often proscribed, a calling under the stigma of the law—the wonder is that, in a free-living and free-spoken age, it should be no worse than it was.

THE RESTORATION RE-ACTION.

The Ordinance apparently was never formally revoked. A year or two after its enactment an attempt was made to give some plays at the Cockpit, Drury Lane, but it was sternly put down. Stray performances took place now and then, surreptitiously a little way from town, or privately at the houses of the nobility. But for all practical purposes the stage for some years ceased to exist. In 1656 Sir William d'Avenant adventured on quasi-classical exhibitions of music and declamation at Rutland House, which were not interfered with, and subsequently he gave similar entertainments at the Cockpit, concerning which, in 1658, Richard Cromwell required a report to be made. It was now, however, the eve of the Restoration. Richard Cromwell resigned the Protectorate in 1659. One Rhodes, a bookseller, who had had some minor theatrical connections, recruited a company, of which two members, apprentices of his, Betterton and Kynaston, were subsequently to become famous. He took the Cockpit. Another company began to act at the Red Bull in St. James's Street. Upon the Restoration, patents were granted to d'Avenant and Thomas Killigrew, whose respective companies, sworn by the Lord Chamberlain as servants of the Crown, became, after some migrations, established at Lincoln's Inn Fields and Drury Lane—the former known as the Duke of York's company, the latter as the King's. Sir Henry Herbert, that judicious scholar of the itching palm, had returned to his post of Master of the Revels; but the real powers of censorship were vested by Charles II., cynically enough, in those libertine wits, d'Avenant and Killigrew, who also, by their patents, had the monopoly of the London stage. Herbert stood out for his rights, and especially for his fees, evidently not without some effect, for an order of the Lord Chamberlain in 1661 required all local authorities to see that players, performers, and the like possessed a license from him, and to disallow all plays and shows without his sanction. But Herbert a few years later gave up the post; then d'Avenant died, and Killigrew became Master of the Revels. Killigrew's considerable reign was partial and corrupt. In 1697 came Jeremy Collier's hot and strong "Short View of the Profaneness and Immorality of the English Stage," a protest that the excesses of the indulgent period of the Merry Monarch—a period now three years at an end—had done much to provoke. Public opinion supported Jeremy Collier. William III., with his Dutch staidness, intervened. Court authority stiffened through the Lord Chamberlain; there were some prosecutions; and the stage, always sensitive to such phenomena, responded to the better conditions of Court life and public taste.

UNDER ANNE : NO EXEMPTION.

Meanwhile, legislation may be said to have stood still. In the next reign a Vagrant Act was passed. This Act—13 Anne, c. 26—otherwise 12 Anne, stat. 2, c. 23—includes as rogues and vagabonds ' all fencers, bearwards, common players of interludes, minstrels, jugglers "; and any person under the Act who has been sent to and wandered from his or her legal settlement is liable to be "stripped naked from the middle upwards and whipped until his or her body be bloody."

The Act repeals 39 Eliz., c. 4, 1 Jac. I., c. 7, and so much of 7 Jac. I., c. 4, as relates to privy search, though privy search is retained in another form. By Acts already repealed exemption from the Vagrant Acts by reason of license of justice and by service under baron or higher personage has ceased; and the new Act makes the position of players yet more unsatisfactory by omitting the words "wandering abroad." About this time the Lord Chamberlain arrogated to himself wide—and vexatious—powers. His proceedings, which were without statutory authority, do not affect the strict legal status of players, which this Act places in an extremely bad case.

WALPOLE'S VINDICTIVE ACT.

However, constitutional force for the Lord Chamberlain as Censor and as Licenser of theatres came about later on. But it arose, not as (in one sense) a measure of justice, but from political motive, and bad political motive. John Gay had satirised venality of politicians in *The Beggar's Opera*, and Henry Fielding in *Pasquin* and other pieces had pitilessly—and not less deservedly—held up Walpole and his corrupt administration to ridicule and contempt. For this wholesome work, done by the effective instrument of the stage, Walpole took a bitter revenge. It lay in the Bill of 1737, for which, in spite of much opposition, and in the face of Lord Chesterfield's brilliant speech, the Minister secured his servile majorities. Chesterfield's speech was chiefly directed against the injury that would be done to drama, wit, the freedom of speech, by placing them, as regards the theatre, under and subject to "the arbitrary will and pleasure of any one man." His lordship appears to have had little concern for the stigma under which the Bill placed the poor players. For how does the title of the Act—10 Geo. 2, c. 28—run? It runs :—

"An Act to explain and amend so much of an Act made in the Twelfth Year of the Reign of Queen Anne, intituled *An Act for reducing the Laws relating to Rogues, Vagabonds, Sturdy Beggars, and Vagrants into One Act of Parliament, and for the more effectual punishing such Rogues, Vagabonds, Sturdy Beggars, and Vagrants, and sending them whither they ought to be sent*, as relates to common players of interludes."

The Act, after reciting that, by 13 Anne, c. 26, all . . . common players of interludes are deemed rogues and vagabonds, and that, some doubts having arisen concerning so much of the said Act as relates to common players of interludes, it becomes necessary to explain the same : therefore be it declared and enacted that "every person who shall for hire, gain, reward, act, represent, or perform, or cause to be acted, represented, or performed, any interlude, tragedy, comedy, opera, play, farce, or other entertainment of the stage, or any part or parts therein, in case such person shall not have any legal settlement in the place where the same shall be acted, without authority by virtue of letters patent from His Majesty, his heirs, successors, or predecessors, or without license from the Lord Chamberlain, shall be deemed to be a rogue and vagabond within the intent of the said recited Act, and shall be liable to and subject to all such penalties and punishments and by such methods of conviction as are inflicted on or appointed by the said Act for the punishment of rogues and vagabonds who shall be found wandering or begging."

Nor is that all. Very few actors, of course, had a legal settlement in the places in which they acted ; yet the statute, as it goes on, takes away nearly all of what little exemption it has given. It further enacts that "no person having or not having a legal settlement as aforesaid shall be authorised by virtue of letters patent, or by the license of the Lord Chamberlain, to act, represent, or perform . . . any interlude, tragedy, comedy, opera, play, farce, or other entertainment of the stage in any part of Great Britain, except in the city of Westminster and within its liberties thereof and in such places as His Majesty, his heirs and successors shall in their Royal persons reside, and during such residence." The London theatres open at this time under one form of authority or another were, I believe, the patent theatres—Drury Lane and Covent Garden, and the Haymarket Theatre. It is not absolutely clear from the wording of the section whether a patent or a license from the Lord Chamberlain waives the matter of the place of settlement. In any case, the bulk of actors and other performers necessarily fell under the stigma of the Act.

Prior to this date a Bill had been brought in for the purpose of restraining the number of houses playing interludes and better regulating the players. Sir John Barnard, then Lord Mayor of London, introduced it to the Commons in 1734, on the grounds that the stage was corrupting the morals and undermining the sober business sense of the country. This severe religionist, however, objected to a proposal to give Parliamentary recognition to the Lord Chamberlain in the affairs of the stage. He disapproved of the exercise of the powers of the office, which he thought had been excessive and wanton, and rather than give Parliamentary effect to one-man rule, he withdrew his Bill. Walpole's Bill followed.

OTHER GEORGIAN ACTS.

Two Vagrant Acts—13 Geo. 2, c. 24, and 17 Geo. 2, c. 5—do not substantially alter the position. The former repealed the statute of Anne, but not 10 Geo. 2, c. 28. 17 Geo. 2, c. 5, which repeals 13 Geo. 2, c. 24, includes all players, except those authorised by law—in the way provided by 10 Geo. 2, c. 28. The Disorderly Houses Act—25 Geo. 2, c. 36—under which London music halls are still largely regulated, has not much bearing on the subject. Theatres run under nominal disguise under this Act were, of course. not duly authorised. In the following reign an Act was passed—28 Geo. 3, c. 30—enabling justices to license theatrical representations occasionally, under restrictions. This statute came into force in 1788, more than fifty years from the passing of 10 Geo. 2, c. 28. In the meantime various provincial cities and towns had by local Acts obtained exemption from the latter Act, which made performances illegal out of Westminster, etc. This Geo. 3 statute enables justices in session, under

MR. EDWARD COMPTON (as DAVID GARRICK).
Facsimile of the Presentation Oil Painting by Hermann Herkomer
Beautifully reproduced in Colour by MESSRS. DAVID ALLEN & SONS, LTD.

certain limitations, to license persons and places for the performance of the regular drama. It leaves offenders to be dealt with under the Vagrant Law. And this law continued in its old style. There were numerous Georgian amending Acts:— 23 Geo. 3, c. 88; 32 Geo. 3, c. 45; 3 Geo. 4, c. 40; and 3 Geo. 4, c. 55. It is unnecessary to go into these, except to say that the last-named—an Act for "ameliorating in one Act the laws relating to idle and disorderly persons, rogues and vagabonds, and incorrigible rogues and other vagrants in England," ordains in s. 3 that "all common stage players and all persons who shall perform or cause to be performed any interlude or entertainment or entertainments of the stage, or any part or parts therein, such persons not being authorised by law, shall be deemed rogues and vagabonds." That was in 1823.

THE RELIEVING ACT.

5 Geo. 4, c. 83, followed almost immediately. It was passed in 1824. It is the statute to the operation of which Lord Russell was referring when he said that up to 1825 actors one and all were vagabonds by Act of Parliament. The preamble sets out that "all provisions hitherto made relative to idle and disorderly persons, rogues, and vagabonds are hereby repealed." In s. 3 of this Act any mention of players is left out.

The Act of 10 Geo. 2, c. 28, with its comprehensive definition of players of interludes, made by Walpole when smarting under the castigation of the stage, was not repealed until the Theatres Act of 1843 ; and some may see a conflict in this fact and the other facts (1) that 5 Geo. 4, c. 83, repeals former Vagrant Acts and (2) does not legislate in any way against players. But the right view would seem to be that while actors—not all, but the great majority—were deemed rogues and vagabonds under Walpole's malicious Act—not to mention others—yet the repeal by 5 Geo. 4, c. 83, of all provisions then in force affecting rogues and vagabonds took them finally and completely out of this charming category in statute law.

ACTORS' ASSOCIATION.

(Incorporated under the Companies Acts, 1862 to 1900.)

The Actors' Association marked the closing of the eventful 1907 year (during which they had faced insolvency by an appeal to their members, which brought in £320) by a removal from 37, King Street, to 409 Strand. Here on Sunday, January 26, 1908, a house-warming dinner was held, with Mr. Cecil Raleigh in the chair. The Association had a well-attended annual general meeting at the Savoy on March 2, when a resolution approving of the £22 minimum and instructing the Council to exert its endeavours towards obtaining the recognition and enforcement of this principle was carried. Mr. Raleigh was in the chair, and the meeting received a stimulus from the presentation of a somewhat outspoken and pungently worded Report, drawn up by the chairman, in which he dealt very severely with the work of the various sub-committees. It was shown at this meeting that by taking less expensive premises, and by reducing salaries, the Association had been able to reduce their expenditure by something like £360 a year. In addition, the outstanding debt for the debentures had been reduced by £125.

The Association during the year were compelled to migrate to new premises (at 353, Strand), as the Queensland Government required their offices at 409, Strand. They are now housed in good, workmanlike offices, and with a healthy increase of membership and an agency which shows a wholesome activity may fairly be said to be gaining ground.

Council :—Mr. Frederick Annerley, Mr. F. J. Arlton, Mr. Cecil Brooking, Mr. Lewis Casson, Mr. C. F. Collings, Mr. Clive Currie, Mr. C. Hayden Coffin, Mr. Clarence Derwent, Mr. Fred Grove, Mr. Edmund Gurney, Miss Agnes Imlay, Mr. Richard A. Greene, Mr. J. Poole Kirkwood, Miss Marion Lind, Mr. Fewlass Llewellyn, Mr. Robson Paige, Mr. Frederick Morland, Mr. J. Sebastian Smith, Mr. Cecil Raleigh, Miss Lucy Sibley, Mr. Franklyn Walford, Mr. Chris Walker, Mr. Jackson Wilcox, and Miss Rose Mathews. Secretary, Mr. Hubert Blount.

Entrance fee, 5s. Annual subscription, payable January 1, 15s., or 4s. 6d. quarterly. The subscription for those elected after April in any year is 4s. 6d. quarterly for the remainder of that year. The election of members is vested in the Council.

ROYALTY AT THE PLAY.

THE KING AT THE THEATRES.

Feb. 18.—*A White Man*—Lyric.
,, 21.—*Malia* (Sicilian Players)—Shaftesbury.
,, 24.—*Diana of Dobson's*—Kingsway.
,, 25.—*Dear Old Charlie*—Vaudeville.
,, 29.—*The Belovéd Vagabond*—His Majesty's.
Mar. 3.—*Lady Barbarity*—Comedy.
May 11.—*La Robe Rouge*—Shaftesbury.
,, 16.—*Jack Straw*—Vaudeville.
,, 18.—*La Loi de l'Homme*—Shaftesbury.
,, 18.—*Le Caprice*—Shaftesbury.
June 25.—*The Flag Lieutenant*—Playhouse.
July 16.—*Mrs. Dot*—Comedy.
Sept. 5.—*The Passing of the Third Floor Back*—St James's.
Oct. 12.—*What Every Woman Knows*—Duke of York's.
,, 26.—*Marriages of Mayfair*—Drury Lane.

THE KING AT THE OPERA.

Jan. 29.—*Siegfried*.
May 8.—*La Traviata*.
,, 9.—*Die Walküre*.
May 23.—*Aïda*.
,, 27.—Gala Performance.
June 2.—*Die Meistersinger*.

THE QUEEN AT THE THEATRES.

Feb. 10.—*Her Father*—Haymarket.
,, 18.—*A White Man*—Lyric.
,, 21.—*Malia*—Shaftesbury.
,, 24.—*Diana of Dobson's*—Kingsway.
,, 25.—*Dear Old Charlie*—Vaudeville.
,, 29.—*The Belovéd Vagabond*—His Majesty's.
Mar. 3.—*Lady Barbarity*—Comedy.
,, 5.—*Her Father*—Haymarket.
,, 6.—*Lady Barbarity*—Comedy.
,, 7.—*A Waltz Dream*—Hicks.
,, 16.—*The Thief*—St. James's.
,, 17.—*Lady Frederick*—Garrick.
,, 18.—*Romeo and Juliet*—Lyceum.
,, 24.—*A White Man*—Lyric.
,, 25.—*The Gay Gordons*—Aldwych.
,, 28.—*The Merry Widow*—Daly's.
April 6.—*The Merchant of Venice*—His Majesty's.
,, 7.—*Jack Straw*—Vaudeville.
,, 10.—*The Mollusc*—Criterion.
June 27.—*The Grey Stocking*—*Matinée* given by Miss Gertrude Kingston at the Royalty.

THE QUEEN AT THE THEATRES—*Continued.*

July 14.—*Matinée* in aid of the King's College Hospital Removal—Lyceum.
,,   16.—*Mrs. Dot*—Comedy.
,,   20.—Miss Isadora Duncan's Dancing —Duke of York's.
Nov. 2.—*Marriages of Mayfair*—Drury Lane.
,,   3.—*Idols*—Garrick.
,,   4.—*The Lyons Mail*—Shaftesbury.
Dec. 9.—*The King of Cadonia*—Prince of Wales.
,,   10.—*What Every Woman Knows*—Duke of York's.
,,   11.—*The Belle of Brittany*—Queen's.
,,   12.—*The Merry Widow*—Daly's.

THE QUEEN AT THE OPERA.

Jan. 29.—*Siegfried.*
Feb. 1.—*Götterdämmerung.*
May 16.—*Tristan und Isolde,*
,,   19.—*La Bohême.*
,,   20.—*Die Meistersinger.*
,,   23.—*Aïda.*
,,   27.—Gala Performance.
Ju'y 6.—*Otello.*
,,   11.—*The Huguenots.*
,,   18.—*La Tosca.*
,,   25.—*Aïda.*

THE PRINCE AND PRINCESS OF WALES.

Feb. 1.—*Stingaree*—Queen's.
,,   21.—*Malia* (Sicilian Players)—Shaftesbury.
,,   22.—*Matt of Merrymount*—New.
,,   27.—*Lady Barbarity*—Comedy.
Mar. 6.—*Dear Old Charlie*—Vaudeville.
,,   7.—*Diana of Dobson's*—Kingsway.
,,   13.—*The Merry Widow*—Daly's.
,,   17.—The Follies—Apollo.
,,   21.—Palace, Shaftesbury Avenue.
May 2.—*Havana*—Gaiety.
,,   7.—*The Thunderbolt*—St. James's.
,,   30.—*Françillon*—Shaftesbury.
June 12.—*Jack Straw*—Vaudeville.
Aug. 13.—*Butterflies*—Apollo.
Oct. 6.—*Idols*—Garrick.
Nov. 4.—*The Sway Boat*—Kingsway.
Dec. 17.—*The Lyons Mail*—Shaftesbury.

THE PRINCESS OF WALES (in addition to above).

Jan. 31.—*Matinée* organised by Mr. George Alexander in aid of the Provision
of Meals for Children Fund—St. James's.
Feb. 17.—*Morte Civile* (Sicilian Players)—Shaftesbury.
,,   20.—*She Stoops to Conquer (matinée)*—Playhouse.
,,   25.—*Matinée* in aid of the League of Mercy—Scala.
May 4.—*The Mikado*—Savoy.
,,   6.—*The Merry Widow*—Daly's.
Oct. 8.—*What Every Woman Knows*—Duke of York's.
,,   10.—*Faust*—His Majesty's.
,,   28.—*The Early Worm*—Wyndham's.
,,   29.—*The Sway Boat*—Kingsway.
Dec. 18.—*Matinée* at the Criterion in aid of the London Poor Children's Boot
Fund.
,,   18.—*Lady Epping's Lawsuit*—Criterion.
,,   19.—*The Merry Widow*—Daly's.
,,   21.—*The Passing of the Third Floor Back*—Terry's.

COMMAND PERFORMANCES.

On Friday evening, November 13, in celebration of the anniversary of the King's Birthday, a command performance of *The Flag Lieutenant* was given at Sandringham by Mr. Cyril Maude and company. The following was the cast :—

Sir Berkeley Wynne .. Mr. Arthur Holmes-Gore	James Sloggett.............. Mr. John Harwood
John Penrose....................Mr. Peter Blunt	Waiter...................... Mr. Edward Coutts
Richard Lascelles............. Mr. Cyril Maude	General Gough-Bogle ...... Mr. Sydney Paxton
Christopher Neats............. Mr. Leo Trevor	Colonel McLeod.............. Mr. E. F. Mayeur
William Theisger.......... Mr. C. Aubrey Smith	Captain Munro...........Mr. Charles Hampden
Walter Crutchley........Mr. Ernest Mainwaring	Michael Palliser........ Mr. Clarence Blakiston
Horatio Hood..............Mr. H Robert Averell	Memeti Salos..............Mr. Daniel McCarthy
Edward Dormer-Lee........ Mr. Spencer Trevor	Mrs. Cameron........... Miss Winifred Emery
Charles Penny..................Mr. Larcombe	Lady Hermoine Wynne..Miss Lilian Braithwaite
George Blockley............. Mr. Lane Crawford	Viola Hood.................. Miss Rosalie Toller
Thomas Steele............. Mr. A. G. Onslow	Mrs. Gough-Bogle........ Miss Emma Chambers
Joshua Borlaise............. Mr. M. Weatherell	Lady Dugdale..............Miss Marie Linden

On Wednesday, November 18, Mr. Martin Harvey and company gave a performance at Windsor Castle of *The Corsican Brothers*. The cast was as follows :—

M. Fabien dei Franchi } Mr. Martin Harvey	Boissec...................... Mr. Percy Foster
M. Louis dei Franchi.... }	Tomaso...................... Mr. Denhoim Muir
M. de Château Renaud....Mr. William Haviland	A Surgeon......................Mr. H. Watson
M. le Baron de Montgiron..Mr. Albert E. Raynor	Servants .... } Mr. R. Allen
M. le Baron Mart-lli......... Mr. George Cooke	} Mr. D. Holm
M. Alfred Meynard........ Mr Alfred Mansfield	Emilie de Lesparre........ Miss Maud Hoffman
M. Favrolles............. M. Charles J. Cameron	Madame Savilia dei Franchi.. Miss Mary Rorke
M. Beauchamp............. Mr. Bernard Sloane	Coralie.................... Miss Maud Rivers
Antonio Sarroie..................Mr. J. Barber	Frisette.................Miss Bessie Elder
Colonna................. Mr. Fred Wright, sen.	Estelle................. Miss Marjorie Field
Orlando.................. M. Philip Hewland	Celestine................. Miss Ethel Patrick
Griffo....................... Mr. Les ie Palmer	Maria................ Miss Madge Fabian

On November 20, Mr. Lewis Waller and company gave a performance at Windsor Castle of *The Duke's Motto*. The cast was as follows :—

Louis XIII................. Mr. Tom Heslewood	Saldagno...................... Mr. Reginald Dane
Louis De Nevers.......... Mr. Owen Roughwood	Pepe...................... Mr. Frank Ridley
Louis De Gonzague.........Mr. Franklin Dyall	Pinto.................. Mr. Cronin Wilson
Marquis de Chavernay. .... Mr. Shiel Barry	Hoel.................... Mr. George Harrington
Comte De Tavannes............. Mr. J. V. Henry	Berichon.................. Master Harry Duff
M. D. Navailles............. Mr. Geoffrey Savile	Landlord of Inn............ Mr. Charles Cecil
M. De Nocé................. Mr. James Harrison	Henri De Lagardère........ Mr. Lewis Waller
M. Oriol..................... Mr. Patrick Digan	Princess Gabrielle De Gonzague
Cocardasse..................Mr. Herbert Jarman	Miss Sybil Carlisle
Passepoil............... Mr. Alec. F. Thompson	Blanche De Nevers............. Miss Valli Valli
Æsop...................... Mr. A. E. George	C dalise................. Miss Gwendolin Floyd
Peyrolles.................... Mr. Hubert Druce	Martine.................. Miss Maud Digan
Staupitz.................... Mr. J. H. Irvine	Brigitte...................... Miss May Chenery
Faenza................... Mr. Caton Woodville	Flora....................Miss Dorothy Minto

Soldiers, Gipsies, Masqueraders, etc.
The performance under the direction of Mr. J. E. Vedrenne.

Manager...................... Mr. Victor Lewis Musical Director............ Mr. Leonard Chalk
Stage Manager..............Mr. C. M. La Trobe

On December 4, at Sandringham, Mr. George Alexander and company gave a performance of Alfred Sutro's play *The Builder of Bridges*, the performance being arranged in connection with the anniversary of the Queen's birthday. The cast was as follows :—

Edward Thursfield........Mr. George Alexander	Dorothy Faringay.........Miss Irene Vanbrugh
Arnold Faringay.......... Mr. Dawson Milward	Mrs. Debney.............Miss Florence Haydon
Walter Gresham.......Mr. E. Harcourt-Williams	Miss Closson............. Miss Babara Hannay
Sir Henry Killick.............Mr. William Farren	Minnie.................... Miss Dora Sevening
Peter Holland.......... Mr. E. Vivian Reynolds	

Manager..... ... Mr. Charles T. H't Helms'ey Stage Manager......... Mr. E. Vivian Reynolds

"HAVANA" AT THE GAIETY.

Principal characters played by: Miss Evie Greene, Miss Jean Aylwin, Mr. W. H. Berry, Mr. Alfred Lester, Mr. Leonard Mackay, Mr. Lawrence Grossmith, Mr. Edward O'Neill, Mr. Robert Hale, Mr. Arthur Hatherton.

[Foulsham & Banfield.

"A WHITE MAN" AT THE LYRIC.

Principals:—Mr. A. G. Paulton, Mr. Lewis Waller, Mr. Manifee Johnston, Mr. Manifee Johnston, Miss Nora Lancaster, and Mr. George Fawcett

Foulsham & Banfield.

"BUTTERFLIES" AT THE APOLLO.

Principals: Miss Louie Cyist, Mr. John Bardsley, Mr. Haydn Coffin, Miss Stella St. Audrie, Mr. Louis Bradfield, Miss Ada Blanche, Mr. Fred
Edwards, Mr. Rexau Lawson, and Miss Iris Hoey.

Mr. Eric Mayne.

"THE LYONS MAIL," AT THE SHAFTESBURY.

Miss Dorothea Baird.

Ellis & Walery.

Mr. H. B. Irving.

BOOKS OF THE YEAR.

A CONSIDERABLE number of books of theatrical and musical interest have been published during the past year, and notice of most of these has been given from time to time. All departments, including fiction, criticism, published plays, and biography, have been fairly well represented, and in the section last named matter of the greatest pith and moment has appeared, controversial points having been raised and some fluttering of the dovecotes caused by some of the volumes of reminiscences put together by hands apparently unable to extenuate anything, even if the second part of the famous sentence has not been followed.

MAINLY ABOUT IRVING.

The keenest attention has been directed to the books referring either directly or indirectly to the late Sir Henry Irving, and there has been a good deal of plain speaking, not all of it in the kindest spirit imaginable, concerning the attributes and achievements of the lamented "Chief." The appearance of the official and authoritative life of Irving—that from the careful pen of Mr. Austin Brereton—for instance, has called forth some rather unreasonable complaints to the effect that the biographer had not given a sufficiently detailed and vivid pen-picture of Irving as a man. It seems to us that Mr. Brereton had endeavoured faithfully, and not without success, to give "a faithful portrait of the head of the stage in the Victorian era." His two large volumes were crammed with details setting forth every phase in his subject's public career, and much new and important matter was published for the first time; though, perhaps, the biographer, in his desire to be judicious before anything else, drew less freely than some might have wished upon Irving's correspondence and the private and secret papers of the spacious days at the Lyceum. For a photographic impression of Sir Henry's "magnetic personality" one may turn with advantage to Mr. Walter Herries Pollock's delightful little volume, aptly styled "Impressions of Henry Irving," which is full not only of personal anecdotes, but also of passages of acute and penetrating criticism.

OTHER MEMOIRS.

A note of a different sort with regard to their dead friend is struck both in "The Story of My Life," by Miss Ellen Terry, and in the most interesting and well-written volume, "Some Eminent Victorians," by Mr. Comyns Carr. Miss Terry's reminiscences gave rise to a good deal of discussion, even before they appeared in book-form, and certainly her tone respecting several of her professional colleagues was less amiable than one would fain have hoped from this charming and distinguished actress. Mr. Comyns Carr has much to say about "Old Friend Toole" and other notable players as well as Irving. Mr. Rutland Barrington, again, as has recently been pointed out, has occasionally dipped his pen in gall in his "Record of Thirty-five Years' Experience on the English Stage." If public performers will hit out when they rush into print they must expect to be hit back again. Other books of an autobiographical nature have lately come from Mr. Hall Caine, Miss Maud Allan, and Mr. Joseph Bennett. This last leads us on to the section of Music.

MUSIC.

From a man who had been chief musical critic of a leading daily and other papers for forty years one might have expected something more exhaustive and less scrappy than the book put together by Mr. Bennett. Further reminiscences, besides a useful little treatise on the Art of Singing, have been written by Sir Charles Santley, the knighthood bestowed upon that celebrated baritone having been as gratifying as the similar honour conferred upon Sir John Hare, whose reminiscences, recently published in the *Strand Magazine,* have also aroused considerable interest. Full of interesting material was Mr. M. Sterling Mackinlay's book about Manuel Garcia. A most inspiring and suggestive book was that entitled "Memories and Music," which, though published anonymously, has been attributed variously to several well-known writers. A further stage towards the completion of a work of reference absolutely indispensable to the serious student of music was reached by the publication of the fourth and penultimate volume of the revised version of Grove's Dictionary. The section Q to S afforded opportunity for the raising of many burning questions, and Mr. Fuller Maitland and his associates have not entirely escaped censure for their method of handling thorny subjects. Mr. E. A. Baughan's essays on "Music and Musicians" should also be mentioned.

SHAKESPEARE AND THE DRAMA.

That facile and long-experienced writer on stage matters, Mr. Percy Fitzgerald, expressed his own, sometimes debatable, opinions pretty plainly in "Shakespearean Representation: Its Laws and Limits," in the course of which stimulating work the author, rather as a *laudator temporis acti* (a position by no means to be deprecated), calls over the coals with much severity various modern managements. Some admirable criticism, fraught with scholarship of the best sort—that is to say, well-informed and sane, without being needlessly pedantic and academic—is to be found in "Types of Tragic Drama," by Prof. C. E. Vaughan. Attention has quite lately been called to the striking merits of Horace Howard Furness, junior's splendid revised version of *Richard III.* in his father's Variorum Edition of Shakespeare; and the Bard has been re-issued in different forms in the course of the year. Other dramatists whose works have appeared in whole or in part include Ibsen and various contemporary writers, including, of course, Mr. G. Bernard Shaw, Mr. St. John Hankin, Mr. Stephen Phillips, and Mr. Comyns Carr, with their *Faust;* Mr. Thomas Hardy, with the last instalment of his great work, *The Dynasts;* and Mr. W. L. Courtney, with his just-published "Dramas and Diversions." A valuable work that came out just before the end of the year was "Annals of the Liverpool Stage," by R. J. Broadbent.

MISCELLANY.

In the domain of fiction Mr. Leonard Merrick has continued to send forth admirable work, Mr. Horace Newte has further improved his position as a delineator of character, and Mr. Dudley Ward has certainly put his foot down firmly with his novel of theatrical life, "View Thy Trespass." Stories of this class always arouse interest, of a somewhat factitious sort, perhaps. Various handbooks on elocution and collections of passages to be used by reciters have been published during 1908, notable among these being "Dramatic Elocution and Action," by Alex. C. Sutherland. Mention should be made of a racy historical sketch of "The Stage Censor," by "G. M. G." Our survey has dealt chiefly with books specially commended to our notice, and any omissions should be attributed to the vagaries of careless publishers or touchy writers. Still, in a frank and friendly manner, we might say, "Let them all come, and the more the merrier."

THE SOCIETY OF DRAMATIC CRITICS.

This Society was formed in October, 1906, with a membership of from 50 to 60. The Society exists for social and professional purposes, to facilitate the exchange of views on the material and intellectual aspects of the calling of dramatic criticism and generally to promote the interests of the calling.

The president of the Society is Mr. A. B. Walkley; the vice-president, Mr. William Archer, and the honorary secretary and treasurer, Mr. F. Moy Thomas. The council, is composed as follows: Mr. A. B. Walkley, Mr. William Archer, Mr. Sidney Dark, Mr. Anthony L. Ellis, Mr. H. Hamilton Fyfe, Mr. J. T. Grien, Mr. G. E. Morrison, Mr. Charles Palmer, Mr. Alfred F. Robbins, Mr. Edward F. Spence, Mr. Bernard Weller, and Mr. F. Moy Thomas, Staple Inn Buildings (South), Holborn, W.C. Membership of the Society is by invitation of the council.

"PETE" AT THE LYCEUM.

The Second Act : Miss Berte Bretton as Kate and Mr. Matheson Lang as Pete.

—"Daily Mirror" Studios.

THE THEATRICAL LADIES' GUILD.

BY AN OUTSIDER.

IT would be difficult to estimate by a bare statement of facts and figures the amount of good that has been effected by the Guild founded in November, 1891, at her private residence in Great Russell Street, by Mrs. C. L. Carson. Anybody having had the opportunity of studying its workings, or realising the benefit conferred on hundreds of the poorer members of the theatrical profession, will agree with me in saying that it was, indeed, a happy inspiration Kittie Carson

MRS. C. L. CARSON.
The Founder of the Guild.

(as she is familiarly called) had, when, with the winter coming on in the year named, she initiated her plan for the relief of distress amongst the more unfortunate members of a very hard-working body of professional people. To form such a plan was one thing, but to carry it out meant the display of a vast amount of energy, and a considerable expenditure of both time and money. Nothing daunted, however, Mrs. Carson set about her self-imposed task and formed a small committee, of which Miss Fanny Brough became President, a position that popular actress has, with singular loyalty and good nature, held ever since. The amount subscribed by this group of Mrs. Carson's friends was not, of course, at the outset very large, so she

THE THEATRICAL LADIES' GUILD.

A COMMITTEE MEETING.

Names reading from left to right.—Miss Fred Wright, Miss Louise Stretrope, Miss Compton, Miss Fanny Brough ('The President, in the Chair), Miss Carlotta Addison, Miss Bishop, Miss Cicely Richards, Miss Harwood (Secretary).

THE THEATRICAL LADIES' GUILD.

A SWARM IN THE HIVE.
A Typical Friday Sewing Bee.

decided to hold weekly Sewing Bees in order that the warm clothing so necessary in maternity cases, or for those requiring assistance whilst temporarily out of employment, could be quickly made. At the earliest Sewing Bees held about a dozen ladies met in Mrs. Carson's dainty little drawing-room, and as from week to week their numbers increased, the observant visitor noticed on arrival that a settee had been removed, or that the arm-chairs had been taken into the adjoining dining-room to make more room for all the kind women desirous of helping. The room, indeed, got almost stripped of its occasional tables, and the walls alone were left untouched, but the mistress of the house cared nothing about her pretty nick-nacks being displaced. She had found an outlet for her superabundant energy, and work for her large heart to do. We had long afternoons in those days, busily plying our needles all the time, with an interval between four o'clock and five o'clock for tea hospitably provided by the lady of the house. And so matters went on for a few years, till one day Mrs. Carson had to acknowledge that with dining and drawing-room both full of bee workers she could hardly let them sit in the hall or on the stairs, but must arrange to have premises that would accommodate them all better than a private residence could. Whilst rejoicing, as everybody must who has followed the history of the Theatrical Ladies Guild, at its rapid and extraordinary growth, I often look back on those first Bee meetings in Great Russell Street as some of the happiest hours my life has known. We were so hospitably treated, and yet had the best that was in us in the way of industry brought out by the founder's own example of industry. The first yearly meeting was held by the courtesy of the late Sir Augustus Harris in the Saloon of Drury Lane theatre, and amongst the many interesting people present was, I remember, the late Mrs. Keeley. Subsequent guests of honour at the annual meetings, held in turn at the Lyceum, the Haymarket, and the St. James's, have included the late Baroness Burdett-Coutts, the late Nellie Farren, Lady Burnand, the Countess of Bective, the present Lady St. Helier, Mrs. Kendal, and Lady Gilbert.

When the Guild with its ever-increasing wardrobe needed to be housed separately, premises were taken in Wellington Street, Covent Garden, and later again the Guild moved to Russell Street, Covent Garden, where it remained for many years. Through overstrain, unfortunately, Mrs. Carson had to retire two or three years ago from the post of Hon. Secretary and Treasurer, and then another move was made, this time to the spacious and commodious offices, 90, Great Russell Street, not far from its first home in Mrs. Carson's residence. The President is still the busy and good-hearted Fanny Brough, and the Vice-Presidents are Mrs. Edward Compton and Miss Carlotta Addison, whilst the Executive Committee working from December, 1908, to December, 1909, are :—Miss Lena Ashwell, Lady Burnand, Miss Phyllis Broughton, Mrs. Alfred Bishop, Miss Lilian Braithwiate, Mrs. E. H. Bull, Miss Ada Blanche, Miss Compton, Mrs. John Douglass, Mrs. Ellis, Miss Vane Featherston, Miss Helen Ferrers, Mrs. A. E. George, Mrs. Synge Hutchinson, and Mrs. Ernest Hendrie, Miss Clara Jecks, and Miss Lindsay Jardine, Miss Gertrude Kingston, Miss Eva Moore, Miss Alma Murray, Mrs. Raleigh, Miss Cicely Richards, Miss Mary Rorke, Miss Louise Stopford, Mrs. Beerbohm Tree, Miss Irene Vanbrugh, Mrs. Fred Wright, and Miss May Whitty. Those unacquainted with the workings of this excellent charity, to which I hope they will some day become subscribers, may be glad to learn a few particulars concerning it. Its object is to assist with maternity cases, to help with clothes for stage or private wear the poorer members (men, women, and children) of the theatrical profession, and the working staff of London and provincial theatres. Some of the rules are as follow :—

Every member to pay not less than 1s. yearly, and to contribute 1s. or more towards buying material.

Candidates for election as Executive Committee must be members of the theatrical profession, paying a yearly subscription of £1 1s., and giving material for clothing, or 5s. to pay for same.

Any lady, theatrical or otherwise, paying not less than £1 1s. yearly may become a member of the General Committee.

The Executive Committee to be elected in November of each year by the General Committee, the new Committee taking office the following January.

The Executive Committee shall have the power to elect the Presidents of Guilds who are working for the Theatrical Ladies' Guild to serve on the Executive Committee. Same to be elected yearly by the Executive Committee.

A Sewing Bee will be held every Friday, from 3 p.m. to 5 p.m., at the offices of the Guild.

Ladies not connected with the theatrical profession can be elected as honorary members of the Guild on payment of a donation of not less than 2s. 6d., and may attend the weekly Sewing Bees, the annual general meeting, and all social functions, but have no voting powers whatever.

Upon Mrs. Carson's enforced retirement from the post of Hon. Secretary, the Committee, with the good luck that has attended all their work, were fortunate in being able to engage a young lady, who, from her previous experience with the Charity Organisation Society, possessed all the aptitudes requisite for dealing with the appeals sent in. For, albeit, the Committee are desirous of assisting every deserving case, they need, of course. to exercise a deal of vigilance to avoid being imposed upon. And it is in the making of the requisite inquiries to guard against this that Miss Millicent Hammond, who received a well-deserved compliment from the chair at the last annual meeting at the St. James's theatre in December, particularly excels. She places before the Committee all the particulars of the families applying for help, and thus their labours are lessened. And this is no mean consideration when it is taken into account that they are all busy women, working hard in a profession that leaves very little time for anything outside the theatre. Think, too, what it must mean at a very busy season of the year, such as December, January, and February, for as many as forty cases a week have to be dealt with by the Committee and their Secretary. The premises in Great Russell Street are both central and convenient, and when I have said that the double first floor room contains over sixty chairs for the bee workers, with only two or three of a more lounging kind for the use of the distinguished visitors who call in from time to time, it will be recognised that interest in the Guild is by no means flagging. If, however, the chairs are put closely together at the Bee Meetings, there is a general air of coziness about the premises. One would, I admit, look in vain for a Reynolds or a Gainsborough on the walls, but they are made bright, nevertheless, by the photographs, often autographed, of a number of stage favourites. First and foremost there is a capital portrait of the founder, Mrs. Carson, over the mantelpiece in the front room, and facing her on the opposite wall is one of Miss Fanny Brough, near whose portrait is one of Miss Vane Featherston. And dotted round the two rooms are portraits of Mrs. Edward Compton, Mrs. Raleigh, Miss Eva Moore, Miss Irene Vanbrugh, Miss Gertrude Kingston, Miss Olga Nethersole, the late Nellie Farren, the late Mrs. Stirling, the centre of a group of artists, and many others. Beyond several tables and a chest of drawers in which materials are stored, the rooms contain little but the chairs. The library books, however, which reach from floor to ceiling in the two niches of the back room, and the handsome photographs that cover all the walls, give the offices a very cheery appearance, and when tea is served at the small charge of a penny, it is only natural that the chatting is increased a little. It would be as well to explain that the tea provided never comes out of the money subscribed by the public. It is a rule for the lady taking the chair to supply the cake required for the meeting, and the penny collected from each visitor defrays the cost of the tea and bread and butter. On the occasion of my last visit I happened quite unintentionally to escape the tea hour altogether. I had been having a chat with Miss Featherston, who was in the chair, and by whose side sat the Countess of Bective, who takes a great interest in the Guild, and, wanting to look over the clothing department upstairs, I asked Miss Hammond as I went on my exploring expedition to accompany me. What a marvellously arranged room the second floor front room is to be sure! For stowed in most perfect order were the 3,000 odd garments sent in a few days previously by Miss Louise Stopford and Miss Margaret Alston, together with the Guild's regular stock of stage costumes and walking dresses, or mantles of varying shapes and sizes. And in a smaller adjoining room were enough men's clothes to last I should think for several weeks' consumption. I could not, of course, resist the temptation to ask whether the secretarial work was heavy just then, and Miss Hammond at once waxed eloquent on the cases she was dealing with that very day. From Belfast a tale of woe had come to the Guild. The husband, who was out of work, had his wife in bed with a baby ten days old, and six other young children all but starving. Clothing was being sent. and by one or two members of the Committee money, too. The rules of the Guild are that clothing, and coal, or soup tickets alone are given, but in exceptional cases,

THE THEATRICAL LADIES' GUILD.

A WELCOME CUP OF TEA ON A BEE DAY.
MISS ALICE GREENWOOD, MISS CARA BENNETT, MISS MAY WARLEY, MISS FREDA LANGFORD.

THE LIBRARY.
MISS COMPTON, MRS. FRED. WRIGHT, MISS CARLOTTA ADDISON, MRS. ALFRED BISHOP, MISS CICELY RICHARDS, and MISS HAMMOND.

MISS FANNY BROUGH, THE PRESIDENT.
Dictating a letter to the Secretary, Miss Hammond.

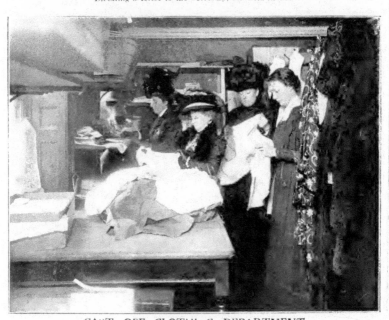

CAST OFF CLOTHING DEPARTMENT.
Miss Fanny Brough, Mrs. Bishop, Mrs. Fred. Wright, Miss Stopford, Miss Hammond.

although the money is not drawn upon, small sums are often subscribed by these charitable women among themselves. An even sadder case was that of a wife who had been in the habit of playing small parts, and had thus provided for her four young children (one of whom is an infant). The husband of this poor woman often "goes wrong," to use her own words, and with an infant that she cannot leave she is reduced now to doing needlework or taking in washing. On inquiry it was discovered that her tale was quite true, and that her father had, as she said, been in a good position in life. Another sad case that has recently received attention is one of an actor who is now in Bedlam, where apparently the authorities insist upon a very ample wardrobe being sent with the patients. The Guild has also for some time been assisting a once very popular clown who is past work, as is an old actress of over seventy years of age. In her zeal, apparently, to make me realise that we could all with advantage to the distressed poor increase our subscriptions, Miss Hammond would have kept me not only past their tea time, as she did, but past my own dinner hour if I had encouraged her to continue her recital of the applicants, including paralytics, that she was then dealing with. But I had to tear myself away. I felt too much of a lump in my throat to be able to return to the busy bee workers, and I got what comfort I could from thinking that the distribution of Miss Stopford's quilts, blankets, and warm underclothing would help to comfort hundreds of poor souls, who can also from the Guild obtain coal and bread tickets as well as medical advice when needed. I certainly had not wasted my afternoon.

"OUR GUILD."

By FANNY BROUGH.

I am glad to have this opportunity of contributing to so admirable an annual as THE STAGE YEAR-BOOK a few words about the Theatrical Ladies' Guild. Sixteen years have passed since Mrs. C. L. Carson came to me with her scheme for assisting the staff of employés of our theatres in London and the provinces. While actors are more or less *en évidence* before the public, the unseen, unknown hands that work "behind the scenes" are rarely given a thought. The staff of a theatre comprises all kinds and conditions of hard-working, deserving men and women, among whom I have met many humble heroes and heroines, bearing their hard struggles for life with exemplary fortitude. The original object of the Guild—to help with necessary clothing and medical aid mother and child in maternity cases—soon extended into various other directions, and has now developed a more widely useful general character, though the basis is always a charitable one. The Theatrical Ladies' Guild has never been obliged to refuse a deserving case, thanks to the ready response of our members, theatrical and non-professional. "A case" nearly always means a whole family—wife, husband, and children. I consider the cast-off clothing branch of the Theatrical Ladies' Guild the most far-reaching charity that was ever formed for helping the less fortunate members of our profession. Scarcely one day in the whole year passes that has not seen one or more made happy by having the means (suitable clothes) provided to look for work, obtain it, and keep it. I have not space or time to enter into all the details of interest I should like to dwell upon, for the Theatrical Ladies' Guild is very dear to me. I would here beg of every member of our profession who reads this little message to start the New Year by joining the Theatrical Ladies' Guild. Remember, it is open to all, the subscriptions ranging from 1s., and if only one single garment, old or new, a pair of boots or gloves, is sent, small as the gift may seem, it will bring a "big bit" of comfort to one of the many deserving applicants who appeal to "Our Guild."

IRVING MEMORIAL.

The site for the Irving statue was in January definitely granted by the Westminster Town Council. The statue is to be erected in the centre of the broad pavement to the north of the National Portrait Gallery, in the Charing Cross Road. The work is in the hands of Mr. Thomas Brock, R.A., and will probably be completed during the year 1909.

SCENE-SHIFTING BY ELECTRICITY.

A NEW electrically-driven equipment has recently been installed at Wyndham's in connection with the scene-shifting arrangements for raising and lowering cloths, sky borders, curtains, and setting ceilings, etc. In the first place the old hempen ropes disappear and give place to wire. This, in itself, is an enormous advantage from the fire-risk point of view. Secondly, it is possible to dispense with the services of at least ten stage-hands in the case of a small theatre like Wyndham's, while this number would be more than trebled at, say, Drury Lane. Further, it expedites the work.

One of the greatest difficulties in the employment of machinery on the stage is that of noise. With the new machinery at Wyndham's this difficulty is overcome to such an extent as to make it negligible. The machine itself is situated in the flies on the prompt side, and occupies nearly the entire length. Only a few inches from the floor of the gallery and supported by iron brackets is a shaft 25 ft. in length and 1¼ ins. in diameter with a key-way cut from end to end. This shaft is rope-driven by a Siemens 4 h.p. electric motor, and carries a number of split bevel gear wheels placed at suitable intervals. Above it and parallel with it are two counter-shafts of the same length and diameter, which can be driven from the main shaft when required through what is termed a "unit." Driving a friction clutch is a raw-hide bevel gear wheel, which engages with a split bevel on the main shaft. The other member of the clutch is fixed to a worm, and is also provided with a spring brake attachment, normally on when the clutch is not engaged. A further raw-hide gearing transmits the power to a sprocket, from which the counter-shaft is driven by a chain. Any number of winding drums can be keyed to this counter-shaft where required.

It is only when it is necessary to raise or lower two or more pieces of scenery at the same time, or to set ceilings, that the counter-shafts are employed. When this is so, the drums are set, and the wire ropes are measured off to the correct length once and for all. It is then simply a matter of raising or lowering, and it will be observed that the relative positions of the pieces are invariable, which is far from being the case with manual labour. For single pieces of scenery a variety of the "unit" is adopted, the only difference being that instead of a chain wheel there is a winding drum, the driving being done, as before, directly from the main shaft. Each unit is provided with a lever which enables the operator to throw it into connection with the main shaft, and therefore wind up; or to disengage it and allow the piece of scenery to drop by its own weight; or, finally, to disengage it and hold it in position by the spring brake. This last-named is the normal condition of affairs. Thus it will be seen that while the machine is running scenery can be raised, lowered, or kept stationary, each winding drum being independent of all the others and of the counter-shafts. There is, of course, no reason why several counter-shafts should not be employed for use in different scenes, although only two have been installed at Wyndham's. Each unit is also provided with an automatic grip device to prevent over-winding. The motor is controlled by a Siemens ironclad automatic starter, while an emergency switch is provided in close proximity to each unit, by which the motor may be stopped at any time. These emergency switches act upon the no-voltage release of the starter.

With these arrangements it is quite possible for one person standing in the prompt corner to set a scene in a few seconds without the slightest asistance from anyone in the flies.

The machine at Wyndham's has been in operation all through the run of *The Early Worm*, in which piece it had to set three different shaped ceilings. It works everything in the flies, including the act-drop, which can be worked at any speed,

MR. EDWARD LYTTON

Watching his invention at work in the Flies at Wyndham's Theatre.

for slow or fast curtains. The cost of electricity is about 8d. a week at 4d. a
unit. At the conclusion of the run of *The Early Worm*, the machines were set
to run *Sir Anthony*, which they are now working, the work of putting machines
in position for a new piece taking about an hour. The saving in using the machines
instead of hand labour is enormous, and Mr. Frank Curzon is fitting up the
Prince of Wales's with an installation, and several other West End theatres will be
fitted up almost immediately.

Mr. Edward Lytton, stage manager at Wyndham's, is the inventor. He holds
over a dozen patents in different countries on the machine. The first experimental
machine was put in at the Coronet by Mr. Edward Lytton to run the act-drop
only. It has now been running over three years, proving its reliability, costing
in electricity only about 1d. per week.

THE PASSING OF THE IMPERIAL.

The history of the Imperial, which was taken down in sections in August and
September, it being understood that the interior decorations would be used
in the reconstruction of the Albert, Canning Town, is not one to inspire
confidence in theatrical enterprise outside the charmed West End radius of a mile
or so. Here was a stately and beautiful theatre, by no means badly situated,
yet it was only occasionally that the depressing cloud of non-success lifted for the
manager who tempted fortune in the house. Mrs. Langtry (who re-opened the
house, over which she had spent so many thousands in beautifying, on April 22,
1901, with *A Royal Necklace*), Miss Ellen Terry, Mr. Herbert Waring, and Mr. Lewis
Waller are among those who at various times gave their best in the seasons they
played there ; but we doubt very much if any management other than Mr. Waller's
came out of the house with its accounts balanced on the right side.

The old Imperial, or the Aquarium Theatre as it was then called, was first opened
in 1876. Miss Marie Litton gave some revivals of old comedies; and in 1877 Samuel
Phelps appeared in *The School for Scandal*. In 1879 the house was renamed the
Imperial. When Mrs. Langtry took over the building only the outer walls were
allowed to remain. An army of workmen in three and a-half months accomplished
wonders, and a stately house of almost severe architectural design, with marble walls
and a comparatively new style in subdued lighting, replaced the old somewhat barn-
looking house. Mrs. Langtry's opening piece, however, did not serve her well, for
on August 21 Mr. Herbert Waring commenced a season with *A Man of His Word*, by
Boyle Lawrence. Mr. Waring's season lasted about a month. On January 25 of
the following year Mrs. Langtry returned with Paul Kester's four-act play,
Mademoiselle Mars, with Mr. Lewis Waller as her leading man, playing Napoleon.
On April 17 she revived Sydney Grundy's *The Degenerates*. *The Crossways*, by Mrs.
Langtry and J. Hartley Manners, was produced on December 8.

Miss Ellen Terry's management at the Imperial commenced on April 15, 1903,
with a production of Henrik Ibsen's *The Vikings*, in which Mr. Oscar Asche was
allotted the part of Sigurd. *The Good Hope* and *Much Ado About Nothing* followed.
Miss Terry in all her productions relied to an extent on the somewhat extreme views
on staging and scenery of her son, Mr. Gordon Craig. On November 3, 1903, the
theatre temporarily passed into the hands of Mr. Lewis Waller, who commenced
with a revival of *Monsieur Beaucaire*. In February of 1904 he produced John
Davidson's wordy version of *Ruy Blas*, entitled *A Queen's Romance*, with Mrs. Patrick
Campbell as the Queen. *Miss Elizabeth's Prisoner* followed on April 16. After a
short revival of *A Marriage of Convenience*, *His Majesty's Servant* was seen in
October. *Hawthorne, U.S.A.*, *The Perfect Lover* (Sutro), *Henry the Fifth*, *Romeo
and Juliet*, *The Harlequin King*, and Conan Doyle's *Brigadier Gérard* were amongst
Mr. Waller's productions at the Imperial. With the last-named piece, produced on
March 3, 1906, he concluded his tenancy, playing at the Imperial for the last time
on Saturday, May 12, and opening at the Lyric with the same play on the following
Monday.

THE BRITISH EMPIRE SHAKESPEARE SOCIETY.

THE society was founded in 1901 by Miss Morritt, with the approval and hearty co-operation of Sir Henry Irving, who became the society's first president. Princess Marie Louise of Schleswig-Holstein is now the president of the society, the vice-presidents being Mr. George Alexander, Mr. Arthur Bourchier, Mr. W. L. Courtney, Lord Howard de Walden, Mr. H. B. Irving, Mr. Alan Mackinnon, Sir Charles Mathews, Mr. Forbes Robertson, and Mr. Lewis Waller. The governing council of the society comprises the president, vice-presidents, hon. secretary, and hon. treasurer. The list of patrons and patronesses includes many other prominent men and women of the day, not only from London, but also from the other great cities of the Empire. The society works not for profit, but for the sole object of making Shakespeare a vital force of the English-speaking race—that is, not only with the cultured, but with the rank and file of the people as well. It is fully appreciated that there are a large number of societies doing excellent work in the Shakespearean cause. Their meetings are, however, generally of a more or less private character, whereas one of the principal rules of the British Empire Shakespeare Society is that (to the majority of meetings) all branches must admit the Press free and the public at a small charge. The public dramatic readings given by the society evoke great interest, the more especially as they are always cast from amongst the local members. Membership of one centre implies membership throughout the Empire, since subscribers may transfer their privileges from one centre to another, as occasion arises. The society's annual essay and elocution competitions (both senior and junior classes) form a further help in spreading the love of Shakespeare. Candidates for the final elocution competition, which takes place annually at a London theatre, with some well-known actor as judge, are only eligible to compete on their having qualified in their respective local competitions. Those desiring to become members or associates of the society should communicate with the hon. general treasurer, Mr. Acton Bond, who, like Miss Morritt, is a joint hon. general director of the society.

The following is a brief summary of the work accomplished in London in 1908 :—

January 19.—Reading of *Cymbeline.* The cast included Mr. Acton Bond, Mr H. A. Saintsbury, and Miss Nora Lancaster.

February 18.—Reading of *Much Ado About Nothing.* The cast included Mr. Acton Bond, Mr. Nigel Playfair, and Miss Dorothy Thomas.

March 17.—Reading of *The Tempest.* The cast included Mr. Acton Bond, Mr. A. E. George, Mr. J. H. Leigh, and Miss Thirza Norman. The orchestra was under the direction of Dr. W. H. Cummings.

April 7.—Reading of *Henry VIII.* The cast included Mr. Acton Bond, Mr. Lyn Harding. Mr. Arthur Bourchier, and Miss Violet Vanbrugh.

May 17.—Reading of *Much Ado About Nothing.* Princess Marie Louise of Schleswig-Holstein was present. The cast included Mr. Acton Bond, Mr. Nigel Playfair, Miss Agnes Brayton, and Miss Helen Haye.

June 2.—Recital of *Hamlet* by Mr. H. B. Irving. Mr. Sidney Lee in the chair.

July 17.—Elocution competition. Judge, Mr. Henry Arthur Jones.

November 6.—Miscellaneous songs, recitals, speeches, etc. Princess Marie Louise of Schleswig-Holstein distributed essay and elocution prizes. Mr. Basil Gill and Mr. Lyn Harding gave a recital of *Julius Cæsar,* act four, scene three. Mr. H. B. Irving, Mr. Henry Arthur Jones, and Mr. J. T. Grein were amongst the speakers.

November 26.—Reading of *Twelfth Night.* Princess Marie Louise of Schleswig-Holstein was present. Mr. Acton Bond read the part of Sir Toby Belch.

SHAKESPEARE MEMORIAL.

THE movement for a memorial to Shakespeare first arose out of an offer of £1,000 made by Mr. Richard Badger to the London County Council. Some meetings were held, and in July, 1905, the Advisory Committee of the Shakespeare Memorial Committee, including Sir E. Poynter, Sir W. Richmond, Sir Aston Webb, Mr. Belcher, Mr. Brock, Mr. Sidney Colvin, and Mr. Hugh Chisholm, met at the Mansion House, and made a report, proposing an architectural memorial, including a statue, and suggesting a site on the south side of the Thames. The matter was then apparently forgotten for a considerable time, but eventually in March of 1908 a meeting was held at the Mansion House, Lord Reay presiding. The Committee then announced that a site in Park Crescent, looking up Portland Place from Crescent Gardens, had been settled upon. with the consent of the Commissioners of Woods and Forests. The Committee proposed to remove the statue of the Duke of Kent from the Portland Place site to " an adjoining spot of equal prominence."

Sir John Hare, with characteristic promptitude, in a letter to the *Times*, demurred to the plans of this Committee. Shakespeare, he urged, had raised the most indestructible monument to his genius by the works he had left us, and required no blocks of stone or marble to keep his memory green. Sir John asked for the founding of a national theatre, and added : " Such an institution would at once remove the existing stigma on our stage, rescue it from the chaos in which it finds itself, raise the position of the drama in this country to the same dignity it obtains in France, Germany, and Austria, and be a noble and lasting tribute."

Some newspaper correspondence then took place, mainly in the columns of the *Daily Chronicle*, in which various opinions were expressed. Mr. Forbes Robertson, Mr. Beerbohm Tree, and Sir Charles Wyndham were inclined to favour the idea of a statue rather than a national theatre, though none expressed commendation of the choice of site. Among those who gave a national theatre the preference, in addition to Sir John Hare, were Mr. George Alexander, Mr. A. W. Pinero, Mr. Henry Arthur Jones, and Mr. G. Bernard Shaw. This eventually culminated in a meeting, held at the Lyceum, on Tuesday, May 19, with Lord Lytton presiding, when the following motion was unanimously carried :—

That this meeting is in favour of the establishment of a national theatre as a memorial to Shakespeare.

It was also arranged to appoint a Committee to draft a scheme; to appoint a Committee inviting the co-operation of the provincial cities, and organising meetings for the formation of a National Theatre Society, and the collection of subscriptions, and that the Committee should appoint a deputation to wait on the Prime Minister and the London County Council with a view to seeking their support for the proposal of a National Theatre.

Previously to the meeting, it had been suggested by Mr. Tree that the two movements should join forces, and a letter was read at this meeting from the Mansion House Committee proposing that there should be a conference between the Committees of the two movements.

A meeting was in consequence held at the House of Lords on May 28 between representatives of the two Committees, and it was resolved "that the two general Committees as they stand at present shall be amalgamated, and that an Executive Committee shall be elected by the Committee thus formed." This resolution was passed on the statement made by Lord Plymouth that the Shakespeare Memorial Committee was prepared to unite with the National Theatre Committee on the understanding that the proposed architectural and sculptural monument should take the form of a Shakespeare Memorial Theatre.

On July 23 a meeting was held of the two Committees at the Mansion House. The Lord Mayor was in the chair. It was decided (1) that the Shakespeare Memorial Committee consist of the members of the Shakespeare Memorial Committee and the members of the National Theatre Shakespeare Memorial Committee, and (2) that an

MISS LENA ASHWELL'S "DIANA OF DOBSON'S" (SOUTH) COMPANY ON TOUR (AUTUMN).

Back Row: Mr. Thomas Pulsford, Mr. Albert Wainright, Mr. Alfred A. Harris, Miss Nancy Goltis, Mr. M. C. Forbu, Mr. Dan Pitt, Mr. R. G. Bartlis. Front Row: Miss Eva Leonard Boyne, Miss Helen Vicary, Miss Georgette de Stradle, Miss Dorothy Green, Miss Max Sitard, Miss Molly Treband, Miss Kate Turnie.

MR. FRANK CURZON'S "MY MIMOSA MAID" COMPANY ON TOUR (AUTUMN).

Top row (left to right): Miss Voland, Mr. Scholes, Miss West, Miss Grapes, Miss Raye, Miss Yeoman, Miss H. Adair, Miss Argent, Miss Sinclair.
Second row (left to right):—Mr. Russell, Miss Ivimy, Mr. Goodwin, Mr. Swoyan, Miss Keeley, Miss Yule, Mr. Winter, Mr. Jackson, Mr. Davis.
Third row (left to right):—Mr. Skinner, Mr. Goldsworthy, Miss Ruby Gray, Mr. Chas. Payton, Miss Eva Sampford, Miss Marie Studholme, Mr. Chas.
McNaughton, Miss May Gorton, Mr. Percy Carr, Mr. Boatwright, Mr. Leonard Hornsby, "Billy," Mr. Warwick.
Sitting down (left to right): Mr. Dent, Mr. Thomas, Miss A. Adair, Mr. Thos. J. Court, Margagte, Mr. Archie McCraig, Miss D. Adair,
Mr. John Wadley, Miss Simpson, Miss O'Connell.

Executive Committee be elected, consisting of 21 members, with the addition of an honorary secretary and a secretary, and with power to add to their number. The following were elected members of the Executive Committee : The Lord Mayor (chairman), the Earl of Plymouth, the Earl of Lytton, Viscount Esher, Sir John Hare, Dr. Furnivall, Mr. William Archer, Mr. H. Granville Barker, Mr. S. H. Butcher, M.P., Mr. J. Comyns Carr, Mr. Sidney Colvin, Mr. W. L. Courtney, Mr. Robert Donald, Mrs. G. L. Gomme, Mr. Edmund Gosse, Mr. Sidney Lee, Mr. H. W. Massingham, the Hon. Mrs. Alfred Lyttelton, Mr. A. W. Pinero, Mr. G. Bernard Shaw, Mr. Beerbohm Tree, and Mr. Forbes Robertson, Mr. I. Gallancz, hon. secretary, and Mr. Philip Carr, secretary. Two sub-committees, one under the chairmanship of Lord Esher, and the other under that of Lord Lytton, held numerous meetings during the autumn of 1908.

ACTORS' BENEVOLENT FUND.

The object of the Actors' Benevolent Fund, which was established in 1882, is to help, by allowances, gifts, and loans, old or distressed actors and actresses, managers, stage managers, and acting-managers, and their wives and orphans.

The President is Sir Charles Wyndham. The Vice-Presidents are Mr. H. Beerbohm Tree, Mr. George Alexander, and Mrs. D'Oyly Carte. Mr. Harry Nicholls is Hon. Treasurer, and Mr. Edward Terry and Mr. Beerbohm Tree the Hon. Trustees.

The Executive Committee are as follows :—

Mr. Morris Abrahams.	Mr. J. Bannister Howard.	Mr. Sydney Paxton.
Mr. J. D. Beveridge.	Mr. Frederick Kerr.	Mr. Lionel Rignold.
Mr. Lionel Brough.	Mr. H. J. Loveday.	Mr. Algernon Syms.
Mr. E. H. Bull.	Mr. Cyril Maude.	Mr. A. B. Tapping.
Mr. Isaac Cohen.	Mr. Akerman May.	Mr. Edward Terry.
Mr. Robert Courtneidge.	Mr. M. R. Morand.	Mr. Arthur Williams.
Mr. Charles Cruikshanks.	Mr. Harry Nicholls.	Mr. Frederick Wright.

Actors' Saturday, held for the benefit of the Fund, is held on the last Saturday in January. The Secretary of the Fund is Mr. C. I. Coltson, and the offices are at 8, Adam Street, Strand.

The annual dinner was held on December 13, 1908, at the Hotel Metropole, with Mr. Cyril Maude in the chair. The subscription list amounted to more than £1,100.

TOURING MANAGERS' ASSOCIATION.

The Touring Managers' Association, Limited, was formed in March, 1900, by a number of leading touring managers, to advance and protect the interests of touring managers, and by the promotion of a system of arbitration to endeavour to avoid litigation between managers and artists.

The Association has one hundred and seventeen members. The Committee, which is elected annually, consists of twenty-seven members. The present Committee is as follows :—President, Mr. Wentworth Croke; Vice-President, Mr. E. Graham Falcon; Honorary Treasurer, Mr. J. Bannister Howard; Honorary Solicitor, Mr. W. Muskerry-Tilson, 25, Southampton Street, W.C.; Mr. A. Clifton Alderson, Mr. Rollo Balmain, Mr. Cecil Barth, Mr. Arthur Bertram, Mr. Louis Calvert, Mr. Silvanus Dauncey, Mr. George Edwardes, Mr. Lionel Glenister, Mr. William Greet, Mr. W. H. Hallatt, Mr. Percy Hutchison, Mr. W. W. Kelly, Mr. G. B. Lambert, Mr. M. V. Leveaux, Mr. E. Lockwood, Mr. F. Cave Maitland, Mr. F. Leslie Moreton, Mr. Norman V. Norman, Mr. Alfred Paumier, Mr. G. Brydon-Phillips, Mr. G. M. Polini, Mr. Herbert Ralland, Mr. Edward Terry, Mr. Brandon Thomas, Mr. H. Beerbohm Tree, Mr. John Tully, and Mr. Frank Weathersby. Secretary, Mr. M. Martin.

During the past year the matters that have chiefly been before the members are the standard form of contract between the resident and touring managers, which has been brought to a successful issue; stage plays in clubs; and kinematograph performances given in dangerous buildings, etc.

Address, Savoy Mansions, Strand, W.C.

THE ACTORS' UNION.

THE birth of the Actors' Union took place early in 1907. It was registered as a Trade Union cn October 8, 1907. The Committee—from which, by a vote of the members themselves, ladies are excluded—is as follows :—

Messrs. Leslie Arthur, Orlando Barnett, J. Hastings Batson, Arthur Bawtree, Henry Bedford, J. W. Braithwaite, W. Ruddle Brown, F. Rawson Buckley, Cecil G. Calvert, Edward Chester, George H. Child, Edwin J. Collins, Fred D. Daviss, H. Tripp Edgar, James English, Lewis Gilbert, Frank Gerald, Campbell Goldsmid, H. Naylor Grimson, Jerrold Heather, George P. Lester, Bruce Lindley, Paul Lovett, Frederick F. Loyd, D. Lewin Mannering, Oswald Marshall, Royce Milton, Harry Paulton, senior, Harry Paulton, junior, Lennox Pawle, Edward S. Petley, Edward Y. Rae, Walter L. Rignold, A. Maitland Stapley, Frank S. Strickland, E. Howard Templeton, Gerald Mirrielees, Clifford Rean, and Langford Reed.

OBJECTS.

The objects of the Union are defined as follow :—

1. To endeavour to establish an equitable minimum salary, and to regulate the relations between members and their employers, and also between member and member.

2. To secure unity of action by organisation and otherwise, in order to improve the position and status of the profession of Actors.

3. To abolish all abuses detrimental to their welfare.

4. To promote industrial peace and progress by all amicable means, and when differences do arise, to assist in obtaining an equitable settlement by reasonable means.

5. To accumulate from the contributions of the members a fund adequate for the protection of their interests, and the provision of the benefits specified.

6. To provide such benefits on the death of a member as herein stated.

7. When the funds of the Union shall permit—

(a) To provide legal assistance to secure the due fulfilment of contracts, the payment of money due under contracts, or compensation due to its members, with all or any of the above objects within the limits allowed by law.

(b) The securing, or assisting in securing, of legislation for the protection of the Union's interests, and for the general and material welfare of its members.

(c) The adoption of any other legal method which may be decided to be advisable in the general interests of the members, declared by a majority of the members of the Executive Committee.

(d) To establish a journal or paper to record the transactions, and be devoted solely to the objects of the Union. The entire profits accruing from such journal (if any) to be added to the general funds of the Union.

(e) To provide a scheme for the establishing of an old-age pension fund.

At the end of 1908 the Union found it necessary to alter their method of subscription. Previously this was 6d. per week for forty weeks in the year. It is now 1s. 8d. paid monthly, or 15s. paid yearly.

Secretary : Mr. Kenneth Blackmore. Office : 49, Bedford Street, Strand, London, W.C.

MISS A. E. F. HORNIMAN'S COMPANY AT THE GAIETY, MANCHESTER.

Inset. Miss A. E. F. Horniman, proprietor and licensee of the theatre.   Schmidt, Manchester.

Back row. Mr. Lewis Casson, Mr. Edward Landor, Mr. Jules Shaw, Mr. Leonard Mudie, Mr. Edwin T. Heys (Acting Manager), Mr. Basil Dean, Mr. Charles Bibby, Mr. Edward Broadley (Stage Manager). 2nd Row, seated.—Mr. Joseph A. Keogh, Miss Sybil Thorndike, Miss Darragh, Mr. B. Iden Payne (General Manager), Miss Penelope Wheeler, Miss Ada King, Miss Lillian Christine. In front. Miss Enid Meek, and Miss Hilda Bruce Potter.

MISS LENA ASHWELL'S "DIANA OF DOBSON'S" (NORTH) COMPANY ON TOUR (AUTUMN).

Back row: MR. W. KINGSFORD PEARCE, MR. EDWARD HARRISON, MR. R. F. BEACH.
Standing: MR. FRANK WOOLFE, MISS E. WILLIAMS, MR. H. B. FITZGIBBON, MISS EVA LONSDALE, MR. STEWART DAWSON.
Seated: MISS DAISY ENGLAND, MISS VIOLET GOULD, MISS EMILIE POLINI, MISS CLARISSA SULWYNNE, MISS GWYNNETH CALTON.
Front: MISS DOROTHY GARTH, MISS OLGA ESMÉ.

MR. J. B. HOWARD'S "WHEN KNIGHTS WERE BOLD" COMPANY ON TOUR (AUTUMN).

Reading left to right. Front row, on ground. Miss Ada Walsh, Mr. Maurice W. Lee, Miss Kitty Carey, Mr. Charles Rapsclose. Second row. Mr. Bert
Benson, Miss Mabel Deville, Miss Edith Aston Laing, Miss Mabel Guthrie, Miss Nora Kingdale, Miss Dorothy Mayhew, Mr. Sydney L. Golding,
Mr. Humphrey Warden, Mr. Arthur Howard. Third row. Mr. Frank Tullick, Mr. Charles Benson, Mr. Alexander Moss, Miss Maud Pescala, Mr.
Myra Stanley. Back row. Mr. Geo. Moss, Miss Emily Billings, Mr. Fred Billings, Mr. Charles Cartwright, Mr. Colin Johnston, Mr. Stanley
Mayd, Mr. Allan Gray.

THE PLAY ACTORS.

THIS Society was formed in June, 1907, amongst several of the more active members of the Actors' Association. The objects of the Play Actors are:—
  1. The production of the plays of Shakespeare and other poetical dramatists without scenery or special costume
  2. The introduction to the public of original plays by English authors.
  3. The representation of adaptations of dramatic works by foreign authors.

From these it will be seen that the objects are in a degree similar to those of other play-producing societies, such as the Incorporated Stage Society, but they go further than these, for in their working details they are so arranged as to bring indirect benefit to the Actors' Association. The membership consists of two degrees —acting membership and ordinary. Only professional players who are members of the Actors' Association are admitted to the first, and from these the various plays presented and produced are cast; £1 1s. and 10s. 6d. are the subscription fees to ordinary members, giving them the right to a couple of seats at each performance of the Society during their season. The £1 1s. subscription carries stall and circle tickets; the 10s. 6d., tickets for the balcony or pit.

During last year thirty-nine plays were submitted to the Council. Of these nine were produced, as follow:—

  The Marquis, sentimental farce, three acts, by Cecil Raleigh and Sydney Dark. Scala, Febuary 9.
  The Philosopher's Stone, phantacy drama, in four acts, by Isaac York. New Royalty, March 1.
  Hannele, a dream poem, by Gerhart Hauptmann, translated from the German by William Archer. Scala, April 12. This play was subsequently produced by Mr. Tree, in conjunction with the Afternoon Theatre, at His Majesty's on
  A Santa Lucia, a two-act play, from the Italian of Goffredo Cognetti, and a scene from *Henry IV.*, Part Two. Scala, May 3.
  The Man Who Won, a three-act play, by A. M. Heathcote. Scala, May 24.
  The Success of Sentiment, play, in three acts, by Hugh Crammer Byng. Court, September 27.
  The Maid's Tragedy, Beaumont and Fletcher's play. Court, October 15.
  The Sentimental Bray, one-act play, by F. D. Bone; *Tilda's New Hat*, one-act play, by George Paston; *Maraquita*, an "incident," by Michael Merrick; and *A Dear Bargain*, one-act play, by F. C. Fenn. Court, November 8.
  The Vagabond, play, in four acts, adapted by M. C. Washburn Freund from the German of Dr. Richard Fellinger. Court, November 29.
  Oop at Kiernstenans, play, in three acts, by Bertha N. Graham. Court, December 20.

The following are the Council of the Play Actors for 1908:—

Mr. Arthur Applin.	Mr. A. M. Heathcote.
Miss Inez Bensusan.	Mr. W. Edwyn Holloway.
Mr. Herbert Bunston.	Mr. Fewlass Llewellyn.
Mr. C. F. Collings.	Miss Rose Mathews.
Mr. Clive Currie.	Mr. Edward Rigby.
Mr. Clarence Derwent.	Mr. Edmund Waller.
Miss Cicely Hamilton.	

Secretary, Miss Winifred Mayo, 3, Bedford Street, Strand, W.C. Hon. Treasurer, Mr. A. M. Heathcote, 81, Albert Bridge Road, Battersea, S.W.

MR. E. S. WILLARD,
In " *The Cardinal*," from the picture by Louis Kronberg.
By permission of Mr. Willard and the Artist.

THE SOCIETY OF WEST END ⟦THEATRE MANAGERS.

The Society of West End Theatre Managers consists of twenty-three members, including two hon. members, Sir Squire Bancroft and Sir John Hare.

The President is Sir Charles Wyndham. The Vice-Presidents are Mr. H. Beerbohm Tree, Mr. George Alexander, Mr. George Edwardes. The Director is Mr. J. E. Vedrenne. The members are Mr. George Alexander, Sir Squire Bancroft, Mr. Arthur Bourchier, Mrs. Helen Carte, Mr. Arthur Chudleigh, Mr. Arthur Collins, Mr. R. Courtneidge, Mr. Frank Curzon, Mr. Tom B. Davis, Mr. George Edwardes, Mr. Charles Frohman, Mr. J. M. Gatti, Mr. William Greet, Sir John Hare. Mr. Frederick Harrison, Mr. Seymour Hicks, Mr. Otho Stuart, Mr. Edward Terry, Mr. H. Beerbohm Tree, Mr. J. E. Vedrenne, Mr. Lewis Waller, Mr. James Welch, Sir Charles Wyndham.

Meetings are held on the first Wednesday of each month at the Society's offices, 52, Shaftesbury Avenue, W. The Committee meet every fortnight.

The theatres controlled by the members are :—Adelphi, Aldwych, Apollo, Comedy, Criterion, Daly's, Drury Lane, Duke of York's, Gaiety, Garrick, Haymarket, Hicks's, His Majesty's, Lyric. New, Prince of Wales's, Queen's, Royalty, St. James's, Savoy, Shaftesbury, Terry's, Vaudeville, and Wyndham's.

THE THEATRICAL MANAGERS' ASSOCIATION.

The Theatrical Managers' Association has ninety-seven members, who represent about 180 theatres.

The President is : Mr. H. Beerbohm Tree.

The Vice-Presidents are :
⟨ Mr. J. Macready Chute.
Mr. J. B. Mulholland.
⟨ Mr. Edward Terry.

The Council, which is elected annually, consists of nine members representing London theatres, and nine members representing country theatres. The present Council is as follows :—

LONDON MEMBERS.

Mr. H. Beerbohm Tree.	Mr. Seymour Hicks.
Mr. Arthur Collins.	Mr. H. G. Dudley Bennett.
Mr. Edward Terry.	Mr. Cyril Maude.
Mr. Ernest Carpenter.	Mr. F. Fredericks.
Mr. J. B. Mulholland.	

COUNTRY MEMBERS.

Mr. J. M. Chute.	Mr. Milton Bode.
Mr. F. W. Wyndham.	Mr. John Hart.
Mr. F. Mouillot.	Mr. T. Sergenson.
Mr. E. Stevens.	Mr. W. B. Redfern.
Mr. T. H. Birch.	

The annual general meeting takes place about the last Tuesday in January. In future the business of the Association will be divided up into sections representing :—Central London Managers, Suburban Managers, Provincial Managers, Touring Managers, and each section will have its own Committee on the General Council ; and fixed dates will be arranged for future Council meetings and general meetings to take place during the year.

Secretary, Mr. H. Blackmore, 11, Garrick Street, London, W.C.

8

THE ACTORS' ORPHANAGE FUND.

THIS FUND, founded in 1896 by Mrs. C. L. Carson, has for patrons the Queen, the Princess of Wales, and the Princess Royal. Mr. Cyril Maude is the President, being elected to that position on the death of the late Sir Henry Irving, the Fund's first President. Vice-Presidents are Lady Bancroft, Mrs. C. L. Carson, Miss Winifred Emery, Miss Ellen Terry, Mr. George Alexander, Mr. Edward Terry, Mr. H. Beerbohm Tree, and Mrs. Beerbohm Tree. Trustees are Mr. Arthur Bourchier, Mr. Charles Cruikshanks, and Mr. Harry Nicholls. Hon. Treasurer, Mr. C. Aubrey Smith, and the Secretary, Mr. A. J. Austin. Mrs. C. L. Carson for many years, since the founding of the Fund, carried on the duties of Hon. Secretary, but three years ago gave up her work on account of illness at the time. The offices of the Fund are at 16, York Street, Covent Garden.

EXECUTIVE COMMITTEE.

Miss Carlotta Addison.	Mr. Lyn Harding.
Miss Lena Ashwell.	Mr. Martin Harvey.
Miss Ada Blanche.	Miss Constance Hyem.
Mr. Arthur Bourchier.	Mrs. A. A. Mangles.
Rev. Arthur Brinckman.	Miss Wynne Matthison
Miss Phyllis Broughton.	Mrs. S. Raleigh.
Mrs. Edward Compton.	Miss Cicely Richards.
Mr. Charles Cruikshanks.	Mr. C. Aubrey Smith
Miss Vane Featherston.	Mr. Fred Terry.
Miss Helen Ferrers.	Miss May Warley.
Mrs. L. Gay.	Mrs. Fred Wright.

The constitution of the Actors' Orphanage Fund is as follows:—

NAME.—The Name of this Institution shall be THE ACTORS' ORPHANAGE FUND.

DESIGN.—To board, clothe, and educate destitute children of actors and actresses, and to fit them for useful positions in after life.

DEFINITION OF DESTITUTE CHILDREN.—By destitute children is meant—

(a) A fatherless and motherless child.

(b) A child, of whom one parent is dead, or incapacitated; the other living, but unable to support it.

(c) A child whose father is permanently and entirely unable, by reason of mental or physical affliction, to contribute to the support of the child, the mother living but unable to support it.

During the year 1908 many of the children have been withdrawn from the homes and schools at which they were, and placed under the charge of Mr. Ansell, at 32 and 34, Morland Road, East Croydon. The houses are run as an orphanage, one house being set aside for the girls and the other for the boys. The children attend the various County Council schools in the neighbourhood.

During the year Mr. Cyril Maude instituted a new "penny-a-week" subscription scheme, which is now in operation in many London theatres and many provincial touring companies. The profits from the Garden Party held on June 30 at the Royal Botanic Gardens were about £1,800.

THE ACTORS' ORPHANAGE.

A DINING ROOM IN ONE OF THE HOMES AT CROYDON.

THE ACTORS' ORPHANAGE.

THE HOMES AT 32 & 34, MORLAND ROAD, CROYDON.

THE ACTORS' ORPHANAGE AT CROYDON.

GIRLS' HOCKEY TEAM.
Athletics are generously encouraged at the Homes.

EIGHTEEN PROMISING FOOTBALL PLAYERS.

THE YOUNGER MEMBERS OF A HAPPY FAMILY.

INDOOR AMUSEMENTS FOR ALL.

FOREIGN SEASONS IN LONDON.

FRENCH.

M. COQUELIN AT HIS MAJESTY'S.

M. COQUELIN opened a season of four weeks at His Majesty's on June 15. The first week he devoted to Sardou's *L'Affaire des Poisons*, the remaining three weeks playing a repertory consisting of *Le Bourgeois Gentilhomme*, *Le Voyage de Monsieur Perrichon*, *Les Romanesques*, *L'Eté de St. Martin*, *Le Mariage de Figaro*, *Cyrano de Bergerac*, *Les Bons Villageois*, *L'Abbé Constantin*, *Tartufe*, *Les Précieuses Ridicules*, *La Joie Fait Peur*, and *L'Anglais tel qu'on le Parle*. The last performance was given on Saturday, July 11.

M. SEVERIN-MARS AND COMPANY AT THE ROYALTY.

A Parisian company headed by M. Severin-Mars opened a short season at the Royalty on Monday, June 29, playing *Octave*, *Un Honnête Homme*, *Fleur d'Oranger*, and *La Dernière Soirée de Brummel*.

MME. BARTET AT THE SHAFTESBURY.

On Monday, May 18, Mme. Bartet opened a fortnight's season at the Shaftesbury. Her programme included *La Loi de l'Homme*, by Paul Hervieu; preceded by *Le Caprice*, by Alfred de Musset, *Le Jeu de l'Amour et du Hasard*, by Marivaux, preceded by *La Nuit de Mai*, by Alfred de Musset; *Françillon*, by Alexandre Dumas Fils; *Le Dédale*, by Paul Hervieu; *Bérénice*, by Racine; and *La Nuit d'Octobre*, by Alfred de Musset.

OFFENBACH AT THE SHAFTESBURY.

On June 1 at the Shaftesbury was commenced an Offenbach season, with Mme. Tariol-Baugé in the principal parts. *La Fille du Tambour Major* was the opening piece.

GRAND GUIGNOL AT THE SHAFTESBURY.

Season commencing March 21. *Rosalie*, *L'Angoisse*, *Un Peu de Musique*, *Le Rouge est Mis*, *Les Nuits du Hampton-Club*, *Monsieur Jean*, *Les 3 Messieurs du Havre*, *La Veuve*, *Gardiens de Phare*, etc. Last performance, April 4.

MME. SUZANNE DEPRES AT THE SHAFTESBURY.

Under the direction of Miss Daisy Andrews a fortnightly season was commenced at the Shaftesbury on May 5, with Mme. Suzanne Depres in *La Rafale* and *Poil de Carotte* (the English version of which Mr. Forbes Robertson and Miss Gertrude Elliott play as *Carrots*), *Le Détour* and *A Doll's House*, *La Robe Rouge*, and *Denise*.

MLLE. THÉRAY AT TERRY'S.

November 2. *Le Grand Soir* and *Le Cœur a ses Raisons*. Transferred to the Court, November 9, where they were played for a few nights.

THE SICILIAN PLAYERS.

The Sicilian Players, headed by Cav. Giovanni Grasso and Mimi Aguglia Ferrau, opened at the Shaftesbury on Monday, February 3, with a play by Luigi Capuana, entitled *Malia*. During their season the Players were seen in the following:—*Cavalleria Rusticana*, *La Zolfara*, *La Figlia di Jorio*, *Juan José*, *Morte Civile*, *Rusidda*, *La Lupa*, *Feudalismo*. Their season ended on March 14.

GERMAN.

HANS ANDRESEN AT THE ROYALTY.

Herr Hans Andresen opened a short season at the Royalty on April 27 with Gustav Kadelburg's farce *Der Weg für Hölle*, followed by Gottbold Ephraim Lessing's comedy *Minna von Barnhelm* on May 2; and by Richard Skowronnek's farce *Panne* on May 4.

THE CHINESE STAGE.

BY THE SHANGHAI CORRESPONDENT OF "THE STAGE."

THROUGHOUT the Empire of China are to be found playhouses. Frequently in smaller towns they are connected with the temples, the priests, as of yore in the West, supervising the dramatic fare. In country places the theatre is often an open-air affair, the audience standing in a temple court-yard, the performance taking place upon a raised platform. In the great cities large substantial theatres are the rule, and these remain open nearly all the year round.

OPEN-AIR THEATRE IN CHEFOO, NORTH CHINA.

They are for the most part quite independent of the priesthood, and in a great many instances the proprietor or lessee plays leading *rôles*. Historical plays are very common, but the impossible things which are supposed to occur suggest that the stories are more legendary than historical. Tragedy, melodrama, domestic comedy (treated with frank sincerity and the broadest humour), and farce are all played.

SHANGHAI THEATRES.

The principal native theatres in Shanghai, the chief centre of European activity in China, are the Chun Kwei Theatre and the Tai Kwei Theatre, both capable of seating about 2,000 persons. These theatres are very similar in interior appearance to the playhouses in other large towns in China. They are rectangular in shape,

THE CHINESE STAGE.

(Photographs specially taken for the STAGE YEAR BOOK.)

SET STAGE IN CHUN KWEI THEATRE, SHANGHAI.

ENTRANCE TO CHUN KWEI THEATRE, SHANGHAI.

THE CHINESE STAGE.

(Photographs specially taken for the STAGE YEAR BOOK.)

VIEW OF STAGE FROM AUDITORIUM OF TAI KWEI THEATRE, SHANGHAI.

HOOPEH ROAD, SHANGHAI, SHOWING ENTRANCE TO TAI KWEI THEATRE.

and the auditorium itself is almost square. Neither back or front is there any rake, and the orchestra sits at one side of the stage. It is a little difficult for an Occidental to understand the uses of the Chinese orchestra, the instruments consisting chiefly of cymbals and gongs (often cracked) and flutes of a peculiarly piercing shrillness. The energies of the performers would seem to be called chiefly into play to drown the despairing cries of hapless victims undergoing execution or torture, or to perform a sort of spontaneous outburst of merriment on the utterance of some choice piece of ribaldry, or on the utter annihilation of some unfortunate misdemeanant.

It is very rarely that women appear on the Chinese stage, the female *rôles* being portrayed by youths of diminutive stature, who walk about upon short stilts which enable them to give their feet the cramped appearance of native ladies.

Scenery there is none, and properties are vague, and leave much to the imagination of the spectators. To a European not understanding the language, and failing to follow the *argumentum*, the only source of interest must be the costumes, which are of the richest texture and most gorgeous appearance.

CHINESE PLAYGOERS.

Chinese playgoers take their meals with them frequently, and sit round little tables and pay but slight attention to the performance, often sitting with their backs to the stage. Frequently also they go to sleep, and sometimes come with their bed (of the Biblical description) and have a refreshing siesta on the floor.

Connecting the auditorium with the stage is a long gangway down which "a robber chief" sometimes comes to hide amongst the audience, and up which sometimes a few members of the audience meander to settle some knotty question of the texture of some admired garment on the leading lady, by a closer inspection. If "she" has left the stage they proceed through the back-cloth in pursuit, or sit down upon a stool (which may be a "castle" or a "mountain") on the stage, until the object of their admiration makes another appearance.

Whether the people enjoy the performance or not it would be hard to say, but theatre-going seems a popular way of spending an evening with one's friends, and the crowded state of the houses bespeaks good business.

THE LYCEUM, SHANGHAI.

The Lyceum Theatre, in the Foreign Settlement of Shanghai, is a handsome playhouse of European construction and design, and is the property of the Shanghai Amateur Dramatic Club. It has a large gallery, a dress-circle, backed by twelve boxes, six stage-boxes, pit and stalls. During the past twelve months the English Amateur Dramatic Club have produced about eight pieces, the German Amateur Dramatic Club and the French Amateur Dramatic Club one or two each. Professional visits have been received from the Bandmann Comedy company, the Bandmann Opera company (with Mr. Henry Dallas), Professor Carter (a magician, hailing from the United States), and the Westminster Glee Singers (under the direction of Mr. Edward Branscombe).

THE REHEARSAL CLUB.

The Rehearsal Club (29, Leicester Square) was founded in 1892 with the view to furnishing a quiet retreat to which minor actresses might resort between the hours of rehearsals and *matinées* and the evening performance.

The member's subscription is 2s. per quarter. The club is open from 11 a.m. to 8 p.m., and contains comfortable reading and refreshment rooms, the former well supplied with books, papers, and magazines. Anyone wishing to see the club will be gladly shown over by one of the committee or the matron.

President, H.R.H. Princess Christian of Schleswig-Holstein; Committee : Chair, Lady Louisa Magenis, Mrs. George Alexander, Lady Bancroft, Mrs. Herbert Brooks, Mrs. Percy Buchanan, Mrs. Chapman, Mrs. Gilmour, Miss Alice Gladstone, Mrs. Max Hecht, Mrs. R. S. Henderson, Mrs. Kendal, Lady Frances Legge, Mrs. George Marjoribanks, Mrs. Cyril Maude, Mrs. Mayne, Mrs. F. M. Paget, Mrs. Pownell, Mrs. Beerbohm Tree, Eleonora Lady Trevelyan, Mrs. Philip Walker, Mrs. W. H. Wharton; Hon Treasurer. Mrs. Mayne, 101, Queen's Gate, S.W.; Hon. Secretary, Mrs. George Marjoribanks, 22. Hans Road, S.W.; Secretary. Miss Davenport Crosier, 88, Vauxhall Bridge Road, S.W.

THE GARRICK CLUB.

The Garrick Club, Garrick Street, Covent Garden, was founded in 1831. Its objects are defined as follows:—"The Garrick Club is instituted for the general patronage of the drama, for the purpose of combining a club, on economic principles, with the advantages of a Literary Society, for bringing together the supporters of the Drama, and for the foundation of a theatrical library with works on Costume. Secretary, Mr. Charles J. Fitch.

THE SAVAGE CLUB.

The Savage Club, 6 and 7, Adelphi Terrace, Strand, London, W.C., is for the association of gentlemen connected professionally with Literature, Art, Science, the Drama, or Music. Trustees :—Mr. E. G. Ravenstein, Mr. A. Gordon Salamon, Sir W. Purdie Treloar, Bart. Committee :—Col. W. J. Bosworth, Mr. F. Bowyer, Mr. F. Franklin Clive, Mr. Conrad W. Cooke, M.Inst.E.E., Mr. Crandon D. Gill, Mr. Reginald Groome, Mr. Fred. Grundy, Mr. Yeend King, V.P.R.I., R.B.A., Mr. Eille Norwood, Mr. Mostyn T. Pigott, Lieut. J. Mackenzie Rogan, M.V.O., Mr. J. Scott Stokes. Hon. Treasurer, Sir James D. Linton, R.I.; Hon. Secretary, Mr. E. E. Peacock; Hon. Solicitor, Mr. R. H. Humphreys; Hon. Counsel, Mr. Rufus Isaacs, K.C., M.P.; Hon. Auditors and Scrutineers, Messrs. Thomas Catling and Achille Bazire; Hon. Librarian, Mr. C. J. Shedden Wilson.

THE ECCENTRIC CLUB.

The Eccentric Club, Limited, 21, Shaftesbury Avenue, W.C., is constituted for the purpose of promoting social intercourse amongst gentlemen connected, directly or indirectly, with Literature, Art, Music, the Drama, the Scientific and Liberal Professions, Sport, and Commerce. The President is Sir Charles Wyndham; Trustees, Mr. Walter J. W. Beard, Mr. J. R. Cleave, Mr. John Woodhouse, J.P.; Treasurers, Mr. Tom Fraser and Mr. William H. White; Hon. Secretary, Mr. J. A. Harrison. Committee:—Major H. Bateman, Messrs. H. Montague Bates, Fred Bishop, Frank Boor, Lionel Brough, Frank Callingham, E. L. Campbell, Alfred Ellis, Walter de Frece, W. E. Garstin, A. E. Gatcombe, Denby Hare, H. J. Homer, Thomas Honey, W. S. Hooper, J. D. Langton, John Le Hay, E. Lockwood, Ernest Stuart, W. J. Dayer Smith, A. J. Thomas, and R. Warner.

THE MANAGERS' CLUB.

The Managers' Club is instituted for the purpose of bringing touring and resident managers, theatrical proprietors, and all interested in theatrical enterprises and business into touch with each other. The club has 190 members, and the annual subscription is £2 2s., except in the case of members of the Touring Managers' Association, Limited, who pay an annual subscription of £1 1s. in addition to their subscription to the Association. The Committee, which is elected annually, consists of twenty-one members. The present Committee is as follows:—President, Mr. M. V. Leveaux; Hon. Treasurer, Mr. J. Banniter Howard; Assistant Hon. Treasurer, Mr. Frank Weathersby; Messrs. A. Clifton Alderson, Rollo Balmain, Cecil Barth, Arthur Bertram, Charles Carey, Edward Compton, Wentworth Croke, Peter Davey, E. Graham Falcon, Walter Howard, W. W. Kelly, Edmund Lockwood, F. H. Pedgrift, G. M. Polini, Alfred Paumier, Herbert Ralland, Edward Terry, H. Beerbohm Tree, John Tully. Secretary, Mr. M. Martin. Address, Savoy Mansions, Strand, W.C.

THE GREEN ROOM CLUB.

The Green Room Club was founded in 1877 for the association of gentlemen of the dramatic profession. Secretary, Mr. T. S. Swann. Address, 46, Leicester Square.

THE YORICK CLUB.

For those connected with Literature, the Drama, Music, and the Arts. Entrance fee, £2 2s.; subscription, £2 2s. Committee: Messrs. E. H. Bull, A. C. R. Carter, C. F. Cazenove, E. Radclyffe Crump, J. Nicol Dunn, Sidney Gandy, W. E. Grogan, Graham Hill, David Hodge, W. W. Jacobs, E. F. Knight, William Mudford. Frank L. Teed, and Standley Wade. Hon. Librarian, Mr. W. Pett Ridge ; Hon. Director of Art, Mr. S. H. Sime ; Hon. Director of Music, Mr. Duncan Tovey ; Master of Revels, Mr. George Parlby; Hon. Secretaries, Mr. A. C. R. Carter and Mr. William Mudford; House Manager, Mr. W. Bradford Smith. Address, 30, Bedford Street. Strand.

Ellis and Walery.

MISS MARIE LLOYD,
From a recent photograph.

THE VARIETY STAGE.

BY W. H. CLEMART.

T HE year 1908 has undoubtedly been one of the most eventful in the annals of
the music hall profession. The old year 1907 had hardly ended with the
successful protest by the Grand Order of Water Rats against the introduction to the variety stage of Wood, of the Camden Town mystery, when the
new year 1908 immediately commenced to make more music hall history. On
January 1 a regulation came into force requiring managers who desired the
gratuitous services of the members of the Variety Artists' Federation at charity
matinées, anniversaries, and managers' benefits, to obtain permission from the
Executive Committee of that body, and also to undertake to give 2½ per cent. of
the proceeds on such performances to the newly formed Variety Artists' Benevolent
Fund. The result of this regulation has been varied, but undoubtedly beneficial,
as it has relieved the members of many a thankless task. In very many cases per-
missions have been asked for and obtained, and in some cases in special circumstances the donation to the Benevolent Fund has been foregone. Anniversaries
have been conspicuous by their absence, and managers' benefits few and far between.
Mr. Oswald Stoll proceeded to promote charity *matinées* at his different halls as
usual. He made application by letter to individual artists, who referred him back
to the Executive. The first took place at the Grand Theatre, Birmingham, on
January 25. Not one of the Federation's members appeared, thus proving that
the loyalty of its members could not be shaken. Mr. Stoll has persevered in the
matter, and periodically has promoted *matinées* in each of his halls. In some cases
he has succeeded in obtaining the services of a few members of the V.A.F., and
these have immediately been expelled for their disloyalty. The Artists'
Protection League, under the generalship of Mr. Frank Gerald, the first ex-general
secretary of the V.A.F., held a meeting to protest against the "Charity Matinée"
policy of the Federation. This was held on March 8, at the New Cross Empire, on
the same evening on which the pick of the music hall profession was holding the
first annual dinner of the Variety Artists' Benevolent Fund at the Criterion
Restaurant, at which £1,000 was subscribed for the sweet cause of charity. *En
passant*, the Artists' Protection League has since been expelled from the Trades
Union Congress.

The next move came from Mr. George Ranken Askwith, the arbitrator, who
invited the representatives of the V.A.F. to meet Mr. Stoll before him to discuss
the matter, and, if possible, to bring it to an amicable settlement. The meeting
was held at the Board of Trade offices on March 27. After listening intently to
both parties, Mr. Askwith drew up a statement to the effect that, in the event of
Mr. Stoll wishing to give a charity matinée, a letter should be written to the
Executive Committee mentioning the fact, and, in the event of the Committee being
satisfied with the bonâ-fides of such charity, the V.A.F. would co-operate with
Mr. Stoll, and further that the 2½ per cent. be foregone, and that Mr. Stoll should
make a suitable donation at his own discretion. On behalf of the V.A.F. its representatives, Messrs. O'Gorman, Pink, and Clemart, signified their acceptance of Mr.
Askwith's proposition. Mr. Stoll preferred to take time to consider it, which he
did, and on April 16 notified Mr. Askwith in diplomatic language that he could not
see his way to give recognition to the Executive, and so the matter remains to this
moment.

Charity *matinées* were undoubtedly becoming so prolific that they were
proving an overwhelming burden to the artist, to whom seldom, if ever,
was any recognition tendered It is a good thing, indeed, to be charitable, but it is interference with the liberty of the subject when one has to
be charitable at the dictation of a third party. The ulterior motive for the

continued promotion of these charity matinées is not hard to discern. They are intended to bring people into the halls who may not otherwise visit them, and thus convert some of them into becoming habitués. It can also be easily understood that at licensing time the authorities may find it harder to refuse a license to, or easier to overlook any little lapse on the part of, a management which has done much for the local charities. It has never been denied that these matinées are bonâ-fide as far as the charities benefiting, but it has always been transparent that they are also a means to an end. Outside the charities themselves the only people who benefit are the managements, who practically do nothing personally except give permission for the use of the theatres. The artists, who do all the work, and who are the attraction, are seldom thanked.

Anniversaries never served any useful purpose whatever. They were merely excuses to extract more gratuitous service from the artists, with the intention of once a year putting more money into the pockets of the management.

Managers' benefits are a scandal, and are the results of the poor salaries as a rule paid to these gentlemen by their employers. It is a system whereby the proprietors force the artists by their labour to contribute to the maintenance of their managers. They put their managers in the degrading position of being paid partly in money, and partly by "benefit," which means they have to cadge from the artists to make up their salaries to living wages. No wonder, then, that the artists should wish to abolish such abuses.

THE AGENTS.

The great event of the year, however, has been the struggle between the V.A.F. and the main body of music hall agents. The agency question was one which sooner or later was bound to come to a head. The methods which have obtained in agency work have been, generally speaking, little short of a scandal, both as regards the amount of commission charged, and the manner in which the business has been conducted. No more evidence to prove the agents have been overpaid is required than the fact that many have in a few years made fortunes. For over two years negotiations, which have proved abortive, have been going on between the parties concerned, but in January, 1908, at the earnest and unanimous demand of the main body of members, the Executive Committee of the V.A.F. appointed a sub-committee, with the full determination to better the conditions under which the music hall profession was being forced to work. After many meetings, much discussion, and a great deal of delay, caused chiefly by the charity matinée dispute, a conference was held between the agents and the sub-committee at 28, Wellington Street, on August 27, at which was discussed a new form of "commission-note," which had been drawn up for the agents' consideration. The first condition to which the agents absolutely objected was a clause, which would have bound them not to offer any contract which was not in strict conformity to the Award, and, as some of them had undoubtedly assisted the managers in keeping the non-award contract on the market for months after the publication of the Award, this point cannot be said to reflect much credit in their direction. Then came the question of the rate of commission. It was agreed this should not exceed 10 per cent., the V.A.F. Sub-Committee requiring that it should apply to all contracts made in England to be played in any part of the world. To this the agents objected, and insisted upon a clause being inserted limiting the rate of 10 per cent. only to contracts to be played in the British Isles ; at the same time, it was plainly stated that it was the intention to charge 15 per cent. on Continental and American business. The question of paying commission on the first or next re-engagement, whether made by the same agent or not, was next discussed, and on the Sub-Committee demanding the entire abolition of this clause, the agents expressed a desire to be allowed to discuss the matter privately, which they did. They finally announced that they were prepared to forego this clause as between agent and agent, but wished to insert a clause to the effect that the same rate of commission should be paid in the event of an artist settling the next engagement direct with a manager within three months of the expiration of the first engagement.

The deduction of the commission by the manager on behalf of the agent was accepted after a little discussion. It will thus be seen the points agreed on were :—
    (1) The rate of commission not to be more than 10 per cent.
    (2) The abolition of the re-engagement clause as between agent and agent.
    (3) The deduction of commission by the managers.
    (4) The guarantee of Award contracts by the agents was forgone.

The points not agreed upon, but to be referred to the general meeting of the V.A.F. on September 6, were :—
  (1) Limitation of the 10 per cent. rate to the British Isles.
  (2) The three months' re-engagement clause on business done direct with a manager.
The general meeting, however, threw out these two points, leaving the conditions at 10 per cent. on work done, and with the right of the manager to deduct the commission in favour of the agents. A meeting was arranged with the agents to receive the report of the General Meeting, but they failed to put in an appearance. The Executive then ordered that payment of all commissions should be suspended, and gave the agents notice that unless the above conditions were accepted within a week, the commission would be reduced to 5 per cent. The agents remaining silent, they were given notice that if 5 per cent. was not accepted all business would be suspended. The agents still remaining silent, a "boycott" was ordered, and this existed to the end of the year. Finding the managers were assisting the agents by refusing to do business with the artists directly, or through any other agencies than those boycotted, the V.A.F. applied to the General Federation of Trade Unions for assistance. Finally a meeting was arranged by them at the House of Commons, at which Mr. Pete Curran, M.P., presided, supported by Mr. John Ward, M.P., and Mr. W. A. Appleton. The V.A.F. was represented by Messrs. Joe O'Gorman, Wal Pink, Geo. B. Sinclair, and W. H. Clemart; and the Agents' Association by Messrs. Hugh J. Didcott, George Barclay, Sydney Hyman, and Emanuel Warner. The terms of reference were drawn up by Mr. Appleton, Secretary to the General Federation of Trade Unions, and each member present had a copy in front of him. They were :—
  1. To determine the powers of the representatives of the two societies.
  2. Re-engagements.
  3. Rate of commission.
  4. Method of collecting commission.
Each party, having stated that they had plenary powers to act, agreed that clauses 2, 3, and 4 covered all points in dispute. The re-engagement clause was discussed for three hours, at which point the meeting adjourned without having arrived at any definite decision.

A week passed, during which Mr. Appleton carried on negotiations with first one party and then the other, and also consulted some of the more important managers. He eventually informed the V.A.F. that the agents refused to discuss the re-engagement clause further until the V.A.F. agreed to 10 per cent. commission, and the deduction by the managers. This the V.A.F. declined to do, and on December 24 called upon the General Federation of Trade Unions to help in a boycott of those managers who were assisting the agents, and who could, by one word, have brought the matter to a conclusion. The General Federation of Trade Unions stated that before proceeding to extremities they must offer arbitration to the agents on all points in dispute. To this the V.A.F. agreed under pressure. On December 30 the agents held a meeting to decide the matter, and late that evening Mr. Appleton communicated the fact to the V.A.F. that the agents had agreed to accept arbitration. Thus everything looked bright for a happy settlement before the old year died. But it was not to be. On the Thursday morning, December 31, the V.A.F. representatives drew up with Mr. Appleton terms of reference similar to those used at the House of Commons. In the afternoon the agents met Mr. Appleton, and at 7 p.m. Mr. Appleton informed the V.A.F. that the agents demanded the insertion of a new clause to the effect "that no person should act as artist and agent at the same time." This was absolutely refused by the V.A.F. representatives as being a point which had not been raised before arbitration had been agreed upon ; a point which was outside the dispute ; and an infringement on the liberty of the subject. Thus the old year closed with a gloomy aspect, and it is feared that the early months of the New Year will see a disruption of the music hall industry on a scale which a year or two ago would never have been thought possible. The verdict is in the hands of the managers, who can by one word to the agents avert disaster. Will they speak that word?

THE GERMAN MUSIC HALL WAR OF 1908.

THIS is the history of a determined struggle on the part of the German Variety Artists for the betterment of their lot; the history of a campaign skilfully carried through by force of solid combination and brilliant leadership, with little or no bloodshed on either side, and with the ultimate happy outcome of perfectly justifiable demands being conceded to the claimants and a lasting peace on a sound basis being concluded to the satisfaction of all concerned.

EARLY ACTIVITY.

During the seven years preceding the recent campaign the International Artists' Lodge, a body corresponding to the British Variety Artists' Federation and the American White Rats, was silently busy in educating its members to that self-conscious *amour propre* and *esprit de corps* without which any concerted action would have been predestined to failure. Many abuses had also been swept away through the instrumentality of the Lodge; irksome imposts, such as the 4 per cent. tax on all salaries earned in the Hanse town of Bremen, were abolished after a long campaign, culminating in an appeal to the Imperial Chancellor; and, on the whole, largely due to the influence of the I.A.L., the status of the variety artist on the Continent had been distinctly improved.

Yet much remained to be done, and the Executive of the Lodge, under the presidency of Mr. Max Berol-Konorah, himself an artist of many years' experience, now retired, attacked their task with quiet determination on well-thought-out lines of action. Their primary object, for which they obtained the hearty co-operation of the members of the V.A.F. and the White Rats of America, was the establishment of a fair and equitable contract between manager and artist. As matters stood, as recently as the month of August, a performer might arrive at Cologne from Chicago or Melbourne only to be coolly informed on the first, second, or third night that, under the three days' cancellation clause, which was exercised entirely at the arbitrary discretion of the manager, his services would no longer be required. This, of course, owing to long and expensive travel, hit the English and American artist even harder than the German. The last-named, moreover, from a more intimate knowledge of the language, was better able to guard against the many pitfalls in which the contract then abounded. All the contracts, though they differed in terms, were entirely in favour of the managements, who, whilst jealously guarding their own rights, bound themselves to nothing beyond the payment of a stipulated sum as salary.

THE FIRST BUGLE CALL.

In pursuance of their plan of campaign, outlined at the second public meeting, which was held at Berlin on July 8, the International Artists' Lodge issued general orders with regard to the boycott of four halls—the Apollo Theatre, Düsseldorf; the Reichshallen Theatre, Cologne; the Kolosseum, Essen; and the Olympia Theatre, Dortmund. According to these orders no member of the Association was allowed to enter into any contract to appear at any of these halls until further notice. Contracts already signed were to be carried out, unless they could be rescinded. At the same time an earnest appeal was issued to the V.A.F. and the White Rats of America, as well as to non-associated variety artists in general, to stand solid, and to prove to the managers and the public their *esprit de corps* and their determination to fight for recognition and a fair contract. It may here be mentioned that the International Variety Theatre Managers' League at first refused to recognise the existence of the I.A.L., and subsequently declined to negotiate with the artists' representative body so long as their Executive, notably Mr. Berol-Konorah, remained in office.

MR. JOE O'GORMAN,
Chairman of the Variety Artists' Federation.

MR. JOE ELVIN,

President of the Music Hall Artists' Railway Association, and also of the Variety Artists' Benevolent Fund.

So far as Great Britain was concerned, the campaign was opened with a meeting on Sunday, August 2, at the Hotel de Provence in Leicester Square, when Mr. William Berol, who attended as a special delegate from the I.A.L. at Berlin, explained to a representative and sympathetic gathering the circumstance under which the Lodge had been compelled to resort to active measures. On that occasion a resolution was moved by Mr. George Gray, and unanimously carried, to the effect : " That this meeting wishes to extend its sympathy and pledges its unstinted support to the I.A.L. in its endeavour to obtain a fair and equitable contract." The defence fund, for the benefit of which a 2 per cent. levy on members' salaries had been made, was considerably increased by Mr. William Berol's appeals at the principal British centres.

THE COMMANDER-IN-CHIEF.

The chief reason why, in spite of seven years' activity, no better results had been obtained was the fact that the Committee consisted of artists who, owing to their different engagements, were unable to devote sufficient time to the affairs of the I.A.L. It was, therefore, decided to entrust the management of the Lodge to some person of international experience, conversant with languages and law, possessed of tact, and in sympathy with the needs of the artistic fraternity. Such a man was found in Mr. Max Berol-Konorah, who was unanimously elected for the post of President. Born forty years ago of German parents, the President is an American, no mean linguist, an experienced lawyer, and a well-known writer on professional topics. That the I.A.L. under his rule has always striven to be impartial is shown by the fact that in several cases where the artist was at fault the cause of the management was espoused. Thus, in two instances (Director Prinz, Königsberg, and Director Busch, Berlin), fines incurred by artists were paid by the Lodge, while commissions due to agencies were collected.

CAUSES OF FRICTION.

An opportunity for attempting to discredit the President with the members of the I.A.L. was supposed to have been found in the following occurrence by some of the directors of variety halls. In a judgment delivered in the court at Dresden it had been held that no playlet or sketch could be performed unless the producer or manager of the company, as well as the director of the hall, held a license for the performing of such entertainments. Since quite a number of such touring companies were without such an official permit, the Lodge, in a circular letter, drew the attention of local directors to this verdict, and requested that great care should be exercised in ascertaining whether such license were held previous to an engagement being made. This, and the fact that a number of trade unions had been approached by Mr. Konorah with a view to enlisting their sympathy with the artists from the paying spectator's point of view, was regarded by the directors, who had convened a Congress of Middle European Variety Directors at Düsseldorf, as an unwarranted, insolent, and impertinent interference with their right of action. Mr. Konorah's reply was to place his resignation in the hands of his Committee, who, however, did not accept it, but forwarded to him a unanimous vote of confidence in writing.

Whilst the Lodge's demand for official recognition was met with a curt refusal on the part of the managers, the latter issued a revised contract, which the members of the Directors' Union were pledged to use from September 1, 1908.

THE LAST PHASE.

Numerous attempts at bringing about a peaceful issue were always wrecked on the obstinate refusal of the directors to recognise the existing Executive of the I.A.L., who, they alleged, had been guilty of gross insults towards the body of directors in general. This the Committee of the Lodge denied repeatedly, offering every *amende honorable*, which, however, was not accepted. Thus matters dragged on for several months, during the course of which a few more boycotted halls were added to the Lodge's black-list. The directors' refusal to recognise the Executive of the Lodge was interpreted by the latter as an infringement of their right of coalition, and by a bold stroke the artists carried the war into the enemy's camp. This was nothing more nor less than an attack on the citadel of the leader of the Directors' Union, Director Bartuschek's Centralhallen in Stettin. At a meeting of the Stettin Branch of the German Trades Unions, which the President of the I.A.L. attended, the following resolution was carried : " This meeting of citizens of Stettin, convened by the local branch of the German Trades Unions, emphatically condemns every attempt at infringing the rights of coalition legally enjoyed by workers of every description. The right of coalition is a sacred right, and must not be tampered with. Therefore, the meeting condemns the attitude of a number of variety directors, among them the management of the Centralhallen Theatre, who are endeavouring to rob the artists of the benefits engendered by the right of coalition. The assembled citizens declare, therefore, their intention of not visiting the Centralhallen until an understanding has been effected between the Directors' Union and the I.A.L."

PEACE AT LAST.

At length, on the occasion of the "Dom" at Hamburg, the gigantic Christmas fair which gathers together artists, directors, and agents from all parts of the Continent, better counsels prevailed, and on Saturday, December 12, there was ratified at Berlin, between representatives of both bodies, a peace, the terms of which are as follows :—

1. The International Artists' Lodge declares that no intention of insulting the Directors' Union had ever been in its mind.

2. The Directors' Union rescinds its resolution of August 22, 1908, acknowledges the entire Executive of the Lodge, and will in future keep in touch with the Lodge for common action.

3. In cases of dispute or arbitration the I.A.L. undertakes the defence of the artist.

4. All boycotts on the part of the directors are raised. It is not intended to take any retributory measures.

5. All boycotts on the part of the Lodge are raised.

6. The minutes of the proceedings drafted conjointly by the President of the Lodge and the Secretary of the Directors' Union will be published without comment in the official organs, *Das Programm* and *Das Organ.*

THE COPYRIGHT-PLAY PROTECTION ASSOCIATION.

The Copyright-Play Protection Association was established in January, 1907. Its objects are to prevent the representation of its members' dramatic property without fee or license; to stop the sale of piratical manuscripts of members' plays, etc.; to advise upon any question of dramatic copyright; to watch over and protect the interests of authors and play proprietors generally; to represent rights in and protect the works of deceased members when authorised so to do. The method the Association adopts is to obtain provincial bills every week, and as these bills come in it first warns those who may be acting the members' pieces without permission. If the offence is persisted in the Association then takes out summonses. During the past year the Association has done much good work. Cases of ordinary piracy taken up are too numerous to mention, as sometimes there have been a dozen in one week. The following cases, occurring during 1908, are examples of the work of the Association :—(1) *The Camden Town Murder*, an unlicensed play found being acted by Broadbent Bell. This, on the Association's information, was ultimately stopped at Canterbury by the Public Prosecutor. (2) The opposition to granting of license for stage plays to Wilson Stacey, at Penrith, on ground that he was not a fit and proper person to hold same. License refused. (3) Prosecution of lessee and proprietor of Hippodrome, Cambridge, for acting plays without a license.

The following is the roll of members:—Messrs. George R. Sims, Wm. Greet, Brandon Thomas, E. Hill-Mitchelson, Walter Howard, W. W. Kelly, W. Lestocq, Harry Nicholls, F. Sutton-Vane, Walter Melville, Fredk. Melville, Chas. Frohman, Arthur Shirley, E. Graham-Falcon, Benjamin Landeck, George Gray, H. A. Saintsbury, Eric Hudson, Herbert C. Sargent, W. Muskerry-Tilson, W. W. Jacobs, Arthur Morrison, Ernest Carpenter, F. Llewellyn, Ernest Martin, J. B. Mulholland, Watson Mill, Wentworth Croke, Henry Chattell, Chas. Macdona, G. M. Polini, A. Clifton Alderson, Henry Bedford, Herbert Leonard, and Miss Harriet Hay, Frank Harvey (Exors.), Geo. Conquest (Exors.), and " French's, Limited." Chairman, Mr. A. Shirley; Secretary, Mr. S. Clare. Office :—11, Newport House, Great Newport Street, W.C.

MR. W. H. CLEMART,
King Rat in the Grand Order of Water Rats (1908), and General Secretary of the
Variety Artists' Federation.

MUSIC HALL ARTISTS' RAILWAY ASSOCIATION.

Founded February, 1897. Head offices, 28, Wellington Street, Strand, London, W.C. Secretary, Mr. C. Douglas Stuart. Glasgow branch offices, Cockburn Buildings, 141, Bath Street, Glasgow; Mrs. Geo. Ripon, agent. Manchester branch offices, All Saints' Chambers, 46, Sidney Street; Fred Slingsby. agent. Officers :— Hon. President, Mr. Joe Elvin; Hon. Vice-Presidents, Sir James Bailey, Mr. Albert Le Fre, and Mr. Fred W. Millis; Hon. Trustees, Mr. J. W. Cragg, Mr. Paul Martinetti, and Mr. G. H. Chirgwin; Hon. Treasurer, Mr. Arthur Rigby; Hon. Solicitor, Mr. Eugene Judge (Judge and Priestley), 10, Warwick Court, Holborn, W.C.; Auditors, Messrs. Jackson, Pixley, and Co. (Chartered Accountants). This past twelve months, if not strikingly eventful as regards this society of performers, has yet been not quite without interest. Over four hundred more new members were enrolled than in the year preceding, and the total number is now close upon 7,000. The annual dinner and dance was this year held in aid of the newly formed Benevolent Fund. Mr. W. H. Clemart, the president, occupied the chair, and more than 300 were present. It was a magnificent success, the profit on the tickets alone being £26, and nearly £900 was obtained for the charity. In April Mr. Douglas White, who had acted as Hon. Treasurer since the foundation of the Association, felt bound, for business reasons, to resign—a fact that was much regretted, and in his place Mr. Arthur Rigby was appointed. At a special general meeting the Executive Committee was increased in number to sixty members, an alteration that has proved very advantageous. During the year branch offices have been opened in Manchester and Liverpool, in addition to that in Glasgow; and this action of the committee has met with considerable favour from the travelling performers. Some little trouble has been caused between the Scotch railways and the Association over the twelve-mile radius limit, but the committee are still hopeful of a peaceful settlement. From April the annual subscription has been raised, on a suggestion from Mr. Joe O'Gorman, by one shilling, that sum being handed over to the Benevolent Fund, and has gained for the latter over £200. Not less a sum than £526 has been distributed during the year between the Railway and Music Hall Charities, increasing thereby the total sum given since the Association was formed to over £3,000. Towards the end of December Mr. W. H. Clemart, the President, tendered his resignation on his appointment as General Secretary of the Variety Artists' Federation, and in his stead Mr. Joe Elvin was appointed to the position. Any information as to joining the Association, and the benefits and advantages to be derived therefrom, can be obtained on application to Mr. C. Douglas Stuart, the Secretary, 28, Wellington Street, W.C.

VARIETY ARTISTS' BENEVOLENT FUND.

This Fund is only just a year old, having been founded on December 7, 1907, but in that brief period it has done a great amount of good work in alleviating the wants of variety performers in need of financial aid by grants and loans. It originated through a suggestion made by Mr. Joe O'Gorman at the 1907 general meeting of the M.H.A.R.A. to start a Fund for artists, to be administered by artists, with a donation of £100. The committee comprise the members of the executive of the M.H.A.R.A., with the addition of a few others, with the same secretary and offices. No better president could have been selected than Mr. Joe Elvin, who has taken a special interest in the Fund, which he has assisted with most liberal donations and a great amount of personal support. At the M.H.A.R.A. Dinner and Dance, held in March in aid of the V.A.B. Fund, over £900 was obtained, and a profit was made on the sports, which were held during the summer. The committee meet every Thursday to consider the numerous applications, and on an average distribute weekly in gifts and loans between £25 and £30. There are thirty-three aged and infirm performers who are in receipt of weekly grants amounting to nearly £10 a week. During the year the funeral expenses of five variety artists—four in London and one in the provinces—have been paid for by the Fund, which has also attended to the needs of the widows or those left behind. Altogether over £1,000 has been given away to the sick, the needy, and the suffering, and in every case strict investigation has been made by the committeemen themselves, in order to ensure that the cases relieved are in every way deserving. The cost of administrating the Fund has been reduced to about 15 per cent., and yet it is efficiently managed. Mr. Elvin, the president, asks us to appeal to every

MR. HARRY LAUDER.

MR. R. A. ROBERTS.

reader of these lines to forward a donation either to himself or to the secretary at 28, Wellington Street, to enable the committee to continue the good work in succouring and aiding those brothers and sisters in the profession who have fallen by the way through misfortune and ill-luck, and are unable to help themselves.

THE TERRIERS' ASSOCIATION.

(Registered pursuant to the Friendly Societies Act.)

This Association has had a most successful year, and is on a sound financial basis, with constantly increasing membership.

The Terriers' Association was formed in 1889 by Mr. Joe Lawrence and other music-hall artists, and their aim was to promote good fellowship and society amongst its members, to assist one another socially, professionally, or financially, to extend the hand of friendship in prosperity or adversity, and be ever mindful of the fact. Should a member meet with misfortune anywhere, he has only to communicate with the Association, and any necessary financial aid is rendered forthwith. If he is taken ill he has but to call in the nearest doctor, and he need have no anxiety whatever regarding the cost. The Association pays all his medical expenses, and also provides him with adequate sick pay. Should he die his wife or nearest relative will receive £20. On the death of his wife he receives £5 towards the expenses. If a Terrier is in urgent need of a loan for any reasonable purpose it is granted, and he can repay it at his convenience.

A ceremonial meet is held in the Kennel, at the "Three Stags" Hotel, Kennington Road, S.E., every Sunday evening, when new members are initiated into the mysteries of the Order, the usual business conducted, and a pleasant hour or two spent in congenial company. During the past year many enjoyable functions have been held, and the dinners, ladies' concerts, suppers, smokers, balls, and the river outing were all successes. The last ladies' concert was held on January 3, 1909, and the annual dinner on January 10, 1909.

President, Mr. Jesse Sparrow; Vice-Presidents, Messrs. J. Alexander, H. Griff, Andie Caine, A. Borelli, Ted Karno, A. Voyce, W. H. Atlas, G. Smythson, H. Wright, G. P. R. Burgess, Leon Bassett, and W. S. Bassett; Executive Committee, Messrs. H. Conlin, Fred Millis, H. Wheatley, Joe Lawrence, T. Burnetti, E. D'Almaine, W. King, H. Herald, F. Neiman, J. Obo, E. Obo, B. Whiteley, T. C. Callaghan, H. Bancroft, J. E. Dunedin, Bert Williams, F. Gee, B. Vox, B. Olrac, W. Wisper, F. Slingsby, A. Dome, Billy Kloof, J. Dwyer, H. Bent, F. Larola, Tony Iveson, W. E. Gillin, T. Maxwell, G. Cooper, G. Pearson, Harry Gage, M. H. McDowall, A. Simmons, E. C. Webb, J. Chas. Moore. John Moore, Fred Gage, and M. Ringham. Hon. Trustees, Messrs. S. N. Salter and J. C. Pratt; Hon. Solicitor, Mr. G. P. R. Burgess; Hon. Treasurer, Mr. Douglas White; Hon. Organist, Mr. Joe Lawrence; Secretary, Mr. Arthur Were.

THE MUSIC HALL HOME.

The Music Hall Home was founded some years ago by certain prominent members of the Terriers' Association. The objects of the Music Hall Home are to afford shelter to deserving members of the variety profession who have fallen on evil times, and to provide a permanent home for poor performers who, through illness, disablement, or old age, are quite unable to find employment.

At present there are a dozen inmates lodged in the Home, which is situated at 31, Wilson Road, Camberwell, S.E.

President, Mr. Thos. Barrasford; Vice-Presidents, Messrs. Harry Barnard, Harry Bawn, Leon Bassett, W. S. Bassett, G. P. R. Burgess, Jas. E. Dunedin, Walter Hassan, Joe Lawrence, Harry Mountford, Fred Neiman, F. H. Pedgrift, C. J. Bartlett Perry, Jesse Sparrow, C. Douglas Stuart, Chas. Weldon, Douglas White; Treasurer, Mr. Harry Barnard; Secretary, Mr. Benj. Woodger; Matron, Mrs. J. J. Fruin. Committee, 1908-9:—Messrs. W. H. Atlas, Harry Blake, John Brandon, Ted E. Box, Bert Chapman, C. C. Cornish, Jim Elmo, Percy Ford, Harry Gage, E. A. Golding, H. Griff, Hamilton Hill, H. Hough, Edward Johnson, Will Johnson, H. Joyner, P. A. Lennon, C. Mannering, Malcolm McDowall, F. W. Millis, Walter Norman, Ben Obo, Jim Obo, George Pearson, Fred Shelley, Arthur Simmons, W. Howard Smith, Geo. H. Smythson, J. Traynor, H. Thacker, E. C. Webb, Horace Wheatley, Squire Windham, Jack Woolf, Harry Wright. Committee meetings are held at the Camberwell Palace first and third Thursdays in the month.

MUSIC HALL SICK FUND.

The Music Hall Sick Fund Provident Society was founded in 1867. Objects :—
to provide, by voluntary subscriptions of the members (who must belong to the
music-hall profession), with the aid of donations, (*a*) For the relief of the members
during mental or physical incapacity; (*b*) On the death of a member, for payment
of ten pounds sterling to nearest relative or nominee. Sick payments : 10s. per
week for subscription of 3d. per week; £1 a week for payment of 6d. per week;
£1 10s. per week for 9d. a week. The Committee of Management meet second
Wednesday in every month, at 4 p.m. President, Fred Karno; Vice-President,
W. J. Wainratta; Trustees, H. Jennings, Jesse Sparrow, and Douglas White;
Treasurer, Pat Carey; Hon. Solicitor, A. O. Clarke; Secretary, R. T. Baines. All
communications to be addressed to the Crown Hotel, Charing Cross Road, W.C.
The chief events which happened in connection with the Society during the year
1908 were the election of Mr. Fred Karno as President, the change of place of
meeting from the York Hotel, York Road, to the Crown Hotel, Charing Cross
Road, W.C., and the death in December of Mr. Frank Heath, the Hon. Treasurer
of the Fund, and one of its oldest members. The late Herbert Campbell was for
many years the President of the Society.

MUSIC HALL LADIES' GUILD.

The Guild was founded in 1905. President, Mrs. Fred Ginnett; Vice-Presidents,
Mrs. Eugene Stratton, Miss Lily Burnand; Hon. Treasurer, Miss Belle Elmore.
Executive Committee :—Mrs. Joe Elvin, Miss Maude Mortimer, Miss Ray Wallace,
Miss Lottie Albert, Miss Irene Rose, Mrs. Lockhart, Mrs. Herbert Shelley, Miss
Freda Sharlotte, Miss Gladys Mavius, Miss Lil Hawthorne, Miss Marie Loftus, Mrs.
Butler, Miss Millie Payne, Miss Kate Vulcana, Mrs. Chas. Best, Mrs. Vernon
Cowper, Miss Louie Davis, Miss Victoria Monks. Honorary Committee:—Mrs.
Lily Bradgate, Mrs. Pettitt, Mrs. H. Maud Gamble (Lady Mayoress of Chelsea).
The above Guild has been formed with the object of assisting the wives of artists
who, through lack of employment, illness, or confinement, are in want of help, by
supplying proper medical aid, food, coal, or other necessaries as may be required.
Also, in cases of confinement, to lend a supply of suitable baby clothes for the first
month, to be returned at the expiration of that time. To assist widows of artists to
find suitable employment; to find employment for children of poor artists and
orphans, as programme sellers, call boys; also office work or other suitable employment, and in cases where possible to assist them in obtaining parts in sketches
where children's parts are included; to supply necessitous artists with free clothing;
to sell stage and other clothing to artists who may require it, at a very small
charge; to visit the sick; to give toys, books, and games to sick children of artists.
During the nine months from October, 1907, to June 30, 1908, as many as 300
cases were helped. £413 was received as income from all sources, and £180 11s. 4d.
was spent in food and clothing and assistance to poor artists, including the giving
of Christmas dinners.
Bee Meetings every Wednesday at the offices, Albion House, 61, New Oxford
Street, London, W. Secretary, Miss Melinda May.

THE GALLERY FIRST NIGHTERS' CLUB.

The headquarters of the Gallery First Nighters' Club are at the Bedford Head
Hotel, Maiden Lane, Strand, W.C. Subscription, 10s. 6d. per annum. President,
Mr. H. S. Doswell; Vice-President, Mr. A. E. Were; Hon. Treasurer, Mr. John
Page; Hon. Secretary, Mr. G. F. Rigden. Committee, Messrs. T. Brandon, A.
W. Haynes, P. L. Jackson, Stanley Jones, Fred Page, W. O. Summers, and H.
F. Whitworth. Hon. Auditor, Mr. Frank H. Long.
The Club was founded in 1896, "to maintain the right of playgoers to give free
and independent criticism in the theatre, and to afford facilities for social intercourse
among gallery first nighters." Genuine gallery playgoers alone are eligible for
membership. The Club holds frequent debates on subjects connected with the
Drama. Other functions include the annual dinner, held at Frascati's in March.
Bohemian suppers, concerts, etc. Ladies are invited to the annual dinner and
the debates.
The Club claims to be the most democratic playgoing club, and one of the last
strongholds of Bohemianism. Its bugbear is "Respectability." Their presidents,

etc., are always genuine gallery "boys," the club having a rooted objection to honorary figureheads. The gallery "boys" number in their ranks some of the oldest and best known playgoers. The famous "man in the white hat" was one of the most active spirits in the founding of the club.

The club had strong associations with the late Nellie Farren, who always spoke affectionately of its members as "her boys." They entertained their never-to-be-forgotten favourite at a dinner on Saturday, April 29, 1899, when Mr. Cecil Raleigh marvelled at the "weird and wonderful enthusiasm." This, however, is a feature which characterises all their dinners. Among the other well-known people who have spoken at their dinner are Miss Ellen Terry, Miss Eva Moore, Miss Kate Rorke, Miss Nina Boucicault, Mlle. Adeline Genée, Sir W. S. Gilbert, Messrs. H. V. Esmond, J. Forbes Robertson, Lewis Waller, Charles Hawtrey, George Alexander, H. B. Irving, Arthur Bourchier, James Welch, Oscar Asche, Cecil Raleigh, Sydney Valentine, Martin Harvey, Louis Bradfield, Spencer Leigh Hughes, T. McDonald Rendle, W. Pett Ridge, James Douglas, Alfred Robins, and the late Mr. C. L. Carson, of THE STAGE—a list of which any club might be proud. During the season 1907-08, in addition to the usual debates held in the Club Room, the Club held its first public debate at Frascati's in November on the old question of disturbances in the gallery on first nights, just then receiving one of its periodical discussions in the columns of the London papers. Mr. Cecil Raleigh presided over an audience of 300 or 400, and Mr. M. Mansell read a paper entitled "Do Playgoers Matter?" An animated discussion followed, the bulk of the speakers being in support of the Club's policy of "calling a spade a spade." The annual dinner was held at Frascati's in March, 1908. The Bohemian functions included a special ladies' supper, "New Year's Eve Revels," "May Day Demonstration," etc.

ACTORS' CHURCH UNION.

The object of the Actors' Church Union is to endeavour to make special provision to meet the needs of those members of the Church who are engaged in the dramatic profession.

The chaplains (nominated by the President with the approval of the Bishop of the Diocese) endeavour to render any service in their power to the theatrical members of the Union, and are glad to be notified of any case of illness or other emergency which may need their help.

The Actors' Church Union is in no sense a mission to the stage. It does not regard actors and actresses as in any way different from other people, nor as needing any "special treatment." It looks upon them simply as members of the Church who, on account of the constant travelling which their profession involves, are deprived of many of those spiritual advantages which are enjoyed by other Churchmen whose mode of life permits them to have a fixed place of residence and to attend some particular church.

In London the Union in many instances, through its chaplains, has been able to co-operate with the Theatrical Ladies' Guild and the Music Hall Ladies' Guild in looking after cases of distress.

Any member of the dramatic profession may become a member of the A.C.U. on payment of an annual subscription of one shilling, which is required to defray the printing and postage expenses connected with the Union.

President, the Right Rev. the Lord Bishop of Southwark; Vice-President and Chairman of Committee, Rev. H. Montagu Villiers, Prebendary of St. Paul's; Vice-Presidents, Right Rev. the Lord Bishop of London. Right Rev. the Lord Bishop of Birmingham. Right Rev. the Lord Bishop of Glasgow. Right Rev. the Lord Bishop of Argyll and the Isles, Right Rev. the Lord Bishop of Stepney. Right Rev. the Lord Bishop of Southampton, Sir Charles Wyndham, Mr. Edward Compton, Mr. Ben Greet, Mr. Martin Harvey, Mr. Charles Manners, Mr. Cyril Maude, Mr. Beerbohm Tree; Committee, Rev. J. Stephen Barrass, Rev. Wm. Cree, Rev. H. F. Davidson, Rev. Wynn Healey, Mrs. Donald Hole, Rev. E. H. Mosse, Rev. Thomas Varney, Mrs. Villiers, Miss C. Chambers, Miss Emily Clarke, Miss Louise Stopford, Miss Phyllis Broughton, Mr. E. H. Bull, Mr. Charles J. Cameron. Mrs. Carson, Mrs. Edward Compton, Mr. Charles Cruikshanks, Miss Anna De Grey, Miss Winifred Emery, Miss Harriet Greet, Mr. Fewlass Llewellyn, Mr. Chris. Walker; Hon. Secretary and Treasurer, Rev. Donald Hole, 20, Woodview Gardens, Highgate, N.; Assistant Hon. Secretary, Miss E. G. Clarke, 22, Kempsford Gardens, Earl's Court, S.W.

THE AMERICAN STAGE.

BY THE NEW YORK CORRESPONDENT OF "THE STAGE."

THE past year has not, on the whole, been quite a satisfactory one, at least as far as the opening was concerned. It had as a legacy the dreadful financial panic of the preceding year, from which it had not recovered, added to which the social and political upheaval, which ever attends a Presidential Election, caused more than the customary depression, owing to the fact that the public was in doubt as to the result of the voting, for on the selection of the chief of the executive depended the trend of the policy of the capitalists, which governs the vitality of America. It was not, therefore, until the certainty of the return of Mr. Taft, which became apparent at the end of the summer, that business revived, and in response to this revival the theatres resumed their accustomed aspect, and the autumn season opened with the greatest promise, which has been fulfilled.

THE OPENING—CLOSING TOURS AND UNEMPLOYED ACTORS.

As the year opened, the Rialto, as that part of Broadway is termed which is most affected by actors, and where most of the agents and managers have their offices, was a most unpleasant sight, for there one could see the hordes of unemployed artists, who had been called in from the road owing to the inability of the public to support the theatres. It was a most unprecedented sight, and later this horde was added to by the premature closing of the theatres on Broadway, while many of those artists who hitherto had been in the habit of taking a summer holiday and enjoying a well-earned rest with the profits derived from their exertions during the season were compelled to go into stock. Even then many failed to realise their anticipations, for numbers of the stock theatres had to close down owing to the want of patronage. Under these circumstances it is not to be wondered at that plays which under ordinary conditions would have turned out financially successful failed to return sufficient to the box-office to warrant their retention in the bills.

THE SPRING SEASON.

The opening of the year was signalled by the failure of Alfred Sutro's *John Glayde's Honour*, and, to fill the vacancy caused by the withdrawal, *The House of a Thousand Candles* was substituted, only to fail also; *Under the Greenwood Tree* received a like fate, or almost as bad, while *Funabashi*, with which Thomas Ryley hoped to make money, was also unsuccessful. In Atlantic City *Miss Hook of Holland* was given a trial, with a favourite comedian in the part of Mr. Hook, but the result was that this part and that of Slink were handed over to others. The New York season of this piece was opened with great promise; but in spite of this the piece did not in any way realise the success anticipated, and for this the unfavourable condition of affairs above referred to was no doubt responsible. *Irene Wycherley* also failed to establish a firm footing, though there is reason to doubt that in ordinary circumstances the result would have been greatly different. *Her Father* had a partial success, which fell far short of what the piece would have attained in a more prosperous season. The plays held over from the previous year, *Polly of the Circus*, *The Merry Widow*, and *The Rose of the Rancho*, continued to attract for the rest of the season. *The Thief*, too, achieved an enormous success. *Peter Pan* was removed early in January to make room for the production of *The Jesters*, and the scene on the final night of the run was one to be remembered. *The Witching Hour* also came over from the previous year as one of the most successful pieces; but, strange to say, although so great a success in New York, it was a partial failure in Chicago. Another great success continuing was *The Man of the Hour*, while *The Girl Behind the Counter* proved to be one of the most acceptable musical pieces of this and the previous year.

Early in January *Paid in Full* was presented for the first time on the road, and the papers referred to it in a humorous way as having handed in its cheques altogether, and being sent into cold storage. Two months later this same play was hailed in this city as "the great play of American contemporaneous life," and the lady who played the heroine was classed among the principal artists of the day, yet the cast was just the same as originally presented on the road, and the piece had not been altered one line. It subsequently turned out to be one of the best of the year, outlasting even the torrid heat of a New York summer.

The Merry Widow caused a run on Viennese operas. One of them, *The Waltz Dream*, did not live up to promise, and died a comparatively early death. *Twenty Days in the Shade* also shared the fate of other pieces not appreciated by the public, and was withdrawn after a short run. On the road in January Denis O'Sullivan created a sensation with *Peggy Machree*, and arrangements were made to bring the piece at once to New York, but very shortly after his first appearance the singer was seized with an illness, which terminated fatally. The piece was then abandoned until the late autumn, when Mr. Joseph O'Mara was brought over by List and Dingwall, and the opera was revived with enormous success.

In February, at the Majestic, *Bandanna Land*, with Williams and Walker, and *The Honour of the Family*, with Otis Skinner, at the Hudson, caught the fancy of New York audiences. In this month Mrs. Patrick Campbell, in *Electra* and *The Flower of Yamato*, at the Garden, assisted by Mrs. Beerbohm Tree, gave a few performances and returned to the road. *The Beloved Vagabond* had a short life at Cincinnati, Ohio. After a few performances, *Toddles*, in March, did not fare well, and *The Easterner*, with which Mr. Nat Goodwin hoped at the Garrick to "scoop the pool" in this city, although apparently satisfactory on the road, disappointed him, and it was removed.

George Ade's *Father and the Boys*, which gave William Crane a fine part and great opportunities, came to the rescue at the Empire. Clyde Fitch's *Girls*, too, which had been tried out in Washington, was brought this month to Daly's, and scored heavily, running out the season and through the summer months.

In Baltimore at this time *The Servant in the House* was given for the first time, and gave rise to much discussion. It was predicted that failure awaited the play in this city, but in spite of these predictions by the clever ones, including the writer of this article, *The Servant in the House* achieved an instantaneous success, and brought wealth to the treasury of Mr. Henry Miller, who had the temerity to produce it, and not only that, had the pluck and foresight to believe that it would succeed in New York. Not only in New York, but in other cities it visited, the play proved a great money-maker. *Nearly a Hero* was presented here at the Casino in March, after a good try out on the road. The success of *Paid in Full* at the Astor drew attention to the author, Eugene Walters, and another of his plays was presented at the Lyric, *The Wolf*, and this also scored. The remainder of the season was devoted to the production of *The Gay Musician*, which was a partial success, and a Revue at the Casino, *The Mimic World*, which drew good audiences during the summer. *The Three Twins*, too, was brought from Chicago, where it had experienced a great success, to the Herald Square, and justified its reputation here.

One of the bright spots of the spring season was the appearance of Mlle. Genée in *The Soul Kiss*, at the beginning of January. Her success was electrical, and led to a contract with Klaw and Erlanger for a period of five years. For the whole period of her engagement, which was only terminated owing to prior contracts at the Empire, London, the vast auditorium of the New York Theatre was absolutely packed.

One of the features of the spring season was the success of Mr. E. A. Sothern in his father's part of Lord Dundreary, which attracted to such an extent as to compel the cancellation of his road dates. Another feature was the taking up the dates usually filled by the late Richard Mansfield by Mr. William A. Brady, for Mr. Robert Mantell, who thus became a first-class legitimate star, in the late popular actor's place.

THE AUTUMN SEASON.

The opening of the autumn season shaped much better, and *The Man from Home*, which had been running in Chicago the whole of the season, was presented at the

Astor, and at once caught the public taste, and attracted crowded houses in spite of the heat of August. Similar success attended the production of *The Travelling Salesman*, which was given at the Liberty, and afterwards removed to the New Gaiety, waich had been built by Messrs. Cohan and Harris for the exploitation of the former's pieces.

In September, George Broadhurst's play, *The Call of the North*, was voted no good, and soon relegated to the store house. This was also the fate of *Diana of Dobson's*, from which were expected great things, and for which Miss Carlotta Nilsson, who had made such a success the previous season in *The Three of Us*, had been specially engaged. The piece, after a few performances, was withdrawn. *The Mollusc*, too, did not reach expectations; Mr. Joseph Coyne had scarcely a part suited to him. *The Like's o' Me*, which was put on as an after-piece, had not a very long life.

Fluffy Ruffles, the production of which had been promised for almost a year, was also given in September, but unfortunately the subject had been worn threadbare in various classes of entertainment for some time previously, and the public did not seem to care for it, though it achieved a certain measure of success. It was founded upon the sketches in the *New York Herald*, by Winson Mackay, with which even Londoners are familiar by means of the "Fluffy Ruffles" hat.

Jack Straw, with John Drew in Mr. Charles Hawtrey's part, caught on at once, and for a considerable time the business at the Empire was quite good. *The Girls of Gottenberg*, too, with Miss Gertie Millar as the bright particular star, made a great hit, and would have achieved a long run had it not been for the fact that Miss Fritzie Scheff had to take the Knickerbocker for her long-promised production of the Henry Blossom-Victor Herbert opera *The Prima Donna*. Another great success produced this month was *Wildfire*, in which Miss Lillian Russell had been touring on the road for the best part of the previous season, under the management of Mr. Joseph Brooks.

October was a very lucky month for productions in New York, for following quickly on one another were *The Fighting Hope*, at the Stuyvesant, the initial work of William J. Hurlburt; *A Gentleman from Mississippi*, at the Bijou; and *Little Nemo*, at the New Amsterdam, which all hit the bull's-eye right in the centre. *Little Nemo*, particularly, turned out to be one of the biggest things in the way of successes Messrs. Klaw and Erlanger have had.

In October, too, Mr. William Gillette appeared in the long-expected Bernstein play *Samson*, but although a partial success it did not approach that achieved by *The Thief;* Mr. Gillette's quiet method, perhaps, not quite suiting the principal character.

November produced a good bunch of successes—*Viâ Wireless* at the Liberty, *The World and His Wife*, with William Faversham at Daly's, and *Lady Frederick* at the Hudson, where Miss Ethel Barrymore made a great hit in the principal part.

In November, *The Patriot*, by Hartley Manners and Willie Collier, was presented by Mr. Charles Frohman at the Garrick Theatre, and achieved success, having been thoroughly overhauled on the road tour previously. At Weber's Theatre, the same date, Miss Annie Russell appeared, under the management of Wagenhals and Kemper, in *The Stronger Sex*, by John Valentine. At this time, too, the Sicilian Players made a bid for popular favour at the Broadway, and found a fair amount of patronage, but *The Winterfeast*, by John Rann Kennedy, a tragedy in five acts, failed to please, though the critics were unanimous regarding the great merit of both play and acting. This month, too, saw the production of *The Prima Donna*, by Henry Blossom and Victor Herbert, at the Knickerbocker, which proved an enormous success, as is customary with any opera with Fritzie Scheff in the cast. Other successful productions were *Miss Innocence*, at the New York Theatre, with Anna Held ; *The Blue Mouse*, adapted by Clyde Fitch from the German of Alexander Engel and Julius Horst, at the Lyric Theatre ; *Mary Jane's Pa*, by Miss Edith Ellis, at the Garden Theatre, with Henry E. Dixey as the star ; and *The Pied Piper*, by Austin Strong, R. H. Burnside, and Manuel Klein, at the Majestic Theatre, presented by the Shubert Brothers, with De Wolf Hopper in the star part.

The year's productions may be said to have concluded with the production, at the Empire, of J. M. Barrie's *What Every Woman Knows* by Charles Frohman, with Miss Maude Adams in the part of Maggie Wylie, which achieved an instantaneous success; *The Battle*, at the Savoy, by Cleveland Moffat, with Wilton Lackaye in the star part; *Mr. Hamlet of Broadway*, by Harry B. Smith and others, with interpolated numbers, at the Casino, with Eddie Foy as the star; and last, but not least, *Peggy Machree*, with Joseph O'Mara as the star, at the Broadway Theatre, which hit the public taste at once.

Two Versions of "The Devil."

A stirring incident took place in the autumn, for at the Belasco Mr. Harrison Grey Fiske produced a version of Franz Molnar's *The Devil*, with George Arliss in the name-part. The preparation had been proceeded with in so secret a manner that Mr. Henry W. Savage, who had already tried a version of the same play out on the road, under the title of *The Cloven Hoof*, did not suspect that there was the least idea of a rival in the field until about forty-eight hours before the first performance took place. Nothing daunted, Mr. Savage took the Garden, and, hastily summoning the people who had taken part in the trial performance, he, too, opened on the same night, and it became a struggle as to which would outlast the other, but there was no doubt as to the favourite from the first. The company headed by George Arliss were very soon left in sole possession of the field.

The Vaudeville Competition.

At the beginning of the year Messrs. Klaw and Erlanger, who had entered the vaudeville field in opposition to Messrs. Keith and Proctor, retired from the contest on the understanding that all outstanding contracts should be taken over by the firm, in whose favour they withdrew. During the "war" a vast amount of money was dropped by both parties, for the event sent up the salaries of artists to a famine point, and English vaudevillians especially reaped the benefit.

Companies and Railway Rates.

A most important event took place at the beginning of the year in the way of the organisation of a Society of Producing Managers, and one of their first effective steps was to procure a reduction of fares in the Southern States, which had been raised by the railway companies to a point which made theatrical ventures absolutely unprofitable. The Society has also done most excellent work since, and many important and vexatious questions have been settled by that body, and others are at the present time under consideration.

Russian Companies.

The success of Mme. Nazimova induced the Russian star actresses to look towards New York as the Promised Land, but unfortunately promise was as far as they got, for two companies who were brought over from Russia went back considerably lighter in pocket than they arrived, and with the least delay possible. They were caviare to the general.

In February the Actors' Society of America removed to their new building, which they had acquired with their own funds, but they had scarcely got settled when the New Amsterdam Bank suspended payment, and locked up quite a considerable amount of their capital, and the result was that they had to appeal to their members for funds, and last, but not least, they found it necessary to raise the subscription from three dollars per annum to five.

The End of Madison Square Theatre.

The Madison Square theatre, after a career of almost half a century, finally closed its doors this year, and will be rebuilt as a commercial structure. The late John Brougham was the first manager of the theatre, though it had been a place of entertainment long before, and both Daniel and Charles Frohman graduated there, under the Mallorys, as did also David Belasco.

A Step Towards a National Theatre.

A step in the direction of a national theatre was made this year by the laying of the foundation-stone of the New theatre, which is to be kept up by private subscription. Mr. Granville Barker was offered the management, but declined it on the grounds that the building was constructed on too large a scale to be of service in the direction intended, whereupon Mr. Winthrop Ames and Mr. Lee Shubert were appointed, and later the announcement was made that Mr. William Archer had been appointed as literary adviser.

10

AMERICAN ORGANISATIONS.

THE ACTORS' SOCIETY.

The Actors' Society of America is the outcome of a meeting of six or seven young actors, which was held fifteen years ago. They conceived the idea that it would be a good thing for the actor to form a society where equity would be their ruling principle. They started in a small hallroom, and to-day they own a handsome four-storey building at 133, West 45th Street, the purchase of this building being the result of years of effort on the part of its members. On the first floor is the office of the society; the secretary or his assistant is present continually at the service of the members. In the rear of this office is the commodious and well-lighted library, which contains several thousand volumes of all classes of books. The mail department is located on this floor.

On the second floor is the ladies' room. The third floor is given over to the men.

The Society gave a reception and a house warming in their new premises, into which they moved in December, 1907, on February 9. They had a benefit at the Hudson Theatre, New York, on April 21, which raised some £400, when they produced a new one-act play by Henry Arthur Jones, entitled *The Goal.*

The annual meeting was held on June 4, when the following were elected:— President, Mr. Thomas A. Wise; Vice-President, Miss Fannie Cannon; Secretary, Mr. Geo. D. Macintyre; Treasurer, Mr. Mark Ellsworth. Directors:—Messrs. Thomas A. Wise, Harold Hartsell, Stokes Sullivan, Mark Ellsworth, Maida Craigen, H. Nelson Morey, Mary Shaw, Georgia Earle, William McVay, Fannie Cannon.

At this meeting a resolution was passed raising the dues from three dollars to five dollars per year.

THE ACTORS' FUND.

President, Mr. Daniel Frohman; First Vice-President, Mr. Jos. R. Grismer; Treasurer, Mr. Henry B. Harris; Secretary, Mr. Frank McKee; Trustees, Messrs. F. F. Mackay, Al. Hayman, Wm. H. Crane, Heinrich Conried, Joseph Brooks, Thomas McGrath, Alf. Hayman, Frank Burbeck.

At the annual meeting, held at the Hudson Theatre, New York, on May 12, addresses were delivered by the President, Mr. Daniel Frohman, by Messrs. F. F. Mackay, W. H. Crane, Milton Nobles, and several other members.

The Actors' Fund had a benefit at the Van Ness Theatre, San Francisco, on July 9.

The Actors' Fund Home is at West New Brighton, Staten Island. Offices of the Fund:—112-114, West 42nd Street, New York.

THEATRE MANAGERS' ASSOCIATION.

A meeting of theatre managers representing a number of houses in different parts of the country was held in New York on August 6 at the offices of Klaw and Erlanger. The object of the meeting was to discuss the possibility of a general betterment of theatrical conditions and a harmonious co-operation toward that end. One of the subjects which the managers discussed was, as their report put it, "that new theatres were constantly being erected for which there were not suitable attractions to fill the time, and that as legitimate theatrical managers did not feel warranted in leasing these additional houses, these theatres usually fell into the hands of over-night speculators who had no permanent or sincere interest in theatricals, and whose tendency in no way contributed to the general welfare of the theatrical situation."

A committee was elected to draw up a plan. The committee included Messrs. Marc Klaw, E. F. Albee, Lee Shubert, Percy G. Williams, Samuel Schribner, Martin Beck, J. H. Havlin, J. J. Murdock, M. C. Anderson, and H. Fehr.

Another meeting was held in the New Amsterdam Theatre Building on September 5, when the Theatre Managers' Association was permanently organised. Mr. A. L. Erlanger was chosen President, and Mr. John H. Havlin Secretary. Messrs. Martin Beck, Marc Klaw, and Mr. Havlin were appointed a committee to draw up bye-laws.

ASSOCIATION OF THEATRE MANAGERS OF GREATER NEW YORK.

Established for mutual protection, and for the advancement of all things appertaining to the theatre, the investigation of all matters appertaining to the theatre to see if the cause of the theatre can be advanced ; the bettering of business methods.

Governed as follows :—President, Mr. Chas. Burnham ; First Vice-President, Mr. Henry B. Harris ; Second Vice-President, Mr. Alf. Hayman ; Treasurer, Mr. Frank McKee. Board of Directors :—Messrs. Daniel Frohman, Heinrich Conried, Marc Klaw, Chas. Burnham, Alf. Hayman, Henry B. Harris, William Harris, George Kraus, Percy Williams, William Keogh.

Secretary, Mr. Leo C. Teller.

NATIONAL ASSOCIATION OF PRODUCING MANAGERS.

Mr. Henry W. Savage was re-elected President at the annual meeting of this body, held on June 9 at the Hudson Theatre, New York. Mr. Hollis E. Cooley was re-elected Secretary, and Mr. Sam A. Scribner Treasurer. Mr. Charles H. Yale was elected to succeed Mr. Charles E. Blaney as Vice-President. Messrs. Daniel Frohman, John A. Himmelein, and Harry Doel Parker were added to the board of directors.

Offices in the *Times* Buildings.

WESTERN THEATRE MANAGERS' ASSOCIATION.

The object of this Association is for the mutual protection and benefit of managers of theatres and travelling theatrical managers, general advancement of business interests, and to keep members advised of matters affecting their interests, and to take action thereon in order to produce harmony in business and to secure the mutual advantages of an organisation.

The jurisdiction of this Association extends to the States of Illinois, Iowa, Nebraska, Missouri, Kansas, Arkansas, Oklahoma, Wisconsin, Indiana, Minnesota, Michigan, North Dakota, South Dakota, Idaho, Montana, Wyoming, Colorado, Oregon, Nevada, California, Utah, and Washington, and the territories of Arizona and New Mexico.

Officers :—President, Mr. C. T. Kindt ; Vice-President, Mr. J. F. Given ; Secretary and Treasurer, Mr. Geo. F. Olendorf, Springfield, Mo. Directors :—Messrs. W. L. Busby, O. F. Burlingame, Roy Crawford, W. M. Hinton, C. A. Holden, C. A. Lick, A. R. Pelton, C. U. Philley, Jos. Rhode, F. C. Smutzer, J. Wingfield, F. C. Zehrung.

WESTERN STOCK MANAGERS' ASSOCIATION.

The Western Stock Managers' Association was formed in Los Angeles, Cal., in February. Mr. Oliver Morosco was elected President, Mr. John H. Blackwood Vice-President, Mr. William Fenn Secretary, Mr. Dick Ferris Treasurer. Mr. George L. Baker was made General Manager for Oregon, Washington, and Colorado, and Mr. Fred Belasco General Manager for Northern California. The directors are :— Messrs. H. W. Bishop, Oakland ; Alexander Pantages, Seattle ; C. W. Alisky, Sacramento ; Harry Haywood, Spokane ; George B. Hunt, San Diego.

The objects of the Association are to do away with certain forms of competition and to deal with the question of extravagant royalties for plays.

NORTH-WESTERN THEATRE MANAGERS' ASSOCIATION.

The Association comprises the managers of twenty-seven theatres in Northern Wisconsin, Minnesota, and Michigan. The object of the Association is to co-operate in improving the bookings. The following are the officers:—President, Mr. C. A. Marshall, Duluth, Minn.; Secretary and Treasurer, Mr. P. B. Haber, Fond du Lac, Wis.; Attorney, Mr. W. J. Powers, Hibbing, Minn. Executive Committee:— Messrs. Jno. D. Cuddihy, Calumet, Mich.; Jno. E. Williams, Oshkosh, Wis.; O. F. Burlingame, Winona, Minn.; Jno. Arthur, Green Bay, Wis.; C. D. Moon, Eau Claire, Wis. The 1908 convention was held in Eau Claire, Wis., on April 17.

MIDDLE WEST THEATRICAL MANAGERS' ASSOCIATION.

The Middle West Theatrical Managers' Association is governed as follows:— President, Mr. Charles T. Kindt, Davenport, Iowa; Vice-President, Mr. J. F. Given, Decatur, Ill.; Secretary and Treasurer, Mr. George F. Olendorff, Sedalia, Mo. Directors:—Messrs. James Wingfield, Chicago, for Illinois; Joseph Rhodes, Kenosha, for Wisconsin; F. C. Zehring, Lincoln, for Nebraska; O. F. Burlingame, Winona, for Minnesota; Roy Crawford, Topeka, for Kansas; C. A. Holden, Wabash, for Indiana; C. U. Philley, St. Joseph, for Missouri; C. A. Lick, Fort Smith, for Arkansas; W. A. Hinton, Muskogee, for Indian Territory.

THE WHITE RATS.

The officers of the White Rats, elected in 1908, were as follows:—Big Chief, Mr. Fred Niblo; Little Chief, Mr. Junie McCree; Secretary, Mr. Harry Mountford; Treasurer, Mr. Harry Hayes; Chaplin, Mr. James F. Dolan; Rap Rat, Mr. Hugh Mack; Gourd Rat, Major Burk; Prop. Rat, Mr. Rube Welch; Nector Rat, Mr. Charles B. Lawlor; Jest Rat, Mr. Bert Leslie; Note Rat, Mr. Fred Hylands; Trustees, Mr. William Carrol, Mr. George Delmore, Mr. John P. Hill? Mr. Colic Lavelle, and Mr. Corse Payton; Board of Directors, Mr. Tim Cronin, Mr. Joseph Callahan, and Mr. William Courtleigh, Mr. Will J. Cook, Mr. Robert Daily, Mr. James F. Dolan, Major Doyle, Mr. George Felix, Mr. Frank Fogarty, Mr. Jack Gardner, Mr. William Gould, Mr. James Harrigan, Mr. Frank Herbert, Mr. Edwin Keogh, Mr. Harry Knowles, Mr. Charles B. Lawlor, Mr. Walter Le Roy, Mr. Bert Leslie, Mr. Mark Murphy, Mr. Sam Morton, Mr. Tim McMahon, Mr. Frank North, Mr. Charles J. Stine, Mr. Ren Shields.

During the year the Rats have established a Political League, an Independent Booking Office, and have had their usual scampers and dance.

VAUDEVILLE COMEDY CLUB.

This Association was incorporated on February 27, 1907. Its stated objects are:— (1) To protect its members, for the procuring of an equitable legal contract. (2) To secure the faithful observance of all contracts signed by both parties thereto. (3) That the members shall keep faith with each other, and that they shall not use an act, in part or whole, or the business of an act, or any mechanical device used therein, or any song, story, or music that is the property of another person, without the written permission of the owner; or allow anyone else to do so, if it is in their power to prevent it. It shall be the duty of every member to at once notify the secretary of the club of any infringement that shall come to his notice. Such notification must be read at the next regular meeting. (4) That the members shall refrain from injuring or attempting to injure any other member of the club, and to prevent others from doing so to the best of their ability. (5) For literary, social, and fraternal purposes."

Officers:—President, Mr. James J. Morton; First Vice-President, Mr. Francis Morey; Second Vice-President, Mr. Howard Truesdell; Third Vice-President, Mr. Lee Harrison; Treasurer, Mr. A. O. Duncan; Secretary, Mr. Gene Hughes.

Board of Governors for 1908:—Messrs. James J. Morton, Francis Morey, Howard Truesdell, Lee Harrison, A. O. Duncan, and Gene Hughes.

Board of Directors for 1908:—Messrs. Will M. Cressy, Carleton Macey, Robert Dailey, Arthur Forbes, Bobby Matthews, and Harry Corson Clarke.

House Committee:—Messrs. Chas. W. Smith, Frank J. Otto, Charles O. Rice, Frank Coombs, Dr. Frank Rodolph, Jules Garrison, and Mr. Gene Hughes (Secretary).

Finance Committee:—Mr. Howard Truesdell, Chairman; Messrs. Bobby North, Charles H. Smith, Charles F. Semon, Marshall P. Wilder.

The Vaudeville Comedy Club exchanges courtesies with the Vaudeville Club of England. The annual benefit, that for the last two years has been held in the New York Theatre, will take place some time in the spring, 1909. "Ladies' Socials" are held every three months, and are very popular. On these occasions the club-house is thrown open to the wives and womenfolk of the members. Smokers are held every two weeks or so, and are the source of many a pleasant evening spent, the members and their friends being invited (no ladies on these occasions). Regular meetings are held every Sunday at 12 noon sharp, and usually are well attended. All business of the club is brought up at these meetings.

Until January 18, 1909, the application (entrance) fee of the club, which is twenty-five dollars, has been reduced to ten dollars, with yearly dues of twelve dollars, payable semi-annually six months in advance, and "lay (outside profession) members" will be admitted to that time (January 18, 1909), with application fee of twenty-five dollars and yearly dues of twelve dollars.

Offices, 147, West 45th Street, New York.

VAUDEVILLE ARTISTS' BENEVOLENT AND PROTECTIVE ORDER.

The founder of this order was Mr. W. H. Stanley, who is now its business manager (443, Central Avenue, Brooklyn, N.Y.). It is a young body, being organised in March, 1908, but it is rapidly gaining members, and early in 1909, the Recording Secretary, Mr. Alan Warren, informs us, will have offices in New York City. The objects of the Order are:—"For the protection of the vaudeville artist. To secure a fair equivalent for our services and sufficient leisure to enjoy the ennobling amenities of life. To adjust differences between managers and performers. To secure an equitable contract for performers. To render legal aid to members when necessary. To help secure engagements and proper recognition of worthy talent. To render assistance in sickness and disability, and to aid in defraying funeral expenses upon the death of a member. Should a member become sick a benefit of six dollars will be paid weekly. Upon the death of a member the sum of a hundred dollars will be paid to his or her legal heirs."

The Order is open to male and female members of the profession. Officers as follows:—President, Mr. Robert Monds; First Vice-President, Mr. Jas. R. Waite; Recording Secretary, Mr. Alan Warren; Treasurer, Mr. Bertram Warren; Chairman Board of Trustees, Mr. Mark Isaacs; Financial Secretary, Mr. Jno. J. Phillips; Guardian, Mr. J. J. Monahan; Business Manager, Mr. Wm. H. Stanley; Chairman Grievance Committee, Mr. J. Aldrich Libby. District Deputies and Organisers:— Messrs. E. Kirke Adams, Wm. Casper, Jess P. Johnson, H. B. Le Clair.

NATIONAL VAUDEVILLE MANAGERS' ASSOCIATION.

The National Vaudeville Managers' Association is governed as follows:—President, Mr. J. E. McCarthy, Hamilton, O.; Vice-President, Mr. William McChaffer, Monessen, Pa.; Second Vice-President, Mr. H. S. Vail, Marion, O.; Secretary, Mr. George C. Shafer, Wheeling, W. Va.; Treasurer, Mr. O. G. Murray, Richmond, Ind. Directors:—Messrs. Proctor Seas, Cleveland; L. H. Ramsey, Lexington, Ky.; H. A. Deardourf, Greenville, O. Amusement Director, Mr. Gus Sun, Springfield, O. Meetings were held during the year at Springfield, O., on April 13, and at Columbus, O., on August 18.

THE PROFESSIONAL WOMAN'S LEAGUE

Is one of the best-known woman's clubs in the United States. The League is one of the charitable organisations of New York, and is composed of the female stars in the theatrical profession, with the leading women doctors, lawyers, journalists, and authors of New York City.

The League had a benefit *matinée* at the New York Theatre on September 24. President, Mrs. Suzanne Westford.

THE DRAMATISTS' CLUB.

The American Dramatists' Club was founded in 1892. Its object is "to promote social intercourse and good fellowship among its members, and to advance the interests of authors and composers whose works are presented on the American Stage." President, Mr. Augustus Thomas; Corresponding Secretary, Mr. Mark E. Swan. Address :—133, West 45th Street, New York.

THE LAMBS' CLUB.

The Lambs' Club is situated at 130, West 44th Street, New York. Object :—"The promotion of social intercourse among persons engaged professionally in the drama, music, authorship, and the fine arts, as well as friends of these professions, and the collection and preservation of objects of interest thereto."

THE GREEN ROOM CLUB.

Members consist of actors, managers, singers, composers, and dramatists, all members of the theatrical profession, and lay members. Its distinct purpose is bringing the actor and manager into close personal relations.

Prompter, Mr. Herbert Hall Winslow; Call Boy, Mr. James O'Neill; Copyist, Mr. Frank G. Stanley; Angel, Mr. James D. Barton. House Committee :—Messrs. Albert Sutherland (Chairman), Eli Cahn, James D. Barton, Will R. Wilson. Scribes : —Mr. Eugene Young and Mr. Nain Grute. Affiliations :—Brooklyn Yacht Club, Brooklyn; Eccentric Club, London.

Offices :—139, West 47th Street, New York.

THE LOTOS CLUB.

Secretary, Mr. George H. Daniels. Address, 558, Fifth Avenue, New York.

BROTHERHOOD OF MAGICIANS.

The Brotherhood of Magicians, an organisation founded by Mr. George E. Closson, in October, 1905, has been established on a solid basis by the election of officers and the location of permanent headquarters at Troy, N.Y.

The following are the officers :—Permanent Chairman, Prof. Mayo; Treasurer, Mr. George E. Closson; Secretary, Mr. Charles D. Chichester; Official Instructor and Chairman Commissioners of Degrees, Mr. Louis Schwartz; Master Representative, Prof. Le Roi; Chairman Reception Committee, Mr. Thomas Beaudry. The Board of Directors includes Messrs. Closson, Le Roi, Beaudry, Mayo, and Schwartz.

The Brotherhood has a membership of over 200 magicians and illusionists in the United States and several in foreign countries. The organisation was formed for the protection and betterment of its members, and its watchwords, exemplified by the spade, diamond, heart, and club, are advancement (the spade that uncovers all mysteries), co-operation (the diamond—results come by united efforts), brotherhood (the heart of fraternity), and protection (the club, or an axe, to use on exposers).

The Brotherhood has an elaborate series of degrees, the highest of which, Grand Sir Knight, B. of M., is conferred only on members who have been students of magic for at least twenty years.

UNITED MUSICIANS.

President, Mr. Sol Beck; Vice-President, Mr. Anton Swoboda; Treasurer, Mr. Chris J. Binzen; Financial Secretary, Mr. Henry Vogeler; Recording Secretary, Mr. G. Edw. Glassing; Almoner, Mr. Frank Hirsh; Sergeant-at-Arms, Mr. Tony White; Assistant Sergeant-at-Arms, Mr. Ernest Huebner; Delegates, Mr. George Biller and Mr. Harry Mandell. Board of Directors :—Messrs. Wm. Blohm, R. N. Seymour, Louis Trenkle, Ernest Mehner, jun., and Harry P. Wolfer.

Offices :—209-219, East 124th Street, New York.

THE WANDERERS.

This club is composed entirely of musical directors, covering every branch of the theatrical field. It is only two years old, with a membership of more than eighty.

Secretary, Mr. Frank Saddler; Treasurer, Joe Nathan. Offices :—Shubert Building, Room 509, 1,416, Broadway, New York.

THE FRIARS.

The officers are:—Abbot, Mr. Charles Emerson Cook; Dean, Mr. Harry G. Sommers; Recording Secretary, Mr. Willard D. Coxey; Corresponding Secretary, Mr. Burton Emmett; Treasurer, Mr. John W. Rumsey. Board of Governors:—Messrs. Philip Mindil, George W. Sammis, W. G. Smyth, A. Toxen Worm, William Raymond Sill, J. M. Welch, Wallace Munro, Walter Floyd, and John B. Reynolds.

Club-house, 107, West 45th Street, New York. New premises opened on May 9, 1908.

SHOW PRINTERS' ASSOCIATION.

The annual meeting of the Show Printers' Association was held in Chicago on May 12-14. The following officers were elected:—President, Mr. Charles W. Jordan, of Chicago; Vice-President, Mr. James Hennegan, of Cincinnati; Treasurer, Mr. H. J. Anderson, of Cincinnati; Secretary, Mr. Clarence E. Runey, of Cincinnati. Directors:—Messrs. E. H. McCoy, E. R. Mackay, Joseph March, C. F. Libbie, L. C. Farrar, Archibald Donaldson, and Walter S. Donaldson.

THE PATHFINDERS' AND TRAILERS' CLUB.

This club was incorporated on February 17. Its membership is composed of theatrical managers, advance agents, and treasurers of theatres. The membership numbers about two hundred. The officers of the organisation are:—President, Mr. W. D. Fitzgerald; Vice-President, Mr. J. B. Isaac; Secretary, Mr. J. A. Daly; Treasurer, Mr. Thos. C. Byers. Messrs. W. B. Irons, J. R. Reymer, Harry Bryant, John P. Daly, and James Weeden constitute the board of governors.

THE PHILADELPHIA CUSHMAN CLUB.

The Cushman Club is composed exclusively of women members of the theatrical profession. It provides rooms at all prices, together with attendance, private use of laundry, sewing-room, etc., and (if desired) table board, including midnight luncheon and afternoon tea to any member of the dramatic or operatic professions.

Quarters:—322, South Tenth Street, Philadelphia.

THEATRICAL PROTECTIVE UNION.

The officers are:—President, Mr. Hugh J. O'Mallon; Vice-President, Mr. John Taylor; Corresponding Secretary, Mr. Joe Meeker; Recording Secretary, Mr. Douglas Gordon; Financial Secretary, Mr. Thomas Dunsworth; Treasurer, Mr. Edward Piersall; Sergeant-at-Arms, Mr. George Hearn. Trustees:—Messrs. Alex. Jandrew (Chairman), Otto Kremm, J. Cohn, Harry Eriverkaer, and Chas. L. Gotson.

Meeting rooms, Yorkville Casino, East 86th Street, New York.

THE DRAMATIC YEAR IN PARIS.

BY THE PARIS CORRESPONDENT OF "THE STAGE."

THERE is reason for satisfaction both as regards the number of plays produced during the past year and the manner of their interpretation on the part of the artists concerned. And commendation must go out to many of the managers for their enterprise, seeing that close upon one hundred new plays, in three, four, or five acts, have been represented, together with a like number of one-act pieces, not to mention revivals. But there are other points to consider besides the number of plays, and, except in two or three special instances, the literary standpoint cannot be said, particularly on the part of the most popular writers, to have been raised. Several of the leading dramatists, too, have been missing altogether. Edmond Rostand, for instance, though his *Chantecler* has long been talked of, has produced nothing for the past two years. Missing, also, are the names of Richepin, Lavedan, Bergerat, Pierre Wolff, Paul Hervieu, and Hermant, only to mention a few amongst the best known. But substantial work has come from Alfred Capus, Eugène Brieux, Paul Bourget, Georges Feydean, Maurice Donnay, Emile Fabre, Henry Bataille, Tristan Bernard, Alexandre Bisson, Paul Gavault, Pierre Veber, Jules Lemaître, Francis de Croisset, Bisson, Thurner, Arthur Bernède, Henry Bernstein, and MM. de Flers and de Caillavet. Those of lesser eminence who have had a certain measure of success include Gabriel Trarieux, Georges Berr, Sacha Guitry, Nozière, Albert Samain, and André Rivoire. Of M. Mirbeau, whose *Affaires sont les Affaires* was such a success, and, who, in collaboration with M. Natanson, wrote *Le Foyer*, produced at the Comédie Française in December, I shall have occasion to speak presently. There has been no marked recrudescence of the lighter form of musical entertainment so popular in Offenbach's time, which has been gradually falling off in recent years, but drama, such as M. Antoine at the Odéon and M. Gémier at the Antoine Théâtre have produced —that is to say, modern drama as distinguished from the old form of melodrama— has met with considerable public support.

ENGLISH PLAYS.

Although Parisian directors, or the critics either for that matter, are not much more fluent with their English or any other language than their own than they were in M. Villemessant's days (when he declared that the fact of an actress's dog being run over on the boulevard was a matter of far more interest to a Parisian than would be the news of an earthquake that had destroyed the rest of the world), they are turning their attention a little to what is going on in the theatrical world of other countries, and, from time to time, they venture upon producing either an English play or a German adaptation. *Sherlock Holmes*, for instance, has had a tremendous run at the Antoine Théâtre, and it has been on tour for months past in the French provinces. Then there was J. M. Barrie's *Peter Pan*, played by the Charles Frohman troupe, headed by Pauline Chase, Hilda Trevelyan, and Robb Harwood, at the Vaudeville, and last, though not least, comes George Bernard Shaw, whose *Candida* was presented at the Théâtre des Arts. The dramatist's *persiflage* was, I am sure, unintelligible to most of the audience, for they laughed when they should have been serious, or looked disconcerted when they ought to have been amused.

What strikes one most on going over the list of the plays produced during 1908 is that several of the leading men have not, as far as popular success goes, maintained their ordinary standard. This remark applies particularly to M. Mirbeau and Henry Bernstein. M. Emile Fabre, on the other hand, with *Les Vainqueurs*, has enormously added to his already great reputation.

Reutlinger.

MLLE. DELZA,

Who made a great success in November as Nodia Meynard, in Maurice Donnay's four act comedy, *La Patronne*.

Reutlinger.

MLLE. ROGGERS,
Who p'ayed Grace Rickerford at the Renaissance.

Reutlinger

MLLE. CASSIVE,

As Amélie in *Occupe-toi d'Amélie!* at the Nouveautés.

[Reutlinger.

MLLE. CÉCILE SOREL

Added another to her many triumphs by her remarkable creation of Jacqueline in *Les Deux Hommes*
by Alfred Capus.

THE SUBVENTIONED HOUSES: THE OPERA.

Turning for a time from the dramatists to the theatres, mention may first be made of the subventioned houses. At the Grand Opéra the change of management from M. Gailhard to MM. Messager and Broussan has resulted in a very welcome improvement in the orchestra. This was particularly noticeable on the production of Wagner's *Götterdämmerung*, which had a magnificent rendering and mounting in October, the Flemish tenor Van Dyck naturally being engaged for the leading *rôle*.

At the Opéra-Comique mention may be made of Massenet's *Werther*, also of *La Tosca*, remounted in October, together with the production, for the first time in France, of Isidore de Lara's *Sanga*, first seen about a couple of years ago at Monte Carlo. M. Albert Carré has, in fact, throughout the year worked hard, by frequent change of programme and careful casting, to maintain the standard of the subsidised house.

THE COMEDIE-FRANCAISE.

And in a still higher degree does this remark apply to M. Jules Claretie, who for more than twenty years has presided over the destinies of the Comédie-Française. There is not, I venture to assert, a more difficult and, at the same time, a more thankless office to fill than that of the director of the house of Molière. He has the traditions of the house to keep up, and he is at the same time anxious to give dramatists of all classes a chance of being heard. His output this year has been quite remarkable. First came Alfred Capus's comedy, *Les Deux Hommes*, written by a man who is always infinitely and delightfully human. His situations are never built up without characters, and his crises are no puzzles in which the men and women are mere pieces. First he invents his men and women, and the situations arise from the clash of their characters. He continues for our benefit to catch them at the critical moment, but we feel that even in their quieter and undramatic moments the characters themselves would have been interesting. In *Les Deux Hommes* the four leading personages are living before us with their atmosphere round them from curtain rise, and when a crisis comes it is not machine made. The whirlpool is composed of several currents running together. Take, for instance, the character of Thérèse Champlin, who becomes jealous of a husband she had not been too fond of, not merely because he is modern, but because another woman has taught him his modernity. The strength of the play lies in the fact that nature seems to have worked it out. Different in style, but of equal interest, was the *Simone* of Eugène Brieux, who, besides being clever, is apparently free from prejudice. Indeed, he gave proof of this on the night of the dress rehearsal of his play in April last by altering the *dénouement* in conformity with the wish of certain friends who were present. Victor Hugo altered his *Marion Delorme* to gratify Mme. Dorval, and Brieux unhesitatingly yielded to the desire of those who wanted to see Simone forgive her father upon learning that he had killed her mother for infidelity. Admitting, for the sake of argument, that the love of a daughter for her mother is the most natural feeling in the world, seeing that Simone was only six at the time of the tragedy, and that she has been living with her father for fifteen years, it must be with her head rather than her heart that she reasons about her mother. The drawback to the alteration the dramatist thought fit to make between the dress rehearsal and the *première* arose from his having started with the thesis that a deceived husband has not the right to kill his faithless spouse, and it was on these lines he built up his play. In the original version the father, on being questioned by Simone, bowed his head with remorse whilst the girl crushed him in a pitiless manner. The second *dénouement* no longer matched the rest of the play, which as a consequence suffers somewhat from a lack of cohesion. Brieux is a man of such resource, however, that great success must come to him if he will only pay more attention to style. He has imagination, warmth of soul, and ideas, and needs merely to conform to the necessary conditions of dramatic art to become a brilliant playwright. Of M. André Rivoire's *Bon Roi Dagobert*, produced in October, I need say little but that the author was fortunate in having his play produced at the Comédie-Française, for he had the advantage of a marvellous interpretation, headed by Georges Berr as the King and Mmes. Leconte, Piérat, Roch, and Provost. M. Rivoire will before long, no doubt, do better than *Le Bon Roi Dagobert*.

LE FOYER.

Of all the plays produced during the year 1908, not only at the Comédie-Française, but probably the whole world over, none certainly had been so much talked about beforehand as MM. Mirbeau and Natanson's *Le Foyer*, concerning which there was a law suit in the spring. M. Claretie cannot, with any justification, be charged with an excess of squeamishness. Theatrical tastes have changed of late years, and he has fully recognised this. Indeed, he has often accepted plays that would formerly have been considered much too daring for the boards of the house of Molière, where tradition still counts for something. M. Mirbeau's previous play, *Les Affaires sont les Affaires*, had, however, been such a success that M. Claretie was not to be blamed for having accepted the scenario of another piece from the same pen. I shall be much surprised if anybody who sees *Le Foyer* is able to condemn this able director for having protested as he did at rehearsal against the leading character (described as a Senator and an Academician) being left as written. Therefore, he asked the authors to modify this character, but as they declined to do as requested, a suit was brought, with the result that M. Claretie was compelled to mount the play. As a matter of fact, M. Mirbeau is a satirist of twenty years' standing, and he evidently delights in the display of anarchist tendencies. But, judging by *Le Foyer*, he seems to consider that in order to have reasons for execrating society, it is his duty to pounce with avidity upon all its sores, examining them, as it were, with a microscope, till a sort of intoxication results from their nauseating odours. And the strange part of the matter is that M. Mirbeau seems to take quite seriously this devastating mission that he has set himself, for, in the third act, we have a perfect avalanche of horrors. All his characters are made to cover themselves with degradation. We are not allowed to feel a shadow of sympathy or pity for any one of them. The husband we have already seen, despite his titles of Baron, Academician, Senator, apostle of charity, Grand Dignitary of the Legion of Honour, and illustrious orator, is able to descend to the ignominy of being a *mari complaisant*, as well as a thief; whilst the wife, after giving up her wealthy and vulgar lover, returns to him, in order that he may set her husband afloat again. And in the third act the leading characters become despicable to the last degree. When the lover. Biron, proposes, as a condition of finding the required 300,000 francs, that the Baroness shall accompany him on a yachting cruise in the Adriatic, bringing her husband and a new young lover with her, because a *ménage à quatre* would be something new for him, it may be imagined with what skill and tact Mme. Bartet interpreted the part for the house not to have risen in revolt against such bestiality. Hissing there was, and on the second performance a small riot took place, the artists being obliged for several minutes to sit still on the stage till calm was restored. But it is not on what is called the first stage of the world that one expects to see such a degrading play, and M. Claretie deserves sympathy for not having been able to prevent its production. By curtain-fall the moral atmosphere of the house had become asphyxiating, and it was a relief to get out even into the winter air of the streets.

It is a pleasure, as well as a relief, to turn from a play like *Le Foyer* to the poet Albert Samain's *Polyphème*. If he invented nothing as regards his story (for since men and women were first created passion has stirred them), the poet has at least put art and sensibility into his work, and also something of himself. And he provides us with fresh emotions. The final episode, in which Polyphemus bids farewell to life, is written in language that is a credit to French literature, and it is a matter for lasting regret that poor Samain had only time to produce this pathetic and perfect little drama before being cut down by death. His *Polyphème* must remain one of the pearls of the repertory of the Comédie-Française, which also during the year saw the reproduction of several more or less interesting plays. These included Favart's *Trois Sultanes*, *Monsieur de Pourceaugnac*, *Arlequin poli par l'Amour*, *La Belle Saïnara*, *Mort de Pompée*, and last, but not least, Georges de Porto-Riche's *Amoureuse*, originally produced at the Odéon some fifteen years ago.

ACTIVITY AT THE ODEON.

At the Odéon M. Antoine has shown the same activity that has characterised him throughout his life. Beginning the year with Gustave Geoffroy's *Apprentie*, he next mounted *Ramuntcho*, which was adapted from Pierre Loti's novel. M. Antoine then produced a three-act play by Gabriel Trarieux, entitled *Alibi*. There is talent displayed in the first act of *Alibi*, where we see the court-martial on Lieutenant Aignevise, who is charged with having murdered Captain Delmas. The interest was excited by the realism of this scene, but it diminished in the second act, and the drama crumbled to pieces, as it were, in the last scene. It is only by compromising a lady he had been visiting at the hour of the murder that the

THE PARIS STAGE.

[Reutlinger.

MLLE. LIFRAUD,

A new comer at the Comédie-Française, made a great hit at the Molière fête as Agnès in *Âmes Mariée*, written specially for the occasion by M. Allou.

THE PARIS STAGE.

[*Reutlinger.*

MLLE. CASSINY,
As Madame Remy in *L'Oreille Fendue* at the Antoine Theatre.

THE PARIS STAGE.

[*Reutlinger.*

MLLE. GABRIELLE ROBINNE,

As Betty in *L'Anglais tel qu'on le parle* at the Comédie-Française.

MLLE. DE MORNAND, [*Reutlinger,*

As Georgette Fargis, in *La Patronne* by Maurice Donnay at the Vaudeville.

lieutenant would have been able to set up an alibi, and this he refrains from doing. Though by no means a great success, *L'Alibi* was not in the least boring, despite the fact that Mme. Jane Hading played in a very artificial manner as the lady who could at once have cleared the falsely accused man. Trarieux will still retain the confidence of his critics, for even the cleverest authors make occasional mistakes.

POETIC DRAMA.

Amongst the poets who have done good work for the stage mention must be made of M. Maurice Magre, the author of *Velléda*, which was given at the end of May. Unfortunately, all his characters do not seem to live before us. To give them the life needed the author would have to be either a Shakespeare or a Goethe. The conception of his tragedy is by no means commonplace, but, for the reasons given, it falls short of being a *chef d'œuvre*. His rhymes also want more attention, for *épaule* and *consolent*, for instance, will not do. It comes like a wrong note in music, and consequently grates on the ear. M. Magre has only to take a little more pains. There is certainly the making of a poet in him.

PLAYS BY LADIES.

Turning to lady dramatists, it may be said that more, if not better, work has been done by them, and Mme. Judith Gautier's *A rare Chinois* may be mentioned quite as much for its brilliant mounting as for its story, which, unfortunately, proved small for a *pièce de résistance* at the Odéon.

A YOUNG AUTHOR.

Always ready to encourage the young, M. Antoine accepted Sacha Guitry's *Petite Hollande*, which was a blend of gaiety, affection, brightness, and sadness. His psychology is that of lovers, and there are always playgoers to welcome this subject. To successfully depict upon the stage the sensations, and joys, or even suffering that many amongst those in front recognise as corresponding to their own feelings, past or present, is a point in any dramatist's favour. Young Guitry is evidently a man of unlimited energy, for upon Desjardins, who was cast for the leading *rôle*, being unable to appear on the occasion of the *première*, he stepped into the breach himself, playing the part really well. The adaptation by MM. Rémon and Valentin of Sudermann's play, with the French title of *Parmi les Pierres*, was interesting in every way. This sober drama is a model of its kind, being strewn throughout with pretty flowers and poetic ideas. It is the sort of play M. Antoine takes a delight in mounting. Nevertheless, as is so often the case at the Odéon, it had soon to make room for another production. Several classical revivals have engaged M. Antoine's attention during the year, one of the most interesting having been that of Félicien Mallefille's comedy, *Le Cœur et la Dot*, in September. This served for the début of Mlle. Renver, a young Conservatoire pupil, who won the only first comedy prize at the July competitions.

THE VAUDEVILLE.

Coming to the theatres on the boulevards, the Vaudeville claims attention as the home of fashionable comedy. It was here that Barrie's *Peter Pan* and Pinero's *His House in Order* were given, with very poor results as regards the last-named play. But early in the year M. Porel produced Paul Bourget's comedy *Un Divorce*, adapted in collaboration with M. André Cury from Bourget's novel. Curiosity was strongly roused to see how the author of *Cruelles Enigmes*, *Mensonges*, and a score of other novels, would come out as a dramatist, for *Un Divorce* happened to be his first essay at the drama. It so often happens that adapted novels are nothing more than a series of tableaux, but these three acts happen to be full of thrilling events. Like the novel, the play expresses the author's ideas respecting the disadvantages of divorce and its effect upon the family, when there are children. One of the strongest scenes occurs between Lucien Chambault and his stepfather, wherein the latter tells the young man that his mother would for certain object to his proposed marriage. "Then let her tell me so." retorts Lucien, "for she was my mother before becoming your wife." The play was well acted by Marthe Brandès and poor Jeanne Heller, who died last month, and not a few of the author's friends have declared it equal to Lavedan's *Duel* or Hervieu's *Course du Flambeau*. In any case, we are all hoping Bourget will devote more of his time to play-writing, though he was certainly not so happily inspired when writing his *Emigré* for the Renaissance. MM. Bisson and Thurner's *Mariage d'Etoile*, which is conceived in the author's lightest vein, pleased the first night audience, as plays generally do when the heroine is a theatrical star. And with Jeanne Granier to play the star who has a marriageable daughter, and who unconsciously excites the admiration of that daughter's *fiancé*, it can be imagined what amusement is provided, especially as the curtain falls upon the prospect of both mother and daughter taking unto themselves husbands. Although space does not permit of an analysis of all the plays produced, Maurice Donnay's *Patronne*, given at the Vaudeville in November, must not be overlooked. In many respects *La Patronne* has been one of the gems of the year. The dramatist has the special gift of always excelling with his heroines, who might one and all adopt Saint Evremond's motto that "none of the pleasures of the world equal the pangs of love." Possessing all the graces of a poet, Donnay has, in turn, shown us all kinds of love—tragic love, conquering love, the love that breathes resignation, as well as that springing from temporary passion. And who better than he can show us the love that suffers, or that which makes others suffer?

THE VARIETES.

The record at the Variétés is good indeed. There was a reproduction in February of Offenbach's *Geneviève de Brabant*, with the imperturbable Max Déarly—whose face never moves a muscle if he does not choose that it should—and in April M. Samuel mounted MM. de Flers, de Caillavet, and Emmanuel Arène's diverting satire, *Le Roi*, which has kept the bill ever since. What a clever trio these dramatists make, to be sure! Arène, poor man, now lies underground in his native Corsica, but the other two, it is hoped, will continue to delight audiences for many years. They have sometimes been charged with having good memories and being able to adapt old scenes, but it has not been with the honey of other bees that these workers have built their hives. *Le Roi* is absolutely original, and the dramatists seem never to lose sight of the fact that they are writing a light comedy, which, be it remembered, in no way resembles an elegy. As to the wit of the dialogue, it would be difficult to over-rate its charm and variety, and, what is more, it is apportioned to everybody, to the psychologists, the moralists, and the journalists of the cast. When I mention that Eva Lavallière, Mlle. Lender, Albert Brasseur, Gay, and Max Déarly are the leading interpreters, it will be understood that the authors were fortunate in this respect. Some of the critics took exception to Brasseur's accent, but, after all, we have not fifty accents. With the Northern and the Marseilles accent, that of the Anglo-Saxon and that of the Latin races, the list is about exhausted. I was forgetting the Belgian accent, and I should have been wrong to do so, and so would Brasseur to have used it.

It is my pleasure now to come to a theatre which, year in and year out, gets a large share of patronage from the more serious-minded members of the community. I refer to the Antoine, which has had M. Gémier at its head since M. Antoine left it to take over the reins of management at the subventioned Odéon. It was at the Antoine that *Sherlock Holmes* had its long run, and amongst the new plays produced may be mentioned Serge Basset's *Auberge Rouge*, Mme. Louise Dartigne's *Repudiée*, Lucien Nepoty's *Oreille Fendue*, with, last month, Emile Fabre's magnificent play, *Les Vainqueurs*. By his *Vie Publique*, *Ventres Dorés*, and *Rabouilleuse* only to mention a few of his successes, M. Fabre has long been recognised as one of the most powerful of present-day dramatists, but with his *Vainqueurs* he has risen to one of the highest rungs in the dramatic ladder. Not only does this writer possess the instinct of the theatre, but he manages always to give relief to the characters he draws. There is so much robust intellectuality about all M. Fabre's work that it is not surprising he should have been compared to Emile Augier. With Gémier's masterful acting in the leading *rôle*, it was no wonder the house resounded with applause at the *première* and that the advance booking has since continued to the extent it has. The director of this popular and interesting theatre will have no need at present to think of rehearsing anything fresh, for *Les Vainqueurs* has undoubtedly started on a long career.

THE RENAISSANCE.

Of the Renaissance, where M. Lucien Guitry's acting is always so justly appreciated, there is less to say this year than usual. With *La Femme Nue*, it is true, there was a success early in the year. Henry Bataille, who had already proved his talent with *L'Enchantement* at the Gymnase, *Madame Colibri* at the Vaudeville, and *Resurrection* at the Odéon, most certainly produced his *chef d'œuvre* at the Renaissance with *La Femme Nue*. Besides being a poet and a psychologist, Henry Bataille possesses that most valuable quality, style. These are rules that need preserving in all stage productions, and nobody understands this better than the author of *La*

Boulanger.

MLLE. RENÉE DESPREY

Made a great success as Vunon in *Paris ou le bon Juge* at the Théâtre des Capucines.

THE PARIS STAGE.

MLLE. RENVER

Took the first prize for Comedy at the last Conservatoire competition and, being immediately
engaged by the director of the subventioned Odéon, made a great success as Georgette in
Molière's *Ecole des femmes*.

THE PARIS STAGE.

Reutlinger.

MLLE. NELLY MARTYL

Created the *rôle* of Lena in Isidore de Lara's opera *Sanga*, produced at the subventioned
Opera-Comique.

MLLE. ARLETTE DORGÈRE,

Nadar.

In the operette *Fraisolis* at the Comédie-Royale. Mlle. Dorgère was engaged for *The Dollar Princess*, produced at Manchester on December 24, 1908, but had to relinquish her part on account of illness.

Femme Nue, in which we are treated to little touches of tenderness and sensibility that savour of genius. And then what acting the dramatist inspired both in Guitry and Mlle. Bady! A most delightful production, too, was that of Alfred Capus's *Oiseau Blessé*, given in December and between which two plays was sandwiched Henry Bernstein's *Emigré*, which in no respect reveals that dramatist at his best. In *L'Oiseau Blessé*, however, Capus, who is invariably good at character drawing, excels himself. It is impossible in a few words to convey even an approximate idea of the beauty of such a play as this, for there is the special quality about Capus's pieces that he appeals to all classes of playgoers, the intellectual as well as the mere pleasure-loving. Therefore with *Les Deux Hommes* at the beginning of the year, and his *Oiseau Blessé* in December, Alfred Capus has done remarkably well.

The Sarah Bernhardt Theatre happens to be another that has no brilliant record to show for the year. In *La Courtisane de Corinthe*, by MM. Michel Carré and Paul Bilhaud, who are young poets, the play was saved from complete failure by the acting of Sarah Bernhardt herself; but neither with *L'Or*, by MM. Peter and Danceny, nor with the Russian drama by Henri Cain and Edouard Adenis, in neither of which did she appear, has the actress mounted plays that have attracted paying audiences. Respecting certain of her revivals, and notably Richepin's *Chemineau* and Dumas' *Dame aux Camélias*, Mme. Sarah Bernhardt would have no cause for complaint from the box-office point of view, but whatever financial success this actress has achieved this year has been achieved touring, and not in Paris. To return to the boulevard, the Nouveautés, like the Variétés, continues to enjoy the good fortune that has attended both these theatres for years, and at comparatively small outlay, for there has been small need for change of programme. Georges Feydeau's *Occupe Toi d'Amélie* was produced early in March, and it held the bills till December, when Berr and Decourcelle's *Dix Minutes d'Auto* took its place. Feydeau in *Occupe Toi d'Amélie* again displays that talent which is all his own for putting before us the most extraordinary people and making us accept them in spite of their failings. This arises from the fact that he can create the right atmosphere. I was discussing his talent with a friend one day in connection with this specific gift, and between us we came to the conclusion that as soon as the curtain rises Feydeau seems to give one two or three blows on the head so as to enable us to follow him to the end. No matter how he does it, there appears always to be a perfect understanding between Feydeau and his audience. Presented as Feydeau has presented *Occupe Toi d'Amélie*, we simply call it amusingly audacious, though the stern moralist who merely read the play might ask whether it was not licentious.

It is with sorrow I refer to the Réjane Théâtre—albeit, Mme. Réjane has spared neither talent nor money. Still I am sure that the result from the managerial point of view must have been disastrous. Pierre Veber's play, *Qui Perd Gagne*, afforded a further proof, if any were needed, that popular novels do not always make good plays. Veber, fortunately, contrived to make his very irresponsible heroine acceptable, but all the little *finesses* of the book were lost behind the footlights, which somehow made most of the characters look despically abject. Emma, on the stage, is little better than a prostitute, and Fayolles, who marries her, is almost as objectionable, owing to their motives not being sufficiently defined. With Bernstein's *Israël* Mme. Réjane hoped in October that she would not have to think of further productions for some time, but the dramatist was not as happily inspired as usual when he sketched the plot of this drama. It was stirring in parts, but it completely failed to move the audience, and the dramatist who does not hold his public is in some way wrong. The writer's aim was high, but he failed to attain it. Still, though not a success, *Israël* contains graces of literature that M. Bernstein will do well to cultivate.

The Gymnase, on the other hand, has fully maintained its reputation, though it has produced no particular play standing out much above the others. Of its *Scandale de Monte-Carlo*, by Sacha Guitry; *Le Passe Partout*, by Georges Thurner; *Le Petit Fouchard*, by Charles Raymond and A. Sylvane; and *Le Bonheur de Jacqueline*; the last-named drew the largest audiences, and had the longest run. Paul Gavault, the author, was fortunate indeed in having Marthe Regnier for the *rôle* of Jacqueline, for without her the story, to begin with, would have seemed short for four acts. Some of the critics found it lacking in originality, but the average playgoer is often content to renew acquaintance with familiar characters, and even to listen to familiar phrases uttered with traditional gestures. I am far from saying that what is commonplace delights, but when the flavouring is daintily prepared, the paying public is not too difficult to please.

The Gaîeté has been given up to popular opera, for which a municipal subvention has been provided, and at the Châtelet a German season of Richard Strauss's *Salomé*, stage-managed by Dr. Lowenfeld, was a feature of very great interest. Of the impressions to be recorded respecting *Salomé*, some of which are subtle, some picturesque, others haunting and terrible, there is one which stands out foremost. It is that of the climax, fearful in the story, and as fearful in the music. The strident strings work on the nerves till the listener thinks he can bear it no longer. Then, after the head has fallen, Salomé's long soliloquy is a wonderful page of music. Her moods are expressed in arresting themes, and her thirst of desire is a magnificent phrase. In short, Paris ratified the verdict that this is the greatest music-drama since Wagner's.

The Porte St. Martin, in addition to its repertory of Coquelin plays, also tried its hand at music with Silvestre and Cain's *Chevalier d'Eon*. Operette, including *Mam'zelle Trompette* and Hervé's *Petit Faust*, likewise served to attract people to the Folies-Dramatiques, and the same kind of fare was provided at the Bouffes-Parisiens, where, under the title of *S. A. R.*, with music by Ivan Caryll , *The Prince Consort* met with considerable success in November.

The Palais-Royal, the Cluny, and the Comédie-Royale produced the average number of light comedies, of which *L'Heure de la Bergère*, by Ordonneau, at the Palais-Royal, and *Les Tribulations d'un Gendre*, by Grenet-Dancourt and Héros, at the Cluny, were of average merit.

A passing mention is all that is called for respecting the theatres devoted more to drama than those already named. These include the Théâtre de l'Œuvre, Les Escholiers, the Athénée, the Théâtre Mévisto, and the Ambigu, at which last-named house *La Bête Féroce*, by Jules Mary and Emile Rochard, and *L'Agence Legris*, by a débutant, Jacques Roullet, met with very fair success.

The Théâtre-des-Arts, where G. Bernard Shaw's *Candida* was given, produced dramas of French and German origin, and several creditable plays were given at the Molière Theatre, the Capucines, the Théâtre Mévisto, at Fémina, as well as at the new building called the Théâtre Michel, where an interesting comedy by Tristan Bernard, entitled *La Poulailler*, served for the inaugural performance in December. Mention must also be made of Jules Lemaître's play, *La Princesse de Clèves*, adapted from the novel by Mme. de la Fayette, and played by the Théâtre d'Action Française. The dramatist, despite his talent, could not, of course, put the whole book on the stage, but he has certainly succeeded in retaining all its sweet perfume, and, in parts, he has even excelled the novel. There has, on the whole, been a good average of interesting and often stimulating plays, and with the exception of *Le Foyer*, which was certainly not in its place at the Comédie Française, and François de Nion's *Angoisse*, and M. Armory's *Monsieur aux Chrysanthèmes*, both of which are absolutely unfit for stage production, the year's productions have been a credit to the city in which they were represented.

OBITUARY.

The obituary in Paris for 1908 has unfortunately been a heavy one, for Ludovic Halévy, Emmanuel Arène, and Victorien Sardou have all joined the majority. So have Taffanel the musician, and amongst others sweet young Jeanne Heller, of the Vaudeville, besides Mme. Favart, who for thirty years remained one of the glories of the Comédie Française.

THE PARIS ORPHELINAT DES ARTS.

IN all her brilliant career as an actress Mme. Marie Laurent did nothing which covered her name with such glory as the foundation of L'Orphelinat des Arts in the month of May, 1880. It would, of course, have been a formidable undertaking for one woman to carry through. Still, the fact remains that the original idea was that of an actress who had lived a busy life, and she was fortunate indeed in finding other generous-hearted people ready to help her with her ambitious scheme. The artists, who, with the late Mme. Marie Laurent, formed the first Committee, were Mme. Krauss, of the Grand Opera ; Mmes. Riquer, Suzanne Reichemberg, Sophie Croizette, Thénard, Sarah Bernhardt, all, at that time, *sociétaires* of the Comédie Française ; Mme. Henry Greville (novelist) ; Mme. Léontine Beaugrand, a dancer at the Grand Opera ; together with Madeleine Zulma Bouffar, also an actress. In arranging their plan of campaign the founders of the orphanage resolved to make it as comprehensive as possible, and, besides admitting the orphans of actors, actresses, and lyric artists, they decided to include all the arts. Thus are admitted without any regard to religious belief within the hospitable walls of the orphanage of Courbevoie, not only the daughters of stage celebrities, but those of painters, sculptors, engravers, architects, musicians, composers, men of letters, and journalists. The boys, taken charge of by this excellent institution are, owing to the foundation by M. Roty of the "Fraternité Artistique," placed as boarders in different schools, whilst the girls form one large family at the Courbevoie orphanage, to which, from its foundation, its actual president Mme. Poilpot, the wife of the painter of that name, has devoted all her energy and almost her whole time. The present committee of administration includes the names of Mesdames Roty and Scalini as vice-presidents ; Mme. Jules Chéret, the wife of the celebrated artist of that name ; together, with amongst others, Mesdames Roger-Marx, Lavedan, Réjane, Edouard Colonne, Chartran, Adolphe Brisson, Paul Nadar, and Blanche Pierson. The lady acting as secretary (an arduous post indeed) is Mme. C. Santon. Although the establishment is entirely managed by ladies, the school directress being Mlle. M. E. Bobe, and the sub-directress Mlle. Gabel, a committee of honour, containing some of the most illustrious names in France, works, when need arises, in the interest of the seventy odd orphans who are now receiving their education at Courbevoie. This committee of honour consists of M. Bonnat, the painter ; Adolphe Brisson, the writer ; Albert Carré ; director of the Opéra-Comique ; Jules Claretie, of the Comédie Française ; M. Constans, French Ambassador at Constantinople : the elder Coquelin, MM. Contan, Detaille, Massenet, and Mercié, all members of L'Institut ; Diémer, Professor at the Conservatoire ; Hébrard, director of *Le Temps;* Mariani ; Albert Maignan, President of the Society of Artists and Sculptors ; Henry Lavedan and M. Mezières, both members of the French Academy ; Mounet-Sully, of the Comédie Française ; Widor and Francis Thomé, both composers ; Rane, the Senator ; Roll, the President of the National Society of Fine Arts ; and Ziem, the honorary President of the Society of Artists. There are ladies also serving on the committee of honour, amongst them being the Duchesse d'Azès, Mesdames Heriot, Barrias, de Selves, Chaminade, and Madeleine Lemaire.

ADMINISTRATION.

The children are admitted at four years of age, and are kept till they are eighteen, unless, for instance, a mother, by remarriage, finds herself in a position to have her child home again. They are also occasionally adopted, but, as Mme. Poilpot and those working with her seek, above all things, the future well-being of their charges, adoption is never sought, and is only consented to under very exceptional circumstances, and then not until money settlements have been legally carried out. It is often, as may be gathered from the foregoing remarks, very heavy work that devolves upon the committee of administration; but the members, and notably Mme. Jules Chéret, and Mesdames Roty, Scalini, and Paul Nadar, give invaluable aid to the president when, as often happens, some momentous question has to be decided. The instruction given to the inmates, it may be added, is very thorough, in order that hereafter they may be fitted for any position in life. The professors include a master for English, a lady for German, and masters both for book-keeping and shorthand. Drawing is taught by three ladies, and the pianoforte by two ladies, as well as a professor. Instruction is given on the violin by M. Hertein-dein, whilst gymnastics are taught by a lady. These teachers, of course, all come on stated days, and at stated hours, whilst there are no fewer than six resident school mistresses. Although actors' children largely predominate at all times in the orphanage, nearly 100 altogether having been admitted, painters, sculptors, archi-tects, and engravers send a considerable contingent, the number of their children having already exceeded 70. Novelists' and journalists' children have totalled thirty in twenty-eight years, and those of composers only eighteen. Concerning those who have left, forty have married, twenty are in business, eighteen are short-hand clerks, whilst two only are actresses.

GOVERNMENT RECOGNITION.

From its foundation in 1880 L'Orphelinat des Arts has by Government and police decree been acknowledged as an "Institution of Public Utility," and yet it was only three years ago, through the intervention of M. Dujardin-Beaumetz, the Under-Secretary of State for Fine Arts, that the Government undertook to support it by an annual subvention of 3,000 francs. Thanks to the legacy of Gustave Doré the Orphanage was some years ago moved to Courbevoie, where the building has recently been much enlarged, and, with the extra pavilion they now have, there is ample accommodation for the present number of seventy-six. The committee depend naturally to a large extent upon their yearly subscribers, but occasionally they have nice legacies left them. The wealthy M. Orisis, for instance, gave the orphanage 25,000 francs free of legacy duty in his will, and from Gustave Doré they had 45,000 francs. The orphanage happily receives a number of substantial subscrip-tions, which help largely to defray the heavy expenses of such an establishment. The Society of French Artists figures on their list for 3,000 francs. The Society of French Architects gives 200 francs, whilst 500 francs each is given by the following societies—that of Dramatic Authors, and also that of Parisian Journalists and of Republican Journalists. M. Bernheim, the president of the society known as Trente ans de Théâtre, gives 500 francs, as does M. Chauchard, whose benevolence is beyond all praise. The Comédie Française gives 200 francs, and the Opéra Comique, the Nouveautés, and Châtelet 100 francs each. Two or three years ago, when money was particularly wanted for the orphanage, Mme. Réjane, through the newspapers, hit upon a happy idea. She suggested that her readers should send something for the orphans in souvenir of some happy date in their own lives, and, as a matter of fact, the public responded in such numbers that a considerable sum passed into the treasurer's funds. The funds are also appreciably augmented at the end of the year by the bazaar held at the official residence of M. Thomson, the ex-Marine Minister. M. Thomson and his wife allow the place to be turned topsy-turvy for about a week. No. 1 stall is that of the president, Mme. Poilpot, who has a tombola of 1,000 tickets every year, and the sale of these tickets is briskly carried on by a score or more of ladies, who include Mesdames Jules Chéret, Hériot, Dettelbach, Rose Caron (the singer), Roger-Marx, and Anna Judic. And every ticketholder, be it remarked, obtains a prize of some sort, many of them being pictures and other works of art. It is no uncommon thing for these ladies at Mme. Poilpot's stall to sell 10,000 francs worth of tickets; and with the money taken at the other stalls the total generally reaches 30,000 francs (or £1,400).

PRIZES AND PRESENTS.

Money prizes are given annually to the pupils with the money subscribed specially for the purpose by ladies on the committee, and all this is taken care of for them till they go out into the world. Many of them thus take away 400 or 500 francs. M. Henri Rothschild has for the last few years given 1,000 francs out of the royalties on his plays, and other generous donors subscribe 1,000 francs for the foundation of a bed. One of the great charms of this very home-like orphanage is that the girls are all brought up to look upon the place as a home to which they can return if ever they want advice or help. Only recently one of the pupils, who had filled the post of governess in a family for some time, found herself homeless, as it were, so she returned to Courbevrie, and spent three months there prior to crossing the sea to take up a position in Senegal. Besides being well educated, the pupils are taught needlework, and brought up to be generally useful. In fact, under the guidance of a good cutter and fitter, they help to make their own dresses. Their jackets or mantles, however, are ordered at the Louvre, and often paid for by some wealthy subscriber like Mme. Hériot, whilst Mme. Roty thinks nothing of making seventy warm petticoats at a time, taking the exact measurement for every child. But though the girls work in this way at times for themselves, they are not brought up to work for a profit, and that this is esteemed an advantage by those who have to inspect orphanages and similar institutions is proved by the following story. At a recent public exhibition in Paris of fancy work, shown as the production of various charitable institutions, a small group of ladies, who had arrived early, were closely examining the exhibits of a public school. Turning to one of her companions, Mme. Chéret said, " We can't hope to get any award with such a poor show as ours ; next year we must try and compete better." A gentleman, who overheard the remark, replied, as he took off his hat, " Never mind about competing, for the Orphelinat des Arts will get the award it deserves for not making its inmates work for their living." The speaker was the Minister, M. Dujardin-Beaumetz. For the most part, of course, the children are fatherless, but in order to provide against all contingencies in cases of a father becoming incurably insane, Mme. Poilpot and her committee look upon the child as an orphan, and accept it at once. Needless to say that a large and efficient medical staff, with numerous specialists, is always at hand to give prompt aid in all cases of illness. It would, in fact, be difficult to point out where any improvement could be made at the Orphelinat des Arts at Courbevoie, whose inmates have recently had added to their number Suzanne and Aimée Desclée, two young nieces of the gifted Desclée, who inspired Alexandre Dumas to write his best plays. Just as Sardou and Sarah Bernhardt were for some years useful to one another, so were Alexandre Dumas and the marvellous Desclée.

AMATEUR PLAYERS' ASSOCIATION.

The Amateur Players' Association was founded in 1905 by Miss Mouillot (present lessee of the Court). Its headquarters are at 92, Victoria Street, S.W. (in the studio of which is a miniature stage, properly equipped), where members meet every first and third Wednesday of the month, when either a dramatic performance— arranged by one of the clubs affiliated to the Association—or a debate or lecture on some subject of interest is given.

The Society issues a monthly diary, giving advance information of the various performances in London and the provinces arranged by the many dramatic and operatic societies connected with the Association.

Every year a Play Competition, confined to members, is held. In 1908 a three-act piece, by Mrs. Clilverd Young, entitled *The House in Green Street*, was staged with success—and three one-act plays have been accepted for production at the Court early in 1909.

The Association was founded in the hope that it might be made the central office and meeting-place of all English-speaking amateur dramatic and operatic societies. It is no part of the aim of the Association to compete in any way with the societies or to interfere with their working. Its object is rather to make the societies better known and their work more effective by combination of interests.

President, 1908-1909, Mr. J. H. Leigh ; Hon. Secretary, Miss Clare Shirley. Committee :—Mr. F. D. Bone, Dramatic Debaters ; Mr. A. C. Chapman, Cripplegate Club ; Mr. Geo. H. Cook, Merrymakers' Dramatic Club ; Miss Aimée Fowler, Dramatic Students ; Mr. F. Foy, Dagonet Dramatic and Operatic Society ; Miss B. N. Graham, Dramatic Students ; Miss Landau, Dagonet Dramatic Club ; Miss Stanley-Clark, Edward Terry Dramatic Club ; Mrs. Clilverd Young.

THE THEATRICAL YEAR IN GERMANY.

By FRANK E. WASHBURN FREUND.

FOREIGN works have again played a great *rôle* in Berlin and the provinces during the last year, but the contribution of new works from England and America has been comparatively small. A Sherlock Holmes is not created every year!

ENGLISH PLAYS.

The new English works which won more or less success were :—In the Berliner Kleines Theater, *Lady Frederick*, in which the critics, perhaps not without truth, "traced the inexhaustible affection of the English public for the aristocracy"; *Truth*, by Clyde Fitch, in the Neues Theater, Berlin; and Shaw's *Philanderer* and *The Doctor's Dilemma*, the former in the Hebbel Theater, where it held the bill for a long time, the latter in Reinhardt's Kammerspielhaus. The criticism on Shaw's works was as divided in Berlin as it was here, and the public equally so; but, nevertheless, he has admirers in plenty in Germany. As is already known, his *Arms and the Man*, under the title of *The Brave Soldier*, has been utilised by Leopold Jakobsohn and Rudolf Bernauer, one of the directors of the Berliner Theater, for the libretto of a musical comedy, the music of which has been written by Oskar Straus, the composer of *A Dream Waltz*. In its new dress this work had great success in Vienna, where its gaiety and freshness were much admired, and the music was said to be full of clever and delicate parody. The critics called it the first successful attempt at elevating the tone of musical comedy, by doing away with the single numbers which have no connection with the plot of the piece. Thus Shaw is helping to raise German musical comedy—and, who knows, perhaps English also!—to a new and better life. Who would have thought that of him!

DANISH WORKS.

Of the numerous French works which have again been given everywhere there need be no mention made here. Some of the French writers have a pretty knack in serving up—never to their pecuniary disadvantage—international theatrical menus which find many patrons. The greatest success of the Berlin theatrical year was reaped by a Danish author, Gustav Wied, with his comedy, *2 x 2 = 5* (agent, Anstalt für Aufführungsrecht, Berlin-Charlottenburg, Hardenbergstr. 14), which ran night after night in the Kleines Theater for a full year, this London style being adopted more and more in Berlin nowadays. And this piece had been refused by several of the best theatres, and had to thank the Dresden Stage Society for its first performance! How often has "the success of the season" the same tale to tell!

Wied has been likened to Shaw, and they certainly have some peculiarities in common, as, for example, their love for applying the lash to the weaknesses of their public. But whereas Shaw does it with a serious object in view, Wied makes fun of everything and everyone, and then turns round and says : "Why excite ourselves about things? It doesn't pay to be earnest! Why not make believe that 2 x 2 = 5? What does it matter?" And so, as an amiable cynic, he shows us in this piece how characterless all people really are, how they turn with every wind that blows like an obedient weathercock, at one time swearing by the Liberals, at another by the Conservatives, seeing in the clouds now a camel, now an elephant. And as his play is very amusing, his public enjoyed themselves thoroughly, and shouted enthusiastically to the new man. With his next piece, *Thummelumsen* (agents, S. Fischer, Berlin W. Bülowstr. 90), which is the story of a small town, his success was not so decided. His weaknesses were recognised

META ILLING,

A well-known German actress of emotional parts, who is going to start an English Theatre in Berlin. She has also played in English in America with great success.

IDA WÜST.

A distinguished member of Brahm's Lessing Theater in Berlin, who has made a name as
ACULINA in Tolstoi's *Powers of Darkness* and also in Ibsen and Hauptmann plays.

more clearly, and the play might have been received less favourably had it not been for the excellent producing of Björn Björnson—the son of Björnson—who is now chief producer at the Hebbel Theater.

Another Danish author, the late Gustav Esman, lives again through his works in Germany. Of his numerous plays, *Vater and Sohn* (Agent, Anstalt für Aufführungsrecht, Berlin), in a version by Rudolf Presber, has made a way for itself. It is a pleasant, well-constructed play, slightly piquant, and with a clever dialogue.

RUSSIAN PLAYS.

Two new Russian writers were introduced to the German public. Dimow's *Nju* was given in Reinhardt's theatre, and achieved an artistic success. It is a drama in quite the Russian style—that is to say, not really a drama, but a succession of well-observed pictures, which are sometimes witty, sometimes sentimental. Nju, the heroine, is a married woman, who makes the acquaintance of a poet, and then the old story begins. After scenes of jealousy with her husband she leaves him and goes to her lover. But happiness does not come to her with him either. Finally, she drowns herself, and the last act shows her old parents reading her diary, where they find the reason of her suicide: She was about to become a mother, but, not knowing who the father was, the horror of bringing a child into the world with such a legacy had unhinged her mind and driven her to her death. The characters are well drawn, and the scenes are clever pictures of the most critical moments in the heroine's life, which contrive finally to give the impression of a whole. It is in reality a novel put on the stage with scarcely any change of technique.

Leonid Andrejew's *Das Leben des Menschen* had its first performance on any stage in Frau Luise Dumont's Schauspielhaus in Düsseldorf. It is a strange kind of mystery play in which, in the truly Russian way, the passivity of man is made the subject of the action. The idea that man is born to an irrevocable fate has hardly ever been treated in a more extraordinary way than this, even in the earlier "fate-dramas," as they were called. The first scene opens with the cries of a woman in child-bed, by whom man is linked to the past he can never escape. Through gloomy scenes the man is followed to his miserable end, accompanied throughout by the dumb and silent "grey shade," the personification of Fate, which finally snuffs out the flickering light of life. From the darkness these scenes seem to come, and to the darkness they return. One hears strange sounds and sees strange sights. All through, it was felt that a poet was at work, and therefore it made a powerful impression in spite of all peculiarities, amongst which are to be reckoned the long speeches to the audience given by the "grey shade," who otherwise has no speaking part in the play itself.

OTHER FOREIGN AUTHORS.

The Hebbel Theater gave a piece, *Hohes Spiel*, by a Swedish author, Ernst Didring, who shows a sure instinct for the theatre in his capacity for keeping up the interest and suspense of his audience. *Hohes Spiel* shows the effect of a sin in thought, and as a piece has much fine shading and characterisation without being theatrical.

Molnar's *Teufel*, which is creating such a sensation in New York, was put on in the Lessing Theater, Berlin, but although Bassermann gave an excellent performance in the title-*rôle*, it did not hold the boards for long. The public saw the common-place plot through all the wit and paradoxical ideas, and felt that the characters were only marionette figures in the hand of the author to show the "Devil" in the desired light. Herr Molnar had miscalculated the effect; even the "Devil" does not draw nowadays in Germany!

Adolf Paul, another Swede living in Germany and writing in the German language, also made the Devil the principal personage in his play *Die Teufels-Kirche* (agent, Anstalt für Aufführungsrecht, Berlin), which had already appeared as a book. This play was received with great favour in Hamburg, then was suddenly prohibited by the censor as "blasphemous." The clergy had complained because in it the Devil builds a church and prevails on a pastor to enter his service, where-upon the good man begins to preach the joys and pleasures of this life. All this, however, only takes place in a dream. The play is fantastic and not clear, the author having failed to seize firmly the idea in his mind, and is therefore himself to blame for a great part of the effect being lost. In earlier works Paul has also tried to embody good and original ideas, but he contents himself with his first rough cast and quickly loses interest in his work, so that it remains, as it were, only a torso.

12

GERHART HAUPTMANN'S FAILURE.

Unfortunately, this has had to be recorded pretty often of Hauptmann's plays in the last few years, and now his latest work, *Kaiser Karl's Geissel*, comes under the same list. It is not the first of his pictures of life in the Middle Ages, but this time he has not imbued it with the full roundness of *Florian Geyer*, nor the tender dreaminess of *Der Arme Heinrich*. Here, man and time are only masks to him. In Karl der Grosse he sees dying old age sacrificing everything to snatch hungrily at youth in the shape of a corrupt young girl. And Karl philosophises over his longing; penetrates his inmost thoughts to find what impels him to this desire; seeks an answer and talks, talks, talks! It seems as if some bitter experience of the poet's own soul has been put into words here, often beautiful, glowing words, like exquisite pearls, but they do not blend into a drama.

FAILURES OF OTHER WELL-KNOWN AUTHORS.

Little of importance has come from other well-known dramatists in the past year. Sudermann has this time written a novel. Frank Wedekind created quite a scandal in Munich with his last play, *Musik*, as several of the characters were suspected to be representations of real personages. The moral of this hazy, obscure piece seems to be : " Girls, beware of the study of music, for music masters are dangerous ! " The motive of the action and forming of the characters show very distinct weaknesses, and there is a decided leaning towards East-end melodrama. A bombastic and wordy drama of Max Halbe's was an absolute failure. It is a would-be symbolic piece, entitled *Blaue Berge* (the Blue Mountains), those distant mountain heights which rise pure and untouched to the sky, whence the longing of all mortals here below is directed. Herrmann Eulenberg again tried in vain to win laurels for himself with his *Ulrich, Fürst von Waldeck*, but it was too full of blood and murder and treason to be a real drama. Even the fact that it was produced by Reinhardt could not help it. In spite of all his evident talent, Eulenburg has not yet found a style of his own. And yet the problem of his work is a fine one—the tragedy of a prince who wishes to be a man among men who are not men but masked figures.

A similar fate awaited Karl Vollmöller with his *Deutscher Graf*, a play full of words and forced scenes and figures, and without real life. The art of words alone does not make a drama.

SUCCESS OF YOUNGER AUTHORS.

On the other hand, another artist in words, Leo Greiner, achieved success in the Mannheim Court Theatre with his one-act play, *Herzog Boccanera's Ende*, which reminds one somewhat of the story of Saul and David. Although it has strong dramatic accents, the play finally ends in thoughts only. Dr. Hagemann, the Intendant, had arranged a beautiful setting—the sea at night in an oppressive, sultry atmosphere.

Richard Fellinger, whose *Unsicherer* was given in London by the Play Actors under the title of *The Vagabond*, won success in Darmstadt with his newest play, *Die Pfarrerin*, a psychological study (agent, Anstalt für Aufführungsrecht; publisher, Vita, Deutsches Verlagshaus; both Berlin-Charlottenburg). Amongst many well-observed types, the finest characterisations are the figures of the young clergyman lost to everything but his parish work, and of his young wife, who is a child of the world, but finally develops into a loving and helpful woman. For the stage, however, the piece was too long-drawn out in places. Ludwig Thoma, the " Peter Schlehmil " of the political comic paper, *Simplicissimus*, and the author of many a satirical comedy full of rich humour, has written another comedy called *Moral*, which was at once a success in Berlin and Munich. It satirises the guardians of morality in Germany, who are themselves, behind the scenes, often very far from spotless. It is a comedy on modern manners, although rather caricatured, and " Serenissimus " (the type of the " little " German Sovereign), who is the target in *Simplicissimus*, at which many of its jokes are levelled, plays a very comic and not at all enviable *rôle*.

Reinhardt began his season last autumn with a revised version of *Die Sozialaristokraten*, by Arno Holz, the " father of the moderns," as he is called. The piece is already twelve years old, and was intended to be the first of a whole series, entitled— " Berlin : The End of a Period, Described in Plays." But it did not find favour at that time, so it remained the first and last of the cycle. It has a certain likeness to Shaw's *Philanderer* in so far as it satirises a literary circle of its time, and contains caricatures of several well-known authors, but it

THE GERMAN STAGE.

ALBERT HEINE

As Mephisto in Goethe's *Faust*.

He is now the Star of the Berliner Theater, Berlin, and made a sensation as Mephisto in the Künstler Theater, München, during the exhibition there last summer. His work was much admired in London when he played during one of the German seasons.

THE GERMAN STAGE.

By permission of Messrs. Becker & Maass, Berlin, W., Charlottenstr., 50/51

ALEXANDER MOISSI

In the rôle of FRANZ MOOR in Schiller's *Die Räuber*.
He is an Italian by birth, but was won by Max Reinhardt for the German stage a few years
ago. He now plays leading character parts in Reinhardt's Deutsches Theater.

seems not much has been lost through the cycle not being completed. This belated *première* was a great first-night success, which, however, was not sustained.

NEW DRAMATISTS.

We come now to the works of new dramatists who had either not had plays performed at all up to last year, or only such plays as had then not established their reputation firmly. These pieces are written in all possible styles—modern society plays, satires on the times, popular pieces, and dramas in the grand style which take events of history or legend for their plot. The peculiar transition period through which Germany is passing just now is clearly shown in these many styles, which often confuse the dramatist himself and make him uncertain as to the one best suited to him. This accounts for the many somewhat faltering, although often very talented, attempts which are made, especially in drama of the grand style, a style demanding a strong and confident personality, a great gift of poetry, and a firm hand in guiding the action. The works of two of these authors had the great distinction of receiving the Schiller prize. These were *Tantris der Narr* (agent, Anstalt für Aufführungsrecht, Berlin; publishers, Inselverlag, Leipzig), a drama by Ernst Hardt, hitherto known as the sympathetic translator of several French works; and *Erde* (agent, S. Fischer, who has also published it in book form), by Karl Schönherr.

THE SCHILLER PRIZE.

The Schiller Prize was created and endowed by the Emperor William I. in the year 1859, and consists of a gold medal and £150, which are given every three years to the best dramatic work performed or published during that time. The decision was given by the Emperor himself, advised by a commission which he had appointed. Amongst the earlier recipients of the prize were Hebbel, for his *Nibelungen*, Ludwig Anzengruber, Adolf Wilbrandt, Paul Heyse, and E. von Wildenbruch. Unfortunately, it has not contributed much so far towards furthering the drama. When, later, the naturalistic period began in the German drama, the Commission was in the painful position of not knowing whom to recommend, and when Fulda's *Talisman*, and later on Hauptmann's *Versunkene Glocke*, were suggested, the present Emperor refused his consent. This caused general disapproval, with the result that the Emperor commanded the prize to be given only every six years with double the amount of money, and dramas of the last twelve years instead of three years were to be valid for the prize. As the result of this command, the prize was awarded on the anniversary of Schiller's birthday—November 10 last year—for the first time in this way, and to the authors already mentioned. Besides this Imperial Schillerpreis, there is another one called the Volksschillerpreis, which was founded as a kind of protest against the Kaiser and his taste. This prize has only been awarded once so far—in 1905—and as no single dramatist was considered far enough above the heads of the others to receive it all, it was divided equally between three authors—Gerhart Hauptmann, his brother Carl, who has also written several pieces, and Richard Beer-Hoffmann for his warm and vivid new version of *Grafen von Charolais*. By a strange coincidence, the Volksschillerpreis was awarded to Hardt's *Tantris der Narr* also, without the two juries having the least cognisance of the fact, whilst Schönherr's *Erde* also received another prize, the Bauernfeld Prize, which is given to Austrian dramatists.

THE STRENGTH OF "ERDE."

Erde had great success both in Berlin and Vienna. It is a peasant play, and draws its strength from the native earth of its milieu, as does the old peasant Grutz also, who is the principal character of the play. It seems as if even Death has no power over him; he lives and works on sturdily, although nearly killed by a kick from an unmanageable horse. Like an old oak struck by lightning, he spreads himself out again and drinks in new life with the coming spring. In spite of his seventy-two years, he is the fittest in the struggle for life, a true son of the soil; therefore the right of the strongest is his and not his soft-hearted and servile-minded son's. Nature wills it so. The play is a modern and genuine drama of the people. If in older plays of this kind the moral were upheld, here it is the recognition of nature and her laws which are emphasised. However realistic these pieces may seem, they still shape themselves to the theme. It was the same with the peasant pieces of Anzengruber; it is the same now with Schönherr's *Erde;* for, judging from the purely realistic standpoint, there are certainly some improbabilities in the work. But probability here is sacrificed for the sake of the higher truth.

In a fantastic play called *Das Königreich* (publisher, J. G. Cotta, Stuttgart) Schönherr has left the sure ground of the peasant drama, not with complete success. There is no such original character in it as in *Erde;* the figures are not moulded so firmly, as if the author were not in his proper element, and the result is a somewhat shadowy work. It was to have been given in the Royal Court Theatre in Vienna, but the subject was a delicate one—the comparison between a prince whose mistresses had ruined his country, and a poor man whose kingdom (Königreich) was the dark cellar where he and his family lived—and so many cuts were thought necessary that finally Schönherr withdrew it altogether. But his sterling piece of work in *Erde* has honestly won for him his prize. It is said that Edmond Rostand intends to adapt the play for France, and will lay the scene in Brittany—an interesting contribution to the problem whether a play should be adapted or merely translated.

A VERSION OF TRISTAN.

A piece in quite another style of drama is *Tantris der Narr.* It was somewhat daring of Hardt to venture on a dramatic version of the Tristan legend after Wagner's masterpiece, but heartfelt enthusiasm and a passionate longing to bring to life those great figures, brooding dimly in his own mind, drove him to the work, and made out of it not a perfect drama, it is true, but a poem from his very heart, full of swelling and powerful rhythms. Tristan has sworn never to see Marke and Isolde again, for if he does he and Isolde are doomed. Nevertheless, something in him drives him back, and when Marke hears of it he determines to give Isolde as a prey to the lepers. In a horribly thrilling scene the lepers come to ravish the queen, but Tristan, disguised as a strange leper, chases them away. Isolde, however, does not recognise him. Again he appears to her and Marke, dressed as a fool, but still she does not know him. Since Tristan has wooed another Isolde in Brittany, he lives in her memory only as the Tristan she once knew. To prove whether he is really Tristan or not, he has finally to go into the kennel of a furious dog. This dog had once belonged to him, and when he disappeared the dog would allow no human being to come near him. Tristan goes to the kennel, and the dog, as in the case of Odysseus, recognises his old master. But Tristan, with his dog, leaves the land, and Isolde is left to cry longingly for him in vain. This play has already been given in Hamburg, and afterwards in Vienna, where Kainz gave an unsurpassable reading of Tristan. It is to be given soon in the Lessing Theater, Berlin.

OTHER RECOMMENDED PLAYS.

Besides these two works of this year, other pieces were recommended for the Volkschillerpreis. Amongst them was *Das Blut*, by Julius Bab (agent, S. Fischer Berlin). Bab had already adopted the verse drama in his former play, *Der Andere* —a tragi-comedy as he calls it—much of which is very fine. His present piece was produced in Stuttgart, and proves him to have both poetic and dramatic power, but it seems to be somewhat forced rather than to come spontaneously from the heart. Nevertheless, everything is at least clear and comprehensible, and his theme is kept well before the audience. His plot is founded on Grimm's fairy tale of the "Goose Maiden" who was really a princess, and may be explained thus:—The man who is born with kingly blood in his veins, but lacks the strength and wisdom of his ancestors, is not the man called upon to rule; the rightful ruler is he who possesses these qualities, be he born peasant or peer. The author's treatment is too rationalistic and not naïve enough for a legendary tale, so that its atmosphere is not maintained. Although there is much fine thought and workmanship in the verse that will remain in the ear, it is yet lacking in that spontaneous passion which springs from living experience.

This childish naïveté is also lacking in the drama of Schmidtbonn, who has worked for several years in connection with the Schauspielhaus in Düsseldorf, where he edited *Die Masken,* an excellent little theatrical paper, with which is incorporated the daily programme of the Schauspielhaus. Another piece of his—*Mutter Landstrasse,* a play of much poetic significance—has already been given in Reinhardt's Theater some years ago. This time he has chosen for his material a story of the Middle Ages, *Graf von Gleichen* (publishers, Egon Fleischel and Co., Berlin). The Graf is a Crusader who is taken prisoner by the Mohamedans, but is at last released, after many years, by a Turkish maiden. He marries her and takes her back to his home, where his Christian wife is still awaiting him. The latter, mad with growing jealousy, kills her rival, and the Graf, torn with love for both, thrusts her from him, mounts his horse, and rides away for ever. The Graf, a slow-blooded dreamer of the Hamlet type, is more a modern figure than one out of the olden times, and the same may be said of the characters of the two wives. As in *Hamlet* the father's ghost appears to the son, so here the figure of Death appears to the Graf, giving the play a note of mysticism and making it into a drama of fate. Schmidtbonn here works on the principle that man is the outcome of his surroundings, his past, his ancestors; and this in poetical speech means simply that man is dependent on Fate. In spite of several weaknesses, the work is full of beauty and dramatic power. His latest piece, *Der Zorn des Achilles*, has as yet only been read to a small circle, but is said to have scenes full of dramatic glow and richness of colour. Schmidtbonn seems to have the materials in him out of which will develop a true dramatist for the German Stage.

Die Merovinger, by Liliencron, the great lyrist, who has also written some dramas, was given in Kiel, but showed that his work is not suited to the stage. It had more the effect of a cycle of ballads, but is, nevertheless, full of deep passion and noble pride.

Another piece which also has much of the ballad material in it is Heinrich Lilienfein's *Der Schwarze Kavalier* (agent, Anstalt für Aufführungsrecht, Berlin-Charlottenburg), a wierd phantom-piece of the Middle Ages, in which the plague, personified in the Black Cavalier, invites the people to a last wild dance. The piece thrills by the power of its language. Lilienfein—who is not a poet by right only of his name (fine as a lily)—has already brought out another piece, in the Dresden Theater, entitled *Der Grosse Tag* (published by Egon, Fleischel, and Co., Berlin), a cleverly written and very effective modern piece on topics of the day, with excellent *rôles*. But better things are hoped and expected from a man of his fine talents.

Dr. Erich Korn has written a very free adaptation of Beaumont and Fletcher's *Maid's Tragedy*, which was produced in Berlin in the Friedrich-Wilhelmstädtische Schauspielhaus, under the name of *Anteros* (Anti-Eros), with great success. Instead of the colourless masque of the original, he has introduced a minor plot, which parodies the main action, and has found great favour because of its ironical tone.

A drama in verse in a very light-hearted vein is *Doktor Eisenbart* (agent and publisher, Georg Müller, Munich), by Otto Falckenberg, the principal character of which is the hero of the old folk song "I am Dr. Eisenbart, who cures folks' ills by special art." The speciality of this Dr. Eisenbart is the cure, somewhat in the manner of Boccaccio—of women who are behindhand in their duty of providing their husbands with an heir. It is an audacious but humorous play of the broad comedy order, although without overstepping certain bounds. There is poetry in it, too, and moments of tragedy, but at the end the laughing rogue wins the day. It was produced first in Mannheim, where in the last few years several new writers have had a first hearing.

NEWCOMERS.

Beside these artists of this new style stand other newcomers, who have tried other ways. I shall only mention here a few from whom much is hoped. Hans Müller has already brought out a cycle of very good one-act plays, *Das Stärkere Leben* (publishers, Egon Fleischel and Co., Berlin), and now in *Puppenschule* (agent, Felix Bloch's Erben, Berlin, N. W. Luisenstr, 21), produced in Munich, depicts a dramatic academy with all its loves and intrigues. There are many peculiar yet true characters in the play, and the acts are firmly constructed, but the typical stage death of suicide by poisoning makes the end theatrical and sentimental. Nevertheless, there is evidence of great talent all through the work. An equally promising writer is Thaddäus Rittner, whose play *Kleines Heim* (publisher, J. G. Cotta, Stuttgart) was brought out in the Deutsches Volkstheater, Vienna. At first sight it seems only the usual theme of a marriage tragedy, but the way in which the actions of the unfaithful wife are made comprehensible stamps the play as a fine work. The wife falls an innocent prey to the evil arts of a selfish, heartless *roué*, and is shot by her husband. At the trial afterwards the husband is acquitted, and finally kills himself. The greatest attribute of the work is the author's unusual power of communicating his feelings to his audience and bringing them into his mood, working on them as a skilled musician who increases his tones to a swelling crescendo, and then lets them die away again. Of quite another style is the modern social picture *Gelbstern* (agent, Anstalt für Aufführungsrecht, Berlin-Charlottenburg), by Jacques Burg and Walter Turszinsky. Its authors call it "a grotesque," because the theme—the unscrupulous measures of a shop girl to get on in the world—is treated in a tone of ironical gaiety. The entire lack of sentimentality and "romancing," such as is to be found in the second part of *Diana of Dobson's*, may almost be called refreshing. The authors are strong enough to have founded their play entirely on a real piece of life, and, moreover, to have made it amusing, although somewhat repulsive, by their ironical side lights. It was much enjoyed by Berlin audiences. *So Sind die Menschen* (agent, A. Langen, Munich), a fine character comedy, by Bernh. Rekse, has an excellently developed *rôle*.

FARCES.

Of course, there has been, as usual, no lack of amusing farces, in more or less good taste. The old-established firm of Blumenthal and Kadelburg appeared punctually with their new work in the Berlin Lustspielhaus, *Die Tür Ins Freie* (agents, Felix Bloch's Erben, Berlin). It is based on the idea that, through the oversight on the part of a civil official in a small town, several marriages are discovered to be not legally binding, out of which results the usual amount of jokes, mostly ridiculous. For they would never risk being risky! That is sufficiently done by A. Engel and T. Horst in *Die Blaue Maus* (agent, Eduard Bloch, Berlin), which now in America also continues its naughty course. It has been a tremendous success. A farce of a better kind was *Wolkenkratzer* (agents, Felix Bloch's Erben, Berlin), by L. Heller and Carl Rössler, whose *Reicher Jüngling* was given in London by Martin Harvey.

That Zeppelin and his airship would give material for the fertile dramatist was to be expected. Even a well-known writer like Otto Ernst has promptly seized the opportunity to write a play on the subject, *Tartüffe, Der Patriot*, which was received with great applause in Stuttgart.

OTHER INTERESTING PRODUCTIONS.

All this does not represent an exactly great yield for a whole year. Besides the many old and modern pieces permanently in the repertory of most theatres, there were, here and there, several specially interesting productions, a few of which I shall mention here shortly. These are:—The magnificently decorated ballet, *Sardanapal*, in the Berlin Hoftheater, on which about £20,000 was spent, but it did not find favour with the public, although the Kaiser himself had superintended the production; and *King Henry VI.*, by Grabbe, a poet of a hundred years ago, and a follower of Shakespeare, also in the Berlin Hoftheater. Dr. Paul Lindau, formerly Intendant of the Meininger Hoftheater and director of the Berlin Deutsches Theater, very well known and much esteemed for his own dramatic as well as managerial work, has been appointed chief literary adviser to this theatre. One may reasonably expect that the Berlin Hoftheater, which has of late confined itself almost exclusively to old classical works, will now open its doors to the new poetical drama, and thus give the movement an impulse forward.

Schiller's first three plays, *Die Räuber, Fiesco*, and *Kabale und Liebe*, were performed in Reinhardt's Theatre, where also *King Lear* was given, making one more addition to Reinhardt's already celebrated Shakespeare productions. It was put on almost without cuts, and the performance lasted more than five hours, but the audience followed every word to the very end, and even seemed for the first time to understand clearly the complicated plot. The scenery and costumes kept well before the audience the semi-barbarous conditions which make much in *King Lear* more comprehensible.

Other important Shakespeare productions to be mentioned are *Antony and Cleopatra*, in the Munich Hoftheatre, in an arrangement by Dr. Eugen Kilian, the literary adviser of the theatre; and the seldom seen *Measure for Measure* in Gera (Principality Reuss), which now possesses a Court Theatre of its own.

Byron's *Cain*, arranged by Baron Berger, was produced by him in his theatre, the Hamburg Deutsches Schauspielhaus.

THE REIGN OF SATIRICAL FARCE.

Reinhardt made use of Aristophanes in a new adaptation of his *Lysistrata*, by Leo Greiner, to which he arranged wonderfully effective pictures. And from that old comedy he went to another by a Viennese writer of "the good old times," Nestroy, with which he made a tremendous hit. In spite of its sixty years, the Berlin people were delighted with the old farce, called, in its new dress, *Die Revolution in Krähwinkel*, and they revelled in its songs and dances, especially in the verses recited with great spirit by their favourite, Harry Walden. The political hits at speeches by well-known personalities in high places were in great favour, and, for a time at least, the stage which is most associated with the great classical drama became the scene of political satire of the lightest kind because the respected public so desired.

And this, to a certain extent, characterises better than anything the Berlin public of 1908, an opinion which is confirmed by the success of *Moral*, the satire by Ludwig Thoma already mentioned, and of an unhackneyed early play by Sardou, *Rabagas*, also a political satire. In Berlin it is the same as in other places; satire and broad comedy are the reigning favourites, while the demand for earnest drama is very limited. The course of events and political doings of the last few months are some of the causes.

THE END OF THE SERIOUS DRAMA.

This turning away from the earnest drama is causing much heart-breaking. In the April number of the *Litterarische Echo* Lilienfein even speaks of the "end of the serious drama." "The predominance of light comedy over serious plays at present is absolute," he writes. "A manager looks at a writer askance if he ventures to bring him a tragedy in his pocket. And a manager even made the reply : ' You must allow your piece to be called a play on the posters instead of a tragedy, otherwise I'll never get my public to come in at all!'" That is the reason for the many "tragi-comedies," as they are called, and satirical pieces, to which conscientious authors resort rather than write farces in order to play the clown for the delectation of the public.

EVIL CONDITION OF BERLIN THEATRES.

In Berlin one circumstance contributes very much to the bad condition of the theatres there. For a long time—too long, in fact—it has been and still is the custom to give free tickets to all possible and impossible people, as well as to allow tickets to be sold at less than half their nominal price at different shops of all kinds. The public will only pay full prices for a "great success." For the free tickets a small payment is exacted, and with this and the half-price tickets the managers fill their theatres, getting at least their expenses paid, although not always even that. But in this way they spoil the public and ruin their own chances of business in the future. The theatres in Berlin have seldom been so energetic as they were last year, every stage having a *première* almost fortnightly, every one searching for the longed-for success, and at last it was found in these satiric-political comedies. But how long these will continue to hit is another question. The condition in Berlin at present is an extremely unhealthy one. Some theatres are even in the habit of sending round "commercial travellers" to private houses to talk people into buying tickets ! It is suggested that performances should begin later in the evening, as they do in London; also to reduce the price of seats and do away with free and cheap tickets altogether. However, so far no change has been made, and whether these changes would help is doubtful.

LENDING ACTORS.

But one step at least has been made towards easing the present conditions of things by breaking through the system of stock companies, which sometimes have their dissatisfactory side. The Berlin stock companies have had hitherto to depend entirely on their own members, and suit them to the *rôles* as well as they could, or else refuse a play with perhaps splendid prospects. But it often occurred that a certain *rôle* was better suited to a member of another company who happened to be "resting" because there was no part for him in his own theatre. Hitherto it was impossible to get such an actor for a certain part ; now, however, it has become the custom for directors to lend their actors to each other in these cases. This is a good arrangement all round ; the director gets the actor he needs and thereby helps the play and its authors ; the actor gets the chance of a good and particularly suitable part, while his director, who has no part for him at the time but would still have to pay his salary, is relieved of this pecuniary loss. The principle of stock companies is broken through, it is true, but the step was a necessary one, and although the "ensemble" sometimes suffers with the newcomer, the advantages far outweigh the disadvantages.

SECOND-RATE CASTS.

Less to be commended is another practice in vogue with Berlin directors in their attempts to lessen expenses. For the first few performances of the piece, the director puts on his best actors in order to make a good impression on the critics and "picked public," then he allows these actors to go on tour in the large provincial towns (when, of course, he does not pay their salaries), and continues the play in Berlin with a very inferior cast, often only of mere beginners. He goes on the assumption that the public who comes after about the twentieth performance does not know much, and only comes for the sake of saying it has seen the play! But this pernicious system is surely a mistake, and has no doubt contributed very much towards keeping away the great public from the theatre. It is quite certain that it does Berlin great harm in the eyes of foreigners and visitors, who in this way often see miserable performances, although *they*, of course, have paid the full price for their tickets.

PROVINCIAL MOVEMENTS.

In the Provinces there are some very praiseworthy movements to record, such as, for instance, the establishment of "Wandertheater," as they are called. These are travelling companies that visit small towns and give performances of good pieces, the expenses being borne partly by private persons or societies, partly by the towns themselves This is not done for the sake of profit, but purely in the service of art, and to help in the education of the people. Such companies have been established in the county of Brandenburg, in Saxony, in Southern Bavaria, and other parts. Dortmund, a middle-sized town, has taken over the theatre there, and made it into a municipal concern, giving the director a salary of £600 a year and 20 per cent. on the possible net profits. Several towns have decided to expend a considerable sum on special popular performances and performances for schools. In Schöneberg, near Berlin, part of the school curriculum of the higher classes now includes attendance of the elder pupils at performances of classical plays. That the theatre retains its old place as the home of refined and artistic pleasure in the heart of the people is shown by the many festival performances and pageants throughout the country.

THE ACTOR'S YEAR AND THE STANDARD CONTRACT.

For the actor the past year brought hopes of a better standard contract, which had been drawn up by committees of the Society of Directors and the Actors' Association. It was, however, unanimously refused by the latter at their general meeting as not satisfactory enough, and it remains for the future to show whether the Association is strong enough to force the Society of Directors to its point of view. At present, the Society of Directors has broken off all official connection with the Association, and there is every prospect of stormy times. On January 1 of the current year, 1909, the Austrian Society for Old-Age Pensions for Actors began operations. It was started last year, and will assuredly prove a great blessing. The income is partly derived from an extra charge put on theatre tickets, so that the public frequenting the theatre provides the funds. The Society also pays premiums for insurance against non-engagement of its members. Almost all the Austrian theatres have joined this society, and send it the extra takings on the tickets, almost £13,000 having been received in this way up to January 1 of this year. A number of theatres have started funds of their own for old or disabled members of their company, and to this number was added the Munich Schauspiel- haus, the directors of which, on the occasion of its tenth anniversary, founded a similar fund, the income to be derived from an extra charge on tickets of 2s. and upwards. To this, the directors have presented a fixed capital of £1,000.

In Augsburg the sum of £2 a month has now been granted to members of the chorus during the summer months when the theatre is shut if they have not been able to find an engagement, so that they may have at least a small income during that time. For this they have to appear at two rehearsals a week from August 1 until the season begins again. Owing to the immense surplus of actors, the Austrian Actors' Association at last found it advisable to issue a warning in the papers to all those who are thinking of taking up the theatrical profession. The Association also addressed a petition to the Government, begging it to institute a special Com- mission to test pupils before entering a school for acting, and to allow to begin only those who have satisfactorily passed their examination. In this way they hope to reduce the great number of half-taught actors.

SOCIETY OF DRAMATIC AUTHORS.

The Society of Dramatic Authors in Berlin, which I mentioned last year, has in the meantime been growing steadily, and has now started an agency of its own for placing pieces, in order to try to do away gradually with the strong agents who have pushed in between authors and directors. One of its objects is to help foreign authors also, by getting them good literary men to translate or adapt their works. The society was probably influenced in this decision by the sudden bankruptcy of one of the largest agencies last year—A. Entsch—which became completely insolvent.

AN ADVISORY COUNCIL FOR THE CENSOR.

In Germany the censorship of plays lies with the police. This sounds bad, but there is a saving clause in the fact that their decision can be appealed against in Court, and that the latter often removes the interdiction. This is at least better than the state of affairs in England, where one Censor can definitely decide the fate of a play according to his lights. In Munich, after years of pressure, a council of experts has at last been instituted to advise the police in their office of censorship, and consists of university professors, authors, artists, actors, etc. It is to be hoped this example will soon be followed elsewhere.

SOME GERMAN THEATRICAL PAPERS.

Deutsche Bühnengenossenschaftszeitung, official organ of the German Actors' Association, which also publishes a year book, "Der Bühnen Almanach," with a directory of all German theatres, their directors and players. Berlin, Charlottenstr. 85. Price for subscription, 4s. a quarter ; 15s. a year.

Die Schaubühne, edited by Siegfried Jacobsohn, an excellent weekly magazine, especially for literary people interested in the stage and dramatic literature. Berlin-Westend, Kaiserdamm, 26, Erich Reiss. Price for subscription, 4s. 1d. a quarter ; 14s. 6d. a year, postage included.

Bühne und Welt, edited by Dr. H. Stümcke, a richly illustrated magazine, appearing every fortnight. It publishes, besides other matter, short biographies of well-known German and foreign actors. Leipzig, Seeburgstr. 100, Georg Wigand. Price for subscription, 3s. 6d. a quarter ; 14s. a year.

Deutsche Theater Zeitschrift, edited by Gustav-May-Hartung and Oberregisseur Karl Ludwig Schröder, a weekly magazine, full of interest for the profession generally. Berlin N. 65, Müllerstr. 38 a/b. Price for subscription, 12s. a year, postage included.

Der Theater-Courier, edited by A. Gaetschenberger, a well-edited weekly magazine. Berlin O27, Ifflandstr. 8. Price for subscription, 3s. a quarter.

Die Masken, an excellent little magazine, published weekly by the Schauspielhaus, Düsseldorf (directors, G. Lindemann and Luise Dumont), as its programme. It can be obtained through the secretary of the Schauspielhaus. Yearly subscription (without postage), 4s.

Die Deutsche Bühne, new official organ of the Society of German Theatre Directors.

Die Bühne, edited by Ernst Neumann-Jötemann and Arthur Langers, a new theatrical paper, appearing every fortnight, and upholding the interests of managers. Berlin W. 15. Uhlandstr. 144. Price for subscription, 2s. 6d. a quarter.

SOME GERMAN PUBLICATIONS OF SPECIAL VALUE ON THEATRICAL MATTERS.

Dr. Karl Hagemann : "Moderne Bühnenkunst " (three volumes).—Berlin, Schuster and Loeffler.

Devrient : "Geschichte der Deutchen Schauspielkunst."—Berlin, Otto Elsner.

J. Savits : "Von der Absicht des Dramas."—Munich, Etzold and Co.

E. Kilian : "Dramaturgische Blätter."—Munich, Georg Müller.

Prof. Dr. Hugo Dinger : "Dramaturgie als Wissenschaft."—Leipzig, Veit and Co.

Max Martersteig : "Das Deutsche Theater im 19 Jahrhundert."—Leipzig, Breitkopf and Härtel.

Theodor Lessing : "Theaterseele."—Priber and Lammers.

Dr. Karl Hagemann : "Theaterbibliothek " (The Theatre, collection of monographs on the theatre, edited by).—Berlin, Schuster and Loeffler.

Julius Bab : "Kritik der Bühne."—Berlin, Oesterheld and Co.

Julius Bab and Willi Handl : "Deutsche Schauspieler."—Berlin, Oesterheld and Co.

Siegfried Jacobsohn : "Theater der Reichshauptstadt " (Berlin).—Munich, A. Langen.

"Schriften der Gesellschaft für Theatergeschichte."—Berlin, Otto Elsner.

"Geschichte der Kostüme."—Munich, Braun and Schneider.

Georg Fuchs : "Die Revolution des Theaters " (Ergebnisse des Münchner Künstler Theaters).—Munich, Georg Müller.

Dr. Christian Gaehde : "Das Theater."—Leipzig, B. G. Teubner.

THE STAGE AND THE ARTS IN GERMANY.

By FRANK E. WASHBURN FREUND.

A BOUT thirty years ago one of the greatest German painters of his time, Anselm Feuerbach, wrote:—
"I hate the modern theatre, because my sharp eyes always see through the cardboard and rouge. From the bottom of my soul I hate the misdeeds committed in the name of decoration and everything that belongs thereto. It spoils the public, frightens away the last remnants of artistic feeling, and encourages barbarisms of taste, from which real art turns away and shakes the dust off its feet. The true work of art has enough power within itself to make its situations visible and real, without unworthy artificial means, which violate all the canons of art. Unobtrusive suggestion is what is needed, not bewildering effects."

TRUE TO NATURE.

Since these lines were written splendour of decoration has increased more and more on the German Stage, the aim striven for being to attain the greatest possible "truth to nature." The public must not think it was watching a scene on the stage, but a real incident in nature; even fairy tales and romantic pieces must be, as it were, "real." That was to a large extent the unintentional legacy bequeathed by the well-known Meiningers. The great and permanent qualities of their performances—the co-operation of all concerned, the ensemble of the smallest as well as the greatest *rôles*, the unity of the production attained thereby, and the correct proportionality of all its parts—all these essentials were, of course, most difficult to bring again and again to life; they demanded great stage management, enthusiasm amongst the performers, and more time than was at the disposal of most repertory theatres. For the reverse side of repertory theatres, which have to change their bills too often, is that the necessary care cannot be given to the many different pieces.

Thus the external qualities of the Meininger were retained—their stage picture and decorations—and this idea was strengthened by the trend of the "Zeitgeist," which at that time, in literature as well as art, was all towards naturalism. "Nature" and "truth to nature" were everywhere the watchwords. As the Meininger had tried to reproduce truthfully every scene of the historical plays they gave, and to have every costume made in the correct style, so every scene, whatsoever it represented, must be "true"—that is, be true—not necessarily make a true impression. And because it was real—of course, only to that point beyond which the theatre cannot go—it left an artificial impression on all gifted with an artistic eye, and to a great extent kept away from the theatre exactly that public which counts in art and is necessary as a kind of sounding board, as it were, in the creation of a new art of the stage and a new drama. What was seen was only a ridiculous, even painful, mixture of deception and truth. And what was heard did not fulfil the expectations one felt entitled to have of an artistic production, because, through emphasising so strongly the outward "milieu," the inward meaning, the real drama, was too often sadly neglected. Only in the representation of modern realistic pictures of life, the acting in at least several of the theatres was equal to the task demanded, and, to their credit be it reckoned, even won for us a new province which can never be lost, but must rather spread and fertilise—that is, the delicate analysis of the soul and the refined play of features and gesture. In Germany Emanuel Reicher, the founder of the realistic style of acting, has done great service in this province.

NEW ART FOR THE STAGE.

But when this era of purely realistic ideas of art came to an end several years ago in Germany, when a vigorous demand and search began after style as the

THE GERMAN STAGE.

Dr. K. Hagemann's scenery for *Hamlet*.

I.—THE TERRACE.

II.—THE BANQUET HALL.

THE GERMAN STAGE.

Dr. K. Hagemann's scenery for *Hamlet*.

III.—THE QUEEN'S CHAMBER.

IV.—THE CHURCHYARD.

expression of the desires and endeavours of our time, and when, after much fighting and many mistakes, that search was finally successful—at least in the arts and crafts in Germany—then the voices became more and more insistent that the time had arrived to find a new style for the art of the stage also. Everyone connected with the stage—architects and artists alike—were in complete accord on the subject, and the direction they should take was clearly given from the beginning. The period of naturalism through which they had just passed had completely revered them from the antiquated, academic rules of deadening convention making a return to them impossible, nor could their education in the school of naturalism and artistic honesty be simply hung away like a Sunday coat. It was clear that a new style and convention had to be sought, and the problem was solved by their remembering the nature and conditions of their art and trying to bring its laws, which were well nigh forgotten, into force again. They found that in obeying the creed "true to nature" on the stage they had got on to quite the wrong track. On the stage the question is, what impression the production makes, not whether it is true or not. By mere suggestion and bringing out the important points, and putting down or rejecting altogether the unimportant ones, far greater and truer effects can be obtained. Instead of a collection of single impressions hardly connected, and often, in fact, only disturbing each other, conveyed to the senses partly by the eye (through "beautiful scenery"), partly by the ear (through "big" scenes), the theatre can now produce a uniform, coherent piece of dramatic art that does not appeal to the eye or ear alone, but goes to the heart of the spectator. The variety element, which, consciously or unconsciously, has crept more and more into the theatre, and has often reduced it to a place of mere amusement, is to be relegated to its rightful place. For this reason architects are striving to suggest, in the building itself, the purpose to which it is dedicated, whether to art or to the mere pleasure of the hour. Most theatres, however, especially in the smaller and middle-sized towns, have to give shelter to both kinds of performances.

WAYS AND MEANS TO THE NEW ART.

Dr. Hagemann's New Illusive and Ideal Stage.

That the real art of the theatre must be clearly separated from mere amusement has been recognised by the clear-sighted and energetic Intendant of the Mannheim Court Theatre, Dr. Karl Hagemann, who has practically applied this principle in the management of his theatre. He gives to each its due. In a short, but valuable pamphlet, entitled "The Stage and Art" ("Bühne und Kunst"), he states his plans explicitly. For the great drama, in so far as it is universal and symbolical (especially Shakespeare's plays), he has invented a new stage, which he calls the "Ideal Stage" (Idealbühne), while for other pieces which grow out of a given period and a distinct milieu, he uses what he calls the "Illusive Stage" ("Illusionsbühne"). But this Illusive Stage he wishes freed from all superfluity of decoration, and made a preparation, as it were, for the higher "Ideal Stage." Instead of minute "truthful details," simplicity and clearness are the key notes, and the important points are always kept in the foreground. Both his ideas spring from the same principles—freeing the scenery of the stage from all disturbing and superfluous details, and, above all, from everything false and ugly, giving the whole as simple and æsthetic a foundation as possible, allowing unlimited opportunities for artistic work of all kinds, and, finally, changing the scenery as quickly and noiselessly as possible. The pauses between the acts must not depend on the mechanical arrangements, as is generally the case at present, but must come about through the dramatic requirements of the piece. Hagemann, as well as many other stage managers also, simplifies the Illusive Stage by doing away with the usual system of rows of wings placed one behind the other, and also with the soffits, which close the scenery from above. All these until now have been painted according to what is called stage perspective—that is, very much shortened towards the back, so that when the figure of the actor stands in relief against this scene supposed to represent a view of the far distance, the perspective is, of course, entirely false. In Mannheim, and also elsewhere now, open spaces are represented in the following way :—Instead of these side wings, a large, round, and very high sky-cloth is used—what is called a "round horizon"—enclosing the stage on all three sides as a permanent part of the scenery. Latterly in Mannheim they have continued this sky-cloth upwards in the form of a cupola or dome of sky, thereby undoubtedly improving the acoustics. Against this round horizon, which can reproduce all shades of day and night, the other parts of the scenery—houses, etc.—are built up, and are easily moved up and down as required by means of perfectly working machinery. It is very necessary that there should be perfectly working traps and hoisting appliances to allow of the quick change of scenery, as well as to permit of the use of the whole depth or a small part of the stage at will. This has been found more important, as giving more freedom than the revolving stage, which in many ways only hinders. For several years such people as Savits in his Shakespeare stage in Munich, Reinhardt in his Berliner Deutschen Theater, Martersteig in Cöln, Frau Dumont in Düsseldorf, lately the Munich people in their Artistic Theatre, and several. others, have all worked at creating a stage for the representation of symbolic drama, all basing their endeavours, to a great extent, on the old ideas of Tieck, Schinkel, and Immermann. Going on similar lines, Hagemann began his "Ideal Stage" with a performance of *Hamlet* staged in the following way :—In the interior scenes, the back-cloth was a Gobelin tapestry, and for the scenes playing in the open air the "round horizon" encircled the stage, while in front of this again only scenery with artistically conventional lines was used for the near distance. For the wings he used two immense, pillar-like towers on each side, placed one behind the other, which remained during the whole piece. Their powerful upward lines gave an impression of great height, and dignity to the scene. These towers are movable, and turn on their own axles, and on them are hung banners, torches, etc., according to the requirements of the scene.

Only the most necessary furniture was used—on a "neutral" floor—in these "ideal" interiors, whilst all the time the important points of space, depth, and plasticity were kept clearly before the audience. On this stage, then, *Hamlet* was given, with a single pause of ten minutes for a rest after the third act, the result being a triumphant success, which also, it may be remarked in passing, showed itself in very satisfactory box-office receipts. We reproduce here the four most interesting scenes :—The Terrace; The Churchyard, with a few straight, conventional poplars; The Banquet Hall; and The Queen's Chamber, showing that the effect of a smaller apartment can also be secured by the same means.

A very important element in this style of ideal decoration is, of course, the lighting, which is used almost with the effect of painting. It is only in their general outlines that these decorations are permanent; they can be made to suit the requirements of any piece that is put on, which is a most important point. It is not a case of a new routine taking the place of an old, worn-out one, but of a new and cultured feeling for style founded on inward understanding, which will constantly endow with new life the great works of dramatic literature. Thus, for example, for Goethe's *Tasso* the staging was of a much more intimate character in order to suit the piece, and for that reason the mighty pillars were used only sparingly. In this kind of staging the fundamental idea is always that the outward scene must point out and support the drama itself as the accompaniment does a song, and that the producer is in the same position as the composer of the song who serves the poem best by losing himself in its spirit instead of overmastering it with something quite new and independent.

MAX MARTERSTEIG.

A similar work was undertaken by Max Martersteig, director of the Cöln Stadttheater, a short time ago, in staging *Herodes und Mariamne*, by Hebbel, of whom I spoke at some length here last year. His idea was not to give a "truthful" representation of a historical play, "truthful" on the naturalistic stage being but a synonym for innumerable details such as are to be seen in the Drury Lane productions. His aim was above all to show the right proportion of man to his surroundings, the idea out of which the spirit of this drama grows, and to make the poetic figures stand out clearly and give them their full value. In a case like this every detail had to be eliminated ; a scene of noble yet simple and artistic convention was necessary to make the heart of the drama live and move, a convention in accord with the antique and Elizabethan stages both in source and intention. But this convention, as Martersteig says also, must not be allowed to become merely a lifeless tradition ; the rhythm of the drama to be produced, not the producer himself, must decide the form of the staging.

MAX REINHARDT.

Reinhart has also presented a Hebbel drama, *Gyges und Sein Ring*, of which the author himself says:—"The action of the play is mystic and takes place in prehistoric times." It is a drama—it may be called *the* drama—of the chaste woman;

THE GERMAN STAGE.

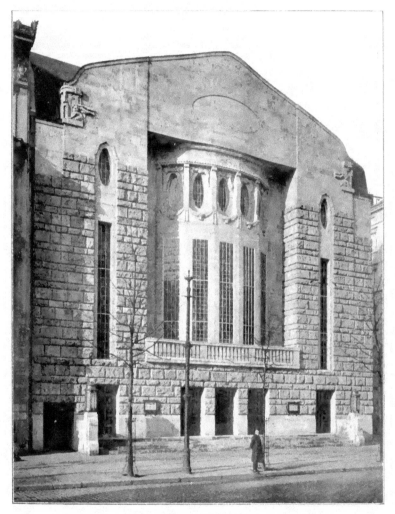

FAÇADE OF HEBBEL THEATRE IN BERLIN.

Architect: OSKAR KAUFMANN.

THE GERMAN STAGE.

THE HEBBEL THEATRE IN BERLIN.

View on to Stage.

it plays nowhere and yet everywhere. Reinhardt's scenes for this play were also based on the ideas I have just described, he being certainly one of the first—if not the very first—who set himself the task of giving every piece its full due, and taking from the work itself the manner and form of the staging. But with Reinhardt this is not only the case with symbolic pieces. Realistic ones also he infuses with a breath of poetry, which frees them from the dust of every day and raises them to works of art. Take, for example, his staging of *Frühlings Erwachen*, although in this case, it is true, the play itself goes over the bounds of realism. His representation of Maeterlinck's *Aglavaine and Selysette* was a rhythmical dream-play; each of his Shakespeare performances an individual solution, although not always entirely successful, of this problem. His latest Shakespearean production, *Julius Cæsar*, illustrates what has been said above. Everything that lives in the names of Rome and of Cæsar, and all the associations they call up, are forcibly suggested by the scenes. In *Twelfth Night* he used the revolving stage—to the annoyance of several of his critics—in a somewhat daring but extremely ingenious way. As the stage revolved, for instance, Malvolio, in ecstasies of delight, was shown changing his costume, and people coming and going, etc.

SAVITS' SHAKESPEAREAN STAGE.

The Shakespearean Stage in Munich owes its conception and practical form to Jocza Savits, the former chief producer of the Munich Court Theatre. It was the outcome, a good many years ago, of the same feeling which Fleuerbach described in the lines quoted at the beginning of this article, and also because Savits, with his love and reverence for the great works of the drama—especially Shakespeare's—could no longer bear to see, and even assist at, the cutting up of the plays into small pieces by pauses which detracted so much from the effect, but were necessary because of the many scenic pictures. A similar theatre had already been in the imagination of Schinkel, the great architect of the beginning of the nineteenth century, Ludwig Tieck, and Carl Immermann; the latter, in fact, gave a trial representation of *Twelfth Night* on such a stage, an attempt which has been described in detail by Dr. Eugen Kilian in his very interesting "Dramaturgischen Blättern" (Georg Müller, München, 1905). The stage was divided into two parts, a broad front one representing a place in the open, and a small back one, somewhat raised, with steps leading up to it and curtains to shut it off. The Munich Shakespearean Stage also consisted of two stages—a front one with a palatial building as permanent background, and a back one also provided with a curtain, as in the case of the Immermann stage. When its curtain was closed the front stage showed an entirely neutral place, which, however, when the curtain was drawn, became part of the room or space indicated in the back-cloth of the back stage. This back-cloth was changed as required. On this simple stage, and in spite of much opposition, Savits has given many artistic and impressive representations of Shakespearean and other dramas.

THE MUNICH ARTISTIC THEATRE.

In Munich, in the summer of 1908, the "Künstlertheater" was one of the sights of the exceptionally fine and artistic exhibition there, which has justly been named the "Exhibition of Good Taste." This special theatre was built to be devoted entirely to the true art of the theatre, and to show it in every part.

The stage is arranged as follows:—It is divided into front, middle, and back stage, and has neither side wings nor soffits. The background, which is a semicircular back-cloth, is always a conventional symbolic picture of an outside scene. In *Twelfth Night*, for instance, it is a beautiful view of wide blue sea, set in a clear Southern atmosphere, with straight up the picture the glittering white sail of a ship. The stage itself is about 57 ft. wide, its opening towards the auditorium about 30 ft., and an entire depth of only 21 ft., which has to suffice for the back, middle, and front stages. As a rule, only the middle stage is used. In front of the front stage is a space for a sunken orchestra, but it can be entirely covered if desired. Instead of side wings, the middle stage is flanked with two towers in a neutral colour, which are permanent parts of the stage, and remain in all pieces. Behind them, again, are two high, movable walls, also in a neutral colour, with door and window, which, by means of lighting, can be made to represent the wall of a house or the inside wall of a room. The two towers are joined by what looks like a stone beam, which can be lowered or raised, according to the height necessary to the apartment represented. Although the action is arranged to appear in "relief," as it were, the spectator is permitted at least a view into the far distance which is given without having recourse to the usual methods of "stage perspective." This is obtained by making an opening all along and in front of the back-cloth, whereby the intersection of the stage floor and the back-cloth is hidden, and the required effect of greater depth is gained. Only the most necessary stage properties are used. Great importance is attached to the lighting, which, with its fine colours —white, red, green, yellow, blue—produces most bewitching shades. Here also an innovation has been made, namely, the lighting is done almost entirely from above instead of by footlights. This style of lighting, however, has not yet proved quite successful, as the faces of the actors were often only in half light, so that the important play of the features was frequently lost to the spectator, in spite of the nearness of the stage to the auditorium.

The necessity of such an Artistic Theatre is treated by Dr. Paul Marsup in a pamphlet entitled "Weshalb brauchen wir eine Reformbühne?" ("The Necessity of a Reformed Stage"), and also by G. Fuchs, the moving spirit of the Artistic Theatre, in "Das Münchner Künstlertheater" (both published by G. Müller, Munich, who also brought out the last-named author's "Deutsche Form," containing the chapter on "Deutsche Form der Schaubühne"), and, finally, in a monograph on "Das Münchner Künstlertheater," by Professor Max Littmann, the architect of the theatre (L. Werner, Munich).

If the Artistic Theatre has not quite succeeded in the most important points of its task—unity of performance in the symbolic drama—it was, nevertheless, a very interesting experiment. Both by its positive, as well as its negative, achievements it can be of great use to the art of the theatre in the future.

Reinhardt is to be director of the theatre during its season next summer, so it may reasonably be expected that the work done will help in marking the new direction.

THEATRE CONGRESS DEMANDED.

These and other questions of stage æsthetics are still not quite solved, and Professor Ferdinand Gregori, of Vienna, one of the best-known and most esteemed producers on the German stage, has come forward with the suggestion that a "Congress for the Æsthetics of the Stage" should be organised, to which all should come who had something to say towards the solution of these questions, and especially as to how practical results might be obtained.

The suggestion was taken up by the newly founded theatrical paper, *Deutsche Theater Zeitschrift* (Berlin N. 6, Müllerstr. 38), edited with much insight by Oberrigisseur Schröder in Hanover. Towards the end of last year a number of interesting letters were published in it in favour of forming an organisation of all the friends of a true art for the theatre, and of arranging a congress later on. Such an organisation will surely come to pass, and should be of great benefit to Germany with her numerous independent theatres.

Most of the ideas and achievements I have mentioned here are already known in England; in fact, with many of them England was first in the field. I need only mention the stage decorations by Gordon Craig, who, although inclined somewhat to force the drama into the shape he wishes, has undoubtedly great talent. He is well known in Germany, where his ideas gave a great impulse to the movement. Other performances I may also mention are some of Mr. Tree's productions, not only his well-known *Hamlet* with curtains, but also some of the scenes of his *A Winter's Tale*, in which the suggestive symbolic element, instead of naturalistic splendour, was clearly seen. Also Mr. Poel's productions with the Elizabethan Society, the performances of the Irish Company, and, finally, the performances of the Vedrenne-Barker Theatre, in which, as with Reinhardt and Hagemann, the poet always received his full measure of justice, and his work the frame most suited to it.

THEATRE ARCHITECTURE.

I come now to the second part of my subject—namely, the newest types of theatre architecture. Under this heading I do not mean to discuss the numerous theatres in large and small towns, which repeat, with more or less taste, the old patterns both inside and outside. It need only be mentioned that in the architecture of the theatres also—although unfortunately still too seldom—new ideas are making headway, and a sure, artistic feeling is visible. Amongst the names which have become known lately as theatre architects, Prof. Max Littmann, of Munich, takes a unique place. Four of his theatres are particularly well known— the Prinz Regenten Theater, Munich, a theatre for Wagner festivals; the popular

THE GERMAN STAGE.

Actors' Dressing Room.

View of Part of Auditorium.

HEBBEL THEATRE IN BERLIN.

THE GERMAN STAGE.

GARTNERPLATZ THEATRE, IN MUNICH, AS IT STANDS AT PRESENT.

HENRY HELBIG'S PLAN FOR ALTERATION OF GÄRTNERPLATZ THEATRE,
IN MUNICH, TO MAKE IT FIRE, OR, RATHER, PANIC PROOF.

playhouse Schiller Theater, Charlottenburg-Berlin; the New Court Theatre in Weimar, and the Artistic Theatre in Munich. In all four theatres the auditorium is arranged on the principle of the amphitheatre except in Weimar, where, on account of the Court, boxes and balconies had to be added for the different classes.

The Amphitheatre Auditorium.

The amphitheatre auditorium had already been planned by Schinkel, then Semper, and finally, as is well known, Wagner put it into practice. Wagner arrived at the idea of an amphitheatre auditorium chiefly through his endeavours to conceal the orchestra from the sight of the spectator; Littmann and others because they wished to gain a free and equally good view of the stage for each spectator alike. The sunken orchestra for Wagner's music-dramas resulted in a space between the stage and the auditorium which he called "the mystic abyss."

The Changeable Proscenium.

In the Court Theatre in Weimar, which has both opera and plays in its repertory, Littmann was confronted with the task of doing justice to the very diverging styles of music-drama and the spoken drama. This problem he has solved in a most satisfactory way by means of his "changeable proscenium," as he calls it. He manages this by simply covering the "mystic abyss" entirely for the spoken drama. This is clearly shown in the accompanying picture. Somewhat the same effect is reached in this way, as in the old Elizabethan theatres, where the stage projected into the auditorium. The lighting is then effected by means of a new kind of apparatus fixed above the auditorium, which acts after the manner of a search-light without any visible beams. From the same picture it will be seen that, although in this theatre the galleries are retained, the side boxes are at least done away with, which alone gives the stage a wider and more imposing appearance, and makes it the most important part of the whole house. It would take too much space to go into more details about it here; suffice it to mention that the stage possesses an arrangement by means of which a great part of its surface can be raised or lowered six feet. The house, which is decorated with the greatest taste and refined simplicity, was built at a cost of about £100,000. And such a theatre belongs to a town of scarcely 40,000 inhabitants!

The Munich Artistic Theatre.

We also reproduce here some views of another of Littmann's theatres—the Artistic Theatre, in Munich. The façade shows at once that the theatre is dedicated to art alone. No unnecessary overloading of decoration, no obtrusive sculpture is to be seen on it, only clearly marked lines of height and breadth. Inside, too, the theatre is purpose-like and unpretending, yet comfortable and refined. The somewhat light colouring of the panelling of the walls and roof gives a characteristic tone. Here, too, the structural lines are strongly marked. The high pilasters at the side give an effect of height to the interior.

A Double Theatre.

Professor Littmann has also just won the competition for the erection of a new Court Theatre in Stuttgart, the old building having been burnt down some years ago. His design has been accepted by the King and will be carried out very soon. Instead of one building for both opera and plays, as in the Weimar Court Theatre, Littmann has this time designed a double theatre—one for opera and one for plays—connected by offices, the exterior having the appearance of a large and noble building. Neither inside nor outside will any concessions be made to the former highly ornamented style of theatre architecture, with its false renaissance forms. Everything—form as well as ornamentation—is developed in accordance with the purpose of the building, and is to be carried out as far as possible on the lines of the old style of the country handed down by tradition, so that the whole building will fit well into the frame of the town. If Littmann's construction of this playhouse justifies itself, then the Stuttgart "Doppel Theater" should bring in a new era in Germany in the building of new theatres in large towns where opera and the spoken drama can be housed separately. It ought also to be of great interest to England, and especially to London.

A Temple of Art.

In Berlin last year a theatre was erected which can rank in many ways as the perfect expression of the architectural art of the present day, in so far as it concerns the theatre. This is the Hebbeltheater, buil. by Oskar Kaufmann, of which some views are given. Every single architectural detail, every ornamental object, with the exception of a few unobtrusive and severely plain reliefs by Hermann Feuerhahn let into the wall here and there, has been designed by the architect himself. The result is a wonderful uniformity in form and combination of colour. As in the façade, where the beautiful rough-hewn stone dominates, so in the auditorium the exquisite panelling of golden brown birch, sparingly framed in rosewood, is the most striking feature. The principal features of modern German industrial art—purity of material and the development of form in accordance with the peculiar nature of the materials and of the task required—are carried out here with the most singular success. Nowhere is the cheap and showy glitter of gilded stucco visible; only the wood in its beautiful natural graining speaks. In this direction also, Reinhardt, with his panelled "Kammerspielhaus," led the way. This kind of auditorium was made possible by the withdrawal of the restrictions laid on the use of wood panelling in theatres on account of the danger of fire, as it was found that, after all, there was not more danger with wood in that respect than with other materials. Rosewood is also used for the huge frame surrounding the opening of the stage, as shown in the photograph. On each side of this frame stands a mighty tower, accentuating the upward lines. Inside these towers are invisible stairs leading to the rigging loft. Side boxes are, happily, avoided. The two balconies are gracefully curved and do not hang too far over the parterre, and behind the first one are seven small private boxes, which make an agreeable break in the uniformity of the wall. Possibly the architect would have also adopted the amphitheatre style had not the piece of ground at his disposal been so very shallow; as it was, he was forced to keep to the old gallery arrangement in order to find sitting accommodation for 800 people. In spite of that, however, the result is a charmingly "cosy" auditorium. The stage itself is about 50 ft. broad and 40 ft. deep, and is provided with a comparatively large revolving stage of about 38 ft. in diameter. The latter is an improved type by which the trap arrangements revolve also, and the loud grating noise and shaking of the whole scene while revolving is avoided. One of the illustrations gives an idea of how thorough, yet simple and hygienic, the dressing-room arrangements are.

Oskar Kaufmann is already busy with the plans for a new theatre, and with his exceptional combination of real "theatre blood" and sure architectural talent some very excellent work may be expected from him again.

PANIC-PROOF THEATRE.

Finally, some words must be said about an entirely new kind of theatre, which, at present, is only on paper, but will, perhaps, soon be a reality. It is what is called a "fire," or, rather, "panic-proof theatre," and has been invented by the German-American architect, Henry Helbig, in Munich, where his designs in the architectural part of the exhibition there last summer found much approval. Helbig's invention—already patented in England—is really aimed, not so much at the fire itself as at the terrible panics that always break out amongst the audience on these occasions. The photographs given here will show how he attempts to make such a disaster impossible. His leading ideas are, in the first place, to divide the spectators into small groups, each separate from the other; secondly, to provide for these groups sufficient and direct exits into the open. The auditorium of this new theatre consists of a cupola-shaped inner shell, containing for each group of spectators an aperture or window-like opening. Behind each of these openings are arranged groups of seats, partitioned off the one from the other. Several tiers of such groups of seats are arranged one above the other. Even the very top of the dome can in this way be utilised for seating spectators, a circular opening at the apex affording a full view of the stage. Further, the pit itself is divided into small groups. But the chief advantage of this new interior—besides being able to seat one-third more spectators than a similar-sized theatre of ordinary construction—is the convenient disposal of the spectators in small groups and the possibility of arranging exits which will preclude all danger from crowding, and, even in the case of a panic, will make a quick and orderly emptying of the house an easy matter. This plan is much more effective than the "outside emergency stairs," added, for instance, to the Berliner Operahaus by command of the Kaiser after the terrible fire in the Chicago theatre, as they would help little in a panic, and are extremely ugly. At the best they are only makeshifts. Helbig provides two broad flights of outside steps, one on each side of the theatre, leading in a straight line, or with only one bend, from the topmost gallery to the street. The

THE GERMAN STAGE.

MUNCHNER KUNSTLERTHEATER.
View on to Stage from Auditorium.
(Architect: Professor Max Littmann.)

MUNCHNER KUNSTLERTHEATER.
View of Amphitheatre Auditorium from Stage, with Private Boxes at back.
(Architect: Professor Max Littmann.

THE GERMAN STAGE.

MÜNCHENER KUNSTLERTHEATER.
Façade. (Architect: Professor Max Littmann.)

WEIMARER HOFTHEATER.
View of Auditorium from Stage. In the foreground the changeable Proscenium.
(Architect: Professor Max Littmann.)

spectators from all tiers and galleries need then only cross the passage or corridor outside their box in order to gain the open air. These flights of steps widen out towards the base, thereby avoiding possibility of crowding. They in no way detract from the beauty of the building; on the contrary, they give it a much more imposing appearance, as will be seen from the photographs reproduced here. The simplicity of this solution is only made possible by the perfect decentralisation of the auditorium.

The visitor to such a theatre, knowing that he is within a few feet of the open, and that he can reach the street without any possibility of hindrance, will, even in the case of real danger, retain his presence of mind. This consciousness of safety should make a panic practically impossible; but even should one ensue, fatal consequences are not to be feared, the broad flights of steps affording an easy and safe road to the ground. These outside flights must not be considered as emergency stairs; they will rather be used on all occasions as the most convenient means of leaving the theatre. Inside stairs are, of course, also provided, and those who prefer to do so can use the latter in bad weather.

The Imperial German Patent Office says of it :—" It cannot be doubted that by these means the safety of the spectators is ensured in a far greater degree than by any of the means adopted heretofore."

CONCLUSION.

All that has been said here goes to prove that amongst the German people in all parts of the land a deep and sympathetic interest is taken in the welfare and future of the theatre. It is felt that this is a most important matter for the culture and development of the country, too important to be allowed simply to "drift." It is true that its progress rests in the meantime on the shoulders of a few individual enthusiasts who have started the idea or are developing it, but if the seed had not found fertile soil it would have ended in isolated attempts of single individuals as in England. Instead of that, however, we see the movement for a real art of the theatre growing visibly; and if only slowly and not always with a sure step it is yet progressing.

ROYAL GENERAL THEATRICAL FUND.

The Royal General Theatrical Fund was instituted January 22, 1839, and incorporated by Royal Charter January 29, 1853. It is for the purpose of granting permanent annuities to actors, actresses, chorus singers, dancers, pantomimists, and prompters; also acting managers, stage managers, treasurers, and scenic artists. Any member who has regularly contributed to its funds for the term of seven years, at any time afterwards, on becoming incapacitated by accident or infirmity from exercising his or her duties, is entitled to receive such annuity for life as the annual available income of the funds shall from year to year afford; such annuity to be, in each case, calculated and apportioned according to the class of subscription which the member has adopted and paid.

If any member die at any period after the commencement of his or her membership, the sum of ten pounds is allowed and paid out of the funds for funeral expenses.

Officers : Mr. Alfred de Rothschild, C.V.O., Sir Squire Bancroft, Mr. George Alexander; Directors, Mr. George Alexander, Mr. Lewis Casson, Mr. Henry Cooper Cliffe, Mr. Charles K. Cooper, Mr. Robert Courtneidge, Mr. Tom Craven, Mr. Dillon Croker, Mr. Alfred H. Elliott, Mr. Henry Evill, Mr. Douglas Gordon, Mr. H. B. Irving, Mr. H. J. Loveday, Mr. M. R. Morand, Mr. Lionel Rignold, Mr. Charles Rock, Mr. Bassett Roe, Mr. F. Percival Stevens, Mr. A. B. Tapping, Mr. Edward Terry, Mr. Hubert Willis; Honorary Treasurer, Mr. Edward Terry ; Secretary, Mr. Charles J. Davies, Savoy House, Strand, W.C.

THE SPANISH STAGE: ITS POSITION TO-DAY.

BY LEONARD WILLIAMS.

THE history of the Spanish Theatre has several points in common with the history of our own. The origin of both these theatres was very nearly simultaneous. Both of them rose to a full splendour through a galaxy of great dramatists—the English drama through the genius of Marlowe, Massinger, Shakespeare, Jonson, and Beaumont and Fletcher ; the drama of Castile through that of Lope de Vega and Moreto, of Rojas, Calderon de la Barca, Tirso de Molina, and Cervantes. The character, too, of both these theatres was at its outset strongly similar ; for the mystery-play of older England is certainly akin to the primitive Spanish *auto*, as well as our sprightly seventeenth-century comedian "of intrigue" to the "cloak and sword" productions of the same Peninsula.

CHARACTERISTICS : ENGLISH AND SPANISH.

But subsequently to that privileged and happy time a swift and solid difference has arisen between the Spanish Theatre and ours. The courses of their several evolutions have become divergent in respective and exact relation with the social and political development of either land. Another cause has also operated to effect this contrast. For it is obvious that the theatre of any nation must unavoidably derive its character from a double source—that is, directly from its national existence proper and, less directly, from the superadded influence of other nations. Now, influence from abroad has not affected English drama very deeply. We are essentially an insular race—perhaps unduly so. We do not lean upon or even look towards the foreigner. We do not live in contact with our extra-territorial neighbours. The sea divides our boundary from theirs, and to this purpose twenty miles of water outvalue a thousand miles of land. Therefore, we live unto ourselves, and in our plays are studious to reflect our national temperament and customs. Our plays exhibit, in the main, a national predilection for the simple joys and quietude of our English home. Their tenor is, above all other qualities, domestic. Therefore, the late T. W. Robertson was one of our most eminently national of playwrights ; just as Constable, Gainsborough, Morland, old Crome, Colman, Girtin, and Joshua Reynolds are our most eminently national of painters; for English landscapes or the portraiture of English people are typical manifestations of our characteristic domesticity. These painters, therefore, have bequeathed to us the plastic expression of our national usages and aspirations. just as Robertson and his successors have bequeathed to us the expression of the same emotions uttered through the medium of the drama.

LAWLESSNESS IN THE DRAMA.

But in the theatre of modern Spain two qualities assert themselves beyond all others. They are a spirit, latent or declared, of sheer hostility towards the written law, and also a mediæval mysticism modified or possibly aggravated by the influence of various foreign playwrights whose mode of viewing life and its ideals is systematically sombre. The English are proverbially a law-abiding people. The spirit of their drama generally manifests this virtue. The Spaniards are proverbially a law-resisting people. The general spirit of their drama manifests this failing. The Englishman is proverbially a model among citizens. He is content to feel himself a factor of the populace, and to co-operate towards the general good. The Spaniard is proverbially a restless, dis-contented unit of a troubled malamalgamated state. He claims the mischievous prerogative to frame and execute his own particular code of law, to be him-self and none other; so that he extracts from the community whatever private benefit he can, yet offers no subservience in return. The Englishman makes an excellent soldier in company with other soldiers. His merit is his inclination to obey. The Spaniard is unrivalled as a *guerrillero*, whose typical ambition is to fight in isolated fashion, each man his own tactician, his own general. His merit, paradoxically stated, is the evasion of obedience.

Again, we English are a constitutionally happy race, because the annals of our commonwealth afford us reason to be happy. Through many centuries our govern-ments have maintained the course of national advancement in its true channel; our land from immemorial time can boast immunity from violent invasion by a foreign foe. Satisfied with what we were and what we are, we relegate the nebulous to-be to rack the brains of other generations. In consequence of this the purpose of our English drama is conspicuously non-didactic and non-speculative. Our preference is with the simple, morally uninvestigative plot and happy curtain. Our audiences demand to be reminded what they are, not lectured as to what they should or might become, rejecting moralist playwrights from our stage, unless they take precautions to administer their theme in miscroscopic doses and beneath a diplomatic form of dialogue.

TRUE TO SOCIAL SPAIN.

But circumstances alter cases—even in the case of an entire nation, together with her art and literature and drama. "Each stage," recently observed a writer in these columns, "must evolve its own character." True to this axiom, the character of the Spanish Theatre has evolved itself in absolute concordance with the character of social Spain. It represents, with great propriety, a proud, impassioned, and penurious race, sprung from a soil where all aspire to rule and none willing to obey; each man mistrustful of his neighbour, hostile to discipline, or trade, or toil; scornful of statutory laws, tinged with the fatalism of the Moor and also with the fanaticism of the Latin Christian, punctiliously polite in speech, but desperate and dark to plot and execute a revolution or a vengeance, hiding a naked dagger in the cordial smile or honeyed sentence, conveying homicidal sneers behind the careless jest; valorous in confronting bodily danger, yet incapable of lasting effort in a sterling and regenerative cause; inherently alert of intellect, endowed with relevant abilities, though stung by constant and humiliating failure by centuries of national misgovernment and wicked waste of golden opportunity.

A TYPICAL SPANISH DRAMA.

Let us consider, very briefly, an example from the older Spanish drama—one that admits of just description as a truthful character-study of the bygone Spanish time, and also, in an equal measure, of the present day. This is the well-known play entitled *The Mayor of Zalamea*, by Calderon. The outline is as follows :—A rugged and unschooled but not dull-witted man named Pedro Crespo, who has attained some consequence and wealth, is chosen by the popular voice to occupy the mayoralty of his native town of Zalamea, an unimportant place upon the Portu-guese or Western Spanish frontier. Crespo has a grown-up daughter, Isabel. A Spanish army, on its way to stifle a revolt in Portugal, pauses awhile at Zalamea, and one of its captains, who is billeted in Crespo's house, abducts the girl and ravishes her. Crespo commands him to be seized and brought before him, and then, brandishing the mayor's staff as haughtily and imperiously as a general his bâton or a king his sceptre, orders him, in a tone of summary resolve, to make atonement for the crime by marrying his child, or vows, if he refuses, to garotte him. The officer, not in the least supposing that the menace is sincere, laughs it to scorn, and as a consequence is promptly strangled. Before the corpse is cold, the king, Philip the Second, hastening to overtake his force, arrives at Zalamea, hears of the act, and entering Crespo's home commands him to appear. Showing him the officer garotted in a chair, Crespo contrives a vigorous defence, maintain-ing, in a rugged peroration, that his mayor's staff empowers him at his sole, supreme and unrestrained discretion to judge and sentence criminals, and, if he chooses, to inflict on them the capital penalty. Philip, appeased, or, as it seems, attracted by this uncouth logic, deigns to approve of Crespo's impudent address and even confirms him for his life-time in the tenure of his mayoralty. The peasant, in a word, subverts at once the national legislation and the authority of the throne. This argument sounds inadmissible enough to any but a Spanish audience, because in every land whose rule is stable and efficient, those only are entitled to apply the law who are themselves responsible for understanding and respecting it. Among the Spaniards, on the contrary, it gives expression, in the form of drama, to their blind and characteristic arrogance, which still continues to demand responsible wisdom of the ruler, coupled with irresponsible and boundless license for the ruled. Crespo's harangue to Philip, while couched apparently in deferential terms, is really turbulent and menacing. Speaking for Spain at large, and at all moments of her history, it constitutes a dangerous apology for high treason and rebellion towards all settled institutions. The doctrine of this drama, which is still vibrating in all Spanish breasts, respires the Spaniard's ancient and incorrigible opposition to the general and controlling system of the law. Another nominally may rule him; he need not ever rule himself. Crespo is thus the advocate and spokesman of a most unhappy people, whose typical and invincible enemy is their very selves; potentially, in truth, a strong, intelligent and admirable race, but yet, with all these misdirected elements of power, a race blown hither and thither by the idle breath of vanity and tumid pride, of selfishness and faction.

Native and Ancestral Influence.

Clearly, a state where such ideals are accepted cannot ever prosper. For in this luckless land of Spain, order is miscontrued as tyranny, and all disorder as a licit instrument of self-defence against such tyranny. Here is indeed a sense of personal dignity run riot, a mischievous and frenzied zeal for freedom from a just control, a popular mind whose balance is inherently unstrung, whose lasting symbol on the Spanish stage is Pedro Crespo, and, in Spanish literature, Don Quixote.

Such is the native and ancestral influence which is manifested both in old and modern Spanish drama. It has a vital value at this moment in the plays of Echegaray, Dicenta, and Galdós—three eminent and eminently Spanish playwrights who express the national ideal by propounding themes of restless violence, which militate invariably against the salutary formal law established by the Cortes and ratified by the Crown. To-day the duellist-protagonist of Echegaray, avenging private quarrels by the gentlemanly foil or silver-mounted pistol; the humbler protagonist of Dicenta, such as the artisan Juan José, plunging with morbid, mock-heroic pride his "cow's tongue" knife into the rich oppressor's heart; or the republican-protagonist of Galdós, scheming by violence to subvert the Church, the Ministry, or the Throne—what are all these but Pedro Crespos of our time, striving to assert the selfish *ego* at all cost, and to set up the perilous and archaic "unwritten"—that is, individual law, in opposition to the healthy and amalgamated civic code of modern equity and modern culture?

Foreign Imitations.

But since the eyes of those who are dissatisfied with their own atmosphere are predisposed to seek example from abroad, and fall more often than not upon the dreariest and the most disquieting of those examples, so, in the case of modern Spain, a number of her living playwrights, such as Rusiñol or Benavente, observe with a pathetic eagerness contemporary masters of the foreign drama—these in their turn expositors of depressing problems which through inability or cynical indifference they do not seek to solve. And since the manner of such foreigners is in general greatly finer and more subtly Machiavellian than the Spanish, the Spaniard also has acquired an added and exotic melancholy from these alien sources, replacing physical by intellectual lawlessness, the primitive knife or sword or pistol by smooth, satiric tongue or clever and corrosive pessimism, harping for ever on the sad and sordid aspects of humanity; the stealthy vengeances of crooked-minded and small-hearted men, the weary woes of ill-sorted marriage, the acrid arguments of *Ghosts* or *Hedda Gabler* or *The Pillars of Society*, the sighs and suicides of *Einsame Menschen* or *Fuhrmann Hentschel*, or frivolous and erring wives and husbands—such as Rovetta's sombre pen depicts with misanthropic realism in *I Disonesti*.

ITS PLAYWRIGHTS TO-DAY.

Who are the most conspicuous and most representative of living Spanish playwrights?

The number of these authors amounts to only seven. I shall consider them in the order following:—Echegaray, Dicenta, Benavente, the brothers Alvarez Quintero, Perez Galdos, and Rusiñol.

ECHEGARAY.

The veteran Echegaray, who won the Nobel prize four years ago, deserves to head the list. His copious labours link another generation with our own. Gifted with a heterogeneous character and prolific and wide-reaching versatility, ne excels alike in writing plays, in practical statecraft, and in mathematics. His lectures on this last subject are delivered, as a rule, to empty benches in the Athenæum of Madrid, because some ten or fifteen students are all that dare to cope with their discouraging abstruseness. His *premières*, on the contrary, attract all classes of society to the pin's-head point of overcrowding. Learned and pedagogic at the lecturer's desk, when he takes office as the national Minister of Finance he is the ruler merely, and the staunch supporter of the Spanish Crown; but when another play slips from his pen he retrocedes once more into the revolutionary. He is at once the Calderon and the Sardou of modern Spain; a master of stage effect, excelling also in the presentation of the old and the recent Spanish character.

Echegaray has given to Spain and to the Spanish-speaking world a long array of celebrated dramas, and in the large majority of these he interprets Spanish human nature very admirably. Many of his earliest works disclose the influence of the violently romantic Spanish playwrights of the first half of the nineteenth century, inherited by him from the Duke of Rivas, author of *The Force of Fate* (a play which from its morbid wealth of weird and grisly episodes would constitute an unmixed melodrama were it not so absolutely Spanish); from Hartzenbusch, author of *The Lovers of Teruel;* and from Garcia Gutiérrez, author of *The Troubadour* (the plot of which is utilised in Verdi's famous opera). And here I would remark that what is melodrama on one stage is not so, of a hard and fast necessity, on another. Thus duelling, which is vitally inseparable from the social life of Spain, is viewed as pure and simple melodrama by the eyes and consciences of northern peoples. Among the fiery Spaniards it is a widespread and inveterate usage, which sums up their typical and absorbing spirit of resistance to a formally administrative system of control. It is with every Latin race a proper and befitting code of personal as distinguished from the general and conventional law. And so in Spain it neither is nor is considered to be melodrama.

Yet even Echegaray is not regarded with an equal measure of enthusiasm by the whole of Spain. His older countrymen continue to applaud him to the echo, to count the moments to his crowded *premières*, to look upon him as an institution, almost as a classic. The younger class, upon the contrary, treat him with some disdain, and call him shallow, artificial, and old-fashioned. Vanity has much to do with this. These juniors do not relish him because he draws their character too well. They grant him fame begrudgingly, slow to detect their likeness save in flattering portraiture.

The truthful definition of his worth resides, of course, between these prejudiced extremes. His plays, such as *The Stigma, A Life of Pleasure and a Death of Pain, The Great Procurer, The Stain that Cleanses, Mariana,* and many more, are not ambitious literature and not an exposition of morality. They are intended to amuse until the curtain falls, and this is all that they pretend to or do achieve. The curtains are constructed mathematically, and the surface of the dialogue is apparently poetic. But the curtain is not pretentious ingenuity, neither is the dialogue pretentious poetry.

A subtle and a singular old man is José Echegaray, whether we view him in the person and the flesh or from the master-portrait of Sorolla—contemplating, enigmatical, sphinx-like. He is a thin, small, fragile figure, with an intellectual head, conical at the apex and extremely bald; and his citrine face, punctured by cold, grey, unemotionally penetrating eyes, is aged into a parchment smoothness, as if the very wrinkles had worn themselves away. He is frigid and yet punctiliously polite with strangers, and his unimpassioned courtesy to these suggests the graceful manners of the old *hidalgo* of Castile. But when he is surrounded by familiar and congenial souls, his speech is confidential, voluble, and ardent; as when, for instance, in the nocturnal *causeries* at his club, he pauses from his facile flow of admirable talk only to light one cigarette upon the unextinguished remnant of the cigarette preceding.

JOAQUIN DICENTA.

Joaquín Dicenta (author of *Aurora, Daniel, The Feudal Lord,* and *Juan José*) is a journalist of great ability and unrestrained and ever-militant ferociousness. All his plays are saturated with this temper, and so, when Grasso and his company were visiting Madrid last winter, the shrewd Sicilian actor seized upon the last-named of those works as being pre-eminently suited to him. The vehemence of the playwright and the vehemence of the actor found their fit association here. Professedly a Republican, Dicenta, in his inmost sympathies, inclines to Anarchism. All of his plays have violent openings, violent developments, and violent endings; yet they are too suggestive of the Spanish character to fall within the well-marked boundary of melodrama. All who are rich, all who exert a definite authority supported by the law, are, in Dicenta's eyes, detestable and evil. The murderer or avenger in his plays is not the villain, but the hero. And yet his clever and effective scenic treatment, yielding magnificent opportunities for realistic acting in the style of Latin peoples, causes his anti-patriotic and fallacious theories to seem almost the opposite of what they are. The celebrated *Juan José* provides us with an instance. The thesis of this drama, recapitulated, not from the garbled adaptation in Sicilian, but directly from the Spanish, shows us a man named Juan José, by trade a bricklayer, who lives with and maintains the frivolous and handsome Rosa, of origin as humble as his own, and also, like himself, a native of Madrid. Juan José is working for a builder named the Señorito Paco—wealthy, amorous, unscrupulous, and under middle age. The Señorito chances to see Rosa, and covets her for himself. Juan José is jealous and shows it, insults his employer, and the latter, in a moment of vindictive rage, dismisses him. He fails to find employment in another quarter; it is the depth of winter, and the times are at their worst. The miserable attic is devoid of furniture and fire and food. Then, for the sake of the complaining girl, her lover steals some trifling thing, is apprehended in the act, and sent to gaol. After a while he there receives a letter from a friend, but he is illiterate, and a fellow-prisoner deciphers it for him. From it he learns that Rosa has surrendered to the Señorito's blandishments, and occupies a comfortable lodging at his charge. Exasperated by this sinister intelligence, the wretched Juan José breaks prison, hastens stealthily to Rosa's new abode, finds the door open, and walks in. Rosa is in her bedroom, posing before the glass and trying on a pretty frock—a gift from her new lord. She is expecting Paco. Hearing a sound, but too absorbed with her toilette to turn her head, she takes the footstep for the Señorito's, and quietly murmurs some endearing term. Then, as the desperate avenger steps up close behind, she sees him in the mirror. Paralysed, like a rabbit by the serpent's murderous look, with eyes distended and an ashy pallor in her cheeks, she turns, and stares at him, and listens. He tells her all. He has no mercy, either for his execrated and triumphant rival, or for Rosa. He has arrived to take the Señorito's life. Finding her tongue at last, Rosa implores, and sobs, and threatens. But tears, prayers, menaces are of no service now. The rabid and discarded lover carries out his threat, plunging his keen *navaja* into Paco's heart, just as he comes upstairs and steps across the doorway.

JACINTO BENAVENTE.

Deeply imbued by foreign pessimism, the plays of Benavente are not openly aggressive, like Dicenta's. His process, on the contrary, is stealthily antagonistic to existing institutions. Choosing his models from the upper and upper middle class of Spain, he probes into their vices with the pitiless imperturbability of the anatomist. While Echegaray is, as I have stated, the Sardou of the Peninsula, Jacinto Benavente is undoubtedly her Ibsen. Various of his plays have been successfully produced in Italy and South America. The titles he prefers are chiefly bizarre and perplexing—for instance, *The Angora Cat, Food for Wild Beasts, Saturday Night, The Motor Car, The Fire-Dragon,* and *The Evil-doers of Good Works.*

Food for Wild Beasts depicts the servants of a household who discover that their master and his wife are on the border of financial ruin, and repay their former liberality with brutishly derisive and aggressive insolence. *The Evil-doers of Good*

JOSE ECHEGARAY,

The leading Spanish dramatist. From the portrait by Sorolla. *Sandez*, which Mr. Martin Harvey produced at Birmingham on December 9, is a version of the dramatist's *El Gran Galeoto*.

SANTIAGO RUSIÑOL,

[*Franzen, Madrid.*

A leading Spanish playwright. He is also an eminent landscape painter, and a popular novelist.

JACINTO BENAVENTE.

A witty and clever playwright

Franzen, Madrid.

THE SPANISH STAGE.

JOAQUIM ALVAREZ QUINTERO.

Franzen, Madrid.

SERAFIN ALVAREZ QUINTERO.

Franzen, Madrid.

They represent the lighter side of Spain's dramatists of to-day.

Works, a typical example of this author's lighter comedy, portrays, in scathing dialogue, those high-born and pretentious dames, greatly addicted to bazaars and raffles and the like, who utilise the veil of charity to prosecute their own self-seeking interests.

The dapper little Benavente is an assiduous haunter of the spacious and luxurious *saloncillo*, or green-room, of the Spanish State-theatre, the venerable and historic Teatro Español, where he sits contributing his share of witty conversation with a meek and diffident air that almost hides his inner and inveterate cynicism. He is an erudite and well-read man, knows English fluently, has closely studied all our classical drama and the British school of acting, and has produced a reverent and graceful adaptation of *Twelfth Night*, titled, in Spanish, Cuento de Amor—"A Love Story."

THE BROTHERS QUINTERO.

The brothers Joaquin and Serafin Alvarez Quintero are two young men, natives of sunny Seville, who have already produced a copious array of full-length comedies, and also of shorter one and two act pieces based upon the model of the old *sainete*. A prominent exception to the general rule in Spain, their plays are commonly facetious and light-hearted, and many of their models are borrowed, with intense fidelity, from the peasantry of Andalusia.

GALDOS.

The talents of Benito Pérez Galdós, like those of José Echegaray, are very varied. He is a noted journalist, a Republican member of the Spanish Parliament, a dramatist, and a writer of historical romances. His "Natural Episodes"—truly a wonderful feat of literature—extending to nearly half a hundred separate volumes, are, so to speak, the Waverley novels of the Spanish people, and differ from Scott's masterpieces only in that their order is continuous and chronological. Throughout the Spanish-speaking world his prestige as a writer is immense, while, as a dramatist, his popularity and fame are scarcely less so. In writing plays his style is sometimes morbidly sarcastic, as in the case of *Doña Perfecta* ("Lady Perfection"), or sometimes, as in that of *Electra*, it is markedly and violently political. His stage work, on the whole, is hyper-literary and prolix, causing three acts to bear a resemblance to three volumes, so that his dialogue is apt to flag, because it is too introspective and polemical.

His celebrated play, *Electra*, was first produced some years ago, just at a moment when the national attention centred, in a hostile manner, on the detention of a young Spanish lady in a convent, in stubborn opposition to the wishes of her family. Therefore, it is a topical play, whose interest, like that of Donnay's *Le Retour de Jerusalem*, is of a circumscribed and special character. It deals with a social question which is isolated and particular—namely, the overwhelming power of clerical and monastic institutions in the land of Torquemada. Triumphing, nevertheless, by reason of its dexterous and novel plot and vigorous and effective character-drawing, it was produced with success at Paris, Buenos Aires, Rome, and other capitals of Europe and of South America.

SANTIAGO RUSINOL.

Santiago Rusiñol provides us with an instance of remarkable versatility. Of handsome and ingratiating person, bearing a close resemblance in his features to the late Lord Leighton (president of our Academy), he is at once an eminent landscape painter, whose canvases receive awards in the leading European exhibitions, a popular novelist, and a playwright of unusual power. His painting is tender, sensuous, dreamy, and poetic. His books and plays, on the contrary, are mordant and sardonic. Among his stage productions are *L'Heroe*, a vigorous and scathing drama in defence of anti-militarism, which was composed originally in the dialect of Cataluña; and his celebrated tragedy, *The Mystic*, certainly the most successful and remunerative play of modern times in Spain. The subject is a realistic study of the altruism of a young Roman Catholic priest, who has relinquished the girl he loves in order to embrace his sacred calling. The girl is lured astray, the "mystic" comforts and reclaims her, no longer as her sweetheart, but as her spiritual guide—as one, in fact, whose mission renders him inherently superior to herself. His life throughout is pure and holy. Although his health is failing, and his troubles bring him to the grave, he dedicates his whole endeavour to the betterment of others. And yet these prove unworthy. Their sordid selfishness pursues him to the end. He gives them all he has to give; and they, in turn, requite him with the cruellest ingratitude.

A GRIM AND UGLY DRAMA.

Such are the leading playwrights of contemporary Spain. Considered as a whole, their work, which bears an obvious correlation to the present state of Spain, is interesting rather than encouraging. Their dialogue, as a rule, is trenchant and concise, although unsympathetic. It is suggestive of the old-time fighting and fanatical *hidalgo*, or (if they draw their model from the humbler classes) of the brigand and the desperado. Their heroes and their villains overlap. Sweetness and domesticity are quite unknown to them. Their sense of genial and wholesome comedy is almost non-existent. Their men are tyrannous and sensual, their women harsh. When the latter are faithful, terror or pride, rather than true affection, compels them to a worthless constancy; or, if not this, passion is substituted by the Spanish playwright for the purer kind of love, and animal propensities for human.

However, in course of time all this may undergo a change, and Spain, though tardily, do justice to her latent capabilities. It would, indeed, be well if new and loftier ideals, if less sordid and self-seeking aspirations, and a sterner sense of civic duty, were to regenerate the inner life of the Peninsula. Then, in immediate and direct response to such a change, the character of the Spanish stage would also be regenerated.

ITS PLAYERS TO-DAY.

Speaking in comprehensive terms, the acting of the Spanish players of to-day is partly excellent and partly the direct reverse of excellent. In common with the national character throughout, it points to the possession of considerable native capability, impeded by an obstinate disinclination to all forms, however salutary, of tuition and control. Because of this, the average Spanish player is the constant and pathetic victim of his own complacent and, indeed, self-sought deficiencies. His creed is egotistically and perversely individual. Industry and obedience are repugnant severally to his racial indolence and his racial pride. He is the creature, not the arbiter, of opportunity. His private sensibilities and impulses alone dictate his margin of success. For if, in his rendering any part upon the stage, his sympathy and intimate emotion happen to be stirred, he not infrequently achieves a great performance, even when his reputation is obscure; but when this happy circumstance does not declare itself upon his side, he is unfailingly a less than mediocre simulator of emotion.

AIDS OF LANGUAGE AND GESTURE.

Language and gesture, too, exert a necessary influence on the theatre of every land. Such influence in the case of Spain is full of interest. The language of Cervantes lends itself with rare or possibly unique effectiveness, to declamation It is, beyond all else, the vehicle of orators—of persons who habitually commit themselves to sonorous and momentary, rather than to written and enduring, forms of utterance. This, I conjecture, was the quality which moved Lord Bacon to record a shrewd suspicion that the French are wiser than they look, and that the Spaniards look wiser than they are; meaning that the Spanish tongue, which tells so weightily upon the hurried medium of the ear, is nugatory and verbose if looked at with the eye; that is, deliberatively.

True to this characteristic failing of his countrymen, the acting of the ordinary Spanish player is declamatory to excess, though it is to some extent redeemed by opportuneness and effectiveness of gesture. And this, I need not say, comes easily to him, for gesture in the Latin races is not empty attitudinising, nor is a Saxon people ever justified in deriding it for such. It is a positive and most powerful aid to conduct and to conversation. Sometimes it wholly stands in lieu of conversation. Thus, when a Spaniard rubs his thumb on his fore-finger, the meaning he conveys is *money;* for by a similar touch we try the goodness of a coin. If, in conjunction with this gesture, he lifts his eyebrows interrogatively, his unarticulated yet most obvious question instantly becomes. "Has he (or she) got any money?"—or further, if he shakes his head and shoots out a disparaging lip, his facial statement signifies, no less explicitly and simply. "The reason why I have (or have not) done such and such a thing is that he (or she) has no money." His *vis-à-vis* reads off these signals rapidly and truly. A whole affair is thus communicated and debated by a trifling movement and a look; and surely no shorthand elaborated on an office stool could be more swift or efficacious, or more simple.

THE SPANISH STAGE.

MARIA GUERRERO,
Spain's most popular and versatile actress,

In an old Spanish Comedy, *La Niña Boba*.   From a painting by Sorolla.

ROSARIO PINO,

Franzen, Madrid.

Leading lady at the Comedia Theatre, Madrid.

FERNANDO DIAZ DE MENDOZA. *Franzen, Madrid*

Leading actor at the Teatro Español, Madrid.

ENRIQUE BORRAS. *Franzen, Madrid.*

Leading actor at the Comedia Theatre, Madrid.

Franzen, Madrid.

BENITO PÉREZ GALDOS,

A noted journalist, a Republican Member of the Spanish Parliament, a dramatist, and a writer of historical romances.

So that, alike upon and off the stage, the value of appropriate and fluent gesture is at least co-equal with the aptest speech. If properly performed, the merest shoulder-shrug interrogates or responds, refuses, acquiesces, or remains between the two. Or gesture may derive a further eloquence from something accessorial. Fluttered by Spanish hands, a fan becomes a very signal-code, with as it were a telepathetic name for each mysterious impulse in a woman's character. Of, if we view more narrowly this most important aid to life, as well as to the counterfeit of life upon the stage, not every gesture needs to be translated to an outward form, and yet subconsciously we feel it to be there. Often a sense of gesture is impressively and happily conveyed without apparent movement, and those who can remember to have watched Le Bargy as he *listens* on the stage will very readily endorse my observation.

THE ELECT.

The players whose names and qualities must now be mentioned (though in briefest terms) as eminently representative of present art in Spain, diverge, of course, from the unhappy rule of ordinary Spanish stagecraft. As in all other quarters of the world, there are the few and fortunate elect among the multitude of failures. Unlike those others whom I spoke of, shipwrecked on the rocks of ineptitude or self-conceit, these have arrived secure in port, because a wiser and more cosmopolitan conception went with them as their pilot. The germ of what their genius has become was in their temper from the first, and, fertilised by well-directed and devoted drudgery, has borne them ample harvest. Study and scrutiny and travel have informed and moulded them, uniting to their own particular grace the best examples of the foreigner. Bernhardt, Réjane, Le Bargy, Bartet, Jane Hading, Antoine Déspres, the Coquelins, and Galipaux, from France; Novelli, Zacconi, Duse, Mariani, Vitaliani, and Tina di Lorenzo, from Italy—all these and many others of the highest rank in their respective spheres or sections of the actor's craft have visited Madrid at frequent intervals, and have been welcomed by the Spanish stars with cordial *camaraderie* for themselves and joyous and solicitous attention to the merits of their labour. Surely an honourable attitude, and tending to a double and substantial benefit—that the strongest players of one land should seek this healthy emulation with the strongest players of another.

MARIA GUERRERO.

The most extensively and favourably known of living Spanish actresses is Doña Maria Guerrero, who as the wife of Don Fernando Diaz de Mendoza, a grandee of Spain, is destined to inherit with him great estates and several titles of nobility. Her portrait by Sorolla, now on view in London at the Grafton Galleries, shows her arrayed in character as the heroine of that laughable old Spanish comedy, *La Niña Boba*. Not yet of middle-age, with large, expressive eyes matching the raven and abundant hair, graceful of figure and of movement, blending a clear contralto voice with perfect diction—such is this noble lady and the queen of living Spanish actresses. She can compete with gifted foreigners on their own ground—witness her passionate and pathetic Paula Tanqueray—and sways the Spanish-speaking world in either hemisphere by her magnificent impersonations of the native Spanish comedy, from Lope, Calderon, and Tirso de Molina to Jacinto Benavente. A versatile and greatly gifted woman is Maria Guerrero, whose art and heart associate the older with the newer Spain. A grand lady in her home domain and social circle, and a grand actress on the historic Spanish stage. What union of two grandeurs could be more desirable?

ROSARIO PINO.

Another lady, also beautiful and talented—this one Rosario Pino, of the Comedy and other fashionable theatres. An all-round actress, but especially distinguished in the milder and domestic vein of modern Spanish drama. A lithe and spiritual creature, exquisitely feminine and suave, her sweet, insinuating air has all the magic of Jane Hading. Nor is persuasion on the losing side when she engages in the task, because her voice is music, and her Spanish eyes achieve the rest.

DE MENDOZA.

As I have said, Fernando Diaz de Mendoza is the scion of a noble house. He is, moreover, the lessee of that historic playhouse, the Teatro Español, and here, except when visiting the provinces or South America, recurring seasons always find him. He is an able manager and first-rate actor, both in comedy and tragedy. Although his voice and stature are not of the best, a natural elegance attends on him:

continually. A type of part he renders perfectly is that of worldly yet ingenuous men (if such a term be not too paradoxical). Whole-hearted and unflagging work have chiefly made him what he is. He took to the profession after meeting her in whom he found at once a wife and a preceptor. A fortunate alliance, since rumour has it that his acting, as an amateur, was most discouraging.

ENRIQUE BORRAS.

A strong and rugged, a deeply personal and interesting actor is Enrique Borras. As he is a native of Cataluña, his only vehicle of speech was formerly the gutteral and harsh, though finely energetic language of that principality. Now that he plays in the romantic language of Castile, his accent, to fastidious ears, is stated to be strained and unmelodious. But this defect is minimised by the overwhelming force and natural ease of his impersonations. He is that dangerous example to the lazy or untalented—a born actor. His grasp of stagecraft is essential and intuitive. It may be truly said that he is most himself when he is simulating others. How many a player, upon the other hand, is reckoned to be most an actor when he solely and inanely simulates himself?

OTHER FAVOURITES.

These four distinguished members of the Spanish stage deprive me of the space to tell, as they deserve, of those most excellent and popular comedians, "Pepe" Santiago and José Rubio; of Emilio Thuillier, the talented, urbane, and handsome Andalusian, and, now that Vico and Perrin are dead, the best impersonator of Dicenta's celebrated Juan José; of José Tallavi and Francisco Morano, actors of pleasing art and presence, if of somewhat curbed originality, who manifestly base their style upon the manifold creations of Zacconi; of Josefina Blanco, the most delightful, delicate, and *petite* of ingenues; of Carmen Cobeña, Nieves Suarez, Conchita Ruiz, and Clotilde Domus, light comedy and vaudeville actresses, who enjoy a privileged and thoroughly deserved position in the eyes of their compatriots.

"GENERO CHICO," SPAIN'S MUSICAL COMEDY.

Another class of Spanish players are those who cultivate the *genero chico* or "diminutive kind" of comedy, consisting of condensed and generally broadly humorous sketches, playing about one hour, as a rule, in which the popular, or topical, or local phases of the national life are sparklingly set forth by means of alternating dialogue and dance and song. The Spaniards stand alone in this particular class of unpretentious yet agreeably entertaining pieces, which are not the fanciful and far-fetched operetta, but a native product of the Spanish soil. For, though the Spaniards are not boisterously gay, life in all quarters of the world produces of necessity innumerable species and degrees of humour; and Spain is no exception to this universal and inevitable law. Indeed, the Spanish wit can fairly hold its own with any that the world can show. It has less inanity than the English or Italian, less indecency than the French, and less heaviness than the German or the Austrian. It is the pungent and spontaneous spirit of the Picaresque translated to our time; unconscious and unstudied humour, exquisitely dry and pointed.

The prototype and parent of the *genero chico* is the Spaniard of the labouring and peasant classes. Never benumbed and rendered brutish by excessive work; never, as in so many lands, debased by passive and unqualified dependence on another's will, he in his method of regarding men and things is quickly and maliciously observant, critical, and haughty. He is at once a rustic and a *caballero*, a scholar and an alphabetic, a clown and a philosopher. He never checks his tongue from false considerations of respect. Shyness or cringing is unknown to him. He always speaks his mind, and mingles wit with wisdom irresponsibly. The rich Castilian idiom fortifies and purifies his humour. The gorgeous range of its vocabulary taught him to be ever ready with the captivating and amusing word; his copious and felicitous turns and similes were engrafted on him by the Moor. And so, directly illustrated from the speech and manners of this most unpedagogic yet distinguished populace, the *genero chico* is a typical and admirable form of lighter Spanish drama.

These liliputian comedies well-nigh construct themselves; and yet they call, perhaps above all other branches of the scenic craft, for truthful and observant words and sympathetic music; nor must their sentiment be overstrained, but eminently simple. If thus employed, with humour, insight, and restraint, the slightest incidents of popular life supply the necessary peg on which to hang a plot—the labours of the fields or of the shore, the rivalries of jealous swains, a sweethearts' tiff, the comic inconveniences of petty tradesmen, the vanity of servants, the swaggering of soldiers, a country fair or wedding, a town or village festival.

As for its representers on the stage, these occupy about the same position as the players of our musical comedy, and constitute a class of whom it may be generally said that they acquit themselves, by reason of their triple attribute of acting, song, and dance, vivaciously and cleverly. Dramatic talent of the loftiest kind is not, of course, vouchsafed to them; but then their genial versatility, which keeps an idle audience well amused throughout an idle hour, is more than self-sufficient for its unassuming purpose.

A GENERAL SURVEY OF ITS WORKING CONDITIONS.

The Spaniards are eminently a playgoing—that is, a play-loving and play-patronising—people, which circumstance enables the prices of admission to their theatres to maintain a reasonable correspondence with the general slenderness of their purses. As with the Italians, their dramatic taste, upon the whole, is more spontaneously and artistically critical than that of Northern races. Melodrama, when it is set before them undisguisedly as such, they readily appreciate, while their impassioned temperament induces them to rise encouragingly to strong and stirring situations. From this cause also they have an eagle eye for trashy yet pretentious pseudo-sentiment, and this, upon the converse side, they visit just as readily with their cordial censure.

OPEN EXPRESSION.

As for their conduct in the theatre, they heartily applaud when pleased, but manifest their displeasure just as heartily—or more so—with their feet or walking-sticks, their theory of breeding in this matter being conspicuously divergent from our own. They hold, in brief, that the money they pay for their seats implies a co-existent right to demonstrate, and not alone inly to feel, their satisfaction or the contrary. Hence, in regard to inexperienced, unresourceful actors, a Spanish audience is a formidable one.

PROTECTIVE ASSOCIATIONS.

The working conditions of the Spanish theatre are broadly similar to those in France and other countries of the Continent. There is a powerful society for protecting the rights and interests of playwrights, and another society—not, perhaps, so powerful, though equally as well-intentioned—for protecting those of actors. There is also, at Madrid, an Actors' Benevolent Fund; and this, together with benefit performances arranged with generous frequency, does much to lessen the distress which cannot but occur from time to time among the lowlier members of this populous profession.

THE LOWER DEPTHS.

About the nethermost rungs of the theatrical ladder the struggle, as in England, is both long and arduous, recalling even now, and in more ways than one, that dreadful epoch of the sixteenth and seventeenth centuries when the Spanish player was treated by society almost as though he were a felon, when he was forced to labour for a wage that often would not serve to buy him bread, and tramp the countryside exposed to all the pitiless and varied rigours of his climate, weathering as best he might the snows and biting frosts of Old and New Castile, the murderous Manchegan or Extremaduran wind, the pelting rainstorms of the northern seaboard, and the tropical and enervating sun of Andalusia.

The wages of the corresponding class of Spanish *comico* in our time are such as he can get—perhaps a couple of shillings daily and his third-class railway fare—this pittance being delivered to him weekly if his *empresario* be an honest and a solvent man, or otherwise being indefinitely "carried over." But if he has indubitable, rock-bed histrionic worth, supported by such necessary qualities as patience, courage, self-assertion, and the rest, his situation must, of course, eventually improve. An influential introduction, too, will commonly expedite his upward path; but, as I stated, Spaniards are intuitive judges of the stage, and ultimately only merit can sustain him in the public eye.

Expenditure in Spanish theatres is generally on a cheaper scale than in our own. The prices of the seats, as I have said, are well below the English average, and range from three to six or seven shillings for a stall, with one *peseta* (ninepence) for the gallery, and intermediate prices for the *anfiteatros*, or upper circles. In many Spanish theatres there is no pit.

A SUBVENTIONED HOUSE.

The handsome and historic Teatro Español at Madrid is the property of the City Council, who cede it to some well-known *empresario* for a term of years. This theatre is in receipt of a subvention yearly of about two thousand pounds, and the lighting is provided free. Strict conditions are imposed by the Madrid Municipality as to the class of plays performed in this fine building. The annual repertory must infallibly include a prescribed number of the classical master-dramas of the older Spanish playwrights, most of whom were nearly or precisely Shakespeare's contemporaries—such as Moreto, Tirso de Molina, Calderon de la Barca, or Lope de Vega, and until about three years ago the production of a work by any foreign dramatist was forbidden absolutely. To-day this species of theatrical protection is removed. One of the first non-Spanish plays to benefit by so happy an extension was *The Second Mrs. Tanqueray*, the *rôle* of Paula being impressively sustained by the eminent Maria Guerrero.

The present holder of the Teatro Español is the celebrated actor-manager Don Fernando Diaz de Mendoza, whose abilities as a player, together with those of Señora Guerrero, his distinguished wife, I have already noted. Under this gentleman's experienced rule the Teatro Español produces year by year a long succession of first-class plays, some old and classical, and others modern, but always excellently acted and luxuriously dressed and mounted.

SEASONS AND TOURS.

As with the generality of the theatres at Madrid, the season of the Español extends throughout the winter and the early spring. During the rest of the year the companies of the metropolis of Spain disperse themselves about the provinces or tour in South America; and here, this quarter of the world being still a Spanish-speaking continent, their almost yearly visits are awaited with the keenest interest and are very handsomely remunerated.

In Spain herself the usual practice, when on tour, is for the actor-manager, who as a rule organises and actively directs the company, to be in all respects the manager and *empresario;* that is, he makes the contracts with his troupe, provides costumes, excepting for the "stars," and rents the local theatre.

THE INCORPORATED STAGE SOCIETY.

This Society was founded in 1899 and incorporated in 1904. Council of Management:—Mr. J. M. Barrie, Mr. Sidney Colvin, the Hon. Everard Feilding, Mr. Almeric W. FitzRoy, C.V.O., Mr. St. John Hankin, Mr. H. A. Hertz, Mr. Alderson B. Horne, Mr. W. S. Kennedy, Mr. W. Lee Mathews, Mr. Gilbert Murray, Sir Sydney Olivier, K.C.M.G., Mrs. W. P. Reeves, Miss Louise Salom, Mr. G. Bernard Shaw, Mrs. Bernard Shaw, Mr. Charles Strachey, Mr. W. Hector Thomson (Hon. Treasurer), Mr. Bernard Watkin, Mr. Charles E. Wheeler, Mr. Frederick Wheelen, Mr. Ernest E. S. Williams. Mr. A. E. Drinkwater, Secretary. Address, 9, Arundel Street, Strand, W.C.

The year's productions of this Society were as follows :—

Cupid and Commonsense, a play, in four acts, by Arnold Bennett, produced at the Shaftesbury. January 26.

The Gates of the Morning, play, in three acts, by Margaret M. Mack, produced at the Shaftesbury. March 1.

The Breaking Point, play, in three acts, by Edward Garnett, at the Haymarket. A license for this play was refused by the Censor. April 5.

Links, play, in four acts, by Herman Heifermans, translated by Howard Peacey and W. R. Brandt, produced at the Scala. May 31.

The Last of the De Mullins, comedy, in three acts, by St. John Hankin, Haymarket. December 6.

THE RUSSIAN STAGE.

By BARONESS BILA and PERCY BURTON.

THEATRES IN ST. PETERSBURG.

THERE are some twenty-three theatres in St. Petersburg all of which are open in winter (the season, of course), and seven in summer. The nightly receipts of the winter theatres average over 24,250 roubles, or about £2,500, and the summer ones, roughly, a quarter of this amount. In addition to these seven summer theatres, there are about a dozen temporary ones. Of the twenty-three regular theatres, two winter and two summer theatres are devoted to light opera, and three winter and two summer to grand opera. The remainder comprise a dozen theatres devoted to the drama pure and simple—one to melodrama and one to farce. The three best theatres—viz., the Alexandra (drama), the Mariensky (opera and ballet), and the Michel (French plays)—are controlled by the Imperial Government, and are subsidised by his Majesty's Court, while the others belong to private people.

The Alexandra Theatre was built according to the plans of the architect Rossi. The first performance took place on August 31, 1832, when a tragedy of Krukovsky, *Count Posharsky,* and a one-act play, called *A Spanish Holiday,* were given. At the beginning of the past century, upon the square on which the Imperial Alexandra Theatre is built, stood a wooden theatre belonging to A. Kasassi (built in 1801 by the architect Brenn), where Italian operas were given. Some years later this theatre was bought by the Government. Since its foundation the Alexandra Theatre has not been rebuilt; only the ventilation and heating apparatus have been modernised. This house holds 2,000 spectators, and is six stories in height, containing boxes to hold six persons, stalls, a balcony, and gallery.

The Mariensky Theatre was opened on October 2, 1860, with Glinka's patriotic opera, *Life for the Czar.* Formerly on this site stood a circus, built in 1847, which was completely burnt down in 1859, the architect of both being A. Kavos. Since that time many improvements have been effected, including the instalment of an electric station, a foyer for the artists, a large atelier for paintings, decorations and photography; storehouses, workshops, and lodgings for the servants. These were carried out by the Imperial architect, Professor Schreter. The auditorium holds 1,900 persons, and has five stories. The foyer and corridors are particularly beautiful in this theatre.

The Michel Theatre was built in 1833, from designs by Professor Bruloff, and rebuilt and enlarged in 1859. This house holds 1,300 spectators. The first performance was a ballet, entitled *Love in a Village,* with a one-act Russian play. It is now a French theatre, the company coming from Paris and being controlled by the Russian Government. Every Saturday a new play is staged, generally a comedy, when the aristocracy of St. Petersburg is sure to be found in force at the Théâtre-Michel.

MOSCOW THEATRES.

In Moscow there are eighteen theatres, ten of which are winter and eight summer theatres. Three of the former are operatic, four dramatic, one for farce, and one for melodrama ; while the summer theatres have mixed programmes, and change their bills of fare to suit the tastes of the public. The receipts and prices are comparatively the same as those in St. Petersburg. Of the ten winter theatres, two belong to the State, viz., the Great Theatre, given up to opera and ballet, and the Maly, or little theatre, devoted to drama, where many of the best Russian actors are to be seen.

The Great Theatre is one of the most ancient Russian theatres, and was formerly known as the Petrovsky Theatre. It belonged first to a private manager, but was bought at the beginning of the last century by the Government. The Great Theatre was burnt down in 1805, and rebuilt in 1822 from designs by Professor Michailoff, the re-opening taking place in 1825, when the ballet, *Cendrillon*, and a prologue called *La Gloire des Muses* were given.

In 1843 a renovation was made, all the wooden walls and ceilings in the corridors being broken down, and stone walls erected in their place. Fate, however, in the form of fire again asserted itself, and once more (in 1853) this beautiful theatre was burnt down, only to spring up phœnix-like in 1856, when it was re-opened with the opera *The Puritans*. The Great Theatre holds about 2,000 spectators, and stands on a large and imposing square.

The Imperial Maly Theatre in Moscow was opened in 1824 by a ballet. It has four stories and holds 1,400 persons.

THE LIBERATION OF THE THEATRE.

In addition to the Imperial Theatres, the ancient capital of Russia, Moscow, can boast one of the best theatres in that vast country—the Artistic Theatre—which recently celebrated its tenth year of existence. In a comparatively short time it has done much for Russian art. Imperial or State theatres have existed for centuries, but no private enterprise was permitted prior to 1883, when a decree was granted by the Czar Alexander III. A few years before this the celebrated composer, Anton Rubinstein, arrived in Moscow to conduct his opera, *Demon*, in the Great Imperial Theatre. For many years Rubinstein tried to get a concession to produce an opera at the St. Petersburg Conservatory, of which he was manager. At the *première* of his opera, *Demon*, in Moscow, he said, laughingly : " We Russians shall obtain a constitution sooner than a concession for private theatres in our capitals."

But theatrical managers and authors at that time worked hard to prepare the artists thoroughly. Many theatrical schools were opened, and the idea of a literary theatre was formed. In Moscow there is a general saying that neither a school, a newspaper, nor a theatre can be founded without a merchant! And so it happened in this case. The proverbial merchant came, but not in the shape of a mere money-grubber, but in himself an artist, and a very good amateur actor to boot. His name was Stanislawsky, and his artistic associate was the well-known dramatist Nemirowitsch-Dantschenko. Their first idea was to create a national theatre, and it proved in time to be the most intellectual theatre of the time, while it ensured its exclusiveness by being the most expensive, surpassing in price the charges made for admission to the Imperial Theatres.

No theatre in the world has probably tried so many new experiments. In Berlin the company of the Moscow Artistic Theatre was received with the greatest respect and cordiality, and their triumphs were almost endless. The German critics wrote that they had never witnessed such artistic ensemble, realistic acting, and genuine talent all round.

For the first few years the repertory of this theatre consisted mostly of Shakespearean plays, such as *Julius Cæsar*, given on a scale of remarkable splendour ; while later Tolstoi, Ibsen, Hauptmann, Hamsun, and other foreign authors were taken up. Tschechoff's plays were cultivated. Nowhere was this famous Russian author better understood or beloved. He passed all his days at rehearsals, and, not unnaturally, perhaps, married one of the young actresses, Miss Knipper. His premature death from consumption was a great loss to the theatre and the drama.

Later on Gorky's plays, with their morbid philosophy, made a great impression. The suffering of all kinds and conditions of people, the dread of pain, the unevenness and injustice of human life, the tragedy—and sometimes the farce and stupidity of death—are dealt with in this Russian theatre. The Moscow Artistic Theatre is ruled by discipline, and has raised itself to an ideal standard.

SUPREMACY OF THE REPERTORY SYSTEM.

In these days every Russian town of any importance at all has several private theatres, all doing good business, and everywhere the repertory system reigns supreme. The prices range more or less from boxes at thirty to six roubles for the five seats ; stalls from six to two roubles ; balcony from three to two roubles ; and gallery from one rouble to thirty kopecks. The rouble, the standard coin, is, roughly, two shillings, and is equivalent to 100 kopecks.

THE RUSSIAN STAGE.

MME. MITSCHURINA
Portia in *The Merchant of Venice* at the Alexandra (Imperial) Theatre, one of the leading comedy actresses, who may shortly appear in *Lady Frederick*.

THE RUSSIAN STAGE.

MADAME PORTSCHINSKAJA,
the charming and clever wife of Mr. Glagolin—both famous Russian artists.

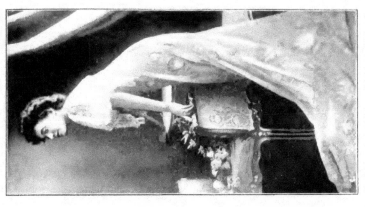

MME. ROSTSCHINA-INSAROVA,

one of the leading comedy actresses at the
Maly Theatre, St. Petersburg.

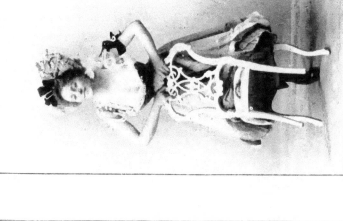

LYDIA YAVORSKAJA

(Princess Bariatinsky) as Zaza.

MR. GLAGOLIN

a well-known actor in parts ranging from Raffles
and Sherlock Holmes to Hamlet) in Mr. James
Welch's part in *When Knights Were Bold.*

V. DALMATOFF,

of the Imperial Theatre, St. Petersburg, who appeared in the title-*rôle* of
The Gay Lord Quex.

Many theatrical schools have opened during the last few years in St. Petersburg and Moscow. The oldest and best are:—The Imperial Dramatic and Ballet School, the Theatrical College of the Maly Theatre, and Rapgoff's.

OTHER TOWNS AND THEATRES.

In Warsaw there are eight winter and six summer theatres, two being under the control of the Russian Government, and in Kieff eleven winter and three summer ones, mostly devoted to drama.

In Riga there are eight theatres, half only open in winter, and the remaining half in summer, while in Odessa there are ten in winter and four in summer, ten of them being taken up with the drama pure and simple.

In Charkoff three theatres in summer and six in winter relieve the monotony of the inhabitants. In five out of the nine drama is played.

There are four or five more theatres in Tiflis (bordering, though it does, almost on Asiatic rule), the chief of which—and said to be one of the best in the world—being under the personal control of the Prince and Princess Bariatinsky, the former a brilliant author, and the latter an actress, who, under the *nom de plume* of Lydia Yavorskaja, has made many triumphs there and in St. Petersburg, Vienna, and Paris. She is a woman of singular charm of personality and great emotional power.

In addition to those mentioned, there are probably about 150 other theatres scattered over the vast area of Russia, some very good ones being found in Siberia, in the towns of Irkutsk, Tomsk, and Omsk, as well as in the Crimea.

CHARACTERISTIC PLAYS.

To turn to Russian plays. These are generally philosophically serious, but are by no means devoid of humour, which is a strong characteristic of the race. As already noted, the repertory system prevails in Russia, and mostly native operas and plays are given, though audiences are broad-minded, and ready to welcome with enthusiasm works of merit from alien countries. The operas of Tschaikowsky, Glinka, and Rimski-Korsakoff are, of course, regarded as classical.

Russian operatic singers have generally clear and powerful voices. Shaliapin is one of Russia's most noted vocalists. He has recently returned from an exceedingly successful tour in America. Russians altogether are a very musical nation, artistic and simple. They are temperamentally bright, with a love of *joie de vivre*, though their national songs, curiously enough, are melancholy and sad to a degree.

The leading dramatists are:—Ostrovsky, Tolstoi, Gorky, Tschechoff, Gneditsh, Prince Sumbatoff (a celebrated author of the Moscow Maly Theatre, who also plays under the name of Yushin), Prince Bariatinsky, Nemirourtsch-Dan, Schenko, and Potapenko.

Shakespeare is produced frequently in every theatre throughout the country. He is intelligently and intellectually translated, artistically depicted and produced, and worshipped by the Russian nation.

In addition, many of the new and most successful plays of France, Germany, England, and other countries are, at various times, included in the repertory of most theatres.

SEASONS AND SALARIES.

The season lasts from September till the beginning of May. Actors and actresses engaged at the Imperial Theatres receive their salaries all the year round—and very good ones they undoubtedly are—while a pension awaits them after twenty years' service, ballet-dancers being excused and duly remunerated after fifteen years in front of the footlights.

During the summer many actors and actresses go on tour, frequently forming their own companies and syndicates. Very good theatres for these purposes are to be found in Charkoff, Kieff, Saratoff, Tiflis (in the Caucasus), Warsaw (Poland), Irkutsk (Siberia), Odessa, and in the Crimea, where the long and sometimes tiring tours extend.

Foreign actors frequently visit St. Petersburg and Moscow. Duse was there last year with her Italian company, and had a magnificent reception, while Sarah Bernhardt has recently played a fortnight, with great success, and also in Moscow, Warsaw, Kieff, and Lods. A permanent German theatre has now been organised, and is doing excellent business. Why does not an enterprising English actor or actress follow suit? A splendid reception awaits the actor who can "make good." And Russia is not a poor country. But she is artistic, discriminating, and critical!

PERSONAL IMPRESSIONS, BY PERCY BURTON.

In Russia, strange to say, the theatre is, in many ways more advanced than in England or America. It is more on a level with France, and in some respects it is on a higher level. In England and America it is first commerce, and then art; in Russia it is art first and commerce afterwards. Nor does this apply only to the State theatres. There is, for instance, the Maly Theatre in St. Petersburg, the leading literary and artistic unsubsidised theatre, the property of Mr. Suworin, who is also editor and proprietor of the *Novoje Vremja*, one of the leading daily papers.

It was at the Maly Theatre that, through the courtesy of the management and the medium of Baroness Bila (herself a distinguished member of the Imperial Theatrical Society, and author and adapter of several successful plays, including *Lady Frederick*, *Jack Straw*, and *When Knights Were Bold*), that I had the privilege of being present on the opening night of this season. I then saw *Twelfth Night* in Russian—an extraordinary fine production and performance (under the direction of Mr. Arbatoff, a Moscow manager). It would be invidious to compare certain London representations of the same play, though it is obvious that the Russians have little to learn from us about Shakespeare, or as regards the theatre generally. Whether they have any such fine or finished actor in modern comedy as Sir John Hare, for instance, I doubt, or whether they can surpass the spectacular achievements to which Mr. Beerbohm Tree and Mr. Arthur Collins have accustomed us I am not sure. Certainly, however, in the *tout ensemble* and *mise en scène* they were not behind us, and always have something artistic to suggest.

It was at the Mariensky Theatre that, through the kindness of Mr. Teliakovsky, the able and amiable director of all the Imperial theatres, I witnessed a *répétition générale* of their superb patriotic opera, *Life for the Tsar*, one of the most beautiful and artistic productions I have ever seen. With Glinka's charming music, its human story, and novel atmosphere, a revival of this operatic play should be a great success in London. The scenes of old Moscow, the Court at Poland, a peasant's home, a wood in mid-winter, and outside the Kremlin, where the assembled troops and populace await the coming of the Tsar (whose " counterfeit presentment " is not, of course, permitted on the stage), were all very artistically and realistically depicted. Fascinating, too, was the Mazurka, danced in the Polish scene with irresistible verve and abandon. Mr. Teliakovsky pointed out to me the most graceful and finished of the male dancers, who seemed to be endowed with the youthful grace of an Adeline Genée, and told me that he was nearly seventy years of age!

As regards the practicability of sending such an opera as *Life of the Tsar* to London, Mr. Teliakovsky told me that the expenses of transit would be too great. Mr. Teliakovsky was very much interested in English plays, and particularly those of Bernard Shaw, who is as great a favourite in Russia as in Germany; while, of course, Shakespeare in Russia is a household word.

It was to the courtesy of Mr Teliakovsky, too, and Baroness Bila that I had an opportunity of visiting the other Imperial theatres, both before and behind the scenes. Apart from the dignity and beauty of the buildings, without and within, the stage arrangements in these houses are wonderfully complete. Roominess is a feature behind the curtain, and there is excellent accommodation for actors and actresses, whose comfort is evidently considered more in Russia than it is in England. At the Alexandra Theatre a rehearsal was proceeding; I was shown all over the theatre, from the stage to the foyer, where stood the busts and pictures of famous actors and authors. The Tsar's box and his private passage behind the scenes were naturally objects of interest. The stage and scene docks were also, they being nearly as large as the auditorium itself, and the flies and set scenes are particularly high and well constructed.

At rehearsal, too, I met several of Russia's well-known actors and actresses, including Mme. Savina. Later at her home I met Mme. Mitschurina, who was the Duchess in the Russian version of *The Gay Lord Quex*, and is shortly to be seen as *Lady Frederick* in St. Petersburg. With the latter lady particularly I had opportunities of exchanging civilities, finding her to be an exceptionally cultivated woman of the world, with a keen sense of humour—and doubtless also a fine actress, for the temperament and charm of the Russian women are a sure index to their ability in that direction.

THE RUSSIAN STAGE

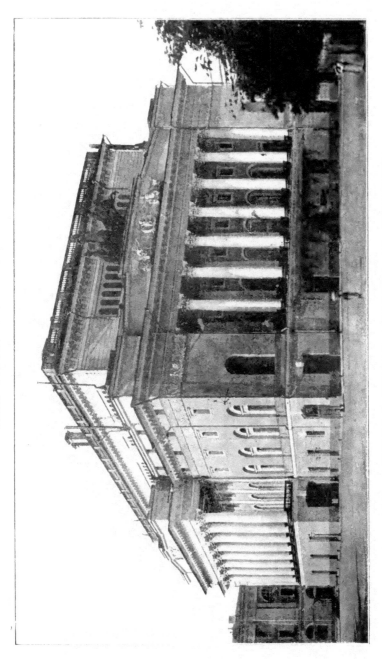

THE ALEXANDRA (IMPERIAL) THEATRE, ST. PETERSBURG.

RAFAEL AND ROBERT ADELHEIM.
Celebrated Shakespearean Actors.

Mme. Portschinskaja (the wife of Mr. Glagolin, himself a well-known young actor of parts ranging from *Raffles* and *Sherlock Holmes* to *Hamlet*) was the charming Olivia on the occasion of *Twelfth Night*, and I had the pleasure of meeting her personally the next evening, when I was present at the Jubilee performance of Tolstoi. To celebrate this event acts from *Anna Karenina*, *Resurrection*, and *The Powers of Darkness* were played, to be followed by tableaux vivants illustrating other of his plays and characters. The most interesting tableaux emblematical and descriptive of Tolstoi and his work were ordered to be eliminated at the last moment, much to the dismay of the justly irate producer, Mr. Glovazsky, in order to obviate any possibility of a demonstration. No fewer than one hundred and fifty detectives were said to be that night amongst the spectators. My visit to Russia gave me the determination to renew acquaintance in the winter time with a most interesting country and some of the most charming and delightful people it has been my privilege to meet. Perhaps the suggestion that I should go down to Tiflis and see Princess Bariatinsky's theatre and witness her performances in her husband's plays may also give me opportunities of ascertaining the theatrical touring possibilities of the Crimea and the Caucasus. At all events, with the few Russian words at my disposal, I would say : " Spaceebo ! Ja skoro vernus ! " " Thank you ! I shall come back soon."

THE THEATRES ALLIANCE.

This Association was formed in the year 1894, under the name of the Suburban Managers' Association. The membership was originally limited to suburban managers, but, it being found desirable to extend the sphere of usefulness of the Association, the scope was enlarged by making eligible for membership all proprietors, lessees, licensees, directors, and responsible managers of theatres receiving touring companies. The name was changed to the present one in 1908.

The objects of the Association are, *inter alia*, the discussion and settlement by arbitration or otherwise of matters of common interest to theatrical managers or proprietors ; the affording to members a central means for inter-communication and encouragement, by meetings or otherwise, of the direct exchange of opinions and ideas regarding theatres ; the taking when necessary of concerted action and the institution or defence of proceedings, legal or otherwise.

The officers of the Alliance are :—President, Mr. J. B. Mulholland ; Vice-President, Mr. H. G. Dudley Bennett ; Hon. Treasurer, Mr. H. G. Dudley Bennett ; Hon. Auditors, Messrs. W. Melville and W. Bailey ; Hon. Secretary, Mr. J. Moverley Sharp, Criterion Chambers, Jermyn Street, S.W.

The members meet every month at Criterion Chambers, Jermyn Street, S.W., on the second Tuesday in the month to discuss and deal with any matters of general or particular interest that may arise.

In 1905 a fund was established to enable the society to assist its members by taking up cases of interest and moment to the general body, either on a defensive or offensive basis, which fund is contributed to by members on an agreed scale, and in this way the Alliance has at call several thousand pounds for any such purposes, which is a great source of strength to the Alliance generally and its members individually. The Alliance is in touch with and works in harmony with all the other theatrical associations.

During the past year the Alliance has been successful in settling with the Touring Managers' Association a standard form of contract between resident and touring managers, which is now in print, and available for all members ; the Alliance has also obtained special exclusive insurance rates for its members, and a special agreement settling in favour of its members many points of difficulty and doubt under the Workmen's Compensation Act, all responsibility under these points being thrown upon the insurance company. It was in direct consequence of the representations of the Alliance that the prohibitive clause with regard to smoking in theatres under the control of the London County Council was removed, and the representations of the Alliance in connection with the standing-room question have caused that matter to be placed upon a more reasonable and favourable basis.

Applications for membership should be made to the Hon. Secretary at the offices as above. Subscription : one guinea per annum for each theatre in respect of which a member is registered.

STAFF ORGANISATIONS.

NATIONAL ASSOCIATION OF THEATRICAL EMPLOYES.

This Association was established on August 20, 1890. It represents those employed in the various stage departments, in the manufacture and use of stage scenery, properties, electrical fittings, animated picture machines, comprising stage managers, heads of departments, carpenters, electricians, kinematograph operators, property men, stagemen, flymen, and others employed in theatres and music halls, or theatrical workshops, resident or touring.

It is affiliated with the General Federation of Trade Unions, the Trade Union Congress, London and Provincial Trades and Labour Councils. The chief office is 29, Wellington Street, Strand, London.

Summary of Objects:—To raise the status of stage employés by maintaining a minimum rate of pay, definite working rules, and the provision of sick, funeral, and benevolent benefits for members. The Association has four branches in London and one in Birmingham, Bradford, Oldham, Newcastle-on-Tyne, Middlesbrough, Stockton-on-Tees, and Greenock. The entrance fees vary according to branch from 2s. 6d. to 10s. The contributions vary, according to branch and benefit desired, from 2d. to 1s. 2d. per week. Each branch has a benevolent fund, and most of them have sick and funeral funds. The constitution of the Association permits any grade or section of employés eligible to join to form a branch, or all sections to combine in one branch in any locality. The aim of the organisation is to enrol all eligible men with touring companies, and those resident in every theatrical centre in the United Kingdom.

The National Executive Committee is selected from the members residing within twenty miles of the chief office, but it is open to any branch to nominate any member to one of the general offices. This Committee organises the London annual theatrical sports and annual concerts, and has charge of the National Open Benevolent Fund, which is maintained from the proceeds of the theatrical sports and donations received to the annual concert funds, for the benefit of non-members, men and women employés, whose case is recommended by a subscriber to the sports or concert funds, or by any theatrical or music hall association whose rules do not permit them to help such applicants.

The funds of the Association on December 31, 1907, amounted to £1,129 14s. 11d., to which date the Association, in addition to the increase of wages, secured and maintained, and the protection afforded to its members, had paid in cash benefits to members:—

	£	s.	d.
At death of Members and Members' Wives	3,149	0	0
To Members supporting the objects of the Society	1,615	11	1
Legal Assistance to Members	226	15	4
Compensation secured for Members	196	0	0
*Sick Pay to Members	103	17	2
Special Grants to necessitous Members, Wages advanced due from Fraudulent and Bankrupt Managers (including sums to Non-Members and their Widows from the Open Benevolent Fund)	308	1	6
Total	£5,599	5	1

*The Sick Fund has only recently been formed.

The present members of the Executive Committee are:—President, Mr. J. Cullen, master carpenter, the St. James's; Vice-President, Mr. G. H. Dyball, stage manager, the London Pavilion; Treasurer, Mr. J. H. Radford, carpenter, the Comedy; Trustees, Mr. William Barbour, chief electrician, the St. James's; Mr. Arthur Palmer, master carpenter, the Comedy; Mr. Charles Thorogood, President, No. 1 Branch; Committee, Mr. C. T. Cory, master carpenter, the Vaudeville; Mr. J. Reid, carpenter (President, Carpenters' Branch); Mr. A. Jones, carpenter, Royal Opera House (Treasurer, Carpenters' Branch); Mr. H. Lane, carpenter (Member Committee, Carpenters' Branch); Mr. H. J. Powell, property master, Hicks's; Mr. Philip Sheridan, electrician, Waldorf; Mr. Edward Stow, stage staff, the Savoy; Mr. George Pickering, stage staff, Duke of York's; Mr. J. N. Hunt, stage staff, the Lyceum; General Secretary, Mr. William Johnson.

During the past year no event of special importance has occurred, but the Association is constantly called upon to intercede on behalf of its members to secure the observance of, or an improvement in, existing conditions of employment, and at the time the Year-Book went to press the General Federation of Trade Unions was acting for the Oldham Branch in negotiations with local managements.

The Committee is now actively engaged in forming a fund of special interest to all sections of employés connected with London theatres and halls, and of particular advantage to those not eligible to join the Association. This fund will be for the purpose of providing sick pay (15s. a week for thirteen weeks and 7s. 6d. a week for a further thirteen weeks), and a sum at death equal to a levy of 6d. per member. The applicants for membership include managers, stage managers, and other heads of stage departments, bill inspectors, box-office keepers, super masters, and there is every prospect of the fund being a success. A meeting was held in Terry's on November 15 by permission of Mr. Forbes Robertson and Mr. Edward Terry. The latter sent his best wishes for the success of the fund. A further meeting will be held in January, 1909, to consider the rules and to establish the fund formally.

Full particulars may be obtained from Mr. Wm. Johnson, at 29, Wellington Street, Strand. W.C.

HEADS OF DEPARTMENTS ASSOCIATION.

This Association is a branch of the N.A.T.E., and was established in November, 1902, and consists exclusively of stage managers, master carpenters, chief electricians, master propertymen, and master gasmen of theatres and music halls. Membership is open to those connected with any theatre, music hall, or touring company in the United Kingdom who have held such positions for at least six months, and are otherwise qualified. The entrance fee is 10s. The contribution varies from 1s. to 4s. 8d. per month, according to benefit desired and age of applicant. Sick pay is assured to those subscribing for same from 10s. to 20s. per week for a number of weeks. On the death of a member £20 is paid to the widow of a member in benefit, and on the death of a member's wife £10 is paid to the member, which sums are partly raised by levies.

The Association has also a benevolent fund, and affords free legal advice to members. An annual dinner has been given each year, at which the following gentlemen have in turn presided:—Mr. J. Comyns Carr, Mr. George Alexander, Mr. H. Beerbohm Tree, Mr. H. B. Irving, and, on the last occasion, Mr. Edward Terry. The Association assists to organise the London theatrical sports and the annual concerts. The present officers are:—President, Mr. James Cullen, master carpenter, the St. James's; Vice-President, Mr. H. J. Powell, property master, Hicks's; Hon. Secretary, Mr. G. H. Dyball, stage manager, the London Pavilion; Financial Secretary, Mr. Wm. Johnson; Committee, Mr. William Barbour, electrician, the St. James's; Mr. Wm. Pulliniger, master carpenter, the Garrick; Mr. Philip Sheridan, electrician, the Waldorf; Mr. John Brunskill, master carpenter, the Savoy; Mr. W. G. Wilton, property master, the Vaudeville; Mr. R. J. Carter, electrician, Terry's; Mr. David Sheridan, electrician, the Scala; and Mr. G. W. Willcox, property master, Mr. Arthur Bourchier's company. Office, 29, Wellington Street, Strand, London.

The annual meeting will take place on January 28, 1909.

NATIONAL ASSOCIATION OF CINEMATOGRAPH OPERATORS
(Branch No. 10. N.A.T.E.).

This Association was established in April, 1907. Its office is at 29, Wellington Street, Strand, London. Its members are qualified operators of animated picture apparatus.

Objects :—(a) To protect and promote the interests of qualified operators, and to raise the status of their profession. (b) To encourage among its members a knowledge of the science of new inventions affecting their business. (c) To establish a standard of proficiency by a qualifying examination or otherwise. (d) To secure the recognition of a minimum rate of pay for each class of work. (e) To establish an employment register, and such other benefits (sick, funeral, or legal aid) as may be hereafter agreed upon.

Entrance fee, 5s. Contribution, 1s. 6d. per month, being for General and Benevolent Funds.

Certificates are issued to members passing an examination, particulars of which are supplied on application.

Present (1909) officers :—President, Mr. J. Wood ; Vice-President, Mr. E. Catlin ; Hon. Secretary, Mr. S. J. Henry ; Financial Secretary and Treasurer, Mr. Wm. Johnson. Committee : Messrs. C. Mayo, J. Lancaster, J. Troup, A. Smith, T. C. Field, C. Hayward, W. Mason, A. Malcolm, and Bowden. Auditors : Messrs. Maloney and Bowden.

During the past year the Association secured the services of representative exhibitors to act as a Board of Examiners, and to issue certificates for members having a knowledge of (a) electric and limelight ; (b) electric only ; (c) limelight only.

The Association appointed a Deputation which was received by the Theatres Committee of the London County Council when the matter of regulations for animated picture exhibitions was under consideration.

Mr. S. J. Henry submitted a statement, containing the following proposals, on behalf of the Deputation :—

1. We beg to ask the committee to recommend to the Council that it be made a condition of a license that any person operating a cinematograph lantern on premises under control of the Council shall be required to show a certificate to prove that he is a qualified operator.

2. We beg to ask the committee to recognise the certificates to be issued by this Association, and, in the event of the committee not being able to recommend the adoption of this suggestion, that you recommend the Council to issue certificates for this purpose.

The reasons for submitting these proposals were :—

1. The inflammable nature of the material used, and the delicate nature of the machine and appliances entrusted to the operator.

2. The enormous increased use of the cinematograph for public and private exhibitions.

3. That modern improvements in the apparatus have not reduced, but tended towards an increase in, the risk of fire.

4. That the business has developed so rapidly that it has been extremely difficult to secure a sufficiency of qualified men, with the result that unqualified men are employed as operators, to the public danger.

5. That the skill and experience of the operator are the main safeguards against fire, and it is desirable, in the public interest, that the Council should support our proposals.

Several satisfactory conferences have taken place between representatives of the operators and the Variety Artists' Federation to secure an agreement as to the rate of pay for operators doing special and extra services for artists requiring slides or films to be shown with their act or sketch. The Committee carefully watches the new appliances and safety devices introduced, and was represented at the exhibitions given during 1908 at the London Hippodrome and elsewhere.

The first annual dinner was given at Anderton's Hotel on April 29, when Mr. C. W. Bowerman, M.P., attended, and presented the certificates awarded to members who had been successful in the examinations held to that date.

The membership is scattered over the United Kingdom, and includes many operators of long experience and holding good positions in the business. The membership is steadily increasing.

PLAYS OF THE YEAR.

B EING a complete list with full casts of new plays and important revivals produced in the United Kingdom during the year 1908.
* Indicates revival.
† Produced at a *matinée.*
‡ Previously produced in the provinces.
∥ Produced by amateurs.
¶ Played only for the purpose of securing the statutory stage right.

JANUARY.

2. *Dear Old Charlie,* comedy, in three acts, adapted from Labiche's old comedy, *Célimare le Bien-Aimé,* by Charles H. E. Brookfield. Last performance, March 22 ; 92 performances.
Charlie Ingleton .. Mr. Charles Hawtrey
Gabriel Peploe .... Mr. Charles Groves
Thomas Dumphie .... Mr. E. H. Clark
Colonel Fishbourne .. Mr. E. Fitzgerald
Purkitt .... Mr. Robert Whyte, jun.
Florist's Boy .... Master Albert Kimber
Agnes .... Miss Muriel Beaumont
Reeve .... Miss Mona Harrison
Mrs. Fishbourne ...... Miss Helen Rous
Vaudeville.

3.∥*Fizzical Culture,* farcical sketch, by Ewart Beech.
Jack Medwin .... Mr. Ewart Beech
Parker .... Mr. Ben Osborne
Thora Kendrick ...... Miss Nellie Peryer
Surrey Masonic Hall.

3.∥*The One-Day Millionaire,* comic opera, in one act, book and lyrics by Francis Reeve, music by Basil Rideaux.
Sir Acton Cherry, Bart .. Mr. F. Knight
Claude Cherry ...... Mr. Francis Reeve
Capt. Elliston, R.N. .. M . W. H. Bishop
Sandy MacPherson Mr. A. F. MacDonald
Johnny Reece .... Mr. H. B. Pride
Mrs. De Fere .... Miss Beatrice Ward
Kitty Camber .... Miss Louie White
Sybil Airn .... Miss Bella Drewry
Surrey Masonic Hall.

4.‡*The Mystery of Edwin Drood,* drama, in four acts, by J. Comyns Carr, founded on Charles Dickens's unfinished novel. Originally produced at the New Cardiff, November 21, 1907. Last performance, February 1 ; 35 performances.
John Jasper .... Mr. Tree
Edwin Drood .... Mr. Basil Gill
Mr. Grewgious ...... Mr. Wm. Haviland
Mr. Crisparkle .. Mr. Claude Flemming
Neville Landless .. Mr. C. Quartermaine
The Dean of Cloisterham.. Mr. R. Atkins
Durdles .... Mr. G. W. Anson
The Deputy .... Mr. Frank Stanmore
A Warder .... Mr. Cyril H. Swarder
A Lascar .... Mr. Henry Morrell
Congo Jack .... Mr. Thomas Weguelin
A Sailor .... Mr. A. C. Grain
Rosa Bud ...... Miss Adrienne Augarde
Helena Landless .. Miss Constance Collier
Mrs. Crisparkle .... Miss Cicely Richards
Miss Twinkleton .. Miss Muriel Alexander
Princess Puffer .. Mrs. F. Wright, sen.
Mrs. Tope .... Miss Augusta Haviland
Servant .... Miss Hilda Moore
His Majesty's.

6. *The Other Woman,* play, in three acts, by Herbert Leonard.
Hon. Michael Dunree Mr. C. B. Vaughan
Barry Dillon, M.P., .. Mr. C. Hairland
Frank Sudley .... Mr. Wentworth Fane
Parkiss .... Mr. Edward P. Walsh
Fencing Referee .... Mr. Frank Adams
Footman .... Mr. Willie James
Myama's Father .... Mr. J. Edgcumbe
Myama's Brother .... Mr. Percy Scott
Servant .... Miss Do Hilda
Myama .... Miss Nora Caston
Daisy Virginia Carlotta .. Miss F. Turner
Nancy Nollid .... Miss Ethel St. Barbe
Dora Marlo .... Miss Maude Fergusson
Pier Pavilion, Hastings.

7. *The Subjection of Kezia,* play, in one act, by Mrs. Havelock Ellis.
Joe Pengilly .... Mr. W. Graham Browne
Kezia .... Miss Beryl Faber
Matthew Trevaskis .. Mr. Arthur Whitby
Court.

9.¶*The City of Mystery,* romantic costume play, in a prologue and four acts, adapted by Lionel Atwill, from the novel of that name by Archibald Clavering Gunter.
Grand, Luton.

10.∥*A Tangled Skein,* by Hugh Tuite—Hall, Nenagh.

11. *A White Man,* romance of the West, in four acts, by Edwin Milton Royle, originally produced in America as *The Squaw Man.* Last performance, June 12; 170 performances.
Earl of Kerhill ...... Mr. Herbert Sleath
Captain Wynnegate .... Mr. Lewis Waller
Sir John Applegate .. Mr. A. G. Poulton
Mr. Chiswick .... Mr. W. Cronin Wilson
Bates .... Mr. Charles Cecil
Malcolm Petrie ...... Mr. Charles Allan
Lieut. Henry George .. Mr. Erik Stirling
Lieut. Alex. Leslie .... Mr. P. Digan
Lieut. Charles Magarth....Mr. R. Dane
The Dean of Trentham .. Mr. H. Vyvyan
Big Bill .... Mr. George Fawcett
Shorty .... Mr. Cecil Yapp
Andy .... Mr. S. J. Warmington
Grouchy .... Mr. Mitchell Lewis
Baco White .... Mr. S. Saville
Tab-y-Wana .... Mr. Wm. Riley Hatch
Cash Hawkins .... Mr. Menifee Johnstone
Nick .... Mr. Dwight Danforth
Bud Hardy .... Mr. A. W. Jack Ellis
Clark .... Mr. D. Bartun
McSorley ...... Mr. A. Caton-Woodville
Parker .... Mr. W. Walshe
Pete .... Mr. A. S. Aspland
Parson .... Mr. H. Ainger

A White Man (continued).

Punk .... Mr. J. Simmonds
Mr. Hiram Doolittle .. Mr. G. Courtney
Little Hal .... Miss Rita Leggiero
Countess of Kerhill....Miss N. Lancaster
Dowager Lady Kerhill....Miss M. Rorke
Lady Wynnegate..Miss Evelyn Beaumont
Mrs. Hiram Doolittle .. Miss Helen Castle
Nat-u-Ritch .... Miss Dorothy Dix
                                        Lyric.

11.‡*Page 97*, play, in one act, by T. K.,
originally produced at the Lyceum, New-
port, December 23, 1907.
Richard Fairfax ...)
Abraham Lovitzski)
Colonel Milward ··· } Mr. Henri de Vries
Timothy Pickering · (
Lord Carleigh .....)
William Briggs .....)
Minnie Fairfax ...... Miss Dorothy Drake
Mary Briggs ...... Miss Mary Pemberton
                                        Garrick.

11.**As You Like It*, Shakespearean revival,
the pastoral comedy, in five acts.
Duke .... Mr. W. F. Stirling
Duke Frederick .. Mr. John Wainwright
Amieus .... Mr. Walter Lawley
Jaques .... Mr. Clifton Alderson
Le Beau .... Mr. Wilfred Beckwith
Charles .... Mr. A. E. Calver
Oliver .... Mr. H. V. Neilson
Jaques de Bois ...... Mr. R. Darnley
Orlando ...... Mr. E. Harcourt Williams
Adam .... Mr. H. Ormby Warburton
Touchstone .... Mr. A. Grenville
Sir Oliver Martex .... Mr. T. E. Daniels
Corin .... Mr. H. F. Fox
Silvius .... Mr. A. Hilliard
William .... Mr. H. K. Ayliff
Hymen .... Mr. W. Lawley
Rosalind .... Miss Margaret Halstan
Celia .... Miss Hilda Druce Potter
Phœbe .... Miss Eleen Kerin
Audrey .... Miss Clare Greet
First Lord .... Mr. Tom Ronald
First Attendant .... Mr. Gordon Kinsley
Second Attendant .... Mr. Vaughan
                                 Queen's, Manchester.

11.¶*The Professor's Vision*, musical playlet, by
Theo Ward.
The Professor .... Mr. T. Howard
Ruth Richardson .... Miss Marie Rosa
                        —Hippodrome, Eastbourne.

13. *A Question of Property*, play, in one act,
by J. Sackville Martin.
Comrade Weaver .... Mr. Henry Austin
Mrs. Weaver .... Miss Louise Holbrook
Comrade Markland .... Mr. Basil Dean
Uncle John .... Mr. Edward Landor
Comrade Pettigrew .... Miss Esmé Filmer
                                Royal, Margate.

18.¶*Sexton Blake, Detective*—King's, Hammersmith.

19. *The Greater Glory*, play, in four acts, by
Estelle Burney. Produced by the Pioneers.
Anthony Sherrard .... Mr. Eille Norwood
Archibald MacEwen .. Mr. E. Gurney
Jack Sherrard .... Mr. Donald Calthrop
Sir Keith Coniston .... Mr. J. E. Pearce
Alexander Wills-Mason Mr. J. E. H. Terry
Dan Stringer .. .. Mr. Jules Shaw
Yardley .... Mr. Arthur Chesney
Purvis .... Mr. Gordon A. Parker
Mary MacEwen ...... Miss Vera Coburn
Hannah MacEwen .... Miss Relph
Mrs. Brown ...... Miss Nora Hastings
A Sister of Mercy .. Miss Gwladys Morris
                                    Shaftesbury.

20. *Only a Woman*, domestic drama, in four acts·
by Percy Ballard.   L ndon production·
April 13, West London.
Courtney Wallace .... Mr. Percy Ballard
Lieut. Richard Sommerfield, .. Fred Green
Lieut. Rodney Sommerfield W. H. Wilson
James Dobson .... Mr. A. Smith
Billy Bumkins .... Mr. George Whillis
Harold .... Miss Kitty Bell
John Bull .... Mr. Norman Plant
Sally Binks .... Miss Nora Williams
Dolly Derelove ...... Miss May Fletcher
Eliza Jane .... Miss Lola Tempest
Grace .... Miss Rosie Fields
Violet Redgrave ...... Miss Flora Leslie
Marie Lestoc ...... Miss Violet Cranford
                                Central, Altrincham.

21. *The O'Grindles*, play, in three acts, by H.
V. Esmond. Last performance, February 22;
33 performances.
Sir Harry O'Grindle .. Mr. Alfred Bishop
Harding O'Grindle .... Mr. K. Douglas
Jim O'Grindle .... Mr. Cyril Maude
Clive Grainger .... Mr. E. Mainwaring
Dr. O'Keefe ...... Mr. Edmund Gwenn
General Fitzgerald .. Mr. D. McCarthy
Major McGee .... Mr. J. H. Ryley
Dan Blake .... Mr. Windham Guise
Captain Jack .... Mr. A. G. Onslow
John .... Mr. John Harwood
Patsey .... Mr. B. Fitzgerald
Larry .... Mr. Patrick Traynor
Brian .... Mr. C. Hampden
Meakin .... Mr. W. Blair
Mrs. O'Grindle ......Miss Winifred Emery
Kathleen Fitzgerald .. Alexandra Carlisle
Miss McGee .... Miss Pollie Emery
Nan Brian .... Miss May Blayney
                                        Playhouse.

22. *Susannah—and Some Others*, comedy, in
four acts, by Mme. Albanesi.   Last per-
formance, January 29; 7 performances.
Sir Edmund Corneston, K.C.
                        Mr. J. Fisher White
Richard Calvert ...... Mr. J. Robertshaw
Adrian Thrale ...... Mr. Dawson Milward
George Harraday .... Mr. Edward Rigby
Lord Herbert Wayne..Mr. J. W. Deverell
Benson .... Mr. F. Powell
Frederick .... Mr. Stanley Logan
Lady Corneston ..Miss Gertrude Kingston
Mrs. Thrale ...... Miss Florence Haydon
Mrs. Harraday ...... Miss Frances Dillon
Susannah Riceland .. Miss Nina Sevening
Duffcey .... Miss Mabel Knowles
Fourth at Bridge...... Miss M. Henderson
                                        —Royalty.

23. *Li 'Iggs*, dramatic sketch, by George S.
Tanner.
Eliza Higgs .... Miss Rose Cazalet
Dare Wraybrooke .... Mr. Gordon Bailey
                        —Bijou, Bayswater.

23. *The Orange Blossom*, farcical comedy, in
three acts, by Victor Widnell.   Last per-
formance, February 5; 15 performances.
Baron Zarony .... Mr. Oscar Adye
Sir Lionel Besby, Bart. .. Mr. A. Stewart
John Hepworth ...... Mr. Sydney Paxton
Raymond Jessell .... Mr. Wilfred Forster
Casadine Zarony ...... Mr. George Silver
Agava .. .. Mr. Owen Steele
Andrews .... Mr. Henry Bute
Harley Hamilton ...... Mr. C. V. France
Cynthia Van Norden ...... Miss G. Bibby
Minnie Westlake .. Miss Esmé Hubbard
Miss Knutsford ...... Miss Rita Milman
Mrs. Harley Hamilton .... Miss Granville
                                        —Terry's.

23.‖*The Lemonade Boy*, play, by Gladys Unger.
                        —Athenæum, Glasgow.

26. *Cupid and Commonsense*, play, in four acts, by Arnold Bennett (produced for stage-right purposes at the Shaftesbury on January 24 by the Incorporated Stage Society).

Emily Boothroyd .... Miss Sybil Noble
Alice Boothroyd ...... Miss Lucy Wilson
Eli Boothroyd ...... Mr. J. Fisher White
Ralph Emery ...... Mr. H. Nye Chart
Willie Beach .... Mr. Walter Pearce
Mrs. Copestick .... Miss Mary Brough
Miranda Finney .... Miss S. Fairbrother
Bessie......Miss Magy Macdonald-Martin
Edna Beach ...... Miss Hazel Thompson
—Shaftesbury.

27. *The Walk*, duologue, by Roy Horniman.
Mr. Westbury ...... Mr. G. D. Burnaby
Mrs. Westbury .... Miss Lettice Fairfax
—Apollo.

27. *Peg Woffington*, arranged by Laurence Irving from Tom Taylor's drama, *Masks and Faces*.
Triplet .... Mr. Laurence Irving
Peg Woffington .... Miss Mabel Hackney
Sir Charles Pomander..Mr. Geo. De Lara
Ernest Vane ...... Mr. Eric Field-Fisher
Snarl .... Mr. J. Crisp
Mabel Vane .... Miss Vera Wallace
Mrs. Triplet .... Miss Beatrice Lett
Triplet Boys .... Miss Dora Crisp
Grand, Birmingham.

27. *Sir George's Folly*, comic opera, in two acts, book by Mr. W. Livingstone, music by Dr. Koeller.
Sir G. Maine .. Mr. Crossley Patterson
Hon. Percy Pomeroy .. Mr. A. Daubency
Harold Smith, M.D...Mr. R. M. Patterson
Major Hector Alisse .... Mr. J. McLean
Duchess of Blankshire..Mdme. Drinkwater
Miss Maine .... Miss Florence Nixon
Mdme. Kooka .... Miss May Savage
Lady Maine .... Miss M. Johnstone
Daisy Meadows .... Miss L. McCann
Royal, Belfast.

28. *Her Father*, play, in four acts, adapted from Albert Guinon and Alfred Bouchinet's *Son Père* by Michael Mort n, produced at Odeon, Paris, October, 31, 1907. Last performance, April 11; 83 performances.
Lord Claremont .. Mr. Arthur Bourchier
Sir C. Trehmayne...Mr. Cyril Keightley
Frank Morris ...... Mr H. Marsh Allen
Mr. Eustace Digby..Mr. C. Leveson Lane
Hon. W. Rigeley-Fane..Mr. E. B. Payne
Simpson .... Mr. E. W. Tarver
Irene Forster .... Miss Marie Löhr
Mrs. Forster .... Miss Henrietta Watson
Hon. Mrs. Rigeley-Fane.Miss A. Vanbrugh
Miss Troubridge .... Miss Gladys Baird
Mary .... Miss Nellie Moore
Mrs. Mason .... Miss Mabel Aldridge
Haymarket.

28. *Foiled*, romantic drama, by Frances M. Kay.
Louis Chatelard .... Mr. Wilfred Harper
Lord Lidderdale .... Mr. Hal Harper
Mark Falworth .... Mr. E. A. Evans
Angus Hamilton ...... Mr. Chas. Mackie
Carrington .... Mr. W. S. Evans
Duncan .... Mr. E. H. Mottershead
Pierre .... Mr. W. S. Evans
Prince Charlie ...... Mr. Wilfred Harper
Trooper .... Mr. W. S. Evans
First Traveller .... Mr. Chas. Mackie
Second Traveller ...... Mr. Chameley Pett
Barbara Lidderdale .... Miss Ida Kay
Beatrix Falworth .. Mrs. G. Mottersheau
—Harborne Inst., Birmingham.

28. *Waste*, tragedy, in four acts, by Granville Barker. *Waste* in its original form was produced by the Incorporated Stage Society on November 24, 1907, after the Censor had refused to license the play. The passages to which the Censor took objection having been deleted, the piece was produced for the purpose of securing stage-right with the following cast:—
Lady Davenport ...... Mrs. W. P. Reeves
Walter Kent .... Mr. Gilbert Cannan
Mrs. Farrant .. Miss Magdalen Ponsonby
Miss Trebell .... Miss Clemence Housman
Mrs. O'Connell ...... Mrs. Bernard Shaw
Lucy Davenport .... Mrs. H. G. Wells
George Farrant .... Mr. St. John Hankin
Russell Blackborough..Mr. J. Galsworthy
A Footman .... Mr. Allan Wade
Henry Trebell .... Mr. Laurence Housman
Simson .... Mrs. Granville Barker
Gilbert Wedgecroft .... Mr. H. G. Wells
Lord Charles Cantelupe
Prof. Gilbert Murray, LL.D.
The Earl of Horsham..Mr. Bernard Snaw
Edmunds .... Mr. Arthur Bowyer
Justin O'Connell .... Mr. William Archer
—Savoy.

29. *Mate in Three Moves*, duologue.
Lady Corkeran .. Miss Dorothy Grimston
Mr. Tudor .... Mr. Chas. Tyrel
—92, Victoria Street, S.W.

29. *His Lucky Star*, play, in one act, by E. Haslingden Russell.
Stella .... Miss Josephine Bennett
Will Lawless .... Mr. Basil Mercer
—92, Victoria Street, S.W.

31. *A New Genevra*, play, in one act, by Frances C. Deverell.
Gabriel Montana .. Mr. H. E. Arkwright
Margaret .... Miss Lucy Evelyn
Beatrice .... Miss Mary Deverell
—Ladbroke Hall, W.

FEBRUARY.

1. *Stingaree, the Bushranger*, play, in four acts, by E. W. Hornung. Last performance, February 22; 25 performances.
Greville Dare, "Stingaree" Mr. H. Ainley
Sam .... Mr. O. P. Heggie
Howie .... Mr. Kenyon Musgrave
Robert Clarkson .... Mr. Athol Forde
Ives .... Mr. Norman Page
Sydney Sid .... Mr. Trevor Lowe
Ah Loo .... Mr. John W. Laurence
Tom Bracy .... Mr. Herbert Waring
Sir Julian Crum .... Mr. A. E. George
James Crum .... Mr. Jules Shaw
Lord Linthorpe, K.C.B..Mr. Fredk. Kerr
Herr Muller .... Mr. Ben Lewin
Supt. Cairns .... Mr. J. J. Bartlett
Sergt. Currie ...... Mr. Richard Fielding
A Trooper .... Mr. Anthony Willard
Attendant .... Mr. Edmund Waller
Jevons .... Mr. Percy Gawthorne
Radford .... Mr. Brian Egerton
King Billabong........Mr. Richard Bodney
Fat Jack..............Mr. Alfred Carlton
Sanderson............Mr. Richard Hatteras
Lady Crum.............Miss Meta Pelham
Mrs. Clarkson .... Miss Ada Ferrar
Hilda Bouverie.........Miss Hilda Antony
—Queen's.

1. *The Maid in the Moon*, "dream fantasy," in two acts and four scenes, by Ralph T. Butler, music by H. Herbert Hart.

MORTALS.

Mr. Elderbury .... Mr. L. M. Howard
Mr. Merryweather .... Mr. S. McQuown
Jack Columbus ...... Mr. A. C. Morgan
Jim Candy .... Mr. H. J. Stokes
Wriggles .... Mr. R. H. Cleverly
Tommy .... Miss Rita Passmore
Winnie .... Miss Mabel Buckland
Mary .... Miss Gertrude Butler
Crystal .... Miss Doris Wilson

PEOPLE OF THE MOON.

The Man in the Moon..Mr. S. McQuown
Terrorcotter .... Mr. Arthur G. Smith
Balloon Attendant .. Mr. Cyril Munford
Sunshine .... Miss Olive Smith
Moonshine .... Miss Dorothy Butler
Silver Cloud .... Miss Violet Smith
Fairy of the Blue Rose..Miss Enid Harries
Crystal .... Miss Doris Wilson
—Bijou, Bayswater.

3. *With Edged Tools*, dramatised version, by H. Armitage, of Henry Seton Merriman's novel. (C. P., February 20, 1907, Gaiety, Ayr. London production, April 6, King's, Hammersmith.)

Sir John Meredith .. Mr. Wm. F. Grant
Jack Meredith ...... Mr. Hamilton Deane
Guy Oscard .... Mr. Seymour Hastings
Victor Durnovo .. Mr. Campbell Goldsmid
Maurice Gordon ...... Mr. Archie Selwyn
Lieut. Conynghame .... Mr. C. Hartopp
Hon. Walter Fordyce..Mr. Bernard Raie
A Doctor .... Mr. Henry Nunn
A Servant .... Mr. B. Ratcliffe
Millicent Chyne ...... Miss Haidee Wright
Lady Cantourne ...... Miss Isabel Grey
Lady Herries .... Miss Frances Irving
Jocelyn Gordon .. Miss Marie Leonhard
Marie .... Miss Mary Raby
First Guest .... Miss Emilee Finch
Second Guest ...... Miss Dorrie Turner
Third Guest ...... Miss Violet Hastings
—Royal, Hull.

3.‡*A Brand from the Burning*, drama, by George S. King. Originally produced at the Rotunda, Liverpool, December 23, 1907.

John Mawle .... Mr. Ronald Grahame
Reginald Dalston .... Mr. Leonard Clarke
Silas Maitland ...... Mr. Leon Ainscliffe
Billy Blossom .... Mr. Harry Wimpenny
George Lawson .... Mr. Walter Clarke
Charles Heather ...... Mr. John F. Owen
Sir Henry Kato ...... Mr. Henry Chatto
Commissioner Jones..Mr. Bernard Temple
James Rogers ...... Mr. Sydney Thompson
Counsel for Plaintiff .. Mr. Ralph Kinton
Detective White .... Mr. James Thompson
Will Neverwork .... Mr. William Beesley
Timmy Flier .... Mr. Charles Watson
Policeman X73 .... Mr. Charles Neal
Daisy .... Miss Elsie Shelton
Ruth Parker .... Miss Alice Mazzoni
Kate .... Miss Alice Trapnell
May Thompson .... Miss Ivy Chandos
Mrs. Pottery .... Miss Olive Mason
Ursula ....Miss Olga Audré
—Royal, Croydon.

3. *Malia*, Sicilian drama, in three acts, by Luigi Capuana.

Ninu .... Cav. Uff. Giovanni Grasso
Cola .... Signor S. Lo Turco
Massaru Paulu ...... Signor F. Cappelli
Mastru Taddarita .... Signor P. Sapuppo
Don Saverio Teri ...... Signor N. Viscuso
1st Suonatore .... Signor V. Galloni
2nd Suonatore ...... Signor V. Balistrieri
3rd Suonatore .... Signor S. Puglisi
Iana ...... Signora Mimi Aguglia Ferrau

Malia (continued).

Nedda .... Signora C. Balistrieri
Za Pina.Signora M. Catelis-Ano Balistrieri
Catarina .... Signora R. Viscuso
A. Caristia .... Signora G. Gragaglia
Mara .... Signora D. Galloni
Vicenza .... Signora S. Aguglia
Rosa .... Signora M. Cappelli
—Shaftesbury.

4.‡*The Beloved Vagabond*, play, in three acts, by William J. Locke (adapted from his own novel of the same name). Originally produced at the Royal, Dublin, October 10, 1907. Last performance, April 4; 62 performances.

Gaston de Nérac (Paragot) ...... Mr. Tree
Asticot .... Mr. Leon M. Lion
Lord Rushworth ...... Mr. W. T. Lovell
Comte de Verneuil.Mr. Chas. Quartermaine
M. Dubois .... Mr. Robert Atkins
President of Villon Club...Mr. D. Calthrop
The Curé .... Mr. William Haviland
Cazalet .... Mr. Harry C. Hewitt
Bonnet .... Mr. Cyril Sworder
Père Ciboulet .... Mr. G. W. Anson
Joanna Rushworth .. Miss Evelyn Millard
Blanquette de Veau .. Miss Hutin Britton
Louisette .... Miss Hetty Kenyon
Lady Rushworth..Miss Augusta Haviland
Madame Leblanc .. Miss Cicely Richards
—His Majesty's.

5. *An Historical Incident*, play, in one act.

Princess Celia Morodas of Koth
Miss Aimée Fowler
King Andrew Folgar of Ouland
Mr. Ashton Pearse
—92, Victoria Street, S.W.

5. *An Alien Star*, play, in one act, by Bertha N. Graham.

Rose d'Etoile .... Miss Elinor Foster
Grace Daly .... Miss Aimée Fowler
Susan ...... Miss Margery Merryweather
Dr. Antony Harwars..Mr. Herbert Burston
—92, Victoria Street, S.W.

6.*Rip Van Winkle*, Dion Boucicault's play, in four acts. (Miss Ine Cameron's season.)

Derrick van Beekman..Mr. W. Raynham
Cockles .... Mr. Montague Wigan
Nick Vedder .... Mr. Gordon Philott
Hendrick Vedder ...... Mr. Philip Tonge
The same (20 years after).....C. E. King
Rip Van Winkle ...... Mr. Fred Storey
Gretchen .... Miss Beatrice Whitney
Meenie .... Miss Nora Thorne
The same (20 years after) .. Mary Lovett
Hendrick Hudson..Mr. Manning Sproston
Nips .... Mr. Jackman
Seth .... Mr. John T. MacCullum
Jacob Steyne .... Mr. Arthur Tinay
Katchen .... Miss Gwladys Faunce
—Royalty.

7. *Cavalleria Rusticana*. The original play. Performed by the Sicilian Players.—Shaftesbury.

7. *La Zolfara*, the first two acts of a Sicilian drama, in three acts, by Giusti Senopole

Vanni .... Cav. Uff. Giovanni Grasso
Japicu .... Signor S. Lo Turco
Fra Filidi .... Signor N. Viscuso
Innaru .... Signor V. Galloni
Crioli .... Signor G. Trovato
Brasi .... Signor F. Capelli
Ntoni .... Signor P. Sapuppo
Peppino .... Signor M. Anselmi
Cola .... Signor D. Balistrieri
Bovodantona ...... Signor G. Calabresi
D. Amilcare Pesacome..Signor V. Galloni
Ingegnere .... Signor A. Girardi
Mara .... Signora Mimi Aguglia
Gna Brigida ...... Signora M. Balistrieri

La Zolfara (continued).
Tudda .... Signora G. Balistrieri
Rosa .... Signora S. Aguglia
Carmela .... Signora R. Viscuso
Santa .... Signora D. Galloni
Maruzza .... Signora V. Balistrieri
Peppina .... Signor M. Capelli
—Shaftesbury.

8. *The Woman of Kronstadt*, play, in three
acts, by Max Pemberton and George
F'eming, being an adaptation of the
former's novel "Kronstadt." The final
performance of the piece took place on
February 29; 25 performances.
Prince Nicolai Stefanoff..Mr. O. B. Clarence
Colonel Bonzo .... Mr. G. S. Titheradge
Capt. Paul Zassoulic..Mr. Charles Bryant
Baron Conrad Muller..Mr. Stratton Rodney
Lieut. Count Talvi..Mr. Leon Quartermaine
Sergeant Seroff .... Mr. Henry Le Grand
Ivan .... Mr. William Burchill
General's Orderly .. Mr. Stafford Hilliard
H. B. Bassett-Holmer .... Mr. B. Forsyth
Clifford Dawkes .... Mr. Douglas Imbert
Marian Best .... Mrs. Russ Whytal
Princess Mary de Hess..Miss Edyth Latimer
Vera .... Miss Marjorie Day
Olga .... Miss Winifred Bateman
Mdme. de Bellegarde..Miss Ethel Matthews
Mdme. de Repnine..Miss Beatrice Lamotte
—Garrick.

8. *Britain's Awakening*, drama, in one act,
by Norman Wrighton.
Lieut. Roberts .. Mr. Norman Wrighton
Scuttler Lee .... Mr. Richard Norton
Orressa Nicolini ..... Mr. Ernest Griffin
Maysell Lee .... Miss Berenice Wrighton
—West London.

9. *The Marquis*, sentimental farce, in three
acts, by Cecil Raleigh and Sidney Dark;
produced by the Play Actors.
Mrs. Rosevere ..... Miss Marie Linden
Miss Levick .... Miss Lillan Tweed
Mrs. Sandes ..... Miss Frances Wetherall
Miss Janet Morice...Miss Sybil Thorndike
Mary .... Miss Vita Spencer
Colonel Hinton Morice..Mr. C. F. Collings
Major Frobisher....Mr. Fewlass Llewellyn
Mr. John M. Golding..Mr. Leonard Calvert
Hon. Reginald Clifton .... Farren Soutar
Mr. Jenkins .... Mr. Walter Hubert
—Scala.

10. *La Figlia di Jorio*, pastoral tragedy, in
three acts, by Gabriele D'Annunzio.
Aligio .... Cav. Uff. Giovanni Grasso
Lazzaro .... Signor S. Lo Turco
Femo di Nerfa .. Signor A. Campagna
Jonia de Midia .... Signor A. Campagna
Le Chercheur de Tresors..Signor V. Galloni
Le Possédé .... Signor G. Campagna
Le Saint de la Montagne Signor F. Capello
Premier Moissonneur Signor D. Quartarone
Deuxième Moissonneur..Signor D. Aguglia
Troisième Moissonneur..Signor G. Aguglia
Quatrième Moissonneur Signor P. Sapuppo
Mila di Codra .... Signora Mimi Aguglia
Candia della Leonessa Signora M. Balistrieri
Splendore .... Signora S. Aguglia
Favetta .... Signora R. Viscuso
Ornella .... Signora C. Balistrieri
Maria di Giave ...... Signora F. Galloni
Vienda .... Signora D. Galloni
Teodula di Cinzio .. Signora R. Marano
La Cinerela .... Signora I. Galloni
Monica de la Cogna Signora V. Balistrieri
Anna di Bova .... Signora S. Algozzino
Felavia Sesara .... Signora M. Calabresi
La Catalane ...... Signora G. Cappelli
Maria Cora ...... Signora G. Sapuppo
Jenna dell'Elfa .... Signora G. Calabresi
La Vieille aux Herbes Signora G. Bragaglio
—Shaftesbury.

10.*†*Rosmersholm*, Ibsen's play, originally pro-
duced at Bergen in 1887, English transla-
tion first played at the Vaudeville, Feb-
ruary 23, 1891.
Johannes Rosmer .... Mr. Eille Norwood
Rector Kroll ...... Mr. Charles Fulton
Ulric Brendal .... Mr. H. R. Hignett
Mortensgore ...... Mr. Edmund Gwenn
Madame Helseth .... Miss Kate Bishop
Rebecca West ...... Miss Florence Kahn
—Terry's.

10. *Lore's Golden Dream*, play, in four acts,
by Frances Delaval.
Harold Tre-Wynne..Mr. Arthur Chisholm
Mrs. Tre-Wynne .... Mrs. Edmund Lyons
Capt. Darrel .. Mr. Wilfred P. Mansfield
Lieut. Tyrone .... Mr. Larry Stokes
Sergt. Muldoon ...... Mr. Charles Ninian
Charity Muldoon ...... Miss Zetta Disney
Gustave de Marconi..Mr. Charles Cameron
Vashti de Marconi .. Miss Alwynne Ermon
Black Mammy .... Miss Minnie Metcalf
Pete .... Master Johnnie Johnson
Mrs. Van-Gruff ...... Miss Adela Herbert
P.C. Penryn .... Mr. Fred Nesbitt
Covey .... Mr. Leslie York
Tommy Tittlemouse ..Tiny Carry Johnson
Margery .... Miss Frances Delaval
—Royal, Stratford.

10.*The Merchant of Venice*, Shakespeare's
comedy. (Miss Ine Cameron's season.)
Shylock .... Mr. Fred Storey
Duke of Venice .. Mr. Rathmell Wilson
Prince of Morocco .... Mr. Clive Currie
Antonio .... Mr. John T. MacCallum
Bassanio .... Mr. Paul Lovett
Salanio .... Mr. Manning Sproston
Salarino .... Mr. Arthur Leney
Gratiano .... Mr. Chas. E. King
Lorenzo .... Mr. William Ross
Tubal .... Mr. Walter Raynham
Launcelot Gobbo .. Mr. Montague Wigan
Old Gobbo .... Mr. Gordon Phillott
Leonardo .... Mr. Allington
Balthazar .... Miss I. Garnet-Vayne
Stephano .... Miss Gwladys Faunce
Nerissa .... Miss Mary Lovett
Jessica .... Miss Beatrice Whitney
Portia .... Miss Ine Cameron
—Royalty.

12. *Juan Jose*, Spanish drama, in four acts, by
Joaquin Dicenta.
Vanni .... Cav. Uff. Giovanni Grasso
Angelo .... N. Viscuso
Bettoliere .... F. Cappelli
Detenuto .... P. Sapuppo
Don Vincenzino .... S. Lo Turco
Carceriere .... V. Galloni
Rosa .... Mimi Aguglia Ferrau
Gna Pidda .... M. Balistrieri
Antoinette .... R. Girardi
—Shaftesbury.

12. *Diana of Dobson's*, comedy-drama, in four
acts, by Cicely Hamilton. Last performance,
June 20; 141 performances.
Miss Smithers ...... Miss Nannie Bennett
Miss Kitty Brant .. Miss Christine Silver
Miss Jay .... Miss Muriel Vox
Miss Diana Massingberd.Miss Lena Ashwell
Miss Morton .... Miss Doris Lytton
Miss Pringle .... Miss Ada Palmer
Mrs. Cantelupe .... Miss Frances Ivor
Walter .... Mr. W. Lemmon Warde
Mrs. Whyte Fraser .. Miss Gertrude Scott
Sir Jabez Grinlay, Bart..Mr. Dennis Eadie
Hon. Victor Bretherton.Mr. C. M. Hallard
Old Woman .... Miss Beryl Mercer
P.C. Fellowes .... Mr. Norman McKinnel
—Kingsway.

13. *Morte Civile* (*La Morte Legale*), drama, in five acts, by P. Giacometti. Adaptation in English by C. F. Coghlan, under the title of *A New Trial*, produced at the Prince of Wales's, December 18, 1880.

Corrado	Cav. Uff. Giovanni Grasso
L'Abbé Ruvo	Signor A. Viscuso
Le Docteur Palmieri	S. Lo Turco
Don Fernando	Signor D. Galloni
Gaetano	Signor P. Sapuppo
Rosalia	Signora Mimi Aguglia
Ada	Signorina V. Balistrieri
Agala	Signora M. Balistrieri

—Shaftesbury.

13. **Romeo and Juliet, Shakespeare's tragedy. (Miss Ine Cameron's season.)

Romeo	Mr. Paul Lovett
Mercutio	Mr. B. A. Pittar
Esculas	Mr. Rathmell Wilson
Capulet	Mr. Clive Currie
Montague	Mr. Geo. Lewis
Tybalt	Mr. Chas. King
Paris	Mr. Manning Sproston
Benvolio	Mr. Gordon Phillott
Friar Laurence	Mr. Walter Raynham
Friar John	Mr. Arthur Linay
Peter and Apothecary	Mr. Montague Wigan
Samson	Mr. Sidney
Gregory	Mr. Wilton Ross
Abraham	Mr. Harold Whatoff
Balthazar	Miss Isla Garnet-Vayne
Page to Paris	Miss Nora Thornton
Lady Montagu	Miss Gwladys Faunce
Lady Capulet	Miss Beatrice Whitney
Nurse	Miss Mary Lovett
Juliet	Miss Ine Cameron

—Royalty.

16. *The Man Who Missed the Tide*, play, by W. F. Casey—Abbey, Dublin.

13. *The Piper*, play, in one act, by F. Noreys Connell—Abbey, Dublin.

14.||*Skittles*, comedy, in three acts, by Paul Rubens and Lechmere Worrall.

William Wiggleshaw	Mr. Henry Bellairs
Lord Roftus (" Vivi ")	Mr. Chas. Whittuck
Captain Pellison	Mr. Derwent Moger
Laurie Cateley	Mr. Lechmere Worrall
Tom Whiteley	Mr. K. N. J. Alves
Adam Beazley	Mr. F. Whittuck
Mrs. Toffin	Miss Constance Adair
Hon. Margaret Atherton	Miss Bay Nicholson
" Skittles "	Miss Hilda Coningham

—Assembly Rooms, Bath.

15. *The Late Ralph Johnson*, comedy, in three acts, adapted from *Le Testament de César Girodot* (a stock piece at the Comédie Française), by Adolphe Bélot.

Joseph Johnson	Mr. T. P. Haynes
Arthur	Mr. Vincent Clive
George Preston	Mr. C. F. Collings
Grantley	Mr. Watty Brunton
Bruton	Mr. Richard Cowell
Frederick Johnson	Mr. Terry Hurst
Mr. Williams	Mr. Henry Pettit
Julia	Miss Alice Hatton
Jemima	Miss Dorothy Marsdin
Amy	Miss Lavinia Kingston

—Scala.

17. **Much Ado About Nothing*, Mr. F. R. Benson's revival. Opening of his season at the Coronet.

Don Pedro	Mr. Murray Carrington
Don John	Mr. Arthur Phillips
Claudio	Mr. George Buchanan
Benedick	Mr. F. R. Benson
Leonato	Mr. Edward Warburton
Antonio	Mr. J. Plumton Wilson
Borachio	Mr. F. G. Hannam Clark

Much Ado About Nothing (*continued*).

Conrad	Mr. Stanley Howlett
Friar Francis	Mr. Arthur Whitby
A Sexton	Mr. J. Moffat Johnston
Dogberry	Mr. George R. Weir
Verges	Mr. H. O. Nicholson
Seacole	Mr. F. G. Worlock
Hero	Miss Olive Noble
Beatrice	Mrs. F. R. Benson
Ursula	Miss Bright Morris
Margaret	Miss Mary Webb
Boy	Miss Lear Hanman
Balthazar	Miss Cissie Saumarez

—Coronet.

17.‡*The Idol of Paris*, drama, in four acts, by Charles Darrell. Originally produced at the O.H., Middlesbrough, August 12, 1907.

Flare-Flare	Miss Annie Bell
Prince Zoreski	Mr. Gordon Robey
Philippe D'Esterre	Mr. J. Boyd Pearson
Gustave Langlois	Mr. Pringle Roberts
Theo. Decline	Mr. Chris Roberts
Guillame	Mr. Harry Jesson
Victor Cashelle	Mr. George Denham
Tarave	Mr. Ellis Carlyle
Bracqueth	Mr. Gerald Travers
Olympe Sosage	Miss Grace Noble
Mdme. Sancterre	Miss Esther Carthew
Ann	Miss Annie Megson

—Dalston.

17.¶*Don Quixote*, play, in four acts, by Justin Huntly McCarthy—Royal, Margate.

17. **Jocelyn the Jester*, comedy, in one act, by Ronald Macdonald. Originally produced Crystal Palace, March 4, 1907.

Jocelyn Savage	Mr. H. A. Saintsbury
Sir Giles Wedderburn	C. H. Croker-King
Percival Kingston, Esq.	C. W. Standing
Chirrup	Mr. Leonard Calvert
Martha Wimpling	Miss Violet Vivian
Lucinda	Miss Dorothea Desmond

—Grand, Croydon.

18. *Rusidda*, drama, in one act, by V. Feiani.

Cieciu	Cav. Uff. G. Grasso
Cosimo	Signor P. Sapuppo
Mastro Cieciu	Signor F. Cappelli
Gna Filomena	Signora M. Balistrieri
Rusidda	Signora C. Balistrieri
Carulina	Signora V. Balistrieri
Un Bambino	Signora C. Balistrieri

—Shaftesbury.

18. *La Lupa* (*The She-Wolf*), drama, in two acts, by G. Verga.

Gna Pina	Signora M. Aguglia-Ferrau
Mara	Signor C. Balistrieri
La Zia Filomena	Signora M. Balistrieri
Grazia	Signora R. Viscuso
Lia	Signora D. Galloni
Nanni Lasca	Cav. Uff. G. Grasso
Bruno	Signor S. Arcidiacono
Cardillo	Signor D. Quartarone
Neli	Signor G. Trovato
Campari Jann	Signor F. Cappelli
Malerba	Signor P. Sapuppo
Nunzio	Signor G. Aguglia

—Shaftesbury.

18.||*Enemies*, Georgian play, in three acts, by John Johnson and Wagney Major.

Ben Bellamy	Mr. E. Brooks
Jack Crawford	Mr. W. Burgess
Sergeant Grindle	Mr. C. Secker
Master Gregory	Mr. F. Howell
Mathew Hobbs	Mr. G. Killick
Natty Miles	Mr. G. Ingrams
Barber Brooke	Mr. H. Hitchcock
Jerry Betts	Mr. W. Pettitt
Joe Bellamy	Mr. G. Ford
First Officer	Mr. H. Neale
Second Officer	Mr. W. May

—Institute, Hildenborough.

19.‖*The Pride of Takahara*, musical comedy, in two acts, by Geo. H. Thompson.
Hon. Grahame Buxton .. C. H. Thompson
Sir Percival Paget .... Mr. R. C. Christie
Archie Paget .... Mr. E. L. Sawyer
Algernon Fitzpopp .. Mr. Brindley Hicks
Godalgo .... Mr. Bert Parish
Ito .... Mr. Fred Carpenter
Tāgo .... Mr. C. Young
Constance Buxton .... Miss Ida Hicks
Beatrice Harringay ...... Miss Freda Tidy
Violet Carlton .. Miss Polly Fairweather
Gladys Verron .... Miss I. Ashmole
Kiku .... Miss Elsie Weller
Sakura .... Miss Ali Moors
Yuki .... Miss May Moors
Haru .... Miss May Peckham
Fuzi .... Miss Florrie Tyler
Irene Clarendon ..... Miss Louie Booker
—Terminus Hall, Littlehampton.

20.‡*Matt of Merrymount*, romantic play in four acts, by B. M. Dix and E. G. Sutherland. Originally produced at the Royal, Newcastle, October 11, 1906. Last performance at the New, April 11; 72 performances.
Matt Compton .... Mr. Fred Terry
George Armitage ...... Mr. A. E. Anson
Gamaliel Frothingham..J. Carter-Edwards
Roger Frothingham..Mr. Alfred Kendrick
Chad .... Mr. C. R. Gibbon
Long Wat .... Mr. Walter Edwin
Firebrace .... Mr. Harvey Braban
Galliard .... Mr. D. J. Williams
Constable Sedgwick....Mr. Fredk. Groves
Bezaleel Peck ....Mr. Jerrold Robertshaw
Lord Buriton ...... Mr. Harry F. Wright
The Earl of Iping .... Mr. George Dudley
Experience Cooper..Miss Claire Pauncefort
Desire Sedgwick .... Miss Kathleen Doyle
Red Jill .... Miss Miriam Lewes
Diantha Frothingham..Miss Alice Crawford
Merrymounters, Edgemouthmen, Serving Maids—Misses Montague, Jennings, Grahame, Manning, Thomas, Vansittart, Freeland, Russell, Innes, and Messrs. Tosh, Powell, Pickering, Schonberg, Elvey, Henry, Robinson, Cooke, Bellew, Stock.
—New.

20.†*Pater Noster*, play, in one act, adapted from the French of François Coppée.
Father Pierre .... Mr. James Hearn
An Officer .... Mr. Douglas Gordon
James Leroux .... Mr. Vincent Sternroyd
Zelie .... Miss Mary Brough
Rose Morel .... Mrs. Cecil Raleigh
—St. James's.

21.‖*The Chosen One*, play, in one act, by Neilson Morris—Albert Hall.

22. *The Whirlpool*, play, in three acts, by Herbert Swears, founded on a short story by Cyrus Townsend Brady. London production, September 21, Marlborough.
Elijah D. Tillottson .... Mr. Kendal
Bertram Livingstone .. Mr. Bassett Roe
Cunningham Cutter..Mr. Wellesley Draper
Hon. Reginald Killiegrew...Mr. T. Holding
Ephraim Johnstone..Mr. Edmund Gurney
Chappin .... Mr. Metcalfe Wood
Parker .... Mr. W. M. Rutherfurd
Gretchen de Kaater..Mrs. A. B. Tapping
Gertrude Van Stuyler....Miss Ethel Dare
Miss Constance Livingstone....Mrs. Kendal
—New, Cardiff.

22.*Fido*, adaptation, in three acts, by Eva Anstruther of *Médor* of M. Malin. Originally produced at the Playhouse at a *matinée* November 26, 1907.—Playhouse. Last performance March 14.

22.*The Golden Wedding*, play, in one act, by Eden Phillpotts and Charles Groves. Originally produced at the Haymarket, June 23, 1898.—Playhouse.

23. *Into the Light*, romantic comedy, in four acts, by Gerald Lawrence. London production, November 30, Court.
Felix Gottlieb .... Mr. Gerald Lawrence
Simon Langley .... Mr. George Mallet
Frederick Ramsden .. Mr. Frank Powell
Peter .... Mr. Walter Cross
Ernest Camp .... Mr. Ernest Cox
Archie Goring ...... Mr. Duncan Yarrow
Dr. Ferris .... Mr. J. Crawford
Lauterback .... Mr. Walter Westwood
Marceau .... Mr. Bernard Ansell
Margaret Ramsden .. Miss Helen Russell
Amy Ramsden .... Miss Joan Ritz
Alice Harley ...... Miss Lillie Leicester
Mary .... Miss Amy Singleton
—Royal, Bradford.

24. *Sexton Blake (Detective)*, drama, in four acts (Stageright performance, King's, W., January 18).
Sexton Blake .. Mr. J. Cooke Beresford
Farmer Blackburn ..Mr. Leonard Calvert
Roger Blackburn .... Mr. William Felton
Squire Lovell .... Mr. H. J. C. Crane
Randolph Lovell .... Mr. E. Maule Cole
Tinker .... Mr. Jack Denton
Simon Faggus .... Mr. W. P. Sheen
Rev. Edward Grey..Mr. Stephen Nicholls
Inspector Widgeon...Mr. H. Ravenscroft
Herbert Clifton .... Mr. Eric Ward
William Smith .... Mr. Edward Boddy
" Major " Tucker ...... Mr. Robert King
Silas Grigg .... Mr. John Leslie
Pedro .... By Himself
Mrs. Blackburn....Miss Ruth Woodhouse
Mrs. Clifton ...... Miss Estelle Despa
Sally Brill .... Mrs. Edwin Palmer
A Homeless Woman..Miss Alice Jameson
Euphemia Pattacake..Miss Agnes Paulton
Philadelphia Kate..Miss Winifred Pearson
Marjorie Lovell....Miss Kathleen Russell
—Crown.

24.‡*A Girl Redeemed from Sin*, drama, in a prologue and four acts, by David Muskerry. Originally produced at Royal, South Shields, on July 15, 1907—Royal, Stratford.

25. *An Episode*, play, in one act, by Marion Roberton.
Nance .... Miss Annie Walden
Kitty .... Miss Dorothy Giles
Nana .... Miss Julie Huntsman
—Guildhall School.

25.‖*A Pageant of Lloyds*, historical, fantastical, and more or less imaginary play, by W. H. Leslie—Savoy Hotel.

26.‖*Metopemania; or, A Sparing Use of Art*, " new musical and dramatic prophecy," performed, under the auspices of the Architectural Association, in the Georgian Hall of the Gaiety Restaurant, the music composed by Claude Kelly.

26.* ‖*A Midsummer Night's Dream* (the O.U.D.S. revival).
FAIRIES.
Oberon .... Mr. G. L. Colmer
Titania .... Miss Janet Alexander
Puck .... Mr. E. Hain
First Fairy .... Miss E. Lomax
Second Fairy ...... Miss Chalker-Pearse
MORTALS.
Theseus .... Mr. J. H. M. Greenly
Egeus .... Hon. G. Charteris
Lysander .... Mr. T. W. Heale
Demetrius .... Mr. C. W. Mercer
Philostrate .... Mr. P. P. Page
Quince...................Mr. J. C. Ledward

A Midsummer Night's Dream (continued).

Bottom .... Mr. H. L. Fletcher
Flute .... Mr. H. G. Farmer
Snout .... Mr. M. E. Hansell
Snug .... Mr. C. Howard-Smith
Starveling ...... Mr. J. N. Oliphant
Hippolyta .... Miss Margaret Ledward
Hermia .... Miss Elsie Goulding
Helena .... Miss Pamela Gaythorne
—New, Oxford.

26.║*Only a Quaker Maid*, play, in one act, dramatised by Fewlass Llewellyn from the late Sir Walter Besant's novel, "A Fountain Sealed." The piece was originally read for stageright purposes at the Grand Fulham, July 19, 1898.
Sir George Le Breton....Mr. F. Llewellyn
Edward .... Mr. W. Adamson
Joseph .... Mr. Ernest Martin
Nancy .... Miss Alice Sharrah
Isabel .... Miss Rees
Molly .... Mrs. Llewellyn
—Assembly Rooms, Putney.

26.;*The Other Side*, play, in three acts, by Clo. Graves. (Originally produced at the Prince's, Manchester, October 25, 1907.
Anthony Redwood, LL.B. .. Mr. Kendal Batch .... Mr. Ernest Hendrie
Sir Wyke Marrabie .... Mr. Bassett Roe
James Whitgift .. Mr. W. M. Rutherfurd
Joshua Snelley .... Mr. F. Charles Pool
Dr. Walson .... Mr. R. Burnett
Bitmead .... Mr. A. N. Phipps
George Comfort .. Mr. Metcalfe Wood
Miss Myrenda Tovey Mrs. A. B. Tapping
Miss Flabella Tovey .. Miss Adah Barton
Anaemia Tubb .... Miss Jessica Thorne
Sister Marie Antoine Miss Sara de Groot
Joy Marrabie .. Miss Gwendolen Wren
Mrs. Stannas ⎱ .... Mrs. Kerda
Lady Marrabie ⎰
—Grand, Croydon.

26. *The Lord of Latimer Street*, play, in four acts, by Oliver Madox Hueffer. Last performance, March 7; 13 performances.
The Earl Latimer .... Mr. H. Nye Chart
The Rev. W. Whittaker..Mr. Geo. Barran
John Reeves .... Mr. Robert Pateman
Alf. Jenkins .... Mr. Edmund Gwenn
Jervis .... Mr. Gerald Ames
The Countess Latimer .. Miss Kate Bishop
The Hon. Mrs. Graeme .. Miss E. Ingram
Cynthia Graeme .... Miss Hilda Dick
Mrs. Reeves .... Miss Elsie Chester
Miss Whittaker..Miss Gladys Bartle-Frere
Miss Boulton .... Miss I. Innes-Ker
Miss Hallswell .. Miss Florence Harwood
Liza Williams .... Miss Katie Johnson
Tilda Reeves ...... Miss Nina Boucicault
—Terry's.

27.║*That Foreigner*. "Tariff Reform play," by Mr. Alan H. Burgoyne—Bijou, Bayswater.

27. *Lady Barbarity*, version, in four acts, by R. C. Carton, of J. C. Snaith's novel of that name. Last performance, April 11. 47 performances.
Earl of Longacre ...... Mr. J. H. Barnes
Captain Grantly .. Mr. Allan Aynesworth
Anthony Dare ...... Mr. Graham Browne
Rev. Mr. Daubery .. Mr. Asheton Tonge
Corporal Flickers ...... Mr. Charles Weir
Snack .... Mr. W. H. Day
Linworth .... Mr. Horton Cooper
Lady Barbara Goessiter .. Marie Tempest
Lady Grimstone ...... Miss Lena Halliday
Polly Emblem .... Miss Dora Barton
—Comedy.

27.†*The Money-Grabber*, Society satire, in three acts, by Hester Stanhope.
Joshua Semeline .... Mr. Ernest Howe
Haidee ....,......... ..Miss Kate Osborne
Johanna .... Lady Clarke-Jervoise
Rebecca .... Miss Cora Lanner
Moses Solomons .... Mr. Robert Castleton
Chamberlaine .... Miss Katherine Talbot
Barthorpe Barnes .... Major H. K. Oram
Stella Steele .... Miss Sylvia Parkyns
Lady Letitia Steele .... Miss Lucia Breen
Dowager Lady Plantagenet Tudor
Miss Clarke-Jervoise
Arthur Plantagenet Tudor..Mr. J. Gelderd
Sir Victor Plantagenet Tudor
Mr. Charles E. C. Thornton
Clara .... Miss Beatrice Ward
Belinda .... Miss Una Dugdale
Vicars .... Mr. Adnam Sprange
—Kingsway.

27. *The Telegram*, Tabloid Company, by Sidney Hamilton.
Capt. Jack Marsfield..Mr. Sidney Hamilton
Peggy Trevors ...... Miss Violet Coombs
—Brinsmead Galleries.

28. *Pride of Regiment*, play, in one act, by F. D. Bone.
Father .... Mr. Charles Rock
Mother .... Miss Cicely Richards
Son .... Mr. Ashton Pearse
—Haymarket.

28. *Feudalismo* Catalonian drama, in three acts, adapted into Italian from the Spanish play, *Tierra Baja*, by Don Angelo Guimera.
Vanni, Pastore..Cav. Uff. Giovanni Grasso
Carlo .... S. Lo Turco
Fra Gaetano .... F. Cappelli
Beppe .... N. Viscuso
Coda .... G. Calabresi
Pudda .... F. Vecchietti
D. Liborio .... O. Quartarone
Turi .... P. Sapuppo
Rocco .... G. Trovato
Un Campieri .... V. Galloni
Ntonia .... R. Girardi
Maria ... . M. Balistrieri
Mica .... T. Aguglia
Filomena .... N. Viscuso
Un Pastore .... V. Balistrieri
Primo Campiere .... E. Bragaglia
Secondo Campiere .... E. Gardenghi
Terzo Campiere .... E. De Pian
Rosa .... Mimi Aguglia Ferrau
—Shaftesbury.

28. *Henry of Lancaster*, romantic drama, by Gladys Unger. London production, April 27, Borough, Stratford.
Henry of Lancaster ... Mr. James Carew
Richard III. .... Mr. Frank Fenton
Sir Pier Gowles .... Mr. Story-Gofton
The Earl of Warwick .. Mr. David Powell
Sir Humphrey Gavin .... Mr. John Hood
Sir Robert Willoughby.Mr. Chas. F. Cooke
Patch .... Mr. Max Montesole
Jasper .... Mr. Frank Powell
Jake .... Mr. Edwin Cushman
Conway .... Mr. Charles Daly
Martin .... Mr. David Hallam
Derick .... Mr. Arthur de Breanski
Thomas .... Mr. Herbert Lomas
A Gipsy Man .... Mr. Chas. French
Two Apprentices,
Mr. Syd. Travers, Mr. Guy Addison
Elizabeth of York ...... Miss Ellen Terry
Iseult of Auvergne....Miss Alison Skinner
Marianne .... Miss Eleanor Hicks
Kate Lee .... Miss Portia Knight
A Gipsy Woman....Miss Lindsay Fincham
Dame Merry .... Mrs. W. Crowe
—Royal, Nottingham.

29.‖*The Lost Dewdrops*, comic opera, in two acts, book by Rev. H. D. Hinde, music by Misses F. Wykes and E. McLean.

FAIRIES.

Queen Asphodel	Miss M. Heyes
Prince Florizel	Miss C. Heyes
Princess Blue Bell	Miss C. Sagrott
Fairy Meadowsweet	Miss D. Taylor
Fairy Speedwell	Miss D. Cole
Fairy Pimpernel	Miss P. Henshall
Bilberry	Miss B. Gales
Will o' the Wisp	Miss Ivy Cunnington
The Spider	Mr. Alan Weight
Fairy Nightshade	Miss F. Fischer

MORTALS.

Sylvie	Miss Kitty Corben
Adolphus	Mr. H. Luetchford
Mademoiselle Stephanie	Miss P. Stooks

FAIRIES OF THE FLOWERS.

Fairy Wildrose	Miss R. Stooks
Fairy Buttercup	Miss L. Cornish
Fairy Pansy	Miss H. Bartholomew
Fairy Daffodil	Miss M. Jackson
Fairy Forget-me-not	Miss N. Jones
Fairy Holly	Miss B. Addison
Fairy Violet	Miss M. Catling
Fairy Poppy	Miss W. Herring
Fairy Honeysuckle	Miss D. Read

—Edmonton Town Hall.

MARCH.

1. *The Gates of the Morning*, play, in three acts, by Margaret M. Mack, produced by Mr. Norman Page (produced by the Stage Society).

Samuel Wilson	Mr. Norman Page
Mill Robyn	Miss Sydney Fairbrother
Alice Wilson	Miss Amy Lamborn
Nancy Larne	Miss Vera Coburn
Henry Mardale	Mr. Athol Stewart
Mrs. Larne	Miss Alice Mansfield
Cook	Miss Lola Duncan

—Shaftesbury.

1. *The Philosopher's Stone*, fantasy-drama, in four acts, by Isaac York, produced by William Burchill (produced by the Play Actors).

David Vaughan	Mr. Laurence Leyton
Blaise Moretti	Mr. Harvey Braban
Osca Elisson	Mr. Lawson Butt
The Hermit	Mr. Frederick Annerley
Ernest	Mr. Spencer Geach
Mimi	Miss Inez Bensusan
Lady Diana	Miss Dorothy Green
Portia Graeme	Miss Marguerite Cellier
Augustine	Miss Joan Pereira

Guests at Moretti's Soiré: Messrs. Topham, Llewellyn, C. F. Collings, Heathcote, Applin, Currie, Bunston, Misses Wetherall, Mayo, Hamilton.

—Royalty.

2.‡*Don Quixote*, play, in four acts, constructed by G. E. Morrison and R. P. Stewart, and written by G. E. Morrison. (Originally produced at Stratford-on-Avon, May 3, 1907.)

The Duke	Mr. Murray Carrington
Don Miguel	Mr. F. G. Worlock
Ecclesiastic	Mr. Guy
Physician	Mr. G. F. H. Clark
Student	Mr. Caine
Steward	Mr. S. Howlett
Courier	Mr. G. Rathbone
Page	Miss N. Robertson
First Servant	Mr. R. McLeod
Second Servant	Mr. Hardy

Don Quixote (continued).

Laundry Maid	Miss Bretherton
Senor Quixano	Mr. F. R. Benson
Sancho Panza	Mr. George R. Weir
Nicolas	Mr. George Buchanan
The Priest	Mr. J. P. Wilson
Pelamque	Mr. E. A. Warburton
Barnabas	Mr. Clark
Samson	Mr. W. R. Haines
Lopez	Mr. M. Johnston
Gomerz	Mr. J. P. Wilson
Juan	Mr. Howlett
Hedrillo	Mr. Haines
First Girl	Miss de Llana
Second Girl	Miss Bright Morris
Puppet Showman	Mr. Johnston
Warder of Convicts	Mr. Wilson
Silk Merchant	Mr. McLeod
Monk	Mr. Caine
Officer of Holy Brotherhood	Mr. Plinge
Fat Man	Mr. Haines
Thin Man	Mr. Owen
Duchess	Miss Cissie Saumarez
Lola	Miss Nash
Roderiquez	Miss Hadwen
Altisidora	Miss Bright Morris
Maraquita	Miss Leah Eanman
Housekeeper	Miss Elinor Aickin
Antonia	Miss Helen Haye

—Coronet.

2.*The Admirable Crichton*, fantasy, in four acts, by J. M. Barrie. (Originally produced at the Duke of York's, November 4, 1902.) Last performance, June 13.

The Earl of Loam	Mr. Eric Lewis
Hon. Ernest Woolley	Mr. G. du Maurier
Rev. John Treherne	Mr. Charles Maude
Lord Brocklehurst	Mr. Carter Pickford
A Naval Officer	Mr. Donald Calthrop
Mr. Crichton	Mr. Lyn Harding
Tompsett	Mr. Compton Coutts
Lady Mary Lasenby	Miss M. Clements
Lady Catherine Lasenby	Miss S. Carlisle
Lady Agatha Lasenby	Miss M. Beaumont
Countess of Brocklehurst	Mrs. E. Saker
Fisher	Miss Margaret Fraser
Tweeny	Miss Hilda Trevelyan

—Duke of York's.

2. *The Romantic Barber*, play, in one act, by Alfred Sutro. London production, March 23, Grand, Fulham.

Jim	Mr. Michael Sherbrooke
Frank Stanley	Mr. Perceval Clarke
Maggie	Miss Alice Arden

—Royal, Dublin.

2.†*Off the Cornish Coast*, play, in one act, by Estelle Burney.

Thomas	Mr. Jules Shaw
Ann	Miss Leah Bateman-Hunter
Ann's Mother	Miss Gladys Jones
A Young Sailor	Mr. Reginald Owen

—Kingsway.

2. *A Desperate Marriage*, drama, by Rosemary Rees. London production, Lyric, Hammersmith, March 16.

Dick Strang	Mr. W. G. Court
Clarence Woolmer	Mr. Riddell Robinson
Dr. Frank Baxter	Mr. Arthur Curzon
Tom Stripe	Mr. Herbert Lloyd
Elijah Boggs	Mr. Frank Coston
Chaplain	Mr. John Walker
Potato Man	Mr. P. V. Booth
Bank Manager	Mr. A. J. Nicholls
Waiter	Mr. A. Desper
Boy	Master Fred Rate
Audrey Howard	Miss Cissie Bellamy
Betty Mackenzie	Miss Lily Annesley
Bertha Onions	Miss May Davies
Miriam Elton	Miss Dorothy Cacey

—Grand, Brighton.

2.‡*A Clever Impostor*, drama, by Emma Litch-
field. (Originally produced at the Royal,
Macclesfield, December 14, 1907.)
Manuel Teixeira .... Mr. Stuart Cleveland
Captain Desmond ...... Mr. Gerald Byrne
Jim Brightside ...... Mr. Harry Liddle
Harris .... Mr. A. Lightfoot
Bob Darnforth .... Mr. Frank Brunell
Matakan .... Mr. William Waring
Sir George Ashwell .... Mr. A. C. Britton
Sergeant Dixon .... Mr. Thomas Fielding
Mexican Sergeant .... Mr. D. Tecke
Stephen Grosvenor .... Mr. Maurice Jones
Maisie Grosvenor ...... Miss Edna Earle
Margaret Grosvenor..Miss Frances Bruce
Annie Pleasant ...... Miss Florence Gomer
Nora Grosvenor ⎫
Sarah Allen   ⎬ Miss Emma Litchfield
Old Rebecca   ⎪
Molly O'Flynn   ⎭
                    —Royal, Stratford.

2. *The Mystery of Edwin Drood*, drama, in
four acts, by C. A. Clarke and S. B.
Rogerson, founded on Charles Dickens's
unfinished novel.
Rosa Bud .... Mrs. Morton Powell
John Jasper .... Mr. Morton Powell
Edwin Drood .. Mr. Walter H. Domoney
Neville Landless .. Mr. J. Henry Twyford
Septimus Chrisparkle..Mr. Richard Harris
Durdles .... Mr. Karl H. Edwards
Chief Constable .. Mr. George J. Clayton
Constable .... Mr. Wm. R. Berry
A Lascar .... Mr. Albert S. Goldburn
A Chinaman .... Mr. Arthur T. Gosport
Deputy .... Miss Jennie Risley
Helena Landless ...... Miss May Beatrice
Princess Puffer .... Miss Addie Addir
Mary Jane .... Miss Alice Glading
                    —Osborne, Manchester.

3.¶*The Three Twins*, farce comedy, in three
acts, by Mrs. R. Pacheco and Charles
Dickson, lyrics by Otto A. Hauerbach,
music by Karl Hoschna—Bijou, Bayswater.

5.¶*Salvation*, drama, in four acts, by Arthur
Shirley.
David Grant ...... Mr. Herbert Pearson
Fred Carnadine ...... Mr. Wilson Coleman
Major Trigg Glinn .. Mr. Harry Reynolds
Kasper Fleece ...... Mr. Dick Winslow
Ernest Diggle .... Mr. Chris Mason
Bob Blare ...... Mr. Walter Walmsley
Mr. Dextible .... Mr. Harry Mann
Denman .... Mr. George Robinson
Doctor .... Mr. McFarlane
Waiter .... Mr. Richard Deccan
A Footman .... Mr. Roofe
A Swell .... Mr. Alfred Mugg
Mary Holford .... Miss Rosslyn Vayne
Louisa .... Miss Alice Lefce
Jane .... Miss Evelyn Shaw
Granny .... Mrs. Forster
                    —Royal, Smethwick.

6.¶*The Goddess of Destruction*, romantic mili-
tary drama, in four acts, by Terence Ner-
rey.
Prince Mierzensky .. Mr. Terence Nerrey
Earl of Kinnerley .. Mr. Wordley Hulse
Lord Lionel Welford .. Mr. Claude Casey
Count Boris Torvineff Mr. H. de Ville
Father Nicholas .. Mr. H. Andrews Fell
Ischar Viborsky .... Mr. Lionel Dicker
Peter Zertov ....Mr. H. Andrews Fell
Griffith Jones Davies Mr. G. St. Oswald
Enid Welford .... Miss Florence Turner
Yenia Poltava .... Miss Maude Fergusson
Carita .... Miss Bessie Renfield
Mrs. Teresa Towzer Miss Beatric Chetwyn
                    —Queen's, Liverpool

7. *A Waltz Dream*, operette, in three acts
music by Oscar Strauss, book by Felix
Doerman and Leopold Jacobson, lyrics
by Adrian Ross. (Last performance,
July 31.)
Count Lothar .. Mr. Geo. Grossmith, jun.
Joachim XIII. .. Mr. Arthur Williams
Lieut. Montschi .. Mr. Vernon Davidson
Wendolin .... Mr. Langford Kirby
Sigismund ...... Mr. Albert Kavanagh
Lieut. Niki .... Mr. Robert Evett
Princess Hélène ...... Miss Mary Grey
Friedrike ...... Miss Florence Parfrey
Fifi .... Miss Luna Love
Hana .... Miss Phyllis Beadon
Franzi Steingruber .... Miss Gertie Millar
Ladies' Orchestra.—Violins: Miss M.
Munro, Miss C. Howard, Miss K. Hayes,
Miss U. Grahame, Miss B. Rayne, Miss
E. Tyser, Miss M. Winifred. Flute: Miss
N. Griffiths. 'Cello: Miss M. Dixon. Bass:
Miss F. Mukle. Piano: Miss D. Dolaro.
Harmonium: Miss C. O'Hara. Bass
Drum: Miss P. Beadon.
                    —Hicks.

8. *The Song of Songs, which is Solomon's*.
arranged for the stage by Nugent Monck.
(Produced by the English Drama Society.)
                    ⎧ Miss W. Borrow
Daughters of Jerusalem ⎨ Miss Nella Po
                    ⎩ Miss Ina Royle
The Shulamite ...... Miss Isabel Roland
The Shepherd .... Mr. Guy Fletcher
The King ...... Mr. Frederick Annerley
                    —Queen's Gate Hall, S.W.

9.‖*Affairs at the Shrubbery*, fantastic comedy,
in two acts, by J. P. Hatherleigh and P.
M. Roberts.
Joseph Bosbury .... Mr. D. W. Crawford
George Benson .. Mr. Archibald Inglis
Theodore Kelvin ...... Mr. H. W. Wilson
S. Legallight .... Mr. William Seggie
Beveridge ...... Mr. Jas. Cormie Speirs
Paxton .... Miss Molly Stevenson
Emily Weston .... Miss Jenny Stirling
Beatrice Ferrier .. Miss Netta C. Addison
                    —Paisley, Paisley.

9. *A Game of Adverbs*, one-act play, by F.
Anstey. London production, March 30,
Grand, Fulham.
Rev. Polyblank..Mr. Leon Quartermaine
Cyril Dormer ...... Mr. Douglas Imbert
Bob Shuttleworth .... Mr. Philip Durham
Mrs. Shuttleworth .. Miss Mabel Knowles
Grace .... Miss Aimée de Burgh
Flossie ...... Miss Frances Titheradge
Connie .... Miss Marjorie Day
Conlin .... Mr. Dion George
Miss Markham .... Miss Laura Barradell
Bowles ...... Mr. John W. Laurence
Charles .... Mr. Stafford Hilliard
                    —Royal Court, Liverpool.

9. *Mrs. Bill*, slight comedy of pleasant people,
in three acts, by Captain John Kendall.
Mr. W. Wilbraham .. Mr. E. W. Garden
Mrs. Wilbraham .. Miss Marie Illington
Miss Mabel Jones .. Miss Beatrice Terry
Lt.-Col. Featherstone..Mr. A. Holmes-Gore
Capt. James Smith .. Mr. Budge Harding
Lieut. Charles Carter .. Mr. Vivian Gilbert
A Native Butler .... Mr. Claude Vernon
                    —Court.

10. *The Doctor's Experiment*, sketch.
Dr. Eames .... Mr. Lynn
Mrs. Eames .... Miss Leigh
Skeleton .... Mr. Biddulph
Policeman .... Mr. Bishop
Burglar .... Mr. Wemyess
Mons. Lamont .... Mr. Conrad Franklyn
                    —Scala.

10.*Lady Frederick. W. Somerset Maugham's comedy, transferred from the Court, where it was produced on October 26, 1907—Garrick.

10.*The Subjection of Kezia. Play, in one act, by Mrs. Havelock Ellis (originally produced at the Court, January 7, 1908.—Garrick.

11. The Royal Mail, domestic play, in four acts, by Eva Elwes.
Sir Fredk. Etherington..Mr. L. E. Eykyn
Daniel Etherington .... Mr. F. K. Reeves
Oliver Trueman .... Mr. J. Ord
James Leighton ....Mr. A. Horton
Det.-Sergt. Catt ...... Mr. H. Goddard
Chike Bobajee ....Mr. F. Gibson
The Notary Public ....Mr. Clarence
Nina Fairholme..Miss Florence Mowbray
Jubilee Bumpstead....Miss Julia Royston
Jane Bumpstead ...... Miss Nellie Driver
Margaret Trueman........Miss Eva Elwes
—Goddard's, Durham.

11. The Farewell Supper, comedy, in one act, by Arthur Schnitzler, translated by Edith A. Browne and Mrs. Alix Grein. (Produced by the New Stage Club.)
Anatol .... Mr. H. B. Hampton
Max .... Mr. Eric Marzetti
Annie .... Mrs. Alix Grein
Waiter .... Mr. Louis F. M. Cohen
—Bijou, Bayswater.

11. Literature, one-act comedy, by Arthur Schnitzler, translated by Edith A. Browne and Mrs. Alix Grein. (Produced by the New Stage Club.)
Margaret .... Miss Louise Salom
Clement .... Mr. W. Lawson Butt
Amandus Gilbert ..... Mr. F. A. Flower
—Bijou, Bayswater.

12.¶True Till Death, melodrama, in three acts, by Enid Edoni—Castle, Brentford.

14.*Romeo and Juliet, Shakespeare's tragedy. (Last performance, May 30.)
Romeo .... Mr. Matheson Lang
Mercutio .... Mr. Eric Mayne
Tybalt .... Mr. Halliwell Hobbes
Paris .... Mr. Gordon Bailey
Benvolio ....Mr. Lauderdale Maitland
Montague .... Mr. George Annesley
Capulet .... Mr. Herbert Grimwood
Friar Laurence.......Mr. Frederick Ross
Friar John.................. Mr. P. Gromer
Kinsman to Capulet..Mr. Alec Weatherly
Apothecary .... Mr. Rothbury Evans
Escalus .... Mr. Herbert Bunston
Peter .... Mr. S. Major Jones
Abram .... Mr. Fred Grove
Gregory .... Mr. Fenn Challis
Balthasar .... Mr. Harold Chapin
Officer of the Guard..Mr. Herbert Dansey
Page to Paris........Miss Joan Harcourt
Lady Montague ...... Miss Rachel Warre
Lady Capulet ....Miss Mary Allestree
Nurse .... Miss Blanche Stanley
Juliet .... Miss Nora Kerin
—Lyceum.

16. The Woman Who Was Dead, four-act drama, by J. W. Sabben Clare. London production, May 29, Royal, Stratford.
Philip Carey..Mr. Montague E. Beaudyn
Denise .... Miss Irene Munroe
Horace Winter .... Mr. G. M. Montanini
Guy Oliphant ...... Mr. Matt Russell
Lord Arthur Dunley .. Mr. Henry Ward
Bransby .... Mr. W. Moate
Commissioner of Police..Mr. F. Holyoake

The Woman Who Was Dead (continued).
Waiter .... Mr. Lionel Carteret
Waiter at Hotel ...... Mr. John Baxter
Marie .... Miss Ethel Baring
Nellie Montague ...... Miss C. Crawford
Helen Tenaire ...... Miss Barbara Fenn
—Gaiety, Dundee.

16.‡A Desperate Marriage, drama, in four acts, by Rosemary Rees (originally produced at the Grand, Brighton, on March 2).
Dick Strang .... Mr. Wallace G. Court
Clarence Woolmer..Mr. Riddell Robinson
Dr. Frank Buxter ....Mr. Arthur Curzon
Tom Stripe .... Mr. Herbert Lloyd
Elijah Boggs .... Mr. Frank Coston
Chaplain .... Mr. John Walker
Potato Man .... Mr. Percy V. Booth
Manager of Club .... Mr. A. J. Nicholls
Waiter .... Mr. A. Desper
Small Boy .... Master Fred Rate
Miriam Elton .... Miss Dorothy Cacey
Bertha Onions .... Miss May Davis
Betty Mackenzie ... Miss Lily Annersley
Audrey Howard .... Miss Cissie Bellamy
—Lyric, Hammersmith.

16.‖The Governor's Bride, light opera, in three acts, by A. S. Manning, composed by Robert A. Smith.
Alonzo the Second ..Mr. T. W. Tomlinson
Manuel de Verena .... Mr. J. E. Jordan
Pedro Romara .... Mr. J. E. Davis
Hernandez .... Mr. H. Muir
Carlos .... Mr. J. E. Orr
Basilio .... Mr. William J. Dodds
Luiz .... Mr. G. Wilkie Holmes
Sancho .... Mr. Nicol Coulson
Sebastian .... Mr. G. E. Heppell
Fillipe .... Mr. G. N. Dalkin
Notary .... Mr. Arnold Smith
Sergeant of the Guard..Mr. G. Macdonald
Margarita de Flavella ..Miss Amy Dunn
Donna Rosella .... Miss Effie Smith
Alina .... Miss Ada Coulthard
Inez .... Miss Alice Smith
Luisa .... Miss Alice Daniels
Maria .... Miss Moira Collier
—Tyne, Newcastle.

16. Mrs. Swallow, farce, in three acts, by E. J. Hart.
Lord Longspur .... Mr. Sydney Lynn
Angus McCrae .... Mr. Dickson Moffat
Silas Martin .... Mr. Arthur McCulloch
Hiram Hazel ...... Mr. W. L. Clitheroe
Garfield Martin .... Mr. Edmund Baker
Bonalti .... Mr. Louis Edmonde
An Irishman .... Mr. Donald Gow
May Martin ...... Miss Margaret Geddes
Helen Hazel ...... Miss Ethel Maguire
An Irishwoman .... Miss E. Huby
—Gaiety, Manchester.

16.¶The House of Rimmon, drama, in four acts, by Henry Van Dyke.
Benhadad .... Mr. George D. Hare
Rezon .... Mr. Chas. Beving
Saballidin .... Mr. M. C. Honnest
Hazael .... Mr. James Stephens
Izdubhar .... Mr. Joseph Franks
Rakhaz .... Mr. Arthur Nelson
Shumakim .... Mr. Gerald Nathan
Elisha .... Mr. Herbert Gush
Naaman .... Mr. Stanley Clifford
Ruahmah .... Miss Laura Scott
Tsarpi .... Mrs. M. Honnest
Khamma .... Miss Marion Hope
Nubita .... Miss Alice Sutherland
—Bijou, Bayswater.

16.¶*Love and the Law*, play, in three acts, by Charlotte Elizabeth Wells.

Simon Dole .... Mr. George D. Hare
Mrs. Dole .... Miss Laura Scott
Gus Kelly .... Mr. Joseph Franks
Hiram Dole .... Mr. J. McHonnest
Annette Kingston .... Mrs. J. McHonnest
Mr. Tellaire .... Mr. Gerald Nathan
Paul Courtenay .... Mr. Arnold Hitchins
Jamison .... Mr. Arthur Nelson
Neil Rimsky .... Mr. Charles Beving
Messenger Boy..Miss Georgie McHonnest
Mrs. Devonport ......Miss Mabel Banfield
Von Schaick .... Mr. Stanley Clifford
Montague Grogan .. Mr. James Stephens
Father Bartholomew....Mr. Herbert Gush
Barbara Rimsky........Miss Marion Hope
A Footman .... Mr. John Kelsey
A Florist .... Miss Francis Clifton
Janitress .... Miss Alice Sutherland
Timmy .... Miss Dorothy Hitchens
Nellie .... Miss Ruby Hitchens
First Labourer ...... Mr. Donald Wilson
Second Labourer ....Mr. Herbert Hutson
—Bijou, Bayswater.

17.¶*The Sin Eater*, play, in one act, by Jean Macpherson.

Sir Roger Moncrieff......Mr. A. E. George
Earl of Hume......... Mr. Cecil Cameron
Letitia Vargrave......Miss Ethel Warwick
Lady Howard......Miss May Leslie Stuart
—Lyric.

17.¶*The Omelette Maker*, musical comedy, in two acts, by Cullen Gouldsbury and Theodore Holland.
—Kingsway.

18. *The Changeling*, farce, in one act, by W. W. Jacobs and H. C. Sargeant.

George Henshaw .... Mr. H. J. Manning
Mrs. Henshaw ...... Miss Helen Palgrave
Ted Stokes .... Mr. George F. Tully
—Wyndham's.

19. *Marjory Strode*, comedy, in four acts, by A. E. W. Mason. Last performance, April 10; 33 performances.

Peter Strode .... Mr. Alfred Bishop
Christopher Strode .... Mr. Cyril Maude
Richard Strode .... Mr. Kenneth Douglas
Parson Cranch .... Mr. E. Mainwaring
Jean, Vicomte de Selac.. Mr. H. Ainley
Captain Desailloud .... Mr. Cecil Wilford
Lieut. Marlot .... Mr. Daniel McCarthy
Zachary Hupkins .... Mr. Sydney Paxton
Dackum .... Mr. John Harwood
Fenner .... Mr. Charles Hampden
Marjory Strode .... Miss Nina Sevening
Mrs. Blacket .... Miss Helen Ferrers
Amelia Blacket ...... Miss Rosalie Toller
Miss Prettiejohn .... Miss Sybil Walsh
—Playhouse.

21. *Un Peu de Musique*, one-act piece, founded by M. Gaston Gronier on a novel by M. Eugene Fourrier.

De Brézieux .... M. R. Bussy
Robillet .... M. Derives
Dr. Maxestown .... M. Hauterives
Julot .... M. Roberty
Le Marquis .... M. Remois
—Shaftesbury.

21. *L'Angoisse*, piece, in one act, by Pierre Mille and C. de Vylars.

Dartez .... M. R. Bussy
Bervil .... M. Boulle
Elise .... Mlle. Jane Meryem
—Shaftesbury

21. *Rosalie*, one-act piece, by M. Max-Maurey.
Monsieur Bol .... M. R. Bertrand
Mdme. Bol .... Mlle. Jeanne Bernon
Rosalie .... Mlle. Barcklay
—Shaftesbury.

21. *Le Rouge est Mis*, piece, in one act, by Johannes Gravier.
Le Médecine des Courses .. MM. Boulle
Le Propriétaire de Savon noir .. Bertrand
L'Infirmier .... Chevil'ot
Le Rédacteur Sportif .... Roberty
Le Commissaire de Police .... Hauterives
Lecourbe .... Nicole
Premier Propriétaire .... Rémois
L'Employé .... Derives
Joe Flaping .... Marquy
Lison de Gisors .... Mlles. Bernon
Alberte Orancini .... Barcklay
Camille d'Orcian ...... Marthe de Deken
—Shaftesbury.

21. *Les Nuits du Hampton-Club*, drama, in three tableaux, by Mouezy-Eon and Armont (adapted from the novel by R. L. Stevenson).
Le Président .... MM. Luguet
Herbert Forbes .... R. Bussy
Professeur Triggs .... Bertrand
Owens .... Chevillot
Sir Archibald .... Derives
Gurnbridge .... Roberty
Rivers .... Hauterives
Dalers .... Nicole
Sam .... Marquy
—Shaftesbury.

22. *Amina*, play, in one act, by Affleck Scott (produced by the Play Actors).
Archie Ford .... Mr. Bertram Forsyth
Campbell .... Mr. Arthur Applin
Doolah .... Mr. Frederick Annerley
Amina .... Miss Ethel Warwick
—King's Hall, W.C.

22. *Breaking It Gently*, play, in one act, by Affleck Scott (produced by the Play Actors).
Grace Hawkins ...... Miss Helena Parsons
George Danby .... Mr. Edward Rigby
Jim Bradford ...... Mr. Herbert Bunston
—King's Hall, W.C.

22. *The Masked Girl*, play, in one act, by Arthur Applin (produced by the Play Actors).
Mimi .... Miss Dora Hole
Despard (Pierrot) .... Mr. Edmund Waller
Ferguson (Clown)..Mr. Fewlass Llewellyn
—King's Hall, W.C.

22. *The Picture of the Year*, play, in one act, by George Paston and Henriette Cockeran (produced by the Play Actors).
Leslie Mackensie .. Mr. Halliwell Hobbes
Mrs. Mackensie ...... Miss Kathleen Rind
Jean Logan .... Miss Winifred Rae
Leslie Logan .... Miss Sylvia Norton
Malcolm Henderson .... Mr. Clive Currie
Maid .... Miss Irene Ross
—King's Hall, W.C.

23.‡*The Romantic Barber*, one-act play, by Alfred Sutro. (Originally produced at the Royal, Dublin, March 2.)
Jim .... Mr. Michael Sherbrooke
Frank Stanley .... Mr. Perceval Clark
Maggie .... Miss Alice Arden
—Grand, Fulham.

23. *A Devil's Bargain*, drama of modern times, in four acts (founded on Florence Warden's novel of that name), by Arthur Onslow, the play produced by Mr. George Unwin.

A Devil's Bargain (continued).

Dick Rutherford ...... Mr. Arthur Burne
Mr. Rutherford ..... Mr. Charles Ashby
Naphtali Pass ...... Mr. H. Lane Bayliff
Vanacker .... Mr. T. Brown-Elliott
Merryweather .... Mr. Leslie Norman
Barry Kelcher .... Mr. Richard Trieve
Banbury .... Mr. Grahame Herington
General Verrion .... Mr. Oswald Marshall
Beverley Wedgwood .. Mr. Frank Manger
Mr. Green .... Mr. L. R. Fergusson
Inspector of Police .. Mr. John Maitland
Detective-Sergeants Barnes and French
         Messrs. Bennett and Hare
Isaac Wedgwood ...... Mr. George Unwin
Consuelo Verrion ...... Miss Rose Temple
Mrs. Rutherford .... Miss Hilda Francks
Dinah .... Miss Gladys Vernon
Mary Barber .... Miss Eileen Ashton
Lady Van Houten .... Miss Hattie Voisey
Lady Emily Goring..Miss Maisie Andrews
Hon. Mrs. Rivers .... Miss M. Stanley
Miss Venters .... Miss Ida Scott
Miss Melville .... Miss Frances Errol
Miss Lennox .... Miss Edith Allen
Naomi Wedgwood...Miss Winifred Pearson
         —West London.

23.*Billy Rotterford's Descent,* revised and renamed version of the sensational farce
entitled *Among the Brigands,* by Robert
Lascelles. Produced at the Royal, Birmingham, October 25, 1907. London production, May 11, King's, Hammersmith.

J. K. Rotterford .... Mr. Murray Carson
Billy Rotterford....Mr. Weedon Grossmith
Aubrey Colpoys .... Mr. W. T. Lovell
Polting .... Mr. Frank H. Denton
Kelly .... Mr. Charles Wemyss
Sir Richard Mulberry .... Mr. A. B. Surd
Drage .... Mr. R. M. Toussaint
Edwards .... Mr. James R. La Fane
Gates .... Mr. George F. Mackarness
Colonel Brazier .... Mr. James Sinclair
Freddy Western .... Mr. John Upham
Lord Dilthorpe .... Mr. H. Tims
Reporter .... Mr. Henry Bosman
Landlord .... Mr. B. Manso
Mrs. J. K. Rotterford..Miss M. Ashworth
Lady Mulberry ...... Miss Harley Connell
Dolly Caterack .... Miss Constance Clive
Popsy Hockett .... Miss Rose Galvin
Mdme. Garvarnavitch .... Miss Annie Hill
Photographer .... Mr. Duncan Druce
Zampassa .... Mr. Frank J. Arlton
Vanderhousan .... Mr. Henry Latimer
Ching Fung .... Mr. Sebastian Smith
Vera Vanderhousan....Miss M. Titheradge
         —O.H., Cork.

23. *The Bride of Lammermoor,* play, founded
on Sir Walter Scott's novel, in three
acts, and a tableau, by Stephen Phillips.
London production under the title of *The
Last Heir.*

Edgar Ravenswood .. Mr. Martin Harvey
Sir Wm. Ashton .. Mr. Albert E. Raynor
Colonel Ashton ...... Mr. Leslie Palmer
Henry Ashton .... Miss Merrie Omar
Hayston of Bucklaw.. Mr. Philip Hewland
Capt. Craigengelt .. Mr. Charles Glenney
Angus of Clydesdale..Mr. C. J. Cameron
Sir John de Bothwell .. Mr. Geo. Cooke
Sir Andrew Murray .. Mr. Denholm Muir
Colonel Murray .... Mr. W. Abbey
James Murray ...... Mr. Henry Watson
Malcolm Rutherford..Mr. Leonard Craske
Caleb Balderstone ...... Mr. F. Cremlin
Landlord of Tod's Den .... Mr. H. Barry
A Notary .... Mr. A. Ruben
Rev. Mr. Bide-the-Bent..Mr. Percy Foster
Ailsie Gourlay .... Mr. Alfred Mansfield
Annie Winnie .... Mrs. Wright
Maggie .... Miss Bessie Elder
Mysie .... Miss Ethel Patrick

The Bride of Lammermoor (continued).

Lady Ashton .... Miss Maud Hoffman
Lucy Ashton .... Miss N. de Silva
         —King's, Glasgow.

23. *Woman's Rights,* comedy, in one act, by
J. Sackville Martin.

John Horrobin ...... Mr. Charles Bibby
Maria Horrobin .... Miss Louise Holbrook
Eveline .... Miss Penelope Wheeler
Edith .... Miss Blanche Horricks
Dr. Fawcitt ...... Mr. Leonard Chatham
         —Royal, Rochdale.

24.†*The Man on the Kerb,* one-act play, by
Alfred Sutro.

Joseph Matthews .... Mr. Seymour Hicks
Mary .... Miss Florence Kahn
         —Aldwych.

26. *Annie Laurie,* play, in one act, by Graham
Moffat.

Annie Laurie .... Miss Kate Moffat
Jamie Cairns .... Miss Madge Ross
Lieut. George Douglas .. Mr. Parry Gunn
Corporal Baillie .... Mr. John M'Kinnon
Sir Thomas Laurie —.. Mr. Alex. Ogilvie
Lady Laurie .. Miss M. Fraser Sanderson
         —Athenæum, Glasgow.

26. *Till the Bells Ring,* humorous comedietta,
in one act, by Graham Moffat.

Aggie Turnbull .... Miss Nellie M'Linden
Janet Struthers .... Mrs. Graham Moffat
John Snodgrass .... Mr. Graham Moffat
Samuel Dowie .... Mr. Alex. Ogilvie
Erchie Dowie .... Mr. Archibald Murray
         —Athenæum, Glasgow.

26. *The High Bid,* comedy, in three acts, by
Henry James.

Chivers .... Mr. Ian Robertson
Miss Prodmore .... Miss Esmé Hubbard
The Young Man .... Mr. Alexander Casey
Mr. Prodmore ...... Mr. Edward Sass
Captain Yule .... Mr. Forbes-Robertson
Mrs. Gracedew .... Miss Gertrude Elliott
         —Lyceum, Edinburgh.

26. *Jack Straw,* comedy, in three acts, by W.
Somerset Maugham. Last performance,
January 1, 1909.

Jack Straw .... Mr. Charles Hawtrey
Count Von Bremer .. Mr. H. R. Hignett
Marquis of Serlo .... Mr. Louis Goodrich
Rev. Lewis Abbott .. Mr. Charles Troode
Ambrose Holland .. Mr. Edmund Maurice
Mr. Parker-Jennings Mr. R. Whyte, jun.
Vincent Parker-Jennings
         Mr. P. R. Goodyer
Head Waiter .... Mr. Vincent Erne
Servant .... Mr. Norman Wrighton
Lady Wanley .. Miss Vane Featherston
Ethel Parker-Jennings Miss Dagmar Wiehe
Rosie Abbott .... Miss Mona Harrison
Mrs. Withers .... Miss Joy Chatwyn
Mrs. Parker-Jennings .. Miss Lottie Venne
         —Vaudeville.

26.¶*Yzdra,* tragedy, in three acts, by Louis V.
Ledoux—Wyndham's.

27. *A Coster Girl's Romance,* play, in one act,
by Edward Jewry.

Capt. Gregory .... Mr. Henry Earlesmere
Jim Murton .... Mr. Will Casey
Matt Naylor .. Mr. R. Wilton Bedford
Policeman .... Mr. Alexander Wills
Lady Mannering .... Miss Winifred Hunt
Elizabeth Sumers Miss Ethel Van Praagh
         —Cambridge, Spennymoor.

27. *Monsieur Jean,* comedy, in one act, by G.
Manteuil.

Lucien de Chaulieu .... M. Luguet
Mr. Jean .... M. R. Bussy
Papavoine .... M. Derives
Paulette .... Mlle. Jeanne Meryem
Eugenie .... Mlle. Jeanne Bernou
         —Shaftesbury.

27. *Les 3 Messieurs du Havre,* a drama, in one act, by Leo Marches and C. Vautel—Shaftesbury.

27. *La Veuve,* a one-act piece by Eugene Heros and Leon Abric—Shaftesbury.

27. *Gardiens de Phare,* a drama, in one act, by Paul Autier and Paul Cloquemin—Shaftesbury.

28.¶*The Home Coming,* tragedy, in one act, by George Unwin. April 22, Queen's, Liverpool.

Herr Krautchen......Mr. H. Lane-Bayliff
Karl Krautchen ....Mr. Oswald Marshall
Frau Krautchen......Miss Hilda Francks
Fraulein Krautchen...Miss Eileen Ashton
—West London.

30.‡*His Dishonoured Wife,* drama, in four acts, by Harry Tilbury—Royal, Stratford.

30.‡*A Game of Adverbs,* play, in one act, by F. Anstey. (Originally produced at the Court, Liverpool, March 9.)

Rev. Polyblank ...... Mr. Arthur Hardy
Cyril Dormer .... Mr. Douglas Imbert
Bob Shuttleworth .. Mr. Stafford Hilliard
Mrs. Shuttleworth....Miss Mabel Knowles
Grace (age 25) ....Miss Aimee De Burgh
Flossie (age 19) ..Miss Frances Titheradge
Connie (age 12) ....Miss Marjorie Day
Colin (age 13) .... Mr. Dion George
Miss Markham ......Miss Laura Barradell
Bowles........... Mr. John W. Laurence
Charles .... Mr. James
—Grand, Fulham.

30. *The Shadow of the Surplice,* new drama, in three acts, adapted from *L'Otage,* by Gabriel Trarieux. Originally produced at the Odéon, Paris, May 14, 1907. Last performance, April 25.

Ernest Brockwell, M.P...Mr. C. F. Collings
Hughes Robertson ....Mr. Henry Pettitt
Fred Wilson, M.P........Mr. T. P. Haynes
Father Honeystones..Mr. Watty Brunton
Alfred Smith .... Mr. Davidson
Dr. Calomel .... Mr. Richard Cowell
Dr. Squills .... Mr. Terry Hurst
Mrs. Brockwell .... Miss Ethel Beale
Veronica .... Miss René Ash
Mrs. Wilson .... Miss Kitty Douglas
Sister Theresa .... Miss Ethel Dancy
—Scala.

30.¶*The Tangled Skein,* play, by the Baroness Orczy and Montagu Barstow—Coronet.

30.‡*The Power of the King,* military melodrama, in four acts, by Mrs. F. G. Kimberley. (Stageright performance. King's, Longsight, October 9, 1907; Junction, Manchester, December 2, 1907.)

Capt. Rupert Langrave .. Mr. A. Hinton
King of Vallombrosa .. Mr. C. Whitlock
Crown Prince Oscar .. Mr. Travis Green
General Stenovie .. Mr. John R. Firmin
Fritz Tarlheim ...... Mr. Wilton Drury
Capella .... Mr. L. W. Lindoe
Carl Segismund .... Mr. George Madden
Alberta .... Mr. John Campling
Michael Zemski .... Mr. Lionel Strong
Hertz Steinberg .... Mr. T. Grandrille
Philippe .... Miss Iza Lyndon
Rosa .... Miss Violet Jason
Marget .... Miss Lydia Audre
Lady Florina .. Miss Georgina V. France
Lady Anastasia .... Miss Leila Zillwood
—Broadway.

APRIL.

2. *The Two Pins,* comedy, in four acts, by Frank Stayton. London production, Aldwych, June 8.

Philip .... Mr. Oscar Asche
Rudolph .... Mr. Vernon Steel
Cyril .... Mr. G. Kay Souper
Francis .... Mr. Courtice Pounds
Elsa .... Miss Lily Brayton
Rosaline .... Miss Muriel Ashwynne
Conrad .... Mr. H. Tripp Edgar
Detrichstein .... Mr. Caleb Porter
Gregory .... Mr. J. Fritz Russell
Karl .... Mr. M. Mancini
Wilhelm .... Mr. J. Tippler
Baron Grunteldell ...... Mr. Henry Kitts
Messenger from Knoden..Mr. A. Whitby
Servant at Knoden ....Mr. Evan Brooke
—Royal, Newcastle.

3.¶*The Lady of Kensington,* play, in five acts, by Sutton-Vane.

George Medfield ,... Mr. Arthur Chisholm
Frank Medfield ......Mr. Clavering Craig
Dr. Barnes .... Mr. Dan Mining
Mr. Gedge .... Mr. Herbert Sydney
Harold Medfield .. Miss R. Dudley Daviss
Reynolds .... Mr. Drew
Evelyn Dare .. Miss Helen Dudley Davies
Ethel Medfield .... Miss Lallah Davis
Evelyn Waters ...... Miss Beatrice Hone
—Lyric, Hammersmith.

3.¶*The Gay Musician,* comic opera, in two acts, book by Edward Seidle, lyrics by Chas. J. Campbell, and music by Julian Edwards.

Eugene Dubois ..... Mr. Hugh Tabberer
Samuel Lyons .... Mr. Clive Currie
Hon. Clarence Beresford....Mr. R. Wilson
Captain George Fish..Mr. Leonard Calvert
A. Corker .... Mr. Orlando Barnett
Hank Hickory .... Mr. Field Fisher
Maude Granville .. Miss Leonora Thomas
Marie Dubois .... Miss Naomi Neilson
Matilda Yager ....Miss Ethel Royale
Hilda Brandon .... Miss Maude Esse
Kitty Connor .... Miss Amy Desmond
Suzanne .... Miss Blanka Stewart
Della .... Miss Vera Wallace
—Bijou, Bayswater.

4.*The Merchant of Venice,* Shakespeare's play, arranged in three acts. (Last performance after the interruption of the Shakespeare Festival, May 29.)

Shylock .... Mr. Tree
Bassanio .... Mr. Basil Gill
Antonio .... Mr. William Haviland
Gratiano .. Mr. Charles Quartermaine
Duke of Venice ...... Mr. Robert Atkins
Prince of Morocco .. Mr. Alfred Brydone
Prince of Arragon ..Mr W. R. Creighton
Salanio .... Mr. Donald Calthrop
Salarino .... Mr. Harry C. Hewitt
Salerio .... Mr. Cyril Sworder
Lorenzo .... Mr. Bertram Forsyth
Tubal .... Mr. Leon M. Lion
Launcelot Gobbo ...... Mr. Norman Page
Old Gobbo .... Mr. G. W. Anson
Leonardo .... Mr. Basil Radford
Balthazar .... Mr. Henry Morrell
Stephano .... Mr. James Smythe
Clerk of the Court .. Mr. A. E. Smithson
Jessica .... Miss Auriol Lee
Nerissa .... Miss Dorothy Minto
Portia .... Miss Alexandra Carlisle
—His Majesty's.

5. *The Breaking Point*, play, in three acts, by Edward Garnett (refused a license by the Lord Chamberlain), produced by the Stage Society privately, before members and friends.
Mr. Lewis Sherrington .. Mr. C. V. France
Mr. Francis Mansell ..Mr. Douglas Gordon
Mary .... Miss M'Aimée Murray
Mrs. Sherrington .... Miss Elaine Sleddall
Miss Grace Elwood ...... Miss Bruce Joy
Miss Dorothy Elwood .. Mrs. C. Maltby
James Elwood .. Mr. William Farren, jun.
Agatha .... Miss Florence Leclercq
Collins .... Mr. William T. Day
—Haymarket.

6.*The Daughter of Herodias*, play, by the Hon. Eleanour Norton. Originally produced at the Comedy for stageright purposes on February 25, 1907; Royalty, June 10, 1907.
Herod .... Mr. Robert Hilton
The Astrologer .... Mr. Philip Desborough
Salome .... Miss Mabilla Daniell
—Midland, Manchester.

6.‡*With Edged Tools*, a dramatic version of Henry Seton Merriman's novel, by Harry Armitage. Originally produced at the Gaiety, Ayr, February 20, 1907 (stageright); Royal, Hull, February 3, 1908.
Sir John Meredith.. Mr. William F. Grant
Jack Meredith .... Mr. Hamilton Deane
Guy Oscard ...... Mr. Seymour Hastings
Victor Durnovo ..Mr. Campbell Goldsmid
Maurice Gordon ...... Mr. Archie Selwyn
Leiut. Conyngham .... Mr. C. Hartropp
A Doctor .... Mr. Henry Nunn
A Servant .... Mr. B. Ratcliffe.
Millicent Chyne ......Miss Haidée Wright
Lady Cantourne ...... Miss Isabel Grey
Lady Herries .... Miss Frances Irving
Jocelyn Gordon .... Miss Marie Leonhard
Marie .... Miss Mary Raby
First Guest .... Miss Emilee Finch
Second Guest .... Miss Dorrie Turner
Third Guest .... Miss Violet Hastings
—King's Hammersmith.

7.¶*A Boy's Best Friend*, domestic drama, in four acts, by G. Roydon Duff.
Edward Ainley .... Mr. A. E. George
Denis Holman ...... Mr. Harry Braban
Teddy Ainley—Act one, Master H. C. Duff; acts two and four, Mr. Malcolm Cherry
Angus Fernie .... Mr. Walter Edwin
Jim Davis .... Mr. Frederick Groves
Margaret Ainley ...... Miss Grace Edwin
Eva Smith .... Miss Annie Webster
Nellie Sutcliffe..Miss M. Wilson Pembroke
—New.

8.¶*The Devil*, play by Franz Molnar—Prince of Wales's, Birmingham.

9 *Lady Lanigan, Laundress*, one-act comedy drama, by J. Russell Bogue.
Mrs. Lanigan .... Mr. Robb Wilton
Bertie Softleigh ...... Mr. R. Seath Innes
Quill Driver .... Mr. Sydney Grant
Sergeant Drill ...... Mr. Harry Tresham
Denny .... Mr. Leo Montgomery
Buggins .... Mr. Cecil Ravenswood
Bridget Lanigan ..Miss Florence Cameron
—Royal, Liverpool.

9.†*Fruit and Blossom*, comedy, in one act, adapted from the French by Clinton Dent —Playhouse.

9.†*The Little Nut Tree*, fairy play, by Annie Dymond and Blanche Penley—Playhouse.

11.‖*Bunkered; or, Too Many Cooks Spoil the Broth*, American comedy-drama, in four acts, by Gerald Ransley.
Jem Thornley ...... Mr. Gerald Ransley
Isaac Kessler .... Mr. George Alsop

Bunkered; or, Too Many Cooks Spoil the Broth (continued).
Bob Dacre ...... Mr. Joseph A .McGrath
Nan Dacre .... Miss Mary Vernon
Terence O'More .... Mr. J. Sidney Gorrie
John Ryder ...... Mr. Jasper G. Ries
Kate .... Miss Vera Moulton
Mamie .... Miss Molly T/ldesley
—Balfour Institute, Liverpool.

11 *Bladud; or, The Swell and the Swineherd*, comic opera, in two acts, written by Edwin Fagg and S. Poole, music by L. D. C. Thomas and C. Wright.
Bladud .... Mr. A. Bertram Fortt
Pitchkin J. Cluster .. Mr. Sid Vaughan
Sadie .... Miss Hilda Blake
The Duke of Shamcastle ..Mr. F. W. Fry
Sir Hampton Rox .... Mr. Stanley Russ
Beau Belvedere .... Mr. Graham Simmons
Baroness Beechen .... Miss Nance Evans
Reggie Rattle ...... Mr. Arthur Taylor
Gertie Greenpark ...... Mrs. F. W. Fry
A Bath Chairman .... Mr. Edwin Fagg
A Bath Beadle .... Mr. S. Poole
Hetling .... Mr. Harold Fortt
—Royal, Bath.

12. *Hannele*, dream poem, by Gerhart Hauptmann (translated from the German by William Archer) (presented by the Play Actors).
Hannele .... Miss Winifred Mayo
Gottwald .... Mr. H. R. Hignett
Tulpe .... Miss Italia Conti
Hedwig (Hete) ....Miss Vita Spencer
Pleschke .... Mr. Fred W. Permain
Hanke .... Mr. Reginald Rivington
Sister Martha ...... Miss Marie Linden
Seidel .... Mr. Fewlass Llewellyn
Berger ...... Mr. Lawrence Leyton
Schmit .... Mr. Montague Wlaye
Dr. Wachler ...... Mr. Lewis Willoughby
There appear to Hannele in her fever dream:
Mattern the Mason .. Mr. C. F. Collings
Female Figure, her Dead Mother
Miss Cicely Hamilton
Great Black Angel
Three Angels of Light { Miss Ethel Warwick
{ Miss Kathleen Rind
{ Miss Dorothy Green
The Sister of Mercy .. Miss Edyth Olive
The Village Tailor .. Mr. A. M. Heathcote
Gottwald .... Mr. H. R. Hignett
A Schoolfellow .... Miss Irene Ross
Preschke .... Mr. Fred W. Permain
Hanke .... Mr. Reginald Rivington
Seidel .... Mr. Fewlass Llewellyn
{ Miss Inez Bensusan
{ Miss Alys Rees
Five Mourners .... { Miss Lucy Beaumont
{ Miss Rita Tomkins
{ Miss Rose Mathews
A Stranger .... Mr. H. R. Hignett
—Scala.

13. *For Love and the King*, drama, in four acts, by C. Watson Mill. London production July 23, Elephant and Castle.
Jarval .... Mr. C. Watson Mill
Michael Obrenovic .... Mr. John Burton
Vladimir-Obrenovic Mr. Henry Earlesmere
Prince Uros Dragomir Mr. J. S. Millward
Duke Fernand Dragomir Mr. Geoffrey Chate
Carl Oppenheim ...... Mr. Jim K. Wools
King Kara Dragomir .. Mr. Frank Lyndon
Kosta Marks .... Mr. Arthur Trail
Vitomir Ladle .... Mr. J. H. Organ
Natilla .... Miss Joan Ellis
Grazia Obrenovic .... Miss Marie Aust
Edith Meredith .. Miss Frances Tierney
Princess Milania .... Miss Laura Munroe
Princess Athene .... Miss Rosalind Tate
—P.O.W., Mexborough

13. *Beatrix*, play, in four acts, adapted from Thackeray's novel, "Esmond," by Alfred Crocker.

Colonel Esmond ...... Mr. O. P. Heggie
Duke of Hamilton .... Mr. Wallis Clark
Viscount Castlewood .. Mr. Ernest Griffin
Prince James Stuart .. Mr. J. Napper
Dr. Atterbury .... Mr. Frank Stone
Tom Lockwood ...... Mr. E. W. Thomas
Captain Steele ...... Mr. Arthur West
Henry St. John .... Mr. J. W. Jordan
Porter at Castlewood .... Mr. T. Hayes
Mr. Graves ...... Mr. Harold Rowlands
Mercer .... Mr. Frank Arthur
Footman .... Mr. L. Rowlinson
Watchman ....Mr. Henry James
Lady Castlewood .. Miss Agnes Knights
Mrs. Steele ....Miss Belle Samer
Lady Masnam .... Miss Isabel Merson
Lucy .... Miss Lilian Rogers
Lace Woman .... Miss Elsie Jones
Beatrix .... Miss Hope Mayne
—Royal, Margate.

13. *The Love of the Princess*, drama, in four acts, by C. Watson Mill.

Prince Conrad Ramona .. Wilson Coleman
Count Nicolas Danillo ..Arthur E. Pringle
King of Ilarnia ...... Mr. E. H. Dobell
Lieutenant Orlans .... Mr. Beckett Bould
Lieutenant Zaroff ..Mr. Graham Winsford
Prince Regent .... Mr. Chas. Osborne
Duke Scarfe .... Mr. George Antley
Boris .... Mr. Charles F. Pick
Stephen .... Mr. Eric Wilde
Carlos .... Mr. James Austin
Lady Irene Ramona .. Miss Nellie Garside
Constantia .... Miss Mona Grey
Princess Idalia .... Miss Theresa Osborne
—Grand, Nelson.

13.‡*Only a Woman*, domestic drama, in four acts, written by Percy Ballard. Originally produced at the Central, Altrincham, January 20.

Courtney Wallace .... Mr. Percy Ballard
Lieut. Richard Summerfield .. Fred Green
Lieut. Rodney Summerfield..W. H. Wilson
James Dobson .... Mr. Victor Silvernie
Billy Bumpkins ...... Mr. E. Edwards
Harold .... Miss Laura Marshall
John Bull .... Mr. Norman Plant
Sally Binks ...... Miss Nora Williams
Dolly Derelove .... Miss May Fletcher
Eliza Jane ...... Miss Maudie Douglass
Grace .... Miss Rosie Fields
Violet Redgrave ...... Miss Flora Leslie
Marie Lestoc .... Miss Violet Craufurd
—West London.

13. *The Likes o' Me*, episode by Wilfred T. Coleby.

Matilda Emms ...... Miss Dorothy Brunt
Billy .... Miss Beryl Mercer
Viscount Worth .... Master Philip Tonge
Joad .... Mr. W. Lemmon Warde
Earl of Whitecliffe .. Mr. T. A. Shannon
—Kingsway.

13.‡*A Soldier of France*, military romantic drama, in four acts, written by Clarence Burnette and C. A. Clarke.

Corporal Jean .... Mr. Leonard Aardale
Judas Delara ...... Mr. Gerald Kennedy
Pollyput Jollyboy .... Mr. David Phillips
Capt. Louis Lorraine } Mr. Edward Hobath
Lieut. Louis }
Duke D'Laval .... Mr. Gilson Brooke
Barnave .... Mr. Lester Charles
Sergeant Flange .... Mr. Arthur Downes

A Soldier of France (continued).

Pirri .... Mr. Robert Mann
Quassi .... Miss Alice Arthur
Rita ..:................. Miss Dora Weber
Margot .... Miss Jennie Clare
Master Louis Lorraine..Miss Ethel Glyde
Zippe .... Miss Phœbe Jones
Pauline Lorraine..Miss Florence Zillwood
—Royal, Woolwich.

14.¶*Receipted*, dramatic sketch by Ellen Wallis and Mrs. Kirkham—Coronet.

15. *The Lady Bandits*, topical and farcical operetta, by Herbert C. Sergeant and Edward Lauri.

Josephus A. Muddifat.. Mr. Edward Lauri
Lady Lilian .... Miss Blanche Astley
Lady Primrose .... Miss Cicely Lowe
Lady Diana Grosvenor..Miss May Beatty
—Royal County, Kingston.

17. *The Torrent*, dramatic interlude, by Sarga.

Batiste .... Mr. Ernest Meade
Valerie .... Miss Mona K. Oram
—Camden.

18. *A Fearful Joy*, farce, in three acts, founded on *Les Plus Heureux de Trois* of Labiche and Gondinet, by Sydney Grundy. Last performance,May 16; 32 performances.

Mrs. Arundel .... Mrs. Langtry
Jack Arundel ...... Mr. Arthur Bourchier
Ernest Campion .. Mr. Allan Aynesworth
Rossiter ...... Mr. Edmund Maurice
Sophy Arundel .... Miss Lily Grundy
Juliette .... Mlle. Marcelle Chevalier
—Haymarket.

18.*Pride of Regiment*, Mr. F. D. Bone's one-act play (originally produced at the Haymarket on February 28).

Father .... Mr. Charles Rock
Mother .... Miss Cicely Richards
Son .... Mr. Ashton Pearse
—Haymarket.

18. *Robinson Crusoe*, pantomime, by Edward Marris and E. H. Bertram.—Royal, Belfast.

18.¶*A Daughter of France*, play, in three acts, by Langford Reed.

Jeanne Lapoux .... Miss Ada Marius
Bernard .... Mr. Clive Currie
Raoul .... Mr. Gordon Smith
Max .... Mr. W. Peel Leslie
Père Gaspard .... Mr. Noel Mackway
Lieutenant Reval..Mr. Taliesyn G. Davies
Loti .... Mr. L. Keith
The Pedler .... Mr. Frank Westfield
Lisette .... Miss Ada Hatchwell
—Kennington.

20. *The Workhouse Ward*, play, in one act, by Lady Gregory.—Abbey, Dublin.

20 *Butterflies*, musical play, in three acts, founded upon the fantastic comedy, *The Palace of Puck*, by William J. Locke, produced at the Haymarket on April 2, 1907, rewritten by the same author, with lyrics by T. H. Read and Arthur Anderson, and music by J. A. Robertson. London production of Butterflies, May 12, Apollo.

Salome .... Miss Gladys Soman
Peter .... Mr. Kenna Lawson
Gilbert .... Mr. John Bardsley
Lalage .... Miss Lucie Caine
Paul .... Mr. Willie Warde
Myra .... Miss Jessie Lonnen
Yarker .... Mr. Lauri de Frece
Christopher Podmore..Mr. Fred Edwards
Elsie Podmore .... Miss Iris Hoey

Butterflies (continued).

Nora Podmore .... Miss Stella St. Audrie
Widgery Blake .. Mr. W. Louis Bradfield
Max Riadore ...... Mr. C. Hayden Coffin
Rhodanthe .... Miss Ada Reeve
Parisiennes: Mesdames   Monkman,
Glynn, Brock, and Gordon.   Parisians:
MM. Giron, Edwarde, Selby, and Rubin.
Chorus of Painters, Sculptors, Artists'
Models, etc., by Misses Carlyle, Florence
Nobbs, Flora McDonald, Gwendoline Hay,
May Foster, Mabel Maartens, Ella Bran-
don, Alice Sands, Maisie Saunby, Olive
Cherry Ella Carlyle, Hilda Saxe, Gladys
Darrell, Raynor Golden, Ivy Moore, Flo-
rence Sinclair, Verona Phyllis, Gladys
Purnell, Florence Manton, Marguerite
Penfold, and Hilda Vining; Messrs. R. A.
Swinhoe, Graham Ainley, Frederick Stret-
ton, Alfred Gresham, Henry Warren,
Cyril Biddulph, Arthur Tregonwell,
Michael Ewart, David Davis, W. R. Per-
cival, Ambrose Primm, and Frank Walsh.
—Tyne, Newcastle.

20. *The Fire Witch*, mystic drama, in four
acts, by Norman Towers.
Pierre Crox .... Mr. Charles East
James Stirling .... Mr. J. B. Murray
Henry Stirling .... Mr. C. J. Vincent
Lloyd Stirling ...... Mr. Arthur D. Mead
Willie Wilks ...... Mr. Freddie Bentley
Jim Spriggs ...... Mr. Harry Wimpenny
The Stranger .... Mr. Preston Moore
P.C. Ellis .... Mr. Geo. Owen
Ebe, the Nubian Imp..Mr. Charles Halling
Jeanette .... Miss Jessie Rutter
Albina Toogood .... Mrs. Sidney Halling
Arline Volmar .... Miss East Robertson
—Royal, Stratford.

20. *The College Widow*, George Ade's American
comedy satire on life in the State of
Indiana. Last performance, May 16; 30
performances.
Billy Bolton ...... Mr. Thomas Meighan
Peter Witherspoon..Mr. Albert Tavernier
Hiram Bolton .... Mr. George S. Trimble
"Matty" McGowan..Mr. John P. Brawn
Hon. Elam Hicks .... Mr. Stephen Maley
"Bub" Hicks .... Mr. Frederick Burton
Jack Larrabee .... Mr. Robert Kelly
Copernicus Talbot ... Mr. Thomas Hoier
"Silent" Murphy....Mr. Thomas Delmar
"Stub" Talmage .. Mr. John A. Butler
Tom Pearson .... Mr. Cyril Raymond
Daniel Tibbetts ...... Mr. E. Y. Backus
Ollie Mitchell ...... Mr. Morton Hidden
Dick McAllister .... Mr. David Locke
"Jimsey" Hopper .... Mr. James McGee
Jane Witherspoon .. Miss Frances Ring
Bessie Tanner ...... Miss Adeline Dunlap
Flora Wiggins .... Miss Gertrude Quinlan
Mrs. Primely Dalzelle..Miss Lida McMillan
Luella Chubbs .... Miss Maud Earle
Josephine Barclay..Miss Anne Butterfield
Sally Cameron ...... Miss Ida Stanhope
Bertha Tyson ...... Miss Clara Tichenor
Ruth Aiken .... Miss Viola Roach
Cora Jenes .... Miss Frances Wedderburn
—Adelphi.

20. *The Fortunes of Fan*, farcical comedy, in
three acts, by H. M. Paull. London pro-
duction, April 20, Lyceum, Edinburgh.
Robert Wigley ...... Mr. George de Lara
Mrs. Wigley .... Miss Janet Hobson
Fan .... Miss Louie Freear
Tom .... Mr. Webb Darleigh
Madame Dobbs .... Miss Gertrude Bibby
Lady Beddington..Miss Maude Henderson
Cecil Ramsden .... Mr. John W. Deverell

The Fortunes of Fan (continued).

Mrs. Maude Gregory..Miss Nellie Redwood
Footman .... Mr. W. J. Rea
—Lyceum, Edinburgh.

20.*The Scarlet Pimpernel, play by Baroness
Orczy (originally produced Royal, Nottingham, October 15, 1903; New, January 5,
1905)—New.

21. *My Mimosa Maid*, Riviera musical inci-
dent, in two acts, chatter by Paul A.
Rubens and Austen Hurgon, jingles and
tunes by Paul A. Rubens. Last perfor-
ance, July 11; 85 performances.
Victor Guilbert ...... Mr. G. P. Huntley
Max Guilbert ...... Mr. George Barrett
Bock .... Mr. Charles McNaughton
Boy .... Master Archie McCaig
M. Emile Gerrard .. Mr. Maurice Farkoa
Groue .... Mr. Windham Guise
Capt. Louis du Laurier ..F. Pope Stamper
Lt. Jean Courmandet..Mr. H. A. Deacon
Lt. Baptiste D'Eranger .. Mr. C. Hillman
Lt. Raoul St. André Mr. H. F. R. Lightfoot
Boss .... Mr. Cecil Burt
Popitte .... Miss Gracie Leigh
Madame de Pilaine ...... Miss Eva Kelly
Granny .... Miss Joan Penrose
Marie .... Miss Clarisse Batchelor
Antoinette .... Miss Gertie Murray
Paulette .... Miss Isabel Jay
—Prince of Wales's.

22. *The Home Coming*, tragedy in one act, by
George Unwin (stageright performance,
West London, March 28).
Herr Krautchen .... Mr. H. Lane-Bayliff
Karl Krautchen .... Mr. Oswald Marshall
Frau Krautchen ...... Miss Hilda Francks
Fraulein Krautchen .. Miss Eileen Ashton
—Queen's, Liverpool.

22. *The Marriage of William Ashe*, play, in
five acts (adapted from the novel of the
same name), by Mary Ward and Margaret
Mayo. Last performance, May 30; 30 per-
formances.
William Ashe ...... Mr. Cyril Keightley
Lord Parham ...... Mr. A. B. Tapping
Lord Grosville .... Mr. George Barran
Geoffrey Cliffe ...... Mr. John W. Dean
Eddie Helston ...... Mr. Spencer Trevor
Dean Winston .... Mr. Ernest Cosham
Count Roche-Fidelio..Mr. Cooke-Beresford
Richard .... Mr. Gerald Ames
Parkin .... Mr. John Cabourn
Footmen .... Messrs. Carlin and Wemyss
Lady Kitty .... Miss Fannie Ward
Lady Tranmore .... Miss Alice Farleigh
Lady Grosville .... Miss Kate Serjeantson
Lady Parham .... Miss Mary Weigall
Mary Lyster .... Miss Nella Powys
Mdme. D'Estrées ..Miss Edith Cartwright
Blanche .... Miss Marguerite Lennox
—Terry's.

23. *Way Down East*. American play, in four
acts, by Lottie Blair Parker, elaborated
by Joseph R. Grismer. Last perform-
ance, May 1; 8 performances.
Anna Moore ...... Miss Phœbe Davies
Squire Amassa Bartlett..Mr. R. A. Fischer
Louise Bartlett .... Miss Josephine Bacon
David Bartlett .... Mr. Ulrie B. Collins
Kate Brewster .. Miss Minnette Barrett
Professor Sterling .... Mr. Frank Currier
Hi Holler .... Mr. John E. Brennan
Lennox Sanderson ...... Mr. Earl Ryder
Martha Perkins .. Miss Ella Hugh Wood
Rube Whipple ...... Mr. Charles Burke
Seth Holcomb .... Mr. Frank Hatch
Dr. Wiggin .... Mr. Oliver Johnson
Sam, the Tenor .. Mr. Fred Freeman

Way Down East (continued).

Zeke, the Bass .... Mr. Robert Wilson
Cynthia, the Soprano ..Miss Estelle Ward
Amelia, the Alto .. Miss Jeanne Millard
Semantha .... Miss Cora Calkine
Priscilla..............Miss Emma Wollcott
Hank .... Mr. Joseph Keefe
Eben .... Mr. John Smith
Jake .... Mr. J. H. Stout
Betsy .... Miss Laura Bennett
　　　　　　　　　　　　—Aldwych.

24. *The House of Clay*, play, in three acts
(adapted from *La Maison d'Argile* of
Emile Fabre), by Herbert Swears. London
production, October 2, Coronet.
Henri Armières .... Mr. Kendal
Pierre Ruchon .... Mr. Bassett Roe
Ternand .... Mr. Ernest Hendrie
Frederic .... Mr. R. Burnett
Julie .... Miss Adah Barton
Valentine .... Miss Jessica Thorne
Marguerite Armières .... Miss Ethel Dane
Madame Rehy .... Miss Sara de Groot
Mdme. Armières, sen..Mrs. A. B. Tapping
Mdme. Armières .... Mrs. Kendal
　　　　　　　　　—O.H., Blackpool.

25.‖*Military Pickle. A*, comedy, in four acts,
by Marjorie Hawkins—Cripplegate Institute.

25. *Havana*, musical play, in three acts, by
George Grossmith, jun., and Graham Hill,
lyrics by Adrian Ross, additional lyrics
by George Arthurs, the music by Leslie
Stuart. Last performance, December 12.
Jackson Villiers .... Mr. Leonard Mackay
Hon. Frank Charteris .. Mr. Robert Hale
Hilario .... Mr. T. C. Maxwell
Alejandro .... Mr. Ernest Mahar
Bombito del Campo ..Mr. A. Hatherton
The Don Adolfo Mr. Lawrence Grossmith
Diego de la Concha Mr. Edward O'Neill
Customs House Officer ..Mr. Lewis Grande
Sentinel .... Mr. J. R. Sinclair
Nix .... Mr. Alfred Lester
Reginald Brown .... Mr. W. H. Berry
Anith .... Miss Jean Aylwin
Isabelita .... Miss Gladys Homfreys
Maraquita .... Miss Kitty Mason
Tita .... Miss Olive May
Pepita ....Miss Mabel Russell
Lolita .... Miss Adelina Baire
Teresa .... Miss Enid Leonhardt
Zara .... Miss Jessie Broughton
Mamie .... Miss Barbara Dunbar
Lola .... Miss Florence Phillips
Signora Verriotti .... Miss Kitty Hanson
Isolda .... Senorita Valencia
Consuela .... Miss Evie Greene
Touring Newspaper Beauties: Misses
Gladys Cooper, Julia James, Frances Kap-
stowne, Daisy Williams, Connie Stuart,
Kitty Lindley, Crissie Bell, and Phyllis
Barker.
Ladies of Havana: Misses Enid Leslie,
Gladys Desmond, Claire Rickards, Eileen
Caulfield, Pauline Francis, Sylvia Storey,
and Pattie Wells.
Gentlemen of Havana: Messrs. H. B. Bur-
cher, Alec Fraser, W. Raymond, J. Red-
mond, and Cecil Cameron.
　　　　　　　　　　　　—Gaiety.

27. *Der Weg zur Hölle*, farce, in three acts, by
Gustav Kadelburg.
Emil Dornwald .... Herr Hans Andresen
Agathe ...... Fräulein Betty L'Arronge
Tilly Bendler ..Fräulein Maria Christoph
Hugo Bendler ..Herr Karl William Büller
Arthur Gernau ...... Herr Max Schlefer
Lola Cornero .... Fräulein Elsa Gademann
Duriano, Impresario Herr Kurt Sakrzenski

Der Weg zur Hölle (continued).

Framelli .... Herr Karl Werner
Marlen .... Fräulein Josefine Gruber
Graf Barakoff .... Herr Max Sylge
Bayer .... Herr Georg l'Orange
Josef .... Herr Rudolf Exner
Ulrich Gröber .. Herr Adolf Walter-Paris
Marta .... Fräulein Valerie Salberg
　　　　　—Royalty, German season.

27. *A Mother's Salvation*, melodrama, in four
acts, by Nita Rae. London production,
May 18, Royal, Stratford.
Reuben Smith ...... Mr. Fred A. Marston
Leslie Mervyne .... Mr. Henry C. Ward
Lynton Desmond .... Mr. John Levey
Joe Turntail .... Mr. T. Newton Cooling
Marmaduke Danby..Mr. J. O. Stephenson
Billy Bumpkin ...... Mr. Fred Gresham
Little Paul .... Miss Mabel Hall
Dan Potter .... Mr. T. Chapman
Guard .... Mr. Harry Oggles
Sergt. Coalville .... Mr. J. Ballard
Gus Durant .... Mr. Fred Daring
Beckey .... Miss Fanny Wallace
Mother Turntail ...... Miss Kate Newton
Naomi Lester 〳
Miriam Mervyne 〵 .....Miss Ada Hender
Daisy Delaval ...... Miss Maud Western
　　　　　　　　　—Royal, Wednesbury.

27.¶*A Sower Went Forth*, play, in prologue
and three acts, by Walter Nixey.
Characters in the Prologue.
Mr. Saxenham .... Mr. Alfred Hollis
Rev. John Mansfield..Mr. Harding Thomas
Richard Lethbridge..Mr. Frank Letheridge
Edith Truscott ...... Miss Elaine Verner
Zachery .... Mr. Donald Gilbert
William .... Mr. Gerald Clarke
George .... Mr. Anthony Robinson
　　　　　　　　The Play.
John Collier (formerly John Mansfield)
　　　　　　　　　Mr. Harding Thomas
Mr. King .... Mr. Alfred Hollis
Made King .... Miss Nellie Freeman
Mrs. Lethbridge (formerly Edith Truscott)
　　　　　　　　　Miss Elaine Verner
Dick Lethbridge....Mr. Frank Letheridge
Rayor .... Mr. Gerald Clarke
Stone .... Mr. Anthony Robinson
Dr. Jones .... Mr. Sydney Hill
Mrs. Gibbon .... Miss Madge Cottier
　　　　　　　　　—Royalty, Llanelly.

27. *Mrs. Dot*, light comedy, in three acts, by
W. Somerset Maugham. Last performance,
December 19; 272 performances.
James Blenkinsop .... Mr. Fred Kerr
Gerald Halstane..Mr. W. Graham Browne
Freddie Perkins .... Mr. Kenneth Douglas
Charles .... Mr. Herbert Ross
Mr. Rixon .... Mr. George Bellamy
Mason .... Mr. Horton Cooper
Mr. Wright .... Mr. Brian Egerton
George .... Mr. H. Gerrish
Lady Sellenger .... Miss Marie Illington
Nellie Sellenger .... Miss Lydia Bilbrooke
Miss Eliza Macgregor..Miss Lena Halliday
Mrs. Worthley ...... Miss Marie Tempest
　　　　　　　　　　　—Comedy.

27.‖*Henry of Lancaster*, romantic drama, in
four acts, by Gladys Unger (originally
produced at the Royal, Nottingham,
February 28).
Elizabeth of York ...... Miss Ellen Terry
Kate Lee .... Miss Portia Knight
Iseult of Auvergne..Miss Allison Skinner
Marianne of Orleans..Miss Eleanor Hicks
Court Ladies ..... 〳 Miss Lizette Cordozo
　　　　　　　　　 〵 Miss Muriel Ellison
King Henry VII. .... Mr. James Carew
Henry of Lancaster, afterwards
A Gipsy Woman .. Miss Lindsay Fincham

Henry of Lancaster (continued).

King Richard III. .... Mr. Frank Fenton
Sir Pier Gowles .... Mr. Story-Gofton
The Earl of Warwick...Mr. David Powell
Sir Humphry Gavin ...... Mr. John Hood
Sir Robert Willoughby....Mr. C. F. Cooke
Sir Henry Doughty .. Mr. Geoffrey Saville
A Courtier .... Mr. Charles Molyneux
Patch, a Jester ...... Mr. Max Montesole
Jasper .... Mr. Frank Powell
Jake .... Mr. Edwin C. Cushman
Conway .... Mr. Charles Daly
Martin .... Mr. David Hallam
Derrick .... Mr. Arthur De-Breanski
Thomas .... Mr. Herbert Lomes
Dame Merry .... Mr. Richard F. Symons
A Gipsy Man .... Mr. Charles French
Two Apprentices .. { Mr. Sidney Travers
                { Mr. Guy Addison
Two Pages .... { Master Roberts
                { Master Thurston
           —Borough, Stratford.

27.‡*The Lancashire Lad*, four-act drama, by G.
Carlton Wallace (originally produced at
the Victoria, Broughton, September 16,
1907).
David Elmore .. Mr. G. Carlton Wallace
Max Carton .... Mr. T. G. Vane
Jem Wincote .... Mr. T. D. Byron
John Willie Wardle .... Mr. Fred Acton
Tum-o'-th'-Swilltub..Mr. J. W. Wilkinson
Inspector Fairclough .... Mr. C. Dudeney
P.C. Peffers ...... Mr. Charles Frankfort
Professor Boulanger .. Mr. Will Brereton
Burly Bil' .... Mr. Louis Weston
Silver Charlie .... Mr. Max Mason
Jessie Wincote ...... Miss Ada Oakley
Lorna Wincote .... Miss V. St. Laurence
Kitty de Vere .... Miss Maudie Grayson
Jane Alice Clitheroe .. Miss Lottie Fearce
Maggie Ramsden...Miss Naomi Wallace
Mary Ann Burns ...... Miss Violet Haye
Mother Wardle .... Miss Harriett Russell
         —Lyric, Hammersmith.

28.*The Mikado, comic opera, in two acts,
written by W. S. Gilbert, composed by
Arthur Sullivan (originally produced at
the Savoy, March 14, 1885).
Mikado of Japan...Mr. Henry A. Lytton
Nanki-Poo .... Mr. Stafford Moss
Ko-Ko .... Mr. C. H. Workman
Pooh-Bah ...... Mr. Rutland Barrington
Pish-Tush .... Mr. Leicester Tunks
Go-To .... Mr. Fred Drawater
Yum-Yum .... Miss Clara Dow
Pitti-Sing .... Miss Jessie Rose
Peep-Bo .... Miss Beatrice Boarer
Katisha .... Miss Louie Rene'
         —Savoy.

29. *Pro Tem.*, adaptation, in three acts, by
Cosmo Hamilton, of Alfred Athi's farce,
Boute-en-Train. Last performance, May
19; 21 performances.
Dodo Brezard .... Mr. Cyril Maude
Victor Radinot .... Mr. Rudge Harding
Albert Malardier .... Mr. E. Lyall Swete
Theodore Poulette....Mr. O. B. Clarence
Hippolyte Vavincourt .. Owen Roughwood
Baron de Dardana ...... Mr. C. Kinnaird
Captain Santeuil ...... Mr. M. Wetherell
George Farja ...... Mr. Daniel McCarthy
Commander Fauconnier .. Sydney Paxton
Campoix .... Mr. Charles Hampden
Gaillardet .... Mr. W. Blair
Pomerel .... Mr. John Harwood
Joseph .... Mr. Edward Coutts
Croupier .... Mr. C. B. Keston
Postman .... Mr. A. Edwards
Gendarme .... Mr. E. Wilfred
Mme. Radinot ...... Miss Rosalie To'ler

Pro Tem. (continued).

Mme. Tasselin .... Miss Mollie Lowell
Mlle. Malardier ...... Miss Hilda Antony
Mme. Vougerolles Miss Emma Chambers
Mme. Fauconnier .... Miss Dorothy Fane
Fanny .... Miss Kitty Melrose
Marie .... Miss Sybil Walsh
Bertha .... Miss de Wilden
         —Playhouse.

30.**The Gay Lord Quex*, comedy, in four acts,
by Arthur W. Pinero (originally produced
at the Globe, April 8, 1899). Last per-
formance, June 13.
The Marquess of Quex....Sir John Hare
Sir Chichester Frayne.....Mr. H. Waring
Captain Bastling .... Mr. Robert Horton
Valma .... Mr. A. Scott Craven
The Duchess of Strood..Miss Ada Ferrar
Julia Countess of Owbridge
              Miss Helen Rous
Mrs. Jack Eden .... Miss Ruth Maitland
Muriel Eden.Miss Jean Sterling MacKinley
Sophy Fullgarney ...... Miss Nancy Price
Miss Moon .... Miss Jean Harkness
Miss Huddle ...... Miss Margaret Busse
Miss Claridge .... Miss Mabel Ada'r
Miss Limbird ...... Miss Morrough Boyle
               { Miss Florence Leclercq
Patrons.......... { Miss Blanchette Grand
               { Mr. Norman Trevor
               { Mr. C. Fancourt
Servants.......... { Mr. Fred W. Permain
               { Mr. C. Ford
         —Garrick.

MAY.

1.‖*The Sakeps*, comic opera, in two acts, book
by Lewis Champion, lyrics by Claude
Selfe, and music by Percy Bowie.
Rhadamant .... Mr. Claude Selfe
Alexis .... Mr. Harold Wilde
Duke Paul .... Mr. Jack Theobald
Melas .... Mr. H. A. Re'l
Nestor .... Mr. Lionel Selfe
Cardinal Poyntz ...... Mr. E. S. Vincent
Countess Zeta ...... Miss Florence Suddaby
Lady Iota .... Miss Ethel Bowie
Herald .... Mr. L. H. Parkin
Maschylis .... Mr. Leonard Willson
Gorgias .... Mr. J. Lewis Champion
Rufo .... Mr. J. S. Berdoe
Charmian .... Miss Bertha Morton
Bitouka .... Miss Stella Phelps
Myra .... Miss Lillie Keen
        —Balham Assembly Rooms.

2. *Minna von Barnhelm*, Gotthold Ephraim
Lessing's comedy in five acts.
Major von Tellheim .. Herr Max Schiefer
Minna von Barnhelm .... Elsa Gademann
Franziska ...... Fräulein Marie Christoph
Just .... Herr Georg L'Orange
Paul Werner ...... Herr Hans Andresen
Der Wirt ...... Herr Adolf Walter-Paris
Eine Dame in Trauer .. Betty L'Arronge
Eine Bedienter ...... Herr Rudolf Exner
Riccaut de la Marliniere
          Herr Kurt Sakrzewski
     —Royalty (German season).

3. *A Santa Lucia*, play, in two acts, from
the Italian of Goffredo Cognetti. Pro-
duced by the Play Actors.
Cillo .... Mr. Herbert Dansey
Totonno .... Mr. Concybeare Gough
Cola .... Mr. Henry Le Grand
Tore .... Mr. Leonard Calvert
Detective .... Mr. Ashton-Jarry
Boy .... Miss Irene Rose
Rosella .... Miss Frances Wetherall

A Santa Lucia (continued).

Giulia .... Miss Italia Conti
Tina .... Miss Rita Tompkins
Carmiella .... Miss Hope Mayne
Filomena .... Miss Sime Seruya
Peppina .... Miss Helen Parsons
Nannina .... Miss Sylvia Norton
—Scala.

4. *Ernestine: The Romance of a Typist,*
play, in four acts, by H. F. Maltby.
Rev. Stanley Kershaw..Mr. Wyn Weaver
Robert Jones .... Mr. H. F. Maltby
Leslie Parkington..Mr. Arthur Claremont
Tommy Kershaw .... Mr. Brember Wills
Mr. Barnes ...... Mr. Reginald Favell
Mr. Bramber ...... Mr. Jas. Willoughby
Jackson .... Mr. J. Clegg
Mrs. Kershaw .... Miss Lizzie Maddocks
Miss Butler .... Miss Katie Johnson
Harper .... Miss Viola Lewis
Ernestine Kershaw .... Miss Mara Maltby
—Royal, Exeter.

4.†_The Bridegroom,_ play, in one act, adapted
from the German of Frau Viebig by
Nigel Playfair, rehearsed by Mr. E. Lyall
Swete.
George .... Mr. Frederick James
Madame Louise..Miss Margaret Hollister
Freda .... Miss Constance Little
Miss Twamley .... Miss Gladys Dale
Miss Dobbin ...... Miss Constance Crook
Ethel Hawkins....Miss Veronica Wootten
Mrs. Henderson .... Miss Hilda Hamilton
Dolly .... Miss Laura Cowie
Lady Sayers .... Miss Mabel Mears
A New Customer..Winifred Fairweather
—Playhouse.

4. *Beau Brocade (the Highwayman),* romantic
play, in four acts, by Baroness Orczy and
Montague Barstow (London production,
Coronet, June 1).
Capt. Jack Bathurst..Mr. Reginald Dance
Duke of Cumberland..Mr. Oswald Griffiths
Earl of Stretton..Mr. Alfred H. Majilton
Sir Humphrey Challoner..Mr. Frank Powell
Squire West .... Mr. A. E. Mayne
Mr. Mittachip .... Mr. Stanley Lathbury
Master Duffy .... Mr. Brisco Owen
John Stich .... Mr. Dalziel Heron
Jock Miggs .... Mr. Edward Irwin
The Sergeant ...... Mr. Henderson Bland
Jeremiah Inch ...... Mr. Harold Carson
Postboy .... Mr. R. Hope
Lady Patience Gascoyne.Miss Ruth Mackay
Betty .... Miss May Brooke
—D. P. Eastbourne.

4. *The Few and the Many,* one-act play, by
H. M. Richardson.
Elsie .... Miss Gladys Morris
Mrs. Ebton-Smith .... Miss Ada King
Mr. Ebton-Smith .... Mr. B. Iden Payne
Maid .... Miss Louise Holbrook
The Hon. Percy Wilton..Mr. Basil Dean
Mary Millington .. Miss Penelope Wheeler
—Gaiety, Manchester.

4. *Panne,* Farce, in three acts, by Richard
Skowronnek.
Heinrich Rösicke....Karl William Büller
Aurelie ...... Fräulein Betty L'Arronge
Franzi .... Fräulein Marie Christoph
Karl Weber, jun..Herr Adolf Walter-Paris
Bodo Graf von Ringerode..Max Schiefer
Arendt .... Herr Georg L'Orange
Malter .... Herr Kurt Sakrzewski
Zernickow .... Herr Hans Andresen
Minchen ...... Fräulein Else Gademann
Lieschen ...... Fräulein Josefine Gruber
—Royalty (German season).

5.°_La Rafale,_ M. Henry Bernstein's play, in
three acts. (Originally produced at the
Gymnase, Paris, October 20, 1905. In
London at the Royalty, January 12, 1906);
also English version, under the title of
The Whirlwind, produced by Mrs. Pat
Campbell, at the Royal, Birmingham,
April 9, 1906, and at the Criterion, May
23, 1906.
Le Baron Lebourg .... M. Marey
Robert de Chacéroy .... M. Chevalet
Amédée Lebourg .... M. Gorieux
Bragelin .... M. Cheron
Le Général duc de Briales .. M. Tramont
De Bréchebel .... M. Savoy
Un Valet de pied .... M. Luxeuil
Un Domestique ....:........ M. Leduc
Hélène de Bréchebel. Mme. Suzanne Depres
Mme. Lebourg .... Mme. Gueret
La Marquise .... Mme. Horden
—Shaftesbury (French season).

5.‖†_Mary Roper,_ duologue, written by John
Douglass.
Mrs. Grayling ...... Miss Jeanne Pierlaux
Miss Champion .... Miss Mary Hope
—Cavendish Rooms.

5.°_The Dairymaids,_ musical comedy, in two
acts and three scenes, by A. M. Thompson
and Robert Courtneidge, lyrics by Paul
Rubens and Arthur Wimperis, music by
Paul Rubens and Frank Tours. (Origin-
ally produced at the Apollo, April 14,
1906.) (Last performance, July 18.)
Lady Brudenell....Miss Phyllis Broughton
Lieut. Brudenell......E. Statham Staples
Lieut. Frank Meredith....Mr. Fred Leslie
Dr. O'Byrne ...... Mr. Ambrose Manning
Tim Capus .... Mr. H. Percival
Lieut. Brereton........ Mr. A. Wyndham
Togers .... Mr. Carr Evans
Joe Mivens .... Mr. Dan Rolyat
Winifred ....Miss Florence Smithson
Helen .... Miss Gladys Ivery
Miss Penelope Pyechase .... Marie Daltra
Eliza .... Miss Florence Lloyd
Lady Hyde .... Miss Dorothy Laine
Mrs. Cheyne...........Miss Maisie Sinclair
Miss Knightsbridge..Miss Edythe Burnand
Peggy.................. Miss Phyllis Dare
—Queen's.

9. *The Thunderbolt,* "an episode in the
history of a provincial family," in four
acts, by Arthur W. Pinero. Last perform-
ance, July 3, 58 performances.
James Mortimore ......Mr. Louis Calvert
Ann .... Miss Kate Bishop
Stephen Mortimore....Mr. Norman Forbes
Louisa .... Miss Alice Beet
Thaddeus Mortimore..Mr. Geo. Alexander
Phyllis .... Miss Mabel Hackney
Joyce .... Miss Mignon Clifford
Cyril .... Master Cyril Bruce
Colonel Ponting.....Mr. Wilfrid Draycott
Rose ....Miss May Palfrey
Helen Thornhill.....Miss Stella Campbell
The Rev. George Trist..Mr. Reginald Owen
Mr. Vallance...........Mr. Julian Royce
Mr. Elkin .... Mr. J. D. Beveridge
Mr. Denyer............. Mr. F. J. Arlton
Heath .... Mr. Richard Haigh
Servant .... Miss Gladys Dale
Two Others at } { Miss Sybil Maurisc
"Ivanhoe" } ···· { Miss Vere Sinclair
—St. James's.

11. *The World and the Woman,* domestic
drama, in four acts, by L. C. Cassidy.
Arthur Burleigh ...... Mr. Carl Rovitelli
Ludlow Burleigh .. Mr. George H. Doyle
Tut Harding ...... Mr. J. Rice Cassidy
Terry C. Harris .... Mr. Ralph Leslie
Sir Francis Chalmers..Mr. Henry Compton

The World and the Woman (continued).

Hike .... Mr. J. Cuthbertson
Hon. Willy .... Mr. Jerold Reed
Old Robert .... Mr. R. Cockroft
John .... Mr. G. Kay
Janitor .... Mr. W. Heeford
Captain Barclay .... Mr. Stanley Wilford
Lady Marion Chalmers .. Roma Tremayne
Gwendoline .... Miss Vara Hern
Libby .... Miss Alice Inman
Nina .... Miss Violet Parker
Martha .... Miss Rita Hestock
Nurse Halton .... Miss Rose Hallas
Nelly .... Mrs. J. Rice Cassidy
              —Palace. Newcastle.

11.‡*Billy Rotterford's Descent*, "sensational farce," by Robert Lascelles. (Originally produced at the Royal, Birmingham, on October 25, 1907, under the title of *Among the Brigands*. Revised and re-named with its present title, it was played at the Opera House, Cork, on March 23, 1908.)

J. K. Rotterford .... Mr. Murray Carson
Billy Rotterford...Mr. Weedon Grossmith
Aubrey Colpoys .... Mr. W. T. Lovell
Mr. Polting .... Mr. Frank H. Denton
Kelly .... Mr. Charles Wemyss
Sir Richard Mulberry.Mr. William Charles
Mr. Drage .... Mr. R. M. Toussaint
Edwards .... Mr. James R. La Fane
Gates .... Mr. Duncan Bruce
Colonel Brazier ...... Mr. James Sinclair
Freddy Western ...... Mr. John Upham
Lord Dilthorpe .... Mr. H. Tims
Reporter. .... Mr. Harold Bosman
Landlord .... Mr. B. Manso
Mrs. Rotterford..Miss Marion Ashworth
Lady Mulberry .... Miss Harley Connell
Dolly Caterack .... Miss Constance Clive
Popsy Hockett .... Miss Rose Galvin
Mme. Garvarnavitch .... Miss Annie Hill
Photographer .... Mr. A. B. Surd
Zampassa .... Mr. Hubert Carter
Vanderhousan ...... Mr. Henry Latimer
Ching Fung ...... Mr. Sebastian Smith
Davitz .... Mr. H. Elphin
Gavonde Vritz .... Mr. Cyril Potts
Age Kingutinsky .... Mr. R. Morton
Baja Linksgentz .... Mr. James Ingersole
Vera Vanderhousan
            Miss Madge Titheradge.
            —King's, Hammersmith.

11. *The Old Home*, domestic drama, in four acts.

Daddy Dean .... Mr. Charles Franmore
Hazel Dean ...... Miss Gertrude Bonser
Rev. Eric Armstrong .. Mr. H. Lonsdale
Bridget Doughan .... Miss Maud Locker
Sam Adams .... Mr. Fred de Vere
Lord Avondale .. Mr. Alexander Bradley
Timothy Twaddle .. Mr. James Lea Hair
Pollie Popp .... Miss Sybil Hare
Warburton .... Mr. Roland Yorke
Jack Warren .... Mr. Walter Osmond
            —P.O.W., Salford.

11. *The Cheerful Knave*, play, in three acts, by Keble Howard.

The Knave .... Mr. George Elton
Lord Bacchus .... Mr. P. Perceval-Clark
Mr. Running Pole .... Mr. Frank Stone
Constable Cogbill .. Mr. Gerald Venning
A Footman .... Mr. J. Napper
Miss Joyce Dartnell....Miss Lilian Rogers
Mrs. Hamp .... Miss Agnes Thomas
Miss Pinto .... Miss Isabel Merson
A Maid .... Miss Haydon Waugh
Lady Bacchus .... Miss Florence Haydon
            —Royal, Margate.

11. *The Last Rose of Summer*, play, in one act, by Percy Robinson.
Taidy Dwyer .... Mr. Wallis Clark
Maureen .... Miss Isabel Merson
            —Royal, Margate.

11. *A Game of Bluff*, one-act play, by H. M. Pauh
Morgan.............. Mr. George de Lara
Danby .... Mr. F. Mason
Bob .... Mr. J. W. Rea
Rosie .... Miss Gertrude Bibby
            —Royal Court, Liverpool.

11. *The Sensible Constanza*, serious comedy, in three acts, by Charles E. O. Thornton.
Bishop of Lundy and Mull..Mr. Guy Lane
Lady Manningtree..Miss Cicely Charlton
Sir Stephen Hollis, K.C.B...Mr. W. Senior
Constanza Marcovitz
            Miss Frances Wetherall
Count de Corrientes..Mr. Herbert Dansey
Lord Manningtree..Mr. Halliwell Hobbes
Servant..............Mr. Geoffrey Douglas
Hon. Henry Sylvester
            Master Haviland Chappell
Hon. Elizabeth Sylvester
            Miss Nancy Bevington
            —Kingsway.

11. *The Boys*, farcical comedy, in three acts, by Henry Seton. Revived at the Court, July 9.
Mortimer Wilberley ...... Mr. Fred Lewis
Brian O'Donaghue.. Mr. Charles Goodhart
Micky Halloran .... Mr. Wilfred E. Shine
Major Robert Rayner..Mr. Herbert Walton
Capt. Hugh Wilson....Mr. Austin Spencer
Peter Tubbs .... Mr. Max Leeds
Ananda ...... Mr. John Brabourne
O'Driscoll .... Mr. J. G. Finley
Colonel Harker...... Mr. Francis Howard
Davies .... Mr. Reginald Craven
Marriot .... Mr. A. Martin Nicholson
Bat .... Mr. Gordon Holmes
Walter ...... Mr. George Handscombe
Miss Petunia Parsons ..Miss Elsie Chester
Miss Patricia O'Donaghue..Maude Thomas
Miss Katherine O'Donaghue
            Miss Vera Beringer
Miss Mary O'Donaghue..Miss May Blayney
Miss Maynard............Miss M. Holford
            —Grand, Croydon.

11. *Nero and Co.*, comic opera, in two acts, libretto by Norman Page, music by Bernard Page.
Nero .... Mr. B. B. Venn
Ethelreduose ......Mr. A. W. Bradshaw
Suetonius ....Mr. A. J. Woodward
Prasutagus ....Mr. Jack Clarke
Thunder .... Mr. L. N. Grover
Boadicea .... Miss Maude Cooper
Poppæa ....Mrs. Arthur Niblett
Phlyte .... Miss Muriel Pratt
            —Mechanics' Hall, Nottingham.

12.‡*Butterflies*, musical play, in three acts, by W. J. Locke (founded on his comedy, *The Palace of Puck*, produced at the Haymarket, April 2, 1907), music by J. A. Robertson, lyrics by T. H. Read and others. (Originally produced at the Tyne, Newcastle, April 20.) Last performance, November 14; 217 London performances.
Salome .... Miss Gladys Soman
Paul .... Mr. Willie Warde
Peter .... Mr. Kenna Lawson
Gilbert .... Mr. John Bardsley
Lalage .... Miss Lucie Cain
Myra .... Miss Jessie Lollen
Yarker .... Mr. Lauri de Frece
Christopher Podmore .. Mr. Fred Edwards
Elsie Podmore .... Miss Iris Hoey
Nora Podmore .... Miss Stella St. Audrie

Butterflies (continued).

Widgery Blake .. Mr. W. Louis Bradfield
Max Riadore ...... Mr. C. Hayden Coffin
Rhodanthe .... Miss Ada Reeve
Parisiennes—Misses Monkman, Glynn,
Brock, and Gordon. Parisians—Messrs.
Giron, Edwarde, Selby, and Rubins.
Chorus of Painters, Sculptors, Artists'
Models, etc
—Apollo.

12. |*Getting Married,* "Conversation," by
George Bernard Shaw. (Put into the
evening bill on June 1.) Last performance,
July 11; 54 performances.
Mrs. Bridgenorth........Miss Mary Rorke
Alderman Collins....Mr. E. Holman Clark
General Bridgenorth..Mr. Charles Fulton
Lesbia Grantham ......Miss Beryl Faber
Reginald Bridgenorth..Wm. Farren, jun.
Mrs. Reginald Bridgenorth..Marie Löhr
The Bishop of Chelsea..Mr. Henry Ainley
St. John Hotchkiss....Mr. Robert Loraine
Cecil Sykes .... Mr. Berte Thomas
Edith Bridgenorth...... Miss Auriol Lee
Rev. O. C. Soames .... Mr. James Hearn
Joseph Wollaston ...... Mr. Albert Sims
Mrs. George Collins....Miss Fanny Brough
—Haymarket.

13. |*The Great Yah Boo,* comic opera, in two
acts, with libretto and songs by the Rev.
H. D. Hinde, music composed by Miss L.
Stooks, Mr. T. R. G. Lyell, and Mr. L.
Phillipson.
Tycho the 47th .. Master Artie Matthews
Kandi .... Miss May Luff
Marcell .... Miss Florrie Conisbee
Zadi .... Master Fred Butcher
Dodo the 1st .. Master Fredk. Hitchcock
The Great Yah Boo .... Mr. Percy Dicks
Duchess of Caviare .. Miss Winnie Wright
Princess Tina .... Miss Julia Dicks
Merle .... Miss Florrie Gledstone
Baron Bonbouche..Mast. Sydney Matthews
Marquis of Cascarel..Master Tom Brooks
Elise. Comtesse d'Aremé...Miss Elsie Tegg
Susanne du Carambert..Miss Ethel Parsons
Jeanne D'Espoir ...... Miss Florrie Tegg
—Southgate Village Hall.

13. |*The House in Green Street,* play, in four
acts, by Mrs. C. Clilverd Young.
Sarah Jenkins ...... Miss C. Coopman
Dick Devereux .. Mr. Albert F. Lawson
Geoffrey Penton ...... Mr. J. Cecil Rowe
Elysia Frobisher .... Miss Gladys Collings
Helena Frobisher .... Miss Dora Landau
Baroness Kitznau .... Miss Louise Salom
Jakes .... Mr. James McGowan
Rudolph Kitznau..Mr. Arthur C. Chapman
Lady Carleton .... Miss Ellie Chester
Baron Kitznau ....Mr. G. H. Cook
Charles .... Mr. George Stanley
Lord Carleton .... Mr. Harry Peach
—King's Hall, W.C.

14. *A Soldier's Daughters,* one-act play, by
Cosmo Hamilton.
Helen Meridith .... Miss Winifred Emery
Pamela .... Miss Beryl Faber
Jane .... Miss Pollie Emery
—Kingsway.

14. *The Flower Girl,* musical play in two acts
(book, lyrics, and music by William T.
Gliddon). London production, November
30, Grand, Croydon.
Lily .... Miss Lily Brammer
Joe Wheeler ...... Mr. Martin Adeson
Billy Wheeler .... Mr. Walter Purvis
Johnny Martin .... Mr. B. Currie
Reginald Rackit .... Mr. Edward Kipling
Alphonse de Racquet .. Mr. Henry Adnes
Lizette de Racquet..Miss Florence Wilton

The Flower Girl (continued).

Miss Spankard .... Miss Jeannie Holmes
Jessie .... Miss Cissie King
Maudie .... Miss Alice King
Kate .... Miss Phyllis Leslie
Dot .... Miss Kitty Hyde
Policeman .... Mr. L. Stanislaus
Mr. Bunker .... Mr. Arthur Carter
Bertie .... Mr. Tom Squire
—Royal, Lincoln.

14. *Lanval,* drama, in four acts, by T. E.
Ellis. (Produced at Mr. Acton Bond's
invitation performance. The first public
performance took place at the Aldwych
on May 21.)
King of Britain............Mr. C. V. France
Duke of Cornwall .. Mr. George Ingleton
Owain .... Mr. Alfred Harding
Geraint .... Mr. Arthur Holmes-Gore
Gawain .... Mr. C. F. Collings
Agravaine .... Mr. Chas. Rock
Meliard .... Mr. Harry Hilliard
Astamor .... Mr. Douglas Imbert
Lanval .... Mr. Harcourt-Williams
Bernardo .... Mr. Robert Forsyth
Gyfert .... Mr. Ashton Pearse
1st Charcoal Burner....Mr. Harry Winton
2nd Charcoal Burner..Mr. Leonard Calvert
Guinevere .... Miss Hutin Britton
Lynette .... Miss Dorothy Scott
Alysoun .... Miss Muriel Mason
Hélène .... Miss E. Howard Ross
Girl .... Miss Evelyn Cockburn
Triamour .... Miss Elaine Inescourt
—Playhouse.

18. |*A Mother's Salvation,* melodrama, in four
acts, by Nita Rae. (Originally produced
at the Royal, Wednesbury, on April 27,
1908.)
Reuben Smith ...... Mr. Monson Thorpe
Leslie Mervyne ...... Mr. Henry C. Ward
Lynton Desmond .... Mr. John Levy
Joe Turntail ...... Mr. Newton Cowling
Marmaduke Danby..Mr. J. O. Stevenson
Billy Bumpkin ...... Mr. Fred Gresham
Little Paul .... Miss Mabel Hall
Dan Potter .... Mr. T. Chapman
Guard .... Mr. Harry Oggier
Sergeant Colville .... Mr. J. Ballard
King of Britain .... Mr. C. V. France
Gus Durant .... Mr. Fred Daring
Beckey .... Miss Fanny Wallace
Mother Turntail ...... Miss Kate Newton
Naomi Lester ....} Miss Ada Hender
Miriam Mervyne ....}
Daisy Delaval ...... Miss Maude Western
—Royal, Stratford.

18. *La Loi de l'Homme,* Paul Hervieu's three-
act comedy.
Le Comte de Raguais........,M. G. Baillet
Monsieur D'Orcieu....M. Jacques Fenoux
Kerbel .... M. Joumard
Le Commissaire de Police....M. Escoffier
Andre D'Orcieu............. M. Bonvallet
Un Valet de Pied..............M. G. Roux
Madame D'Orcieu..............Mme. Dux
Isabelle de Raguais....Mme. Flore Mignot
Henriette Kerbel............Mme. Arlette
Laure, Comtesse de Raguais..Mme. Bartet
—Shaftesbury (French season).

18. *The Girl from Over the Border (A Prince's
Dream),* musical extravaganza.
Prince Carl .... Mr. Leslie Stiles
Dandy Pearsop.......... Mr. T. W. Volt
Tubby Wiggles ....Mr. Bertie Wright
Wee McGregor ....Mr. George Carroll
Sandy McAlpine..........Mr. Cecil Frere
A Student....Mr. Herbert Standing, jun.

The Girl from Over the Border (continued).
Lady Clancarty..Miss Winifred Hart-Dyke
Lady Joan Campbell..Miss Marion Marler
Margaret Helen......Miss Gladys Ffolliott
Jeanie .... Miss Nellie Bouverie
Jessie .... Miss Amy Fanchette
Mary McAlpine........Miss Norah Walker
Stella .... Miss Gay Silvani
—King's, Hammersmith.

18. *Dingle's Double,* farcical sketch, by Edward Marris.
James Dingle, Esq....Mr. Heller Le Maistre
Archie Framland......Mr. Walter Nugent
Jim Stent..........Mr. George Brentwood
Major Podmore....Mr. Leonard Dalrymple
Mrs. Stent .... Miss Lillian Drake
Mrs. Dingle............Miss Grace Lester
—O.H., Jersey.

18. *The Simple Life,* one-act farce, by an anonymous author.
Gwendoline Welch-Mannering
Miss Margery Chard
Margaret Moody-Gibson
Miss Edith Deverell
Cripps .... Mr. E. Boddy
The Village Postman..........Mr. B. Noel
P.C. Swigley .... Mr. Edward Thirlby
—County, Kingston.

19. The Lady Mayoress,* comedy, " in three odd tricks," written by Harry D. Rowan.
Amy Denswell........Miss Evelyn Buckley
Tom Warefield ....Mr. Gerald A. Hall
Irene Fosdyck....Mrs. Walter Champneys
Bessie Denswell .... Mrs. W. S. Hall
John Denswell...... Mr. Arthur A. Coles
Kidder............ Miss Beatrice Hawkins
Sir Arthur Forde, Kt.....Mr. Percy White
Molyneux Montgomery..Mr. Hy. D. Rowan
Florence Denswell......Miss Ethel Fowler
Adolphus ....Master R. Tackley
—All Saints' Parish Hall, East Finchley.

19. *Charlotte on Bigamy,* play, in one act, by Edward A. Parry
Charlotte Garvice .. Miss Gertrude Scott
Peter Garvice....Mr. Michael Sherbrooke
Lancelot Bragby ...... Mr. Dennis Eadie
John McIntyre ...... Mr. C. M. Hallard
—Kingsway.

19. *A Nocturne.* play, in one act, by Anthony P. Wharton.
Martha Blackburne..Miss Haidée Wright
Cecilia Hope .... Miss Mary Barton
James Trantbridge .... Mr. Ernest Young
Mrs. Gaul .... Miss Ada Palmer
Man in Grey Tweeds....Mr. T. A. Shannon
—Kingsway.

19. *The Latch,* play, in one act, by Mrs. W. K. Clifford.
Mme. Pilleau ...... Miss Nannie Bennett
Harcourt Wilson...Mr. Norman McKinnel
Charlotte .... Miss Constance Collier
—Kingsway.

19. *The Whirligig,* play, in one act, by Eva Anstruther
Lady Lee .... Miss Marion Terry
Footman .... Mr. W. Lemmon Warde
Sir Antony Culgaith, M.P.
Mr. Henry Vibart
Sir Richard Lee ...... Mr. Eric Maturin
The Other Woman....Miss Muriel Wylford
—Kingsway.

19. *An Evening at the Detective's,* play, in one act, by J. F. Cooke.
—Prince of Wales's, Birmingham.

20.†*Breaking it Gently,* play, in one act, by Affleck Scott.
Jim Bradford .... Mr. Robert Whyte, jun.
George Danby ...... Mr. Charles Troode
Grace Hawkins .... Miss Mona Harrison
—Vaudeville.

20.**Toddles,* farce, in three acts, adapted by Clyde Fitch from *Triplepatte,* by Tristan Bernard and André Godfernaux (originally produced at Duke of York's, September 3, 1906)—Playhouse.

21. *Lanval,* drama, in four acts, by T. E. Ellis (first public performance). See under date 14 for cast, etc.—Aldwych.

21.¶*The End of the World; or, Tablitsky Says,* playlet, by Aaron Hoffman.
Abraham Levy .... Joe Hayman
Sammy .... George Sachs
Esther .... Mildred Franklin
—Hippodrome, Eastbourne.

23. *The Secretary's Wedding Present,* play, in one act, by Henry Allen Ashton.
Lady Eileen Margatroyd..Miss Hope Mayne
Gordon Henderson .... Mr. Edmund Lee
Cyril Raymond .... Mr. S. Courtney
John .... Mr. G. Goodwin
—Rehearsal, W.C.

23. *The King of Borneo,* farce, in one act, by Henry Allen Ashton.
Sir Harry Bombay .. Mr. Marius Girard
Dr. Lansdowne .... Mr. S. Teversham
Hon. Reggie Fairfax..Mr. Wentworth Fane
Lieut. Edgar Jarvis .... Mr. Robert Grey
Grayson .... Mr. R. Van Cortlandt
Letty .... Miss E, Desmond
Milly .... Miss Violet Pickworth
Alice .... Miss Amy Randolph
—Rehearsal, W.C.

23. *The Savage Beneath,* drama, in one act, by Godfrey Dean.
Charles Rivers ...... Mr. William Dexter
Mrs. Rivers .... Miss Dora Heritage
Jack Wilson .... Mr. G. Goodwin
—Rehearsal, W.C.

24. *The Man Who Won,* drama, in three acts, by Arthur M. Heathcote (founded on the novel of the same name by Mrs. Baillie Reynolds).
Bert Mestaer .... Mr. Norman Trevor
Rev. Carol Mayne....Mr. Cecil Brooking
Otis .... Mr. Cecil A. Collins
Harry Helston .... Mr. Fewlass Llewellyn
Sir Lancelot Burmester.Coneybeare Gough
General Ayres .. Mr. Reginald Rivington
Shepherd .... Mr. Spencer Geach
Arnie Lutwyche ...... Miss Lilian Tweed
Melicent Lutwyche .. Miss Rose Mathews
Tante Wilma .... Miss Lilian Tweed
Brenda Helston ...... Miss Elinor Foster
Sybil Ayres .... Miss Mary Deverell
Theo Cooper ...... Miss Beatrice Chester
—Scala.

24. *Feed the Brute,* " an uninstructive conversation," in one act, written by " George Paston," produced by the Pioneers.
Samuel Pottle ...... Mr. Edmund Gwenn
Susan Pottle .... Miss Clare Greet
Mrs. Wilks .... Miss Agnes Thomas
—Royalty.

24. *Nan,* play, in three acts, by John Masefield, produced by the Pioneers. (A public performance of this piece was given at the Haymarket on June 2.)
Jenny Pargetter .... Miss Mary Jerrold
Mrs. Pargetter ...... Mrs. A. B. Tapping
William Pargetter .. Mr. Horace Hodges
Nan Hardwick .... Miss Lillah McCarthy
Dick Gurvil .... Mr. A. E. Anson
Artie Pearce ...... Mr. Percy Gawthorn
Gaffer Pearce .... Mr. H. R. Hignett
Tommy Arkel .... Mr. Allan Wade
Ellen .... Miss Marion Nugent
Susan .... Miss Bokenham
Rev. Mr. Drew ...... Mr. Edmund Gurney
Captain Dixon ..... Mr. H. Athol Forde
The Constable ..... Mr. Christmas Grose
—Royalty.

25.†*The Chalice*, tragic episode, By Harry and Edward Paulton.
Père Oller .... Mr. Harry Paulton
Marie .... Miss Lucy Verrier
Féron .... Mr. Duncan McRae
Martha .... Miss Wynne-Hanley
—Daly's.

25.‡*The Fortunes of Fan*, three-act farcical comedy, by H. M. Paull (originally produced on April 20 at the Royal Lyceum, Edinburgh).
Robert Wigley ...... Mr. George de Lara
Mrs. Wigley .... Miss Janet Hodgson
Tom Hudson .... Mr. Robert Whitworth
Fan .... Miss Louie Freear
Madame Dobbs .... Miss Gertrude Bibby
Lady Beddington..Miss Maude Henderson
Cecil Ramsden .... Mr. John W. Deverell
Mrs. Gregory (Maud)..Miss Nellie Redwood
Footman .... Mr. W. J. Rea
—Crown, Peckham.

25. *Le Dédale*, Paul Hervieu's four-act drama.
Max de Pogis .. M. Albert Lambert, fils.
Guillaume Le Breuil..M. Jacques Fenoux
Vilard Duval .... M. Joumard
Hubert de Sainte Eric ...... M. Escoffier
Le Docteur .... M. Deroy
Un Jeune paysan .... M. Henriot
Un Domestique .... M. Roux
Madame de Pogis .... Mme. Dux
Madame Vilard-Duval..Mme. Jeanne Even
Paulette .... Mme. Flore Mignot
Marianne .... Mme. Bartet
—Shaftesbury (French season).

25.‡*Send Him Victorious*, drama, in four acts, by Herbert Skardon. (Originally produced at the Prince's, Horwich, December 30, 1907.)—Royal, Stratford.

28.‖*The Key of Life*, phantasy written and arranged by Viscountess Maitland. The music of the prologue and epilogue composed by Reginald Somerville—Scala.

28.‖*The Masque of War and Peace*—Scala.
28.¶*The Scarlet Highwayman*, drama, by Max Malcom—Lyric, Hammersmith.

28.†*The Grey Stocking*, comedy, in four acts, by Maurice Baring.
Miss Farrer .... Miss May Pardoe
Lady Sybil Alston..Miss Lilian Braithwaite
Mrs. James .... Mrs. Beerbohm Tree
Footman .... Mr. E. H. Brooke
Mrs. Simpson.............. Miss Pattison
Miss Rennett............ Miss Annie Hill
Mrs. Willbrough..Miss Gertrude Kingston
Henry Alston.............Mr. C. V. France
Basil Alston ....Mr. Lewis Willoughby
Robert Macfarlane....Mr. Arthur Eldred
Charles Meriot ......Mr. George Ingleton
Wilfred Beenham......Mr. Ashton Pearse
Count Velichkovsky..Mr. Harcourt-Williams
Tommy Connybeare..Mr. Wilfred Forster
Hugo Willbrough.....Mr. J. Fisher White
—Royalty.

28.¶*He's a Jolly Good Fellow*, play, in four acts, by Arthur Shirley and E. Vivian Edmonds—West London.

29. *The Monarch of the World*, domestic drama, produced by Alfred B. Cross—Royal, Barry Dock.

29.‡*The Woman Who was Dead*, melodrama, in four acts, by J. W. Sabben Clare. Originally produced March 16, Gaiety, Dundee.
Philip Carey......Mr. Montague Beaudyn
Denise .... Miss Irene Munroe
Horace Winter ......Mr. G. M. Montanini
Guy Oliphant ....Mr. Frank Holyoake

The Woman Who was Dead (continued).
Lord Arthur Dumley......Mr. James Bert
Bransby .... Mr. Harry Oates
Commissaire of Police..Mr. Frank Walton
Waiter at the Casino..Mr. Lionel Carteret
Waiter at Hotel de Paris..Mr. John Baxter
Marie .... Miss Netta Mitchell
Nellie Montague........Miss C. Crawford
Helen Terraire ....Miss Marie Robson
—Royal, Stratford.

29.‖*The Head of the Family*, play, in one act, by B. Knollys.
Bobs Durant ....Mr. Andrew Shanks
"Skittle" Durant.....Miss Eva Rowland
Mimie Mayne........Miss Florrie Moss
Dick Maynard ....Mr. Arthur Lorimer
Servant.............Miss Margaret Ismay
—Royal Academy of Music.

31. *Links*, play, in four acts, by Herman Heijermans, translated by Howard Peacey and W. R. Brandt. (Produced by the Stage Society.)
Jacob Dulk ....Mr. H. Murgatroyd
A Book-keeper ......Mr. W. H. Rotheram
A Messenger ....Mr. Burton Cooke
Sally .... Mr. Ivan Berlyn
Henk .... Mr. Hubert Harben
A Telegraph Boy ....Mr. Frank Kingston
Pancras Duif .... Mr. J. Fisher White
Sister .... Miss Cicely Charlton
Marianne........... Miss Edyth Latimer
Dirk .... Mr. Kenyon Musgrave
Jan .... Mr. Robert Atkins
Toon .... Mr. Leon Quartermaine
Hein Duif ....Mr Edmund Gwenn
Gerritje .... Miss Clare Greet
Coba .... Miss Margaret Bussé
Elsie .... Miss Iris Hawkins
Margriet .... Miss Lilian M. Revell
Dr. Van Rijn .... Mr. Vincent Clive
A Maid-Servant....Miss Dora E. Clements
—Scala.

JUNE.

1.°*La Fille du Tambour-Major*, opera-comique, libretto by MM. Chivot and Duru, music by Jacques Offenbach (produced in Paris in 1879; English version at the Alhambra, April 19, 1880), revived by French company, headed by Mme. Tariol-Baugé—Shaftesbury

1.‡*Beau Brocade*, romantic play, in four acts by the Baroness Orczy and Montagu Barstow (originally produced at D.P., Eastbourne, May 4).
Capt. Bathurst .... Mr. Reginald Dance
Duke of Cumberland..Mr. Oswald Griffiths
Earl of Stretton..Mr. Alfred H. Majilton
Sir Humphrey Challoner..Mr. Frank Powell
Squire West .... Mr. A. E. Mayne
Mr. Mittachip ...... Mr. Stanley Lathbury
Master Duffy .... Mr. Brisco Owen
John Stich .... Mr. Dalziel Heron
Jock Miggs .... Mr. Edward Irwin
The Sergeant ...... Mr. Henderson Bland
Jeremiah Inch .... Mr. Harold Carson
Postboy .... Mr. R. Hope
Lady Gascoyne ...... Miss Ruth Mackay
Betty, her Maid ...... Miss May Brooke
—Coronet.

2.†*Nan*, first public performance of the three-act tragedy by John Masefield, which was produced by the Pioneers at the Royalty, May 25—Haymarket.

2.†On the Right Road, play, in one act, by Mrs. de Courcy Laffan.
Lord Dangerfield .... Mr. Henry Doughty
Major Urquhart .. Mr. Julian L'Estrange
Gillingham .... Mr. P. L. Julian
Lady Dangerfield .... Miss Vera Leslie
Somers .... Miss Armine Grace
—Court.

2.†*Guinevere*, adaptation of Tennyson's poem, by Vera Leslie.
King Arthur ...... Mr. Henry Doughty
Guinevere .... Miss Vera Leslie
A Novice .... Miss Thyrza Norman
Chorus of Nuns: Misses A. Grace, E. Kitson, E. Knight. H. Leith, B. McHoul, J. McHoul, M. Nicholson, A. Riste, and A. Rind.
—Court.

2. *Flo Rigg,* play, in one act, by Estelle Burney.
Flo Rigg .... Miss Agnes Hill
Kate Granger .... Miss Marie Linden
Jim .... Mr. Howard Sturge
Millie Miers .... Miss Begbie
Nelly Kirby ...... Miss Vera Longden
Susie Price ...... Miss Ruth Heathcote
Gerty Winter .... Miss Hilliard
—Royal Albert Hall.

4. *Darkness and Light.* Pageant in four episodes by John Oxenham, music by Hamish McCunn, produced by Hugh Moss.
—Royal Agricultural Hall.

5.¶*Aunt Gabrielle,* three-act comedy, by J. C. New—Straithblaine Hall, St. John's Hill.

3. *The Prince and the Beggar Maid,* romantic drama, in four acts, by Walter Howard. Last performance, August 26 ; 84 performances.
Prince Olof .... Mr. Lauderdale Maitland
Hildred .... Mr. Eric Mayne
Michael .... Mr. Halliwell Hobbes
Capt. Hector .... Mr. Frederick Ross
Lieut. Karl Stromberg..Mr. Reg. Sheldrick
Col. Wellenberg .... Mr. S. Major Jones
Capt. Karsburg .... Mr. Sidney Vautier
Capt. Schwartz .... Mr. Ernest Cresfan
Capt. Sudermann .. Mr. Alec Weatherley
Lieut. Welder .. Mr. Wynfred Williams
Lieut. Schultz ...... Mr. Harry Hilliard
The Bishop of Illyria .. Mr. Fenn Challis
Nathan .... Mr. Herbert Dansey
Viola .... Miss Dido Drake
Camiola .... Miss Lillian Digges
Princess Monica of Illyria Miss Nora Kerin
—Lyceum.

8. *Loyalty House; including the Siege of Manchester,* historical play, in four acts.
ROYALISTS.
Earl of Derby .. Mr. Seymour Hastings
Capt. Hercules Hartfield .. Mr. L. Atwill
Capt. Frank Standish..Mr. W. Beckwith
Major Ffarington .. Mr. Julian J. Gallier
Sir Thomas Tyldesley .... Mr. E. Farrell
Sir Edward Mosley..Mr. J. Coulston Ross
Sir Tristan Audley..Mr. Fred Lillywhite
Master Peter Crump .. Mr. Hargreaves
Col. Chisenhale .... Mr. J. Foster
Sir Gilbert Houghton .. Mr. D. Lawson
Sir Alexander Radcliffe .. Mr. J. Emsley
Col. Molineux .... Mr. P. Newell
Countess of Derby .... Miss Mary Raby
Isobel Lafont .... Miss Lalla Shelton
Gertrude Rosworm ...... Miss B. Doyle
Dame Partlett .... Miss Laura Ray
Ruth .... Miss Clare O'Sullivan
ROUNDHEADS.
Col. Alexander Rigby..Mr. Roy Fortescue
Capt. Ralph Markland..Mr. F. Etheridge
Col. Rosworm .... Mr. T. G. Bailey
Capt. Bootle .... Mr. David Curtis

Loyalty House (continued).
Col. Holland ...... Mr. Harry Bannister
Capt. Robert Bradshaw..Mr. E. P. Neville
Col. Birch .... Mr. J. Hilton
Col. Holcroft .... Mr. T. Grayson
—Queen's, Manchester.

8. *Old Virginia,* original musical comedietta, libretto by Kennedy Allen and Edwin Adeler, lyrics by Kennedy Allen, Frank Dunlop, and Arthur W. Parry.
Col. Cyrus P. Van Buren
Mr. H. G. Buckland
Sadie Van Buren .. Miss Mildred Bryan
Mamie May ...... Miss Odeyne Spark
Sallie Potts .... Miss Joey Ellis
Rastus .... Mr. Kit Keen
Chloe .... Miss Nellie Sheffield
Fraham Falconer .. Mr. Leonard Russell
Archie Marjoriebanks .... Mr. Bert Errol
Hiram P. Dooley .. Mr. William Pringle
—Olympian Gardens, Rock Ferry.

8. *A Lucky Spill,* new one-act comedy, by H. A. L. Rudd.
John Charlton .... Mr. Eustace Burnaby
William .... Mr. Drelincourt Odlum
Gaffer Hollis .... Mr. Reginald Eyre
Mildred Burnside .. Miss Elaine Inescort
—Criterion.

8. *The Two Pins,* comedy of the Middle Ages, by Frank Stayton. Originally produced April 2, Royal, Newcastle. Last performance, June 20; 14 performances.
Philip .... Mr. Oscar Asche
Rudolph .... Mr. Vernon Steel
Cyril .... Mr. G. Kay Souper
Francis .... Mr. Courtice Pounds
Elsa .... Miss Lily Brayton
Rosaline .... Miss Muriel Ashwynne
Conrad .... Mr. H. Tripp Edgar
Detrichstein .... Mr. Caleb Porter
Gregory ....Mr. J. Fritz Russell
Karl .... Mr. M. Mancini
Wilhelm .... Mr. J. H. Tippler
Baron Gruntendell ..... Mr. Henry Kitts
Messenger from Knoden....Mr. A. Whitby
Servants, Messengers, Men - at - Arms, Huntsmen, etc.: Messrs. Harker, Davis, Brooke, Turner, Trantom, Weekes, Uttridge, Bramble, Digues, Horscroft, Lewys.
—Aldwych.

10 *The Three of Us,* play, in four acts, by Rachel Crothers (originally produced in America). Last performance, July 11.
Stephen Townley .... Mr. John W. Dean
Louis Beresford .... Mr. Cyril Keightley
Clem Macchesney ...... Mr. J. A. Butler
Sonnie Macchesney..Mr. E. J. Morris, jun.
Rhy Macchesney .... Miss Fannie Ward
Tweed Bix .... Mr. Spencer Trevor
Mrs. Bix .... Miss Edith Cartwright
Maggie .... Miss Pattie Browne
Lorimer Trenholm....Mr. Cooke-Beresford
Hop Wing .... Mr. A. B. Tapping
—Terry's.

11.*La Grande Duchesse de Gerolstein,* operacomique, libretto by Meilhac and Halévy, music by Jacques Offenbach (English version produced 1867 at Covent Garden), revived by French company headed by Mme. Tariol-Baugé—Shaftesbury.

13. *The Explorer,* play, in four acts, by William Somerset Maugham. Last performance, July 25; 48 performances.
Alexander Mackenzie .. Mr. Lewis Waller
Richard Lomas .... Mr. A. E. George
Dr. Adamson .... Mr. Charles Rock
Sir Robert Boulger Mr. Owen Roughwood
George Allerton .... Mr. Shiel Barry
Rev. Jas. Carbery..Mr. S. J. Warmington
Capt. Mallins....Mr. A. Caton Woodville

The Explorer (continued).

Miller .... Mr. Charles Cecil
Charles .... Mr. P. Digan
Mrs. Crowley .... Miss Eva Moore
Lady Kelsey .... Miss Mary Rorke
Lucy Allerton ...... Miss Evelyn Millard
                              —Lyric.

13. *The Head of the Firm*, comedy, in four
acts, adapted from the Danish of Hjalmar
Bergstrom by Leslie Faber.
George Heymann ...... Mr. Leslie Faber
John Lydford...... Mr. Ernest H. Ruston
Philip Lydford ...... Mr. Richard Neville
James Browne ...... Mr. Fredk. Morland
Edward Dalby ...... Mr. F. G. Thurstans
Butler .... Mr. Albert Coe
Helen Lydford....Miss Henrietta Leverett
Betty Lydford .... Miss Muriel Pope
Mrs. Dalby .... Miss Beatrice Ainley
                              —O.H., Buxton.

14. *Englands Throne:* A History—Chandos
Hall, W.C.

15. *He's a Jolly Good Fellow*, play, in four
acts, by Arthur Shirley and E. Vivian Ed-
monds. (C.P. May 28, West London.)
Lord Vernon .... Mr. J. Milne Taylor
Harold Vernon .. Mr. E. Vivian Edmonds
Vincent Vernon .... Mr. Charles Aldred
Sampson .... Mr. Richard A. Greene
Baron Levertz .... Mr. Riddell Robinson
Bertie Splashington..Mr. Edwin T. Kisby
Pierre Pasha ...... Mr. Cyril Price Evans
Jean Crac .... Mr. Frank Sutherland
Duplay .... Mr. Stanley Hoban
Père Lacome .... Mr. J. M. Ward
Gaiot .... Mr. Richard Slater
La Bossu .... Mr. Chris Dashwood
Mufle .... Mr. John Mansley
Torquade .... Mr. T. H. Suthers
Secretary .... Mr. George Currie
Landlord .... Mr. Arthur Jackson
Marion Brooklyn .... Miss Dorothy Casey
Lizette ...... Miss Winifred Williamson
Julia Flonflon .... Miss Hilda Gray
Little Harold .... Miss Ella Gillette
Concierge .... Miss Nellie Hayes
Hester Danvers .... Miss Mary Austin
                              —Dalston.

15. *Judith*, dramatic sketch, in one act, by
Augusta Tullock.
Judith Sartoris .... Miss Augusta Tullock
Jack Carrington .... Mr. James Musgrove
Eugen Darville .... Mr. E. Vivian
Silas Norriss .... Miss D. Kirk
Percy Hackmansmite....Mr. Will de Lacy
Walter .... Mr. Chas. R. Collins
                              —Central, Altrincham.

15. *A Wonderful Woman*, romantic costume
comedy, in three acts, founded on the
original play by George Dance as to plot,
entirely re-written by Sydney Spenser,
with incidental music arranged by Mr.
Wilfred E. Cotterill.
Marquis de Frontignac...Mr. S. Spenser
Viscount d'Esparre..Mr. F. T. Freeman
Alphonse .... Mr. Harry T. Butler
Pierre Larolle .. Mr. Edward Rawlinson
Dechelette .... Mr. John Porter
Jules .... Miss Lillie Smith
Lacquey .... Mr. Henry Thompson
Cecile .... Miss Olive Downes
Franchette ...... Miss Amy Rogerson
Marcelle .... Miss Lizzie Hall
Mme. H. Delauney .. Miss Ada Champion
                      —Pier Pavilion, St. Leonards.

15. *The Real Mr. Jonathan*, farcical comedy,
in three acts, by Mr. C. Vernon Proctor.
James James ...... Mr. Pennington Gush
Jonathan James .... Mr. Frank Medhurst
John.............. Mr. C. Vernon Proctor
Ned Hail .... Mr. Martin B. Pedler
Count de Coutte ...... Mr. Robin Shiels
Maria James .... Miss Florence Mitchell
Lily James .... Miss Ethel Bracewell
Jane .... Miss Amy Rudd
William Wiggins ...... Mr. Fred Barnes
The Inspector .... Mr. Edgar Stanley
                      —Pier Pavilion, Paignton.

15. *L'Affaire des Poisons*, play, in a prologue
and five acts, by Victorien Sardou (origin-
ally produced at the Porte-St.-Martin, De-
cember 7, 1907).
Abbé Griffard .... M. Coquelin, ainé
Colbert .... M. Jean Coquelin
Louvois .... M. Dorival
Monsieur de la Reynie........M. Monteux
Louis XIV. .... M. Capoul
Hector de Tralage .... M. D'Auchy
Desgrez .... M. Chabert
Carloni .... M. Fabre
De Pommayrac .... M. Magnard
De Brionne .... M. Latour
D'Acquin .... M. Nargeot
Lulli .... M. Dannequin
Chef de Patrouille .... M. Tournier
Zamar .... M. Picard
Sagot .... M. Clerville
De Seissac .... M. Totah
Lesage .... M. Lebrun
De Visé .... M. Person
L'Abbé Guibourg .... M. Adam
Un Huissier .... M. Stebler
Gilbert .... M. Galland
Maître d'Hôtel ....M. Leroy
La Voisin .... Mme. de Renot
Mlle. d'Ormoise..Mlle. Carmen de Raisy
Mlle. Descœillets .... Mlle. Bouchetal
Fille Voisin .... Mlle. Goldstein
Mme. d'Humière .... Mme. Merle
Mme. de Nevers .... Mme. Guerraz
Mme. de Brissac .... Mme. Moore
Mlle. de Fontanges .... Mme. Vallet
Mme. de Dancourt .... Mme. Bouyer
Margot .... Mme. Labarre
Mme. de Montespan ..Mlle. Gilda Darthy
                      —His Majesty's (French season).

15. *A Miracle*, a one-act play, by George de
Lara.
Martin Greville ......Mr. George de Lara
George Winston .. Mr. Robert Whitworth
Mr. Bond .... Mr. W. T. Rea
Servant .... Mr. T. Mason
Molly Greville ...... Miss Nellie Redwood
                              —Royal, Brighton.

15.*Afterthoughts, episode, in one act, by
A. E. Drinkwater (originally produced
June 12, 1899, at the Bijou, Bayswater,
and reproduced on November 22, 1905, at
the Coronet).
Philip Deane-Nichol ..Mr. Robert Horton
Mike Toddy .... Mr. Bertram Steer
Hodges .... Mr. Chas. Fancourt
Margaret Deane-Nichol...Miss F. Leclercq
                              —Garrick.

15.**A Pair of Spectacles*, comedy, adapted by
Sydney Grundy from Labiche and Dela-
cour's *Les Petits Oiseaux* (originally pro-
duced at the Garrick on February 22, 1890).
(Last performance and closing of Sir
John's season at the Garrick on July 10.)
Mr. Benjamin Goldfinch .. Sir John Hare
Uncle Gregory .... Mr. Charles Groves
Percy .... Mr. Chas. R. Maude
Dick .... Mr. Bertram Steer

A Pair of Spectacles (continued).

Lorimer .... Mr. Robert Horton
Bartholomew .... Mr. J. H. Brewer
Joyce .... Mr. Fred W. Perma'n
Another Shoemaker..Mr. Claude Edmonds
Mrs. Goldfinch..Miss Sterling MacKinlay
Lucy Lorimer..Miss Amy Brandon Thom is
Charlotte .... Miss Blanche Grand
                    —Garrick.

16. *The Flag Lieutenant,* naval comedy, in four
acts, by Major W. P. Drury and Leo
Trevor.
Vice-Admiral the Hon. Sir Berkeley
  Wynne, K.C.B...Mr. Arthur Holmes-Gore
John Penrose ...... Mr. Lewis Broughton
Richard Lascelles ...... Mr. Cyril Maude
Christopher Neate ...... Mr. W. Percival
William Thesiger .. Mr. C. Aubrey Smith
Walter Crutchley..Mr. Ernest Mainwaring
Horatio Hood .... Mr. H. Robert Averell
Edward Dormer-Lee .... Mr. Eric Maturin
Charles Penny .... Mr. Larcombe
George Blockley ...... Mr. Lane Crawford
Thomas Steele .... Mr. A. G. Onslow
Joshua Borlaise .... Mr. M. Wetherell
James Sloggett ...... Mr. John Harwood
General Gough-Bogle..Mr. Sydney Paxton
Colonel McLeod .... Mr. Eugene Mayeur
Captain Munro .... Mr. Charles Hampden
Michael Palliser .. Mr. Clarence Blakiston
Memeti Salos ...... Mr. Daniel McCarthy
Mrs. Cameron ...... Miss Winifred Emery
Lady Wynne .... Miss Lillian Braithwaite
Viola Hood .... Miss Rosalie Toller
Mrs. Gough-Bogle .. Miss Emma Chambers
Lady Dugdale .... Miss Marie Linden
                    —Playhouse.

16.†*The Chinese Lantern,* fairy play, in three
acts, by Laurence Housman, music by
Joseph Moorat.
Olangtsi .... Mr. O. B. Clarence
Mrs. Back of the House
                 Mrs. A. B. Tapping
Yunglangtsi ...... Mr. Frederick Volpé
Pee-Ah-Bee .... Mr. Allan Wade
Han-Kin .... Mr. Walter Creighton
Tee-Pee .... Mr. O. P. Heggie
Hiti-Titi .... Mr. Norman Page
New-Lyn .... Mr. Gerald Jerome
Nau-Tee ....Mr. Donald Calth'op
Li-Long .... Mr. Leslie Hamer
A Crier .... Mr. Richard Andean
A Bailiff .... Mr. Kingsford Pearce
Josi Mosi .... Mr. Michael Sherbrooke
Cosi Mosi .... Mr. James Hearn
Tikipu .... Mr. Henry Ainley
Mee-Mee .... Miss Irene Clarke
Wiowani .... Mr. E. Lyall Swete
                  —Haymarket.

18.‖*Bulmer's Threat,* drama, in one act, by
Alex. M. Lee
Henry Bulmer .... Mr. Alex. M. Lee
Rowlands .... Mr. P. Reynard
The Nurse .... Miss Poppy Sheffield
                  —Bijou, Bayswater

22.**The Taming of the Shrew,* revived by Mr.
Oscar Asche at the Aldwych.

22. *Convict 99,* drama, in four acts, adapted
by Jack Denton from a story.
Lawrence Gray .... Mr. Frank Beresford
Ralph Vicars ...... Mr. E. Maule Cole
Christopher Lucas .. Mr. Francis Hawley
James Stinchcombe .. Mr. Jack Denton
Charles Kesteven .. Mr. Henry Nelson
Doctor .... Mr. William Hadley
Foreman of the Jury .. Mr. W. Lester
Jim Lacy .... Mr. Fred Epitaux
The Judge .... Mr. Percy Hall
Warder Gannaway .. Mr. Harry J. Crane

Convict 99 (continued).

Council for Prosecution .. Mr. Fred Kollan
Warder Hewitt ...... Mr. P. L. Julian
Counsel for the Defence .. Mr. F. Harold
Inspector Jennings .. Mr. Roland Chester
Captain Podmore .... Mr. Ulick Burke
Clerk of the Court .... Mr. W. Langford
Major Walsh .... Mr. F. Sidney
Visiting Magistrate ...... Mr. H. DeToe
Chief Warder .... Mr. Daniel Dobell
Mrs. Smedley .... Miss Florence Lovell
Maggie Mason .... Miss Elly Helene
Geraldine Lucas .. Miss Margaret Murch
          —Crown, Peckham.

22. *The Gay Deceivers,* musical absurdity, in two
acts.
Colonel Dewar .. Mr. George Delaforce
Lieut. Frank Dewar .. Mr. Guy Williams
Major Kurrie .... Mr. Clive Currie
Lord Reggie Muddleton..Mr. F. Stanmore
Pinch .... Mr. J. W. Wood-Ingram
Mons. Kiraffe .... Mr. Pat Eden
P.C. Parker .... Mr. Will Capers
Joseph .... Mr. Mark Lester
Mrs. Dewar .... Miss Kate Chard
Winnie Winter ...... Miss Cicely Stucky
Rosie .... Miss Pauline Prim
Mimi .... Miss Mina Goss
Balette .... Miss Brenda Gulden
Fluffy .... Miss Nellie Day
Gladys .... Miss Violet Darling
Mabel .... Miss Maud Leslie
Birdie .... Miss Hilda Ward
Molly .... Mlle. de Taillebon
Dora Dartrey ...... Miss Dorothy Chard
           —Royal, Margate.

22. *Geoffrey Langdon's Wife,* play, in four
acts, by Fred C. Somerfield.
Felix Beverley .. Mr. Fred C. Somerfield
Jack Stirling .. Mr. Edward E. Louis
Geoffrey Langdon .. Mr. Wilson Summers
Colonel Miles .... Mr. Marcus Grey
Thomas .... Mr. Percy Brown
Charles .... Mr. Percy Dawsone
Arthur Bellairs ...... Mr. Ivan Mavis
Detective Banks .. Mr. Harland Brookes
Inspector Froest .... Mr. John Turnbull
The Hon. Mrs. Sands..Miss Cissie Bellamy
Sweet Nancy .... Miss Kate Lever
Mary Langdon ...... Miss Cecilia Dare
           —Rotunda, Liverpool.

22. *The Better Land,* four-act drama, by
Dorothy Granville.
Philip Radcliffe ...... Mr. G. M. Newall
Hubert Radcliffe .. Mr. Stanley Radcliffe
George Grant .... Mr. J. D. Geddes
Tom Tadlepole ...... Mr. Albert Rogers
William White .... Mr. Herbert M. Kink
Bill Bones .... Mr. F. Christian
Mercedes .... Miss Ella Thornton
Polly Perkins .... Miss Jennie Hallworth
Aunt Jemimah .... Mrs. S. Wybert
Harry .... Miss Reni Bentley
Tessa .... Miss Emilie Entwistle
Doris .... Miss Pattie Hastings
          —Queen's, Liverpool.

22. *A Woman's Love,* domestic drama, in five
scenes, by Nita Rae.
Ronald Beaufort ..Mr. Stanley S. Gordon
Jasper Orme........Mr. Alfred D. Adams
Dr. Langton .... Mr. Cyril Grier
Albert Alonby .... Mr. Alfred Grenville
Dick .... Mr. Tom H. Solly
Mary Beaufort .... Miss Nina Vaughton
Lillian Langton .... Miss Kathleen Magee
Anna Maria ...... Miss Louie Heathfield
Jess Smith .... Miss Effie Macintosh
          —Muncaster, Bootle.

23.†*The Mill*, play, in three acts, by Nugent Monck (presented by the English Drama Society).

Ada .... Miss Clare Greet
Frank Benville ...... Mr. Arthur Eldred
Ralph Cooperson .... Mr. Eric Maxon
The Pedlar ...... Mr. Courtenay Thorpe
Virtue Preece .... Miss Isabel Roland
Mr. Preece .... Mr. Arthur Dennis
—Scala.

23.†*The Drums of Doom*, impressionist drama, in one act, by Gerald Villiers-Stuart (presented by the English Drama Society).

Mrs. Fitzgerald ......Mrs. Beerbohm Tree
Delaney .... Mr. Arthur Goodsall
Billy Buckstone ...... Mr. Gordon Bailey
Hotel Manager .... Mr. Geoffrey Douglas
—Scala.

23.†*The Voice of Duty*, duologue, by H. F. P. Battersby—Comedy.

24. *Pierrette's Birthday*, episode, with music, words by Colin Nell Rose, music by Clement Locknane.

Pierrette .... Miss Elaine Inescort
Harlequin .... Mr. Reginald Eyre
Pierrot .... Mr. Robert Cunningham
—New.

25. *The Outcast of the Family*, drama, in four acts, by Harry Foxwell.

Sir H. Thorne, Bart...Mr. F. C. Leighton
Harry Thorne .... Mr. Harry Cullenford
Richard Martin ...... Mr. C. H. Coleman
Stephen Barry .... Mr. H. Bentone
Joe Bushell .... Mr. Bert Atherton
Abram Wasper .... Mr. E. W. Cudd
Uncle Sam .... Mr. M. Platting
Seth Sleeke .... Mr. E. Jeffs
Parkins .... Mr. Murray Maude
Tom Strutt .... Mr. Harold Holmes
Inspector Johnson .. Mr. Heaton Lodge
Nancy Bray .... Miss Vera Neville
Grace Redburn .... Miss M. Tueskie
Little Bob .... Little Dorothy
Ruth .... Miss Gertrude Morella
P.O.W., Salford.

26.‖*Peggy Doyle*, play, in three acts, by Mirabel Hillier.

Peggy Doyle .. Miss Marguerite Adamson
Mrs. Osbourne .... Miss Grace Sheffield
Milly Osbourne ...... Miss Alex Verces
Kitty Osbourne .. Miss Gladys Mackadam
Miss Johnson .... Miss Mary Wilson
Laura Grennall .... Miss Mirabel Hillier
Jack Davies ...... Mr. Valentine Glynn
Tom Osbourne ...... Master Jack Hobbs
Hugh Osbourne .... Mr. Herbert Darran
—Rehearsal, W.C.

26.‖*An April Fool*, comedietta, by Marguerite Adamson.

Alamanda Sniffkins .. Miss M. Adamson
Liza Smith .... Miss Mirabel Hillier
Harry Maynard .... Mr. Valentine Glynn
Richard Browning ...... Mr. J. L. Dale
—Rehearsal, W.C.

26.¶*His Sacrifice*, three-act play, by Donald F. Buckley—Ladbroke Hall, W.

29. *The Yarn-Spinner*, Tom Craven's comedy duologue.

Mr. Yapper .... Mr. Lionel Brough
Mrs. Cackle .... Miss Mary Brough
—Pier Pavilion, Southend.

29. *A Princess in Bohemia*, comedy, in four acts, by Gilbert Dayle.

Sir Philip Templeton..Mr. Charles Boult
Hamilton Quirk .. Mr. Fred A. Marston
Jimmy Ludlow .. Mr. Edgar Stevenson
Mr. Heathcote .. Mr. Fred Castleman
Vickery .... Mr. Edward Petley
Judson .... Mr. George Fisher
Crayley Carr .... Mr. Ernest E. Norris
Miss Joan Herepath..Miss Lena Delphine
Mrs. Rainsford .... Miss Bessie Harrison
Miss Alma Maxwell..Miss Edith Coleman
Lady Delia Kingsfield Miss Rosemary Rees
—Royal, Bradford.

29. *Octave*, by Mirande et Henri Geroule.

Octave .... M. Gouget
Henri .... M. Laurysse
Jean .... M. Rémongin
L'employé des pompes funèbres..M. Raoul
Suzanne .... Mlle. Dariel
—Royalty (French season).

29. *Un Honnête Homme*, De Mme. Camille Clermont.

Pierre Caissier ...... Mr. Séverin-Mars
Léon .... M. Schultz
Morasson .... M. Rémongin
Emma .... Mlle. Lavernière
Marie .... Mlle. Renetty
—Royalty (French season).

29. *Fleur d'Oranger*, by Jean Sery, music by Mérril.

Louison .... Mlle. Lavernière
Paul ....Mlle. Little Chrysia
—Royalty (French season).

29. *La Dernière Soirée de Brummel*, by Georges Maurevert.

Georges Brummel ...... M. Séverin-Mars.
Francis .... M. Gouget
Lord Hefton .... M. Schultz
Le Docteur Moisant .... M. Laurysse
Fichet .... M. Rémongin
Lady Fersey .... Mlle. Jane Doé
Marie Jeanne .... Mlle. Dariel
—Royalty (French season).

JULY.

2. *The Absentee.*

Sir Ulick de Burgo....Mr. Warren Wynne
David McClutchy .... Mr. A. S. Aspland
Jack Bracebridge .... Mr. J. M. Napper
Michael Mulcahy ⎫
Postman ...... ⎬ Mr. James R. La Fane
Jeremy Joyce ...... Mr. Jerome Murphy
Paddy O'Rafferty...Mr. D. Byndon Ayres
Jacob Grimes ...... Mr. Brendan Stewart
The Schoolmaster .. Mr. Sebastian King
Sheriff's Officer ...... Mr. S. Carpenter
Sergeant of R.I.C. .. Mr. William Walshe
An Old Man .... Mr. Owen Gilbert
Nora Joyce .... Miss Magrath
Mrs. Joyce .... Miss Maud Shelton
Kate Joyce .... Miss Mab Aspland
Mrs. O'Connor ...... Miss Maud Waller
Flora Brewster .. Miss Evelyn Vernham
Lady Betty Brabazon .. Miss Sybil Noble
—Court (Irish season).

2.‡*Leap Year in the West*, play by Johanna Redmond—Court (Irish season).

3.*The Postbag, comedietta by A. P. Graves—Court (Irish season).

3. *The Quest of the Holy Grail*, by Ernest Rhys, with music by Vincent Thomas.
King Arthur ...... Mr. Wingfield Heale
Sir Galahad ...... Miss Gwendolien Lally
Sir Percival ...... Mr. Launcelot Crane
Sir Gawain .... Mr. C. Court Treatt
Sir Launcelot .... Mr. C. F. Barrett
Sir Kay .... Mr. Allan Gomme
Sailor .... Mr. W. H. Nicholson
Court Minstrel .... Mr. Dixon
Timor Mortis ...... |
Arch Druid ....| Mr. Joseph Payne
Hermit |
Arch Druidess..Miss O'Auvergne Upcher
Queen Quenever .... Miss Doule
Nimuè (Vivian) .... | Miss Edith Rhys
Tradition .... |
Tradition's Child .... Miss Esther Tilley
—Court (Irish season).

4.†‡*Rhys Lewis*, drama, adapted by T. Morgan Edwards from Daniel Owen's novel—Court (Irish season).

4.‡*An Uadhact (The Will)*, by Padraic O'Conaire—Court (Irish season).

6.**Cyrano de Bergerac*—His Majesty's.

6.**A Vision of the Twelve Virgin Goddesses*, masque, by Samuel Daniel (originally presented at Hampton Court, January 8, 1604)—Botanic Gardens, Regent's Park.

7.†*The Anarchists*, tragedy, in one act, by Rowan Orme.
Vasilissa .... Miss Esmé Beringer
Micholitch Tarhov....Mr. Godfrey Tearle
The President .... Mr. Charles Vane
Agrafena .... Miss Agnes Hill
Lenotchka .... Miss Dorothy Bell
Markelov .... Mr. Hubert Carter
Ivanoff .... Mr. Charles Gelderd
Teliegin .... Mr. Charles Bruce
—Court.

7.†*On the East Side*, play, by Christopher St. John.
Lucia Bandino......Miss Brineta Browne
John Anthoulis....Mr. Herbert Grimwood
Henry Green.............Mr. O. P. Heggie
Rosa Anthoulis............Miss Auriol Lee
George Anthoulis..Mr. Harcourt-Williams
Sandro .... Mr. W. K. Pearce
—Court.

7.†*The Sentence*, tragedy, in one act, by Rowan Orme.
The Judge .... Mr. Hubert Carter
The Woman .... Miss Granville
—Court.

7.†*A Modern Daughter*, comedy, by Mrs. Tom Godfrey.
Enid Burne............Miss Dorothy Heal
Dick Burne........Mr. Hugh B. Tabberer
Claire Chester ......Miss Brineta Browne
Violet Young......Miss Winifred Clayton
Mrs. Chester......Miss Frances Wetherall
Jack Longley........Mr. Geoffrey Douglas
—Court,

8.¶*The Undercurrent*, play, in four acts, by Herbert Chorley—Grammar School Hall, Dedham, Essex.

9.¶*The Reptile's Devotion*, by Cecil H. Taylor —Queen's, Leeds.

9.†*The Boys, farcical comedy, in three acts, by Henry Seton. (Originally produced at the Grand, Croydon, May 11, 1908.)
Brian O'Donaghue....Mr. Chas Goodhart
Mortimer Wilberley....Mr. Fred Lewis
Micky Halloran........Mr. Wilfred Shine
Major Robert Rayner...Mr. E. S. Staples
Capt. Hugh Wilson.....Mr. George Silver

The Boys (continued).
Peter Tubbs .... Mr. Max Leeds
Ananda .... Mr. John Brabourne
O'Driscoll .... Mr. John Fairway
Colonel Harkner........Mr. Chas. Towson
Bat ....Mr. Ellis Carlyle
Waiter .... Mr. Eden Potts
Bobbie Davies........Mr. Reginald Craven
Lane-Marriot..........Mr. Douglas Imbert
Miss Petunia Pareons......Miss C. Zerbini
Patricia O'Donaghue..Miss Florence Lloyd
Katherine O'Donaghue..Miss V. Beringer
Mary O'Donaghue......Miss May Blayney
Miss Maynard............Miss M. Holford
—Court.

10. *Trixie*, comedy, in three acts, by John Strange Winter.
Mrs. Desmond......Miss Betty Stannard
Capt. Wilson-King..Mr. Laurence Leyton
Lieut.-Col. Tonkinson..Mr. C. F Collings
Bishop of Blankhampton...Mr. Fred Lewis
Lord St. Barbe....Mr. Herbert H. Herbert
Wilfred Parker.........Mr. Charles King
Lady Agnes ...... Miss Audrey Stannard
Lady Idleminster ......Miss Millie Donati
Lieut. George Drummond....Mr. L. Grove
Margaret Chatfield ....Miss Sylvia Morris
Capt. Richard Vernon..Mr. Gordon Bailey
Trixie Armytage......Miss Gladys Mason
Chaplain O'Rafferty...Mr. Chas. Danvers
Nolan .... Mr. Victor Brook
James .... Mr. Francis Drake
—Scala.

10. *The White Lady*, play, by Isabel Alexander.
Sir Francis Mavius..Mr. Henley Attwater
Jennings .... Mr. Francis Drake
Jessamine Hope .... Miss Helen Child
—Scala.

14.†*A Matter-of-Fact Husband*, comedy, in one act, by John Cutler, K.C.
Bella .... Miss Ella Dixon
Henry .... Mr. J. Gelderd
—Lyceum.

14.**H.M.S. Pinafore; or, The Lass that Loves a Sailor*, comic opera, in two acts, by W. S. Gilbert and Arthur Sullivan (originally produced May 25, 1878, at the Opera Comique).
Sir J. Porter, K.C.B...Mr. C. H. Workman
Capt. Corcoran...Mr. Rutland Barrington
Ralph Rackstraw......Mr. Henry Herbert
Dick Deadeye .... Mr. Henry A. Lytton
Bill Bobstay ...... Mr. Leicester Tunks
Bob Becket .... Mr. Fred Hewett
Josephine .... Miss Elsie Spain
Hebe .... Miss Jessie Rose
Little Buttercup ...... Miss Louie Rene
—Savoy.

15. *A Welsh Sunset*, operetta, by Frederick Fenn, with music by Philip Michael Faraday.
Jenny Jones .... Miss Beatrice Meredith
Griffith David .... Mr. Strafford Moss
Mrs. Jones .... Miss Ethel Morrison
Mary Fewlass ...... Miss Mabel Graham
Nancy Raine ...... Miss Beatrice Boarer
Gwenny Davis ...... Miss Bertha Lewis
Owen Rhys .... Mr. Leo Sheffield
John Lloyd ...... Mr. Sydney Granville
Morgan Llewellyn ......Mr. Allan Morris
—Savoy.

16. *A Scheme that Failed*, play, in four acts, by Fred Green.
Harry Vaughan .... Mr. Stanley Bedwell
Reggie Hardy .. Mr. Sydney C. Cranston
George Vaughan .... Mr. Charles Sydney
Will Smith ...... Mr. Allen Carruthers

A Scheme that Failed (continued).

Mark Rudge .... Mr. W. E. Melrose
James .... Mr. Louis Edmonde
Philip Norton ...... Mr. Robert Faulkner
Jem Rudge .... Mr. J. G. Maine
Paperhanger ....Mr. Williams
Sis Vaughan ...... Miss Maud Townsend
Mary .... Miss Violet Temple
Barbara Dane..Miss Francesca Strickland
Doris Vaughan .... Miss Nellie Lewis
Kate Norton .... Miss Mabel Mannering
                    Prince's, Accerington.

17.‖*Penelope's Lovers*, play, in one act, by
George P. Bancroft.
Lord Colbeck ...... Mr. Wilfred Fletcher
Jack Meredith ...... Mr. Lane Crawford
Bertram Ashbrook ..Mr. Frederick James
A German Waiter .... Mr. Lyonel Watts
Muriel March ...... Miss Phyllis Davey
Penelope March .... Miss Athene Seyler
                    —Rehearsal, Maiden Lane.

20. *Happy Hooligan*, musical play, in three
acts.
Happy Hooligan .. Mr. Wm. H. Lester
Donald Macgregor .. Mr. Jos. J. Sullivan
Max Guggenheimer Mr. John K. Hawley
Charley Flipp ...... Mr. Harry Emeric
Widow Johnson .... Miss Lottie Wilson
Rose .... Miss Rose Lyndon
Nettie .... Miss Blanco Moure
Daisy .... Miss Lilian Lilyan
Oiki San and Cowboy .. Mr. Jack Henry
Constable .... Mr. A. R. Galloway
Mr. "Notsowell" Mr. J. W. Woodbridge
President of Tram Co. Mr. H. A. Hewitt
Nurse Girl .... Miss Lily Callen
Mrs. Phat .... Miss Clara Pierse
Yo San .... Miss May Yorke
Wot Guy .... Miss Nan Ainslie
Yoco Mey .... Miss Beatrice May
Chop Suey .... Miss Doris Hartley
Oyama .... Miss Doris Ainsley
Newsboy .... Mr. M. McCluskey
                    —Empire, Oldham.

20. *The Lady of the Pageant*, farcical comedy,
in three acts, by Max Pemberton and
Cyril Wentworth.
Prosper Vandelay .. Mr. Louis Calvert
Sir Titus Eastrey .. Mr. Edward Rigby
Harry Eastrey ...... Mr. Ernest Graham
Mr. Honeyspinner .. Mr. Frank T. Arlton
The Rev. Arthur Sheldon
                    Mr. G. Elphinstone
Ali Ben Hassan .... Mr. Sandymenn
Wallace .... Mr. Leonard Calvert
Sandwichmen
    Messrs. Brodie, Macklin, and Harman
Police Officers
    Messrs. Chas. Bishop and W. Penning
Footmen.... Messrs. Colmer and Doreen
Claudine Dawn ...... Miss Daisy Fisher
Mrs. Marris ...... Miss Nelly Griffin
Lady Violet Deane .. Miss Vere Sinclair
Molly Gibbs ....Miss Gladys Dale
The Countess .... Miss Maud Henderson
Sara .... Miss Marion McCarthay
Betty .... Miss Edith Brent
Phyllis .... Miss Violet Fenton
Lady Eastrey ...... Miss Ernita Lascelles
                    —D.P., Eastbourne.

20 *A Play Without a Name*, society drama,
by T. M. Paule.
Eric Duncombe .. F. Forbes Robertson
Captain Clive .... Mr. Sydney Hawton
John Scott, M.D. .. Mr. Jack Allerton
Hon. Bertie Symkins .... Mr. Tom Leeson
Sir Richard Temple .. Mr. Rich. Beaton
Barrington Selmore Mr. A. D. Scudamore
Marcus Selmore ...... Mr. Claude Agnew
Wilkins .... Mr. Edmond Beresford

A Play Without a Name (continued).

P.C. Browne .... Mr. Robert West
P.C. Keene .... Mr. Henry Millgate
Dixon .... Mr. Austen Milroy
Esther Leroy .... Miss Eva Fryett
Stella .... Miss Margaret Collins
Vera Desmond .... Miss Avice Meredith
                    —East Oxford, Oxford.

20.‡*For Love and the King*, romantic drama,
in four acts, by C. Watson Mill. (Ori-
ginally produced at the P.O.W., Mex-
borough, on April 13.)
Jarval .... Mr. C. Watson Mill
Michael Obrenovic .... Mr. John Burton
Vladimir Obrenovic .. Mr. H. Earlesmere
Prince Uros Dragomir
                    Mr. T. W. Dunscombe
Duke Ferdinand Dragomir Mr. G. Chate
Carl Oppenheim .... Mr. Jim K. Woods
King Kara Dragomir Mr. Frank Lyndon
Kosta Marko .... Mr. Arthur Trail
Vitomir Ladie .... Mr. G. H. Organ
Corporal Reston .... Mr. A. H. Leslie
Vadoe .... Mr. D. Adams
Natila .... Miss Joan Ellis
Grazia Obrenovic .... Miss Marie Ault
Edith Meredith .. Miss Frances Tierney
Princess Milania .... Miss Laura Munroe
Princess Athene .... Miss Rosalind Tate
                    —Elephant and Castle.

23. *Three Weeks*, private performance of play
by Elinor Glynn, founded on her book of
the same name—Adelphi.

25.¶*The Woman from Russia*, domestic play
of "passion, virtue, and humour," in
four acts, by Fred G. Ingleby.
Frank Haldane .. Mr. Robert Ayrton
Hon. Reginald Fitzgerald..Mr. B. Mitchell
Captain Alexis Yarviski..Mr. F. G. Ingleby
James Haldane .... Mr. Richard Pitt
Jerry Moriarty .... Mr. F. Wheatcroft
Ezra Caroni .... Mr. Harry Elliston
Wun-hi .... Mr. G. M. Hancock
Dr. Chetwode .... Mr. T. Wyndham
Sergeant Petroff ...... Mr. John Vernon
Corporal Trevitch ....Mr. Tom Carew
Smirkoff .... Mr. Steve Parker
Feritski .... Mr. Jack Gillett
Edith Haldane ....Miss Ethel Patrick
Mary Ann Smith....Miss Maude St. John
Wanda Sonorovitch......Miss Adria Hill
                    —Royal, Jarrow.

27. *The Belle of the Ball*, musical play, in
three acts, by A. Norden, music by E. T.
De Banzie and Michael Dwyer. (London
production, October 19, Crown, Peckham.
Sir Francis Lake ...... Mr. Robert Hyett
Bobbie Fletcher ......Mr. L. C. Hughes
Farmer Jones .... Mr. J. Chippendale
James Forster .... Mr. E. W. Chewd
William .... Mr. Jack Hale
Timothy Timkins ...... Mr. J. Schofield
Showman Jack..........Mr. Frank Collins
Footman .... Mr. E. Osborne
Queenie Trevor .... Miss Maud Terry
Lucy .... Miss Vera Grafton
Alice .... Miss Mary Earle
Mary .... Miss L'Estrange
Marie ....Miss Penrhyn
Irene .... Miss Cartwright
Red Riding Hood ...... Miss Clara Casey
San Toi .... Miss May Hawthorne
Poppy .... Miss Gertrude Melville
                    —O.H., Southport.

27. *Man or Beast*, romantic drama, in four
acts, by Charles H. Phelps (London production, November 30, Royal, Stratford)—
Star, Swansea.

27. *For Love of a Woman*, drama, in four
acts, by Nita Rae.
Ned Merrick ....Mr. Arthur Chisholm
Guy Manor .... Mr. Fred Lloyd
Allen Paget..............Mr. Eustace ...ay
Major Hulmes........Mr. Charles Ninian
Albert St. Everamond
           Mr. Leonard Harrison
Sam Holland..........Mr. Fred Ramsdale
Tom Jones............Mr. Ernest Yandel
Warder ....Mr. Brook Leicester
Nell Paget ... . Miss Dorothy Rough
Marjory Hulmes........Miss Elsie Shelton
Jane Manor ....Miss Eva St. Vincent
Nance Manor.......... . ..Miss May Day
           —Lyceum, Stafford.

27. *The Power of Lies*, domestic drama, in
four acts, music by Michael Connelly, pro-
duced by Mr. Marshall Moore.
Lady Margaret Harden...Miss Mary Ford
Charlotte Barton......Miss Ella Anderson
Phyllis Harden..Miss Gladys Ford-Howitt
Ruth Carson ....Miss Lillian Williams
Mrs. Elkington..............Mrs. Williams
Kattilana Flyblow .... Miss Davie
Nurse Blair...........Miss Mary Farmer
Servant .... Miss Ida McKenna
Sir George Harden, ⎱
   Bart, M.D.   ⎰ ....Mr. Otto Minster
Geoffrey Carson ⎰
Mr. Isaacs.................Mr. T. W. Ford
Dr. Bletchley........Mr. Marshall Moore
Joe Barton ....Mr. Herbert Russell
Lord Robert Gordon...Mr. Dudley Stuart
Ring Master ....Mr. Ivan P. Gore
Detective Hamilton...Mr. Harcourt Bailey
Warder.................Mr. W. H. Ordish
Hospital Porter.......Mr. James Admans
Tommy ....Mr. Chantry
           —Shakespeare.

27. *The Man of Her Choice*, play, in four acts,
written by Ada G. Abbott (Mrs. Ernest
P. Abbott).
Everard Hilderson........Mr. John ...ester
Berkley Hilderson..Mr. Ernest R. Abbott
Kingsley Hilderson...Mr. Herbert Morgan
Barry Hilderson......Mr. Frank Stephens
Morris ....Mr. Edwin Keene
Miss Penelope Hilderson
           Miss Blanche Stanley
Mrs. Manx ....Miss Marjorie Tennant
Eliza ....Miss Florence North
Napoleon .... " Billy "
Barbara Linley .... Miss Ada Abbott
           —Broadway

30. *The New Tenants*, comedy, in three acts,
by Geoffrey Wilkinson.
Jane.................Miss Dorothy Elliston
Groves............Mr. Geoffrey Wilkinson
William Ludlow....Mr. Archibald McLean
Henry Armstrong..Mr. Clifford Heatherley
Audrey Armstrong......Miss Mavis Clare
Lady Montrose......Miss Madge Whiteman
Lord Gerald Montrose...Mr. Lyonel Watts
Mrs. Hunter ....Miss Violet Hearson
           —Rehearsal, Maiden Lane.

AUGUST.

1. *A Country Girl in London*, drama, in four
acts, by Frank Price.
John Hamilton ...... Mr. J. B. Sheridan
Frank Gordon ...... Mr. W. V. Garrod
Godfrey Clinton .... Mr. M. Williams
Job Smithers .... Mr. Clifford Marle

A Country Girl in London (continued).
Heinrich Oppenheim....Mr. E. W. Avery
Wilberforce Puddyphat .... Mr. S. Perry
Joe Button .... Mr. Edward Ashton
P.C. Brown .... Mr. C. Mitchell
P.C. Green .... Mr. T. E. Evans
Gwendoline Gordon ...... Miss J. Colona
Adelaide Puddyphat ...... Miss L. Adair
Marjorie Hamilton .... Miss B. Kingston
           —Royal, Macclesfield.

3. *The Gutter of Time*, play, in one act, by
Alfred Sutro.
Mrs. Transford .. Miss Violet Vanbrugh
Sir Harry Jardine ...... Mr. B. Forsyth
           —Pier, Eastbourne.

3. *A Merry Maid*, musical comedy.
Larry O'Hooligan ...... Mr. V. Wakeman
Hon. Cecil Taft .... Mr. Niel Hardy
Thady Clancy ...... Mr. Ireland Cutter
Von Swank .... Mr. Phil Goldie
Sharpe Scrivener ...... Mr. H. Hillerby
Angelina Vere de Vere....Miss F. Adamson
Bertie .... Wee Geo. Wood
Biddy O'Hooligan..Mr. W. S. Hutchinson
Flossie Kixie .... Miss Ray Watson
Peggy O'Hooligan .... Miss May Gibson
           —Grand, Chorley.

3. *The Way Out*, one-act play, by George
Unwin.
The Man .... Mr. Fred Conyers
The Boy .... Mr. Legal Robinson
The Woman ...... Miss Lorna Lawrence
Maid .... Miss Ida Scott
           —Royal, Newcastle.

3. *Admiral Peters*, comedy, in one act, by
W. W. Jacobs and Horace Mills, adapted
from W. W. Jacobs's story of the same
name.
George Burton ...... Mr. Arthur Whitby
Joe Stiles ...... Mr. Leon Quartermaine
Mrs. Dutton .... Miss Mary Weigall
           —Pier, Eastbourne.

3. *Straight from the Shoulder*, play, in four
acts (London production August 10, at
the Broadway).
CHARACTERS IN ACT ONE.
Dr. Francis Bedford .... Mr. M. Boulton
David Gleeson ...... Mr. Leonard Clarke
Jim Green .... Mr. Fred Beck
Donald Macgregor ...... Mr. C. Dennison
Henry M. Grant .. Mr. Franklin McAvoy
Millicent Grant ....Miss Beatrice Burdett
Mary Gleeson ...... Miss Frances Bruce
Sergt. Bright .... Miss Bertram Carlton
CHARACTERS IN SUBSEQUENT ACTS (SIX
           YEARS AFTER).
Harry Bletchley .. Mr. Matthew Boulton
Major Lucas .... Mr. Leonard Clarke
Rev. John Armitage .. Mr. Geo. H. Child
Jim Green .... Mr. Fred Beck
Fred Stafford .... Mr. George Fisher
Millicent Grant .. Miss Beatrice Burdett
Miss Brittle .... Miss Edie Casson
Gladys Brittle ...... Miss Beatrice Moore
           —Grand, Brighton.

3. *London with the Lid Off*, drama, in four
acts, by Arthur Shirley.
Rev. Allen Gorden....Mr. Stanley Carlton
Gratton Gale....Mr. William G. Marshall
Mr. Templeton.......Mr. Marshall Meade
Collini .... Mr. James Hart
Percy Plunker ....Mr. Lancelot Usher
Sam Rendall...........Mr. Edward Vincent
Trencher .... Mr. Tom Murray
Flickster .... Mr. Fred Coutts
Cousin Peter .... Mr. Alfred Deane
P.C. Sharpe .... Mr. Dan Warden

London with the Lid Off (continued).

Inspector Conway.......Mr. Percy Roland
P.C. Morton .... Mr. Fred Garth
P.C. Gordon .... Mr. Bert Garrett
Messenger Boy....Master Charles Buxton
Mord Emily .... Miss Rose Morton
Clara Jane ....Miss Emily Marshall
Peppermint Poll ....Miss Grace King
Julie .... Miss Mildred Chapman
Jane Wilson .... Miss Alice Thorne
Sally Perkins...........Miss Julia Martin
Mary Elliott ....Miss Annie Montague
Mrs. Fordyce...........Miss Muriel Ross
Dolly .... Miss Emily Lewis
Mrs. Glendale..Miss R. Hamilton Balesco
Sarah Shafto..Miss Charlotte E. Bellinger
Madge Rendall...........Miss Amy Ellam
Astra Bell .... Miss Rubie Maude
               —Royal, Stratford.

3. *The Girl with the Angel Face,* "mystery drama," in five acts, by James Willard.
Sir John Wentworth. ⎰ Mr. Naylor Grimson
Thomas Wentworth ⎱
Stephen Arkwright..Mr. Austin Mortimer
Mark Fenning ......Mr. Fenton Wingate
Jasper Death..........Mr. Fred G. Evison
Martin Flood .... Mr. Dobell Lyle
Rev. Gordon Cross..Mr. Cecil Mannering
Hon. Percy Paget.......Mr. Allen Charles
Jim Bates .... Mr. Dicky Bird
Matthew Crupps.....Mr. Forbes Leighton
Inspector Lane........Mr. David Morgan
James Govett .... Mr. Henry Lee
Bill Muggs ....Mr. Robert Dore
Ena Wentworth ......Miss Phyllis Dailley
Nellie ....Miss Winifred Delevanti
Mollie Maitland ....Miss Mildred Carr
Pollie ....: Miss Ormonde
Angel Leigh .... Miss Florrie Green
               —Shakespeare.

3. *Married to the Wrong Man,* drama, in four acts, by Frederick Melville.
Jack Gladwin ....Mr. Oswald Cray
Captain Deering......Mr. H. Lane Bayliff
Sergeant Manners ....Mr. Joe Livesey
Doctor Brandon.......Mr. Henry Eustace
Landlord .... Mr. Claude Vernon
Brown.............Mr. Charles Darton
Henry .... Mr. Lewis McMahon
Usher of the Court....Mr. Henry Fielding
Timothy Clinker........Mr. Syd Claydon
Jasper Skinner........Mr. Charles Vivian
Hugh Brown .... Mr. F. Somerset
Archie Bird..........Mr. Paige Lawrence
Sir James Flint........Mr. Gatenby Bell
Frank Aylesbury......Mr. Harry Milding
Bertie Swanker .... Mr. C. Leopold
Lord Hawke ....Mr. Vernon
Nurse Harmsworth.........Miss Beamish
Nurse Manners......Miss Rosalie Natrelle
Mother Snaggs.........Miss Amy Vickers
Jane Seaweed ....Miss Clare Henry
Dolly Fritter .... Miss May Davis
Rose O'Connor......Miss Maisie Hanbury
Ruth ....Miss Gertrude Boswell
            —Elephant and Castle

5.†*The Philosopher's Diamond,* comedy of marvels, by Nevil Maskelyne.
Sir Grimley Greensward..Nevil Maskelyne
Huckaback .... Mr. E. Morehen
Bottles .... Mr. Arnold Mussett
Lady Greensward..Miss Helen McCulloch
Ali Ben Slobur.............Mr. E. S. Elton
Djinn al Kohl.......Mr. Charles Glenrose
Moonsheen .... Miss Cassie Bruce
            —St. George's Hall.

6 *The Man on the Box,* light comedy, in three acts, by Grace Livingstone Furniss, founded on Harold McGrath's novel of the same name.
Lord Kintire........Mr. Arthur Bourchier
Hon. Chas. Henderson..Mr. Chas. Vernon
Col. Annesley, U.S.A...Mr. Doré Davidson
Count Karloff........Mr. Bertram Forsyth
Major Frank Raleigh..Mr. L. Quartermaine
Judge Watts ....Mr. Stafford Hilliard
Pierre Flageot.......Mr. Arthur Whitby
O'Brien .... Mr. Philip Ascot
Cassidy .... Mr. William Burchill
Martin .... Mr. F. Cecil
William .... Mr. R. Hope
June Annesley....Miss Pamela Gaythorne
Mrs. Conway.........Miss Mary Weigall
Nancy Henderson..Miss Winifred Bateman
Cora .... Miss Eva Killick
           —Pier, Eastbourne.

10.‡*Straight from the Shoulder,* drama, in four
      CHARACTERS IN ACT ONE.
Dr. Francis Bedford....Mr. Matt. Boulton
acts. (Originally produced, Grand, Brighton August 3.)
David Gleeson........Mr. Leonard Clarke
Jim Green .... Mr. Fred Beck
Donald MacGregor..Mr. Cuthbert Dennison
Henry M. Grant..Mr. Franklin McAvory
Millicent Grant....Miss Beatrice Burdett
Mary Gleeson ....Miss Frances Bruce
Sergeant Bright.....Mr. Bertram Carlton
    CHARACTERS IN SUBSEQUENT ACTS.
Harry Bletchley (formerly Dr. Bedford) .... Mr. Matthew Boulton
Major Lucas (formerly David Gleeson)
             Mr. Leonard Clarke
Rev. John Armitage..Mr. Geo. H. Child
Jim Green ....Mr. Fred Beck
Fred Stafford..........Mr. George Fisher
Millicent Grant ....Miss Beatrice Burdett
Miss Brittle ....Miss Edie Casson
Gladys Brittle ......Miss Beatrice Moore
            —Broadway.

10. *Light in the Darkness,* domestic drama, in four acts, by W. Watkin-Wynne. (C.P., Queen's, Birmingham, June 25, 1902.)
Will Mortimer ....Mr. Alfred Beaumont
Sir Chas. Mortimer..Mr. H. Elmore Frith
Raymond Frere.......Mr. Arthur Rodney
Denis O'Brien ....Mr. Charles L. Ludlow
P.C. Jarvis ....Mr. Bert Lloyd
Joe Stack ....Mr. Norman Clark
Evans .... Mr. Frank Sturt
Det.-Serget Seymour..Mr. Watkin-Wynne
May Mortimer......Miss Maud Buchanan
Agnes Green......Miss Beatrice Western
Nora Power..........Miss Agnes St. Clair
Jack Mortimer..Little Marjorie Lawrence
          —Lyric, Hammersmith.

10.*The Girls of Gottenberg,* musical comedy, written by George Grossmith, jun., and L. E. Berman, music by Ivan Caryll and Lionel Monckton, lyrics by Adrian Ross and Basil Hood (originally produced at the Gaiety, May 15, 1907). Revived for a special fortnight.
Otto .... Mr. Lawrence Grossmith
Margrave of Saxe-Nierstein..Mr. J. Hope
Albrecht ....Mr. Fred Allandale
Brittlbotti .... Mr. Fred Payne
Colonel Finkhausen .... Mr. Arnold Lucy
Fritz .... Mr. J. Redmond
Hermann .... Mr. Arthur Whitehead
Franz .... Mr. Lawrence Robbins
Karl .... Mr. Ellis Holland
Burgomaster .... Mr. Douglas Munro
Kannenbier .... Mr. A. Chentrens
Adolf .... Mr. Charles Brown

The Girls of Gottenberg (continued).

Policeman .... Mr. D. Logum
Walters ....⎰ Mr. W. Garrett
⎱ Mr. D. Goodban
Corporal Reithen .... Mr. H. Glyn
Max Moddelkopf ......Mr. Edmund Payne
Clementine .... Miss Maisie Gay
Elsa .... Miss Thelma Raye
Lucille .... Miss Florence Phillips
Eva .... Miss Kitty Sparrow
Lina .... Miss Nancy Rich
Freda .... Miss Dora Dent
Anna .... Miss Peggy Paton
Katrina .... Miss Florence Melville
Barbara Briefmark .... Miss May Weston
Betti Berncastler ...... Miss Ethel Wilson
Mitzi ...:............ Happy Fanny Fields
—Adelphi.

12. *Sweet Peggy O'Neill*, musical comedietta, in
one act, written by George E. Cornille-
Pescud, music composed by George E.
Cornille-Pesoud and arranged by Vladimir
Brodo.
Sweet Peggy O'Neill ....Miss Elaine Cliffe
Lady Carteret .... Miss Victoria Carman
Phoebe .... Miss Ellie Verriere
Lord Carteret ..Mr. G. E. Cornille-Pescud
Captain Carless ...... Mr. Harry Marvello
The McIntosh of Intosh Mr. Sam Thomson
The Bishop of Tunbridge Wells
Mr. Harry Griffiths
Terence O'Rell ...... Mr. Michael Kemble
—Tower Pavilion, Portobello.

13. *The Postern Gate*, one-act play, by B. Iden
Payne.
Capt. Ambrose Underwood..Mr. L. Casson
Sir Thomas Ambergate....Mr. E. Lander
Sophia Ambergate .. Miss Doris Horrocks
Ensign Dermott Enderby....Mr. L. Mudie
—P.O.W., Birmingham.

17. *Dark Deeds of the Night*, drama, in four
acts, by Edward Thane.
Dr. Mortimer Caine .. Mr. F. Eaglesfield
Philip Bardsley .... Mr. T. W. Ford
Jack Brandon ...... Mr. Lewis De Burgh
Captain Tom Cornish .. Mr. Alfred Terriss
Nicholas Pickles .... Mr. Fred Richards
Joe Norton .... Mr. W. Treloar
Tim O'Mallory .... Mr. Albert Hayzen
P.C. Norton .... Mr. Harry Sidney
Mrs. Brandon ...... Miss Jennie Bostock
Ruth Maitland ...... Miss Gwen Stuart
Polly Prince .... Miss Edith Bottomley
Dora Bardsley ...... Miss Hilda Merrilise
—Royal, Stratford.

17. *The Passing of the Third Floor Back*,
"idle fancy," in a prologue, a play and
an epilogue, by Jerome K. Jerome. (London
production, Terry's, September 1.)
Joey Knight .... Mr. Ernest Hendrie
Christopher Penny.... Mr. H. Marsh Allen
Major Tompkins ...... Mr. Ian Robertson
Mrs. Tompkins ...... Miss Kate Carlyon
Vivian .... Miss Alice Crawford
Jape Samuels .... Mr. Edward Sass
Harry Larcomb ...... Mr. Wilfred Forster
Miss Kite .... Miss Haidée Wright
Mrs. Percival de Hooley....Miss K. Bishop
Stasia .... Miss Gertrude Elliott
Mrs. Sharpe .... Miss Agnes Thomas
The Third Floor Back....Mr. F. Robertson
—O.H., Harrogate.

17.‡*The Conscience of a Judge*, play, in four
acts, by Mrs. Sam Duckworth and Ridge-
wood Barrie (originally produced at the
Royal, Tonypandy, December 23, 1907).
Herbert Granstone ...... Mr. K. Musgrave
Cecil Bentley ...... Mr. Reginald Maurice

The Conscience of a Judge (continued).

Sir Edward Mervin .... Mr. Sam Courtney
Geoffry Granstone ...... Mr. L. Stevenson
John Summers .... Mr. Frank Ayrton
Horatio Winters ...... Mr. Walter Clarke
Old Jervis .... Mr. Ford Edwards
Carter Ben .... Mr. Tom Carter
Officer .... Mr. Charles Benson
Mrs. Draycott ...... Miss Mona Dalwish
Ethel Vaughn ...... Miss Mabel Coleman
Mary Rostron ...... Miss Madge Seymour
Little Kitty .... Miss Elsie Isaacs
Jessica Draycott ...... Miss Nellie Howitt
—Elephant and Castle.

17. *The Old Firm*, farce, in three acts, by Ed-
ward and Harry Paulton (originally pro-
duced in America). (London production,
Wyndham's, September 4.)
Daniel Hake ....Mr. Richard Golden
Mr. Nichol ......Mr. Jerrold Robertshaw
Harrison .... Mr. Clayton Greene
Herbert Wardley ......Mr. Frank Tennant
Jabez Vennamy .. Mr. Ernest A. Douglas
Merrick .... Mr. George West
Deffner .... Mr. Atheling Farrar
Rosalie .... Miss Beatrice Ferrar
Lila Hake .... Miss Gladys Mason
Judy Hake .... Miss Alice Beet
Lucy Upton .... Miss Constance Hyem
Fay Lofty .... Miss Florence Lloyd
—Royal, Newcastle.

17. *The Meturef*, drama, in four acts, by Jacob
Gordin
Malkiel Garber .... Mr. J. Fineberg
Frima .... Mme. R. Waxman
Chazkel .... Mr. M. D. Waxman
Ben-Zion .... Mr. Jacob P. Adler
Izrael-Jacob .... Mr. S. Aurbach
Sarah-Eve .... Mme. Chizisk
Milka .... Miss Gladstone
Abraham Rosenberg .... Mr. H. Fineberg
Misha .... Mr. M. Gusofsky
Lizah .... Mme. F. Waxman
Yeruchem-Zalmen ...... Mr. B. Fischman
Rachel .... Miss Jonkel
—Pavilion (Jewish season).

18.*The Dumb Man*, drama, in four acts—
Pavilion (Jewish season).

21. *Uriel Acosta*, Carl Gutzkow's tragedy.
Mehasha .... Mr. S. Aurbach
Judith .... Mme. F. Waxman
Ben Yucha .... Mr. M. Gusofsky
De Silvia .... Mr. H. Fineberg
Ben Akibo .... Mr. D. Fishman
Uriel Acosta .... Jacob P. Adler
Esther .... Mme. R. Waxman
Reuben .... Mr. David Reitz
Rabbi de Santes..........Mr. J. Fineberg
Servant .... Mr. Goldstein
—Pavilion (Jewish season).

21.¶*The Melting Pot*, drama, in four acts, by
Israel Zangwill—Terminus Hall, Littlehampton.

24. *Broken Hearts*, play, by Z. Lubin.
Nochum Ostron...... Mr. Jacob P. Adler
Mechle .... Miss Gladstone
Gitele .... Mme. Fr. Waxman
Feige .... Mme. R. Waxman
Benjamin............ Mr. M. D. Waxman
Vigdor .... Mr. S. Aurbach
Seprincy .... Mme. Lowenwirth
Glotkin .... Mr. D. Fishman
Dr. Applebaum ....Mr. D. Reitz
Nurse Janel .... Miss Jonkel
—Pavilion (Jewish season).

24.‚ *The Tyrant*, play in four acts, by Fred C. Somerfield (adapted from Victor Hugo's *Angelo*). (Originally produced at the Osborne, Manchester, December 17, 1900.)

Homodei .... Mr. Fred C. Somerfield
Angelo .... Mr. Roy Fortesque
Rudolph .... Mr. Ed. E. Louis
Pan .... Mr. T. Ashmore
Victor .... Mr. Frank Etheridge
Nobbo .... Mr. Willie Barrett
Lieut. Tasker .....Mr. James Sherwin
Arch Priest ....Mr. Stanley Whyte
Doctor .... Mr. Kurson Proctor
Dean of St. Anthony..Mr. Geo. Rathbone
Abrossi .... Mr. Rowland Wade
Roderic .... Mr. Charles E. Geary
Usher .... Mr. Sidney
First Night Watchman......Mr. G. Bynge
Second Night Watchman..Mr. C. Williams
Lady Katherine ....Miss Margaret Frame
Eulie .... Miss Cherry Vehenye
Daphne .... Miss Vida Halsewood
Reginella .... Miss Nellie Freeland
Tisbe .... Miss Marie Dagmar
—Dalston

24. *Idols*, play, in four acts, adapted from the novel of W. J. Locke, by Roy Horni- ‚) (London production, September 2, Garrick.)

Irene Merriam........Miss Evelyn Millard
Minna Hart ....Miss Edyth Latimer
Mrs. Harroway....Miss Augusta Haviland
Anna Josephs ....Mrs. Harry Cane
Maid to the Merriams..Miss Ethel Ingram
Gerard Merriam....Mr. Herbert Waring
Saunders............ Mr. C. W. Somerset
Jacob Hart ....Mr. Alfred Brydone
Counsel for Prosecution..Mr. Chas. Rock
Counsel for Defence..Mr. Arthur Wontner
Mr. Harroway ......Mr. C. Leveison-Lane
The Judge ....Mr. Evelyn Vernon
Dr. Fenwick ....Mr. Heath Haviland
The Clerk of Assize....Mr. Guy Fletcher
An Usher .... Mr. Frank Danby
P.C. Rivington..........Mr. Albert Sims
Hugh Colman ....Mr. Allan Aynesworth
—Royal, Birmingham.

24. *His Life for Her Love*, play, in four acts, by Geo. S. King.

Jacob Trewitt .. Mr. Douglas C. Phelps
Seth Shaw .... Mr. Francis Roberts
Abel Trewitt .... Mr. Herbert Lawrence
Jimmy Newsome Mr. Sydney Humphreys
Mattie Corncraike .... Mr. Fred Watson
Rev. Stephen Addison .. Mr. Geo. Gessop
Betty Crawley .... Miss Hazel Hood
Dolly Newsome .... Miss Dolly Gilroy
Ruth Tempt ..... Miss Phyllis Gibbon
Lena Shaw .... Miss Helen Lowther
—Metropole, Devonport.

25.¶*My Californian Sweetheart*, musical comedy drama, the book, lyrics, and music by A. Bardwell-Challier.—Town Hall, Burnham.

26.¶*In the Nick of Time*, drama, in five acts, by Della Clarke.—Haymarket.

26.¶*The Fighting Hope*, play, in three acts, by William J. Hurlbut.—Elephant and Castle.

28. *Solomon the Wise*.
Cardinal Richelieu....Mr. M. D. Waxman
Burney, his secretary....Mr. H. Fineberg
Jerbelieu, his spy.......Mr. J. Fineberg
Janet, his sister........Mme. R. Waxman
Lord Worcester.........Mr. M. Gusofsky
Jack Traville................Mr. S. Bloom
Solomon the Wise.......Jacob P. Adler
Shushna, his wife......Mme. F. Waxman
Poet Sasiskin........Mr. Ferdinand Staub

Solomon the Wise (continued).
Doctor Benha..............Mr. S. Oerbach
Griza....................Mr. D. Reitz
Officer....................Mr. J. Goldstein
—Pavilion (Jewish season).

29. *Pete*, play, in four acts, by Hall Caine and Louis N. Parker, dramatised from Hall Caine's novel, "The Manxman." (Last performance, December 12; 120 performances.)
Pete Quilliam ..... Mr. Matheson Lang
Philip Christian ..... Mr. Eric Mayne
Ross Christian .. Mr. Wilfred E. Payne
Cæsar Cregeen .... Mr. Frederick Ross
Black Tom .... Mr. S. Major Jones
Jonaique Jelly .... Mr. Chas. L. Ludlow
Postman Kelly .... Mr. H. K. Ayliff
William .... Mr. Sydney Young
Constable Nipilghtly.. Mr. Joseph O'Brien
Dr. Mylochreest .. Mr. Sydney Vautier
The Lieut.-Governor .. Mr. Henry Brooks
Adam Quirk ...... Mr. Ernest Cresfan
Johnny Dumbell .... Mr. Charles Terric
Clerk of the Court Mr. Henry Armstrong
Nancy .... Miss Rita Tomkins
Mary .... Miss Lillian Digges
Grannie .... Miss Blanche Stanley
Meg .... Miss Dora Clements
Sarah .... Miss Lillian Tweed
Kate Cregeen .... Miss Hutin Britton
—Lyceum.

29. *The Wild Man*, a drama in four acts.
Schmuel Leiblich......Mr. M. D. Waxman
Zeldy....................Miss Gladston
Lemech...............‚........Jacob P. Adle
Liza....................Mme. F. Waxman
Simon...................Mr. Gusofsky
Alexander................Mr. S. Aurbach
Spreh................Mme. R. Waxman
Valadimir Vorobeitchik..Mr. H. Fineberg
—Pavilion (Jewish season)

29. *When the Devil Was Ill*, original comedy in four acts, by Charles McEvoy.
Godfrey Rawlings .. Mr. B. Iden Payne
Martin Leatherhead .. Mr. Charles Bibby
Mrs. Rawlings .... Miss Sybil Thorndike
Walter King .... Mr. Basil Dean
Owen Davis .... Mr. Jules Shaw
Isobel .... Miss Penelope Wheeler
Lady Mendle-Parrish .... Miss Ada King
Chauffeur .... Mr. Leonard Mudie
Fanny Goldstone .. Miss Louise Holbrook
—H.M., Carlisle.

31. *The Duke's Motto*, new version, by Justin Huntley McCarthy, of the drama. (London production, September 8, Lyric.)
Louis XIII...........Mr. Tom Heslewood
Louis de Nevers....Mr. Owen Roughwood
Louis de Gonzague ..Mr. Franklyn Dyall
Cocordasse .....Mr. Herbert Jarman
Passepoil..............Mr. Alec Thompson
Peyrolles ....Mr. Hubert Druce
Æsop................Mr. A. E. George
Staupitz.................Mr. J. H. Irvine
Faenza.............Mr. Caton Woodville
Saldango..............Mr. Reginald Dane
Pepe.....................Mr. Frank Ridley
Pinto...................Mr. Cronin Wilson
Hoel ....Mr. Geoffrey Saville
Charvernais..............Mr. Shiel Barry
Tavannes.................Mr. J. V. Henry
Navailles...........Mr. George Harrington
Noce..............Mr. James Harrison
Oriol..................Mr. Patrick Digan
Berichen...........Master Harry Duff
Bonnivet ....Mr. D. Bartun
Landlord of Inn........Mr. Charles Cecil
Grieveau ....Mr. Paul Sutcliffe
Henri de la Gardere....Mr. Lewis Waller
Blanche de Nevers........Miss Valli Valli

Duke's Motto (continued).

Gabrielle Gonzague .. Miss Sybil Carlisle
Flora................Miss Dorothy Minto
Cidalis ....Miss Gwendolin F'oyd
Martine................Miss Maud Digan
Brigitte...............Miss May Chenery
—Royal, Birmingham.

‡*The Best of Her Sex*, domestic drama, in
four acts, by William A. Armour and
Robert Cheval (originally produced at
the Colosseum, Oldham, May 13, 1907).
Sir Stanton Faringdon .... H. J. Walton
Philip Faringdon........Mr. Percy Horton
Leslie Verney............Mr. Henry Lloyd
Vera Delorme...........Miss Dora Price
Ruth Raeburn........Miss Alvina Mining
Rev. Stephen Maxwell .. W. A. Armour
Jake Smith..........Mr. Herbert de Ville
P.C. Peter Jorkins....Mr. J. W. Hooper
Holy Joe................Mr. Dan Mining
Polly Perkins........Miss Alice Buckland
Simon Downy..........Mr. Hume Fergus
Warder....................Mr. H. Ashton
Little Phil............Miss Dorothy Love
Detective Grey........Mr. Vincent Hales
Drunken Man.........Mr. James Morgan
—Royal, Stratford.

SEPTEMBER.

.‡*The Passing of the Third Floor Back*, idle
fancy in a prologue, a play and an epi-
logue by Jerome K. Jerome (originally
produced at the O.H., Harrogate, August
13, 1908). Transferred to Terry's on Novem
ber 9.
Joey Knight .... Mr. Ernest Hendrie
Christopher Penny..Mr. H. Marsh Allen
Major Tompkins .... Mr. Ian Robertson
Mrs. Tompkins .. .. Miss Kate Carlyon
Vivian .... Miss Alice Crawford
Jake Samuels .... Mr. Edward Sass
Harry Larcomb ...... Mr. Wilfred Forster
Miss Kite .... Miss Haidée Wright
Mrs. Percival de Hooley.Miss Kate Bishop
Stasia .... Miss Gertrude Elliott
Mrs. Sharpe .... Miss Agnes Thomas
The Third Floor Back
Mr. Forbes Robertson
—St. James's'

2.‡*Idols*, play, in four acts, adapted from the
novel of that name, by W. J. Locke, by
Roy Horniman. (Originally produced August
24, Royal, Birmingham.) Last performance
January 2, 1909.
Irene Merriam ...... Miss Evelyn Millard
Minna Hart .... Miss Edyth Latimer
Mrs. Harroway .. Miss Augusta Haviland
Anna Josephs .... Mrs. Harry Cane
Maid .... Miss Ethel Ingram
Gerard Merriam .... Mr. Herbert Waring
Saunders .... Mr. C. W. Somerset
Jacob Hart .... Mr. Alfred Brydone
Counsel for Prosecution.Mr. Charles Rock
Gardiner .... Mr. Arthur Wontner
Mr. Harroway ...... Mr. C. Leveson-Lane
The Judge .... Mr. Howard Sturge
Dr. Fenwick .... Mr. Heath Haviland
The Clerk of Assize....Mr. Guy Fletcher
An Usher .... Mr. Frank Danby
P.C. Rivington .... Mr. Albert Sims
Hugh Colman .... Mr. Allan Aynesworth
—Garrick.

3. *The King of Cadonia*, musical play, in
two acts, the book by Frederick Lonsdale, with lyrics by Adrian Ross, and
music by Sidney Jones.
Duke of Alasia .... Mr. Huntley Wright
Alexis .... Mr. Bertram Wallis
General Bonski..Mr. Roland Cunningham

The King of Cadonia (continued).

Captain Laski .... Mr. F. Pope Stamper
Lieutenant Jules .... Mr. Harold Deacon
Lieutenant Saloff .... Mr. Cameron Carr
Panix .... Mr. Arthur Laceby
Laborde .... Mr. Akerman May
Bran .... Mr. George Barrett
Militza .... Miss Gracie Leigh
Stephanie .... Miss Peggy Bethel
Natine .... Miss Queenie Merrall
Wanda .... Miss Gladys Beech
Ottaline .... Miss Claire Lynch
Fridoline .... Miss Gladys Anderson
Duchess of Alasia .... Mme. Amy Martin
Princess Marie .... Miss Isabel Jay
—Prince of Wales's.

3. *What Every Woman Knows*, comedy, in
four acts, by J. M. Barrie, transferred to the
Hicks on December 21.
John Shand .... Mr. Gerald du Maurier
Alick Wylie .... Mr. Henry Vibart
David Wylie ...... Mr. Sydney Valentine
James Wylie ...... Mr. Edmund Gwenn
Maggie Wylie .... Miss Hilda Trevelyan
Mr. Venables ...... Mr. Norman Forbes
Comtesse de la Brière .... Mrs. Tree
Lady Sybil Lazenby.Miss Lallah McCarthy
Maid .... Miss Madge Murray
—Duke of York's.

4.‡*The Old Firm*, eccentric comedy, in three
acts, by Harry and Edward Paulton.
(Originally produced at the Royal, New-
castle, August 17, 1908.) Last performance
; 31 performances.
Daniel Hake .... Mr. Richard Golden
Mr. Nichol ...... Mr. Jerrold Robertshaw
Harrison .... Mr. Clayton Greene
Herbert Wardley .... Mr. Frank Tennant
Jabez Vennamy ..Mr. Ernest A. Douglas
Deffner .... Mr. George West
Merrick .... Mr. Atheling Farrar
Rosalie .... Miss Beatrice Farrar
Lila Hake .... Miss Gladys Mason
Judy Hake .... Miss Alice Beet
Lucy Upton ...... Miss Constance Hyem
Fay Lofty ...... Miss Florence Lloyd
—Queen's.

5 *Faust*, new adaptation of portions of the
First Part of Goethe's *Faust*, in a pro-
logue and four acts, by Stephen Phillips
and J. Comyns Carr. [Last performance
December 12 ; 114 performances.]
Mephistopheles .... Mr. Tree
Faust .... Mr. Henry Ainley
Valentine .... Mr. Godfrey Tearle
The Witch .... Mr. Charles Quartermaine
Altmayer .... Mr. G. W. Anson
Hans .... Mr. Norman Page
Fritz .... Mr. W. Cleighton
Siebel .... Mr. Cyril Sworder
Frosch .... Mr. Compton Coutts
Albrecht ...... Mr. J. Cowley Wright
Brander .... Mr. John Deverell
Adolf .... Mr. Henry Morrell
Burgomaster .... Mr. Robert Atkins
Heavenly Messenger...Elizabeth Valentine
Raphael .... Miss Isabel Merson
Gabriel .... Miss Muriel Alexander
Michael .... Miss Sylvia Buckley
Anna .... Miss Shelley Calton
Hedwig .... Miss V. Sinclair
Laine .... Miss Laura Cowie
Elsa .... Miss Pauline Bredt
Lisbeth .... Miss Ethel Hodgkins
Magda .... Miss Juliet Hardinge
A Witch .... Miss Maud Leslie
Lisa .... Miss Madge Titheradge
Martha .... Miss Rosina Filippi
Margaret .... Miss Marie Lohr
—His Majesty's.

7. *The Sailor's Wedding*, romantic drama, in
five acts, by H. Brinsley Hill.
Gordon Drake ...... Mr. C. W. Standing
Sir Victor Lascelles .... Mr. Cecil Klein
Count Bellini .... Mr. Frank Stone
Giovanni Ferici .... Mr. Hodgson Taylor
Giacomo ...... Mr. F. Finch Smiles
Jack Hawkins .... Mr. Walter Pemberton
Bill Burns .... Mr. Huntly Gifford
Father Gianelli .... Mr. Frederic Jacques
Luigi Polti .... Mr. Walter Emsdale
Manservant .... Mr. Chas. Childs
Countess Bellini ...... Miss Maud Linden
Mary .... Miss Dulcie Greatwich
Lenore de Grésac..Miss Winifred Pearson
Ninette .... Miss Celestine Bertram
Polly Clarke .... Miss Belle Travers
—Marlborough.

7.*Filby the Faker*, play, in one act, adapted
from a story by Tom Gallon by Leon M.
Lion. (Originally known as *The Fairy
Uncle*, produced at the New, November
28, 1907, and also on the halls.)
John Griffin .... Mr. W. Brandon
Lucy Winwood .... Miss Mary Leslie
Dr. Arthur Wakefield Mr. Forbes Dawson
Timothy Filby .... Mr. Ben Nathan
—Wyndham's.

7. *The Early Worm*, farce, in three acts, by
Frederick Lonsdale. [Last performance
November 21; 77 performances.]
Duke of Tadcaster...Mr. A. E. Matthews
Lord Steyne .... Mr. Alfred Bishop
Sir William Mayton .. Mr. W. Draycott
Allan Marchmont..Mr. Weedon Grossmith
Captain Baxter .. Mr. Henry Stephenson
Tom .... Mr. A. W. Baskcomb
Boatman .... Mr. E. W. Laceby
Sailor .... Mr. Gerald Malvern
Naylor .... Mr. Edgar B. Payne
Sybil Annesley .. Miss Muriel Beaumont
Lady Steyne .... Miss Fanny Brough
—Wyndham's.

7. *The Proof*, one-act play, by Alice Clayton
Greene.
Jim Patterson .... Mr. Dalziel Heron
Sydney Ross .... Mr. A. E. Mayne
Elizabeth K. Binns .. Miss Mildred Orme
Brenda .... Miss May Brooke
—O.H., Southport.

7. *Next Door*, "tragic farce," in three acts,
by Eardley Turner.
Mr. Thackeray Jellyby.Mr. M. R. Morand
Hector Pennicuick .. Mr. Arthur Soames
Reuben Quilten .... Mr. Frank G. Bayly
Mr. Minnikin .... Mr. Arthur Dennis
Andrew Kinch .... Mr. Dennis Bryan
Bill Yarrow ...... Mr. Eardley Turner
"Man Next Door".Mr. Robert D. Taylor
Sergeant of Police..Mr. A. Morrice Seaton
Mrs. Jellyby .... Miss Lilian Dundas
Kitty Maygrove .. Miss Dorothy Rundell
Ann .... Miss Katie Johnson
"Woman Next Door" ......Alice A. Cook
—Royal, Newcastle.

7. *Marriages Are Made in Heaven*, one-act
episode, by Basil Dean.
John Abel .... Mr. Lewis Casson
Mrs. Hannah Abel..Miss Louise Holbrook
Bessie Taylor ...... Miss Sybil Thorndike
Samuel Carter ...... Mr. Edward Landor
—Gaiety, Manchester.

8. *Paid in Full*, play, in four acts, by Eugene
Walter. Last performance, September 26;
20 performances.
Joseph Brooks ...... Mr. Robert Loraine
Emma Brooks .... Miss Hilda Antony
James Smith .... Mr. Paul Arthur
Captain Williams .... Mr. Louis Calvert

Paid in Full (continued).
Mrs. Harris .... Miss Kate Serjeantson
Beth Harris ...... Miss Daisy Markham
Sato .... Mr. John Arthur
—Aldwych.

8.;*The Duke's Motto*, melodrama, adapted
from the French of Paul Féval, in four
acts, by Justin Huntly McCarthy (origin-
ally produced at the Royal, Birmingham,
August 13, 1908.) Last performance Novem-
ber·21; 86 performances.
Louis XIII. ...... Mr. Tom Heslewood
Louis de Nevers .. Mr. Owen Roughwood
Louis de Gonzague....Mr. Franklyn Dyall
Marqu's de Chavernay .. Mr. Shiel Barry
Comte de Tavannes .... Mr. J. V. Henry
M. de Navailles .... Mr. Geoffrey Saville
M. de Nocé .... Mr. James Harrison
M Oriol .... Mr. Patrick Digan
Cocardasse .... Mr. Herbert Jarman
Passepoil .... Mr. Alec F. Thompson
Æsop .... Mr. A. E. George
Peyrolles .... Mr. Hubert Druce
Staupitz .... Mr. J. H. Irvine
Faënza .... Mr. Caton Woodville
Sa'dagno .... Mr. Reginald Dane
Pepe .... Mr. Frank Ridley
Pinto .... Mr. Cronin Wilson
Hoël .... Mr. George Harrington
Berichon .... Master Harry Duff
Bonnivet .... Mr. D. Bartun
Landlord of Inn ...... Mr. Charles Cecil
Henri de Lagardère .... Mr. Lewis Waller
Princesse Gabrielle .. Miss Sybil Carlisle
Blanche de Nevers .... Miss Valli Valli
Cidalise .... Miss Gwendolin Floyd
Martine .... Miss Maude Digan
Brigitte .... Miss May Chenery
Flora .... Miss Dorothy Minto
—Lyric.

9.¶*Her King*, romantic play, in four acts, by
Harold Whyte—Crown, Peckham.

9.‡*The Conspiracy*, play, in one act, by
Robert Barr and Sidney Lewis-Ransom.
(Originally produced at the Royal,
Dublin, November 8, 1907.)
King Konrad of Polavia..Martin Harvey
Baron Brünfels .... Mr. Charles Glenney
Count Staunn .... Mr. Albert E. Raynor
Herr Von Steinmetz..Mr. Alfred Mansfield
Nobles of Polavia: Messrs. George Cooke,
Philip Hewland, Leonard Craske, Percy
Foster, Leslie Palmer, Denholm Muir,
and Henry Watson.
—Adelphi.

9.*The Corsican Brothers*, new version of *Les
Frères Corses*, adapted from the novel of
Alexandre Dumas. (Originally produced
at the Royal, Birmingham, October 10,
1906; Adelphi, June 17, 1907)—Adelphi.

14.‡*The House of Pierre*, play, in one act, by
Julie Opp Faversham and Kate Jordon.
(Originally produced at the Royal,
Dublin, November 8, 1907.)
Pierre .... Mr Martin Harvey
M. Crapeau .... Mr. Charles Glenney
Jaques .... Mr. Alfred Mansfield
Cora .... Miss Maud Rivers
Blanche .... Miss Bessie Elder
Lizette .... Miss N. de Silva
—Adelphi.

14.‡*The Love of the Princess*, play, in four
acts, by C. Watson Mill. (Originally produced at the Grand, Nelson, April 13,
1908.)
Prince Conrad Ramona...Wilson Coleman
Count Nicholas Danillo..Ernest E. Imeson
Josef, King of Ilarnia..Mr. E. H. Dobell

The Love of the Princess (continued).

Lieut. Orians .... Mr. Beckett Bould
Lieut. Zaroff ...... Mr. Graham Winsford
Prince Regent of Narava..W, F, Stirling
Duke Scarfe .... Mr. George Antley
Boris .... Mr. Edgar Morgan
Stephen .... Mr. Eric Wilde
Carlos .... Mr. James Austin
Lady Irene Ramona..Miss Nellie Garside
Constantia ....Miss Ellen Elmar
Princess Idalia .... Miss Ward
    —Elephant and Castle.

14.‡*At the World's Mercy*, musical comedy-
  drama, in four acts, by Carr Loates.
Captain Frank Manley..Mr. Leo Rodway
Jabez Barber .... Mr. Carr Loates
Morris Goldstein ...... Mr. G. D. Knight
Charley Smart .... Mr. Jess Boxer
Slouching Sam .... Mr. Will Griffin
Dan .... Mr. W. Leonard
Alice Lloyd .... Miss Molly Bee
Skittles and Kitty Knott..Cissie Milford
Mrs. Rouke .... Miss Clara Hall
Dot .... Miss Kathleen Saunders
Rosie .... Miss Alice Hunter
    —Royal, Stratford.

16. *The Emperor Commands*, musical comedi-
  etta, written and composed by George
  Cornille-Pescud.
Napoleon Bonaparte .... Mr. M. Kemble
Comte de Chatillon .... Mr. H. Marvello
Talleyrand ...... Mr. G. Cornille-Pescud
Fouché .... Mr. Harry Griffiths
Marshal Macdonald....Mr. Sam Thomson
Josephine .... Miss Victoria Carmen
Eugénie .... Miss Ellie Verriers
Mme. Romolino Bonaparte..Miss J. Jeune
Mlle. St. Cyr .... Miss Elaine Cliffe
    —Tower Pavilion, Portobello.

17. *The Bells of Old York*, drama, in five acts,
  by Rass Challis.
Rev. Philip Gordon ... Mr. Rass Challis
Captain Romney Kent...William Carriden
Colonel Kent ...... Mr. Frank Cavanah
Trooper Jigger Popkins .. Mr. Fred Davis
Peter Pluggitt ...... Mr. Tommy Cough
Corporal Spatchcock...Mr. Dick Eckersley
Jules Pomponnett .... Mr. Rupert Vane
Gasconne .... Mr. George Ranter
Robert Entwistle .... Mr. G. B. Rawlings
Constable Cluiken...Mr. Harry Harbourne
Angel Grantham, "Boy," and Young
  Romney Kent .... Miss Rose Moncrieff
Lady Angela Grantham and Angela
  Grantham .... Miss Maud Hastings
Judith Puison ...... Miss Gussie Everitt
Mary Ellen Ramsbottom..Miss D. Robins
Aunt Diana .... Miss Lucy Courtenay
Jane Richeux and Kittie Flash
                Miss Lillie Ray
    —Globe, Deal.

17.‖*Fate and the Footman*, "song salad in
  three helpings," by Olive Tulloch.
Lady Tissypate ...... Miss Helen Hulme
Clarissa Tissypate..Miss Sylvia Armstrong
Anne Tissypate ...... Miss R. Armstrong
Sybil Cassandra de Cumae..Miss. H. Hulme
Sir Timothy Tipathy Mr. G. F. Armstrong
Rev. Cornelius Meakhart..Mr. M. Brothers
Lieut. Tollemache .. Mr. Clive Armstrong
Eppie Cure .... Miss S. Armstrong
Jane Print .... Miss M. Armstrong
Sara Gubbins ...... Miss Olive Tulloch
Sam Sprangle .... Mr. G. Armstrong
    —Terminus Hall, Littlehampton.

17. *Lady Dolly and the Decalogue*, play, in
  three acts, by Joseph Fletcher and
  Marcus Ellis.
Sir John Markham...Mr. Pennington-Gush
Lord Deveril .... Mr. Chas. Sewell
Hamilton Dereham .... Mr. Robin Shiels
Hon. Reginald Anstey..Mr. F. Medhurst
Captain Stacey .... Mr. M. B. Pedlar
Malmaison .... Mr. F. Barnes
Rogers .... Mr. Edgar Stanley
Hon. Margaret Anstey....Miss F. Mitchell
Mrs. Audrey Braun....Miss Sara Dudley
Fanchette .... Miss Eileen Constance
Dolly, Lady Markham.. Miss E. Roberts
    —Pier Pavilion, Paignton.

18.¶*In the Gloaming*, play, in four acts, by
  Loie Esmond—Royal, Goole. Production
  September 29, Exchange, Wellingborough.

21.°*Hands Across the Sea*, drama, by the late
  Henry Pettitt. (Originally produced at
  Royal, Manchester, July 30, 1888; Prin-
  cess's, November 10, 1888.)
Jack Dudley ....Mr. Rawson Buckley
Joseph Stillwood ...... Mr. A. Alexander
Robert Stillwood ...... Mr. G. C. Boyne
Tom Bassett ...... Mr. Cecil A. Collins
Jean de Lussac .... Mr. Clive Currie
Dick Melford .... Mr. Frank Woodville
Captain Lane ...... Mr. Robert Hunter
Count Paul de Renai—Mr. E. Beresford
Governor ...... Mr. Forrester Harvey
Lieut. Victor .... Mr. John Wilson
The French Minister..Mr. L. Hutchinson
Hiram Hickory .... Mr. A. L. Burke
French Walter .... Mr. Arthur Blair
First Mate .... Mr. Stanley Brew
Inspector Thompson .. Mr. Henry Willis
Lieut. Mayne ...... Mr. Olfred Ritson
Port Official ...... Mr. Hugh Grimshaw
Lillian Melford .... Miss B. Whitney
Lucy Nettleford ...... Miss Lilla Nordon
Mme. Vallerie..Miss Marjorie Davenporte
Polly .... Miss Kirsteen Græme
    —Dalston.

21. *The Cheat*, drama, in four acts, by Edward
  Ferris and B. P. Matthews. London pro-
  duction September 28, Crown, Peckham.
Lieut. Blanchard .... Mr. Edward Ferris
General Blanchard .... Mr. R. Keith
Admiral Bruce-Hardy ...... Mr. W. Guise
Captain Philip Rivers ... Mr. E. O'Neill
Dr. John Vorland ...... Mr. C. Goodhart
Colonel Paget .... Mr. Edward Y. Rae
Lieut. Brabazon .... Mr. Max Leeds
Lieut. Neyland .... Mr. C. Crawford
La Sing .... Mr. S. A. Cookson
Sergeant Mack ...... Mr. Duncan Druce
Larry O'Brien .... Mr. Littledale Power
Native Hospital Orderly..Mr. F. Manners
Stephen Blanchard ...... Mr. F. Cooper
Ethel Hardy .... Miss Helen Russell
Joan Fielding .. Miss Eugenie Francklyn
Marjorie Vorland .. Miss Daisy Atherton
    —Grand, Wolverhampton.

21. *The Marriages of Mayfair*, drama of
  modern life, in four acts, by Cecil Raleigh
  and Henry Hamilton, produced by Arthur
  Collins, incidental music composed by
  J. M. Glover.
Lord Adolphus Villiers..Albert Chevalier
Jim Callender .... Mr. Lyn Harding
Nigel Villiers .... Mr. Basil Gill
Dudley Gore .... Mr. Vincent Clive
Duke of Exmoor .. Mr. Charles V. France
Julian Merrowdale ...... Mr. Oscar Adye
Sir Antony Gore ...... Mr. Arthur Poole
Andrew McBroader .... Mr. Fred Grove

17

The Marriages of Mayfair (continued).

Percy Hosfield	Mr. Frank Bradley
Dorothy Gore	Miss Eva Moore
Bess Bissett	Miss Marie George
Lady M. Villiers....Mrs.	Lancaster-Wallis
Mrs. Bissett	Miss Lucy Sibley
Lily de Mario	Miss Marie Pera
Mrs. Clayson	Mrs. Edwin Palmer
Mrs. Anstruther	Miss Muriel Langley
Elise Dubernay	Miss Olive Palmer
Lady Mab Middleton...Miss	D'Arcy Lane
Mary Bandeleur	Miss Marjorie Day
La Bébé Bax	Miss Irene Smith
Lady Fordyce	Miss Marjorie Doré
Prudence	Miss Gertie Britton
Yeoman Warder	Mr. John Archer
Father Felix	Mr. Clarence Vincent
Captain Carlyon........Mr.	Guy Williams
Matthew Elkins ...	Mr. Howard Russell
Jeffreys	Mr. Edward Morgan
Lord Tenby	Mr. Fred Penley
The Rector	Mr. Richard Norton
Policeman	Mr. Arthur Leigh
Schweitzer	Mr. Archibald McLean
Sir Nicol Eardley	Mr. Kenelm Foss

Messrs. James Capel, Seymour Richards, Percy West, W. Walsh, A. Melford; Stedman's Choir Boys; Misses Florence Hooton, Edith Russell, M. Cooper, Ethel Lennard, fl. Varre, May Hannam, De Soolem, Joan Burton.

—Drury Lane

21.*Ib and Little Christina*, the revival of " a picture in three panels," by Basil Hood. (Originally produced at the Prince of Wales's, May 15, 1900.)

Ib	Mr. Martin Harvey
Ib's Father	Mr. Albert E. Raynor
Little Ib	Master Bobbie Andrews
Old Heinrik	Mr. Philip Hewland
John	Mr. George Cooke
The Gipsy Woman	Miss Mary Rorke
Christina	Miss Coleridge
Little Christina	Miss Rita Leggiero

—Adelphi.

21.‡*The Whirlpool*, play, in three acts, by Herbert Swears, founded on a short story by Cyrus Townsend Brady. (Originally produced at the New, Cardiff, February 22, 1908.)

Elijah D. Tillottson	Mr. Kendal
Bertram Livingstone	Mr. Bassett Roe
Cunningham Cutter.Mr.	Wellesley Draper
Hon. Reginald Killiegrew..Mr .T.	Holding
Ephraim Johnstone..Mr.	Edmund Gurney
Chappin	Mr. Metcalfe Wood
Parker	Mr. W. M. Rutherfurd
Elise	Miss Sara de Groot
Gretchen de Kaater..Mrs. A. B.	Tapping
Gertrude Van Stuyler....Miss	Ethel Dane
Constance Livingstone	Mrs. Kendal

—Marlborough.

21. *His Wife No Longer*, drama, in four acts, by Stephen Pritt.

Anthony Merivale ..	Mr. Clavering Craig
Harold Medworthy ..	Mr. E. Paul Neville
Rev. F. Willacy ..	Mr. C. Worldley Hulse
Daniel Trench	Mr. David Donaldson
Tommy Oglethorpe. Mr. C.	Vivian Charles
P.C. Michael Flanagan..Mr. D.	McFarlane
Warder Cunningham..Mr. Norman	Clifton
Chambers	Mr. J. E. Baines
Detective	Mr. Douglas Bute
Prison Gate Missioner....Mr. T.	Wheeler
Marion Jeffries	Miss Louie Peebles
Lucy Hooper	Miss Nellie Lawson
Mrs. Merivale	Miss Rosa Mervyn

—Royal, Preston.

21.*The Merchant of Venice*, arranged in three scenes.

Shylock	Mr. Fred Storey
Portia	Miss Lilian Holmes
Antonio	Mr. A. Maitland Stapley
Bassanio	Mr. Wilfred Blair
Gratiano	Mr. Bevan
The Duke	Mr. Booth Conway

—Grand, Birmingham.

22 *The Woman from Russia*, drama, in four acts, by Fred G. Ingleby. (C.P. July 25, Royal, Jarrow.)

Frank Haldane	Mr. Robert Ayrton
Reginald Fitzgerald ..	Mr. Basil Mitchell
Alexis Yarviski	Mr. Fred G. Ingleby
James Haldane	Mr. Richard Pitt
Jerry	Mr. Frank Wheatcroft
Baroni	Mr. G. M. Hancock
Wun-Hi	Mr. H. Elliston
Dr. Chetwede	Mr. T. Wyndham
Petroff	Mr. John Vernon
Trevitch	Mr. Tom Carew
Smirkoff	Mr. Steve Parker
Peritski	Mr. J. Gillette
Edith Haldane	Miss Maggie Hobart
Mary Ann	Miss Maude St. John
Wanda	Miss Adria Hill

—Alexandra, Sheffield.

27. *The Success of Sentiment*, play, in three acts, by Hugh Cranmer Byng (produced by the Play Actors).

Rupert Shires	Mr. Frank G. Bayly
Cuthbert Kennet	Mr. Edward Rigby
Hon. Arthur Frieton..Mr.	Edmund Waller
Major Graves	Mr. Herbert Bunston
Walter .... ⎫	Mr. Murri Moncrieff
Gondolier ..... ⎭	
Official	Mr. Harold Chapin
Lady Mary Kennet ..	Miss Kate Carlyon
Vera Shires	Miss Valerie Salberg
Lucy Kennet	Miss Gillian Scaife
Lady Marcham	Miss Alys Rees
Malcolm	Miss Dora Hole
Disset	Miss Inez Bensusan

—Court.

28.*A Tragedy of Truth*, play, in two scenes, by Rosamund Langbridge (originally produced at the Royal, Manchester, November 2, 1906, under the name of *The Spell*; at the Adelphi, with the present title, on June 17, 1907).

Michael Hennessy ...	Mr. Martin Harvey
Mrs. Riordan	Miss Mary Rorke
Mary Riordan	Miss N. de Silva

—Adelphi.

28.*Dorothy*, comic opera, by B. C. Stephenson and Alfred Cellier (originally produced at the Gaiety, September 25, 1886).

—Broadway.

28.‡*The Cheat*, drama. in four acts, by Edward Ferris and B. P. Matthews (originally produced at the Grand, Wolverhampton, on September 21, 1908).

Lieut. Richard Blanchard...Mr. E.	Ferris
Gen. Blanchard	Mr. Royston Keith
Admiral Bruce-Hardy	
	Mr. Windham Guise
Capt. Philip Rivers..Mr. Edward	O'Neill
Dr. John Vorland..Mr. Charles	Goodnart
Colonel Paget	Mr. Edward Y. Rae
Lieut. Brabazon	Mr. Max Leeds
Lieut. Neyland	Mr. Charles Crawford
La Sing	Mr. S. A. Cookson
Sergt. Mack	Mr. Duncan Druce
Larry O'Brien	Mr. Littledale Power
Native Orderly	Mr. Fred Manners
Stephen Blanchard ....Mr. Frank	Cooper
Ethel Hardy	Miss Helen Russell
Joan Fielding ..	Miss Eugénie Francklyn
Marjorie Vorland..Miss Daisy	Atherton

—Crown, Peckham.

28. *Cold Mutton*, farce, in one act, by H. W.
Mince.
Dick Middleton .... Mr. Ralph Hutton
Mabel .... Miss Evelyn Cecil
Mr. Morley .... Mr. Claud Haviland
—Brixton.

28. *If We Only Knew*, romantic play, in four
acts, by Harry Nicholls and Charles
Ross.
Dick Steen .... Mr. P. A. Gawthorn
Ensign John Willmott..Mr. Ernest Young
Mr. Bignell .... Mr. J. Benedick Butler
Samuel Scarper ...... Mr. Harry Nicholls
Crampton .... Mr. William Amos
Naylor .... Mr. Henry Jessop
Jackson .... Mr. George Page
Partlett .... Mr. Alfred Wynne
Mr. Wilkins .... Mr. F. Rosse
Mr. Finch .... Mr. H. W. Parkinson
Mr. Piper .... Mr. F. Thorpe Tracey
Mr. Gossage .... Mr. Albert Bernard
Ruth Steen..Miss Margaret Van Hollister
Barbara Wentworth..Miss Sylvia Morris
Miss Priscilla Tompkins..Miss K. Kearney
Mrs. Thornhill ...... Miss Violet Langley
Hebe .... Miss Cicely Nicholls
Avice .... Miss Saffie Kingsford
—Grand, Fulham.

28. *Reaping the Whirlwind*, play, in one act,
by Allan Monkhouse—Gaiety, Manchester.

29. *In the Gloaming*, domestic play, in four
acts, by Loie Esmond (C.P., September
18, at the Royal, Goole).
Ross Heatherston..Mr. F. Douglas Howard
Clyne Quiller ...... Mr. E. Holland Day
Theophilus Thistlewood...Edward Neville
Holmes Thistlewood .. Mr. Claude Casey
Alfred Hummock .. Mr. Edwin Ramsdale
Captain Tollbrook .... Mr. J. Le Fleming
Adolphus .... Mr. Fred White
Policeman .... Mr. W. Frederick
Ella Tollbrook .... Miss Hilary Burleigh
Smudge .... Miss Loie Esmond
Kate Horton .... Miss Mary Askew
Brenda Thistlewood .. Miss Rosie Neville
—Exchange, Wellingborough.

OCTOBER.

2.‡*The House of Clay*, play, in three acts,
adapted by Herbert Swears from *La
Maison d'Argile* (produced at the
Comédie Française, February 25, 1907) of
E. Emile Fabre. (Originally produced April
24, Opera House, Blackpool.)
Henri Armières .... Mr. Kendall
Pierre Ruchon .... Mr. Bassett Roe
Fernand .... Mr. Edmund Gurney
Frédéric .... Mr. R. Burnett
Valentine .... Miss Jessica Thorne
Marguerite .... Miss Ethel Dane
Mme. Reny .... Miss Sara de Groot
Mme. Armières, sen...Mrs. A. B. Tapping
Mme. Armières .... Mrs. Kendal
—Coronet.

3. *The Hon'ble Phil*, musical piece, in two
acts, book by G. P. Huntley and Her-
bert Clayton, music by Harold Samuel,
additional numbers by Ralph Nairn,
lyrics by Harold Lawson, additional
lyrics by Bertrand Davis and Claude
Aveling. [Last performance December 12
—1 performances.]
Capt. Phil. Giffard....Mr. G. P. Huntley
Capt. Jules de Valery.Mr. Herb't Clayton
Mons. Marinet ...... Mr. O. B. Clarence
Buckle .... Mr. Horace Mills
Lieut. Montpensier....Mr. Charles Brown
Counort ..:........ Mr. Charles Seguin

The Hon'ble Phil (continued).
Dubois .... Mr. Hubert Willis
Homard .... Mr. T. M. Hickton
Jerome .... Mr. Frank Perfitt
Gascon .... Mr. Carlton Brough
Gobert .... Mr. J. Herbert
Courriol .... Mr. H. Hulcup
Marie .... Miss Denise Orme
Didine .... Miss Eva Kelly
Brigette .... Miss Elsie Spain
Mme. Lascelles....Miss Barbara Huntley
Annette .... Miss Nellie Francis
Fleurette .... Miss Dorothy Dunbar
Fanchette .... Miss Alice Kay
Suzanne .... Miss Julia Sanderson
—Hicks.

5. *Makeshifts*, comedietta, by G. L. Robins.
Miss Caroline Parker .... Miss Ada King
Miss Dolly Parker..Miss Louise Holbrook
Mr. Thompson ...... Mr. Leonard Mudie
Mr. Albert Smythe....Mr. Charles Bibby
—Gaiety, Manchester.

5. *Bringing It Home*, one-act play, by H. M.
Richardson.
Mrs. Unwin .... Miss Darragh
Mrs. Bent-Bullough..Miss Louise Holbrook
Simpson .... Mr. Henry Austin
Jeanette .... Miss Lilian Christine
Cyril Unwin .... Mr. Basil Dean
Maid .... Miss Enid Meek
—Gaiety, Manchester.

5.‡*The Old Folks at Home*, drama, in four
acts, by J. A. Campbell. (Originally pro-
duced at the Junction, Manchester, Sep-
tember 30, 1907.)
Lord Howard Kenilworth .. Mr. F. Liston
Andrew Ross .... Mr. Aidan Lovett
Christopher Robin .... Mr. Henry Nelson
Hugh Lovell .... Mr. Vernon Proctor
Ben Jolly .... Mr. Frank Caffrey
Joe Chaff .... Mr. Leslie Crowther
Jock .... Mr. Arthur Dudley
Musillo .... Mr. William Speke
William .... Mr. William Myers
Robert .... Mr. Harold Shuter
A Policeman .... Mr. Henry Strong
Sam .... Mr. Richard Loft
Johnson .... Mr. H. Danby
Martha .... Miss Clara Santley
Susan Giles .... Miss Nellie Hook
Patricia Bathurst .... Miss Kate Fronde
Bonita Durham .... Miss Amy Rudd
Dinah .... Miss Lillian Francies
A Nurse .... Miss Helene Cronie
Dorothy Robin (afterwards Lady Howard
Kenilworth) .... Miss Mary Fulton
—Lyric, Hammersmith.

5.‡*The Last Heir*, play, in prose, in four acts
and a tableau, adapted from Sir Walter
Scott's novel, " The Bride of Lammer-
moor," by Stephen Phillips. (Originally
produced at the King's, Glasgow, March
23, 1908, under the title of *The Bride of
Lammermore*. [Last performance October 24 ;
21 performances.]
Edgar Ravenswood...Mr. Martin Harvey
Sir Wm. Ashton .. Mr. Albert E. Raynor
Colonel Ashton ...... Mr. Leslie Palmer
Henry Ashton .. Master Bobbie Andrews
Hayston of Bucklaw.Mr. Philip Hewland
Captain Craigengelt..Mr. Charles Glenney
Angus of Cyldesdale..Mr. C. J. Cameron
Sir John de Bothwell..Mr. George Cooke
Sir Andrew Murray .. Mr. Denholm Muir
Colonel Murray .... Mr. Alfred Mansfield
James Murray ...... Mr. Henry Watson
Malcolm Rutherford..Mr. Leonard Craske
Caleb Balderstone ...... Mr. F. Cremlin
Landlord of Tod's Den .. Mr. H. Barry

The Last Heir (continued).

A Notary	Mr. A. Ruben
Rev. Mr. Bide-the-Bent	Mr. Percy Foster
Ailsie Gourlay	Miss Mary Rorke
Annie Winnie	Mrs. F. Wright
Maggie	Miss Bessie Elder
Mysie	Miss Ethel Patrick
Lady Ashton	Miss Maud Hoffman
Lucy Ashton	Miss N. de Silva

—Adelphi.

5. *A Long Journey*, one-act play, by Marie Muggeridge.

Rex Hardy	Mr. Christmas Grose
Bobby	Mr. Ernest Graham
Mme. Bontemps	Miss Estelle Despa
Constance Ford	Miss Lucy Milner

—Royal, Birkenhead.

6. *Bellamy the Magnificent*, social extravaganza, in five acts, from which the novel of the same name was adapted, by Roy Horniman. [Last performance December 12 90 performances.]

Lord Bellamy	Sir Charles Wyndham
Stephens	Mr. Robert Loraine
Mr. Spottit	Mr. Paul Arthur
Hon. Reg. Vandeleur	A. Vane-Tempest
Mr. Dawlish	Mr. Yorke Stephens
Lord Porchester	Mr. Richard Lambart
Lord Petersfield	Miss Rita Leggiero
Curtis	Mr. Edmund Waller
Lord Bellamy	Miss Fortescue
Hon. Mrs. Challoner	Miss Sarah Brooke
Lady Charlotte Blount	Miss Alice Beet
Duchess of Havant	Miss Marguerite Leslie
Miss Pamela Gray	Miss Gladys Mason
Miss Williams	Miss Catherine Dupont
Mme. Henriette	Miss Kate Cutler

—New.

6. *John Daintry*, melodrama, in three acts, by J. R. Cobbing.

Isaac Douroff, alias John Daintry	
	Mr. J. R. Cobbing
Henry Stone	Mr. L. G. Carley
Sam Roberts	Mr. Dan Scase
Black Arthur	Mr. H. V. Nuthall
Joe Bright	Mr. D. Sara
David White	Mr. A. T. Wicks
Sir James Doughty	Mr. J. H. Cousins
Sergius von Helper	Mr. E. Cooke
Count Henri de Fabriquin	Mr. C. Murfitt
Bessie Douroff	{ Miss K. Abbott / Miss C. Abbott
Hon. Mary Doughty	Miss B. Summers
Baroness van Helper	Miss D. Deer

—Castle Hall, Framlingham.

9. *The Sway Boat*, play, in three acts, by Wilfred T. Coleby. [Last performance November 21; 45 performances.]

Mrs. George Lomax	Miss Kate Rorke
Dench	Mr. Ernest Cosham
Jim Maitland	Mr. C. M. Hallard
Freddy Cartwright	Master Philip Tonge
Lady Kilross	Miss Lena Ashwell
Countess of Churnside	Miss Frances Ivor
Lord Kilross	Mr. Dennis Eadie
Cresswell Barker, M.D.	Mr. E. W. Garden
George Lomax, K.C.	Mr. N. McKinnel

—Kingsway.

9. *The Treasure*, play, in one act, by Elisabeth Kirby, founded on a story by L. N. Becke in *The Smart Set*.

Algernon Ifley	Mr. T. A. Shannon
Mary	Miss Dorothy Brunt
Mrs. Van Buskirk	Miss Mary Barton
Charles James Jenkins	Mr. O. P. Heggie
Isaac Cohen	Mr. W. Lemmon Warde

—Kingsway

12. *Lady Epping's Lawsuit*, satirical comedy, in three acts, by Hubert Henry Davies (rehearsed and produced under the direction of Sir Charles Wyndham). Last performance.

Countess of Epping	Miss Mary Moore
Lady Lucy Lester	Miss Elfrida Clement
Lady Beacroft	Miss Anne Cleaver
Mrs. Paul Hughes	Miss Grace Lane
Mrs. Olivia Vanderhide	Miss N. Whalley
Miss Berengeria Mortimer	Mrs. S. Sothern
Miss Ferris	Miss Frances Vine
Earl of Epping	Mr. John Toke
Lord Bruce-Bannerman	Mr. W. Pearce
Mr. Justice Wray	Mr. Eric Lewis
Mr. Craven, K.C.	Mr. Berte Thomas
Mr. Clinton Perry	Mr. F. Gottschalk
Mr. Paul Hughes	Mr. Sam Sothern
Rev Dr. Gull	Mr. Cooper
Mr. Hickory	Mr. Arthur Hare
Mr. Pearson	Mr. Reginald Besant
Henry	Mr. Lawrence White
Associate	Mr. Thomas Braidon
Usher	Mr. Toosé

—Criterion.

12.‡*For Her Husband's Sake!* play, in four acts, by Millar Anderson. (Originally produced at the St. James's, Manchester, May 20, 1907.)

Lieut. J. Seymour, R.N.	Mr. R. Faulkner
Herbert Grey and Samuel Gorgans	
	Mr. Millar Anderson
Joseph Dene	Mr. Fred Elvin
Abraham K. Silas	Mr. Albert Rogers
Terry O'Neill	Mr. Finn Doyle
Pietro	Mr. Walter Long
Alphonse de Pom-Pom	Mr. C. Williams
Richards	Miss Grace Dean
Maria Dene	Miss Margaret Murch
Vi	Gem Lloyd
Eileen Silas	Miss Olive Lloyd
Estelle Beaudet	Miss Mabel Mannering

Royal, Edmonton.

14. *Fanny and the Servant Problem*, "quite possible" play, in four acts, by Jerome K. Jerome. [Last performance November 14; 33 performances.]

Fanny	Miss Fannie Ward
Vernon Wetherell	Mr. Leslie Faber
Martin Bennet	Mr. Chas. Cartwright
Susannah Bennet	Miss Kate Phillips
Jane Bennet	Miss Alma Murray
Ernest Bennet	Mr. Benedict
Honoria Bennet	Miss Mabel Garden
The Misses Wetherell	{ Miss Carlotta Addison / Miss Adela Measor
Dr. Freemantle	Mr. Chas. Sugden
England	Miss Esmé Beringer
Scotland	Miss Jean Harkness
Ireland	Miss Barbara Vivian
Wales	Miss Lydia Flopp
Canada	Miss Margaret Hastings
Australia	Miss Miriam Miner
New Zealand	Miss Vera Beringer
Africa	Miss May Straker
India	Miss Marion Ashley
Newfoundland	Miss Patsy McCulloch
Malay Archipelago	Miss Stewart Dawson
Straits Settlements	Miss Daisy Markham
Geo. P. Newte	Mr. John W. Dean

—Aldwych.

15.*The Lyons Mail*, play, in three acts, by Charles Reade, from *Le Courrier de Lyon*, by MM. Moreau, Siraudin, and Delacour. (Originally produced Paris Gâité, March 16, 1850; Princess's, June 26, 1854; St. James's (in French), May, 1859.)

Joseph Lesurques	{ Mr. H. B. Irving
Dubosc	
Courriol	Mr. Eric Maxon
Choppard	Mr. Chas. Dodsworth

The Lyons Mail (continued).

Fouinard .... Mr. Tom Reynolds
Durochat .... Mr. Norman MacOwan
Jerome Lesurques ...... Mr. Frank Tyars
Dorval .... Mr. Frank Cochrane
Didier .... Mr. Frank Randell
Joliquet .... Mr. Arthur Curtis
Guerneau .... Mr. Stanley Howlett
Lambert .... Mr. J. Patrick Curwen
Postmaster of Montgeron.Mr. B. A. Pittar
Coco .... Mr. H. R. Cook
Commissary of Police .... Mr. W. Graham
Postillion .... Mr. W. Cass
Guard .... Mr. Geo. Silver
Walter .... Mr. S. Beaumont
Julie .... Miss Phyllis Embury
Marie .... Miss May Holland
Niece to Postmaster.Miss E. Frances Davis
Janette .... Miss Dorothea Baird
                           —Shaftesbury

15. *An Outsider*, three-act comedy, by Mayne
Lindsay and Robert Marshall.
General Mortimer .... Mr. Bourchier
Hon. Richard Caldwell..Mr. Chas. Bryant
Sir Thomas Farleigh..Mr. Arthur Whitby
Sir Aubyn Burdicott.Mr. L. Quartermaine
Capt. Ferningham..Mr. Bertram Forsyth
Right Hon. Sir John Craven..Mr. F. Cecil
Westbury Allison, M.P. .. Mr. D. Imber
Jervis .... Mr. Charles Vernon
Landlord .... Mr. Alfred Bristowe
Margaret Hepplestone .. Miss H. Watson
Elsie Farleigh .... Miss Pamela Gaythorne
Lady Vereker .... Miss Eva Killick
Lady Helen Caldwell.Miss Violet Vanbrugh
                           —Royal, Manchester

18.*The Maid's Tragedy*, by Beaumont and
Fletcher. Produced by the Play-Actors.
King .... Mr. A. E. Warburton
Lysippus .... Mr. Le Grand
Amintor .... Mr. W. Edwyn Holloway
Melantius .... Mr. H. A. Saintsbury
Diphilus .... Mr. P. Perceval Clark
Calianax .... Mr. Leonard Calvert
Cleon .... Mr. Harold Chapin
Strato .... Mr. Rathmell Wilson
Servant to Amintor .. Mr. Robert Taylor
Evadne .... Miss Esmé Beringer
Aspatia .... Miss Kathleen Rind
Dula .... Miss Marion Lind
                           —Court

19. *Griffith Gaunt; or, Jealousy*, romantic cos-
tume play, in five acts, adapted from
Charles Reade's novel, by Freeman Wills
and the Rev. Canon Langbridge.
Griffith Gaunt.. Mr. W. Edwyn Holloway
Sir George Neville....Mr. Penn Hamilton
Captain Peyton .... Mr. Byron Douglass
Parson Oldbury ...... Mr. Ellis Carlyle
Father Leonard ...... Mr. Arthur Byrne
Tom Leicester .... Mr. Reg. H. Stephens
Major Rickards .... Mr. A. C. Thornhill
Mr. Hammersley ...... Mr. Lionel Barton
Dr. Islip .... Mr. Frank Stone
Mr. Housman ...... Mr. Leonard Calvert
Solomon Ryder ...... Mr. William Looze
Enoch Hump .... Mr. L. S. Yorke
Joram Monk .... Mr. Louis Palgrave
Roger .... Mr. A. Poulett
Brockbank .... Mr. H. Ainger
Pycroft .... Mr. S. F. Rankin
Hayes .... Mr. M. R. Bell
Jane Ryder .... Miss Nona Hoffe
Miss Penfold ...... Miss Dorothy Hullah
Mrs. Dickson ...... Miss E. M. Jessel
Septima Dickson .. Miss Jessie Lothian
Kate Gaunt .... Mrs. Rita Trekelle
                           —Royal, Margate.

19. *The Blackmailers*, three-act drama, by
Mrs. T. P. O'Connor and R. Henderson
Bland.

PROLOGUE.—DATE 1870.
Marquis de Marsay....Mr. Frank Collins
Gaston .... Mr. Hubert Harben
Louis .... Mr. J. Fisher White
Pierre Latour ...... Mr. John A. Howitt
Jean .... Mr. Alfred J. May
Sergeant of Gendarmes..Mr. C. Wood
Henriette de Lambelle..Miss R. Barton

THE PLAY.—DATE 1893.
Louis de Marsay .... Mr. J. Fisher White
Gaston de Marsay .. Mr. Hubert Harben
M. Dubois .... Mr. Jack Haddon
Henri Bertram..Mr. R. Henderson Bland
Lucien de Lagors .... Mr. S. Wentworth
Leroy .... Mr. Rudge Harding
Peter Fanfarlot .... Mr. John A. Howitt
Casaillon .... Mr. Alfred J. May
Charles .... Mr. W. Bannister
Alphonse .... Mr. James Ellis
Henriette Dubois .... Miss Roxy Barton
Madeleine ...... Miss Elizabeth Wieland
Julie Cliquet .... Miss Kitty Carteret
Sophie .... Miss Audrey Vaughan
                           —R.C., Kingston.

19.‡*East Lynne*, Miss Grace Warner's version.

Sir Francis Levison...Mr. George Gordon
Archibald Carlyle .... Mr. C. D. Pitt
Richard Hare .... Mr. Roy Rhind
Mr. Dill .... Mr. E. W. Brettou
Lord Mountsevern .... Mr. T. Vyner
Detective Perryfoot .. Mr. Artie Francis
Justice Hare .... Mr. Robert Arnold
Wilson .... Miss Cora Patey
Billie .... Mr. C. F. Evans
Barbara Hare .... Miss K. Stewart
Cornelia Carlyle..Miss Kathleen Cranston
Joyce .... Miss A. Corri
Susanne .... Miss Phyllis Massey
Little Willie ...... Little Norah Bretton
Lady Isabel Vine ... Miss Grace Warner
                           —Royal, Edmonton.

19.‡*The Belle of the Ball*, musical comedy, in
three scenes, by A. Norden, music by
E. T. de Banzie and Michael Dwyer.
(Originally produced at the O.H., South-
port, July 27, 1908.)
Sir Francis Lake .... Mr. Robert Hyett
Gussie Maitland..Mr. Llewellyn C. Hughes
Bobbie Fletcher .. Johnnie Schofield, jun.
Farmer Jones .... Mr. Charles Adeson
James Foster .... Mr. E. W. Chewd
William .... Mr. Jack Hale
Timothy Timkins...Mr. Johnnie Schofield
Showman Jack ...... Mr. E. H. Bertram
Footman .... Mr. E. Osborne
Queenie Trevor .. Miss Florence Watson
Lucy .... Miss Vera Grafton
Alice .... Miss Ethel Bertram
Mary .... Miss Corona L'Estrange
Marie .... Miss Sydney Penrhyn
Irene .... Miss Gwenneth Penrhyn
Red Riding Hood ...... Miss Rosie Wade
San Toi .... Miss May Hawthorne
Poppy .... Miss Gertrude Melville
Cabin Girls—Misses Maisie May, Gertie
Bryan, G. St. Clair, May Hawthorne,
Edie Leslie, Rosie Wade, Marion Vyner,
Alice Bradbury. Villagers—Misses Jennie
Bradbury, Phyllis Castleton, Flo Leslie,
Ethel Penrhyn, Gwenneth Penrhyn, Molly
Ford, Rose Rogers, Elsie Moor.
                           —Crown, Peckham.

19. *The Beggar Girl's Wedding,* drama, in four acts, by Walter Melville.

Jack Cunningham	Mr. Otto Minster
Dr. Millbank	Mr. James C. Taylor
Dicky Storm	Mr. Willie Garvey
Norman Marsh	Mr. Ernest G. Batley
P.C. Phillips	Mr. George Vernon
Rev. Mr. Melsom	Mr. David Cartwright
Thompson	Mr. C. Brown
Davis	Mr. B. Elton
Lizzie	Miss Anita Playfair
Tina Torkington	Miss Eva Dare
Maud Villiers	Miss Olive Warne
Gilbert Lindsay	Mr. Herbert Morgan
Joe Webster	Mr. Harry Playfair
The Dodger	Mr. Horace Kenny
Robert Grimshaw	Mr. Ellis J. Preston
Old Cloe	Mrs. Wilson
Jim Rothschild	Mr. George Bates
Corky	Mr. J. Clark
Elsie Cunningham	Miss Doris Whyte
Bessie Webster	Miss Vashti Wynne

—Elephant and Castle.

19. *The Kiss of Judas,* drama, in four acts, by Herbert Leonard.

Philip Dunree	Mr. Howard Templeton
Capt. Silas Brandon	Mr. J. H. Darnley
Jake Long	Mr. Herbert Leonard
Rev. Barry Dillon	Mr. Herbert De Ville
Frank Sudley	Mr. Chas. V. Sandford
Timothy Parkis	Mr. Henry C. Moreton
Little Jack	Miss Bertha Hanbury
Myama	Miss Isabel De Cresse
Myama's Brother	Brant Sero
Daisy Virginia Carlotta	Miss L. Dyson
Nancy Nollid	Miss Katherine Clarke
Dorothy Marlow	Miss Jess Dorynne

—Royal, Aston.

19.**Iolanthe,* fairy opera, in two acts, by W. S. Gilbert and Arthur Sullivan. (Originally produced November 25, 1882.) Last performance November 28.

The Lord Chancellor	Mr. C. H. Workman
Earl of Mountararat	Mr. R. Barrington
Earl Tolloller	Mr. Henry Herbert
Private Willis	Mr. Leo Sheffield
Strephon	Mr. Henry A. Lytton
Queen of the Fairies	Miss Louie Réné
Iolanthe	Miss Jessie Rose
Celia	Miss Dorothy Court
Leila	Miss Beatrice Boarer
Fleta	Miss Ethel Lewis
Phyllis	Miss Clara Dow

—Savoy.

19.¶*Wireless,* drama, in three acts, by Paul Armstrong and Winchell Smith.

--Royal. York.

23.¶*The Wreathed Dagger,* drama, in three acts, by Margaret E. M. Young.

—St. James's.

24. *The Belle of Brittany,* musical play, by Leedham Bantock and P. J. Barrow, lyrics by Percy Greenbank, music by Howard Talbot, with aditional numbers by Marie Horne.

Baptiste Boubillon	Mr. Walter Passmore
Raymond de St. Gautier	Mr. L. Rea
Comte V. de Casserole	Mr. D. Burnaby
Poquelin	Mr. M. R. Morand
Old Jacques	Mr. E. W. Royce, sen.
Pierre	Mr. Frank Melville
Bertrand	Mr. Vere Mathews
Eugene	Mr. John Montague
Philippe	Mr. Harry Leslie
Vivien	Mr. Hamlyn Hamling
Marquis de St. Gautier	Mr. G. Graves
Toinette	Miss Maudi Darrell
Mlle. Denise de la Vire	Miss Lily Iris
Mme. Poquelin	Miss Maud Boyd

The Belle of Brittany (continued).

Luville	Miss Blanche Stocker
Miquette	Miss Cora Carey
Adele	Miss Alice Hatton
Mirette	Miss Blanche Carlow
Christine	Miss Minnie Baker
Rosalie	Miss Gladys Saqui
Babette	Miss Ruth Vincent

—Queen's.

26.‡*The Nursery Governess,* play, in one act, translated and adapted by Mr. P. G. Duchesne from *La Gouvernante* of M. Provins.

Captain Trent	Mr. Harcourt Williams
Mrs. Trent	Miss J. Sterling Mackinlay
Simpson Brigge	Mr. Ashton Pearse
Wilson	Miss Barbara Hannay

—Kennington.

26. *A Question of Time,* comedy, in one act, by F. Matthias Alexander and Evelyn Glover (suggested by an old English recitation).

Jacob Rimmer	Mr. Harold Carson
Mary Rimmer	Miss Helen Palgrave
Esther	Miss Daisy Cordell
James Hassall	Mr. George Tully

—Coronet.

26.*The Only Way—Adelphi.

27.†*Mrs. Bailey's Debts,* comedy, in three acts, by Charles Eddy (founded on his novel of the same name).

Peter Browser	Mr. Edward Sass
Sir John Basing	Mr. Sydney Paxton
Dick Currie	Mr. P. H. Clayton Greene
Mr. Chattock	Mr. W. R. Staveley
Bone	Mr. E. H. Wynne
Wilkins	Mr. Charles Cecil
Kitty Bailey	Miss Hilda Antony
Mrs. Hammersley	Miss E. Cruickshanks
Julia Hammersley	Miss Esmé Hubbard
Laura Vansittart	Miss Florence Lloyd
Mrs. Ellis	Miss May Holford
Dawson	Miss Dorothy Edwards

—Garrick.

27. *The Burglar Who Failed,* comedy, in one act, by St. John Hankin.

Mrs. Maxwell	Miss Kate Wingfield
Dolly	Miss Elfrida Clement
Bill Bludgeon	Mr. Ferdinand Gottschalk

—Criterion.

27.†*The Waif,* one-act piece, by Frank Dix.

Auriol Raynor	Miss Elsie Evelyn Hill
Jasper White	Mr. Frank Dix
Mark Ellerton	Mr. George W. Cockburn
Jimmy Collins	Master Bobbie Andrews

—Kennington

29. *The Flag Station,* one-act drama, by Eugene Walter.

Dick Anderson	Mr. J. W. Dean
Charlie	Mr. J. Cook Beresford
Mary Anderson	Miss Fannie Ward

—Aldwych.

31. *The Troth,* play, in one act—Crown, Peckham.

31.¶*A March Hare,* comedy by Mr. Harold Smith—Royal, Birkenhead.

31.**The Boatswain's Mate,* one-act piece by W. W. Jacobs and H. C. Sargent—Wyndham's.

NOVEMBER.

2.¶*Vera the Medium*, play, in four acts, by Richard Harding Davis—Garrick.

2. *Le Grand Soir*, French version by Robert d'Humières of the three-act play, by Leopold Kampf (originally produced at the Des Arts, Paris, December 22, 1907), transferred to the Court, November 9.

Vasili	M. Karl Roger
Anton	M. Duree
Tantale	} M. Carl Bac
Gregor	}
Ivan Pavlowich	} M. Saulieu
Le Capitaine de Gendarmerie	}
Sasha	M. Martinet
Le Docteur	} M. Lietry.
Le Commissaire de Police	}
L'Etudiant	M. Dallet
Le Portier	M. St. Ober
Le Banquier	M. Dufrény
Masha	} Mlle. Marie Kalf
Arina	}
Sofia	} Mlle. Arnous Riviere
Barbara	}
Maria	Mlle. Suzanne Théray
Nathalia	Mme. Montout
Tanya	Mlle. Hélène Florise
Anna	Mlle. Vera Sergine
	—Terry's.

2.†*A King's Hard Bargain*, play, in one act, by Major W. P. Drury.

James Vinnicombe	Mr. Fisher White
John Collins	Mr. E. W. Tarver
Mrs. Pagett	Miss Mary Brough
Harry Quick	Mr. Frederick Volpe
Joseph Pagett	Mr. Louis Calvert
Loveday Yeo	Miss Beatrice Ferrar
Pincher Martin	Mr. Orlando Barnett
Albert Shillitoe	Mr. Philip Knox
William Wix	Mr. Clarence Derwent
Seth Penhelligan	Mr. Guy Cary
	—Court.

2.†*Private Nobody*, play, in one act, by F. D. Bone.

The Corporal	Mr. Halliwell-Hobbes
'Arry	Mr. Morris Harvey
Billy	Master Francis Walker
Clara	Miss Beatrice Terry
	—Court.

2. *Le Cœur a ses Raisons.*

Jacques Artenay	M. Savoy
Lucien de Jullianges	M. Saulieu
Françoise Vernières	Mlle. Suzanne Théray
Femme de Chambre	Mlle. Hélène Florise
	—Terry's.

2. *The Dear Departed*, comedietta, by Stanley Houghton.

Mrs. Slater	Miss Ada King
Victoria Slater	Miss Enid Meek
Henry Slater	Mr. Henry Austin
Mrs. Jordan	Miss Louise Holbrook
Ben Jordan	Mr. Joseph A. Keogh
Abel Merryweather	Mr. Edward Landor
	—Gaiety, Manchester.

3.†*The Topside Dog*, one-act play, by F. D. Bone.

Pensioner Robert Boiler	Mr. E. Rigby
Pensioner James Bates	Mr. E. Gwenn
Mrs. Boiler	Miss Agnes Thomas
	—Court.

3. *Dolly Reforming Herself*, comedy, in four acts, by Henry Arthur Jones.

Mrs. Harry Telfer (Dolly)	Miss E. Irving
Harry Telfer	Mr. Robert Loraine
Matthew Barron	Mr. C. M. Lowne

Dolly Reforming Herself (continued).

Capt. Wentworth	Mr. C. R. Maude
Peters	Miss Ada Webster
Criddle	Mr. Gilbert Porteous
Rev. James Pilcher	Mr. Herbert Bunston
Professor Sturgess	Mr. E. Lyall Swete
Mrs. Sturgess	Miss Margaret Halstan
	—Haymarket.

4.†*Playlets, Ltd.:* or, *Percy's Proposal*, musical comedietta, in one act, by Victor Stevens.

Molly Millington	Miss Margaret Lynhart
Percy Vere	Mr. Clevedon Woods
	—Rehearsal, W.C.

5. *Henry of Navarre*, romantic play, in four acts, by William Devereux. (London production January 7, 1909. New.)

Charles IX.	Mr. Malcolm Cherry
Henry of Navarre	Mr. Fred Terry
Henry (Duc de Guise)	Mr. A. E. Anson
Henry (Duc d'Anjou)	Mr. H. F. Wright
Arthur de Mouhy	Mr. Walter Edwin
Cosmo Ruggieri	Mr. Horace Hodges
Marshal de Tavannes	J. Carter-Edwards
Duc de Biragues	Mr. George Dudley
Duc de Retz	Mr. Maurice Tosh
Duc de la Rochefoucauld	C. R. Gibbon
M. des Valles	Mr. Maurice Elvey
M. de Besme	Mr. Philip Merivale
Nançay	Mr. Sydney Porter
Page	Mr. R. Eastern Pickering
Catherine de Medici	Miss Marion Sterling
Marie Belleforèt	Miss Kathleen Doyle
Charlotte de Sauve	Miss Gladys Gardner
La Belle Dayole	Miss Mary Jennings
Mlle. de Montmorenci	Miss Gwen Thomas
Mlle. de Torigni	Miss Beatrice Manning
Marguerite de Valois	Miss Miriam Lewes
	—Royal, Newcastle.

7. *Mr. Riggles Joins the Choir*, one-act play, by E. Rynd and Amy Nankivell. (The Pivot Club's performance.)

Mrs. Riggles	Miss Sylvia Dawson
Mrs. Smith	Miss Helena Kentley Moore
Miss Margaret	Miss Ruby Ginner
The Curate	Mr. Jack Hulbert
Mrs. Williams	Miss Dorothy Topham
	—Royal Albert Hall.

7. *St. John's Eve*, fantasy, in two acts, by Gabrielle Festing and Dorothy Hart. (The Pivot Club's performance.)

Duke Silvio	Mr. Alec. Dyer
Gualdrado	Mr. Jack Hulbert
Zapata	Mr. Walter Armstrong
Countess Anna	Miss Chick
Princess Primavera	Miss Joan Edridge
Attendant	Mr. Hockin
Silence	Miss Doris Matzetti
Dawn	Miss Isobel English
Dusk	Miss Vivienne Honey
Summer	Miss Ruby Ginner
Echo	Miss Irene Hayter
	—Royal Albert Hall.

8. *The Sentimental Bray*, one-act play, by F. D. Bone. (Produced by the Play Actors.)

Sergeant-Major Hunter	Mr. W. L. Butt
Colour-Sergeant Bray	Mr. J. Wilcox
Sergeant Best	Mr. Reginald Rivington
Sergeant Sparkes	Mr. Harold Chapin
Sergeant Dash	Mr. P. Percival Clark
Sergeant Renny	Mr. Norman Trevor
Coxswain	Mr. Norman MacOwan
Cerizola	Mr. Ivan Berlyn
Azopardi	Mr. A. E. Filmer
Sis	Miss Sybil Ruskin
	—Court.

8. *Tilda's New Hat*, one-act play, by George Paston. (Produced by the Play Actors.)
Mrs. Fishwick ...... Miss Agnes Thomas
Tilda .... Miss Mabel Hackney
Daisy Meadows .... Miss Lorna Laurence
Walter Emerson .... Mr. Ashton Pearse
—Court.

8. *Maraquita*, an incident, by Michael Merrick. (Produced by the Play Actors.)
Miguel Carmeno ..Mr. Norman MacOwan
Pedro .... Mr. Edmund Waller
Avaristo .... Mr. P. Percival Clark
Señorita Inez ...... Miss Nancy Grogan
Maraquita .... Miss Rita Milman
—Court.

8. *A Dear Bargain*, one-act play, by L. C. Fenn. (Produced by the Play Actors.)
Mr. Armstrong ...... Mr. Edward Rigby
Mrs. Armstrong ...... Miss Ida Phillips
Marla .... Miss Rita Tomkins
A German Rug-seller...Mr. M. Moncrieff
A Police Sergeant....Mr. Patric Curwen
—Court.

9. *The Man from Mexico*, farcical comedy, in three acts, by H. A. du Souchet. (Originally produced in America and Australia. London production, Coronet, November 23.)
Benjamin Fitzhugh .. Mr. Stanley Cooke
Roderick Majors..Mr. George Willoughby
William Loveall ...... Mr. Walter Gay
Von Bulow Bismark Schmidt....F. Lewis
Edward Farrar ...... Mr. Hugh Ardale
Richard Dornton .. Mr. Rupert Stutfield
Timothy Cook .. Mr. Ernest A. Douglas
O'Mullins .... Mr. James Schnapper
Googan .... Mr. Arthur Cornell
Louis .... Mr. Walter Champney
Clementine Fitzhugh..Miss Emily Fitzroy
Sally Grace .... Miss Fyfe Alexander
Nellie Majors .... Miss Amy Francis
Miranda .... Miss Doris Digby
—D.P., Eastbourne.

9. *The Dragon*, operetta, in one act, by James M. Gallatly.
The Enchanter .... Mr. John Le Hay
Gaoler .... Mr. Reginald Compton
Prince ....Mr. Frank G. Dunn
Princess .... Miss Ruby Melbon
The Dragon Launcelot is heard and not seen.
—Royal, Margate.

9.¶*The Princess and the Vagabond*, romantic play, in seven scenes, by Olive Fulton—Gaiety, Dundee.

9. *How Women Ruin Men*, domestic drama in four acts, by T. G. Bailey — Victoria, Broughton. (London production, December 28, Royal, Stratford.)

10.†*The Builders*, play, in three acts, by Norah Keith.
Adrian White, K.C. Mr. C. Aubrey Smith
David Gilbert .... Mr. A. E. George
Mrs. Cray .... Miss Evelyn D'Alroy
Celia White .... Miss Maude Millett
Edith Haines .... Miss Vane Featherston
Nini .... Miss Doris Walker
Lady Sarah Sparkes .. Mrs. H. Nye Chart
The Hon.Mrs. Trent Miss Irene Fitzgerald
James .... Mr. Heath Haviland
Perkins .... Miss Haviland
—Criterion

10.†*The Bacchae* of Euripides, translated into English rhyming verse by Gilbert Murray.
Dionysis .... Miss Lillah McCarthy
Cadmus .... Mr. R. A. Eeator
Pentheus .... Mr. Esmé Percy
Agave .... Miss Winifred Mayo
Teiresias .... Mr William Fazan

The Bacchae (continued).
A Soldier .... Mr. George Ellis
A Messenger .... Mr. Anstey
A Herdsman .... Mr. Sivori Levey
Chorus .... { Miss May Saker
{ Miss Juliet Hardinge
{ Miss Florence McHardy
{ Miss Helen Macdonald
Maiden .... Miss Edith Rhys
Dancers .... { Miss Male Hoey
{ Miss Rubini
{ Miss Ruth Bower
—Court.

11. *The Builder of Bridges*, play, in four acts, by Alfred Sutro.
Edward Thursfield..Mr. George Alexander
Arnold Faringay .. Mr. Dawson Milward
Walter Gresham Mr. E. Harcourt Williams
Sir Henry Killick .. Mr. William Farren
Peter Holland .. Mr. E. Vivian Reynolds
Dorothy Faringay .. Miss Irene Vanbrugh
Mrs. Debney ...... Miss Florence Haydon
Miss Closson .... Miss Barbara Hannay
Minnie .... Miss Dora Sevening
—St. James's.

12. *The Arab Gardener*, one-act play adapted from the French by Gladys Unger.
Mahamoud .... Mr. H. R. Hignett
Ramdan Ben Ramdan..Mr. Percy Goodyer
El Hadj Salah Ben Hassin..R. Whyte, jun.
Abdallah Ben Attig .. Mr. Chas. Troode
Ali .... Mr. E. Maturin
Messaouda .... Miss Mona Harrison
—Vaudeville.

12.†*A Bridge Tangle*, Society comedy, in four acts, by Mrs. Frank Wright and Mrs. Caleb Porter.
Lord Baintree .... Mr. Frank Cooper
Sir Charles Dereham .. Mr. Edward Ferris
Colonel James .... Mr. Charles Goodhart
Captain Bell .... Mr. Max Leeds
Wolf Steinbach ...... Mr. S. A. Cookson
Jim Travers .... Mr. Arthur Wontner
Parker .... Mr. J. Willes
Lady Dereham .. Miss Gertrude Kingston
Hon. Mrs. Desmond ..... Miss Granville
Mrs. Blaine ...... Miss Claire Hamilton
Mamie Vanderfelt..Miss Violet K. Cooper
Mignon .... Miss Phyllis Embury
—Court.

13.†*The Witches of Macbeth*. Adapted from Shakespeare's *Macbeth* by Mr. J. N. Maskelyne.
Macbeth .... Mr. Gordon Bailey
Lennox .... Mr. E. S. Elton
First Witch ...... Mr. J. N. Maskelyne
Second Witch .... Mr. Chas. Glenrose
Third Witch .... Mr. E. Morehen
Hecate .... Miss Cassie Bruce
—St. George's Hall.

13.‡*A Reformed Rake*, comedy, in three acts, by Pelham Hardwicke and Walter E. Grogan. (Originally produced at the Lyceum, Edinburgh, on February 14, 1902.)
Harry Jasper .... Mr. Edward Compton
Mr. Thornton ...... Mr. Henry Crocker
Adolphus Thornton .... Mr. Ivan Leslie
Frederick Adderley...Mr. Henry Worrall
Andrew Wylie ... Mr. Wallace Johnston
Matthew .... Mr. Philip Gordon
Binks .... Mr. J. W. Austin
Markham .... Mr. Neville Clifford
Mrs. Constance Thornton..Miss C. Merton
Joyce Thornton .... Miss Kathleen Leigh
Miss A. Mountstuart...Miss V. Compton
—Coronet.

13.†*Jealousy*, wordless play, by Marc Aubry, with music by Lucien de Flagny (produced by the Argonauts).
Pierrot .... Mr. Quentin Ayrault
Le Beau Léandre .... Mr. Erik Stirling
Sylvette .... Miss Sheba Brozel
—Rehearsal, W.C.

13.†*The Renewal*, comedy, in one act, from the Italian, by Ben Phillips. (Produced by the Argonauts.)
Donna Paola Monteforte.Miss M. Magrath
Maria .... Miss Maimie Stuart
Gaspare .... Mr. Alexander
Count Malatesta .. Mr. Herbert Dansey
Umberto .... Mr. Quentin Ayrault
—Rehearsal, W.C.

13.†*The Black Devil*, Sicilian tragic episode, by Carlo Broggi, translated by Herbert Dansey. (Produced by the Argonauts.)
Toto .... Mr. Lauderdale Maitland
Don Luigi ...... Mr. Herbert Dansey
Police Officer .... Mr. A. Thompson
Tresa .... Miss Janet Alexander
—Rehearsal, W.C.

13.†*An Action for Breach*, play, in one act, by M. E. Francis. (Produced by the Argonauts.)
Fred Baverstock .. Mr. Frederick Volpe
Sally Baverstock .... Miss Minnie Griffin
Maria Frizzell.....Miss Florence Harwood
—Rehearsal, W.C.

13.‖*A Pot of Caviare*, dramatised by Mrs. Arthur Mortimer, by special permission of Sir Arthur Conan Doyle.
Professor Mercer........Mr. A. G. Somers
Colonel Dresler .... Mr. A. Mortimer
Ainslie .... Mr. F. de Carteret
Ralston .... Mr. T. Cockburn-Mercer
Mr. Patterson ....Mr. Goodwyn
Père Pierre ....Mr. Dickson
Commodore Whyndham, R.N.
Mr. Harold Fairweather
Nurse Sinclair ....Miss Nancy Lindsell
Mrs. Patterson .... Miss Goodwyn
Jessie Patterson .. Mrs. Arthur Mortimer
—O.H., Jersey.

16. *Old Maid's Corner*, one-act piece, by Maud Thompson.
Miss Letitia ...... Miss Adelaide Grace
Miss Sophia ...... Miss Viola Garland
Irene .... Miss Rita Johnson
Emma .... Miss Rita Narcelli
Briggins .... Mr. G. P. Polson
Rev. Mr. Thursfield .. Mr. E. H. Paterson
Dick Thursfield ...... Mr. Wilton Ross
—Royal, Plymouth.

16. *The Empty Cradle*, domestic drama, in four acts.
Kenneth Bloodworth ...Mr. C. H. Seaton
Carnaby Bloodworth Mr. St. Claire Forbes
Sir Carnaby Bloodworth Mr. D. Urquhart
James Boswell ...... Mr. Fred Wells
Hon. St. Clair Selby ..Mr. Kenneth Scott
Misery .... Mr. Wallace Black
Mary Barton .. Miss Florence Trelvoir
Sarah Puddicombe Miss Connie Meadows
Martha Boswell .... Mrs. Tom Wilson
Ida Boswell ...... Miss Nance Battersby
—Royal, Bilston.

17.†*A Pastoral Postponed*, playlet, by Mr. Creagh-Henry.
Lady Julia Lavender Miss Creagh-Henry
Colonel Cavanagh .. Mr. Creagh-Henry
—Queen's Gate Hall.

17.†'*Liz*, playlet by May Creagh-Henry.
'Liz .... Miss Creagh-Henry
Jim Dodson }
Gerald Howard } .... Mr. Creagh-Henry
—Queen's Gate Hall.

17.†*Nell Gwynne, the Player*, one-act comedy, by Catherine Lewis.
Nell Gwynne .... Miss Jean Aylwin
Charles II. .. Mr. Charles Quartermaine
Duchess of Portsmouth .. Miss E. Olive
Call Boy .... Mr. Basil Osborne
—New.

17.†*Diogenes and the Damsel*, playlet, by May Creagh-Henry.
Diogenes .... Mr. S. Creagh-Henry
The Damsel .... Miss Creagh-Henry
—Queen's Gate Hall.

18. *God Save the King*, one-act costume play.
Rawdon Wolfe ...... Mr. Junius Booth
King Charles I. ...... Mr. C. W. Crowe
Harding .... Mr. Conrad Heywood
Widney .... Mr. John Crimmins
Buckley .... Mr. H. Bannister
Stanmore .... Mr. H. Colley
Mistress Marion Wolfe ..Miss Alice West
—Alhambra, Stourbridge.

18.†*Winter Sport*, one-act play, written by D. Brandon.
Rex Gascoigne .... Mr. Patrick Kirwan
Harold Johnson .... Mr. Gerald Venning
Jessie Pickering .... Miss Isabel Fladgate
—Court.

18.‖*The Trumpet Major*, play, in four acts, adapted by A. H. Evans from Thomas Hardy's novel of that title.
John Loveday .... Mr. H. O. Lock
Bob Loveday .... Mr. H. A. Martin
Miller Loveday ...... Mr. W. R. Bawler
Squire Derriman ...... Mr. E. J. Stevens
Festus Derriman ...... Mr. A. H. Evans
David .... Mr. R. C. Barrow
Cripplestraw .... Mr. T. H. Tilley
Corporal Tullidge .... Mr. T. Pouncy
Sergeant Stanner ...... Mr. W. J. Fare
Cornick .... Mr. R. N. Dawes
Press-gang Officer .... Mr. W. B. Fussell
Sergeant of Hussars .... Mr. A. S. Hill
Widow Garland .... Miss Rowston
Anne Garland .... Miss E. Lock
Matilda Johnson .... Miss A. Tilley
—Corn Exchange, Dorchester.

19. *The New Governess*, farcical comedy, founded by Mr. Walter Frith upon a short story written by Mr. G. S. Layard.
—Assembly Rooms, Malvern.

19.*For Wife and Kingdom*, romantic drama, in four acts, by Ward Bailey—Grand T., Brighton.

21. *A Wolf in Sheep's Clothing*, farce, adapted from a story which appeared in the *Covent Garden Magazine*, conducted by W. H. C. Nation.
John Morris .... Mr. Davidson
Mr. Price .... Mr. Watty Brunton
Mr. Crafty Trixter .. Mr. T. P. Haynes
Mrs. Easy-to-Blind .. Miss Kitty Douglas
Kitty Trueheart Miss Margaret Webster
—Royalty.

21.*The Shadow of the Surplice*, Mr. W. H. C. Nation's adaptation of Gabriel Trarieux's *L'Otage*, which, was originally produced at the Scala on March 30.
Ernest Brockwell ...... Mr. Claude King
Hughes Robertson .... Mr. Hicks
Fred Wilson .... Mr. T. P. Haynes
Father Honeytones .. Mr. Watty Brunton
Servant .... Mr. Lancaster
Alfred Smith .... Mr. Alec Davidson
Dr. Calomel .... Mr. Matt Gordon
Dr. Squills .... Mr. Terry Hurst
Mrs. Brockwell .... Miss Olive Wilton
Mrs. Wilson .... Miss Kitty Douglas
Veronica .... Miss Rene Ash
—Royalty.

23. *When a Lass Loves*, melodrama, in four acts, by Tom Craven.
Caleb Crass .... Mr. Frank Stone
Dr. Allan Crass .. Mr. W. Edwyn Holloway
Anthony Greig ...... Mr. A. C. Thornhill
Bertram Bridge ...... Mr. Arthur Burne
Slack .... Mr Louis Palgrave
Reggie Stapleton ... Mr. R. H. Stephens
Calvin Chase .... Mr. H. Ainger
Policeman .... Mr. Lional Barton
Nina May .... Miss Jessie Lothian
Cynthia Bridge ...... Miss Rita Trekelle
Constance Lane ...... Miss Nona Hoffe
—Royal, Margate.

23.‡*The Man from Mexico*, farcical comedy, in three acts, by H. A. du Souchet (original English production at D. P., Eastbourne, November 9; originally produced in America and Australia).
Benjamin Fitzhugh .. Mr. Stanley Cooke
Roderick Majors..Mr. George Willoughby
William Loveall .... Mr. Walter Gay
Von Bulow Bismark Schmidt Mr. F. Lewis
Edward Farrar ...... Mr. Hugh Ardale
Richard Dornton .. Mr. Rupert Stutfield
Timothy Cook .... Mr. Ernest A. Douglas
O'Mullins .... Mr. James Schnapper
Googan .... Mr. Arthur Cornell
Louis .... Mr. Walter Champney
Clementine Fitzhugh ..Miss Emily Fitzroy
Sally Grace .... Miss Fyfe Alexander
Hettie Majors .... Miss Amy Francis
Miranda .... Miss Doris Digby
—Coronet.

23. *His Living Image*, one-act musical playlet, by Stanley Cooke, music by Arthur Wood.
The Figure and Jan .... Mr. Lytton Grey
Jake .... Mr. Fred Lewis
Gretchen .... Miss Amy Francis
—Coronet.

23.¶*The Love that Conquers*, play, in four acts, by Dudley Beresford—Bijou, Bayswater.

23.*The Corsican Brothers*—Adelphi.

23.*The Conspiracy*—Adelphi.

24. *Enid*, opera, in two acts, the music by Vincent Thomas, and the book by Ernest Rhys.
Geraint .... Mr. Gwynne Davies
Earl Dwrm .... Mr. Ian MacKobert
Earl Ynwl .... Mr. Joseph Payne
The Dwarf .... Mr. John Dixon
The Herald ...... Mr. Ernest Muriel
The Chief Armourer .... Mr. Tim Evans
The Lady Emmelin }
The Countess Ynwl } Miss Gurney Jones
Olwen ..../
Enid .... Miss Laura Evans
—Court.

24. *Grit*, play, in four acts, by H. Herman Chilton.
Erith Winter ...... Miss Lena Ashwell
Dick Travers .... Mr. C. M. Hallard
Mrs. Winter .... Miss Frances Ivor
Mr. Winter ...... Mr. H. Athol Forde
William .... Mr. Douglas West
Mr. Norreys ...... Mr. Ernest Cosham
Jim Barr ...... Mr. Norman McKinnel
Mr. Percival .... Mr. Dennis Eadie
Nora .... Miss Mercia Vaucelle
Sarah .... Miss Olivia
Mrs. Percival .... Miss Kate Rorke
Miss King ...... Miss Margaret Murray
Charles .... Mr. W. Lemmon Warde
Suzanne .... Miss Nannie Bennett
Nelson .... Mr. Patrick Grey
—Kingsway.

24.¶*The Earl of Iona*, musical comedy, in two acts, by H. Gerald Ransley—Balfour Inst., Liverpool.

25.*Henry V.*, Shakespeare's play. (Originally staged by Mr. Martin Harvey and Mr. Wm. Mollison at the Lyceum, December 22, 1900, and revived by Mr. Harvey at the Imperial, January 21, 1905.)
King Henry V. .... Mr. Lewis Waller
Duke of Gloucester .. Mr. Patrick Digan
Duke of Bedford ... Mr. J. H. Napper
Duke of Exeter .... Mr. Franklyn Dyall
Duke of York .. Mr. Hugh Cunningham
Earl of Westmoreland .. Mr. Reg. Dane
Archbishop of Canterbury
Halliwell Hobbes
Bishop of Ely .... Mr. J. H. Irvine
Earl of Cambridge Mr. H. Cronin Wilson
Lord Scroop .... Mr. Shiel Barry
Sir Thomas Grey .... Mr. Cecil du Gue
Sir Thomas Erpingham
Mr. H. Cronin Wilson
Captain Gower .... Mr. Frank Ridley
Captain Fluellen .... Mr. A. E. George
Captain McMorris .. Mr. Herbert Maule
Captain Jamy ...... Mr. J. H. Irvine
John Bates ...... Mr. Caton Woodville
Alexander Court .... Mr. St. A. Bentley
Michael Williams .. Mr. Herbert Jarman
Boy .... Master Harry Duff
Nym .... Mr. Alec F. Thompson
Bardolph .... Mr. Robert Bolder
Pistol .... Mr. Louis Calvert
Charles VI. .... Mr. Hubert Druce
The Dauphin .... Mr. Owen Roughwood
Duke of Burgundy .... Mr. Cecil du Gue
Duke of Orleans .... Mr. J. R. Sinclair
Duke of Bourbon .. Mr. A. J. Gade
Constable of France .. Mr. W. Devereux
A French Soldier .... Mr. Shiel Barry
Montjoy .... Mr. Halliwell Hobbes
Governor of Harfleur Mr. C. Branscombe
Isabel .... Miss May Chevalier
Katherine ...... Miss Madge Titheradge
Alice .... Miss Dora Hole
Hostess of Tavern .... Miss Minnie Griffin
Chorus .... Miss Fay Davis
—Lyric.

26.†*The Toyshop of the Heart*, play, in one act, by Ella Hepworth-Dixon.
Philip Altanmore Mr. Harcourt Williams
Edward Poyning ...... Mr. Leslie Faber
Danvers .... Mr. P. Blunt
Rosie Rosalba .. Miss Lilian Braithwaite
—Playhouse.

27.†*Deirdre*, legendary verse, in one act, by W. B. Yeats.
First Musician .... Miss Sara Allgood
Second Musician .... Miss Olga Ward
Third Musician .. Miss Violet Luddington
Fergus .... Mr. H. R. Hignett
Deirdre ...... Mrs. Patrick Campbell
Naisi .... Mr. Claude King
A Messenger .... Mr. Dennis Cleugh
Conchubar .... Mr. Arthur Holmes-Gore
—New.

27.‖*Let Furnished*, play, by G. S. Tanner—County Hall, Guildford.

27.¶*The White Prophet*, play, in four acts, by Hall Caine—Garrick.

27.¶*Victoria*, "story with songs," in three acts, by George V. Hobart, music by Victor Herbert—Bijou, Bayswater.

27.†**Electra**, one-act original tragedy, founded on the old Greek story by Hugo Von Hofmannsthal, and translated into English by Arthur Symons.
Clytemnestra .... Miss Florence Farr
Electra .... Mrs. Patrick Campbell
Chrysothemis .... Miss Sara Allgood
Ægisthus ...... Mr. Arthur Holmes-Gore
Orestes .... Mr. Vernon Steel
Foster-Father of Orestes...H. R. Hignett
The Waiting Woman...Miss Olga Ward
The Train-bearer .... Miss Ethel Morison
Young Serving-Man..Mr. A. P. Campbell
Old Serving-Man ...... Mr. Edgar Kent
The Cook .... Mr. H. Willis
The Overseer ...... Miss Florence Wells
1st Serving Woman .... Miss M. Lennox
2nd Serving-Woman..Miss V. Luddington
3rd Serving-Woman......Miss V. Salberg
4th Serving-Woman .. Miss R. De Vaux
5th Serving-Woman..Miss S. P. Campbell
—New.

28 **The Earl of Iona**, musical comedy, in two acts, by H. Gerald Ransley.
Gordon Bruce ...... Mr. Gerald Ransley
José Gonzaga .... Mr. George Alsop
Cholmondeley Chunks...Mr. Jo. McGrath
Freddy Wood ...... Mr. Arthur Terry
Thompson Tadpole ...... Mr. A. Philips
Claude Dumas .... Mr. Alex. Richardson
Derrick Van Winkle.Mr. J. Sidney Gorrie
Number 22 .... Mr. Fred C. Dare
Gus Freeman .... Mr. Geo. Parry
Arthur Green .... Mr. Victor Farquhar
Marie Dalmay ...... Miss Vera Moulton
Carmen Pastia .... Miss Stella Raine
Countess of Helsby .. Miss Mary Vernon
Hon. Lucy Coverdale..Miss Mariel Harris
Sadie Chunks .... Miss Maude Barry
—Florence Institute, Liverpool.

28. **Sir Anthony**, comedy, in three acts, written by C. Haddon Chambers.
Clarence Chope .. Mr. Weedon Grossmith
Mrs. Chope ...... Miss Henrietta Cowen
Victoria Chope .. Miss Nina Boucicault
Olive Bruton ..... Miss Christine Silver
Percy Guy Bulger ..Mr. Edmund Maurice
Rev. Wilkin Delmar..Mr. J. D. Beveridge
Robert Morrison .. Mr. Evelyn Beerbohm
Mrs. Bulger ..... Miss Suzanne Sheldon
Emily .... Miss Mignon Clifford
Matilda .... Miss Mary Leslie
—Wyndham's.

28. **The Antelope**, musical comedy, adapted from the French by Adrian Ross, music by Hugo Felix, lyrics by Andrian Ross. (Last performance, December 19.)
Bennett Barker .. Mr. Fred Wright, jun.
Hon. Guy Daubeney .. Mr. Farren Soutar
Joe Derrick .... Mr. Fred Emney
Montagu Mosenstein .. Mr. John Brabourne
Loïsi Huber .... Mr. Jack Cannot
Vincent Clive .... Mr. Charles R. Rose
Gerald Grosvenor .. Mr. Arthur Grover
Peter .... Miss Maudie Thornton
Gwendoline .... Miss Florence Lloyd
Araminta .... Miss Hilda Stewart
Iris Fenton .... Miss José Collins
Gladys .... Miss Vivienne West
Stella Smithson .... Miss Beatrice Read
Theodora Thompson .. Miss Ethel Oliver
Celia Corinth .... Miss Lily Mills
Violet Vivian .... Miss Dorothy Monkman
Camilla Claude .... Miss Nancy Hervyn
Della De Vere ...... Miss Lily Maxwell
Speranza .... Miss Kitty Gordon
Ladies and Gentlemen, Clients of the Antelope Agency. Artists' Models, Artists, etc.—Misses Ashcroft, Madeley, Darrell, Dale, Lillington, Levine, de Lacey, Dolaro, Lee, Muret, Ismay, Mann, Grey,

The Antelope (continued).
Kipling, Bland, Bride, Barbour, O'Brien, Germaine, Gosling, Herbert, and Hartopp; Messrs. Hugh Crosse, A. Harris, Richard Long, Andrew Paice, Murri Moncrieff, Baker Ker, Ernest Hine, E. Marton, H. Wingrove, and Alec Turnbull. —Waldorf.

29. **The Vagabond**, play, in four acts, adapted from the German of Dr. Richard Fellinger by M. C Washburn Freund. (Produced by the Play Actors.)
Harry Kibblewhite .. Mr. Norman Trevor
Mary .... Miss Ethel Warwick
John Hoskyns .... Mr. Frank Cochrane
Stone .... Mr. Philip Knox
Brown .... Mr. Jackson Wilcox
Tomkins .... Mr. Arthur Webster
Driver Waters .. Mr. J. Benedict Butler
Driver Billings ...... Mr. Patric Curwen
Driver Hall ...... Mr. Arthur L. Burke
Driver Taylor ...... Mr. H. Edwards
Driver Molony .... Mr. William Pringle
Driver Walker ...... Mr. Harold Chapin
Driver Jackson .... Mr. Lawrence Grove
Boy .... Mr. Walter Cross
Cook at the Depôt..Mr. Herbert Sidney
Orderly Sergeant .. Mr. Arthur Marini
1st Recruit .... Mr. Gordon Carr
2nd Recruit .... Mr. Ernest Marini
Scottie .... Mr. Basil Osborne
Peter Lane .... Mr. Edmund Gwenn
Zillah .... Miss Irene Ross
—Court.

30.‡**Man or Beast?** drama, in four acts, by Chas. H. Phelps. (Originally produced at the Star, Swansea, July 27.)
Lord Newton ...... Mr. Fred Newland
The Hon. Jack Newton..Mr. J. W. Boyling
Sir Richard Tremere..Mr. Ernest Vaughan
Col. Bruce Anderson..Mr. Chas. D. Pitt
Capt. Donald Macdonald..Mr. C. H. Phelps
Christopher Sharp ...... Mr. Fred Boyes
Lothario Sinclair ...... Mr. Alf Kitson
Dr. Watson .... Mr. Frank Rogers
Pat O'Brien .... Mr. Fred Gresham
Inspector Gresham .. Mr. John C. Gray
Annita .... Miss Phyllis Elton
Marie .... Miss Marie Pemberton
Lottie Fairfax ...... Miss Teresa Phelps
Lady Winscope .... Miss Winifred Lester
Bella Newton .... Miss Irene Carrington
Rosie Newton .... Miss Madge Douglas
—Royal, Stratford.

30.¶**The Marble Pallas; or, The Mannikins,** comic opera, by R. T. Nicholson and A. Wimperis.
—Lopping Hall, Loughton.

30.‡**The Flower Girl**, musical comedy, in two acts, the book, music, and lyrics by William T. Gliddon. Originally produced at the Royal, Lincoln, May 14.
Lily .... Miss Dorothy Firmin
Joe Wheeler .... Mr. Martin Adeson
Johnny Wheeler .. Mr. Alfred Donoghue
Hon. Billy Greenhill.. Mr. R. H. Howard
Reginald Rackit .... Mr. Norman Bowyer
Alphonse de Racquet...Mr. Henry Adnes
Lizette de Racquet..Miss Florence Wilton
Miss Greenhill ..... Miss Jennie Holmes
Maisie Flirtington......Miss T. Laurence
Jessie .... Miss Cassie King
Maudie .... Miss Alice King
Kate .... Miss Phyllis Leslie
Dot .... Miss Kitty Hyde
Policeman .... Mr. P. Prujean
Mr. Bunker .... Mr. Arthur Carter
Bertie .... Mr. F. Williams
—Grand, Croydon.

30.‡*Into the Light*, romantic comedy, in four acts, by Gerald Lawrence. (Originally produced at the Royal Bradford, February 23.)

Simon Langley .... Mr. J. Fisher White
Felix Gottlieb .... Mr. Gerald Lawrence
Frederick Ramsden.Mr. Kenyon Musgrave
Archie Goring .... Mr. Duncan Yarrow
Dr. Ferris .... Mr. Henry Stephenson
Peter .... Mr. Walter Cross
Ernest Camp ...... Mr. Courtenay Foote
A Postman .... Mr. J. Weyman
Lauterbach .... Mr. Lionel Brough
Marceau .... Mr. Owen Gwent
Servant .... Miss Madge Snell
Margaret Ramsden..Miss Elaine Inescourt
Amy Ramsden .... Miss Joan Ritz
Mary .... Miss Mary Brough
Alice Harley ...... Miss Beryl St. Leger
—Court.

DECEMBER.

1.**The Pirates of Penzance; or, the Slave of Duty*, comic opera, in two acts, written by W. S. Gilbert, composed by Arthur Sullivan (originally produced at Paignton, December 30, 1879; Opera Comique, April 3, 1880).

Major-Gen. Stanley .. Mr. C. H. Workman
The Pirate King .. Mr. Henry A. Lytton
Samuel .... Mr. Leo. Sheffield
Frederic ....Mr. Henry Herbert
Sergeant of Police Mr. Rutland Barrington
Mabel .... Miss Dorothy Court
Edith .... Miss Jessie Rose
Kate .... Miss Beatrice Boarer
Isabel .... Miss Ethel Lewis
Ruth .... Miss Louie Rene
—Savoy.

1.¶*Her Secret Lover*, new play, in four acts, by Mrs. F. G. Kimberley—O.H., Dudley.

2. *The Little Devil Chooses*, by Kate Goddard and F. A. Stanley—St. John's Hall, Wembley.

4.‖*The Sentimentalist*, new one-act play, by J. M. Cuthbertson.

Cecil Dorrincourt ...... Mr. Parry Gunn
Mr. Gregson .... Mr. J. Hill Rogers
Tom Gregson .... Mr. Wylie Dick
A Manservant .... Mr. Main Edmond
Lady Carton ...... Miss Jean S. Macile
Mabel Carton ...... Miss Edith Fairbairn
Mrs. Mostyn .. Miss M. Fraser Sanderson
—Athenæum, Glasgow.

5. *Yaid a Nain*, play, by Richard Williams—Hulme Town Hall.

6. *Isaac's Wife*, drama, in three acts, by F. D. Bone and Teignmouth Shore, presented by the Dramatic Productions Club.

The Quartermaster....Mr. Hy. Stephenson
Quartermaster Parker......Mr. C. L. Lane
Quartr.-Sergt. Isaac Hunter..Mr. C. Rock
George Mayhew..Mr. Arthur Holmes-Gore
Tom Bradbury........Mr. Ashton Pearse
Lieut. Jack Benton....Mr. John Cabourn
Lieut. Harry Draycott..Mr. Basil Mercer
Manager of Hotel ....Mr. Wallett Waller
Pim-Lum............Master George Burton
Chinese Waiter ....Mr. H. Attlay
Norah Parker........Miss Margaret Yarde
Alice Hunter ....Miss Lucy Wilson
—Court.

6. *The Last of the De Mullins*, comedy, in three acts, by St. John Hankin. Presented by the Incorporated Stage Society.

Hester De Mullin......Miss Amy Lamborn
Mr. Brown..............Mr. Nigel Playfair
Jane De Mullin........Miss Adela Measor
Mrs. Clouston .... Miss M'Aimée Murray
Dr. Rolt.............. Mr. Ernest Young
Hugo De Mullin....Mr. H. A. Saintsbury
Ellen ....Miss Jean Bloomfield
Janet De Mullin..Miss Lillah McCarthy
Johnny Seagrave..Master Bobbie Andrews
Miss Deans...............Miss Clare Greet
Monty Bulstead.........Mr. Vernon Steel
Bertha Aldenham.....Miss Jean Harkness
—Haymarket.

7. *The Woman Who Sinned*, domestic drama, in four acts, by Augusta Tullock.

Silas Norris .... Mr. Edward Vivian
Jack Carrington....Mr. James Musgrove
Eugene Darville......Mr. Lionel Yeomans
Bill Scamp ....Mr. Will Kirk
Percy Hogg ....Mr. Will de Lacy
Sergeant Jones ......Mr. Blake Thornton
Counsel for Defence....Mr. Tom Seamour
Fritz .... Mr. Alf Davis
Waiter .... Mr. Tom Shaw
Hester Norris ......Miss Eva K. Cobridge
Blind Meg ....Miss Dorothea Vivian
Lady Munro ....Miss Marie O'Brien
Maudie Green..........Miss Rosie Watson
Judith Sartoris....Miss Augusta Tullock
—Palace, Boston.

7.**King René's Daughter*, arranged for the stage by Sir Henry Irving from the adaptation by the Hon. Edward Phipps of the Danish of Henrik Hertz. (Originally produced at the Lyceum, May 20, 1880.)

King René.............. Mr. Frank Tyars
Tristan de Vaudemont
Mr Gerald Lawrence
Ebn Jahia...........Mr. Frank Cochrane
Count Geoffrey......Mr. Stanley Howlett
Sir Almeric ....Mr. Frank Randell
Bertrand ....Mr. J. Patric Curwen
Martha ....Miss E. Frances Davis
Iolanthe .... Miss Dorothy Baird
—Shaftesbury.

7. *Her Marriage Vow*, sensational domestic drama, in four acts, by Owen Davis (originally produced at the Royal, Blyth, August 5, 1907).

Gilbert Carlton .. Mr. Charles B. Bedells
Ned Benton .... Mr. J. Forbes Knowles
Daffy Dan .... Mr. Vincent Wardle
William Walters .... Mr. John W. Ryder
Larry Leary .... Mr. H. Vernon
Eben Chubb .... Mr. Wilford Bailey
Jim Burke .... Mr. Walter Wilby
Jenks .... Mr. W. Brooks
Hester Norton .... Miss Nellie Shirley
Almira .... Miss Grace Garside
Maggie Clair ...... Miss Winifred Barton
Kate Walters .... Miss Lillian Herries
—Pavilion.

8.†*Zanetto*, opera, in three scenes, by Mascagni, given for the first time in costume publicly in England.

Sylvia ....Miss Barwell-Holbrook
Zanetto .... Miss Gilderoy-Scott
—St. James's.

8.*†*Hannele*, dream poem, by Gerhart Hauptmann, translated by William Archer.

Tulpe .... Miss Clare Greet
Hedwig (Hete) .... Miss Muriel Alexander
Pleschke .... Mr. Norman Page
Hanke .... Mr. Halliwell Hobbes
Gottwald ....
The Stranger .... } Mr. Henry Ainley

Hannele (continued).

Hannele .... Miss Marie Lohr
Seidel .... Mr. Robert Atkins
Schmidt .... Mr. Cyril Sworder
Berger .... Mr. Charles Quartermaine
Dr. Wachler .... Mr. J. Fisher White
Sister Martha .... } Miss Marie Linden
Hannele's Mother .. }
Mattern .... Mr. Edward Saes
Angels of Light { Miss Elizabeth Valentine
{ Miss Isabel Merson
{ Miss Sylvia Buckley
Angel of Death .. Mr. Hugh B. Tabberer
The Village Tailor .. Mr. Compton Coutts
—His Majesty's (The Afternoon Theatre).

8.†*Emily*, play, in one act, by Margaret M.
Mack.
Emily .... Miss Sydney Fairbrother
Miss Brown .... Miss Agnes Thomas
George Goodwin .. Mr. A. Holmes-Gore
—His Majesty's (The Afternoon Theatre).

9. *Slander*, English version of José Eche-
garay's *El Gran Galeoto*, adapted by C. F.
Nirdlinger.
Don Ernesto .... Mr. Martin Harvey
Don Julian .... Mr. William Haviland
Don Severo .... Mr. George Cooke
Captain Beaulieu ...... Mr. Ben Webster
Pepito .... Mr. Percy Foster
Genero .... Mr. Leonard Craske
Servants   D. Holm and H. Comberbach
A Surgeon .... Mr. W. Abbey
Donna Teodora .... Miss N. de Silva
Donna Mercedes ...... Miss Mary Rorke
—Royal, Birmingham.

10.‖*Past and Future; or, Three Times on
Earth*, a serio-comic opera, words and
music by Dr. H. A. Speed—Douglas Hall,
N.

13. *Mademoiselle Fifi*, one-act piece, adapted
from the French of Guy de Maupassant,
by Joan Pereira (produced by Le Cercle
Artistique).
Colonel, the Count Von Folsberg
Mr. Benedict Butler
Captain, Otto Von Grossling
Mr. Lawrence Grove
Captain, the Marquis Von Eyrich (Nick-
named Mlle. Fifi)..Mr. Gerald Mirrielees
Armande .... Miss Rosetta Maclaren
Blondine .... Miss Alys Rees
Rachel .... Miss Joan Pereira
—Rehearsal, W.C.

14.‡*Love Rules the World*, domestic drama, in
four acts, by T. G. Bailey (originally pro-
duced at the Star, Liverpool, July 1,
1907).
Harold Kingston ...... Mr. Richard Vane
Stephen Blight ......Mr. Stephen Langton
Paul Carruthers..Mr. Alex. Wilson Wynne
Billy Binks .... Mr. Matt Russel
Jim Dixey ....Mr. Sidney Rennef
Farmer Carruthers ......Mr. A. Fitzhugh
Sir Edward Wybrow ....Mr. G. H. Langley
Inspector Ferritt ....Mr. Fred Astley
Maud Carruthers .... Miss Grace Murielle
Flo Merton .... Miss Doris Brookes
Mother Grimble .... Miss Annie Brunette
Kitty Snowdrop ...... Miss Kitty Russell
—Elephant and Castle.

14.¶*The Pickpockets*, play, in four acts, by
C. M. S. McLellan—Garrick.

14.‖*The Haunted Man*, dramatic version of
Charles Dickens's Christmas story, by E.
Clarence Boielle.
Mr. Redlaw .... Mr. E. C. Boielle
The Phantom .... Mr. R. L. Smith
Philip Swidger....Mr. W. V. D'Authreau
William Swidger ......Mr. Max Le Feuvre
Adolphus Tetterby ..Mr. C. F. Snellgrove

The Haunted Man (continued).

George Swidger .... Mr. R. Le Geyt
Edmund Longford..Mr. C. H. D'Authreau
Mr. Longford .... Mr. R. Grandin
City Walf ...... Master Lester O'Brien
Adolphus Tetterby, jun.
Master C. G. Fox
Johnny Tetterby ...... Master W. Vicars
Jimmy Tetterby
Master E. G. D'Authreau
Harry Tetterby
Master C. J. D'Authreau
Georgie Tetterby .... Master E. G. Boielle
Billie Tetterby .... Master R. C. Boielle
City Outcast .... Miss L. Oldridge
Madge .... Miss A. Adams
Mrs. Tetterby .... Mrs. E. C. Boielle
Millie Swidger .... Miss C. Oldridge
—Oddfellows' Hall, St. Heliers, Jersey.

15. *Love, the Conqueror*, romantic play, in five
acts, by Frank Lindo.
William of Orange .. Mr. Albert Sefton
Brian Norval .... Mr. Frank Lindo
Sir John Mortimer .. Mr. Norton Shields
Count Leon Lascelles
Mr. D. Lawrence Doyle
Captain Rupert Armadale .. Mr. H. Lloyd
Andrew Albertree .. Mr. Harry Belford
Peter .... Mr. Richard Walsh
Dame Norval .... Miss Nellie Benson
Susan Shortly .. Miss Maude Leslie-Cudd
Mistress Mortimer Miss Marion Wakeford
—Palace, Newcastle.

17. *Olivia's Elopement*, comedy, in one act, by
Affleck Scott.
Olivia Fielding .... Miss Beatrice Wilson
Lucy .... Miss Ethel Coleridge
Sir James Fielding .... Mr. Alfred Gray
—King's, Hammersmith.

18.†*Notre Edouard*, a one-act play in French,
by Constance Meredyth—Criterion.

18. *Estrella*, musical wordless play, written and
composed by Marguerite Barrellier (Mrs.
Barnett), Student G.S.M.
Estrella .... Miss Marguerite Barrellier
Paolo .... Miss Hilda M. Brooker
Marquis de Monte Fiasco (and Gipsy)
Miss Gertrude Ketchell
Guglielmo .... Miss Anais Holbrook
Footman .... Mr. B. Hatton-Sinclair
—Guildhall School.

19. *Pinkie and the Fairies*, fairy play, in
three acts, for children and others, by W.
Graham Robertson, music by Frederic
Norton, produced by Mr. Herbert Beer-
bohm Tree.
Aunt Imogen .... Miss Ellen Terry
Aunt Caroline .. Miss Augusta Haviland
Tommy .... Master Philip Tonge
Pinkie .... Miss Iris Hawkins
Molly .... Miss Stella Patrick Campbell
Uncle Gregory ...... Mr. Frederick Volpé
Elf Pickle ...... Master Sidney Sherwood
Elf Whisper ...... Miss Kathleen Yorke
Herald .... Miss Hermine Gingold
Prince Frog .... Master William Parke
The Queen of the Fairies
Miss Elsie Craven
Cinderella .... Miss Marie Lohr
Jack the Giant Killer .. Master F. Walker
Jack of the Beanstalk .. Master F. Varna
Sleeping Beauty .... Miss Viola Tree
Beauty ....Miss Winifred Beech
The Beast .... Mr. Walter R. Creighton
Mr. Irons ....Mr. Smithson
The Butcher .... Mr. Henry Mather
—His Majesty's.

19.¶*Paying the Debt*, play, in one act, by Harold B. Lewis—Royal, Ashton-under-Lyne.

20. *Management*, comedy, in four acts, by Curtis Brown (presented by the English Play society).

Lady Culthorne ...... Miss Kate Phillips
Chambers .... Mr. Stewart Dawson
Maid .... Miss Dorothy N. Edwards
Ellice Harborough .. Miss Elaine Inescort
Arthur Somerville .. Mr. H. A. Saintsbury
Jessamine Harborough .. Miss D. Desmond
Robert Harborough .. Mr. Sydney Paxton
Hon. Barclay-Wallace .. Mr. R. Harding
—Kingsway.

20. *Mumby*, one-act play, by George H. Blagrove (presented by the English Play Society).

Geo. Fairholm (Mumby).. Mr. A. Thomas
Norah ....Miss Frances Dillon
Cicely .... Miss Dorothy N. Edwards
Clarence Hartopp ...... Mr. Claude King
—Kingsway.

20. *Oop at Kierstenan's*, play, in three acts, by Bertha N. Graham (presented by the Play Actors).

Mrs. Kierstenan .... Miss Inez Bensusan
Ada Rowbotham..Miss Marguerite Cellier
George Kierstenan ..Mr. Clarence Derwent
Bessaria .... Miss Beryl Faber
Ada Raby .... Mr. Fewlass Llewellyn
Zebra Reynard ...... Miss Elinor Foster
Edith Reynard .... Miss Lorna Laurence
—Court.

21.**Dorothy.* Comedy opera, in three acts, by B. C. Stephenson and Alfred Cellier (originally produced at the Gaiety, September 25, 1886). Transferred to the Waldorf, January 4, 1909.

Phyllis Tuppitt..........Miss Corali Blythe
Tom Strutt ....Mr. Herbert Strathmore
John Tuppitt ....Mr. F. J. Vigay
Dorothy Bantam ..Miss Constance Drever
Lydia Hawthorn ......Miss Louie Pounds
Geoffrey Wilder ......Mr. John Bardsley
Harry Sherwood ....Mr. C. Hayden Coffin
Lurcher ....Mr. Arthur Williams
Squire Bantam ....Mr. Lempriere Pringle
Mrs. Privett ....Miss Emily Spiller
Lady Betty ....Miss Betty Hardress
—New.

21. *Dick Whittington*—Coronet.

21. *The Eyes of the World.* Conflict of sex, in three encounters, by Charles Darrell.

Achille Fanfarade..Mr. J. Edward Whitty
Hector de L'Orme..Mr. George D. Dalper
Gaston de Carnac..........Mr. Will Casey
Paul Roqueville..............Mr. W. Rowe
Octave................Mr. Charles Stirling
Brigard..................Mr. Bert Hendley
Mme. Esme de Carnac
Miss Beatrice Fitzhugh
Mlle. Susanne Pomfleure
Miss Nellie Garside
Avice...................Miss Irene Stanhope
Antoinette..............Miss Ivy Courtney
Hélène de L'Orme..Miss Ethel Van Praagh
—P.O.W., Grimsby.

22.‖*Dot.* New version of Charles Dickens's Christmas story, "The Cricket on the Hearth," by William Shore.

Dot ....Mrs. J. T. Grein
Tilly Slowboy ....Miss May Daniel
John Peerybingle
Mr. W. Teignmouth Shore
The Stranger ....Mr. H. C. M. Reeve
Caleb Plummer ....Mr. Louis Rihll
Tackleton ....Mr. Fredk. T. Harry
Bertha Plummer ......Miss Vera Grenville
Mrs. Fielding ....Miss Connell
May Fielding ....Miss Kathleen Marriott
—Cripplegate Institute.

23. *Little Red Riding Hood*—Lyceum.

23.**Peter Pan.* Revival of the fairy play, in five acts, by J. M. Barrie, music by John Crook—Duke of York's.

24. *Robinson Crusoe*—Crystal Palace.

24. *Red Riding Hood*—Dalston.

24.**The Knight of the Burning Pestle*, Beaumont and Fletcher's satirical burlesque.

Speaker of the Prologue
Miss Carmen Woods
A Citizen .... Mr. Edward Landor
His Wife .... Mrs. Theodore Wright
Ralph .... Mr. Esmé Percy
Venturewell .... Mr. Jules Shaw
Humphrey .... Mr. Leonard Mudie
Merrythought ...... Mr. Charles Bibby
Jasper .... Mr. Basil Dean
Michael .... Miss Beatrice Chetwyn
Tim .... Mr. Joseph A. Keogh
George .... Miss Enid Meek
Host .... Mr. Frank Radcliffe
Tapster .... Mr. J. H. Etherdo
Barber .... Mr. A. Percival
William Hemmerton .... Mr. John Beech
George Greengoose .. Mr. Charles Loraine
Jasper's Boy .... Mr. Gerard Wynne
Servant to Venturewell
Mr. Kingston Trollope
Luce, daughter of Venturewell
Miss Hilda Bruce Potter
Mistress Merrythought .. Miss Ada King
Pompiona, daughter of the King of Moldavia .... Miss Lilian Christine
—Gaiety, Manchester.

24. *The Dollar Princess*, new play, with music from the German of A. M. Willner and F. Grünbaum.

Freddy Fairfax .... Mr. Robert Michaelis
John, Earl of Quorn..Mr. Vernon Davidson
Dick .... Mr. Howard Cridland
Tom .... Mr. Harry Parker
Lady Augusta Broadstairs
Mr. Robert St. George
Sir James McGregor .. Mr. Willie Warde
Sir Antony Phipps .. Mr. Philip Simmons
Vicomte de Champignou.Mr. Wm. Guilbert
Phineas Q. Condor....Mr. Richard Golden
Alice .... Miss Hilda Moody
Daisy .... Miss Alice Pollard
Lady Augusta Broadstairs
Miss Mabel Duncan
Hon. Edith Dalrymple..Miss Doris Dewar
Lady Dorothy Datchet...Miss May Sarony
Dulcie Dobbins ...... Miss Alice Moffat
Olga .... Miss Kitty Gordon
—Prince's, Manchester.

26.**Little Lord Fauntleroy*, Mrs. F. H. Burnett's version of her story of the same name. (Originally produced at Terry's, May, 1888)—Court.

26. *A Repentant Sinner*, domestic play, in five acts.

Daniel Debenham..Mr. Archie W. Chappell
John Merryweather..Mr. Herbert Robinson
Stephen Lorridale ....Mr. A. Lovett
Mark Witherley
Mr. Stewart Quartermayne
Ezekiel Progg.......Mr. Charles Howarth
Blind Peter............Mr. Evan Benton
Ben Bowser.......Mr. Willie H. Vernon
Major Tillock ....Mr. James Lewis
Flappy .... Mr. Holman Harris
Hon. Pethwick Bray
Mr. Archie W. Chappell
Bullet ....Mr. Wyndam Jackson
Inspector of Police....Mr. Geo. Harrison
Bill Tarpot.............Mr. Bert Tomlins
Village Boy ....Master George Nash
Dora .... Miss Amy Dalby
Araminta ....Miss Jenny Bostock

A Repentant Sinner (continued).

Fanny Jiggs......Miss Beatrice Reynolds
Mary .... Miss G. Lillian
Winnie Haughtington..Miss Lilleth Gabriel
Sybil Merlscord........Miss Bertha Deene
La Belle Estelle......Miss Marie De-Roce
—Alhambra, Stourbridge.

26.*Antony and Cleopatra. Mr. Richard
Flanagan's fourteenth annual Shake-
spearean production.
Cleopatra..................... Miss Darragh
Mark Antony.....Mr. Jerrold Robertshaw
Octavius Cæsar......Mr. Hamilton Deane
M. Æmilius Lepidus....Mr. J. H. Atkinson
Sextus Pompelus ..Mr. John Wainwright
D. Ænobarbus ...... Mr. Frank Woolfe
Ventidius .... Mr. J. Sheldon
Eros .... Mr. Leonard Robson
Scarus .... Mr. Ellerslie Pyne
Philo .... Mr. D. Davis
Agrippa .... Mr. W. F. Stirling
Proculeius ....Mr. Gordon Kingsley
Thyreus .... Mr. Jack R. Darnley
Menus .... Mr. A. D. Anderson
Candius ....Mr. H. Marston Clifford
Soothsayer ....Mr. George Fitzgerald
Mardian .... Mr. Alfred Hilliard
Diomedes ......Mr. Hornby Warburton
A Clown .... Mr. J. F. Fox
1st Soldier .... Mr. Leslie Bennett
2nd Soldier ....Mr. Walter T. Clifford
3rd Soldier ....Mr. Vaughan
Octavia .... Miss Madge Raper
Charmian ....Miss Phyllis Relph
Iras .... Miss Ella Thornton
—Queen's, Manchester.

26. The Kingdom of Kennaquhair, new musi-
cal and satirical play, in three scenes, by
V. Park, in which several songs written
by W. H. C. Nation are introduced.
Squire Addlepate ......Mr. T. P. Haynes
Sophron ....Mr. Watty Brunton
Ernest Wilmot.......Mr. Alec Davidson
Flutter .... Miss Una Bruckshaw
Bouncer .... Miss Mabel Funstan
Aminta .... Miss Angela Hope
Beatrix .... Miss Margaret Webster
Domestics and Harvesters by Misses
Patricia Musgrave, Mayse Scott, Jennie
Ansell, Beatrice Gomez, Marie Brand,
Dareen Drew, and Winifred Hanes.
—Royalty.

26.*Charley's Aunt, comedy, in three acts, by
Brandon Thomas—Aldwych.

26. Aladdin—Borough
26. Dick Whittington—Brixton.
26. Humpty Dumpty—Broadway.
26. Blue Beard—Camden.
26. Dick Whittington—Croydon Grand.
26. Dick Whittington—Drury Lane.
26. The Babes in the Wood—Elephant and
Castle.
26. Cinderella—Fulham.
26. Red Riding Hood—Kennington.
26. The Babes in the Wood—King's.
26. Cinderella—County, Kingston
26. Red Riding Hood—Lyric, Hammersmith.
26. The House that Jack Built—Marlborough.
26. Cinderella—Pavilion.
26. The Babes in the Wood—Shakespeare.
26. Cinderella—West London.

28.‡How Women Ruin Men, domestic drama,
in four acts, by T. G. Bailey. (Originally
produced at the Victoria, Broughton.
November 9, 1908.)
Jack Fairclough...... } Mr. Sydney Rennef
Maurice Fairclough... }
Bruno Schlag...........Mr. Richard Vane
Major Bagstock.....Mr. Stephen Langton
Freddy Fonheart..Mr. Alex Wilson Wynne
Jimmy Chucket.......... Mr. Fred Elvin
Dr. Methvin .... Mr. Matt Russell
Karl Swarts .... Mr. Fred Astley
Earl's Court Attendant....Mr. John Blyth
Sylvia Grey ....Miss Doris Brookes
Mercy Grey ....Miss Gracie Jones
Belle Plantin........Miss Annie Brunette
Mrs. Meadows ....Miss Lily Stanley
Jennie Chucket........Miss Kitty Russell
—Royal, Stratford.

28. Her Fatal Marriage, play, in four acts, by
C. Brunette and A. Hinton.
Zaco Malletto.........Mr. Arthur Hinton
Wilfred Grey.......Mr. Victor Millward
Colonel Crichton
Mr. Percy Morton Wright
Jim Rogers ....Mr. Fred Hewitson
Paul....................Mr. Gerald Byrne
Detective Smart....Mr. Henry Emmerson
Peter Pimple...........Mr. Frank Brunell
Sergeant Wiggins....Mr. Laurence Grove
P.C. Jenkins..........Mr. William Bailey
Lily...................Miss Lydia Audre
Polly Dimple..........Miss Laura Wright
Myra Malletto........Miss Ruth Zillwood
—Royal, Aston.

INDEX TO PLAYS

ALPHABETICAL LIST OF PLAYS PRODUCED IN THE BRITISH ISLES DURING THE YEAR 1908.

Full particulars and casts will be found in the foregoing.

LONDON.

The particulars in parentheses refer to a prior production in the country.

Absentee, The—July 2. Court.
Action for Breach, An—November 13. Rehearsal, W.C.
Affaires des Poisons, L'—June 15. His Majesty's.
Alien Star, An—February 5. 92, Victoria Street, S.W.
Amina—March 22. King's Hall, W.C.
Anarchists, The—July 7. Court.
Angoisse, L'—March 21. Shaftesbury.
Antelope, The—November 28. Waldorf.
An Uadhacht (The Will)—July 4. Court.
April Fool, An—June 26. Rehearsal, W.C.
Arab Gardener, The—November 12. Vaudeville.
At the World's Mercy—September 14. Royal, Stratford (originally produced in the provinces).
Aunt Gabriel—June 5. Strathblane Hall, S.W.
Bacchae, The, of Euripides—November 10. Court.
Beau Brocade—June 1. Coronet (May 4, D.P., Eastbourne).
Beggar Girl's Wedding, The—October 19. Elephant and Castle.
Bellamy the Magnificent—October 6. New.
Belle of Brittany, The—October 24. Queen's.
Belle of the Ball, The. October 19. Crown, Peckham (July 27, 1907, O.H., Southport).
Beloved Vagabond, The—February 4. His Majesty's (October 10, 1907, Royal, Dublin).
Best of Her Sex, The—August 31. Royal, Stratford (May 13, 1907, Colosseum, Oldham).
Billy Rotterford's Descent—May 11. King's, Hammersmith. Produced O.H., Cork, March 23, 1908, under title of *Among the Brigands* (October 25, 1907, Royal, Birmingham).
Black Devil, The—November 13. Rehearsal, W.C.
Blackmailers, The—October 19. R.C., Kingston.
Boy's Best Friend, A (C.P.)—April 7. New.
Boys, The—May 11. Grand, Croydon; July 9. Court.
Brand from the Burning, A—February 3. Royal, Croydon (Rotunda, Liverpool, December 23, 1907).
Breaking it Gently—March 22. King's Hall, W.C.; May 20, Vaudeville.
Breaking Point, The—April 5. Haymarket.
Bridegroom, The—May 4. Playhouse.
Bridge Tangle, A—November 12. Court.
Britain's Awakening—February 8. West London.
Broken Hearts—August 24. Pavilion.
Builder of Bridges, The—November 11. St. James's.
Builders, The—November 10. Criterion.
Bulmer's Threat—June 18. Bijou, Bayswater.
Burglar Who Failed, The—October 27. Criterion.

Butterflies—May 12. Apollo (April 20, Tyne, Newcastle).
Cavalleria Rusticana—February 7. Shaftesbury.
Chalice, The—May 25. Daly's.
Charlotte on Bigamy—May 19. Kingsway.
Cheat, The—September 28. Crown (September 21, Grand Wolverhampton).
Chinese Lantern, The—June 16. Haymarket.
Chosen One, The—February 21. Albert Hall.
Clever Impostor, A—March 2. Royal, Stratford (December 14, 1907, Royal Macclesfield).
Cœur à ses Raisons—November 2. Terry's.
Cold Mutton—September 28. Brixton.
College Widow, The—April 20. Adelphi.
Conscience of a Judge, The—August 17. Elephant and Castle (December 23, 1907, Royal, Tonypandy).
Conspiracy, The—September 9; revived November 23. Adelphi (November 8, 1907, Royal, Dublin).
Couvict 99—June 22. Crown, Peckham.
Cupid and Commonsense—January 26. Shaftesbury.
Dark Deeds of the Night—August 17. Royal, Stratford.
Darkness and Light—June 4. Royal Agricultural Hall.
Daughter of France, A (C.P.)—April 18. Kennington.
Dear Bargain, A—November 8. Court.
Dear Old Charlie—January 2. Vaudeville.
Dédale, Le—May 25. Shaftesbury.
Deirdre—November 27. New.
Dernière Soirée de Brummel, La—June 29. Royalty.
Desperate Marriage, A—March 16. Lyric, Hammersmith (March 2, Grand, Brighton).
Devil's Bargain, A—March 23. West London.
Diana of Dobson's—February 12. Kingsway.
Diogenes and the Damsel—November 17. Queen's Gate Hall.
Doctor's Experiment, The—March 10. Scala.
Dolly Reforming Herself—November 3. Haymarket.
Don Quixote—March 2. Coronet (Stratford-on-Avon, May 8, 1907).
Dot—December 22. Cripplegate Institute.
Drums of Doom, The—June 23. Scala.
Duke's Motto, The—September 8. Lyric (August 31, Royal, Birmingham).
Early Worm, The—September 7. Wyndham's.
East Lynne (Miss Grace Warner's new version)—October 19. Royal Edmonton.
Electra—November 27. New.
Emily—December 8. His Majesty's.
England's Throne—June 14. Chandos Hall, W.C.
Enid—November 24. Court.
Episode, An—February 25. Guildhall School.
Estrella—December 18. Guildhall School.
Explorer, The—June 13. Lyric.
Fanny and the Servant Problem—October 14. Aldwych.
Farewell Supper, The—March 11. Bijou, Bayswater.
Faust—September 5. His Majesty's.

Fearful Joy, A—April 18. Haymarket.
Feed the Brute—May 24. Royalty.
Feudalismo—February 28. Snaftesbury.
Fighting Hope, The (C.P.)—August 26. Elephant and Castle.
Figlia di Jorio, La—February 10. Shaftesbury.
Fire Witch, The—April 20. Royal, Stratford.
Fizzical Culture—January 3. Surrey Masonic Hall.
Flag Lieutenant, The—June 16. Playhouse.
Flag Station, The—October 29. Aldwych.
Fleur d'Oranger—June 29. Royalty.
Flo Rigg—June 3. Royal Albert Hall.
Flower Girl, The—November 30. Grand, Croydon (May 14, Royal, Lincoln).
For Her Husband's Sake—October 12. Royal, Edmonton (May 20, 1907, St. James's, Manchester).
For Love and the King—July 20. Elephant and Castle (April 13, P.O.W., Mexborough).
Fortunes of Fan, The—May 25. Crown (April 20, Lyceum, Edinburgh).
Fruit and Blossom—April 9. Playhouse.
Game of Adverbs, A—March 30. Grand, Fulham (March 9, Court, Liverpool).
Gardiens de Phare—March 27. Shaftesbury.
Gates of the Morning, The—March 1. Shaftesbury.
Gay Musician, The (C.P.)—April 3. Bijou, Bayswater.
Getting Married—May 12. Haymarket.
Girl from Over the Border, The—May 13. King's, Hammersmith.
Girl Redeemed from Sin, A—February 24. Royal, Stratford (July 15, 1907, Royal, South Shields).
Girl With the Angel Face, The—August 3. Shakespeare.
Grand Soir, Le—November 2. Terry's.
Greater Glory, The—January 19. Shaftesbury.
Great Yah Boo, The—May 13. Southgate Village Hall.
Grey Stocking, The—May 28. Royalty.
Grit—November 24. Kingsway.
Guinevere—June 2. Court.
Hannele—April 12. Scala; December 8, His Majesty's.
Havana—April 25. Gaiety.
Head of the Family, The—May 29. Royal Academy of Music.
Henry of Lancaster—April 27. Borough Stratford (February 28, Royal Nottingham).
Her Father—January 28. Haymarket.
Her King (C.P.)—September 9. Crown, Peckham.
Her Marriage Vow—December 7. Pavilion (August 5, 1907, Royal, Blyth).
He's a Jolly Good Fellow (C.P.)—May 28. West London (June 15, Dalston).
His Dishonoured Wife—March 30. Royal. Stratford (originally produced in the provinces).
His Lucky Star—January 29. 92, Victoria Street, S.W.
His Sacrifice—June 26. Ladbroke Hall, W.C.
Historical Incident, An—February 5. 92, Victoria Street, S.W.
Homecoming, The (C.P.)—March 28. West London (April 22, Queen's, Liverpool).
Hon'ble Phil, The—October 3. Hicks'.
Honnête Homme, Un—June 29. Royalty.
House in Green Street, The—May 13. King's Hall, W.C.
House of Clay, The—October 2. Coronet (April 24, O.H., Blackpool).
House of Pierre, The—September 14. Adelphi (November 8, 1907, Royal, Dublin).
House of Rimmon, The (C.P.)—March 16. Bijou, Bayswater.
How Women Ruin Men—December 28. Royal, Stratford (November 9, 1908, Victoria, Broughton).

Idol of Paris, The—February 17. Dalston (August 12, 1907, O.H., Middlesbrough).
Idols—September 2. Garrick (August 24, Royal, Birmingham).
If We Only Knew—September 28. Grand, Fulham.
In the Nick of Time (C.P.)—August 26. Haymarket.
Into the Light—November 30. Court (February 23, Royal, Bradford).
Isaac's Wife—December 22. Court.
Jack Straw—March 26. Vaudeville.
Jealousy—November 13. Rehearsal, W.C.
Juan Jose—February 12. Shaftesbury.
Key of Life, The—May 28. Scala.
Kingdom of Kennaquhair, The—December 26. Royalty.
King of Borneo, The—May 23. Rehearsal, W.C.
King of Cadonia, The—September 3. Prince of Wales's.
King's Hard Bargain, A—November 2. Court.
Lady Bandits, The—April 15. R.C., Kingston.
Lady Barbarity—February 27. Comedy.
Lady Epping's Lawsuit—October 12. Criterion.
Lady Mayoress, The—May 19. All Saints' Hall, Finchley
Lady of Kensington, The (C.P.)—April 3. Lyric, Hammersmith.
Lancashire Lad, The—April 27. Lyric, Hammersmith (September 16, 1907, Victoria, Broughton).
Laurel—May 14. Playhouse.
Last of the De Mullins, The—December 6. Haymarket.
Last Heir, The—October 5. Adelphi (March 23, King's Glasgow, as *The Bride of Lammermoor*).
Latch, The—May 19. Kingsway.
Late Ralph Johnson, The—February 15. Scala.
Leap Year in the West—July 2. Court.
Light in the Darkness—August 10. Lyric, Hammersmith
Li 'Lyys—January 23. Bijou, Bayswater.
Likes o' Me, The—April 13. Kingsway.
Links—May 31. Scala.
Literature—March 11. Bijou, Bayswater.
Little Nut Tree, The—April 9. Playhouse.
Liz—November 17. Queen's Gate Hall.
Loi de l'Homme—May 18. Shaftesbury.
London with the Lid Off—August 3, Royal, Stratford.
Lord of Latimer Street, The—February 26. Terry's.
Lost Dewdrops, The—February 29. Town Hall, Edmonton.
Love and the Law (C.P.)—March 16. Bijou, Bayswater.
Love of the Princess, The—September 14. Elephant and Castle (April 13, Grand, Nelson).
Love Rules the World—December 14. Elephant and Castle (July 1, 1907, Star, Liverpool).
Love that Conquers, The (C.P.)—November 23. Bijou, Bayswater.
Love's Golden Dream—February 10. Royal Stratford
Lucky Spill, A—June 8. Criterion.
Lupa La—February 18. Shaftesbury.
Mademoiselle Fifi—December 13. Rehearsal, W.C.
Maid in the Moon, The—February 1. Bijou, Bayswater.
Malia—February 3. Shaftesbury.
Management—December 20. Kingsway.
Man from Mexico, The—November 23. Coronet (November 9, D.P., Eastbourne).
Man of Her Choice, The—July 27. Broadway.
Man on the Kerb, The—March 24. Aldwych.
Man or Beast—November 30. Royal. Stratford (July 27, Star, Swansea).
Man Who Won, The—May 24. Scala.

Maraquita—November 8. Court.
Marquis, The—February 9. Scala.
Marriage of William Ashe, The—April 22. Terry's.
Marriages of Mayfair, The—September 21. Drury Lane.
Married to the Wrong Man—August 3. Elephant and Castle.
Mary Roper—May 5. Cavendish Rooms.
Masked Girl, The—March 22. King's Hall, W.C.
Masque of War—May 28. Scala.
Mate in Three Moves—January 29. 92, Victoria Street, S.W.
Matter-of-Fact Husband, A—July 14. Lyceum.
Matt of Merrymount—February 20. New. (Royal, Newcastle, October 11, 1906).
Metopemania—February 26. Gaiety Restaurant.
Meturef, The—August 17. Pavilion.
Military Pickle, A—April 25. Cripplegate Institute.
Mill, The—June 23. Scala.
Minna von Barnhelm—May 2. Royalty.
Modern Daughter, A—July 7. Court.
Money Grabber, The—February 27. Kingsway.
Monsieur Jean—March 27. Shaftesbury.
Morte Civile—February 13. Shaftesbury.
Mr. Riggles Joins the Choir—November 7. Royal Albert Hall.
Mrs. Bailey's Debts—October 27. Garrick.
Mrs. Bill—March 9. Court.
Mrs. Dot—April 27. Comedy.
Mumby—December 20. Kingsway.
My Mimosa Maid—April 21. Prince of Wales.
Mystery of Edwin Drood, The—January 4. His Majesty's (New, Cardiff, November 21, 1907).
Nan—May 24. Royalty (private). June 2, Haymarket (public).
Nell Gwynne, the Player—November 17. New.
New Genevra, A—January 31. Ladbroke Hall.
New Tenants, The—July 30. Rehearsal, W.C.
Nocturne, A—May 19. Kingsway.
Notre Edouard,—December 18. Criterion.
Nuits du Hampton-Club, Les—March 21. Shaftesbury.
Nursery Governess, The—October 26. Kennington.
Octave—June 29. Royalty.
Off the Cornish Coast—March 2. Kingsway.
O'Grindles, The—January 21. Playhouse.
Old Firm, The—September 4. Queen's. (August 17, Royal, Newcastle.)
Old Folks at Home, The—October 5. Lyric, Hammersmith. (September 30, 1907, Junction, Manchester.)
Olivia's Elopement—December 17. King's.
Omelette Maker, The (C.P.)—March 17. Kingsway.
One-Day Millionaire, The—January 3. Surrey Masonic Hall.
Only a Quaker Maid—February 26. Assembly Rooms, Putney.
Only a Woman—April 13. West London. (January 20, Central, Altrincham.)
On the East Side—July 7. Court.
On the Right Road—June 2. Court.
Oop at Kierstenan's—December 20. Court.
Orange Blossom, The—January 23. Terry's.
Other Side, The—February 26. Grand, Croydon (October 25, 1907, Prince's, Manchester.)
Pageant of Lloyds, A—February 25. Savoy Hotel.
Page 97—January 11. Garrick.
Paid in Full—September 8. Aldwych.
Panne—May 4. Royalty.
Passing of the Third Floor Back, The—September 1. St. James's. (August 13, O.H., Harrogate.)
Past and Future—December 10. Douglas Hall, N.

Pastoral Postponed, A—November 17. Queen's Gate Hall.
Pater Noster—February 20. St. James's.
Peggy Doyle—June 26. Rehearsal, W.C.
Penelope's Lovers—July 17. Rehearsal, W.C.
Pete—August 29. Lyceum.
Peu de Musique, Un—March 21. Shaftesbury.
Philosopher's Diamond, The—August 5. St. George's Hal¹, W.
Philosopher's Stone, The—March 1. Royalty.
Picture of the Year, The—March 22. King's Hall, W.C.
Pickpockets, The (C.P.)—December 14. Garrick.
Pierrette's Birthday—June 24. New.
Pinkie and the Fairies—December 19. His Majesty's.
Playlets, Ltd.—November 4. Rehearsal, W.C.
Power of Lies, The—July 27. Shakespeare.
Power of the King, The—March 30. Broadway (C.P., October 9, 1907, King's, Longsight; produced Junction, Manchester, December 2, 1907).
Pride of Regiment—February 28. Haymarket. (Revived April 18.)
Prince and the Beggar Maid, The—June 6. Lyceum.
Private Nobody—November 2. Court.
Pro Tem—April 29. Playhouse.
Question of Time, A—October 26. Coronet.
Quest of the Holy Grail, The—July 3. Court.
Receipted (C.P.)—April 14. Coronet.
Reformed Rake, A—November 13. Coronet (February 14, 1902, Lyceum, Edinburgh).
Renewal, The—November 13. Rehearsal, W.C.
Rhys Lewis—July 4. Court.
Romantic Barber, The—March 23. Grand, Fulham (March 2, Royal, Dublin).
Rosalie—March 21. Shaftesbury.
Rouge est Mis, Le—March 21. Shaftesbury.
Rusidda—February 18. Shaftesbury.
Sailor's Wedding, The—September 7. Marlborough.
St. John's Eve—November 7. Royal Albert Hall.
Sakebs—May 1. Balham Assembly Rooms.
Santa Lucia, A—May 3. Scala.
Savage Beneath, The—May 23. Rehearsal, W.C.
Scarlet Highwayman, The (C.P.)—May 28. Lyric, Hammersmith.
Secretary's Wedding Present, The—May 23. Rehearsal, W.C.
Send Him Victorious—May 25. Royal, Stratford (December 30, 1907, Prince's, Horwich).
Sensible Constanza, The—May 11. Kingsway.
Sentence, The—July 7. Court.
Sentimental Bray, The—November 8. Court.
Sexton Blake, Detective (C.P.)—January 18. King's, Hammersmith (February 24, Crown).
Shadow of the Surplice, The—March 30. Scala (revived November 21, Royalty).
Simple Life, The—May 18. County, Kingston.
Sin Eater, The (C.P.)—March 17. Lyric.
Sir Anthony—November 28. Wyndham's.
Soldier of France, A—April 13. Royal, Woolwich (originally produced in the provinces).
Soldier's Daughters, A—May 14. Kingsway.
Solomon the Wise—August 28. Pavilion.
Song of Songs, The—March 8—Queen's Gate Hall, S.W.
Stingaree—February 1. Queen's.
Straight from the Shoulder—August 10. Broadway (August 3, Grand, Brighton)
Subjection of Kezia, The—January 7. Court.
Susannah and Some Others—January 22. Royalty.
Success of Sentiment—September 27. Court.
Sway Boat, The—October 9. Kingsway.
Tangled Skein, The (C.P.)—March 30. Coronet.
Telegram, The—February 27. Brinsmead Galleries.

That Foreigner—February 27. Bijou, Bayswater.
Three of Us, The—June 10. Terry's.
Three Twins, The (C.P.)—March 3. Bijou, Bayswater.
Thunderbolt, The—May 9. St. James's.
Tilda's New Hat—November 8. Court.
Topside Dog, The—November 3. Court.
Torrent, The—April 17. Camden.
Toyshop of the Heart, The—November 26. Playhouse
Treasure, The—October 9. Kingsway.
Trixie—Ju'y 10. Scala.
Trois Messieurs du Harre, Les—March 27. Shaftesbury.
Troth, The—October 31. Crown, Peckham.
Two Pins, The—June 8. Aldwych (April 2, Royal, Newcastle).
Tyrant, The—August 24. Dalston (December 17, 1906, Osborne, Manchester).
Uriel Acosta—August 21. Pavilion
Vagabond, The—November 29. Court.
Vera the Medium (C.P.)—November 2. Garrick.
Veuve, La—March 27. Shaftesbury.
Victoria (C.P.)—November 27. Bijou, Bayswater.
Voice of Duty, The—June 23. Comedy.
Waif, The—October 27. Kennington.
Walk, The—January 27. Apollo.
Waltz Dream, A—March 7. Hicks.
Waste (C.P.)—January 8. Savoy.
Way Down East—April 23. Aldwych.
Welsh Sunset, A—July 15. Savoy.
Weg Zur Holle, Der—April 27. Royalty.
What Every Woman Knows—September 3. Duke of York's.
Whirligig, The—May 19. Kingsway.
Whirlpool, The—September 21. Marlborough. (February 22, New Cardiff.)
White Lady, The—July 10. Scala.
White Man, A—January 11. Lyric.
White Prophet, The (C.P.)—November 27. Garrick.
Wild Man, The—August 29. Pavilion.
Winter Sport—November 18. Court.
Witches of Macbeth, The—November 13. St. James's Hall.
With Edged Tools—April 6. King's, Hammersmith. (C.P. February 26, 1907, Gaiety, Ayr; produced February 3, 1908, Royal, Hull.)
Wolf in Sheep's Clothing, A—November 21. Royalty.
Woman of Kronstadt, The—February 8. Garrick.
Woman who was Dead, The—May 29. Royal, Stratford. (March 16, Gaiety, Dundee.)
Woman who Sinned, The—December 7. Palace, Boston.
Yzdra (C.P.)—March 26. Wyndham's.
Zanetto—December 8. St. James's.
Zolfara, La—February 7. Shaftesbury.

PROVINCIAL.

The particulars in parentheses refer to the London production.

Admiral Peters—August 3. Pier, Eastbourne.
Affairs at the Shrubbery—March 9. · Paisley, Paisley.
Annie Laurie—March 26. Athenæum, Glasgow.
Beatrix—April 13. Royal, Margate.
Beau Brocade—May 4. D.P., Eastbourne (June 1, Coronet).
Belle of the Ball, The—July 27. O.H., Southport (October 19, Crown, Peckham).
Bells of Old York, The—September 14. Globe, Deal.

Better Land, The—June 22. Queen's Liverpool.
Billy Rotterford's Descent (originally, *Among the Brigands*, October 25, 1907, Royal, Birmingham)—March 23. O.H., Cork (May 11, King's Hammersmith).
Bladud—April 11. Royal, Bath.
Bride of Lammermoor, The—March 23. King's, Glasgow (London production, October 5, at the Adelphi, under the title of *The Last Heir*).
Bringing It Home—October 5. Gaiety, Manchester.
Bunkered—April 11—Balfour Institute, Liverpool.
Butterflies—April 20. Tyne, Newcastle (May 12, Apollo).
Cheat, The—September 21. Royal, Wolverhampton (September 28, Crown, Peckham).
Cheerful Knave, The—May 11. Royal, Margate.
City of Mystery, The—January 9. Grand, Luton.
Coster Girl's Romance, A—March 27. Cambridge, Spennymoor.
Country Girl in London, A—August 1. Royal, Macclesfield.
Dear Departed, The—November 2. Gaiety, Manchester.
Desperate Marriage, A—March 2. Grand, Brighton (March 16, Lyric, Hammersmith).
Devil, The (C.P.)—April 8. P.O.W., Birmingham.
Dingle's Double—May 18. O.H., Jersey.
Dollar Princess, The—December 24. Prince's, Manchester.
Don Quixote—February 17. Royal, Margate.
Dragon, The—November 9. Royal, Margate.
Duke's Motto, The—August 31. Royal, Birmingham (September 8, Lyric).
Earl of Iona, The (C.P.)—November 24. Balfour Inst., Liverpool. Production, November 28, Florence Inst., Liverpool.
Emperor Commands, The—September 16, Tower Pavilion, Portobello.
Empty Cradle, The—November 16. Royal, Bilston.
End of the World, The (C.P.)—May 21. Hippo., Eastbourne.
Enemies—February 18—Institute, Hildenborough.
Ernestine—May 4. Royal, Exeter.
Eyes of the World, The—December 21. P.O.W., Grimsby.
Evening at the Detective's, An—May 19. P.O.W., Birmingham.
Fate and the Footman—September 17. Terminus Hall, Littlehampton.
Few and the Many, The—May 4. Gaiety, Manchester.
Flower Girl, The—May 14. Royal, Lincoln (November 30, Grand, Croydon).
Foiled—January 28. Harborne Inst., Birmingham.
For Love and the King—April 13. P.O.W., Mexborough (July 20. Elephant and Castle).
For Love of a Woman—July 27. Lyceum, Stafford.
Fortunes of Fan—April 20. Lyceum, Edinburgh (May 25, Crown, Peckham).
For Wife and Kingdom (C.P.)—November 19. Grand, Brighton.
Game of Adverbs, A—March 9. Royal Court, Liverpool (March 30, Grand, Fulham).
Game of Bluff, A—May 11. Royal Court, Liverpool.
Gay Deceivers, The—June 22. Royal, Margate.
Geoffrey Langdon's Wife—June 22. Rotunda, Liverpool.
Goddess of Destruction, The—March 6. Queen's, Liverpool.
God Save the King. November 18. Alhambra, Stourbridge.

Governor's Bride, The—March 16. Tyne, Newcastle.
Griffith Gaunt—October 19. Royal, Margate.
Gutter of Time, The—August 3. Pier, Eastbourne.
Happy Hooligan—July 20. Empire, Oldham.
Haunted House, The—December 14. Oddfellows' Hall, St. Heliers, Jersey.
Head of the Firm, The—June 13. O.H., Buxton.
Henry of Lancaster—February 28.—Royal, Nottingham (April 27, Borough, Stratford).
Henry of Navarre—November 5. Royal, Newcastle (New, January 7, 1909).
Her Fatal Marriage—December 28. Royal, Aston.
Her Secret Lover (C.P.)—December 1. O.H., Dudley.
High Bid, The—March 26. Lyceum, Edinburgh.
His Life for Her Love—August 24. Metropole, Devonport.
His Wife No Longer—September 21. Royal, Preston.
Home Coming, The—April 22. Queen's Liverpool (C.P., West London, March 28).
House of Clay, The—April 24. O.H., Blackpool (October 2, Coronet).
How Women Ruin Men—November 9. Victoria, Broughton. (December 28, Royal, Stratford).
Idols—August 24. Royal Birmingham (September 2, Garrick).
In the Gloaming (C.P.)—September 18. Royal, Goole. Production, September 29, Exchange, Wellingborough.
Into the Light—February 23. Royal, Bradford (November 30, Court).
John Daintry—October 6. Castle Hall, Framlingham.
Judith—June 15. Central, Altrincham.
Kiss of Judas, The—October 19. Royal, Aston.
Lady Dolly and the Decalogue—September 17. Pier Pavilion, Paignton.
Lady Lannigan, Laundress—April 9. Royal, Liverpool.
Lady of the Pageant, The—July 20. D.P., Eastbourne.
Last Rose of Summer, The—May 11. Royal, Margate.
Lemonade Boy, The—January 23. Athenæum, Glasgow.
Let Furnished—November 27. County Hall, Guildford.
Little Devil Chooses, The—December 2. St. John's Hall, Wembley.
Long Journey, A—October 5. Grand, Birkenhead.
Love of the Princess, The—April 13. Grand, Nelson (September 14, Elephant and Castle).
Love the Conqueror—December 15. Palace, Newcastle.
Loyalty House—June 8. Queen's, Manchester.
Makeshifts—October 5. Gaiety, Manchester.
Man from Mexico, The—November 9. D.P., Eastbourne (November 23, Coronet).
Man on the Box, The—August 6. Pier, Eastbourne.
Man or Beast?—July 27. Star, Swansea (November 30, Royal, Stratford).
Man Who Missed the Tide, The—February 13. Abbey, Dublin.
Marble Pallas, The—November 30. Lopping Hall, Loughton.
March Hare, A—October 31. Royal, Birkenhead.
Marriages Are Made in Heaven—September 7. Gaiety, Manchester.
Melting Pot, The (C.P.)—August 21. Terminus Hall, Littlehampton.
Merry Maid, A—August 3. Grand, Chorley.
Miracle, A—June 15. Royal, Brighton.
Monarch of the World, The—May 29. Royal, Barry Dock.

Mother's Salvation, A—April 27. Royal, Wednesbury (May 18, Royal, Stratford).
Mrs. Swallow—March 16. Gaiety, Manchester.
My Californian Sweetheart (C.P.)—August 26. Town Hall, Burnham.
Mystery of Edwin Drood, The—March 2. Osborne, Manchester.
Nero and Co.—May 11. Mechanics' Hall, Nottingham.
New Governess, The—November 9. Assembly Rooms, Malvern.
Next Door. September 7. Royal, Newcastle.
Old Firm, The—August 17. Royal, Newcastle (September 4, Queen's).
Old Home, The—May 11. P.O.W., Salford.
Old Maid's Corner—November 16. Royal, Plymouth.
Old Virginia—June 8. Olympian Gardens, Rock Ferry.
Only a Woman—January 20. Central, Altrincham (April 13, West London).
Other Woman, The—January 6. Pier Pavilion, Hastings.
Outcast of the Family, The—June 25. P.O.W., Salford.
Outsider, An—October 15. Royal, Manchester.
Passing of the Third Floor Back, The—August 17. Opera House, Harrogate (September 1, St. James's).
Paying the Debt (C.P.)—December 19. Royal, Ashton-under-Lyne.
Peg Woffington—January 27. Grand, Birmingham.
Piper, The—February 13. Abbey, Dublin.
Play Without a Name, A—July 20. East, Oxford.
Postern Gate, The—August 13. P.O.W., Birmingham.
Pot of Caviare, A—November 13. O.H., Jersey.
Pride of Takahara—February 19. Terminus Hall, Littlehampton.
Princess and the Vagabond, The (C.P.)—November 9. Gaiety, Dundee.
Princess in Bohemia, A—June 29. Royal, Bradford.
Professor's Violin, The—January 11. Hippodrome, Eastbourne.
Proof, The—September 7. O.H., Southport.
Question of Property, A—January 13. Royal, Margate.
Real Mr. Jonathan, The—June 15. Pier Pavilion, Paignton.
Reaping the Whirlwind—September 28. Gaiety, Manchester.
Repentant Sinner, A—December 26. Alhambra, Stourbridge.
Reptile's Devotion, The (C.P.)—July 9. Queen's, Leeds.
Romantic Barber, The—March 2. Royal, Dublin (March 23, Grand, Fulham).
Royal Mail, The—March 11. Goddard's, Dublin.
Salvation—March 5. Royal, Smethwick.
Sentimentalist, The—December 4. Athenæum, Glasgow.
Scheme that Failed, A—July 16. Prince's, Accrington.
Sir George's Folly—January 27 Royal, Belfast.
Skittles—February 14. Royal, Margate.
Slander—December 9. Royal, Birmingham.
Sower Went Forth, A—April 27. Royalty, Llanelly.
Straight from the Shoulder—August 3. Grand, Brighton (August 10, Broadway).
Sweet Peggy O'Neill—August 12. Tower Pavilion, Portobello.
Taid A Nain—December 5. Hulme Town Hall.
Tangled Skein, A—January 10. Hall, Nenagh.
Till the Bells Ring—March 26. Athenæum, True Till Death—March 12. Castle, Brentford.

Trumpet Major, The—November 18, Corn Exchange, Dorchester.
Two Pins, The—April 2. Royal, Newcastle (Aldwych, June 2).
Undercurrent, The (C.P.)—July 8. Grammar School, Dedham, Essex.
Way Out, The—August 3. Royal, Newcastle.
When a Lass Loves—November 23. Royal, Margate.
When the Devil Was Ill—August 29. H.M., Carlisle.
Whirlpool, The—February 22. New Cardiff (Septe nber 21. Marlborough).
Wireless (C.P.)—October 19. Royal, York.
With Edged Tools—February 3. Royal, Hull (C.P., February 20, 1907, Gaiety, Ayr; London production, April 6, 1908, King's, Hammersmith).
Woman from Russia, The (C.P.)—July 25. Royal, Jarrow (September 22, Alexandra, Sheffield).
Woman's Lore, A—June 22. Muncaster, Bootle.
Woman's Rights—March 23. Royal, Rochdale.
Woman who Sinned, The—December 7. Palace, Boston.
Woman Who Was Dead, The—March 16. Gaiety, Dundee (May 29, Royal, Strat'ord).
Wonderful Woman; A—June 15. Pier Pav., St. Leonards.
Workhouse Ward, The—April 20. Abbey, Dublin.
World and the Woman, The—May 11. Royal, Newcastle.
Yarn Spinner, The—June 29. Pier Pavilion, Southend.

PRINCIPAL REVIVALS.

Admirable Crichton, The—March 2. Duke of York's.
Afterthoughts—June 15. Garrick.
Antony and Cleopatra—December 26. Queen's, Manchester.
As You Like It—January 11. Queen's, Manchester.
Boatswain's Mate, The—October 31. Wyndham's.
Charley's Aunt—December 26. Aldwych.
Corsican Brothers, The—September 9 and November 23. Adelphi.
Cyrano de Bergerac—July 6. His Majesty's.
Dairymaids, The—May 5. Queen's.
Daughter of Herodias, The—April 6. Midland, Manchester.

Dorothy—September 28. Broadway. December 21. New.
Dumb Man, The—August 18. Pavilion.
Filby the Faker (originally *The Fairy Uncle*)—September 7. Wyndham's.
Fille du Tambour Major, La—June 1. Shaftesbury.
Fido—February 22. Playhouse.
Gay Lord Quex, The—April 30. Garrick.
Girls of Gottenberg, The—August 10. Adelphi.
Golden Wedding, The—February 22. Playhouse.
Grande Duchesse de Gerolstein, La—June 11. Shaftesbury.
Hannele—December 8. His Majesty's.
Hands Across the Sea—September 21. Dalston.
H.M.S. Pinafore—July 14. Savoy.
Henry V.—November 25. Lyric.
Ib and Little Christina—September 21. Adelphi.
Iolanthe—October 19. Savoy.
Jocelyn the Jester—February 17. Grand, Croydon.
King René's Daughter—December 7. Shaftesbury.
Knight of the Burning Pestle, The—December 24. Gaiety, Manchester.
Little Lord Fauntleroy—December 26. Court.
Lyons Mail, The—October 15. Shaftesbury.
Maid's Tragedy, The—October 18. Court.
Merchant of Venice, The—April 4. His Majesty's.
Merchant of Venice, The—February 10. Royalty.
Merchant of Venice, The—September 21. Grand, Birmingham.
Midsummer Night's Dream, A—February 26. New Oxford.
Mikado, The—April 28. Savoy.
Much Ado About Nothing—February 17. Coronet.
Only Way, The—October 26. Adelphi.
Pair of Spectacles, A—June 15. Garrick.
Peter Pan—December 23. Duke of York's.
Pirates of Penzance, The—December 1. Savoy.
Postbag, The—July 3. Court.
Rafale, La—May 5. Shaftesbury.
Rip Van Winkle—February 6. Royalty.
Romeo and Juliet—February 13. Royalty.
Romeo and Juliet—March 14. Lyceum.
Rosmersholm—February 10. Terry's.
Scarlet Pimpernel, The—April 20. New.
Taming of the Shrew—June 22. Aldwych.
Toddles—May 20. Playhouse.
Tragedy of Truth, A—September 28. Adelphi.
Vision of the Twelve Virgin Goddesses, A—July 6. Botanic Gardens.

PRINCIPAL NEW SKETCHES

PRODUCED IN THE VARIETY THEATRES DURING THE YEAR 1908.

† Indicates *matinée* performance.　‡ Indicates first performance in London.

JANUARY.

6. *Till Sunday; or, The Girl Who Took the Wrong Towing Path*, produced by Arthur Roberts—Tivoli.
6. *The Violin Girl*, by Edgar Dereve, music by Henry W. May—Richmond.
6. *The Passing of Paul*, by Leonard Mortimer —Sadler's Wells.
6. *The Sleigh Bells*, a new version, by E. Hoggan-Armadale of *Le Juif Polonais*— Camberwell Empire.
13. *A Man in Motley*, duologue, by Tom Gallon—Grand, Birmingham. Coliseum, London, January 20.
13. *Law and Order*, farcical duologue, by Tom Gallon—Palace.
13. *His Shop Girl Bride*, musical comedietta, by Roland Oliver, music and lyrics by Louis La Rondelle—Camberwell Palace.
13. *I Want to Go On the Stage*, by F. R. Yeulett—Stoke Newington Palace.
20. *Hearts of Gold*, one-act drama, presented by W. T. Ellwanger—Camberwell Palace.
27. *Black Against White*, "sporting and dramatic sketch," in one scene, written by Worland S. Wheeler—Paragon.
27. *The Wreckers*, sketch, by Geraldine Campbell—Richmond.
27. *Cupid Wins*, divertissement, arranged by Alfredo Curti, with mus.c by Geo. W. Byng—Alhambra.
31. *Wearing the Apron*—Greenwich Palace.

FEBRUARY.

3. *Charlie, the Sport*, produced by Maurice H. Hoffman and company, a racing sketch (presented originally at the Haymarket)—Camberwell Empire.
3. *The Devil's Mate*—London Coliseum.
10. *The Post Office Girl*—The Granville.
10. *My New Cook*, sketch, by Seymour Hicks —London Pavilion.
14. *Sciatica*, comedy sketch, produced by Mr. H. P. Oven—Barnard's Palace, Greenwich.
17. *A Nice Quiet Morning*—Tivoli.
17. *The Burglar's Ball*, musical sketch, by Geo. Dance—Richmond.
17. ‡*Peg Woffington*—London Coliseum.
17. *Singing Servants*—Holborn Empire.
17. *The Three Thieves*, playlet, by Maurice Vernon—Hackney Empire.
24. *Honour Among Thieves*, drama, by Gladys Hastings Walton—Paddington Palace, Liverpool.
24. *The Convict Ship*—Camberwell Empire.
24. ‡*My Lady*, "dramatic play," in three scenes, written by Arthur Shirley—Holborn Empire.
24. *Now On*, sketch, in two scenes and a "lot more trouble," written and composed by Harry Leighton and Gilbert Wells—Empress, Brixton.

MARCH.

2. *An Amateur Raffles*, musical duologue, written by Herbert Clayton, lyrics by Arthur Anderson, music by Ralph Nairn— London Pavilion.
2. *Murphy's Affinity*—The Surrey.

2. *For England's Glory*, military spectacle, by W. J. Mackay—Canterbury.
7. *Oh, Indeed!* revue, by George Grossmith, jun., lyrics by C. H. Bovill, music by Cuthbert Clarke—Empire.
9. *Her Princely Betrayer*, romantic episode, in one act, by Robt. Wilton—Stoke Newington Palace.
9. *Hawksley's Luck*, dramatic episode, in four scenes, by F. Maxwell—Bedford.
16. *The White Bride*, dramatic sketch, in a prologue and an episode—Standard.
16. *The King's Portrait*, dramatic sketch, by James Malam—Camberwell Empire.
16. *A Disturbed Rendezvous*, burlesque pantomime, in one scene—Islington Hippodrome.
23. "*Trial Scene*" from Hall Caine's *The Eternal City*—Crouch End Hippodrome.
23. *Cromwell or the King*, historical episode, by Worland S. Wheeler—Paragon.
23. *Dreamland*, musical fantasia—Camberwell Empire.
30. *The House of Terror*, sketch, in one act, by John G. Brandon—Islington Palace.
30. *The Last Command*, dramatic episode, written by Frederick Maxwell—Bedford.
30. *Nance Arden; or, the Woman Who Did*, sketch, in one scene, written by Cecil Raleigh—Empress.
30. *A Disgrace to the Force*—Holborn Empire.
30. *England, Mistress of the Seas*, musical scena, invented and written by Sydney Blow, music by Edward Jones—Camberwell Empire.
30. *The Casuals*, sketch, written by Fred Karno and Tom Tindall, with music by A. E. Wilson—Stoke Newington Palace.
30. *The New Boarder*, farcical musical absurdity, written by Frank Stanmore, with music by F. A. Armstrong—Paragon.
30. *Our Master*, farcical comedy sketch, in one scene—Queen's, Poplar.

APRIL.

1. *The Ten O'Clock Squad*, musical sketch by H. M. Vernon—Shepherd's Bush Empire.
6. *The Power of the Idol*, by Laura Leycester —Richmond.
6. *The Magic Cloak*, by Espinasse and Turman—Camberwell Empire.
6. *Brokers Ahead*—Paragon.
9. *The Motor Man*, farcical sketch, by Clare Shirley—Cleveland Hall, Brotton.
13. *The Dulcie Darenda Affair*, by Harry Lowther—Bow Palace.
13. *Fat and Fair*, by Wal Pink—Rotherhithe Hippodrome.
13. *The Mystery of the Red Web*, sketch, written by Fergus Hume and Newman Harding—Olympia, Liverpool. Canterbury, London, May 18.
13. *No Cats*, farcical sketch, by Gilbert Wells— Camberwell Empire.
13. *The Irony of Fate*, dramatic episode, by J. G. Levy—Bedford.
13. *The Tuppenny Tube; or, The Flying Machine*, sketch, in two scenes, written by Tom Terriss—Islington Empire.
18. *My Butler*, by Ivan Gore—Crouch End Hippodrome.

20. *The Magic Eye*, miniature grand opera—Metropolitan.
20. *The Volcano*, sensational spectacle, in one scene, written by Aliela Ramsey and Rudolph de Cordova, with music composed by Carl Kiefert—London Hippodrome.
21. *Grandfather's Clock*, by Lionel Scudamore—Empress.
27. *A Royal Heart*, by A. Scott Craven and J. D. Beresford—Empress.
27. *The Lady Bandits*—Holborn Empire.
27. *Blind*, one-act drama, adapted from the French *Aveugle* of Messrs. Charles Hellem and Pol d'Estoc, by Mr. Edmund Maurice.—New Cross Empire.

MAY.

2. *My Wife's Husband*—Oxford.
6. *A Lost Chance*, by Bertha N. Graham—Empress, Brixton.
11 *That Did It!* "tabloid musical comedy," written by Eustace Burnaby and H. S. Browning, with music by Eustace Burnaby and lyrics by George Grossmith, jun., and Ralph Roberts—Crouch End Hippodrome.
11. *The Pixies' Revel*—Empress, Brixton.
11. *An Interrupted Elopement*—Islington Hippodrome.
12. *A Tooth for a Wife*—Middlesex.
15. *When Women Rule*, athletic scena—Palace, Bradford
15. *A Belfrey Dream*—Camberwell Palace.
18. *Parker, P.C.*, by Chas. Austin and Chas. Ridgwell—Islington Hippodrome.
18. *Sweet Mistress Dorothy*, by Roy Redgrave—Foresters'.
18. *The Sultan*—Stoke Newington Palace.
18. *The Partner of My Joys*—Crouch End, Hippodrome.
20. *The Sergeant-Major*, by F. D. Bone—Middlesex.
22. *A Woman's Reputation*—Middlesex.
25. *His Living Image*, by Stanley Cooke, music by Arthur Wood—Canterbury.
25. *The Futurity Winner*—Shepherd's Bush
25. *Who's Who*—Alhambra, Brighton.
25. *The Girls in Scarlet*—Royal Standard.
25. *Shop Hours*, by Edgar Dereve, music by Henry W May—Richmond.
25. *The Two Flags*, Franco-British *divertissement*, in three scenes, arranged and produced by Alfredo Curti, with music composed and arranged by George W. Byng.—Alhambra.

JUNE.

1. *The Sword of Justice*, by Percy Ford—Camberwell Empire.
1. *The Adventures of 101*—Camberwell Empire.
1. *Sky High*, by Wal Pink, music by J. S. Baker—Islington Empire.
1.‡*The Tea Shop Strike*, by H. M. Vernon—Hackney Empire.
1. *What Happened to Flannigan*—Middlesex.
3.†*The Death Waltz*—Queen's, Leeds.
4.†*Desperate Difficulties*, by Mabel Archdall and Jem Aitken—Empress, Brixton.
8. *Fa(u)st and Loose*, by J. J. Hewson—Hippodrome, Glasgow.
15. *The Police Trap*, by Cecil Raleigh—Tivoli.
15. *Paying Guests*, farce, by H. Leslie Bell and Charles D. Hickman, with lyrics by Hickman and Woodin, and music by Richard E. Lawson—Islington Hippodrome.
15. *The Beggars' Hotel*, by G. R. Sims—Sadler's Wells.
15. *Five Years Later*—Holborn Empire.
15. *Goody Two Shoes*—Chelsea Palace.

15. *Prince Arthur*—Walthamstow Palace.
16. *The Gambler's Wife*—Middlesex.
22. *Her Country's Enemy*—Bedford.
22. *The Usurer*, by Sydney Mason—Middlesex.
22. *The Poor Fiddler's Windfall*—Tivoli, Bar row.
22. *Billiards*—Oxford.
22. *The Toast of the Town*, by Luke Jennings—Crouch End Hippodrome.
23. *The Sheriff and the Rosebud*—Hippodrome, Manchester.
24.†*After Balaclava*—Empress, Brixton.
25. *Where Woman Loves*—King's, Longsight.
29. *The Major's Manœuvre*—Bedford.
29.‡*The Admiral's Lady*—Holborn Empire.
29. *The Top of the Bill*—Standard.
29. *The Strike*—Paragon.
29. *The Little Ascot Hero*, by Tom Petrie—Sadler's Wells.
29. *Almighty Gold*—Empress, Brixton.

JULY.

4. *Find the Lady First*—Standard.
6. *'Twixt Dawn and Daylight*, by V. L. Granville and Fred Russell—Stoke Newington Palace.
6. *A Friend in Need*, by Richard Purdon—Sadler's Wells.
6.‡*A Baby's Shoe*—Bedford.
6. *The Belle of Andalusia*, spectacular ballet extravaganza, in three scenes; libretto lyrics by G. R. Sims and Charles Fletcher; music by Herman Finck. The whole invented and arranged by J. R. Huddlestone and John Tiller—Winter Gardens, Blackpool.
6. *La Double Epouvante*, by Paul Franck—Tivoli.
6. *The Shadow on the Blind*, by Stafford Smith—Standard.
6. *A Shakespearean Lunatic* — Camberwell Palace.
13. *The Last Muster*, by J W. Tate and J. P. Harrington, music by Orlando Powell—Oxford.
13. *An Uninvited Guest*—Camberwell Palace.
13. *The Musician's Daughter*—Canterbury.
20. *A Woman's Way*, by Mollie Laney—Hippodrome, Manchester.
20. *The Money-Spider*, by E. Phillips Oppenheim—London Coliseum.
20. *Corkscrew*—Paragon.
20. *Otake*, by W. Shiko and Loie Fuller—London Hippodrome.
20. *The Moreton Pearls*, by Russell Vaun—Hammersmith Palace.
20. *The Coster's Christmas Eve*—Queen's, Poplar.
27.‡*The Sheriff and the Rosebud*, adapted by W. J. T. Collins—Shepherd's Bush Empire.

AUGUST.

3. *Lucky Jim*—Walthamstow Palace.
3. *A Timely Awakening*—Tivoli.
3. *Pat and the Genie*—Alhambra.
3. *The Professor's Secret*, by Louis Dagmar—Ealing Hippodrome.
3. *The Governor's Nephew*—Holborn Empire.
3. *The Queen of Music*—Middlesex.
10. *Behind the Scenes*—London Coliseum.
10. *The Brigands of Tarragona*—Shepherd's Bush Empire.
10.‡————, sketch without a name, by T. M Paule—Holloway Empire.
17. *The Alchemist*, by Wm. Warden and Fredk. Lloyd—Bedford.
17. *A Woman of Paris* (new version)—Canterbury.
17. *Are You a Socialist?*—Bedford.

17. *Greater London,* spectacle, by Herr Rousby
—Hackney Empire.
22.†*Princess Aurora,* sixteenth-century " grand
opera tabloid," written by Tom S. Jones,
and composed by R. M. Harvey—Tivoli.
24.‡*The Local Amateurs.* George Dance's
musical comedy sketch—Richmond Hippodrome.
24. *At England's Command,* "revolutionary
episode," in one scene, written by Edward
Thane—Queen's, Poplar.
24.‡*The Organ Grinder,* sketch, in four scenes,
by Alicia Ramsey and Rudolph de Cordova—New Cross Empire.
31. *Having a Dip,* musical extravaganza, in one
scene, by W. E. Phillips, with music by
Joseph Tabrar—Canterbury.
31. *Cavalleria Rusticana*—Richmond Hippodrome.
31. *The Black Devil,* translated from the
Italian by Lauderdale Maitland—Hammersmith Palace.
31. *Dick's Sister,* by Norman McKinnell—
Tivoli.
31. *The Sands o' Dee,* a "sensational aquatic
hippodrama," by Alicia Ramsey and Rudolph de Cordova, music composed by
Carl Kiefert, produced by Frank Parker—
London Hippodrome.

SEPTEMBER.

7. "Visions of Wagner," produced by Charles
Wilson—London Coliseum
7. *A Fighting Chance,* by Barry Williams—
Euston.
7. *Captured by Brigands*—Empress.
7. *My Lady's Bower*—Canterbury.
14.‡*Lift'ems, Limited,* by Chris Davis—Holborn
Empire.
14. *Old Knockles,* by Arthur Law, music by
A. J. Caldicott—Empress.
14. *Peter's Picture,* by C. C. Horton—B dford.
14. *A Ride to Win,* by Max Goldberg—Empire, Croydon.
16. *The Willow Pattern Plate,* by Eugenic
Magnus—Empire, Camberwell.
21. *The Prima Donna*—Holborn Empire.
21. *The Fatal Error,* by Hall Caine—Queen's,
Poplar.
21. *Coward or Hero?* by R. Cameron Matthews
—Camberwell Empire.
28. *The Unforeseen*—Empress, Brixton.
28. *The White Hand of a Woman,* in three
scenes, by George R. Sims—Sadler's
Wells.

OCTOBER.

5.‡*Pigs in Clover,* by J. J. S. Sutcliffe—Putney Hippodrome.
12. *Paquita,* romantic ballet, in three scenes,
arranged and produced by Alfredo Curti,
with music by George W. Byng—Alhambra.
12.‡*High Jinks*—Holborn Empire.
12. *Is Life Worth Living?* monologue, by Paul
Pelham—Empress.
12. *Life and Love,* by E. Dalvery—Palace,
Stoke Newington.
14. *Thicker than Water*—Empress, Brixton.
16. *Bouncing a Burglar*—Barnard's, Greenwich.
19. *A Day in Paris,* ballet, in five scenes, by
Lieut.-Col. N. Newnham-Davis, with
music composed and arranged by Cuthbert Clarke—Empire.
19. *The Gates of Dawn,* in one scene, by
Arthur O'Keene—Canterbury.

19. *The Mountain Belle,* musical sketch, by
Laurence Anarto and Harry Rushworth—
Richmond Hippodrome.
19. *The Old Willow Plate,* operatic phantasy,
by Mark Strong—Camberwell Empire.
19. *The G.P.O.,* burlesque, by Fred Karno—
Empire, Sheffield.
26. *The Actors*—Hippodrome, Hastings.
26. *Sweet Innisfail*—Richmond Hippodrome.

NOVEMBER.

2. *The Cert*—Queen's, Poplar.
2. *The Little Peacemaker,* by Ivan P. Gore
and Ronald Bayne—Bedford.
2. *The Hankey-homey Showman,* "operatic
agony," with lyrics by George Burnley—
The Oxford.
9. *All About a Bout,* sketch, in three scenes,
by Irving B. Lee, under direction of
Frank Beal—New Cross Empire.
9. *The Deputy,* by Ivan P. Gore—Olympia,
Shoreditch.
16.‡*The G.P.O.*—Paragon.
16. *Poor Arthur,* farcical comedy, adapted
from Sydney Grundy's version of *The
Arabian Nights*—Richmond Hippodrome.
16. *The Last Halt*—Queen's, Poplar.
16. *My Lancashire Wife*—Middlesex.
16. *The Afrikander Maid*—Middlesex.
23. *Chums Till Death,* in three scenes by
Albert Marsh—Canterbury.
23. *The Kiss*—Canterbury.
23. *A Modern Galatea,* by Luke Jellings and
George Bellamy—The Middlesex.
23. *A Kiss*—Canterbury.
23. *A London Galatea*—Middlesex.
30. *Amid Northern Lights*—Bedford.
30. *Ladies Only,* by Chas. Darrell—Greenwich
Palace.
30. *The Duchess of Deptford,* by John Rid-
ding—Standard.
30. *First Stop, London,* by Edward Morris—
Sadler's Wells.
30.*The Experiment,* by Mrs. Albert Bradshaw
—Battersea Palace.
30. *My Dear Old Dutch*—South London.

DECEMBER,

5. *In the Studio*—Middlesex.
5.†*The Abiding Power of Love*—Shoreditch
Empire.
7. *The King and the Vagabond,* adapted from
Theodore de Banville's *Gringoire,* by
Laurence Irving—London Coliseum.
7.‡*The Yap Yaps,* sketch, in three scenes, by
Fred Karno and J. Hickory Wood (originally produced at the Hippodrome, Margate, November 30)—Paragon.
7. *A Bottled Request*—Empress, Brixton.
7. *Gay Dogs,* by Messrs. Stanmore, Leslie, Hawkins, and Mark Lester—Stoke Newington
Palace.
7. *The Major's Niece,* farcical sketch, in one
scene, by John Beauchamp—Hammer-
smith Palace.
7. *Mazeppa,* equestrian spectacle—East Ham
Palace.
7. *Ring Up 735 East,* by E. S. France—Willesden Hippodrome.
7. *A Man's a Man for a' That*—Hippodrome,
Belfast.
7. *Puss in Boots*—Canterbury.
9. *An Old Man's Darling,* by John Chandler
—Middlesex.
14. *Slippery Jim,* by Luke Jellings and Geo.
Bellamy—Holloway Empire.
14. *Fun on a Racecourse*—Camberwell Empire.
14. *Scenes on the Mississippi*—Queen's, Poplar.
14. *That Girl Carrots*—Standard.

14.†*The Reptile's Daughter*, by Robert Trebor
—Battersea Palace.
14. *The Fly by Night*, by Paul A. Rubens—
Palace.
14. *The Conquering Hero*, by Frederick Fenn
—Metropolitan.
14. *The Leaves of Memory*—Euston.
14. *In the Midst of Life*, by H. E. Terry—
Shoreditch Empire.
14. *The Case of the Kidnapped King*, by C.
Douglas Carlile—Sadler's Wells.
16. *A Blank Cheque*, by W. J. Locke—Empire.
21. ‡*Truth in Absence*—Shepherd's Bush Empire.

21. *The Rain Dears*—London Hippodrome.
21.‡*A Man's a Man for a' That*—Oxford.
21. *Polly Pickle's Pets in Petland*—London
Coliseum.
21. *My Princess of Japan*—Holborn Empire.
22. *The Suffragettes*, by George Thorne—Middlesex.
24. *To-Morrow*, by Bolossy Kiralfy—London
Hippodrome.
28. *Why the Third Floor Passed*, by J. J.
Spencer—Metropolitan.
28. *Blind Musician*, by John Jackson—Empress,
Brixton.

RECITALS.

PRINCIPAL RECITALS DURING THE YEAR 1908.

JANUARY.

6. Mr. Geo. Grossmith's Recital (and during
the week)—Steinway Hall.
8. Miss Elsie Gesper's Pianoforte Recital—
Bechstein Hall.
11. Kruse Quartet—Bechstein Hall.
20. "Apollo and the Seaman" and "The
Shepherd"—Queen's Hall.
22. Miss D. Hanseel's Violin Recital—Bechstein
Hall.
22. Ladies' Concert of the Royal Amateur Orchestral Society—Queen's Hall.
23. Joachim Memorial Concert—Queen's Hall.
23. Broadwood Concert—Æolian Hall.
24. Chappell Ballad Concert—Queen's Hall.
24. "Caractacus," by the Alexandra Palace
Choral Society—Alexandra Palace.
24. "Night wi' Burns"—Albert Hall.
30. Mr. Willy Burmester's Recital—Bechstein
Hall.
30. Royal Choral Society's Fourth Concert—
Albert Hall.

FEBRUARY.

1. Queen's Hall Symphony Concert.
1. Dulwich Philharmonic Society's performance of "Athalie," Crystal Palace.
6. Willy Burmester, violin recital, Bechstein
Hall.
6. Dramatic and musical recital by Mrs. May
Belcher and Percival Garratt, Steinway
Hall.
7. Pianoforte recital by Mrs. George Swinton and Miss Ella Spravka, Æolian Hall.
10. Miss Hilda Saxe, pianoforte recital, Æolian
Hall.
11. Kathryn Comber, vocal recital, Bechstein
Hall.
11. Nora Hastings, dramatic recital, Steinway
Hall.
12. London Choral Society, Queen's Hall.
12. Helene Young and Roger Thynne, vocal
and pianoforte recital, Bechstein Hall.
13. Philharmonic Society Concert, Queen's Hall.
13. Willy Burmester, violin recital, Bechstein
Hall.
13. Emily Greenyer, dramatic recital, Steinway Hall.
14. Royal Amateur Orchestral Society's Concert, Queen's Hall.
14. Joska Szigeti, violin recital, Bechstein Hall.
14 Marion Dyke, vocal recital, Æolian Hall.
14. Dunhill Chamber Concert, Steinway Hall.
15. London Ballad Concert, Albert Hall.
15. Queen's Hall Orchestra, Queen's Hall.

15. Brinsmead Chamber Concert, Cavendish
Rooms.
17. London Symphony Orchestra, Queen's Hall.
17. Edith Muriel Compton, vocal recital,
Bechstein Hall.
17. Archy Rosenthal, pianoforte recital, Æolian
Hall.
17. Students' invitation concert, Trinity College.
18. Emil Sauer, pianoforte recital, Queen's
Hall.
18. Henry Gurney, vocal recital, Bechstein
Hall.
18. J. Campbell McInnes, vocal recital, Æolian
Hall.
18. Concert in aid of the Clergy Rest, Margate, Steinway Hall.
18. Edith Allen, ballad concert, Steinway
Hall.
18. Rose Koenig's Wagner recital, Suffolk
Street Galleries.
19. Royal Academy of Music, Queen's Hall.
19. Moritz Moszkowski, orchestral concert,
Queen's Hall.
19. Gwendoline Pelly, evening concert, Bechstein Hall.
19. Donald Francis Tovey, chamber concert,
Chelsea Town Hall.
19. Harold Ketèlbey, violin recital, Trinity
College.
20. Bohemian Concert, Queen's Hall.
20. Willy Burmester, violin recital, Bechstein
Hall.
20. Mildred Marks and Alfred Moyles, pianoforte and 'cello recital, Æolian Hall.
20. Broadwood's Chamber Concert, Æolian
Hall.
21. Mabel Paice and Paul Edmond, 'cello and
vocal recital, Æolian Hall.
21. Thomas Dunhill, chamber concert, Steinway Hall.
21. Joseph Holbrook, chamber concert, Salle
Erard.
22. Chappell's Ballad Concert, Queen's Hall.
22. Marmaduke Barton, pianoforte recital,
Bechstein Hall.
22. Dora Gilpin, vocal recital, Bechstein Hall.
22. Myra Hess, pianoforte recital, Æolian
Hall.
22. Brinsmead Chamber Concert, Cavendish
Rooms.
23. Fifth annual grand concert in aid of the
Theatrical Employés' Benevolent Fund,
London Coliseum.
23. Concert Club concert, Bechstein Hall.
24. Musical soirée, Criterion Grand Hall.
24. Anna Hirzel, pianoforte recital, Æolian
Hall.

24. Strings Club chamber concert, Salle Erard.
25. Margaret Horne, orchestral concert, Queen's Hall.
25. Adelaide Rind, vocal recital, Bechstein Hall.
25. Charles Clark, vocal recital, Æolian Hall.
25. Maude Aldis, violin recital, Æolian Hall.
25. Alvilde Rasmussen, pianoforte recital, Steinway Hall.
25. Concertgoers' Club: "Joachim as a Composer," Royal Academy of Music.
25. Students' concert, Royal College of Music.
26. New Symphony Orchestra, Queen's Hall.
26. Gwladys Cronie, vocal recital, Bechstein Hall.
26. Dorothy Wiley, vocal recital, Bechstein Hall.
26. Hugh Langton, recital, Æolian Hall.
26. Donald Francis Tovey, chamber concert, Chelsea Town Hall
26 Sonata recital, Guildhall School.
27. Philharmonic Concert Society, Queen's Hall.
27. Brussels String Quartet, Bechstein Hall.
27. Eileen Russell, vocal recital, Æolian Hall.
27. Mabel Marx and Joseph Schofield, vocal and 'cello recital, Steinway Hall.
27. The Worshipful Company of Musicians concert, Stationers' Hall.
28. Ruth Troward, pianoforte recital, Bechstein Hall.
28. Invitation concert, Æolian Hall.
28. Walenn Quartet chamber concert, Æolian Hall.
28. Pauline Theurer and Thorold Waters, vocal recital, Steinway Hall.
28. Welsh Choral Festival, St. Paul's.
29. London Ballad Concert, Albert Hall.
29. Orchestral Symphony concert, Queen's Hall.
29. Florence and Bertha Salter, vocal recital, Bechstein Hall.
29. Miss Sydney Martin, vocal recital, Bechstein Hall
29. Concert in aid of Paddington and St. Marylebone Nursing Association, Æolian Hall.
29. John Wilmot, concert, Steinway Hall.
29. Dorothy Martin, vocal recital, Salle Erard.
29. Brinemead Chamber Concert, Cavendish Rooms.

MARCH.

2. London Symphony Orchestra, Queen's Hall.
2. Dorothea Walenn, Æolian Hall.
3. Busoni and Arrigo Serato pianoforte and violin recital, Bechstein Hall.
3. Hegedüs subscription concert, Æolian Hall.
3. Ethel Berry pianoforte recital, Steinway Hall.
4 Royal Choral Society, "The Dream of Gerontius," Albert Hall.
4. Wessely Quartet, Bechstein Hall.
5. Maud Nimer's concert, Queen's Hall.
5. Brussels String Quartet, Bechstein Hall
5. Westminster Orchestral Society, Kensington Town Hall.
6. London Trio, Æolian Hall.
7. Chappell ballad concert, Queen's Hall.
7. Barns-Phillips' chamber concert, Bechstein Hall.
7. Elderhorst Quartet, Cavendish Rooms.
10. Adelaide Dodgson pianoforte recital, Bechstein Hall.
10. Ferencz Hegedüs chamber concert, Æolian Hall.
10. Giulia Strakosch evening concert, Steinway Hall.
11 New Symphony Orchestra concert, Queen's Hall.
11. Charity concert, Bechstein Hall.
11. Hilda Saxe pianoforte recital, Æolian Hall.

12. Winifred Davis vocal concert, Bechstein Hall.
12. Carlo Erici vocal recital, Bechstein Hall.
12. Marjorie Wigley pianoforte recital, Æolian Hall.
13. Plunket Greene vocal recital, Æolian Hall.
13. Susan Metcalfe vocal recital, Bechstein Hall.
14. London Ballad Concert, Albert Hall.
14. Queen's Hall Orchestra, Symphony concert, Queen's Hall.
14. Brinsmead's chamber concert, Cavendish Rooms.
16 Susan Metcalfe vocal recital, Bechstein Hall.
16. Welte-Mignon concert, Steinway Hall.
16 Oriana Madrigal Society, Portman Rooms.
17. Irish festival concert, Albert Hall.
17. Charles Clark vocal recital, Æolian Hall.
17. Irish ballad concert, Steinway Hall.
17. Musical Association, King's Rooms.
18. Bach Choir, Queen's Hall.
18. Jeanne Raunay and Gabriel Fauré recital, Bechstein Hall.
18. Orchestral concert, Caxton Hall.
19. Queen's Hall Orchestra concert, Queen's Hall.
19. Carlo Erici vocal recital, Bechstein Hall.
19. Arthur Goodsall dramatic recital, Steinway Hall.
21. Chappell's ballad concert, Queen's Hall.
21. Kruse Quartet, Bechstein Hall.
21. E. Milman and L. Percival Clark vocal and dramatic recital, Steinway Hall.
21. Brinsmead's chamber concert, Cavendish Rooms.
23. London Symphony Orchestra, Queen's Hall.
23. May Harrison violin recital, Bechstein Hall.
23. Concert, Royal College.
23. Maria Capoccetti pianoforte recital, Salle Erard.
24. Cyril Scott concert, Bechstein Hall.
24. Herbert Fryer pianoforte recital, Steinway Hall.
24. Theodora Macalster vocal recital, Steinway Hall.
24. Harold Frome and Hermann Vezin, Salle Erard.
25. Stock Exchange concert, Queen's Hall.
25. Société de Concerts d'Instruments Anciens, Bechstein Hall.
26. Philharmonic concert, Queen's Hall.
26. Iona Robertson dramatic and musical recital, Bechstein Hall.
26. Le Mar and Hener Skene vocal and pianoforte recital, Æolian Hall.
26. Charles Bennett vocal recital, Æolian Hall.
26. Evelyn Ingleton chamber concert, Broadwood's.
27. Jean Waterson vocal recital, Bechstein Hall.
27. Joseph Holbrooke chamber concert, Salle Erard.
28. Choral and Orchestral Society, Alexandra Palace.
28 Symphony Orchestra, Queen's Hall.
28. Arthur Broadley sonata recital, Bechstein Hall.
30. Mischa Elman orchestral concert, Queen's Hall.
30. May Harrison violin recital, Bechstein Hall.
31. Royal Academy of Music students' orchestral concert, Queen's Hall.
31. Mr. Beecham's third orchestral concert, Queen's Hall.
31. Arrigo Serato violin recital, Bechstein Hall.
31. Frederic Brandon pianoforte recital, Æolian Hall.

31. Frida Dancyger vocal recital, Steinway Hall.
31. Herbert Fryer pianoforte recital, Steinway Hall.

APRIL.

1. London Choral Society, Queen's Hall.
1. La Société de Concert d'Instruments Anciens concert, Bechstein Hall.
1. Mme. Frickenhaus concert, Bechstein Hall.
2. Royal Choral Society, Albert Hall.
2. Kathleen Purcell's concert, Bechstein Hall.
2. Chastian violin recital, Bechstein Hall.
2. Hugo Heinz vocal recital, Æolian Hall.
2. Marie Valerie concert, Steinway Hall.
3. Plunket Greene, Æolian Hall.
3. London Trio, Æolian Hall.
3. Benefit concert for Mme. Sinico, 79, Eaton Square, S.W.
4. Chappell's ballad concert, Queen's Hall.
4. Edward Mason Choir and New Symphony Orchestra, Queen's Hall
4. Lamond pianoforte recital, Bechstein Hall.
7. Horace Keateren, pupils' concert, Bechstein Hall.
7. May Harrison violin recital, Bechstein Hall.
7. Cleaver Simon and Ingo Simon vocal recital, Æolian Hall.
8. La Société de Concert d'Instruments Anciens, Bechstein Hall.
8. Josephine Wareka recital, Bechstein Hall.
8. Alma Haas pianoforte recital, Steinway Hall.
8. Alan Macwhirter folk-song recital, Steinway Hall.
8. Valerie Knoll violin recital, Æolian Hall.
8. York Bowen pianoforte recital, Æolian Hall.
9. Vera Jacobsen 'cello recital, Bechstein Hall.
9 Adelaide Dodgson pianoforte recital, Æolian Hall.
9. Sape'lnikoff pianoforte recital, Steinway Hall
9. Jaxon-Yuill vocal recital, Steinway Hall.
10. Julia Culp, vocal recital, Bechstein Hall.
10. Dorothy Cheetham vocal recital, Æolian Hall.
10 Christine D'Almayne vocal recital, Æolian Hall.
10. Nadia Sylva violin recital, Steinway Hall.
11. Ferencz Hegedüs concert, Æolian Hall.
12 Queen's Hall Orchestra and Sheffield Choir, Queen's Hall.
12. Dorothy Normandy vocal recital, Bechstein Hall.
12. Mons. Nicolay vocal recital, Steinway Hall.
27 Henry Gurney and Marie Novello concert, St. James's Hall.
27. Thorpe Bates vocal recital. Æolian Hall.
27. Marion Sydney vocal recital, Steinway Hall.
28. Kathleen Parlow and Florence Monteith with Queen's Hall Orchestra, Queen's Hall.
28. Royal Amateur Orchestral concert, Queen's Hall.
28. Agnes Osman and Henry Gurney, St. James's Hall.
28. Elena Gerhardt and Arthur Nikisch vocal recital, Bechstein Hall
28. Gwladys Lewis violin recital, Bechstein Hall.
28. Sara Susman vocal recital. Æolian Hall.
28. Lillian Ginnett dramatic recital, Salle Erard.
29. Sydney Martin, Grace Wounacott, and Nico Poppelsdorff, St. James's Hall.
29. Bokken Lassou vocal recital, Bechstein Hall.
29. Philip Simmons concert, Æolian Hall.
29. Grace Smith soirée musicale, Doré Galleries.

30. Hilda Paull and Thudichum concert, St. James's Hall.
30. Lois Barker pianoforte and vocal recital, Bechstein Hall.
30. Audrey Richardson violin recital, Æolian Hall.
30. Xenia Beaver and Richard Brinkman vocal and violin recital, Æolian Hall.
30. John Powell pianoforte recital, Steinway Hall.

MAY.

1. May Harrison violin recital, Bechstein Hall.
1. Dr. Ludwig Wüllner vocal recital, Bechstein Hall.
1. A. Welton Fordham and C. Finucane Draper concert, Æolian Hall.
2. London Symphony Orchestra, conducted by Mr. Nikisch, Queen's Hall.
2. Godowsky pianoforte recital, Bechstein Hall.
2. Backhaus pianoforte recital, Æolian Hall.
2. Grossmith dramatic recital, Steinway Hall.
3 Concert Amalgamated Musicians' Union, London Coliseum.
4. Eveline Gerrish vocal recital, St. James's Hall.
4. Marian van Duyn vocal recital, Bechstein Hall.
4. Sigmund Beel violin recital, Bechstein Hall.
4. Joska Szigeti violin recital, Æolian Hall.
4 Mr. and Mrs. Thomas Meux's concert, Æolian Hall.
5. Gerhardt and Nikisch vocal recital, Bechstein Hall.
5. Ruby Bond vocal recital, Bechstein Hall.
5. José Gomez, Æolian Hall.
5. Maja Kjohler and Muriel Davenport Folksong recital, Æolian Hall.
5 Muriel Warwood violin recital, Steinway Hall.
6. Albani's concert, Queen's Hall.
6. Ada Tierney vocal recital, St. James's Hall.
6. Marjorie Evans violin recital, Bechstein Hall.
6. Jan Hambourg violin recital, Æolian Hall.
7. Charlotte Lund vocal recital, Bechstein Hall.
7. Mlle. de St Andre vocal recital, Bechstein Hall.
7. Antonia Dolores's vocal recital, Æolian Hall.
7. Carmen Vardou vocal recital, Æolian Hall.
7. Percy French dramatic recital, Steinway Hall.
8. Violet Anderson vocal recital, Bechstein Hall.
8. Dr. Ludwig Wüllner vocal recital, Bechstein Hall.
8. Catherine Aulsebrook concert, 24, Park Lane.
8. Alexander Heinemann vocal recital, Æolian Hall.
9. Mark Hambourg pianoforte recital, Albert Hall.
9. Emile de Vlieger 'cello recital, St. James's Hall.
9. London Symphony Orchestra, Mr. Nikisch, Queen's Hall.
9. Tina Lerner pianoforte recital, Bechstein Hall.
9. Backhaus pianoforte recital, Æolian Hall.
11. Ysaye and Pugno violin and pianoforte recital, Queen's Hall.
11. Le Mar vocal recital, Bechstein Hall.
11. Elizabeth O'Callaghan vocal recital, Bechstein Hall.

11. Amy Woodford-Finden concert. Æolian Hall.
11. Alexander Heinemann vocal recital, Æolian Hall.
12. Kussewitzky and London Symphony Orchestra, Queen's Hall.
12. Wilhelm Sachse orchestral concert, Queen's Hall.
12. Elena Gerhardt vocal recital, Bechstein Hall.
12. Frederic Austin and Howard Jones vocal and pianoforte recital, Bechstein Hall.
12. George Mackern concert, Æolian Hall.
12. Fermina Hoffmann and Marie Bender vocal and pianoforte recital, Æolian Hall.
12. Marie Roberts vocal recital, Steinway Hall.
13. Katie Parker and Isador Epstein violin and pianoforte recital, St. James's Hall.
13. Robin Overleigh vocal recital, Bechstein Hall.
13. Ida Kopelschny vocal recital, Bechstein Hall.
13. Alma Haas pianoforte recital, Steinway Hall.
13. Alma Stinzel pianoforte recital, Steinway Hall.
13. Jan Hambourg violin recital, Æolian Hall.
14. Philharmonic Concert, Queen's Hall.
14. Dettmar Dressel violin recital, Bechstein Hall.
14. Dorothea Crompton vocal recital, Bechstein Hall.
14. Tora Hwass pianoforte recital, Æolian Hall.
14. Agnes Stewart Wood violin recital, Æolian Hall.
15. Benno Schönberger pianoforte recital, Bechstein Hall.
15. Geza de Kresz violin recital, Bechstein Hall.
15. Marie Dubois pianoforte recital, Æolian Hall.
15. Vera French and London Symphony Orchestra, Æolian Hall.
15. Pattie Hornsby recital, Steinway Hall.
15. Paul Graener concert, Steinway Hall.
16. Mischa Elman and New Symphony Orchestra, Queen's Hall.
16. Sven Scholander vocal recital, Bechstein Hall.
16. Sergei Kussewitzky, Bechstein Hall.
16. Backhaus pianoforte recital, Æolian Hall.
18. Ysaye and Pugno violin and pianoforte recital, Queen's Hall.
18. Tilly Koenen vocal recital, Queen's Hall.
18. Marian Jay violin recital, Bechstein Hall.
18. Noel Fleming and Dorothy Ewens's vocal and violin recital, Bechstein Hall.
18. Ernest Sharp recital, Æolian Hall.
18. Alexander Heinemann vocal recital, Æolian Hall.
18. Bach Choir, Royal College of Music.
19. Elena Gerhardt vocal recital, Bechstein Hall.
19. Ella Ivimey violin recital, Bechstein Hall.
19. Irene St. Clair vocal recital, Æolian Hall.
19. Muriel Carryer vocal recital, Æolian Hall.
19. Barbara Battishill and Ruby Cobbett vocal recital, Steinway Hall.
20. Hegedüs's orchestral concert, Queen's Hall.
20. Hugo Heinz vocal recital, Bechstein Hall.
20. Dorothy Wiley vocal recital, Bechstein Hall.
20. Jan Hambourg recital, Æolian Hall.
20. Edith Wynne-Agabeg and Jessie Field vocal and pianoforte recital, Steinway Hall.
20. Emilia Conti vocal recital, Steinway Hall.
20. John Wilmott pianoforte recital, Salle Erard.
20. The Misses Eyre concert, Chelsea Town Hall.

20. Sarah Fennings violin recital, Suffolk Galleries.
21. Marie Hall and Queen's Hall Orchestra, Queen's Hall.
21. Willy Burmester violin recital, Bechstein Hall.
21. Ernest Groom vocal recital, Æolian Hall.
21. Mme. Larkcom pupils' vocal concert, Steinway Hall.
21. Mrs. Julian Clifford's *matinée*, Bridgewater House.
22. Dohnanyi and Dr. Hassler recital, Queen's Hall.
22. Victor Busst pianoforte recital, Bechstein Hall.
22. Rudolf Bauerkeller violin recital, Bechstein Hall.
22. Jeanne Blancard pianoforte recital, Steinway Hall.
22. Anita Sutherland vocal recital, Steinway Hall.
22. Joseph Holbrook chamber concert, Salle Erard.
23. "Empire Day" concert, Albert Hall.
23. London Choral Society, Queen's Hall.
23. Zimbalist orchestral concert, Queen's Hall.
23. Emile de Vliege's 'cello recital, St. James's Hall.
23. Last promenade concert of present series, St. James's Hall.
23. Helene Staegemann vocal recital, Bechstein Hall.
23. Backhaus pianoforte recital, Æolian Hall.
23. Marguerite Loriot violin recital, Steinway Hall.
25. Ysaye and Pugno violin and pianoforte recital, Queen's Hall.
25. London Symphony Orchestra, Tchaikovsky concert, Queen's Hall.
25. Martucci pianoforte recital, Bechstein Hall.
25. Mathilde Verne pianoforte recital, Bechstein Hall.
25. Ernest Sharpe vocal recital, Æolian Hall.
25. Folk song Quartet, Æolian Hall.
25. John Powell pianoforte recital, Steinway Hall.
25. Eugenie Boland vocal recital, Steinway Hall.
25. Meyer van Praag's benefit concert, Caxton Hall.
26. Wilhelm Ganz's Jubilee Concert, Queen's Hall.
26. London Symphony Orchestra under Kussewitsky, Queen's Hall.
26. Elena Gerhardt vocal recital, Bechstein Hall.
26. Jean Fyans vocal recital, Bechstein Hall.
26. Reinhold von Warlich vocal recital, Æolian Hall.
26. Eugenie and Virginie Sassard vocal recital, Æolian Hall.
26. Florence Etlinger recital, Steinway Hall.
26. Ethel Duthoit vocal recital, Steinway Hall.
26. Kitty Woolley and Florence Smith chamber concert, Salle Erard.
26. Jan Mulder's annual concert, Broadwood's.
27. Handel Society concert, Queen's Hall.
27. Phyllis Lett vocal recital, Bechstein Hall.
27. Roland Jackson vocal recital, Bechstein Hall.
27. Jan Hambourg violin recital, Æolian Hall.
27. Lois Knollys and Helen Egerton vocal and violin recital, Steinway Hall.
28. Queen's Hall Orchestra Concert, Queen's Hall.
28. Philharmonic Concert, Queen's Hall.
28. Julia Culp vocal recital, Bechstein Hall.
28. Hilda Barnes violin recital, Bechstein Hall.
28. Grace Thynne violin recital, Æolian Hall.
28. Gabrilowitsch pianoforte recital, Æolian Hall.
28. Sivori Levey musical reciter, Steinway Hall.

29. Kathleen Parlow orchestral concert, Queen's Hall.
29. Mme. Menzies vocal recital, Bechstein Hall.
29. Myrtle Meggy pianoforte recital, Bechstein Hall.
29. Johannes Tomscha violin recital, Æolian Hall.
29. Marie Stark, Herbert Fryer, and Oscar Eve evening concert. Æolian Hall.
30. London Symphony Orchestra, "The Wreckers," Queen's Hall.
30. Anna El-Tour vocal recital, Bechstein Hall.
30 Master Maurice Mirsky vocal recital, Bechstein Hall.
30. Backhaus, Æolian Hall.
30. The Misses Eyres' concert, Chelsea Town Hall.

JUNE

1. William Willes orchestral concert, conducted by Nikisch, Queen's Hall.
1. The Cologne Choral Union, Queen's Hall.
1. Mavel Crow and Emil Sauret vocal and violin recital, Bechstein Hall.
1. Susan Strong vocal recital, Bechstein Hall.
1. Cecil Fanning vocal recital, Æolian Hall.
1. Helen Mars *matinée*, Steinway Hall.
1. Evelyn Keepe dramatic recital, Steinway Hall.
2. Katherine Goodson and London Symphony Orchestra, Queen's Hall.
2. Oxford House Musical and Dramatic Association choral and orchestral concert, Queen's Hall.
2. Willy Burmester violin recital, Bechstein Hall.
2. Helene Staegemann vocal recital, Bechstein Hall.
2. Richard Buhlig pianoforte recital, Æolian Hall.
2. Mme. Svardström recital, Æolian Hall.
3. Arthur Shattuck pianoforte recital, Bechstein Hall.
3 Carlotta de Feo vocal recital, Bechstein Hall.
3. Jan Hambourg violin recital, Æolian Hall.
3. Arthur Helmore and Ulph Smith special recital, Steinway Hall.
4 South Hampstead Orchestra, Queen's Hall.
4. Gregory Hast vocal recital, Bechstein Hall.
4. Julia Culp vocal recital, Bechstein Hall.
4. Ernest Sharpe vocal recital, Æolian Hall.
4. Marie Wadia vocal recital, Æolian Hall.
4. Margaret Omar dramatic recital, Steinway Hall.
5. Cologne Choral Union concert, Queen's Hall.
5. Armando Lecomte morning concert, Bechstein Hall.
5. Boris Hambourg 'cello recital, Æolian Hall.
5. Donald Baxter recital, Æolian Hall.
5. Florence Etlinger vocal recital, Steinway Hall.
6. Tina Lerner pianoforte recital, Bechstein Hall.
6. Ethel Leginska pianoforte recital, Æolian Hall.
9. Clodia de Toussaint vocal recital, Bechstein Hall.
9. Jean Pyne vocal recital, Bechstein Hall.
9. Maria Theresa Maggi vocal recital, Æolian Hall.
9. George F. Boyle pianoforte recital, Steinway Hall.
10. Alys Lorraine vocal recital, Bechstein Hall.
10. William Willis pianoforte recital, Bechstein Hall.
10. Ethel Marsh and Reginald Davidson vocal and violin recital, Æolian Hall.

10. Harrison Hill's entertainment, Steinway Hall.
11. Miss Louis von Heinrich orchestral concert, Queen's Hall.
11. Ernst Lengyel pianoforte concert, Bechstein Hall.
11. Dr. Lulek vocal recital, Bechstein Hall.
11. Ernest Sharpe vocal recital, Æolian Hall.
11. Katherine Eggar concert, Æolian Hall.
12. Julia Culp, Bechstein Hall.
12. Charles Tree and Herbert Fryer vocal and pianoforte recital, Bechstein Hall.
12. Fanny Davies pianoforte recital, Æolian Hall.
12. Mme. Mackenzie Fairfax concert, Æolian Hall.
12. Earle Douglas concert, Steinway Hall.
12. Marie Roberts vocal recital, Steinway Hall.
13. Thomas Beecham orchestral concert, Queen's Hall.
13. Szigeti and Myrta Stubbs violin and pianoforte recital, Æolian Hall.
15. Saint-Saëns concert, Queen's Hall Orchestra, Queen's Hall.
15. La Société des Concerts d'Instruments Anciens, Bechstein Hall.
15. Cafetto vocal recital, Bechstein Hall.
15. Katherine Jones vocal recital, Æolian Hall.
15. Charles Clark vocal recital, Æolian Hall.
15. Nora and Frederica Conway dramatic and musical recital, Steinway Hall.
16. Clara Clemens and Marie Nichols vocal and violin recital, Bechstein Hall.
16. Marie O'Connor vocal recital, Bechstein Hall.
16. Percy Grainger pianoforte recital, Æolian Hall.
16. Dora Becker violin recital, Æolian Hall.
16. Sofie Menter pianoforte recital, Steinway Hall.
17. William Willis pianoforte recital, Bechstein Hall.
17. Marjorie Wigley pianoforte recital, Bechstein Hall.
17. Brabazon Lowther recital, Æolian Hall.
17. Alfred Kastner harp recital, Salle Erard.
18. Mary Layton's Ladies' Choir concert, Queen's Hall.
18. Ida Kopetschny vocal recital, Bechstein Hall.
18. Elise Kutscherra vocal recital, Bechstein Hall.
18. Ernest Sharpe vocal recital, Æolian Hall.
18. The Sisters Svärdström concert, Æolian Hall.
18. Ada Thomas and Dorothy Bridson pianoforte and violin recital, Steinway Hall.
18. Louise Desmaisons pianoforte recital, Salle Erard.
19. Sara Davies concert, Bechstein Hall.
19. George Menges concert, Æolian Hall.
19. Dr. Lierhammer vocal recital, Æolian Hall.
19. Reginald Dawson concert, Steinway Hall.
19. Eugenia von Klemm vocal recital, Steinway Hall.
20. "Golden Legend," with Handel Festival Choir, Crystal Palace.
20. Mischa Elman concert recital, Queen's Hall.
20. Sobrino vocal recital, Bechstein Hall.
20. Vera French violin recital, Æolian Hall.
20. Arthur Barbour vocal recital, Salle Erard.
22. Julia Culp and Paul Reimers vocal recital, Bechstein Hall.
22. Gertrude Peppercorn pianoforte recital, Bechstein Hall.
22. Lily West's pupils pianoforte recital, Æolian Hall.
22. Jeanne Blancard and Joseph Hollman sonata recital, Steinway Hall.
23. Paderewski pianoforte recital, Queen's Hall.

23. Arthur Friedlander choral and orchestral concert, Queen's Hall.
23. Kirkby Lunn vocal recital, Bechstein Hall.
23. Charles Normand vocal recital, Bechstein Hall.
23. British Musical Society concert, Æolian Hall.
23. Rheinhold von Warlich vocal recital, Æolian Hall.
23. Nora and Frederica Conway dramatic and musical recital, Steinway Hall.
23. Rev. Dr. Collisson recital, Steinway Hall.
23. Edith Allen ballad concert, Queen's Hall.
23. Sterling Mackinlay's pupils' concert, Salle Erard.
24. Melba's anniversary *matinée,* Covent Garden.
24. Royal Academy of Music orchestral concert, Queen's Hall.
24. Carlo Erici vocal recital, Bechstein Hall.
24. Louis van Hes vocal recital, Bechstein Hall.
24. Marguerite Tilleard pianoforte recital, Æolian Hall.
24. Sofie Menter pianoforte recital, Steinway Hall.
24. Emma Barnett pianoforte recital, Broadwood Rooms.
25. George Meader vocal recital, Bechstein Hall.
25. Halsted Little and Dora Becker vocal and violin recital, Bechstein Hall.
25. Ernest Sharpe vocal recital, Æolian Hall.
25. Heinemann vocal recital, Æolian Hall.
25. Decima Moore and Frank Haskoll musical *matinée,* Steinway Hall.
25. Ida Parry vocal recital, Steinway Hall.
26. Blanche Marchesi's pupils' operatic performance, Albert Hall.
26. Theo Crozier violin recital, Bechstein Hall.
26. Elise Kutscherra vocal recital, Bechstein Hall.
26. Dora Eshelby vocal recital, Steinway Hall.
27. Clara Butt and Kennerley Rumford concert, Albert Hall.
27. Pachmann pianoforte recital, Queen's Hall.
27. Leo Lossy violin recital, Bechstein Hall.
27. Clara Addison and Mary Craven vocal recital, Æolian Hall.
29. Rosa Olitzka vocal recital, Bechstein Hall.
29. Sigismond Stojowski pianoforte recital, Æolian Hall.
29. Irene Scharrer pianoforte recital, Æolian Hall.
29. Marie Mely concert, Steinway Hall.
29. Olivia Sconzia concert, Steinway Hall.
29. Marguerite Casalonga soirée musicale, Salle Erard.
30. Eva Katarina Lissmann and Carlotta Stubenrauch vocal and violin recital, Bechstein Hall.
30. Reinhold von Warlich vocal recital, Æolian Hall.
30. Julius du Mont pianoforte recital, Æolian Hall.
30. Emelie Lewis annual concert, Steinway Hall.
30. Richard Epstein annual concert, Salle Erard.

JULY.

1. Nicolay vocal recital, Bechstein Hall; Tilly Koenen vocal recital, Bechstein Hall.
1. The four Svärdström Sisters' vocal recital, Æolian Hall.
2. Sybil Lonsdale concert, Bechstein Hall.
2. Concert in aid of the Church Army League of Friends of the Poor—Æolian Hall.
3. Dorothy Wiley vocal recital, Bechstein Hall.
3. Bertha Scholefield concert, Æolian Hall.

OCTOBER.

1. Mr. Harold Bauer, pianoforte recital—Bechstein Hall.
3. Marie Hall, violin recital—St. James's Hall.
3. Mme. Carreño, pianoforte recital—Bechstein Hall.
3. Strings Club recital—Salle Erard.
5. Miss Madge Whittaker's vocal recital—Æolian Hall.
9. Mr. Joseph O'Mara, farewell concert—Bechstein Hall.
10. Miss Ellen Beck, vocal recital—Æolian Hall.
10. Mr. Rowsby Woof, violin recital—Bechstein Hall.
10. *Elijah,* by the Alexandra Palace Choral Society.
13. Mr. Albert Spalding's violin recital—Bechstein Hall.
15. Mr. Theodore Byard's song recital—Bechstein Hall.
15. Miss Foster-Salmond and Mr. Otto Meyer's vocal and pianoforte recital—Æolian Hall.
17. Mme. Carreño, pianoforte recital—Steinway Hall.
17. Miss Jessie Peake, pianoforte recital—Steinway Hall.
17. Mr. Frederick Moore, pianoforte recital—St. James's Hall.
17. Queen's Hall, Symphony concert.
19. Mr. Hans Brousil's chamber music concert—Bechstein Hall.
19. Mr. W. Higley's song recital—Æolian Hall.
20. Mr. A. Spalding's violin selections—Bechstein Hall.
20. Miss Janet Wheeler's evening with the pianoforte—Æolian Hall.
20. Miss Marthe Marcelli's violin recital—Bechstein Hall.
21. Wessely String Quartet—Bechstein Hall.
21. M. Ysaye's violin *matinée*—Queen's Hall.
21. Chamber Music Concert—Bechstein Hall.
22. Messrs. S. Webbe and Hans Neumann's sonata recital—Steinway Hall.
22. Miss Christine Brooks' vocal *matinée*—Bechstein Hall.
22. Miss Gwendolen Griffiths' 'cello selections—Æolian Hall.
22. Mr. E. Kreuz and Miss F. Kreuz's lyric evening—Salle Erard.
22. Chamber music by Miss Helen Egerton—Æolian Hall.
22. Misses M. Wadia and Myra Hess's vocal and pianoforte recital—Hampstead Conservatoire.
23. Miss E. Altemus's pianoforte *matinée*—Bechstein Hall.
24. Lyric selections by Misses L. and C. Arkandy—Steinway Hall.
24. Mr. Rudolph Ganz's pianoforte recital—Bechstein Hall.
24. Chappell ballad concert—Royal Albert Hall.
24. Vaughan Grey *matinée*—Æolian Hall.
26. London symphony concert—Queen's Hall.
26. Messrs. J. Powell and F. Harford's piano and vocal recital—Æolian Hall.
26. Miss D. Moggridge's evening with the pianoforte—Æolian Hall.
26. Mr. S. Master's concert—Assembly Rooms, Surbiton.
27. London Trio—Æolian Hall.
27. Miss Madge Murphy's violin *matinée*—Æolian Hall.
27. Lyrics by Miss E. Broughton—Steinway Hall.
28. Chamber Music Concert—Bechstein Hall.
28. Mr. H. R. Bird's recital—Bechstein Hall.
29. Broadwood concert—Æolian Hall.
29. Miss E. Digby O'Neill's entertainment in aid of University College Hospital—Bechstein Hall.

29. Mr. Hugo Heinz's vocal *matinée*—Æolian Hall.
29. Mr. Rudolph Ganz's pianoforte recital—Bechstein Hall.
30. Miss Jolanda Méró's pianoforte *matinée* Steinway Hall.
30 Concert by Albion Trio—Steinway Hall.
30. Pianoforte selections by Miss Lucy Polgreen—Æolian Hall.
31. London ballad concert—Royal Albert Hall.
31. Mischa Elman's violin *matinée*—Queen's Hall.
31. Misses A. McKenzie and Alys Turner's musical and dramatic recital—Steinway Hall.
31. Messrs. Rudolph Weinman and E. Goll's violin and pianoforte *matinée*—Bechstein Hall.
31. Chamber music by Mr. E. H. Thorne—Queen's Hall.
31. Miss A. Ellis's orchestral concert in aid of Hospital for Women—Æolian Hall.
31. Mme. E. O'Callaghan and Miss J. Heymann's vocal and pianoforte recital—Salle Erard.
31. Concert by Miss Liza Lehmann—Crystal Palace.
31. Devon and Cornish musical evening—Queen's Hall.

NOVEMBER.

1. Queen's Hall Orchestra, Queen's Hall.
1. London Symphony Orchestra, Royal Albert Hall.
2. Mr. Howard-Jones's Bach-Chopin Recital, Bechstein Hall.
2. Recitations by Mme. Lorraine-New, Æolian Hall.
2. Miss Elsa Delmar's Vocal *matinée*, Bechstein Hall.
3. Miss Agnes Nicholls's Vocal Evening, Bechstein Hall.
3. Barn-Phillips' Concert, Bechstein Hall.
3. Miss K. Eggar's programme of own compositions, Æolian Hall.
3. Lyric Selections by Miss Violet Defries, Broadwood Rooms.
3. Miss Lilian Evans's Violin Recital, Steinway Hall.
4. Mr. Ysaye's Violin *matinée*, Queen's Hall.
4. Father Vaughan's Charity Entertainment, Royal Albert Hall.
4. "Omar Khayyam" (1st part), by London Choral Society, Queen's Hall.
4. Chamber Music Concert, Bechstein Hall.
4. Mme. Perelli's lyric selections, Bechstein Hall.
5. *Elijah*, by Royal Choral Society, Royal Albert Hall.
5. Brinsmead Popular Concert, St. James's Hall.
5 Miss E. Altemus's Pianoforte *matinée*, Bechstein Hall.
5 Mr. Godfrey Nutting's programme of own compositions, Æolian Hall.
5. Mr. C. Roff's Vocal Recital, Bechstein Hall.
5. Broadwood Concert, Æolian Hall.
5. Miss Leonora Russell's Musical Evening, Steinway Hall.
5. Strolling Players' Amateur Orchestral Society, Queen's Hall.
6. Mrs. H. Hutchinson's Song Recital, Bechstein Hall.
6. Concert by Albion Trio, Steinway Hall.
6. Lyrics by Mr. W. Higley, Æolian Hall.
6. Miss Jolanda Méró's pianoforte *matinée*, Steinway Hall.
6. Mr. Theodore Spiering's Violin Programme, Æolian Hall.

7. Mme. Melba's Farewell Concert, Royal Albert Hall.
7. Miss Fanny Davies and Mr. Gervase Elwes' *matinée*, Crystal Palace.
7. Miss Evelyn Suart's Pianoforte Recital, Bechstein Hall.
7. Miss Elvira Gambogi's Lyric Evening, Bechstein Hall.
7. Chappell Ballad Concert, Queen's Hall.
8. Queen's Hall Orchestra, Queen's Hall.
8. London Symphony Orchestra, Royal Albert Hall.
9. London Symphony Concert, Queen's Hall.
9. Messrs. André Mangeot and P. Augiéras' Violin and Pianoforte Recital, Steinway Hall.
9. St. Petersburg String Quartet, Bechstein Hall.
9. O'Neil Phillips's Pianoforte *matinée*, Æolian Hall.
9. Cine-matinée, London Pavilion.
10. Miss E. Double and Mr. S. Gardner's Lyric Recital, Bechstein Hall.
10. Miss Aimée Nugent's Dramatic and Musical Entertainment, Steinway Hall.
10. Misses W. Hooke and D. Densham's Piano and 'Cello Concert, Public Hall, Croydon.
11. Messrs. S. Webbe and Hans Neumann's Sonata Recital, Steinway Hall.
11. Miss Feilding Roselle's Vocal *matinée*, Bechstein Hall.
11. Chamber Music Concert, Bechstein Hall.
11. Lyric Selections by Miss Marie Altona, Æolian Hall.
11. Misses Kato van der Hoeven, N. Gunning, and J. Heymann's Recital, Steinway Hall.
12. Concert by Philharmonic Society, Queen's Hall.
12. Miss Bramley Taylor's Vocal *matinée*, Steinway Hall.
12. Songs by Mme. Le Mar, Æolian Hall.
12. Mr. C. Crabbe and Misses M. Law and A. Fenning's Recital, Bechstein Hall.
13. Misses D. Swainson and Marjorie Howard's Pianoforte and Violin Recital, Æolian Hall.
13. Mr. C. W. Clark's Vocal *matinée*, Æolian Hall.
13. Pianoforte Selections by Mr. Edward Goll, Bechstein Hall.
13. Hampstead Chamber Music Concert, Hampstead Town Hall.
13. Mr. Basil Gauntlett's Pianoforte Recital, Steinway Hall.
14. Queen's Hall Symphony Concert, Queen's Hall.
14. Kubelik's Violin *matinée*, Crystal Palace.
14. Mr. Busoni's Pianoforte Programme, Bechstein Hall.
14. London Ballad Concert, Royal Albert Hall.
14. Mr. L. Denza's Musical Evening, Bechstein Hall.
14. Pianoforte Recital, by Mr. W. Willis, Æolian Hall.
14. *Judith*, Alexandra Palace.
15. London Symphony Orchestra, Royal Albert Hall.
15. Queen's Hall Orchestra, Queen's Hall.
15. Vocal and Instrumental Concert in aid of Playgoers' Club Pantomime Fund, His Majesty's.
16. Mr. R. Newman's Annual Concert, Queen's Hall.
16. Messrs. J. Powell and F. Harford's Piano and Vocal *matinée*, Æolian Hall.
16. Vocal Selections by Miss Henriette Schmidt, Bechstein Hall.
16. Mr. R. Burnett's Vocal Recital, Æolian Hall.
16. Myrtle Meggy's Orchestral Concert, Croydon Public Hall.

17. Violin Selections by Miss M. Bentwich, Bechstein Hall.
17. Mr. R. Buhlig's Pianoforte Programme, Æolian Hall.
17. Mr. J. Lindner's 'Cello Recital, St. James's Hall.
17. English Lyrics, by Mr. Gervase Elwes, Bechstein Hall.
17. Miss Vera Margolies' Pianoforte *matinée*, Steinway Hall.
17. Miss Myra Hess's Pianoforte Recital, Æolian Hall.
18. Wessely String Quartet, Bechstein Hall.
18. Miss Haidée Voorzanger's Violin *matinée*, St. James's Hall.
18. Misses R. Borowski's and Grosholz's Pianoforte and Vocal Programme, Steinway Hall.
18. Concert by R.A.M., Queen's Hall.
18. Imperial Quartet, Queen's Hall.
18. Pianoforte Selections by Miss Marian Gilhooly, Queen's Hall.
18. Classical Concert Society, Bechstein Hall.
18. Dramatic Programme by Miss Mary Levien, Steinway Hall.
19. Broadwood Concert, Æolian Hall.
19. Miss E. Leginska's Pianoforte *matinée*, Æolian Hall.
19. Misses Griffiths and Poole's Chamber-Music Recital, Steinway Hall.
19. Lyrics by Miss Miriam Wohl, Bechstein Hall.
20. Miss C. Butt and Mr. Kennerley Rumford's Concert, Royal Albert Hall.
20. Mr. W. O'Donnell's 'Cello Programme, St. James's Hall.
20. Miss K. R. Heyman and Mr. H. Connell's Pianoforte and Vocal Recital, Æolian Hall.
21. St. Petersburg String Quartet, Bechstein Hall.
21. Chappell Ballad Concert, Queen's Hall.
21. Mr. A. Cortot's Pianoforte *matinée*, Æolian Hall.
21. Misses Iona Robertson and J. Glynn's Evening Concert, Æolian Hall.
21. College of Violinists' Annual Recital, Queen's Hall.
21. Brighton Municipal Orchestra, St. James's Hall.
22. Queen's Hall Orchestra, Queen's Hall.
22. London Symphony Orchestra, Royal Albert Hall.
23. London Symphony Orchestra, Queen's Hall.
23. Mr. Stuart Edwards's Vocal *matinée*, Æolian Hall.
23. Miss Helen Troye's Recital, Æolian Hall.
23. Operatic Selections by Mme. Perelli, Bechstein Hall.
23. Miss G. Azulay's Pupils' Concert, Steinway Hall.
24. Mr. R. Buhlig's Pianoforte Recital, Æolian Hall.
24. The London Trio, Æolian Hall.
24. Pianoforte *matinée* by Mr. Sapellnikoff, Steinway Hall.
24. Grimson String Quartet, St. James's Hall.
24. Messrs. Cyril Scott and F. Austin's Piano and Vocal Concert, Bechstein Hall.
25. Mischa Ehman's Violin Recital, Queen's Hall.
25. Mr. Backhaus's Pianoforte *matinée*, Queen's Hall.
25. Chamber Music Concert, Bechstein Hall.
25. Pianoforte Selections by Mr. A. Cortot, Æolian Hall.
25. Mr. Mugellini's Pianoforte Recital, Bechstein Hall.
25. Mr. H. Hodge's Musical Evening, Steinway Hall.
26. Concert by Philharmonic Society, Queen's Hall.

26. Mr. Wladimir Cernikoff's Pianoforte Recital, Æolian Hall.
26. Lyrics by Mme. Le Mar, Æolian Hall.
26. St. Petersburg String Quartet, Bechstein Hall.
26. Miss Hugolin Haweis's Dramatic and Musical Entertainment, Steinway Hall.
26. Miss E. Holmstrand's Vocal Programme, Bechstein Hall.
27. Mme. Donalda's Charity Concert, Queen's Hall.
27. Misses C. Trask and J. Field's Vocal and Pianoforte Recital, Æolian Hall.
27. Vocal Selections by Mrs. G. Swinton, Bechstein Hall.
27. Mr. A. Broadley's 'Cello Programme, St. James's Hall.
27. Hampstead Chamber Concert, Hampstead Town Hall.
27. Misses M. A. Case and W. Hunter's Vocal and Pianoforte Recital, Æolian Hall.
27. Mr. P. Elliott's *matinée* of his own compositions, Steinway Hall.
28. Queen's Hall Symphony Orchestra, Queen's Hall.
28. Mr. Frederic Lamond's Beethoven *matinée*, Bechstein Hall.
28. Hambourg Subscription Concert, Æolian Hall.
28. Mme. E. O'Callaghan and Miss J. Heymann's Vocal and Pianoforte Recital, Salle Erard.
28. Misses Perkins and May's Pupils' Demonstration, Broadwood Rooms.
28. London Ballad Concert, Royal Albert Hall.
29. London Symphony Orchestra, Royal Albert Hall.
29. Queen's Hall Orchestra, Queen's Hall.
29. Concert in aid of Benevolent Funds of the N.A.T.E., His Majesty's.
30. Mr. J. Linden's 'Cello Recital, St. James's Hall.
30. Mr. Vernon Warner's Pianoforte *matinée*, Æolian Hall.
30. Lyrics, by Miss Winifred Mayes, Bechstein Hall.
30. Scotch Musical Festival, Royal Albert Hall.
30. Recitations by Miss M. Irene Simpson, Æolian Hall.
30. Reeves Quartet, Steinway Hall.

DECEMBER.

1. Mr. R. Buhlig's pianoforte *matinée*, Æolian Hall.
1. Vocal programme by Miss Irene Spong, Bechstein Hall.
1. Pianoforte selections by Miss Phyllis Emanuel, Steinway Hall.
1. Mr. Arturo Tibaldi's violin recital, Æolian Hall.
1. Mr. Sapellnikiff's Concert, Steinway Hall.
2. Classical Concert Society, Bechstein Hall.
2. *Samson and Delilah*, by London Choral Society, Queen's Hall.
2. Mr. John Munro's vocal *matinée*, Æolian Hall.
2. Songs by Mr. Roland Jackson, Bechstein Hall.
2. Chamber music concert, Steinway Hall.
3. *Francesca*, by Royal College of Music, His Majesty's.
3. *The Golden Legend*, by Royal Choral Society, Royal Albert Hall.
3. Brinsmead concert, St. James's Hall.
3. Miss E. Leginska's recital of American music, Æolian Hall.
3. Operatic and dramatic entertainment in aid of house of shelter, Bechstein Hall.
3. Violin selections, by Miss M. Bentwich, Bechstein Hall.

S. Broadwood concert, Æolian Hall.
3. Lyrics by Miss Agnes Coates, Steinway Hall.
4. Mme. Blanche Marchesi's farewell recital, Bechstein Hall.
4. Recitations by Miss Dorothea Spinney, Steinway Hall.
4. Mr. and Mrs. A. Hobday's viola and pianoforte programme, Æolian Hall.
4. Stock Exchange Orchestral and Choral Society, Queen's Hall.
5. Chappell Ballad Concert, Queen's Hall.
5. Mrs. George Swinton's recital, Bechstein Hall.
5. Miss Marie Hall's violin *matinée*, Crystal Palace.
5. Hambourg subscription concert, Æolian Hall.
5. Mr. Christian Carpenter's pianoforte programme, Steinway Hall.
5. Barns-Phillips combination, Bechstein Hall.
7. London Symphony Concert, Queen's Hall.
7. Misses Myra Hess and M. Wadia's piano and vocal recital, Æolian Hall.
7. Chamber music by Misses Griffiths and Poole, Steinway Hall.
7. Pianoforte selections by Mr. J. Powell, Æolian Hall.
7. Mr. W. G. Alcock's organ programme, Brixton Independent Church.
7. Royal College of Music Patron's Fund concert, Bechstein Hall.
8. Mr. R. von Warlich's lyric *matinée*, Æolian Hall.
8. Miss Dorothy De Vin's violin recital, Bechstein Hall.
8. Marion Scott Quartet, Æolian Hall.
8. Miss Scialtiel's musical afternoon, Steinway Hall.
8. Mme. Norman Salmond's programme, Bechstein Hall.
9. Concert by Société D'Instruments-Anciens, Bechstein Hall.
9. Grimson String Quartet, St. James's Hall.
9. Miss D. Grinstead's pianoforte recital, Bechstein Hall.
9 West Ham Philharmonic Society, Stratford Town Hall.
9. Chamber music concert, Queen's Hall.
9. Miss K. R. Heyman's Chopin programme, Steinway Hall.
9. Miss Margel Gluck, Æolian Hall.
10. Messrs. S. Webbe and Hans Neumann's sonata recital, Steinway Hall.

10. 'Cello selections by Miss Maud Bell, Æolian Hall.
10. Lyrics by Miss Dorothy Wiley, Bechstein Hall.
10 Recitations by Miss Tita Brand, Æolian Hall.
10. Miss Mary Winifred's violin recital, Salle Erard
10. Strolling Players' Amateur Orchestral Society's concert, Queen's Hall.
11. Concert by Philharmonic Society, Queen's Hall.
11. Pianoforte selections by Miss Tosta de Benici, Æolian Hall.
11. Miss Carmen Hill and Mr. M. Thompson's vocal programme, Bechstein Hall.
11. Recitations by Miss Dorothea Spinney, Steinway Hall.
11. Selections from *Carmen* and *The Magic Flute*, by Operatic Class of R.A.M.
11. Wagner recital, St. Stephen's, Walbrook.
11. Chamber music, Hampstead Town Hall.
11. Bach's "Christmas Oratorio," St. Anne's, Soho.
11 Miss Berthe Duranton and Mr. F. Mesnier's pianoforte and violin concert, Salle Erard.
12. Queen's Hall Orchestra—Queen's Hall.
12. Mr. Benno Schonberger's pianoforte *matinée*—Bechstein Hall.
12. Miss Mary Field's dramatic recital—Steinway Hall.
12. Hambourg subscription concert—Æolian Hall.
12. *Hiawatha*, Alexandra Palace.
14. Mr. Arthur Newstead's pianoforte *matinée*—Bechstein Hall.
14. Misses A. Rolda and E. Altemus's vocal and pianoforte recital—Bechstein Hall.
14. Lyric and instrumental concert, by Messrs. Gervase Elwell and James Friskin—Æolian Hall.
15. London Trio—Æolian Hall.
15. Audrey Chapman orchestra—Queen's Hall.
15. Welte-Mignon *matinée*—Steinway Hall.
16. Grimson String Quartet—St. James's Hall.
16. Smoking concert by Royal Amateur Orchestral Society—Queen's Hall.
16. Misses Griffiths' recital—Salle Erard.
17. Broadwood concert—Æolian Hall.
19. Elgar's new symphony, by London Symphony Orchestra—Queen's Hall.
19. Hambourg subscription concert—Æolian Hall.
19. Miss Rosamond Ley's pianoforte *matinée*—Bechstein Hall.

OBITUARY.

Alexander, Annie Emma. February 5.
Alwyn, Vivian. Aged 18 months. July 16.
Arrandale, Gilbert. Aged 39. June 4.
Arthur (Geary), Samuel. Aged 39. July 17.
Aston, George. Aged 22. March 1.
Baily, Harrington. December 14.
Ballard, Thomas. September 13.
Bare, Emma. June 1.
Bare, Thomas. June 1.
Barker, Annie Alpha. November 23.
Barrett, Eliza. December 20.
Barrett, Henry J. May 7.
Barrington, H. H. August 1.
Baugh, Alice Lydia. Aged 43. June 15.
Beagle, G. H. April 20.
Beattie, Mrs. Nancy. Aged 61. July 13.
Beckwith, J. W. November 14.
Belding, Henry. January 18.
Benone, Alfred. October 4.
Benson, George. Aged 83. February 17.
Berte (Bryant), Charles Herbert. Aged 33.
  May 26.
Bion, Victor. Aged 66. March 17.
Blake, Minnie. October 5.
Blamphin, Stephen. Aged 54. January 6.
Bolton, Charles. Aged 79. July 29.
Booker (Dingle), George. Aged 49. March 25.
Bourke, George Arlington. Aged 48. March
  30.
Bowden (Delavante), John Walter. Aged 83.
  April 16.
Boyle, Herbert. Aged 43. January 21.
Brabourne, John. December 10.
Bradford, Thomas. May 13.
Brinsmead, John. Aged 93. January 17.
Brodie, Matthew. Aged 45. January 3.
Brown, Isabella. February 6.
Bruce, Mary Ann. February 24.
Brull (Pepi). Joseph. Aged 36. December 9.
Burnett, Joan. March 9.
Burroughs, Jane. March 18.
Byrt, Wilfred Grantly. Aged 32. April 29.
Caddick, Sophia. February 15.
Carlin, Charles. Aged 49. July 6.
Carlyon, Frank. Aged 36. November 22.
Chadwick, Thomas. September 3.
Chadwick, William Thorpe. Aged 57. June
  22.
Chichester (Baker), Henry. April 1.
Chute, W. C. Macready. Aged 25. January
  12.
Cinquevalli, Adelina. March 3.
Clark, Allan. June 26.
Clarkson, Dot. March 17.
Clay, Edwin. Aged 56. January 6.
Clifford, Charles. Aged 29. July 16.
Clinton, Dudley. October 1.
Closs, William F. August 8.
Cole, Jennie. March 12.
Comber, Mrs. April 25.
Congo, William. October 18.
Cook, James A. March 27.
Coppée, Francois. Aged 66. May 23.
Corri, Mme. Ida Gilliess. Aged 67. March 2.
Cory-Thomas, Lambert. November 14.
Courteney, Neville. Aged 48. January 11.
Cousins, Rosie. Aged 31. September 20.
Crane, Jessie (Mrs. H. J.). November 25.
Craston, Annie. June 3.
Curzon, Beatrice. November 2.

Cuthbert, Edmund. September 13.
Danter, John. Aged 64. February 19.
Darnley, Mrs. J. H. October 22.
Davenport, Clara. Aged 68. January 1.
Davis, Miss Ada. Aged 64. March 10.
De Frece, Hettie. Aged 33. December 23.
Denville, Alice. June 7.
De Pinna, David. February 15.
De Rees, James. December 2.
Dodd, William. March 23.
Doyle (Gould), Lila. October 11.
Dvas, Ada. Aged 64. March 10.
Edouin, Willie. April 14.
Elcock, Mary. September 9.
Elsmore, Arthur. July 12.
Evans, Eliza. January 6.
Fairbanks, Robert. January 15.
Farren, William. Aged 82. September 26.
Favert, Mme. November 11.
Fell, Thomas Kennedy, M.R.C.S. Aged 56.
  June 26.
Fernandez (Jig), Tom. March 8.
Firth, Harriet. January 15.
Fischer, Harry. November 20.
Fleming, Herbert Aged 52 October 23.
Florence, Tom. December 11.
Foot, John (George Conway). Aged 27. Feb-
  ruary 3.
Forde, Mrs. H Athol. June 26.
Forrest, Arthur. October 2.
Forth, Eric. November 4.
Fowler, Elizabeth. January 9.
Francis, William. Aged 62. January 10.
Franklin, John Campbell. June 30.
Fuller, Frank. Aged 64. January 29.
George (Ratcliff), Henry. Aged 60. April 26.
Gilbert, Michael George. Aged 77. February
  15.
Gillam, J. W. E. (Dudley Clinton). October 1.
Gillin, Delia. January 19.
Glover, Eleanor. Aged 25. May 29.
Clyn, Gertrude. Aged 52. August 3.
Goddard, Harry. Aged 57. June 16.
Grace, Edmund. Aged 62. December 18.
Graham, Gertrude. January 18.
Graham, Nixon. January 13.
Greaves, Thomas. Aged 71. July 9.
Griffiths, William. Aged 77. September 26.
Guest, Rosa Annie Aged 58. August 3.
Halévy, Ludovic. Aged 74. May 8.
Hamilton, David. January 7.
Hanbury, Lily (Mrs. Herbert Guedalla). Aged
  34. March 5.
Hanbury, Pattie. July 10.
Hardyman, Elizabeth. August 10.
Hargreaves, Mrs. John. Aged 51. July 13.
Hart, Jerry. jun Aged 23. April 30.
Harvey, John. Aged 62. December 26.
Hayes, Eva May. September 23.
Hayes, Percy. Aged 42. May 22.
Haynes, Rosetta (Rosie Lewis). October 19.
Hayward, Arthur (A H. Ward). January 7.
Hazlehurst, Jack. Aged 19. November 26.
Heath, Frank. Aged 52. December 16.
Henderson, William. June 6.
Hilton, Alec (Alexander Torrie). July 31.
Hindson, Violet. January 26.
Hoare, Ryton. Aged 24. November 24.
Howard, Sydney Lester. November 28.
Howe, J. B. Aged 78. March 9.

Hudspeth, Matilda (Marie Bramah). February 16.
Hunter (Smith), Agnes Emma. Aged 52. May 2.
Hunter, Jane. March 8.
Jarvis, Ernest Herbert. Aged 27. August 21.
Jefferson, Mrs. Arthur (Madge Metcalfe). December 1.
Johnson, Ottilie. January 6.
Keats, Sydney Carl. Aged 24. November 77.
Keith (Hayden), Madoline Marie. Aged 24. November 9.
Kemble, John. June 11.
Kilburn, Harry. Aged 42. November 29.
Lanner, Mme. Katti. Aged 80. November 15.
Lee (Tasker), Edgar. Aged 57. December 14.
Lees, Herbert Thomas. Aged 27. November 23.
Leighton, Margaret (Mrs. Margaret Alcott). March 3.
Leith, Leslie. Aged 32. January 22.
Lennon, John. April 17.
Lester, Harry. October 5.
Lewis, Elsie. February 2.
Lichtenstein, Ethel C.M. November 16.
Lockwood, Thomas. March 27.
Loller, Charles P. Aged 28. September 19.
Longmore, Mrs. S. A. March 24.
Lovel, Gertrude. Aged 40. November 12.
Lovesey, A. F. (Frank). Aged 33. February 20.
Lundy, Harry Aged 45. July 29.
Lyon, Margaret. January 20.
Lyons, Robert. November 28.
Macarte, Adelaide. July 26
Macmahon, George. November 28.
Macmillan, Alick. Aged 21. June 14.
Macready. Mrs. Cecile Louise Frederica. Aged 81. September 19.
Mann, David. May 22.
Marchesi, Salvatore. February 20.
Marinelli, Mme. Buettner. November 9.
McCann, Mary Jane. December 2.
McNally, J. P. Aged 49. September 20.
Melford, Austin. Aged 53. January 23.
Melville, John. October 15.
Merritt, James. Aged 57. March 30.
Metcalfe, George Taylor. Aged 24. March 10.
Minter, Mrs. Hal. November 5.
Mitchell, Josephine. June 25.
Molloy, Joseph Fitzgerald. March 19.
Monteith, Benjamin. February 5.
More (Robertson), Tom. Aged 37. July 30.
Morgan, Clifford. April 20.
Morrell, Daisy. September 8.
Mosedale, Edward. Aged 74. November 17.
Moss, Mrs. M. August 2.
Nelson, Eliza (Mrs. H. T. Craven). Aged 81. March 21.
Nelson, Harry G. January 30.
Noakes, Richard John. Aged 33. April 24.
Norman, Alfred D. September 20.
Novello, Mme. Clara. Aged 89. March 12.
O'Flynn, Michael. Aged 60. August 21.
O'Gorman, Mrs. Joe (Jessica Grace). Aged 34. May 22.
O'Shea, John. Aged 76. April 19.
Osrani, Jean. Aged 49. May 26.
O'Sullivan, Denis. February 1.
Palmer, Harriett Ann (Mrs. A. P. Boswell). Aged 52. November 15.
Parker, Mrs. Jane. Aged 74. July 13.
Parkes, W. S. March 31.
Pateman, Bella. Aged 64. January 30.
Paulus (Paul Hahans). Aged 63. June 1.
Peach, George Robert. September 3.
Pike (Devereux), Ernest Lingard. Aged 29. December 25
Pook, Seth. March 4.
Potter, Joseph. Aged 64. October 10.

Price, Henry Perkins. November 21.
Prince, Mrs. December 6.
Quick, John William (Jess Jean). May 10.
Richardson, Nell. February 11.
Ripon, George. May 26.
Robbins, Rose Jane. March 29.
Robertson, James. Aged 46. July 14.
Rochelle, Edward. April 16.
Rogerson, Miss Amy. July 6.
Romilli, Alexander. November 5.
Roper, Susannah. January 17.
Rorke, John. April 26.
Rosalind, Myra (Mrs. J. J. Lloyd). Aged 40. April 6.
Rowden, Elizabeth Isabella. July 30.
Russell, Countess. September 22.
Samwells, Roland. Aged 49. December 25.
Sarasate, Señor Pablo. September 20.
Sardou, Victorien. November 8.
Saville, George. March 10.
Scott, Louie. April 20.
Shaw, Robert. Aged 55. January 10.
Shelton, Mrs. George. June 15.
Shenton, F. S. June 23.
Sheppard, Edwin James. Aged 76. December 7.
Shervell, Emma. February 2.
Simmons, William Arthur (Little Jimmy). November 9.
Sivado (Brown), Robert. October 25.
Slaughter, Walter. Aged 48. March 2 .
Soutar, Robert. Aged 81. September 28.
Spence, Beatrice (Charlotte Beatrice Cooton). Aged 44. November 3.
Statham, Francis Reginald. Aged 64. March 4.
Stephens, Tom. January 8.
Stephens, Tom. January 15.
Sullivan, Mary. August 16.
Sutton, Frank Cane. Aged 42. May 6.
Swanborough, Edward. Aged 67. December 21.
Swan, Charles. Aged 80. June 2.
Symon, Rev. T. H. (St. Bernard Wyntour). Aged 27. August 22.
Tansley, Emma. Aged 71. March 22.
Taylor, Henry Esher. January 7.
Tempest Ada (Mrs. Charles Darrell). June 16.
Temple, Ellen. January 14.
Thompson, Lydia. Aged 72. November 18.
Thornton, Louis Edmund. March 9.
Titherington, Eli. December 9.
Tomkinson, Annie. Aged 57. November 4.
Toms, Cuthbert Imric. Aged 27. September 27.
Topham, Frederic Aged 50. November 10.
Tucker, Harold Herbert Christol. July 16.
Varley, Louisa Rose. Aged 75. February 6.
Verno, Jess. Aged 38. February 22.
Verren, Milner. Aged 34. July 29.
Wade, Tom. Aged 47. October 25.
Wallace, Mary. Aged 42. January 25.
Waller, John. Aged 59. March 30.
Wardroper, Walter. Aged 60. March 4.
Ware, Hibbert. Aged 36. September 14.
Warner (Pratt), Harry. October 21.
Watkin-Wynne, Mrs. W. July 31.
Watson, Paddy. Aged 62. December 12.
Weight, Hannah Louisa. Aged 56. November 14.
Westcott, John Smith. January 16.
Weston, John. October 1.
White, Mrs. V. C. July 31.
Wigglesworth, Hugh. Aged 44. January 6.
Wilson, Ada (Mrs. Gordon). November 20.
Williams, Edward. Aged 64. March 27.
Willson, F. Stuart. Aged 37. July 4.
Wilson, Robert Thorpe (Thorpe Sheffield). Aged 42. April 20.
Winstanley, Annie Nadine. December 5.
Wood, Arthur O. January 5.
Wray, Albert George. Aged 26. January 19.

LONDON GUIDE.

PARTICULARS OF THE PLACES OF ENTERTAINMENT IN THE COUNTY OF LONDON
AND THE SUBURBS.

PRINCIPAL THEATRES.

ADELPHI THEATRE, Strand.—Proprietors, Messrs. A. and S. Gatti; Manager, Mr. Herbert Rolland.

ALDWYCH THEATRE, W.C.—Proprietors, Hicks, Ltd. Mr. Brandon Thomas's season. Manager, Mr. Cecil Barth.

APOLLO THEATRE, Shaftesbury Avenue, W. —Proprietor, Mr. Henry Lowenfeld; Lessee and Manager, Mr. Tom B. Davis; Acting-Manager, Mr. A. C. Belsey. Holding capacity, 1,500. Prices of seats, 1s. to £5 5s. Depth and width of stage, 26ft. by 73ft. 30ft. opening. 17 dressing-rooms.

ARTILLERY THEATRE, Woolwich. — Managers, Messrs. Arthur Carlton and Sam Duckworth; Acting-Manager, Mr. Chisholm Taylor; Musical Director, Q.-M.-Sergt. G. Dawes. Holding capacity, 900. Prices of seats, 21s., 3s., 2s. 6d., 2s., 1s. 6d., 1s., 6d. Depth and width of stage, 40ft. by 70ft. 30ft. opening. 10 dressing-rooms. Printing required: 900 lithos., 450 sheets, walls, 3,000 circulars. Thursday matinée. Band rehearsals, 12.30 p.m. Adjacent theatre barred, T.R., Woolwich. Electricity, 210 volts. No kinematograph box.

BOROUGH THEATRE, Stratford, E.—Proprietress, Mrs. C. Ellis Fredericks; Manager, Mr. Fred Fredericks; Acting-Manager, Mr. Frank Rothsay; Box Office, Mr. Arthur Barnes; Musical Director, Mr. Ben Barrow; Master Carpenter, Mr. George Saunders; Scenic Artist, Mr. Arthur Hillyard. Holding capacity, 3,000. Prices of seats, 6d. to 4s.; boxes, £1 1s., £1 11s. 6d., £2 2s. Depth of stage, 40ft., 15ft. dock; width of stage, 65ft.; proscenium, 30ft. wide by 24ft. high. 18 dressing-rooms. Printing required, 3,500 sheets and 1,000 lithos., etc. Wednesday matinée, 2.30 Band rehearsals, Monday, 11.0.

BRITANNIA THEATRE, Hoxton, N.—Lessee and Manager, Mr. Thomas Barrasford.

BRIXTON THEATRE, S.W.—Proprietors, Messrs. W. and F. Melville; Manager, Mr. Will S. Taylor.

BROADWAY THEATRE, New Cross, S.E.—Lessees, Moss's Empires, Ltd.; Managing Director, Mr. Oswald Stoll; Acting-Manager, Mr. Bertram Iles; Musical Director, Mr. S. Clarke Richardson; Booking Circuit, Moss's Empires Theatres; Scenic Artist, Mr. John Leonard. Holding capacity, 2,500. Prices of seats, 6d. to 3s. Depth and width of stage, 36ft. by 75ft.; proscenium; width, 30ft. by 24ft. high. 12 dressing-rooms. Printing required, 2,500 pictorial, 1,000 d.c. letterpress and pictorial, 1,000 circulars. Wednesday matinée, 2.30. Band rehearsals, 11 a.m. Theatres or halls within three miles' radius barred. Electric light: Continuous current, 100 volts. Kinematograph box established.

CAMDEN THEATRE, Camden Town, N.W.—Proprietors, London Theatres of Varieties, Limited. Managing Director, Mr. Walter Gibbons. Manager, Mr. Leslie Hughes. Booking circuit, Gibbons—Barrasford. Holding capacity, 2,500. Depth of stage, 35ft. 10in. to iron, 38ft. 6in. to floats; width, wall to wall, 73ft. 11in.; proscenium, 32ft. wide. 19 dressing-rooms. Time of band rehearsals, 1 p.m. Electric light, 220 voltage direct. Kinematograph box established.

CASTLE THEATRE, Richmond. Opens occasionally. Holds 700.

COMEDY THEATRE, Panton Street, Haymarket, S.W.—Lessee and Manager, Mr. Arthur Chudleigh; Acting-Manager, Mr. Leonard Lillies; Musical Director, Mr. H. E. Haines. Holds about 800. Prices, boxes, £4 4s., £3 3s., £1 11s. 6d.; other seats, 10s. 6d., 7s. 6d., 5s., 4s., 2s. 6d., 1s. Depth of stage, 24 ft. 4 ins. Width of opening, 24 ft. 4 in. Height, without frame border, 24 ft. Distance between side walls, 47 ft.; between fly rails. 30 ft. Dressing-rooms, 12.

CORONET THEATRE, Notting Hill, W.—Proprietors, Robert Arthur's Theatres Co., Limited. Manager, Mr. Eade Monteflore.

COURT THEATRE, Sloane Square, S.W.—Licensee and Manager, Mr. J. H. Leigh; Lessee, Miss Mouillot.

COVENT GARDEN THEATRE (Royal Opera House).—Proprietors. The Grand Opera Syndicate Ltd.; General Manager, Mr. Neil Forsyth; Acting-Manager. Mr. Percy Eales; Musical Director, Mr. Percy Pitt. Holding capacity over 2,000. Prices of seats for English season, January-February. 19·9: 1s. 6d. to £4 4s.

CRITERION THEATRE, Piccadilly, W.—Proprietors, Messrs. Spiers and Pond; Lessee, Sir Charles Wyndham; Manager, Mr. A. F Henderson; Stage Manager, Mr. Reginald Walter; Musical Director, Mr. E. Lockwood Holding capacity, 500. Prices of seats. 10s 6d., 7s. 6d., 5s., 4s., 2s. 6d.; boxes, £6 6s. to £1 1s. Depth of stage, 21ft. 6in.; width between side walls, 48ft.; proscenium opening, 25ft. 10 dressing-rooms and a greenroom, also small office for stage manager. Electric light, direct and alternating, 220 volts.

CROYDON GRAND THEATRE.—Manager, Mr. Roland Daniel; Musical Director, Mr. V. Chalder. Double license. Holding capacity: Number of persons, 1,800; amount, £140. Stage measurements: Depth, 50ft.: width, 44ft.; width between fly rails, 32ft. 6in.; height to grid, 55ft.; proscenium opening, 27ft. 6in. Electric light. Amount of printing required, 1,500 sheets and 600 d.c. lithos. Usual matinée day, Thursday. Voltage 110. All halls and towns within five miles barred.

CROYDON THEATRE ROYAL. — Lessees, Moss's Empires, Limited. Managing Director, Mr. Oswald Stoll. Double license. Holding capacity: Number of persons, 1,500 (about); amount, £85 (about). Stage measurements, 50ft. by 25ft. Electric light. Amount of printing required, 600 wall sheets, 500 lithos. Usual matinée day, Wednesday. Time of band rehearsal, 1 p.m.

CRYSTAL PALACE THEATRE, S.E.—Proprietor, Mr. J. Bannister Howard; Manager, Mr. J. E. Sharpe; Musical Director, Mr. Leonard Gautier. Holding capacity, about 2,300. Prices of seats, 3s., 2s., 1s. 6d., 1s., 6d. Depth and width of stage, 27ft. by 38ft.; proscenium opening, 24ft. 6in. 10 dressing-rooms. Particulars of printing required, 24, 18, 12, 6, and d.c. Wednesday matinée. Band rehearsals, 12. Electric light, 100 voltage. Kinematograph box established.

DALSTON THEATRE, N.E.—Lessees and Managers, Messrs. Milton Bode and Edward Compton; Acting-Manager, Mr. W. R. King. Holding capacity, 4,000. Thursday matinée.

DALY'S THEATRE, Cranbourn Street, W.C. —Proprietors, Executors of late Augustin Daly; Lessee and Manager, Mr. George Edwardes; Acting-Manager, Mr. G. E. Minor; Musical Director, Mr. Harold Vicars. Holding capacity, 1,300. Prices of seats: Private boxes, 2½ to 5 guineas; stalls, 10s. 6d.; balcony, 7s. 6d.; upper circle (front), 5s.; other rows, 4s.; pit, 2s. 6d.; gallery, 1s. Depth and width of stage, 70ft. by 60ft.; proscenium width, 30ft.; height, 31ft. 20 dressing-rooms. Electric light, 100 volts.

DRURY LANE THEATRE ROYAL, W.C.—Patent theatre. Proprietors, Theatre Royal, Drury Lane, Limited; Managing Director, Mr. Arthur Collins; Acting-Manager, Mr. C. H. Taylor; Musical Director, Mr. J. M. Glover. Holding capacity, about 3,000. Prices of seats, 1s. 6d. to £7 7s. Depth of stage, about 100ft.; width from wall to wall, about 100ft.; proscenium, 50ft. to 50ft. (about). Electric light, 100 volts continuous current.

DUKE OF YORK'S THEATRE, St. Martin's Lane, W.C.—Proprietors, Mr. and Mrs. Frank Wyatt; Lessee and Manager, Mr. Charles Frohman; General Manager for Mr. Charles Frohman, Mr. W. Lestocq; Business Manager, Mr. James W. Mathews; Musical Director, Mr. John Crook. Holding capacity, 1,100. Prices of seats, from 1s. to £4 4s. Depth of stage, 33ft.; width between walls, 43ft.; proscenium width, 26ft. 6in. Electric light, 100 volts continuous current.

EDMONTON NEW THEATRE ROYAL AND OPERA HOUSE.—Proprietor, Mr. Joseph Lewis Samuel Moss; Manageress, Mrs. A. H. B. Moss; Musical Director, Mr. Arnold B. J. Moss. Double license; full excise. Holding capacity: Number of persons, about 1,000; amount, over £40. Prices of seats, 4d. to 1s. 6d. Depth of stage, 35ft.; width, 45 ft.; proscenium, 25ft. by 25ft. 5 dressing-rooms. Printing required, 600 sheets, walls, 400 window lithos. Thursday matinée. Band rehearsals, Monday, 6 p.m. All theatres and halls in Edmonton and Tottenham barred. Lighted by gas.

ELEPHANT AND CASTLE THEATRE, S.E.—Proprietor, Mr. Chas. Barnard; Manager, Mr. Sidney Barnard; Musical Director, Mr. Wm. Stephenson; Booking Circuit, Barnard. Holding capacity, 3,000. Prices of seats, 4d., 6d., 1s., 1s. 6d., 2s. Depth of stage, 35ft.; width, 70ft.; proscenium, 31 ft. wide. 11 dressing-rooms. Thursday matinée, 1 p.m. Electric light, 220 volts. Kinematograph box established.

FULHAM THEATRE, S.W.—Lessee and Manager, Mr. Robert Arthur; General Manager, Mr. Frederick Merer; Musical Director, Mr. A. M. Moon. Holding capacity, 2,000. Prices of seats, 6d. to 5s. Depth of stage, 31ft. working; width, 73ft. 6in.; proscenium, 29ft. 6in. 9 dressing-rooms. Printing required, 2,000 d.c. sheets. Wednesday matinée

at 2.30. Band rehearsals, 1.30 p.m. No adjacent theatres or halls barred. Electric light, alternating and 200.

GAIETY THEATRE, Strand, W.C.—Managing Director, Mr. George Edwardes; Manager, Mr. W. H. Dawes.

GARRICK THEATRE, Charing Cross Road.—Proprietor, Sir W. S. Gilbert; Lessee and Manager, Mr. Arthur Bourchier; Business Manager, Mr. Thomas Stevens; Musical Director, Mr. Edmund Rickett. Holding capacity, 1,120. Prices of seats: Boxes, 2gs. to 4gs.; stalls, 10s. 6d.; balcony stalls, 7s. 6d.; dress circle, 6s.; upper circle, 5s. and 4s.; pit, 2s. 6d.; gallery, 1s. Depth of stage, 32ft.; width, 52ft.; proscenium, 28ft. by 30ft. 15 dressing-rooms. Electric light, 100 volts continuous.

GREENWICH THEATRE, S.E.—Licensee, Mr. Arthur Carlton; Managing Director, Mr. Edward Fish. L.C.C. licence for stage plays.

HAYMARKET THEATRE, Haymarket, S.W.—Lessee and Manager, Mr. Frederick Harrison; Acting-Manager, Mr. Horace Watson; Musical Director, Mr. Claude Fenn-Leyland. Holding capacity, 1,000. Prices of seats, 2s. 6d. to 10s. 6d. reserved, 1s. and 2s. 6d. unreserved. Depth and width of stage, 42ft. by 55ft.; proscenium, 27ft.; 15 dressing-rooms. Electric light, 100 volts.

HICKS THEATRE, Shaftesbury Avenue, W.—Lessee and Manager, Mr. Charles Frohman; Acting-Manager, Mr. Oscar Barrett, junr. Holding capacity, 1,100. Prices of seats: Boxes, £3 3s. and £2 2s.; stalls, 10s. 6d.; dress circle, 7s. 6d. and 6s.; upper circle, 5s. and 4s.; pit, 2s. 6d.; gallery, 1s.

HIS MAJESTY'S THEATRE, Haymarket, S.W.—Proprietor and Manager, Mr. H. Beerbohm Tree; General Manager, Mr. Henry Dana; Musical Director, Mr. Adolf Schmid. Holding capacity, 1,500. Prices of seats, from 1s. to £3 3s. Depth and width of stage, 50ft. by 90ft.; proscenium, 34ft. 6in. 18 dressing-rooms. Electric light. Two independent circuits.

HOXTON VARIETY THEATRE, Pitfield Street.—Proprietor, Mr. J. G. Stubbs; Lessee, Mr. Matt Raymond; Manager, Mr. Fred Boustead; Musical Director, Mr. T. Young. Holding capacity, 1,800. Prices of seats, 2d. to 1s. Depth and width of stage, 14ft. by 23ft. 5 dressing-rooms. Matinées, Monday and Saturday. Band rehearsals, 12 noon. No adjacent theatres or halls barred. Electric light, 240. Kinematograph box established. Running pictures only at present, and probably for next two years.

KENNINGTON THEATRE, S.E.—Proprietors, Robert Arthur Theatres Co., Ltd.; Manager, Mr. H. B. Brandreth; Musical Director, Mr. Jullien H. Wilson; Scenic Artist, Mr. McKie. Full license. Holding capacity, 2,000; amount, £247. Stage: Depth, 40ft.; width, 60ft.; between fly rails, 40ft.; proscenium, 30ft. Electric light, 100 volts, direct current. Amount of printing required varies from 2,000 to 3,500. Usual *matinée* day, Thursday.

KILBURN THEATRE ROYAL, N.W.—Licensee, Mr. Richard Chadwick.

KING'S THEATRE, HAMMERSMITH.—Proprietor, Mr. J. B. Mulholland; Acting-Manager, Mr. Norman Walters; Musical Director, Mr. Horace Middleton. Holding capacity, about 2,400, representing just over £250. Prices of seats: Stalls, 5s., 4s.; circles, 4s., 3s.; pit stalls, 2s. 6d.; promenade, 2s.; amphitheatre, 1s.; pit, 1s.; gallery, 6d. Depth and width of stage, 40ft by 72ft., proscenium opening, 34ft. 13 dressing-rooms. Thursday matinée at 2.30. Electricity; alternating voltage, 110.

KINGSWAY THEATRE, Gt. Queen Street, W.C.—Proprietress and Manageress, Miss Lena Ashwell; Acting-Manager, Mr. Walter Maxwell; Stage-Manager, Mr. Maitland Dicker; Musical Director, Mr. S. Hawley. Holding capacity, 567. Prices of seats: Boxes, £2 12s. 6d., £1 11s. 6d.; orchestra stalls, 10s. 6d.; dress circle, 7s. 6d. and 5s.; pit stalls, 5s.; upper circle, 4s.; amphitheatre, 3s., 2s.; pit, 2s. 6d. All seats may be booked. Proscenium measurements, 25ft. by 18ft.; width of stage, 38ft. 7 dressing-rooms. Electric light; voltage, 200.

LYCEUM THEATRE, Wellington Street, Strand, W.C.—Popular Playhouses, Ltd.; Managing Directors, Messrs. H. R. Smith and Ernest Carpenter; Acting-Manager, Mr. W. F. Crowe.

LYRIC OPERA HOUSE, Hammersmith, W.— Licensee and Manager, Mr. Wentworth Croke.

LYRIC THEATRE, Shaftesbury Avenue, W.— Lessee, Mr. William Greet; Manager, Mr. Tom B. Davis; Acting-Manager, Mr. A. C. Belsey; Musical Director, Mr. Leonard Chalk; Holding capacity, 1,500. Prices of seats, 1s. to £5 5s. Depth and width of stage, 40ft. by 70ft.; proscenium, 29ft. 6in. 20 dressing-rooms.

MARLBOROUGH THEATRE, Holloway Road, N.—Proprietors, Messrs. Stevens and Buchanan; Manager, Mr. Murray Herriot; Treasurer, Mr. Ambrose Taylor; Musical Director, Mr. C. Elcock. Prices: Boxes, £2 2s., £1 1s.; other seats, 5s., 4s., 3s., 2s. 6d., 2s., 1s. 6d., 1s., 6d.

NEW ROYALTY THEATRE. — Proprietress, Miss Kate Santley; Lessee, Mr. Tom B. Davis; Manager, Mr. A. C. Belsey. Holding capacity about £60 people (£250). Prices of seats, 2s. 6d. to £4 4s. (English seasons). Depth of stage, 24ft.; width, 45ft.; proscenium, 24ft. by 22ft. 16 dressing-rooms.

NEW THEATRE, St. Martin's Lane, W.C.— Proprietor, Sir Charles Wyndham; Manager, Mr. H. Armitage; Musical Director, Mr. A. Maclean. Holding capacity, approximately 1,000. Prices of seats: Stalls, 10s. 6d.; dress circle, 7s. 6d. and 6s.; upper circle, 5s. and 4s.; boxes, £3 3s. and £1 11s. 6d.; pit, 2s. 6d.; gallery, 1s. Depth of stage, 42ft. in the centre, but is greater at P.S. and less at O.P.; width of stage, 55ft. 9in., wall to wall. Proscenium measurements: Width, 31ft. 6in.; height, 26ft. 9in.; under fly floor, 23ft. 3in.; fly, rail to rail, 42ft. 18 dressing-rooms. Electric light, voltage 100.

THE PLAYHOUSE, Northumberland Avenue.— Lessee and Manager, Mr. Cyril Maude; General Manager, Mr. Alfred Turner; Musical Director, Mr. John Ansell. Holding capacity, 640. Prices of seats: Stalls, 10s. 6d.; balcony stalls, 7s. 6d.; balcony, 5s.; upper boxes, 2s. 6d.; gallery, 1s. Every seat can be booked. Depth of stage, 26ft.; proscenium opening, 26ft. 6in. 14 dressing-rooms. Electric light, 200 volts.

PAVILION THEATRE, Mile End Road, E.— Lessee, Mr. Laurence Cowen; Manager, Mr. Gordon; Stage Manager, Mr. George Taylor; Musical Director.

PRINCE OF WALES THEATRE.—Proprietors, The Executors of the late Mr. Edgar Barnes; Lessee and Manager, Mr. Frank Curzon; General Manager Mr. J. B. Vaughan; Musical

Director, Mr. J. A. de Orellana. Prices of seats, 1s. to £4 4s. Depth of stage, 25ft. 6in.; width, 70ft.; proscenium, 30ft. by 27ft. 11 dressing-rooms.

QUEEN'S THEATRE, Shaftesbury Avenue.— Sole Manager, Mr. Tom B. Davis; Acting-Manager, Mr. A. C. Belsey.

ROYAL COUNTY THEATRE, Kingston-on-Thames. — Proprietors, the Kingston-on-Thames Theatre Co., Limited; Managing Director, Mr. Peter Davey; Musical Director, Mr. Hugh Rignold; Resident Scenic Artist, Mr. George Miller. Holding capacity, about 1,200. Prices of seats: Dress circle, 3s.; orchestra stalls, 2s. 6d.; pit, 1s.; gallery, 6d.; private boxes, 21s. During variety seasons the prices are reduced. Depth of stage, 42ft.; width, 58ft.; proscenium, 23ft. by 24ft. 10 dressing-rooms. Particulars of printing required: About 1,000 sheets, which are posted on the theatre's reserved stations. Wednesday matinée at 2.30. Band rehearsals, Monday at 11. No first-class theatre is barred, but the small theatres and fit-up halls in the neighbourhood are absolutely barred. Electric light, 105 alternating. Kinematograph box established. During the off seasons the theatre is run with high-class varieties (twice nightly). (No barring.)

ROYAL STRATFORD, E.—Proprietress, Mrs. C. Ellis Fredericks; Manager, Mr. Fred Fredericks; Acting-Manager, Mr. Sam Fredericks; Musical Director, Mr. Ben Barrow; Master Carpenter, Mr. Wm. Alders; Scenic Artist, Mr. Wm. Hillyard. Holding capacity, 1,200. Seats, 4d. to 1s. 6d.; boxes, 10s. 6d. and £1 1s. Depth and width of stage, 30ft. by 40ft.; proscenium, 22ft. 8 dressing-rooms. Printing required, 1,000 sheets, 500 lithos. Band rehearsal, Monday, 11 a.m.

ST. JAMES'S THEATRE, S.W.—Sole Lessee and Manager, Mr. George Alexander; General Manager, Mr. Charles T. H. Helmsley; Stage Manager, Mr. E. Vivian Reynolds; Musical Director, Mr. William Robins. Holding capacity, 1,130. Prices of seats: Stalls, 10s. 6d.; dress circle, 7s. 6d.; upper circle, 5s. and 4s.; pit, 3s.; gallery, 1s.; boxes, £4 4s. Depth of stage, 53ft.; width, 54ft. in front, 31ft. at back; proscenium, height 26ft., width 26ft. 6in. 16 dressing-rooms. Electric light, direct current, voltage 107.

SAVOY THEATRE.— Proprietress and Manageress, Mrs. D'Oyly Carte; Acting-Manager, Harry P. Towers; Musical Director, Mr. François Cellier; Stage Manager, Mr. Albert James; Box Office, Mr. Richard Weaver. Holding capacity, 1,100. Prices of seats, £5 5s., £2 2s., 10s. 6d., 7s. 6d., 5s., 4s., 2s. 6d., and 1s. Depth of stage, 30ft.; width, 62ft.; proscenium measurements, 30ft. by 30ft. 18 dressing-rooms. Electric light, voltage, 100 direct.

SCALA THEATRE, Charlotte Street, W.—Proprietor, Dr. E. Distin-Maddick. Holding capacity, 1,500. Prices of seats: Boxes, £4 4s.; stalls, 10s. 6d.; staircase stalls, 7s. 6d. and 5s.; balcony, 4s. and 3s.; pit, 2s. 6d.; gallery, 1s. Depth of stage, 54ft.; width, 59ft.; proscenium, 30ft. 4in. 20 dressing-rooms. Electric light, continuous, 220.

SHAFTESBURY THEATRE.—Lessee, Mr. H. B. Irving; Proprietors, The Lancaster Trustees; Manager, Mr. W. T. Cunningham; Acting-Manager, M . J. B. Glover; Musical Director, Mr. J. Meredith Ball; Stage Manager, Mr. Tom Reynolds; Box Office, Mr. J. W. Sheppard. Prices of seats, 1s. to 3 guineas. Depth of stage, 32ft.; width, 64ft. 12 dressing-rooms.

SHAKESPEARE THEATRE, Clapham, S.W.—
Lessees, Messrs. Wm. Bennett and H. G. D
Bennett; Manager, Mr. H. G. Dudley Ben
nett.

TERRY'S THEATRE, Strand, W.C.—Pro-
prietor, Mr Edward Terry; Lessee, Mr.
Forbes Robertson; Manager, Mr. Shad
Frost; Stage Manager, Mr. Ian Robertson.

VAUDEVILLE THEATRE, Strand, W.C.—Proprietors and Managers, Messrs. A. and S
Gatti; Acting-Manager, Mr. Herbert Clark;
Musical Director, Mr. Edward Jones. Holding capacity, 770. Prices of seats: Stalls,
10s. 6d.; boxes, £4 4s. and £3 3s.; dress
circle, 7s. 6d.; lower circle, 5s.; upper circle,
4s.; pit, 2s. 6d.; gallery, 1s. Depth of stage,
22ft. 8in.; width, between walls 40ft., between fly rails, 27ft.; proscenium, width
21ft. 8½in., height 17ft. 8 dressing-rooms.
Electric light, continuous, 100 volts.

WALDORF THEATRE, Aldwych, W.C.—Proprietors, Waldorf Productions, Limited;
Managing Director, Mr. Henry R. Smith;
Musical Director, Mr. J. Steir. Holding
capacity, £328 at full West End prices, £256
at present prices. Prices of seats: Boxes,
£4 4s. and £2 2s.; stalls, 10s. 6d. and 7s. 6d.;
dress circle, 6s.; upper circle, 4s.; pit, 2s.;
gallery, 1s. Depth and width of stage, 35ft.
by 70ft.; proscenium, 31ft. 6in. wide.
Electric light, 200 volts; two separate supplies. Re-opened on November 28, 1908,
after being closed for sixteen months.

WEST LONDON THEATRE, Edgware Road.—
Proprietor, Mr. William Bailey; Manager,
Mr. William Bailey, jun.; Musical Director,
Mr. Percy Kurntz; Scenic Artist, Mr. William
Charles. Holding capacity, about 1,800.
Prices of seats, 6d., 9d., 1s., 1s. 6d., 2s.,
Boxes 7s. 6d. and 10s. 6d. Depth and width
of stage, 60ft. by 34ft.; proscenium, 24ft. 9
dressing-rooms. Printing required, two 24-
sheets, four 18's, forty 6's, 600 upright double
crown, pictorial lithos. Letterpress supplied
by management. No matinées except during
pantomime. Band rehearsals, six o'clock
Monday. No adjacent theatres or halls
barred. Gas, but electricity for kinematograph. Kinematograph box established.

PRINCIPAL MUSIC HALLS.

THE ALHAMBRA, Charing Cross Road, W.C.
—Proprietors, the Alhambra Co., Limited;
Managing Director, Mr. Alfred Moul; Business Manager and Secretary, Mr. H. Wood-
ford; Musical Director, Mr. G. W. Byng;
Scenic artist, Mr. E. H. Ryan. Prices of
seats, 6d. to £4 4s. Depth and width of
stage, 40ft. by 62ft.; proscenium, 36ft. by
29ft. 17 dressing-rooms. Band rehearsals,
Monday, 12 o'clock. Electric light, 100 volts
continuous. Kinematograph box established.
Barring as per arrangement.

BALHAM EMPIRE, S.W.

BATTERSEA PALACE, S.W.—Proprietors, the
Macnaghten Vaudeville Circuit; Director-
General, Mr. Frank Macnaghten. Band re-
hearsal, 12 noon. Bars Balham Hippodrome
(Duchess), Chelsea Palace, Grand (Clapham),
Granville (Walham Green), and Putney Hip-
podrome.

BEDFORD PALACE, Camden Town, N.W.—
Licensee and Managing Director, Mr. B. P.
Lucas. Band rehearsal, 1 p.m. Bars Isling-
ton Hippodrome, Euston, Islington Empire,
Holloway Empire, Metropolitan, and Sadler's
Wells.

BOW PALACE.—Proprietors, The Macnaghten
Vaudeville Circuit; Director General, Mr.
Frank Macnaghten. Bars Paragon, Poplar
Hippodrome, Queen's (Poplar), and Stratford
Empire.

CAMBERWELL EMPIRE, S.E.—Proprietors,
Empire, Camberwell, Limited; Managing
Director, Mr. Jesse Sparrow; Manager, Mr.
Percy Ford; Acting-Manager, Mr. Gus Dau-
ter; Musical Director, Mr. Frank Hurst.
Holding capacity, 2,000. Prices of seats, 2d.,
4d., 6d., 9d., 1s., 1s. 6d., boxes 7s. 6d., 10s. 6d.
Depth and width of stage, 30ft. by 32ft.;
proscenium, 70ft. 8 dressing-rooms. No
matinee. Band rehearsals, 2 p.m. Adjacent
hall barred, Palace, Camberwell. Electric
light, alternating, voltage 220. Kinematograph box established. Bars Camberwell
Palace, Peckham Hippodrome (late Crown),
Empress, South London, Star (Bermondsey),
and the Surrey.

CAMBERWELL PALACE, S.E.—Proprietors,
London Theatres of Varieties, Ltd.; Manag-
ing Director, Mr. Walter Gibbons; Manager,
Mr. A. W. Deer. Band rehearsal, 2 p.m.
Bars Camberwell Empire, Peckham Hippo-
drome (late Crown), Empress (Brixton),
South London, Star (Bermondsey), and the
Surrey.

THE CANTERBURY THEATRE OF VARIE-
TIES, Westminster Bridge Road.—Proprietors, the Canterbury and Paragon, Limited;
Manager, Mr. Chas. W. Adams; Acting-Manager, Mr. H. C. Robbins; Musical Director
Mr. Horace Sheldon. Booking circuit, Syn
dicate halls. Prices of seats: Boxes for four
10s. 6d.; fauteuils, 1s. 6d. (bookable in advance 3d. extra); stalls, 1s. (bookable 3d.
extra); pit, 9d.; balcony, 6d.; gallery, 3d.
Depth of stage, 34ft. 6in.; width, wall to
wall, 60ft., between fly rails 42ft.; proscenium, height 31ft. 6in., width 29ft. 6in.
6 dressing-rooms. No matinées. Band rehearsals, two o'clock Mondays. Adjacent
halls barred, Surrey and Camberwell Palace.
Electric light, alternating, 110 voltage. Kinematograph box established. Bars Star (Bermondsey) and Surrey.

CHELSEA PALACE, King's Road, S.W.—Managing Director, Mr. Henri Gros; Manager,
Mr. J. Norman Berlin; Acting-Manager, Mr.
George B. Andrews. Booking circuit, Henri
Gros. Prices of seats, 3d. to 10s. 6d. Depth
and width of stage, 31ft. 3in. by 80ft., wall
to wall; proscenium opening, 29ft. 6in.;
wings, 18ft. 9 dressing-rooms. Band rehearsals, 12 noon. Electric light, 100 alternating and 200 direct. Kinematograph box
established. Bars Battersea Palace, Grand
(Clapham), and Granville (Walham Green).

CROUCH END HIPPODROME, N.—Licensee,
Mr. W. H. Burney. Middlesex County
Council licenses for music and dancing and
stage plays. Booked in conjunction with
the Syndicate Halls. Band rehearsal, 1.30.
Bars Finsbury Park Empire and Holloway
Empire.

CROYDON EMPIRE PALACE.—Proprietors,
the London Theatres of Varieties, Limited.
Holds 2,000. Band rehearsal, 1 p.m.

DUCHESS PALACE, Balham, S.W. (Balham
Hippodrome).—Proprietors, London Theatres
of Varieties, Ltd.; Managing Director, Mr.
Walter Gibbons. Booking circuit, Gibbons-
Barrasford. Band rehearsals, 1.30. Bars
Battersea Palace.

EALING HIPPODROME, W.—Licensee, Mr.
Walter Gibbons. Middlesex County Council
license for music and dancing and stage
plays. Band rehearsal, 1.30 p.m.

EAST HAM PALACE, E.—Proprietors, United Varieties Syndicate, Limited; Directors, Messrs. Henri Gros, Henry Tozer, and Joseph Davis; Manager, Mr. Albert E. Hill; Acting-Manager, Mr. Harry B. Wincote; Musical Director, Mr. W. S. Bassett. Holding capacity, 2,000. Prices of seats: Stalls, 1s. and 1s. 6d.; circle, 1s.; pit, 6d.; gallery, 3d. Depth and width of stage, 31ft. by 64ft. 6in.; proscenium, 30ft. 6in. wide, 27ft. 9in. high. 9 dressing-rooms. Electric light, 480 direct. Double license. No hall within barred area.

EMPIRE, Leicester Square, W.C.—Manager, Mr. H. J. Hitchins; Acting-Manager, Mr. A. M. Aldin. Barring as per arrangement.

EMPRESS THEATRE OF VARIETIES, Brixton, S.W.—Proprietors, The Empress Theatre of Varieties, Ltd.; Manager, Mr. Nelson Francis; Acting-Manager, Mr. Francis Winchcombe; Musical Director, Mr. R. Allington; Booking Circuit, Gibbons, Barrasford. Holding capacity, 1,500. Prices of seats, 4d. to 2s. Depth and width of stage, 40ft. to 30ft.; proscenium, 40ft. 7 dressing-rooms. Wednesday and Saturday matinées, pictures only. Band rehearsals, Monday, 1 o'clock. Electric light, 110 voltage. Kinematograph box established. Bars Camberwell Empire.

EUSTON PALACE, Euston Road, N.W.—Proprietors, The Variety Theatres Consolidated, Ltd.; Manager, Mr. Fred McAvoy; Acting-Manager, Mr. Arthur Opferman; Musical Director, Mr. Victor Opferman. Holding capacity, 2,500. Prices of seats: Boxes, 10s. 6d. and 7s. 6d.; stalls, 2s. and 1s. 6d.; circle, 1s.; pit, 6d.; gallery, 3d. Depth and width of stage, 50ft. by 60ft.; proscenium, 29ft. 6in. 12 dressing-rooms. Monday matinée. Band rehearsals, 12 o'clock. Electric light, 220 continuous. Kinematograph box established. Bars Bedford, Islington Empire, and Sadler's Wells.

FINSBURY PARK EMPIRE, N.—Proprietors, Moss's Empires, Ltd.; Licensee, Mr. Oswald Stoll. In course of construction on a site at the junction of St. Thomas's Road and Prah Road, Finsbury Park, N. Bars Crouch End Hippodrome, Islington Hippodrome, and Stoke Newington Palace.

FORESTERS MUSIC HALL, E.—The Macnaghten Circuit; Director-General, Mr. Frank Macnaghten. Bars Hackney Empire, Paragon, Poplar Hippodrome, Rotherhithe Hippodrome, Shoreditch Hippodrome, Shoreditch Empire, Shoreditch Olympia, and Star (Bermondsey).

GATTI'S PALACE, Westminster Bridge Road, S.E.—Licensees, Giacomo Corazzi and Luigi Corazzi. Closed. Will probably re-open during 1909.

GRANVILLE, WALHAM GREEN, S.W.—Manager, Mr. R. W. Duce. Band rehearsal, 2 p.m. Bars Battersea Palace, Chelsea Palace, Grand (Clapham), Hammersmith Palace, and Putney Hippodrome.

GRAND PALACE OF VARIETIES, Clapham Junction, S.W.—Proprietors, London Theatres of Varieties, Ltd.; Manager, Mr. A. W. Deer; Acting-Manager, Mr. A. J. Taylor; Musical Director, Mr. W. Silverman; Booking Circuit, Gibbons, Barrasford; Scenic Artist, Mr. A. Berlin. Prices of seats: Private boxes, 10s. 6d., 7s. 6d., 5s.; orchestra stalls, 1s.; grand circle, 6d.; pit, 4d.; gallery, 2d. Seats reserved, 3d. extra. Depth of stage, from back wall to footlights, 30ft.; width of stage, from wall to wall, 67ft.; proscenium opening. 30ft. by 28ft. 9in.; width of stage, from wall to wall, 67ft.; 7 dressing-rooms. Band rehearsals, Monday, at 1.30. Electric light; continuous current;

voltage, 110. Kinematograph box established. Bars Battersea Palace, Chelsea Palace, and Granville.

GREENWICH PALACE, S.E.—Bars New Cross Empire and Queen's (Poplar).

HACKNEY EMPIRE, N.E. Proprietors, Moss's Empires, Limited; Manager, Mr. Percy Percival; Musical Director, Mr. Grecco. Rehearsal, 1 p.m. Bars Foresters', Paragon, Shoreditch Empire, Shoreditch Hippodrome, Shoreditch Olympia, Bow Palace, and Stoke Newington Palace.

HAMMERSMITH PALACE, W.—Booked in conjunction with the Gibbons tour (this hall will probably be rebuilt at the end of the spring season, 1909). Bars Granville and Shepherd's Bush Empire.

HENGLER'S CIRCUS, Argyll Street, W.—Proprietors, London Theatres of Varieties, Ltd.; Managing Director, Mr. Walter Gibbons; Manager, Mr. Foster C. Marner; Musical Director, Mr. James Sales. Holding capacity, 2,000. Prices of seats, 6d. to 5s.; private boxes, 1 to 3 guineas. 42-ft. circus ring. 25 dressing-rooms. Matinées daily. Band rehearsals, Monday, 12.0. Electric light, 210. Kinematograph box established. This hall will be re-constructed and opened as the London Palladium on August Bank Holiday. Bars Alhambra, London Coliseum, Empire, London Hippodrome, Middlesex, Oxford, Palace, London Pavilion, and Tivoli.

HOLBORN EMPIRE, W.C.—Proprietors, London Theatres of Varieties, Ltd.; Managing Director, Mr. Walter Gibbons; Manager, Mr. Leslie Conroy. Music and dancing license. Stage, 24ft. deep, 29ft. wide. Proscenium, 29ft. Electric light, own plant. Bars Alhambra, Coliseum, Empire, London Hippodrome, London Pavilion, Middlesex, Oxford, Tivoli, and Palace.

HOLLOWAY EMPIRE, Holloway Road, N.—Proprietors, Moss's Empires, Ltd.; Manager, Mr. Bertie Ralland; Musical Director, Mr. Fred Camp; Booking Circuit, Moss-Stoll. Prices of seats: 10s. 6d., 7s. 6d., 5s., boxes; 1s. 6d., 1s., 6d., 4d., 3d. No matinée. Band rehearsals 1 o'clock. Kinematograph box established. Bars Bedford, Crouch End Hippodrome, and Islington Hippodrome.

ILFORD EMPIRE, E.—In course of construction.

ISLINGTON EMPIRE, Upper Street, N.—Proprietor, Mr. Walter Gibbons; Manager, Mr. B. Adams; Acting-Manager, Mr. T. Murray; Musical Director, Mr. A. Petersen; Booking Circuit, Gibbons-Barrasford; Scenic Artist, Mr. Birling. Holding capacity, 3,000. Prices of seats: Fauteuils, 1s.; stalls, 8d.; circle, 6d.; pit, 4d.; gallery, 2d. Depth and width of stage, 30ft. by 70ft.; proscenium, 32ft. 9 dressing-rooms. Band rehearsals, 1 o'clock. Adjacent halls barred: Collins', Bedford, Shoreditch Hippodrome, Olympia, and Empire, Stoke Newington Palace, Euston, and Sadler's Wells. Electric light, 110 volts. Kinematograph box established.

ISLINGTON HIPPODROME, Islington Green, N. Booked in conjunction with the Syndicate Halls. Bars Bedford, Euston, Finsbury Park Empire, Islington Empire, Sadler's Wells, Shoreditch Empire, Shoreditch Olympia, and Stoke Newington Palace.

KILBURN VAUDEVILLE THEATRE, N.W.—Licensee, Mr. H. W. S. Chilcott. Now in course of erection on a site at 7-11, The Parade, Kilburn High Road, N.W. Bars the Metropolitan.

LEWISHAM HIPPODROME, S.E.—Licensee, Mr. A. A. W. Grist. In course of erection on a site at 135-9, Rushey Green, Lewisham

LONDON COLISEUM, St. Martin's Lane, W.C. —Proprietors, The London Coliseum Syndicate, Ltd.; Managing Director, Mr.· Oswald Stoll; Manager, Mr. C. Dundas Slater; Acting-Manager, Mr. H. Pryme; Musical Director, Mr. Louis La Rondelle; Stage-Manager, Mr. H. Crocker; Booking Circuit, Miss-Stoll. Prices of seats, from 21s. to 6d. Depth of stage, 88ft.; width, 133ft. front, 85ft. back; proscenium, width, 54ft. 6in., height, under drapery, 34ft. 24 dressing-rooms; one rehearsal and two wardrobe. Matinée every day. Band rehearsals, Mondays, 10 o'clock. Electric lights (continuous), 200 volts. Two kinematograph boxes established. Bars as per arrangement.

LONDON HIPPODROME.—Proprietors, Moss's Empires, Ltd.; Managing Director, Mr. Oswald Stoll; Manager, Mr. Fred Trussell; Assistant Manager, Mr. A. Coleman Hicks; Stage-Manager and Producer, Mr. Frank Parker; Musical Director, Herr Henry Erhorn; Booking Circuit, Moss's Empires; Scenic Artists, Messrs. Joseph Harker and Bruce Smith. Holding capacity, 4,000. Prices of seats, 1s. to £4 4s. Matinée every day. Band rehearsals, Monday, at 12 noon. Electric light, 100 volts. Kinematograph box established. Bars as per arrangement.

LONDON PAVILION, Piccadilly, W.—Proprietors, The London Pavilion, Ltd.; Manager, Mr. Frank Glenister; Assistant-Manager, Mr. William Cobbett; Musical Director, Mr. A. Bond-Sayers; Stage-Manager, Mr. George Dyball; Booking Circuit, Syndicate Halls; Scenic Artist, Mr. W. T. Hemsley. Holding capacity, 1,200. Prices of seats: Orchestra stalls, 5s.; reserved first circle, 4s.; unreserved first circle and stalls, 3s.; second circle, 1s. 6d.; pit, 6d. Depth of stage, 30ft.; width, 42ft. between walls; proscenium, 23ft. 6in by 27ft. 7 dressing-rooms. Saturday matinée at 2.15; rehearsal 12.0. Current of electricity and voltage, alternating and direct, 107 volts. Bars Alhambra, London Coliseum, Empire, Hengler's Circus, London Hippodrome, Holborn Empire, Middlesex, Palace, and Standard.

METROPOLITAN, 267, Edgware Road, W.— Managing Director, Mr. Henri Gros; Manager, Mr. J. W. Edgar; Acting-Manager, Mr. G. L. Gooch; Musical Director, Mr. D M. Trytell; Booking Circuit, Syndicate Halls. Prices of seats, 3d. to 1s. 6d. Depth and width of stage, 24ft. by 45ft.; proscenium, 30ft.; 8 dressing-rooms. No matinée. Band rehearsals, 12.45 Mondays. Adjacent hall barred, Kilburn. Electric light, alternating 100 voltage. Kinematograph box established. Bars Bedford and Kilburn (in course of construction).

MIDDLESEX, Drury Lane, W.C. Proprietor, Mr. J. L. Graydon. Band rehearsal. 2 p.m. Bars Alhambra, London Coliseum, Empire, Hengler's Circus, London Hippodrome, Oxford, Holborn Empire. London Pavilion, Palace, and Tivoli.

NEW CROSS EMPIRE, London.—Proprietors, Moss's Empires, Ltd.: Managing Director, Mr. Oswald Stoll; Acting-Manager, Mr. Ernest Bridgen; Musical Director, Mr. Forbes Russell; Booking Circuit, Moss-Stoll. Holding capacity, 3,000. Prices of seats, 3d., 4d., 6d., 1s., 1s. 6d., 2s., 7s. 6d., and 10s. 6d. Depth and width of stage, 34ft. by 84ft.; proscenium, 32ft. wide and 32ft. high. 8 dressing-rooms. No matinée. Band rehearsals, 1 o'clock Mondays. Electric light, 105 volts, alternating. Kinematograph box established. Bars Greenwich Palace, Rotherhithe Hippodrome, and Peckham Hippodrome (late Crown).

OXFORD MUSIC HALL, Oxford Street, W.— Proprietors, The Oxford, Ltd.; Manager, Mr. C. Blyth-Pratt; Acting-Manager, Mr. A. L. Edwards; Musical Director, Mr. Leon Bassett; Booking Circuit, Syndicate Halls. Prices of seats, 5s., 4s., 3s., 2s., 1s. Proscenium: width, 28ft. 6in.; height, 24ft. 9 dressing-rooms. Saturday matinée. Band rehearsals, 12.30 Monday. Electricity, voltage, 240 and 220. Kinematograph box established. Bars Alhambra, London Coliseum, Empire, Hengler's Circus, London Hippodrome, Holborn Empire, Middlesex, and Palace.

PALACE THEATRE, Shaftesbury Avenue, W. —Proprietors, Palace Theatre, Ltd.; Managing Director, Mr. Alfred Butt; Acting-Manager, Mr. E. A. Pickering; Musical Director, Mr. Herman Finck. Holding capacity, 1,400 seated; 2,000 in all. Prices of seats, from 1s. to 7s. 6d.; boxes, £1 1s. to £3 3s. Depth and width of stage, 47ft. by 67ft.; between fly rails, 51ft.; proscenium, 34ft. 6in. 23 dressing-rooms. Matinée Saturday. Band rehearsals, 12 o'clock Mondays. Electric light, 100 volts. Kinematograph box established. Barring as per arrangement.

PARAGON, Mile End Road, E.—Proprietors, The Canterbury and Paragon, Ltd; Manager, Mr. Chas, Marté; Acting-Manager, Mr. Pierre Cohen; Musical Director, Mr. Arthur Grimmett. Booking Circuit, Syndicate Halls. Holding capacity, 4,500 have been in. Depth of stage, 45ft.; width, 60ft., wall to wall; dock to dock, 102ft. Proscenium opening, 36ft. 3 dressing-rooms. No matinée. Band rehearsals, 12 o'clock Monday. Electric light direct, 240 volts. Kinematograph box established. Bars Bow Palace, Foresters' Hackney Empire, Poplar Hippodrome, Queen's (Poplar), Rotherhithe Hippodrome, Shoreditch Empire, Shoreditch Hippodrome, Shoreditch Olympia, Star (Bermondsey).

PECKHAM HIPPODROME, S.E. (late Crown Theatre).—Proprietors, The Crown Theatre, Ltd.; Manager, Mr. Cecil Paget; Musical Director, Mr. Alfred Wigley. Music and dancing license. Holding capacity, 2,500 persons, £60. Stage 34ft. by 32ft. Electric light and gas. Band rehearsal, 12.30. Booking circuit, Gibbons-Barrasford. Bars Camberwell Empire, New Cross Empire, and Star (Bermondsey)

POPLAR HIPPODROME.—Proprietors, London Theatres of Varieties; Managing Director, Mr. Walter Gibbons; Manager, Mr. E. Austin Anderson. Holding capacity, 2,500. Prices of seats: Boxes, 7s. 6d.; seats in boxes, 2s.; fauteuils, 1s.; orchestra stalls, 6d.; grand circle, 6d.; pit, 3d.; gallery, 2d. Depth and width of stage, 42ft. by 54ft.; proscenium opening, 30ft.; height, 26ft. 14 dressing-rooms. Rehearsals, 1 p.m. Monday. Electricity voltage, 230, continuous current. Kinematograph box established. Bars Bow Palace, Foresters', Paragon, Queen's (Poplar), and Star (Bermondsey).

PUTNEY HIPPODROME, S.W.—Proprietors London Theatres of Varieties. Limited; Managing Director, Mr. Walter Gibbons; Manager, Mr. Louis G. Goldsmith. Music and dancing license. Holding capacity, about 2,000. Fine stage. Proscenium, 40ft. Gas and electric light. 200 volts, alt. Band rehearsal, 1 p.m. Booking circuit, Gibbons-Barrasford. Bars Battersea Palace and Granville (Walham Green).

QUEEN'S PALACE OF VARIETIES, Poplar, E.—Proprietors, Messrs. F. and M. Abrahams; Managers, Messrs. Morris Abrahams and Chas. Hector; Musical Director, Mr. Fred V. Venton. Prices of seats, 2d. to

18*

1s. 3d. Depth of stage, about 40ft.; proscenium, about 32ft. Thursday matinée. Band rehearsals, 1 o'clock Monday. Electricity and voltage, 230 volts. direct. Kinematograph box established. Bars Bow Palace, Greenwich Palace, Hippodrome, Poplar, and Paragon.

RICHMOND HIPPODROME AND THEATRE. —Proprietor, Mr. George Dance; Manager, Mr. Frederick H. Terrell; Musical Director, Mr. G. W. Richardson; Booking Circuit, Gibbons-Barrasford. Holding capacity about 1,600. Prices of seats: Boxes, 10s. 6d., 6s.; stalls, 1s. 6d.; circle, 1s.; pit, 6d.; gallery, 3d. Depth and width of stage, 30ft. by 50ft.; proscenium, opening, 27ft.; height, 50ft. 7 dressing-rooms. Thursday matinée. Band rehearsals, 1 o'clock. Kinematograph box established. No hall within barred area.

ROTHERHITHE HIPPODROME, S.E.—Proprietors, The London Theatres of Variety, Limited; Managing Director, Mr. Walter Gibbons. Booking circuit, Gibbons-Barrasford. Band rehearsal, 1 p.m. Bars F ters', Paragon, Shoreditch Empire, Star (Bermondsey). Shoreditch Hippo.

ROYAL ALBERT MUSIC HALL, Canning Town, E.

ROYAL COUNTY THEATRE, Kingston-on-Thames. Run in the off season as a variety house. For particulars see London Theatres.

ROYAL STANDARD MUSIC HALL, Victoria, S.W.

SADLER'S WELLS THEATRE, Rosebery Avenue, E.C.—Proprietor, Mr. Frank Macnaghten; Manager, Mr. Pete Murray; Musical Director, Mr. F. Payne; Booking Circuit, Macnaghten; Scenic Artist, Mr. T. Baker. Holding capacity, 2,000. Prices of seats, 3d., 4d., 6s., 1s. Depth and width of stage, 50ft. by 45ft.; proscenium, 30ft. 10 dressing-rooms. Monday matinée. Band rehearsals, 12 o'clock. Electricity and voltage, 104 amps. Kinematograph box established. Bars Bedford, Euston, Islington Empire, Islington Hippodrome, Shoreditch Empire, Hippodrome, and Olympia.

SEBRIGHT THEATRE, Hackney Road, N.E — At present run as a picture palace.

SHEPHERD'S BUSH EMPIRE, W.—Proprietors, the Hackney and Shepherd's Bush Empire Palace, Limited; Managing Director, Mr. Oswald Stoll; Manager, Mr. E. P. Morgan; Acting-Manager, Mr. Herbert Mack; Musical Director, Mr. Henry W. May; Scenic Artist, Mr. F. L. Schmitz. Depth and width of stage, 53ft. by 65ft. 4in.; proscenium opening, 30ft. 8in. No matinées. Band rehearsals, 1 o'clock. Electricity and voltage, alternating (220) and continuous (80). Motor generator. Bars Hammersmith Palace.

SHOREDITCH EMPIRE, N.E.—Booked in conjunction with the Syndicate Halls. Bars Foresters', Hackney Empire, Islington Empire, Paragon, Rotherhithe Hippodrome, Sadler's Wells, Shoreditch Olympia, Star (Bermondsey), and Stoke Newington Palace

SHOREDITCH OLYMPIA, N.E.—Proprietors, the London Theatres of Varieties, Limited; Managing Director. Mr. Walter Gibbons; Manager, Mr. H. Kettemann. Booking Circuit, Gibbons-Barrasford. Band rehearsal, 12.30. Bars Cambridge, Foresters', Hackney Empire, Islington Empire, Islington Hippodrome, Paragon, Sadler's Wells, Shoreditch Empire, and Star (Bermondsey).

SHOREDITCH HIPPODROME, N.E.—Closed. When open is booked in conjunction with the Syndicate Halls. Bars Foresters', Hackney Empire, Islington Empire, Islington Hippodrome, Shoreditch Olympia, Paragon, Sadler's Wells, Star (Bermondsey), Surrey, and Rotherhithe Hippodrome.

SOUTH LONDON PALACE, S.E.—Manager, Mr. Wm. Payne; Musical Director, Mr. Chas. Howells. Band rehearsal, 12 noon. Booking circuit, Syndicate Halls. Bars Camberwell Empire, Camberwell Palace, Star (Bermondsey), and Surrey.

STAR PALACE, Bermondsey, S.E.—Licensee, Mr. John Hart. Bars Camberwell Palace, Canterbury, Foresters', Paragon, Peckham Hippodrome (late Crown), Poplar Hippodrome, Rotherhithe Hippodrome, Shoreditch Empire, Hippodrome, and Olympia, South London, and Surrey.

STOKE NEWINGTON PALACE.—Managing Director, Mr. Walter De Frece; General Manager, Mr. Jack De Frece; Acting-Manager, Mr. T. J. Robinson; Musical Director, Mr. Amos Parker. Booking circuit, De Frece. Holding capacity, about 3,000. Prices of seats, 2d. to 1s. 6d. Depth of stage, 47ft., curtain line to back stage: width, 65ft.; proscenium, width 30ft., height 32ft. 15 dressing-rooms. Band rehearsals, 1 o'clock. Electricity and voltage, continuous, 240. Kinematograph box established. Bars Finsbury Park Empire (in course of construction), Islington Empire, Islington Hippodrome, Hackney Empire, Shoreditch Empire, and Olympia.

STRATFORD EMPIRE, E.—Proprietors, Moss's Empires, Limited; Managing Director, Mr. Oswald Stoll; Manager, Mr. E. J. Macdermott. Booking Circuit, Moss-Stoll. Band rehearsal, 1 p.m. Bars Bow Palace.

THE SURREY VAUDEVILLE THEATRE, S.E.—Proprietors, Surrey Vaudeville Theatre, Limited; Managing Director, Mr. Frank Macnaghten; General Manager, Mr. Frederick Baugh; Acting-Manager, Mr. Roy Cochrane; Musical Director, Mr. Rattray. Booking circuit, Macnaghten. Scenic Artist, Mr. Lancy Beltran. Holding capacity, 3,500. Prices of seats, 2d., 4d., 6d., 1s., 2s. Depth and width of stage, 65ft. by 84ft.; proscenium, 32ft. wide, 40ft. high. 14 dressing-rooms. Monday matinée, 2.30. Band rehearsals 12 o'clock. Electricity and voltage, 100, alternative. Kinematograph box established. Bars Camberwell Empire, Camberwell Palace, Canterbury, South London, Shoreditch Hippodrome, Star (Bermondsey).

THE TIVOLI, Strand, W.C.—Proprietors, New Tivoli, Limited; Manager, Mr. Joseph Wilson; Acting-Manager, Mr. James Howell; Musical Director, Mr. Walter Johnson. Booking circuit, Syndicate Halls. Price of seats from 1s. to £3 3s. Depth and width of stage, 24ft. by 38ft.; proscenium, 21ft. 7 dressing-rooms. Saturday matinée. Band rehearsals, 12 o'clock. Bars all West End halls. Electricity and voltage, 100. Kinematograph box established. Bars Alhambra, London Coliseum, Empire, Hengler's Circus, London Hippodrome, Holborn Empire, Middlesex, and Palace.

TOTTENHAM PALACE THEATRE OF VARIETIES, N.—Managing Director, Mr. Henri Gros; Manager, Mr. T. S. Mayne; Musical Director, Mr. William Burgess. Booking circuit, Syndicate Halls. Holding capacity, 3,000. Prices of seats, 3d., 6d., 1s., 1s. 6d., boxes 10s. 6d.; Depth and width of stage, 40ft. by 60ft.; proscenium, 30ft. wide, 36ft. cloths, 21ft. wings. 10 dressing-rooms Band rehearsals, 2 p.m. No halls barred. Electricity and voltage, 500 amps. and 120 volts, alternating current. 110 amps. and 60 volts, direct current. Kinematograph box established.

WALTHAMSTOW PALACE, N.E. — Proprietors, Varieties Consolidated, Limited; Manager, Mr. Arthur J. Barclay; Acting-Manager, Mr. Harry V. Mann; Musical Director, Mr. H. Petersen. Booking circuit, Syndicate Halls. Holding capacity, about 3,000. Prices of seats, 3d. to 10s. 6d. Depth and width of stage, 36ft. by 36ft.; proscenium. 32ft. 7 dressing-rooms. Band rehearsals, 3 o'clock. Electric light voltage, 230. Kinematograph box established.

WILLESDEN HIPPODROME, N.W.—Proprietors, London Theatres of Varieties, Limited; Managing Director, Mr. Walter Gibbons. Booking circuit, Gibbons-Barrasford. Band rehearsal, 12 noon.

WOOLWICH HIPPODROME, S.E. — Proprietors, London Theatre of Varieties, Limited; Manager, Mr. Herbert H. Laidman; Acting-Manager, Mr. E. P. Delevanti; Musical Director, Mr. Douglas Ross. Booking circuit, Gibbons, Barrasford. Holding capacity, 2,200. Prices of seats, 2d., 4d., 6d., 9d., 1s. Depth and width of stage, 42ft. by 76ft. 6in.; proscenium opening, 33ft. 13 dressing-rooms. Thursday matinée. Band rehearsals 1 o'clock. Electricity and voltage, 210. continuous. Kinematograph box established.

OTHER HALLS, ETC., POSSESSING LICENSES.

NORTH.

· N., N.E., and N.W. DISTRICTS.

BETHNAL GREEN, N.E.

ROYAL VICTOR ASSEMBLY ROOMS, 234, Old Ford Road.—Licensee, Edwin Stephens. L.C.C. license for music.

ST. JOHN'S SCHOOLS, Peel Grove.—Licensee, D. T. Keymer. L.C.C. license for music and dancing.

EXCELSIOR HALL AND BATHS, Mansford Street.—Licensee, A. P. Charles. L.C.C. license for music and dancing.

HACKNEY, N.E.

PUBLIC BATHS (KING'S HALL).—Proprietors, the Mayor, Aldermen, and Councillors of the Borough; Manager, the Town Clerk, acting under the directions of the Baths Committee. Music and dancing license. Holding capacity, 900. Portable stage, 20ft. by 15ft., curtained all round and well lighted. Electric light, direct current, 100 and 210 voltage (two separate machines). Terms of hiring on application. Deposit required on booking, £1 1s.

MORLEY HALL —Hon. Secretary, Mr. C. W. Garrard. Music license. Holding capacity, 1,000. Good platform. Gas and electric light, 240 volts direct current and for power 240 and 480 direct. Terms subject to arrangement.

FINCHLEY, N.

WOODSIDE HALL.—Licensee, Miss M. S. Chignell. Music and dancing and stage plays licenses.

ALL SAINTS' PARISH HALL.—Licensee, C. M. Woolsey. Music and dancing and stage plays licenses.

HACKNEY.

ST. JAMES'S PARISH HALL, Powell Road, Clapton.—Licensee, Rev. John Gardner Brown. L.C.C. license for music and dancing.

STOKE NEWINGTON LIBRARY HALL, Edwards Lane, Church Street.—Proprietors, the Borough Council. Licensee, Geo. Webb, Town Clerk. L.C.C. license for music.

HAMPSTEAD, N.W.

DRILL HALL AND ASSEMBLY ROOMS, Holly Bush Vale.—Licensee, Sutton Sharpe L.C.C. license for music and dancing.

TOWN HALL, Haverstock Hill.—Licensee, O. E. Winter, Borough Engineer. L.C.C. license for music and dancing.

WEST HAMPSTEAD TOWN HALL, Broadhurst Gardens.—Licensee, H. G. Randall. L.C.C. license for music and dancing.

HAMPSTEAD CONSERVATOIRE, Eton Avenue. — Licensee, Ralph Beauchamp, L.C.C. license for music and dancing.

HORNSEY, N.

ALEXANDRA PALACE THEATRE. — Proprietors, The Alexandra Park Trustees; Manager, Mr. Edwin Goodship. Holding capacity, 5,000. Prices of seats, 2s. 6d. to 6d. Depth and width of stage, 50ft. by 80ft.; proscenium, 36ft. 20 dressing rooms. Gas. Kinematograph box established.

ATHENÆUM, Muswell Hill.—Licensee, James Edmondson. Music and dancing and stage-plays licenses.

NATIONAL HALL.—Licensee, Chas. Jenkins Music and dancing and stage-plays licenses.

IRON ROOM, Granville Road, Stroud Green.—Licensee, Rev. R. Linklater. Music and dancing and stage-plays licenses.

HOLY INNOCENTS' MISSION ROOM.—Proprietor and Manager. Vicar of Holy Innocents', Hornsey, N. Dramatic and music and dancing licenses. Holding capacity: Number of persons, 209. No proper stage. Gas. Used only for charitable purposes.

HOXTON, N.

PUBLIC BATHS, Pitfield Street.—Licensees, the Borough of Shoreditch. L.C.C. license for music and dancing.

SHOREDITCH TOWN HALL.—Licensee, Hugh M. Robinson, Town Clerk of Shoreditch. L.C.C. license for music and dancing.

ALMA MUSIC HALL. Alma Street.—Licensee. W. H. Page. L.C.C. license for music and dancing.

ISLINGTON, N.

NORTHERN POLYTECHNIC, Holloway Road. Licensee, Wm. Murdoch Macbeth. L.C.C. license for music.

ROYAL AGRICULTURAL HALL, Liverpool Road.—Licensee, John Jeffery. L.C.C. license for music and dancing.

CAMDEN ATHENÆUM, Camden Road.—Licensee, A. A. Beale, L.C.C. license for music and dancing.

HOLLOWAY HALL, Holloway Road.—Proprietor, F. R. Griffiths; Manager, Richard Ralli; Operator. Charles A. Hitchcock. Music and dancing license. Holding capacity: Number of persons, 750. Gas and electric light, 200, 40 amps. Run as a picture palace.

PARKHURST THEATRE. Holloway Road.—Run as a picture palace.

STANLEY HALL. Junction Road.—Proprietor, Walter Lewis Lewis; Manager, W. J. Dowling. Music and dancing license. Holding capacity, 550. Proper stage, 23ft. by 15ft.; draw curtain. Gas and electric. 200 volts; alternating current. Terms for hiring, 4gs. per night. Deposit required on booking, 2gs.

MYDDLETON HALL, Almeida Street.—Licensee, H. W. Lawrence. L.C.C. license for music and dancing. Used for theatrical performances, concerts, and dances.

BEALE'S ASSEMBLY ROOMS, Holloway Road. Licensee, W. E. Beale, L.C.C. license for music and dancing. (Only let for private entertainments.)

HIGHBURY ATHENÆUM, Highbury New Park.—Licensee, W. M. Bradbear, L.C.C. license for music and dancing. (Only let for private entertainments.)

NORTHAMPTON HOUSE, Compton Road.—Licensee, R. O. Smith. L.C.C. license for music and dancing.

CALEDONIAN ROAD BATHS.—Licensee, the Borough Council. L.C.C. license for music and dancing.

DROVERS' HALL, Cattle Market.—Licensee, Leonard Vaughan Williams. L.C.C. license for music and dancing.

LEYTON, ESSEX, N.E.

TOWN HALL, Leyton.—Proprietors, Urban District Council. Music and dancing license. Holding capacity: Number of persons, 700. Platform. Electric current, voltage, 150. direct. Terms, £3 3s. per night to ratepayers; 20 per cent. more to others. The amount must be prepaid, together with a deposit of £2.

ST. JOHN'S WOOD.

WELLINGTON HALL.—Proprietor, C. B. Murless; Manager, A. J. Barrell. Dramatic and music and dancing licenses. Holding capacity, 500. Made-up stage, 30ft. by 35ft. Electric light, 240 voltage. Terms for hiring, from £5 5s.

ST. PANCRAS, N.W

PRINCE OF WALES' HALL, St. Pancras Baths, Prince of Wales' Road.—Proprietors, the Borough Council. L.C.C. license for music and dancing.

ST. MARY'S HALL, York Rise, Dartmouth Park.—L.C.C. license for music and dancing.

ALBERT ROOMS, Whitfield Street.—Licensee, James Windus. L.C.C. license for music and dancing.

PASSMORE EDWARDS SETTLEMENT. Tavistock Place.—Licensee, G. E. Gladstone. L.C.C. license for music and dancing.

SOUTHGATE. N.

THE INSTITUTE, High Road.—Licensee, A. E. Bages. Music and dancing license.

VILLAGE HALL.—Licensee, J. T. Camp. Stage plays and music and dancing licenses.

PARISH HALL AND INSTITUTE, Winchmore Hill.—Licensee, W. T. Paulin. Stage plays and music and dancing licenses.

TOTTENHAM. N.

GLENDALE HALL, South Tottenham.— Licensee, Frank Brooking. Music and dancing license.

STANSTEAD HOUSE, High Road.—Licensee, Clara Chard. Music and dancing license.

PUBLIC BATHS.—Licensee, Edward Crowne. Music and dancing license.

BERESFORD HALL. Green Lanes.—Licensee. Wm. Denchfield. Music and dancing license.

FAIRFAX HALL.—Licensee, Albert Victor Greenfield. Music and dancing license.

ALLHALLOWS' CHURCH HALL.—Licensee. Rev. D. Jones. Music and dancing and stage-plays licenses.

HOLCOMBE HALL.—Licensee, James Meadmore. Music and dancing and stage-plays licenses.

ST. ANN'S PARISH HALL.—Licensee, Rev. F. Rice. Music and dancing and stage-plays licenses.

WALTHAMSTOW, N.E.

VICTORIA HALL.—Proprietor, Mr. Matt. Raymond. Holding capacity, 1,700. Kinematograph box established. At present used as a picture palace.

PUBLIC BATHS.—Proprietors, Urban District Council. Music and dancing license. Holding capacity, 1,600. Stage width, 35ft.; depth, 22ft.; no proscenium. Electric light, continuous, 230 volts lighting; 460 volts power. Terms for hiring, from 3½gs. per evening. Deposit required on booking, £1.

WOOD GREEN, N.

ASSEMBLY ROOMS.—Proprietor and Manager, Mr. Geo. Henry Thurston. Dramatic and music and dancing licenses. Holding capacity, 500. Depth of stage, 17ft.; width, 25ft.; proscenium, 21ft. Gas. Terms of hiring, £2 12s. 6d., including grand piano; limelight, £1; Stage, £2 extra. Half fees required on booking.

CANNING HALL, Canning Crescent.—Licensee, W. A. Lambert. Music and dancing licenses.

ST. MARK'S HALL. Gladstone Avenue.— Licensee, Rev. J. T. Thomas. Music and dancing and stage plays licenses.

SOUTH.

S.E. and S.W. DISTRICTS.

BARNES, S.W.

BYFELD HALL.—Proprietor and Manager, Mr. F. W. Dunkley. Dramatic and music and dancing licenses. Holding capacity, 500. Proper stage. Electric light, direct current, 210 voltage. Terms on application.

BATTERSEA.

POLYTECHNIC, Battersea Park Road.— Licensee, Joseph Harwood. L.C.C. license for music.

TOWN HALL, Town Hall Road.—Licensee, the Town Clerk. L.C.C. license for music and dancing.

BERMONDSEY, S.E.

TOWN HALL, Spa Road.—Licensee, Frederick Ryall, town clerk. L.C.C. license for music and dancing.

BRIXTON, S.W.

AVONDALE HALL, Landor Road.—Licensee, E. M. Hayward. L.C.C. license for music and dancing.

BRIXTON HALL, Acre Lane.—Licensee, Eliza Chard. L.C.C. license for music and dancing.

HAMMERTON HALL, Lingham Street.— Licensee, Rev. W. H. Longsdon. L.C.C. license for music and dancing.

CAMBERWELL, S.E.

CAMBRIDGE HOUSE HALL, 1, Addington Square.—Licensee, Rev. W. J. Conybeare L.C.C. license for music and dancing.

LONGFIELD HALL, Knatchbull Road.— Licensee, William Minet. L.C.C. license for music and dancing.

SURREY MASONIC HALL, 295, Camberwell New Road. Licensee, L. C. Venables. L.C.C. license for music and dancing.

OLD KENT ROAD PUBLIC BATHS.— Licensees, the Borough Council. L.C.C. license for music and dancing.

CHELSEA, S.W.

TEMPERANCE HALL, Pond Place.—Licensees, H. J. Kimmins and F. Turney. L.C.C. license for music and dancing.

TOWN HALL, King's Road.—Licensee, the Town Clerk. L.C.C. license for music and dancing.

QUEEN'S PARK HALL, First Avenue.—Lessee, S. A. Blackwood. L.C.C. license for music and dancing.

SOUTH-WESTERN POLYTECHNIC, Manresa Road.—Licensee, H. B. Harper. L.C.C. license for music and dancing.

CLAPHAM, S.W.

CHRIST CHURCH PAROCHIAL HALL, Union Grove.—Licensee, the Rev. P. D. Hedges. L.C.C. license for music and dancing.

NINE ELMS BATHS (PEOPLE'S HALL).—
Licensees, the Battersea Borough Council.
L.C.C. license for music and dancing.
ASSEMBLY ROOMS, Gauden Road.—Licensee,
Jenry Boddington. L.C.C. license for music
and dancing.

DEPTFORD, S.E.
AMERSHAM HALL, Amersham Vale.—
Licensee, C. E. Seaman. L.C.C. license for
music and dancing.
NEW CROSS HALL, Lewisham High Road.—
Licensee, William Miller. L.C.C. license for
music and dancing.

DULWICH, S.E.
LORDSHIP LANE HALL, Wood Vale.—
Licensee, H. F. Hann. L.C.C. license for
music and dancing
CONSTITUTIONAL HALL, East Dulwich
Grove.—Licensee, Alfred Oliver. L.C.C.
license for music and dancing.
PUBLIC BATHS, East Dulwich Road.—
Licensees, the Camberwell Borough Council.
L.C.C. license for music and dancing.
IMPERIAL HALL, Grove Vale.—Licensee, W.
G. Newman. L.C.C. license for music and
dancing.
LAVA SKATING RING.—Licensee, A. E.
Chapman. L.C.C. license for music and danc-
ing.

FULHAM, S.W.
KING'S HALL, 163, New King's Road.—
Licensee, Wm. West. L.C.C. license for
music and dancing.
ST. CLEMENT'S PARISH HALL, Fulham
Palace Road.—Licensee, Rev. R. W. Free.
L.C.C. license for music and dancing.
ST. THOMAS'S CLUB, 36, Kelvedon Road.—
Licensee, John Cossins. L.C.C. license for
music and dancing.
LONDON EXHIBITIONS BUILDINGS, Earl's
Court. — Licensee, Herman Hart. L.C.C.
licenses for music and dancing and stage
plays.
TOWN HALL.—Proprietors, Fulham Borough
Council; Manager and licensee, Mr. J. Percy
Shuter. Music and dancing license. Hold-
ing capacity: Large hall, 780; concert hall,
330. Electric light, alternating, 200 volts.
Terms for hiring, four guineas per night.
LILLIE HALL, Lillie Road.—Licensee, C. W.
Gardner. L.C.C. license for music and danc-
ing.

GREENWICH, S.E.
CONCERT HALL and RINK, Blackheath Village.—Licensee, W. T. le Santeur. L.C.C.
license for music and dancing.
BOROUGH HALL.—Licensee, F. S. Robinson,
town clerk. L.C.C. license for music and
dancing.
CHARLTON ASSEMBLY ROOMS, Old Charlton Village.—Licensee, Rev. J. H. Bridgwater. L.C.C. license for music and dancing.

KENNINGTON, S.E.
HORNS ASSEMBLY ROOMS, Kennington Park
Road. Licensee, A. A. Moore. L.C.C.
license for music and dancing.

LAMBETH, S.E.
ROYAL VICTORIA HALL, 143, Westminster
Bridge Road. Licensee, Emma Cons. L.C.C.
license for music and dancing.
PUBLIC BATHS.—Licensees, the Borough
Council. L.C.C. license for music and danc-
ing. '

LEWISHAM, S.E.
FOREST HILL PUBLIC BATHS, Dartmouth
Road.—Licensees, the Borough Council
L.C.C. license for music and dancing.
LADYWELL PUBLIC BATHS.—Licensees, the
Borough Council. L.C.C. license for music
and dancing.

SPORTSBANK HALL, 31, Sportsbank Street,
Catford.—Licensees, H. T. Taylor and George
Taylor. L.C.C. license for music and danc-
ing.

NORBURY, S.W.
PUBLIC HALL.—Proprietor, Mr. Charles
Spencer, 7, Elmwood Road, Croydon; Manager, Mr. G. Spencer, 16, Tylecroft Road,
Norbury. Dramatic and music and dancing
licenses. Holding capacity, 700. Depth and
width of stage, 20ft. by 15ft. (about to be
enlarged. Electric light, 200, alternating.
Terms for hiring, £3 3s. per night. Half fee
required on booking, balance before doors
open. Fine lawn at rear suitable for garden-
parties, receptions, open-air concerts, etc.

NORWOOD, S.E.
WEST NORWOOD PUBLIC HALL, Knight's
Hill Road.—Licensee, Elizabeth R. Blake.
L.C.C. license for music and dancing.

PECKHAM, S.E.
PUBLIC HALL, Rye Lane.—Lessee, W. L. Dow-
ton. L.C.C. license for music and dancing.

PENGE, S.E.
TOWN HALL.—Proprietors, the Penge Urban
District School; Manager, F. W. Hood.
Dramatic and music and dancing licenses.
Holding capacity, 300. Depth and width of
stage, 17ft. by 27ft.; proscenium, 21ft. Gas.
Terms for hiring, £3 3s.; concerts, £4 4s.;
dramatics, reduction for consecutive nights.
Whole fee required before performance.

ROTHERHITHE, S.E.
TOWN HALL, Lower Road.—Licensee, the
Town Clerk. L.C.C. license for music and
dancing.
ST. OLAVE'S AND ST. JOHN'S INSTITUTE,
Fair Street, Tooley Street.—Licensee, J. P.
Chadwick. L.C.C. license for music and
dancing.

SOUTHWARK, S.E.
BOROUGH POLYTECHNIC, Borough Road.
Licensee, W. M. Richardson. L.C.C. license
for music and dancing.

WALWORTH, S.E.
ROBERT BROWNING HALL, York Street.
Licensee, J. C. Mather. L.C.C. license for
music.
MONTPELIER ASSEMBLY HALL, Montpelier
Street. Licensee, Frederick Stephens. L.C.C.
license for music and dancing.

WANDSWORTH, S.W.
HIGH SCHOOL HALL, Pinfold Road, Streat-
ham. Licensee, the Rev. Isaac H. Bland.
L.C.C. license for music and dancing.
PUTNEY ASSEMBLY ROOMS, 113, High
Street. Licensee, H. B. Durbin. L.C.C.
license for music and dancing.
ASSEMBLY ROOMS, Spread Eagle Hotel,
Garratt Lane. Licensee, Frances E. Stuart.
L.C.C. license for music and dancing.
STREATHAM HALL, 152, High Road.—
Licensee, F. C. J. Astbury. L.C.C. license
for music and dancing.
WANDSWORTH TOWN HALL, High Street.—
Licensee, the Town Clerk. L.C.C. license for
music and dancing.
BALHAM ASSEMBLY ROOMS, High Road.
—Licensee, J. H. Beare. L.C.C. licenses for
music and dancing and stage plays.
CROMWELL HALL (Putney Baths), Putney
Bridge Road.—Licensee, William Bishop.
L.C.C. license for music and dancing.
BEEHIVE ASSEMBLY ROOMS, Streatham
Common.—Licensee, W. H. Stanborough.
L.C.C. license for music and dancing.

WESTMINSTER, S.W.

CAXTON HALL, Caxton Street.—Licensee, John Hunt, town clerk. L.C.C. license for music and dancing.

LONDON SCOTTISH DRILL HALL, Buckingham Gate.—Licensee, Colonel J. W. Greig. L.C.C. license for music and dancing.

ROYAL HORTICULTURAL HALL, Vincent Square.—Licensee, Rev. W. Wilks. L.C.C. license for music and dancing.

TREVELYAN HALL, St. Ann's Lane.— Licensee, H. B. Thompson. L.C.C. license for music and dancing.

WIMBLEDON, S.W.

PUBLIC BATHS HALL.—Proprietors, Corporation of Wimbledon; Manager, Town Clerk, Town Clerk's Office, Wimbledon. Dramatic and music and dancing licenses. Holds 1,000. Temporary stage about 20ft. deep by 30ft. wide. Electric light, alternating current, 220 volts. Scale of charges on application. Fees payable in advance. Kinematograph chamber.

MASONIC HALL, Merton.—Proprietors, Merton Park Estate Co., Limited; Manager, Bertram T. Rumble. Dramatic and Music and dancing licenses. Holding capacity 460. Stage, depth, 14ft.; width, 20ft.; proscenium, 20ft. wide by 16ft. deep. Electric light, 220 voltage to body and 25 voltage to footlights. Terms for hiring, £2 2s. per evening. Whole of the fee required on booking.

EAST.

EAST AND E.C. DISTRICTS.

BOW AND BROMLEY, E.

PEOPLE'S PALACE (Bow and Bromley Branch), Bow Road.—Licensee, Clarence Brandon. L.C.C. license for music.

BROMLEY PUBLIC HALL.—Licensee, Leonard Potts, town clerk. L.C.C. license for music and dancing.

BOW BATHS, Roman Road.—Licensees, the Poplar Borough Council. L.C.C. license for music and dancing.

CITY OF LONDON, E.C.

CANNON STREET HOTEL (Great Hall), Cannon Street.—Licensee, C. H. Ritter. L.C.C. license for music and dancing.

CRIPPLEGATE INSTITUTE, Golden Lane.— Licensee, H. W. Capper. L.C.C. license for music and dancing. Also licensed for stage plays.

HAMILTON HALL (Great Eastern Hotel).— Licensee, H. C. T. Amendt. L.C.C. license for music and dancing.

BISHOPSGATE INSTITUTE, Bishopsgate Street.—Licensee, C. W. F. Goss. L.C.C. license for music and dancing.

EALING, W.

GIRTON HALL.—Licensee, Miss B. Grylls. Music and dancing license.

DRILL HALL, Churchfield Road.—Licensee, E. D. W. Gregory. Music license.

VICTORIA HALL, Uxbridge Road.—Licensee, J. E. Kemp. Music and dancing license.

PRINCE'S HALL.—Licensee, J. E. Kemp. Music and dancing license.

LECTURE HALL, Public Buildings.—Licensee, J. E. Kemp. Music and dancing license.

PUBLIC BATHS.—Licensee, H. P. Sharpe. Music and dancing license.

VESTRY HALL, Ranelagh Rad.—Licensee, W. J. Tidy. Music and dancing license.

EAST HAM, E.

TOWN HALL.—Proprietors, Corporation of East Ham; Manager, Mr. C. E. Wilson. Dramatic and music and dancing licenses.

Holding capacity, 1,000. Stage, depth, 19ft. clear back to organ loft, 23ft. 9in. back to wall under organ loft; width, 29ft. 4in.; height of proscenium, 27ft. 3in. Electric light, continuous, 240 voltage. Terms for dramatic performances, 6 guineas per night.

FINSBURY, E.C.

NORTHAMPTON INSTITUTE, St. John Street. —Licensee, R. M. Walmsley. L.C.C. license for music.

TOWN HALL, Rosebery Avenue.—Licensee, G. W. Preston, town clerk. L.C.C. license for music and dancing.

FOREST GATE, E.

EARLHAM HALL.—Proprietors, New Metropolitan Academy of Music; Manager, Mr. A. R. Jaques. Dramatic and music and dancing licenses. Holding capacity, about 400. Stage, 40ft. by 15ft.; proscenium opening, 22ft. Electric light, voltage 115. Terms for hiring, £3 3s., or as arranged. Amount of deposit required on booking, 10s. 6d. Several excellent rooms to let for rehearsals from 2s. 6d.

ILFORD, E.

TOWN HALL.—Proprietors, Urban District Council; Licensee and Responsible Manager, Mr. John Wheeldon Benton, clerk to the council. Dramatic and music and dancing licenses. Holding capacity, 848. Stage, 33½ft. wide by 17ft. deep; proscenium, 25ft. wide. Electric light. Terms for hiring, £5 5s. per evening, £12 12s. three nights. Amount of deposit required on booking, £1 1s. on each book, proportionately for series of bookings.

LIMEHOUSE, E.

TOWN HALL, Commercial Road.—Lessee, G. W. Clarke. L.C.C. license for music and dancing.

YE OLDE GREEN DRAGON MUSIC HALL, Grosvenor Street.—Licensee, Chas. Feist. L.C.C. license for music and dancing.

MILE END, E.

ASSEMBLY ROOMS, Cottage Grove, Stepney. —Licensee, C. T. King. L.C.C. license for music and dancing.

PEOPLE'S PALACE.—Proprietors, the Governors; Manager, Mr. Clarence Brandon. Music license. Holding capacity, 2,500. Concert platform, with curtain fit-up and footlights. Electric light, direct, 112. Terms for hiring, from £5 5s., according to purpose for which required. Half-fee required on booking.

POPLAR, E.

TOWN HALL, Newby Place.—Licensee, Leonard Potts, Town Clerk. L.C.C. license for music and dancing.

ST. GEORGE-IN-THE-EAST, E.

TOWN HALL, Cable Street.—Licensee, G. W. Clarke, Town Clerk. L.C.C. license for music and dancing.

PRINCESS HALL, Commercial Road.— Licensee, Lazarus Greenberg. L.C.C. license for music and dancing.

SILVERTOWN, E.

TATE INSTITUTE.—Secretary, Geo. G. Rickwood. Dramatic and music and dancing licenses. Stage, 26ft. 9in. wide; 19ft. deep. Gas. Terms for hiring on application. 50 per cent. required on booking.

WHITECHAPEL, E.

PUBLIC BATHS, Goulston Street.—Licensees, the Stepney Borough Council. L.C.C. license for music and dancing.

WEST.

W. AND W.C. DISTRICTS.

CHISWICK, W.

TOWN HALL.—Proprietors, Chiswick Urban District Council; Manager, Mr. A. George. Dramatic and music and dancing licenses. Holding capacity, 540. Depth and width of stage, 24ft. by 16ft. Electric light, 220 volts direct. Terms, £3 18s. 6d. per night. All fees at time of booking.

HAMMERSMITH, W.

ATHENÆUM, Godolphin Road.—Licensee, J. C. Platt. L.C.C. license for music and dancing.
TOWN HALL, Broadway.—Licensee, Horatio Thompson, Town Clerk. L.C.C. license for music and dancing. Holding capacity, 668. Terms £5 5s. per night.
ST. LUKE'S HALL, Hadyn Park Road.— L.C.C. license for music and dancing.
OLYMPIA.—Licensee, F. H. Payne. L.C.C. license for music and dancing.
PUBLIC BATHS, Lime Grove.—Proprietors, the Borough Council. Holding capacity, 1,284. Terms £5 5s.

HANWELL, W.

PARK HALL.—Manager, Mr. W. Stephens. Dramatic and music and dancing licenses. Holding capacity, 500. Stage: Depth, 18ft.; opening, 22ft. Gas. Terms for hiring on application.

HOLBORN, W.C.

HOLBORN TOWN HALL, Gray's Inn Road.— Licensee, L. J. Walford, town clerk. L.C.C. license for music and dancing.
KING'S HALL (Holborn Restaurant).—Licensee, A. G. Chifferiel. L.C.C. license for music and dancing.
BLOOMSBURY HALL, Hart Street.—Licensee, B. I'Anson Beech. L.C.C. license for music.

KENSINGTON, W.

LADBROKE HALL, Addison Road. Licensee, H. B. Hartnell. L.C.C. licenses for music and dancing and stage plays.
VICTORIA HALL, Archer Street.—Licensee, Ann S. George. L.C.C. licences for music and dancing and stage plays.
ADDISON HALL, Addison Road.—Licensee, G. F. Johnson. L.C.C. license for music and dancing.
TOWN HALL, High Street.—Licensee, W. C. Leete, town clerk. L.C.C. license for music and dancing.
BLECHYNDEN HALL, Blechynden Street.— Licensee, Harry Lewis. L.C.C. license for music and dancing.
EMPRESS ROOMS.—Proprietors, the Palace Hotel, Limited; Manager, Mr. E. W. Booth. Music and dancing license. Holding capacity, 600-700. No proper stage. Electric light, 200 volts. Terms: According to arrangement. Amount of deposit required on booking: Half.

MARYLEBONE, W.

BECHSTEIN HALL, Wigmore Street.—Licensee, Max Lindlar. L.C.C. license for music.
MME. TUSSAUD'S EXHIBITION, Marylebone Road. Licensee, J. I. Tussaud. L.C.C. license for music.
REGENT STREET POLYTECHNIC (Marlborough Hall).—Licensee, L. H. Harris. L.C.C. license for music.
QUEEN'S HALL, Langham Place.—Licensee, William Boosey. L.C.C. license for music and dancing.
ST. JAMES'S HALL, Great Portland Street. Licensee, H. C. Lock. L.C.C. license for music.

EYRE ARMS ASSEMBLY ROOMS (Wellington Hall), Finchley Road. Licensee, C. B. Murless. L.C.C. license for music and dancing.
STEINWAY HALL, Lower Seymour Street. Licensee, Edwin Eshelby. L.C.C. license for music.
CAVENDISH ROOMS, Mortimer Street.— Licensee, Edward Humphrey. L.C.C. license for music and dancing.

PADDINGTON, W.

PUBLIC BATHS, Queen's Road, Bayswater.— Licensees, the Borough Council. L.C.C. license for music and dancing.
ST. GEORGE'S, HANOVER SQUARE, W.
ÆOLIAN HALL, New Bond Street.—Licensee, R. J. Mason. L.C.C. license for music.
GROSVENOR HALL, Buckingham Palace Road.—Licensees, Sir H. B. Praed and Baron Weardale. L.C.C. license for music and dancing.
DRILL HALL (9th County of London Regiment), Davies Street.—Licensee, Col. Wm. Morris Tanqueray. L.C.C. license for music and dancing.
ST. GABRIEL'S PARISH HALL, Caledonia Street.—Licensee, Rev. R. H. Morris. L.C.C. license for music and dancing.
ST GEORGE'S HALL, Mount Street. Licensee, John Hunt, town clerk. L.C.C. license for music.

STRAND, W.C.

INNS OF COURT HALL, Drury Lane.— Licensee, F. S. Cooper. L.C.C. license for music and dancing.
NEW GALLERY, Regent Street.—Licensee, C. E. Hallé. L.C.C. license for music and dancing.
SALLE ERARD, Great Marlborough Street.— Licensee, W. Adlington. L.C.C. license for music.

RECOMMENDED APARTMENTS.

BATTERSEA, CLAPHAM JUNCTION, S.W.
Mrs. Holder, 15, Lavender Road. 2 bed, 2 sitting, 2 combined. Also baggage contracted for.

FULHAM, S.W.
Mrs. A. Frost, 38, Fulham Park Gardens. 2 sitting rooms, 2 bedrooms, 1 combined, 2 pianos, bath h. and c.

LONDON, N.W.
Mrs. A. Wilson, 53, Gloucester Crescent, Regents Park, N.W. 2 bedrooms, 2 sitting rooms, 2 combined, 2 pianos, 1 bath.

LONDON, S.E.
Mrs. H. M. Parker, 39, Doddington Grove. Kennington Park Sitting room (piano), 2 bedrooms, very large bed-sitting, and smaller bed-sitting.

LONDON, W.
Mrs. Berry, 6, Aynhoe Road, Brook Green, Hammersmith. Sitting and 2 bedrooms, piano, bath, and W.C. in house.

LONDON, W.C.
Mrs. Dubois, 16, York Chambers, York Buildings, Charing Cross. Bed-sitting, double-bedded and single rooms.
Mrs. Jacobs, 21, Guilford Street, Russell Square. Combined rooms and sitting rooms.

STRATFORD, E.
Mrs. E. Stone, 76, Romford Road, Stratford, E. 2 sitting rooms, 4 bedrooms, 1 combined, 2 extra beds. Piano, bathroom.
Mrs. King, 38 and 40, Grove Crescent Road. 4 bedrooms, 2 sitting rooms, 3 combined, piano.

WEST HAM, E.
Mrs. Marsh, 61, Mark Street, Stratford, E. 2 bedrooms, 1 sitting, 1 combined, piano.

OPERA SEASONS AT COVENT GARDEN.

CARL ROSA OPERA SEASON.

Jan. 1. *The Marriage of Figaro.*
,, 2. *The Merry Wives of Windsor.*
,, 3. *Esmeralda.*
,, 6. *Carmen.*
,, 7. *Il Trovatore.*
,, 8. *Faust.*
,, 9. *Cavalleria Rusticana* and *Pagliacci.*
, 10. *Tannhäuser.*
,, 11. *Faust.*

SYNDICATE.

,, 27. *The Rheingold.*
,, 28. *The Valkyrie.*
,, 29. *The Siegfried.*
Feb. 1. *Götterdämmerung.*

REGULAR SEASON.

April 30. *Die Walküre.*
May 1. *Die Walküre.*
,, 2. *Lucia de Lammermoor.*
,, 4. *Cavalleria Rusticana* and *Pagliacci.*
,, 5. *Götterdämmerung.*
,, 6. *La Traviata.*
,, 7. *Tannhäuser.*
,, 8. *Rigoletto.*
,, 9. *Die Walküre.*
,, 11. *Tannhäuser.*
,, 12. *Lucia di Lammermoor.*
,, 13. *Götterdämmerung.*
,, 14. *Rigoletto.*
,, 15. *Cavalleria Rusticana* and *Pagliacci.*
,, 16. *Tristan und Isolde.*
,, 18. *Rigoletto.*
,, 19. *La Bohême.*
,, 20. *Die Meistersinger.*
,, 21. *Lucia di Lammermoor.*
,, 22. *Tristan und Isolde.*
,, 23. *Aïda.*
,, 25. *Die Meistersinger.*
,, 26. *Cavalleria Rusticana* and *Pagliacci.*
,, 27. Gala Performance. First act of *Pescatori di Perle*, and the Garden scene of *Faust.*
,, 28. *Tristan und Isolde.*
,, 29. *Madame Butterfly.*
,, 30. *La Traviata.*
June 1. *Rigoletto.*
,, 2. *Die Meistersinger.*

REGULAR SEASON *(continued).*

June 3. *Die Walküre.*
,, 4. *Der Fliegende Holländer.*
,, 5. *Lucia di Lammermoor.*
,, 6. *Armide.*
,, 8. *Der Fliegende Holländer.*
,, 9. *Rigoletto.*
,, 10. *Armide.*
,, 11. *Il Barbiere di Siviglia.*
,, 12. *Aïda.*
,, 13. *La Bohême.*
,, 15. *Il Barbiere di Siviglia.*
,, 16. *Madame Butterfly.*
,, 17. *La Traviata.*
,, 18. *Manon Lescaut.*
,, 19. *Pescatori di Perle.*
,, 22. *Aïda.*
,, 23. *Il Barbiere di Siviglia.*
,, 24. *Manon Lescaut.*
,, 25. *Pescatori di Perle.*
,, 26. *La Bohême.*
,, 27. *Carmen.*
,, 29. *Pescatori di Perle.*
,, 30. *Madame Butterfly.*
July 1. *Otello.*
,, 2. *Carmen.*
,, 3. *Manon Lescaut.*
,, 4. *Il Barbiere di Siviglia.*
,, 6. *Otello.*
,, 7. *Fedora.*
,, 8. *Cavalleria Rusticana* and *Pagliacci.*
,, 9. *Il Barbiere di Siviglia.*
,, 10. *Carmen.*
,, 11. *The Huguenots.*
,, 13. *La Bohême.*
,, 14. *The Huguenots.*
,, 15. *Faust.*
,, 16. *Otello.*
,, 17. *Il Barbiere di Siviglia.*
,, 18. *La Tosca.*
,, 20. *Lucia di Lammermoor.*
,, 21. *Otello.*
,, 22. *Il Barbiere di Siviglia.*
,, 23. *Faust.*
,, 24. *La Traviata.*
,, 25. *Aïda.*
,, 27. *The Huguenots.*
,, 28. *La Tosca.*
,, 29. *La Bohême.*
,, 30. *La Traviata*
,, 31. *Otello.*

NEW THEATRES AND MUSIC HALLS OPENED.

Feb. 24.—Pavilion Music Hall, Liverpool.
Mar. 23.—Palace, Maidstone.
April 25.—New St. James's Hall, Great Portland Street.
Aug. 3.—Pavilion Northwich.
,, 12.—New South Parade Pier and Pavilion, Southsea.
,, 17.—New Hippodrome, Middlesbrough.
,, 24.—The Metropolitan, Edgware Road (re-constructed).
,, 31.—New Tottenham Palace.
Sept. 7.—New Palace, Ebbw Vale (formerly Central Hall).
,, 14.—Hippodrome, Devonport.
,, 14.—Grand, Lancaster.

Sept. 14.—Gaiety (formerly Criterion), Worksop.
,, 28.—Hippodrome, Nottingham.
Oct. 5.—New Todmorden Hippodrome.
,, 12.—New, Oxford.
,, 12.—New Hippodrome, Rochdale.
,, 14.—New Public Hall, Cirencester.
Nov. 2.—Gilbert's Palace and New Hippodrome, Exeter.
,, 16.—New Rochdale Hippodrome.
Dec. 7.—New Hippodrome, Birkenhead.
,, 7.—New Hippodrome, Aston.
,, 14.—New Grand and Hippodrome, Leigh.
,, 21.—New Hipp drome, Accrington.
,, 24.—New Weymouth Pier Pavilion.
,, 24.—New Grand Opera House, Oldham.
,, 25.—New Edmonton Empire.

LECTURES AND ADDRESSES OF THE YEAR.

January 3.—Mr. Martin Harvey lectured at the Society of Arts (under the auspices of the Ethnological Society) on "Character and the Actor."

January 12.—Mr. Sidney Lee gave an address to the members of the English Association at the University College on "The Teaching of Shakespeare in Secondary Schools." Mr. Lee argued against making Shakespeare simply a school study. He thought that some such book as "Lamb's Tales from Shakespeare" should be brought to children's notice at the earliest age at which they could comprehend what they read.

January 17.—Professor Ernest Gardner gave an address on "The Greek Theatre and the Development of the Drama" at the University College. The theatre in Greece, said the lecturer, was quite a different thing from what the theatre is to us to-day. The theatre in the early times was a religious institution connected with the State. It was an institution established by the State, and it was a public duty to attend it.

January 19.—Miss Margaret Halstan, in the New Islington Hall, Manchester, gave to the Ancoats Brotherhood an address, entitled "An Actor's Notes on Acting." People nowadays, Miss Halstan said, did not go to the theatre to see a great play. They went to see Mr. X or Miss X, who happened to be playing some particular part. The public had no conception of their own of the characters they saw on the stage; they only associated those characters with the individuals who played them. Notoriety was really the ruin of the art. In illustration of her point Miss Halstan quoted a conversation between two ladies in the stalls at a performance of *His House in Order*. At the end of the scene where the hero persuaded one of the characters to surrender some letters one of the ladies asked the other, "Would *you* have given up the letters?" "No," she replied, "not to George Alexander. But I would to Charles Wyndham."

January 26.—Mr. Bransby Williams read a paper on "Actors and Versatility" to the members and friends of the O.P. Club at the Criterion. All acting was, or should be, character acting; but the present age was an age of personality, and personality upon the stage contributed at least 50 per cent. towards success. Character acting, pure and simple, was, in his opinion, upon the decline, not as regards quality, but as the natural result of authors having to write parts to suit the personality of the actor. He deplored the absence of any chance of the young actor acquiring experience nowadays to be compared with that of the player of the older generation, who passed through the valuable stock season school. He had no faith in academies. Acting could not be taught. The young actor was severely handicapped by the long-run system, or the necessity or habit of copying someone else in a "big London success."

February 9.—Mr. R. A. Roberts lectured to the O.P. Club members, entitling his subject "Twenty Years' Hard," at the Criterion Restaurant. Mr. Roberts detailed his early struggles and adventures.

February 21.—Miss Cicely Hamilton addressed the members of the Actors' Association on the subject of "Why Should Actresses have the Vote?" In the course of her speech Miss Hamilton said:—"We may appear ridiculous when we ring the bells of Cabinet Ministers' houses while they stand inside in their pyjamas listening, but we have a principle."

March 14.—Mr. Alfred Sutro delivered an address on the subject of "The Playwright and the Public" at the Working Men's College, Crowndale Road. Mr. Sutro said the writers of plays should be regarded as entertainers. The dramatist must recognise the fact that he had to write for the crowd. He was in the nature of things an observer standing between the philosopher and the crowd. To have influence on his generation the dramatist might lift one eye to heaven, but the other must be squinting at the box-office. Woman was the autocrat of the theatre.

March 25.—Mr. H. B. Irving read his lecture on "The Shakespearean Actors of the Eighteenth Century" at the Birmingham University.

March 26.—Miss Gertrude Kingston gave the first of two lectures on the subject of "The Drama and the Public" at 20, Hanover Square. The first part she entitled "A Chapter in the History of Prejudice." She had often thought that if an actor were permitted to ask his audience "Is it the play or my acting to which you take exception?" it would make for a more cordial *entente* between the stage and the auditorium. If an actor could sometimes address his audience in this manner it would, perhaps, solve the mystery of what was affecting the drama at the present day. The history of the British stage, she said, was one long story of unceasing struggle between the drama and the public. Almost every decade had seen the drama engaged in a struggle for bare existence against an inherited prejudice of the people. Miss Kingston went on to trace the history of the drama in England.

The second lecture, given on the following Tuesday, dealt with the drama from the beginning of the eighteenth century.

April 5.—Mr. T. P. O'Connor, M.P., delivered an address to the O.P. Club at the Criterion on "Things in General, and Some Reference to the Drama."

April 5.—Mr. Hubert Druce lectured to the Playgoers' Club on "The Dramatic Instinct" at the Gaiety Restaurant.

May 17.—Mr. Gilbert Hudson read a paper before members of the Actors' Association on the subject of "Beaumont and Fletcher."

October 18.—Mr. J. Fisher White read a paper to the Playgoers' Club on "The Actor's Art"—Hotel Cecil.

November 1.—Miss Cicely Hamilton read a paper on "The Rights and Wrongs of the Critic" to the O.P. Club—Criterion.

November 8.—Mr. Philip Carr read a paper to the Playgoers' Club on "Theatre Prices and Seating"—Hotel Cecil.

November 15.—Mr. Philip Carr read a paper to the Manchester Playgoers' Club on "Historical Costumes."

November 13.—Mr. Frederick Whelen lectured before the Glasgow Stage Society at the Athenæum Hall on the subject of "The New Drama."

November 24.—Mr. Arthur Bourchier delivered a lecture in the Medical Theatre of the Birmingham University on "William Shakespeare, Maker of Men."

November 30.—Mr. Fred Farren read a paper before the members of the O.P. Club on "Ballet and the Ballet Public" at the Criterion Restaurant.

November 30.—Mr. Bransby Williams lectured before the Manchester Playgoers' Club on "The Actor and Personality"—Albion Hotel.

December 9. — Mr. G. Albert Smith, F.R.S., lectured at the Royal Society of Arts, on Colour Kinematography.

DINNERS, BANQUETS, ETC., OF THE YEAR.

Jan. 1. New Year's Party of the Music Hall Ladies' Guild at the Horns, Kennington.

Jan. 5. The Terriers' Annual Dinner and Social. Mr. Jesse Sparrow presided. Dover Castle Hotel.

Jan. 7. The Showmen's Annual Supper and Ball at Bolton.

Jan. 19. Complimentary Banquet to Mr. Carl Hentschel. Mr. H. Beerbohm Tree in the chair. Hotel Cecil.

Jan. 26. Annual Dinner of the National Association of Theatrical Employés. Salisbury Hotel, St. Martin's Lane.

Jan. 30. Annual Ball and Supper of the Grand Order of Water Rats. Trocadero Restaurant.

Feb. 2. Dinner to Sir W. S. Gilbert. The Earl of Onslow in the chair. Savoy Hotel.

Mar. 8. V.A.B.F. Dinner. Mr. Joe Elvin in the chair. Criterion Restaurant.

Mar. 22. Dinner to Sir John Hare and Sir Charles Santley. Criterion Restaurant.

Mar. 29. Eleventh Annual Dinner of the Gallery First Nighters. Frascati's Restaurant.

April 12. Heads of Departments Dinner. Mr. Edward Terry in the chair. Criterion Restaurant.

April 29. National Association of Kinematograph Operators' Luncheon. Anderton's Hotel.

May 10. Twenty-fourth Annual Dinner of the Playgoers' Club. Mr. Cyril Maude in the chair. Hotel Cecil.

May 28. Sixty-third Annual Dinner of the Royal General Theatrical Fund. Alderman Sir Henry E. Knight in the chair. Hotel Métropole.

June 14. Dinner and Presentation to Mr. H. Beerbohm Tree to celebrate the twenty-first year of his management. Savoy Hotel.

July 12. Dinner and Presentation to Mr. Joe O'Gorman, Mr. Wal Pink, and Mr. W. H. Clemart at the Boulogne Restaurant.

Sept. 20. Mr. Arthur Bourchier and Miss Violet Vanbrugh were the principal guests at dinner given by the members of the Liverpool Stage Club at the Exchange Hotel.

Nov. 22. Annual Dinner of the Eccentric Club. Sir Charles Wyndham in the chair. Hotel Cecil.

Dec. 12. Annual Dinner of the Savage Club. Mr. William Senior in the chair. Hotel Cecil.

Dec. 13. Annual Dinner of the Actors' Benevolent Fund. Mr. Cyril Maude in the chair. Hotel Métropole.

Dec. 19. Annual Dinner of the Kit Marlowe A.D.C. Mr. Martin Harvey in the chair. Gaiety Restaurant.

Dec. 20. Playgoers' Club's Ladies' Christmas Dinner. Miss Ethel Irving principal guest. Hotel Cecil.

GENERAL MEETINGS OF SOCIETIES, FUNDS, ETC.

Jan. 19. Third Annual General Meeting of the Variety Artists' Federation. Mr. Joe O'Gorman presided. Camberwell Empire.

Jan. 30. First General Meeting of the Variety Actors' Benevolent Fund. Bedford Head.

Feb. 9. Annual Meeting of the London Branch of the National Association of Theatrical Employés. King's Hall.

Feb. 11. Annual Meeting of the Actors' Benevolent Fund. Sir Charles Wyndham in the chair. Criterion.

Mar. 2. Annual Meeting of the Actors' Association. Mr. Cecil Raleigh in the chair. Savoy.

Mar. 8. Meeting of the Artists' Protection League. New Cross Empire.

Mar. 19. Annual Meeting of Actors' Day Fund. Mr. Laurence Irving in the chair. Kingsway.

Mar. 20. Annual Meeting of the Royal General Theatrical Fund. Mr. Edward Terry in the chair. Terry's.

April 5. Special General Meeting of the Music Hall Artists' Railway Association. Subscription increased by 1s., the extra money to be devoted to the V.A.B.F. Camberwell Empire.

April 15. Annual General Meeting of the Travelling Theatres' Managers' Association. P.O.W., Birmingham.

April 21. Actors' Union Meeting. Hummum's Hotel.

May 21. Annual Meeting of the Rehearsal Club. St. James's.

May 26. Actors' Union. General Meeting. Rehearsal Theatre, Maiden Lane.

May 28. Special General Meeting of the M.H.A.R.A. at the Bedford Head.

May 29. Annual Meeting of the Actors' Orphanage Fund at the Playhouse.

July 8. Annual Meeting of the Music Hall Sick Fund at the York Hotel.

Aug. 2. Meeting at the Hotel Provence in connection with the I.A.L. Boycott in Germany.

June 16. Annual General Meeting of the Actors' Church Union. Kennington Theatre.

Oct. 25. Annual General Meeting of the Music Hall Artistes' Railway Association at the Bedford Head.

Oct. 25. Special General Meeting of the Variety Artists' Federation. Bedford Head.

Dec. 1. Special General Meeting of the Actors' Union, at which it was decided to alter the method of subscription from 6d. per week for forty weeks in the year to 1s. 3d. per month, or 15s. per year.

Dec. 18. Annual General Meeting of the Theatrical Ladies' Guild. Miss Fanny Brough, the President, in the chair. St. James's.

MISCELLANEOUS EVENTS OF THE YEAR.

May 25. The Guild of Catholic Actors and Musicians gave a *Matinée*, by permission of Mr. George Edwardes, President of the Guild, at Daly's, in aid of Poor Catholic Missions in and around London.

May 27. The Music Hall Ladies' Guild gave a *Matinée* at the Oxford. The programme consisted of some seventy items, all contributed by ladies, the chief attraction being Mr. Fred Ginnett's equestrian sketch *Dick Turpin*, with Miss L. Ginnett in the title-*rôle*.

June 16. The Theatrical Sports arranged by the National Association of Theatrical Employés were held at Stamford Bridge. Mrs. Langtry presented the prizes.

June 21. The Terriers and their friends, numbering over 100, held their annual River Outing, journeying to Windsor for that purpose.

June 25. A *Matinée*, organised by Miss Rose Mathews to aid in clearing off the debenture debt of the Actors' Association, was given at the Scala. On this occasion the winning verses in a competition organised by THE STAGE for a prize for three verses on the subject of Actors' Unity were sung, the words of Mr. Rathmell Wilson being set to music by Mr. Arthur Fagge. They were as follows:—

I.

For those who wage in the footlights' glare the strenuous fight of life,
Smiling when all the world seems dark, strengthened by endless strife;
For the sometimes-paid, and the never-paid, and for those whose pay is slight,
For all who know Life's tragedy we cry to-day, UNITE!

II.

For those who work without reward eight weeks for a fortnight's "run,"
For those who find " all parts are gone " to the frauds who act for fun,
For the undersold and all who fail, pushed down by Premium's might,
For Blacklegs' victims one and all we cry to-day, UNITE!

III.

For those who dress in filthy rooms, where Death is wont to stay,
Ready to spring at a father's throat or steal a wife away;
For those our comrades who are wronged we seek the torch to light;
For the children who are yet unborn we cry to-day, UNITE!

June 28. A motor-car run to Brighton of the Grand Order of Water Rats and their friends, organised by Mr. Harry Tate, took place. Before a start was made two pictures, the original painting, " Popularity," by " Lydia Dreams," and an enlarged photograph of all the members of the Order of Water Rats, were unveiled in the Vaudeville Club. On the journey down a halt was made at Crawley, where scenes were acted for the purpose of taking a kinematograph record. Luncheon was served at the York Hotel, Brighton, Mr. W. H. Clemart, as King Rat, occupying the chair, after which a parade of cars took place.

June 30. The Theatrical Garden Party in aid of the Actors' Orphanage Fund. Fine weather again favoured the party, which was held in the Botanic Gardens, Regent's Park, a return being made to these after a trial in 1907 of the Chelsea Hospital Grounds. In the Theatre Royal the usual exciting drama was acted by Mr. Cyril Maude and company. The Hat Trimming Competition, Jarley's Waxworks, the Eldorado Palace, the Lecture Tent, the Gipsy Encampment were other features. Some 7,000 or 8,000 people were present, and the net profit came to nearly £1,800. Kinematographic records were taken by the Gaumont Company, and shown at the London Hippodrome and the Coliseum on the same evening.

July 16. The Annual Cricket Match between an eleven of actors and another eleven of authors, in aid of the Actors' Benevolent and the Actors' Orphanage Funds, was commenced at Lord's, but owing to the inclement weather was abandoned after a little play.

July 21. The Annual Cricket Match between London and Provincial actors, in aid of the Actors' Benevolent and the Actors' Orphanage Funds was played at the Oval. The London eleven, captained by Mr. C. Aubrey Smith, won.

Aug. 12. Music Hall Sports at Herne Hill in aid of the Variety Artists' Benevolent Fund.

Aug. 28. Variety Artists' Benevolent Fund River Outing.

*INTERNATIONAL COPYRIGHT CONVENTION.

REVISED CONVENTION OF BERNE FOR THE PROTECTION OF LITERARY AND ARTISTIC WORKS.

An International Conference for the revision of the Berne Convention, held under the auspices of the Emperor of Germany, was opened in Berlin on October 14. The British delegates were Mr. George Ranken Askwith, K.C., and the Count de Salis. Sir Henry Bergne had been appointed the principal British delegate, but was unable to attend all the sittings on account of illness. The articles were signed on November 13.

Mr. Askwith has supplied us with a copy of the Convention, which, as is customary ,is in French, the International diplomatic language. The following is our translated version of the Convention :—

I.

The contracting countries are hereby constituted into a union for the protection of the rights of authors in their literary and artistic productions.

II.

The expression "literary and artistic works" includes all productions of the literary, scientific, or artistic domain, whatever may be the mode or form of their reproduction, such as : books, pamphlets, and other written works; dramatic or dramatico-musical works, choregraphic works and pantomimes, the "mise-en-scène" of which is fixed by writing or otherwise; musical compositions, with or without words; works pertaining to drawing, painting, architecture, sculpture, engraving, and lithography; illustrations and geographical maps; plans, sketches, and plastic works relating to geography, topography, architecture, or sciences.

The following are protected as original works, without detriment to the rights of the original author :—Translations, adaptations, arrangements of music and other transformed reproductions of a literary or artistic work, and likewise collections† of various works.

The contracting countries are bound to ensure the protection of the works enumerated above.

Works of art applied to industry are protected to the extent permitted by the home legislation of each country.

III.

The present Convention applies to photographic works and other productions obtained through a process analogous or kindred to photography. The contracting countries are bound to assure their protection.

IV.

Authors under the jurisdiction of any one of the countries composing the Union enjoy, in contracting countries outside that in which the work originated, for their productions, either unpublished, or published for the first time in one of the countries belonging to the Union, the rights which the respective laws at the time grant, or will, in the future, grant to natives, as well as the rights specially granted by the present Convention.

The enjoyment and use of these rights are not subordinated to any formality; this enjoyment and this use of rights are independent of the protection existing in the country of origin of the work. Consequently, apart from the stipulations of the present Convention, both the extent of the protection and the means of redress

---

† The term "recueils," used in the text of the Convention, would apply to compilations of all kinds, catalogues, works of reference, etc.—ED.

assured to the author for the safeguard of his rights are determined exclusively according to the legislation of the country in which the claim for protection is made.

The consideration upon which the country of origin of a work rests is : for unpublished works, the country of origin is that to which the author belongs; for published works, the country in which the first publication takes place; and for works published simultaneously in several countries of the Union, that in which the period of protection granted is the shortest. Should works be published simultaneously in a country outside the Union and in a country belonging to it, the latter shall be exculsively considered as the country of origin.

By published works it must be understood that in the sense of the present Convention printed works are meant. The performance of a dramatic or dramatico-musical work, the execution of a musical composition, the exhibition of a work of art, and the construction of a work of architecture, do not constitute a publication.

V.

Authors under the jurisdiction of one of the countries belonging to the Union who, for the first time, publish their works in another country of the Union, have, in the latter country, the same rights as native authors.

VI.

Authors not subject to the jurisdiction of one of the countries belonging to the Union who publish their works for the first time in one of the united countries enjoy in that country the same rights as the native authors, and in the other countries the rights granted by the present Convention.

VII.

The duration of the protection granted by the present Convention comprises the author's lifetime and a period of fifty years after his death.

However, in case of this duration not being uniformly adopted by all the contracting countries to the Union, the period will be determined according to the law of the country where protection is claimed, and it shall not exceed the duration fixed in the country of origin of the work. Consequently, the contracting countries will only be bound to apply the disposition stipulated in the preceding paragraph to the extent to which it can be reconciled to their home rights.

In the instance of photographic works and works executed by a process analogous to photography, of posthumous works, of anonymous or pseudonymous works, the duration of the protection is settled by the law of the country where the protection is claimed, with the reservation that this protection shall not extend further than the duration fixed in the country of origin of the work.

VIII.

The authors of unpublished works subject to the jurisdiction of one of the countries in the Union, and the authors of works published for the first time in one of these countries, enjoy, in the other countries of the Union, and during the whole period of their right in the original work, the further and exclusive right of authorising the translation of their works, or translating them themselves.

IX.

Serials, novels, and all other works, whether literary, scientific, or artistic, whatever their object may be, published in newspapers or periodical publications in one of the countries of the Union, may not be reproduced in the other countries without the consent of their authors.

Excluding serials and novels, any newspaper article may be reproduced in another paper, provided the reproduction has not been expressly forbidden. However, the source of it must be stated ; the sanction of this obligation is to be determined by the legislation of the country where the protection is claimed.

The protection established by the present Convention does not apply to daily news or miscellaneous intelligence having the character of mere Press information.

X.

In respect of the faculty of borrowing lawfully from literary or artistic works for the purpose of publications intended for education, or having a scientific character, or for the compilation of chrestomathies (or collections of extracts), the legislation of the countries of the Union and the particular arrangements existing or to be made hereafter between them will alone come into effect.

XI.

The stipulations of the present Convention apply to the public performance of dramatic or dramatico-musical works, and to the execution in public of musical compositions, whether these works have been published or not.

The authors of dramatic or dramatico-musical works are, while their right in the original production lasts, protected against the unauthorised performance in public of the translation of their works.

In order to enjoy the protection secured by the present article, authors, at the time of publication of their works, are under no obligation to prohibit their performance or execution in public.

XII.

Specially included among the illicit reproductions aimed at by the present Convention are : The indirect and unauthorised appropriations of a literary or artistic work, such as adaptations, arrangements of music, transformation of a work of fiction, novel, or poetry, into a play, or *vice versâ*, etc., if they be merely a reproduction of the original work in the same or in another form, with only unessential alterations, additions, or curtailments, and devoid of the character of an original work.

XIII.

Authors of musical compositions have the exclusive right to authorise : (1) the adaptation of these works to instruments devised to reproduce them mechanically; (2) the public execution of the same works by means of these instruments.

Reservations and conditions relating to the application of this article will be liable to determination according to the internal legislation of each country, in so far as that country is concerned, but all reservations and conditions of such nature will, in their effect, be strictly limited to the country in which they have been established.

The disposition of paragraph 1 has no retro-active effect, and consequently is not applicable in a country belonging to the Union to works which in that country have been licitly adapted to mechanical instruments before the coming into force of the present Convention.

Adaptations made in virtue of paragraphs II. and III. of the present article and imported without authorisation from the interested parties into a country where they are not licit, will be liable to seizure.

XIV.

Authors of literary, scientific, or artistic works have the exclusive right to authorise the public reproduction and representation of their works by means of kinematography.

Kinematographic productions are protected as literary or artistic works, whenever, owing to the devices of the "mise-en-scène," or the combinations of the incidents represented, the author shall have imparted to the work a personal and original character.

Without any detriment to the rights of the author of the original work, the reproduction by kinematography of a literary, scientific, or artistic work is protected as an original work

The preceding dispositions apply to the reproduction or production obtained through any other process analogous to kinematography.

XV.

So that authors of works protected by the present Convention should be, until proof to the contrary, considered as such, and therefore admitted before the tribunals of the various countries to institute lawsuits against plagiarists, pirates, etc., it is sufficient that their names be indicated on their works in the customary manner.

In the case of anonymous or pseudonymous works, the editor whose name appears on the work is empowered to safeguard the rights belonging to the author. He is, without other proofs, deemed to be the assign of the anonymous or pseudonymous author.

XVI.

Every counterfeited work may be seized by the competent authorities of the countries of the Union in which the original work carries the right to legal protection.

In those countries (*i.e.*, belonging to the Union), the seizure may also be applicable to reproductions originating from a country where the work is not, or has ceased to be, protected.

The seizure is carried out in conformity with the home legislation of each individual country.

XVII.

The dispositions of the present Convention cannot be permitted to act in any way whatever detrimentally to the rights which belong to the Government of each of the countries of the Union, to permit, or to interdict, through measures of legislation or home police, the circulation, the representation, the exhibition of any work or production in respect of which the competent authority should be called upon to exercise this right.

XVIII.

The present Convention is applicable to all works which, at the time of its coming into force, have not yet become public property in the country of their origin, through the period of protection having expired.

However, in the event of a work having, through the expiration of the term of protection previously granted, become public property in the country where protection is claimed, such work will not be protected anew in that country.

The application of this principle will be effected according to the stipulations contained in the special conventions already existing between countries of the Union, or to be hereafter concluded for that purpose. Failing such stipulations having been formulated, the respective countries shall settle, each in so far as it is concerned, the modalities relative to this application.*

The dispositions which precede apply equally in case of new accessions to the Union, and in the event of the duration of the protection being extended through application of article 7.

XIX.

The dispositions of the present Convention do not prevent a claim to the application of dispositions of a larger scope, should such be edicted by the legislation of a country of the Union in favour of foreigners generally.

XX.

The Governments of the countries of the Union reserve to themselves the right to enter between each other into particular arrangements, in so far as these arrangements should confer on authors more extensive rights than those granted by the Union, or should contain other stipulations non-prejudicial to the present Convention. The dispositions of existing arrangements which agree with the fore-mentioned conditions remain applicable.

XXI.

The international office instituted under the name "Bureau de l'Union internationale pour la protection des œuvres littéraires et artistiques" is maintained.

This Bureau is placed under the high authority of the Government of the Swiss Confederation, which regulates its organisation and superintends its working.

The official language of the Bureau is the French language.

XXII.

The International Bureau centralises information of all kinds relative to the protection of the rights of authors in their literary or artistic works. It arranges and publishes them. It prosecutes studies of general utility interesting the Union, and draws up with the help of documents placed at its disposal by the various Administrations a periodical paper in the French language on all questions furthering the object of the Union. The Governments of the countries of the Union reserve to themselves to authorise by common consent the publication by the Bureau of an edition in one or more languages, should experience eventually demonstrate the need thereof.

The International Bureau is bound to be constantly at the disposal of the members of the Union to furnish them with any special information they might require on questions relating to the protection of literary and artistic works.

The Director of the International Bureau makes a yearly report on his administration, which is communicated to all the members of the Union.

---

* Will consider from the particular circumstances connected with [the [fact the]questions] of possibility or necessity.—ED.

XXIII.

The expenses of the International Bureau of the Union are borne in common by the contracting countries. Until further decision, they shall not exceed the sum of sixty thousand francs (£2,400) per annum. This sum may be increased if need be by a simple decision of one of the conferences foreseen in Article XXIV.

In order to determine the share of contribution of each of the countries towards the sum total of expenses, the contracting countries and those which may subsequently join the Union are divided into six classes, each contributing in proportion to a certain number of units, namely :—

First Class	...	...	...	...	...	...	25 units.
Second Class	...	...	...	...	...	...	20 units.
Third Class	...	...	...	...	...	...	15 units.
Fourth Class	...	...	...	...	...	...	10 units.
Fifth Class	...	...	...	...	...	...	5 units.
Sixth Class	...	...	...	...	...	...	3 units.

These co-efficients are multiplied by the number of countries included in each class, and the sum of the products thus obtained supplies the number of units by which the total expenditure must be divided. The quotient gives the amount of the unit of expenses.

Each country shall declare, at the time of its accession, in which of the above-mentioned classes it wishes to rank.

The Swiss Administration prepares the budget of the Bureau and supervises its expenses, supplies the necessary advances and establishes the annual account to be communicated to all the other Administrations.

XXIV.

The present Convention is liable to be submitted to revisions, with a view of introducing in it improvements of a nature to perfect the system of the Union.

Questions of this nature, and likewise any questions which, in other respects, may be of interest to the development of the Union, are to be dealt with at Conferences which will take place in succession in the countries belonging to the Union between delegates from the said countries. The Administration of the country where a Conference is to sit is entrusted, jointly with the International Bureau, with the preparation of the labours of the assembled delegates. The Director of the Bureau attends the sittings of the conferences and takes part in the discussions, without, however, having the right to vote.

No alteration to the present Convention can be considered as valid by the Union unless it be unanimously assented to by the contracting countries which compose it.

XXV.

States outside the Union which ensure the legal protection of the rights which the present Convention has for object to secure can, on their demand, obtain accession to it.

This accession will be notified in writing to the Government of the Swiss Confederation, which will undertake to notify it to all the others.

It will carry as a matter of course adhesion to all the clauses and admission to all the advantages stipulated in the present Convention. However, it may include the indication of the dispositions of the Convention of September 9, 1886, or of the additional Act of May 4, 1896, which they should deem necessary to substitute, at least temporarily to the corresponding dispositions of the present Convention.

XXVI.

The contracting countries have, at any time, the right to accede to the present Convention on behalf of their colonies or foreign possessions.

They may, to this end, either make a general declaration, by which all their colonies or possessions are included in the accession, or expressly mention by name those which are comprised, or confine themselves to indicate those which are to be excluded.

This declaration will be notified in writing to the Government of the Swiss Confederation, which will undertake to notify it to all the others.

XXVII.

The present Convention shall, in the relations between the contracting States, take the place of the Berne Convention of September 9, 1886, including the additional Article and the protocol of closure of the same day, as well as the additional Article and the interpretative Declaration of May 4, 1896. The Conventional Acts fore-mentioned will remain in force in the relations with States which should abstain from ratifying the present Convention.

The signatory States to the present Convention will, at the time of exchange of the ratifications, be at liberty to declare that they intend, on some point or other, to hold themselves still bound by the dispositions of the Conventions to which they have previously subscribed.

XXVIII.

The present Convention will be ratified, and the ratifications exchanged at Berlin on July 1, 1910, at latest.

Each contracting party shall remit for the exchange of ratifications one single document, which will be deposited with those of other countries in the archives of the Government of the Swiss Confederation. Each party will receive in return a copy of the " procès-verbal," or official report of the proceedings of the exchange of the ratifications, bearing the signatures of the Plenipotentiaries delegated to take part in it.

XXIX.

The present Convention will be carried into effect three months after the exchange of ratifications, and will remain in force during an indeterminate time, until the expiration of one year dating from the day on which its denunciation was tendered.

This denunciation will have to be addressed to the Government of the Swiss Confederation. It will only take effect in regard of the country from which it emanates, the Convention remaining executory for the other countries forming the Union.

XXX.

States introducing in their legislation the fifty-years period of protection statutable according to article 7, paragraph 1, of the present Convention, shall impart the fact to the Government of the Swiss Confederation by a written notice which will be forthwith communicated by that Government to all the other States forming the Union.

The same proceeding will be followed in respect of States renouncing reservations made by them in virtue of Articles 25, 26, and 27.

In witness and testimony whereof the respective Plenipotentiaries have signed the present Convention and affixed their seals thereto.

Made in Berlin on the 13th day of November, the year one thousand nine hundred and eight, in one single copy, which will be deposited in the archives of the Government of the Swiss Confederation, and of which copies certified to be true will be transmitted through diplomatic channels to the contracting States.

FIRES AND ACCIDENTS IN THEATRES AND HALLS.

Jan. 11. Accident at the Harvey Institute, Barnsley, owing to children congesting the stairways and not being under adequate control. Sixteen children lost their lives.

Feb. 1. Athenæum, Lancaster, destroyed by fire.

Feb. 18. Fire at the Royal, Windsor.

Mar. 25. Fire at Drury Lane. Stage and flies destroyed. The auditorium was practically undamaged, being saved by the fire-resisting curtain.

June 13. Hippodrome, Maidstone, destroyed by fire.

June 26. Hippodrome, Accrington, destroyed by fire.

Dec. 17. Fire at the Irving, Seacombe. Auditorium damaged.

Dec. 26. Fire at Gale's Picture Show, Stratford. Eighteen persons injured in the rush for the exits.

ACTRESSES' FRANCHISE LEAGUE.

This League was founded by Mrs. Forbes Robertson, Miss Winifred Mayo, Miss' Sime Seruya, and Miss Adeline Bourne. The first meeting, which was in the nature of an " At Home," was held on Thursday, December 17, at the Criterion Restaurant, when between 300 and 400 actresses and actors were present. Mr. Forbes Robertson was in the chair. The following resolution was passed : —

That this meeting of actresses calls upon the Government immediately to extend the franchise to women; that women claim the franchise as a necessary protection for the workers under modern industrial conditions, and maintain that by their labour they have earned the right to this defence.

Mrs. Kendal is the President of the League, and the Vice-Presidents are Miss Violet Vanbrugh, Miss Gertrude Elliott, Mrs. Langtry, Miss Irene Vanbrugh, Miss Eva Moore, Mme. Marie Brema, and Mrs. Lucette Ryley. The Committee are as follow : —Miss Granville, Miss Edith Craig, Miss Winifred Mayo, Miss Bessie Hatton, Miss Sime Seruya, Miss Tita Brand, Miss Mary Martyn, Miss Beatrice Forbes-Robertson, and Miss Adeline Bourne. Among the members already enrolled are Miss Ellen Terry, Miss Fanny Brough, Miss Decima Moore, Miss Lilian Braithwaite, Miss Compton, Miss Mouillot, Miss Violet Hunt, Miss Cicely Hamilton, and Miss Christine Silver. The Hon. Secretary is Miss Adeline Bourne, of 19, Overstrand Mansions, Battersea Park, S W. Green and pink are the colours of the League.

CIRCUITS.

WHERE AND TO WHOM TO WRITE FOR ENGAGEMENTS.

BARRASFORD-GIBBONS TOUR.—Mr. Thomas Barrasford, Adelphi Terrace House, Robert Street, Adelphi, W.C. (for Provincial and Continental Halls only) ; Mr. Walter Gibbons (for London Halls only). (1668, 1669, 3184, and 3183 Gerrard.)

BOSTOCK TOUR.—Mr. E. H. Bostock, Zoo Hippodrome, Glasgow.

BROADHEAD TOUR.—Mr. Percy B. Broadhead, Hippodrome, Hulme.

HARRY DAY TOUR.—Mr. Harry Day, 1, Effingham House, Arundel Street, Strand, London, (Gerrard 6915.)

DE FREECE CIRCUIT.—Mr. J. De Freece, 178, Charing Cross Road, W.C. (Gerrard 1739.)

T. ALLEN EDWARDS TOUR.—Mr. T. Allen Edwards, Palace Theatre, Derby.

GROS, HENRI (Mr. Leon Zeitlin).—1, Durham House Street. W.C. (Gerrard 2035.)

GRAHAM TOUR.—Mr. Alfred Graham, Hippodrome, Hull.

MACNAGHTEN TOUR.—Mr. Frederick Baugh, Oakley House, Bloomsbury Street, W.C. (Avenue 5954.)

PEPI TOUR.—Signor Pepi, Tivoli, Carlisle.

ROBINSON TOUR.—Mr. Wm. Robinson, Theatre Royal, Halifax.

STOLL TOUR.—Mr. Oswald Stoll, Cranbourne Mansions, Cranbourne Street, London, W.C. (Gerrard 1399.)

SYNDICATE TOUR (Mr. Will Collins).—1, Durham House Street, London, W.C. (Gerrard 2619.)

UNITED COUNTY THEATRES, LTD.—Messrs. Rosen and Bliss, 12 and 13, Henrietta Street, London, W.C. (Gerrard 7623.)

WILMOT TOUR.—Mr. Fred Wilmot, 156, Islington, Liverpool.

THE AMERICAN STAGE.

PRINCIPAL PLAYS PRODUCED IN AMERICA, JANUARY TO THE END OF NOVEMBER, 1908.

Agnes, play, in four acts, by George Cameron—Opera House, Providence, R.I., September 28; Majestic, New York, October 5.

Algeria, musical comedy, in two acts, by Victor Herbert and Glen MacDonough—Apollo, Atlantic City, N.J., August 24; Broadway, New York (F. McKee), August 31.

All for a Girl, farce comedy, in four acts, by Rupert Hughes—Plainfield Theatre, Plainfield, N.J., August 17; Bijou, New York, August 22.

American Heiress, An, musical comedy—Ennis, Tex., September.

American Idea, The, musical comedy, by George M. Cohan—Star, Buffalo, New York, September 7; New York Theatre, New York, October 5.

Angels and Devils of Philadelphia, melodrama—Philadelphia, April 6.

And the Greatest of These—, drama, by George Earle and Fanny Cannon—Orpheum, Salt Lake City, U., July 20.

Around the Clock, piece, in three acts, book by Steve Cassin, music by Lee Orean Smith—American Theatre, New York, January 6.

Aunt Cynthy's Homestead, comedy drama, in four acts, by Ulie Akerstrom—Yorkville, New York, November 23.

Awakening, The, play, in three acts, from the French of Paul Hervieu, produced by Olga Nethersole—Daly's, New York, February 10.

Awakening of Helena Ritchie, The, dramatised from a novel by Margaret Deland by Charlotte Thompson—Parson's, Hartford, Conn., February 19; Adelphi, Philadelphia, February 24.

Battle of Port Arthur, melodrama, in one act, by Owen Davis—Hippodrome, New York, January 6.

Bandanna Land, in three acts, book by J. A. Shipp and Alex. Rogers, music by W. M. Cook (Williams and Walker)—Majestic, New York, February 3.

Bandbox, The, one-act play, by Marie B. Schrader—Fifth Avenue, New York, May 10.

Battle in the Skies, spectacle, in four scenes, by Arthur Voegtlin and R. H. Burnside—Hippodrome, New York, September 10.

Battle, The, play, by Cleveland Moffett—Duluth, Minn., September 18.

Bachelor and the Maid, The, farce comedy, in three acts, by Claude L. N. Norrie—Gottschalk Theatre, Aberdeen, S.D., October 3.

Barber of New Orleans, The, by Edward Childs Carpenter—Garrick, Chicago, October 17.

Baucis; or, The Children's Paradise, one-act play, dramatised from Hawthorne's "Wonder Book" by Rose O'Neill—Chicago, July.

Beloved Vagabond, The, play, by W. J. Locke—Cincinnati, February 23.

Big Stick, The, comedy, in three acts, music by G. V. Hobart—West End, New York, February 24.

Blockhead, The, comedy, in five acts, by Ludwig Fulda—German Theatre, New York, January 1.

Blue Grass, drama, in three acts, by Paul Armstrong (Liebler and Co.)—Majestic, New York, November 9.

Blue Mouse, The, adaptation by Clyde Fitch—Hyperion, New Haven, Conn., November 25; Lyric, New York, November 30.

Bluffs, comedy, by Leo Ditrichstein—Plainfield, New Jersey (Wagenhais and Kemper), February 17; Bijou, New York, March 19.

Boys and Betty, The, play, by George V. Hobart and Silvio Hein—Broadway, Norwich, Conn., October 1; Wallack's, New York, November 2.

Broken Idol, A, musical play, by Hal Stephens and E. Van Alstyne—Chatterton Opera House, Springfield, Ill., August 16; Whitney Theatre, Chicago, August 22.

Busy Izzy's Boodle, musical comedy, in two acts, book by Frank Kennedy, songs by W. J. McKenna—West End, New York, April 6.

By Order of the Court, three-act play, by Mary Roberts Rinehart—Hoyt's Theatre, South Norwalk, Conn., August 1.

By Order of the President, melodrama, by Polly Pry—Curtis Theatre, Denver, June 28.

Calverts of Louisiana, The, play, by Sadie Calhoun—Fourot Theatre, Lima, O., February 22.

Call of the North, The, play, by George Broadhurst—Opera House, Providence, April 23; Hudson, New York, August 24.

Captain Clay of Missouri, four-act play, by David Higgins and his brother—Majestic Theatre, Fort Wayne, Indiana, August 13.

Cameo Kirby, play, by Booth Tarkington and Harry Leon Wilson—Great Southern Theatre, Columbus, November 16.

Captain Walrus, comedietta, in one act, by Alexander Laidlaw, jun. (Academy matinée)—Empire, New York, February 20.

Cash Girl, The, play—Dover, N.J., October 10.

Castle in Spain, A, melodrama, in one act, by Grenville Vernon (Academy of Dramatic Arts and Empire Theatre Dramatic School)—Empire, New York, January 23.

Chaperon, The, three-act comedy, by Marion Fairfax—Majestic, Boston, November 30.

Cloven Foot, The, a version of *Der Teufel* (The Devil), adapted by Oliver Hereford—Parson's Theatre, Hartford, July 6 (afterwards produced as *The Devil*, by H. W. Savage, at the Garden, New York, August 18).

Colonial Days, operetta, by B. A. Rolfe—Freebody Park Theatre, Newport, R.I., August 3.

Commencement Day, comedy, in four acts, by Margaret Mayo—Belasco, Los Angeles, January 26; Colonial, Boston, August 31.

Cora, play by Mme. Fred de Gressac—Cincinnati, October 26; Chicago, November 30.

Cowpuncher's Sweetheart, A, playlet, by Guy Dailey—Hiland Theatre, Pittsburg, November 2.

Creole Slave's Revenge, The, melodrama, in four acts, by Walton Lawrence—Grand Street Theatre, New York (A. H. Woods), September 14.

Cupid and the Dollar, comedy—Savannah, Ga., August 29.

Daughter of America, musical comedy, in two acts, by John Saunders, music by N. Harris Ware—Plainfield Theatre, Plainfield, N.J., August 25.

Daughter of the People, A, drama, in four acts, by J. Searle Dawley—Lincoln Square, New York, June 8.

Devil, The, drama, in three acts, by Franz Molnar, adaptation by Alexander Konta and W. T. Larned (H. Grey Fiske)—Belasco, New York, August 18.

The Devil, drama, in three acts, by Franz Molnar, adaptation by Oliver Hereford (H. W. Savage), first entitled *The Cloven Foot*—Parson's, Harford, July 6; Garden, New York, August 18 (originally produced, Deutsches Volkstheater, Vienna, February 15).

Diana of Dobson's, four-act play, by Cicely Hamilton—Savoy, New York, September 5.

Divorce, A, Stanislaus Stange's version of Paul Bourget's *Un Divorce*—Montreal, November 2.

Dolls, The, sociological comedy, by Julius Hopp—Socialist Theatre, New York, March 27.

Don Quixote, play, in four acts, by Paul Kester, from Cervantes' novel (Lee Shubert)—Lyric, New York, April 8.

Duellist, The, one-act play, by Cecil de Mille, by students, at a *matinée*—Hacket, New York, March 31.

Easterner, The, melodrama, in four acts, by George Broadhurst—Garrick, New York, March 2.

Electra, tragedy, in one act, by Arthur Symons, from the German version by Hugo Von Hofmannsthal (Liebler and Co.), Mrs. Patrick Campbell and Mrs. Tree in the east Garden, New York, February 11.

End of the Day, The, one-act play, by A. H. Laidlaw, junior — Students' *matinée*, Hacket, New York, March 31.

Energetic Mr. West, The, play, by Edgar Selwyn—Belasco, Los Angeles, February 10.

Enigma, The, play, in two acts, by Paul Hervieu, produced by Olga Nethersole—Daly's, New York, February 19.

Esther, the Queen, play, in four acts, by the Rev. Leon H. Elmaleh—New Columbia Hall, Philadelphia, May.

Ethical Demand, An, comedy, in one act, by Otto E. Hartleben—New German Theatre, New York, November 11.

Falling Leaves, comedy drama, by Signor Giacosa—Lyric, Philadelphia, May 18.

False Friends, melodrama, in four acts, by Robert Norton—Third Avenue, New York, September 7.

Fair Co-Ed, The, play, by George Ade—Opera House, Detroit, Mich., September 28.

Father and Son, comedy, in three acts, by Gustav Esmann—German Theatre, New York, November 24.

Father and Son, play, by Edward Selwyn—Belasco Theatre, Washington, September 14; Majestic, New York (F. Ray Comstock), September 24.

Father and the Boys, four act play, by George Ade—Empire, New York (Chas. Frohman), March 2.

Fighting Chance, A, melodrama, in four acts, by Theodore Kremer—American Theatre, New York, January 13.

Fighting Hope, The, play, by William J. Hurlbut—Belasco Theatre, Washington, September 5; Studvysant, New York (Belasco), September 22.

Fifth Commandment, The, folk play, in four acts, by Ludwig Anzengruber—German Theatre, New York, March 3.

Fifty Miles from Boston, musical play, in three acts, George M. Cohan—Previously produced outside New York; Garrick, New York, February 3.

Florette and Patapon, farce, in three acts, by Maurice Hennequin and Pierre Veber—German Theatre, New York, March 13.

Flower of the Ranch, The, musical comedy melodrama, in three acts, by J. E. Howard—West End, New York.

Flower of Yamato, The, one act Japanese tragedy, translated from the original by Comte Robert d'Humière (Liebler and Co.)—Garden, New York, February 11.

Fluffy Ruffles, musical comedy, by John J. McNally, music by W. T. Francis—Star Theatre, Buffalo, New York, August 24; Criterion, New York (Chas. Frohman), September 7.

Folly, comedy, by Wilbur Underwood—Ford's Theatre, Baltimore, July 27.

Follies of 1908, The, review, by F. Ziegfeld—Apollo, Atlantic City, N.J., June 8; Roof Garden, New York, June 15.

Fool's Gold, dramatic act, by Edward Brandt—Fifth Avenue Theatre, New York, August 16.

Fool Hath Said There is No God, The, play, five acts, by Laurence Irving, on Dostoieffski's novel, " Crime and Punishment " (Lee Shubert)—Lyric, New York, March 9.

Forger, The, drama, in three acts, by Joseph Byron Totten—Auditorium, Burlington, N.J., September 10.

Freckles, one act play, dramatised by J. Frank Davis and Robert Hilliard from a short story by P. E. Browne, entitled " Proof "—Colonial, New York, September 29.

Funabashi, musical comedy, in three acts, book by Irving S. Cobb, music and lyrics by Safford Waters—Casino, New York, January 6.

Gates of Eden, The, play, by the Rev. William Nanforth—Garrick, Chicago, July 6.

Gay Musician, The, musical play, book and lyrics by E. Siedele, music by Julian Edwards—Academy, Baltimore, April 20; Philadelphia, April 27; Wallacks, New York, May 18.

Gauntlet, The, emotional drama, in two acts, by Björnsterne Björnson (Academy *matinée*)—Empire, New York, February 20.

Gentleman Convict, The; or, The Secret Wedding, melodrama, in four acts, by C. Verner Findlay—Lyric, Portland, Ore., June 22.

Gentleman from Mississippi, A, by Thomas A Wise and Harrison Rhodes—Nationa Theatre, Washington, September 21; Bijou, New York, September 29.

Girls, three act comedy, by Clyde Fitch—Belasco, Washington, March 9; Daly's, New York, March 23.

Girl and the Detective, The, melodrama, in four acts, by Chas. E. Blaney and J. Searle Dawley—Blaney's, New York, May 11.

Girl at the Helm, A, musical play, by Robert B. Smith and Raymond Hubbell—La Salle Theatre, Chicago, September 5

Girl's Best Friend, A, comedy drama, in four acts—first time in New York, Fourteenth Street Theatre, New York, September 14.

Girl from Hamburg, The, one act play, by Harlan E. Babcock—Majestic, Kalamazoo, May 4.

Girl from Texas, The, comedy drama, in four acts, by C. T. Dazey and Charles E. Blaney —Lincoln Square, New York, June 1.

Girls of Gottenberg, The, musical comedy, in two acts, by Geo. Grossmith, jun., and L. E. Bernan; music by Ivan Caryll and Lionel Monckton—Knickerbocker, New York (Chas. Frohman), September 2.

Girl Question, The, musical comedy, in three acts, by Messrs. Hough and Adams; music by J. E. Howard—Wallacks, New York, August 3 (previously produced in the country).

Gloria, by James Fagan—Opera House, Providence February 24.

Glorious Betsy, comedy, in four acts, by Rida Johnson Young (Shubert Bros.)—Lyric, New York, September 7.

Governor and the Boss, The, play, by G. F. Blagdon and W. Postance—Blaney's Theatre, New York, April 27.

Goal, The, one act tragedy, by Henry Arthur Jones—Actors' Society *matinée,* Hudson, New York, April 21.

Going Some, comedy, in four acts, by Paul Armstrong and Rex Beach (Liebler and Co.)—Waterbury, Conn., March 16.

Golden Butterfly, The, three act light opera, by Reginald de Koven and Harry B. Smith —National Theatre, Washington, September 28; Broadway, New York, October 12.

Graustark, five act play, by Grace Hayward, adapted from George Barr McCutcheon's novel of the same name—Haarlem Opera House, New York, January 20.

Great Passion, The, comedy, in three acts, by Raoul Auernheimer—German Theatre, New York, April 16.

Great Question, The, play, by Frederick Paulding—Lyceum, Rochester, September 24; Majestic, New York, October 26.

Great Secret, The, comedy, in three acts, by Pierre Wolf—New German Theatre, New York, November 3.

Her Father's Honour, melodrama, by Robert Goodman—Lyceum, Troy, June 22.

Hertha's Wedding, comedy, in four acts, by Max Bernstein—German Theatre, New York, January 28.

His Soul's Mate, comedy drama, in four acts, by Arthur Griffin—Taylor Opera House, Danbury, Conn., October 16.

His Wife's Family, comedy, in three acts, by George Egerton—Wallacks, New York, October 6.

Honour of the Family, The, play, in four acts, by Emile Fabre, adapted by Paul N. Potter (Chas. Frohman)—Hudson, New York, February 17.

Honeymoon Trail, The, musical play, by Messrs. Adams, Hough, and Howard—Alhambra, Milwaukee, March 16.

Hotel Clerk, The, musical comedy, by Robert B. Smith and A. Aarons—Walnut Street, Philadelphia, April 27.

House of Cards, A, four act play, by Ivey Ashton Root—Star, Buffalo, November 28.

House of a Thousand Candles, The, dramatised version of Meredith Nicholson's novel of the same name, melodrama, in four acts, by George Middleton—Daly's, New York, January 6.

Husband's Rights, A, one-act comedy, by Hermann Adeler and Meyer Schwartz—People's Music Hall, New York, June 19.

Hussarenfieber, Das, comedy, in four acts, by Gustav Kadelburg and Richard Skowronnek—Irving Place, New York, October 1.

I Take This Man, comedy, by Edith Ellis Baker—Court Square Theatre, Springfield, Mass., July 20.

Idol of the Hour, The, one-act play, by Virginia Harned—Suburban Theatre, St. Louis, Mo., June 13.

Imperial Divorce, The, play by John G. Wilson and W. J. Humphrey—Auditorium, Burlington, N.J., November 5.

Imposter, The, play by R. N. Beach—Washington, April 11; Philadelphia, April 13.

In Carolina—Dauphine Theatre, New Orleans, February 3.

Inconsistent, one-act play, by Clara Ruge—Berkeley, New York, May 20.

Indian's Secret, The, melodrama, by Lincoln Carter—Alhambra, Chicago, August 17.

In the Nick of Time, play, in five acts, by Thomas Morris and Florence Bindley—Fourteenth Street Theatre, New York, September 21.

In the House of the Priest, emotional drama, in one act, adapted from an incident in *Les Miserables*

Intruder, The, drama, by Thompson Buchanan—*Matinée,* Tremont Theatre, Boston, April 9; Empire, New York, November 5.

International Marriage, An, play, in three acts, by Geo. H. Broadhurst—Parson's Theatre, Hartford, Conn., November 2.

Invader, The, play, in four acts, by Walter Hackett—Pabst Theatre, Milwaukee, May 18.

Irene Wycherley, play, in three acts, by Anthony P. Wharton (Liebler and Co.)—Astor, New York, January 20.

Jack Sheppard, melodrama, in four acts, by Olive Harper (A. H. Woods)—Grand Street Theatre, New York, November 16.

Jack Straw, comedy, in three acts, by W. Somerset Maugham—Empire, New York (Chas. Frohman), September 14.

Jane, of Nevada, dramatic act, by Robert Drouet—Fifth Avenue Theatre, New York, August 16.

Jesters, The, play, in four acts, by John Raphael, from the French of Miquel Zamacois—Empire, New York, January 15.

Jet, four-act comedy-drama, by Louise Lovell—Columbia Theatre, Washington, September 5.

Jewel Regained, A, one-act play, by George Bachus—Students' *matinée,* Hacket, New York, March 31.

Jewish Heart, The, four-act play, by Joseph Latimer—Kessler's Thalia Theatre, October 16.

Joy is Dangerous, comedy-drama, in one act, by Mme. Emilie De Girardin (Academy of Dramatic Arts and Empire Theatre Dramatic School)—Empire, New York, January 23.

Just Like John, farce-comedy, by Mark E. Swan—Albaugh's Theatre, Baltimore, April 6.

Kate Barton's Temptation, melodrama, in four acts, by Thomas H. Sewell—Thalia, New York, April 20.

Kate Shannon, play, by Mrs. Gertrude Nelson —Andrew's, Los Angeles, January 6.

Kentucky Boy, A, play, in three acts, by Pauline Phelps and Marion Short—Apollo Theatre, Atlantic City. N.J., November 19.

Kingmaker, The, comic opera, written by Waldemar Young, W. C. Patterson, and Race Whitney, music by R. H. Bassett—Princess's, San Francisco, June 22.

Ladies' Battle, The, comedy, in two acts, translated from the French of A. E. Scribe (Academy *matinée*)—Empire, New York, February 20.

Lady Frederick, three-act comedy, by W. Somerset Maugham—Poughkeepsie, N.Y., September 15; Hudson, New York (Chas. Frohman), November 9.

Lady in the Kimono, The, farce, in three acts, by Helen Bagg—Studebaker, Chicago, April 23.

Land of Birds, The, ballet, in two tableaux, by R. H. Burnside—Hippodrome, New York, September 10.

Lasso Land, romantic comic opera, by John N. Edwards and W. V. Brumby, music by E. J Novy—Casino, Lake Cliff, Dallas, Tex., September 28

Last of Smith, The, a sketch—Lyceum, Englewood, N.J., October 20.

Libation Pourers, The, Greek music drama, by Æschylus, in one act, translated by Anna H. Branch, music by R. O. Jenkins (Academy of Dramatic Arts)—Empire, New York, March 26.

Like Father Like Son, farce, by Mrs. Jean Pardee Clark—Polis Theatre, New Haven, Conn., October 19.

Likes o' Me, The, one-act play, by Wilfred T. Colby—Garrick, New York (Chas. Frohman), September 1.

Little King, The, comedy, in one act, by Leon Xanrof and Gaston Guerin—New German Theatre, New York, November 12.

Little Nemo, musical comedy, by Harry B. Smith, music by Victor Vernon—Forrest Theatre, Philadelphia, September 28; New Amsterdam, New York, October 20.

Lily and the Prince, The, drama, in four acts, by Carina Jordan—Yorkville, New York, May 4.

Li'l Mose, musical play, in three acts, by Fred G. Nixon-Nirdlinger and Chas. H. Brown, music by A. Baldwin Sloane—Atlantic City, N.J., April 20.

Literary Sense, The, translation by Charles Harvey Genung of Arthur Schnitzler's one-act satire, *Literatur* (first produced in America at the German Theatre, New York, on October 29, 1907)—Madison Square, New York, January 13.

Lonesome Town, musical comedy, in two acts, by Judson D. Brusie, music by J. A. Raynes (Kolb and Dill)—New Circle, New York, January 20.

Lost Trail, The, melodrama, in four acts, by Anthony E. Wills—West End, New York, January 27.

Love's Comedy, Ibsen's three-act comedy—Hudson, New York, March 23.

Love Waltz, The, musical play, libretto by Paul West, lyrics by Mr. Lasky, music by Charles Berton—Fifth Avenue, New York, April 21.

Love Watches, comedy, in four acts, by R. de Flers and G. Caillavet, adapted by Gladys Unger (Chas. Frohman)—Lyceum, New York, August 27.

Luck of MacGregor, The, romantic comedy, in four acts, by Edward Vroom—Garden, New York, April 20.

Lucky Jim, melodrama, in four acts, by W. G. Beckwith, music by Joseph Santley—Grand Street, New York, August 10.

Maid of Japan, The, musical comedy—Airdome Theatre, Palisades Amusement Park, New York, June 22.

Making of Maddalena, The, modern play, in four acts, by Samuel Lewis—Scranton, Pa., November.

Malia, tragedy, in three acts, by Luigi Capuana—Sicilian players, Broadway, New York, November 23.

Mallet's Masterpiece, one-act play, by Edward Peple—Shea's Theatre, Buffalo, July.

Man and His Mate, A, play, by H. R. Durant, adapted by the author from his novel of the same name—Danbury, Conn., November 24.

Man Down Stairs, The, play, by Paul C. Willard—Majestic, Utica, N.Y., July 13.

Man from Home, The, four-act play, by Booth Tarkington and Harry Leon Wilson—Astor Theatre, New York, August 17.

Man Who Stood Still, The, drama, in four acts, by J. E. Goodman (W. A. Brady)—Circle, New York, October 15.

Marcelle, operetta, in two acts, by Frank Pixley and Gustave Luders (Shubert's)—Casino, New York, October 1.

Marigold, comic opera, three acts, by Barclay Walker—Court Theatre, Wheeling, W. Va., September 15.

Marriage, A, comedy drama, in two acts, by Björnsterne Björnson, translated by Grace Isabel Colbron (Academy of Dramatic Arts and Empire Theatre Dramatic School)—Empire, New York, January 23.

Marrying Mary—Grand Opera House, New Haven, August 24.

Marshall, The, one-act play, by T. H. Davis—One Hundred and Twenty-fifth Street, New York, August 17.

Marta of the Lowlands, drama, in three acts, by Angel Guimera, translated by Wallace Gillpatrick and Guido Marburg—Revived, Garden, New York, March 24.

Mary's Lamb, musical comedy, in three acts, adapted from the French by Richard Carle—New York Theatre, New York, May

Mater, comedy, in three acts, by Percy Mackaye—Van Ness Theatre, San Francisco, August 3; Savoy, New York (H. Miller), September 25.

Meadowbrook Farm, melodrama—Columbus, Chicago, August 17.

Melting Pot, The, play, in four acts, by Izzael Zangwill—Columbia, Washington, October 5.

Merry-Go-Round, The, musical travesty, in three acts, book by Edgar Smith, music by Gus Edwards—Lyric, Philadelphia, April 13; New Circle, New York, April 25.

Merry Grafters, The, musical comedy, by Harold Orlob—Salt Lake Theatre, Salt Lake City, June 16.

Merry Widow Burlesqued, The, book by G. V. Hobart, original music of Franz Léhar—Weber's, New York, January 2.

Merry Widow and the Devil, The, burlesque—West End Theatre, New York, November 14.

Messenger Boy No. 42, melodrama—Holliday Street Theatre, Baltimore, August 31; Grand Street, New York, October 12.

Mexican Honeymoon, A, musical comedy, in two acts, by T. B. Donaldson—Able Opera House, Easton, Pa., February 20.

Mice at Play, play, by Helen Merci Schuster—New Richmond O., September.

Midas; or, The Golden Touch, dramatised from Hawthorne's "Wonder Book," by Rose O'Neill—Chicago, July.

Mimic World, The, farce, by Edgar Smith, lyrics by Addison Burkhardt, music by Carl Rehman and Seymour Furth—Atlantic City, June 15; Lyric, Philadelphia, June 22; Casino, New York, July 9.

Miss Innocence, book and lyrics by Harry B. Smith, music by Ludwig Englander—Chestnut Street Opera House, Philadelphia, November 23; New York Theatre, New York, November 30.

Miss Innocence Abroad—Atlantic City, October 26.

Mll^e. Mischief, Viennese operetta, in three acts, by Kraatz and Van Steck, adapted by Sidney Rosenfeld, music by G. M. Ziehrlehr —Lyric Theatre, Philadelphia, September 12; Lyric, New York (Shubert), September 28.

Molly Bawn, play, by Beulah Poynter, dramatised from the novel, "The Duchess"— Gerard Avenue Theatre, Philadelphia, February 7.

Mollusc, The, comedy, in three acts, by Hubert Henry Davis—Garrick, New York (Chas. Frohman), September 1.

Montana, Limited, The, melodrama, by Charles Ulrich—Alhambra, Chicago, May.

Moon Hunters, The, opera, book by Herbert Farrar, music by Robert S. Bearman— Academy of Music, Baltimore, May 18.

Moral Demand, The, one act play, translated from the German of Otto Erich Hartleben —Socialist Theatre, New York, March 27.

Morning, Noon, and Night, musical farce, in two acts, by J. W. Herbert, William Jerome, music by Jean Schwartz—Hartford Opera House, Hartford, Conn., August 31.

Mr. Clay of Missouri, by David Higgins—McVickers's Theatre, Chicago, August 15.

Mr. Hamlet of Broadway, musical play, by Edgar Smith and Edward Madden; music by Ben Jerome—Lyric, Philadelphia, October 1.

Mrs. Peckham's Carouse, playlet, by George Ade—Garrick, New York, September 29.

Music Lesson, The, playlet, by Marie Hubert Frohman—Garrick Theatre, Chicago, July.

Muttburg Life Insurance, farce, by James Crawford—Belasco Theatre, Los Angeles, August 17.

My Lord Chesterfield, romantic drama, by Asa Steele and Walter Percival—Davidson Theatre. Milwaukee, July 29.

My Mamie Rose, play, in four acts, by Owen Kildare and Walter Hackett—Pole's Theatre. Waterbury, Conn., February 1.

Myself Bettina, by Rachel Crothers (produced by Miss Maxine Elliott)—Academy, Baltimore, February 3; Daly's, New York, October 5.

Mysterious Burglar, The, melodrama, in four acts, by Joseph Lebrandt—New Star, New York, January 6.

Naked Truth, The, one-act play, by Edward A. Paulton—Keith and Proctor's Fifth Avenue, New York, June 15.

Nearly a Hero, musical farce, in three acts, book by Richard Grant, music by Reginald de Koven—Trenton, N.J., February 1; Adelphi, Philadelphia, February 3; Casino, New York, February 24.

New Generation, The, play, in four acts, by Jules Eckert Goodman—Opera House, Chicago, September 6.

Night of the Play, The—Casino, Toledo, O., September 6.

Night with the Devil, A, one-act play, by Ulysses Davis—Majestic, Chicago, June.

Offenders, The, four-act play, by Elmer Blaney Harris—Parson's Theatre, Hartford, Conn., September 21; Hudson Theatre, New York (H. B. Harris)—September 28.

On Trial for His Life, melodrama, in four acts, by Owen Davis—Grand Street Theatre, New York (A. H. Woods), October 26.

On the Road, one-act play, by Clara Ruge—Berkeley, New York, May 20.

Our American Cousin, Tom Taylor's four-act comedy, revived by Mr. E. H. Sothern—Lyric, New York, January 27.

Our Children, three-act play, translated from the French of Maurice Biollay by E. S. Belknah, produced by the American Academy of Dramatic Arts—Criterion, New York, January 9.

Out all Night, musical farce, book by J. E. Green and Marion A. Brooks, music by J. T. Brymn—Pekin, Chicago, January 5.

Paid in Full, drama, in four acts, by Eugene Walter (Wagenhals and Kemper)—Astor, New York, February 25.

Pagliacci, I, two-act dramatic version, by C. H. E. Brookfield, produced by Olga Nethersole—Daly's, New York, February 19.

Panic, The, four-act drama—Providence Opera House, Providence, October 15.

Panne, three-act comedy, by Richard Skowronnek—Irving Palace Theatre, New York, November 19.

Pandora, dramatised from Hawthorne's "Wonder Book" by Rose O'Neill—Chicago, July.

Papa Lebonnard, comedy, in four acts, by Jean Aicard, translated by Iva Merlin and C. A. de Lima, adapted by Kate Jordan— Poll's Theatre, Waterbury, Conn., April 17; Bijou, New York, April 28.

Paradise of Lies, A, romantic drama, in prologue and three acts, by Matthew Barry— Yorkville, New York, June 1.

Paradise of Mahomet, The, music by Robert Planquette and Louis Genee, the book Americanised by Harry B. and Robert Smith (Shubert's) — Lyric, Philadelphia, January 24.

Path of Thorns, The, romantic drama, by Otis Colburn—Bush, Philadelphia, April 6.

Patriot, The, opera, in one act, lyrics by Stanislaus Stange, music by Julian Edwards—Fifth Avenue, New York, Nov. 23.

Patriot, The, three act play, by William Collier and J. Hartley Manners—Columbia Theatre, Washington, September 28; Garrick, New York, November 23.

Pelleas and Mélisande, Claude Debussy's opera —Manhattan Opera House, New York, February 26.

Pierre of the Plains, founded on Louis N. Parker's "Pierre and His People," by Edgar Selwyn—Broad Street Theatre, Pittston, Pa., September 18; Hudson, New York, October 12.

Pioneers, The, four act drama, by Julius Hopp —Socialist Theatre. New York, October 20.

Pipe of Peace, The, play, by Sedely Brown— Shubert Theatre, Milwaukee, September 21.

Price of Power, The, one-act piece, by H. D. Cottrell—125th Street Theatre, New York, August 26.

Prima Donna, The, comic opera, by Henry Blossom and Victor Herbert—Studebaker Theatre, Chicago, Ill., October 5; Knickerbocker, New York, November 30.

Prince Humbug, musical comedy, by Mark Swan—Court Square Theatre, Springfield, Mass., August 31.

Prince of Spendthrifts, The, melodrama, in four acts, by Owen Davis—Grand Street Theatre, New York (A. H. Wood's), August 31.

Prize, The, one act play, by John Bargate— Criterion, New York, January 9.

Provider, The, drama, four acts, by Matthew Barry—Yorkville, New York, May 11.

Queen of the Moulin Rouge, The—Chestnut Street Opera House, Philadelphia, November 18.

Rabensteinerim Die (The Executioner), four act drama, by Ernest von Wildenbruch— New German Theatre, New York, October 1.

Ragged Robin, by Rida Johnson Young—Broadway Theatre, Saratogo Springs, New York, August 14.

Rector's Garden, The, comedy, in four acts, by Byron Ongley—Bijou, New York, March 3.

Redemption, The, sociological play, in four acts and prologue—Chestnut Street, Philadelphia, April 13.

Reformer, The, play, by Benjamin Legere and Walter Woods—Boston, Mass., June.

Regeneration, play, in four acts, from the novel "My Mamie Rose," by Owen Kildare and Walter Hackett—Studebaker, Chicago, March 8; Wallack's, New York (Liebler and Co.), September 1.

Revelation, The, four act play, by the Rev. Henry Knott—Fine Arts Theatre, Chicago, November 24.

Revizor, farce, in five acts, by Nicholas V. Gogol, translated from the Russian—Waldorf-Astoria, New York, April 20.

Richard Lovelace, new version of Laurence Irving's play—Macauley's Theatre, Louisville, Ky., November 20.

Richest Girl, The, four act comedy, by Messrs. Gauvolt and Morton—Park Theatre, Boston, Mass., September 21.

Right to Live, The, play, by Jules Eckert Goodman—Academy, Richmond, Va., July 13; Columbia, Washington, October 26.

Rising of the Moon, The, by Lady Gregory—Savoy, New York (Chas. Frohman), February 24.

Rose of the Wind, one act play, by Anna Hempstead Beach—Criterion, New York, January 9.

Royal Divorce, A, play, by John Grosvenor Wilson—Colonial, Cleveland, November 7.

Royal Mounted, The, by Cecil B. and William C. de Mille—Garrick, Philadelphia, March 16; Garrick, New York, April 6.

Salvation Nell, play, by Edward Sheldon—Providence, November 12; Hackett, New York, November 17.

Samson, William Gillette's adaptation of Henri Bernstein's play—Lyceum, Rochester, N.Y., October 9; Criterion, New York, October 19.

School Days, musical comedy, by Aaron Hoffman; lyrics by Vincent Bryan and E. Gardiner; music by Gus Edwards—Savoy Theatre, Atlantic City, August 25; Circle Theatre, New York, September 14.

Searchlight, The, play, by Richard Barry—Auditorium, Los Angeles, November 16.

Sergeant Devil McCare, play, by Cecil de Mille —Philadelphia, October 19.

Servant in the House, The, play by C. Rann-Kennedy—Academy, Baltimore, March 5; Savoy, New York (Henry Miller's Associated Players), March 23.

Shadowed by Three, play, in four acts, by Lem B. Parker, music by Clarence Sinn (W. F. Mann)—American Theatre, New York, January 20.

Sheriff of Angel Gulch, The, melodrama, in four acts, by Chas. E. Blaney—Third Avenue, New York, August 1.

Sinner, The, by George Middleton and Leonidas Westerveldt—Chestnut Street O.H., Philadelphia, January 2.

Ski-Hi, musical comedy, in two acts, by Charles Alphin—Madison Square Roof, New York, June 20.

Society and the Bulldog, three act comedy, by Paul Armstrong—Daly's, New York, January 18 (previously produced in Baltimore).

Society Plot, The, play by Oliver Morosco and C. Williams Bachman—Burbank Theatres, Los Angeles, June.

Soldier of the Cross, A, religious melodrama, in four acts, by Eugene Thomas (Cohan and Harris)—West End, New York, February 5.

Soul Kiss, The, extravaganza, in two acts, book and lyrics by Harry B. Smith, music by Maurice Levy (E. Ziegfeld, manager)—Chestnut Street O.H., Philadelphia, January 20; the New York, New York, January 28.

Sporting Days, spectacular melodrama, in five scenes, by R. H. Burnside—Hippodrome, New York, September 10.

Star Bout, The, play, in four acts, by Taylor Granville—National Theatre, Philadelphia, August 1; Fourteenth Street Theatre, New York, September 7.

Stronger Sex, The, comedy, in three acts, by John Valentine—Weber's, New York, November 23.

Strugglers, The, one-act play, by Clara Ruge—Berkeley, New York, May 20.

Struggle, The, play, by Edward Tilton—Providence Opera House, Providence, R.I., November 2.

Stubbord Cinderella, A, musical comedy, in three acts, by Messrs. Hough, Adams, and Howard—Alhambra, Milwaukee, May 24.

Substitute, The, by Beulah M. Dix and Evelyn G. Sutherland—Metropolitan, Minneapolis, September 27.

Sure Shot Sam, four act play, by Lem B. Parker—Henck's Opera House, Cincinnatti, O., August 9; Grand Street, New York, November 23.

Swindler, The, society drama, in four acts, by Howard Russell—Baker Theatre, Portland, Ore., June 14.

Tears, comedietta, in one act, from the French by Chas. J. Bell (Academy of Dramatic Arts and Empire Theatre Dramatic School) Empire, New York, January 23.

Temptress, The, comedietta, in one act, from the German of Gustav von Moser, by Florence Frederick Beryl (Academy of Dramatic Arts), Empire, New York, March 6.

Tess of Tennessee, melodrama, in four acts, by C. E. Blaney—Fourteenth Theatre, New York, August 10.

Test, The, play, by Jules Eckert Goodman—Auditorium, Los Angeles, Cal., September 28; Opera House, Bayonne, N.J., October 29.

That Little Affair at Boyd's, comedy, in four acts, by William Gillette—Columbia, Washington, June 15; Liberty, New York, December 18.

Thief of Destiny, The, drama, in one act, by Campbell MacCullough (Academy of Dramatic Arts)—Empire, New York, March 6.

Their Daughter, one act satire, by André Fridon—Socialist Theatre, New York, March 27.

Their Honeymoon, play, by George Randolph Chester and Edna Mannheimer—Auditorium, Cincinnati, April 28.

Three Twins, adaptation from *Incog*, by Chas. Dickson, lyrics by O. A. Hauerbach, music by Carl Hoschna—Herald Square, New York, June 15.

Third Degree, The, play, by Charles Klein—Atlantic City, N.J., November 16.

Ticker Ticks, The, playlet, by E. C. Ranck—Mannion's Park, St. Louis, July 12.

Too Many Wives, musical comedy, by Chas. Horwitz, music by Frederick Bowers—Van Curler Opera House, Schenectady, N.Y., August 29; Metropolis, New York, November 2.

Toddles, adaptation, by Clyde Fitch, from the French of Tristan Bernard and André Godferneaux—Baltimore, February 24; Savoy, New York (Chas. Frohman), March 16.

Too Young to Know, by George O. Holt—Savoy Theatre, Fall River, Ma., August 17.

Traitor, The, play, by Thomas Dixon, jun., and Channing Pollock—Norfolk, Va., September 28.

Travelling Salesman, The, four-act comedy, by James Forbes—Washington, March 16; Liberty, New York, August 10.

Twelfth Night, Shakespeare's comedy, presented in German under the secondary title of *What You Will (Was Ihr Wollt)*—German Theatre, New York, February 11.

Twenty Days in the Shade, adaptation, by Paul Potter, of French farce by Hennequin and Veber—Hyperion Theatre, New Haven, January 16; Savoy, New York, January 20.

Two Dollar Bill, farce, music by James T. Brymm and H. Laurence Freeman—Pekin, Chicago, March 2.

Under the Bear Flag, drama—American, San Francisco, August 17.

Undesirable Citizen, The, drama, by Lee Arthur—Lee Avenue Theatre, Brooklyn, March 9.

Vacuum, The, one-act play—Belasco, New York, June 15.

Vampire Cat, The, a legend of Old Japan—German Theatre, New York, November 12.

Vera, the Medium, four-act play, by Richard Harding Davis—Harmanus Bleecker Hall, Albany, N.Y., November 2.

Via Wireless, four-act play, by Paul Armstrong—National Washington, October 19; Liberty, New York, November 2.

Village Lawyer, A, comedy by Will M. Cressy and James Clarence Harvey (Nixon and Zimmerman)—Opera House, Wilmington, Del., February 7; The Garden, New York (Shubert's), February 29.

Waltz Dream, The, operetta in three acts, English book by Joseph W. Herbert, by Oscar Strauss—Chestnut Street, O.H., Philadelphia, January 6; Broadway, New York, January 27.

Wall Street Detective, The, melodrama, in four acts, by Howard Hall—Fourteenth Street Theatre, New York, August 17.

Wandering Musician, The—Girard Avenue Theatre, Philadelphia, April 21.

Wanted by the Police, melodrama, in four acts, by Langdon McCormick—Metropolis, New York, November 16.

We Are King, comedy, in three acts, by Lieutenant Gordon Kean (A. W. Cross)—Metropolis, New York, April 13.

What Happened Then! musical fantasy, by Austin Strong, music by Edward Corliss—Majestic, Montreal, September 14.

What Every Woman Knows, J. M. Barrie's four-act comedy—Apollo, Atlantic City, N.J., October 16; Empire, New York, December 23.

When Old New York Was Dutch—Plainfield, N.J., September 3.

Where Was Simon! by G. H. Trader—Shubert, Milwaukee, September 28.

White Pilgrim, The, Herman C. Merivale's play, by pupils of Chicago School of Acting—Studebaker, Chicago, February 25.

White Lily, The, comedietta, one act, from the French of Alphonse Daudet, by Fane Randolph White (Academy of Dramatic Art)—Empire, New York, March 6.

Wildfire, first time in New York, three-act racing comedy, by George Broadhurst and George V. Hobart—Liberty Theatre, New York, September 7.

Winning Miss, A, in two acts, by Harold Ottendye, music by W. F. Peters—Auditorium, South Bend Road, November 4; Garden, Chicago, November 23.

Winterfeast, The, mystic play, in five acts, by Chas. Rann Kennedy—Savoy, New York (Henry Miller), November 30.

Wolf, The, melodrama, in three acts, by Eugene Walter Belasco—Washington, March 30 (Sam. S. and Lee Shubert); Bijou, New York, April 18.

Woman of the West, A, melodrama, by Father L. J. Vaughan—Bush Temple Theatre, Chicago, May 4.

Woman's Hour, The, three-act comedy, by Frederick Paulding—Academy of Music, Norfolk, Va., October 2.

Woman Who Understood, The, one-act play—Fifth Avenue Theatre, New York, June 21.

World and His Wife, The, drama, three acts, by C. W. Nirdlinger, from the Spanish *El Gran Galeoto* of Jose Echegaray—Belasco Theatre, Washington, September 21; Daly's, New York, November 2.

World Without Men, The, farce, in three acts, by A. Engel and Julius Horst (the original of Clyde Fitch's *Girls*)—German Theatre, New York, October 15.

Worth of a Woman, The, drama, in four acts, by David Graham Phillips (W. N. Laurence)—Madison Square, New York, February 12.

Yankee Prince, The, musical play, in three acts, by George M. Cohan—Parson's Theatre, Hartford, Conn., April 2; Knickerbocker, New York, April 20.

2 × 2 = 5, comedy, in four acts, by Gustav Wied—New German Theatre, New York, October 27.

AMERICAN OBITUARY.

FROM JANUARY TO END OF NOVEMBER, 1908.

Adams, Jessie, vaudeville artist. January 28.

Albaugh, Mrs. (M Mitchell), retired actress. Aged 77 years. Long Branch, N.J., May 31.

Alexander, Albert Thomas, actor. Pittsburg, Pa. April 14

Alexander, John C., master mechanic. Aged 64 years. Denver, Col., May 4.

Alto, Clara, vaudeville artist. New York, February 12.

Allen, William, stage carpenter. Aged 67 years. Brooklyn, June 29.

Appletou, Aaron, manager. Brooklyn, N.Y., August 10.

Apel, Lillian (Emery), pianist. New York City, July 7.

Armour, Hamilton, actor. Seattle, Wash., April 7.

Arnold, Mrs. A. (Madame La Salle), one time operatic artist. April 13.

Armbruster, Otto H., scenic artist. Mamaroneck, N.Y., August 15.

Arthur, Robert, manager. New York City, October 11.

Atkinson, Wilbur, manager. Morrilton, Ark., September 26.

Aubrey, Harriet (Powell), actress. Aged 37 years. New York City, August 10.

Austin, William, theatrical manager. Aged 75. years. Duxbury, Mass. January 15.

Baker, Katie. New York City, February 17.

Baetens, Charles, musician. Aged 82 years. Omaha, Neb., January 15.

Bailey, J. W., coloured performer. New York City, March 9.

Baird, I. W., circus manager. Aged 60 years. Portland, Ore., January 16.

Baisly, Jas. A., comedian. Danbury, Conn. February 11.

Ballenberg, Louis, impressario. Cincinnatti, May 29.

Balneau, James (Murphy), clown. May 24.

Bangs, Frank C., actor. Aged 74 years. Atlantic City June 12.

Banks, "Billie," minstrel. Los Angeles, Cal., July 5.

Barratt, Joseph, manager. Aged 60 years. Portland, Ore., May 3.

Barton, Harriett, actress. Nashville, Tenn., May 3.

Bates, Mrs. F., Wren, mother of Blanche Bates. Newcastle, near Ossington, N.Y., May 30.

Beamer, Ida, actress. Alameda, Cal., November 3.

Benden, Helen, M., vaudeville artist. Aged 57 years. Exeter, N.H., February.

Bendix, William, composer. Aged 72 years. Arlington, Mass., September 27.

Bernard, Jack, actor and vaudeville artist. Aged 46 years. New York, January 12.

Bernard, Mrs .Mollie, actress. New York, February 17.

Berwick, Alice, actress. Aged 36 years. Bron, New York City, August 5.

Beverley, Frank, vaudeville artist. Aged 51 years. Seattle, Wash., November 19.

Bimberg, Meyer R., theatre builder. New York City, March 25.

Blair, Hal, black face comedian. Ogden C., 13.

Blanchard, C. C., actor. Aged 30 years. Litchfield, February 4.

Bloom, M. M., manager. New York, February 13.

Boardman, Mrs. C. T., elocutionist. San Francisco, July 30.

Bond, Charles H., theatre proprietor. Boston, July.

Bondrow, J. H., vaudeville manager. Bay Ridge, N.Y., August 10.

Bonnell, Joseph, vaudeville artist. Aged 34 years. New York, May 20.

Bossard, Violet. New York, August 1.

Bowers, Mrs. S. E. Philadelphia, February 5.

Bowman, Peter, bagpipe player. Brooklyn, June 7.

Bradfield, Wayne, black-face comedian, Columbus, O., May 8.

Bradley, Alfred, general manager. New York, April 10.

Bratton, Chas., musician. Aged 38 years. Cleveland, February 9.

Brock, E. H., business manager. Buffalo, N.Y., March.

Brown, Chas. E., actor. Ft. Dodge, Iowa, January 17.

Brown, Geo. H., manager.. New York. City, February 25.

Bruno, Christopher, comedian, Aged 31 years. Menlo Park, N.J., January 30.

Brusie, Judson D., dramatist. Los Angeles, Cal., June 10.

Bryan, William Henry, actor. New York, February 26.

Bryant, Henry L., manager. Aged 73 years. April 22.

Burr, Professor O. V., magician. Detroit, Mich., January 10.

Burke, Henry E., scenic artist. New York City, February 21.

Burrell, Thomas, black-faced comedian. Rochester, N.Y., February 15.

Byars, W. Minor, musical director. Aged 37 years. Waco, Tex., January 26.

Calice, Myron, actor. Aged 61 years. New York, October 3.

Callimore, Vincent, clarinet player. Aged 21 years. Atlantic City, N.J. August 12.

Campbell, E. C., stage hand. Aged 45 years. March 13.

Carey, John J. (Joe J. Mackie), vaudeville artist. Punxsutawney, Pa., January 16.

Carter, Mrs. John (Jennie Coburn). Aged 53 years. Atlantic City, N.J., July 3.

Carlstedt, Viola Ashton, actress. Chicago, August 22.

Carlyle, Hal Newton, actor. Aged 65 years. Grand Junction, Colo., February

Carter, Leslie. Chicago, September 25.

Cathers, John, showman. Aged 55 years. Philadelphia, February 18.

Cash, Thomas H., circus artist. Aged 54 years. Lynn, Mass., October 19.

Chaffin, W. E., manager. Mt. Hope, W. Va., March 3.

Chambers, Will H., minstrel. Boston, March 2.
Chaplin, Geo. D. (Inglis), actor. Aged 76 years. New York, October 24.
Clifton, Mrs. Harry, singer. Aged 65 years. Yonkers, August 28.
Cole, Charlotte (Mrs. C. C. Dowell), soprano. Aged 34 years. Louisville, Ky., October 4.
Cole, Elisha B., theatre proprietor. Springfield, Mass., April 11.
Cole, Mrs. Minnie F., actress. Boston, Mass., July 17.
Collins, John, vaudeville comedian. Aged 34 years. Bloomfeld, N.J. November 28.
Condit, Mrs. G. B. San Antonio, Tex., January 6.
Cook, Charles E., manager. San Francisco, January 29.
Cooke, Wallace E., comedian. Aged 36 years. New Haven, Conn., February 29.
Cotton, Ben., minstrel. Aged 80 years. New York, February 14.
Couran, John H. Philadelphia, July 1.
Courtleigh, Mrs. William, wife of a former President of the Actors' Society. New York, January 16.
Coveney, Jessie West, actress. Brooklyn, July 16.
Cowper, Mrs. Eleanor Merron, actress and playwright. New York City, November 30.
Coyle, Hugh. Chicago, September 12.
Cunningham, W. S., vaudeville artist. Aged 41 years. Cleveland, March 26.
Curtis, Edward, actor. Aged 51 years, Sandusky, O. January 30.
Curtis, Edwin, actor. Oak Harbour, O. August 3.
Dale, Dallas, vaudeville artist. Cincinnati, September 19.
Dailey, Peter, F., comedian. Chicago, May 23.
Daly, W. H., song writer. Aged 43 years. Somerville, Mass., March.
D'Arville, Estelle, actress. New York, May 3.
Davey, Robert E., manager. Coney Island, N.Y., October 1.
Davis, John J., actor. Boston, May.
Davis Ivan L., musical director. Aged 42 years. Chicago, February 13.
Day, E. Murray, actor. Aged 74 years. Long Branch, N.J., March.
Deagle, George J., manager. Aged 86 years. Port Washington, May 5.
De Haven, William, manager. Chicago, Ill., February 25.
Delamatto, Miro, tenor. Aged 40 years. Chicago, February 4.
Denny, Will, singer. Seattle, Wash., October 2.
Devere, Annie (Daly). New York, May 30.
Devine, Catherine. Aged 42 years. January 3.
Devine, James, vaudeville artist. Auburn, Cal., October 2.
Dickson, Henry, manager. Kenton, January 27.
Dingeon, Helene, comic opera singer. San Francisco, July 26.
Dixon, Henry, stage manager. Woodcliff, N.J., October 4.
Dobson, Henry C., banjo instructor. Aged 77 years. New York City, May 27.
Dolan, William A., actor. New York City, November 10.
Donnolly, Robert J., dramatic critic. Aged 45 years. Brooklyn, February 8.
Donaldson, Rose Ellis, soubrette. Cincinnati, February 14.
Doyle, Mrs. Thomas M. Aged 66 years. New York, March 6.
Dreux, Loraine, actress. Aged 35 years. New York City, November 12.
Duffy, Edward S., bandmaster. Brooklyn, N.Y., April 11.

Dunne, Chas. P., one time vaudeville manager. Aged 45 years. Brooklyn, N.Y., November 24.
Dyas, Ada, actress. Seaton, March 10
Eby, Eunice, soubrette. Eagle Pass, Tex., March 30.
Edward, Alice, coloured performer. Chicago, January 6.
Edwards, William Bruce. Hartford, Conn., March 7.
Edwards, Jas. S., vaudeville artist. Cincinnati, O., September 6.
Elmore, Mrs. Julia, actress. Yonkers, N.Y., July 10.
Emmett, Mrs. Chas., retired actress. Paterson, N.J., July 28.
Enright, Agnes, actress. Buffalo, N.Y., April 18.
Estes, Marie L., vaudeville artist. Chicago, January 23.
Etherington, Arthur E., comedian. Providence, R.I., May 16.
Evans, Ollie (Mrs. C. J. Stine), vaudeville artist. New York City, January 20.
Falk, Wolf, manager. St. Louis, August 28.
Farnworth, Dudley, actor. Aged 49 years. New York City, July 3.
Fax, Reuben, actor. Aged 46 years. New York City, August 14.
Fay, Frank C., actor. Baltimore, February 12.
Fernandez, Harry, actor. Aged 52 years. Phillipsburg, Kan., February 8.
Ferry, Estella (Mrs. G. P. Haines), actress, Grand Rapids, February 13.
Fessenden, William, actor, Forth Worth, Tex., October.
Finn, Joseph, actor. Aged 37 years. Brooklyn, Mass., September 20.
Fischer, Marie, violinist. Aged 23 years. Philadelphia, August 1.
Fisher, Chas. (Noble), vaudeville artist. Bloomington, Ill., January 20.
Fitzgerald, Hildebrand, manager.—Philadelphia, June 1.
Floyd, Bessie, vaudeville artist. Buffalo, N.Y., August 19.
Folsom, Harry, staff, Keeth's, Boston. Boston, February 28.
Fonda, Chas. W., manager. Worcester, Mass., October 22.
Forbes, Grace Carroll, vaudeville artist. Cincinatti, O., October 22.
Frank, Don C., actor and dramatist. Wellington, Mo., May.
Frederick, Oscar, vaudeville artist. Brooklyn, June 3.
French, Chas., jun. New York City, July 30.
Galligan, John F., musician. Aged 33 years. Taunton, Mass., June 30.
Getz, Chas., S. scenic artist. Aged 86 years. Baltimore, January 15.
Gibbons, Thomas, stage manager. May.
Gibney Morgan, actor. Aged 64 years. Chicago, November 30
Gilmore, Edward, manager. New York, November 5.
Goldberg, Henry, manager. Lynn, Mass., April 14.
Goldfadden, Abraham. New York, January 9.
Goodman, Henry S., showman. Aged 72 years. Friendship, N.Y., May 14.
Gorey, Arthur, musician. Memphis, Tenn., March 7.
Gotthold, Philip H., vaudeville comedian. Asheville, N.C., March 16.
Graham, Thomas E., actor. Aged 45 years. New York City, March 30.
Graham, Harold, actor. Eugene, Ore, February 6.
Graves, Mrs. Emily L., actress. Aged 52 years. Columbus, O., June 20.
Guy, Maimie (Mrs. S. B. Call), singer. Springfield, Mass. February 29.

Hafey, John, actor. Columbus, O., February 29.

Hall, Frankie, vaudeville artist. Spokane, Wash., May 6.

Hamilton, Maude, actress. Toronto, Can., May 19.

Hamlin, John A., manager. Aged 73 years. Chicago, May 20.

Harlow, Ed., showman. Aged 40 years. Horse Cave, Ky., March 1.

Harold, Robert, actor. Aged 42 years. Philadelphia, March 5.

Harper J. Brook, manager. Aged 75 years. Reading, Pa., October 8.

Harrington, Jas. A., actor. Aged 88 years. Brooklyn, N.Y., October.

Harris, Alexander, manager. Aged 44 years. New York, May 24.

Harris, Chas. M., September 11.

Harris, Mrs. Rachael. Aged 80 years. Chicago, November 16.

Harrison, Henry, actor. Aged 29 years. Portsmouth, O., August 21.

Hathaway, James, diver. Coney Island, Cincinnati, O., July 4.

Hart, Terry, jun. Aged 23 years. Milwaukee, Ars., March 30.

Hart, Timothy, J., actor. Providence, R.I., January 14.

Hazelton, Little Grace. Aged 13 years. Abilene, Tex., February 8.

Haven, G. G., a director of Metropolitan Opera House, New York. Aged 72 years. New York City, March 19.

Heartel, Pauline, vaudeville artist. Aged 28 years. Memphis, Penn., August 4.

Heaverley, Bert J., comedian. San Francisco, October 31.

Heck, William S., circus proprietor. Aged 49 years. June 30.

Heckler, Frank, manager. Larchmont, N.Y., March 14.

Hedrix, Harry, vaudeville artist, Kansas City, Mo., April 8.

Hedges, Morris B., character actor. Aged 37 years. Portland, Ore., February 21.

Heed, John C., musician. Aged 46 years. Newark, February 12.

Hegeman, Dr. W., father of Mrs. Richard Mansfield. Aged 81 years. Troy, New York, February 12.

Heineman, Georg, director German theatre, St. Louis. In that city, February 2.

Heiser, Maria Chatzel. New York, January 6.

Henderson, David, manager. Aged 54 years. Chicago, Ill., May 27.

Higby, William, clown. Aged 66 years. New York City, June 17.

Higgins, Gerald F., actor. Richmond, Va., August 8.

Hiss, Wm. Aged 56 years. Baltimore, March 26.

Hogan, Gus W., clog dancer. Aged 50 years. Fair Haven, N.J., May 30.

Holcombe, Herbert, vaudeville performer. Aged 41 years. January 4.

Hooker, Mrs. Fred, actress. St. Louis, September 12.

Horn, John, musician. Zanesville, O., April 6.

Horn, Williamson W. Aged 57 years. Nashville, Tenn., July 9.

Howard, Alfred C., vaudeville artist. Paterson, N.J., November 20.

Howard, Alice (Mrs. Warren), actress. Chicago, November 4.

Howard, Bronson, dramatist. Aged 65 years. Avon-by-the-Sea, N.Y., August 4.

Howard, jun., Joseph, journalist. New York, March 31.

Howard, Mrs. George C., actress. Cambridge, Mass., October 15.

Hoyt, George B., actor. About 38 years. Des Moines, Ia., May 6.

Hubinger, J. C., theatrical manager. Aged 54 years. Keokuk, In., January 28.

Huddy, Alfred, musician. Aged 58 years Trenton, N.J., November 26.

Huffman, Nellie D. September 6.

Hunt, Alice Treat, actress. Los Angeles, Cal., June 8.

Huntoon, Col. J. K., scenic artist. Aged 68 years. Lawton, Okla., April 6.

Hurd, Isabel, vaudeville artist. New York City, May 8.

Hurdle, Geo., coloured performer. Anderson, Ind., May 18.

Hurley, W. J., actor. Aged 62 years. New York, June 9.

Intropidi, Frederick, musical conductor. New York, January 26.

Irving, Joe, stage manager. Ft. Worth, Tex., April 18.

Jackson, Chas. J., actor. Aged 45 years. New York, January 11.

Jacques, Philip M., advance agent. Aged 34 years. New York, April 11.

Jakob, J., high diver. Jamaica Bay, June 15.

Jefferson, C. B. (son of Joseph Jefferson), actor. Aged 58 years. New York, June 23.

Jennings, John W., actor. Aged 79 years. Montvale, N.J., May 19.

Jepson, Eugene, actor, Cleveland, Ohio, June 1.

Jones, Helen, actress. Aged 54 years. Sioux City, Ia., October 15.

Jones, Laura, whistler. Indianapolis, February 4.

Jones, L. E., aeronaut. Aged 27 years. Springfield, Ill., June 7.

Kellog, Mrs. Anna, April 30.

Kempton, Joseph, circus rider. San Francisco, September.

Kenfield, Mildred, vaudeville artist. New York City, October 24.

King, Edward H., musician. Aged 64 years. New York, January 17.

Kinsey, M. L., actor. Aged 50 years. January.

Kiralfy, Arnold (brother of Imre Kiralfy), dancer. New York City, May 3.

Klaw, Louis (brother of Marc Klaw). Aged 60 years. New York, April 26.

Kline, Lewis, actor. Grand Island, Neb., September 26.

Knoll, Harry M., musician. Los Angeles, Cal., January 10.

Knorr, musician. Philadelphia, August 22.

La Blanche, circus artist. November 29.

La Rose, Harry (Lawrence O'Neill), acrobat. New York, January 13.

La Vere, Pansy, musician. Cleveland, February 9.

Laidlaw, A. H. (Jun), dramatist. New York, July 11.

Lamberti, Elizabeth, vaudeville artist. Aged 24 years. Green Point, N.Y., October 24.

Lamson, Ernest, actor and dramatist. St. Louis, Mo., May 31.

Landis, W. H., vaudeville artist. Aged 53 years. Keo, Kuk., March 25.

Langley, Louise W., vaudeville artist. Brooklyn, N.Y. April 9.

Latourelle, Jas., musical director. Aged 30 years. St. Paul, Minn., September 20.

Leckie, W. T., manager. Kalamazoo, April 19.

Lee, Elmore, song writer. Aged 33 years. Denver, September 1.

Lee, Richard Kenneth, sketch writer. Aged 43 years. New York, January 22.

Lennox, George, manager. Colfax, Wash., March 21.

Leonard, John F., Irish comedian. Aged 48 years. Philadelphia, July 1.

Leonard, Mrs. Chas. E., mother of Lillian Russell. Rutherford, N.J., April 9.

Leslie, Jennie, vaudeville artist. Chicago, January.

Levick, Mrs. Ada, actress. Aged 56 years. Frankfort, June 22.

Lindsay, R. F., musical conductor. Aged 43 years. Boston, January 18.

List, Philip, violinist. Aged 86 years. Brooklyn, November 30.

Livingstone, Edward H., vaudeville artist. New York, June 17.

Lloyd, Henry T., manager, Cincinnatti. April 15.

Long, Chas. G., theatrical manager. Aged 81 years. Mobile, Ala., January 30.

Long, Frank, circus clown. Bristol, Tenn., June 2.

Lo Mier, Chas., actor. Aged 37 years. April 8.

Looney, Mrs. Viva. F. September 9.

Lorene, George F., comedian. Aged 35 years. April 24.

Lynn, R. Fuller, piano player. Chicago, April 24.

Mackay, Charles, actor. January 5.

MacDowell, Edward A., composer. New York. January 23.

McFarland, Phil. Aged 45 years. New York City, July 29.

McGann, William, actor. Providence, June 6.

McNulty, J. A., ventriloquist. Bellingham, Wash., September 24.

Maccart, Adelaide. Catskill Mountains, July 26.

Mackie, Joe J., vaudeville artist. (See John J. Carey.)

Mack, Johnny, Irish comedian. Baltimore, Md., July 14.

Manley, Clifford, E., stage carpenter. Wichita Falls, Tex., April 18.

Mannion, Patrick, manager. St. Louis, Mo., April 24.

Marsh, Lillian (Drumgold). Saranac Lake, N.Y., June 1.

Martine, Ella. New York, March 10.

Masterton, John A., stage-manager. Providence, R.I., June 21.

Mason, William, musician. New York City, July 14.

Mayo, Carl, clown. Cincinnatti. O., April 10.

Meder, J. P., manager. Nevada, March 1.

Melville, Frank, equestrian director. New York, November 23.

Merritt, Frank T., manager. Beamsville, Ont., March 20.

Meyer, Alphonse J., sometime manager. Buffalo, N.Y., May 30.

Merkeley, Harry C., acrobat. St. Johnsville, N.Y., August 2.

Meyers, Amos, old-time showman. Sparta, N.Y., September 27.

Michael, M. C., manager. Aged 48 years. Waukesha, Wis., June.

Miller, Chas. L., actor. Memphis. Tenn., February 4.

Miller (Arizona Jack), rifle shooter. Aged 47 years. September 25.

Miles, H. J. January 1.

Minott, Maggie, midget. Aged 48 years. Chicago, February.

Mitchell, O. M., ventriloquist. Las Animas, Col. May 30.

Miner, Mrs. Helen, actress. Aged 36 years. New York City, August 11.

Mix, Jas. E., manager. Aged 24 years. Kokomo, Ind., September 21.

Mollenhauer, Mrs. Pauline. Aged 70 years. Brooklyn, N.Y., March 3.

Montgomery, Henry W., actor. Aged 65 years. Actors' Home, Staten Island, June 20.

Morris, Hattie, actress. New York City, January 7.

Morrison, George W., character actor. Aged 67 years. Buffalo, N.Y., March 13.

Mothersole, George, manager. September 27.

Muscat, William, agent. Denver, March 11.

Munzer, J. L., agent. San Francisco, February 24.

Murdoch, Mortimer, author and actor. Aged 86 years. Bridgewater, Mass., March 31.

Murphy, Mrs. M. J. S., retired actress. Oakland, Cal., October 1.

Nedham, Thomas Stanley, violinist. Aged 90 years. New York, March 23.

Neelans, Belle. Westmont, N.J., April 1.

Neidling, Edward, living skeleton. Aged 35 years. Ansonia, Conn., January 20.

Neilson, Nesta (Mrs. Axtell), actress. New York City, July 1.

Nelson, Mrs. Millie Willard, manageress. Aged 62 years. Denver, August 16.

Nelson, Miss Shirley, actress. Chicago, May 29.

Nett, Maud, actress. Burlington, Ia., June 12.

Newton, W. W., actor. Elmira, N.Y., October 31.

Newell, Ulysses D. ("Yank"). New York, March 10.

Noble, Charles, aerial acrobat. Aged 40 years. Bloomington, January 20.

Noble, William Lee Louisville, Ky., July 12.

Nunn, James, actor. Portland. Me., July 4.

Nuno, James, composer. Aged 84 years. Aubarndale, July 17.

O'Brian, Mrs. Hackett. Aged 84 years. Forrest Home. Holmsburg, May 18.

O'Brien, Mrs. Dan. New York City, April 1.

Ogden, Mrs. John Cleveland, February 1.

Ol'ver, James, theatre proprietor. South Bend, Ind. March 2.

Oliver, William, aeronaut. Jackson, Mich., July 30.

Oldner, P. A., retired circus performer. Minnesota, October.

Ome, William H. De., black face comedian. Omaha, Neb., October 22.

O'Sullivan, Denis, singer and actor. Columbus, Ohio, February 1.

Oskara, Harry, vaudeville artist. Aged 36 years. Raleigh, N.C., February 27.

Ott, W. C., vaudeville artist. Bayonne, N.J., March 27.

Padovani, Frank, singer. Los Angeles, Cal., May 11.

Page, May, actress. Aged 26 years. New York City, November 1.

Paige, Mrs. Dora, manageress. Aged 61 years. New York, January 17.

Palmer, William, J., one time manager. New York City, August 4.

Palmer, Mrs. Alice. Aged 72 years. Brooklyn, N.Y., March 5.

Parker, Richard, manager. Actors' Home, Staten Island, August 28.

Pastor, Tony, manager. Aged 71 years. Long Island, August 26.

Pascoe, William H., actor. Amityville, L. I. August 7.

Patterson, George, theatrical printer. Aged 61 years. November 7.

Payne, Mrs. Myrtle, actress. Aged 25 years. Zanesville, O. April 21.

Payton, Senter, actor. Aged 53 years. Selma, Ala., October 24.

Payton, Henry, stage director. Centerville, Ia. November 1.

Pearl, William, dancer. Aged 42 years. June 24.

Pembroke, Edmund (Davis), actor. Boston, May 10.

Perry, Francis, M. S. Portland, Me., September 1.

Peters, Emma, vocalist and dancer. Aged 42 years. Saginaw, Mich., June 2.

Peyser, Julius H., advance agent. August 8.

Plack, Louis, manager. Aged 80 years. September 20.

Plaisted, Gracie, one time vaudeville actress. Alameda, Cal., August 24.

Powell, Joseph, trick cyclist. Minneapolis, February 9.

Poor, Charles B., actor. San Francisco, July 22.

Port, Fred, vaudeville pianist. May 21.

Prince, Floretia, dancer. El Pasco, Tex., March 4.

Putnam, Boyd, actor. Irvington-on-the-Hudson May 24.

Quinn, Charles C., stage manager. Aged 28 years. New York, April 14.

Ramsey, Mrs. J. M., actress. Gahagan, La., May 22.

Randolph, Jessie Lee, retired actress. Aged 50 years. Waldoboro, Me., March 2.

Redon, Marsh, manager. New Orleans, October.

Reeve, Clifford C., theatrical manager. New York, February 16.

Reboul, Arthur, flautist. Philadelphia, June 16.

Rench, Chas., clown. Columbus, O., June 25.

Revell, Dorothy, actress. Aged 28 years. New York City. July 6.

Rhodes, Joseph, piano player. Ellenville, N.Y., June.

Ricard, Carlita (Maxwell), vaudeville artist. Yonkers, N.Y., October 5.

Rice, Mrs. Glen, singer. Aged 24 years. New York, October 21.

Rich, Isaac B., manager. Aged 81 years. Boston June 10.

Richards, Lamont W., manager. Bay City, Mich., October 10.

Rice, Mrs. Marcel. San Antonio, Texas, April 16.

Rigby, Mrs. Cora Strong (Cora Strong). New York City, January 25.

Ritzel, J. W., comedian. Aged 38 years. Atlanta, Ga., March 24.

Robbins, Burr, circus manager. Aged 70. Chicago, January 30.

Robinson, James, old showman. Aged 97 years. Cincinnati, O., February 3.

Rogers, Bertha, actress. Boston, Mass., September 20.

Rogers, Gus, comedian. New York City, October 19.

Roscoe, Harry J., hypnotist. Seattle, Wash., April 23.

Runnells, Burnel R., circus artist. Aged 82 years. Philadelphia, February 2.

Ryse, Ellis, actor and opera singer. New York City, July 8.

Ryse, Mrs. Ellis, opera singer. Aged 64 years. New York City, November 24.

Sanders, Arthur, comedian. Milwaukee, Wis., September 5.

Sanford, John Shanley, manager. Aged 45 years. New York, February 21.

Saville, Gus H., vaudeville artist. Philadelphia, May 9.

Sayre, Theodore H., dramatist. Aged 67 years. New York City, March 22.

Scobie, George, tenor. Buffalo, March 23.

Setaro, Frank, violinist. Philadelphia, May 9

Sells, William, circus artist. Aged 42 years. New York, February 21.

Senac, Regis, fencing master. New York City, August 16.

Setaro, Giovanni, harpist. Vineland, N.J., April 5.

Shannon, Irene, actress. Mass., September 3.

Shay, Jessie D., pianist. June 21.

Shine, William H., manager. Bedford, Mass., March 12.

Siegrist, William, acrobat. Aged 40 years. New York City, June 23.

Simmons, Edward, electrician. New York City, July 1.

Simonds, Alvin H., one-time manager. Boston, November 14.

Sindis, Joseph. New York, February 11.

Smith, S. Decatur, musician. Philadelphia, March 19.

Smith, Arthur Ward, actor. Aged 32 years. San Angelo, Texas, March 16.

Somers, Vernon, actor. Buffalo, February 15.

Sousa, Mrs. E., mother of J. P. Sousa. Aged 82 years. Washington, August 23.

St. Clair, W. S. actor. Aged 50 years. New York City, August 17.

Stanton, Stella, actress. Aged 48 years. Reading, Mich., May 26.

Stevens, Mrs. Elizabeth, circus performer. Aged 84 years. Bridgeport, Conn., May 30.

Stange, John R., manager. Annapolis, Md., July 13.

Stine, Mrs. C. J. (Ollie Evans), vaudeville artist. New York, January 19.

Stork, Mrs. T., trick cyclist. Boston, Mass., September 14.

Stotchen, Frank W., manager. Aged 65 years. Oakland, Cal., November 18.

Strickland, Mrs. F. B., actress. Aged 79 years. Benton Harbour, Mich., February 12.

Stronse, Horace, singer. Philadelphia, September 10.

Suter, Henry, singer. Aged 58. New York City, January 29.

Sutherland, Harry. Nashville, Tenn., March 10, 1908.

Switzer, Jule F., actor. Aged 56 years. Ray, N.D., September.

Taylor, Edward, manager. Aged 65 years. Dorchester, Mass., February 22.

Taylor, John C., actor. Del Rio, Texas, March 21.

Taylor, Chas S., composer. Utica, N.Y., March 23.

Taylor, James, actor. New York Harbour, Me., May 12.

Terry, F. W., actor. Toronto, Canada, February 25.

Toland, Hugo, actor. Germantown, Pa., May 18.

Townsend, George R., piano player. Pittsburg, Pa., July 18.

Traynor, William W., vaudeville artist. Aged 35 years. St. Paul, Minn., March 29.

Truean, Augustus H. (Saville). Philadelphia, May 3.

Turner, "Happy Dick," vaudeville artist. Aged 58 years. Brooklyn, N.Y., January.

Van, Dee William, vaudeville performer. Aged 85 years. Atlanta, Ga., January 7.

Vernon, Daniel S., circus man. Aged 54 years. Cincinnati, O., May 9.

Verney, Harry. Actors' Home, August 20.

Vendig, Stephen, vaudeville artist. Aged 45 years. Brooklyn, November 4.

Vianesi, August, musical conductor. New York City, November 3.

Vickers, Geo. M., song writer. Aged 68 years. Wynnewood, Pa., February 19.

Vincent, John. New York City, April 3.

Virginia, Paul. Philadelphia, May 13

Von Olden, Kate, operatic contralto. Aged 43. Alleghany, Pa., January 7.

Vokes, Margaret Daly, dancer. Revere, August 27.

Wagner, Mitzi, circus artist. New York City, March 3.

Waite, Henry T., trick violinist. Boston, Mass., February.

Wallack, James H., actor-manager. Aged 64 years. Middletown, N.Y., May 1.

Waltone, Lillian, vaudeville artist. Chicago, June 13.

Walters, Mrs. Della. Aged 39 years. St. Louis, Mo., October 15.

Ward, Pembroke, bandmaster. Milwaukee, July 22.

Webb, Sophie Welsch. New Orleans, La. March 24.

Weber, Ernest, musician. Aged 75 years. Boston, November 4.

Welch, Artie, trap drummer. Baltimore, March 18.

Wellington, Emily (Mrs. J. F. Peachey), actress. Woodbury, N.J., September 15.

Wessells, George W., actor. Denver, Colo., February 20.

Westford, Robert Owen, actor. New York, February 19.

Wheeler, J. W., musician. Belfast, Me., June 13.

Wheelock, Joseph, actor. September 29.

Whiston, John Ware, actor-manager. Aged 81 years. Washington, March 22

Whytal, Thomas G. Aged 83 years. Bayside, L.I., November 19.

Wiggins, Thos., coloured pianist. Hoboken, June 13.

Wigle, Fred, actor. Cleveland, February 11.

Wiley, Clarence, pianist. Chicago, March 3.

Williamson, Mrs. Laura, actress. Seattle, Wash., April 6.

Wilson, George H., manager. Aged 54 years. Pittsburg, March 18.

Wilson, "Fearnaught," cyclist. Killed doing " the circle of death." Coshocton, August 3.

Wister, Mrs. Owen Jones (a granddaughter of John Kemble). Philadelphia, June 9.

Wood, Will B., manager. Lost at sea off Mexico, February 20.

Wood, Fred L., aeronaut. Newark, N.J., May 31.

Wood, Minnie. Aged 49 years. Chicago, June 14.

Woodville, Jas. S. August 17.

Woodward, Will, music publisher. August 2.

Young, Fanny, actress. San Francisco, October 6.

Young, Marion, actress. Buffalo, May 1.

Zeb, Jolly, comedian. Brooklyn, September 29.

Zehrung, John. Aged 77 years. Los Angeles, Cal., March 11.

AMERICAN THEATRES DESTROYED OR DAMAGED BY FIRE.

FROM JANUARY TO END OF NOVEMBER, 1908.

Jan. 13.—Rhoades Opera House, Boyertown, Pennsylvania. Burnt out. One hundred and sixty-seven lives lost.

Feb. 4.—Greenup theatre, Greenup, Illinois. Destroyed.

March 18.—Olympic, Springfield, Ill. Destroyed.

March 18.—Opera House, New London, Mo. Destroyed.

April 17.—Nixon, Tarentum, Pa. Dessing-rooms and back destroyed. Auditorium saved by safety curtain.

April 24.—Miller Opera House, Starbuck, Wash. Used as a skating rink. Ground floor damaged.

May 20.—Fairyland Park, Memphis, Tenn. Damaged.

June 8.—Keith's, Cleveland. Damaged.

June 20.—Ridgeway, Colfax, Wash. Damaged.

July 8.—Clayton's Music Hall, Surf Avenue, Coney Island, N.Y. Destroyed.

Aug. 9.—Royal, Tampa, Fla. Destroyed.

Aug. 17.—Majestic, Houston, Texas. Damaged.

Sept. 3.—Colonnade Opera House, Sullivan, Ont., Canada. Destroyed.

Sept. 16.—Opera House, Newcastle, Del Damaged.

Oct. 14.—Opera House, Bisbee, Arizona.

Nov. 12.—The Park, Brooklyn.

NEW THEATRES OPENED IN AMERICA.

FROM JANUARY TO END OF NOVEMBER, 1908.

January 20.—Shubert's New Theatre, Joplin, Mo.

March 3.—New Illinois, Urbana, Ill.

March 16.—White's, McKeesport, Pa.

April 20.—New Majestic, Milwaukee.

May 9.—Flood's New Park, Curtis Bay, near Baltimore.

May 10.—Lyric, Memphis, Tenn.

June 1.—Princess's, Chicago.

June 8.—Vaudeville, Clinton, Ill.

July 27.—Holler, Port Townsend, Wash.

August 1.—Lyceum, Chicago.

August 24.—Empire, Schenectady.

August 24.—New Grand, New Haven.

August 31.—Hollis, Boston; New Gaiety, New York City.

September 7.—Valencia, San Francisco; Grand Opera House, Amarillo, Tex.

September 26.—Fulton, Brooklyn, N.Y.

September 28.—Arts, Chicago; Hayden Pike-Gadsen, Alabama.

October 3.—New Majestic, Cedar Rapids, Ia.

October 10.—Greenpoint, Greenpoint, Brooklyn, N.Y.

October 12.—Broadway, Elk City, Okla.

October 22.—New National, Panama.

October 26.—Union, Bangor, Me.; New Garden, Ottumwa, Ia.

November 16.—New Jefferson, Memphis, Tenn.

November 21.—New Garden, Chicago.

November 23.—New Jefferson, Auburn, N.Y.; Mozart, Elmira, N.Y.; New Gaiety, Boston, Mass.; New Majestic, Los Angeles.

c

PARIS STAGE.

PRINCIPAL PLAYS AND IMPORTANT REVIVALS DURING THE YEAR 1908.

* Indicates Revival.

JANUARY.

3.*Les deux écoles, comedy, in four acts, by M. Alfred Capus—Variétés.

3.**Coralie et Cie.*, comedy, in three acts, by MM. Albin Valabrègue and Maurice Hennequin—Nouveautés.

7. *L'Apprentie*, historical drama, in four acts and ten tableaux, by M. Gustave Geffroy—Odéon.

8. *Malia*, Sicilian drama, in three acts, by L. Capuana, produced under the auspices of the Théâtre de l'Œuvre by a Sicilian troupe—Marigny.

10.**Le Pré aux clercs*, comic opera, in three acts, by Planard, with music by Hérold——Trianon-Lyrique.

14. *Ce renard de Bridache*, vaudeville, in three acts, by MM. Hugues Delorme and Francis Gally—Cluny.

19. *Chapeau! Chapeau! révue*, in two acts, by MM. Ernest Depré and Jacques Bousquet—Comédie-Royale.

20. *Deux Hommes*, comedy, in four acts, by Alfred Capus—Comédie-Française.

20.*Le Grand Mogol, opera-bouffe, in three acts and four tableaux, by MM. H. Chivot and A. Durn, with music by Audran—Trianon-Lyrique.

22. *Le plus beau corps de France*, military operette, in two acts and six tableaux, by MM. Trébla and Codey—Parisiana.

27. The re-opening, under the management of MM. Messager and Broussan, with Gounod's *Faust*, took place of the—Grand Opéra.

27. *Un divorce*, a comedy, in three acts, by MM. Paul Gavault and André Cury—Vaudeville.

29. *Tourtelin s'amuse*, vaudeville, in three acts, by MM. Henri Kéroul and Albert Barré—Folies-Dramatiques.

30. *Boute-en-Train*, comedy-vaudeville, in three acts, by Alfred Athis—Athénée.

FEBRUARY.

4. *Le Bonheur de Jacqueline*, comedy, in four acts, by Paul Gavault.—Gymnase.

13.**Jean-Gabriel Borkman*, drama, in five acts, by Ibsen, with French adaptation by Count Prozor.—Réjane.

14. *La Bête Féroce*, drama, in five acts and eight tableaux.—Ambigu.

16. *Tu Parles! revue*, in two acts and eight tableaux, by Georges Arnould and Jacques Bousquet.—Cigale.

17.**Arlequin Poli par l'Amour*, comedy, in two acts, by Marivaux, and *Les Trois Sultanes*, comedy, in three acts, by Favart.—Comédie-Française.

18. *Le Dernier Jour de Toupin*, comedy, in one act, by Alfred Delilia; *Pour être Heureux*, comedy, in two acts, by Charles Desfontaines and Paul Arosa; *Les Rendez-vous Strasbourgeois*, operette, by Romain Coolus, with music by Charles Cuvillier.—Comédie-Royale.

19. *Les Tribulations d'un Gendre*, comedy vaudeville, in three acts, by Grenet-Dancourt and Eugène Héros.—Cluny.

20. *Aux Bouffes, on Pouffe, revue*, in three acts and seven tableaux, by Rip, Wilned, and Fargue.—Bouffes-Parisiens.

21.**Geneviève de Brabant*, operette, in three acts and five tableaux, by Hector Crémieux and Etienne Tréfeu, with music by Jacques Offenbach.—Variétés.

21. *L'Homme de Proie*, play, in three acts, by Lefévre and C. de la Porte—Molière.

24. *Une Poire pour la Soif*, comedy, in one act, by M. Henry Falk; *Isidore*, comedy, in one act, by M. Jean-José Frappa; *Le Postiche*, operetta, in one act, by MM. Samson and Pradels, with music by Léo Pouget; and *L'Amour s'Amuse*, comedy, in two acts, by M. Daniel Jourda.—Capucines.

25. *Acquitté*, one-act comedy, by Camillo Antona-Traversi, translated from the Italian by M. Lecuyer; and *Hypatie*, antique drama, in two acts, by M. Paul Barlatier, given under the auspices of the Théâtre de l'Œuvre.—Marigny.

26. *La Habanera*, lyric drama, in three acts, by M. Raoul Laparra, and *Ghyslaine*, lyric drama, in one act, by MM. Gustave Guiches and Marcel Frayer, with music by M. Marcel Bertrand.—Opéra-Comique.

27. *Le Revisor*, comedy, in three acts, by Nicolas Gagol, the French translation by M. E. Gothi.—Réjane.

27. *La Femme Nue*, comedy, in four acts, by Henry Bataille.—Renaissance.

28. *Ramuntcho*, drama, in five acts and eleven tableaux, by Pierre Loti, with incidental music by Gabriel Pierné.—Odéon.

29.**La Mariée du Mardi Gras*, vaudeville, in three acts, by MM. Grange and Lambert-Thiboust.—Cluny.

MARCH.

1.*Aiglon, drama, in four acts, by Edmond Rostand—Sarah-Bernhardt.

12.**La Mort de Pompée*, tragedy, in five acts, by Corneille—Comédie Française.

14. *Qui Perd Gagne*, comedy, in five acts, by M. Pierre Veber, adaptation from a novel by Alfred Capus—Réjane.

17. *Les Jumeaux de Brighton*, comedy, in a prologue and three acts, by MM. Tristan Bernard. Produced under the auspices of the Antoine at the Femina.
19. *Occupe toi d'Amélie*, vaudeville, in three acts, by Georges Feydeau—Nouveautés.
24. *Son Altesse l'Amour*, operette, in three acts, by MM. Victor de Cottens and Pierre Veber—Moulin-Rouge.
25. *La Poudre aux Moineaux*, vaudeville, in three acts, by MM. Maurice Desvallières and Lucien Gleize—Palais-Royal.
25. *La Petite Hollande*, comedy, in three acts, by Sacha Guitry; *La Comédie des Familles*, comedy, in one act, by M. Paul Geraldy; and *Le Chauffeur*, comedy, in one act, by M. Max Maurey—Odéon.
27. *Nos Magistrats*, drama, in four acts, by M. Arthur Bernède—Molière.

APRIL.

4. *Qui qu'a vu Ninette*, a vaudeville-operette in three acts and four tableaux, by Jules Oudot and Jean Drault, with music by M. Lebailly—Cluny
4. *Ma Générale*, a comedy, in one act, by Jules Claretie, and *La Revue de Paques*, by M. Adrien Vély, performed on the occasion of the benefit given to M. Baillet on his retirement from the Comédie Française.
5. *Le Grillon*, adapted by M. L. de Grandmesnil from Dickens's "Cricket on the Hearth," with music by Massenet—Réjane.
9.*Le Trou d'Almanzor*, an operette in one act, by MM. Rip and Wilned, with music by M. Willy Redstone, produced as a curtain-raiser to *Aux Bouffes on Pouffe*—Bouffes-Parisiens.
6.*Rip*, a comic opera, in four acts and seven tableaux, by MM. Meilhac, Gille, and H. Farnie, with music by Robert Planquette—Trianon-Lyrique.
8. *La Courtisane de Corinthe*, a drama, in five acts and a prologue, by MM. Michel Carré and Paul Bilhaud, with incidental music by M. Charles Levadé—Sarah-Bernhardt.
10 *Le Chevalier d'Eon*, a spectacular comic opera, in four acts, by MM. Armaud Silvestre and Henri Cain, with music by Rodolphe Berger—Porte-St.-Martin.
11. *Les Pierrots*, a military drama, in five acts and seven tableaux, by M. Gustave Grillet—Ambigu.
13. *La Fille de Pilate*, a sacred drama, in three acts in verse, by M. René Fauchios—des-Arts.
13. *Simone*, a comedy, in three acts in prose, by M. Eugène Brieux—Comédie-Française.
16. *Le Coup de Foudre*, a vaudeville, in three acts, by M. Léon Xanrof—Folies Dramatiques.
17. *La Course à l'Amour*, a fantaisie, in two acts and six tableaux, by M. André Matieux—Cigale.
18.*Les Pilules du Diable*, a féerie, in three acts and thirty-two tableaux, by MM. Ferdinand Laloue, Anicet Bourgeois, and Laurent—Châtilet
22. *Le Scandale de Monte Carlo*, a comedy, in three acts, by M. Sacha Guitry; with *L'Incendiaire*, a comedy, in one act, by M. Heyersmaus, with French adaptation by M. Schumann—Gymnase.
22. *Le Noël de M. Moutton*, a comedy, in three acts, by Félicien Champsaur—Comédie-Royale.

24. *La Loi*, a comedy, in three acts, by M. Daniel Jourda, given under the auspices of the Théâtre de l'Œuvre—Fémina.
24. *Le Roi*, a comedy, in four acts, by MM. G. A. de Caillavet, Robert de Flers, and Emmanuel Arène—Variétés.
25. *Alibi*, a drama, in three acts, by M. Gabriel Trarieux—Odéon.
26. *En Bonne Fortune*, a comedy, in one act, by MM. Xanrof and Pierre Veber; *Un Épisode sous la Terreur*, by M. Mozlère; *Jujules*, a comedy, in one act, by MM. Auguste Germain and Pantlan; *Les Trois Masques*, a drama, in one act, by M. Charles Méré; and *Méphisto, Chez Méfisto*, a drama, in one act, by MM. Trébar and Mainger—Méfisto.
27. *Saul*, a lyric tragedy, in five acts, by M. Alfret Poizat, adapted from Alfieri, with music by Letorey—Gaîté.
29. *Madame Gribouille*, a comedy-vaudeville, in three acts, by MM. Abel Tarride and Adolphe Chenevière—Palais-Royal.

MAY.

6.*L'Autre Danger*, comedy, in three acts, by Maurice Donnay—Comédie-Française.
8. *Candida*, comedy, in three acts, by G. Bernard Shaw, adapted by Augustin and Henriette Hamon—Théâtre-des-Arts.
8. *Mariage d'Etoile*, comedy, in three acts, by MM. Alexandre Bisson and Georges Thurner—Vaudeville.
9. *La Conquête des Fleurs*, comedy, in three acts, by M. Gustave Grillet—Athénée.
12. *Auteur de la Lampe*, comedy, in three acts, by M. André Ibels—Femina.
13. *Hippolyte et Aricie*, tragedy, in five acts and a prologue, by Pellegrin, with music by Jean-Philippe Rameau—Grand Opera.
15. *Le Crime d'un Autre*, drama, in five acts, by MM. Lecomte Arnold and Léonce Renault—Ambigu.
16. *Chérubin*, comedy, in three acts, by M. Francis de Croisset, with incidental music by M. Edmond Diet—Femina.
18.*Jeunesse*, comedy, in four acts, by M. André Picard—Gymnase.
18.*Le Chemineau*, drama, in five acts, by M. Jean Richepin—Sarah Bernhardt.
19. *Boris Goudounow*, opera, in three acts and seven tableaux, adapted from the drama of Pouchkine, with music by Modeste Moussorgsky—Grand Opera.
21. *Paris ou le Bon Juge*, operette, in two acts, by MM. Robert de Flers and G. A. de Caillavet, with music by Claude Terrasse—Des Capucines.
22.*Une Nuit de Noces*, vaudeville, in three acts, by MM. Henri Kéroul and Albert Barré—Palais-Royal.
22. *Snegourotchka*, opera, in four acts and a prologue, adapted from the Russian by M. Pierre Lalo, music by M. Rimsky-Karsakon—Opéra-Comique.
22. *Le Nirvana*, dramatic poem, in four acts, by M. Paul Vérola, with incidental music by Tiarko Richepin; also *La Voix Frêle*, comedy, in one act, by MM. Augustin Thierry and Eugène Berteaux—Odéon.
27. *Velléda*, tragedy, in four acts, in verse, by M. Maurice Magre, with *L'Autre*, comedy, in one act, in verse, by M. André Dumas—Odéon.
29.*La Basoche*, comic opera, in three acts, by M. Albert Carré, with music by André Messager—Gaîté.

20. *Le Chant du Cygne*, comedy, in three acts, by MM. Georges Duval and Xavier Roux —Athénée.

30. *Les Mystères de Paris*, drama, in five acts, and ten tableaux, adapted from the novel of Eugène Sue by Ernest Blum—Ambigu.

30. *Paris Tout Nu*, revue, by MM. de Gorsse and Nanteuil, with music by Claude Terrasse—Ambassadeurs.

JUNE.

4. *Les 28 Jours de Clairette*, an operette in four acts, by MM. Raymond and Antony Mars, with music by Victor Roger—Porte-St.-Martin.

5. *L'Amoureuse*, Georges de Porto-Riche's comedy, in three acts, originally produced at the Odéon, with Mme. Réjane as the heroine—Comédie-Française.

6. *Au Palais-Cardinal*, an *à propos*, written for the occasion of the Corneille anniversary, by M. Tancrède Martel—Comédie-Français.

7. *Væ Victis*, a drama in three acts and four tableaux, by Mlle. M. Duterme, and *Les Amours d'Ovide*, a comedy, in two acts in verse, by M. Mouezy-Eon, produced under the auspices of the Théâtre de l'Œuvre—Femina.

12. *Salammbo*, an opera, in four acts, by Ernest Reyer—Grand Opera.

13. *Pelléas et Mélisande*, an opera, in three acts, by Claude Dubussy—Opéra-Comique.

15. *Peter Pan*, a comedy, in five acts, by J. M. Barrie with music by John Crook, produced under the management of Mr. Charles Frohman—Vaudeville.

17. *Le Monsieur aux Chrysanthèmes*, a comedy, in three acts, by M. Armory, given under the auspices of the Théâtre d'Art—Palais-Royal.

22. *La Belle Sainara*, a Japanese comedy, in one act, by M. Ernest d'Hervilly; *L'Ecran Orisé*, a comedy, in one act, in prose, by M. Henry Bordeaux; with Molière's *Misanthrope*—Comédie-Française.

JULY.

5. *Les Ouvriers*, comedy, in three acts, by M. Eugène Manuel, originally produced in 1870—Comédie Française.

12. *Le Berger aux Trois Déesses*, comedy, by Mme. Lucie Delarue-Mardrus; *Le Manonais Grain*, by M. Maurice de Taramond; and *Le Guérisseur*, comedy, by M. Jules Princet, performed at the Théâtre aux Champs at Aulnay-sous-Bois.

12. *Andromaque*, tragedy, in four acts, by Racine, performed by Mme Cora Laparcerie at the open-air theatre at Pré-Catalan.

23. *Hernani*, tragedy, in five acts, by Victor Hugo, with Mlle. Madeleine Roch for the first time as Doña Sol—Comédie Française.

26. *Dalila*, tragedy, in five acts, by Mme. G. Constant Lounsbury, French adaptation by M. Gabriel Nigond, with music by M. Tiarko Richepin, at the de Verdure at Pré-Catalan.

26. *Les Hommes de Proie*, tragedy, in four acts, by M. Charles Meré, given at the Théâtre Antique de la Nature at Champigny-la-Bataille.

AUGUST.

1. *Trois Femmes pour un Mari*, a farcial comedy, by M. Grenet Dancourt—Palais-Royal.

1. *As-tu vu mon nu?* a revue, in three tableaux, by M.M. Max Viterbo and Jules Moy, with music by R. Beretta—Ambassadeurs.

2. *La Revue Nouvelle*, a revue by M.M. Jules Oudot Léo Lellèvre, and Emile Codey—Marigny.

8. *L'Abbé Constantin*, a comedy in three acts, adapted from Ludovic Halévy's novel of the same name by Hector Frémieux and Pierre Decourcelle—Porte-St.-Martin.

9. *Le Roi Charmant*, a play in two acts, by M. L. Michaud d'Humiac, produced in the Theatre Antique de la Nature at Champigny-la-Bataille.

14. *L'Homme de la Montagne*, a vaudeville in three acts, by M.M. Claude Roland and Kraatz, the French adaptation by M. A. de Mauprey—Cluny.

21. *Electra*, Sophocles's three act tragedy, with French translation by M. Alfred Poizat—Comédie-Française.

26. *L'Etoile*, a ballet, by M.M. André Wormser and Aderer—Grand Opera.

SEPTEMBER.

2. The re-opening, under the management of MM. Charles Debasta and L. Rozenberg, took place of the Apollo Music Hall.

3. The re-opening, under the management of MM. Victor de Cottens and Marinelli, took place of Olympia.

5. *Roger la Honte*, drama, in five acts, by MM. Jules Mary and Georges Grisier—Ambigu.

10. *Patachon*, comedy, in four acts, by MM. Maurice Hennequin and Félix Duquesnil—Vaudeville.

10. *Marie Stuart*, drama, in five acts, by MM. Charles Samson and L. Cressonnois—Moncey.

10. *Chanteclairette*, operette, by MM. G. P. Lafargue and Jean Roby, with music by Willy Redstone—Scala Music Hall.

12. *Le Major Ipéca*, vaudeville, in three acts, by MM. Mouezy and E. Joullot—Cluny.

15. *Paul et Virginie*, opera, in three acts, by MM. Michel Carré and Jules Barbier, with music by Victor Massé—Gaieté.

15. *Mam'zelle Trompette*, operette, in three acts, by MM. Maurice Desvaillères and Paul Moncousin, with music by M. T. Hirlemann—Folles-Dramatiques.

17. *L'Amour Brule*, spectacular operette, in five tableaux, by Daniel Riche—Casino-de-Paris.

19. *Hayaée*, comic opera, in three acts, by Eugène Scribe, with music by Adam—Trianon-Lyrique.

21. *La Muette de Portici*, opera, in four acts and five tableaux, by Scribe and Casimir Delavigne—Trianon-Lyrique.

25. *Madame Bluff*, comedy, in three acts, by M. Alexandre Debray—Bouffes-Parisiennes.

24. *Le Cœur et la Dot*, comedy, in four acts, by Félicien Mallefille—Odéon.

24. *L'Or*, drama, in five acts, by MM. Robert Peter and Robert Danceny—Sarah-Bernhardt Theatre.

28. *Le Roi*, comedy, in four acts, by MM. A. de Caillavet, Robert de Flers, and Emmanuel Arène—Variétés.

30. *Le Petit Fouchard*, comedy, in three acts, by MM. Charles Raymond and André Sylvane—Gymnase.

OCTOBER.

1. *La Maison en Ordre*, adaptation by MM. Bazalgette and Bienstock of A. W. Pinero's four-act comedy, *His House in Order*—Vaudeville.
1. *L'Auberge Rouge*, adaptation in two acts, by M. Serge Basset, of Balzac's *Auberge Rouge;* and *Répudiée*, drama, in three acts, by Mme. L. Dartigne—Antoine
2. *Pantaloon*, comedy, in two tableaux, by J. M. Barrie, with Miss Pauline Chase in the leading *rôle*—Des Arts.
3. *Paris-Voyeur*, *féerie révue*, in two acts and seventeen tableaux, by MM. Alévy and Eugène Joullot—Parisiana.
5.*Jean de Nivelle, comic opera, in three acts, by MM. Edmond Gondinet and Philippe Gille, with music by Léo Delibes—Opéra-Comique.
7. *Le Bon Roi Dagobert*, comedy, in four acts, in verse, by M. André Rivoire—Comédie-Française.
7. *La Révue de Cluny*, révue, in three acts and ten tableaux, by MM. Paul Ardot and Albert Laroche—Cluny.
9. *L'Emigré*, play, in four acts, by Paul Bourget—Renaissance.
10. *Parmi les Pierres*, drama, in four acts adapted from the German of Hermann Sudermann by MM. Remon and Valentin—Odéon.
13. *Israël*, drama, in three acts, by Henry Bernstein—Réjane.
14. *V'la l'Potin Mondain*, révue, by MM. Fargue and Charon; *L'Après-Midi-Byzantine*. comedy, in one act, by M. Nozière; *La Petite Femme Forte*, comedy, in one act, by MM. A. Germain and Trebor; and *Madame est de Bois*, comedy, by M. E. G. Gluck—Comédie-Royale.
16. *L'Agence Legris*, drama, in six acts, by M. Jacques Roullet—Ambigu.
16. *L'Oreille Fendue*, drama, in four acts, by M. Lucien Népoty—Antoine.
23.*Götterdämmerung, libretto and music by Richard Wagner, with French version by M. A. Ernst—Grand Opéra.
24. *L'Heure de la Bergère*, comedy, in three acts, by Maurice Ordonneau—Palais-Royal.
25.*Napoléon, drama, in five acts, by MM. Fernand Meynet and Gabriel Didier—Porte-St.-Martin.
28. *Arsène Lupin*, play, in three acts and four tableaux, by F. de Croisset and Maurice Leblanc—Athénée.
28. *Monsieur Mésian*, farce, one act, by Pierre Veber—des Arts.
29. *L'Eveil du Printemps*, comedy, in three acts and fifteen tableaux, by Frank Wedeking, with French version by Robert d'Humières.—Théâtre des Arts.
30. *Le Passe-Partout*. comedy, in three acts, by M. Georges Thurner.—Gymnase.
31.**La Famille Pont-Biquet*, comedy, in three acts, by Alexandre Bisson—Palais-Royal.

NOVEMBER.

4. *La Chatte Blanche*, a féerie, in three acts and twenty-three tableaux, by the Brothers Cogniard, with music by M. Marius Baggers—Châtelet.
6. *Plumard et Barnabé*, vaudeville, in three acts, by MM. Henry Moreau and Charles Quinel—Cluny.
6. *La Patronne*, comedy, in four acts, by M. Maurice Donnay—Vaudeville.
7. *Vera Violetta*, spectacular Viennese operette, adapted for the French stage by M. Redelspeyer—Olympia.

11. *S. A. R.*, operette, in three acts, by MM. Xanrof and Chancel, with music by Ivan Caryll—Bouffes-Parisiens.
12. *L'Enfant de ma Sœur*, comedy, in three acts, by MM. Monezy-Eon and Francheville—Déjazet.
13. *Dix minutes d'Auto*, farce, in three acts, by MM. Georges Berr and Pierre Decourcelle—Nouveautés.
16. *Petite Babouche*, comedy, in one act, by M. Grafferi; *Feu la mère de Madame*, comedy, in one act, by M. Georges Feydeau; and *Fraisidig*, operette, in one act, by MM. Jacques Redelspeyer and Lattès.—Comédie Royale.
19. *Le Heurt*, comedy, in three acts, by M. Paul Granet; *La Logique du Doute*, comedy, in two acts, by M. A. Mortier—Le Nouveau d'Art.
20. *Les Révoltés*, drama, in five acts and six tableaux, by MM. Henry Cain and Edouard Adenis—Sarah Bernhardt.
22. *Nuit d'Illyric*, play, in two tableaux, by MM. E. M. Saumann and Paul Olivier; *La Première Misa*, comedy, in one act, by M. Léon Frapié; *Cent lignes émues*, comedy, in one act, by M. Charles Torquet; and *Une présentation*, comedy, in one act, by M. Ilie de Bassan—Grand Guignol.
24. *Kaatje*, play, in four acts, in verse, by Spaak—Des Arts.
25. *Electra*, play, in two acts, adapted by MM. Epstein and Paul Strozzi from the play by Hugo de Hoffmannstahl—Femina.
25. *Les Vainqueurs*, drama, in four acts, by Emile Fabre; *Le Mufle*, comedy, in two acts, by Sacha Gintry—Antoine.

DECEMBER.

1. *Le Petit Faust*, an operette, in three acts and four tableaux, by MM. Jaime and Crémieux, with music by Hervé—Folies-Dramatiques.
2. *La Boscotte*, a drama, in five acts and six tableaux, by Mme. Georges Maldagne—Ambigu.
3. *Le Poulailler*, comedy, in three acts, by Tristan Bernard; *Après . . .*, a revue, in one act, by Sacha Guitry; and *Asseyez Vous*, a farce, in one act, by MM. Pierre Mortier and André Mycho—Michel.
4. *Bienheureuse*, comedy, in two acts, by Jean Bouchar; *Le Poussin*, a comedy, in three acts, by M. E. Guiraud; *Pylade*, a comedy, in one act, by M. Louis Legendre—Odéon.
5. *La Revue des Folies-Bergère*, a Franco-English revue, in twenty-two tableaux, by M. P. L. Flers, with music by M. Patusset—Folies-Bergère.
5. *Le Tasse*, a drama, in five acts in verse, by M. Paul Souchon—Fémina.
7. *Le Foyer*, a comedy, in three acts, by MM. Octave Mirbeau and Thadée Natanson—Comédie Française.
9. *Sanga*, a lyric drama, in four acts, by MM. Eugène Morand and Paul de Choudens, with music by Isidore de Lara—Opéra-Comique
9. *L'Oiseau Blessé*, a comedy, in four acts, by M. Alfred Capus—Renaissance.
11. *L'Affaire des Variétés*, a comedy, in three acts, by M. Gabriel Timmory; and *Leurs Maîtres*, a comedy, in once act, by M. Jacques Terni—Mevisto.
11. *Les Vieux*, a comedy, in three acts, by MM. Rameil and Saisset—De l'Œuvre.
13. *Quart d'Œil*, a vaudeville, in three acts, by M. Camille Audigier, and *L'Examen de Florent*, a comedy, in one act, by M. Robert Oudot—Montrouge.

15. *La Femme X.*, a drama, in five acts, by M. Alexandre Bisson—Porte-St.-Martin.
16. *La Dame qui n'est Plus aux Camélias*, a comedy, in three acts, by M. de Faramond; *Les Vieux*, a comedy, in three acts, by MM. P. Rameil and F. Saisset; *La Madone*, a comedy, in two acts, by M. Spack—De l'Œuvre.
16. *Jeanne qui Rit*, a comedy, in·three acts, by MM. Solué and Darantière—Réjane.
17 *Le Lys*, a comedy, in four acts, by MM. Pierre Wolff and Gaston Leroux—Vaudeville.
19. *L'Année en l'Air*, a revue, in two acts and ten ·tableaux, by MM. André Mouezy and Henri Bataille—Apollo.

20. *La Revue de Noel*, a spectacular revue, in two tableaux, by M. Jacques Brindjont-Offenbach—Fémina.
21. On the occasion of the Racine anniversary an à-propos, in one act, by M. Maurice Olivaint, entitled *La Champmeslé au Camp*, was recited at the—Comédie-Française.
23. *Pastorale de Noel*, a fifteenth-century mystery, by M. Arnould Greban, adapted by MM. Leonel de La Tourrasse and Gailly de Taurines, with music by Reynaldo Hahn—Des Arts.
23. *La Beauté du Diable*, a drama, in five acts and eight tableaux, by MM. Jules Mary and Emile Rochard—Ambigu.

GERMAN STAGE.

ALPHABETICAL LIST OF PRINCIPAL GERMAN PLAYS PRODUCED FOR THE FIRST TIME IN GERMANY, AUSTRIA, AND SWITZERLAND, DURING THE YEAR, 1908.

Blaue Band, das, comedy in three acts, by A. Lippschitz and G. Okonkowski—Hannover, Residenztheater. January 21.
Blaue Maus, die, farce in three acts, by Alexander Engel and Julius Horst—Vienna, Raimundtheater. February 15. (Agent: Eduard Bloch.)
Blut, das, drama in five acts, by Julius Bab—Stuttgart, Hoftheater, November 26. (Agent and Publisher: S. Fischer, Berlin.)
Brautnacht, a play by Hermann Kienzl—Graz, Stadttheater. December 12.
Bretzenburg, farce by R. Skowronnek and R. Wilde—Berlin, Lessing Theater. December 25. (Agent: Felix Bloch's Erben, Berlin.)
Dame mit den Lilien, die, comedy in three acts, by Rudolf Presber—Berlin, Neues Schauspielhaus. February 15.
Doktor Eisenbart, comedy in four acts, by Otto Falckenberg—Mannheim, Hoftheater. March 14. (Agent and Publisher: Georg Müller, Munich.)
Ein Königreich m. b. H., farce by Wagh—Nuremberg, Intimes Theater, December 25.
Ein unverstandener Mann, comedy in three acts, by E. v. Wolzogen — Wiesbaden, Residenztheater. October 31.
Entweder—oder, farce in three acts, by Emil and Arnold Golz — Vienna, Raimundtheater, October 17.
Erde, comedy in four acts, by Karl Schönherr—Düsseldorf, Schauspielhaus. January 13. (Agent and Publisher: S. Fischer, Berlin.)
Ernte, die, play in three acts, by Felix Philippi—Vienna, Deutches Volkstheater. January 4. (Agent: F. Bloch's Erben, Berlin.)
Ersten Menschen, die, a mystery in two acts, by Otto Borngräber—Berlin, Neues Theater. May 23.
Frau Juttas Brautfahrt, comedy by G. Schätzler-Perasini—Posen, Stadttheater, December 25.
Fremdling von Murten, der, tragedy in three acts, by E. von Bodman—Zurich, Stadttheater. May 29.
Gelbe Nachtigall, die, comedy, by Hermann Bahr—Breslau, Schauspielhaus.
Gelbstern, grotesque in three acts, by Jacques Burg and Walter Turszinsky—Berlin, Deutsches Theater. (Agent: Anstalt für Aufführungsrecht, Berlin—Charlottenburg; Publisher: Vita, Deutsches Verlagshaus, Berlin—Ch.)
Georgina, comedy by Franz v. Schönthan—Vienna, Deutsches Volkstheater, December 25.

Glücklichen, die, comedy, by T. E. Poritzki—Karlsruhe, Hoftheater. October 24. (Agent: E. Bloch, Berlin.)
Glücklichste Zeit, die, comedy by Raoul Auernheimer—Berlin, Lustspielhaus. December 23.
Graf von Gleichen, der, play in four acts, by W. Schmidtbonn—Düsseldorf, Schauspielhaus. February 3.
Gute König, der, comedy in three acts, by R. Auernheimer — Vienna, Deutsches Volkstheater. March 24.
Herzog Boccaneras Ende, a drama by Leo Greiner —Mannheim. November 21.
Hinterm Zaun, comedy in three acts, by Karl Roessler—Vienna, Lustspiel-Theater. Feb. 17.
Hochzeit, drama in five acts, by Emil Strauss—Berlin, Kammerspielhaus. January 23.
Junge Welt, die, comedy in four acts, by Frank Wedekind—Munich, Schauspielhaus. April 22.
Kaiser Karl's Geissel, play in four acts, by Gerhart Hauptmann—Berlin, Lessing Theater. January 11. (Agent: F. Bloch's Erben, Berlin.)
Kaisertoast, der, comedy in three acts, by Baron von Schlicht and W. Turszinsky—Norderney, Kurtheater. August 4. (Agent: F. Bloch's Erben.)
Kampf, play in three acts, by Ludwig Heller and Bernhard Rehse—Crefeld, Stadttheater. February 4.
*Ketten, drama by Arno Hagen—Königsberg, Stadttheater. October 20. (Agent: Anstalt für Aufführungsrecht, Berlin—Charlottenburg.)
Kimiko, tragedy, by W. von Gersdorff—Dresden, Hoftheater. March 26.
Kleine Heim, das, play in three acts, by Thaddäus Rittner—Vienna, Deutsches Volkstheater. May 23. (Publisher: J. G. Cotta'sche Buchhandlung, Stuttgart.)
Kuss, der, play in one act, by Ludwig Huna—Vienna, Deutsches Volk-theater. October 10.
Liebe, comedy in three acts, by Paul Apel—Berlin, Hebbeltheater. March 28.
Lokomotivführer Claussen, play in four acts, by A. Waldemar Müller—Eberhart. Berlin, Friedrich-Wilhelmstädt, Schauspielhaus. February 27.
Lori Pollinger, comedy in three acts, by F. v. Schönthan and R. Oesterreicher — Vienna, Bürgertheater. (Agent: F. Bloch's Erben, Berlin.)

Luftleutnant, der, farce by G. Schätzler-Perasini and R. Kessler — Heidelberg, Stadttheater, December 27.

Lysistrata, comedy in two acts (after Aristophanes), by Leo Greiner—Berlin, Kammerspielhaus. February 27.

Maria Arndt, play in five acts, by Ernst Rosmer—Munich Schauspielhaus. October 17. (Agent: S. Fischer, Berlin.)

Masken, three one act plays, by Konrad Falke—Zürich, Stadttheater. January 28.

Mausefalle, die, farce in three acts, by A. Engel and J. Horst—Munich, Volkstheater. February 20. (Agent: F. Bloch's Erben, Berlin.)

Menschenopfer, play by W. Henzen—Leipzig, Stadttheater. December 17.

Merovinger, die, tragedy in five acts, by D. v. Liliencron—Kiel, Stadttheater. October 23. (Agent: Anstalt für Aufführungsrecht, Berlin —Charlottenburg.)

Moral, comedy in three acts, by Ludwig Thoma—Munich, Schauspielhaus. November 21.

Musik, play in four acts, by Frank Wedekind —Nuremberg, Intimes Theater. January 11.

Niemand weiss es, play by Theodor Wolff—Berlin, Kammerspielhaus.

O diese Leutnants !, comedy in three acts, by Kurt Kraatz—Hanau, Stadttheater. November 1.

Panne, comedy in three acts, by R. Skowronnek —Berlin, Lustspielhaus. January 10. (Agent: F. Bloch's Erben.)

Pfarrerin, die play by Richard Fellinger—Darmstadt — Hoftheater. October 25. (Agent: Anstalt für Aufführungsrecht, Berlin— Charlottenburg.)

Puppenschule, die, play in four acts, by Hans Müller—Munich. Residenz-Theater. January 25. (Publishers: Egon Fleischel and Co., Berlin.)

Rantzau und die Pogwisch, die, play in five acts, by Detlev v. Liliencron—Berlin, Friedrich Wilhelmstädt, Schauspielhaus. March 21. (Agent: Anstalt für Aufführungsrecht, Berlin —Charlottenburg.)

Schwarze Kavalier, der, drama by Heinrich Lilienfein—Berlin, Schillertheater. November 7. (Agent: Anstalt für Aufführungsrecht, Berlin —Charlottenburg.)

Seine Kleine, farce in three acts, by A. Engel and J. Horst —Vienna, Raimundtheater. Mar. 14.

So sind die Menschen, comedy in three acts, by Bernhardt Rehse—Breslau Sommertheater. Augus 26. (Agent: A. Langen, Munich.)

Sozialaristokraten, comedy, by Arno Holz—Berlin, Kammerspielhaus.

Start, comedy in three acts, by Leo Feld—Vienna, —Kleines Schauspielhaus. February 13.

Sünde, die, comedy by Max Bernstein—Berlin, Neues Schauspielhaus, December 30.

Tantris der Narr, drama in five acts, by Ernst Hardt—Cologne, Schauspielhaus. January 23. (Agent: Anstalt für Aufführungsrecht, Berlin—Charlottenburg. Publisher: Inselverlag, Leipzig.)

Tartuffe, der Patriot, comedy by Otto Ernst—Stuttgart, Hoftheater. December 12. (Agent: E. Bloch, Berlin.)

Teufel, der, play in three acts, by Franz Molnar—Vienna, Deutsches Volkstheater. February 15.

Teufelskirche, die, comedy in three acts, by Adolf Paul — Hamburg. November 26. (Agent: Anstalt für Aufführungsrecht, Berlin—Charlottenburg.)

Tessa, tragedy in five acts, by Wilhelm Weigand —Breslau. (Publisher: Georg Müller, Munich.)

Thalea Bronkema, play in three acts, by Johannes Wiegand — Strassburg, Stadttheater. September 16. (Agent: Eduard Bloch, Berlin.)

Thersites, drama by Stefan Zweig—Dresden, Hoftheater. November 26. (Agent: F. Bloch's Erben.)

Traum des Glücklichen, der, play in one act, by Ludwig Fulda—Hamburg, Deutsches Schauspielhaus. March 31. (F. Bloch's Erben.)

Ulrich, Fürst von Waldeck, play in five acts, by Herbert Eulenberg—Cologne, Stadttheater. April 15.

Unbekannte, der, play by Oskar Bendiner—Berlin, Neues Theater. December 31.

Unsichere, der (The Vagabond), play in four acts, by Richard Fellinger—Berlin, Kleines Theater. January 22. (Agent: Anstalt für Aufführungsrecht, Berlin—Charlottenburg.)

Unverbesserlichen, die, play in one act, by Georg Hirschfeld—Leipzig, Schauspielhaus, Dec. 22.

Verflixten Frauenzimmer, die, four one-act plays, by M. Burckhart—Vienna, Deutsches Volkstheater. Nov. 28.

Wolkenkratzer, farce in three acts, by Karl Rössler and Ludwig Heller—Berlin, Neues Schauspielhaus. January 18. (Agent: F. Bloch's Erben, Berlin.)

Wolkenkuckuksheim, comedy in 3 acts, by Josef Ruederer—Munich, Künstlertheater. July 3.

Wunderliche von Bevern, der, tragedy in five acts, by Fritz Hartmann—Brunswick, Hoftheater. September 21.

LEGAL CASES OF THE YEAR.

JANUARY.

THE PREMIUM FRAUD.—ALFRED KENNEDY SENT TO GAOL.

6 At the West Hartlepool Police Court, before the Mayor (in the chair), Ald. Suggitt, Ald. Sargeant, and Mr. A. S. Purdon, Alfred Kennedy was brought up on remand charged with having obtained telegraph money orders, of the value of £1 and £4, from Nellie Burnand, a music hall artist, by means of certain false pretences.

Formally charged, prisoner pleaded guilty. The Mayor said they would take a lenient view of the case, and prisoner would have to go to gaol for three months with hard labour.

READINGS AND RECITATIONS.—A QUESTION OF LICENSE.

11 A case of importance to entertainers was heard in the Liverpool City Police Court, before Messrs. W. E. Willink, A. Shelmerdine, and C. H. Hayhurst. Mr. Lancelot Lowder, elocutionist, was summoned for "being the occupier of a room and using it for the purpose of a public entertainment without a license."

Mr. G. S. Clayton, who prosecuted in behalf of the police, said he thought there was no dispute about the facts. The defendant was a teacher of elocution, and he rented some rooms in Colquitt Street for the purpose of giving what he said was an entertainment of a religious character, "The Christmas Carol," from Charles Dickens. People paid an admission to hear the performance, and he (Mr. Clayton) submitted that that constituted the keeping of a place for a public entertainment within the meaning of the Act, and the premises ought to be licensed. Defendant contended that because there was no music and dancing, his entertainment did not require a license.

Defendant was fined 1s. and 1s. costs.

DEAL v. SHAKESPEARE THEATRE.

13 Frederick Deal, of Simpson Street, Battersea, a painter and decorator, brought an action at the Wandsworth County Court to recover damages from the proprietors of the Shakespeare Theatre, Clapham Junction, Mr. Moyses appeared for plaintiff, and Mr. Lincoln Read for defendants.

It was stated on behalf of plaintiff that, being out of work, he was selling bananas outside the pit door of the theatre on the night of October 14, 1907, when a box used for putting the checks in fell from a third or fourth storey window on to him and injured him seriously.

The jury finally awarded the plaintiff £15.

BOYLE v. DAVY.—CLAIM FOR COMMISSION.

15 In the Westminster County Court the case of Boyle v. Davy was tried, and was an action by the plaintiff, who described himself as a dramatic agent carrying on business at Dean Street, Soho, to recover the sum of five guineas, which he alleged was due to him as commission from the defendant, Miss R. Davy, a music hall artist, living at Brompton Square, S.W. The plaintiff's case was that he met the defendant in May of last year and procured two dates for her, but she declined to fulfil them, and now refused to pay him his commission.

The defendant appeared, and said it was quite true she agreed to pay plaintiff commission if he procured her engagements for vacant dates, but in both cases the dates were identical with those for which she had previously fixed up, and therefore she could not accept them.

In the result judgment was given for the defendant, but without costs.

HARRIS v. GOULD.—CLAIM FOR SCENERY.

15 Before his Honour Judge Woodfall, in the Westminster County Court, the case of Harris v. Gould was heard, and was a claim by the plaintiff, a theatrical property dealer, carrying on business at Long Acre, to recover the sum of £3 9s., balance of account in respect of certain scenery let out to the defendant, James Morpass, for the production of a sketch on tour in the North of England.

Plaintiff said the defendant had paid him some sums on account, but now refused to pay the balance.

The defendant appeared in person, and said he went into partnership with a man named Boyce for the tour of the sketch in question, and that after the tour was over the latter ran away with all the takings, and left him to pay the debts.

His Honour said it was an extremely unfortunate state of affairs for the defendant, but he was liable for the partnership debts, and, therefore, there must be judgment for the plaintiff for the amount of his claim, with costs.

On defendant's application, an order was made for payment at the rate of 10s. a month.

ROSEN AND BLISS v. HARDEN.

16 In the King's Bench Division, before Mr. Justice Jelf, was continued the hearing of the case in which Messrs. Rosen and Bliss, music hall proprietors, sued Mr. Theo. Harden, "the handcuff king," to recover damages for breach of contract. It appeared that Harden entered into an agreement under which he was to appear at music halls in Aberdeen, Dundee, and Sunderland in the early part of 1907. Shortly before he was due to appear at Aberdeen he telegraphed that he was too ill to travel, and sent a doctor's certificate to the effect that he was unable to follow his employment. He did not fulfil his engagements at Aberdeen or Dundee, and the plaintiffs would not allow him to appear at Sunderland. The plaintiffs contended that the defendant's failure to perform his engagements was not due to his health, but to his fear that his salary would be attached by the Scottish Court in respect of proceedings for slander, which had been taken against him by a lady with whom he lodged during a former visit to Aberdeen. They further said that at the time the defendant alleged that he was unwell he was supporting the music hall artists on strike and addressing meetings. The defendant, on the other hand, denied that he abstained from going to Scotland because he was afraid of having his salary attached, or that he had had an action brought against him in that country. He said he was unable to fulfil his engagements as he was suffering from nervous breakdown.

Defendant counter-claimed for salary for a week when he was not permitted to appear at Sunderland.

Mr. Frank Dodd appeared for the plaintiffs; Mr. E. H. Cannot and Mr. Arthur Woolf for the defendant.

Mr. Justice Jelf, in giving judgment, said that the contract to appear at Aberdeen, Dundee, and Sunderland was all one engagement, and one of the terms was that if the artist was unable to attend to his duties through illness he was to send a medical certificate, and if he was unable to attend to them for three consecutive performances the management might terminate the engagement. The defendant's real reason for not going to Aberdeen was not because he was ill, though there might have been a slight illness, but to avoid service of process in the Scotch Courts. The defendant had suffered no damage by not being allowed to appear at Sunderland, as he had got another engagement, which was at least quite as good, and, therefore, in respect of that, he could not recover on the counter-claim. There having been a breach of contract by the defendant the only question on the claim was one of damages. His Lordship gave judgment for the plaintiffs on the claim for £100, with costs, and judgment for £36 on the counter-claim, without costs.

EMPLOYMENT OF CHILDREN.

At the Manchester City Police Court, Charles Caban, a Frenchman, who was performing **17** with a circus at the Manchester Tivoli, was summoned for employing two boys under thirteen years of age after nine o'clock in the evening without a license. Caban offered a sum of money to anyone who kept his legs on the revolving table used in his performance. A constable stated that he visited the hall and found two boys, named Wall, of Chester Street, Hulme, making the attempt on the table. To prevent them from falling they had a rope attached to their waists. After the performance the boys told him that the defendant's groom had promised them sixpence a night. This was, however, contradicted, and the defendant's wife said that the boys were challenged to try the table, and came from the gallery to the stage. They were only promised a medal. Bigger boys were preferred, she said, because it was better fun. In each case a fine of five shillings was imposed.

EMPLOYMENT OF CHILDREN.

At the Westminster Police Court Mr. T. S. Dickie, licensee of the Standard Music Hall, **17** and his manager, Mr. Maurice Volny, appeared to summonses charging them with causing a child under the age of ten to perform. Against Nellie Bowden, aged nineteen, the elder sister of the child in question, there was another summons for allowing the performance.

Mr. Curtis-Bennett thought it would only

be necessary in Mr. Dickie's case to tell him that he must be more careful in future. He should allow the summons against Mr. Dickie to be withdrawn. The defendant, Mr. Volny, would be fined £8. and £7 7s. costs, and the girl Bowden would have to pay 23s. costs.

MARTINE v. NICHOLSON.—BILL MATTER.

At Stockton County Court, Albert A. Martine sued G. and R. Nicholson, proprie **21** tors of the Hippodrome, Stockton, for alleged breach of contract. Counsel for plaintiff explained that his client was a music hall artist, who, with his son, appeared under the name of the American Singing Picture Artists. The contract proposed that the plaintiff should enter into an engagement commencing November 11, 1907, for one week, for £12 per week. The defence, he understood, was that the plaintiff did not comply with the terms of the contract, which stated that he must forward his bill matter within fourteen days of the commencement of the engagement. Plaintiff wrote a letter with reference to the bill matter on October 26, but did not post it until October 28, because he wanted to enclose a special bill which he had in London. He contended that the bill matter was sent within the prescribed time, and would be received by the first post on October 29.

Mr. Robert Nicholson said he had been repeatedly disappointed by artists not complying with the terms of the contract, and he was determined it should be stopped. He received plaintiff's bill matter on October 29, which was not within the prescribed fourteen days.—In reply to Mr. Woolf, defendant stated that two artists disappointed him the same week as Mr. Martine. As a matter of fact, those two never came at all.—Mr. Woolf: And you wanted to make a scapegoat of Mr. Martine.—Defendant: Nothing of the kind. Proceeding, defendant stated that on the 29th, when he did not receive the bill matter by the morning post, he proceeded to Newcastle, and on the way he engaged a Hindoo contortionist for £6 a week.—Mr. Woolf suggested that the defendants were trying to get out of the contract by a mere quibble.—His Honour thought not. He was of the opinion that defendants had a real grievance.—Mr. Woolf said, assuming the defendants' case was true, there was from Tuesday, October 29, to November 11 fourteen days, because there was the whole day on the Tuesday on which the bill matter was received, and the performance was not to commence until Monday evening, November 11.

His Honour gave judgment for the defendants, with costs. A counter-claim for an amount for which, according to the terms of the contract, plaintiff rendered himself liable by any breach of agreement, was withdrawn.

MORGAN AND MORGAN v. MACNAGHTEN. RINGING DOWN A CURTAIN.

In the Shoreditch County Court, before his Honour Judge Smyly, K.C., the hearing **21** was resumed and concluded of the claim brought by the Misses Elsie and Annie Morgan, of 112, Holmleigh Road, Stoke Newington N.E., to recover damages from Mr. Frank Macnaghten, of Bedford Court Mansions, W.C.

Mr. Doughty, barrister, appeared on behalf of the plaintiffs, and Mr. Martin O'Connor for the defence.

PLAINTIFF'S CASE.

At the opening of the case it was stated that the plaintiffs were engaged in what was called the Macnaghten Tour for six weeks, having to appear in Lincoln, Bath, Halifax, Hartlepool, Blackburn, and Southampton. When they reached Hartlepool in the fourth week they rehearsed during the day the song, "San Antonio," and no objection was taken to it, but at the end of the first house, owing, it was alleged, to the caprice of a hasty-tempered stage manager, they were told they must not sing it in the second house. They pointed out that the notice was too short to alter the song, but he was obdurate, and said they must not sing it. In their dilemma, before going on for the second house, they asked the stage manager if there was any change in the programme, and on being informed "No," proceeded to sing "San Antonio," but before they had quite finished, or, anyway, before they had had time to make their bow to the audience, the curtain was rung down in their faces. They were not allowed to perform the rest of the week, and this, they suggested, had caused them a great deal of harm in the profession, although they admitted they were in pantomime at Birmingham at £30 a week at Christmas. Judge Smyly said he did not think he could have much to say as to the £100 claim, as it appeared to be in the nature of a libel or slander, but he adjourned for other evidence that the £8 was tendered to the plaintiffs for their week's work, as they alleged they were turned out of the theatre bag and baggage with no money.

In resuming the case Mr. Doughty said he hoped his Honour would be able to award him damages for the breach of contract, as it was palpable the harm that must have been caused his clients by the action of the defendant's manager in ringing down the curtain. There was no doubt it had been rung down intentionally.

Judge Smyly: I understood they had really finished singing when the incident occurred.

Mr. Doughty: The main point of my objection to the treatment is that they could not make their exit properly before a critical audience. They had actually finished singing —at least, your Honour signified that you would hold so at the last hearing—but they had not gone off when the curtain was rung down; and can one imagine a more heartless act on the part of a manager?

Judge Smyly: I must ask you to confine yourself to the contract.

Mr. Doughty: I am afraid I am obliged to if your Honour holds that he has no jurisdiction as to the other.

Mr. Frank Wm. Macnaghten was then called as to the question of the tender of the £8.

Mr. O'Connor: Your Honour will remember that the plaintiffs agreed that £8 was offered them at Blackburn, but Mr. Macnaghten refused to make any reparation by offering an apology to be inserted in the theatrical papers.

Judge Smyly: I have looked through the evidence, and cannot find any note as to any tender made at Blackburn, but I see the note that they admitted finishing singing.

Mr. O'Connor: But they did admit having the £8 tendered to them.

Judge Smyly: And I tell you I haven't got it on my notes.

THE DEFENCE.

Mr. Macnaghten then gave his evidence.

Mr. O'Connor: Did you hear of the dispute that had occurred with the plaintiffs at Hartlepool?

Defendant: Yes, I was in Sheffield at the time, and went specially across to Blackburn to see the plaintiffs. I saw them in my office, and we chatted over the matter of the disagreement they had had with Mr. Simpson, my manager, at Hartlepool. They said they felt very deeply insulted over the matter, and wanted an apology from Mr. Simpson. I reasoned with them, and said that I could not think of asking my manager to apologise, as he had nothing to apologise for, and suggested a settlement by my paying a week's money, which I offered them.

Mr. O'Connor: And they refused?

Defendant: Yes, they refused to accept the £8 unless I got a letter of apology from Mr. Simpson for insertion in all the theatrical papers, and as I saw they meant at that moment what they said I told them the interview was closed and the matter ended.

Mr. Doughty: You knew when you went from Sheffield to Blackburn what the plaintiffs had been stopped in their performance for?

Defendant: Most certainly—for the singing of "San Antonio."

Mr. Doughty: What was there against the singing of it? Was it a suggestive song?

Defendant: Oh no, certainly not, it was quite harmless; in fact, it was an empty and meaningless song.

Mr. Doughty: And although it was such a meaningless and empty song you still allowed it to be sung at Blackburn?

Defendant: I did.

Mr. Doughty: Never made any effort to stop it there or the rest of the tour?

Defendant: I did not. What might have suited one town would not suit another.

Judge Smyly: What I understand is that she was asked to change her song for the second house, but declined to do so, as she said the band was so bad.

Defendant: She had three songs, and could have sung the third. All songs are perfectly rehearsed; or if she had have liked she could have had a rehearsal between the first and second house with a new song.

Judge Smyly: Could that have been done?

Defendant: It is often done.

Mr. Doughty: Why were they stopped for a week?

Defendant: I was not there, so cannot say.

Mr. Doughty: Was it reasonable to refuse to allow them to perform?

Defendant: I was not there, so I don't know the full circumstances.

Judge Smyly: If a man is prepared to pay for the engagement there is nothing in it; they must be there whether they sing or not. But to suppose that they can compel a manager to let them sing is quite wrong. It is just the same as going to a dentist—you can pay him for pulling a tooth, but he cannot compel you to have it pulled. (Laughter.)

Mr. Doughty: But suppose he goes to the dentist and says he won't have it pulled because the dentist is incompetent?

Judge Smyly: But that does not enter into this case, as that would be slander, and we are not trying that case.

In answer to Mr. Doughty, Mr. Macnaghten said he was sure a second tender of the £8 was made in his presence by his general manager, Mr. Baugh. Mr. Monte Bayly, of the Variety Artists' Federation, called down with three cases to settle, two of which were settled, and this third one would have been, only Mr. Bayly did not seem to be quite sure whether he was acting for the plaintiff or not.

This closed the case for the defence, and Mr. Doughty asked leave to recall Miss Annie Morgan on the question of the tender which was agreed to. She said that they were performing at Blackburn after the Hartlepool incident, and on the Wednesday evening, as they came out of the theatre, they met Mr. Macnaghten by accident, and he asked them to come to his office. There they discussed the matter, and Mr. Macnaghten agreed that his manager was in the wrong.

Mr. O'Connor: You really suggest that he said you were entitled to a week's money and reparation?

Miss Morgan: Yes, but he never offered to pay.

Judge Smyly: In fact, he never offered anything?

Miss Morgan: No; but he used the words that we were entitled to it.

Mr. O'Connor: Didn't he say he was ready and willing to pay?

Miss Morgan: No, he certainly did not.

Mr. O'Connor: What you really wanted was an apology in the papers?

Miss Morgan: Only what was right and just after what had occurred.

Judge Smyly: Then that was why the matter went off—because there was no apology?

Miss Morgan: I suppose so: he refused to do any more when we talked about apologies.

Mr. Doughty: Was it ever brought to your knowledge before the issue of the summons that the £8 would be paid if desired?

Miss Morgan: Never at any time.

Mr. Doughty: Do you think it is at all likely you would have accepted the £8 in Blackburn if you had seen it?

Miss Morgan: Well, when we left Hartlepool we had to borrow to pay our way on to Blackburn, so we were not in the best of positions financially. You see, our salary was so small for the expenses we had to meet.

Judge Smyly: I think I might as well say now that I do not think the tender was made. It is a very difficult thing under the circumstances to prove a legal tender, and I am by no means convinced that one was made.

Mr. Doughty: I thank your Honour, and might I ask if there is any intention to insist that a legal tender was made to Mr. Bayly, as, if so, I shall have to call evidence as to that?

Mr. O'Connor: Oh, no.

Judge Smyly: As to the tender supposed to be made to Mr. Bayly, there is nothing in it one way or the other, as it is admitted that he was not quite clear whether he was entitled to act for the parties or not. I don't think the tender by Mr. Macnaghten is proved in this case, as it is a most difficult thing for an unprofessional gentleman to make a legal tender. There are so many technicalities which, admittedly, he knows nothing about before it could be upheld in law. For instance, he may have put his hand in his pocket and jingled some coins, saying as he did so that the plaintiffs had better settle the case, as it would be better by far for all parties if they did so. But, supposing he did, and even supposing he put the money down, then that would not be a legal tender in such a case as this, even if they had taken it. When people are fighting in such a case as slander, where an apology is required as well as the salary, then he would have to put the £8 down, and say, I don't care about your action for slander; you can do what you like about that afterwards, but here is the money for your wages. It would have to be an absolute tender, and I think it very unlikely if it was done legally.

Mr. O'Connor: But I submit, directly they refused to accept, except with an apology, that proves a tender.

Judge Smyly: I don't think so.

Mr. O'Connor: Anyway, I submit to your Honour that my client was justified in the course he took, as he had had an irritating, if not a bogus claim brought against him by two artists for slander and all sorts of things, and he was anxious to settle on the best terms, as he knew that he could never ultimately get any costs from them if they lost, which he had no doubt they would do.

Judge Smyly: I do not see that a breach of contract can be made out.

Mr. Doughty: For the way these ladies had been treated and their reputations imperilled, I submit to your Honour that they are entitled to some measure of damages. Is it the right way to treat a lady, to turn her out into the streets to walk about for a week, with no money in her pocket, or, if she had, the manager of the hall had made no effort to supply her with it, whilst everyone knew that for some reason she was not appearing at the hall. I think, if I prove that the place was not reasonably and properly conducted, I am entitled to damages.

Judge Smyly: But I think it was reasonably and properly conducted. I don't think a young lady is entitled to sing a song if the manager says she is not to. Surely he is the one to look after his audience, and not the artist.

Mr. Doughty: She gives a reasonable cause for not being able to sing anything else at a moment's notice—because the band was not good enough; and you have to bear in mind that the manager had seen the songs a fortnight in advance.

Judge Smyly: She rehearsed three, and the artist must be content with two that she can sing to the satisfaction of the management. Do you really mean to suggest that the manager or proprietor of a hall, having made a contract, cannot say what shall be sung or what shall not be sung? Because if you do I am afraid you are wide of the mark, from my opinion.

Mr. Doughty: But there is also a grave responsibility resting on the manager. These ladies had been extensively billed throughout the town, and their non-appearance at once excites the greatest curiosity and conjecture. It is, therefore, for the manager to see, after he has made her name public, that she does appear, otherwise her reputation is sadly imperilled.

Judge Smyly: Such a matter as that is a question for another court. I have nothing to say regarding it, except that I consider a manager entitled to insist on the songs that are sung.

Mr. Doughty: But he stops her from performing. I submit that he should justify his reason for doing so, which has not been done here. All he raised objection to was a song which he had seen two weeks before, and for that they are sent away, with every appearance of deliberate insult and no money in their pockets.

JUDGMENT.

In giving judgment, Judge Smyly said that in his opinion there had been no breach of contract at all. When a person engaged artists he had to be ready to pay them for that engagement, or the manager, but he was not compelled to let them appear. An artist in one town who was a great success would not suit another. High intelligence in one place would be a frost of a decided character in another. It was absurd to say that a manager was compelled to put on the stage for five nights artists who were singing songs not suited to his audience just because they suited in another place. Continuing, Judge Smyly said: "I don't consider an artist has any right, or is entitled to insist on appearing. In this case, they sang in the first house songs which they thought suitable, but at the conclusion they were rightly, in his opinion, told by the manager that they must stop one of them and sing something in its place, but they sang the song very wrongly again." Continuing, his Honour said he therefore thought the manager was right in stopping them for good, and quite within his rights as one looking after his audience. "Therefore, I say there has been no breach of contract, and as to the questions of libels and slander, or insult, which have arisen during the hearing of the claim, I say nothing, as I am not competent to try the matter. Regarding the £8 claimed for wages, I consider they are entitled to recover, as, although the manager was right in stopping a song, they were willing to go on with other songs, and as they were prevented they are entitled to their salary. I do not consider that the tender was sufficient. I shall therefore enter judgment for the plaintiffs for £8 and costs."

WILLEY v. CLARKE.—ATTACHING AN ARTIST'S SALARY.

In the Westminster County Court his Honour Judge Woodfall had again before him **21** the case of Willey v. Clarke (Dickee garnishee), in which a question arose as to whether the salary of an artist could be attached by a judgment creditor. It appeared that the plaintiff in the original action had recovered judgment against Miss Dorothy Clarke, and failing to get payment of his money he caused a garnishee order to be served on the management of the Standard Music Hall, where she was then appearing. An order nisi was made against her, but it afterwards transpired that she had assigned her salary to a firm of solicitors to whom she owed a bill of costs.

Mr. Cannot (barrister) again appeared on behalf of the defendant, Miss Dorothy Clarke, and said he was now before the Court on a question of costs. He contended that when the garnishee order was set aside an order was made providing for his costs as against the creditor, but the Registrar on taxation had refused to allow them, in spite of the fact that they had to pay the costs of the garnishee for appearing as their witness at the first trial of the action. In further support of his argument Mr. Cannot said he had before him a copy of THE STAGE newspaper, which contained a very good report of the case, and he would just like to read to his Honour the following extract from it:—

Mr. Cannot (barrister) appeared on behalf of the judgment debtor, and submitted that the garnishee summons could not stand on the ground that the salary of an artist could not be anticipated before it was actually earned and was due and payable. His case was that when the garnishee summons was served upon the management of the Standard Music Hall there was really no salary due to Miss Dorothy Clarke,

His Honour: Yes, but you cannot have two sets of costs. You can either have the order for costs against the garnishee or else against the judgment creditor.

Mr. Cannot: This is what your Honour said on the last occasion, according to the report which appeared in THE STAGE:—

After hearing the arguments of counsel, his Honour said he had come to the conclusion that the salary of an artist could not be attached before it was actually due and payable, and, that being so, it followed that the garnishee order could not stand, and must be dissolved with costs.

His Honour: I think the best thing will be to give you costs as against the garnishee, and the costs of this application will go against the judgment debtor in the action.

LECKIE v. WATTS.—THE BARRING CLAUSE.

A note of suspension and interdict was presented in the Bill Chamber of the Court of **24** Session, Edinburgh, at the instance of John Leckie, proprietor and manager of the Alhambra Theatre of Varieties, Edinburgh, against Clive Watts, variety artist, then appearing in the Pavilion Theatre, Glasgow. The respondent, Watts, had undertaken to appear at the Alhambra, Edinburgh, for the week commencing Monday, January 27, but afterwards asked and obtained permission to be released from this engagement, that he might be able to accept an offer for pantomime. The complainer, Mr. Leckie, now found that in place of playing in pantomime the respondent was advertised to perform in a variety entertainment at the King's, Edinburgh, during the week commencing January 27. He therefore asked that the respondent be interdicted from doing so. Lord Guthrie ordered answers to be lodged within twenty-four hours, and that the parties be heard in the Bill Chamber on the 27th.

On the 27th Lord Guthrie passed the note for the trial of the cause, but refused interim interdict, being of opinion that as the agreement was not stamped it could not be founded on, and also that the complainer, in letting the respondent off from his engagement, did not make it a condition of the release that the respondent was to be engaged for pantomime alone.

FRANCIS, DAY, AND HUNTER v. THE EVANTOSCOPE PUBLISHING COMPANY, LIMITED.

In the King's Bench Division, before Mr. Justice Jelf, Mr. Walter Payne moved for **25** judgment against the defendants in the terms of the statement of claim—namely, for an injunction restraining them from infringing the plaintiffs' copyright in a song called "Stop yer tickling, Jock," by printing and selling copies of it without authority, and for damages.

His Lordship granted an injunction, and 40s. damages, and costs.

GRANVILLE THEATRE OF VARIETIES v. MAYO.—THE BARRING CLAUSE.

In the King's Bench Division, before Mr. Justice Jelf, Mr. Maurice Gwyer moved for **25** judgment, on the ground of default in delivery of defence, in Granville Theatre of Varieties v. Mayo, which was an action for breach of a contract by the defendant not to appear while engaged at the Granville at any other music hall within two miles within a specified period. Originally the claim was for an injunction and damages, but as the contract had expired there was no need now for an injunction.

His Lordship entered judgment for the plaintiffs, with 40s. damages and costs.

Motion for judgment on similar grounds was made on behalf of the plaintiffs by Mr. Vaughan Williams in Hackney, etc., Empire Palaces v. Mayo. The action in that case was for damages for breach of an agreement An injunction had been obtained after the first breach by the defendant.

Judgment was entered for the plaintiffs for 40s. damages and costs.

HOOPER AND MOORE v. THE EVANTO-SCOPE PUBLISHING COMPANY, LTD.

In the King's Bench Division, before Mr. Justice Jelf. Mr. Walter Payne moved for judgment against the defendants in the terms **25** of the statement of claim—namely, for an injunction restraining them from infringing the plaintiffs' copyright in two songs, " Don't tell your pals your troubles " and " I wish I had a pal like you," and for damages.

His Lordship granted an injunction, and 40s. damages in respect of each song, and costs.

MELFORD v. MOSS'S EMPIRES, LIMITED

In the King's Bench, before Mr. Justice Bray and a jury, was heard the case of Melford v. **29** Moss's Empires, Limited, in which Mr. Mark Melford sued the defendants for £37 10s., which he claimed to be due as a week's salary. The defence was that plaintiff had been guilty of vulgarity, and that by the contract under which he was performing defendants were justified in dismissing him and forfeiting his salary.

Mr. Ward appeared for the plaintiff and Mr. Eldon Bankes, K.C., and Mr. E. E. Bankes for the defendants.

Mr. Ward said the plaintiff had been for something like thirty-five years before the public, and to-day held a position in the front rank of comedians. In addition to being a comedian, he was a dramatic author of some repute, and had written about 100 sketches and pieces. In 1905 he entered into a contract with the defendants by which he engaged to appear at Newcastle, Liverpool, Birmingham, and most large towns where the defendants had music-halls, commencing at Liverpool in September, 1906, at a salary of £37 10s. per week. Amongst the rules of Moss's Empires, Limited, was one to the following effect:—

" No artist shal' introduce the slightest obscenity or vulgarity into his or her business, and any artist committing a breach of this rule shall be instantly dismissed, and shall forfeit the whole of the salary due. Artists are to carefully observe this rule, as the management are determined to rigidly enforce it."

Mr. Melford selected for performance at the Empire, Liverpool, a piece called *Only a Widow*, a sketch written by himself, and adapted from a well-known farce called *Turned Up*, which had been performed at theatres all over the country.

At one of the performances a gentleman who acted as agent for the chairman of the licensing magistrates was present, and he was the one person, counsel asserted, who was horrified at some words used. He communicated with the managers of the theatre, and the matter was reported by the local manager to headquarters. Mr. Allen, of Moss's Empires, then wrote to him:—

" Words cannot express my surprise and indignation when I heard of the disgusting matter you had introduced into your sketch, filling the audience with astonishment.

" We cannot allow such offensive words to be used on the stage in our theatres. . .

" We have always tried to present a good, clean entertainment to the public. . . . You deliberately abuse our confidence. . . .

" A gentleman present said it made his flesh creep. You must give an undertaking that the words objected to will in future be omitted."

Mr. Melford replied :—

" Acting on the fanatical zeal of your local district manager, you are doing me an outrageous injustice.

" The line mentioned was an inadvertence introduced in response to a cue by my wife.

" I ask you whether you intend to deprive me of my salary, as well as ruin my reputation."

In a subsequent letter Mr. Allen said :—

" We will not allow any double meaning on our stage, and a clever man like yourself has no need of anything of the kind."

Mr. Melford, giving evidence, denied that the line introduced had any double meaning. There was some dialogue about somebody adopting the disguise of a nurse. The cue given was " Tom will find you out," and the line objected to was " Not if he doesn't search me."

This, the witness declared, was perfectly innocent and harmless.

The cue and criticised line had been omitted from the first performance for shortening purposes, but Mrs. Melford gave the line accidentally.

In cross-examination by Mr. Eldon Bankes, K.C., Mr. Melford said that he did not utter objectionable lines in his performances. He knew it was the object of the defendants to present to the public a good, clean entertainment, and he quite approved of it. He did not keep one version of his sketches for one management and another version for another not so particular. They were all particular, and he was particular. He kept elastic sketches which could be stretched to oblige the management.

For the defence, Mr. A. W. Young, joint superintendent of Moss's Empires, said he witnessed the second performance, and at the words complained of there was a convulsion in the house—" a mixed convulsion of amazement, disgust, and, possibly, delight." He protested to Mr. Melford, who replied that he saw nothing in it.

Cross-examined, the witness said the piece might be a popular one on the stage at the present time. With the exception of the objectionable matter, Mr. Melford's performance was a success in making people laugh.

Mr. Horace Cole, acting-manager of Moss's Empire at the time of the incident said he had many complaints from ladies and gentlemen as they left the theatre about the words.

Mr. Turton, surveyor to the Licensing Justices of Liverpool, said he heard the words, and objected to them, and considered it his duty to report them to the justices.

THE VERDICT.

The jury found for the plaintiff for the amount claimed.

Judgment accordingly, with costs on the High Court scale.

JOSEPH v. BRIXTON EMPRESS OF VARIETIES.

At the Lambeth County Court, an auctioneer named Joseph Joseph, of Brixton Road, sued the Empress Theatre of Varieties for **30** £9 9s. for stage furniture supplied in July, 1907, to the Brixton theatre. Mr. Walter Williams appeared for the plaintiff, and Mr. Walter Payne (instructed by Messrs. Kingsbury and Turner) for the defendants.

Mr. Williams said that on March 22 Mr. Allum asked plaintiff to supply the theatre with furniture, and from then until July 22 furniture was supplied week by week. Mr. Allum told him every week what furniture was required, and it was by Mr. Allum's order that the articles were sent Up to July 22 no notice was given to the plaintiff that Mr. Allum was engaged in any different capacity to that which he held in March. Plaintiff was paid fortnightly by cheque up to the end of June. Each cheque was signed by Mr. Grimes, a director, and countersigned by Mr. Nelson Francis, who was the secretary of the company.

Plaintiff gave evidence bearing out counsel's statement, and in cross-examination denied that he was told in June that Mr. Maclean was to have a short season at the theatre, and that Mr. Walter Melville was taking the theatre after Mr. Maclean's season. Mr. Allum told him on July 19 that no more furniture would be required because Mr. Melville was going to have a season. Three days later he "cleared out" his furniture.

Mr. William John Grimes, called for the defence, said he was managing director of the Empress Theatre of Varieties and also landlord of the Brixton Theatre. In conversation with Mr. Joseph in June last year he told him that they were going to give up the theatre at the end of June, and that the theatre had been let for two years to Mr. Walter Melville, with the option of taking the theatre for two years more, subject to a two weeks' season by Mr. Maclean from July 1, with the option of two further weeks. Witness told plaintiff that he must make his arrangements with these people.

Judge Emden: Where is Mr. Maclean?—At Newcastle.

Is he solvent?—I am afraid not, your Honour. He has "let in" the billposters and a lot of them.

Mr. Richard Allum said he was manager for the defendant company up to the end of June, and then for Mr. Maclean after that. He ordered the furniture up to the end of June, but did not order the furniture for Mr. Maclean for the three weeks in July. Plaintiff knew that Mr. Maclean was the tenant.

Mr. Gerald James stated that he saw Mr. Joseph in June with reference to the change of tenancy, and that he selected the furniture for the three weeks' season under Mr. Maclean. As far as he knew, Mr. Maclean had not paid the Empress Theatre Company or any other accounts at all.

Mr. Williams asked his Honour to accept plaintiff's evidence. Mr. Joseph knew nothing about the new arrangement until the third week in July.

Judge Emden summed up, and said that from the weight of evidence he thought the action must be dismissed.

FEBRUARY.

ROYSTON v. KARNO.—BREACH OF CONTRACT.

In the King's Bench Division, Mr. Justice Darling and a special jury heard an action, **3** brought by Mr. Harry Royston, comedian, residing at 47, Coldharbour Lane, Camberwell, against Mr. Fred Karno, to recover damages for breach of contract. The defendant denied the alleged breach of contract.

Mr. R. W. Turner and Mr. J. R. Bell appeared for the plaintiff, and Mr. Dickens, K.C., and Mr. Charles Doughty for the defendant.

Plaintiff said that in July, 1906, he received a letter from Mr. Karno, asking him to call upon him. He did so, and then the defendant said that he wanted him to go to America to play in his sketch called *The Mumming Birds.* The plaintiff finally agreed to go to America at a salary of £15 a week, his travelling expenses out and home to be paid. The defendant said that he could engage the plaintiff for twelve months, but was only booked up to May 6, 1907, which the witness said he would accept. Mr. Karno said, "We will call that the tour," and plaintiff would get his money, whether he worked or played. The contract was signed, and it was stated that the tour should start in August, 1906, and that the engagement was for the period of the tour in America. On July 25, 1906, the plaintiff sailed for America and played with the company there in *The Mumming Birds.* Eventually Mr. Reeves, the defendant's manager in America, dismissed him on November 24, 1906.

The defendant's case was that the whole of the contract was contained in the written document of July 23, 1906, and that there were no verbal terms. The agreement, he said, fixed no date, but was for the tour, which ended at the Doric Theatre, Yonkers, on November 26, 1906, when the company in which the plaintiff was engaged were disbanded.

The mischief arose, said Mr. Dickens, through a system prevailing in America whereby a company could steal a sketch and produce it in a town before the owner of the sketch arrived with it. Consequently, when the defendant came with his sketch it had lost its novelty, and managers refused to confirm the pencil bookings. There was no guarantee that the tour would last until May, 1907, and therefore defendant was not liable.

Defendant gave evidence, and stated that he did not promise plaintiff that the tour would last until May, 1907. Several of his "boys" had left his company and joined the opposition company. It was a very strong opposition, "especially when some of the company worked for half the price." He told the plaintiff he had engagements booked up to May, 1907, but he pointed out that American managers were liable to cancel them. It was therefore agreed to make the contract out "for the tour."

The jury found for the plaintiff, and assessed the damages at £75.

KELSON TRUEMAN v. GOODALL.

At the Westminster County Court, before his Honour Judge Woodfall, a claim was made by **4** Mr. Kelson Trueman, of 233, Regent Street, dramatic agent, against Miss Edyth Goodall in respect of £5 commission alleged to be due by him for procuring her an engagement in Mr. Peter Davey's pantomime of last year. Messrs. Amery Parkes and Co. appeared for the plaintiff, and Mr. W. H. Bulbeck for the defendant.

It appeared by the evidence that Mr. Davey wrote Miss Goodall in September, 1907, that he wished to transfer her to Mr. Denton's pantomime at Leicester, as he had no suitable part for her. Mr. Denton subsequently repudiated the engagement, and Mr. Davey also wrote to the defendant that he would not carry out the agreement. The judge held that the plaintiff was not entitled to recover, as the contract was never carried out, and that Mr. Trueman might possibly only have a claim for damages, and he was therefore nonsuited.

GROSSMITH v. "VANITY FAIR."

In the King's Bench Division, before Mr. Justice Channell and a special jury, Mr. George Grossmith brought an action for alleged libel against the proprietor of *Vanity Fair* and Messrs. W. H. Smith and Son, the printers.—Sir Edward Clarke, K.C., said that in April, 1907, a young woman called at Mr. Grossmith's door and told him that her parents were dead, that her father had been a cutler, and she was endeavouring to dispose of the stock he had left her. Mr. Grossmith was touched by her story, and as a matter of charity he bought three pairs of scissors and a nail trimmer, which came to 10s. 6d. He handed the girl a sovereign, and asked her to bring back the change, but instead of doing so she kept the sovereign, scissors, and nail trimmer, and never returned. The plaintiff said nothing about the matter until he saw that people in the same profession and others were being victimised in a similar manner. He then wrote a letter to the newspapers, in which he stated how he had been victimised, and warned the public against the girl's story. About three weeks afterwards the following paragraph appeared in *Vanity Fair*:—

"A short time ago Mr. George Grossmith wrote to the Press in great indignation because he had been victimised by a red-haired girl, who sold him a pair of scissors, by a plausible tale, which turned out to be untrue.

"Most of us are induced to buy things in shops by false stories, but it seems a pity to hound a girl to misery.

"Is truth any element of the patter which Mr. Grossmith gives us from the stage, we wonder?"

thereby suggesting, said counsel, that Mr. Grossmith was on the same level as fraudulent tradesmen and as the girl who cheated him and told him an untrue tale. In a further passage, *Vanity Fair* continued that they thought it would have been better to put up with a small loss than act in such a way towards a girl who wanted to get some sort of a decent living.

After counsel's opening, the case was settled, the proprietor of *Vanity Fair* agreeing that judgment should be entered in favour of the plaintiff, with costs as between solicitor and client.

SPURIOUS THEATRE TICKETS.

William Frederick Cooper (28), of 25, Creek Street, Deptford, was charged before Mr. Hutton, at Greenwich, with "unlawfully and knowingly, by false pretences—*i.e.*, presentation of a false ticket—attempting to obtain admission to the gallery of the Broadway, New Cross, to witness the performance, with the intent to defraud Mr. Frederick Mouillot to the value of sixpence." It appeared that the prisoner handed in a metal check similar to those used by the theatre, but bearing different letters. Carter, a check-taker, admitted him, and called Mr. T. N. Walter, the manager, who said that, in consequence of many spurious tickets having been brought to the theatre of late, he was determined to find where they came from.

Mr. Hutton (quoting from the Act): Is admission "a chattel, money, or valuable security"?

Inspector Trafford: It is money's worth.

Mr. Hutton: Suppose he did not think it worth the sixpence? What did he attempt to obtain? The Act says "a chattel, money, or valuable security." Mr. Hutton added that no offence had been made out. The statute did not say this was a crime. The ticket might or might not have been given to the prisoner, and whether he was legally in custody was not for him (the magistrate) to decide. No offence had been disclosed, and the prisoner would be discharged.

STAGE PLAYS IN MUSIC HALLS.—BIRMINGHAM HIPPODROME FINED.

At the Birmingham Police Court, before the Stipendiary, Mr. Morton Brown, the licensee of the Birmingham Hippodrome was summoned, at the instance of the United Theatres of Birmingham (Theatre Royal, Prince of Wales, and Alexandra), for producing stage plays without having a license. There were three summonses issued, the first being against Mr. Percival Drayton Elbourne, licensee of the Hippodrome, for keeping the Hippodrome for the performance of stage plays, to wit, a pantomime called *Cinderella*. A second summons was against Mr. Sid Baynes, manager for Mr. John Tiller, for allowing the piece to be produced, and the third was against Christopher Baker for acting in the piece.

The Stipendiary, summing up, found the piece was a stage play, and imposed a fine of £5 and costs.

The other two cases were withdrawn by the prosecution.

NEALE v. DENTON AND NEALE.—QUESTION OF ASSIGNMENT OF PROFITS.

In the Westminster County Court, before his Honour Judge Woodfall, the case of Neale v. Denton and Neale was tried, and was an action by the plaintiff, Miss Dora Beatrice Neale, as assignee, to recover a share of profits arising out of the production of an aerial ballet at the King's, Hammersmith, which was produced by her brother, Mr. Wm. Vaughan Neale.

The facts of the case were opened by the plaintiff's counsel at some length, and it appeared that his client had lent her brother, Mr. Wm. Vaughan Neale, a certain sum of money, and that as security for it she took an assignment from him, of half his share of the profits which might accrue from his production of an aerial ballet. Her case now was that the ballet in question had been produced at the King's, Hammersmith, and that the defendant, Mr. St. John Denton, had failed to pay her the share of profits which she was entitled to under the assignment given to her by her brother, who was the co-defendant in the action.

On behalf of Mr. St. John Denton, it was urged that he had no desire to keep any money back which ought to go to the plaintiff, but the contention was that what was left of Mr. Vaughan Neale's share of the salary was expended upon the artists in order to keep the show going.

His Honour, in giving judgment, said this case had occupied the time of the Court considerably, but he did not think it would take him long to decide it, as so many of these theatrical disputes came before him. He (the judge) did not for a moment make any suggestion against the defendant Denton, but at the same time he thought he had paid moneys out under a misapprehension, and that he must suffer for it. After having gone carefully through the figures, he had come to the conclusion that Denton had wrongfully, or under a mistaken idea, paid out the sum of £53 12s. 2d. which should have gone to the plaintiff, and therefore judgment would be in her favour for that amount with costs.

Counsel for the defendant Denton asked for a stay of execution pending notice of appeal.

His Honour said there would be the usual stay of fourteen days, but if the defendant decided to appeal an application could be made in the usual way.

COLLINSON v. UNITED COUNTIES THEATRES CO.

11 In the Westminster County Court his Honour Judge Woodfall had before him the case of Collinson v. The United Counties Theatres Co., in which the plaintiff, Mr. Jack Collinson, who is the proprietor of a sketch entitled *The Club Raid*, sued the defendants to recover a balance of salary due in respect of the production of the sketch at the King's, Aberdeen.

The defendants disputed the plaintiff's claim, and set up a counter-claim for damages, on the ground that the sketch produced was not the one for which they had contracted to pay.

His Honour, in giving judgment, said he had not the slightest hesitation in coming to the conclusion that the plaintiff must recover. It had been suggested that the company which he had produced was not the one which was provided for in the contract, and that it was an incompetent company. He (the judge), after having heard the evidence called on behalf of the plaintiff, was quite satisfied that he did present his No. 1 company, and that it was a thoroughly competent company. The defendants had suggested that the performance drove the people out of the house, but it might well be that as Christmas was at that time approaching the people of Aberdeen were saving up their money and not going to music halls. On the whole he (the judge) was quite satisfied that the plaintiff had properly performed his contract, and therefore he would recover judgment for the amount claimed with costs, and there would also be judgment for him on the counter-claim, with costs.

TATE v. FULLBROOK.—IMPORTANT PLAYRIGHT APPEAL.

13 In the Court of Appeal, before Lords Justices Vaughan Williams, Farwell, and Kennedy, the case of Tate v. Fullbrook was heard. It was an appeal by the defendant from a judgment of Mr. Justice Phillimore on July 22, 1907.

The question was largely whether a dramatic idea or plot, plus the manual and physical actions of the persons who acted it, could constitute a " dramatic piece " within the meaning of the Copyright Act, although there was little or no actual taking of the dialogue, and as a dramatic piece was entitled to be protected.

In the present case the plaintiff sued for an injunction to restrain the defendant from infringing his right in the sketch *Motoring* or *The Motorist* by presenting *Astronomy*, which, he alleged, was a colourable imitation of his piece.

Mr. Justice Phillimore held that the plaintiff had established his case, and accordingly directed an injunction to restrain the defendant from playing *Astronomy* in a form to infringe *Motoring*.

Mr. Hohler, K.C., and Mr. G. A. Scott (instructed by Messrs. Amery-Parkes, Macklin, and Co.) appeared for the appellant, and Mr. McCall, K.C., and Mr. R. W. Turner (instructed by Messrs. Burton, Yeates, and Hart) for the respondent.

CASE FOR APPELLANT.

Mr. Hohler, K.C., explained that the action was brought by Mr. Harry Tate, the comedian, against his client, Mr. William Fullbrook, also a comedian, to restrain him from presenting *Astronomy*, which the plaintiff alleged was a colourable imitation of his sketch *Motoring*. It was admitted by the defendant at the trial that he had played in *Motoring* with the plaintiff; that his make-up was similar to that of the plaintiff; that certain incidents of the two sketches in respect of commonplace business were similar; but he denied that there was any intention to imitate or infringe the plaintiff's entertainment, and pleaded that substantially the two sketches were dissimilar.

Lord Justice Vaughan Williams: Did the judge find against you on a question of fact?

Mr. Hohler replied that a number of theatrical witnesses were called on both sides, who differed as to whether the defendant's entertainment could be reasonably regarded as a colourable imitation of the plaintiff's sketch. The judge's view was that there was a substantial similarity.

" And he granted an injunction? "

" Yes." Continuing, counsel said there was no case in which an injunction had been granted by any Court to restrain a person from imitating another, and the appeal was brought from the decision of the judge on a pure question of law. The plaintiff, he should submit, had not brought himself within the statutes of 3 and 4 Will. IV., c. 15, and 5 and 6 Vict., c. 45—the Copyright Acts—as there was no literary element in the plaintiff's entertainment, it being merely a collection of nonsensical remarks calculated to provoke laughter.

Lord Justice Farwell: Is the claim here based upon the Copyright Acts?

Mr. McCall, K.C., who appeared with Mr. R. W. Turner for the plaintiff, said that his contention was that the plaintiff had a right of action independently of the Copyright Acts, but he also relied upon the Acts.

Mr. Hohler said the plaintiff had done no literary work, and was not the proprietor of the copyright, and the only person protected by the statutes was the person who put the idea into language. Mr. Pink was solely responsible for the whole of the dialogue, and Mr. Pink was not the plaintiff.

Lord Justice Vaughan Williams: Then it is a question of which is the more important—the business or the dialogue?—Yes, and I submit there is no copyright in business until it is put into literary form.

The learned counsel said he would read the two sketches in order to substantiate his contention that they were quite dissimilar. He was proceeding to read *Motoring* when

Lord Justice Vaughan Williams said that he saw the characters were a motorist, a chauffeur, a street urchin, a son of the motorist, a drunken man, and a policeman; and that the opening dialogue was between an " Aside " and the " Motorist." Which character did Mr. Hohler propose to read?

Mr. Hohler said he would take whichever his lordship liked if his lordship would take the other.

His lordship said he could not undertake a part. Perhaps Mr. M'Call would oblige.

Mr. McCall declined.

Mr. Hohler therefore read the manuscript, which ended up with a general knockabout scene and an explosion on the motor-car.

Lord Justice Vaughan Williams pointed out that the first word of Section 1 of the Copyright Act, 1833, defining things which could be registered was "tragedy." "Is this piece a tragedy?" he asked.

Mr. Hohler thought not. It was simple nonsense.

The learned counsel then read the other piece, which he explained turned mainly on various things which could be seen by the aid of a big telescope. One of the characters (the Major) inquired of his son Dudley if he knew the names of all the "stars." Dudley: "Oh, yes, daddy. George Robey, Little Tich, Harry Randall, and Marie Lloyd." The Major: "Here, halt a minute; I've never heard of them before. Recent discoveries, I suppose." Another character, looking through the telescope, which was pointed then towards a window, asked if the lady he saw was Venus. On hearing that an elderly man called out, "That's not Venus; that's my wife taking a bath." (Laughter). The play also ended in general confusion.

Lord Justice Vaughan Williams: Mr. M'Call will not, I am sure, say that similarity in action or dress is material. The similarity must be a similarity in something that can be printed.

Mr. McCall: It must be some substantial taking of the invention of the brain.

Lord Justice Vaughan Williams: You cannot print dress.

Mr. McCall: In the terms of the statute it must be a representation of the whole or part of the plaintiff's piece.

Mr. Hohler: At the trial great stress was laid by the plaintiff on the fact that my client had a policeman, as he also had, but I thought a policeman was common property. Another thing he laid stress upon was that in my sketch, as in his, a boy exploded a cracker under a man's foot. I thought the cracker was a very ancient property, used from time immemorable.

Lord Justice Farwell: Could the late Mr. Sothern have restrained anybody from appearing in Dundreary whiskers? (Laughter.) This seems more like a passing-off case than anything else.

Mr. Hohler said that those were the things which influenced the learned judge.

The case was then adjourned until the following day, February 14.

Mr. Hohler, resuming his argument for the appellant on Friday, described the plaintiff's sketch as a series of nonsensical observations about a motor-car, and asked how that could be said to be within the meaning of the Act a dramatic piece.

Lord Justice Kennedy: Suppose it had been called 'Follies Round a Motor-car,' it might have been a dramatic sketch, might it not?

Mr. Hohler: Surely not.

Lord Justice Kennedy: The dramatic element is sufficient; you do not need a plot.

Mr. Hohler: I think that is right. But I submit this is neither a tragedy, comedy, play, nor musical sketch. Further, no piece can come within the Copyright Acts as a dramatic piece unless it is capable of being printed.

Mere imitation of make-up or gestures is not a subject-matter of protection under the Copyright Acts. The action here is like a passing-off action, where the resemblance between two things is a material element. There has never been a case where mere imitation of a person, his make-up, his facial or other gestures, is held to be the subject of protection under the Acts of 3 and 4 Will. IV., c. 15, and 5 and 6 Vict., c. 45. Unless a thing is capable of being registered it cannot be the subject of copyright. It is impossible to register scenic effects, facial expression, and gesticulations of an actor or the clothes which he might choose to wear.

Lord Justice Kennedy: There are in both sketches bad jokes and the elements of horseplay, a knock-kneed boy, a policeman, a so-called musical—or sounding—instrument, and tumbling over each other.

Mr. Hohler: And a cracker, my lord.

Lord Justice Kennedy: I think you might almost say that every pantomime—the clown with sausages, for instance—would be a copy of the others.

Mr. Hohler: Quite so. Counsel further argued that Mr. Tate was not the author of Motoring, but merely supplied suggestions for the sketch to Mr. Wal Pink, who put them in writing.

Lord Justice Vaughan Williams: It is not suggested that the words in Motoring are that which gives artistic merit to the production. The words do not seem to involve any great skill in composition. What makes the sketch go is the way in which it is acted. Assuming that, who is the author?

Mr. Hohler: I submit that in those circumstances there is no author within the meaning of the Act.

Lord Justice Vaughan Williams: Does not Mr. Justice Phillimore mean that a person who produces very striking scenic effects and situations in a play may be protected as the author of a dramatic piece quite apart from any similarity of words?

Mr. Hohler contended that such a person would not be protected as the "author" within the Copyright Acts, nor would he be protected at common law.

Lord Justice Vaughan Williams: Take the Colleen Bawn—there you have a scenic effect, with a bridge crossing a chasm, and the heroine crosses the bridge. The villain, I think, is drowned, and the heroine is saved by the activity of the hero. People used to go to see that particular scene. I think what Mr. Justice Phillimore meant was that if you have got a piece which contains such a scenic effect as that you may become an author so as to be protected within the Act if other people, without taking the words, adopt the scene. If you have the scenic effect and the situation I take it that an injunction might be granted.

Mr. Hohler: If your words are original, there is nothing to prevent you putting on any scene you like.

Lord Justice Kennedy: Suppose a man sees a Shakespearean play and produces one like it himself, with similar scenery and directions, is there any Act or common law right to prevent him doing so?

Mr. Hohler: I submit none at all.

Lord Justice Kennedy: May not the test be that unless it is something which can be registered and protected there is no right of action?

Mr. Hohler: I submit it is so. It is the work alone that can be protected, not the scenic effects.

Lord Justice Kennedy: Suppose a person copied the scenery, dresses, etc., from a performance of a play of Shakespeare or Sheriuan, the words of which are not protected by copyright, would an action lie?

Mr. Hohler said that an action would certainly not lie. There must be the taking of a substantial part of the author's written work—Chatterton v. Cave.

Lord Justice Farwell: If Shakespeare's works were now protected by copyright, could anyone be prevented from introducing a gravedigger and a skull?

Mr. Hohler: Certainly not. It would have to be taken into account as an element to be considered, with other circumstances, in seeing whether the play itself was copied. There might be certain written directions in the play as to the action and situations in the performance which might be protected. There was nothing of the sort here.

The learned counsel having dealt with several cases,

Mr. G. A. Scott addressed the Court on the same side.

Lord Justice Vaughan Williams: Suppose you had a sketch the subject matter of which is finding out the fraud of some medium who professes to hold conversation with the dead, and there are certain scenic accessories. Another music hall manager seeing that it draws very much produces a similar sketch, called by a different name, and with different words, but with the same action and dénouement—what would you say?

Mr. Scott: I should say that if the man who composed the first sketch had reduced it to writing, and had given directions from which it was produced on the stage, he would be entitled to protection under the Act.

Lord Justice Vaughan Williams: What would you say if he had not reduced it to writing and had not given stage directions?

Mr. Scott: Then I should say he had no right under the Act, because the Act contemplates something produced by an author which is capable not only of writing, but of assignment.

CASE FOR RESPONDENT.

Mr. McCall, K.C., for the plaintiff, said that it seemed to him that the questions in the case were largely questions of fact, and it was desirable to have the evidence read. The evidence was, accordingly, read.

Mr. McCall argued that, under the Copyright Acts, the title of the sketch was registered, and the sketch as represented was protected. The protection was not confined to the words alone. The words, plus the dramatic action and make-up, were protected. The words might be of very little importance. By registration under Section 11 of 5 and 6 Vict., c. 45, the person whose title was registered had the sole liberty of representing the dramatic piece. That was shown by the observations of Mr. Justice Brett in Chatterton v. Cave and of Lord Blackburn in the same case in the House of Lords. The test, therefore, was, Were the parts taken, whether of dialogue or of dramatic situation, material parts of the piece? Mr. Justice Phillimore decided the questions of fact in favour of the plaintiff, and the Court would not disturb his finding. The question whether Mr. Tate or Mr. Pink was to be regarded as the author of *Motoring* was also one of fact. The judge had decided that Mr. Tate was the author. It was proved that he had suggested to Mr. Pink that a good music hall sketch could be written on the lines he mentioned, and Mr. Pink had carried out his idea. But what Mr. Pink wrote

was not the piece as it appeared on the music hall stage. It was merely the skeleton upon which the sketch as performed was hung.

Lord Justice Vaughan Williams: Suppose a China correspondent sent a telegram of six words to a newspaper in London. That message appeared in the paper occupying twenty-five lines of ten words a line. Who is the author of the news—the correspondent or the sub-editor who padded it out?

Mr. McCall said that would be a question of fact in each case. If the sub-editor added to it from his imagination or of his own knowledge no doubt he would be; but if he merely put in words which were omitted on the ground of expense in the telegram and worked it up so as to read intelligently, he thought the man who supplied it could claim to be the author. The thing protected by the statute was the play as it was presented.

Mr. Turner followed. He submitted that there was a finding of fact that the defendant's piece was a colourable imitation of the plaintiff's sketch. That decision was based, not on a sentence here and there being alike in the two sketches, but a general resemblance in the plot and the make-up and dress of the principal actors, which entitled the plaintiff to say that his play had been "cribbed." Dress was only one incident which went to support the plaintiff's case.

Lord Justice Farwell: What legal right has an author in the get-up of an actor who plays his piece?—he has not registered it. Who Sothern took the character of Lord Dundreary in *Our American Cousin* that character was quite a small part. But his gag made it. It became the part in the play. Do you say that Sothern could have claimed the right to stop the play being produced?

Lord Justice Vaughan Williams: If you say so, then you will have to admit that there is copyright in patter. (Laughter.)

Mr. Turner: Patter or gag may vary from night to night.

Lord Justice Vaughan Williams said he thought the defendant was entitled to succeed.

THE JUDGMENT.

He would first deal with a question which had given him some difficulty. Whatever else the Act of 3 and 4 Will. IV., c. 15, might have been passed to accomplish, it was passed for the benefit of authors of dramatic pieces. Before, therefore, applying that Act, it ought to be ascertained whether the plaintiff was the author of this sketch called *Motoring* or *The Motorist*. He had considerable doubt about that as a matter of fact. No doubt Mr. Justice Phillimore had found that the plaintiff was the author; but he (the Lord Justice) could only say that, upon looking at the evidence upon that point, he had great doubt. Mr. Pink, in his evidence, spoke of the piece as "my play," and he was inclined to think that Mr. Pink was the author. It was true that the plaintiff suggested to Mr. Pink the ideas upon which the sketch was written; but that did not make the plaintiff the author of the sketch. Suppose a music hall artist suggested to a writer a sketch founded upon anything at all—say, the suffragettes—that would not make him the author of the sketch which he paid a literary man to write for him. If the present case had come before him in the first instance he would probably have said that Mr. Pink, and not the plaintiff, was the author of the sketch. Having stated that doubt which he felt, he now came to the Act 3 and 4 Will. IV., c. 15. His lordship read the preamble and Section 1, and said that that was an Act which dealt with words—that was to say, with those things which went to make up a book, and which were essential to a composition. The subject-matter of the section was a composition which, though not printed and published, was capable of being printed and published. That was the true subject-matter of the section. He would have felt no doubt upon the matter but for some words used by Mr. Justice Brett in Chatterton v. Cave, in the report in the *Law Times* (33 *L.T.*, 255), upon which Mr. Justice Phillimore probably acted. Those words seemed to suggest that there might be a property in scenic representations and dramatic situations. Those words, however, did not appear in his judgment in the Law Repofts (L.R., 10 C.P., 572), a judgment which may have been revised by the learned judge himself. It looked as if Mr. Justice Brett, when he came to revise his judgment, thought that the words were rather rash, and struck them out. Those expressions did not appear in the judgments of the other judges. But, however that might be, the observations were not binding upon this Court. The conclusion he (the Lord Justice) came to was that the subject-matter in which the author acquired a property was one which was capable of being printed and published, and the greater part of that which was held by Mr. Justice Phillimore to be the subject-matter of protection under the Act was not the subject-matter of protection at all. Sometimes the learned judge did not put the matter quite in that way. Sometimes he spoke of the written production, and also of other matters, such as the similarity of make-up and facial expression, and spoke of the latter as ancillary to the words. If his judgment had proceeded on that ground he would have proceeded on a right basis. Once one got words capable of protection, and the question was raised whether the property in those words had been infringed, one must not merely take the two sets of words and compare them together, one must take the words with the dramatic surroundings; one must take the stage situations and scenic effects; and then, taking them with the words, one must say whether there was such a similarity between the two plays as to lead to the conclusion that the defendant's play was an infringement of the proprietary right of representation of the plaintiff's play. That was his view of the Act. It was admitted that the similarity in the words of the two sketches here was of a trifling character. The matters principally relied upon as showing an infringement were such things as a certain likeness in the stage situations and in the scenic effects, and in the make-up, matters which ought not to be taken into consideration in a case where there was no real similarity in the words. In his opinion the appeal must be allowed.

Lord Justice Farwell and Lord Justice Kennedy delivered judgment to the same effect.

A stay of execution was granted on an undertaking to repay the taxed costs if an appeal were lodged and proved successful.

CORRI AND CRICHTON v. WILLIAMS. WHAT IS MUSICAL COMEDY?

Proof was led in the Sheriffs' Court, Dundee, before Sheriff Campbell-Smith, in an action at the instance of Mr. Clarence Collingwood Corri and Mr. Haldane Crichton, against Mr. R. A. P. Williams, lessee and manager of the Gaiety, Dundee.

Mr. Douglas (for Mr John M. Soutar) appeared for the pursuers, and Mr. James Buchan for the defenders.

The action was for £55, the balance alleged to be due by the defender to the pursuers, in respect of a contract between them for the production of "the musical comedy" *The Dancing Girls of Spain* and the "pantomimic absurdity" *Office Hours* at the Gaiety, Dundee, for the week beginning December 30, 1907. The contract bore that the pursuers were to provide a full and efficient company for the proper representation of the pieces specified, and the certainty agreed to be paid was £755. Mr. Williams had paid £100 and refused to pay more, on the ground that the pursuers had broken their contract by failing to provide a full and efficient company for the proper representation of the plays, and he counterclaimed for £100 on account of loss of business.

THE DEFENCE.

For the defence, Mr. Williams stated that when he booked a musical comedy he expected a company of at least thirty. He would never have given £155 certainty to *The Dancing Girls of Spain* company if he had known what it was like. The public at the Gaiety did not like the piece, and Mr. Williams heard many adverse comments. His drawings were nearly £100 less than in the corresponding week of the previous year, when the holding capacity of the theatre was less. For the following week he had to add £40 to his bill in order to restore the public confidence in the entertainment he provided.

The Sheriff took the case to *arizandum*, recommending a settlement. He did not think that any of the parties were intentionally dishonest, but Mr. Williams had bought a "pig in a poke" and had got a dead cat, or something like it.

JUDGMENT

Written judgment was delivered a fortnight later in the following terms :—

"The Sheriff Substitute having considered the proof led, and whole process, finds that the pursuer, Haldane Crichton, who is the chief or manager of a migratory or circulating theatrical company, on behalf of the pursuers, entered into a joint adventure with the defender, who is proprietor of the Gaiety Theatre, Dundee, to play in said theatre for the first week of 1908, and to furnish amusement for Dundee by the acting of *The Dancing Girls of Spain* and a pantomime sketch *Office Hours;* finds that the pursuers sent a company of artists to carry out their part of the joint adventure, and that they did attempt to carry out the pursuers' part of the joint adventure; finds that their attempt in the Gaiety Theatre was a total failure; finds that the failure was owing to want of consultation, of co-operation, and of skill on the part of both pursuers and defender, and was due to the fault of both of them; that the failure of the joint adventure being due to their joint faults, the loss, injury, and damage due by each partner, in the fault or faults, ought to be proportional to capital interest of each, and the capital loss that has fallen upon each should be in proportion to their respective interests and actual outlays; finds that the proof does not contain information for settling the capit of each involved in the joint adventure and the loss sustained by each; finds that the pursuers obtained a payment of £100 as subsistence money for the artists, and that the proof does not show that they have not obtained enough, or that they have obtained more than they ought to have obtained, out of which they can pay damages to their co-partner, in their proportion in the fault that was disastrous to the joint adventure. Therefore assoilzies the defender from the conclusions of the petition or writ, and finds no expenses due to or by either party.

"(Sgd.)　J. C. SMITH.

"Note.—The pursuer, the said Haldane Crichton, is the chief and manager of a circulating play-acting company that travels over Great Britain, and gives temporary entertainments on such terms, pecuniary and otherwise, as may be agreed on. In the end of last year it was arranged that about New Year time Dunfermline and Dundee should have the benefit of the pursuers' æsthetic missionary enterprise. The bargain with the proprietor of the Gaiety Theatre, Dundee, was that he should, for the first week of the year, have the experience of this missionary theatrical skill for £155. The company came and performed in *The Dancing Girls of Spain* and *Office Hours*. £100 was paid to account about the beginning of the week, and the present action has been raised to recover the £55 of balance, the defender having refused to pay, on the ground that the pursuers and their company did not duly fulfil their part of the contract, and that their performance in Dundee was, in the matter of dramatic art and theatrical profit, an unprecedented failure. I think it is proved to have been a decided failure, whether unprecedented or not. I have not the means of forming an opinion as to all or even the chief causes of it. My impression is that the theatre,going and vagrant imagination of Dundee does not extend its excursions very much to *The Dancing Girls of Spain*, or even of India, who have been more frequently heard of in Scottish sea-faring towns. My most clear conviction as to the causes of failure is now, and is likely to remain, that it was the want of consultations, adjustment, and settlement of plans, and arranging what and how much was to be done, and what artists were to do, and amid what scenery, whether Dundee, Cockney, or Spanish, also whether the Spanish girls were to play with their fans, show their beauty and their teeth, or dance the Highland fling or Irish jigs, or only to scatter the kind of arrows of long ago furnished by their great grandmothers during Childe Harold's pilgrimage at bull-fights by the abounding of dames skilled in the ogle of a roguish eye. The evidence shows that the result of this somewhat blind bargain has been a loss to the defender, even if the state of his payment to the pursuers should remain at £100; the pursuers have failed to show that they have lost anything if they retain the £100. I am clearly of opinion that, as matter of justice, the two parties to a bargain, based on or worked out under joint essential error, should make profit or share loss in proportion to their shares in it. What profit or loss the pursuers made has not been proved. The defender has proved, at least stated, details that he lost £100 fully, and in that state of the evidence I think he has lost enough, and that without further evidence it would be impossible to apportion the loss each ought to bear. The result is that the defender has made nothing out of this disastrous joint adventure; therefore I do not see why he should pay anything further to his partners in error, and therefore in consequent misfortune; at all events, I cannot now determine the share of the loss or want of profit on each side.

"(Intd.)　J. C. S."

(See reports, March 30 and November 10.)

EDELSTEN v. BELL.—QUESTION OF SPLIT COMMISSIONS.

At the Darlington County Court, before his Honour Judge Templer, Mr. Willie Edelsten, trading as Messrs. Willie Edelsten, variety agents, Lorn Road, Brixton, sued Joseph Bell, proprietor of the Royal, Darlington, for £4 13s., balance of certain commissions deducted, it was alleged, unlawfully by the defendant from artists' salaries. Mr. W. Bevan, solicitor, of Stockton, appeared for the plaintiff, and Mr. G. G. Plant, solicitor, Darlington, for the defendant.

Mr. Bevan explained that commission was due to Mr. Edelsten at the rate of 10 per cent. from artists whose engagement he had secured for the theatre, and Mr. Bell deducted 5 per cent. for himself. He sent a cheque to Mr. Edelsten for £2 5s. 6d., only half the commission.

His Honour: Is the arrangement a matter of contract or custom?

Mr. Bevan: Both.

Plaintiff said he booked certain artists for Mr. Bell in April, 1906, and Mr. Bell collected 10 per cent. on the total salaries of Cyclo, Fred Keelon, Collins and Rice, Arthur Stacey, Lena Dudley, and Henriques, and 5 per cent. from Frazer's Iona. The latter would not at first allow that to be taken. His (plaintiff's) arrangement with the artists was that he should have 10 per cent. commission on their salaries. This was sent on to him unless he asked the proprietor of the theatre to collect it for him. In the present case he had not asked the defendant to collect the commission, but he had done so, and claimed 5 per cent. of it for himself. He did not ask defendant to stop the money from the artists, though defendant stated that one of them refused to allow him to do so as money was owing to him. He afterwards discovered, however, that the money had been stopped from that artist. There was no reason why defendant should deduct 5 per cent. He had never authorised him to do so, and he knew of no custom to entitle him to deduct the 5 per cent.

Replying to Mr. Plant, plaintiff admitted the receipt of a letter (put in) from Mr. Bell, who, on September 4, replied to Mr. Edelsten that he was more than surprised at the contents of his letter, because he (Mr. Edelsten) distinctly stated that if Mr. Bell would duly confirm some of his contracts he would allow 5 per cent. of the commission, and it was on this understanding, and this alone, that he agreed to confirm some of Mr. Edelsten's bookings. He admitted that Mr. Bell sent a cheque for £2 15s., but that didn't settle the matter in his eyes. Shown a contract form, plaintiff said he had signed contracts with artists, but he could not say whether they were in the form of the one produced.

His Honour asked why the contracts had not been produced.

Mr. Plant replied that defendant had not got them with him. It was not usual to keep them.

His Honour said he could not allow the contract to be proved by the form presented. The original contract must be produced.

THE DEFENCE.

For the defence Mr. Plant submitted as a matter of law that their cheque was sent in settlement, and having kept the cheque the plaintiff was precluded from coming there and raising any question of fact.

Mr. James Bell said his father, Joseph, was the lessee. But they were the same for the purposes of that suit. He said the arrangement with Mr. Edelsten was that if he collected the commission and confirmed certain "pencillings"—provisional bookings—he would allow 5 per cent., or half of the commission,

The Judge: Was this verbal?

Mr. Bell: Yes.

What were you going to do with this 5 per cent.—was it for yourself?—Yes.

Not for the theatre?—No.

"This secret commission was not in the interests of the theatre in the least?" observed the judge.

"It was not a secret commission: it was for the theatre," replied Mr. Plant. "Mr. Bell represents the theatre. He is the man himself. It is not taking a secret commission as against himself."

Mr. Bevan: He is only the manager.

In reply to Mr. Plant, the defendant said that after sending the cheque for the 5 per cent. he received no further intimation until he received the summons. The arrangement for the commission was made in his office, in the presence of his clerk, who made out the agreements signed by the artists.

In answer to Mr. Bevan, he said it was the custom of the profession that the manager should obtain 5 per cent. It was so as far as he was concerned.

Mr. Bevan: That would have been obtaining a commission of 5 per cent. unknown to Mr. Joseph Bell. You are only the manager?—I am the manager.

Is there any reason why he should pay you 5 per cent.?—He offered to do it.

Mr. Plant: As to the suggested secret commission, are not you and your father one in this matter?—Yes.

The Judge said he did not understand why the contracts with the artists were not produced, and ultimately the case was adjourned for half an hour to allow Miss Ethel Selby, Mr. Bell's clerk, who was then in the witness-box, to find one or two of them.

Miss Selby said when they commenced the variety business at the theatre in April, 1906, several agents came to see Mr. Bell, including Mr. Walter Bentley and Mr. Edelsten. She heard the plaintiff tell Mr. Bell that if Mr. Bentley had promised him 5 per cent. of the commission he would do the same.

The Judge looked at the copy of the contract that Miss Selby had brought. "Nothing in here as to taking half of the commission," he said. "Did you prepare these forms of contract?" he asked Miss Selby.

"Yes, before Mr. Edelsten left the office," was the reply.

"Why didn't you put in that Mr. Bell was to be entitled to half of the 10 per cent. commission?" inquired Mr. Bevan.

"I wasn't told to do so," witness responded.

JUDGMENT FOR PLAINTIFF.

His Honour said that on the whole he preferred the evidence of the plaintiff. It was a pity this unfortunate conflict of evidence had arisen, but he did not say it was perjury. He dared say Miss Selby had given her evidence very fairly, but he thought at the time these contracts were made it should have been defined if defendant was to receive half of the commission. He should give judgment for plaintiff, with costs. To avoid disputes some record should be made. Mr. Bell had only himself to thank. He should have made it perfectly clear—stated it in black and white on the contract itself.

WILLIAMS v. MOORE.—RIGHTS IN "LES CLOCHES DE CORNEVILLE."

In the King's Bench Division on February 21 and 25, before Mr. Justice Phillimore, Joseph Williams, Ltd., who **21** claimed to be the assigns of the copyright of the music in *Les Cloches de Corneville*, sued Augustus M. Moore, of Sack-

ville Street, Piccadilly, to recover penalties for alleged infringement. They also asked for an injunction restraining the defendant from further infringement. Defendant set up a plea of inadequate registration of copyright, and denied that he had produced the plaintiffs' composition, or one substantially identical.

Mr. Scrutton, K.C., and Mr. F. Dodd appeared for the plaintiffs, while Mr. H. Kisch represented the defendant.

After hearing the evidence and arguments, Mr. Justice Phillimore held that there had been no registration of the performing rights in England of which the plaintiffs could avail themselves. But he held that they claimed through the author within the meaning of Sections 6 and 11 of the International Copyright Act, 1886, and, if the rights of performance were existent in France, the plaintiffs were entitled to similar rights in England, unless the defendant could avail himself of the exception granted in the proviso to Section 6 in the case of those who had acquired valuable interests. On reviewing the facts, he held that there was no such valuable interest in Mr. Moore. In his opinion, defendant was not the producer of the version of *Les Cloches de Corneville* in question, but was the employé of Mr. Phillips. He did not think anybody could have been said to have lawfully produced it, and he was still stronger in the opinion that it was not produced by Mr. Moore. The result was that the plaintiffs made out their case, and there would be judgment for them for £50 and costs, and an injunction restraining the defendant from any further infringement.

GIBBONS v. SHIELDS.—INCONVENIENT TURN TIME AND SMALL BILLING.

The case of Gibbons v. Shields came before his Honour Judge Woodfall in the Westminster County Court, on a claim by Mr. Walter **24** Gibbons, proprietor of the Holborn Empire and controller of other music halls, against Miss Ella Shields, music hall artist, for damages for breach of contract to appear at the Holborn Empire and the Duchess, Balham. Miss Shields counter-claimed for damages she alleged she sustained through being billed in small type for a performance at the Holborn.

Mr. Walter Payne was counsel for the plaintiff, and Mr. Cannot for the defendant.

In giving a somewhat lengthy judgment, his Honour said:—I am perfectly satisfied in this case that the plaintiff is entitled to recover as to breach of contract. In my opinion there is absolutely no defence to the breach of contract to perform at the Holborn Empire. I have rarely listened to a more idle claim than that put forward by the defendant in this case. Her case is that her name should be printed in large type on the bills at the places where she is engaged to perform, but if her contention was allowed to prevail just think what the consequences would be to managers and proprietors of music halls! What was there, his Honour continued, to prevent any artist from bringing an action against the management for failing or refusing to place the name of any particular artist in a conspicuous position on the bills and in any particular size of type? If such a claim as this was recoverable every artist might make a similar one, and life would be simply intolerable to the managers of music halls and theatres. In his opinion there was no implied contract on the part of the plaintiff to print the defendant's name in large type on the Holborn Empire bills. The defendant had no right whatever to break her contract, either at the Holborn Empire or the Duchess Balham, and therefore judgment would be for the plaintiff for the amount claimed in each case, with costs.

EDWARDES v. PELISSIER.—POTTED PLAYS.

In the Chancery Division, the Gaiety Theatre Company and Mr. George Edwardes moved respectively, before Mr. Justice Warrington and Mr. Justice Eve, for injunctions against Mr. Pélissier, proprietor of The Follies troupe, who were performing "Potted Plays" at the Apollo.

28

The plaintiffs complained that Mr. Pélissier has been playing musical numbers from *The Girls of Gottenberg* and *The Merry Widow*.

Both motions were adjourned until March 6 for evidence to be filed, Mr. Pélissier undertaking not to perform the parts complained of in the meantime.

On March 6 it was stated that the defendant had agreed to a perpetual injunction in the terms of the writ.

BURNS v. LUCAS.

In the King's Bench Division, Mr. Justice Bray heard an action brought by Mr. Tommy Burns, the heavy-weight boxing champion, to recover from Mr. B. Pierce Lucas, a music hall proprietor, the sum of £221 10s. 1d., which the plaintiff alleged was due upon an agreement, dated January 7, 1908, under which he appeared for a week at the Bristol Empire music hall. The defendant paid £200 18s. 9d. into Court.

29

Mr. Schiller appeared for the plaintiff, and the defendant was represented by Mr. Payne.

Mr. Schiller said that under the agreement the plaintiff was to give boxing entertainments at the Bristol music hall for a week, commencing on January 13. For these exhibitions he was to receive 55 per cent. of all receipts, and the total receipts amounted to close upon £630. The defence was that the defendant was entitled to deduct from the amount certain advertising expenses, and there was a question as to whether the commission should be charged on gross receipts or net receipts.

Mr. Harry Day, the agent who made the contract between Mr. Burns and the Albemarle Syndicate, in answer to his Lordship, said the word "receipts" had a special meaning in the profession; it meant the gross amount an artist was paid.

His Lordship said he was not satisfied there wa⁻ any special meaning. He held that "receipts" meant the money received after deducting the £115. He was satisfied there was no agreement as to the advertising, and he gave judgment for the plaintiff for £20 11s. 4d., plus £200 18s. 9d., paid into court, with costs.

MARCH.

MELFORD v. CROSSMAN.—ALLEGED WRONGFUL DISMISSAL.

In the King's Bench Division, before Mr. Justice Jelf and a common jury, Mr. Mark Melford, comedian, sued Mr. Robert Crossman, theatrical manager, of the Shakespeare, Clapham Junction, to recover damages for an alleged wrongful dismissal.

2

Mr. Powell, K.C., and Mr. D. Warde appeared for the plaintiff; while Mr. Rose-Innes represented the defendant.

Mr. Powell, in opening the case for the plaintiff, said that in the early part of 1906 the defendant engaged the plaintiff to write a pantomime entitled *Aladdin*, to be produced at the Shakespeare, Clapham Junction, the following Christmas. The plaintiff wrote the pantomime and received his fee of £100. It was arranged that the plaintiff should play the part of Widow Twankey, and receive a salary of £60 a week, with extras for certain *matinées*. Miss Winifred Hare was appearing at another theatre under the defendant's management, and as that theatre was turned into a music-hall it was arranged that she should take the part of the principal boy in *Aladdin*. That, apparently, was the cause of all the trouble.

When she came there were, of course, two star artists at this suburban theatre, and he (the learned counsel) suggested that the theatre would not bear the expense, and that the management looked round for some pretext to get rid of the plaintiff. His part had been cut down from occupying some fifty to thirty minutes. The pantomime went well on the first night, but, notwithstanding this, the defendant at a rehearsal said to the plaintiff, "You had better resign, old boy; you are outweighted." The plaintiff protested that there was nothing the matter with him except a cold. The following Saturday the defendant suggested that the plaintiff should resign his part, remarking that he could do it by giving his recent illness as a reason. The defendant also said that the plaintiff was the only person who did not trouble to perfect his part. The plaintiff again protested, and said that he should continue to play the "fragment" of the widow. The defendant then wrote to the effect that he should not require the plaintiff's services any longer. He (the learned counsel) submitted that the reason for dismissing the plaintiff was that the defendant could not afford to pay two artists £60 a week each.

Mr. Powell stated that Mr. Dan Lindon was afterwards engaged to fill the *rôle* of Widow Twankey at a week's salary that was not equal to what plaintiff received for one night. Counsel said he supposed the reason for the change was that defendant could not afford to have two "star" artists at £60 a week, and, having "cut down" Mr. Melford's part to half an hour, he thought he could do without plaintiff. The latter subsequently received two weeks' salary in lieu of notice.

THE DEFENCE

Mr. Rose-Innes, for the defendant, admitted that the plaintiff was a man of great artistic taste, but said that at this particular period, and for this particular pantomime, he was not up to the warranty he had given in the contract, and, therefore, the defendant was entitled to dismiss him. The plaintiff at the time seemed to be in a sleepy, drowsy condition. There was no ground for the suggestion that the defendant got rid of the plaintiff in order to make the pantomime pay.

JUDGMENT FOR PLAINTIFF.

His Lordship, in summing up the case to the jury, pointed out to them that the question they had to decide was not the general reputation of the plaintiff as an actor, which was admittedly high, but whether upon this particular occasion, for some reason or another, the plaintiff failed to maintain his reputation to such an extent as to justify the defendant in discharging him.

The jury returned a verdict for the plaintiff for £390, the amount claimed.

Judgment was given accordingly.

(See appeal heard on May 4.)

BLACKMORE v. HUXLEY.

Before his Honour Judge Woodfall, in the Westminster County Court, the case of Blackmore's Agency v. Gladys Huxley was tried, and was an action by the plaintiffs to recover the sum of £45 as commission due to them from the defendant, Miss Gladys Huxley, in respect of engagements procured for her at various music halls and theatres.

The defendant disputed the claim, with the exception of a sum of £9, which she had paid into Court.

Mr. Cannot (barrister) appeared on behalf of the plaintiffs, and said that his clients had succeeded in obtaining a number of engagements for the young lady in question, including contracts with Mr. Robert Arthur and the late Mr. Adney Payne, and other well-known people in the profession. She had paid various sums since, but she appeared to dispute her liability in respect of the present claim on the ground that she ought not to pay for re-engagements arising out of the plaintiffs' introduction.

Mr. Lionel Wallace was called, and said he was a partner in the plaintiff firm, and had obtained commission notes from the defendant in respect of various engagements. He negotiated engagements for her with Mr. Robert Arthur for pantomime, and also with Messrs. Tiller and Soames for music halls, the latter being at the Woolwich for ten weeks. He also negotiated for her with Messrs. King and Clarke, and in December, 1905, made an engagement for her with Mr. Robert Arthur for 1906 and 1907 at a salary of £12 a week for six weeks and £15 a week for seven weeks. In respect of these engagements his firm had not been paid any commission whatever.

In cross-examination the witness said he considered an agent was entitled to commission on renewals of engagements so long as he represented the artist as her agent, but he would not claim commission in a case where the management of a theatre refused to negotiate with an artist through his agency. He was aware that Mr. Hugh Jay Didcott had acted for the defendant since the contracts in question had been entered into. Before this action was commenced he sent repeated applications to the defendant for payment of the account, but to no purpose. His impression was that owing to the illness of Mr. Masters, who acted as manager for the late Mr. Payne, a number of contracts which should have been carried through by his (witness's) firm were dealt with by Mr. Payne in error as to the agency. He could, as agent for the defendant, have done all that Mr. Didcott had done, and was prepared to do so. In the event of artists absenting themselves through illness, he did not claim to be paid commission, but if through any fault of their own they failed to appear, then, of course, he should claim it, whether they were paid their salary or not.

Mr. Masters was called, and said he was secretary to the late Mr. Adney Payne, and, owing to his unfortunate death, matters in respect of artists' contracts became somewhat mixed up. In his opinion the plaintiffs were entitled to the commission which they now claimed.

Mr. Walter Payne, on behalf of the defendant, submitted that the sum which had been paid into Court was sufficient to cover the plaintiffs' claim, and that they had totally failed to prove their claim to anything further.

At this stage of the case his Honour adjourned the further hearing until the following day, March 4.

When the hearing was resumed,

Miss Gladys Huxley was called, and said that with regard to the Tiller engagement she had paid the plaintiffs all that was due to them, and that in consideration of the sum of £9 odd which she had paid into Court she contended that she owed them nothing more.

In cross-examination by Mr. Cannot, she said that it was in March of 1906 that she gave up the plaintiffs as her agents and went to Mr. Hugh Jay Didcott. She did so because she was out of work, and Mr. Didcott quickly found her engagements. She did not tell Mr. Blackmore that she was going to Mr. Didcott, but simply said that she must employ another agent to find her some work. She could not say what amount of salary she had received under the Payne contracts, but it might have been as much as £190. In some cases she admitted that she did not fulfil her contracts, owing to illness, but she considered she had paid the plaintiffs all that was due to them. The first engagement which was procured for her by Mr. Didcott was in 1906 at the Euston, and she gave him a commission note for that and other engagements, but she had not got them in Court.

His Honour, in giving judgment, said on the whole he had come to the conclusion that the amount which had been paid into Court was all that the plaintiffs had proved their title to, and it therefore followed that there would be judgment for the defendant with costs subsequent to the payment into Court.

BROOKS v. KIRBY—AGENT'S CLAIM FOR COMMISSION.

In the Westminster County Court, before his Honour Judge Woodfall, the plaintiffs, who carry on business as Brooks's Dramatic Agency, brought an action to recover a sum of £37 which they alleged to be due to them as commission from Mr. George Kirby for procuring him an engagement with Mr. Fred Karno to appear in pantomime at Glasgow. Mr. Druequer was counsel for the plaintiffs, and Mr. Cannot appeared on behalf of the defendant.

Counsel for the plaintiffs, in opening the facts of the case, said that as a result of his clients' introduction the defendant obtained an engagement with Mr. Karno at Glasgow, and that as a result of his introduction a contract was entered into between the defendant and Mr. Fred Karno, on March 11, 1906, for a ten weeks' engagement, at a salary of £37 10s. per week, and it was upon that engagement that the plaintiffs now sought to recover their commission. When the plaintiffs first put forward their claim for commission, however, the defendant wrote them to the effect that neither he nor Mr. Karno considered that they were entitled to it, but that, under all the circumstances, they could have £1 a week on the engagement if they were prepared to accept it. The plaintiffs at once declined that offer, and they now sought to recover their 10 per cent. commission.

THE DEFENCE.

For the defence Mr. George Kirby said it was true he made an offer to the plaintiffs to pay them £1 a week on the engagement in question, but he only did so in order to save any trouble, and never considered that he was legally liable to pay them anything, as they took no part in the making of the contract between himself and Mr. Fred Karno.

JUDGMENT FOR PLAINTIFFS.

In giving judgment, his Honour said it was quite clear in this case that there must be a

verdict for the plaintiffs, and the only question was as to how much they were entitled
to recover. The defendant had said that he
never agreed to employ the plaintiffs to act
as his agents, but it was perfectly clear that
his memory was at fault on that point. He
was put out of court by his own witness (Mr.
Karno), who had admitted that the defendant
was introduced to him by the plaintiff firm,
and that something was said about the plaintiffs' commission. It was true that the contract was fixed up between Kirby and Karno
between themselves, but it did not preclude
the plaintiffs from claiming their commission.
Then, again, the defendant had made the
plaintiffs an offer of £1 a week, thus showing
that he knew they were entitled to payment.
On the whole, he (the Judge) was of opinion
that the plaintiffs were entitled to 5 per cent.
commission on the contract, on the footing
that the defendant had heavy expenses to pay
out of his salary, and, therefore, judgment
would be for the sum of £20 12s. 6d., with
costs.

ATKINSON v. THE SURREY VAUDEVILLE THEATRE, LIMITED.

CURTAIN RUNG DOWN TOO SOON.

In the King's Bench Division, before Mr.
Justice Lawrence and jury, the Sisters
Atkinson, known on the music-hall stage
as the Sisters Worth and the Two
Primroses, sued the Surrey Vaudeville Theatre,
Limited, for damages for injuries asserted to
have been sustained by them while perform-
ing at the Surrey.

Mr. Dobbs, for the plaintiffs, stated that although the accident happened two years ago,
the younger sister—Edith—was now a helpless
cripple, and would always continue to be so.
While performing they came under the notice
of Mr. Macnaghten, well known in music-hall
circles, and an engagement for four or five
halls, at £3 a week, was the result. The performances were to be at different dates. The
sisters met with the accident, counsel went on,
while performing at the Surrey as the Two
Primroses. The drop-curtain, he said, was let
down upon them a: they were finishing their
turn. The curtains were of heavy plush and
weighted with lead.

Miss Florence Atkinson, the elder of the
two plaintiffs, said that their performance
consisted of acrobatic dancing and upright
contortions. When the curtain came down it
struck her on the right side of the head and
spun her round into the right-hand wings. On
turning round she saw her sister lying in a
heap at the back of the stage. She was picked
up and carried home. On the following day
she went to the theatre and asked to be allowed to go on with a song and dance, but the
manager, she said, refused unless she signed
a paper saying that the theatre was not to
blame for the accident. This she declined to
do.

In cross-examination by Mr. Brandon, the
witness said that an action was brought in
respect of the accident in 1905.

Mr. Justice A. T. Lawrence said that the
doctrine of common employment must prevail, and that on the pleadings as they stood
judgment must be given for the defendants.

Mr. Dobb then asked for leave to amend
the statement of claim by substituting for
the words "agreement made with the defendants" the words "made with the Macnaghten Vaudeville Circuit."

Mr. Rawlinson submitted that the amendment ought not to be allowed. This defence
of common employment had been before the
plaintiffs for some months, no application to

amend being made, and the defendants had
come into court prepared to fight the case as
pleaded. If allowed, the defendants would be
in a very unfavourable position, for Mr. Macnaghten, who could prove that the suggested
amendment would not be correct, and that
the contract was, in fact, made with the defendants, had gone to America, as he was told
that his presence was unnecessary.

Mr. Justice A. T. Lawrence said he could
not allow the amendment, because if he did
the defendants would be deprived of a legal
right. He would give judgment for the defendants, without costs, and without prejudice
to the plaintiff's right to bring another
action

[See report of case November 9.]

CLINTON v. BRINKLEY AND OTHERS.— ENTERTAINMENT HALL DISPUTE.

At Lambeth County Court, before his Honour
Judge Emden, Miss Edith Leyland Clinton, of
10 Kennington Park Road, brought an action against the proprietors of the Horns
Assembly Rooms, Kennington, for £100
damages for breach of contract. The defendants were Elizabeth Isabella Brinkley,
William Dennis Palmer, and Alfred John Cope.

Plaintiff's case was that she arranged to
hire the Assembly Rooms for a concert and
dance, arranged for her benefit, for the night
of December 19, 1907. She paid 5s. deposit, and
nothing definite was said as to when the
balance was to be paid. At six o'clock on the
night of the entertainment permission to open
the doors was refused unless the full amount
was paid. Plaintiff offered £2, saying the remainder should be paid immediately out of
the box-office takings, but the offer was refused, and the benefit performance never took
place, with the result that a great number of
people were disappointed, and plaintiff's professional reputation was damaged. His Honour
gave judgment for the plaintiff for £10, with
costs.

CLYDE v. GRANT.—CLAIM FOR SALARY IN LIEU OF NOTICE.

In the Auckland County Court, before his
Honour Judge O'Connor, K.C., Miss Evelyn
10 Clyde claimed from Mr. Alexander C.
Grant the sum of £2 1s. 8d., a portion of
one week's salary, and also two weeks' salary,
amounting to £5, in lieu of notice.

Mr. A. B. Allen (for Mr. H. P. Douglas,
Crook) appeared for the plaintiff, and Mr.
Thos. Jennings defended.

In opening the case, Mr. Allen said the
plaintiff entered into an engagement with the
defendant in the summer of 1907 as leading lady in The Woman from Scotland Yard.
The plaintiff had remained with the defendant
for a period of nearly six months, taking
the leading part in that play. The very
fact of her being with the defendant for six
months showed the plaintiff was perfectly competent and played the part in a proper manner. In February Mr. Grant's company was
engaged for the week at Crook. During that
week Mr. Grant arranged to represent two
plays, the one in which the plaintiff played a
leading part, and another A Master of Millions. It appeared that the previous week the
company had been at Waterhouses, and during
that period a lady of the company made an
accusation against the plaintiff. The latter
was rather hurt about the matter, and on the
fourth day they were at Crook she walked
over to Waterhouses to make inquiries about
the assertions made. She was unwell at the
time, and upon arriving at Waterhouses became very ill, and medical assistance was ob-

tained. She had to stop at Waterhouses that night, and owing to being unable to get a message to Crook by telegraph could not let Mr. Grant know. The following morning the plaintiff went back to Crook, and on seeing Mr. Grant he forthwith discharged her, telling her he had engaged another lady to take up the position. At the interview the defendant also intimated her absence had been a loss to him, but as a matter of fact he was not playing *The Woman from Scotland Yard*, in which the plaintiff took a leading part.

The plaintiff, in her evidence, stated that the contract was for £2 10s. per week, subject to a fortnight's notice on either side. Her engagement was to play the title-*rôle* in *The Woman from Scotland Yard*, and there was no engagement to play any other part, although she was willing to play a minor part in *A Master of Millions.*

Cross-examined, witness said there was no understudy for her part in *A Master of Millions*; still, her absence would not be serious, but would be inconvenient.

Mr. John Elliott, printer, of Esh Winning, and part lessee of the Waterhouses Theatre, said that on Thursday, February 6, plaintiff went to his shop after having walked from Crook. She said she was ill. He visited several places to try and get a trap to take Miss Clyde back to Crook, as she was ill, and eventually succeeded. When they got about two miles on the way they had to turn back, owing to plaintiff being so ill.

Dr. McLeod, medical practitioner, of Esh Winning, stated he prescribed for plaintiff, and gave her a certificate.

For the defence, Mr. Jennings submitted that defendant had to do what he did, absolutely through circumstances. The custom of the profession was that if any member of the company did not appear when billed to do so without having given reasonable cause and notification that terminated the contract.

Evidence was given in support of this contention by Mr. Grant and Mr. A. Loftus.

His Honour, in summing-up, said he was bound to give plaintiff judgment. Whatever might be the custom—if there was any definite custom—custom, like everything else, had to give way before the intervention of that which was beyond the power of both parties to control. If what is called an act of God, or anything of that kind, interposed in the execution of the part of the contract, that did not entitle the other side to all the advantages or rights which otherwise the contract might have secured. Now, he thought it was clear that it was physically impossible for the plaintiff to deliver a medical certificate at Crook that night, and that impossibility discharged her from the obligation of sending it. As to the medical certificate, it was written on the night when it was required. The plaintiff appeared to have made all reasonable efforts for the purpose of presenting herself at the theatre in time. Judgment was given for the plaintiff for the amount claimed, with costs.

PROSECUTION OF ROBERT FROEST.—A DEAL IN FILMS.

At Aberdeen, Robert Froest, photographer, 5, Canal Street, Aberdeen, was charged with fraud. The indictment set forth that **14** on February 27, by means of an advertisement inserted by him in THE STAGE of that date under the false name and address, Moir, 41½, Union Street, Aberdeen, he pretended that he had for sale certain kinematograph films at the price of £5 10s., but which were really worth double the price, and which would be sent to likely purchasers on approval on receipt of a deposit in security. The advertisement having come under the notice of Carl Mannheim, variety entertainer, 22, Wesley Street, Prudhoe-on-Tyne, Froest thereby induced him to send him by post a letter addressed " Moir," etc., containing a cheque for £5, being deposit in security for the inspection or approval, with a view to the purchase or return of the films, and failing purchase to return the cheque, which sum Froest appropriated. He did send on certain films, but these were not value for the money, and Froest thereby defrauded Mannheim.

Froest pleaded guilty.

The Sheriff passed sentence of forty days' imprisonment on Froest.

STARLING v. GAUMONT.—AN ECHO OF THE NEWMARKET DISASTER.

Before his Honour Judge Woodfall, in the Westminster County Court, an action was **16** brought by Mr. Ephraim Starling, who described himself as a groom residing at Newmarket, to recover damages against Gaumont Company, at Sherwood Street, Regent Street, W., for the loss of his wife owing to the alleged defective working of a kinematograph machine at the Newmarket Town Hall.

The jury, after a short consultation, found a verdict for the plaintiff for £50, and judgment was so entered, with costs.

THORPE v. BARSTOW.—ROYALTIES ON " THE SCARLET PIMPERNEL."

In the King's Bench Division, before Mr. Justice Darling and a special jury, was commenced an action brought by Mr. Courte- **16** nay Thorpe against Mr. Montague Barstow and Mrs. Barstow (Baroness Orczy) to recover moneys alleged to be due under an agreement in connection with *The Scarlet Pimpernel.* Mr. C. F. Gill, K.C., and Mr. McCardie (instructed by Mr. J. D. Langton) were for the plaintiff, and Mr. Rawlinson, K.C., and Mr. H. Dobb (instructed by Mr. E. R. Wood) for the defendants.

Mr. Gill explained that the question in dispute was what was the agreement between the plaintiff and defendants with regard to the work he did and the assistance he gave in the circumstances under which the play was placed. The defendants said that the agreement was that he should have 20 per cent. of the royalties received from March 2, 1903, to March 2, 1906. Mr. Thorpe was an actor who had been on the stage for twenty-five years, he had had large experience, had written plays himself, and had acted for people who had written plays in placing them. He met the defendants in September, 1902, at the house of a mutual friend. Mr. Thorpe offered, if she liked to try, to help and advise her in connection with writing plays. She and her husband wrote *The Scarlet Pimpernel*. It was finished about the end of January, 1903, and after many interviews and suggestions by the plaintiff it was practically rewritten. It was agreed that he should have 20 per cent. of the royalties, and at the beginning of May he submitted it to Mr. Fred Terry and Miss Julia Neilson. He went to Cheltenham and read it to them. On May 8 Mr. Fred Terry provisionally accepted the play, and on May 29 it was finally accepted.

The play was produced at Nottingham and afterwards, at the beginning of 1905, in London, by Mr. Terry, and made a very great success. Mr. Thorpe did all he could with regard to three or four other plays by the defendants,

Mr. Justice Darling: Have the defendants produced any other plays?

Mr. Gill: After they got dissatisfied with Mr. Thorpe they found somebody whom they thought would serve their requirements. They did produce a play called *The Sin of William Jackson*, which ran for five or six nights, and cost them over £2,000.

Counsel went on to say that the defendants wrote *The Millionaire*, *The Tangled Skein*, and *Voltaire*, but though Mr. Thorpe did what he could with them he did not succeed in placing them, and defendants became dissatisfied. On March 3 Mr. Barstow wrote enclosing returns at the New and cheque, saying:— "This brings our three years' agreement to a close, and as you seem either unable or unwilling now to further our interests in any way whatever, we have no desire to continue so one-sided an arrangement." The sum actually received by the defendants for the play was £5,980.

Mr. Rawlinson: And plaintiff was paid £500 or £600 for reading the play once—a couple of hours' work.

Mr. Gill: Now we know what the defence is.

Mr. Justice Darling: The question here is, what was the contract?

Mr. Gill: That's the whole question—whether Mr. Thorpe was entitled to 20 per cent. of the royalties received for *The Scarlet Pimpernel* for whatever period it might run, or whether it was for three years only.

The hearing was adjourned till Wednesday, the 18th.

The Defence.

Mrs. Barstow said she had written a number of books, and also contributed to magazines. She wrote under the title of Baroness Orczy. "The Scarlet Pimpernel" and "I Will Repay" had been translated into twelve foreign languages, and both had a circulation of about a quarter of a million each. When she met the plaintiff he suggested she should write a play, which she did. He, however, disapproved of it, and then she wrote *The Scarlet Pimpernel*.

Mrs. Barstow, continuing, said that, wishing to put the matter on a business footing, she suggested to Mr. Thorpe that he should have a percentage on her dramatic work. He said that Mr. Paul Kester paid him 15 per cent., but she and her husband suggested that he should have 20 per cent. on all dramatic work for a period of three years. She confirmed the arrangement on March 2, 1903. That was the only arrangement they had for work done by Mr. Thorpe. She denied that she ever wrote to him concerning all future plays.

Cross-examined by Mr. Gill, Mrs. Barstow said that before she was married she carried on business in High Street, Kensington. At the beginning of 1906 she was in communication with Mr. Murray, who was to place her plays with managers.

With reference to the production of a play entitled *The Sin of William Jackson*, the witness said that £700 was paid for the rent of a theatre, over £300 for other expenses, and also a sum of £560. She added that, with Mr. Tom B. Davis, she was sued by Mr. Boucicault and other actors who appeared in the play, but, on the advice of her lawyers, the case was settled out of Court for £350.

Judgment for Plaintiff.

The jury found for the plaintiff.

His Lordship gave judgment accordingly, and, as a result of the verdict, directed an account to be taken.

GETTMANN v. GOODSHIP AND COLLINI.—CONTRACT AND A SEQUEL.

At Wood Green County Court, before Judge Edge, Walter Gettmann, musician, of Newbold Street, Commercial Road, E., sued Edwin Goodship, secretary of the Alexandra Palace Trustees, and Ernest Collini, musician, of Warwick Road, Upperton Edmonton, for £25. The claim was made partly for services rendered and partly for damages for alleged breach of agreement. Mr. H. Nield was counsel for Mr. Goodship.

17 Mr. Collini said he arranged with Mr. Goodship to provide a band for the Alexandra Palace circus for three weeks, and he entered into a contract with the plaintiff for providing the necessary music.

Judge Edge: You contracted with Mr. Goodship to provide a band for £14 5s. Then you made arrangements with plaintiff to provide it for £12 10s. You were making a profit.

Collini: That was my commission.

Mr. Nield: He gives a receipt for the first week for £14 5s. (produced). Then the band struck and would not perform.

The Judge: There is clearly no case against Mr. Goodship, and I must find a verdict in his favour.

A verdict was entered for plaintiff as against Collini for the amount claimed.

MORTIMER v. V.A.F.—CLAIM RESULTING FROM THE MUSIC HALL WAR.

Before his Honour Judge Woodfall, in the Westminster County Court, Mr. Leonard Mortimer, music hall artist, brought an action to recover the sum of £40 from the Variety Artists' Federation in respect of loss of salary owing to the music hall strike, or, in the alternative, damages for that amount.

27 Mr. R. Storrey Deans was counsel for the plaintiff, and Mr. Chas. Doughty appeared for the defendants.

Mr. Storrey Deans, in opening the plaintiff's case said that in January, 1907, his client was engaged to appear at the Canterbury and other music halls, his engagement being for a salary of £80 a week, but he was instructed by the secretary of the defendant Federation not to appear on account of the strike, which was at that time going on, and as a result he was compelled to break his contract. He had been paid a sum of money by the Federation, but he now claimed the further sum of £40 in respect of his loss on the Canterbury engagement alone, they having agreed to recoup him for any loss of salary which he might sustain by breaking his engagements.

The plaintiff, Mr. Leonard Mortimer, was called, and said he was a member of the Variety Artists' Federation in 1907 when the strike took place. He received a letter from Mr. Frank Gerald, who was the secretary of the Federation, informing him that he was forbidden to carry out his engagements at the Canterbury, and as a result he was compelled to break his contract and lose his salary. When he spoke to Mr. Gerald on the subject the latter told him not to bother himself about his salary as he would get it in another way. His engagement at the Canterbury was for six nights at a salary of £46 a week, but he had also engagements at the Euston, Brixton, Balham, South London, and Croydon. His present claim was only in respect of the Canterbury, over which he had suffered a loss of £40, after giving the defendants credit for a sum of £6, which they had already paid. As a matter of fact he lost five weeks' engagements at the instance of the Federation, under whose instructions he refrained from appearing at any of the Payne or Gibbons halls, and he considered that by so doing he had lost about £235 in salary, but he was only claiming now in respect of the Canterbury.

In cross-examination, the witness said that he had done work inside on behalf of the defendant Federation in the day time, and that he also assisted them outside at night. When he found that he could not get his money from the Federation he consulted Messrs. Morriss and Rickards on the subject, and they advised him to make a claim for it, but they did not suggest to him that Mr. Frank Gerald was liable.

At this point of the case counsel for the defence submitted as a point of law that the plaintiff was not entitled to recover as against the Federation as a body, as the Federation was not registered until March 26, 1907, and that in any event he could not recover without adding Mr. Frank Gerald as a party to the action. He said that the Federation could not be sued, and that in order for the plaintiff to succeed in this action he must bring an action against each member personally.

His Honour said he felt that in any event Mr. Gerald ought to be joined as a defendant to the action.

Mr. Storrey Deans asked for an adjournment in order that he might consider his position.

His Honour said the plaintiff could sue the members of the Federation personally, and he was much disposed to adjourn the case, but if he did so the costs would be the defendants' in any event.

Mr. Doughty, on behalf of the defendant Federation, said he had a complete and perfect answer to the claim, but on the point of law alone he submitted that he was entitled to judgment.

His Honour agreed. He would, however, adjourn the case on the plaintiff undertaking to pay the defendants' costs of the day within fourteen days, otherwise there would be a non-suit.

Counsel for the plaintiff asked for leave to appeal if his Honour was against him.

His Honour said he felt some difficulty in this case, but, after carefully considering it and having struggled to help the plaintiff all he could, he felt he must non-suit him, with costs. His action was brought against a body of people who were not registered at the time when the cause of action arose, and therefore he (the judge) did not think he could recover.

Counsel for the plaintiff asked for a stay of execution pending appeal, but his Honour said there would be the usual stay of fourteen days, with leave to apply for a further stay if an appeal were decided upon.

CORRI AND CRICHTON v. WILLIAMS.—APPEAL SUSTAINED.

The following interlocutor, dated Dundee, March 30, was issued by Sheriff Principal James Fergusson:—

30 The Sheriff, having considered the cause, sustains the appeal, recalls the interlocutor of the Sheriff substitute of March 4, 1908, complained of, finds, in fact (1) that in August, 1907, the defenders entered into a contract with the pursuers under which the latter, who are theatrical managers, undertook with the touring theatrical company of which they are managers to perform an engagement at the Gaiety Theatre, Dundee, during the week commencing December 30, 1907; (2) that by said contract the pursuers undertook to provide a full and efficient company

as per bill, matters, and correspondence for the proper representations of the musical comedy *The Dancing Girls of Spain* and the pantomime sketch *Office Hours*, and the defender undertook to pay to the pursuers for said representation "a certainty of £155"; (3) that pursuers brought their company to Dundee and performed the plays named during the stipulated period; (4) that defender has failed to prove that the company was not full and efficient, or that he has sustained damage through the fault of the pursuers; (5) that defender has failed to pay the stipulated sum of £155, having only made a payment of £100, and refuses to pay the balance of £55; finds, in law, that the pursuers are entitled to receive and the defender is bound to pay the whole sum of £155 in terms of the contract, therefore sustains the pursuers' plea in law, repels the defences and counter-claim made by defender, ordains the defender to pay to the pursuers the sum of £55, with legal interest thereon and decerns; finds the pursuers entitled to expenses, including those of the appeal; appoints an account thereof to be given in, and remits the same to the auditor to tax and report, and remits the cause to the Sheriff Substitute.

(Signed) JAMES FERGUSSON.

[NOTE.—This is a simple case of contract in which there is no element of joint risk or participation in profits. The pursuer Crichton says that he would have preferred and proposed an engagement on the footing of sharing profits, but that the defender declined this, and he ultimately agreed to accept a fixed sum considerably less than he had asked in correspondence. That being so, the question of whether the defender suffered loss or not is irrelevant, unless the pursuers were guilty of a breach of contract subjecting them in damages for loss caused thereby. The defence is that pursuers did not fulfil their contract because they did not produce a musical comedy, but only a comedy with music, and that their company was not full and efficient. To the ordinary mind a musical comedy is just a comedy with music, and it is curious that while in the document headed "Artists' Contract" and on letter paper *The Dancing Girls of Spain* is called a musical comedy, it is, in the bills used elsewhere, and particularly in the specimen bill sent to defender before its production, described as a comedy with music, and was so billed at Dundee. To satisfy a Court that descriptive words which in ordinary use mean the same thing have in the theatrical world acquired distinct special esoteric significance, the evidence must be clear and substantially uncontradicted. On a mere balance of opinion the ordinary meaning will not be superseded. The defender defines a musical comedy as "a comedy with music, full chorus, and special scenery." But it is clear that the expression has been used for plays which had neither a "full"—by which is meant a large chorus—or special scenery. Thus, in programmes, *Somebody's Sweetheart* is described as a musical play, *A Trip to Chinatown* as a musical farcical comedy, and *My Sweetheart* as a charming pastoral play, with music, all of which seem to be various, but not contradictory, modes of describing a certain class of performances.

The pursuers' witnesses do not agree that a large chorus is essential to a musical comedy. They also affirm that the practice is for the local theatre to supply its ordinary scenery, and for the performing company only to bring something special. If a manager of a theatre, in engaging a company, is in doubt as to either of these points, he can clear the matter up by inquiring, and if he makes no inquiry, it is not the fault of the person providing the company. The onus of inquiring is specially strong, when, as in this case, he is sent a bill of previous perform-ances in which the other expression is used, and where a fortnight before the company comes down he receives, as here, communica-tion in which the scenery he is expected to provide, and the scenery the company will bring is specified. I am clearly of opinion that defender has failed to establish his con-tention that the pursuers' company did not perform a musical comedy.

I am also of opinion that he has failed to prove that the company was not full and efficient. He engaged an existing and acting company. It is, I think, proved that the company which played at Dundee was the company which had been playing in England, and which afterwards played at other places in Scotland. He made no stipulation as to numbers, and none as to chorus. The pursuers' evidence is that there were nineteen all told, of whom sixteen were on the stage, and of these sixteen, six acted as chorus. Two of the company were ill for a night or two, but that is an accident to which all are liable. As to their qualifications my impression is that they were a fair average company for the boards at least of a provincial theatre. They are "crabbed" by the defenders' wit-nesses, and it is said that the ladies were badly made up; that it was "the rottenest so-called musical comedy," and that the per-formance was too "weird for words." But these phrases are merely flowers of histrionic rhetoric, and in three if not more cases, when tested, the performers get a good character, and in at least one an offer of engagement, from the defender and his witnesses. The play appears to have given satisfaction not only in England, but at Paisley, Glasgow, Perth, and Inverness. It does not seem to have been so popular in Dundee, Dunfermline, Methel, and Kirkcaldy. Whether it be that something in it awakens a sympathetic chord in the hearts of the descendants of the Mile-sian Scots, who are said to have found their way to central Scotland by way of Ireland and Spain, which does not vibrate in the organism of the progeny of the Picts in Angus and Fife, or that east of the Ochills and the Sidlaws, souls chilled by the east wind are less responsive to the associations of orange groves and castanets, nothing more is proved than a difference of taste on the part of the local public. It is impossible to predict what particular play will or will not take on at a particular locality, and in this case the de-fender took the whole risk, and indeed drew some £50 more than he undertook to pay to the pursuers. On the whole evidence it is impossible to affirm that the pursuers did not fulfil their contract according to its rea-sonable interpretation. If so they are en-titled to be paid the stipulated sum, and there can be no claim against them for damages.

(Intd.)   J. F

[For appeal see report, November 10.]

APRIL.

KARNO v. PATHE FRERES, LIMITED.— FILMS AND PLAYRIGHT.

Mr. Justice Jelf, in the King's Bench Divi-sion, had this action before him on April 3 and 6. Mr. Fred Karno, the well-known music-hall sketch artist, sued Pathé Frères, Limited, London, to recover damages for hav-ing infringed the plaintiff's sole right of per-forming, or permitting to be performed, the dramatic sketch, *The Mumming Birds; or, Twice Nightly,* by producing the sketch on kinematograph films and selling them for the purposes of representation. The plaintiff fur-ther asked for an injunction restraining the defendants from continuing the infringement. The defendants denied that the manufacture and sale of films for use in a kinematograph or a reproduction by a kinematograph was in law a performance or representation of a dra-matic piece or an infringement of the right of performance. They also denied that the piece in question was a dramatic piece within the meaning of the Statutes 3 Wm. IV., c. 15, or 5 and 6 Vict., c. 45.

Mr. Scrutton, K.C., and Mr. Mackinnon ap-peared for the plaintiff; while Sir R. Finlay, K.C., and Mr. C. A. Bennett represented the defendants.

THE JUDGE AT THE OXFORD.

After the hearing of the case and arguments by counsel King's Bench VII. was transferred to the Oxford Music Hall in the afternoon of April 6 to obtain further evidence of a novel kind in judicial proceedings.

Mr. Justice Jelf having signified his inten-tion of seeing for himself the sketch and the picture, a small and select company awaited his lordship's arrival. By the judge's direction the green-covered table and the armchair which stood behind it were brought down from the dress-circle and set in the centre of the gangway near the front of the stalls. When all was ready, his lordship, devoid of all outward semblance of his judicial rank, quietly took his seat about half-past four. The word to begin the performance was given, the orchestra struck up the lively accompanying music of the sketch, and almost before one was aware of the fact *The Mumming Birds,* with its rollicking fun, was in full swing by Mr. Fred Karno's company. Every movement in the sketch was keenly followed by the judge, with the aid of a large pair of opera-glasses. Then the kinematograph show which was complained of was thrown on the screen. The kinematograph representation lasted just five minutes by the clock, and the audience at the close was about to depart, when the learned judge indicated a desire to witness the kinematographic display again. His lordship's desire was at once complied with. Judgment was reserved, and delivered on April 29, and was to the following effect:—

FULL JUDGMENT.

Mr. Justice Jelf said: This action, which was tried before me without a jury on the 3rd and 6th instant, was brought by the plaintiff, Mr. Fred Karno, who is the author and pro-prietor of various music-hall sketches, against the defendants, Messrs Pathé Frères (London), who are makers of and dealers in kinemato-graphs and films, to recover damages for an alleged infringement by them of his alleged copyright in or sole liberty of representing at any place of dramatic entertainment a certain dramatic piece, being a farce or pantomimical sketch, *The Mumming Birds; or, Twice Nightly,* by an imitation of it being thrown upon a screen by means of a film; and for an injunction to restrain the defendants from a continuance of such infringement.

IMPORTANT QUESTIONS RAISED.

The case raises important questions under

the Dramatic Copyright Act, 1833, commonly known as Bulwer-Lytton's Act, 3 William IV., c. 15, s. 1, which I have to construe by the light of the recent decision of the Court of Appeal in Tate v. Fullbrook, 1908, 1 King's Bench, page 821, in the current April number of the Law Reports.

The defendants contended (1) that the sketch in question was not such a dramatic piece as to be entitled to protection under the Act; (2) that the alleged kinematographic reproduction was not in fact or in law a "representation" of the plaintiff's sketch within the meaning of the Act; (3) that the defendants by merely selling the film were not "causing" the plaintiff's sketch to be represented.

DESCRIPTION OF "THE MUMMING BIRDS."

In order to determine these points, it is necessary to state somewhat minutely the facts which were admitted or proved before me.

The plaintiff carries on a lucrative business by composing humorous sketches, training his companies to play them, and sending them round the country and abroad to be performed in music halls and theatres. One of such sketches is called *The Mumming Birds; or, Twice Nightly,* which is entered by that name under date January 15, 1906, as a pantomimical sketch in the Book of Registry of Copyrights and Assignments at the hall of the Stationers' Company. The plaintiff's name, with his address, appears therein as the author and composer, and also as the proprietor of the sole liberty of representation or performance so far as Great Britain and Ireland are concerned, and the time and place of the first representation or performance is stated to be April 14, 1904, at the Star Music Hall, Bermondsey.

In teaching his company the plaintiff instructs them orally what to do and what to say. He has not got written down the words which the actors are to speak. The plaintiff, in his evidence, confirms the particulars of *The Mumming Birds* which he had delivered in the action pursuant to an order of the Master. From these it appeared that the plot —if such it can be called—consists in a representation of a music hall performance, as viewed by a stage audience, and the humour depends on the frequent interruptions and interferences by the audience. The performers who appear are (1) the spectators or audience of the performance, (2) the performers and artists, (3) the stage attendants. Amongst the audience the principal characters are a boy dressed in an Eton suit and his guardian in the bottom box on the left, and a "swell" in evening dress in a state of semi-intoxication in the opposite box on the right. The various turns of the artists are announced by a card put into a frame on the right—No. 1, No. 2, etc. The artists are a male vocalist, a lady vocalist, a conjurer, a quartet of singers, a soubrette, and a wrestler. The piece is acted mainly in pantomime, and the "fun" consists in the incompetence of the performers, the disgust of the audience, the pranks of the boy who shoots peas or throws buns at the artists and members of the audience, especially the swell, and who spoils the conjuring tricks, etc., the general free fights on the stage, in which most of the company take part, and the bye-play between the soubrette, the swell, a female programme attendant, and others.

NO SUSTAINED DIALOGUE.

There is no sustained dialogue, but from time to time a few words are spoken. There is no written copy of stage directions used in this country, but copyright has been obtained

in America, and a book of stage directions, written by the plaintiff and used in the United States was produced and sworn by the plaintiff to be a substantially correct description of the piece as played in England and of the dialogue, such as it is. The dialogue comprised such remarks as the following by the male vocalist: "Ladies and Gentlemen,— Will any members of the audience give me a subject, and I shall be pleased to extemporise upon it. Any subject, please, if you know of any"—whereupon various names, such as Lord Roberts, Deadwood Dick, etc., are suggested, and the extemporising follows, but always in the same way, and without reference to the particular subject suggested by the audience.

The plaintiff's evidence was that, substantially, the same words were used throughout at each performance, but I was satisfied by the evidence of witnesses called for the defendants, and by a comparison of the particulars in the action with the stage directions in the United States, that in connection with the "extemporising" incident and many others the words used vary in detail from one performance to another, and that it would be difficult, if not impossible, to write down in the form of a libretto the exact words used from time to time by the various actors. The general idea of "fun" and "ragging," with plenty of business and a considerable amount of gag, is carried through the piece, but there is no connected story or plot capable of being written down in a literary form. The fun (however nonsensical it may be) has been remarkably successful in London, in the provinces, and abroad, and, having been brought out at considerable expense, has, nevertheless, put thousands of pounds into the plaintiff's pocket, and still attracts crowded audiences and provokes roars of laughter wherever and whenever it is produced.

WHAT THE DEFENDANTS DID.

Now, what the defendants have done is this: They have manufactured a kinematograph film, photographed from living persons whom they have placed on a stage to act got up like the plaintiff's players, and these figures, when their pictures are thrown upon the sheet, appear to go through the same antics, the same succession of pranks, and the same scenic business as that portrayed in the plaintiff's sketch, the incidents being presented substantially in the same order and by the same characters. The boy in the Eton suit and his guardian are in the same left-hand lower box, and do almost exactly the same things; the swell is in the opposite box, precisely as in the plaintiff's sketch; the turns come in the same order; the numbers are put up and knocked out on the same right-hand side of the stage, and in the same succession; the artists follow the example of those in *The Mumming Birds,* and the general get-up is the same throughout. There are, no doubt, some additions and variations, but the parts in which the two pantomimes agree largely exceeds those in which they differ.

ESSENTIALLY COPIED.

At the request of the parties, and in order the better to judge as to the alleged plagiarisms. I attended a special private performance at the Oxford on the 6th instant, at which the plaintiff's sketch was performed, and was followed immediately by the film of the kinematograph, twice repeated, and I have no hesitation in finding, as a fact, whatever the result may be in law, that the one piece is copied in all essential particulars from the other. It was moreover proved to my satisfaction that when the plaintiff is about to give a performance in a provincial town the purchasers from the defendants of the film in question habitually anticipate such performance by giving an exhibition of the "living pictures," and so destroy or damage the success of the plaintiff's show, people refusing to go to the latter, on the ground that they have seen it before.

In selling these films to these purchasers the defendants well knew that they were bought for the purpose and with the intention on the part of the purchasers of exhibiting the "living pictures" in places of entertainment, and they obtain large prices for them on the ground that they will be in this way profitable to the purchasers.

The defendants advertise these animated pictures as follows:—"The Pathé Company, convinced that their kinematographic work would revolutionise showmen's entertainments, at once applied their energies to the development of this new industry," adding, "it is at once the theatre, the school, and the newspaper of to-morrow." And again they say: "To the directors of kinematograph entertainments. The possessors of our material, profiting by the prestige attached to the kinematograph . . . will have at hand the best entertainment. We can only prophesy for them the largest profits." And in an illustrated catalogue they publish amongst others the following item: " At the music hall . . . about 330 ft., the film £5 10s," with a picture and a description which show clearly that the film will produce a substantial imitation of the plaintiff's sketch.

The defendants do not, however, take any part in the actual use of the films, and have no control over the purchasers thereof after the purchase.

THREE CONTENTIONS—(1) NOT A STAGE PLAY. On this state of facts I have to deal with the three contentions of the defendants above mentioned: (1) Their first point was *The Mumming Birds* is not a "dramatic piece or entertainment" within the meaning of the 3rd William IV., chapter 15, Section 1, and is, therefore, not within the protection of the Act. That section, after reciting that by 54 George III., chapter 156, it was enacted that the author of any book or books composed, and not printed or published, or which should thereafter be composed and printed and published, and his assignee or assigns should have the sole liberty of printing and reprinting such book or books for twenty-eight years from the day of first publishing the same, and also if the author should be living at the end of that period, for the residue of his natural life, and reciting that it was expedient to extend the provisions of the said Act, proceeds as follows:—

Be it therefore enacted that from and after the passing of this Act the author of any tragedy, comedy, play, opera, farce, or any other dramatic piece or entertainment composed and not printed and published by the author thereof or his assignee, or which hereinafter shall be composed and not printed or published by the author thereof or his assignee, or the assignee of such author, shall have as his own property the sole liberty of representing or causing to be represented at any place or places of dramatic entertainment whatsoever in any part of the British dominions, any such production as aforesaid, not printed and published by the author thereof or his assignee, and shall be deemed and taken to be the pro-

prietor thereof; and the author of any such production printed and published within ten years before the passing of this Act by the author thereof or his assignee, or which shall hereafter be so printed and published, or the assignee of such author, shall from the time of the passing of this Act or from the time of such publication respectively until the end of twenty-eight years from the day of such first publication of the same, and also if the author or authors, or the survivor of the authors, shall be living at the end of that period, during the residue of his natural life have as his own property the sole liberty of representing or causing to be represented the same at any such place of dramatic entertainment as aforesaid, and shall be deemed and taken to be the proprietor thereof.

Now, if the matter were *res integra*, I should have thought there were some strong reasons for holding that the piece in question is a dramatic piece within the protection of the Act. Looking to the object of the statute, which is evidently to protect the results of independent labour and composition in dramatic work and to extend to dramatic compositions the same protection as that already given to books, I see no reason in the nature of things why a dramatic composition, which is entirely pantomimic or performed in dumb show, and neither reduced or reducible into writing, should not be protected against piracy as being a piece "composed"—namely, "put together"—by its author. For example, why should not the clever and touching French piece *L'Enfant Prodigue* be so protected?

In the Law Journal Report of the case of Chatterton v. Cave, 44 Law Journal, Common Pleas, 386, Lord Esher, then Mr. Justice Brett, in the Divisional Court, is reported to have said:—

The first point argued was that what was proved to have been borrowed was not the subject-matter of property at all, inasmuch as it consisted not of the text of the play, but of theatrical situations. I am aware that theatrical situations may be sometimes expressed wholly by dramatic action and without the aid of words, but it seems to me that of whatever kind they may be, they are in every instance entitled to the protection afforded by law to dramatic literary property.

And the Law Times report, 33 Law Journal, page 255, is to the same effect:—

Now, it was first said that the subject-matter of the action was not the subject of copyright—that the Act gives a property in words but not in situations and scenic effects, but I think these latter are more peculiarly the subject of copyright than words themselves.

It seems, however, that this opinion was extra-judicial, and the passage does not appear in the report in the Law Reports, 10 Common Pleas, page 572. The suggested reason for this omission is given by Lord Justice Vaughan Williams in Tate v. Fullbrook, Law Reports, 1908 (1), King's Bench, at page 828, which I will deal with presently; and this latter case being a decision of the Court of Appeal, must, of course, if there is a conflict, prevail. Nevertheless, such an utterance by Lord Esher as that quoted above, whether afterwards corrected by him or not, cannot be left out of account.

Again, the words of the section, involved and clumsy as they are, do not, in my humble judgment, necessarily imply that the pieces to be protected must be capable of being printed and published. The first part, it might be argued, apparently deals with pieces composed, but not printed and published by the author, and might, I should have thought, include pieces not capable of being printed and published at all; and, though the second part, which deals with pieces which have been printed and published by the author within ten years, or which should thereafter be printed and published by him, would not apply to pantomimes or pieces performed in dumb show, this may not be inconsistent with such argument because the apparent object was to exclude from protection pieces which have been more than ten years before deliberately thrown open by their authors by printing and publication, which exclusion would be unnecessary as applied to pieces incapable of being printed and published. Note, too, the antithesis between the liberty of "printing and reprinting" in the first part of the section, and the liberty of "representing or causing to be represented" in the second part.

On the other hand, the 5 and 6 Victoria, Chapter 45, Section 20, recites that the Act in Question 3, William IV., Chapter 15, was passed to amend the law relating to dramatic literary property, which word "literary" might raise a presumption against its application to any piece incapable of being printed and published. To which again it might be answered that the Act was to amend the then existing law in this very particular. The United States authorities are collected in "Scrutton on Copyrights," 4th Edition, 1903, pages 86 to 87; but as the cases are contradictory and the American Act different, I do not refer to them further.

My decision, however, must depend not upon a priori reasoning, nor upon my own construction of the Statute, but upon the view which I take of the ratio decidendi in the case of "Tate v. Fullbrook," 1908, 1 King's Bench, 821, for if the principle there laid down by the Court of Appeal governs the present case, I am, of course, bound by it.

Now in "Tate v. Fullbrook" the defendant's dramatic piece, which was alleged to be an infringement of the plaintiff's copyright in his dramatic piece was, as regards verbal composition, in substance entirely different from it; but Mr. Justice Phillimore had found that there was such a similarity in the performances in respect of certain accessories such as the number and character of the dramatis personæ, the scenic effects, and the comic business and gags that the one was a copy and infringement of the other.

Each of the Lords Justices, however, seems to have held that the subject matter protected by the Dramatic Copyright Act, 1883, is a composition capable of being printed and published; and although they said in effect that when it is doubtful whether the words of the one piece are a plagiarism from the words of the other you may look at the accessories, such as the general "get up" of the characters, the scenic effects, and all the dramatic surroundings to see whether, taken as a whole, the one piece is a piracy from the other, yet you must have to begin with words constituting a dramatic piece which are capable of protection under the Act, and that the similarity of stage situations ought not to be taken into consideration at all when there is no appreciable similarity between the words of the two productions, or when there is no dialogue or literary composition to be compared.

Their Lordships seem to me to have distinctly excluded from the protection of the Act every mere pantomime or any piece which

is acted entirely in dumb show, however much or however little merit there may be in the composition, and however clear and damaging the plagiarism may be.

Applying this principle to the present case I cannot doubt that the Lords Justices would have held that The Mumming Birds had no real foundation in the way of dialogue or literary composition as to bring it under the Act. There could, of course, be stage directions in writing such as those printed in the United States, but that does not make the piece itself capable of being printed and published, and even if the words in "inverted commas" in the American book are collected together they fall far short of a book of words or any connected literary work. In indeed it could be shown that in the present case there are words capable of being printed and published as a literary piece, then I think it ought to be held that the kinematograph reproduction is a representation of a substantial part of the whole piece, though, of course, no words are reproduced, and "Tate v Fullbrook" might, on that ground, be distinguishable on the facts; but as I have said, I do not think there is really any literary substratum on which to found this contention.

The defendants' first objection, therefore, prevails.

Inasmuch, however, as "Tate v. Fullbrook" and the present case may some day be reviewed by the House of Lords, I think it best to state shortly, for what it is worth, my opinion on the other two points taken by the defendants.

(2) FILMS AND PLAYRIGHT.

In my opinion, if The Mumming Birds were within the protection of the Act, the kinematograph reproduction of it, such as I find this to be, would, in fact and in law, be a representation of the plaintiff's sketch within the meaning of the Act. It is represented to the eyes of the spectator. If the parts were played by living persons the spectators would see them moving about and copying what is done in The Mumming Birds. Mere pictures, or even stationary tableaux vivants, would not, I think, infringe the right of sole representation; but as the kinematograph shows the figures just as the living persons, I think this reproduction would be held to be within the language as well as within the mischief of the Act.

(3) CAUSING TO REPRESENT.

As to the defendants' third point, I was at first inclined to think that, by selling the film to other persons in the manner with the knowledge, and under the circumstances already described, the defendants were "causing" the plaintiff's sketch "to be represented" within the meaning of the Statute.

But on further consideration, and after perusing the case of Russell v. Bryant, 8 Common Bench, page 836, and comparing it with Marsh v. Conquest, 17 Common Bench, New Series, page 418, I have come to the opposite conclusion, and I think there is no evidence on which I could properly hold the defendants liable.

In the former case Chief Justice Wilde says:—"No one can be considered as an offender against the provisions of the Act so as to subject himself to an action of this nature unless by himself or his agent he actually takes part in a representation which is a violation of copyright," and the same view is taken in Lyon v. Knowles, 3 Best and Smith, page 556. It might indeed be plausibly argued that the defendants who make and sell the infringing instrument without which the infringement could not take place, and do so with the knowledge and intention that it will and shall be used for that purpose, do take an important part in the infringement itself, but I think, on the whole, the inference would be held to be too remote, and too far-reaching in its consequences to be accepted. If this view is correct, then, even if the action were otherwise maintainable, it ought to have been brought not against the defendants, but against the actual proprietors of the piratical performance impugned.

DECISION

For these reasons I must give judgment for the defendants, with costs.

HARCOURT v. HOLLOWAY.—CLAIM FOR SALARY.

At the Walsall County Court, before Judge H. Smith, Cecil Harcourt sued William Holloway, proprietor of the Empire Theatre, Hednesford, for £2 12s., balance of wages. There was a counter-claim for a fortnight's wages on the ground that plaintiff left Mr. Holloway's employ without giving the necessary notice.

Plaintiff, it was stated, was engaged at one guinea per week, but on a few occasions he was only paid part of his wages. He now claimed the deficiency. Plaintiff contended that he had been insulted by the proprietor's wife, and Mr. F. Cooper, who represented the plaintiff, contended that plaintiff was perfectly justified in leaving his employ instantly, in view of the accusations which had been made and the abuse he had received.

The judge gave a verdict in favour of the plaintiff on the claim and counter-claim.

NATHAN v. ASHTON.—ALLEGED BREACH OF CONTRACT.

In the King's Bench, before Mr. Justice Lawrence and a special jury, Mr. Benjamin Nathan sued Messrs. Ashton and Mitchell, Limited, Bond Street, for damages for a breach of contract and wrongful dismissal, and for an account of commission alleged to be due. Defendants denied the alleged breach of contract and wrongful dismissal, and counter-claimed for certain sums of money which plaintiff said were not due. Mr. Duke, K.C., and Mr. Colam (instructed by Messrs. Hicks, Arnold, and Mozley) appeared for the plaintiff; and Mr. Dickens, K.C., Mr. Low, K.C., and Mr. C. Doughty (instructed by Messrs. Stanley, Woodhouse, and Hedderwick) represented the defendant company.

After the case had been opened counsel consulted, and eventually Mr. Duke said the parties had come to terms, which were mutually satisfactory, and the action would be withdrawn. He understood from Mr. Dickens that there was no intention to reflect on the good faith or character of the plaintiff. Mr. Dickens had asked him to say that, although plaintiff did not receive his expenses in advance, the failure to do so was not due to any want of financial ability on the part of the defendant company. He had only to ask that in case of need there should be a judge's order for the parties on the terms agreed to.

Mr. Dickens remarked that there was no suggestion to reflect on the personal honour of the plaintiff. It was obviously a question for settlement, and they had, he was glad to say, arrived at a fair settlement to both sides.

ROTHERY v. NATION.

At Bloomsbury County Court, in the case of an action by Mr. Rothery, an author, against Mr. W. H. Nation, of the Scala, which was set down for hearing on a Friday, counsel applied for an adjournment. He mentioned that the dispute arose over the production of a play at the Scala called *A Lucky Star*, and the claim was for £50. He added that his Honour would know that Friday was "treasury day." It would not be possible for the defendant and his manager to attend on that day, and they are essential witnesses.—The case was adjourned by Judge Bacon.

[This case was eventually settled out of court, Mr. Nation informing us on May 18 that the plaintiff "accepted £9 for certain fees for *A Lucky Star*."]

McDONALD AND HUNTINGTON v. ROSEN AND BLISS.

Before his Honour Judge Woodfall, in the Westminster County Court, the case of McDonald and Huntington v. Rosen and Bliss was tried, and was an action by the plaintiffs, who are sketch artists, to recover damages against the defendants, Messrs. Rosen and Bliss, for alleged professional negligence in respect of an engagement at the Alhambra, Leicester Square.

Mr. Woolf, counsel for the plaintiffs, said that in January, 1908, his clients had two engagements, one at Woolwich and one at the London, Shoreditch; but in consequence of a letter which they received from the defendant, they were induced to give up their engagement at the Woolwich Empire, in order to take one at the Alhambra. They found out afterwards, however, that the time at the Alhambra clashed with their Shoreditch engagement, and, as a result, they were unable to appear at the Alhambra, and in the meantime had lost their engagement at Woolwich, and it was for negligence on the part of the defendant that they now sought to recover damages.

Counsel for the plaintiffs said Miss Huntington was at the present time in Liverpool, and, therefore, he should have to ask for an adjournment, in order to get her here.

The Judge: Very well, then, the case is adjourned on your paying the costs of the day; otherwise, there will be judgment for the defendants.

FALSE PRETENCES.—A. E. HUNT CHARGED.

At Clerkenwell, Albert Edgar Hunt, alias Bert Gaythorn, was charged with obtaining on false pretences sums of 10s. 6d. and 8s. from Cyril Stanley Button, similar amounts from Norman Irving, and 5s. from Myrtle King.

Mr. Ricketts appeared for the defendant.

Cyril Button, a clerk, of New North Road, said he saw an advertisement and went to prisoner's address in City Road with his friend, Norman Irving. The prisoner said he would be willing to put them into a sketch at 25s. or 30s. per week wages at the London Music Hall, for a fee of a guinea.

Complainant told him he could not raise the money just then; and prisoner agreed to accept 10s. 6d. on the Saturday and the same the following Saturday. The first sum was paid, and witness was given a part in a sketch called *Fate*. On the following Thursday complainant called for the purpose of rehearsing, but prisoner said there would be no rehearsal, as the young lady had not turned up. Witness then said that he could not pay the other 10s. 6d., and prisoner suggested 8s., and the balance of 2s. 6d. the next week. On a subsequent occasion when complainant called to rehearse he did not see prisoner, and had not seen him since until his arrest.

Norman Irving and Myrtle King also gave evidence.

The case was committed for trial, bail in £20 being allowed.

[See report May 1.]

HARDY v. BOWDEN.—CLAIM FOR COMMISSION.

In the Westminster Country Court, before the Registrar, the case of Hardy v. Bowden **15** was disposed of It was a claim by the plaintiff, a variety agent of Charing Cross Road, to recover commission for procuring an engagement for the defendant, Miss Florence Ellen Bowden, to appear for a fortnight in pantomime at Hull.

The plaintiff's case was that he got the defendant an engagement, and that for reasons of her own she declined to fulfil it, and therefore he now claimed his commission.

The defendant appeared, and said it was true the plaintiff did obtain an engagement for her, but she was not able to accept it, as she afterwards obtained a better one, and could not fulfil both. She was willing to pay him something for his trouble, but she thought the amount claimed (£2) was too much.

Judgment was given for the plaintiff for the amount claimed, with costs.

WILLIS v. BRADFORD.—AGENT'S COMMISSION ON RE-ENGAGEMENTS.

Before his Honour Judge Woodfall, in the Westminster County Court, the case of Willis **15** v. Bradford was tried, and was an action by the plaintiff, a dramatic agent, carrying on business at New Oxford Street, to recover the sum of £6 7s. 6d. commission on renewals of engagements obtained for the defendant, Miss Clara Bradford, a variety artist, living at 193, Kennington Road.

The plaintiff's manager said that in the latter part of 1906 they obtained for the defendant an engagement at Brighton, and in due course they were paid their commission. They afterwards discovered, however, that she had fulfilled several other engagements in other towns as a result of their introduction, and it was in respect of those engagements that they now claimed to be paid their commission.

The defendant denied that plaintiff was entitled to charge her on the subsequent engagements, as she got them through another firm of agents.

In cross-examination the witness admitted having written to the plaintiff promising· to pay his claim, but said she did so quite under a misapprehension as to her liability.

His Honour said he thought the plaintiff had made out his case, and gave judgment for the amount claimed, with costs.

THE WALDORF AND ITS RATES.

In the Chancery Division, before Mr. Justice Swinfen Eady, a summons was applied for by **29** the Corporation of Westminster for leave to issue a distress to recover rates in regard to the Waldorf, in the hands of a receiver appointed by the Court.

His Lordship made·an order that, notwithstanding the appointment of the receiver, the applicants were at liberty to take proceedings in the due course of law, before a court of summary jurisdiction, to enforce payment of the

rates, without prejudice to any question as to who might be liable for them.

FALSE PRETENCES.—D. G. D. PHAIR SENT TO PRISON

At Lambeth Police Court, David George Douglas Phair was charged, on remand, be- **30** fore Mr. Cecil Chapman, with being in the unlawful possession of some postal letters. He was further charged with obtaining postal orders of the value of 10s. each from John Henry Eames, Reginald Williams, and Alfred Rhodes by false pretences.

Mr. Cecil Chapman, remarking that the fraud was a bad one, sentenced him to three months' hard labour.

ROLLASON v. BARRASFORD.

In the Westminster County Court, before his Honour Judge Woodfall, on April 30 and **30** May 1, the case of Rollason v. Barrasford was tried, and was an action by the plaintiff, a theatrical advertising agent, of Moorgate Street Chambers, E.C., to recover the sum of £54 in respect of electrical advertisements supplied to the defendant, Mr. Thomas Barrasford, trading as Barrasford, Limited.

Counsel for the plaintiff said the action was brought to recover the sum of £54 in respect of the hire of a number of electric advertising boards supplied to the defendant for use in connection with his various halls at Brussels, Brighton, Liverpool, and other places. The principal question in dispute would be as to whether the advertisements were supplied for one month certain in each case, or whether, as the defendant was going to contend, they were only supplied as from week to week on approbation.

The defence was that they were supplied on terms of payment from week to week, and that in some cases they were faulty, and that in some instances they were not delivered in time to be of much use.

His Honour, after having heard the evidence on both sides, said he had come to the conclusion that the plaintiffs had made out their claim subject to certain deductions, and having gone carefully into the figures, he had decided that they were entitled to £48 12s 6d, and for that amount there would be judgment with costs

PACEY AND REEVES v. THORPE AND COE.—CLAIM FOR COMMISSION.

At Lambeth County Court, before his Honour Judge Emden, Thorpe and Coe, a man and **30** his wife, sketch artists, were sued by Messrs. Pacey and Reeves, agents, of Brixton Road, for £3 14s., commission due on engagements procured.

Mr. Pacey stated the engagements referred to were at Attercliffe, Middlesbrough, Derby, and the Middlesex Music Hall.

The male defendant said his defence was that his wife became ill and was unable to play on the dates concerned; consequently, no money was earned, and, therefore, no commission was due, the commission being paid upon money earned.

Judge Emden: Your explanation seems quite reasonable. I hardly think this case should have been brought into court.

Mr. Pacey stated that in conversation with him at Grimsby the man said he "would not work for cheap contracts," and he was "going to get out of it." Defendants performed at the London Pavilion on September 23 when they should have been carrying out an engagement plaintiffs obtained for them. He could not say where Thorpe and Coe performed during the week they should have been at Attercliffe—perhaps they were at Brighton; neither could he say where they were when they were to have performed at Derby, but he believed they performed at Middlesbrough.

The Judge: They allege you were performing at other places when you might have been fulfilling their engagements. Is that so?

Defendant: Only in one case, and I agree to pay commission for that. I earned £16 that week, and the commission is 16s.

His Honour gave judgment for 16s. commission, observing that defendants' answer to the remainder of the claim appeared to be perfectly reasonable.

CRUELTY TO A LIONESS.

30 A fine of £1 was imposed upon Richard Sedgwick, animal trainer, at Exeter Police Court, for cruelty in infuriating a lioness at a menagerie at Exeter during the Easter holidays.

Defendant entered the cage with the animal, fired off a revolver four or five times, and beat the beast with a stick in order to make the animal roar.

An inspector of the Society for the Prevention of Cruelty to Animals considered that the beast was caused unnecessary pain.

Defendant said the lioness "revelled" in the performance. He denied beating the beast, remarking that the blows were either against the cage or floor—not for the purpose of exciting the animal, but to make the public believe that she was going to eat the trainer.

MAY.

CURZON v. ARTHUR.—THE CAMDEN AS A MUSIC HALL.

1 In the Chancery Division, before Mr. Justice Joyce, Mr. Younger, K.C., applied on behalf of Mr. Curzon, lessor of the Camden, for an injunction restraining Mr. Robert Arthur, the lessee, from using the theatre as a music hall. The lease contained a stringent covenant that the premises should be used as a theatre, and nothing else.

Upon Mr. J. C. Matthews consenting, Mr. Justice Joyce granted a perpetual injunction with costs.

On the same evening Mr. Sidney Marler and Mr. Robert Arthur arranged the matter with Mr. Curzon, who surrendered his lease of the theatre, thereby rendering the injunction inoperative. The Camden opened on the Monday, May 4, as a music hall on the two-houses-a-night principle.

(See reports May 12 and June 19.)

FALSE PRETENCES.—A. E. HUNT (BERT GAYTHORN) SENT TO PRISON.

1 Before Mr. Loveland, K.C., at the Clerkenwell Sessions, Albert Edgar Hunt, otherwise Bert Gaythorn, 21, gilder, surrendered to his bail indicted for having obtained 18s. 6d. from Cyril Stanley Bulton and Norman Irving, clerks, and 5s. from Miss Myrtle King, Mr. Leonard Kershaw prosecuted.

The prisoner was found guilty, and ordered nine months in the second division.

(See report April 10.)

FALSE PRETENCES.—FLORENCE AND ALMEDA HARDAKER CONVICTED.

1 At the Bradford City Court, Florence and Almeda Hardaker, alias Freear, aged respectively twenty-four and twenty-two years, of 2, Well Hill Yard, Yeadon, were charged with having obtained divers sums of money by false pretences. It was stated that the accused advertised for a number of young women to constitute a troupe of vocalists and dancers, and after receiving from applicants sums of money varying in amount from 4s. 6d. to £4 10s., they absconded, taking the proceeds with them. From Elizabeth Ann Wilson they were alleged to have obtained £3 6s. between February 1 and April 1, from Nellie Fortune £3 15s. between March 14 and April 7, from Lily Jackson £2 12s. 6d. between February 7 and April 1, from Maud Brow 10s. between January 4 and February 28, from Ethel Bean and Florence Bean 4s. 6d. each between January 24 and March 14, and from Dinah French £3 0s. 7d. between February 7 and April 3.

The Bench committed the prisoners for one month each in the second division.

MELFORD v. CROSSMAN—APPEAL DISMISSED.

4 In the Court of Appeal, the case of Melford v. Crossman was heard. It was an appeal by the defendant Crossman from a verdict and judgment entered for the plaintiff at trial before Mr. Justice Jelf and a common jury.

The defendant was Mr. Robert Crossman, a theatrical manager, who had engaged the plaintiff, Mr. Mark Melford, to play the part of Widow Twankey during the run of *Aladdin* at the Shakespeare, Clapham. After the play had been running a fortnight, Mr. Crossman dismissed the plaintiff on the ground that he could not act the part. He admitted, in defence to the action, that the plaintiff had been dismissed, but he denied liability to the claim for salary during the run of the piece, which amounted to £390, on the ground that the plaintiff's acting was so bad that he was justified in the course he had taken.

Sir Gorell Barnes: But the contract was to act during the run of the piece.

Counsel: Yes; but when an actor undertakes a part there is an implied warranty by him that he is fit to play the part well. We called several witnesses, and they all agreed that, if Mr. Melford had not been dismissed, he would have wrecked the play.

Sir Gorell Barnes: Is not all that a question for the jury—they heard the evidence you rely on?

Counsel: True, but the verdict was against that evidence. There was such overwhelming testimony in our favour that there should be a new trial.

The learned counsel having read the evidence,

Without calling on Mr. Powell, K.C., and Mr. D. Warde, who appeared for the plaintiff,

Sir Gorell Barnes said the appeal failed. It was impossible in the face of the evidence to say that the verdict was against the weight of evidence. It was entirely a case for the jury.

The Lords Justices concurred.

The appeal was accordingly dismissed, with costs.

(See original case heard March 2.)

FIANA v. ARTHUR.

In the Brompton County Court, before Sir William Selfe, Antonio Fiana, an Italian, sued Mr. Robert Arthur, lessee of the Grand, Fulham, to recover the sum of 5s. in respect of the week's hire of an organ, and an additional sum for damage alleged to have been caused to the instrument while in the possession of the defendant.

Plaintiff said the organ was hired from him by the stage manager of the Grand, Fulham, for six weeks, at five shillings a week, being required to play in the pantomime. He alleged that the organ was in good condition when delivered at the theatre, but that when it was returned it was broken, and would not play.

Several witnesses said the instrument was in as good condition when returned as when received, but his Honour gave judgment for 26s., and costs.

GURNEY v. VANE.—CLAIM FOR SALARY.

At the Lambeth County Court, before his Honour Judge Emden, Mark Gurney, actor, **7** of Vauxhall Bridge Road, sued Mrs. Hutchinson Ratcliffe, professionally known as Rose Vane, residing at Corrance Road, Acre Lane, for a week's salary.

Plaintiff stated that on March 12 he answered the following advertisement in THE STAGE:—"Wanted, at once, Four Gentlemen for Sketch in London. One suitable for Heavy, one Juvenile, one Detective, one Butler. Preference in the former to those who can use foils." With three other artists, he was engaged verbally. It was said that the first performance was to be given in the Empress, Brixton, on March 23. Miss Vane told him that there would be a seven or eight weeks' run in London, followed by a long provincial tour. Plaintiff bought a dinner jacket for the part, and attended the rehearsals. Everything was ready, but there was no performance. He applied for salary, and the lady merely tossed her head. In order to be at liberty, he tendered a week's notice, and this was accepted. The other three artists were " in the same boat," one of the men having had to walk about two nights owing to the lack of salary. Plaintiff described the engagement as " a base deception," because there had been no show.

Miss Rose Vane, the defendant, denied that plaintiff was given specific dates of performances when engaged. He was informed that the agents were arranging bookings. She considered plaintiff was at liberty to perform anywhere until he got a written contract.

Judge Emden: That is something new!

Miss Vane: It is the custom of the profession.

Plaintiff: Your Honour, this lady knows very little about the profession. Had I entered into another engagement she would have " advertised " me.

Miss Vane: Certainly not. She added that she was not responsible for the delay in obtaining books, but plaintiff was certainly not told there was to be a performance at the Empress after the first week's rehearsals.

In giving judgment, his Honour described as unreasonable and unjust an arrangement whereby plaintiff was verbally engaged for this entertainment, was to give the benefit of his services at rehearsals—there had been eight—and was to wait indefinitely for a written agreement and performance. Under such a verbal agreement plaintiff could be held to be engaged for ever, because even if he were allowed to take another engagement until dates were fixed he would have to cancel that directly defendant called upon him. Judgment must be for plaintiff for the amount claimed, with costs.

SHOWMEN AND MITCHAM FAIR.

Before Mr. Justice Neville, in the Chancery Division, Mr. Pattison, for the Conservators of **8** Mitcham Common, applied for an injunction. He stated that there were originally forty-five defendants against whom these proceedings were taken to restrain them from encroaching on the Common with shows, exhibitions, and appliances for amusements. Of these forty-one had applied for leave to withdraw their defences, and had submitted to a perpetual injunction. He now asked for an injunction against the other four.

The defendants did not appear, and his Lordship granted the injunction asked for.

FRENCH v. WHITMEE.—INFRINGEMENTS IN PORTABLES

In the King's Bench Division, before Mr. Justice Jelf, Samuel French, Limited, moved **9** to enter judgment against Mr. Alfred Whitmee, general manager of a portable theatre, for having infringed their sole right of producing the play entitled *Lost in London*.

Mr. Morton Smith, who appeared for the plaintiffs in support of the motion, said the defendant had produced the play at Great Missenden without the plaintiffs' consent. He asked that there should be judgment for the plaintiffs for 40s., and that the interim injunction restraining the defendant from repeating the offence should be made perpetual.

His lordship entered judgment for the plaintiffs for 40s. and costs, and made the injunction perpetual.

In a second case the learned judge granted an injunction restraining the defendant, Mr. Whitmee, from producing *The Private Secretary*, and directed an inquiry as to the damages sustained by Messrs. W. F. Fladgate and W. Muskerry Tilson, the proprietors of the rights of representation of the play.

MOSS EMPIRES v. WILLS.—THE BARRING CLAUSE.

In the King's Bench Division, before Mr. Justice Jelf, Mr. Holman Gregory, on behalf **9** of the plaintiffs, the Moss Empires, Ltd., proprietors of the Olympia Theatre of Varieties, Liverpool, asked for an injunction restraining Mr. H. O. Wills, music-hall artist, from appearing at the New Pavilion Hall, Liverpool, or at any place of amusement within a certain area, as specified in his contract, until the contract with the plaintiffs had been completed.

The defendant did not appear, and his lordship granted a perpetual injunction, and directed him to pay nominal damages, with costs.

THE WALDORF.

In the Chancery Division, before Mr. Justice Swinfen Eady, the case of the Waldorf Theatre **9** Syndicate v. Shubert came on. The plaintiffs asked for judgment in default of the defendant's appearance.

The Judge: The defendant, I understand, has left the theatre and gone to America.

Mr. Crossman: That is so. But he may come back any day and take possession of the theatre and re-open it, and do considerable injury to our property, and we desire to prevent that.

The Judge said that, under the circumstances, he would grant an injunction restraining the defendant from committing waste or damage during the residue of his tenancy, and from committing any act of his own which was an offence against the laws and regulations of the London County Council, or other local authorities, Mr. Morgan, the receiver appointed, to be continued until further order.

BOSTOCK v. BERMINGHAM.—THE BARRING CLAUSE.

In the Hamilton Court, N.B., before Sheriff Thompson, Mr. E. H. Bostock, Glasgow, proprietor of the Hamilton Hippodrome, petitioned for interim interdict against Peter Bermingham, comedian, Bridgeton, to prevent him from appearing at the New Century, Motherwell in respect that he had entered into an agreement with the pursuer not to appear at any place of entertainment within a distance of ten miles of Hamilton Hippodrome prior to November, 1908.

Mr. Archd. Campbell, writer, Glasgow, produced on behalf of the pursuer the contract.

Mr. C. K. Murray, writer, Motherwell, who appeared for Mr. Bermingham, held that the contract was not valid, because it did not bear the signature of both parties, and was not attested.

Having heard both agents, Sheriff Thompson refused interim interdict. The document produced, he said, did not bear the signature of pursuer, nor the admitted signature of defender, and it was not attested by witnesses. Had the case been one for damages or permanent interdict, and a proof taken on the specific document, if a binding contract, his Lordship said it might have been different.

Pursuer's agent thereafter intimated an appeal to the Sheriff-Principal.

STAGE PLAY LICENSES AND VARIETY PERFORMANCES.—THE CAMDEN.

An application at Clerkenwell Police Court was made by Mr. T. M. Knight against the Camden, which, he alleged, was being carried on as a music-hall, although the management had not obtained the necessary license from the London County Council. He was instructed by the New Bedford Palace of Varieties, which was likely to be injurious'y affected by that change, and therefore wished to take action against the Camden. The latter was licensed for plays by the Lord Chamberlain, but it had not the London County Council license for music and dancing, and, incidentally, smoking. The conversion from theatre to music hall took place a fortnight ago. There was, perhaps, an important point involved—i.e., as to whether the Lord Chamber'ain's license covered a variety programme.

Mr. Bros said that the application was made under an old Act, and the procedure laid down in that Act must be followed. He declined to grant summonses on information. The applicants must apply to "the parish constable."

(See report June 19.)

MOSS EMPIRES v. MARIE LLOYD—THE BARRING CLAUSE.

At Glasgow the Moss Empires sought to interdict Miss Marie Lloyd from continuing her appearance at the Glasgow Pavilion. Counsel argued that she was under a £1,000 contract with them not to appear within ten miles of Glasgow from May to October.

The Sheriff refused an interdict, as the contract was not signed by both parties.

(See report May 16.)

GIBBON v. KITTS.—A BREACH OF CONTRACT.

Before his Honour Judge Woodfall in the Westminster County Court the case of Gibbon v. Kitts was tried.

The plaintiff was Miss Phyllis Gibbon, a variety artist. She sued the defendant, Mr. Chas. Kitts, a dramatic agent, carrying on business at 3, Bedford Street, Strand, to recover the sum of £36 damages for breach of contract.

Mr. May was counsel for the defendant, and said his case was that the plaintiff was engaged on the basis of no play, no pay.

Counsel on behalf of Miss Gibbon said that in October of 1907 his client was engaged by the defendant to take a leading part in a sketch called *The Cuckoo*. It was arranged that she should appear in it for three weeks in London, and that after that she should go with the defendant and his wife on a fifteen weeks' tour in America. A contract was signed, and the plaintiff went to America, where the sketch was produced, but at the expiration of six weeks the defendant told her that he could not go on with the tour, as it was not a success, but that if she would return to England he would reproduce it there, and find her engagements for the other nine weeks. She did return to her home, and subsequently she received a letter from the defendant to the effect that he saw no chance of going on with the sketch, but that he had mentioned her name in respect of another engagement.

His Honour, in giving judgment, said that, so far as he could see, the action against the defendant was entirely undefended. It was upon him to show that he was entitled to put an end to the contract with the plaintiff, and he had totally failed to do so. The plaintiff was engaged for fifteen weeks under a contract at a salary of £4 a week, and, after appearing for six weeks, she was informed by the defendant that he was not going on with the tour. Whatever his reasons might have been for adopting that course did not affect the plaintiff's case, and she was entitled to recover her nine weeks' salary by way of damages. It was admitted that she had been paid £1 16s. on account of the amount now claimed, and therefore judgment would be for the sum of £34 4s., with costs.

RUSHBROOK v. GRIMSBY PALACE.—WHEN IS A STAGE-MANAGER A WORKMAN?

In the King's Bench Division, before Mr. Justice Phillimore and Mr. Justice Darling, came on the case of Rushbrook v. the Grimsby Palace, as an appeal from the Grimsby County Court (see STAGE Year-Book, 1908, page 199).

In January, 1907, the plaintiff's son, Mr. Frank Rushbrook, entered the employment of the defendants as stage-manager under a written agreement, and in the following month he was killed by the curtain falling and striking him on the head. The plaintiff brought an action to recover damages under the Employers' Liability Act, and the jury awarded her £150. The learned county court judge, however, held that the deceased was not a workman within the meaning of the Act, and entered judgment for the defendants. By the agreement the deceased was appointed stage-manager, and he had to attend to the electric plant and to the billing. But evidence was given that the deceased also attended to the raising and lowering of the curtain, which was worked by a lever, and removed furniture between the turns.

Mr. Giveen, for Mrs. Rushbrook, submitted that under these circumstances the deceased was a workman within the meaning of the Act, and that the plaintiff was entitled to recover.

Mr. Justice Darling, in delivering judgment, said that as to whether the deceased man was a "workman" within the meaning of Section 8 of the Employers' Liability Act, 1880, he thought that the principles applicable were quite plain. They were laid down in the case of "Morgan v. the London General Omnibus Company." They must look and see what was the substantial employment of the deceased man. They could not say deceased was not a workman simply because he was called a stage-manager in the contract of employment. He thought they must look at the evidence to see what work the deceased man had to do to see whether he was substantially employed in manual labour. The evidence showed that as part of his duty he shifted the furniture and the side scenes. He did these things not as a volunteer, but as part of his duty. The matter had been left to the Court as a matter of law, and it appeared from the facts that the deceased man was employed in manual labour. The appeal, therefore, would be allowed, with costs.

Mr. Justice Phillimore said that in the contract it appeared that deceased was employed as a stage-manager, to shift scenery and furniture, to do some rough carpentering, and certain work to the electric plant. His work might be compared to that of a foreman. In his opinion, therefore, the deceased man was a "workman" within the meaning of the section.

Judgment was entered for the plaintiff for £150, with costs.

MOSS EMPIRES v. MARIE LLOYD.—THE BARRING CLAUSE.

An application was made in the Court of Session, Edinburgh, to have Miss Marie Lloyd **16** interdicted from appearing at the Pavilion Theatre, Glasgow, in that she had entered into a contract with the Moss Companies, Limited, not to appear within so many miles of the Moss theatres.

On the preceding Wednesday, May 13, an application was made at the Glasgow Sheriff's Court, but it was pleaded that the lady repudiated her signature, and the Court declined to grant an interdict.

Counsel now submitted that the contract left no loophole, and it was of the greatest importance that the sanctity of these contracts should be maintained.

Lord Guthrie refused to grant an interim interdict, and intimated that the case would be heard on the Monday. His lordship stated that if the validity of the signature was to be denied he expected Miss Lloyd to be present.

On the Monday, May 18, there was no appearance for Miss Lloyd, and Mr. Allan, of Messrs Menzies, Bruce-Low, and Thomson, W. S., agents for the complainers, moved for interim interdict.

Lord Guthrie passed the note, granted interim interdict, and ordered answers in eight days. (See report July 5.)

SCOTT (BRODIE) v. MACNAGHTEN—CONTRACTS FOR SKETCHES.

At the Bloomsbury County Court, before Judge Bacon, Mr. George Scott, trading as **18** Matthew Brodie and Co., Tavistock Hotel, W.C., sued Mr. Frank Macnaghten, of the Foresters', E., for the sum of £35.

Mr. Henn Collins, barrister, appeared for the plaintiff, and Mr. Martin O'Connor was counsel for the defendant.

The case had been remitted from the High Court, the claim being for one week's salary for performances at Sadler's Wells, as per contract dated November 1, 1907. The performances were to have taken place between December 23 and 28 last. A special defence had been entered in behalf of Mr. Macnaghten, in which it was contended that the contract sued upon was an illegal contract, as the sketch which the plaintiff was to produce was a stage play, and defendant's music hall was not licensed for the production of stage plays. The defendant relied upon the provisions of the Theatres Act, 1843 (Sec. 11). The sketch which led to the litigation was entitled *The Drummer of the 76th*, in which the late Matthew Brodie, Plaintiff's partner, enacted the part of Napoleon Bonaparte and Miss Dorothea Vivian that of Charles Bonaparte Corvont, the drummer. The other characters represented included Marshal Lannes, the scene being a cottage outside Ulm in the year 1805.

Mr. Henn Collins explained that the contract made between the parties was for a series of performances beginning at the Palace, Bow, followed by other weekly engagements at other music halls controlled by defendant. The salary was fixed at £35 a week in London and £37 in the provinces, and it was arranged that the Surrey, Sadler's Wells, and the Foresters' should follow, the company subsequently going to Southampton. At the defendant's desire, plaintiff's company performed on December 16, the second week, at the Foresters' instead of at the Surrey, and the following week plaintiff was asked to substitute Southampton for Sadler's Wells. Mr. Scott pointed out that such an alteration would put him to additional expense, whereupon Mr. Fredk. Baugh, defendant's manager, told him that if his company did not play at Southampton as he desired they should not perform anywhere else. When the company presented themselves at Sadler's Wells defendant refused to admit them to the theatre. The next week they performed at the Surrey, and eventually defendant declined to pay for the week between December 23 and 28, and gave notice of the defence now relied on.

Mr. O'Connor said both parties knew perfectly well that the halls were not licensed for the production of stage plays, and the contract had been entered into with this knowledge.

THE DEFENCE.

Mr. O'Connor submitted the contract was an illegal one. Plaintiff had admitted the sketch was a stage play. He did not admit he knew the houses were music halls, but he knew perfectly well sketches were produced in music halls and not in theatres.

Judge Bacon: What is sauce for the goose is sauce for the gander. I don't mean by that that any of these parties are easily taken in; but it does not lie in Macnaghten's mouth to say "Scott knew all about it, but I am an innocent child." I daresay there are evasions of the law, and there is such a thing as not being found out.

Mr. O'Connor said that Macnaghten would have been liable to fines amounting to £60 a week.

Mr. Fredk. Baugh said he did not know that the troupe belonged to the plaintiff: the contract was signed by the late Mr. Brodie. Mr. Brodie told him the sketch had been produced at the Coronet.

Judge Bacon: Then you knew it had been

produced in a theatre. You agreed to produce it, meaning to risk it or what?

Witness: We are liable to any common informer who comes up and prosecutes. It was to avoid the risk of a prosecution—having two sketches in the bill for the same week—that Mr. Scott was asked to go to Southampton.

Mr. Baugh continued that he told Mr. Scott he was compelled to pay the extra expenses under the provisions of the Arbitrator's Award. Every week he was paying artists extra money on the basis of the Award.

In cross-examination, witness said that in twenty years' experience he had known of only two prosecutions which had not been instituted by the theatrical managers. There was an agreement with the theatrical managers that there should be no prosecution if only one sketch appeared in the bill at the same time, and another sketch was billed that week.

Witness: I was between a police-court on one side and a breach of contract on the other.

Judge Bacon: Between the devil and the deep sea.

JUDGMENT.

His Honour held that, on the authority of the decision in De Begnis and Armistead, it was impossible for either party to recover upon a contract which was known to be illegal to both contracting parties. In this case, no matter what his suspicions might be, he did not think it had been proved that Mr. Brodie's partner, Mr. Scott, knew that it was a contract in breach of the law. There was no such evidence. He could not hold that this had been a contract to perform an illegal act, and there must be a judgment for the plaintiff.

Mr. O'Connor asked for a stay of execution for fourteen days with a view of an appeal, which his Honour granted.

(See report, November 24.)

KARNO v. BRABOURNE.
ALLEGED BREACH OF CONTRACT.

In the King's Bench, before Mr. Justice Lawrance and a special jury, Mr. Fred **20** Karno claimed damages from Mr. John Brabourne for breach of a contract dated June 29, 1907, under which the defendant had agreed to play the principal part in a sketch which was variously described as *The Tragedy of Errors* and *Up the Pole*, for five weeks. His salary was to be £20 a week. He played for four weeks in the provinces, and in the fifth week the sketch was to be played for the first time in London at the Holborn Empire and the London, Shoreditch. But the defendant declined to appear at these houses, alleging that it was an implied condition of the contract that he should only be required to appear at one music hall on the same day.

The case was continued on the following day, May 21.

The jury returned a verdict for the defendant on the claim, and awarded him £20 damages on his counter claim.

On the following Monday, May 25, his Lordship gave judgment for the defendant in accordance with the verdict, putting the same construction upon the contract as the jury—namely, that it was an implied term that the defendant was only to play at one hall a day.

Mr. G. Doughty asked for a stay of execution, but his lordship refused to grant the application.

SUMMER ENTERTAINMENTS SYNDICATE
v. CAMPBELL.
SEQUEL TO A BROKEN CONTRACT.

Before Mr. Under Sheriff Burchell and a jury at the London Sheriff's Court the case **20** of the Summer Entertainments Syndicate v. Campbell came on for the assessment of damages for breach of contract.

Mr. R. V. Bankes appeared for the plaintiffs, and the defendant was not represented.

Mr. Bankes stated the case was one in which the defendant, a variety artist, had flagrantly broken his contract, and he asked the jury to award such damages as would show artists that they could not break their contracts with impunity. The plaintiffs carried on business by providing summer entertainments at Bognor, Eastbourne, Hastings, Lowestoft, Cromer. In 1903 it appeared the plaintiffs "discovered" the defendant and brought him out. The plaintiffs gave him an agreement under which he was to appear in the plaintiffs' companies. He appeared in 1906-1907, was under agreement to appear from Whitsun to September again in 1909, with an option for 1910. He was paid £6 10s., with music, dresses, etc., found. During 1906 and 1907, when he appeared at, among other places, Eastbourne and Hastings he was a great success, so much so, said counsel, that by special request he was engaged by the plaintiffs to appear at Eastbourne in the season this year. He asked to be released from his contract, but this was impossible. Subsequently it was discovered that he had sailed for Australia, where he had accepted a contract to appear at a salary, it was stated, of £20 per week. Counsel said that as a result of the excellent turns provided by the defendant the profits of the plaintiffs went up very considerably from £756 to £1,015 at Bognor in 1907. The people at Eastbourne were so delighted with the defendant's performances that they made it a *sine quâ non* that in accepting plaintiffs' contract the defendant should appear. "Instead," said counsel, "defendant levanted to Australia and left plaintiffs in the lurch. The contract was a very important one, and £300 would not represent the plaintiffs' loss by reason of defendant's breach.

Mr. Wallis Arthur, the managing director of the Summer Entertainments, Co., Limited, gave evidence in support of counsel's statement. He said his company found the defendant in 1903. In 1905 at Eastbourne he was a great success, and also at Hastings and Eastbourne in 1906. By special request he appeared at Eastbourne in 1907, and it was by special request he was to appear at Bognor in 1908.

At Eastbourne for 1908 he got his contract on condition that he engaged Mr. Campbell. There was no written agreement. He gave his word and they relied on his producing the defendant. Plaintiff added that £250 would not cover his loss if he lost the Eastbourne contract.

There was no defence, and the jury assessed the damages at £100, judgment being entered with costs.

RICHARDS, BURNEY, AND CO. v. SYD MAY.

In the Shoreditch County Court, before his Honour Judge Bray, Richards, Burney, and **21** Co. were the plaintiffs in an action to recover from Mr. Syd May, a music hall artist, £12, being damages at the rate of one week's salary for a breach of contract made on February 5, 1908, to appear on May 10, 1908 at the Cambridge.

Mr. Whetton, barrister, who appeared for the plaintiffs, said the claim was for a breach of a contract made to appear at the Cambridge Music Hall, but as a fact defendant failed to put in an appearance on the first night. He said he would prove his case.

Mr. Richards was then called, and said that he engaged the defendant to appear, but he did not.

Judge Bray: Did it affect the receipts of the house at all?

Witness: There is no doubt as to that.

Judge Bray: Tell me how you make out that it would affect your house.

Witness: Well, you see, having engaged an artist, you freely advertise that he is to appear on such and such nights, and people who know him naturally come to the house to see their favourite, and if he is not appearing they go and tell others, and it cannot do the house any good, that is certain.

Judge Bray: Very well, on that evidence I will award the plaintiffs £12 damages and costs.

Judgment was entered accordingly.

BATTEN v. REES.—SKETCH PARTNERSHIP PROFITS.

A sketch produced at Middlesbrough formed the subject of an action heard by Judge **25** Templer at the Middlesbrough County Court. The defendant was Phil Rees, music hall artist, and a claim for £11 13s. was brought against him by Wm. S. Batten, of St. Paul's Road, Middlesbrough. Mr. A. Forbes appeared for the plaintiff, and Mr. F. W. Bain, of Sunderland, for the defence.—Mr. Forbes explained that the action concerned the sketch *Stable Lads*. A partnership was discussed and entered into between Rees, Batten, and a third person by which Batten was entitled to one-fifth of the profits in respect of the sketch. Until January last defendant paid the money, but then he suddenly stopped payment.

For the defence it was submitted that there were a number of conditions not embodied in the agreement.—His Honour gave judgment for plaintiff for the amount claimed.

JUNE.

GANDILLOT v. EDWARDES AND ANOTHER —ALLEGED INFRINGEMENT—RIGHT OF TRANSLATION.

Mr. Justice Bigham, sitting without a jury in the King's Bench Division, had before him **2** the case of Gandillot v. George Edwardes and another. This was an action brought by M. Gandillot, French dramatic author, to recover damages for infringement of copyright.

Mr. Eldon Bankes, K.C., and Mr. E. F. Spence appeared for the plaintiff, and Mr. Scrutton, K.C., Mr. Gill, K.C., and Mr. R. J. Willis represented the defendants.

Mr. Bankes, in opening the case, said it was an action brought by the plaintiff against three gentlemen, one of whom, Mr. James Davis, had since died, for infringement of copyright. The two surviving defendants were Mr. George Edwardes, and Mr. George Dance, an equally well-known manager of provincial theatrical companies. Mr. James Davis was a dramatic author who wrote under the name of "Owen Hall." The plaintiff complained that the defendants had infringed his copyright in his play, *La Mariée Récalcitrante*. The action was brought under William IV., chapter 15, giving an author of a dramatic piece the liberty of representation in any place of dramatic entertainment, and placing under

a penalty any person who, during the continuance of the liberty, caused any representation to be made without the consent of the author.

Under the Convention of Berne, and the International Copyright Act, the provisions of the enactment were extended to persons who wrote plays in France. The only point, therefore, was whether or not the plaintiff did, within the meaning of that section, give his consent in writing to the production in the United Kingdom of his play by Mr. Edwardes and afterwards by Mr. George Dance in the provinces under the title of *The Girl from Kay's*. It was now admitted that *The Girl from Kay's* was an adaptation of the plaintiff's work.

It was submitted by Mr. Scrutton that the plaintiff, not having complied with the statute, 49 and 50 Vic., under which he must produce a translation within ten years in the United Kingdom, his right to prevent representation had ceased.

Mr. Bankes, in reply, contended that an adaptation or version was not a translation, and that the section cited did not, therefore, apply. He referred to "Wood v. Chart" (L.R., 10, Eq., 193). Article 10 of the Berne Convention he relied upon as giving protection against adaptations.

Mr. Scrutton having replied.

Mr. Bankes said that he was glad to say it would not be necessary to trouble his lordship any further. As the result of his learned friend's argument, his client thought it was better to come to an arrangement with the other side. Both sides had acted very reasonably, and it was agreed the action should be dismissed, each party paying their own costs. Mr. Edwardes and Mr. Dance had said, as far as they were able to do so, that they would, in any future representations of the play, state that it was an adaptation from M. Gandillot's play. He ought to repeat that this was one of those cases in which the plaintiff, having seen the documents, quite accepted the view that Mr. Edwardes was not personally responsible for the plaintiff's play having been utilised .

Mr. Gill said that the point the defendants took up, and, had it been necessary, would have taken to the House of Lords, was that the point raised by his learned friend Mr. Scrutton was conclusive.

The action, therefore, was dismissed, each side paying their own costs.

ANTONY v. DE FRECE—CLAIM FOR SALARY.

In the Westminster County Court his Honour Judge Woodfall tried the case of Antony v. **3** De Frece, in which the plaintiff, a professional conjuror, sued Mr. Jack De Frece, theatrical agent, of Imperial Mansions, W.C., to recover the sum of £4 balance of salary due to him.

The plaintiff conducted his case in person, and said that, so far as Mr. De Frece was concerned, the action was quite a friendly one. The fact was that some time ago he (plaintiff) became a bankrupt, and all his creditors, with the exception of a Mr. Swanson, a moneylender, were passed as creditors. Swanson, however, refused to come in under the bankruptcy, and chose to make a claim against Mr. De Frece in respect of his (plaintiff's) salary, and when he applied to Mr. De Frece for payment of his salary, a sum of £4 was deducted in respect of Swanson's claim. He (plaintiff) was wanting money at the time, and agreed to sign for the amount due to him less £4, which had been claimed by Swanson, but he signed the receipt without prejudice to his claim for the balance.

For the defence, a witness was called on behalf of Mr. De Frece, and said that when the plaintiff was paid the balance due to him, after deducting Swanson's claim, he agreed to accept it in settlement.

His Honour said he could not see that the plaintiff had made out any case, and gave judgment for the defendant with costs.

POCKNILL v. GIBBONS.—AN EXPLOSION ON THE STAGE.

Before his Honour Judge Woodfall, in the Westminster County Court, the case of Pocknill v. Gibbons was tried. It was an **3** action by the plaintiff, Robert Pocknill, an electrician, to recover damages against Mr. Walter Gibbons for personal injuries sustained owing to the alleged negligence of the defendant's electrician at the Croydon Empire. Mr. W. Clark Hall, instructed by Mr. C. F. Appleton, solicitor, appeared for the plaintiff. The plaintiff was called, and said he was formerly employed in Mr. Wal Pink's sketch *The Beacon Bell.* A cannon had to be introduced, which was actuated by an electrical current. At the Croydon Empire, Mr. Wells, who was in charge of the electrical apparatus, put on the power before plaintiff was ready, and the result was that the gun went off and his eyes were seriously injured. His charge of negligence against the defendant was that his electrician ought not to have put on the power until he received notice to do so, and that had it not been for that the accident would never have happened.

In cross-examination, the witness said that when he first made this claim he told his solicitors that his salary was £2 a week. As a matter of fact, it was thirty shillings a week, but it resulted in an average of £2 a week with what he "picked up."

His Honour, after having heard evidence on behalf of the defendant at some length, gave judgment for the plaintiff for £30 damages, with costs.

MUSICAL COPYRIGHT—TEST CASE.

At Bow Street Police Court James Connor, Neal Street, Shaftesbury Avenue, was summoned, before Sir Albert De Rutzen, **4** for unlawfully offering for sale the pirated copy of a musical work, to wit, a perforated music roll, being the reproduction of a pianoforte accompaniment of a song called "Bandelero."

Mr. Muir, who appeared in support of the summons said this was an action brought for the purpose of deciding a point of law of great public interest. The persons for whom he appeared, who were interested, as composers or owners of copyrights in certain musical works, desired to raise the question as to whether their rights extended to perforated rolls for reproducing their music on pianolas and similar machines. For this purpose it was arranged that proceedings of a perfectly friendly character should be taken in order that the question of law might be raised. The defendant, who was a perfectly respectable hawker, was supplied with a perforated roll, and offered it for sale to a police officer who was waiting outside Bow Street Police Court armed with a request in writing from the owner of the copyright to seize the roll. This was done, and the defendant was taken before Mr. Fenwick, who was then sitting at Bow Street, and a summons was granted. The hearing of the summons was fixed for July 15 last, but it was adjourned for the convenience of counsel.

The long vacation intervened, and Mr. Fenwick's long illness, resignation, and lamented death accounted for the further delay.

Mr. Muir proceeded to say that his friend, Mr. Scrutton and other gentlemen who appeared on the other side would be pleased if his view of the law as to musical copyright was upheld. They agreed with him that it was an absolute injustice that manufacturers of pianolas should be able to reproduce—without paying a penny for the right to do so—the music which the genius and labour of other men had created. Manufacturers of these and similar instruments were making enormous fortunes without paying a farthing to the composer or the owner of the copyright of the music they reproduced, and he (counsel) contended that it was not the intention of the Legislature that such a state of things should exist. Mr. Muir went on to quote cases in support of his contention that the Musical Copyright Act was intended to apply to all kinds of musical reproduction, whether on paper or on metal. Many people, he said, were labouring under a just sense of wrong in being deprived of the fruits of their labour, and it was hoped that the existing state of things would be remedied by the magistrate's decision.

Formal evidence as to the sale having been given, Mr. Scrutton, K.C., who (with Mr. George Elliott) appeared for the defendant, said he did not agree with Mr. Muir. The sale of this perforated roll seemed to have been arranged, and he considered it an abuse of the process of the Court.

Mr. Muir read correspondence to show that it had been arranged to bring this action in a friendly way, and said that the late Mr. Fenwick was fully acquainted with all the circumstances.

At a late hour all the summonses were adjourned.

The same course was pursued in connection with a second summons against the defendant for offering a talking machine disc for sale. In that case Mr. Travers Humphreys appeared for the defendant, and intimated that the case would be fought out on a point of law.

(See report of judgment June 29.)

ROLT v. BEECHER.

In the Shoreditch County Court, before his Honour Judge Smyly, K.C., Mr. Henry Garnet **4** Rolt, of Christleton, Chester, described as a theatrical manager, sought to recover £50 damages against Mr. Trevor St. John Beecher, of the Sebright Arms and Regent Theatre, 26 and 28, Coate Street, Hackney Road, N.E., a licensed victualler and theatre proprietor. The hearing of the action had been remitted from the High Court by order of the Master under Sec. 45 of the County Court Act.

The claim, as set forth, was that whereby the defendant agreed to provide a first-class combination of competent artists for the performance of a pantomime, entitled *The Babes in the Wood,* at the Kursaal, Bexhill-on-Sea, for six nights and three *matinées,* commencing January 6, 1908, and whereas the defendant failed to do so on Saturday evening, January 11, the plaintiff claimed as liquidated damages the sum of £50, being the amount in the agreement mentioned as damages in the event of any failure on the part of the defendant to perform his portion of the contract.

Mr. Groser, barrister, appeared for the plaintiff, and Mr. Turrell was counsel for the defence.

In opening the case for the plaintiff, Mr. Groser said the trouble that had arisen was due to the failure on the part of the defendant to pay the artists on the Saturday evening before the last performance, with the result that no performance could be carried out. So far as he knew, the defence were setting up a legal technical defence that the £50 was a penalty and not liquidated damages, which would have to be argued before his honour. By reason of the unhappy position created by the fact that no salaries were paid, two of the principal artists, Munro and Wilson, refused to play. They were the leading comedians playing the part of the robbers, and it would be easily seen that serious consequences would arise. The defendant's representative, Mr. St. John, who was the manager of the company, then, to make matters worse, tried to leave the town with his portmanteau, but he was haled back by the aggrieved artists from the station. The girls who were in the cast were absolutely stranded, and, by the generosity of the plaintiff, were given enough money to get back to London, or otherwise the consequences might have been more serious still. He based his case that it was agreed that a sum of money should be paid in the event of anything untoward happening, and this had happened, causing financial loss to the plaintiff.

The first witness called was Mr. Henry Garnett Rolt, the plaintiff, who said he was the manager of the theatre at Bexhill on the occasion in question. On the Saturday, however, he was laid up, so that he was not in a position to say too positively what did occur. He had seen the play during the week. It would be impossible to play the piece without the principal comedians, Munro and Wilson.

Mr. Groser: When you heard what had occurred and that the girls were stranded, what did you do?—Witness: I gave them £4 11s. 3d. to get them all out of the town.

Mr. Groser: Did you ever hear from anyone that the performance could have been carried out by understudies?—Witness: There was absolutely no mention of understudies to me. If I had known that it was possible to perform the play with first-class artists I should have had no objection to their going on.

Mr. Robert Welch was the next witness; and he said he had been the superintendent of the Kursaal for the past twelve years. *The Babes in the Wood* pantomime had been at St. Leonards-on-Sea the week prior to coming to Bexhill. The theatre was quite ready for the performance on the Saturday night, but he heard that Munro and Wilson would not play, and that Mr. St. John—who was responsible for the salaries—had paid them 5s. each. When he returned from his tea there was a row in progress about it.

Mr. Groser: Did you hear it in front of Mr. St. John that he had been brought back from the station? Witness: Yes, several times. Mr. Groser: And what was the reason assigned for bringing him back? Witness: I understood they were afraid he was going to run away without paying them. Mr. Groser: Were some of the artists willing to perform? Witness: Yes, most anxious to do so; they seemed to want to come to some amicable arrangement, so that they could get their salaries, but Munro and Wilson stopped in the buffet and declined to have anything to do with it on principle.

Mr. Edgar Benjamin Willett, a solicitor practising at Bexhill-on-Sea, said he was called to the theatre shortly before eight o'clock on the Saturday evening to see what could be arranged.

Mr. Groser: Did you see Mr. St. John? Witness: No; he had apparently disappeared, from what I could gather. Mr. Groser: You being there in the capacity of a solicitor, what did you think as to the closing of the doors? Witness: I considered it a very right and proper thing to do; in fact, it would not have been proper to have done otherwise.

DEFENCE.

Mr. Chas. Trevor, a witness for the defendant, said when Munro and Wilson refused to perform there were still twenty-three left, and it would have been quite easy to have played *The Babes in the Wood*. He himself was quite willing to act the part of Friar Tuck, his original part, and one of the Robbers, whilst Mr St John would have played the other, but Mr. Rolt would not allow it.

Judge Smyly: A great deal depends on this; had the parts been understudied by anyone at all? I mean, had you got regular understudies? You cannot fence with the term, you know, because an understudy is one who is always there watching how his or her chief performs, so as to be able to follow as nearly as possible in their footsteps. Witness: There was no actual understudy, because there was no necessity, as there were others who knew the parts so well.

Judge Smyly: If there was no understudy it would seem to me that he had a right to close his theatre instead of running any risks.

Mr. Groser: Do you not think that it was the proper thing to do to close the theatre, as two of the artists would not appear, as their salaries were not paid? Witness: We were not given the chance to perform, and then, again, there was very little salary owing; most of them had "subbed" the majority of their money during the week.

Judge Smyly: It seems to me that it might have been a very dangerous precedent to try and play a pantomime with two people in it who had not played it before; anyway, not at that place.

Mrs. Trevor, the wife of the last witness, was called, and said she acted the part of the principal boy in the pantomime. She quite well remembered the circumstance of Wilson and Munro refusing to go on, because the salaries were not paid in full, but, all the same, the others were quite willing and able to give a show if Mr. Rolt had allowed them to.

Miss Harper was called last for the defence, and bore out the statements of the last two witnesses.

Mr. Groser then asked for permission to recall his client to deny the statement made that any mention had been made to him that the piece could be easily performed, as there were some who knew the parts, and that in face of that he refused to open the theatre. Mr. Rolt went into the box and denied absolutely that any such suggestion had been made to him. He pointed out also that the many wild propositions that were put to him could not be acceded to, as the defendant was looking to him for 65 per cent. of the takings, or his manager, and he would have been responsible for that sum had he opened up.

Mr. Turrell then addressed his Honour, and said that he submitted that if a person agreed to put on a first-class company at a theatre to play a certain piece, because one of the actors played a certain part on the Monday, Tuesday, and Wednesday, there was nothing binding on him that that particular actor should appear on any other day of the week, or, again, even if you liked, so long as another just as competent artist was provided. In this case there were two actors there who were perfectly willing to perform the parts vacated by two "strikers," and he wished to point out that there was nothing binding upon a person to provide an understudy to carry out such an agreement as the present one. If it was well known that there was someone who could take the part at a pinch. The whole point as to the question of the breach was were the artists, Trevor and St. John, capable of taking the places of Munro and Wilson, and he submitted that it was for the plaintiff to prove that they were not. There had been a great deal of prejudice imported into the case, as the salaries had not been paid, but he asked his Honour to treat the case as one of illness on the part of two actors. In conclusion, Mr. Turrell said his friend must fail, as he had brought his action for liquidated damages, whereas it was clearly a penalty, under which circumstances his friend would be out of Court.

In reply, Mr. Groser said he was confident his action laid as liquidated damages, and as to the breach being on the plaintiff's side he had only to point out that the whole question arose only upon a breach of the defendant, and that was in not paying the salaries of the artists.

Judge Smyly said the question was too important to give a hurried decision, and he would look up the authorities and deliver judgment on some future date.

(See report of reserved judgment June 23.)

METROPOLE, GLASGOW, LTD., v. HARD-ACRE. — "BULLOCK" VERSION OF "EAST LYNNE."

Before the Lord Justice-Clerk and Lords Stormonth-Darling, Low, and Ardwall, in the
9 Court of Session, Edinburgh, the Division disposed of a reclaiming note against the interlocutor of Lord Guthrie in the action raised to decide the question of playright in the "Bullock" version of *East Lynne*. The playright was claimed by the pursuer, John Pitt Hardacre, Ferndene, Sydney Road, Staines, Middlesex, and his complaint was that the defenders, the Metropole Theatre, Limited, Glasgow, had been presenting the drama without his permission. Accordingly, Mr. Pitt Hardacre asked declarator of his rights in the play, and that the defenders should be interdicted from producing it or any colourably altered or modified version. He also sued for £250 in name of damages. Lord Guthrie found the pursuer entitled to the declarator and interdict sought, with expenses, but held that, in view of his having assigned his rights to another party, who was not a party to the action, no damages could be awarded.

The Division adhered to the interlocutor of the Lord Ordinary, with expenses.

The Lord Justice-Clerk said that as regarded the facts he was satisfied that it was made out (1) that one Chute produced what was called the Bullock version at Doncaster in 1866; (2) that the policeman part in that edition was written up into a substantial character part such as admitted of proprietary of copyright in it, which might be infringed by anyone having a version performed in which this character part was introduced similarly to what was done in the Chute version; (3) that the version produced by the defenders was of the nature of an infringement, in respect of which the pursuer was entitled, if he had the right by assignation from Chute and thereby held the right of production, to have the defenders interdicted from infringing his right. The real question, assuming that view of the facts to be right, was whether Hardacre was so put in Chute's place as the holder of the right that he was entitled to a judgment, as Chute would have been entitled to a

judgment had he not divested himself by selling to Hardacre. It was in respect of the special circumstances surrounding the registration of Hardacre that the defenders maintained that whatever the facts were as to the existence of the right, Hardacre could not prevail as having been duly put in the right by assignation. It appeared that in June, 1888 Chute granted the assignation to Hardacre, and his Lordship assumed that that assignation was a valid one. Now it appeared that the pursuer, through his law agent, was desirous to get himself on to the official register as proprietor so as to publish himself as such. To that end it was arranged that Chute should register himself as the proprietor, and should then enter Hardacre on the register as his assignee. Accordingly, on August 22, 1888, Chute did register himself as sole proprietor, and at the same time registered himself as assigner and Hardacre as his assignee. To his Lordship it appeared that whatever was done in June, 1888, was entirely a matter between Chute and Hardacre. No one else had any right to found on the assignation of June. Hardacre might found upon it if he pleased. He could destroy it or could give it up to Chute, and thus render it nugatory. What then was to prevent Hardacre agreeing that Chute should treat the assignation of June as a mere agreement to sell, and carry that out by registering himself as having power to assign and assigning by entry of assignation on the Register? The purpose was to give Hardacre the advantages as assignee which the Act of Parliament conferred on a registered assignee. His Lordship could see nothing to bar the procedure which was taken, which truly carried out the wishes of both parties, and which no one else had any interest to interfere with. If the evidence in regard to that matter was not so complete as it might have been, it must be remembered that no notice of this objection, which was one to title, was given by the defenders. Therefore the evidence was not to be examined too closely, but it seemed to justify what had been said. If Hardacre was duly registered he was entitled to found on the registration as *prima facie* evidence of his right. That that right referred to the Bullock version was quite clear.

Lord Ardwall, while agreeing with the majority in the result, was of opinion that the registration in 1888 was a bad registration, and would have been fatal to the pursuer's case but for the want of notice on record.

Counsel for the Pursuer and Respondent, Mr. Thomson and Mr. Morton. Agent, Norman M. Macpherson, S.S.C.

Counsel for the Defenders and Reclaimers, Mr. M'Clure, K.C., and Mr. Jameson. Agent, D. Hill Murray, S.S.C.

CONNOLLY v. RUSSELL.—SALARY IN LIEU OF NOTICE.

A case involving the question of notice required to artists engaged at a portable was
15 heard at Poole County Court, Dorset, where Edmund and John Connolly, musicians, claimed £5 wages, in lieu of notice, from Jesse Russell, proprietor of the Empire, a portable theatre at Poole. Plaintiffs are father and son, and were engaged as pianist and violinist by the defendant, at a joint salary of 50s., the engagement being by wire. On May 9 defendant gave all his company a week's notice, nine days later asking plaintiffs to come on for another week. Plaintiffs and others gave evidence that plaintiffs, being in the band, would be, according to custom, engaged on a fortnight's notice, although the artists might perhaps be on a

weekly notice. For the defence Ernest Stephens, manager for defendant, said the custom was a week's notice, and Alice Digby, an artist at present at the theatre, stated that her engagement was subject to a week's notice, but the latter admitted that the custom was a fortnight's notice.

Judge Philbrick gave judgment for plaintiff for one week's salary, 50s., remarking that plaintiffs had had the offer by defendant of another week's work.

JACOBS v. COTTON.—CLAIM FOR COMMISSION.

16 In the Westminster County Court, before his Honour Judge Woodfall, Miss Jessie Jacobs, an agent, of Shaftesbury Avenue, sued Miss Ada Reeve to recover the sum of £16 10s. as commission on a re-engagement at the Pavilion, Glasgow.

Mr. E. F. Lever was counsel for the plaintiff, and said his client was a dramatic agent, and her claim was in respect of a renewal of an engagement procured for the defendant, Miss Ada Reeve, at the Pavilion, Glasgow, at a salary of £300 a week, and £25 for *matinées*. The defence, he understood, would be that the engagement in question was not procured by the plaintiff, but was effected through a Mr. Lloyd, who was the manager of the Glasgow Pavilion. The facts of the case were that in 1906 the plaintiff procured an engagement for Miss Reeve at the Pavilion, Glasgow, at a salary of £300 a week, and upon that transaction she was duly paid her commission; but the present claim was based on a renewal engagement which the defendant fulfilled in January, 1908, and which, the plaintiff contended, was the result of her introduction. As a matter of fact, Miss Reeve gave so much satisfaction at Glasgow on the first engagement that Mr. Lloyd, the manager of the hall, wrote a letter to the effect that her re-engagement was a foregone conclusion. The plaintiff, in due course, sent Miss Reeve a form of contract to sign, offering her various dates at Glasgow, but in spite of that she signed a contract which was sent to her by Mr. Lloyd in his capacity as manager of the hall, and now refused to pay the plaintiff's commission.

Miss Jennie Jacobs was called, and said she had carried on business in London for seven years past as a théatrical and variety agent. In 1906 she obtained an engagement for Miss Reeve with Mr. Lloyd at the Glasgow Pavilion, and was paid her commission on it. In May, 1907, she was in communication with Mr. Lloyd as to a further engagement of Miss Reeve, but a question arose as to whether he would agree to pay her so high a salary. He afterwards wired to her agreeing to the terms, and she then sent a form of contract to the defendant for her signature, embodying the terms of £300 a week and £25 extra for *matinées*. She afterwards discovered, however, that Miss Reeve subsequently signed a contract with Mr. Lloyd direct, but she contended that that did not preclude her from claiming her commission, as, according to the usages of the profession, she was entitled to her full 5 per cent. commission on the first renewal engagement.

In cross-examination the witness said she had since heard that Mr. Lloyd had claimed 5 per cent. commission on the engagement in question. and, as a matter of fact, she (plaintiff) had to give him half her commission on the first engagement.

At this point of the case his Honour adjourned the further hearing until Friday, June 19.

On Friday, June 19, Mr. Barry Cohen, solicitor, appeared on behalf of Miss Ada Reeve, and in the course of a lengthy argument submitted that the plaintiff had totally failed to show that she was the means of bringing about the contract between the parties, and, therefore, she was driven back to the alleged custom which, she contended, prevailed in the profession, by which agents were entitled to charge commission on re-engagements. It was a well-known fact, he said, that in cases of this kind, where artists such as Miss Reeve could command very high salaries, they were much sought after by agents, and there was considerable competition on their part to act for them. It was admitted that the plaintiff approached Miss Reeve in this matter, and obtained for her an engagement at the Pavilion, Glasgow, at a salary of £325 a week, upon which she was paid a commission of 5 per cent., but that was a special contract, and did not in any way provide for payment of commission on return engagements. In November of last year Mr. Samuel Lloyd, the manager of the Glasgow Pavilion, wrote a letter to plaintiff, in which he stated that the re-engagement of Miss Reeve was a foregone conclusion, but he (Mr. Cohen) contended that that was not sufficient to entitle the plaintiff to claim commission on a re-engagement. Some time subsequently Miss Reeve received a letter from Mr. Lloyd offering her a re-engagement, and enclosing a form of contract, which she signed and returned to him. The engagement was duly fulfilled, but the defendant's case was that it was carried through between herself and Mr. Lloyd, and that, therefore, she was not liable to pay commission to the plaintiff. either on the point of introduction or of custom of the profession. The plaintiff, in order to prove her case, must show that there was a special contract to pay commission on re-engagements, and that she had totally failed to do. She relied to a large extent on a letter which she had received from Mr. Lloyd, but if that gentleman could have given satisfactory evidence in her favour, why was he not called in support of her case?

Miss Ada Reeve said she knew of no custom in the profession by which an artist was bound to pay commission on re-engagements unless a special contract was made to that effect, and in her experience she had only had one exception. Mr. Hugh Jay Didcott some time ago obtained for her an engagement at the Palace, upon which she paid commission, but although his introduction resulted in her having a number of return engagements he never claimed a penny from her in respect of them.

Mr. Louis Bradfield was called, and said that in his experience there was no custom in the profession to pay commission on re-engagements unless a special contract was entered into.

Mr. Lauri De Frece gave evidence to the same effect

In giving judgment, his Honour said it was upon the plaintiff to make out her case either upon the contract or on the alleged custom of the profession, but she had totally failed to do so. She might have called Mr. Lloyd to give his version as to how the contract was entered into, and he might have proved her case if she was right, but she had not done so, and on the evidence which had been placed before him he (the judge) was quite satisfied that the engagement in question was procured by Miss Reeve quite apart from anything which the plaintiff did, although it might to some extent have been influenced by the first engagement, which was brought about by the plaintiff. Then with regard to the alleged custom to pay commission on renewals, the plaintiff had quite failed to prove that any such custom prevailed, and even if it had been proved it might not avail her in this case, as the agreement between the parties was for payment of a commission of 5 per cent. on that particular contract, and no agreement whatever was made as to future engagements. There would be judgment for the defendant with costs.

BRANDON v. MANNING—THE PRINCESS'S.

17 In the King's Bench Division, before Mr. Justice Channell, Mr. Jocelyn Brandon, of Messrs. Brandon and Nicholson, solicitors, sued Mr. William Herbert Manning, as representative of the Princess's Theatre Syndicate, Limited, to recover £190, balance of £210, stated to be costs for procuring an agreement for a lease of the Princess's, Oxford Street.

Mr. Rose-Innes, counsel for the plaintiff, said that Mr. Brandon had procured the agreement for the lease, and did all that was necessary in connection with the registration of the company, but the shares had not gone to allotment.

His Lordship: Does it seem likely that they will go to allotment?

Mr. Rose-Innes said the application money had been returned to the various applicants for shares. The sum of £1,000 had been paid as deposit towards the cost of the lease by Sir A. Conan Doyle, but that amount had been forfeited.

Mr. Brandon, in his evidence, said the company was registered in June, 1907. In his opinion the company did not go to allotment because shareholders were not prepared to subscribe £40,000, of which £20,000 was to go to the vendor.

Mr. Manning, examined, stated that, at Mr. Brandon's suggestion, a resolution was passed by the company relieving the witness from the liability of the plaintiff's charges.

Cross-examined, he said he was the promoter of the company, but he was not a director.

His Lordship, deducting a certain amount which had already been paid and a guinea for unexecuted work, gave judgment for the plaintiff for £158 8s. 4d., with costs.

MORTIMER v. O'GORMAN.

17 In the Westminster County Court his Honour Judge Woodfall tried the case of Mortimer v. O'Gorman and others, in which the plaintiff, a sketch artist, sued Mr. Joe O'Gorman and other officers of the Variety Artists' Federation to recover the sum of £24 5s., balance of loss of salary owing to his having been called out on strike during the music hall war in 1907.

Mr. R. Storry Deans was counsel for the plaintiff. Mr. Doughty appeared for the defendants.

Counsel for the plaintiff said that a previous action had been brought by his client, but he was non-suited on the ground that the Federation was not a registered body at the period of the transaction in dispute, and he therefore now brought his action against the defendants personally.

The plaintiff was called, and said that at the time of the strike he was producing a sketch at the Canterbury and Euston halls,

and in January he received a letter from Mr. Frank Gerald informing him that he was forbidden to appear at the halls on that night. He was informed by Mr. Gerald that he would be indemnified as to his salary, and consequently he broke his contracts and did not appear. At that time he was in receipt of a salary of £46 a week for himself and his company. He subsequently saw Mr. Gerald again, and was told by him that he need not bother his head about the salary, as it would be all right, and, acting upon his instructions, he (plaintiff) went to see Mr. Percy Murray, and, on behalf of the Federation, offered him full salary to break his contract and go out on strike.

Counsel for the defence argued at some length that this was an action which could not be maintained in law.

His Honour said that before deciding that that was so he should prefer to hear the whole of the evidence, and as the case would take some time he should adjourn the further hearing.

The case was continued on the following day.

The plaintiff was recalled, and said that at the time when the strike took place he was running a sketch at the Canterbury, for which he was receiving a salary of £46 a week, and it was upon Mr. Frank Gerald's letter, in which he informed him that he was not to appear at that hall, that he was induced to break his contract with Mr. Payne. He subsequently was served with a writ from the proprietors of the Canterbury, and at once took it to the office of the Federation, but was told that he was not to bother himself about it, and that they would see to it, and, as a matter of fact, he heard no more about it, and understood that the Federation had dealt with the matter.

Cross-examined: He admitted that he was liable to the management for £46 a week for breach of contract, but his case was that the Federation had indemnified him against that. He further admitted that he had appealed to the Federation for money with which to pay his company and that on one occasion they paid him £50, but he looked to them for payment of his own personal salary, which he had lost in consequence of his having acted upon their instructions, by which he broke his contract.

Judge Woodfall: What I should like to know is, what induced you to break your contract with the Canterbury Music Hall?

The plaintiff: Because the Federation were fighting the proprietors, and said I must do so. I was a member of the Federation, and had I not done as they asked me to do it might have been bad for me afterwards.

Judge Woodfall: You knew that your breach of contract with Mr. Payne would put him to great inconvenience?

The witness: Yes, I knew that.

In re-examination by Mr. Doughty, the plaintiff admitted that after he went out on strike he made speeches in public on behalf of the Federation, but those speeches were made to the general public, and not to the profession in particular. He also admitted having endeavoured to induce Mr. Percy Murray to break his contract, but he did so on behalf of the Federation, and was not successful. He did not at that time know that Mr. Mountford and Mr. Gerald were the originators of the strike, and that both of them had since ceased to be members of the Federation. From first to last he trusted to Mountford and Gerald, and thought they had authority to act on behalf of the Executive Committee.

At this point of the case his Honour interposed, and said the case for the defendants was that the indemnity, if given, to the plaintiff, was given for an illegal act, and that it could not be sustained in a court of law. The real question was whether the indemnity was against public policy, and on that point he (the judge) was disposed to non-suit the plaintiff, but it was a question of great importance, and he was disposed to adjourn the case in order that it might be thoroughly argued out before him, but he could only do that on the terms that the plaintiff paid the defendants' costs of the day.

Mr. Storrey De ins, on behalf of the plaintiff, said he regretted that he had not had an opportunity since the adjournment of looking into the authorities on the point, but if he was given an opportunity of so doing he hoped to be able to put another complexion on the case.

The Judge: I have gone very carefully into the question, because, as I said before, it is one of great importance, and as the matter at present stands I am prepared to direct a non-suit, but if you, on behalf of the plaintiff, agree to pay the costs of the day I will give you an adjournment in order to give you an opportunity of arguing the question thoroughly.

Mr. Doughty said that he had another point under Section 4 of the Trade Union Act of 1871, that a member of a trade union cannot bring an action for a benefit under the rules of the Union.

The case was adjourned to July 20. (See report of judgment on that date.)

THEATRES AND VARIETY PROGRAMMES.

Before Mr. Robert Wallace, K.C., at the Clerkenwell Sessions Robert Arthur, Walter Gibbons, A. W. Dear, and F. H. Terrell **19** were indicted for having "on and between May 4 and 23 last unlawfully kept the Camden Theatre of Varieties as a place for public dancing, music, and other public entertainment of the like kind, within twenty miles of the City of London and Westminster, without a license for that purpose from the Licensing Sessions of the County of London."

Mr. Horace Avory, K.C., and Mr. W. S. Knight appeared for the prosecution. Mr. R. D. Muir represented Mr. Robert Arthur, and Mr. George Elliott was counsel for the three other defendants

Mr. Wallace intimated that it was unnecessary for the defendants to enter the dock or be subjected to the customary search when surrendering in Court, and they were accommodated on the bench beneath counsel.

There was great delay before the case was commenced, owing to the non-appearance of Mr. Walter Gibbons. It was stated that he had left Epsom in a motor-car, and probably had broken down on the way.

Mr. Wallace: Starting from Epsom in a motor-car he might be anywhere—perhaps in a ditch. He should estreat Mr. Gibbons's recognisances. Mr. Gibbons's name was called three times in the corridor, and as there was no response his recognisances were estreated.

Mr. Avory proceeded against the three other defendants, the case of Mr. Gibbons to be considered later.

In opening, Mr. Avory, K.C., said the case raised a question of great public interest and importance—whether a theatre holding a theatrical license is entitled to be conducted as a music hall and to present an entertainment of the ordinary music hall character which is not a stage play Although in form it was a criminal proceeding, the case had been in-

stituted for the sole purpose of obtaining a decision on the matter. Theatres and music halls in the metropolis had been for a great many years past governed respectively by two different statutes. The Theatres Act, 1843, prohibited any theatre being opened for the performance of stage plays in the metropolis without the license of the Lord Chamberlain. On the other hand, music halls were regulated by an Act which provided that no house should be opened for public music and dancing or for an entertainment of the like kind without the license of the London County Council. In recent years a serious conflict had been going on between the theatres and music halls. Those who produced the legitimate drama found that the counter-attractions of the music hall, where things were much more free and easy, were drawing away a considerable number of people, who otherwise would go to the theatre. That had led to proceedings being taken in the Courts against music halls for performing stage plays, and fines and other penalties had been inflicted on persons for encroaching on the rights of the theatres in presenting stage plays instead of a legitimate music-hall performance. This was a case of the opposite character. The Camden was opened in 1900, and it had been licensed by the Lord Chamberlain year by year ever since, the place being carried on legitimately as a theatre up to May last. Whether it was that the management found that their attendance was falling off or whether it was that they thought they could make greater profits by turning it into a music hall did not matter. What they did, in fact, was to turn it into a music hall. The question which had to be decided was whether they were entitled to do so by law, seeing that the license of the Lord Chamberlain only was held. Mr. Robert Arthur held this license, and an application by him for a license from the London County Council was refused.

The defence probably was that the performance given was a stage play within the meaning of the Theatres Act, and if that was so it was covered by the Lord Chamberlain's license. If it was not in the nature of a stage play, it was an entertainment requiring the license of the London County Council. A stage play was defined in these terms:—"The words 'stage play' shall be taken to include every tragedy, comedy, farce, ballet, burletta, interlude, melodrama, pantomime, or other entertainment of the stage, or any part thereof." An entertainment off the stage might be different to a performance on the stage, and acrobatic turns had been held not to be stage plays. If a music hall performance could be given under the Lord Chamberlain's licence, it would be idle to compel people to get the licence of the L.C.C. The defendants, Dear and Terrell, were actual managers of the theatre at the time in question.

Mr. Muir said that so far as the trial before the jury was concerned, Mr. Robert Arthur would take no part, but he wanted it stated that he authorised no performance other than that which came within the definition of a stage play of the Theatres Act.

While witnesses were being called, Mr. Gibbons came into Court. On being called forward, he said, "I am extremely sorry. Unfortunately, I depended on a motor to bring me to town. It has been very faithful up to now, but I burst a tyre, and came to a stop away from station, cab, or anything else."

Mr. Wallace: After that apology and explanation the forfeiture of your recognisances will be removed.

Mr. Joslyn Godefroi, residential clerk, Lord

Chamberlain's Department, St. James's Palace, said that the Lord Chamberlain's license did not author'se or permit smoking.

On Mr. Avory objecting to a question, Mr. Elliott said his case was that the proper person to interfere in a case of this kind was the Lord Chamberlain, and not the people Mr. Avory represented.

Mr. Wallace: That is a question to be determined on law.

Alfred Squire, auctioneer and surveyor, of High Street, Camden Town, said he was one of the persons who gave notice commencing these proceedings. When he visited the Camden he saw a music hall entertainment. One man gave imitations of animals and all sorts of things.

Mr. Avory: Then I see there was a comedy entertainment, entitled *There's Hair*, "The Dusky Comedy Queen," and Fred Earle, the popular comedian of "Seaweed" fame. Was there anything of a smell of Margate about it? There was also Geo. Mozart, the popular and favourite comedian, in one-man drama, playing hero, heroine, villager, villain, and villainess, and 100 other characters.

Mr. Muir: That was clearly a stage play.

Mr. Avory elicited that another item was "Whir'ing the Whirl; or, Motoring in Mid-air."

Mr. Elliott: Did you give notice in writing to the parish constable? I did not personally.

You never saw the parish constable? I should not know him if I saw him. (Laughter.)

The witness said that on each occasion he visited the theatre a stage play was also given. He did not think the turns were of the kind seen in a pantomime. They were separate turns of a few minutes each, and a pantomime was continuous. Gunner Moir boxed once to "slow music."

Myer Lee, furniture dealer, said he was the second person who had instituted the proceedings. He gave similar evidence.

Mr. Huntly Jenkins, for Mr. Robert Arthur, submitted that he had no case to answer. The specific allegation was that he had "kept and maintained" the theatre, and there was no evidence of that.

Mr. Avory replied that the existence of the license in Mr. Arthur's name was sufficient, and the judge overruled the objection.

Mr. Elliott said that since 1750 he could trace no case of the kind of this prosecution, and the cases which had come before the Courts were entirely distinct. He submitted that the defendants were protected in the performances they gave by the Lord Chamberlain's license.

Mr. Wallace: Supposing in a place l'censed in this way you gave a performance of no kind except a tumbling performance accompanied by music, do you say that would be covered by the license of the Lord Chamberlain? Yes; I put it as high as that.

Mr. Elliott argued that if either before or after a stage play there was introduced music alone, dancing alone, or music and dancing combined, or any possible variation of the two things, that so long as there was a proper entertainment, which the Lord Chamberlain had sanctioned, and the holder was not carrying on anything which the Lord Chamberlain had forbidden, then the mere fact that music or dancing was carried on was cleaned and protected by the original virtue of the license and the proper entertainment under it. So long as the Lord Chamberlain did not actively interfere, the license was not withdrawn or determined.

Mr. Wallace: So far as I can gather, that has never arisen.

Mr. Elliott: If under this general license, granted once a year, my clients have been guilty of a breach of the regulations in the sense that they may have performed a particular play, notice of which had not been sent to the Chamberlain, and he took no notice of it, and sanctioned the next play they produced, it seems clear that the license remains valid the whole time.

Mr. Wallace: If an offence was committed which destroyed the license then you would be liable for that offence. The question is whether this was a variety entertainment in the music hall sense or stage play under the Theatres Act.

Mr. Elliott: I am not going to contend that it was not a variety entertainment. I prefer to rely on the legal position. I say that having regard to the position we were in under the Lord Chamberlain's license it does not matter if the performance could be described in that way. Counsel added that if his clients had given in the form of a pantomime a connected entertainment of exactly the same items, there would be a complete answer. It was for the Lord Chamberlain to say whether his license had been used or abused, and for him to say, "This is not the sort of entertainment I intend you to have, and I withdraw my license." Then, of course, the lessees would be at once at the mercy of anyone who prosecuted them, because they would have no license; but so long as the Lord Chamberlain does not choose to interfere or prohibit any particular performance he submitted that his license prevented a prosecution.

Mr. Wallace, K.C.: Is it not possible to have a double license?

Mr. Elliott: I have never heard of it. We sometimes hear of jealousy in high places, and whether the Lord Chamberlain would withdraw the license if the London County Council conferred one I do not know.

Mr. Wallace decided against the argument. The question left to the jury was, "Has this theatre been kept for music and dancing or other entertainment of the like kind without a license?"

The jury answered in the affirmative, and found the defendants guilty.

Mr. Wallace said that as this was the first case of the kind he should only pass a nominal judgment, but he wanted the fact to be affirmed that this could not be done.

Mr. Avory said he should be satisfied if recognisances were entered into so as to prevent a repetition of the offence.

Mr. Elliott said his clients would undertake not to give any performance outside the Chamberlain's license, but in the end the defendants were bound over to be of good behaviour in the sum of £10 each.

JONES v. SAPHRINI AND BELL.
"THE SILVER KING."

Two motions by the proprietors of ⊥he *Silver King* were heard. The plaintiff asked in each **20** case for an injunction perpetually restraining the defendant during the continuance of the performing right from announcing for representation and from representing or causing to be represented the copyright play called ⊥he *Silver King*, or any other dramatic piece in which the words, scenes, characters, or incidents were copied, imitated, or colourably altered from those of the plaintiffs' play, and also from announcing or representing under that name, or any name colourably altered therefrom, any play not being the plaintiffs' said play without distinguishing the same from such play. The defendant Bell was proprietor and manager of a travelling company, and the defendant Saphrini was the proprietor and manager of the Palace, Boston. Damages of 40s. under the Dramatic Copyright Act, 1833, were also asked against the latter for an unauthorised performance at the place named, and against the former for performances at Maldon in Essex, and March, in Cambridgeshire.

Mr. Justice Swinfen Eady gave judgment accordingly

GRAND, GLASGOW, v. GLASGOW "EVENING TIMES"—ALLEGED LIBEL.

23 A reclaiming note by the pursuers in the action by the Grand Theatre and Opera House, Glasgow, Limited, against the proprietors of the Glasgow *Evening Times* for £2,500 damages for alleged slander, was disposed of by the Division. In November, 1907, the pursuers stated, a petition for the judicial winding-up of the pursuers' company was boxed to the First Division, the petitioners being two shareholders of the company. On the date on which intimation, advertisement, and service of the petition was ordered the defenders published a paragraph with a heading, "Glasgow Theatre Surprise—Grand to be Wound Up." The pursuers said that by the heading the defenders falsely and calumniously represented that the Grand Theatre was insolvent. The pursuers lodged answers to the petition, and in January last it was refused, the company being found entitled to expenses. The defenders denied having slandered the pursuers, and explained that the paragraph was an accurate report of the wider statements in the petition and of what occurred in the Court in connection with the petition

Lord Guthrie, in the Outer House, dismissed the action with expenses.

Without calling on counsel for the respondents their Lordships now affirmed the Lord Ordinary's interlocutor, refused the reclaiming note, and found the respondents entitled to additional expenses.

Lord M'Laren thought any reasonable reader when he came to the words "Petition in Court" would at once see that this was a question still undecided. The words "Petition in Court" clearly limited the meaning of what came before to this extent, that there was a proceeding in Court which might result in the Grand being wound up. Lord Kinnear said the question was whether the head-line contained a statement which falsely represented that the pursuers' company had become bankrupt, and that the Court of Session had pronounced an order for the winding-up of the pursuers' company. He did not think any reasonable reader could have come to such a conclusion upon the words. What the words really meant was perfectly plain, that there was a petition in Court for the winding-up of the Grand Theatre, and that to the newspaper there was something surprising in that. There was nothing injurious in saying that the paper was surprised that there was a proposal to wind up the theatre. All that the heading itself contained was that there was a petition for winding-up, and that was perfectly true. To put upon these words the inuendo that the pursuers' company had become bankrupt, and that not only was there a petition in Court, but that the order for winding-up had been pronounced was, to his mind, going altogether beyond what was justified by the words themselves.

ROLT v. BEECHER—VERDICT FOR DEFENDANT ON POINT OF LAW.

In the Shoreditch County Court, his Honour Judge Smyly, K.C., gave his considered judgment in the action "Rolt v. Beecher," **23** in which Mr. Henry Garnett Rolt, described as a theatrical manager, of Christleton, Chester, was the plaintiff, to recover from Mr. Trevor St. John Beecher, of the Sebright Arms and Regent Theatre, 26 and 28, Coate Street, Hackney Road, N.E., a theatrical proprietor, the sum of £50 as liquidated damages in connection with an alleged breach of contract. The case was fully reported in THE STAGE of June 11. Mr. Groser, barrister, appeared for the plaintiff, and Mr. Turrell was counsel for the defence.

Judge Smyly said: This is a case which has reference to a performance which should have taken place at the Kursaal at Bexhill-on-Sea, and which, it is admitted, did not take place on the Saturday evening, and that is alleged to be from various causes, which, however, I do not at the moment propose to go into, as I hardly think it will be necessary to do so under the circumstances. It was admitted to me by counsel that it was essential that the plaintiff should prove that the sum he claimed, the £50, was liquidated damages, and not a penalty, and if it was a penalty, then he would fail under the form he had brought it. That has cleared the air a great deal, I am pleased to say, and has enabled me to arrive at a clear decision much easier than I should have been able to do had all the facts so placed before me been in dispute. What I have to determine is whether this £50 is a penalty or liquidated damages, and I do not see that I can come to any other conclusion than that it is clearly a penalty in law. In the House of Lords it has been held that such a sum is a penalty, and there are a great many decisions following which do nothing but emphasise it. In the case of "Elphinstone v. the Musson Iron Company" the decision of the learned lords must govern such a case as this and any case like it—that is quite clear. In a more recent case —"The Clydebank Engineering Company v. Donejone Ramos"—the law in the Elphinstone case was referred to, and although the learned lords in the latter case said it did not quite fall within the scope of penalty cases, they did not in any way attempt to upset the Elphinstone decision. Then, again, Lord Davey quoted a part of the Elphinstone decision, and agreed that where a lump sum was agreed upon it was a penalty; whilst the late Master of the Rolls was also in perfect agreement with it. The question has also been considered by Lord Bigham in "Higham v. the Automobile Association," and he admitted he is not in agreement with the Master of the Rolls, but he agrees with the principle of the penalty in most parts, and even if he does not agree in all the essential points, then the decision must go to the wall in face of the Elphinstone judgment, which is most clear on all the points. There did not seem to be much doubt in the minds of the learned lords as to the point that if one sum was agreed upon as a settlement of a certain breach, then it was by no means a liquidated or arrived-at sum, but was, by the very nature of the arrangement, a penalty pure and simple, with no other interpretation. I have to consider this agreement and see if the terms of it come within the propositions as laid down in law, and I think there is not a reasonable shadow of doubt that it does, because the memorandum of agreement goes on to say that the defendant in the present case was to provide a first-class combination of artists to

perform a pantomime, *The Babes in the Wood.*
That was one part of the agreement, and, it
could readily be seen, a very material part of
the contract, going as it does to the root of
the whole matter. Then, again, he was to
supply the whole of the necessary scenery; it
did not, under the circumstances, go for much,
because, if he only supplied 19-20ths of the
scenery and the other 1-20th part was missing,
he would not obviously perform his contract;
but that breach would not go to the root of
the matter, as it could not be said that such
a small thing would go to the non-fulfilment
of the whole of the contract. Then, again,
the defendant had agreed to pay all the
author's fees, but it still less goes to the root
of the matter, as it would be absurd to suppose that the performance or the takings would
be influenced in the slightest degree by the
fact that the defendant forgot to pay them.
Then there is special printing to be taken
into consideration, as in the agreement 500
circulars had to be supplied. He would have
broken the contract if he had printed less
than these 500 special circulars, and equally
broken it if he had only printed 400, but it
would be absurd to say that if 500 were not
supplied much harm would have been done.
It is mentioned expressly, too, in another
portion of this agreement that it is stipulated
that neither the manager, nor any of the artists, nor one of the artists, I presume, for
that matter, is to appear at any time in any hall
in Bexhill during the period that the company
was in Bexhill for the purpose of performing
the pantomime *The Babes in the Wood.*
Would it not be absurd to suppose that if
one member of the company appeared at
another performance it would have any
material effect on the performance given by
the defendant at the Kursaal, under different
circumstances, with the full complement of
artists that were actually engaged? There
are a number of things which the defendant
undertook to do, some of them of a most
trivial character, some of them very material,
and it was agreed that on the breach of any
one of these he (the defendant) should indemnify the plaintiff in the sum of £50 as
liquidated damages. Under the circumstances,
it would be impossible to say that this was
not a penalty pure and simple and not
liquidated damages, although it was clearly
set out as liquidated damages in the agreement. That has been settled for many years—
I might say many, many years—before the case
that I have referred to in the House of Lords.
Still, that case, of course, disposes of the
present case, and it is, under the circumstances, useless to go into the further and
much more complicated and difficult questions
and issues that arise in the agreement and in
the hearing of the case. Therefore, on the
ground that this was a penalty and not
liquidated damages, and that on both sides
it was admitted that unless it could be shown
to be liquidated damages, the action could not
be maintained, I give judgment for the defendant, with the usual consequences as to costs.
Mr. Groser (who appeared for the plaintiff):
I ask for a stay whilst *he position of affairs
is considered by the parties concerned. Judge
Smyly: You do not need my leave. You can
have your appeal, if you desire it, without me.
Mr. Groser: But I am only asking your Honour
to give leave. Judge Smyly: No, if you pay
the amount of the costs into court you get
your leave without my having to express an
opinion one way or the other, which I do not
wish to do as it happens. So far as I am
concerned, though, I might say that I should
not give leave to appeal myself, because I
have not a shadow of a doubt as to the ulti-

mate result after the authorities I have read.
Judgment was then entered for the defendant with costs.

(See report of case on June 4.)

SPRAGUE v. MURRAY CARSON—A THEATRE PROJECT.

24 In the King's Bench Division, before Mr.
Justice Channell, William George Robert
Sprague, architect, carrying on business
in Jermyn Street, Piccadilly, sued
Murray Carson, actor and dramatic author,
for £2,006 for professional services rendered in
connection with procuring a site and drawing
up of plans for a proposed new theatre.

The defence was that the plaintiff undertook the work as a speculation.

Eventually the case was settled on terms
agreed between the parties, his Lordship
stating that the plaintiff was entitled to a
substantial sum, but whatever his legal rights
were he should grant the defendant an abate-
ment.

FRASER v. ARTHUR AND McCREA.

25 In the Chancery Division, before Mr. Justice
Joyce, Mrs. Fraser (Miss Ruth Vincent) applied for an injunction to restrain the
defendant Arthur and the defendant
McCrea, from announcing by advertisement or
otherwise that the plaintiff had been engaged
to appear or perform in any theatrical or other
entertainment without the authority of the
plaintiff previously had or obtained.

It appeared that the defendants had without
any authority from the plaintiff announced by
means of bills or advertisements that the plaintiff would appear and act in certain dramatic
pieces to be performed at Ilfracombe, and also
her appearance on various dates at Taunton
and Newquay. The plaintiff complained that
such unauthorised use of her name was calculated to do her serious damage professionally,
and she accordingly claimed an injunction.

Mr. Hughes, K.C., who, with Mr. Stokes, appeared for the plaintiff, stated that the defendants were now prepared to give an undertaking until the trial in the terms of the notice of motion.

Mr. Robertson appeared for the defendant
McCrea, who, he said, had acted innocently in
the matter as the local agent of his co-defendant. He was willing to undertake as above
stated.

The defendant Arthur appeared in person
and also gave the necessary undertaking.

In these circumstances his Lordship made no
order on the motion.

THE VARIETY ASSAULT CASE.

26 Before Mr. Curtis Bennett at Bow Street,
Mr. Joe O'Gorman appeared to answer a summons for an assault against Mr. Leonard
Mortimer, alleged to have been committed in the Wellington Hotel, Strand, on the
afternoon of June 18.

The prosecution was conducted by Mr. Kenneth Poyser (instructed by Messrs. Morris and
Rickards), and Mr. Charles Doughty (instructed
by Messrs. Judge and Priestley) appeared for
defendant.

Mr. Curtis Bennett said there appeared to
have been provocation on both sides. Defendant had straightforwardly admitted he
did strike at complainant, but he did not
think he succeeded in reaching him. He (the
magistrate) was inclined to think he did not
succeed in his purpose.

Mr. Curtis Bennett added that in his opinion
plaintiff himself did not come out of the case

as a Simon Pure. He would bind both complainant and defendant over in the sum of £20 to keep the peace towards each other for the next twelve months.

MECHANICAL MUSIC ROLLS.—A TEST CASE.

29 At Bow Street, Sir Albert De Rutzen gave his considered decision in the case in which James Connor, a hawker, was summoned for offering for sale a pirated copy of a musical work—namely, a perforated music roll—being the pianoforte accompaniment of a song called "The Bandolero."

Mr. R. D. Muir (instructed by Mr. Percy H. Beecher) appeared on behalf of Messrs. Chappell and Co. in support of the summons; Mr. Scrutton, K.C. (with him Mr. George Elliott), defended.

This was a test case brought for the purpose of deciding the rights of composers and owners of copyright in relation to mechanical devices for the reproduction of music. A similar summons against the defendant in respect of a talking-machine disc was not gone into.

Sir Albert now said that, in the case of "Boosey v. Wight," it was decided by the Court of Appeal in 1900 that a perforated roll was a part of an organ, and was not a copy of a sheet of music within the Copyright Act of 1842. Since then two new Acts had been passed—one in 1902 and the other in 1906—to amend the law relating to musical copyright, and it was contended that those Acts had altered the law with regard to perforated rolls, and had defined them as being copies of a musical work. The prosecution relied for their contention upon the words of the section, "To make any new adaptation, or arrangement, in any system," but he found nothing to lead him to suppose that the Legislature in so defining musical copyright intended those words, which in their ordinary and unstrained interpretation seemed to him to apply to written or printed copies of musical works, to cover these perforated rolls. He therefore dismissed the summons, but he made no order as to costs.

Mr. Muir asked for a case to be stated, and his worship, in readily agreeing to do so, said he should not be at all sorry if his decision was held to be wrong.

(See report of the case, June 4.)

LONDON MUSIC HALL, LIMITED, v. EVANS —AN UNFULFILLED ENGAGEMENT.

30 In the Shoreditch County Court, before his Honour Judge Bray, the London Music Hall, Limited, were the plaintiffs in an action to recover from Mr. Will Evans, music hall artist, £45 damages for breach of contract. The full claim was that the plaintiffs claim damages for breach of an agreement in writing made on October 14, 1904, between the plaintiffs of the one part and the defendant of the other part, whereby the defendant agreed to perform at the London Music Hall, High Street, Shoreditch, E., for one week commencing March 11, and one week commencing March 18, 1907, at £22 10s. a week, and failed to do so. Mr. A. Engelbert (instructed by Messrs. Strong, Mercer, and Co.) was counsel for the plaintiffs, and Mr. Walter Payne (instructed by Amery, Parkes, Macklin, and Co.) appeared for the defence.

In opening his case for the plaintiffs Mr. Engelbert said that so far back as 1904 the plaintiffs entered into a contract for him to appear at the London Music Hall and Collins's Music Hall at various dates, amongst which were the weeks commencing March 11 and 18. Shortly

their case was that Mr. Evans took a trip to America to fulfil an important and no doubt lucrative appointment out there, and failed to put in an appearance at the London.

The first witness called was Mr. Richards, of the London Music Hall, Limited, who proved the arranging of the contract with Mr. Evans. When Mr. Evans returned from America witness wrote to him reminding him that he was under contract to appear at the London in July, and asking what he intended to do with regard to the other dates. An interview took place on June 29, at which it was agreed that Mr. Evans should perform at the London Music Hall twice nightly instead of once at a salary of £30 instead of £22 10s., and also he was to try and arrange with Mr. Oswald Stoll as to what dates he could give in reparation for the dates he had failed to appear in March. There was no suggestion made that the engagement of March had been cancelled. As the defendant did not put in an appearance in March, witness said he had to engage other turns.

Witness was cross-examined at length by Mr. Payne, as to certain dates which Mr. Evans had since filled, doing two houses at the London and Collins's for £60 the lot, instead of £90, which, witness declared, was not a reduction made by Mr. Evans to wipe off the matter of the dates which he did not fulfil when away in America, at the end of which Judge Bray asked if they could not come to some arrangement.

A consultation then took place between the parties, at the end of which Mr. Engelbert said he was sorry, but the case would have to go on, as they could not come to terms.

Mr. Will Evans then went into the box. He admitted the contract which had been handed in. In the early part of 1906 he was approached as to his going to America in 1907. At the time he had a number of contracts which would have prevented him going, and he arranged that they should be cancelled, including the plaintiffs, on the telephone. On June 29 he saw Richards, and it was suggested that his contract was for one house a night, and what did he suggest to do? He said he would fulfil the contract for one house a night. Then it was suggested that he had not had permission to go to America, and that he could be sued for breach of contract, and he said he couldn't, as they had let him off. As it was awkward for them to play him one house a night, if they played him at all, they suggested he should play the two houses, and he agreed at double salary. They said he ought to let them down lightly, as he never had permission to go to America, and at the finish it was agreed that he should take £33 for the two houses, and that would settle the March dispute. The only reference to Mr. Stoll was that when his next two weeks' engagement came round he should split them, and so it was quite reasonable, as it would never pay to keep one turn two weeks in a twice-nightly house, he said he would see what he could arrange with Mr. Stoll. In cross-examination, he said the permission was granted on the telephone, and, although it was of great importance to him, he did not trouble to confirm the telephone conversation. As it was a favour on their part to let him go, he offered to make it up to them, and he had done so, and wiped it out by making them a £30 allowance. He thought it was quite an adequate compensation considering they never lost anything, as they did not bill him. In re-examination, he said that if his letters did not convey up to the hilt all he was now saying he could only say that he was a comedian and not a lawyer.

JUDGMENT.

Judge Bray, in giving judgment, said: I have to determine two things—was there a communication on the telephone and what took place in June. I have to be guided, to a very large extent, by the correspondence, and unless it is a fraudulent correspondence then I have to find for the plaintiffs. In the last two letters the plaintiffs wrote to the defendant they pointed out that he had broken his contract without apparent reason, and that they failed to understand what had caused him to act in such an unbusinesslike way as to go to America without first making an arrangement with them. It would have been pure bounce to have written such a letter if an arrangement had been come to, and then, again, one would have thought that he would have immediately sat down and written an indignant letter repudiating the suggestion, but he did not, and therefore I am forced to the conclusion that the correspondence is genuine. All that happened was that he had an interview, at which he arranged to cut down his price from £45 to £30, but I have come to the conclusion that that only had reference to those dates, and had nothing to do with March. I don't suppose they have lost a penny over the matter, but that they are entitled to a verdict is my conclusion, and I shall enter judgment for the plaintiffs for £45. Mr. Engelbert asked for costs, which was agreed to, and judgment was then entered for the plaintiffs for £45 and costs.

JULY.

JONES v. LA RONDELLE.—A SKETCH DISPUTE.

2 Mrs. La Rondelle, professionally known as Roland Oliver, was the defendant in an action at Lambeth County Court, before Judge Emden. The plaintiffs were Miss Grace Jones and Mr. Ellerslie Pyne, residing in Cowper's Road, Stoke Newington, and they each sought to recover £3, a week's salary.

Miss Grace Jones stated that defendant approached her with a view to reproducing her sketch *Her Last Dance*, and expressed a desire that Mr. Pyne might also be engaged to take the part in the duologue. A trial week at the Middlesex, Drury Lane, was arranged to commence on June 1, and it was agreed a salary of £3 each should be paid for the week. Plaintiffs duly appeared in the sketch. It went very well, and the curtain was three times raised. In response to a letter received on the following morning Miss Jones visited defendant, and was given another dress, which Mrs. La Rondelle wished her to wear, saying she wanted a more brilliant dress than the one Miss Jones wore. No complaint was made about the action. They were ready to play again on the Tuesday, but were not allowed to go on. The manager said the sketch was too dangerous.

Judge Emden: Why dangerous?

Miss Jones explained that the story of the sketch turned on a quarrel, in which flower pots and chairs were thrown about. The manager said the orchestra were in danger.

Mrs. La Rondelle contended that the sketch was badly played. She hardly recognised her own sketch.

Evidence was given that the fight was not at all dangerous.

Judge Emden said that the question whether the performance was or was not a success did not affect the fact that an agreement had been made for the payment of a certain salary for the week. Judgment would therefore be given for the plaintiff.

GORDON v. MACDONA.—"A COUNTRY GIRL" ON TOUR.—BROKEN WEEKS.

3 In the Westminster County Court, before Judge Woodfall, the case of Gordon v. Macdona, Limited, was tried. It was an action by the plaintiff, Mr. Antony Gordon, actor, to recover the sum of £9 1s. 6d., being a fortnight's salary, in lieu of notice.

Mr. Gordon said he was engaged to go on tour with the defendants' *A Country Girl* company, and they appeared at various towns in the provinces. On March 14, however, whilst they were on tour Mr. Lloyd called the whole of the company, and informed them that they must submit to deduction of 15 per cent. from their salaries, and that if they did not accept that proposition the tour must come to an end on the following week. He (plaintiff) did not agree to the suggested reduction of salary, and as he had a wife and family to support he looked about for and obtained another engagement, but he considered that by the usages of the profession he was certainly entitled to a fortnight's salary in lieu of notice.

Mr. Harry Paulton, jun., was called to give evidence as to custom with regard to notice. He said the usual procedure was to give a fortnight's notice by posting it at the stage door of the theatre, and he was not prepared to say that broken weeks in a tour could be counted as part of the fortnight's notice.

For the defence, Mr. Lloyd said he was the manager of the tour in question, acting in behalf of the defendant firm, and it was quite true that he suggested a reduction of salaries to the extent of 15 per cent., and told the company that if they would not accept those terms the tour would have to be brought to a close. The plaintiff, among others, raised an objection, and finally left the company at Croydon and took another engagement. He (witness) contended that in this case there was a "broken" notice, which was included in the various nights on which the plaintiff did not play whilst on tour, and that in any event he could not claim more than three days' pay.

In giving judgment, his Honour said it was true that the contract between the parties provided for a fortnight's notice on either side, but he thought that broken weeks whilst on tour could be regarded and counted as a part of the notice after the company had been given an intimation that the tour was coming to an end, and inasmuch as the plaintiff left the company and obtained another engagement, there would be judgment for the defendants, with costs.

PAYNE AND GIBBONS v. PAYNE.—A DISPUTED WILL.

3 Mr. Walter Payne and Mr. Walter Gibbons, son and son-in-law of the late George Adney Payne, music hall proprietor, who met his death in a motor-car accident in 1907, sought in the Probate and Divorce Division probate of the deceased's will, dated May 1, 1904, dividing his fortune amongst his four children.

The will was contested by the widow, Mrs. Clara Agnes Payne, known on the stage as Ethel Earle. She put forward a will which she said was made by her husband between May and September, 1904, under which she was to receive one-fifth of the estate absolutely.

In opening the case, Mr. McCall, K.C., said Mr. Payne in 1898 met and became very much attached to Miss Ethel Earle, marrying her in November of that year. Mr. Payne was induced to make a codicil to his will of 1899, striking his wife out of all benefits. But a fresh will was made in the wife's favour. It was frequently referred to by Mr. Payne. On his death-bed Mr. Payne told his wife and the doctor of the contents of the will, saying that he had made good provision for Mrs. Payne. Since her husband's death she had been refused access to anything in the house, Mr. Walter Payne taking possession.

A settlement was suddenly arrived at, Mr. McCall saying it had been agreed that Mrs. Payne's case should not be pressed, and that all imputations would be withdrawn. The will of May, 1904, was formally pronounced for, and it was understood that Mrs. Payne's costs were to come out of the estate.

MOSS'S EMPIRES v. MARIE LLOYD.

3 Lord Guthrie had before him the note of suspension and interdict for Moss's Empires, Limited, proprietors of the Empire and the Coliseum, Glasgow, against Miss Marie Lloyd. The respondent appeared at the Pavilion, Glasgow, during the week beginning May 11, 1908. The complainers averred that she did so in contravention of a condition of contract which she had with the complainers that she was not with certain exceptions to perform at any place of amusement or public place within a radius of ten miles of the complainers' theatres, and they were granted interim interdict. Under her agreement with the complainers she was to appear at the complainers' Coliseum. Empire, or Zoo Theatres, Glasgow, during the week beginning October 12, 1908, at a salary of £130 per week. The action passed into the Court of Session, and on July 3, on the motion of counsel for the complainers, Lord Guthrie made the interdict perpetual and found the respondent liable in expenses.

(See report, May 16.)

COFFIN v. FRASER—ECHO OF "THE CINGALEE" CASE.

5 In the King's Bench Division, before Mr. Justice Darling, in the action of Coffin v. Fraser, Mr. E. F. Spence, on behalf of the defendant, asked for judgment dismissing the action and for costs as between party and party down to December 8, and as between solicitor and client after that date.

Mr. Daldy, who appeared for the plaintiff, the well-known actor-singer, said the action had reference to the action brought by Major Fraser to recover from Mr. George Edwardes damages for having taken a play of his, altered it, and produced it under the name of *The Cingalee.* In the course of the evidence at the trial it was suggested that the introduction to Mr. George Edwardes, given to Major Fraser by Mr. Hayden Coffin, was given for a valuable consideration. Mr. Coffin was indignant at the suggestion that it was an introduction for a reward, and brought this action.

Mr. Justice Darling: It seems to me a complicated way of arriving at a simple result.

Mr. Spence agreed, but Mr. Coffin wished to have the wrong impression that had got abroad corrected in a public way.

Mr. Justice Darling: Well, he has done that now. Everyone seems to be satisfied that in introducing Major Fraser Mr. Coffin did it as a matter of friendship and not for reward,

and anybody who thinks otherwise has no ground for so doing

The action was therefore dismissed with costs.

ADVERTISING THEATRE CURTAINS

6 Some important questions in connection with the interpretation of contracts for notices on advertising curtains in theatres arose at Wandsworth County Court, when Judge Harrington, K.C., heard an action in which the Expert Advertising Company, of Sheffield, were the plaintiffs and Mr. A. Gasson, optician, of Battersea Park Road, the defendant. The case for the plaintiffs was that defendant signed a contract for his advertisement to appear on the advertising curtain at the Shakespeare, S.W., the amount being £3 and the stipulation being that the advertisement should be shown "three times during each performance." Evidence was given by James Solly, fireman, and J. H. Armsworth, flyman, as to the exhibition of the curtain, the three times to be once before the performance, once during the interval, and once at the end of the performance. A paper to this effect was signed after each performance

Defendant's solicitor said the words of the contract were "three times during each performance." If given before the play commenced, would that be "during the performance"?

His Honour: You would not have the curtain lowered in the middle of a scene?

The Solicitor: No, but there are two or three acts in most pieces.

Defendant, giving evidence, said that on signing the contract he was told that the pantomime season was worth all the money, for then there would be two shows a day. On two occasions in February and October he went to the theatre, and only saw the curtain once during the performance. It was lowered when the early doors were opened, but it was so dark nobody could read it. At the close they turned out the lights and the people at the same time, and so it could not be seen. He complained to the plaintiffs in November, and they said they had never had a complaint before.

Mr. Corfield, another advertiser, deposed to visiting the Shakespeare on June 1 and to the curtain not being shown. He did not wait till the end. Two other witnesses gave similar evidence.

His Honour said this was a very unsatisfactory case. The plaintiffs appeared to carry on their business at Sheffield. They obtained orders from people in London, but had no power over the stage managers, and appeared to take no steps to see that the contracts were carried out. He was not satisfied that the contract in this case had been carried out, and there would be judgment for the defendant.

HANDS v. COURTNEIDGE.—TEST ACTION: MUSICIANS AND REHEARSALS.

9 In the Westminster County Court Judge Woodfall tried the case of Hands v. Courtneidge, in which a question of importance was dealt with as a test action as to the right of managers to retain the services of the members of the orchestra for purposes of rehearsal after the ordinary hours. The plaintiff was Mr. Harry Arthur Hands, flautist, and he sued the defendant, Mr. Robert Courtneidge, lessee of the Queen's, Shaftesbury Avenue, for damages for wrongful dismissal. Mr. Ricardo, in opening the case, said that in April his client who was a member of the Orchestral Association, was engaged as a flautist in the orchestra in *The Gay Gordons* at the Aldwych, and early in May he received a postcard from Mr. Chapman, acting in behalf of Mr. Wood, the conductor of the orchestra at the Queen's, offering him an appointment as second flute for *The Dairymaids.* The plaintiff accepted the appointment, and on May 4 attended at the Queen's for a full-dress rehearsal at seven o'clock. The rehearsal continued until 12.25 midnight, when the plaintiff appealed to Mr. Wood to let him go in order that he might catch the last train to his home at Barnes. Mr. Wood, however, directed him to go back to his seat in the orchestra, and he did so, but about ten minutes later he left the theatre in order to catch his train, as he had only a shilling in his pocket at the time, and had he lost his train he would have had to walk home. On the following day he went to the theatre, and was told that his place had been filled up. He now sought to recover damages for wrongful dismissal. He (counsel) submitttd that, inasmuch as the plaintiff had been playing at an afternoon performance that day, it could not be expected of him to continue playing at the rehearsal until the early hours of the following morning, as it required great skill to manipulate a flute.

The plaintiff said that on the night in question he remained in the orchestra until about 12.25, when he got up with the intention of asking Mr. Wood to allow him to go in order to catch the last train. Mr. Wood told him to go back to his seat, and he did so, and remained there until the last moment that would leave him time to catch his train.

The Judge: Did you tell Mr. Wood that you had only a shilling in your pocket, and that if you lost the last train you would have to walk home?

Plaintiff: Yes.

The Judge: What happened when you went to the theatre on the following day?

Plaintiff: I saw Mr. Wood, who told me that my place had been filled up, but in spite of that I went to the theatre in the evening, but was not allowed to take my place in the orchestra.

DEFENCE.

For the defence, Mr. A. Wood said that he was musical director in the employ of the defendant. On the night of May 4 he saw the plaintiff leaving the orchestra, and stopped him at the door. He asked him where he was going, and he replied that he was going home. He (witness) told him that he must go back to his place in the orchestra, and that if he did not do so he would be dismissed. Plaintiff then went back to his seat and stayed there about ten minutes; then he got up and left the theatre, after having told witness that he was quite as independent as he was. On the following day he called at the theatre and apologised for his conduct, but he was told that he had been dismissed. Upon that ne asked for a week's salary, which was refused. So far as the question of working late was concerned, he (witness) agreed that the men should be allowed a cab fare, but at the same time the non-payment of it did not justify him in committing a breach of discipline. As to the question of notice, he considered the plaintiff's contract was subject to fourteen days' notice on either side.

Cross-examined: He did not hear the plaintiff say that he had only a shilling in his pocket. In any event he contended that he

had a right to keep the members of the orchestra until the rehearsal was finished.

In giving judgment, his Honour said the first point was as to what was the contract and what was a reasonable notice to put an end to it. The second point was, Was the plaintiff engaged for the run of the piece? The further question arose as to whether the order given by Wood was a reasonable one 1) keeping the plaintiff at the theatre until such a late hour. He (the judge) thought it was not a reasonable order unless a cab fare was provided. He thought the plaintiff's engagement was subject to a fortnight's notice, according to the custom of the profession, and for that sum judgment would be given in his favour, with costs.

GOWER v. BELL.—"MILL OF TIFTIE'S ANNIE."

In the Peterhead Sheriff Court proof was led before Sheriff Begg in an action at the instance of Mr. James Gower, actor, Peterhead, against Mr. W. R. Bell, theatre proprietor, Peterhead, and Mrs. Bell, his wife, concluding for £20 from each for loss and damage sustained by pursuer, the author and proprietor of the copyright drama *Mill of Tiftie's Annie; or, The Trumpeter of Fyvie,* in respect that the defenders, without having obtained the license or authority of the pursuer, or made any payment to him of royalty, played that drama at Bervie on or about April 9, 1908.

Mr. David Troup, solicitor, Peterhead, who appeared for Mr. and Mrs. Bell, said that his defence was a denial that the defenders had performed any play belonging to the pursuer. He suggested that one proof should suffice for both cases. This was agreed to.

Mr. Gower, who conducted his own case, called as his first witness Mr. W. R. Bell. In answer to Mr. Gower, Mr Bell said he admitted that pursuer was the author of the drama *Mill of Tiftie's Annie.* He likewise admitted that he performed the play in the Music Hall, Peterhead, four years ago; but he denied having performed Mr. Gower's play in Bervie on April 9 last. At this stage pursuer demanded a letter signed by his daughter, who was a member of Mr. Bell's company at Bervie. A discussion took place between pursuer and Mr. Bell, and the Sheriff had to intervene, remarking that Mr. Gower ought to put questions, and not quarrel with the witness. The evidence had not proceeded much further when angry words again passed between the parties, and the Sheriff reminded Mr. Gower that that was a court of justice.

Mrs. Bell, the next witness, denied having performed Mr. Gower's play of *Mill of Tiftie's Annie* at Bervie on April 9 last. She never asked Mr. Gower's daughter to give a performance of the play. She had the manuscript of *Mill of Tiftie's Annie* twelve years ago, but she had no manuscript now.

The Sheriff: Have you got any more witnesses regarding the piece being performed at Bervie? We cannot waste the time of the Court in this manner.

Mr. Gower: I have no more witnesses.

Mr. Gower then went into the witness-box, and in answer to the Sheriff, said he was not present at Bervie on April 9 when *Mill of Tiftie's Annie* was performed. His daughter was with Mr. Bell's company on that occasion.

The Sheriff gave judgment in favour of defenders, and assoilzied them with expenses,

BAINES v. WITHERS.—BREACH OF CONTRACT.

Before Mr. Justice A. T. Lawrence and a jury, at the Nisi Prius Court at the Staffordshire Assizes, Cecil Hamilton Baines, proprietor of the Burslem Hippodrome, brought an action against Alfred Withers for breach of contract.

11

According to Mr. V. G. Milward, who appeared for the plaintiff, the defendant at the beginning of the year was travelling an excellent pantomime. On January 1 a telegram was sent by plaintiff to the defendant offering a date to the latter to bring his pantomime to Burslem. Some correspondence passed between the parties, and defendant ultimately contracted to present his performance at Burslem on January 27. On January 20, a week after defendant had entered into the contract, he wired repudiating it, and said he did not intend to open on the terms arranged. It was alleged that in addition to material damages, which the plaintiff had suffered through the defendant's company not appearing at Burslem, he had lost prestige, and his takings had gone down.

Plaintiff in evidence said that he wrote to the defendant stating that his company could "play to £150." The terms on the contract were that the defendant should have 65 per cent. of the gross takings.

Cross-examined by Mr. W. J. Disturnal, who defended, plaintiff said that he knew that Mr. Withers was managing director of the South Wales Entertainments, Limited. So far as this pantomime was concerned, he had dealt with Mr. Withers, and nobody else.

Mr. Disturnal, for the defence, submitted that there was never any agreement, and therefore there could be no contract.

The jury found that there was a contract, and awarded the plaintiff £45 damages.

ARTISTS AND ILLNESS.—UNITED COUNTIES THEATRES v. CHANTI.

The case of the United Counties Theatres, Limited, v. Chanti came before Judge Woodfall in the Westminster County Court by way of a claim for damages by music hall proprietors against an artist for breach of contract. Mr. Walter Payne was counsel for plaintiffs, and Mr. Doughty for the defendant.

20

The case for the plaintiffs was that defendant was engaged to perform at their Plymouth hall, and wrote that he was too ill to fulfil his contract. He wrote that he had a slight attack of rheumatic fever, but sent no medical certificate. Plaintiffs had put him at the top of the bill, and had to go to considerable trouble and expense to get another turn to take the place. There was a clause in the contract that a medical certificate must be supplied in cases of inability to perform through illness.

Mr. Doughty said the only person who had suffered was Chanti, who lost his salary. Illness, he submitted, was an excuse in law.

His Honour said the contract was a binding one, and had been partly performed by each side, defendant having supplied the bill matter and plaintiffs having put it in the bill. What damages had plaintiffs sustained? What was the cause of the contract being broken? The illness, not the absence of the certificate. Plaintiffs would have suffered the same had defendant sent the certificate, and they would have had to engage another artist just the same. He quite understood the necessity for a certificate, and here the artist agreed to supply one if he fell ill and was unable to perform. Plaintiffs were entitled to nominal damages, which he assessed at 40s.

LAKE GRANGE v. SAVILE.—ACTORS AND FREE REHEARSALS.

At Brompton County Court, before Judge Bray, Mr. George Lake Grange, actor, of New King's Road, Fulham, sued Mr. W. H. Savile, proprietor of a music hall sketch, residing at Bishop's Mansions, to recover 25s. in respect of a week's salary.

20

Plaintiff's wife appeared, and stated that her husband had recently been engaged in kinematograph work. He asked her to look at the columns of THE STAGE, and if she saw anything that was likely to suit him to reply to the advertisement. She did so, and saw among the advertisements one from the defendant for a tall gentleman, and, her husband being a man 6 ft. 2½ in. in height, she sent her little boy round to the defendant, and in her husband's behalf asked for 35s. per week. Subsequently an interview took place between her husband and the defendant, and the latter arranged to pay her husband 25s. weekly, and fixed a rehearsal for the following Saturday, thus confirming the agreement.

Defendant, in evidence, said that he was producing a new sketch with seven people in it. It was customary for the actors in such a production to give their services free at one week's rehearsals, and six out of the company of seven did. Mr. Grange told him he did not see his way to pay his expenses to and from Fulham to the Surrey, where the sketch was to be produced. Witness thereupon agreed to pay out-of-pocket expenses. The production of the sketch was, however, postponed.

In reply to his Honour, the defendant said that he had no witnesses to prove the custom to which he had referred. He added that he considered the plaintiff's claim a most improper one; a promise to pay his out-of-pocket expenses had been twisted into an agreement to pay salary.

His Honour said the onus rested with the defendant to show that it was customary for artists to give their services for a week, but no witnesses were present to prove this, and in the circumstances he could not find that such custom was proved. There would be judgment for the plaintiff for 25s., the amount claimed.

MORTIMER v. O'GORMAN AND OTHERS.—JUDGMENT.

In the Westminster County Court, Judge Woodfall decided the case of Mortimer v. O'Gorman and others, in which the plaintiff sued the defendants, in their capacity of officers of the Variety Artists' Federation, to recover damages by way of indemnity for breach of contract.

20

Mr. Doughty contended that under the Trade Union Act, 1871, Section 4, a member of a trade union could not recover damages.

His Honour said the question that he had to consider was as to whether the defendants induced the plaintiff to break his contracts with Mr. Payne and Mr. Gibbons, and agreed to indemnify him for any loss which he might sustain by so doing; and, if so, was it a legal contract? It was stated at the trial that a sort of ambassador of the defendants went to the plaintiff at the Canterbury armed with a letter from the defendants forbidding him to take his part in the performance, and agreeing to make good any loss which he might sustain. But what was the object of the defendants in acting as they did? He (the Judge) had no doubt that their object was to injure Mr. Payne, and they did injure him, because they caused him to close his house on that particular night. The act of the defendants was both malicious and illegal, and it followed, therefore, that their contract with the plaintiff was bad in consequence of its illegality, and that he could not recover under it. The strike in question could not be regarded as a trade one, as it was only directed against Mr. Payne and Mr. Gibbons, and, therefore, it did not come under the Trades Disputes Act. Defendants must have judgment. "I make no order as to costs," said his Honour. "The reason for defendants' success is their own illegality."

Mr. Doughty raised a question as to some costs being defendants' in any event.

His Honour: I will reserve the question of costs, then, and let you know.

(See report of case June 17.)

WALDORF THEATRE RATES.

At Bow Street Police Court, the Waldorf Theatre Syndicate, Ltd., Broad Street Avenue, E.C., and Mr. George Frederick Hughes **20** Morgan were summoned before Sir Albert De Rutzen for the non-payment of rates amounting to £1,253 due in respect of the Waldorf.—Mr. H. C. Ryde supported the summonses in behalf of the Westminster City Council; Mr. Cunningham Glen appeared for the defendants.

Mr. Ryde said that Mr. S. Shubert entered into negotiations with the Waldorf Theatre Syndicate, Limited, for taking over the lease of the theatre, which had at that time just been erected at Aldwych; but unfortunately he died before the matter was completed. His executor, Mr. Lee Shubert, was afterwards granted a lease of the theatre for twenty-one years, dating from March 12, 1907. The venture was not successful, and in July, 1907, Mr. Shubert shut up the theatre, sent the keys to the syndicate, and left this country. Since then he had had nothing further to do with the theatre. The police subsequently reported that the place was insecurely fastened—in fact, someone had feloniously entered it—and an application was made to the High Court. In consequence, Mr. Morgan, who now appeared as one of the defendants, was appointed to act as receiver. He at once appointed a caretaker and a fireman to look after the property. The curtains, carpets, seats, and all the fittings of a modern theatre —which belonged to the syndicate—still remained. After Mr. Shubert had left this country the name of the receiver and that of the syndicate were put upon the rate books, and he (Mr. Ryde) submitted that either or both of them were liable for the rates.

Mr. A. W. Peckham, solicitor to the syndicate, said that the Duke of Bedford was the ground landlord, and that the syndicate were the lessees.

In reply to Mr. Glen he said that in his opinion Mr. Shubert would be entitled to use the theatre to-morrow if he wished to do so. He believed that Mr. Shubert left a safe and a few articles of furniture at the theatre.

Mr. Morgan, the receiver, gave evidence as to appointing a caretaker and fireman. Water welled up in the basement of the theatre, and when he was first appointed he found that it was costing something like £80 a year to pump it away. He had, however, arranged to have a hydraulic pump which automatically discharged the water into the main when it reached a certain point, and only cost about £6 a year. That and the provision of some new locks was all he had had done to the theatre since his appointment.

Mr. Robert Stokes, rate collector, said that the name of Mr. Lee Shubert was still on the rate-books, and the names of Mr Morgan and the syndicate had been added.

Mr. Glen, in the course of a long legal argument, contended that the receiver was an officer of the Court of Chancery, and that neither he nor the syndicate were liable for the rates. He submitted that the syndicate were in the same position as a man who let a furnished house to someone who went away without paying.

Sir Albert De Rutzen reserved his decision until July 23, when, in giving his judgment, the magistrate said in March, 1907, Mr. Lee Shubert was granted a twenty-one years' lease of the Waldorf Theatre, Aldwych, but the venture was not a success, and a few months afterwards he shut up the place and left the country. Owing to the insecure state in which the theatre had been left, proceedings were taken in Chancery, and Mr. Morgan, one of the defendants in this case, was appointed to act as receiver. It had been argued by the defence that the appointment of the receiver did not constitute a change of occupation, and in support of that contention counsel quoted the decision of Lord Justice Lopes in the case of marriage, "Neave and Co." He (the magistrate) was bound by that decision, and therefore the summons must be dismissed. He felt sorry for the Westminster City Council that it should be so, and if he were asked to state a case for the High Court he would be pleased to do so.

Mr. Cunningham Glen applied for costs, but the application was refused.

THE "LESSER COLUMBUS" CASE.— PROSECUTION WITHDRAWN.

Laurence Cowen, of Great Portland Street, W., again appeared before Mr. Denman, at **27** Marlborough Street Police Court, to answer an adjourned summons which alleged that he obtained valuable securities, worth about £320, with intent to defraud Ella Amelia Crispin, a married lady, residing in Nottingham Place, W.

Mr. Arthur Newton, solicitor, prosecuted, and Mr. R. D. Muir, barrister, instructed by Mr. Freke Palmer, appeared for the defence.

Mr. Arthur Newton now said that the case had been before the Court for about two months. He mentioned in his opening statement that a lady had written to the Public Prosecutor complaining about Mr. Cowen having obtained £500 from her. He (Mr. Newton) wished to say that the lady had now repudiated the letter she wrote to the Public Prosecutor, and had stated that she was quite satisfied with the treatment she had received at the hands of Mr. Cowen. With regard to the debenture for £3,500 which had been referred to, Mr. Crispin admitted in cross-examination that he had actually filled up some of the forms connected with the debenture. Then, too, Mrs. Crispin was seriously ill, and it was imperatively necessary that she should go for a sea voyage. Another point he (Mr. Newton) relied upon was that Mr. Cowen had put £30,000 into St. James's Hall, but it had been shown by his friend Mr. Muir that a mistake had been made with regard to that matter, and that there was merely a mortgage on the hall for that sum.

Before the prosecution was launched, he continued, the defendant had offered to buy back from Mrs. Crispin the shares she had in the company, and it would be recollected that the certificate with regard to the profits was unfortunately mislaid. As the case had gone on it dwindled, and he could not fail to notice that the evidence of some of the witnesses did not come up to the proofs they had made. Mr. Cowen had offered to buy back the shares Mrs. Crispin had in the company on his receiving back the money he had paid her and her husband, and on condition that she should pay the law expenses he had been put to in connection with the present prosecution. His (Mr. Newton's) application was that the Court should allow the prosecution to be dropped, and allow Mr. Cowen's offer to be accepted.

Mr. Muir said that he was sure the magistrate would not be surprised at the course taken by the prosecution, as there was not a single point on which they could establish a case. No terms would satisfy Mr. Cowen except an unconditional withdrawal. Prior to the prosecution Mr. Cowen had offered to buy Mrs. Crispin's shares in the company from her, and he was now prepared to offer her just and equitable terms, namely, that she should have back the money she paid for the shares, less the sum taken out of the company by her and her husband, Mrs. Crispin undertaking to pay the legal expenses Mr. Cowen had been put to in connection with his defence. These terms had been accepted, and his (counsel's) submission was that there would be no difficulty whatever in allowing the prosecution, which had absolutely failed, to be withdrawn.

Mr. Denman said that allowing a prosecution to be withdrawn was no part of his duty. The prosecution, half-way through the preliminary inquiry, withdrew, and all he could do was to mark the case as withdrawn. He would, however, as part of his duty, have to lay the facts before the Public Prosecutor.

VERNON v. HICKS.

In the Westminster County Court, Miss Millicent Vernon, then playing in Manchester, **29** sued Mr. Seymour Hicks for a fortnight's salary in lieu of notice. Miss Vernon was one of the Gibson Girls at the Vaudeville, and was engaged as singer and dancer for Mr. Seymour Hicks's Continental tour of *The Dress Rehearsal*.

Mr. Cosmo R. Cran, plaintiff's solicitor, explained that the tour broke down at Paris, and the company were summarily dismissed. Plaintiff had made a special journey from Manchester to give evidence in support of her claim, and now defendant did not appear, nor did anyone represent him.

Mr. C. R. Cuff, senior registrar, gave plaintiff judgment with costs, but was unable to include plaintiff's costs of coming from Manchester, as her address on the summons was a London one.

KINEMATOGRAPH ENTERTAINMENTS WITH MUSIC.

At Tottenham Petty Sessions, John Wood, of the People's Palace, Tottenham, and James **30** Philip Beavan, 8, Bruce Grove, Tottenham, were summoned for "unlawfully using for public music and other public entertainment of the like kind a certain place there called the People's Palace, without having a license for the purpose, contrary to the Music and Dancing Licenses (Middlesex) Act, 1894."

Mr. M. F. Wrottersby prosecuted for the Middlesex County Council; Mr. S. Lambert represented the defendant Wood, and Mr. Beavan conducted his own defence.

Mr. Wrottersby, in opening the case, said the defendant Beavan in 1907 applied for a singing and dancing license, which was granted subject to certain conditions—viz., structural alterations, as recommended by the Engineer to the County Council. These conditions, however, were not complied with, and the Council felt themselves obliged to refuse the license. In spite of that, Beavan, as the owner of the premises, and Wood, as manager of the company which was giving performances there, permitted entertainments accompanied by music. The entertainment was a kinematograph one, accompanied by music, which therefore came within the Statute. The only defence could be upon a point of law, but he submitted that a kinematograph entertainment which was accompanied by the playing of the piano was sufficiently within the Statute to justify the Bench convicting. The reason the County Council refused the license originally was entirely with a view to the safety of the public—the fixing of hydrants, removing the barriers, and so forth, which were absolutely necessary.

Gustav Perrin, contractor, of London Road, Enfield, stated that he visited the Palace on June 5, 9, and 11. The entertainment opened with a pianoforte solo, and while the pictures were shown the piano was played continuously. During the interval of five minutes the instrument was played. There was no singing and no dancing. He, however, heard some noises at the back of the hall.

Cross-examined by Beavan, witness said he was not a contractor under the County Council, and was in no way connected with that body. The reason he attended the Palace was because he received a letter from Sir Richard Nicholson, the clerk to the County Council, asking him to go.

Cross-examined by Mr. Lambert, witness said he did not know why it was that a Mr. Potter laid the information; witness was merely asked to report. He had not been paid for his services, but he hoped to be.

Mr. Lambert advanced a point of law as to the occupation of the premises, which the Bench upheld, and the summons against Wood was therefore dismissed.

The defendant Beavan said that that was another instance of the persecution he had been subjected to by the County Council. About twelve months before the withdrawal of the license the County Council insisted on all sorts of alterations, necessitating an expenditure of £500 or £600. The place was rendered perfectly fit for stage music and dancing purposes. He wrote to the County Council asking whether a kinematograph entertainment would be allowed. They replied in November, 1906, stating that no objection would be taken to that in view of the fact that the hall was no longer licensed for music, dancing, and stage purposes. There would be "no objection raised to a piano."

Mr. Wrottersby said he was not aware that such a letter was sent by the County Council, but he contended that it was superseded by subsequent correspondence, and was therefore rendered obsolete.

The Magistrates looked upon the letter as a definite grant. "On the face of that letter," the Chairman (Dr. Daly) said, "we are bound to dismiss the summons."

Mr. Wrottersby wished to withdraw the letter.

The Clerk: Then you must write and tell him so.

RENO v. THE OXFORD, LIMITED.

In the Westminster County Court, his Honour Judge Woodfall tried the case of Reno v. The Oxford, Limited. It was an action by **31** the plaintiff, Mr. George Lawrence Reno, who was described as a burlesque artist, to recover from the defendants the sum of £40, being one week's salary for appearing at the Oxford Music Hall.

Mr. Doughty was counsel for the plaintiff, and Mr. Payne appeared for the defence.

It appeared from the opening of counsel that in April, 1908, Mr. Wilkie Bard was engaged at the Oxford, but on the 25th of that month he was unable to appear owing to illness, and Mr. Collins, acting on behalf of the defendants, appealed to Messrs. Marinelli to supply him with a turn to take the place of Mr. Wilkie Bard. It was arranged at very short notice that the plaintiff should fill up the vacancy at a salary of £40 a week, but after appearing for one night he was informed that Mr. Wilkie Bard was coming back, and that he would not be required. His contention now was that the plaintiff was engaged for one week at a salary of £40.

On behalf of the defence, it was contended that the plaintiff was not engaged for a week, but that he was to be paid at the rate of £40 a week. As a matter of fact, he only appeared for one night, and in respect of that the salary had been paid into court.

On the other hand, it was urged on behalf of the plaintiff that it would be absurd to suppose that he would agree to take about a thousand pounds worth of properties to the theatre in order to give a one-night show on the basis of one night's pay.

His Honour, in giving judgment, said the question was as to whether Marinelli's acting as agents on behalf of Mr. Collins had exceeded their instructions in engaging the plaintiff for a week. The probabilities of the case were of equal weight on both sides. He (the judge) did not think the plaintiff ever agreed to take a one-night engagement, and on the other hand he did not think Mr. Collins ever intended that he should be engaged for a week. He was prepared to give judgment for the plaintiff for a week's salary, but if the defendants chose to pay the costs of the day he would give them a fresh trial, and have the case tried by a jury.

After a consultation it was decided to have the case disposed of at once, and accordingly his Honour gave judgment for the plaintiff for £40, to include the sum paid into court.

FREER v. THOMPSON.—SCENIC RAILWAY ACCIDENT AT THE WHITE CITY.

Before his Honour Judge Woodfall, in the Westminster County Court, the case of Freer **31** v. Thompson was disposed of. The plaintiff when at the White City decided to take a trip on the scenic railway. The train stopped for a time owing to a defect in the running, and the plaintiff and other persons alighted whilst it was being put right. When the signal was given for the passengers to take their seats again the plaintiff, among a number of others, endeavoured to do so, but before he could get on to the car the train was set in motion, and the result was that he was thrown violently to the ground, and sustained injuries.

The defence was that the plaintiff endeavoured to get on the car whilst it was in motion, and that the accident was brought about by his own negligence. It was alleged that a proper signal was given for the restarting of the train, and that ample time was allowed for the passengers to take their seats.

His Honour, in giving judgment, said his view of the case was that the defendants must at all costs make such provisions as were necessary to prevent a passenger from entering a car whilst it was in motion, and if they failed to do that they were guilty of negligence. In this case he had come to the conclusion that the plaintiff had established his case as to negligence on the part of the defendant, and therefore it was now only a question of damages. The plaintiff had no doubt received very nasty injuries, and he (the Judge) thought the justice of the case would be met if he gave him a verdict for fifty guineas, and for that sum there would be judgment, with costs.

AUGUST.

ROGERS v. WITHERS.—UNAUTHORISED PERFORMANCE OF PANTOMIME.

At West Bromwich County Court, before Mr. Registrar Walker, a case was heard in which **7** Stanley Rogers, pantomime writer, of North Shields, claimed £10 damages from Albert J. Withers, of the New Hippodrome, West Bromwich, for the infringement by unauthorised performances of the plaintiff's pantomime entitled *Aladdin.* In the alternative the plaintiff claimed £10, or his fee for license to perform the said pantomime for the season 1907-8. Mr. A. A. Millichip appeared for the plaintiff, the action being undefended. Mr. Millichip explained that the plaintiff had written a pantomime entitled *Aladdin.* Last Christmas this pantomime was produced at the West Bromwich Hippodrome, where it ran for two weeks. No application was made to the plaintiff for the use of the pantomime, and the production was quite unauthorised. It was now stated that the defendant had sent a letter to the Registrar saying that he had decided not to defend the action, and offering to pay the claim by monthly instalments. The Registrar gave judgment for plaintiff for the full amount claimed, and an order was taken for the payment of £2 down and £2 a month.

WILKES v. WALLER.

Before his Honour Judge Woodfall, in the Westminster County Court, the case of Wilkes **7** v. Waller was tried. It was an action by the plaintiff, a dramatic agent carrying on business in the Strand, to recover the amount of £16 5s. as commission for procuring a week's engagement for Mrs. Waller at the Pavilion, Glasgow.

Mrs. Waller conducted her case in person, and contended that by the terms of her contract with the plaintiff she was to be paid for two *matinées* at the rate of £12 10s. for each, whereas Mr. Lloyd, the manager of the hall, only paid her for one.

His Honour told Mrs. Waller that she was in a difficult position in not having been legally represented, although she was perfectly entitled to conduct her own case if she chose. If, as she suggested, the plaintiff had improperly altered the terms of the contract, her remedy was by way of a counterclaim for damages. In any event, Mr. Lloyd ought to have been called to give his version of the affair, and if she (defendant) chose to pay the costs of the day, together with the amount of the claim, into Court, he (the judge) would adjourn the case for the attendance of Mr. Lloyd; otherwise, he was prepared to give judgment for the plaintiff for the amount of his claim.

Mrs. Waller agreed to adopt his Honour's

suggestion to pay the debt and costs into Court, and accordingly the case was adjourned. (See report, October 7.)

KINEMATOGRAPH ENTERTAINMENTS.— THE INCLUSION OF MUSIC.

The application for a music and dancing license for the Gem, on the Marine Parade, **8** Great Yarmouth, where a kinematograph entertainment was given with music, refused by the Yarmouth Bench on Friday, July 31, had a sequel on August 8 in the Yarmouth Police Court, when Charles Blake Cochrane, manager of the Gem, was summoned for keeping open this hall for public singing without having first obtained a license, and also for causing an obstruction on the footpath by the playing of a gramophone from the balcony. The Town Clerk prosecuted; Mr. G. Elliott (London), instructed by Messrs. Ferrier and Ferrier, defended.

The magistrates retired, and were absent ten minutes. On their return the Chairman said there could be no doubt that a public entertainment was given at the Gem, and a majority of the magistrates were of opinion the music and singing were not merely subsidiary, but formed a substantial part of the entertainment. On the first summons defendant would be fined £5 and £1 each on the other four.

The obstruction summons was adjourned *sine die.*

On the following Friday, August 13, an application for a music and dancing license was refused by the magistrates.

CLAYTON v. HOLLAND—WHAT ARE P TO-DATE FILMS?

An action of interest to kinematograph proprietors and proprietors of places of enter-**13** tainment where the kinematograph is an attraction came before Judge Benson in the Sheffield County Court.

The plaintiff was Elisha Charles Clayton, kinematograph proprietor, of 276, Western Bank, Sheffield, and the defendant was William Holland, of the St. James's, Manchester. Plaintiff sought to recover £25 damages, representing two weeks' engagement in lieu of notice, for breach of contract, and 10s. for the use of a special film of the Grand National race.

Mr. T. E. Ellison, instructed by Mr. Kesteven, appeared for the plaintiff, and Mr Meunier represented the defendant

His Honour, in summing up, said the question to be considered was, What was an up to-date picture? No two witnesses in the case appeared to have specifically agreed as to what really constituted an up-to-date picture. It seemed to be purely a matter of opinion as to the length of time during which a picture might be so described. He came to the conclusion that there had been no substantial breach of the agreement to justify the sudden termination of it not in accordance with the terms of the contract. But his Honour held that the plaintiff was entitled to recover only the damage that he had suffered on account of the loss of two weeks' employment.

Accordingly he gave judgment for the plaintiff for £6 10s.

CHILDS v. THOMPSON.—A CURIOUS COUNTER-CLAIM.

Before Judge Parry in the Salford County Court, Wallace Childs, of Mill Lane, Leigh, **14** claimed £12 0s. 10d. from Peter Thompson, of Monton Road, Eccles, as the balance of salary due to him as manager, and as the balance of money paid by him in defendant's behalf in connection with a pantomime, *The Babes in the Wood.* The defendant admitted the claim, but counter-claimed for twelve guineas for board and lodgings, with which, he said, he provided the plaintiff at his request in 1906 and 1907.

In reply to this counter-claim, the plaintiff denied that he owed anything, as he was an invited guest on each occasion.

Judge Parry said the matter was difficult to decide, because theatrical people were not so distinctly businesslike as other business folk. With regard to the first part of the counter-claim, it seemed that Mr. Thompson asked the plaintiff to dinner, and he stayed six weeks. He was afraid he must be considered an invited guest on that occasion. The defendant could not invite a person for six weeks, and then a year or two afterwards send in a bill. If that were upheld there would be a danger of that kind of thing happening everywhere. With regard to the second part of the counter-claim, however, there was a difference. The plaintiff knew that the defendant owed him money and was in difficulties for the time being, and even if he misunderstood the terms on which he was staying in the house, he ought not to have taken advantage of the defendant's friendship. There would consequently be judgment for the plaintiff for £6 0s. 10d., with costs.

RELPH (TICH) v. LONDON ANIMATED PICTURE COMPANY.—ALLEGED MIS-REPRESENTATION.

In the Vacation Court Mr. Justice Eve had before him the case of Relph v. the London **14** Animated Picture Company and Gooes, in which the plaintiff, known as Little Tich, sought an injunction to restrain the company from displaying bills which might lead people to believe that he was personally going to appear at a certain place of amusement. Mr. J. Fulton Carr said that the defendant company had, during Bank Holiday week, billed Southsea with a statement that there would be a special attraction, Little Tich, London's great comedian, running at enormous expense at the music hall. The plaintiff's case was that, although in fact the defendant company were only representing him in pictures, the public might be led to believe that he personally would appear. The plaintiffs were billing Hove for next week with similar bills, and he desired that this should be stopped. Mr. Matthews said the defendants had no desire to misrepresent the facts, and would give an undertaking in any terms his Lordship thought fit. but they were sure when they had time to answer the affidavit his Lordship would agree that this was not a case for an injunction. Mr. Carr replied that a music-hall artist held a peculiar position. being often under contract to appear only with the consent of managers. The plaintiff, therefore, was entitled to all the assistance that the law could give him to stop a person representing that he was going to appear at a music hall when in fact he was not. After considerable argument his Lordship said there must be an undertaking by the defendants until the following Wednesday. when the matter could be argued before him on its merits, not to make use of bills which would be likely to suggest that Little Tich was going to appear at any music hall at which they were under contract to give a kinematograph representation. Mr. Matthews said that if the plaintiff had approached the defendants he had no doubt neither he nor his friend would have been in court that day.

On August 19 the hearing again came before Mr. Justice Eve. Mr. Matthew, on behalf of the defendants, stated that they did not wish to issue any posters of the same sort again, and would give a perpetual undertaking to that effect, provided that no order as to costs be made against them. Plaintiff's counsel would not agree to forego the costs, and the hearing was again adjourned until August 26, when plaintiff was awarded his costs.

PORTABLES AND THE LAW.—A STAGE-PLAYS LICENSE.

At Reigate a portable theatre proprietor, named A. J. Barden, who for the preceding month had been giving dramatic performances in a canvas erection off the Brighton Road, Redhill, was summoned for "that on July 29, at Redhill, he did act and present from a certain building, known as the Royal Pavilion, a stage play, *Convict 99*, the said building not being licensed for stage plays."

Defendant pleaded not guilty.

Inspector Lee said that on July 29, from 9.30 p.m. to 10 p.m., he visited the Royal Pavilion, off High Street, Redhill, where he saw a play being acted named *Convict 99*. Witness produced an announcement bill, similar to others exhibited on the building, giving information as to the plays to be performed. He saw the public admitted by payment, the defendant being at the door and his wife in the pay-box. Witness did not pay when he went in. The audience numbered something over a hundred. He did not see the defendant acting. Witness had seen the defendant, and he told him he had not got a license, but he had been to the County Council, and they had given him a letter saying a license was not necessary. The letter was not shown to witness.

The Head Constable, in reply to the Mayor, said he could not produce any evidence that the defendant had acted himself.

The summons was dismissed.

Another summons for causing to be acted, at the same time and place, a stage play named *Convict 99*, in an unlicensed theatre, was then proceeded with.

Inspector Lee repeated the evidence he gave on the previous summons.

Defendant said he went to Kingston, and was told a license was not required, as the place did not have a foundation. He made an application to the Town Clerk of Reigate, and was referred to Kingston.

Charles Elliston, stage manager to the defendant, said when they left Dorking he made application to the Reigate Council for a license. There were portable theatres in other places in Surrey without licenses, and it was understood that so long as they were not a nuisance they were allowed to continue. They did not act stage plays, as they were only a small band of strolling players, simply giving sketches. *Convict 99* was taken from a penny book, "Simon Lee," and was "boiled" down, not being really a stage play. Witness produced a letter from the County Council. in which it was stated, as they were strolling players, that the Council had no power to license the building. The defendant had written to the Chief Constable asking him if there was any objection to give them reasonable time, and they would go away.

Defendant asked why he could not get a

license in the town. He had been granted one by the magistrates at Horsham.

The Mayor said the justices had decided to convict.

There were two other summonses for alleged offences on August 19, similar to those on which summonses were granted for July 29.

Head Constable Metcalfe said he would withdraw both of these, as so long as there was a conviction the object was attained.

A fine of £1 and costs was imposed for the offence of causing acting in an unlicensed theatre on July 29.

SEPTEMBER.

CRUELTY TO A CHILD.

At Bow Street, before Mr. Curtis Bennett, Mary O'Neil, aged 42, described as an elocutionist, of Little James Street, Bloomsbury, was charged with assaulting and ill-treating Mary Lynas, aged 7, by beating her about the body, arms, and legs in a manner likely to cause her unnecessary suffering and injury to her health.

Mr. Harry Wilson prosecuted on behalf of the National Society for the Prevention of Cruelty to Children.

Dr. Thomas B. Brooke, divisional surgeon, detailed the result of his examination of the child. He said he found a large number of severe bruises, caused for the most part by a stick or heavy cane.

The Magistrate: To cause the bruises you saw, must considerable violence have been used or not?

The Witness: Extreme violence. Continuing, he said that on one portion of the back there was severe and extensive bruising, caused by some flat instrument used with extreme violence. There was another terrible bruise 2½ins. by 1½ins. caused by a blow or a succession of blows inflicted with a heavy stick or cane. On the back of the legs there were weals and scars 4ins. or 5ins. long. In some cases the blows had been severe enough to cut the skin, as though done with a knife. On the left forearm there were two severe weals, one of them 2½ins. long and an inch wide. From the waist to the feet at the back there were no fewer than twenty-four severe contusions, and a long weal extending right across the shoulders. There were other weals on the arms, which had probably been caused on the day of the examination.

The hearing was adjourned until Saturday, September 12, the prisoner being remanded in custody. (See report, September 12.)

ALLEGED BOGUS THEATRICAL AGENCY.—W. C. WATSON CHARGED.

At the Guildhall, before Alderman Sir Walter Wilkin, William Cecil Watson, twenty-five, alias F. J. Benson, who described himself as a dramatist, of no fixed abode, was charged, on a warrant, with having, on or about October 15, 1907, unlawfully carried on a theatrical employment agency without having registered his name, address, and other particulars required by Sections 45 and 48 of the London County Council (General Powers) Act, 1905.

The prisoner, it was stated, having been served with a summons to answer this charge last January, absconded to America, returning to England on Wednesday, September 2. He was arrested at Hackney on September 5, and his reply to the charge was that he never carried on an agency, but was the actual employer.

For the purposes of a remand the sworn information of Frank Fenton, a barman, of the Royal Hotel, Mile End Road, was read. Fenton said that in September last, having answered an advertisement in a daily paper, he received a letter, in consequence of which he went to Broad Street House, where he saw a person calling himself F. J. Benson. This individual stated that he was forming a company to produce *East Lynne*, and offered him (Fenton) a part, on payment of two guineas for "stage tuition." He paid the money and was given a part to learn. Later on, receiving a guarantee of employment, he handed Benson a further sum of £5. Benson never, in fact, procured him employment, but returned him £3 15s. by cheque.

Detective Nicholls said that the police had received numerous complaints concerning prisoner's business, and there would probably be charges of obtaining money by false pretences.

Sir Walter ordered a remand in custody. (See report, September 16.)

CRUELTY TO A CHILD.

At Bow Street Police Court, Mary O'Neil was charged, on remand, before Mr. Curtis-Bennett, with assaulting and ill-treating **12** May Lynas, aged seven, by beating her about the arms, body, and legs, in a manner likely to cause her unnecessary suffering and injury to health.

Mr. Harry Wilson prosecuted on behalf of the National Society for the Prevention of Cruelty to Children ; Mr. Crawshay defended.

Dr. Brook stated that on the preceding Thursday he further examined the child at her mother's house in the presence of Dr. Ryan, who was there on behalf of the defence. What he saw on Thursday confirmed the opinion he had previously formed, that great violence must have been used to inflict such injuries. There were still eighteen distinct marks of injury below the child's waist line. Portions of two wounds behind the knees were still unhealed. On Thursday the child complained of internal pains.

The child's mother, Madge Lynas, the wife of an engineer, living in Clapham Road, was the next witness. She said that she was an actress, and sometimes went in the name of Moon. A short time ago she saw the following advertisement in THE STAGE:—

Wanted, a pretty, refined little girl for small part in drama. Beginner not objected to.

The witness wrote in reply : "I have a little girl aged seven. Very quick and old-fashioned. Can be of a serious turn of mind, and very funny. Would make a good boy." An interview ensued, and it was eventually agreed that the child should go to live with the prisoner at her flat in Bloomsbury, and be trained for the theatrical profession. The child was quite healthy when she left home.

The witness said she did not see the child again until her husband brought her from Gray's Inn Road Police Station.

Cross-examined, the witness said that she had been twice married. The child in question was by her first husband. She did not tell the prisoner that the child had given her a great deal of trouble. She told the prisoner to see that the child obeyed her, but she did not mean that she was to beat her. The witness had sometimes slapped her hands, but her husband (the child's stepfather) had never beaten her. It was not true that she had pulled the child round the room by the hair of her head. There was no ground for suggesting the child was bruised when she went to reside with the prisoner.

May Lynas was then called, and said that the prisoner told her that she was going to teach her to "do the splits" and also to become an acrobat. Shortly after her arrival at the flat on the Monday night she saw some sweets in a dish on the table, and took some. For this the prisoner beat her with a cane on the wrists and also on her back. When she was practising the "splits" the prisoner threatened to beat her with a cane if she did not do them properly. During the five days she was with the prisoner she was beaten every day except one. Sometimes she was slapped with the hand, sometimes the cane was used, and occasionally a slipper.

Police-constable 94 E, said he found the child in the street crying bitterly, surrounded by a crowd. She appeared to be very much frightened, and he took her to Gray's Inn Road Police-station. She had her nightdress with her, and said she wanted to go home to her mother, as she had been ill-treated by a woman with whom she had been living.

Mr. Curtis-Bennett said that the case had occupied a great deal of time, but he did not regret that, as he was very anxious to get at the truth of the matter. When the case first came before him he declined to grant the prisoner bail, and found now that what he did then was absolutely right. The woman in the dock told the children she hoped to make money out of them. She demanded three things from them—honesty, truthfulness, and obedience. But what example did she set them? She was certainly not honest in her dealings, and she had admittedly told lies as to the ages of the children placed in her charge. Had it not been for the kindness of the police—and he had always found them kind during the twenty-three years he had been a metropolitan police magistrate—this poor little child might still have been in the power of the unmerciful woman now in the dock. How she, as a woman and a mother, could thrash a poor little mite while she was lying face downwards on a sofa ; how she could hit her harder and harder because she would not cry, and at the same time hold her head down so as to stifle any noise she might make, he could not conceive, but that she had done so there could be no doubt. Moreover, she had got her living out of poor children who had worked for her, and had neglected them in every way. It was an infamous trade, and it was time that the prisoner and others like her should know that it would be tolerated no longer. The prisoner had shown the child no mercy in this den of hers, and she would be sent to hard labour for six months without the option of a fine. In all probability any other cruel person who trafficked in the earnings of children would be sent for trial in order that they might be more severely dealt with.

Mr. Robert Dunston, barrister, said that some people, reading the report of the last hearing, might suppose that the proprietors of THE STAGE were to blame for inserting the prisoner's advertisement. He was asked by the proprietors of the paper to point out that there was nothing in the advertisement to lead them to suppose that it was intended or an improper purpose.

Mr. Wilson said he had no complaint to make, THE STAGE being a paper of good repute.

21

ALHAMBRA COMPANY, LIMITED, v. LOFTUS—MOTION TO RESTRAIN.

14 Mr. Bischoff, in the Vacation Court, applied, ex parte, in behalf of the Alhambra Theatre Company, for leave to serve Miss Cissie Loftus with notice of motion for an injunction to restrain her from appearing at the Coliseum, or any other theatre in London, in alleged breach of her contract with the Alhambra Company. Counsel also asked for an interim injunction over the next Wednesday restraining Miss Loftus in the terms of the notice of motion. He stated that she, in May, 1898, entered into a contract with the plaintiffs for an engagement for twelve weeks, and for a further engagement for a period of four weeks, at their option, her engagement to commence May 15, 1899. Her salary was to be £85 a week. Before the date of the performance of the contract Miss Loftus had a very good offer to go to America, and she applied to the plaintiffs to be released in some way from the contract. After some correspondence they agreed to her going to America, on condition that she performed her contract when she returned, before appearing at rival establishments in London. She returned to England in 1902, and appeared with Sir Henry Irving in *Faust.* The subject of the old contract was again revived, and there was an interview between Miss Loftus and the plaintiffs' manager. It was arranged that the date of the old contract should remain in abeyance, because she intended to go again to America, and it was also arranged, counsel added, that if she returned to the music hall stage she should fulfil her engagement with the plaintiffs. She had since come back to England, and had entered a contract with the Coliseum Company at a salary of £250 a week. The plaintiffs accordingly asked for the injunction.

Mr. Justice Coleridge: You can have leave to serve your notice of motion, but you cannot have your injunction. (See report, September 30.)

PIRATED MUSIC.

14 Samuel Lubinski, 22, was charged, at Old Street, with being in possession of a number of pirated copies of copyright musical publications.

Frank Maybee, an agent of the Association of Music Publishers, proved that shortly after midday the prisoner had a stall with music in Whitecross Street, and the witness sent a woman to make a purchase, she returning with a copy of a song called, "Love me and the world is mine." He then called a constable and gave the prisoner into custody, and on searching the stock on the stall and a quantity hidden found forty-one pirated copies of songs.

Witness produced the copyright certificates of some of these, and Mr. Cluer made an order condemning the copies. He ordered the prisoner, who offered no defence, to pay a fine of £5, or suffer a month's imprisonment.

ALLEGED BOGUS AGENCY.—WILLIAM CECIL WATSON DISCHARGED.

16 Before Mr. Alderman Johnston, at Guildhall, William Cecil Watson, 25, alias F. J. Benson, was charged, on remand, with having, in October last, carried on a theatrical employment agency at Broad Street House without having the same duly registered.

Mr. T. G. Vickery, appearing on behalf of the City Solicitor (Sir Homewood Crawford),

said the evidence which it had been proposed to put before the Court had been carefully sifted, and it seemed that he was not so much an agent as a person who himself offered employment to people who wished to go on the stage.

That he did form a company to play *East Lynne* now seemed clear, and he (Mr. Vickery) did not feel that he would be justified in taking up the time of the Court by calling his witnesses. The accused had been remanded till the following day, but, having arrived at the conclusion he (Mr. Vickery) had indicated, after a consultation with the Chief Clerk, he had had the prisoner brought up that day so that he should not be kept in custody a day longer.

The accused was discharged.

CRUELTY TO ELEPHANTS.—TRAINER AND ATTENDANT FINED.

18 At West London Police-court Mr. Garrett heard three summonses taken out by the Royal Society for the Prevention of Cruelty to Animals against Gustave Hagenbeck, elephant trainer, of the Ceylon Village, Franco-British Exhibition, William Schreida, trainer, and Havadia, elephant attendant, in respect of alleged cruelty to an elephant. Schreida and Havadia were summoned for "cruelly abusing and terrifying an elephant contrary to the Wild Animals in Captivity Protection Act"; and Mr. Hagenbeck for permitting the cruelty.

The cruelty, it was stated, consisted in the manner in which this elephant was driven down a steep declivity into a tank of water.

The magistrate imposed on Schreida a penalty of £5 with seven guineas costs, and on Havadia a penalty of 40s. As regards Hagenbeck, he was going to take a certain course in the hope that he would now realise that his elephants must not be treated in the fashion described, and that a stop would be put at once to that form of cruelty. He should order him to enter in his own recognisances in £10 to appear for judgment when called upon.

"CHARLEY'S AUNT" INFRINGEMENT.—W. G. BELL COMMITTED.

23 Mr. Justice Coleridge, sitting as Vacation Judge in the Chancery Division of the High Court, made an order to commit Mr. W. G. Bell to prison for contempt of court in performing *Charley's Aunt* at Hawkhurst, Kent, in August, in breach of an injunction made by the Court in April, 1907. Mr. Bell did not appear, and his lordship directed that the order should lie in the office for fourteen days.

RETURN OF POST—AN IMPORTANT POINT ON CONTRACTS.

24 At Lambeth County Court Percy E. Barkshire sued Joseph Blaschek, proprietor of The Dagonets concert company, to recover £3 10s. for breach of engagement.

Mr. W. Sparks, solicitor for the plaintiff, said his client was a baritone singer, and in July, 1908, in reply to an advertisement for an artist to appear with The Dagonets at Tunbridge Wells, he applied for an engagement, and received a postcard from the defendant offering him £3 10s. for his services during the following week. Plaintiff replied by return of post accepting the engagement, but was then told that he was not wanted.

Defendant said he wrote to plaintiff offering him the engagement on July 10, and not having received a reply from him by the night of the 11th he wired to another artist who had applied for the post and engaged him.

His Honour said the defendant in his postcard had requested a reply by return of post, and plaintiff had complied with that condition by writing on the day he received the defendant's communication. There would be judgment for the plaintiff, with costs.

ARTISTS AND BETTING MATTER ON HAND-BILLS—PROSECUTION AT COLCHESTER.

26 At Colchester Police Court, Charles Baldwin, manager of a troupe of artists performing at the Colchester Hippodrome in *Bank Clerks*, was summoned for that he did on September 22 "cause to be published a certain handbill, whereby it was made to appear that Thomas Henry Dey, of 406, Old Bond Street, London, W., would on application give information with respect to the receipt of money by the said Thomas Henry Dey as and for the consideration of securing the paying and giving by the said Thomas Henry Dey of certain sums of money on the happening of certain events and contingencies of and relating to horse races."

Mr. F. S. Collinge appeared for the defendant.

The Chief Constable said he had brought this case before the Bench in consequence of a number of complaints that had been received in reference to the matter.

Police-constable Hurren deposed that whilst in High Street he saw the defendant throw a number of handbills from a cab, in which he was driving with another gentleman and a lady. There were a number of foundrymen and boys near by at the time, and witness saw some of them pick up the handbills and read them.

The Bench retired for consultation, and, on their return, the Chairman said, looking at the bills, there could be no doubt as to what their meaning was. Even if defendant did not really know he was breaking the law, he must have known he was sailing near the wind. He was liable to a fine of £30, but this being the first case of the kind in that Court they imposed a fine of £1 only, with 11s. costs.

PERFORMING AN UNLICENSED PLAY.—W. G. BELL AND THE LESSEE FINED.

26 A case of considerable interest to the theatrical world, and more particularly to theatre lessees, was heard at St. Augustine's Petty Sessions, Canterbury, when W. G. B. Bell, who did not appear, and R. B. Reeves, the lessee and owner of the Assembly Rooms, Whitstable, were summoned by the director of public prosecutions, at the instance of the Lord Chamberlain, for producing a play, entitled *The Mysterious Drama: The Camden Town Murder*, at Whitstable on September 5. the same not having been licensed by the Lord Chamberlain.

Mr. Pearce prosecuted on behalf of the Treasury, and A. K. Mowll, of Dover and Canterbury, represented Mr. Reeves.

In opening the case Mr. Pearce said those proceedings were taken with the object of stopping what the authorities considered a most objectionable play, which enacted some of the principal incidents in the well-known murder trial which took place some few months back in London. This the authorities considered was extremely undesirable, for reasons which, he was sure, would be appreciated by the Bench. Those proceed-

ings were taken under Section 15 of 6 and 7 Vic., cap. 8, under which a penalty of £50 could be inflicted for producing an unlicensed play; while the license of the place in which it was produced would become absolutely void. Now, the performance in question really re-enacted the salient features of the now famous trial, and it was thought that a play of that kind could only pander to a morbid taste for sensationalism, and was in every way undesirable as being likely to bring the administration of justice into contempt. No sanction had been obtained from the Lord Chamberlain to perform the play, and had there been an application for sanction there was every reason to suppose that the Lord Chamberlain would have withheld it. In regard to the summons against the lessee of the theatre, there was no desire on the part of the prosecution to press this, because it could be assumed for the purposes of that prosecution that he had very little, if any, opportunity of ascertaining the nature of the play, although, of course, the person who so let his theatre came within the meaning of the section and rendered himself liable. Of course, if he was deceived in the matter and a fraud was practised upon him that might be a matter of defence. In that case, however, he did not press the summons, and he did not ask, under the circumstances, that the license should become void.

The Bench fined Bell £5 and the costs, or one month's imprisonment in default of distress, and in regard to Reeves said they could quite understand that it was a very serious thing for him, but as the owner of the hall he could not get away from his responsibility, and would have to pay a fine of 5s. and 7s. 10d. costs.

ALHAMBRA COMPANY v. LOFTUS.
INJUNCTION REFUSED.

30 In the Vacation Court, Mr. Justice Coleridge again had before him the application of the Alhambra Company for an interim injunction restraining until after the trial or further order Miss Cissie Loftus from committing an alleged breach of contract she had entered into with the plaintiffs' company by appearing at the Coliseum.

His Lordship, without calling upon Mr Bramwell Davis, K.C., for the defendant, in giving judgment, said he thought the terms of the contract were disputable, and in these circumstances he did not see why the matter should not be left to the trial, as damages would be sufficient remedy for any breach, if breach were proved. (See report, September 16.)

RELPH v. GILMORE.
INJUNCTION GRANTED.

30 In the Vacation Court the case of Relph v. Gilmore and Bainbridge came before Mr. Justice Coleridge upon the application of the plaintiff, Mr. Harry Relph, professionally known as "Little Tich," for an interim injunction restraining, until the trial, the defendants, Barry Gilmore and J. Bainbridge, from representing that the plaintiff was acting for them at the Waterloo Theatre, Whitby. The plaintiff also asked for an injunction restraining, until the trial, the defendant Gilmore from representing that he was "Little Titch."

His Lordship granted both injunctions in the terms asked for.

OCTOBER.

BETTING MATTER ON HANDBILLS.
PROSECUTION AT YARMOUTH.

3 At Yarmouth, Nat Travers was summoned for distributing handbills containing betting announcements. Travers' name appeared on the front of the bills with the programme of a pier entertainment, but at the foot and on the back were intimations by a betting agent of Flushing inviting business. The magistrates held that it was a distinct breach of the Betting Act, and, accepting defendant's plea of ignorance, inflicted a penalty of 19s., but cautioned him against any repetition of it in Yarmouth.

DOUGHTY v. MEREDYTH.

5 At the Marylebone County Court, before his Honour Sir William Selfe, Miss Ada Marian Doughty, professionally known as Vera Leslie, sought to recover ten guineas damages for breach of contract from Miss Constance Meredyth, playwright and actress, of Montague Street, Portman Square.

Mr. R. Cartwright, solicitor for the plaintiff, said the action arose practically out of an arrangement come to between the parties for the production, on June 2, at a *matinée*, at the Court, of a piece called *Notre Edouard*, which was written by the defendant, and in which that lady was also to appear. The plaintiff induced Mlle. Jane May to come to London to appear in the defendant's piece. In connection with the production an agreement was drawn up to the effect that the defendant should take ten guineas' worth of tickets, but at the last moment Miss Meredyth wrote saying that her piece could not be played on the day named, as it would be courting disaster to produce it at a few days' notice.

Miss Meredyth, in defence, said she had been abroad, and she made a mistake as to the date of the play's production, and then found that it could not be put on on the day named.

His Honour said it was an unfortunate transaction, but the defendant had entered into an agreement, and there must be judgment for the plaintiff for the ten guineas claimed and costs.

PIRATED MUSIC.

At Lambeth, Ernest Gibbs, 28, described as a costermonger, was charged with exposing and offering for sale thirty-five copies of pirated music at Ferndale Road, Brixton, on Saturday evening.

Mr. Hopkins ordered him to pay a fine of £5, and he made an order for the destruction of the music.

DEFRAUDING ACTORS' DAY FUND.

7 Bertha Chambers, an actress, was sentenced to three months' hard labour before Mr. Curtis Bennett at Bow Street for obtaining money by false pretences from the Actors' Day Fund.

PRIOR v. BALMAIN.

7 At the Cardiff County Court, George Prior, late business manager of the Royal, Cardiff, claimed £100 damages from Rollo Balmain, lessee of the Royal, for alleged wrongful dismissal. Mr. F. H. Gaskell was for the plaintiff, and Mr. Maurice Moseley for the defendant.

Plaintiff said in August defendant summarily dismissed him, and he did not at that time allege improper conduct as his reason.

He denied that he was so drunk on one occasion that Mr. Balmain advised him to go and take a rest.

The defendant said he discharged Mr. Prior for incompetency, for drunkenness, for disobedience, and neglect of duty. It was true he did not assign a reason in his letter of dismissal; that was because he wanted to let Mr. Prior down lightly.

In giving judgment for the defendant, with costs, his Honour said that if a man was drunk it was a serious matter to the public and to the owners of the theatre.

WILKES v. WALLER.

7 In the Westminster County Court his Honour Judge Woodfall had before him the adjourned case of Wilkes v. Waller. An application was now made by counsel for a further adjournment of the case, on the ground that they had not succeeded in getting Mr. Lloyd to come up to London and give his version of the transaction.

His Honour said the case involved a somewhat serious question, as it had been suggested at the previous hearing that the plaintiff had altered the terms of the contract without the knowledge of the defendant. It was a serious charge to make against the plaintiff, and on the evidence of Mrs. Waller he (the judge) gave her an adjournment in order that she might file a counterclaim and produce Mr. Lloyd as a witness. However, Mr. Lloyd was not here, and, therefore, he should further adjourn the hearing of the case for his attendance, and reserve the question of costs.

LONDON MUSIC HALL v. KITTS AND WINDRUM.—BREACH OF CONTRACT.

8 In the Shoreditch County Court, before his Honour Judge Smyly, K.C., the London Music Hall, Limited, sued Chas. S. Kitts and Rhoda Windrum, music hall artistes, to recover £10 damages for breach of contract. Mr. Profumo, barrister, appeared for the plaintiffs, and Mr. Martin O'Connor was counsel for the defence. In opening the case Mr. Profumo said that the defendants entered into a contract in 1904 to appear at the London in June, 1907, and a fortnight before they were to have appeared they sent in billing matter. They, however, did not put in an appearance on the date. He supposed the cause of the whole thing was that they got better and more remunerative engagements, and therefore did not bother about the first one.

Judge Smyly said the fact was two contracts had been made, one with Mr. Stoll and one with the plaintiffs. That should not be, as no business firm or a music hall could be run on such lines. If an artist signed a contract to appear on a certain date, then he had to perform to that contract or else suffer the consequences. There must be judgment for the plaintiff, with costs.

LONDON MUSIC HALL v. SINCLAIR.—BREACH OF CONTRACT.

8 In the Shoreditch County Court, before his Honour Judge Smyly, K.C., the London Music Hall, Limited, sued Messrs. Sinclair and Whiteford for breach of contract. Mr. Profumo, barrister, appeared for the plaintiffs, and Mr. Nicholson was counsel for the defence. In opening the case Mr. Profumo said it was another case of an artist having signed a contract to appear and failing, though he sent his billing matter along. Mr. Richards was called to prove the making of the contract, and said that since the date that they should have appeared he had not seen nor heard of the defendants.

Mr. Sinclair then went into the box, and said that he heard from Mr. Stoll that he was barred. He at once communicated with Mr. Richards with the idea of arranging fresh dates. These could not be agreed upon at the moment, and the matter was left until he was next in London. Then he received a summons, much to his astonishment, so he rang up Mr. Richards on the telephone and explained how the matter stood, and Mr. Richards said, "All right, let the matter drop," and that was the end of the business so far as he knew until he received another summons.

Mr. Nicholson: As a matter of fact, there was a special endorsement on the back of your Stoll contract which would have allowed you to have carried out this contract?

Defendant: Yes.

Mr. Nicholson: You made a mistake, and did not notice it.

Defendant: That is so; it was an oversight on my part.

Judge Smyly: A rather unfortunate one for you, too. There is no defence to this; there must be judgment for the plaintiffs, with costs.

DAMAGES FOR PERSONAL INJURIES.

In the Westminster County Court, his Honour Judge Woodfall had before him the case of Partait v. the Law Land **14** Guarantee Trust Society, in which the plaintiff sued the defendant society, in their capacity of debenture holders of the Pavilion Theatre, Whitechapel Road, to recover damages for personal injuries, which, he alleged, he had sustained owing to a notice-board at the theatre having fallen upon his head as he was passing the building.

After hearing the evidence of a number of witnesses, his Honour said he had no doubt that the plaintiff was injured by the canvas frame falling upon him, but he thought the amount he claimed was very excessive, and should give him judgment for the sum of £8, with costs.

STANSFIELD v. BOLTON.

At the Hyde County Court, before Judge Reginald Brown, K.C., Mr. Wilbraham Stansfield, proprietor of the Hyde Hippo- **14** drome, sued Horace Bolton, a bioscope operator, for the recovery of £12 damages alleged to have been suffered through defendant leaving plaintiff's employ without notice. The defendant brought a counter-claim for £40, for hire of his bioscope to the plaintiff from last December to September 26, at £1 a week. Mr. H. Bostock, solicitor, appeared for the plaintiff, and Mr. Joe Cooke, solicitor, for the defendant.

His Honour said he had come to the conclusion that the plaintiff had established his right to recover something from the defendant. He gave judgment for Mr. Stansfield on the claim for the full amount, £12, with costs. He also gave judgment for Mr. Stansfield on the counter-claim, with costs.

DENTON v. HILDYARD.—AGENTS' CLAIM FOR COMMISSION.

Before his Honour Judge Woodfall, in the Westminster County Court, the case of Denton **15** v. Hildyard was tried. Mr. Scott was counsel for the plaintiff, and Mr. Hugh Rose Innes appeared for the defendant.

Mr. St. John Denton said on July 2 of last year he wrote to Miss Hildyard with reference to an engagement in Australia. In reply he received a wire from her, making an appointment at his office. She duly kept the appointment, and he (plaintiff) introduced her to Mr. Meynell, theatrical manager, who engaged her under a contract of August, 1906, to appear in Australia for forty weeks at a salary of £50 a week, subject to it being raised to £80 a week in respect of her dramatic rights. She duly fulfilled the engagement, and his claim now was for 10 per cent. commission on the first ten weeks of the engagement, as was allowed by the custom of the profession.

In reply to a question put to him by the Judge, the witness said that if the engagement lasted over ten weeks he was entitled to charge 10 per cent. commission on the first ten weeks.

For the defence Miss Maud Hildyard said that with regard to the engagement in question she considered she took it direct from Mr. Meynell, and in fact he told her he would settle with Mr. Denton and send her on the contract direct. He did so, and she signed it and returned it to him. On the day before she sailed for Australia she received a letter from the plaintiff claiming commission, but her husband replied to it to the effect that the contract was not obtained through him, and that therefore she (defendant) was not liable for the commission.

In cross-examination the witness said she did not at that time know that her husband was getting work through the plaintiff's agency, nor did she seek the engagement in question, but she took it through Mr. Meynell. Her contention was that the plaintiff acted on behalf of Mr. Meynell and not as her agent, as she could always get engagements without the intervention of agents at all.

His Honour, in giving judgment, said the defendant could not get out of her liability. It was true she had not made any express agreement to pay the plaintiff his commission, but she had accepted his services, and therefore there was an implied agreement to pay for them. Acting upon her own evidence, it was clear that the engagement was brought about by the plaintiff's introduction, and that he was expecting to be paid his commission, and the only question now was as to what amount he was entitled to. He (the judge) should give him judgment for the sum of £50, being 10 per cent. commission for the first ten weeks of the engagement, on the footing of the salary being £50 a week, and excluding the question of dramatic rights.

CADBURY v. BEARDMORE AND OTHERS.

An application was made before Mr. Justice Bucknill, in the above action, when the learned judge granted an injunction restraining **16** the defendants, John Pope Beardmore and Violet Hope, until the trial of the action, from using the name of Mlle. Sahara in connection with any public performance at any public place of entertainment or elsewhere, and also restraining the defendants Pooles' Theatres, Limited, from allowing the other defendants to perform at any of their theatres under that name.

INJUNCTION AGAINST ELLA RETFORD REFUSED.

Lord Skerrington, in the Glasgow Bill Chamber, disposed of a note of suspension and interdict at the instance of the Glasgow **16** Pavilion, Limited, against Ella Retford, comedienne, Glasgow Coliseum Theatre, to have her interdicted from performing at the Coliseum, Glasgow, during that week, or at any other place of entertainment within a radius of ten miles from the Pavilion between October 9, 1908, and October 19, 1909. The complainers averred that on February 18 last they entered into a contract with the respondent, whereby she contracted to appear at the Pavilion Theatre during the week commencing August 30 next and also during the week commencing September 5, 1910, and that the respondent in breach of the agreement had contracted to appear in the Coliseum Theatre for the present week. The respondent pleaded that no validly executed or binding agreement was ever entered into between the parties. Although the document in possession of the complainers, as signed by her, bore to be a mutual agreement between them and her it was not signed by the complainers, and the agreement signed by the complainers' managing director, which was in her possession, also bore to be a mutual agreement, was not signed by the respondent, and was unstamped and undated. The respondent admitted that she was engaged to appear at the Coliseum for the present week, but she averred that the complainers were aware that she was under contract to appear in the Coliseum on that date.

Lord Skerrington refused to grant interim interdict, and as it was intimated by the complainers' counsel that he did not desire to have the note passed if interim interdict were not granted, his lordship refused the note, with no expenses.

MACDONALD v. SEEBOLD.—ALLEGED INFERIOR COMPANY ON RETURN DATE.

At the Worthing County Court an action was brought by Mr. Macdonald, theatrical agent, London, against Mr. Adolf Seebold, lessee of the Royal, Worthing, to recover the sum of £6 8s., alleged balance due on an agreement. Mr. Webb, solicitor, Brighton, appeared for plaintiff, and Mr. Buckland Dixon for defendant. Defendant counterclaimed for £9 9s. for loss sustained by alleged breach of agreement

Mr. Dixon explained the circumstances. In 1906 Mr. Seebold booked through Mr. Macdonald *The Dairymaids*, which the latter represented as the "A" company, that only visited firstclass theatres, and consisted entirely of artists of the highest merit. After some negotiations, it was settled the company should come to Worthing on certain terms. These terms were 67½ per cent. of gross returns to the visiting company, such terms being largely in excess of those paid to ordinary companies, and only paid to companies that went to the Royal, Brighton, not to companies that only went to smaller towns as fit-up companies. The company came to Worthing in September, 1907, and did excellent business, the returns being very good indeed. In the spring of the present year Mr. Seebold went to London and saw Mr. Macdonald's representative, who asked him if he would like to have a return visit of *The Dairymaids*. Mr. Seebold replied that he would be pleased to do so, and would give a better date—a date in August, which was the best month in the year for that class of entertainment. The company came in August, and directly they arrived Mr. Seebold realised they were not so good a company as he had before. There were not so many artists in it, and only fit-up scenery was carried—14-ft. scenery, which looked very inferior on the Worthing stage, which took 18 ft. Mr. Seebold

also found fault with the company, but he was assured by the manager that he would find them all right. On the third night, when settling up accounts, Mr. Seebold deducted from the company's share £6 8s., more by way of protest than as any compensation for the loss sustained in having such an inferior show. He considered it was not right in the circumstances that he should be "palmed off" with a company that would not bear comparison with that of the previous year.

Mr. Seebold, in the witness-box, bore out his counsel's statements, and produced certain correspondence relating thereto. When the question of terms was mentioned, he wrote that he only gave high percentages to companies like Miss Ellen Terry, *The Prince of Pilsen*, etc., and that he received a reply that the company would be quite equal to any of these. The terms eventually agreed on were 67½ per cent. On the occasion of the first visit of *The Dairymaids* he took £150 15s. 9d. in four performances on September 2, 3, and 4. When he entered into the contract for the return visit this year the same terms were agreed upon, and he fully expected the company and the scenery and everything else would be fully equal to that of the first visit.

At the close of Mr. Seebold's examination, Mr. Webb asked for the production of the contract, which, however, could not be produced. It was stated to be in the hands of Mr. Seebold's London solicitor.

His Honour Judge Scully said he could not decide the case in the absence of the contract. Mr. Dixon asked for an adjournment. Mr. Webb objected, and pointed out the expense of bringing a lot of witnesses a long distance. Eventually the Judge entered a non-suit against Mr. Seebold.

PERFORMING STAGE PLAYS IN AN UNLICENSED BUILDING—GERALD LESLIE AND OTHERS FINED.

At Cambridge Police Court Gerald Leslie was summoned for that on September 16 he did act or present part of a stage play called *Sally in Our Alley*, at the Hippodrome, Cambridge, a building not licensed for the performance of stage plays; further, with a similar offence on September 19, in respect of a play called *True as Steel*, also with performing a play *True as Steel* which had not been licensed by the Lord Chamberlain. Miss Violet Lisle was also charged with similar offences, and Thomas Askham, the proprietor of the building, was charged with keeping a place for the public performance of stage plays without a license on September 16 and 19.

Mr. Bodkin, instructed by Messrs. Stanley, Woodhouse, and Hedderwick, of Essex Street, London, prosecuted on behalf of the Theatrical Managers' Association, whilst Leslie and Miss Lisle were represented by Mr. H. St. J. Raikes, instructed by Mr. Ernest Vinter. Askham was not represented by counsel.

The case of Askham was taken first, and Mr Bodkin, in opening, said that Askham had on three occasions since 1902 been refused a theatrical license on application to the County Council. The performance of *Sally in Our Alley* was in eight scenes, with six speaking parts, and occupied thirty-five minutes in presentation. *True as Steel* was in seven scenes, with six speaking parts. Regarding the latter piece, the book had never been submitted to the Lord Chamberlain, nor any license obtained for its performance; and this was not the only instance in which plays had been performed under titles which were well-known and popular plays at the present time. It was a piracy of titles.

The magistrates, numbering ten, retired, and on their return expressed their unanimous opinion that Askham had allowed the Hippodrome to be used for the performance of stage plays on those dates without authority, but they reserved their imposition of a penalty until they had heard the charges against Leslie and Lisle. The cases of Leslie and Lisle were then taken, and most of the evidence given in Askham's case was repeated.

The magistrates decided that in each case the offence alleged had been committed, and after being in consultation for some time they announced the following penalties:—Askham, fined five guineas; Leslie, fined two guineas on the first count and one guinea on each of the two other counts, making four guineas in all; and Miss Lisle, one guinea. The Bench added that they had imposed very low penalties, but it must be distinctly understood that any further offences of a similar kind would be met by heavy fines.

PIRATED MUSIC.

19 At Lambeth, Charles Bradley, 45, a licensed pedlar, was charged with having in his possession and offering for sale eighteen copies of pirated music at Camberwell Green.

The offence was proved by Mr. Arthur Preston, chief agent to the Music Publisher-' Association.

Mr. Hopkins (to the prisoner): It is a traffic we are all concerned to stop. I always fine the same amount. It is £5.

AN ASSAULT.

24 At the Jersey Royal Court, Harry Carlo, music-hall artist, was presented by the Crown Officers charged with having committed a violent assault on the person of Mr. Stanley Hope, manager of the Opera House, Jersey, and St. Julian's Hall, Guernsey, the assault having taken place outside the Opera House. Jersey, early on the morning of September 19.

The accused pleaded guilty, and was sentenced to three months' imprisonment with hard labour.

THE CAMDEN CASE.—KINEMATOGRAPH PICTURES WITH MUSIC.

27 Before Mr. Wallace, K.C., at the Clerkenwell Sessions, the case of the Camden Theatre was mentioned. In June Mr. Robert Arthur, Mr. Walter Gibbons, and Mr. W. H. Terrell were bound over at the Clerkenwell Sessions, a jury having found them guilty of having carried on a music-hall entertainment at the Camden without having a music and dancing license from the London County Council. It was now alleged that the terms of the recognisances of the parties had been broken, and therefore notice had been served upon them to attend the court to show why they should not be forfeited.

Mr. George Elliott and Mr. Basil Watson represented Mr. Gibbons and Mr. Terrell; Mr. R. D. Muir was counsel for Mr. Robert Arthur; and Mr. Horace Avory, K.C., and Mr. W. H. M. Knight appeared to support the contention that the recognisances had been broken.

Mr. Horace Avory, K.C., said the defendants were convicted on June 19, 1908, for having kept the Camden for public music and dancing without any license from the London County Council. The prosecution then stated

that they only desired to establish the law, and the Court adopted that view and bound the defendants over in £10 to come up for judgment if called upon, and to be of good behaviour in the meantime. The house was closed after the conviction until Monday, September 14, when, without any license having been obtained from the London County Council, the theatre was opened for public entertainment, the license of the Lord Chamberlain (since surrendered by Mr. Robert Arthur) then being in existence. It was re-opened with an entertainment consisting of animated pictures accompanied by music.

The music, counsel argued, was not incidental to or subsidiary to the entertainment, but was independent and substantial. These performances, said Mr. Avory, K.C., had been carried on ever since in breach of the Act of Parliament and of the recognisances of the defendants, and in defiance of the law apparently. The Sunday performances was a serious matter because that was a fresh offence, as if they (the defendants) had held a license under the London County Council that would not have allowed them to open the house on Sunday. The statute which forbids that was 21st George III., c. 49.

It was stated that Mr. Arthur surrendered the Lord Chamberlain's license on September 17, and

Mr Muir, arguing that these proceedings were to punish contumacious persons, asked that, as Mr. Arthur had no desire to offend he might be allowed to go.

Mr. Wallace, K.C.: Certainly.

Witnesses were called by Mr. Elliott to prove that the music was a subsidiary part of the entertainment only.

Mr. Walter Gibbons, called on his own behalf, said he opened with this entertainment after consultation with his solicitor. He was not conscious at any time of having violated his recognisance. The public came to see the bioscope; the electrical piano never played more than half the evening, and was not part of the performance. The witness said arrangements had been made to give appropriate pictures on Sunday.

Mr. Wallace, K.C. (to Mr. Elliott): Is it intended to keep this place open if the decision of the Court is against you?

Mr. Elliott: Of course, we shall stop the music at once.

Mr. Wallace, K.C.: That is what I mean. I am of opinion that you have violated the law. I think the defendants Gibbons and Terrell have broken the law in connection with the matter and the terms of their recognisances, and I think they are liable to the penalty imposed in the particular case. I do not think they deliberately intended to violate their obligation, and I should not propose to impose a heavy penalty. The Sunday performances must cease. It is a burlesque of words to say "sacred performances."

Mr. Elliott said his clients would undertake to cease the music at the week-day performances and to give up the Sunday entertainments.

Mr. Wallace, K.C., said that on these undertakings he would fine the defendants 40s. each. He thought the defendants should pay something towards the costs of the other side.

Mr. Elliott replied that they were being sued for penalties of £400, and Mr. Wallace said the matter would be left where it was.

Mr. Wallace, K.C., pointed out, in answer to Mr. Elliott, that it was open to the defendants to appeal to the Court of Criminal Appeal for their decision in the matter.

ST. CLAIR v. EDWARDES—BARRING AND BREACH OF CONTRACT.

27 At the Derby County Court, before his Honour Judge Walter Lindley, Thomas St. Clair, one of a trio of trick football cyclists, brought an action against Mr. Thomas Allan Edwardes (Derby), proprietor of music halls, for £20 wages for breach of contract at the Derby Palace of Varieties and the Stoke-on-Trent Hippodrome, while Mr. Edwardes counter-claimed for £10 for breach of contract with reference to the Attercliffe Palace of Varieties (Sheffield).

Mr. Doughty (instructed by Messrs. Judge and Priestley, London) appeared for the plaintiff, and Mr. J. R. Clifford (Derby) defended.

In detailing the case Mr. Doughty said that plaintiff, with colleagues, gave a turn under the name of St. Clair Brothers, and on October 17, 1907, an agreement was entered into through an agent between defendant and plaintiff, for the latter to perform in three consecutive weeks in August, 1908, at Attercliffe (Sheffield), Derby, and Stoke respectively. Before the contracts were signed, plaintiff wrote to the agent pointing out that he would be unable to accept the Attercliffe engagement, unless Mr. Edwardes was prepared to risk plaintiff being " barred " at Attercliffe by Mr. Stoll. Receiving no reply to that communication, St. Clair telephoned the agent on the subject, and was informed that it would be all right. On that guarantee plaintiff signed the contracts. Nothing more was heard until August 11, 1908, when Mr. Edwardes acknowledged plaintiff's " billing " matter. The Saturday previous to the Monday, however, St. Clair received a telegram from Mr. Stoll, and then telegraphed to Mr. Edwardes: " Sorry, cannot open Monday, Palace, Attercliffe, on account of Stoll threatening injunction." Mr. Edwardes replied: " You must open and risk injunction. I will indemnify you against all legal expenses, otherwise shall cancel all engagements and sue you for breach of contract. Wire definitely your intentions." Plaintiff further replied: " Sorry, impossible to open at Attercliffe on Monday. Will give another date in lieu of same." However, plaintiff decided to act in accordance with Mr. Edwardes last telegram, and on the Monday presented himself at the Palace, Attercliffe, but although permitted to rehearse in the afternoon, he was not allowed to perform at night. He afterwards received a letter from Mr. Edwardes asking for the date on which he signed Stoll's contract at Sheffield, and also stating that when such information was given the proposal of another date would be considered. As a matter of fact, stated Mr. Doughty, Stoll's contract was signed before Mr. Edwardes' and was not to be fulfilled until May, 1909; therefore, Mr. Stoll had the power to bar plaintiff at Attercliffe. Later, when plaintiff said he would be at Derby, defendant wrote stating that he regretted he would be unable to entertain St. Clair at Derby or the following week at Stoke, the contracts having been cancelled, after the telegram respecting plaintiff's statement that he would be unable to open at Attercliffe, also in accordance with Rule 14 on the back of the contract. Such, stated Mr. Doughty, was considered as a repudiation of the contract.

The Judge found that there had been a breach in respect to the Attercliffe contract, and that defendant was perfectly justified in cancelling the Derby and Stoke engagements. He pointed out however, that Rule 14, which was added to the regulations respecting the theatre, might well

be placed on the front of the agreement. The action was therefore dismissed, judgment being given for the defendant on the claim, with costs, and also on the counter claim, with costs.

JOSEPH v. GREEN.—BREACH OF CONTRACT.

27 At the Arundel County Court, before his Honour Judge Scully, the case of Harry Joseph v. Bruce Green was a claim for £40 damages for breach of contract.— Mr. W. J. Boycott appeared for the plaintiff, and Mr. G. W. Cutts for the defendant.—An agreement was put in, dated October, 1906, engaging the defendant by the plaintiff for a year, which contained an option to prolong for another year. This, plaintiff said, he exercised a fortnight before the close of the first year, when it was alleged defendant verbally agreed to continue. Defendant appeared in *The Blue Coat Boy* at the close of the alfresco concerts, and was billed to appear and take the leading part in *Sinbad the Sailor* for the Dover Christmas pantomime. Plaintiff alleged that it was impossible adequately to replace the defendant, who did not fulfil the engagement, and the result was a loss on the takings at Dover of from £80 to £100.—The defence was that plaintiff made it so uncomfortable for defendant that he could not continue to work with him, and he accordingly gave fourteen days' notice on November 23 that he should terminate the agreement, and pleaded that this was a custom in the profession. He further stated that plaintiff assaulted him in the dressing-room, and literally threw him out of same.—The Judge remarked that the defendant could not for any trivial matter put an end to a contract of the nature in question, and there must be judgment against him, and he assessed the amount at £30, with costs, payable at the rate of £6 per month.

CARLTON v. BESTIC.

28 At the Lambeth County Court, Miss Dorothy Carlton, of Fairfax Road, Bedford Park, claimed damages from Mr. Charles Bestic, theatrical manager, for dismissal. The plaintiff stated she had performed by agreement for the defendant in a musical play, *The Flower Girl*. During a rehearsal at Birkenhead the stage manager accused her of smiling, and ordered her off the stage.

She became stranded at Oldham, having refused to apologise to the stage manager, and, consequently, not being allowed to play.

The judge awarded the plaintiff £3 damages and a week's salary.

COCHRAN v. LONDON PAVILION, LTD.

29 In the King's Bench Division, Mr. Justice Ridley, sitting with a special jury, concluded the hearing of the action for breach of agreement brought by Mrs. Evelyn Cochran, the wife of Mr. Charles Blake Cochran, against the London Pavilion, Limited. The alleged breach was the termination of an agreement for the appearance of Zbysco, the wrestler. The defendants pleaded justification, and said that the contract was with Mr. Cochran.

Mr. Rawlinson, K.C., and Mr. Tindal Davis appeared for the plaintiff; and Mr. Horridge, K.C., and Mr. Greer for the defendants.

Mr. Justice Ridley, in summing up, said the questions were:—(1) Was the contract the plaintiff's or her husband's? (2) If it was her contract did the defendants wrongfully determine it? And (3), if so, what were the damages? As to (1), when the contract was made the plaintiff was without means except such as she could get from her friends, and had no business habits; while her husband had been engaged in furnishing wrestlers before, and well understood the business. If the jury held it was the plaintiff's contract, the next question was—Did the defendants wrongfully terminate it? As to that, if they considered that the uproar took place owing to the announcement of a time limit and that the defendants never consented to that time limit, they would find for the defendants.

The jury, in answer to the first question, found that the contract was not that of the plaintiff, but of her husband, and, in answer to the second question, found that there had been no negligence on the part of Mr. Cochran, and the defendants had no right to terminate the performances. Damages were fixed at £170.

Mr. Justice Ridley said that on the findings he must give judgment for the defendants with costs. The costs to be taxed on the solicitors' undertaking to return if notice of appeal were given within fourteen days.

NOVEMBER.

COHEN v. AUGARDE.

6 In the Court of Appeal, before Lords Justices Moulton and Farwell, came on the case of Cohen v. Augarde, which was an appeal by the defendant, Miss Amy Augarde against an order granting the plaintiff, Mr. Louis Cohen, an interim injunction restraining her from performing a sketch called *La Carmencita*, which had been adapted from the opera *Carmen* for the music-hall stage by the plaintiff, without his name appearing on the play-bills and programmes as the author.

Mr. Doughty, in support of the appeal, said that the plaintiff had sold the copyright in the sketch to the plaintiff for £50, and this sum had been paid. It was possible that by an oversight Mr. Cohen's name as author had been omitted from some of the bills or programmes. He submitted, however, that as the result of the agreement lately entered into at the close of the variety artists' strike, managers of music halls could no longer be dictated to by artists as to the position, size of the type, and the like that the artist's name was to appear in on the programme in the description of the turn. There was no ground on which the interim injunction, which had been granted by Mr. Justice Coleridge at chambers, could be supported, and he asked that it should be discharged.

Mr. Watson having been heard for Mr. Cohen,

The Court held that this was not a case in which an interim injunction should have been granted, and accordingly discharged the order, directing that the costs of the application should be costs in the action.

ATKINSON v. THE SURREY VAUDEVILLE THEATRE, LIMITED.

9 In the King's Bench Division, Mr. Justice Ridley and a special jury commenced the hearing of an action for damages against the Surrey Vaudeville Theatre, Limited, for personal injuries, the plaintiffs being Miss Edith Mary Atkinson and Miss Florence Elizabeth Atkinson, two sisters, known under the name "Two Primroses."

Mr. Harry Dodd and Mr. F. E. Wynn WerD-wick appeared for the plaintiffs, and Mr. Rawlinson, K.C., and Mr. Harold Brandon for the defendants.

The plaintiffs' case was that they were performing at the Surrey Theatre in October, 1905, when the drop curtain was suddenly lowered. They were struck by the curtain and flung to the back of the stage. Miss Edith Mary Atkinson sustained serious injuries to the spine, and will, it was stated, be a cripple for life. The defendants denied all the allegations, and said that the plaintiffs were not hit by the curtain.

The case was continued on the 10th, when Mr. Rawlinson, K.C., for the defence, said that neither of the girls was struck by the curtain. Miss Edith Atkinson was exhausted by three performances and a rehearsal on the day of the accident. What happened was that the sisters stepped back at the end of their turn, after making their bow, and Miss Edith fell backwards.

Mr. Frank Macnaghten, managing director of the Surrey Vaudeville Theatre, said he engaged the stage employés and the artists on behalf of the defendant company. He did not pay any of them; that was done out of the company. He engaged the plaintiffs on behalf of the company as agent. He received a salary from the company, and his duties included the engagement of artists for them. He never received any commission for the engagements.

During the cross-examination of the witness by Mr. Dobb his lordship said that there was no doubt at all that Mr. Macnaghten, acting as agent for the theatre company, engaged the plaintiffs on the company's behalf. The artists and the other employés at the theatre were all in common employment.

Mr. Dobb asked his lordship to leave the question of employment to the jury.

His lordship replied that he should not do so, there was no question of fact in dispute. He should only leave the question as to the cause of the accident to the jury, as he was anxious to hear their opinion on that.

Dr. Dennis McCarthy, who examined Miss Edith Atkinson after the accident, said there were no physical appearances of any injury to the spine. She was very frail and hysterical, and seemed ill-nourished. Witness had examined her since, and was of opinion that she never had any concussion of the spine.

The hearing was adjourned until the following day (Wednesday), when, before counsel addressed the jury, his lordship said he would direct the jury on the question of the agency of Mr. Macnaghten, who, it was contended, engaged the plaintiffs in his capacity as agent to the defendant company, the girls thereby being in common employment with the servants of the company. Counsel might deal with the merits of the case.

The foreman added that they found that the accident was caused by the curtain falling, but they were not satisfied that Florence received any injury. They found, however, that she lost employment through her sister's accident. They gave a verdict for the plaintiffs, assessing the damages for Edith at £705, and for Florence at £12 16s. 3d.

Mr. Dodd asked for judgment for the plaintiffs.

His lordship said he thought it ought to be for the defendants. He must hear counsel on the point of law relating to common employment, but not that day.

On Friday, November 12, his lordship said

it was clearly proved, beyond possibility of doubt, that Mr. Macnaghten engaged the plaintiffs on behalf of the theatre company, and that he was acting as the agent of the company. There was, therefore, a common master for all those who were employed in the theatre, and where there was a common master the servants who were in that employment took the risks of each other's injuries. He agreed with the following passage from the judgment of Lord Justice Collins in the case of Burr v. Theatre Royal, Drury Lane :—"It is a fundamental principle of law that, wherever the relation of employer and employed exists, there is this limitation of the liability of the employer as regards injury occasioned by the negligence of a fellow-servant. That is the rule of law which applies to contracts of employment, whether written or unwritten, at any rate unless it is expressly excluded by the terms of the contract." The principle, his lordship added, would apply to actors and actresses. He was of the opinion that he had held from the very beginning of the case, that if this agency were proved to exist the action could not be maintained. Therefore there would be judgment for the defendants.

Mr. Dobb asked for a stay of execution, in view of an appeal.

Mr. Rawlinson intimated that if there were no appeal the defendants would not tax the costs.

His lordship remarked that he was sorry the action went on so far, because it must have cost a great deal of money. It seemed to him that the point was quite clear.

Judgment was accordingly entered for the defendants.

CORRI v. WILLIAMS

There was before the First Division an appeal by the defender in an action raised in the Sheriff Court at Dundee by Clarence **10** Collingwood Corri and another against R. A. P. Williams, lessee and manager, Gaiety, Dundee.

Sheriff-Substitute Campbell Smith, when the case came before him in February, found that the performances were a failure, and that both parties were to blame, and he gave the defendant (Williams) absolvitor, with no expenses to either party. This judgment was reversed on March 30 by Sheriff-Principal Fergusson, who gave judgment for the balance of £55 against the plaintiffs, dismissing the counter-claim.

The First Division now affirmed the decision of the Sheriff. In the opinion of the Lord-President the case was wholly based upon the allegation that the pursuers had not fulfilled their contract. The defender alleged various particulars in which he regarded the company as not full or efficient, but the points so raised by the defender were chiefly concerned with scenery and chorus, regarding which there was no stipulation in the contract which could be said to have been broken by the pursuers. It was clearly a case of contract, and not, as the Sheriff-Substitute had put it, of joint adventure, and there was no proof of breach of contract. The pursuers were allowed expenses.

KELSO v. BATTY—ALLEGED BREACH OF CONTRACT—A TEST CASE.

At the Stockton County Court, his Honour Judge Templer heard the case in which Tom Kelso and Company sued John Batty, **10** of the Grand, Stockton, for £14 breach of contract. Dr. Doughty, barrister, London,

appeared for the plaintiffs, and Mr. Reuben Cohen for the defendant.

The case for the plaintiffs was that they agreed in October, 1907, to perform in August, 1908, at the defendant's theatre. During the engineers' strike the theatre was closed, and, in accordance with the agreement between Mr. Batty and his artists, he issued a notice that through trade depression the theatre was closed, and that, therefore, all contracts were null and void. The defendant was entitled to close his theatre and cancel the contracts for the time it was closed, but it was opened in August with drama. The theatre being opened, plaintiffs, Mr. Doughty argued, were entitled to fulfil their contract.

Mr. Cohen stated that when the theatre was opened it was by a Mr. Montgomery, who had leased it for twelve months with the option of renewal for another twelve months. According to the contract the plaintiffs could only be allowed to fulfil their contract "subject to the theatre being in the occupation and possession of the management."

Mr. Batty was called to show that the theatre was not in his occupation or possession, and stated that there were altogether 130 artists who were satisfied with the notice they received of the closing of the theatre.

His Honour said he could not see that plaintiffs had any case.

Mr. Doughty said the case which he had brought before his Honour was not an attack upon Mr. Batty but a test case. This sort of thing was taking place all over the country, and music hall artists were seeking to put a stop to the practice of music hall proprietors engaging artists at long dates, barring them from appearing within a certain radius, and at their own will saying, "Oh, I shall not go on with this business; I shall close the theatre, and all contracts must be off."

His Honour said when the artists put their names to the agreement they did so with their eyes open and a full knowledge of what they were doing, and could not, therefore, have anything to complain of if they were treated according to the terms of the contract. He, therefore, gave judgment for defendant, with costs.

Mr. Doughty asked for leave to appeal, which was refused.

DE ROSE AND HAWTREY v. ROTHERHAM HIPPODROME, LTD.—MANAGERIAL DEDUCTION OF AGENT'S COMMISSION.

At the Rotherham County Court, before Judge Benson, the first action in connection with the dispute between the V.A.F. **11** and the agents came on for hearing. De Rose and Hawtrey sued the Rotherham Hippodrome for £1 6s., deducted by the defendants from their salary of £13. Mr. Chas. Doughty, instructed by Messrs. Judge and Priestley, appeared for the plaintiffs, and Mr. Thomas E. Fox, the managing director of the company, appeared to defend in person. After Mr. Doughty had stated his case, Mr. Fox admitted the deduction because he had received notice from the agents, with whom the contract was made, to do so. Eventually Mr. Fox applied for an adjournment, and the hearing was fixed for December 11.

FRAZER v. WILLIAMS.—ALLEGED WRONGFUL DISMISSAL.

At Westminster County Court Carrie Frazer, sued Philip Williams for damages for wrongful dismissal. Mr. Douglas Hogg, for the **11** plaintiff, said his client was an accompanist and vocalist, playing in London during the winter and at the seaside in the summer. She was introduced to defendant, and subsequently engaged by him to sing at Hythe for July, August, and September at £2 10s. per week. Plaintiff did not start singing until July 25, but claimed her salary from the date of the agreement, July 15. This was refused, but she continued to fulfil her engagement. His client, he contended, was badly treated in consequence of the claim she made. She was given second "turn" on the programme when the "house" was practically empty, and was therefore not successful. In the first-night performance she was given a turn in the second half of the programme, and was encored. At subsequent performances she was cut out of the second part of the programme, and was later dismissed as incompetent. She was now accompanying Miss Loftus at the Coliseum. It was a serious thing for her to be dismissed as incompetent.

Judge Woodfall found for plaintiff for £21 9s. 7d. His Honour said that perhaps Miss Frazer failed to "catch on" with Hythe audiences, but that was not sufficient to break the agreement on the ground of incompetency.

CLAXTON v. STOCKELLE.—CLAIM FOR COMMISSION ON BREACH OF CONTRACT.

In the Westminster County Court his Honour Judge Woodfall decided the case of Claxton v. Stockelle. Mr. Thomas Claxton, dramatic agent, carrying on business at Charing Cross Road, sued to recover the sum of £5 12s. 6d. commission, at the rate of 5 per cent., for procuring an engagement for the defendant, Miss Nora Stockelle, for nine weeks for South Africa.—The plaintiff said he booked the defendant to appear in South Africa for nine weeks at a salary of £12 10s. a week, and she duly signed the contract, but at the last moment she refused to go out, and consequently he now claimed to be paid his commission on the engagement.—For the defence the mother was called. She said that her daughter was an infant, and that as soon as she heard that her daughter had signed a contract with the plaintiff to go to South Africa she objected to it on account of her being so very young, and at once went to the plaintiff's office and told him that she should not allow her to go.

His Honour said he thought it was quite clear that the plaintiff was entitled to judgment for the commission due to him on the contract. The case raised a question of very considerable difficulty, inasmuch as the Court could not hold that it was desirable for a young girl who was little better than a child to be sent to South Africa, but it was extremely difficult to say where the line was to be drawn. The question at issue was a very wide and a very serious one, but the Court must look at each case, and deal with it on its own merits, and he (the judge) knew of no authority which would justify the Court in interfering with the contract in question. He did not know that even the Court of Chancery would interfere in such a case. In any event, so far as this action was concerned, he had come to the conclusion that the defendant was quite capable of acting for herself in the making of a contract. It was true that her mother interfered in the matter, and very properly so, but that did not affect the plaintiff's right to his claim for commission, and therefore judgment would be for the plaintiff for the amount claimed, with cost.

A stay of execution was asked for, pending notice of appeal on behalf of the Variety Artists' Federation.

His Honour granted a stay for fourteen days on condition that notice of appeal was given.

STUBBS v. RAYMOND.—SUNDAY THEATRE PERFORMANCES.

In the Chancery Division, before Mr. Justice Eve, Mr. Jessel, K.C., moved for an injunction restraining the sub-lessee of a theatre of varieties at Hoxton from using the house on the Sunday for a kinematograph performance.

The motion was made on behalf of the lessee, who is the holder of the license. The Lord Chamberlain, counsel said, desired to prevent the use of theatres for Sunday performances, except under exceptional circumstances, and the lessee did not care to have his license jeopardised by the performance taking place without the sanction of the Lord Chamberlain.

His lordship said that these performances having gone on for a considerable time, it did not seem desirable to suspend them the next Sunday.

The motion was adjourned in order that the parties might have an opportunity of, if possible, arriving at an agreement about sureties.

At the close of the day's sitting, Mr. Jessel said he had arranged with Mr. Lawrence that no performance should be given on Sunday, and that the motion should stand over until to-morrow (Friday). In the meantime, the parties would visit the Lord Chamberlain's office together, and see whether matters could not be satisfactorily arranged.

OTTO AND OLGA v. PEPI.—ALLEGED BREACH OF CONTRACT.

At Middlesbrough County Court, before his Honour Judge Templer, Otto and Olga sued Mr. Pepi, managing director of the Hippodrome, Middlesbrough, for £18 in respect of a contract.

Mr. Charles Doughty appeared for the plaintiffs. Plaintiffs, it was stated, were engaged to perform during the week commencing August 3, but on that date the hall, a new one, was not completed, and consequently plaintiffs could not perform there. Mr. Doughty handed in a form of contract, which was not stamped, and which contained the words "In the event of the hall closing for any purpose whatever it is distinctly understood that this agreement should be immediately cancelled." The point was whether those words justified Mr. Pepi in repudiating the contract. Mr. Mundhal, for the defence, submitted that the terms of the engagement must be taken to imply "Contingent to the hall being ready for use." Mr. Doughty urged that from May, 1907, to July, 1908, the two artists had been kept by the "Barring clause" out of Middlesbrough and Stockton entirely, and that was a serious limitation. His Honour gave judgment for defendant with costs, and gave leave to appeal.

CRAMER v. STUART.

At Bloomsbury County Court, before Judge Bacon, the case of Cramer and Co. v. Otho Stuart was heard. The plaintiffs, Messrs. J. B. Cramer and Co., of Oxford Street, sought to recover from Mr. Otho Stuart, theatre proprietor, the sum of £21 17s. 6d. for 1,500 librettos of *Tales of Hoffmann*, supplied by them in April, 1907.

Mr. McCaskie was counsel for the plaintiffs and Mr. Bucknill for the defendants.

The defence was a denial of liability, the order, it being alleged, being given on behalf of Herr Gregor.

Judge Bacon said the plaintiffs had put forward their claim, but it had been repudiated by the defendant, and that repudiation had been supported by evidence. He gave judgment for the defendant, with costs.

EDWARDES v. BERESFORD.

20 Before Mr. Justice Warrington, in the Chancery Division, Mr. Cave, K.C., moved on behalf of the plaintiff, Mr. George Edwardes, for an injunction to restrain the defendant, Miss Kitty Gordon, from singing any song or musical piece taken from the play *The Merry Widow*. For the defence it was stated that the lady did not assert any right to sing the song, and she was willing to give an undertaking not to do so pending the trial of the action. No intimation not to sing the song was given to her before the action was begun. An undertaking as suggested was given and agreed to.

SHOOLBRED v. WYNDHAM AND ALBERY.

20 In the King's Bench, Mr. Justice Darling and a special jury commenced the hearing of an action by Messrs. James Shoolbred and Co., of Tottenham Court Road, to recover from Sir Charles Wyndham and Mrs. Albery (Miss Mary Moore, the actress) a sum of £267 6s. 7d., balance alleged to be due on a contract for work done at the Criterion Theatre in April, 1907. The defendants' case was that the work done was not in accordance with contract, and counter-claimed for damages.

Mr. English Harrison, K.C., and Mr. R. J. Willis appeared for the plaintiffs, and Mr. Spencer Bower, K.C., and Mr. Albery for the defendants.

Mr. Harrison explained that what the defendants really complained of was that the work was not done to their satisfaction or their approval. In 1899 the plaintiffs d'd a great deal of work for the defendants at Wyndham's which was satisfactory, and in 1907 a contract was entered into with regard to the Criterion. The total cost of this work was £1,398, and that sum had been paid with the exception of the balance, which was now sued for. The work included a yellow drop curtain and yellow upholstering for the stalls, renewing the arm-rests, curtains for the boxes, and pelments for the proscenium and boxes. Blue satin trimmings had to be put on the curtains and round the family circle. There had been interviews with regard to the shades of the colours, but it was now complained that the colours did not match. There was also a complaint about a carpet which was for the stalls bar. The carpet in the stalls was a Saxony carpet, and complaint was made that it did not match the one in the bar, which was a Wilton pile carpet. It was his submission that the carpets were well matched, that the blue satin was an excellent match, and the velvet was as good as could be made, and a great deal better than the sample.

Among those who gave evidence were Miss Mary Moore, Sir Charles Wyndham, and Mr. Frederick Shoolbred.

The case was resumed on November 23 and 24. On the 24th the jury inspected the materials at the Criterion.

The Judge left several questions to the jury. In answering these the jury found that the blue satin was the same shade as sample as regards the face, but not as regards the back; the velvet as regards the face was the same shade in certain lights, but in other lights it was not. They disagreed on another question of shade, but found two slight defects in the curtain. They found that the defendants were honestly and in good faith dissatisfied with the work, but disagreed on the question as to whether the dissatisfaction was reasonable, and agreed that the defendants had proved no damage.

The discussion on the effect of these findings was adjourned to December 1 (see report).

RICHMOND v. SHEPHERD'S BUSH EMPIRE.

21 At the Brompton County Court, before Sir William Selfe and a jury, Israel Richmond, an insurance agent, of Cromwell Grove, Shepherd's Bush Road, sued the Shepherd's Bush Empire to recover £5 1s. 6d. damages for alleged unjustifiable ejectment from the theatre and assault.—Mr. W. S. Knight, barrister, appeared for the defendants.

His Honour, in summing up, said there could be no doubt that the plaintiff was entitled to the eighteenpence which he paid for admission, inasmuch as he was ejected before any performance commenced. The jury would have to judge from the evidence as to whether they considered any unnecessary violence had been used, or whether the plaintiff had brought the trouble upon himself by exercising a high-handed manner.

The jury deliberated for some time, and on returning into Court the foreman said: We award the plaintiff £5 for breach of contract and eighteenpence, the money paid for admission to the theatre.

Judgment was accordingly entered for the amount claimed, and costs.

SCOTT v. MACNAGHTEN.—APPEAL SUSTAINED.

24 In the King's Bench Division, before Mr. Justice Bigham and Mr. Justice Walton, sitting as a Divisional Court, Mr. Frank Macnaghten appealed against the decision of Judge Bacon at Bloomsbury County Court in an action. "Scott v. Macnaghten," arising out of his (Mr. Macnaghten's) refusal to produce a sketch, entitled *The Drummer of the 76th*, at Sadler's Wells.

Mr. Hugo Young, K.C., for the appellant, said that Mr. George Scott was interested in a music-hall sketch, which was being played by Mr. Matthew Brodie and others. Mr. Brodie had since died. Mr. Scott arranged with Mr. Macnaghten to produce this sketch at Sadler's Wells, but a week before the time of opening Mr. Macnaghten said that there was another sketch on the bill, and he should not allow *The Drummer of the 76th* to be performed. He did, however, offer a week in lieu of this at Southampton, but Mr. Scott refused this offer, and brought an action for a week's salary, and obtained judgment. Mr. Macnaghten now appealed, on the ground that the contract was illegal, and the claim should have been one for damages, and not for salary, and no damages had been proved.

Mr. M. Lush, K.C., on behalf of respondent, submitted that in the circumstances the county court judge was right in his decision.

Mr. Justice Bigham, giving judgment, said he was satisfied that both parties were aware of the illegality of performing stage plays at music halls, and there would be judgment for the appellant.

Mr. Justice Walton concurred.

The appeal was accordingly allowed. Leave to further appeal was granted.

ROBERTI v. ELPHINSTONE.—IMPORTANT DISPUTE ON CONTRACT.

In the Westminster County Court his Honour Judge Woodfall tried the case of Roberti v. **26** the Hanley Theatres Co., in which the plaintiff, who is the proprietor of the Roberti's Troupe of jugglers, sued the defendant company to recover the sum of £5, balance of salary due. Mr. Doughty was counsel for the plaintiff, and Mr. Randolph appeared for the defence. It was understood that the proceedings were being brought at the instance of the Variety Artists' Federation.

Counsel for the plaintiff, in opening the case, said on April 27, 1907, a contract was entered into by which the plaintiff agreed to produce his sketch at Hanley for one week at a salary of £27 10s. The plaintiff and his troupe were to appear on September 14, and a fortnight before that date they sent in their bill matter in the usual way, and appeared on the scene at Hanley on the day for their opening performance. One of the members of the troupe, however, was a boy of tender age, who was a son of Mr. and Mrs. Roberti, and for whom it was necessary that they should procure a license from the local magistrate before he could perform. An application was made for the license on the day of the opening of the performance, but the plaintiff was told by the police that he must wait until the following day, but in the meantime the boy was allowed to go on the stage on the Monday night. On the following day (Tuesday), when the license was applied for, it was refused by the magistrate, and as a result the plaintiff and his wife, together with an assistant, had to carry out the performance for the rest of the week without the assistance of the boy. When treasury day arrived it was found that Mr. Elphinstone, manager to the defendant company, had deducted £5 from the plaintiff's salary, on account of the boy not appearing, and it was in respect of that amount that this action was brought. He also deducted further the agent's commission, but as there was a case pending in the High Court on that question it was agreed that they should withdraw the claim for that until the result of the High Court case was known.

In giving judgment, his Honour said his own view of the case was that the defendants might have set up a claim for damages against the plaintiff by way of counterclaim for breach of contract, but that had not been done, and therefore he had to deal with the case as it came before him. Mr. Elphinstone had constituted himself his own jury, and had assessed his own damages, but the question was as to whether or not his terms could be upheld. He (the judge) was rather inclined to think that the onus of procuring a license for a child of tender age to appear on the stage was on the proprietor of the house at which it was to appear, but he would not express any opinion, as he was not quite certain on the point. In any event, the defendants entered into the contract with the knowledge of the possibility of a license being refused by the magistrate, and therefore they took a certain amount of risk in the matter. He did not think in this case that there had been such conduct on the part of the plaintiff as to justify the defendants in deducting £5 from his salary, and it therefore followed that there would be judgment for the plaintiff for the sum of £5, with costs.

SHEA v. TREE.—WORKMEN'S COMPENSATION ACT.

In the Westminster County Court his Honour Judge Woodfall had before him the case of **30** Shea v. Tree, by way of an action for an award under the Workmen's Compensation Act, in respect of injuries sustained by the plaintiff, a scene shifter, whilst engaged at His Majesty's.

Mr. Firminger was counsel for the plaintiff, and Mr. Duckworth appeared on behalf of Mr. Tree.

For the defence, it was not denied that the accident happened, and that the plaintiff was entitled to an award under the Act, but it was contended that he had based his claim on a scale of salary far in excess of that which he was paid at the defendant's theatre. It was admitted that the plaintiff was properly entitled to a sum of eight shillings a week on the footing that his earnings as a scene shifter would have been sixteen shillings a week if he had worked the whole of the week round.

After a lengthy discussion by counsel on both sides, his Honour, in giving judgment, said he was sorry to have to find against plaintiff, but he was satisfied that he had no alternative but to do so. He had no doubt as to the law on the subject, and had come to the conclusion that the applicant was engaged casually on night work, which would work out at sixteen shillings a week for a full week with *matinées*, and that he was not entitled to take into consideration what he had previously earned at other theatres, or what he might have subsequently earned had it not been for the unfortunate accident. He must find that the average wages of the applicant were sixteen shillings a week, and therefore this application must be dismissed.

SCHOLZ v. AMASIS, LIMITED, AND FREDERICK FENN. — ALLEGED INFRINGEMENT OF COPYRIGHT.

In the King's Bench, before Mr. Justice Jelf and a common jury, was commenced the **30** hearing of an action brought by W. H. Scholz (W. Gunn Gwennett) against Amasis, Limited, and Frederick Fenn. Plaintiff alleged that *Amasis* was a copy of his own work, *The Son of the Sun*, and asked for damages and an injunction. Mr. Lawrence Hales and Mr. Whitfield appeared for the plaintiff, and Mr. E. F. Spence and Mr. Norman Craig for the defendant.

Mr. Lawrence Hales explained that in 1897 his client completed a comic opera, *The Son of the Sun*. It was based upon the Egyptian legend that whoever took away the life of a cat would be in danger of sudden death. The play was sent round to various managers. In 1906 the plaintiff saw a notice of the forthcoming production of *Amasis*. He gathered that the play to be produced was very similar to his own, and he accordingly wrote to Mr. Calvert, who was producing it, pointing out that he had written a play with a similar plot. Mr. Calvert replied saying that the Egyptian opera he proposed to produce was written four years before, and was copyrighted two years ago; to which the plaintiff replied that his play was written in 1897. When he saw *Amasis* at the New he found it was similar in many respects to his own.

THE DEFENCE.

Mr. Spence (for the defence) said *Amasis* was Mr. Fenn's own idea, and it was his own knowledge of Egyptology which enabled him to carry it through. He (Mr. Spence) should submit that for the plaintiff to succeed there must be deliberate piracy.

Mr. Hales cited two cases, "Lee *v.* Simpson" and "Reichardt *v.* Sapte," and contended that he need do no more than show the fact of similarity.

His Lordship said there must be a definite taking and piracy.

The hearing was adjourned.

Yesterday (Wednesday), Mr. Spence, the defendant's counsel, continuing his address, said the basis of the two plays was a feature of the old Egyptian law whereby the killing of a cat was a capital crime, but he denied that the plaintiff's plot was used in *Amasis.* Counsel explained to his lordship the necessity of a happy ending to such a piece as *Amasis,* which meant, he said, the inclusion of a wedding between the hero and heroine.

The judge directed attention to the apparent similarity between the incidents in the first acts of the two plays, where the sacred cat is supposed to be killed, and also to the fact that both authors subsequently employed the phrase in a rhyme, "Nine lives at least."

The judge reserved his decision.

DECEMBER.

SHOOLBRED AND CO. v. WYNDHAM AND ALBERY.

In the King's Bench Division Mr. Justice Darling delivered judgment in this case. The jury found that Sir Charles Wyndham and Miss Mary Moore were honestly and in good faith dissatisfied with the work, but found that they had proved no damage.

Mr. Justice Darling, in giving judgment, said the defendants were not satisfied with the work in the way it had been carried out. Plaintiffs had undertaken to satisfy Miss Moore, but they did not give her the thing she wanted. He was sorry for the plaintiffs, because he thought they undertook to do a very difficult thing—to satisfy a lady who was very fastidious—who had discovered a colour scheme, and would not be satisfied with anything which came near it, but with the precise thing. As they failed to satisfy her, she was entitled to judgment. Therefore, upon the claim, defendants would have judgment with costs. On the counter claim, which failed, he gave judgment for the plaintiffs with costs.

MARKS v. TIVOLI, MANCHESTER.

At the Manchester Assizes, the Tivoli Music Hall Co., Limited, of Manchester, were the defendants in an action brought by Harry Marks, Chumley Road, Pendleton, to recover damages for an injury which he alleged was caused by the defendant company's negligence. Mr. Tobin, K.C., who, with Mr. Whitley, appeared for the plaintiff, said Mr. Marks and his wife, with her father and mother, visited the Tivoli Music Hall on August 15. They took seats in the stalls, and to get to them they had to descend two flights of stairs in direct descent. Between the two flights of stairs—with eight steps in each flight—there was a landing. The stairs were carpeted, and there was a rough cloth above the carpet to protect it. This had been rucked up owing partly to there being no stair rod below the last step of the first flight. Mr. Marks caught his foot on the cloth and fell down the second flight of steps with his arm beneath him.

The jury returned a verdict for plaintiff, awarding £60 damages.

BARCLAY v. GRAY.

In the Official Referee's Court, before Mr. Pollock, a settlement was arrived at in this action. The action was one against Mr. George Gray, brought by Mr. George Barclay, for commision on third and subsequent re-engagements.

The amount of the claim was £404 18s., being the balance alleged to be due for engagements obtained for the defendant between September, 1903, and February, 1906.

Mr. Turrell said they had come to an agreement by which judgment would be given for the plaintiff for £250 and costs.

It was agreed that if the amount be paid within six weeks, and the costs within fourteen days of taxation, or within six weeks from the present time, the plaintiff should give up all outstanding claims against the defendant in respect of commission then due, or that might become due under any existing contract.

HEWITT v. PORTEOUS—PROFITS ON "LADY FREDERICK."

In the Chancery Division, before Mr. Justice Swinfen Eady, the case of Hewitt v. Porteous came on. The case arose out of an agreement between plaintiff and defendant to finance *Lady Frederick.* This commenced when the piece was transferred to the Garrick. It was a term of the agreement that should the run continue beyond April 25, to which period the Garrick was available, plaintiff should have the option to withdraw. He took advantage of this, and now alleged that he had been induced by misrepresentation on the part of the defendant to do so.

It was now stated that the plaintiff and defendant had agreed to terms. These were as follows:—Judgment for the plaintiff for £485 in Court, and judgment for balance to be ascertained. Plaintiff withdrew all charges against the defendant.

Mr. Justice Swinfen Eady entered judgment accordingly.

HASSELMAN v. POOLE AND OTHERS.

In the Court of Appeal, before the Master of the Rolls and Lords Justices Moulton and Farwell, was the case of Hasselman and another v. Poole and others, which was an appeal from a decision of the judge of the Gloucester County Court, sitting as arbitrator under the Workmen's Compensation Act, 1897. The applicants for compensation were the dependents of a man named Hasselman. The County Court held that the respondents were not liable, hence the present appeal.

Mr. Sturgess, in support of the appeal, said that Hasselman was employed by the lion tamer Mme. Ella. On Sunday, July 28, at the Palace, Gloucester, a lion escaped into a dressing-room, and in trying to drive it back Hasselman was killed.

Mr. Tyfield, for Mme. Ella, contended that Hasselman had been guilty of serious and wilful misconduct, and therefore could not recover.

The Master of the Rolls, in giving judgment, said that he saw no evidence of serious and wilful misconduct on the part of Hasselman, whose duty it was, when the lion escaped, to try and get it back into the cage. For these reasons he thought the accident arose out of, and in the course of, the deceased man's employment, and that Mme. Ella was liable to pay compensation under the Act. The case must therefore go back to the county court judge for him to assess the amount of compensation due to the applicants from her, and the appeal, so far as Mme. Ella's liability was concerned, would be allowed, and so far as Messrs. Poole were sought to be made liable dismissed.

The lords justices concurred.

GRAY v. THE V.A.F.

In the King's Bench Division, Mr. Justice Darling and a special jury heard the action **14** brought by Mr. George Gray to recover damages for alleged libel and slander against the Variety Artists' Federation, Mr. C. C. Bartram (the editor), and Messrs. Odhams (the printers of the *Performer*), and Mr. Edmond Edmonds, Mr. Joe Elvin, and Mr. Paul Martinetti (the trustees of the Federation). The statements complained of were in an issue of the *Performer* of February 20, 1908. The defendants admitted publication, and relied on Section 4 of the Trades Disputes Act. They said that the words did not bear the meaning complained of, and were a report of a public meeting held for discussing matters of public concern; part of the words were true in substance and in fact, whilst the other part consisted of fair and *bonâ-fide* comment.

Mr. Hume Williams, K.C., Mr. Walter Payne and Mr. J. D. Cassels appeared for the plaintiff, and Mr. Marshall Hall, K.C., Mr. Doughty, and Mr. Nicholson for the defendants.

Mr. Gray, the plaintiff, gave evidence, after which a consultation took place between counsel.

Mr. Hume Williams, K.C., then announced that the case had been settled. Mr. Gray had never been anxious to make money out of these proceedings, and it was only the attitude assumed towards him which made it necessary to bring the action. The defendants agreed to pay £100 to any theatrical charity which Mr. Gray should name, pay his costs, and unreservedly withdraw and apologise for the statements complained of.

Mr. Justice Darling said Section 4 of the Trade Disputes Act, 1906, provided that an action against a trade union for any tortious act alleged to have been committed by or on behalf of a trade union should not be entertained by any Court. This meant that courts of law had been absolutely deprived of any jurisdiction to hear a claim against a trade union for any wrong which they do in the course of a trade dispute, and even if they consent to make some reparation the statute made it impossible for a court of law to enter any judgment whatever in a cause it was forbidden to entertain. The defendant O'Gorman had been dismissed from the action, and the others were sued as trustees and officers of the union. Whether witnesses could have been prosecuted for perjury if uttered in the course of such an action he did not know; he should say not. He could give no judgment, nor make the Court a party to any sort of arrangement.

The record was withdrawn.

EDWARDS v. LOFTUS.

In the King's Bench Division, Mr. Justice Lawrence and a special jury heard an action **15** brought by Mr. Thomas Allan Edwardes, a music hall proprietor, to recover damages from the defendant, Miss Marie Loftus, a comedienne, for breach of contract in respect to her engagement to appear at the Empire Music Hall, Stoke-on-Trent, in November last year. Mr. Shearman, K.C., and Mr. Charles A. M'Curdy appeared for the plaintiff,

and the defendant was represented by Mr. Marshall Hall, K.C., and Mr. Charles Doughty.

The defence was that the defendant was very ill, and on her doctor's advice she took a voyage to South Africa. She telegraphed to the plaintiff and received a telegram, " All contracts are off." Other managers released her from her engagements, and she put an advertisement in the theatrical papers thanking them for their kindness. It was submitted, therefore, that there had been no breach, and that the plaintiff's action failed.

The jury returned a verdict for the defendant.

Judgment was given accordingly.

LONDON MUSIC HALL, LIMITED, v. AUSTIN.

In the Chancery Division, before Mr. Justice Eve, the London Music Hall, Limited, sought **15** for an interim injunction to restrain Mr. Charles Austin from performing a sketch called *Parker, P.C.*, at the Palace, Stoke Newington, in contravention of an agreement with the plaintiffs.

His lordship granted the application.

MILBURN v. ROGERS. — COMMISSION ON RE-ENGAGEMENTS.

In the Westminster County Court his Honour Judge Woodfall disposed of the case of Milburn v. Rogers. The plaintiff was Mr. **15** Hartley Milburn, a dramatic agent carrying on business at Leicester Square, and he sued the defendant, Mr. Harry Rogers, who is the proprietor of a music-hall sketch, to recover the sum of £60 10s. as commission for procuring him an engagement with the Moss and Stoll Empires.

The defence was that the defendant procured his own engagements, and that therefore the plaintiff was not entitled to claim commission.

In giving judgment his honour said it was upon the plaintiff to prove his claim to commission, and he was afraid he had failed to do so. The defendant had sworn that he had refused to pay commission on renewals, and there was no evidence to show that he did agree to do so; therefore judgment must be for the defendant, with costs.

PROTECTION OF SONGS.—THE QUESTION OF SUMMARY POWERS.

Before Alderman Sir T. Vansittart Bowater, at Guildhall, Edward Solomon, of Assam **15** Street, Commercial Road, E., was charged on remand, with selling and having in his possession for sale a quantity of pirated copyright " musical works "—*i.e.*, " Will you love me in December as you do in May? " and " Love me and the world is mine."

The Alderman dismissed the charge, observing that he had not been convinced that words alone constituted a " musical work." Had the music and words been published together it would have been different. As it was an important question to the trade, he would willingly state a case.

RICKARDS v. THE V.A.F.

Before Mr. Justice Darling and a special jury, in the King's Bench Division, Mr. A. R. **15** Rickards, a member of the firm of Morris and Rickards, solicitors, sued the Variety Artists' Federation and its trustees— Mr. Edmond Edmonds, Mr. Joe Elvin, and Mr. Paul Martinetti—and Mr. C. C. Bartram, the editor, and Messrs. Odhams, the printers.

of the *Performer*, for damages for an alleged libel contained in the paper. The paper contained the report of a meeting at which the position of the paper was discussed, and these words were used:—" In connection with the unfortunate libel action into which we were precipitated by the ill-advice of our former legal representatives."

Mr. Hume Williams, K.C., Mr. M. O'Connor, and Mr. J. D. Cassels appeared for the plaintiff, and Mr. Marshall Hall, K.C., and Mr. Charles Doughty represented the defendants.

Mr. Justice Darling, in summing up, said it had been submitted, on behalf of the defendants, that the action would not lie under the Trades Disputes Act. He held, however, that a trade union was amenable if they committed certain wrongs, unless they did them in contemplation or furtherance of a trade dispute. If acts were committed by a trade union in contemplation or furtherance of a trade dispute, Parliament had enacted that it should enjoy absolute immunity. He had ruled on this point against the defendants because there was no suggestion that the words which were alleged to be a libel were in any way connected with a trade dispute. It was in that respect that it differed from the subject matters of the action which had been brought by Mr. Gray on the previous day. In the present case there was no doubt the article by "Buckeby" appearing in the *Performer* was libellous. The question was, Did Mr. Rickards advise that the article was not libellous? Someone must be deliberately saying what was not true. It was for the jury to decide.

The jury, after a long consultation in private, awarded the plaintiff £25 damages. In reply to a question put by the Judge, they found that the libel was published without malice.

Answering further questions, they found that the words published by the defendants concerning the plaintiff were a matter of public concern, but that the publication of them was not for the public benefit.

His lordship entered judgment for the plaintiff for £25 and costs.

BEGGS v. COLLIS.

In the King's Bench Division, before Mr. Justice Jelf and a jury, Mr. William Begg claimed damages from Mr. Edward Kenyon Collis, alleging breach of agreement to produce a play entitled *For the King*.

16

It appeared that in consideration of the plaintiff transferring his rights in the play to the defendant for three years Mr. Collis agreed to produce it " at a London theatre as early as possible. The play, however, had not been produced.

The jury returned a verdict for the plaintiff, assessing dmaages at £200, and judgment was entered accordingly.

McCALLAM v. DOVE.—ACTION FOR BREACH OF CONTRACT.

Before his Honour Judge Woodfall, in the Westminster County Court, Mr. F. F. McCallam, a baritone singer, sued to recover £100 damages for alleged breach of contract on the part of the defendant, Mr. Alfred Dove, musical director.

16

Mr. Emile Canot was counsel for plaintiff, and Mr. Power represented the defendant.

The plaintiff said that on August 28 he received a communication from a Mr. Campbell Bishop, who, he thought, was acting on behalf of Mr. Dove, and as a result of it he was engaged to sing the baritone parts in *Caval-*

leria Rusticana. There was a short tour. After that there was an interval of a week, and he found by THE STAGE that the next show was booked for Hull. He thereupon wired to Mr. Dove asking him for a train call, and in reply he received a message to the effect that, with regret, his services were not required.

For the defence, Mr. Alfred Dove said Mr. Bishop was not in his employ and had no authority to make contracts with any artists on his behalf.

His Honour, in giving judgment, said he thought the plaintiff was entitled to recover, and that Bishop was the agent of both parties in the matter. He thought the contract was for a tour. He awarded the plaintiff 25 guineas as damages, with costs.

EDELSTEN v. SHIELDS.

At Lambeth County Court, before his Honour Judge Emden, Mr. Willie Edelsten, variety agent, of Brixton Road, brought an action against Sammie Shields, music-hall artist, to recover money due upon engagements procured and performed. The amount of the original claim, £20 3s., was, by consent, reduced to £14 7s.

17

Judge Emden gave judgment for plaintiff for £13 7s.

ABRAHAMS v. HOWARD.—ADVERTISING ON THEATRE CURTAINS.

In the City of London Court, before his Honour Judge Lumley Smith, K.C., an action was brought by Mr. Abram E. Abrahams, 26, Great Eastern Road, Stratford, against Mr. J. Bannister Howard, proprietor of the Theatre Royal, King's Lynn, to recover the sum of £83, being damages for breach of agreement entered into between the plaintiff and defendant, dated November 4, 1904, by which the defendant agreed to show the plaintiff's advertising curtain and to let to the plaintiff part of the programme of the Royal, King's Lynn, for a definite period and for a definite number of nights.

18

Judge Lumley Smith, K.C., gave judgment for the plaintiff on the claim, and referred the matter of damages to the Registrar for assessment, with liberty to report to the Court.

SHAW v. MOSS EMPIRES AND ANOTHER. THE ASSIGNMENT OF AGENTS' COMMISSION.

In the King's Bench Division, before Mr. Justice Darling, Moss Empires, Limited, with Mr. George Bastow, the comedian, were the defendants in an action brought by Messrs. Tom Shaw and Co., agents, to recover commission deducted from the artist's salary by the management and held by the management. There was another case in the list—Ashton and Mitchell v. Moss Empires, Limited, and Goldin—and Mr. Duke, K.C. (for the plaintiffs, in opening the case, said the two cases were similar, and the second would be settled according to the judgment given by his Lordship in the first.

19

Mr. Duke added that the case was much in the nature of a test, and the question arose from the controversy which had taken place between variety artists and the agents who had been accustomed to arrange their engagements for them. The plaintiffs were claiming for five sums which were now in the hands of Messrs. Moss. Mr. Bastow, it appeared, entered into an agreement with the plaintiffs as follows:—

" In consideration of your having procured

for me an engagement with Messrs. Moss, Limited, to appear as comedian, I hereby agree to pay to you or your assigns 10 per cent. commission on the salary above referred to—seven weeks at £40 a week and twelve weeks at £45 a week—and all money which shall accrue from the said engagement or a prolongation of the same, and like commission on the salary at the next engagement. I hereby authorise Messrs. Moss, Limited, to deduct and pay the said amount from my salary in any manner you may deem expedient."

His lordship said the question was whether Mr. Bastow's contract with Messrs. Moss amounted to an equitable assignment in favour of the plaintiffs. He thought it did, and that it came within the authorities. In the circumstances he would give judgment for the plaintiffs for the amount claimed, with costs against the defendant Bastow.

PERFORMANCE IN UNLICENSED PREMISES AT WINKLEIGH.

Arising out of the visit of a company to Winkleigh, N. Devon, police-court proceedings took place at Chulmleigh, when Frederick Beckett was charged with causing a play to be represented on unlicensed premises, and the Rev. Henry Bremridge (Vicar of Winkleigh) was charged with allowing the acting.

Police-constable Tozer stated that on November 13 last the company of which Mr. Beckett was manager gave *The Private Secretary* in the Board Schoolroom, and the following day (Saturday) they presented *Maria Martin; or, The Murder in the Red Barn.* The license had not been obtained for the room, the company having for several nights previously occupied another schoolroom, which, however, was licensed.

The Bench, after some consideration, by a majority inflicted a fine of 1s. and costs in in each case.

INDEX TO LEGAL CASES.

Plaintiff.	efendant.	Date.	Nature of Case.
Abrahams	Howard	December 18....	Curtain advertising. Breach of contract
Alhambra Co., Ltd.	Loftus	September 14 & 30	Motion to restrain
Antony	De Frece	June 3	Claim for salary
Atkinson	Surrey Vaudeville Theatre, Ltd.	March 4 and November 9	Claim for damages for injuries (two cases)
Baines	Withers	July 11	Breach of contract
Barclay	Gray	December 4	Claim for commission
Barkshire	Blaschek	September 24	Question of contract
Batten	Rees	May 25	*Re* profits in partnership
Beg	Collis	December 16....	Breach of agreement
Blackmore	Huxley	March 3	Claim for commission
Boyle	Daly	January 15	Claim for commission
Bostock	Bermingham	May 11	Question of barring
Brandon	Manning	June 17	*Re* the Princess' Theatre
Brooks	Kirby	March 3	Claim for commission
Burns	Lucas	February 29	Claim for balance on a contract
—	Baldwin	September 26	Betting matter on handbills
—	Barden	August 27	Stage play in an unlicensed building
—	Beckett	December 22....	Stage play in an unlicensed building
—	Bell and another	September 26	An unlicensed play in a licensed building
—	Bell	September 23	Contempt of Court
—	Bradley	October 19	Pirated music
—	Brown	February 7	Stage play in a music hall
Cadbury	Beardmore	October 16	Injunction to restrain
Carlton	Bestic	October 28	Wrongful dismissal
Childs	Thompson	August 14	Claim for salary
Claxton	Stockelle	November 12	Commission on broken engagement
Clayton	Holland	August 13	Breach of contract
Clinton	Brinkley and others	March 10	Hiring of a hall
Clyde	Grant	March 10	Salary in lieu of notice
Cochran	London Pavilion, Ltd.	October 29	Alleged breach of agreement
Coffin	Fraser	July 5	To disclaim an imputation
Cohen	Augarde	November 8	Appeal against injunction
Collinson	United Counties Theatres	February 11	Claim for balance of salary
Connolly	Russell	June 15	Claim for salary
Corri and Crichton	Williams	February 19, March 30 and November 10	Claim for balance on a contract
Cramer	Stuart	November 19....	Claim for payment for goods
Curzon	Arthur	May 1	The Camden as a Music Hall
—	Caban	January 17	Illegal employment of children
—	Camden	June 19	Variety performances under a stage plays license
—	Camden	October 27. ...	Kinematograph entertainment with music
—	Carlo	October 24	Assault
—	Connor	June 4 and 23	Musical copyright in perforated rolls
—	Cooper	February 7	Spurious theatre tickets
—	Cowen	July 27	Alleged fraud
Deal	Shakespeare Theatre	January 13	Damages for injury
Denton	Hildyard	October 15	Claim for commission
Doughty	Meredyth	October 5	Breach of contract
—	Dickie and others	January 17	Illegal employment of a child
Edelsten	Bell	February 19	Split commissions
Edelsten	Shields	December 17	Commission on engagements
Edwards	Loftus	December 15	Alleged breach of contract
Edwardes	Pelissier	February 28	Injunction—infringement of playright
Edwardes	Beresford	November 20....	Motion for injunction to restrain
Expert Advertising Company	Gasson	July 6	*Re* advertising on curtain

INDEX TO LEGAL CASES—*Continued.*

Plaintiff.	Defendant.	Date.	Nature of Case.
Fiana................	Arthur.............	May 5 ....'	Claim for hire of an organ
Francis, Day, and Hunter	Evantoscope Co....	June 25	Injunction for infringement of copyright
Fraser	Arthur and McCrea	June 25	Announcing the apearance of an artist without authority
Frazer	Williams...........	November 11....	Wrongful dismissal
French	Whitmee	May 9	Playright infringement in portables
Freer.....	Thompson	July 31	Claim for damages in consequence of accident
	Froest	March 14	Fraud
Gandillot	Edwardes	June 2..........	Alleged infringement of copyright
Gettmann............	Goodship and Collini	March 17	Breach of agreement
Gibbon	Kitts..............	May 14	Breach of contract
Gibbons	Shields	February 24	Breach of contract
Glasgow Pavilion....	Retford	October 16......	Application for injunction.
Gower	Bell	July 10	Alleged infringement of playright
Gordon	Macdona..........	July 3	Broken weeks and the fortnight's notice
Grand. Glasgow......	Glasgow *Evening News*	June 23	Alleged libel
Granville Theatre....	Mayo	January 25	The barring clause
Gray	Variety Artists' Federation	December 14....	Libel
Grossmith	*Vanity Fair*	February 5 ...	Libel
Gurney.............	Vane	May 7	Claim for salary
—	Gem (Yarmouth) ..	August 18	Kinematograph entertainment with music
—	Gibbs	October 5	Pirated music
Hands	Courtneidge	July 9	Claim for damages for wrongful dismissal
Harcourt	Holloway	April 4.........	Claim for salary
Hardy	Bowman...........	April 15	Claim for commission
Harris	Gould	January 15	Claim for balance due for scenery
Hasselman	Poole and others....	December 8	Workmen's compensation
Hewitt	Porteous..........	December 4	Claim for profits on *Lady Frederick*
Hooper and Moore ..	Evantoscope Co.....	January 25	Injunction. Infringement of copyright
—	Hagenbecker and others	September 18 ..	Cruelty to elephants
—	Hardaker	May 1	False pretences
—	Hant	April 10 & May 1	False pretences
Jacobs	Cotton	June 16	Claim for commission
Jones..............	Saphrini and Bell ..	June 20	Infringement of playright
Jones..............	La Rondelle	July 2	Breach of contract
Joseph	Green	October 27.....	Breach of contract
Joseph	Empress, Brixton ..	January 30.....	Claim for goods
Karno	Brabourne........	May 20	Alleged breach of contract
Karno	Pathé Frères.......	April 3.........	Films and playright
Kelso	Batty	November 10 ..	Alleged breach of contract
	Kennedy...........	January 6	Premium fraud
Lake Grange	Saville............	July 20	Claim for salary
Leckie	Watts	January 24.....	The barring clause
London Music Hall..	Austin	December 15....	Motion to restrain
London Music Hall..	Evans	June 30	Breach of contract
London Music Hall..	Kitts	October 8	Breach of contract
London Music Hall..	Sinclair	October 8	Breach of contract
—	Leslie and others ...	October 19.....	Stage plays in a music hall
—	Lowder	January 11.....	Entertainment without a license
—	Lubinski	September 14 ..	Pirated music
Macdonald	Seebold	October 19.....	Claim for balance due on agreement
Martine	Nicholson	January 21.....	Alleged breach of contract
Marks	Tivoli, Manchester,.	December 3	Damages for personal injuries
McCallam	Dove	December 16....	Breach of contract
Melford.............	Crossman	March 2 and May 4	Wrongful dismissal. The run of the piece
Melford.............	Moss Empires	January 29.....	Claim for salary
Metropole, Glasgow, Limited	Hardacre	June 9	Question of playright .
Mitcham Common Conservators	Showmen	May 8	Injunction. Question of Mitcham Fair
Milburn	Rogers	December 15 ..	Commission on re-engagement
Morgan	Macnaghten	January 21.....	Claim for salary and alleged breach of contract
Mortimer	O'Gorman and others	June 17 and July 20	Claim for loss of salary during music hall war
Mortimer	Variety Artists' Federation	March 27	Claim for loss of salary during music hall war

INDEX TO LEGAL CASES—*Continued.*

Plaintiff.	Defendant.	Date.	Nature of Case.
Moss Empires	Lloyd	May 13 and 16, and July 3	The barring clause
Moss Empires	Wills	May 9	The barring clause
Nathan	Ashton	April 6	Alleged breach of contract
Neale	Denton and Neale	February 10	Assignment of profits
Otto and Olga	Pepi	November 16	Alleged breach of contract
—	O'Gorman	June 26	Question of assault
—	O'Neill	September 5 & 12	Cruelty to a child
Pacey and Reeves	Thorpe and Coe	April 30	Claim for commission
Partait	LawLand Guarantee Trust Society	October 14	Damages for personal injuries
Payne	Gibbons and Payne	July 3	Dispute *re* will
Pocknill	Gibbons	June 3	Damages for injuries through negligence
Prior	Balmain	October 7	Alleged wrongful dismissal
—	Phair	April 30	False pretences
Relph	London Animated Picture Company	August 14	Alleged misrepresentation
Relph	Gilmore	September 30	Injunction restraining
Reno	Oxford, Limited	July 31	Claim for salary
Rickards	Bartram and others	December 15	Libel
Richards, Burney, and Co.	May	May 21	Breach of contract
Richmond	Shepherd's Bush Empire	November 21	Claim for damages for ejectment from theatre
Robertis	Elphinstone	November 26	Claim for balance of salary
Rogers	Withers	August 7	Infringement of playright
Rollason	Barrasford	April 30	Claim *re* electrical advertising
Rolt	Beecher	June 4 and 23	Alleged breach of contract
Rosen and Bliss	Harden	January 16	Damages—Breach of contract
Rothery	Nation	April 8	*Re A Lucky Star*
Royston	Karno	February 3	Breach of contract
Rushbrook	Grimsby Palace	May	For damages under the Employers Liability Act, 1880
Scholtz	*Amasis*, Limited, and Fenn	November 30	Alleged infringement of copyright
Scott	Macnaghten	May 18 and November 24	Breach of contract
Shoolbred	Wyndham and Albery	November 20 and December 1	Claim for payment for goods
Shaw	Moss Empires and another	December 19	Assignment of commission
Shea	Tree	November 30	Workmen's compensation
Sprague	Carson	June 24	Payment for theatre plans
Starling	Gaumont	March 16	Damages for loss of wife
Stansfield	Bolton	October 14	Damages for leaving employment
St. Clair	Edwardes	October 27	Breach of contract
Stubbs	Raymond	November 13	Movement for injunction to prevent Sunday performance
Summer Entertainments Syndicate	Campbell	May 20	Breach of contract
—	Sedgwick	April 30	Cruelty to a lioness
—	Solomon	December 15	Protection of songs
Tate	Fullbrook	February 13	Playright appeal
Thorpe	Barstow	March 16	Claim for royalties
Trueman	Goodall	February 4	Claim for commission
—	Travers	October 5	Betting matter on handbills
United Counties Theatres	Chanti	July 20	Breach of contract
Vernon	Hicks	July 28	Salary in lieu of notice
Wa dorf Syndicate	Shubert	May 9	Injunction *re* the Waldorf
WestminsterCorporation	Waldorf Theatre	April 29	In regard to rates
Williams	Moore	February 21	Infringement of copyright
Willey	Clarke	January 21	Attaching an artist's salary
Wilkes	Waller	August 7 and October 7	Claim for commission
Willis	Bradford	April 15	Commission on re-engagement
—	Waldorf Syndicate	July 20	Summons for non-payment of rates
—	Wood	July 30	Kinematograph entertainment with music
—	Watson	September 7 & 16	Alleged bogus agency

IN THE BANKRUPTCY COURTS.

FEBRUARY.

MR. SAM REDFERN.

In the Bankruptcy Court, the statutory first meeting of creditors was held before Mr. Egerton S. Grey, official receiver, under the failure of Samuel Redfern Phillips, music-hall artist, professionally known as Sam Redfern, and described as of St. George's Road, Southwark.

The debtor states that he has followed his profession for forty years. He returned his liabilities at £244 and his assets at nil, and attributes his failure to losses in connection with a poultry farm and a public-house, and to an accident which befell him at a Coventry music hall.

There was no offer of composition before the meeting, and the matter remained in the official receiver's hands.

MR. MARSHALL MOORE.

In the Bankruptcy Court, before Mr. G. Chapman, under the failure of Robert Moore Marshall, formerly general manager of the Coliseum, the first meeting of the creditors was held, and in the absence of any offer the case was left with the Official Receiver to be wound up in bankruptcy. The accounts showed liabilities £803, and no available assets.

The debtor, it was stated, had been in the theatrical line for twenty-seven years, and had respectively acted as stage manager at Drury Lane Theatre, general manager of the Coliseum, and manager of a suburban pantomime. He had also taken part in dramatic sketches at London music halls, and had managed a touring comic opera company.

The failure was attributed, among other causes, to the unexpected closing of the Coliseum in April, 1906.

MR. SAM POLUSKI.

The statutory first meeting of creditors was held before Mr. W. G. Williams, assistant receiver, in the Bankruptcy Court, under the failure of Samuel Thomas Govett, comedian, known as Sam Poluski, and described as of St. Quintin Avenue, North Kensington.

The debtor stated that he has followed his profession for the last twenty-five years, and works with his brother as the Poluski Brothers. He estimated his liabilities at between £700 and £800, and his assets at £600, chiefly represented by a motor-car, the ownership of which is, however, disputed.

There was no proposal before the meeting, and the matter remained in the Official Receiver's hands.

MARCH.

MR. NORMAN ROE.

At the Bankruptcy Court, the creditors met under the failure of James Norman G. Roe, who lately carried on business at the Royalty.

The Chairman reported that according to the debtor's statements he left school six years ago, and afterwards went to Canada. Having studied medicine at Liverpool, he came to London in 1906, and in the following year became connected with the stage, investing money in a play running in the provinces. In December last he entered into an agreement to take the Royalty and produce the *Sphinx* and other plays. Another person agreed to finance him, but the play was never produced. He, however, did produce *Susanna—and Some Others*, but the play only ran for a week, and he attributed his present position to the breaking down of the arrangements to finance his enterprise and to his having lived beyond his means. A statement of affairs had been lodged disclosing unsecured liabilities £2,149, and estimated assets £240.

The case went into bankruptcy.

MR. SAM POLUSKI.

At the Court of Bankruptcy, at a sitting before Mr. Registrar Hope, S. T. Govett, known as Sam Poluski, was examined. Liabilities were £2,419, of which £961 are stated to be unsecured, and assets £772.

The debtor stated, in reply to the Official Receiver, that his income has averaged £500 a year, and that his insolvency was due to his wife's extravagance. He had not lived extravagantly himself, although his principal liability was in respect of the purchase of a motor-car. The car was bought by his wife, and presented by her to him at his expense. He was sued for the balance of £468 due on the car, with the result that he was now without a car and in the Bankruptcy Court.

The examination was closed.

MR. FRANK RUBENS.

In the Bankruptcy Court, before Mr. Registrar Hope, the examination was held and concluded of Herbert Francis Ellis, variety artist, professionally known as Frank Rubens, the accounts showing debts £113 14s. 6d., and assets £13.

The debtor attributed his insolvency to lack of engagements and to his liability for damages and costs under a judgment recovered against him in an action for infringement of copyright.

MR. MARSHALL MOORE.

In the Bankruptcy Court, before Mr. Registrar Brougham, the examination was concluded **20** of Mr. Robert Moore Marshall, a theatrical manager, professionally known as Marshall Moore. The liabilities were returned at £803, but no available assets were disclosed.

It was stated that the debtor had been engaged in theatrical business since 1880, principally as stage manager and actor. From 1898 until 1904 he was stage manager at Drury Lane, and from the latter year until 1906 general manager at the London Coliseum. He attributed his insolvency to the closing of the London Coliseum, to the subsequent non-fulfilment of important contracts, and generally to his expenditure having exceeded his income.

APRIL.

Mr. J. H. WEBSTER.

In the Court of Bankruptcy, an application for discharge was made before Mr. Registrar Linklater by John Hampden Webster, **7** who was adjudicated bankrupt in December, 1903, when he was described as of an address in Portsdown Road, W.

Mr. Egerton S. Grey appeared as official receiver, and reported that the liabilities amounted to £12,322, and that a sum of £160 had been realised in respect of the estate, but it was insufficient to pay the preferential claims. The bankrupt, from 1892 until 1899, followed his profession of an actor in the name of George Sheldon. In March of the latter year he purchased for £2,000 a half-share in a theatrical training school, he subsequently putting £4,000 capital into the business; but he and his partner failed to agree, and eventually he (the bankrupt) took over the management of a touring company, playing *High Jinks*. In March, 1903, he took the *Rose of the Riviera* on tour, but it involved him in a loss of £700, and had partly brought about his failure. The applicant attributed his bankruptcy to loss in connection with the partnership business previously mentioned. The Official Receiver opposed the application on statutory grounds, adding that since his failure the bankrupt had been engaged in writing for newspapers, composing and producing plays, etc. Certain creditors opposed the application on the ground that they had received no dividend.

After hearing Mr. Tindal Davis, who represented the bankrupt, his Honour suspended the order of discharge for two years.

MAY.

MR. MARTIN ADESON.

At the Liverpool Bankruptcy Court, before his Honour Judge Thomas, application for his **8** discharge from bankruptcy was made by Martin M'Hale, otherwise known as Martin Adeson, described as a comedian, of 14, Seymour Street, Liverpool, and lately residing at 15, Electric Mansions, Brixton.

Applicant, in answer to questions, stated that since the receiving order had been made he had obtained very few engagements. He had no money at the present time; "in fact," he added, "I will go further than that. This thing has been hanging over me, and it has thrown me out of employment."

His Honour granted the discharge, subject to a suspension of two years.

AUGUST.

MR. ELLIS DAGNALL.

The first meeting of creditors was held under a receiving order made against Ellis Dagnall, described as of 103, Regent **19** Street, W., theatrical manager.

Debtor states that in April, 1907, he leased the Shaftesbury for twenty-one years. He afterwards granted a sub-lease to the New Shaftesbury, Limited, by whom the theatre was carried on until the end of July, 1907, when it was closed. In the following September the debtor, with the consent of the company, took possession, and ran the theatre with various attractions from December, 1907, until the beginning of July last, when the landlord took possession for arrears of rent. The debtor states that in April, 1907, he had £400 or £500 capital, apart from his holding of £1,000 shares in the New Shaftesbury, Limited, and no liabilities. He attributes his present position to loss in connection with the working of the Shaftesbury. The accounts showed liabilities £3,012, against assets of uncertain value.

In the absence of any proposal, the case was left in the hands of the Official Receiver as trustee.

MR. ARTHUR HARE.

A first meeting of creditors was held, under a receiving order made in the case of Arthur Hugh Hare, who stated that he was an **28** actor, and had been the proprietor and manager of touring companies in England. He estimates his liabilities at about £500 or £600, and attributes his present position to losses on theatrical speculations and on the Stock Exchange and to extravagance in living. It was stated that the debtor hoped to pay his creditors in full, and the meeting was adjourned for three weeks.

MR. B. H. WHITCOMB.

The first meeting of creditors was held at the Bankruptcy Court, under a receiving order **31** made in the case of Beresford W. Whitcomb, who states that he is an actor, and has been on the stage for twenty-one years, having acted principally in the provinces. He attributes his insolvency to the failure of his theatrical productions owing to bad seasons. The debts were returned at £204, the assets at £6.

No offer was submitted, and the chairman reported that the debtor had already been adjudicated bankrupt.

SEPTEMBER.

MR. NORMAN J. NORMAN.

The case of Norman John Norman, theatrical manager, of Ridgmount Gardens, came **15** before the Bankruptcy Court at a sitting for public examination. The accounts showed liabilities £5,487, of which £4,162 was expected to rank, and assets £3,602.

In answer to Mr. W. G. Williams, Assistant Receiver, the debtor said that he was an American, and came to England in 1898. In 1901 he commenced business as a tourist agent and theatrical manager at 33, Haymarket, S.W., but later discontinued the theatrical business owing to the growth of the tourist agency. In January, 1906, he removed to 23, Haymarket, and continued business as "Normans" down to December, 1907. He then sold his connection to a company in consideration of £250 in cash and a commission on all business derived from his customers. Early in 1907 he joined another person, who had taken a lease of the Shaftesbury, and agreed to work with him and share the profits equally. In April, 1907, the "New Shaftesbury, Limited," was registered, with a nominal capital of £14,000, to take over the lease, etc., he (debtor) being appointed business manager at a salary of £10 a week, but the company only ran for a short period. From December, 1907, to July, 1908, he acted as manager of the theatre, and was to receive a half-share of the profits and £5 per week for expenses, but the business was not a success. He attributed his failure to want of capital, heavy expenses of the premises, 23, Haymarket, and slackness of trade. The examination was closed.

MR. ARTHUR HARE.

Before Mr. G. W. Chapman, official receiver, in the Bankruptcy Court, the creditors met **18** by adjournment under the failure of Arthur Hugh Hare, comedian, described as late of an address in Jermyn Street, W.

The chairman reported that a statement of affairs had been filed showing liabilities £1,297, of which £897 was unsecured, and estimated assets £840. The debtor for the last nine years had been proprietor and manager of touring companies, some of which proved successful and others failures. His liabilities chiefly represented money advanced for touring, or theatrical and personal requirements.

The debtor submitted no offer of composition, and his estate remained in the hands of the Official Receiver as trustee.

MR. GEORGE ABEL.

In the Bankruptcy Court, the case of George Abel, described as of Greycoat Gardens, Westminster, came before the Court at a **22** sitting for public examination. The unsecured liabilities were returned at £2,690, and there appeared to be no available assets.

The debtor formerly managed the Opera House, Cheltenham, and from July, 1901, to December, 1903, performed on the music hall stage with his wife, who is professionally known as Ethel Arden. In April, 1905, a company called Ethel Arden and George Abel, Limited, was registered, to which they sold the right of producing certain sketches for a consideration payable in shares. The debtor afterwards assisted his wife in the production of a music hall sketch in the United States, and promoted the George Abel Motor Transfer Company, of which he became president. He

attributed his present position to the cancellation of contracts for the production of musical sketch, in consequence of proceedings instituted by the Theatrical Managers' Association.

The examination was closed.

OCTOBER.

MR. ARTHUR HARE.

At the London Bankruptcy Court, Arthur Hare, comedian, appeared to pass his public **6** examination upon accounts showing liabilities £1,297 and assets £840. He attributed his failure to loss on his theatrical enterprises, extravagance in living, and Stock Exchange speculation. The examination was concluded.

MR. WILLIAM BAILEY.

The creditors met at the London Bankruptcy Court under the failure of William Bailey, proprietor of the West London, Marylebone. **6** The Chairman reported that the debtor, with two partners, acquired the theatre in 1892, with a capital of £2,400. He paid his partners out, the last one, in 1906, receiving £4,000, and he had since carried the business on alone. He attributes his present position to depreciation in trade, caused by the removal of so many thousands of families from the neighbourhood on the completion of the Great Central Railway. The liabilities are returned at £5,494, of which £855 is unsecured, and assets showing a surplus of £1,250. A trustee was appointed to wind up the case in bankruptcy.

NOVEMBER.

MR. WILLIAM BAILEY.

Before Mr. Registrar Giffard, in the Bankruptcy Court, the examination was held of **4** Mr. William Bailey, theatre proprietor, of Church Street, Marylebone. Accounts were lodged showing liabilities £5,940, of which £855 were stated to be unsecured, and an estimated surplus in assets of £1,240.

The debtor was, it was stated, a music-hall manager prior to January, 1893, and then, in partnership with two other persons, he purchased for £8,000 (of which £6,000 remained on mortgage to the vendor) the lease of the Marylebone, which they renamed the West London. The partners retired in 1896 and 1901 respectively, and the debtor then carried on the theatre alone.

He attributed his failure to competition, to general depression in trade, to falling off in takings, and to pressure by one of the mortgagees.—The examination was concluded.

THE STAGE PROVINCIAL GUIDE.

ABERAVON, Port Talbot, Glam.

Population, 7,553. Miles from London, 192.
PUBLIC HALL.—Secretary, Mr. M. Tennant.
Dramatic license. Holding capacity: Number
of persons, 800. Fixed stage, capable of being
enlarged. Proscenium opening, about 21ft.
wide. Lighted by gas. Terms for hiring:
First night, £2 2s.; after, £1 1s. per night;
piano, 7s. 6d. Amount of deposit required on
booking, £1 1s. Gas, 3s. 6d., or per meter
Early closing day, Thursday; market days,
Tuesday and Saturday.
Agent.—M.H.A.R.A.: F. Jones, Red Lion
Hotel.

ABERCARN, Mon.

Population, 12,607. Miles from London, 169.
VICTORIA PUBLIC HALL.—Manager, Mr.
John Sykes. Dramatic and music and dancing
licenses. Holding capacity: Number of persons, 800. Stage, 29ft. wide by 15ft. deep.
Lighted by gas. Amount of printing required,
200 sheets. Terms for hiring, three nights,
£4 17s. 6d. Amount of deposit required on
booking, £1.
The population is an industrial one, miners
and tinplate workers, there being two collieries and two tin works, employing approximately 3,500 men.
There are no local fairs. Portables have
visited the place, but not for the past few
years, although there does not appear to be
any difficulty in obtaining a license from the
County Council. There is no site now available for circus pitches.
Early closing day, Wednesday; market day,
Saturday.

ABERDARE, Glam.

Population, 43,365. Miles from London, 185.
NEW THEATRE.—Proprietors, Theatre and
Billposting Co., Limited; Manager and Secre-
tary, Mr. Z. Andrews; Acting - Manager,
Mr. B. Richards. Booking circuit, Llan-
elly. Musical Director, Mr. Everard Ash-
ton. Dramatic license. Holding capacity:
Number of persons, nearly 2,000; amount, £60.
Stage, 25ft. deep, 50ft. wide; proscenium open-
ing, 26ft. Lighted by gas. Time of band re-
hearsal, 1 p.m. No matinée day. The sur-
rounding halls are not barred.
Early closing day, Thursday; market day,
Saturday.
Agent.—M.H.A.R.A.: R. W. Bentley, Crown
Hotel.

RECOMMENDED APARTMENTS.

Mrs. Morgan, 54, Dean Street.—1 sitting-room
and bedroom.

ABERDEEN, N.B.

Population, 160,780. Miles from London, 558.
HIS MAJESTY'S THEATRE.—Proprietors,
the Robert Arthur Theatres Co., Limited;
Managing Director, Mr. Robert Arthur; Act-
ing-Manager, Mr. H. Adair Nelson; Musical
Director, Mr. A. W. Loseby; Scenic Artist,
Mr. Joseph Hogg. Full dramatic license.
Holding capacity: Number of persons, 2,500,
producing with early doors £250. Proscenium
opening, 31ft.; stage depth, 41ft.; width, 75ft.;
from stage to grid, 60ft. Electric light.
Amount of printing required: Walls, 1,000 d.c.
sheets; windows, 1,600. Usual matinée day,
Saturday, at 2.15. Band rehearsal, 11 a.m.

PALACE. — Proprietors, United County
Theatres Co.; Managing Director and Chairman, Mr. Alfred Moul; Manager, Mr. Walter
Gilbert. Band rehearsal, 1 p.m. Electric
light, direct current, voltage 220.

ROYAL ALBERT HALL.—Managers, Messrs.
Storie, Cruden, and Simpson, 9, Golden Square,
Aberdeen; Hall-keeper, Mr. Adam Matthew, 53,
Huntly Street, Aberdeen. Music and dancing
license. Holding capacity: Number of persons,
900. Platform, 23ft. by 10ft. Electric light,
direct current, voltage 220. Terms for hiring,
£5 per night; per week, £24. Amount of deposit required on booking, one-fourth. Special
quotations on application to the managers.

THE UNION HALL.—Secretary, Mr. A. Neil
MacDonald, solicitor, 129, Union Street, Aberdeen; Hall-keeper, Mr. H. E. Humphries, 13,
Spa Street, Aberdeen. Available for music,
dancing, kinematograph, and dramatic entertainments. Seating capacity, 650. Fitted
stage. Proscenium opening, 23ft. Electric
light, direct current, voltage 220. Terms for
hire from £2 12s. 6d. per night. Special terms
for continuous engagements.

MUSIC HALL.—Secretaries, Messrs. Fraser
and Duguid, 57, Crown Street, Aberdeen; Hall-
keeper, Mr. G. Rettie, Music Hall Buildings,
Union Street, Aberdeen. Large Concert Room,
available for music, dancing, kinematograph
entertainments, and concerts. Seating capacity: Number of persons, 2,500. Platform,
41ft. 7ins. by 19ft. 9ins. Electric light, direct
current, voltage 220. Spacious fireproof apartment for kinematograph. Terms for hire,
£10 10s. per night. £40 to £50 per week.
Special terms for continuous engagements on
application to secretaries.

ALHAMBRA AND WINTER ZOO.—Proprie-
tor, Mr. John Sinclair; Manager, Mr. Geo. B.
Lee. Animals, pictures, and variety.
There is no local fixed fair. The town is
visited periodically by portables, sites for

which there is little or no difficulty in obtaining. A good circus pitch in a central position is available. Concerts are held in the Beach Pavilion Hall (owned and managed by Mr. D. Thomson, a local entertainer) during the summer months, and various public halls throughout the town are available and suitable for such entertainments. The population of Aberdeen is mostly industrial. There is a large fishing community, which comprises a class of people who are regular theatre and music hall goers. Granite workers (i.e., masons, sculptors, etc.) and persons employed in the manufacture of paper, wool, linen, and combs form a large proportion of the inhabitants.

Early closing days, Wednesday and Saturday; market day, Friday.

Medical Officers.—A.A.: Dr. McKerron, 1, Albyn Place; A.U.: The same.

Agents.—A.U.: J. McGregor, Bon Accord Hotel, Market Place; V.A.F.: The same; M.H.A.R.A.: Mrs. McMillan, "Mac's" Bar, Bridge Street.

RECOMMENDED APARTMENTS.

Mrs. Innes, 255, Union Street.—3 sitting, 5 bedrooms; 2 pianos; bath (h. and c.); electric light; 4 minutes from theatre.

ABERGAVENNY, Mon.

Population, 7,795. Miles from London, 165.

TOWN HALL.—Proprietors, the Town Council; Manager, Mr. W. Llewellin. Not licensed at present, but temporary music license may be had. Holding capacity: Number of persons, 800. Amount, £45. Stage measurements, 15ft. by 36ft., but can be made larger; no proscenium. Gas. Terms for hiring: One night, £2 4s.; two nights, £3 17s.; three nights, £4 19s. Amount of deposit required on booking, £1.

MARKET HALL.—Proprietors, the Town Council; Manager, Mr. W. Llewellin. Music license. Holding capacity, 2,000. No proper stage. Market hall is too cold for use in winter months.

Dates of local fairs, May 14 and September 25.

Sites available for portables, alfresco concerts, and circuses. Castle Grounds, Cattle Market, Bailey Park.

Early closing day, Thursday. Market days, Tuesday and Friday.

ABERTILLERY, Mon.

Population, 21,945. Miles from London, 175.

METROPOLE THEATRE.—Lessee and Manager, Mr. C. J. Seaborn; Musical Director, Mr. Joseph Collier. Stage dimensions, 43ft. by 26ft. Clear 18ft. Bioscope.

PAVILION THEATRE OF VARIETIES.—Proprietor, Mr. A. Tilney; Lessees, Messrs. E. and H. Tilney; Manager, Mr. E. Pryce; Musical Director, Mr. Fred Drake. Full dramatic license. Holding capacity: Number of persons, 1,500. Stage measurements: Depth, 30ft. by 50ft.; proscenium opening, 26ft. Own installation for electric light, direct current, 220 voltage; also gas. Amount of printing required, 1,000 and 500 lithos. No regular matinée day. Band rehearsal, 12.30 p.m. Two performances nightly.

Early closing day, Wednesday; market day, Saturday.

Agent.—M.H.A.R.A.: Mrs. Evans, Station Hotel; V.A.F.: The same.

ABERYSTWYTH, Cardigan.

Population, 8,013. Miles from London, 243.

COLISEUM.—Proprietor and Manager, Mr. David Phillips. Holding capacity: Number of persons, 1,400; amount, £80 to £100, popular

prices. Dramatic license. Stage measurements: Opening, 24ft.; depth, 14ft.; flats, 15ft. to 18½ft. by 6ft. wide. Electric light, direct current, voltage 220. Amount of printing required, 250 sheets. Terms for hiring, sharing.

ROYAL PIER PAVILION.—Lessee, Mr. C. W. Jenkinson. Holds 2,000. Amount, £100 to £120, popular prices. Dramatic license. Stage measurements: Opening, 30ft.; depth, 26ft.; flats, 14ft. to 16ft. Electric light, direct current, 220 voltage. Terms for hiring, sharing.

MARKET HALL.—Proprietors, the Corporation; Manager, Mr. W. Edwards. Holding capacity, 400; amount, £20 to £30. Stage measurements, 21ft. by 13ft. Concert or kinematograph. Terms for hiring, £2 2s. first night, and following nights £1 1s.

Summer population, about 60,000.

Early closing day, Wednesday; market day, Monday.

Agent.—A.U.: J. P. Savin, Hotel St. George, Queen's Square; V.A.F.: The same.

RECOMMENDED APARTMENTS.

Mrs. H. Jones, 3, Terrace Road.—2 sitting-rooms, 4 bedrooms.

ABINGDON, Berks.

Population, 6,480. Miles from London, 60.

CORN EXCHANGE.—Manager, Mr. J. H. Viner, The Guildhall, Abingdon. Dramatic and music and dancing licenses. Holding capacity: Number of persons, 700. No proscenium or scenery. Stage measurement, 33ft. by 21ft. Gas. Terms for hiring: £2 17s. 6d. first night; half this amount each night following, gas extra. Amount of deposit required on booking, £1.

Fairs: Monday and Tuesday before October 11; also Monday after October 11.

Early closing, Thursday; market, Monday.

ACCRINGTON.

Population, 43,122. Miles from London, 209.

PRINCE'S THEATRE.—Proprietor and Manager, Mr. J. B. Ormerod; Acting-Manager, Mr. J. E. Barnes.

NEW HIPPODROME.—Proprietors, Messrs. Willmot, Vandy, Potter, and Weisker; Manager, Mr. Walter Mould; Director, Mr. Fred Willmot. Booked in conjunction with Thos. Barrasford tour. Music and dancing license. Electric light. Band rehearsal, 2 p.m.

TOWN HALL.—Hall Superintendent, Mr. W. Prescott. Let for all kinds of entertainment. Holding capacity: Number of persons, 1,200. Open platform, 30ft. by 18ft. Terms for hiring: Meetings and concerts, per night, 42s.; entertainments where scenery is used, one week, £17 10s.; kinematograph exhibitions, one week, £16; extras, electric light (direct current, 230 voltage), per meter, and piano. Amount of deposit required on booking: Three days' rent; if for one day, £2 2s.

LIBERAL CLUB ASSEMBLY ROOM.—Secretary, Mr. John W. Barlow. Music and dancing license. Holding capacity: Number of persons, 500. No proper stage. Electric light and gas. Terms on application to secretary.

Accrington has two general fairs—one always the week before Easter and one the first Thursday in August. Both fairs last five days.

Early closing day, Wednesday; market day, Tuesday.

Medical Officers. — A.A.: Dr. Greenhalgh, 151, Blackburn Road; A.U.: The same; M.H.A.R.A.: Dr. Greenhalgh, 1, Brunswick Terrace.

Agents.—A.U.: J. McGregor, Commercial Hotel; M.H.A.R.A.: Thomas Bentley, Blockade Hotel; V.A.F.: The same.

ADDLESTONE, Surrey.

Population, 6,073. Miles from London, 20.
VILLAGE HALL.—Proprietors, Addlestone Village Hall Co., Limited; Manager, Mr. J. Bower-Binns. Double license. Holding capacity: Number of persons, 300; amount, £20-£30, according to arrangement of seats. Stage measurements, 20ft. by 14ft.; proscenium opening, 15ft. 9ins. Gas. Terms for hiring: £2 2s. first night, £1 1s. each following. Amount of deposit required on booking, half fees; balance to be paid before doors are opened.
Early closing day, Thursday.

AIRDRIE, Lanark.

Population, 22,288. Miles from London, 396.
PUBLIC HALL.—Manager, Mr. William Ferguson. Dramatic license. Seated for 1,200, with platform fitted up with scenery and sidewings. Gas fully and part electric. Terms for hiring: Saturday or Monday, single, £3 3s.; Saturday and Monday consecutive, £5; Friday and Saturday consecutive, £4 10s.; whole week, £8. Hall let on condition that the lowest charge for admission shall be 3d.
Market day, Tuesday. There are no fairs. For sites for portables, alfrescos, concerts, and circuses, apply, John Gibson, bill-poster, Broom Kroll Street.

ALCESTER, Warwick.

Population, 2,303. Miles from London, 121.
CORN EXCHANGE.—Secretary, Mr. E. A. Jephcott. Dramatic license. Holding capacity: Number of persons, 400. No proper stage. Platform, 30ft. by 12ft. Lighted by gas. Terms for hiring, £1 7s. 6d., or £2 2s. for two successive nights. Amount of deposit required on booking, 10s.
Early closing, Thursday; market day, Wednesday.

ALDEBURGH, Suffolk.

Population, 2,405. Miles from London, 99.
JUBILEE HALL.—Apply Miss Ethel T. Wightman. Holding capacity: Number of persons, 350 to 400. Lighted by gas. Terms for hiring, £2 2s. for one night, £1 1s. each subsequent night. Amount of deposit required on booking, half amount.
Early closing, Wednesday.

ALDERSHOT, Hants.

Population, 30,974. Miles from London, 33.
ROYAL AND HIPPODROME. — Proprietor and Manager, Mr. Clarence Sounes; Resident Manager, Mr. Jack Gladwin; Musical Director, Mr. Herbert Harrison. Full dramatic license. Gas and electric light. Amount of printing required: 750 sheets posting, 500 lithos. Usual matinée day, Saturday. Band rehearsal, 1.30 p.m.
There are one or two pitches where circuses and fairs are held, but no portable theatrical companies visit here. If they did no opposition or difficulty in getting licenses, etc., is expected.
Aldershot relies principally on the military camps, which are very extensive—the largest in the world—with about 20,000 troops permanently quartered there, and there are several large military colleges in the close vicinity where officers are trained. These and the military generally are large patrons of amusement at the local playhouse. Each brigade, however, has a canteen, where a variety perform-

ance is given each evening by music hall artists. Within easy distance of Aldershot there are several towns and villages. It might be mentioned that new camps are now formed around Aldershot, and every opportunity is given by the railway companies and motor-bus company in joining up with a theatre train service.
Early closing day, Wednesday.
Medical Officer.—A.A.: Dr. Kyngdon, Cargate Lodge (hours, 9-11 and 7-7.30).
Agent.—M.H.A.R.A.: A. J. Clement, Wellington Hotel; V.A.F.: The same.

RECOMMENDED APARTMENTS.

Mrs. H. E. East Irvine, Halimote Road.—3 bedrooms, 2 sitting-rooms; piano; bath.

ALFORD, Lincs.

Population, 2,478. Miles from London, 130.
CORN EXCHANGE.—Manager, Mr. S. B. Carnley, solicitor and secretary. Double license. Holding capacity: Number of persons, 300; amount, £20. Platform: 15ft. by 9ft. wide; 3ft. high. A proper stage can be put up by arrangement with caretaker. Lighted by gas. Very little printing required. Terms for hiring: 12s. 6d. first night, 9s. second, and 7s. succeeding nights; gas and fires extra. Amount of deposit required on booking, 10s.
Early closing, Thursday; market, Tuesday. Alford Bull Fair, November 6. In addition there are the May and November fairs.

ALFRETON, Derbyshire.

Population: Town, 6,500; district, 17,505.
Miles from London, 136.
TOWN HALL.—Proprietor, Mr. Fredk. Lee. Double license. Holding capacity: Number of persons, 600. Proper stage. Stage measurements, 32ft. by 16ft.; 17ft. high; proscenium, 21ft. Lighted by gas. Terms for hiring: For 1 night, 37s. 6d.; 2, £3 10s.; 3 £5 0s. 6d.; 4, £6 15s.; 5, £7 17s. 6d.; 6, £9; 7, £10 2s. Amount of deposit required on booking, £1, or by arrangement.
Early closing day, Wednesday; market day, Friday.

ALLOA, Clackmannan.

Population, 14,458. Miles from London, 420.
TOWN HALL.—Hall-keeper, Mr. D. Campbell. License: Dramatic and Music and Dancing. Holding capacity: Number of persons, 1,000. Stage, 16ft. deep, 24ft. wide; open stage; can be extended at an extra fee of 12s. 6d. Electric light, 4d. per unit. Terms for hiring: 1 night, £2 17s.; 2, £5 3s. 6d.; 3, £6 19s. 6d.; exclusive of charges for heating and lighting. Amount of deposit required on booking, £1.
EXCHANGE HALL.—Manager, Mr. John Crawford. Dramatic and music and dancing license. Holding capacity: Number of persons, 500 to 600; amount, £10 to £15. Stage measurements: 15ft. deep, 34ft. wide; width between proscenium, 18ft.; height, 11ft. 6ins. Gas and electric light. Amount of printing required: 2,000 handbills, 150 posters. Terms for hiring: From 20s. to 40s. for one day, cheaper for period. Amount of deposit required on booking, 20s. Two dressing-rooms.
Early closing day, Tuesday.

ALNWICK, Northumberland.

Population, 6,716. Miles from London, 313.
CORN EXCHANGE.—Licensee, Mr. Joseph Sanderson. Licensed for nine months. Holding capacity: Number of persons, 1,200. Stage

measurements: Stage, 30ft. by 25ft.; proscenium, 21ft. by 16ft. Gas and electric light (voltage 230).

TOWN HALL.—Manager, Mr. W. T. Hindmarsh, clerk of the Council, Corporation Offices, Alnwick. Not licensed. Holding capacity: Number of persons, 400. Platform. Stage measurements: 9ft. by 40ft. Inverted gas lamps. Terms for hiring: Concerts, 10s. inclusive. Amount of deposit required on booking: No deposit, as a rule. There are two radiators, which may be used at a small charge, and two ante rooms. The hall is well lighted and ventilated.

Hiring for hinds and shepherds, first Saturday in March; Entire Horse Show, first and second Mondays in April; hirings for single servants, first Saturday in November and first Monday in May; lamb and wool fair, second Monday in July; horses and cattle, second Monday in July and first Monday in October. Sites: Market Place and Recreation Ground. Early closing day, Wednesday; market day, Monday.

ALTON, Hants.

Population, 5,479. Miles from London, 47.

ASSEMBLY ROOMS.—Manager, Mr. W. B. Trimmer. Holding capacity: number of persons, 506; amount, £30. Proper stage. Measurements: 19ft. 15in. deep, 26ft. wide, 19ft. high. Gas. Terms for hiring: One night with gas, £2 15s.; two nights, £4 14s.; three, £6; after, £1 5s. per night. One night without gas, £2 7s. Extras: License fees, 5s. for each evening. Two firemen always on duty at a charge of 6d. per hour per fireman. Deposit required on booking, 10s. Only one company booked in each week.

Early closing day, Wednesday; market, day, Tuesday.

ALTRINCHAM, Cheshire.

Population, 16,831. Miles from London, 186.
CENTRAL THEATRE.—Sole Lessee and Manager, Mr. Chas. A. Seymour. Dramatic license, restricted. Holding capacity: Number of persons, 900; amount, £35. Stage measurements: 21ft. deep, 30ft. wide, take 18ft. flats, etc. Lighted by gas. Amount of printing required: 300 sheets, 750 lithos, circulars, etc. Usual matinée day, Saturday. Time of band rehearsal, 12 p.m.

PUBLIC HALL.—Owned by the Urban Council; Secretary, Mr. F. Beckett. Dramatic and music and dancing licenses. Holding capacity: Number of persons, 600 (seating). Stage measurements: 36ft. wide by 19ft. deep; proscenium opening, 21ft. by 14ft.; height of frame, 19½ft. Gas and electric light. Terms for hiring on application.

The district of Altrincham and Bowdon is generally estimated for theatrical purposes as containing a population of 35,000.

The population of Altrincham is trading and industrial; of Hale and Bowdon, residential. Altrincham and Bowdon have separate urban district councils. Hale is also independently governed.

Portables rarely frequent the town. No visit from a portable for two years or more. Their licenses are usually granted, and no serious interference offered. Show day is generally the last Wednesday in September. A fair circus pitch is obtainable. Alfresco concerts are not given here.

Sale is a separate district as regards local government, but geographically is part of

Altrincham, to which it is connected by tram (fare 1d., five to seven minutes service) and train. Sale and Altrincham mutually rely on each other for audiences at dramatic performances. Sale is a good residential district for Manchester business men.

Broadheath Station (L.N.W. Railway) is almost as convenient as Altrincham for touring companies.

Early closing day, Wednesday.

ALVA, Clackmannanshire, N.B.

TOWN HALL.—Secretary, Mr. Wm. Cochrane. Fully licensed. Holding capacity: Number of persons, 800. Stage measurements, 35ft. by 11½ft. Lighted by gas. Terms for hiring. £1 1s., and gas per night. Amount of deposit required on booking, 10s. 6d. Wednesdays and Thursdays best nights.

Early closing, Wednesday.

ALYTH, Perth.

Population, 1,965. Miles from London, 465.
TOWN HALL.—Manager, Mr. A. Robertson. No license: one can be obtained. Holding capacity: Number of persons, 800. Stage measurements, 33ft., 11ft. No proscenium. Lighted by gas. Amount of printing required: 150 day bills and 8 16-sheets. Terms for hiring: Dramatic, £1 17s. 6d.; concert, £1 5s. Amount of deposit required on booking, 10s.

Early closing, Wednesday; market, Tuesday.

Dates of local fairs: Third Tuesday in May; first Wednesday after November 12. Sites in market square available for portables; market muir available for circuses.

AMBLE, Northumberland.

Population, 3,000. Miles from London, 303.
CENTRAL HALL.—Proprietor and Manager, Mr. Thomas Gibson; Musical Director, Mr. F. Stokoe. Double license. Holding capacity: Number of persons, 1,250; amount, £50. Stage: Depth, 22ft.; width, 33ft.; opening, 18ft. Gas. The surrounding halls which it bars are Ashington, Morpeth and Alnwick.

AMBLESIDE, Westmorland.

Population, 2,536. Miles from London, 263.

ASSEMBLY ROOMS.—Manager, Mr. Edward Tyson. Dramatic license. Holding capacity: Number of persons, 500 to 600; amount, £35 (about). Stage measurements: 18ft. 9ins. from flooring of stage to top of arch, and 14ft. 3ins. to beginning of rise; depth, 12ft.; width, 19ft. 5ins.; 2ft. 6ins. wider behind arch: an additional 4ft., 8ft., or 12ft. extension on premises can be had at extra cost. Lighted by gas. Terms for hiring: £2 10s. for one night, which includes light. Amount of deposit required on booking, 10s.

THE PAVILION is licensed for drama, but since the Assembly Rooms were built about fifteen years ago it has only been used for the proprietor's own purposes in connection with his hotel.

Local fairs: Cattle and sheep, Whit Wednesday—sheep, October 13; cattle, October 29. There are no sites available for portables, alfresco concerts and circuses.

Early closing day, Thursday; market day, Wednesday.

AMMANFORD, Carm.

Population, 4,000. Miles from London, 213.

IVIROTES HALL.—Manager, Mr. Thomas Davies. Holding capacity: Number of persons, 600. Stage measurements, 36ft. by 12ft. Lighted by oil. Terms for hiring, £3 for three nights, £1 5s. for one night. Amount of deposit required on booking, 10s.

AMPTHILL, Beds.

Population, 2,177. Miles from London, 41.

There are in Ampthill three small rooms available for concerts, etc.—viz., the Court Room, the Wesleyan School, and the Church room. All these rooms are unlicensed, and in none of them is there a proper stage; all are lighted with gas. For any travelling company the Court Room is practically the only room which would be serviceable, unless the hirer was prepared to make all arrangements down to the last detail, including the provision of seating accommodation, and the Court Room would not hold more than about 250 people. The proprietors are H.M. Office of Works, and the charge is £1 1s. a night. There are no local pleasure fairs, but cattle fairs are held on May 4 and November 30 in each year.

There is a field available for circuses, etc., known as "Canal Close"; applications to Messrs. H. and C. Stanbridge, Ampthill.

Early closing day, Tuesday; market day, Thursday.

ANDOVER, Hants.

Population, 6,509. Miles from London, 67.

ASSEMBLY ROOM.—Manager, Mr. Jas. Blackmore. Dramatic and music licenses. Holding capacity: Number of persons, 450. Stage measurements: 26ft. by 16ft. deep; proscenium, 16ft. wide by 10ft. Lighted by gas. Terms for hiring: One night, £2 12s. 6d.; two nights, £3 13s. 6d. Amount of deposit required on booking: 10s. one night; 20s. two nights. Piano may be hired.

Early closing, Wednesday; market, Friday.

ANNAN, Dumfries.

Population, 5,804. Miles from London, 400.

VICTORIA HALL.—Manager, Mr. R. P. McDougall. Dramatic license. Holding capacity: Number of persons, 500-600; amount, £30. No proper stage, but permanent platform, capable of enlargement; depth, 13ft. to 19ft.; width, 24ft. to 38ft., as required. Lighted by gas. Amount of printing required, 200 sheets, 100 d. bills. Terms for hiring: £3 per night, including piano. Amount of deposit required on booking, £2.

GOOD TEMPLAR HALL, Lady Street.—Manager, Mr. Joe Bonner, 64, High Street. Dramatic and music and dancing licenses. Holding capacity: Number of persons, about 400; amount, £20. Stage is 4ft. deep by 9ft. wide. Footlights. Lighted by gas. Amount of printing required, about £1 5s., including billposting. Terms for hiring: 12s. 6d. per night, including one anteroom. Hall engaged every Thursday. Amount of deposit required on booking, 8s. Remarks: Suitable for small concert companies, kinematograph and variety entertainments.

Fairs: First Friday in May and third Friday in October. Site available for portables, alfresco concerts, etc., Annan Town Merse.

Market day, Friday.

ANSTRUTHER, Fife.

Population, 1,663. Miles from London, 417.

TOWN HALL.—Hallkeeper and bill-poster, Mr. H. Elliot. Dramatic license. Holding capacity: Number of persons, 600. Stage measurements: 20ft. width, 10ft. depth; can be extended when required at small cost. Lighted by gas. Amount of printing required, from 100 to 150 sheets, exclusive of day bills, etc. Terms for hiring: Dramatic £2 first night, £1 every succeeding night; concerts, £1 15s. first night, £1 every succeeding night. Gas extra. Amount of deposit required on booking, 10s.

Early closing, Wednesday; market, Friday.

APPLEBY, Westmoreland.

Population, 1,764. Miles from London, 276.

MARKET HALL.—Proprietors, The Corporation of Appleby; Manager, Mr. J. T. Alderson). Dramatic, music and dancing licenses. Holding capacity: Number of persons, 400. No proper stage. Platform 22ft. by 13ft.; 17ft. from platform to beam. Lighted by gas. Terms for hiring, 15s. Amount of deposit required on booking, 15s.

Dates of local fairs, second Tuesday and Wednesday in June.

Early closing day, Thursday; market day, Saturday.

ARBROATH, Forfarshire.

Population, 22,372. Miles from London, 473.

ARBROATH THEATRE.—Manager and Lessee, Mr. Geo. J. Melvin; Acting-Manager, Mr. Alexander Melvin; Musical Director, Mr. D. W. Jackson. Fully licensed. Holding capacity: Number of persons, 1,000. Stage measurements: 17½ft. deep, 35ft. wide; proscenium opening, 22ft. Electric lighting. Band rehearsal, 2 p.m. Usual matinée day, Saturday. No surrounding halls barred.

PUBLIC HALL.—Manager, Mr. A. Joiner. Dramatic and music and dancing license. Holding capacity: Number of persons, 1,000; seat, 900; amount, £50, ordinary prices. Concert stage, 11ft. deep, 24ft. wide; can be extended to 19ft. by 45ft. Bare stage. Frame can be fitted up; 20ft. opening, act drop, proscenium, gas fittings. Lighted by electricity, plug for kinematograph. Amount of printing required, 400 sheets. Terms for hiring: Dramatic—1 night, 63s.; 2 nights, 105s.; week, £12 12s.; Concerts—1 night, 42s.; 2 nights, 74s. 6d. Gas extra, as per meter. Amount of deposit required on booking, £1.

Population is industrial, flax mills and iron trade preponderating. There is also a certain amount of shipping.

There is an admirable beach for alfresco entertainments, and no difficulty is experienced as to ground for portables and obtaining licenses.

Early closing day, Wednesday; market day, Saturday.

ARDROSSAN, Ayrshire.

Population, 6,045. Miles from London, 405.

ASSEMBLY HALL.—Holding capacity: Number of persons, 500. Stage measurement, 30ft. by 11ft.; can be extended to 30ft. by 18ft. Lighted by gas. Terms for hiring: Dramatic, £2 2s.; concerts, £1 10s. Amount of deposit required on booking, £1.

No local fairs, and no sites available for portables or circuses.

ARDWICK.

See Manchester.

ARKLOW, Co. Wicklow.

Population, 5,294. Miles from Dublin, 51.

MARLBOROUGH HALL.—Manager, Mr. A. O. Hood, Estate Office. No dramatic license. Holding capacity: Number of persons, 600. Hall, 80ft. by 40ft.; stage, 40ft. by 9½ft.; also ante-room for dressing, etc. Lighted by gas. Terms for hiring: £1 6s. per night, including gas and caretaker's fee. Amount of deposit required on booking, £5 as security against damage.

Local fairs, second Tuesday of each month. Market, Thursday.

ASHBOURNE, Derby.

Population, 4,039. Miles from London, 147.

TOWN HALL.—Manager, Mr. H. Wright. Dramatic and music and dancing licenses. Holding capacity: Number of persons, about 600. Stage measurements: 14ft. by 26ft.; hall, 67ft. by 26ft. Lighted by gas. Terms for hiring: 40s. first; 30s. second; 25s. subsequent nights. Amount of deposit required on booking, 10s. each date booked.

Dates of local fairs: February 13, May 21, August 16, October 20, November 29, December 15.

Early closing, Wednesday; market, Saturday.

ASHBURTON, Devon.

Population, 2,628. Miles from London, 227.

MARKET HALL.—Managers, Messrs. Rendell and Sawdye. Fully licensed. Holding capacity: Number of persons, about 400. Concert platform measurements: Depth, 22ft.; width, 10ft. 6in.; height, 3ft. Lighted by gas. Terms for hiring, 30s. for one night. Amount of deposit required on booking, 10s. 6d.

Fairs: March 4, June 3, August 10, and November 11.

Early closing, Wednesday; market, Friday.

ASHBY-DE-LA-ZOUCH, Leicester.

Population, 4,726. Miles from London, 118.

TOWN HALL.—Proprietors, Urban Council; Manager, Mr. Hy. Baggott. Dramatic and music and dancing licenses. Holding capacity: Number of persons, 500. Proper stage, 18ft. high, 19ft. between pillars, 15ft. back to front, 6ft. can be added to front, 3ft. 6in. each side extra. Lighted by gas. Terms for hiring: 1 day, £1 10s.; 2 days, £2 12s. 6d., gas included. Amount of deposit required on booking, one-third.

Ashby-de-la-Zouch is a compact town, with an excellent train and tram service, the latter tapping populous centres of industry, the last tram out of Ashby running about eleven p.m. to Woodville, Swadlincote, etc. Ashby is a residential town, and good companies have been well patronised. Mr. C. St. E. Hussey, printer, stationer, newsagent, and tobacconist, opposite the Town Hall, is theatrical agent. Telephone 598. Portables only occasionally visit the town. They pitch at the Statues or Fair. These are held on the first Tuesday after September 21. There are admirable sites for alfresco concerts and circus pitches.

Early closing day, Wednesday; market day, Saturday.

ASHFORD, Kent.

Population, 12,808. Miles from London, 54.

CORN EXCHANGE.—Lessee and Manager, Mr. C. Creery. Dramatic and music and dancing licenses. Holding capacity: Number of persons, over 1,000. Stage measurements: 41ft. by 23ft. 6in.; height to grid, 22ft.; proscenium opening, 24ft. Cloths worked on rollers. Has some scenery. Lighted by gas. Amount of printing required: 300 sheets for walls, 100 lithos for windows. Terms for hiring: Sharing or rental. Apply to lessee.

Population chiefly industrial. Employees of the S.E.R. works about 2,500 men.

There is no fixed date for local fair. The town is not visited by portables. Licenses for these are not granted.

There is a good site for alfresco concerts called "The Paddock," where a permanent stage and dressing-rooms are erected. Circus pitches are obtainable in a large field adjoining the Victoria Hotel; or in "The Paddock."

Early closing day, Wednesday; market day, Tuesday.

ASHINGTON, Northumberland.

Population, 20,000. Miles from London, 290.

MINERS' THEATRE.—Lessee and Manager, Mr. Fred Gould. Holds 2,500. Electric light. direct current, 230 volts; also gas.

There is a little difficulty in reaching the town by train (ordinary), because there are so many junctions. There are the Co-operative Hall and others which can be booked for variety shows. The chief industry is mining, and miners receive their pay fortnightly. Blyth is the nearest town where there is a theatre. Ashington is 18½ miles from Newcastle Station (New Bridge Street).

No market day; early closing day, Wednesday.

ASHTON-UNDER-LYNE, Lancs.

Population, 43,890. Miles from London, 184.

THEATRE ROYAL.—Proprietor and Manager, Mr. Charles Revill; Acting-Manager, Mr. Chas. Revill, jun.; Musical Director, Mr. W. Halton; Scenic Artist, Mr. Alfred Crocker. Full dramatic license. Holding capacity: Number of persons, 3,000; amount, £145. Stage measurements: 45ft. deep, 75ft. wide, 29ft. proscenium opening. Electric light.

EMPIRE.—Proprietor, Messrs. W. H. Broadhead and Son; Manager, Mr. Percy B. Broadhead; Resident Acting-Manager, Mr. W. Leech; Booking Circuit, Messrs. W. H. Broadhead and Son; Musical Director, Mr. Robert Peel. Stage measurements: 90ft. by 45ft.; proscenium opening, 36ft. Gas and electric light. Time of band rehearsal, 11 a.m. Usual matinée day, Monday.

ODDFELLOWS HALL.—Manager, Mr. John Jenkins. Music and dancing license. Holding capacity: Number of persons, 800. No proper stage. Gas and electric light. Terms for hiring, £1 per day.

TOWN HALL.—Apply, Secretary.

CENTRAL HALL.—Apply, Secretary.

CO-OPERATIVE HALL.—Apply, Secretary.

The town itself is surrounded by smaller towns and villages within a radius of, say, 2½ miles, making up a total population of about 150,000, each place being connected by an excellent service of electric trams. The annual holidays or wakes are held the week following August 15, when all works are closed for ten days.

There is a large market ground on which portables can be erected, but they only stay for short periods. No difficulty in obtaining licenses.

Large circuses, such as Sanger's and Buffalo Bill's, call here occasionally, and find excellent pitches in the fields adjoining the town. Pierrots are numerous in the summer months, and have cosy sites in country places adjoining. The population is residential and industrial. Cotton spinning, engineering, mining, and allied trades.

The town has excellent railway accommodation, being served by the London and North-Western, Great Central, Lancashire and Yorkshire, North-Eastern, and Midland Railway Companies.

Early closing day, Tuesday; market days, Monday and Saturday.

Medical Officer.—A.A.: Dr. Mann, 222, Katherine Street; A.U.: The same; M.H.A.R.A.: The same.

Agent.—M.H.A.R.A.: T. Cropper, White Hart Hotel; V.A.F.: The same.

RECOMMENDED APARTMENTS.

Mrs. Christian, 4, Fletcher Street.—2 bedrooms 1 sitting-room, and large combined room ; piano.

ASHTON-UPON MERSEY, Cheshire.

Population, 5,563.　Miles from London, 190.

SALE PUBLIC HALL.—Manager, Mr. Joseph Toft, " Skernedale," Lyon's Fold. Fully licensed. Holding capacity: Number of persons, 800. Stage, 16ft. high, 52ft. wide, 33ft. deep; opening, 22ft. Gas and electric light. Terms for hiring: Vary as to circumstances.

ASPATRIA, Cumb.

Population, 2,885. Miles from London, 319.

PUBLIC HALL.—Proprietors, Aspatria Public Hall Co., Limited; Manager, Mr. Cephas Bouch. Dramatic, music and dancing licenses. Holding capacity: Number of persons, 400. Stage, 30ft. by 12ft. Lighted by gas. Terms for hiring, £1 per day. Amount of deposit required on booking, 10s. Site available for portables and circuses, public ground.

Early closing day, Tuesday; market day, Thursday.

ASTON.

See Birmingham.

ATHERSTONE, Warwick.

Population, 5,248.　Miles from London, 102

CORN EXCHANGE.—Manager, Mr. Harry Charnell. Dramatic license. Holding capacity: Number of persons, about 500. Stage measurements: 26ft. by 20ft. Proscenium. Three dressing-rooms Lighted by gas. Amount of printing required, up to 200 sheets. Terms for hiring on application to Manager. Other particulars upon application. Bill-poster, J. H. Calladine, Long Street.

Early closing day, Thursday; market day, Tuesday.

ATHERTON, Lancs.

Population, 16,211. Miles from London, 195.

VOLUNTEER HALL.—Manager, Mr. V. A. Hodder. Full license. Holding capacity: Number of persons, 1,000. Stage (without proscenium, etc.) measurements, 46ft. by 14ft. 6ins. Gas and electric light (alternating cur-

rent, voltage 230). Lighting free. For kinematograph charge according to use. Terms for hiring: One night, £2 2s.; each succeeding night, £1 1s. Amount of deposit required on booking, £1 1s.

Annual wakes, first Saturday October to following Wednesday. Market-place only available for portables.

Early closing, Wednesday; market, Saturday.

ATTERCLIFFE.

See Sheffield.

AYLESBURY, Bucks.

Population, 9,243. Miles from London, 35.

TOWN HALL.—Proprietors, Urban Council; Manager, Mr. Percy A. Wright. Fully licensed. Holding capacity: Number of persons, 600; amount, £40 is about the maximum. No proper stage; platform made of tables. Lighted by compressed gas. No piano, stock scenery, or fit-up. Terms: One performance, £2 2s., with £1 deposit; for every succeeding performance, £1 5s., with 2s. 6d. deposit. Gas extra by meter. There is seating accommodation for 450. The Corn Market is held on Saturday. On that day no afternoon performance may be held (except after 4.30 by special arrangement), but possession can be given at six o'clock in the evening.

The town is visited by portables. The County Council have always granted licenses very readily. There is not any site suitable for alfresco concerts, but circuses can always find a suitable meadow. The dates of the fairs are second Saturday in May, third Saturday in June, fourth Saturday in September, and second Saturday in October, the two last being the best ones. The population is chiefly industrial and agricultural. The industries are two large printing works and a Swiss milk factory, which employs a large number of hands.

Early closing day, Thursday; market days, Wednesday and Saturday.

AYLSHAM, Norfolk.

Population, 2,471. Miles from London, 120.

TOWN HALL.—Proprietors, Parish Council; Manager, Mr. H. F. Proudfoot. Dramatic or music and dancing license can be obtained. Holding capacity: Number of persons, 400. A permanent platform measures 29ft. by 15ft.; 2ft. 10ins. high. Lighted by gas. Terms for hiring: £1 5s. one night; £3 three nights; £5 six nights. All fees must be paid in advance when hall is booked.

Dates of local fairs: March 23 and last Tuesday in September in every year.

Early closing, Wednesday; market, Tuesday.

AYR, Ayrshire, N.B.

Population, 31,000. Miles from London, 393.

NEW GAIETY. — Proprietors, the New Gaiety Theatre, Limited; Managing Director, Mr. R. C. Buchanan; Acting-Manager, Mr. Harry W. Day; Musical Director, Mr. W. G. Burgoyne. Full dramatic license. Holding capacity: Amount, £120. Stage measurements: Depth, 30ft. by 32ft.; width between fly rails, 35ft.; grid, 42ft.; proscenium opening, 24ft. Electric lighting, voltage 250. Amount of printing required: 900 sheets walls, 500 lithos. Band rehearsal, 1.30 p.m.

TOWN HALL.—Manager, Mr. A. B. Mac-Callum, Town Chamberlain. Used for concerts, etc. Holding capacity: Number of persons, 1,100. Stage measurements: 33ft. by 11ft. Extended platform in front of ordinary, 45ft. by 9 ft. Gas and electric light. Terms for hiring, £3 3s. one night, £2 2s. every subsequent night.

Early closing day, Wednesday; market day, Tuesday.

Medical Officer.—A.A.: Dr. Walter F. Brown, 57, Belle Vue Crescent, Ayr.

BACUP, Lancashire.

Population, 25,000. Miles from London, 204.

NEW COURT THEATRE.—Lessee and Manager, Mr. Frank Denman-Wood; Musical Director, Mr. P. Woodroffe; Scenic Artist, Mr. T. Clarke Lockett. Licensed for drama and variety. Holding capacity: Number of persons, 2,000; amount, £100. Stage measurements: 55ft. deep, 33ft. wide; proscenium opening, 26ft. Lighted by gas; electric light by arrangement. Amount of printing required: 500 wall, 500 window, 1,000 circulars. Usual matinée day, Saturday. Band rehearsal, 2 p.m. Monday. Electric current, 110 volts.

Population industrial, with a few residential. Owners of industry or property-system of co-operation is strong here. Situation, 20 miles north-east of Manchester. In addition to the Court there are two halls—Central Store Hall and Mechanics' Institute—situated centre of town. Can be hired by day or week. Lighted by gas; stage, piano, and two dressing-rooms, but no scenery kept. Seating capacity of the Store Hall, 950. That of the Mechanics' Institute, 800. Industries: cotton-spinning and weaving, with large stone quarries in and around the borough; also a few small collieries. Local fair is held once each year in Whit-Week. Stands can be taken up after market on Wednesday, and must be clear to allow market to continue as usual the following Wednesday. Markets are held every Wednesday and Saturday. The fair is held on the Market Ground and in Union Street on private property. All industries close down two days for the fair, either Friday and Saturday or Saturday and Monday. The last week in July industries close down the whole week for Midsummer holidays; other holidays do not exceed two days at one time. Portables do not visit the town. Circus pitches are obtainable, but sites for outdoor alfresco concerts are not available. No difficulty in obtaining a license. One kinematograph show visits the town during fair week; also a few kinematograph shows visit the town during winter, taking one or other of the local halls.

Early closing day, Tuesday.

Agent.—V.A.F.: J. Lee, Waterworks Inn.

BAKEWELL, Derbyshire.

Population, 2,850. Miles from London, 152.

TOWN HALL.—Secretary, Mr. E. Morewood Longsdon. Dramatic license obtained as required on proper notice. Holding capacity: Number of persons, 400. Height of stage to ceiling, 20ft.; width, 15ft., and 31ft. long; height of proscenium, 13ft. Lighted by gas. Two dressing-rooms. Terms for hiring, £2 2s. for the first night and 30s. for each night after. Amount of deposit required on booking, £1.

Local fairs: Easter Monday, Whit Monday, Monday before August 26 (when the 26th falls on Monday it will be held on that day), 1st Monday after October 10, 1st Monday after November 11.

Early closing, Thursday; markets, Monday and Friday.

BALLINA, Co. Mayo.

Population, 4,846. Miles from Dublin, 166.

OPERA HALL.—Manager, Mr. Arthur Mullaney. Double license. Holding capacity: Number of persons, 900. Proper stage Stage, 30ft. by 12ft., with newly-erected waiting and dressing rooms Lighted by gas (incandescent). Terms for hiring: £2 10s. single night, £3 10s. two nights, £9 per week. Amount of deposit required on booking, one fourth cash.

There are 16 fairs yearly, and abundant places for portables

Market, Monday.

BALLINASLOE, Co. Galway.

Population, 4,642. Miles from Dublin, 91.

FARMING SOCIETY HALL.—Managers, Messrs. F. A. Harpur and Son. No dramatic license. Holding capacity: Number of persons, 300; gallery, 100. 18ft. by 13ft. stage. Stage and ceiling, 20ft.; stage 3ft. from ground. Lighted by gas. Terms for hiring: £5 for week, £1 a night.

Dates of local fairs: January 8 and 11, March 11 and 14, April 8 and 11, May 6 and 7, July 3, September 2, October 6, 7, 8, 9, 11, November 4. Sites available for portables, al fresco concerts, and circuses

Markets, Wednesday and Saturday.

BALLYMENA, Co. Antrim.

Population, 12,000. Miles from Dublin, 145.

PROTESTANT HALL.—Manager, Mr. Alexander Cairns. Seating capacity: Number of persons, about 1,000. Size of platform, 40ft. by 20ft. Two dressing-rooms. Letting terms: 15s. per night. Lighted by gas. Grand piano on premises for hire.

TOWN HALL.—Manager. Ballymena Estate Office, Seating capacity, 700. Platform, 21ft. by 15ft. Dressing-rooms. Letting terms, 15s. per night. Lighted by gas. Piano on premises for hire.

Early closing day, Wednesday; market day, Saturday.

BALSALL HEATH, (Birm.), Warwick.

Population, 38,820. Miles from London, 113.

MOSELEY AND BALSALL HEATH INSTITUTE.—Proprietors, The Committee; Licensee, Mr. Thomas Parsons. Dramatic, music, and dancing licenses. Holding capacity: Number of persons, 600. Proper stage. Lighted by gas. Terms for hiring: 3 guineas per night, payable on booking.

Early closing day, Wednesday; market day, Thursday.

BANBRIDGE, Co. Down.

Population, 5,000. Miles from Dublin, 87.

TEMPERANCE HALL.—Manager, Mr. Frank Weir, Dromore Street, Banbridge. No license required. Holding capacity: Number of persons, 500. Depth and width of stage, 12ft. by 27ft. Can be extended. Lighted by gas. Terms for hiring: 15s. per night, £4 per week. Amount of deposit required on booking, £1. Two dressing-rooms.

Local fairs last Monday of each month. Early closing, Thursday; markets, Monday and Friday.

BANBURY, Oxon.

Population, 12,968.　Miles from London, 86.

ROYAL AND CORN EXCHANGE.—Proprietor, Mr. A. J. Kilby).—License, restricted dramatic. Holding capacity: Number of persons, 700-800. Stage measurements, 24ft. by 36ft.; proscenium, 18ft. by 18ft. Gas and electric light.

TOWN HALL.—Address Mr. Wincott. Holding capacity, 700. Platform. Gas; electric light laid on.

CHURCH HOUSE.—Lessee, Mr. E. C. Fortescue. Holds 700. Well-fitted stage.

Early closing day, Tuesday; market day, Thursday.

BANFF, Banffshire.

Population, 3,730. Miles from London, 592.

ST. ANDREW'S HALL.—Secretary, Mr. Peter Lyon. Fully licensed. Holding capacity: Number of persons, 500; amount, 28s. 6d. No proper stage. Lighted by gas. Amount of deposit required on booking, 5s.

Early closing, Wednesday; market, Friday.

BANGOR, Carn. •

Population, 12,000. Miles from London, 240

PENRHYN HALL.—Manager, Mr. W. A. Roberts. Dramatic license. Holding capacity: Number of persons, about 500. Movable platform. 27ft. long, 21½ft. wide, 3½ft. high. Lighted by electricity (continuous current, voltage 200). Terms for hiring: £2 2s. first night, and £1 1s. for every consecutive night, and 5s. each night for lighting. Amount of deposit required on booking, £1 1s.

CENTRAL HALL.—Variety and picture entertainments are conducted by Mr. Will Summerson. Holds about 150. Electric light. Continuous current. Kinematograph charged as per meter.

Early closing day, Wednesday; market day, Friday.

RECOMMENDED APARTMENTS.

Mrs. W. G. Evans, "Old London House," High Street.—2 private, 2 public sitting-rooms; 6 bedrooms used for visitors; bath.

BARNARD CASTLE, Durham.

Population, 4,421. Miles from London, 249.

VICTORIA HALL.—Manager, Mr. Tom Borrowdale. Full dramatic license. Holding capacity: Number of persons, 1,000. Permanent stage, 24ft. deep, 36ft. wide: proscenium and act-drop. Dressing-rooms. Lighted by gas.

MUSIC HALL.—Seats 700. No stage fittings. Chief event: Whitsuntide North of England Cyclists' Meet. Town has a good number of visitors in the summer. Alfresco concert pitch could be arranged for; circus pitches ditto. Portables occasionally visit.

Early closing day, Friday; market day, Wednesday.

BARNOLDSWICK, Colne.

Population, 9,000. Miles from London, 230.

QUEEN'S HALL. — Manager, Mr. Frank Perry. Double license. Holding capacity: Number of persons, 500 (seating). Proper stage, 33ft. by 21ft. Lighted by gas. Amount of

printing required: 300 daybills, 250 sheets letterpress and lithos for posting, comprising 18, 16, 12, and 6 sheets. Terms for hiring: Shares, 50 and 60 per cent. Amount of deposit required on booking, 5s. per day.

Early closing day, Tuesday.

BARNSLEY, Yorks.

Population, 41,086. Miles from London, 177.

THEATRE ROYAL. — Proprietors, Barnsley Theatre Royal Co., Limited; General Manager, Mr. A. C. Mitchell. Holding capacity, 1,200. Gas and electric light, voltage 230. Band rehearsal, 1 p.m.

PUBLIC HALL.—Proprietors, Mayor and Burgesses, Borough of Barnsley; Manager, Mr. E. Cheesman. Double license. Holding capacity: Number of persons, 2,500. Full stage. Gas and electric light. Band rehearsal, 1 p.m.

EMPIRE PALACE.—Proprietors, the Barnsley Empire Palace Co., Limited; Managing Director, Mr. Will Smithson; Assistant Manager, Mr. J. T. Tennant. Full stage. Electric light, direct current, voltage 230, reduced to 90 for arcs and kinematograph. Holding capacity, 2,200. Band rehearsal, 1 p.m. No matinées.

NEW EMPIRE PALACE.—Proprietors, the New Empire Palace, Limited; Managing Director, Mr. Will Smithson.

[Town voltage for electricity in all cases, 230.]

Surrounding districts (within two miles radius) bring available population for theatrical purposes up to 100,000. Industrial class of people; mostly mines and ironworks. The local fairs are February 14, May 13, and October 11. There are two sites suitable for circuses and menageries—one, the Queen's Ground, about 25 acres, letting to be obtained from Mr. A. Senior, Park House, Ardsley, near Barnsley; the other from the Barnsley Corporation, Market and Fairs' Department, Barnsley. This site is called "The Nook." No alfresco pitches are available.

Early closing day, Thursday; market days, Wednesday and Saturday.

Agents.—A.U.: Frank Bedford, Three Cranes Hotel; M.H.A.R.A. and V.A.F.: The same.

RECOMMENDED APARTMENTS.

Mrs. Dickinson, 5, Blucher Street. — 4 bedrooms, 1 sitting-room, 2 combined; piano.

BARNSTAPLE, Devon.

Population, 14,137. Miles from London, 211.

THEATRE ROYAL.—Proprietors, Barnstaple Bridge Trust; Manager, Mr. H. Ashton; Scenic Artist, Mr. Arthur Page. Restricted dramatic license. Holding capacity: Number of persons, 818 (seating); amount, £50. Stage measurement: 22ft. deep, 34ft. wide; proscenium opening, 19ft. by 19ft. Lighted by gas and electricity, direct current, 230 voltage; electric plugs. Amount of printing required: 300 circulars for post, 18 6-sheets and 3 18 or 24-sheets, 75 window lithos. Theatre closed May, June, and July.

ASSEMBLY ROOMS.—Secretary, Mr. F. Adams. Music and dancing license. Holding capacity: Number of persons, 300. Lighted by gas. Small movable platform.

ALBERT HALL.—Proprietors, the Town Council; Manager, Mr. Oliver J. Nicklin, The Square; Booking Offices, Nicklin's Music Warehouses. License, music and dancing. Platform, 9ft. by 41ft., may be extended to 15ft. by 41ft. Length of hall, 80ft.; clear floor space, 60ft. by 41ft. Side recess, height 20ft. Balcony, 19ft. by 9ft. Movable seats throughout. Six ante-rooms. Electric light, continuous current, voltage 460. Gas in the hall only.

Barnstaple Annual Fair, nearest Wednesday to September 19, three days' fair.

Early closing day, Wednesday; market days, Tuesday and Friday (big market Friday).

BARRHEAD, Renfrew.

Population, 9,855. Miles from London, 400.

PUBLIC HALL.—Secretary, Mr. Jos. Watson. Double license. Holding capacity: Number of persons, large hall, 700; lesser hall, 150. Stage, 9ft by 24ft., with extension 15ft. by 24ft. Lighted by gas. Terms for hiring: £2 concerts; dramatic entertainments, £2 11s. 6d. Amount of deposit required on booking, £1.

BARROW-IN-FURNESS, Lancs.

Population, 57,586. Miles from London, 266.

ROYALTY THEATRE AND OPERA HOUSE. —Lessee and Manager, Mr. Hugh Robertson; Resident Manager, Mr. George Stone; Musical Director, Mr. W. Armer. Full dramatic license. Holding capacity: Number of persons, 1,500; amount, £90. Stage measurements: 35ft. deep, 40ft. wide; proscenium, 21ft. 6in. Lighted by gas, electric if required. Amount of printing required: 650 sheets walls, 650 lithos, circulars, etc. Usual matinée day, Thursday or Saturday. Time of band rehearsal, 1.30 p.m.

HIS MAJESTY'S THEATRE.—Lessees and Managers, Mr. and Mrs. Calvert Routledge; Scenic Artist, Mr. D. Edwardes. Full dramatic license. Holding capacity: Number of persons, 1,500; amount, £80. Stage measurements: Depth 30ft., width 60ft.; proscenium, 24ft. Electric light and gas throughout. Amount of printing required: 700 sheets for walls, 600 window bills. Usual matinée day, Saturday. Time of band rehearsal, 1.30 p.m.

TIVOLI.—Lessees and Managers, Messrs. Laban and Pepi. Rehearsal 2 p.m.

NEW HIPPODROME.—Proprietors and Managers, Mr. and Mrs. Calvert Routledge; Musical Director, Mr. Storey. License, music and dancing. Holding capacity, 2,500. Bookings, animated pictures and varieties.

Early closing day, Thursday; market days, Wednesday and Saturday.

Agent.—M.H.A.R.A.: Mrs. Tyson, Majestic Hotel. V.A.F.: The same.

RECOMMENDED APARTMENTS.

Mrs. Williamson, 63, School Street, 1 sitting, 5 bedrooms (7 beds), 1 combined; piano, bath.

BARRY, Glam.

Population, 31,342. Miles from London, 178.

THEATRE ROYAL AND HIPPODROME.— Proprietors, Tours, Limited; Managing Director, Mr. Arthur Carlton; Acting-Manager, Mr. Arthur Brogden. Double license. Holding capacity: Number of persons, 1,500; amount, £80. Stage measurements: Depth 35ft., width 62ft.; proscenium opening, 27ft. Gas and electric light. Amount of printing required: 1,000 walls, 500 lithos. Usual matinée day, Saturday. Time of band rehearsal, 1 p.m.

The playgoing population of the Barry district is drawn from four neighbourhoods— viz., Cadoxton, Barry Dock, Barry, and Barry Island—and is an industrial population. Barry possesses two magnificent docks, and the shipping industry is of importance, the export of coal comparing favourably with that of other sea ports, whilst there is also a big import of pitwood for the South Wales Collieries, also timber for building purposes, and an import of foreign meat, etc. There are also ship-repairing yards. The average arrivals and sailings of steamers weekly are about fifty, and these bring and take away about 1,250 officers and seamen. Portables visit the town. The Gasworks grounds, Barry Dock, which is in the centre of the town, is a site where travelling living picture shows visit, also various other kinds of shows. The big circus owners usually pitch at the Witchill Grounds, Cadoxton, a ground of considerable size. The Romilly Hall, Barry, is always available for fit-up touring, dramatic, and variety companies; whilst the Masonic Hall, Barry, is occasionally utilised for pierrot entertainment. Barry Island is an important watering-place, the sands, Whitmore Bay, being about a mile in length. In the summer months this place is daily visited by from 5,000 to 15,000 excursionists. Pleasure steamers ply from Barry to Bristol, Weston-super-Mare, and Ilfracombe, and other important pleasure resorts in the Bristol Channel.

Early closing day, Wednesday.

Medical Officer.—A.U.: Dr. Brewer, The Griffins, Tynewydd Road.

Agency.—M.H.A.R.A.: Windsor Hotel.

RECOMMENDED APARTMENTS.

Mrs. Thompson, 33, Newlands Street.—2 bedrooms, 2 sitting-rooms; bathroom (hot and cold).

BARTON-ON-HUMBER, Lincs.

Population, 5,671. Miles from London, 174.

ODDFELLOWS' HALL.—Manager, Mr. F. Thompson. Double license. Holding capacity: Number of persons about 500. Stage, 7ft. wide, 35ft. long; can be enlarged to 14ft. wide. Proscenium measurements, 18ft. Lighted by gas. Amount of printing required: 100 window bills, 10 six sheets. Terms for hiring on application. Amount of deposit required on booking, 10s.

Early closing, Thursday; market, Monday.

BASINGSTOKE, Hants.

Population, 11,000. Miles from London, 47.

CORN HALL.—Lessee, Mr. S. E. Walford. Seating accommodation, about 600. Lighted by gas. Terms: £2 10s. first night, £2 per night after. Gas and heating extra. Proscenium. Fit-up stage, 17ft. by 29ft.

DRILL HALL.—Manager, Mr. A. E. Grant. Double license. Seating capacity: Number of persons, 500. Lighted by gas. Terms: First night, £2 18s.; second, £2 7s. 6d.; third, £2 7s. 6d.; including four sets of scenery, 500 chairs, gas, heating, etc. Stage, 23ft., 23ft. open; height, 18ft.; wings, 16ft. £1 deposit on final booking. Lowest charge for admission, 1s., except for children.

Early closing day, Thursday; market day, Wednesday.

BATH, Som.

Population, 49,839. Miles from London, 106.

THEATRE ROYAL.—Proprietors, The Bath Theatre Royal Co., Ltd.; Lessee and Manager, Mr. Egbert Lewis; Acting-Manager, Mr. L. A. Long; Musical Director, Mr. W. F. C. Schöttler. Full dramatic license. Holding capacity: Number of persons, 1,200; amount, £125. Stage measurements: Proscenium opening,

22

28ft.; depth of stage, 43ft.; width, 53ft.
Electric light, continuous current, voltage 220.
Amount of printing required: 600 sheets, 600
d.c.'s, 1,000 circulars. Usual matinée day,
Saturday. Time of band rehearsal, 11 a.m.

PALACE THEATRE.—Proprietor, Mr. Frank
Macnaghten; Manager, Mr. Chas. Schuberth.
Music and dancing license. Rehearsal 12 noon.

THE BATH ASSEMBLY ROOMS.—Manager,
Mr. Lawson A. Howes. License: Music and
dancing; no dramatic license. Holding capa-
city: Number of persons: Large concert hall,
800; smaller concert hall, 400; card room, 200;
club room, 200. Staging to suit requirements.
Electric light, continuous current, voltage 220.
Terms for hiring: Apply, the Manager.
Amount of deposit required on booking, one
quarter. Use of company's billposting stations
in town and district free.
Early closing day, Thursday; market day,
Wednesday.
The town has no local fair, and portables
do not visit. Circus pitches are available.
The population is largely residential, the in-
dustrial class not being greatly represented.
Medical Officer.—Dr. Curd, 6, Gay Street
(hours 2 to 3); A.U.: The same; M.H.A.R.A.:
The same.
Agents.—A.U.: A. Ashman, Seven Dials
Hotel; M.H.A.R.A.: The same. V.A.F.: The
same.

BATHGATE, Linlithgowshire.

Population, 9,000. Mil s from London, 417.

CORN EXCHANGE HALL.—Manager, Mr.
Wm. Russell. Fully licensed. Holding capacity: Number of persons, 1.000. Stage, 22ft.
by 24ft. Lighted by gas. Terms for hiring:
£3; license, 2s. 6d. Amount of deposit required on booking, 20s. Four days should be
allowed between each entertainment. Hall
recently enlarged and redecorated.
Dates of local fairs first Monday after May
28 and first Monday after November 28.
Early closing, Wednesday; market, Monday.

BATLEY, Yorks.

Population, 30,321. Miles from London, 183.

THEATRE ROYAL.—Proprietor and Manager, Mr. J. Edward Whitty; Acting-Manager,
Mr. A. A. Taylor; Musical Director, Mr. F.
Hime; Scenic Artist, Mr. R. Young. Restricted
dramatic license. Holding capacity: Number
of persons, 2,100; amount, £80. Stage measurements: 32ft. deep, 50ft. wide; grid, 50ft.; fly
floor, 20ft.; proscenium opening, 26ft. Gas
and electric light. Amount of printing required: 500 sheets wall, 500 lithos. No regular matinée day. Time of band rehearsal,
1 p.m.

VICTORIA HALL.—Secretary, Mr. John
Hopkinson Dramatic and music and dancing
licenses. Holding capacity: Number of persons, about 1,000. Not proper stage—platform.
Full size of platform, 45ft. by 21ft. 6ins.
Electric light. Terms for hiring: One night,
£2 2s.; two nights, £4; three nights, £5 5s.;
four nights, £6 6s.; five nights, £7 7s.; six
nights, £8 8s. Electric light to be paid for
in addition according to quantity consumed.
Amount of deposit required on booking: One-
fourth rent; balance, if required, in advance
or from day to day
TOWN HALL.—Manager, Mr. Jas. Warden.
Let for concerts. Holding capacity: Number
of persons, 400. Platform only. Electric light.
Terms for hiring: Concert, 25s. per night;
2s. 6d. per hour lighting. Amount of deposit
required on booking, one half.

Electric light for all halls, 220 voltage.
Site available for portables and circuses,
Market Place.
Dates of local fairs, Saturday on or before
September 17 to following Tuesday night.
Early closing day, Tuesday; market days,
Friday and Saturday.

BECCLES, Suffolk.

Population, 6,898. Miles from London, 109.

PUBLIC HALL.—Proprietors, the Borough;
Hall Keeper, Mr. G. Fiske. Dramatic license.
Holding capacity: Number of persons, 400.
Fixed stage, 26ft. deep by 16ft. wide; pros-
cenium, 23ft. Lighted by gas. Terms for
hiring: £1 13s. 6d. first day; each day after,
£1 3s. 6d.; gas and heating extra. All moneys
for the hall to be paid in advance.
Early closing day, Wednesday; market day,
Friday.

BECKENHAM, Kent.

Population, 26,331. Miles from London, 10.

PUBLIC HALL.—Proprietors, A Company;
Manager, Mr. T. W. Thornton. Fully licensed.
Holding capacity: Number of persons, 250 to
300. No proper stage. Electric light alternating. Terms for hiring: From £3 3s. miscellaneous to £5 5s. dramatic.
No local fairs. No sites available for portables, etc.
Early closing day, Wednesday; no market
day.

BEDFORD, Beds.

Population, 35,144. Miles from London, 50.

ROYAL COUNTY THEATRE.—Proprietor,
Mr. Edward Graham-Falcon; Manager, Mr.
Walter R. Wilson; Musical Director, Mr. H.
Elphinstone Stone; Scenic Artist, Mr. J. Tam-
lin. Double license. Holding capacity: Num-
ber of persons, 1,500; amount, £120. Stage
measurements: Depth 26ft., width 46ft.; pros-
cenium opening, 26ft. Gas and electric light.
Amount of printing required, 732 sheets d.c.
Usual matinée day, Saturday. Time for band
rehearsal, 1 p.m.
Early closing day, Thursday; market day,
Saturday.

BELFAST.

Population, 380,000. Miles from Dublin, 113.

THEATRE ROYAL.—Proprietors, Warden,
Limited; Managing Director, Mr. Fred W.
Warden; Acting-Manager, Mr. J. M McCann;
Musical Director, Mr. S. P. Swanton. Double
license. Holding capacity: Number of per-
sons, 2,500; amount, £160. Stage measure-
ments: Depth 40ft, width 60ft.; proscenium
opening, 21ft. Electric light. Time of band
rehearsal, when called. Usual matinée day,
Friday.
PALACE.—Proprietors, Warden, Limited;
Managing Director, Mr. Fred W. Warden;
Acting-Manager. Mr. A. Salmond; Booking
Circuit, Mr. Walter De Frece; Musical Direc-
tors, Mr. S. P. Swanton and Mr. H. A. Knight;
Scenic Artist, Mr. G. Jansen. Double license.
Holding capacity: Number of persons, 3.500;
amount, £100 (prices, 2d. to 1s. 6d.). Stage
measurements: Width 89ft., depth 60ft.; pros-
cenium opening, 30ft. Electric light. Time of
band rehearsal, 1 p.m.
EMPIRE (Victoria Square). — Proprietors,
Belfast Empire Theatre of Varieties, Limited;
Manager, Mr. Frank Allen; Resident Manager, Mr. John A. Walker; Booking Circuit,

Moss's Empires, Limited; Musical Director, Mr. Wm. L. Richards. Music and dancing license. Holding capacity: Number of persons, 2,250; amount, £70. Stage measurements: Depth 26ft., width 50ft.; proscenium, width 29ft. 8in.; height of grid, 50ft. Electric light. Time of band rehearsal, 1 p.m. Usual matinée day, Saturday. Bars the Palace and the Hippodrome. Twice nightly, 7 and 9.

Bars other Managements' Halls in Belfast and the following towns: Carrickfergus, Comber, Lisburn, Hillsborough, and Saintfield.

ALHAMBRA.—Proprietors, The Belfast Alhambra, Limited; Manager, Mr. Will White; Musical Director, Mr. P. H. Boyle. Electric light.

WELLINGTON HALL (Y.M.C.A.).—Manager, Mr. D. A. Black, J.P. No dramatic license. Holding capacity: Number of persons, 1,800. Large platform. Electric light. Terms for hiring on application.

ULSTER HALL.—Manager, The Town Clerk. No dramatic license. Holding capacity: Number of persons, 2,000. No proper stage. Electric light. Terms for hiring: By arrangement. Amount of deposit required on booking: 25 per cent. of rent fixed. Not suitable for theatricals. It is a concert hall with grand organ.

Electric light voltage in all cases, 220.

Local fair first Wednesday each month. No good sites for portables.

Market days, Tuesday and Friday.

Medical Officer.—A.A.: Sir P. R. O'Connell, M.D., 9, College Square.

Agent.—M.H.A.R.A.: Mrs. Stamford. Shakespeare Hotel: V.A.F.: E. Randewicke, Abercorn Hotel, Castle Street.

BELPER, Derbyshire.

Population, 10,934. Miles from London, 134.

PUBLIC HALL.—Manager, Mr. Joseph Pym. Dramatic license. Holding capacity: Number of persons, 650. Proper stage. Stage measurements, 18ft. deep by 21ft. wide. Lighted by gas. Terms of hiring: £2, one night; £3 15s., two nights; £5, three nights; £7 10s., six nights. Amount of deposit required on booking, one-half.

Early closing day, Wednesday; market day, Saturday.

BELTON, Lincs.

Population, 1,500. Miles from London, 168.

PUBLIC HALL. (Grey Green).—Hon. Secretary, Mr. John W. Ross, The Poplars, Belton, Doncaster. No dramatic license. Holding capacity: Number of persons, 450. Platform measurements, 22ft. by 10ft. Terms for hiring, 5s. to 7s. 6d. per night.

Dates of local fairs, September 24 and 25. Sites available for portables, etc., Pye Lidgell Croft.

BERWICK-ON-TWEED, Northumberland.

Population, 13,437. Miles from London, 342.

QUEEN'S ROOMS.—Lessee and Manageress, Mrs. W. M. Mather. Double license. Holding capacity, 900. Stage measurements, 40ft. by 18ft. Stock of scenery and fit-up kept. Gas and electric light. Amount of deposit required on booking, £1.

CORN EXCHANGE.—Manager, Mr. A. L. Miller. Dramatic license. Holding capacity: Number of persons, 1,500. Temporary stage,

32ft. deep, 15ft. wide. Gas and electric light. Terms for hiring: One night, £3; two, £5; three, £6 10s.; six, £10 10s. Amount of deposit required on booking, 20 per cent.

Berwick Fairs are held on the first Saturday in March and the last Saturday in May.

For sites for portables, alfresco concerts, and circuses, apply, the Borough Surveyor.

Early closing day, Thursday; market day, Saturday.

BEVERLEY, Yorks.

Population, 13,183. Miles from London, 181.

ASSEMBLY ROOMS.—Secretary, Mr. Francis Mills. Fully licensed. Holding capacity: Number of persons, 1,000. Proper stage. Stage measurements: 32ft. deep, 16ft. wide; no proscenium. Lighted by gas. Terms for hiring: 1 night, £2; 6 nights, £6. Payment required in advance.

Early closing day, Thursday; market day, Saturday.

BEXHILL-ON-SEA, Sussex.

Population, 15,500. Miles from London, 71.

THE KURSAAL.—Lessee, Mr. J. M. Glover. Double license. Holding capacity: Number of persons, 900; amount, £100 at 4s., 3s., 2s., and 1s. Stage measurements: Depth, 21ft.; width, 29ft.; opening, 19ft.; scenery, 22ft. at outside. Electric light. Matinée day, Wednesday or Saturday. Three nights is the usual run for one piece.

Bexhill-on-Sea is one of the quiet, fashionable, rising watering-places. The Earl de la Warr did much to develop the attractions of the place. The Kursaal formerly belonged to him. There is no local fair, and the town and Council discourage portable shows or any entertainment of this type. The greatest difficulty is experienced in obtaining from the Council pitches in the parks or on the beach. There is a fine motor track, and motor races are much encouraged.

Early closing day, Wednesday.

BEXLEY HEATH, Kent.

Population, 12,918. Miles from London, 13.

PUBLIC HALL.—Manager, Mr. Thos. Jenkins. Double license. Holding capacity: Number of persons, 500. No proper stage. Measurements: Depth and width of platform, 16ft. 6in. by 34ft. No scenery. Electric light. Terms for hiring: 1 night, £3 3s.; 2 nights, £5 5s.; 3, £6 6s. Amount of deposit required on booking, £1 1s. Hall not let on sharing terms. Three dressing-rooms. Electric trams pass hall.

Early closing day, Wednesday

BICESTER, Oxon.

Population, 3,023. Miles from London, 66.

CORN EXCHANGE.—Manager, Mr. J. Peacock Drover. Double license. Holding capacity: Number of persons, 350 seated, 400 standing. The dimensions of the permanent platform are 12ft. long by 8ft. deep, in front of it is erected the extension in three sections, 18ft. by 6ft. each, which make a stage 18ft. square. There are three dressing rooms at the back and sides of the permanent platform. Lighted by gas. Terms for hiring: 30s. for first night and 20s. for succeeding nights. Special arrangements must be made for *matinées*. Amount of deposit required on booking, 10s. The hall is used as the Bicester Corn Exchange, and the market stallholders have the right to the entire hall space on Fridays, market day, from 10 a.m. to 5 p.m.

Markets: Corn, Friday; cattle, alternate Fridays from January 10, with Christmas fat stock on Friday after December 11. Fairs: August 5 (sheep, cattle, and horses) and August 6 (pleasure), Friday before October 11, and two following Fridays (pleasure).

Sites available for portables, alfresco concerts, and circuses, Market Square and field in vicinity of station.

Early closing day, Thursday.

BIDEFORD, Devon.

Population, 8,754. Miles from London, 220.

PUBLIC ROOMS.—Managers, Messrs. Caleb Squire and Son. Double license. Holding capacity: Number of persons, 700; amount, £50. Proper stage. Depth, 20ft. 6in.; 27ft. wide; within the fit-up, 16ft.; 21ft. wide; 15ft. high. Lighted by gas. Amount of printing required, 500 sheets. Terms for hiring: Sharing, or £3 10s. per day. Amount of deposit required on booking, £1.

Early closing day, Wednesday; market day, Tuesday.

Medical Officers.—A.A.: Dr. Pearson, Strand House; A.U.: The same.

BIGGLESWADE, Beds.

Population, 5,120. Miles from London, 41.

TOWN HALL. — Secretary, Mr. Henry Channdler. Dramatic license. Holding capacity: Number of persons, 300. Proper stage. Stage measurements, 19ft. 8ins. deep by 12ft. wide. Lighted by gas. Terms for hiring: First night, £1 10s.; subsequent nights, £1 1s. Amount of deposit required on booking, £2.

Early closing day, Thursday; market day, Wednesday.

BILSTON, Staffs.

Population, 24,034. Miles from London, 139.

ROYAL.—Proprietors, Bent's Brewery Co. Lessee and Manager, Mr. John M. Dawson. Double license. Holds 1,400 at £50. Stage opening, 24ft., 50ft. wide, 36ft. deep. Fly cloths, 28ft. by 24ft. Fly floor, 22ft. Grid, 48ft. Gas and electric light. Printing 700 walls, 400 lithos, and plenty of circulars.

AL FRESCO PAVILION.—Situated at the rear of the Theatre Royal.

TOWN HALL.—For concerts and entertainments. Application must be made to the District Council through the caretaker.

DRILL HALL.— Available for concerts, entertainments, animated pictures, etc.

The Annual Fair, which falls about the week preceding August Bank Holiday, is held on a piece of ground opening off Mount Pleasant, and known locally as the Bull Holes. This piece of land is also used at times as a circus pitch. Another piece of ground which may be used for this purpose is the Football and Recreation Ground, Willenhall Road.

Population.—Industrial. Tinplate and japanned hollow ware, steel and ironworkers, and coal miners.

Early closing day, Thursday; market days, Monday and Saturday.

BINGLEY, Yorks.

Population, 18,449. Miles from London, 207.

ASSEMBLY ROOMS.—Proprietors, Co-operative Society. No dramatic license. Holding capacity: Number of persons, about 600. Stage measurements: About 9 yds. by 4 yds.;

height of stage from floor, about 3 ft. Incandescent gas. Terms for hiring: £1 per night; six nights charged as five. Amount of deposit required on booking, half.

Local Feast held last week in August. Gas Field is available for portables and circuses. Early closing, Tuesday.

BIRKDALE, Lancs.

Population, 20,250. Miles from London, 214.

TOWN HALL AND LECTURE HALL (separately or combined).—Proprietors, Birkdale Urban District Council; Clerk of the Council, Mr. J. F. Keeley. Music and dancing license. Holding capacity: Number of persons, Town Hall 350; Lecture Hall, 500. Two stages. Electric light: voltage 230, continuous current. Terms for hiring: £1 2s., £2s. 2s., cash in advance.

No local fairs.

Early closing day, Tuesday; market day, Wednesday.

BIRKENHEAD, Ches.

Population, 110,915. Miles from London, 194.

NEW THEATRE ROYAL.—Lessee and Manager, Mr. W. W. Kelly; Acting-Manager, Mr. Reginald Grant; Secretary, Miss Isabel Morris; Musical Director, Mr. Joseph Callaghan; Scenic Artist, Mr. Walter P. Warren. Full dramatic license. Holding capacity: Number of persons, 1,750; amount, £100. Electric light. Amount of printing required: Walls, 1,750; d.c. lithos, 1,000; d.c. letterpress, 500. Usual matinée day, Thursday at 2.30. Time of band rehearsal, 1.10 p.m.

HIPPODROME (Managing Director, Mr. W. De Frece; Acting-Manager, Mr. Harry Ball.

ARGYLE THEATRE OF VARIETIES.—Proprietor and Manager, Mr. D. J. Clarke; Acting-Manager, Mr. J. Keating; Musical Director, Mr. E. Denny. Time of band rehearsal, 2 o'clock. Usual matinée day, Thursday. Dramatic license.

Early closing day, Thursday; market day, Tuesday.

Medical Officers.—A.A.: Dr. Wilkinson, 4, Hamilton Square; 'Phone: 41; A.U.: The same.

BIRMINGHAM, Warwick.

Population, 522,204. Miles from London, 113.

PRINCE OF WALES'S THEATRE.—Proprietors, Messrs. Rodgers, Limited; Manager, Mr. J. F. Graham; Acting-Manager, Mr. Henry Johnston; Musical Director, Mr. William Southworth; Scenic Artist, Mr. W. K. Young. Full dramatic license. Holding capacity: Number of persons, 3,000. Amount, £350. Gas and Electric light. Amount of printing required, 1,500 sheets. Usual matinée day, Thursday.

THEATRE ROYAL.—Proprietors, Theatre Royal, Birmingham, Limited; Managing Director, Mr. Tom B. Davis; Acting-Manager, Mr. Philip Rodway; Musical Director, Mr. Guy Jones. Full dramatic license. Holding capacity: Number of persons, 3,500. Amount, £330. Stage measurements: Depth 46ft.; width, 72ft.; opening of proscenium, 34ft. Electric light, latest installation. Amount of printing required, 2,000 sheets. Usual matinée day, Thursday, at 2. Time of band rehearsal, 12 noon.

METROPOLE THEATRE.—Proprietor and Manager, Mr. Andrew Melville; Acting-Manager, Mr. J. Hindle Taylor; Musical Director, Mr. Edward Reeves; Scenic Artist, Mr. Alfred

Whyatt. Restricted license. Holding capacity: Number of persons, over 3,000. Amount, £128. Stage measurements: 30ft. deep by 30ft. wide; 28ft. proscenium opening. Gas and electric light (voltage 220). Amount of printing required, 2,000 walls, 1,000 d.c. windows. Matinées on Bank Holidays. Time of band rehearsal, 12 noon.

ALEXANDRA THEATRE.—Proprietor and Manager, Mr. Lester Collingwood; Acting-Manager, Mr. W. T. Guest; Musical Director, Mr. Francis Knowles; Scenic Artist, Mr. R. A. Hall. Restricted dramatic license. Holding capacity: Number of persons, 2,000. Amount, £130. Stage measurements: Depth, 35 ft.; width, 54 ft.; proscenium opening, 28 ft. 6 ins. Gas and electric light. Amount of printing required, 1,000 lithos, 1,500 wall printing. Usual matinée day, Wednesday, at 2.30. Time of band rehearsal, 1 o'clock.

BORDESLEY PALACE.—Proprietors, Moss' Empires, Limited; Managing Director, Mr. Oswald Stoll; Acting-Manager, Mr. W. G. Woodward. Dramatic house.

THEATRE ROYAL, ASTON.—Proprietor, Mr. Charles Barnard; Manager, Mr. Edward Hewitson; Acting-Manager, Mr. Chas. Lake; Musical Director, Mr. George Daw. Full dramatic license. Holding capacity: Number of persons, about 2,500. Amount, £120. Stage: Depth, 36 ft.; width, 52ft.; proscenium, 28ft. Gas and electric light, voltage 230. Amount of printing required: 2,500 sheets, 700 lithos. Time of band rehearsal, 1 p.m. No towns or theatres barred.

CARLTON THEATRE, SALTLEY.—Licensee and Manager, Mr. James Alexander; Musical Director, Mr. Percy Heap. Full license. Holding capacity: Number of persons, 2,000. Electric light, voltage 110. Time of band rehearsal, 1 o'clock.

EMPIRE PALACE.—Proprietors, Moss' Empires, Limited; Managing Director, Mr. Oswald Stoll; Acting-Manager, Mr. A. W. Matcham. Booking circuit: Stoll's. Band rehearsal, 2 p.m.

Bars other Managements' Halls in Birmingham and the following towns: Wednesbury, Didley, Darlaston, Oldbury, West Bromwich, Coleshill, Bilston, Solihull, Brierley Hill. Halesowen, Tipton, Smethwick, Handsworth, Saltley, Erdington, and Kings Norton.

GRAND THEATRE OF VARIETIES, Corporation Street. - Proprietors, Moss' Empires, Limited; Managing Director, Mr. Oswald Stoll; Acting-Manager, Mr. Edward Foster: Musical Director, Mr. J. H. Whittaker. Pros. opening, 33ft. Stage depth, 30ft. Electric light, 220 volts. Barring as per Award. Time of band rehearsal, 1 p.m.

Bars other Managements' Halls in Birmingham and the following towns: Wednesbury, Didley, Darlaston, Oldbury, West Bromwich, Coleshill, Bilston, Solihull, Brierley Hill, Halesowen, Tipton, Smethwick, Handsworth, Saltley, Erdington, and Kings Norton.

BARRASFORD'S HIPPODROME.—Proprietors, The Birmingham Hippodrome, Limited; Resident Manager, Mr. Harry Lyons. Booking Circuit, Barrasford's. Musical Director, Mr. W. Crabtree. Music and dancing license. Electric light, own engines. Time of band rehearsal, 12 o'clock noon. Usual matinée day, Thursday, at 2.30.

GAIETY THEATRE.—Proprietor, Gaiety Theatre of Varieties, Limited; Manager, Mr. Albert Bushell; Musical Director, Mr. Fred Camp. Music and dancing license. Holding Capacity: Number of persons, 3,800. Stage measurements: 30 ft. deep by 30 ft. wide. Gas and electric light. Time of band rehearsal, 1 o'clock. Usual matinée day, Thursday.

KING'S HALL (Late Old Central Hall).—Proprietors and Managers, Messrs. J. P. Moore and B. Kennedy.

The following is a list of the halls which may be hired for theatrical entertainment. Most of them are already licensed for the performances of stage plays, and no difficulty is experienced in getting a temporary license for the others. Those marked with an asterisk have a fixed stage, proscenium, scene dock, etc. In brackets are the approximate seating capacities:—

MIDLAND INSTITUTE (800), Paradise Street.—Proprietors, the Council of the Institute; Secretary, Mr. Alfred Hayes, M.A. Double license. Holds 1,000. No proper stage. Fittings can be hired. Gas and electric current, 220 volts. Terms, £6 6s. per night, with reduction for series. Rent to be paid in advance.

*ACOCK'S GREEN INSTITUTE (200), Dudley Park Road, Acock's Green (5 miles from city). —Secretary, Mr. Offley Wade.

ALEXANDRA HALL, Hope Street.

ASSEMBLY ROOMS, Bell Barn Road.—Proprietor, Mr. Arthur Bufton.

ASSEMBLY ROOMS, Exchange, New Street. —Secretary, Mr. W. F. Haydon.

*ASSEMBLY ROOMS, Edgbaston, Hagley and Francis Roads (500).—Secretary, Leigh H. Elkington. (Fashionable part of the city.)

BINGLEY HALL, King Alfred's Place (suitable for a large covered-in fair or exhibition). —Apply, Secretary.

*CURZON HALL, Suffolk Street.—Proprietors, The Curzon Hall Company, Limited, Secretary, Edmund W. Beech, 37, Temple Street. Terms for letting (exclusive of gas and cleaning): For 1 night, £10; for 2 nights, £18; for 3 nights, £25; for 4 nights, £30; for 5 nights, £35; for 6 nights, £40; for 2 weeks £75; for one month (4 weeks), £110; for season of 12 weeks, £360. Special arrangements for longer periods.

The hall is suitable for concerts, theatrical entertainments, &c. It is also admirably adapted and seated for an equestrian circus, and there is stabling under gallery for a stud of horses.

The dimensions of the hall are about 103ft. 6ins. by 91ft. The chairs, seats and lower promenade will accommodate about 2,000 persons, and with upper promenade about 3,000 persons, or with extra gallery on the promenade about 4,000.

The stage is 44ft. deep by 91ft. wide; the proscenium is 33ft. 8ins. wide. When occupied by an equestrian company a gallery is erected upon the stage calculated to hold about 900 people.

*MOSELEY AND BALSALL HEATH INSTITUTE (600).—Apply, the Secretary.

*KING'S HEATH INSTITUTE (600).—Apply, the Secretary.

MASONIC HALL, New Street (600).—Apply, the Secretary.

*KYRLE HALL, Sheep Street (800).—Secretary, H.M. Mackintosh, New Street.

*SUTTON COLDFIELD TOWN HALL (600).--Secretary, Town Clerk, Sutton Coldfield.

SUTTON COLDFIELD MASONIC HALL (300),—Nine miles from city.

ERDINGTON PUBLIC HALL (300).—Apply, the Secretary.

STECHFORD MASONIC HALL.—Seats 300. Apply, Secretary.

There is only one fair (the Onion Fair) held near the centre of the city. The site is the Old Pleck, Aston. The ground available now is very small, owing to the neighbourhood being constantly built up. There are several available spaces for fairs in the adjoining districts of Erdington, Sutton, Aston, Olton, Solihull, etc., and no difficulty is experienced with the licensing authorities by the managers of portables and circuses who appear from time to time.

The population of the adjoining borough of Aston is 77,310. The chief industries of Birmingham are gunmaking, jewellery, saddlery, brassfoundry, electric fittings, ironfoundry, glass-blowing, brewing, coach and motor-making, buttons, toys, electroplate goods, and electroplating.

Medical Officers.—A.A.: Dr. Rutherford, Broxash, Valentine Road, King's Heath. Telephone, 04676. Wire, "Dunkley, King's Heath." Hours, 9-10.45 and 7-8 (summer), 6-8 winter. Dr. Hawkins, 241, Birchfield Road. Hours, 9.15-10, 2-3, and 6.30-8. Dr. Kirby, 106, Hagley Road, Edgbaston, and 10, Victoria Square. Telephone 5690. Dr. Trout, 412, Monument Road. 9-10, 2-2.30, and 6-8. Telephone 01692. A.U.: Dr. Kirby and Dr. Trout as above. M.H.A.R.A.: Dr. Trout as above; Dr. Walker, 362, Moseley Road; Dr. Walsh, Queen's Hospital. Agents: A.U.: Bert Wilson, White Lion Hotel, Horsefair. M.H.A.R.A.: The same. V.A.F.: The same.

RECOMMENDED APARTMENTS.

Mrs. Dunkley, 6, King Alfred's Place.—2 front and 2 back rooms, with pianos.

Mrs. Lloyd, 91, Cato Street, Saltley.—2 bedrooms, 1 sitting-room, 1 combined floor piano.

BIRR, or PARSONSTOWN, King's Co.

Population, 4,313. Miles from Dublin, 89.

OXMANTOWN HALL.—Assistant Secretary, Mr. R. George Sheppard. Holding capacity: Number of persons, 850. Good stage. Lighted by gas. Terms for hiring on application.

Market, Saturday.

BISHOP AUCKLAND, Durham.

Population, 11,969.

EDEN THEATRE.—Proprietors, Messrs. R. Addison, Limited; Manager, Mr. J. Huntley; Musical Director, Mr. J. Young; Scenic Artist, Mr. J. Vinning. Full dramatic license. Holding capacity: Number of persons, 2,000; amount, £70. Stage measurements: 40ft. by 70ft. by 26ft. Proscenium opening: Stage to grid, 40ft.; stage to fly floor, 20ft.; fly rail to rail, 32ft. Gas and electric light, voltage 250. Amount of printing required, 600 sheets, 700 lithos. Usual matinée day, Saturday. Time of band rehearsal, 1 o'clock. Sixteen dressing-rooms. Theatre heated throughout (hot-water pipes).

TEMPERANCE HALL.—Manager, Mr. John W. Robson. Music and dancing license. Holding capacity: Number of persons, 650. Platform size, 24ft. by 15ft. Gas and electric light. Amount of printing required, 50 posters, 2,500 handbills. Terms for hiring: 20s. per night inclusive (reduction for consecutive lettings), payable in advance. Electric current, continuous, voltage 250.

Early closing day, Wednesday; market days, Thursday and Saturday.

RECOMMENDED APARTMENTS.

Mrs. Wilson, 50, Fore Bondgate.—1 sitting, 2 bedrooms.

BISHOP'S STORTFORD, Herts.

Population, 7,143. Miles from London, 33.

GREAT HALL.—Owners, Committee of Working Men's Club; Secretary, Mr. W. H. Glasscock. Double license. Holding capacity: Number of persons, 600 to 800; amount, according to setting of chairs and price of seats. Fixed stage, 40ft. wide, 17ft. front to back; height from stage to tie rod, 14ft. 6ins. at 20ft. wide for grid. Lighted by gas. Amount of printing required, 4 18-sheet, 10 6-sheet, 25 d.c. Terms for hiring: One night, 40s.; two nights, 70s.; three nights, 90s.; six nights, 120s. Fire and gas extra. Amount of deposit required on booking: 10s. one night, 20s. two or more nights. A charge of 5s. extra each night if used after 12 o'clock midnight. Two dressing-rooms and lavatories and property-room. No proscenium or fit-up. Hall-keeper, Mr. S. J. Bull.

Early closing day, Wednesday; market day, Thursday.

BLACKBURN, Lancs.

Population, 133,000. Miles from London, 216.

ROYAL AND OPERA HOUSE.—Proprietor, Mr. Harry Yorke; Manager, Mr. Reginald Yorke. This theatre is being at present re-built, and will re-open early in 1909 as the Hippodrome, with variety, two performances nightly, and occasional theatrical companies.

NEW PRINCE'S THEATRE.—Proprietor, Mr. E. H. Page; Manager, Mr. C. E. Clarkson.

PALACE.—Proprietor, Mr. Frank Macnaghten; Manager, Mr. Will Murray. Double license. Holds 3,500. Electric current, 220 volts, direct. Rehearsal, 12 noon.

EXCHANGE HALL.—Lessee, Mr. William Kenyon. Music and dancing license. Holding capacity: Number of persons, 2,000. No proper stage; platform. Measurements: 52ft. width, 38ft. in depth. Gas and electric light. Amount of printing required, 1,000 sheets and upwards. Terms for hiring, £15 15s. per week. Amount of deposit required on booking, £5 5s.

The large pleasure fair of this town commences Saturday (day after Good Friday) and concludes Wednesday in Easter Week. The town is rarely visited by portables, and they are not encouraged by the Council. Circus pitches are easily obtainable. The population is mostly industrial, cotton-weaving being the principal industry; next to that, ironworks and breweries.

Early closing day, Thursday; market days, Wednesday and Saturday.

Medical Officers.—A.A.: Dr. Pollard, Hollyville, Preston New Road. 'Phone 142. Hours, 2-3 and 7-8.30. A.U.: The same. M.H.A.R.A.: The same.

Agents.—A.U.: Geo. Rigby, Bay Horse Hotel; M.H.A.R.A.: The same; V.A.F.: The same.

RECOMMENDED APARTMENTS.

Mrs. Cheetham, 66, Regent Street.—2 bedrooms, sitting, combined room; piano.

BLACKHILL, Co. Durham.

ST. AIDAN'S CHURCH HALL.—Proprietors, The Trustees; Manager, Mr. Joseph Hamilton, The Lodge, Blackhill. Music and dancing license; dramatic can be obtained if required. Holding capacity: Number of persons, 600. Depth and width of stage, 18ft. by 30ft. Gas. Terms for hiring: £1 per night and gas (about 2s. 6d. per night). Size of hall, 70ft. by 40ft. by 22ft. high. Situation of hall, at Blackhill, midway between Consett and Sholley Bridge, and one minute from Blackhill Station (the principal station in the district).

BLACKPOOL, Lancs.

Population, 62,420. Miles from London, 227.

HER MAJESTY'S OPERA HOUSE.—Proprietor, the Blackpool Winter Gardens and Pavilion Co., Limited; Manager, Mr. Jno. R. Huddlestone; Secretary and Treasurer, Mr. A. E. Peace; Musical Director, Mr. Ralph Harwood; Scenic Artist, Mr. Bernoscomi. Fully licensed. Holding capacity: Number of persons, 2,500; amount, £250. Stage measurements: Depth, 40 ft.; width, 60 ft.; proscenium, 30 ft.; between fl rails, 40 ft.; under fly beam, 20 ft.; height to grid, 48 ft. Electric light. Amount of printing required, 1,600 sheets. Usual matinée days Saturdays and Bank Holidays. Time of band rehearsal, 10.30 a.m.

GRAND THEATRE.—Proprietor and Manager, Mr. Thos. Sergenson; Responsible Manager, Mr. T. Allan Edwardes; Acting-Manager, Mr. Harry Hunter.

WINTER GARDENS (including Floral Hall, Empress Ballroom, and Pavilion).—Manager, Mr. John R. Huddlestone.

PALACE.—Proprietors, Blackpool Tower Co., Limited; Manager, Mr. G. H. Harrop; Acting-Manager, Mr. Fred Waller; Musical Director, Mr. F. H. Jepson. Double license. Holding capacity: Number of persons, 4,000. Stage measurements: Depth: 37 ft. by 75 ft.; proscenium, 28 ft. 6 ins. Gas and electric light. Time of band rehearsal: October to July, 2 p.m.; August to September, 11 a.m. Usual matinée day, Saturday. Bars ten miles round Blackpool.

THE TOWER.—Manager, Mr. G. H. Harrop.

VICTORIA PIER.—Proprietors, Blackpool South Shore Pier and Pavilion Co., Limited; Manager and Secretary, Mr. George Roberts; Musical Director, Herr Arnold Blomie. Holding capacity: Number of persons, 1,600. Gas and electric light (alternating current, 200 volts).

PAVILION, NORTH PIER.—Manager, Mr. J. Walker. Double license. Holds 1,900. Gas and electric light, alternating current, 200 volts.

CENTRAL PIER.—Manager and Secretary, Mr. Cyril Chantler. Music and dancing license. Holds 1,000. Has platform. Electric light.

HIPPODROME.—Lessee, Mrs. Fioni.

Blackpool, the popular northern seaside resort, enjoys a world-wide reputation for its lavish entertainment all the year round, but more particularly in the summer season, when it is the Mecca of holiday-makers from all parts of the kingdom. The pleasure beach at South Shore has been aptly styled the English Coney Island. A huge open-air combination of shows. Place no good for portables. Plenty of sites and good prospects for alfresco entertainers and circuses. There are no local fairs or holidays that are calculated seriously to affect theatres, except Tradesmen's Holiday, one day, usually in June. During winter months Wednesday afternoon is recognised by tradespeople as half-holiday, but usually this benefits theatres.

Market day, Saturday.

Medical Officers.—A.A.: Dr. Butcher, Warley Road (hours, 2—4; 'phone, 72). A.U.: Dr.

Butcher, Waverley House. M.H.A.R.A.: The same as A.A.

Agents.—A.U.: J. Blackhurst, Adelphi Hotel. M.H.A.R.A.: The same; V.A.F.: The same.

RECOMMENDED APARTMENTS.

Mrs. Wilson, 3, Dickson Road.—2 sitting-rooms, 5 bedrooms, 2 combined rooms; pianos; bath.

Mrs. R. Butcher, 56, Elizabeth Street.—4 bedrooms, 2 sitting-rooms, 1 combined room; bath.

BLACKROCK, Co. Dublin.

Population, 8,719. Miles from Dublin 7.

ASSEMBLY ROOM, TOWN HALL.—Town Clerk, Mr. R. Finlay Heron, M.A. No dramatic license. Holding capacity: Number of persons, 500. Proper stage; no traps; head and foot lights; back and side entrances; stage depth, 10ft. 6ins.; width, 20ft.; proscenium, 18ft. by 9ft. Lighted by gas. Terms for hiring, £2 10s. per night. Amount of deposit required on booking, ditto. Two large dressing and green rooms; 4ft. passage at back of stage on level of same; stage sloped.

BLAENAVON, Mon.

Population, 12,000. Miles from London, 155.

TOWN HALL.—Has dramatic license. Holds about 800. Apply, the Secretary.

WORKING MEN'S INSTITUTE.—Has dramatic license. Holds about 1,400. Apply, the Secretary.

BLAINA, Mon.

Population, 14,000. Miles from London, 174.

EMPIRE THEATRE. — Proprietors, the Blaina Theatre Co.; Manager, Mr. W. R. Lee; Stage Manager, Mr. Fred Lewis; Musical Director, Mr. Sam Brown. Holding capacity, 1,200. Stage, 22ft. deep by 43ft. wide. Proscenium opening, 20ft. Lighted by gas. Printing required, 500 walls, 500 lithos.

PUBLIC HALL.—Manager, Mr. T. W. Allen. Dramatic license. Holding capacity: Number of persons, 1,200. Platform, 19 ft. by 30 ft. Gas and electric light. Terms for hiring: £7 per week. Amount of deposit required on booking, £1 1s.

Mining district; big pays fortnightly.

Early closing day, Wednesday; market day and workmen's half holiday, Saturday.

BLAIRGOWRIE, Perth.

Population, 3,337. Miles from London, 465.

PUBLIC HALL.—Manager, Mr. Jas. McLevy. No dramatic license, but all travelling companies appear here. Holding capacity: Number of persons, 650. Stage, depth, 14ft. 9ins. by 36ft. width. Lighted by gas. Amount of printing required: See Andrew Gowans Billposter, High Street. Terms for hiring: One night, £1 15s. 6d. inclusive. Amount of deposit required on booking, 10s.

Dates of local fairs: 4th Tuesday in July is Fair o' Blair Day and Highland Games. The ground is let every year for shows.—Apply to Town Clerk.

Early closing, Thursday; market, Tuesday

BLYTH, Northumberland.

Population, 5,472. Miles from London, 283.

NEW THEATRE ROYAL. — Proprietors, Theatre Royal Co.; Manager and Lessee, Mr. Arthur C. Moody; Acting-Manager, Mr. Lacy Lyne; Musical Director, Mr. James Evans; Scenic Artist, Mr. William Francotte. Full dramatic license. Holding capacity: Number of persons, 2,500; amount, £85. Proscenium opening, 28ft. by 28ft. Stage measurements: Depth, 40ft.; width, 56ft.; height to grid, 50ft.; between rails, 42ft.; stage to fly floor, 21ft. Gas and electric light. Amount of printing required, 800 sheets. Usual matinée day, Saturday. Time of band rehearsal, 1 o'clock.

HIPPODROME.—Proprietor and Manager, Mr. W. Tudor; Manager, Mr. J. Fraser. Holding capacity, 1,700. Gas and electric light, voltage 460.

GAIETY MUSIC HALL.—Proprietor, Mr. J. Grantham; Manager, Mr. John Storm. Holding capacity, 1,000. Stage 36ft. wide, 18ft. deep. Electric light, 460 volts, direct current.

NEW EMPIRE.—Manager, Mr. A. C. Moody. Holding capacity, 800. Early closing day, Wednesday; market, Saturday.

Industries: Mining, fishing, shipbuilding, docks. Miners are paid fortnightly. Population within four miles radius, 70,000.

Sites for portables, alfresco concerts, etc., Market Square.

Medical Officer.—A.A., Dr. Newstead; M.H.A.R.A., The same.

Agent. M.H.A.R.A.: J. O'Connell, Ship Hotel V.A.F.: The same.

BODMIN, Cornwall.

Population, 5,353. Miles from London, 273.

PUBLIC ROOMS.—Secretary, Mr. Mark Guy. Fully licensed. Holding capacity: Number of persons, 500. Lighted by gas. Terms for hiring: Scale on application. Amount of deposit required on booking, £1 1s.

Early closing day, Wednesday; market days, Wednesday and Saturday.

BOGNOR, Sussex.

Population, 6,180. Miles from London, 66.

ASSEMBLY ROOMS.—Manager, Mr. E. L. Wood. Double license. Lighted by gas. Usually visited for three nights, except by concert companies in the summer season. 23ft. 6ins. opening, depth 17ft., width 26ft., fly rail 16ft., grid 35ft. Printing, 300 sheets.

PIER PAVILION.—Proprietors, Urban District Council. Let for concerts.

OLYMPIAN GARDENS.—Proprietors, the Summer Entertainments Syndicate. On the parade. Alfresco concerts are given here during the season.

Sites for alfresco concerts may be obtained, while the fine sands provide excellent pitches for pierrots and other entertainers. Circus pitch behind the gasworks. Bognor is a seaside town on the south coast, largely visited by families on account of the extensive sands. Outdoor entertainments do well in the season.

BOLTON, Lancs.

Population, 185,358. Miles from London, 196.

THEATRE ROYAL.—Proprietors, The Bolton Theatre and Entertainments Co., Ltd.; Managing Director, Mr. J. F. Elliston; Acting-Manager, Mr. John Moncur; Musical Director, Mr. J. Ainscorth; Scenic Artist, Mr. J. E. Griffiths. Full dramatic license. Holding capacity: Number of persons, 2,200; amount, £120. Proscenium, 28ft. 6in.: between fly rails, 40ft.; stage to grid, 48ft.; curtain line to back wall, 50ft.; wall to wall, 50ft. 6in.; stage to underfly floor, 24ft.; front back, 22ft. Electric and gas. Amount of printing required: 1,200 sheets, 1,000 lithos., 1,000 circulars, 10,000 handbills. Time of band rehearsal, 12.30.

GRAND THEATRE.—Proprietors, the Bolton Theatre and Entertainments Co., Limited; Managing Director, Mr. J. F. Elliston; Acting-Manager, Mr. Harry Kenyon; Musical Director, Mr. A. Braddock. Double license. Holding capacity: Number of persons, 2,800. Gas and electric light. Amount of printing required, 1,600 sheets. Time of band rehearsal, 11.30 prompt. Usual matinée day, Monday, at 2.30. Voltage, 110, direct, own manufacture.

EMPIRE AND HIPPODROME.—Proprietor and Manager, Mr. T. Hargreaves; General Manager, Mr. T. Hargreaves, jun.; Assistant Manager, Mr. A. R. Harrison; Musical Director, Mr. A. E. Wilson. Holding capacity, 2,500. Gas and electric, 230 voltage, direct. Printing, 1,600 sheets. Band rehearsal, 11 a.m. Matinée, Monday, at 2.30.

TEMPERANCE HALL.—Music license. Holding capacity: Number of persons, 2,500; amount, according to prices.

Local fair, January 1, held on the Wholesale Market, Victoria Square, and in the Drill Hall. The town is visited by portables. No difficulty in obtaining licenses from council. These sites are available for alfresco concerts or circus pitches. Population chiefly industrial. Mill and foundry operatives. The fair is well patronised, and there is a good opening for a revival of the ghost show, which was formerly tremendously popular, and which has not been seen here for some years past.

Early closing day, Wednesday; market days, Monday and Saturday.

Medical Officers.—A.A.: Dr. Ferguson, 53, Manchester Road. M.H.A.R.A.: The same.

Agents.—A.U.: Golden Lion Hotel, Churchgate. M.H.A.R.A. and V.A.F.: Joiners' Arms, Deansgate.

BO'NESS, Linlithgow.

NEW TOWN HALL.—Proprietors, The Corporation; Clerk, Mr. A. Stewart Jamieson, solicitor. Holding capacity: Number of persons, 1,100; amount, £80 or so. Proper stage. Electric light; plug for kinematograph. Printing required for seven or eight large bill-posting stations. Terms for hiring: Letting; no shares. Amount of deposit required on booking, generally 20 per cent.

Dates of local fair: Second Friday in July; Show Ground, Corbiehall.

Early closing, Wednesday.

BOOTLE.

See Liverpool.

BOSCOMBE.

See Bournemouth.

BOSTON, Lincs.

Population, 15,667. Miles from London, 107.

SHODFRIARS HALL.—Manager, Mrs. B. Storr. Fully licensed. Holding capacity: Number of persons, 800. Proscenium opening, 19ft. 3ins. Footlights to proscenium, 4ft. Proscenium to wall, 16ft. Lighted by gas. Amount of deposit on booking, £1.

PALACE THEATRE.—Lessees, Messrs. Holloway and Fountain; Manager, Mr. E. Cass; Musical Director, Mr. Bert Mortimer. Double license Holding capacity: Number of persons, 1,200; amount, £40. Stage measurements: 26ft. deep, 23ft. 6in. wide; proscenium opening, 30ft.; 16ft. wings; full width of stage, 46ft. Lighted by gas. Time of band rehearsal, 2 p.m. Usual matinée day, Saturday. Bars no surrounding halls. Population residential, also fishing and seafaring. District agricultural.

Local Fair, May 3, 4, and 5. Town is not visited by portables; used to be about twenty years ago.

Alfresco Concerts.—Good pitches obtainable in the Oldrid's Park, right in centre of town. Circus pitches are to be obtained near the town.

Early closing day, Thursday; market days, Wednesday and Saturday.

Agent. — M.H.A.R.A.: H. Fountain, Corn Exchange Hotel. V.A.F.: The same.

BOURNE, Lincs.

Population, 4,361. Miles from London, 97.

CORN EXCHANGE.—Apply, The Secretary. Early closing day, Wednesday; market day, Thursday.

BOURNEMOUTH, Hants.

Population, 65,000. Miles from London, 108.

THEATRE ROYAL.—Proprietors, Messrs. David Allen and Sons; Lessee and Manager, Mr. F. Mouillot; Manager, Mr. Robert Dunbar; Musical Director, Mr. A. D. Weatherstone; Scenic Artist, Mr. Percy Selby. Full dramatic license. Holding capacity: Number of persons, 1,500; amount, £150, ordinary prices. Stage measurements: Mean depth, 35ft.; mean width, 42ft. 6ins.; proscenium opening, 24ft. Gas and electric light. Amount of printing required: 600 sheets, 600 lithos, 2,000 circulars, 1,000 throwaways. Usual matinée day, Saturday, at 3 p.m. Time of band rehearsal, 11 a.m.

GRAND HALL.—Proprietor, Mr. Fredk. Mouillot (in connection with the Theatre Royal).

WINTER GARDENS.—Proprietors, The Bournemouth Corporation; Manager, Mr. Dan Godfrey; Assistant Manager, Mr. W. T. Skeates. Music license. Holding capacity: Number of persons, 1,700. Platform only. No proscenium. Electric light. Cannot be hired; in constant use by Municipal Orchestra. Twice daily, except Sundays. Reading-room and refreshment-room. Alfresco concerts in summer.

SHAFTESBURY HALL.—Committee of the Y.M.C.A. Music and singing licenses. Holding capacity: Number of persons, 850. Platform; no proscenium. Gas and electric light. Usually engaged for lectures, pictures, etc.

PIER.—No theatre. The Corporation Band (Dan Godfrey's) plays morning and evenings, and in the summer the Corporation usually engages a concert party in addition.

BOSCOMBE PIER.—The Bournemouth Corporation Band (Section) plays in the summer. Concert parties are occasionally engaged.

BOSCOMBE HIPPODROME (late Grand Theatre).—Proprietors, Messrs. Mouillot and De Freece; General Manager, Mr. Jack De Freece; Booking Circuit, Mr. De Freece; Musical Director, Mr. F. Leake. Double license, restricted. Holding capacity: Number

of persons, about 1,600. Time of band rehearsal, 1 p.m. Two houses a night.

Early closing day, Wednesday.

Agents.—M.H.A.R.A.: J. H. Mouflet, London Hotel, and C. D. Smith, Palmers on Hotel, Boscombe. V.A.F. Pa merston Hotel. Boscombe. A.U.: C. Parsons, Salisbury Hotel, Boscombe.

RECOMMENDED APARTMENTS.

Mrs. C. Sellick, 112, Commercial Road.—1 sitting, 1 combined, 2 bedrooms; bath and piano.

BOVEY TRACEY, Devon.

Population, 2,693. Miles from London, 216.

TOWN HALL.—Manager, Mr. Henry J. W. Heath. Fully licensed. Holding capacity: Number of persons, about 400. Proper stage. Lighted by gas. Terms for hiring, 15s. per night. There is no piano in the hall.

Early closing day, Wednesday; no market day.

BRACKLEY, Northamptonshire.

Population, 2,467. Miles from London, 68.

TOWN HALL.—Manager, Mr. Samuel Sawford. No dramatic license. Holding capacity: Number of persons, 250 to 300. Stage, 15 ft. by 28 ft. Lighted by gas. Terms for hiring: For hall and dressing-room, 17s. 6d. each day. Amount of deposit required on booking, 17s. 6d.

Local fair, Dec. 11. Fields adjoining town are available for portables and circuses.

Early closing day, Tuesday; market day, Wednesday.

BRADFORD, Yorks.

Population, 279,767. Miles from London, 196.

THEATRE ROYAL.—Lessee, Mr. John Hart; Manager, Mr. T. F. Doyle; Acting-Manager, Mr. Jas. Richardson.

PRINCE S THEATRE.—Proprietor, Mr. F. Laidler; Acting-Manager, Mr. W. Hepworth; Musical Directors, Mr. W. Hudson for drama, Mr. H. Rushworth for pantomime. Full license. Electric light. Printing required, 2,300 d.c. sheets and 1,200 d.c. lithos.

PALACE.—Proprietor, Mr. Frank Macnaghten; Manager, Mr Edward Harrison; Booking Circuit, Macnaghten's.

EMPIRE.—Moss's Empires, Limited; Managing Director, Mr. Oswald Stoll; Acting-Manager, Mr. Percival Craig; Booking Circuit, Moss and Stoll tours; Musical Director, Mr. Jas. H. Pearson. Double license. Holding capacity: Number of persons, 2,500. Stage measurements: Depth, 38 ft.; width, 54 ft.; proscenium, 30 ft. Electric light. Band rehearsal, 2 p.m.

Bars all other Managements' Halls in Bradford and the following towns: Batley, Keighley, Ilkley, Shipley, Cleckheaton, Heckmondwike, Elland, and Bingley.

ST. GEORGE'S HALL.—Seats 3,400, with orchestra for 300 performers. Electric light.

MECHANICS' INSTITUTE.—Seats 1,350, and a Saloon holding 350. Electric light.

TEMPERANCE HALL.—Seats 900. Electric light.

CENTRAL HALL.—Seats 1,000. Smaller Room, 500. Electric light.

CENTRAL BATHS HALL.—Seats 1,240 Standing room for 300. Electric light. Apply to the Secretary.

Early closing day, Tuesday; market day, Thursday.

This city has fairs on first Monday (and following days of that week) in January and first Monday in July, besides which various districts within the city boundaries have local feasts. Portables frequently visit the outlying parishes, and a license is readily obtained. With regard to alfresco shows, at the meeting of the Bradford City Council, July 14, 1908, the Chairman of the Licensing Committee said: "The Committee are virtually agreed that no more such licenses shall be granted." There are numerous small towns and boroughs round about with a trade similar to that of the city—viz., the worsted industry, of which Bradford is the world's centre.

Medical Officers.—A.A.: Dr. Lodge, 110, Preston Street, Listerhills ('phone, 02,702; Dr. Rabagliati, 1, St. Paul's Road; Dr. Forshaw, 20, Otley Road (dental). A.U.: Drs. Lodge and Forshaw, as above. M.H.A.R.A.: Dr. Lodge, as above.

Agent.—A.U.: F. G. Schultz, Alexandra Hotel. M.H.A.R.A.: The same. V.A.F: The same.

BRAINTREE, Essex.

Population, 5,330. Miles from London, 45.

THE INSTITUTE.—Hon. Secretary, Mr. W. H. Tilston. Double license. Holding capacity: Number of persons, 400 to 500. No proscenium. Stage, 32ft. by 11ft. deep, with extension to 17ft. Lighted by gas. Terms for hiring, £2 2s. first night, £1 1s. second night. Amount of deposit required on booking, £1 1s.

CO-OPERATIVE HALL.—Proprietors, Braintree and West Essex Co-operative Society, Limited; Manager, Mr. B. S. Wood. Holds 300. Stage, 10ft. by 16ft. Gas.

Site available for portables and circuses at Fairfield. Fair day, October 4.

Early closing day, Thursday; market day, Wednesday.

BRAMPTON, Cumberland.

ST. MARTIN'S HALL.—Manager, Mr. C. Cheesbrough. Full license. Holding capacity: Number of persons, 550; amount £20 to £25. Proper stage, and permanent. Depth and width of stage and proscenium measurements: 15ft. deep; width, 35ft.; 25ft. high; 18ft. opening. Gas. Amount of printing required: 150 daybills, 400 handbills. For terms for hiring: Apply C. Cheesbrough. Amount of deposit required on booking, 10s.

BRECHIN, Forfarshire.

Population, 8,941.

CITY HALL.—Manager, Mr. Ed. W. Mowat, City Chamberlain. Fully licensed. Stage measurements, 25ft. 6in. by 17ft. 11in Can be extended forward by 5ft. or 8ft. 4in. if required, on payment of 2s. 6d. extra. Lighted by gas. Terms for hiring:—Drama: First night, £2 10s.; second night, £1 10s.; every subsequent night, £1. Gas extra. Amount of deposit required on booking one-fourth of rental.

Dates of local fairs: May 28 and November 27. Feeing markets, if 28th on a Tuesday, or Tuesday following. Fair ground for circuses at Strachan's Park.

Early closing, Wednesday. Market, Tuesday.

BRECON, Brecknock.

Population, 5,901. Miles from London, 183.

GUILDHALL.—Proprietors, The Town Council; Manager, Mr. W. H. Dowdeswell. Dramatic and Music and Dancing licenses. Holding capacity, about 700. Stage. 23 ft. by 21 ft. Proscenium, 19 ft. by 19 ft. Gas. Printing required for 6 stations, none very large. Terms for hiring entertainments, First night, £1 10s.; second, 5s.; third, 10s., besides gas and fee for Hallkeeper of 2s. 6d. per night. Amount of deposit required on booking, £1.

Dates of local fairs: First Tuesday in May and November, extending over the week in both cases. Sites available for Portables, Alfresco Concerts and circuses, The Green. Apply for latter to the Lessee of Tolls.

Early closing, Wednesday; markets, 1st and 3rd Tuesdays and Fridays.

BRENTFORD, Middlesex.

Population, 15,171. Miles from London, 11.

PUBLIC BATHS.—Proprietors, Brentford Urban District Council; Manager, Mr. T. Peters. Dramatic, music, and dancing licenses. Holding capacity: Number of persons, 455. Temporary stage. Lighted by gas. Terms for hiring: For a concert or other entertainment, from 7 to 11 o'clock p.m., £2 2s. (includes lighting and one attendant). Special terms for engagements for more than two consecutive nights. Full amount required on booking. Swimming bath boarded over during winter.

Dates of local fairs, May 17, 18, and 19, and September 13, 14, 15. Site available for portables, alfresco concerts, and circuses, Market Place, New Brentford.

Early closing day, Thursday; market days, Tuesday and Saturday.

BRENTWOOD, Essex.

Population, 4,932 Miles from London, 18.

TOWN HALL.—Proprietors, Brentwood Town Hall, Company, Limited; Chairman of Directors, Mr. J. J. Crowe; Secretary, Mr. Geo. C. Barkham. Holding capacity: Number of persons, about 500. Plain platform, with footlights; about 40ft. wide and 16ft. deep. Gas, incandescent Amount of printing required, 100 day bills, 30 large posters. Terms for hiring: One night, £2; two nights, £3; three nights, £4, etc. Amount of deposit required on booking, 10s for each night booked. Only available large hall in district; stands in very heart of town, in the High Street. Warley Barracks near by

No local fairs.

Early closing day, Thursday. No market day.

BRIDGEND, Glam.

Population, 8,000. Miles from London, 183.

TOWN HALL.—Proprietors, the Town Hall Trust Committee; Agent, Mr. Walter Hughes, Town Hall Chambers. Dramatic license. Seats about 500. Gas-lighted, but electric current alternating 200 voltage is available by arrangement with District Council. Stage, 16ft by 18ft. Terms, £2 5s. first night; £2 second Deposit, £1.

The population is largely residential. Portable theatres occasionally visit the place, but prefer to go to the neighbouring Llynvi, Ogmore, and Garw mining valleys, where there is a very large collier population, which, especially on Saturday evenings, visits this town in large numbers. Circus pitches are available, but there is no site for alfresco concerts. Early closing day, Wednesday; market day, Saturday.

BRIDGNORTH, Shropshire.

Population, 6,052. Miles from London, 149.

AGRICULTURAL HALL.—Proprietors, The Crown and Raven Hotels, Limited; Managers, Messrs. Nock, Deighton, and Kirkby. Dramatic license. Holding capacity: Number of persons, 600. This building measures 78ft. in length by 30ft. in width; exclusive of raised platform at west end, 21ft. 6in. by 10ft. 6in. (capable of extension to 30ft. by 24ft. full stage, or 30ft. by 18ft. half stage), and balcony at east end, 20ft. by 9ft. Lighted by gas. Terms for hiring: Hire of hall (exclusive of balcony), with seats, tables, etc., and two dressing rooms, £1 5s. per day; balcony (with separate entrance), 10s. 6d. per day; stage extension, 10s 6d.; dressing room fires, 1s. each per day; gas (as per meter, which is accessible to each company), 4s. per 1,000 feet. A deposit of £1 for one day, 20s. for two days, and £2 for three or more, must always be paid at time of engaging the hall, otherwise it will not be reserved.

N.B.—The hall is at all times reserved on Saturday from 10 a.m. until 6 p.m., for Corn Exchange purposes, which does not interfere with evening performances.

Early closing, Thursday. Market, Saturday.

BRIDGWATER, Som.

Population, 15,300. Miles from London, 151½.

TOWN HALL.—Manager, Mr. Charles Chard. Dramatic license. Holding capacity: Number of persons, about 1,200; amount according to prices of admission. Terms for hiring: First day, morning or afternoon £1, evening only £2 5s., day £2 15s.; including gas; for each succeeding consecutive engagement after the first day, 20 per cent. off; for six consecutive days, £10; for fit-up or rehearsal, when not otherwise engaged, each day (in addition to gas actually consumed), 5s. For kinematograph entertainments the hirer will be charged in addition 5s. each performance for insurance. Amount of deposit required on booking, £1.

VICTORIA HALL.—Apply Mr. C. Mockridge, Victoria Road, Bridgwater.

HALSWELL HALL.—Apply Mr. L. Hayter, Conservative Association, Bridgwater.

Population, industrial (mostly brickmaking). Fair: Last Wednesday in September and two following days. Portables visit the town. No difficulty with Council regarding license. For circuses, alfresco concerts, world's fair, etc.: Bridgwater's Club Football Ground, apply J. Locker; Albion Club Football Ground, apply H. Hutchins, Taunton Road, are available.

Early closing day, Thursday; market day, Wednesday.

BRIDLINGTON, Yorks.

Population, 15,500. Miles from London, 215.

SPA THEATRE AND OPERA HOUSE.—Proprietor, New Spa and Gardens, Limited; Manager and Secretary, Mr. Harry Tunbridge. Full license. Holding capacity: Number of persons, 1,500. Amount, £100. Stage measurements: 35ft. deep, 30ft. wide, 27ft. high; total width, 55ft. 6ins. Electric light, continuous current, 220 and 440 voltage. Best dates: August and September.

GRAND PAVILION.—Proprietor, The Brid-

lington Corporation; Manager, Mr. C. Palmer. Full license. Holding capacity: Number of persons, nearly 2,000. Stage measurement: 37ft. deep, 36ft. wide. Electric light. Amount of printing required: 300 posters, 300 window bills. No matinée day. Time of band rehearsal, 1 p.m. Best dates: July, August, and September.

PALACE AND WINTER GARDENS THEATRE.—Manager, Mr. John W. Delmar. All licences. Holding capacity: Number of persons, 1,500. Stage measurements: opening, 29ft. by 20ft.; depth, 20ft. Electric light. Amount of printing required: 200 window lithos, 300 sheets. Terms of hiring: £12 per week or shares. Amount of deposit required on booking, 50 per cent.

ROYAL VICTORIA ROOMS, at south end of Royal Prince's Parade.—Proprietors, The Corporation; Manager, Mr. C. Palmer. Has dramatic license. Electric lighting. Holds 700 people. Stage, 26ft. wide, 24ft. deep. Musical comedy is most popular. Best houses during the season (July, August, and September).

No industrial population, except fishermen. At both Spa Gardens and Prince's Parade, in the season, pierrots and entertainers in addition to orchestras appear. Small fairs in October and April.

Early closing, Thursday; market days, Wednesday and Saturday.

Medical Officer: A.A., Dr. A. E. Whitehead, Manor House, Manor Street; A.U., the same; M.H.A.R.A.. The same.

Agent: M.H.A.R.A.: J. Gillett, Albion House. V.A.F.: C. Loveday, Hilderthorpe Hotel.

RECOMMENDED APARTMENTS.

Mrs. Dove, 26, Quay Road.—Good attention, splendid cook, and very clean.

BRIDPORT, Dorset.

Population, 5,710. Miles from London, 154.

RIFLE DRILL HALL.—Manager, Lieut. Whetham. Dramatic and music and dancing license. Holding capacity: Number of persons, 700 seating. Proper stage: depth, 18ft.; width, 33ft. Gas. Terms for hiring: One night, £2 12s. 6d.; two nights, £3 17s. 6d.; six nights, £7 7s. Amount of deposit required on booking, half rent. Five dressing rooms, lavatories, etc.

Early closing day, Thursday; market days, Wednesday and Saturday.

BRIGHOUSE, Yorks.

Population, 22,117. Miles from London, 194.

ALBERT THEATRE.—Proprietors, The Albert Theatre Co., Limited; Lessees, Messrs. Beanland and Emerson; Manager, Mr. Chas. H. Beanland. Holding capacity: Number of persons, 1,500. Stage measurements, 50ft. wide, 30ft. deep; 20 to fly, 40 to grid. Gas and electric. Amount of printing required: 600 walls, 500 lithos. Time of band rehearsal: 12. Voltage 110. Bars Halifax and Huddersfield.

TOWN HALL.—Manager, Mr. T. Washington Chambers, Solicitor, Brighouse. Dramatic and music and dancing licenses. Holding capacity: Number of persons, 900. Stage measurements: 17ft. 6in. deep by 26ft. wide; 10ft. 8in. wings. Lighted by gas. Electric light available if required. Terms of hiring: £2 10s. one night, £4 10s. two nights, three or more nights £2 per night; piano, etc., extra. Amount of deposit required on booking: one-third of rent (£1 minimum).

ODDFELLOWS' HALL.—Address the Caretaker. Music and dancing license. Holding capacity: Number of persons, 500. No proper stage. Lighted by gas. Terms for hiring: Entertainments of every kind, 12s. one night; entertainments, for two nights and upwards, 10s. per night. Amount of deposit required on booking, half fees. The hall belongs to a Friendly Society, not a private company.

Cattle fair, first Monday after October 12. Brighouse Feast, August 12, 13, and 14, 1909. Fair grounds, The Lees, Wakefield Road and Bull Field.

Since the opening of the theatre portables have not visited the town, but kinematograph shows occasionally open in the large room of the Town Hall. There are admirable sites for alfresco concerts, and also good circus pitches, the latter shows always doing well when they visit this district. The population are largely engaged in the textile trades—silk, cotton, and woollen—and are keenly appreciative of good shows.

Early closing day, Tuesday; market day, Saturday.

Agent. — M.H.A.R.A.: J. Sutcliffe, Anchor Hotel, Briggate; V.A.F.: The same.

BRIGHTON, Sussex.

THEATRE ROYAL.—Resident Manager, Mr. Lawson Lambert.

Population, 123,478. Miles from London, 50.

GRAND THEATRE. — Proprietors, Grand Theatre Limited; Managing Director, Mr. Ernest,Gates; Resident Manager, Mr. Ben Court.

COURT THEATRE (late The Coliseum).— Proprietress and Manageress, Mrs. M. Barrasford; Manager and Secretary, Mr. Thos. Barrasford, jun. Animated Picture show all the year: "The World n Motion."

WEST PIER.—Proprietors, The Brighton West Pier Co.; Secretary and Entertainment Manager, Mr. A. W. Scholey; Assistnt Secretary, Mr. F. J. Blight; Musical Director, Mr. J. Quinlan; Scenic Artist, Mr. G. Shepherd Full license. Holding capacity: Number of persons, 1,109; amount, £70. Stage measurements: Opening 2 f., height 24ft., depth 23ft. Electric light. Amount of printing required: 26 18-sheets, 200 lithos, circulars, etc. Time of band rehearsal, 10 a.m.

HIPPODROME.—Proprietors, Messrs. Barrasford and Smith; Managing Director, Mr. Thos. Barrasford; Resident Manager, Mr. B. J. Brown; Stage Manager, Mr. Harry Clark; Musical Director, Mr. Chas. Johns n; Electrician, Mr. Wm. Faulkner. Band rehearsal, 12 noon.

ALHAMBRA.—Lessee and Manager, Mr. Alfred Smith. Band rehearsal 1 o'clock.

THE AQUARIUM. — Owned by the Corporation.

NEW PALACE PIER. — Proprietors, the Palace Pier Company; Entertainment Manager, Mr. Cowell.

MELLISON'S GRAND HALL AND SKATING RINK. — Manager, Mr E. Heathcote. Stage measurements: 160ft. by 45ft., with spacious gallery all round. Holding capacity: Number of persons, 2,000. Let for concerts, entertainments, exhibitions, panoramas, etc.

Early closing days, Wednesday, Thursday, and Saturday; market days, Tuesday and Thursday.

Medical officers.—A.A.: Dr. F. A. Stewart Hutchinson, 32, Brunswick Place. Hours, 2.30 to 4 p.m., except Wednesdays. Tel. 2649 Hove; Dr. Spurgeon (Dental Surgeon), 8, Pavilion

Parade. A.U.: Dr . W. W. Dunkley, The Chalet, Rottingdean. 'Phone 12 X.

Agents.—A.U.: D. G. Clarke, The Unicorn, North Street; M.H.A.R.A.: J. Cowey; Coach and Horses, North Street; V.A.F.: W. Marlow, Lord Nelson, Russell Street.

RECOMMENDED APARTMENTS.

Mrs. Deane, Denmark House, 7, Buckingham Street, 4 bed, 1 sit., 1 comb.; piano.

Mrs. E. Read, 49, Kensington Place.—2 sittingrooms, 3 bedrooms, 1 combined; 2 pianos.

Mrs. Gibbons, 8, Buckingham Street.—2 bedrooms and sitting-room; also combined; piano.

BRIGHTLINGSEA, Essex.

Population, 4,501. Miles from London, 63.

FORESTERS' HALL. — Proprietors, the Foresters; Manager, Mr. E. C. Atkins, 8, Green Street. Mr. W. Ainger, caretaker. Dramatic and music and dancing license. Holding capacity: Number of persons, 450. Stage width, 31ft.; depth, 12ft. No fit-up Gas. Small amount of printing required. Terms for hiring: One day, £2 2s.; two days, £3 19s.; three days, £5 11s.; four days, £6 18s.; week, £9. Amount of deposit required on booking, from 10s. upwards.

Dates of local fairs, July 14, 15, 16, and October 9.

Fields can be hired for portables and circuses.

Early closing day, Thursday. No market day.

BRISTOL, Glos.

Population, 328,945. Miles from London, 118.

PRINCE'S THEATRE.—Proprietor and Manager, Mr. James Macready Chute; Acting-Manager, Mr. F. S. Green; Musical Director, Mr. G. R. Chapman; Scenic Artist, Mr. George Jackson. Full license. Holding capacity: Number of persons, 2,700; amount, £270. Proscenium opening, 30ft.; curtain to back wall, 54ft.; side wall to side wall, 65ft.; fly rail, 40ft.; opening; cloths, 39½ft. by 27ft. Gas and electric, 105 voltage, alternating. Usual matinée day, Thursday. No barring.

THEATRE ROYAL.—Lessees, Carpenters' Theatres, Limited; Managing Director, Mr. Ernest Carpenter; Acting-Manager, Mr. Henry C. Alty; Musical Director, Mr. Edwin Jacobs. Full license. Holding capacity: Number of persons, 1,500. Electric light.

PEOPLE'S PALACE.—Proprietor, United County Theatres, Limited; Manager, Mr. Horace Livermore. Booking circuit, Aberdeen, Dundee, Sunderland, Gateshead, Plymouth. Musical director, Mr. N. Fey. Music and dancing license. Holding capacity: Number of persons, 3,000; amount, £90. Stage measurements: 32ft. opening, 24ft. deep. Gas and electric light. Time of band rehearsal, 1 o'clock. Usual matinée day, Thursday. Bars no hall but the local Empire.

EMPIRE AND HIPPODROME.—Managing Director, Mr. B. Pearce Lucas; General Manager, Mr. Harry Day; Resident Manager, Mr. Sid Macaire. Musical director, Mr. H. E. Hatley. Music and dancing license. Gas and electric light. Time of band rehearsal, 12 noon. Usual matinée day, Wednesday.

COLSTON HALLS.—Proprietors, Colston Hall Co., Limited. No dramatic license. Apply to Secretary,

VICTORIA ROOMS, CLIFTON.—Secretary, Mr. Charles H. James. Double license. Holding capacity: Number of persons, 1,500 large room; small room, 400; Daniel room, 110. Stage, 30ft. by 30ft. in large room. Electric light. Terms for hiring: According to what purpose rooms are used for. Amount of deposit required on booking, quarter. Has grand organ.

There are no local fairs, and the town is not visited by portables. No alfresco concert parties visit the town, but at the local Zoological Gardens there are band concerts two or three times a week. Occasionally a circus visits the town, and the Volunteer Drill Hall forms an excellent place for this class of entertainment. A tent circus may find an excellent pitch either at Eastville or Horfield, two of the suburbs of the city, to both of which there is a good connection of trams from all parts. The population of the city is both residential and industrial. The former principally reside in Clifton, Westbury and Redland (all these suburbs are well served by motor 'buses and electric trams)—three charming districts—the two first mentioned adjoining the well-known Clifton Downs, which possess much picturesque scenery, and on which many theatricals enjoy the game of golf, with an occasional cricket match in the summer.

Early closing days, Wednesday and Saturday; market day, Thursday.

Medical officers.—A.A.: Dr. Carter, 28, Victoria Square, Clifton; M.H.A.R.A.: Dr. Wintle, 24, Gloucester Road, Bishopston.

Agent.—A.U.: D. Crombie, Crown and Dove, Bridewell Street; M.H.A.R.A.: The same; V.A.F.: The same.

RECOMMENDED APARTMENTS.

Mrs. A. Barnes, 6, Upper Berkeley Place, Clifton Road.—1 combined, 2 sitting, 4 bedrooms; bath; 2 pianos.

Miss Merchant, Elton House, 59, St. Michael's Hill.—2 sitting-rooms, 4 bedrooms; pianos; bathroom (h. and c.); terms moderate and inclusive.

BRIXHAM, Devon.

Population, 8,092. Miles from London, 222. TOWN HALL.—Manager, Mr. J. S. Arlidge, Clerk to the Urban District Council. Dramatic, music, and dancing licenses. Holding capacity: Number of persons, 800; amount, £30. Proper stage, fitted with proscenium and drop-piece. Depth, 22ft.; width, 25ft. clear from sides of proscenium; height from stage to ceiling, 20ft. clear; full width, 31ft. Large incandescent gas lights. Terms for hiring: Dramatic entertainments, £2 10s. first night, £2 5s. second and third nights. Above three nights as may be arranged. Other than dramatic, £2 first nights, £1 5s. second and third nights. Above three nights as may be arranged. Amount of deposit required on booking, half rental.

Fair or regatta, Friday and Saturday, August 20 and 21.

Early closing, Wednesday. Market days, Tuesday and Saturday.

BROADSTAIRS, Kent.

Population, 6,466. Miles from London, 77. VICTORIA ASSEMBLY ROOMS.—Now used as a club. THE GRAND PAVILION.—Manager and Lessee, the Rev. F. T. Mills, The Rectory, Broadstairs. Fully licensed. Holding capacity: Number of persons, 450. Stage: 18ft. by 20ft. Lighted by gas. Terms for hiring: £1 10s. for single night; 10s. for three or more. Amount of deposit required on booking, 10s. Special terms arranged for a week or more.

Early closing and market day, Thursday.

BROMLEY, Kent.

Population, 27,354. Miles from London, 10. LYRIC THEATRE.—Closed. Early closing day, Wednesday; market day, Thursday.

BROMSGROVE, Worcestershire.

Population, 8,418. Miles from London, 144. DRILL HALL.—Manager, Harry J. Phelps. Fully licensed. Holding capacity: Number of persons, 1,500. Properly equipped stage; depth, 23ft.; full width, 32ft.; opening, 21ft.; height to grid, 14ft. Lighted by gas. Amount of printing required, 350 to 400 sheets. Terms for hiring: One night, £2 10s.; two, £4 5s.; three, £5 10s. Amount of deposit required on booking, 20 per cent. All communications to H. J. Phelps, "Stonycroft," Handsworth Wood, Birmingham.

ASSEMBLY ROOMS THEATRE.—Proprietors, W. Watton and Son. Accommodation, 500; balcony for best seats. Stage: 27ft. by 19ft.; opening, 19ft. by 13ft. Stock scenery; heated with hot water. Lighting, gas.

Early closing day, Thursday; market day, Tuesday.

BROUGHTON.

See Salford.

BRYMBO, Denbigh.

Population, 4,610. Miles from London, 203. PUBLIC HALL.—Brymbo Public Hall Company, Limited; Manager, the Secretary. No license. Holding capacity: Number of persons, 500. Proper stage. Gas. Small amount of printing required. Terms for hiring: One day, 15s.; two days, £1 5s. Amount of deposit required on booking, 10s.

No local fairs.

Good sites available for portables, alfresco concerts, and circuses.

Early closing day, Wednesday. No market day.

BRYNAMMAN, Carm.

Population, 4,500. Miles from London, 217. PUBLIC HALL.—Manager, Mr. Thomas H. Thomas; Secretary, Mr. Evan W. Evans. Dramatic license. Holding capacity: Number of persons, 1,100; amount, £50 to £70. Permanent stage (no proscenium); 45ft. wide, 16ft. deep. Electric light. Amount of printing required, 400 sheets. Terms for hiring: Six guineas per week. Amount of deposit required on booking, 50 per cent. Electric current, 220 volts continuous.

Early closing day, Thursday.

BRYNMAWR, Brecon.

Population, 6,855. Miles from London, 159. MARKET HALL.—Secretary, Mr. William Evans, 42, Worcester Street, Brynmawr. Dramatic license. Holding capacity: Number of persons, 1,400. Proper stage. Stage measurements, depth, 56ft. by 23ft. Temporary baize proscenium. Lighted by gas. Amount of printing required: More the better. Terms for hiring: 1 night, £2 10s.; 2, £4 10s.; 3, £6; 4, £7; 5, £8; 6, £9. Amount of deposit required on booking, £1.

TOWN HALL.—Available for small entertainments. Has not dramatic license.

Population.—Chiefly coalminers. There are two fairs in the year—Whit Monday and the third Monday in September. Town occasionally visited by portables, and no difficulty with Local District Council about licenses.

Circuses often visit, and pitches available.

Early closing day, Wednesday; market day, Saturday.

BUCKFASTLEIGH, Devon.

Population, 2,520. Miles from London, 230.

TOWN HALL AND INSTITUTE.—Mr. W. H. Furneaux, Hon. Sec. Fully licensed. Holding capacity: Number of persons, about 400. Stage measurements, 15ft. to ceiling; 21ft. by 13ft.; 3ft. extra if required. Lighted by gas. Terms for hiring: £1 1s. per night, 3 nights, 50s. Amount of deposit required on booking, 25 per cent. Two ante rooms.

Early closing, Wednesday.

BUCKHURST HILL, Essex.

Population, 4,786. Miles from London, 10.

PUBLIC HALL.—Proprietors, the Trustees; Manager, Mr. E. H. Bally, Palmerston Road, Buckhurst Hill. Dramatic, music and dancing licenses. Holding capacity: Number of persons, 300. Depth and width of stage, 24ft. by 16ft. Gas. Terms for hiring for dramatic entertainments, £1 11s. 6d.; reduction for series. Amount of deposit required on booking, £1.

Early closing day, Wednesday. No market day.

BUDLEIGH SALTERTON, Devon.

Population, 1,883. Miles from London, 190.

PUBLIC ROOM.—Proprietors, Public Room Company, Limited; Manager, Capt. T. M. Cregory. Dramatic, music, and dancing licenses. Holding capacity Number of persons, 350. Stage, 23½ft. long, 10ft. wide, 2½ft. height from floor, 14ft. from stage to ceiling. Gas, incandescent. Amount of printing required, 75 double crown posters. Terms for hiring: One day, £1 10s.; two days, £2 5s.; hallkeeper, 3s. 6d. per day, and gas extra. Full payment required on booking.

Early closing day, Thursday. No market day.

BUILTH WELLS, Brecknock.

Population 2,000. Miles from London, 188.

ASSEMBLY ROOMS.—Secretary, Mr. H. V. Vaughan, solicitor. Fully licensed. Holding capacity: Number of persons, 600. Stage measurements, 32ft. by 15ft. Lighted by gas. Terms for hiring: 30s. first night; 21s. subsequent nights. Amount of deposit required on booking, 10s.

Dates of local fairs, February 1, 17, April 16, May 11, June 26, July 17, August 31, September 21, October 2, 16, and December 7.

Early closing, Wednesday; market, Monday.

BULWELL, Notts.

Population, 14,767. Miles from London, 133.

PUBLIC HALL.—Manager, Mr. H. Widdowson, The Hall House, Bulwell. Double license. Holding capacity: Number of persons, 800 to 1,000. Stage about 18ft. deep by 22ft. Frontage opening. Lighted by gas. Terms for hiring: £1 10s. single night; less for more than one night. Amount of deposit required on booking, £1 10s.

Dates of local fairs first Monday and Tuesday after first Sunday to be held in November.

Vacant land to be let for circuses, etc., in Main Street, Bulwell. Area, 1,500 square yards.

Early closing, Thursday; market, Saturday.

BURNHAM, Somerset.

Population, 2,897. Miles from London, 145.

TOWN HALL.—Manager, Mr. D. S. Watson. Double license. Holding capacity: Number of persons, about 400. Stage measurements: 30ft. wide, 16ft. deep; tableaux curtains open to 20ft. Lighted by Gas. Terms for hiring: £1 10s. first night and £1 a night after. Full amount required on booking.

Alfresco concerts on sands.

Early closing, Wednesday.

BURNHAM-ON-CROUCH, Essex.

Population, 2,919. Miles from London, 43.

PUBLIC HALL.—Proprietor, Mr. Alfred Newman. Dramatic license. Holding capacity: Number of persons, 300. Gas.

Early closing day, Wednesday. No market day

BURNLEY, Lancs.

Population, 97,043. Miles from London, 216.

VICTORIA OPERA HOUSE.—Proprietor, Mr. W. C. Horner; Musical Director, Mr Hayes. Restricted license. Holding capacity, Number of persons, 2,500. Stage measurements, 61ft. by 32ft. from curtain line. Gas and electric light. Amount of printing required: 1,000 sheets minimum, and 600 window bills. Time of band rehearsal, 1.30 p.m.

GAIETY THEATRE.—Proprietress, Mrs. T. Culeen; Manager, Mr. James E. Culeen; Musical Director, Mr. A. Nuttall; Scenic Artist, Mr. H. Grant. Dramatic license. Holding capacity: Number of persons, 3,500. Depth of stage, 46ft.; width, 65ft.; proscenium opening, 30ft. Gas and electric light. Amount of printing required: 400 pictorial posters and 600 lithos. Band rehearsal, 1 o'clock. Electric current, 220 volts.

EMPIRE.—Lessee and Manager, Mr. W. C. Horner; Acting-Manager and Treasurer, Mr. Harry Horner. Restricted license. Holding capacity: Number of persons, 2,100. Stage measurements, 48 ft. by 24 ft. Gas and electric light. Band rehearsal, 2.30.

PALACE AND HIPPODROME.—Proprietors, Burnley Palace and Hippodrome Co., Limited; Manager, Julius Simpson. Dramatic and music and dancing licenses. Holding capacity: Number of persons, 2,750. Gas and electric light.

MECHANICS' INSTITUTION. — Manager, Mr. John R. Marsden, Librarian. Music and dancing license only. Holding capacity: Number of persons, 1,350; amount depends on charges. Stage measurements: 31ft. by 22ft. Electric light. Terms for hiring:

£3 3s. per night, £12 10s. per week. Amount of deposit required on booking, 25 per cent.

Date of local fair, second Thursday in July until Monday following.

Cattle market available for circuses, etc.—Apply Markets Superintendent, Burnley.

Early closing day, Tuesday; market days, Saturday and Monday.

Medical Officer.—A.A.: Dr. Rodgers, Stone-clough. A.U.: The same.

Agent.—A.U.: Stephen Jackson, Rose and Thistle Hotel. M.H.A.R.A.: The same. V.A.F. The same.

RECOMMENDED APARTMENTS.

Mrs. Chorlton, 23, Belgrave Street.—Bed and sitting-room; piano.

Mrs. Hawkins, 92, Manchester Road.—2 sitting-rooms, 1 combined, 4 bedrooms.

Mrs. Menzies, 105, Curzon Street.—1 sitting-room and 1 bedroom.

BURNTISLAND, Fife.

Population, 4,726. Miles from London, 435. MUSIC HALL.—Proprietors, the Corporation; Hallkeeper, Mr. Robert Kinnel. Seats about 340. The hall is small and not suitable for large companies. Double license. Stage, 19ft. by 11ft. Gas.

Local Fair, first Monday in July. No portable sites. Alfresco pitches on beach. Circus pitch on links.

Early closing day, Wednesday.

BURSLEM, Staffs.

Population, 38,776. Miles from London, 150. HIPPODROME (LATE WEDGWOOD THEATRE).—Proprietor, Mr. R. Colins; Musical Director, Mr. Gus Foulkes. Full license. Holding capacity: Number of persons, 1,600; amount, £60. Electric light. Usual matinée days, Monday and Saturday. Time of band rehearsal, 1 p.m.

TOWN HALL.—Manager, Mr. Arthur Ellis, Town Clerk. Dramatic license. Holding capacity: Number of persons, 700. No proper stage. Electric light. Terms for hiring: £1 15s. per evening. Amount of deposit required: According to period of booking, £1 1s. to £3 3s.

DRILL HALL.—Manager, Borough Accountant, Town Hall. Dramatic license. Holding capacity: 1,400 persons. No proper stage. Electric light. Terms for hiring: £2 15s. per evening. £12 for a week. Amount of deposit required according to period of booking, £1 1s to £3 3s.

Early closing day, Thursday; market days, Monday and Saturday.

BURTON-ON-TRENT, Staffs.

Population, 50,386. Miles from London, 127. NEW THEATRE AND OPERA HOUSE.—Proprietors, W. and H. G. Dudley Bennett; Manager, Mr. E. de Hague Body; Musical Director, Mr. F. Leslie; Scenic Artist, Mr. Rudolph List. Full double license. Holding capacity: Number of persons, 1,800. Electric light, alternating current, 110 volts. This house has a season as THE HIPPODROME.

TOWN HALL.—Proprietors, The Corporation; Manager, Mr. J. W. Sherratt. Dramatic license. Seats about 1,000. Contains organ. Gas and electric light, alternating 100 volts. Terms, with any scenery. £21; for picture shows, £7 10s., light extra.

Burton is a county borough, with a fairly substantial residential population and a large industrial population, engaged principally in the brewing trade.

The Opera House and Town Hall are easily accessible by tramcar and railway from the neighbouring populous districts of Swadlincote, Gresley, and Newhall. Musical comedy, high-class drama, and first-class concerts are always successful attractions. There is an annual pleasure fair held in the centre of the town on the Monday after September 29. This lasts one day only, and the entertainments are of the usual mixed variety. Portable theatres do not visit the town, but pitches can be obtained either for circuses or menageries. Alfresco concerts are held during the summer months on the banks of the river (which is very pretty here), either in a meadow or one of the gardens, and in the Recreation Ground of the Corporation (which is also on the side of the river). Band concerts are given during the summer months. Early closing day, Wednesday; market days, Thursday and Saturday.

Agent.—A.U.: F. J. Hingley, Staffordshire Knott Hotel. M.H.A.R.A.: The same.

BURY, Lancs.

Population, 58,029. Miles from London, 199. THEATRE ROYAL AND PALACE.—Proprietors, The Northern Theatres Co., Limited; Manager, Mr. Otto C. Culling; Musical Director, Mr. Harry Bridge; Scenic Artist, Mr. F. G. Venimore. Stage measurements: Depth, 40 ft.; width, 60 ft.; proscenium, 30 ft. Gas and electric light, volts 220. Double license. During 1908 had seasons as theatre and music hall. Bars for five miles.

HIPPODROME.—Proprietors, Messrs. W. B. Broadhead and Sons; Acting-Manager, Mr. J. S. Garner. Music and dancing license. Band rehearsal, 11 a.m. Booking circuit, Broadhead's.

CIRCUS OF VARIETIES.—Proprietors, Northern Theatres Co., Limited; Manager, Mr. Otto C. Culling. Double license. Stage measurements: 30 ft. deep, 40 ft. wide, proscenium, 25 ft. Gas and electric light. Time of band rehearsal, 11 o'clock. Usual matinée day, Monday.

Early closing day, Tuesday; market day. Saturday.

Medical Officer.—A.A.: Dr. I. W. Johnson, Brook House, Barnbrook. A.U.: The same.

Agent.—A.U.: Robert Gregson, Knowsley Hotel. M.H.A.R.A.: The same; V.A.F.: The same.

BURY ST. EDMUNDS, Suffolk.

Population, 16,255. Miles from London, 87.

THEATRE ROYAL.—Run by shareholders under a directorate, with Mr. Auguste A. Penleve as general manager. Holds 800. Gas and electric, 200 volts.

ATHENÆUM HALL.—Resident Manager, Mr. E. A. Crack. Has dramatic license, and holds 550. Movable stage. Gas and electric, 200 volts. Printing: 300 window bills, 50 posters, 500 circulars. Concerts do well here.

CONSTITUTIONAL HALL. Seats 300 Secretary, Mr. C. H. Nunn. Dramatic license. Movable stage. Gas and electric, current 200 volts. Terms, 25s. per night, including light and use of piano. Deposit 10s. Fit-up scenery can be hired.

County town of West Suffolk, and depôt of the Suffolk Regiment.

There is no local fair. The Abbey Gardens, etc., are available for circuses, and Angel Hill and Market Hill for menageries, etc. No portable theatres have been here for years. Licenses are difficult to obtain. Animated picture shows have done well.

The chief drawback to every class of professional entertainment is the increasing competition of local amateur performances, which are much more extensively patronised. There are local operatic and musical societies, which secure a great share of public support. At the theatre musical plays draw best. This house is also sometimes used for two-night variety entertainments at cheap prices.

Early closing day, Thursday; market day, Wednesday and Saturday.

BUXTON, Derbyshire.

Population, 10,181. Miles from London, 163.

OPERA HOUSE.—Proprietors, The Buxton Gardens Co., Limited; Manager, Mr. Arthur Willoughby. Restricted license. Holding capacity: Number of persons, 1,250; amount, £120. Stage measurements: Back to front, 40ft.; width, 58ft. 6in.; opening, 30ft.; stage to fly-rail, 22ft.; stage to grid, 49ft. Electric light. Amount of printing required: 3 18-sheet, 4 12-sheet, 12 6-sheet, 130 d.c.'s, 1,000 circulars. Usual matinée day, Wednesday, and Saturday in the summer. Time of band rehearsal, 1 o'clock. Electric current, 230 volts.

WINTER GARDENS PAVILION and OLD THEATRE (for Concerts and Lectures only).— The property of Buxton Gardens Co., Limited.

ASSEMBLY ROOM, TOWN HALL.—80ft. long by 40ft. wide; platform, 31ft. by 11ft. 6in., with dressing-room adjoining. Accommodation for 500. No gallery. The hall is not licensed for stage plays, and there is no scenery, curtains, or footlights. Electricity is supplied, voltage 230, continuous current. Kinematograph entertainments are subject to special conditions, for particulars of which apply to the Council Electrical Engineer (Mr. W. J. Leeming). All other particulars obtainable from Mr. J. Willoughby, Town Hall, Buxton.

Population, chiefly residential; surrounding district extensive; fashionable health and pleasure resort.

Situation: Central; well served by Midland and North-Western Railways.

Distances: Manchester, 24 miles; Sheffield, 30 miles; Derby, 36 miles.

Fairs: Whit Thursday, Friday, Saturday; also well-dressings (June). Town visited by portables; local council favourable to licensing them. Season extends from Easter to middle of October.

Private and public sites obtainable for alfresco concerts; Council now more favourably inclined. Arrangements possible with Buxton Gardens Co., present directors very progressive. Good pitches obtainable for circus and menagerie.

Market day, Saturday.

Medical Officer.—A.A.: Dr. John Braithwaite, 2, Hardwick Mount. Hours, 11-1 and 5.30-6.30.

RECOMMENDED APARTMENTS.

Mrs. Cowburn, 2, Barlbro Cottage, Spring Gardens.—1 combined, 1 sitting, 2 bedrooms; piano.

Mrs. Ball, 27, South Avenue.—2 bedrooms and 1 sitting-room, or 1 bedroom and 1 combined room; bath.

Mrs. Harvey, 3, Brooklyn Place.—3 sitting 6 bedrooms, and bathroom.

CAHIR, Co. Tipperary.

Population, 2,046. Miles from Dublin, 128.

TOWN HALL, Cahir.—Manager, Mr. Joseph Walsh, Castle-street. Double license. Holding capacity: Number of persons: 300; amount, £20. Stage (movable benches), 23 ft. wide, 10 ft. deep. Can be added on to if necessary. Gas throughout, with two dressing-rooms equipped with gas and fire-grates. Amount of printing required: 150 bills for windows, etc. A large private hoarding attached, for pictures, etc., let on very reasonable terms during time. Terms for hiring: From three guineas per week (gas, piano, and hoarding extra).

Market, Friday.

CARISBROOKE, Isle of Wight.

Population, 3,993. Miles from London, 88.

There are no halls in Carisbrooke suitable for dramatic entertainment.

Early closing day, Thursday. No market day.

CALLANDER, Perthshire.

Population, 1,458. Miles from London, 433.

PUBLIC HALL.—Manager, Mr. Peter Buchanan, solicitor, Callander. Holding capacity: Number of persons, 600. Platform, 24ft. by 10ft. Lighted by gas. Terms for hiring: £2 2s. per night. Amount of deposit required on booking, 10s. 6d.

Market day, Thursday.

CAMBERLEY, Surrey.

Population, 5,249. Miles from London, 30.

DRILL HALL.—Manager, Colour-Sergeant Instructor T. Coltman. Fully licensed. Holding capacity: Number of persons, 600. Stage measurements: Depth, 30ft.; width, 40ft.; proscenium, 22ft. Lighted by gas. Terms for hiring, one night: Musical comedy, £4; pantomine, £3; dramatic, £2 2s.; ball, £3; auction sale, £2; £2 2s. for each subsequent night. Amount of deposit required on booking, £1. The above terms include gas and 400 seats. Scenery let if required. Building heated by hot air.

Dates of local fairs.—November 7 and 8 (Blackwater). Sites available for portables, alfresco concerts, and circuses. Mr. G. Doman's meadow, Frimley Road, Yorktown.

Early closing, Wednesday; no market day.

CAMBORNE, Cornwall.

Population, 14,726. Miles from London, 307.

PUBLIC ROOMS.—Manager, Mr. T. H. Cadwell. Dramatic license. Holding capacity: Number of persons, 1,500. Stage, 30ft. wide by 20ft. deep. Gas and electric light. Terms for hiring: One night, £3 3s.; two nights, £5 5s. Amount of deposit required on booking, £1. Current, 240 volts direct.

ASSEMBLY ROOMS.—Secretary, Mr. H. Burrow. In centre of town. Gas and electric light, voltage 240, for kinematograph 480. Fit-up and scenery. Seats 800.

Connected with Redruth (3 miles) by tramway; district population, 30,000. Industrial, mining and engineering. Best nights, Monday, Tuesday, Wednesday, and Thursday. Fairs, March 7, Whit Tuesday, June 29, and November 11. Ground available for portables and circuses at Fair Meadow. Apply J. Wales.

Early closing day, Thursday; market day, Wednesday and Saturday.

CAMBRIDGE, Cambs.

Population, 47,731. Miles from London, 58.

NEW THEATRE.—Proprietors, Limited Liability Company; Managing Director, Mr. W. B. Redfern; Secretary, Mr. Herbert Hall; Musical Director, Mr. T. G. Briggs. Full dramatic license. Holding capacity: Number of persons, about 1,500; amount, about £100. Stage measurements: Depth, 37ft.; width, 56ft.; proscenium, 28ft. wide by 27ft. high; wings, 22ft.; width of cloths, 34ft.; height to grid, 54ft. Gas and electric light. Amount of printing required, 500 d.c.'s, 36 6-sheet panels, 8 18-sheet, 600 circulars. Usual matinée day, Saturday. Time of band rehearsal, 1 o'clock. Closed from middle June to middle September. Electric current, 200 volts.

THE GUILDHALL.—Proprietors, the Corporation; Manager: Apply to the Hallkeeper. Seats about 1,000. Electric current, 200 volts alternating. Has dramatic license.

HIPPODROME.—Proprietor, Mr. W. Askham. Seats 600. Small stage; dramatic license. Circus ring if required.

CORN EXCHANGE.—Seats 2,000, but no seating supplied by lessees.

CENTRAL HALL, CONSERVATIVE CLUB.—Seats 300. Small permanent stage, with Scenery. Licensed for theatrical performances.

VICTORIA ASSEMBLY ROOMS.—Seats 300.

BEACONSFIELD HALL.—Seats 300.

ALEXANDRA HALL, Y.M.C.A.—Seats 200.

Circus pitches on Midsummer Common on application to Corporation officials. Fairs: Midsummer Fair, June 24 (four days); Stourbridge Fair, September 25 (three or four days). Early closing day, Thursday; market day, Saturday.

Medical Officer.—A.A.: Dr. W. W. Wingate, 60, St. Andrew's Street.

Agent.—M.H.A.R.A.: J. Fuller, Foresters' Arms, City Road.

CANTERBURY, Kent.

Population, 24,899. Miles from London, 61.

THEATRE ROYAL.—Proprietor, Mr. E. Graham-Falcon; Musical Director, Mr. W. T. Harvey. Double license. Holding capacity: Number of persons, 900; amount, £75. Stage measurements: Depth, 21ft.; width, 38ft.; proscenium opening, 22ft. Gas (electric light, 220 volts, direct, by arrangement). Amount of printing required, 350 sheets d.c. Usual matinée day, Saturday. Time of band rehearsal, 1 p.m.

ST. GEORGE'S HALL.—Let for concerts, balls, plays (temporary license). Holds about 450. Platform, 20ft. by 16ft. Electric, 220 volts. Apply, Manager, 39, St. George's Street.

ST. MARGARET'S HALL.—No dramatic license. Holds 600. Platform 30ft. by 15ft. (can be extended). Apply, the Secretary.

FORESTERS' HALL.—Has dramatic license. Holds about 400. Proscenium opening 22ft. by 12ft., width of platform 30ft. Apply, the Secretary.

Local fair commences October 11.

Stage play licenses (occasional) are frequently issued for the various halls.

Sites easily obtainable for circuses and alfresco concerts.

Population mainly residential. Garrison of about 1,000 men.

Early closing day, Thursday; market day, Saturday.

CARDIFF, Glam.

Population, 164,338. Miles from London, 163.

NEW THEATRE.—Proprietor, Mr. Robert Redford; Musical Director, Mr. A. H. Mabbett. Full license. Holding capacity: Number of persons, 2,000; amount, £250. Stage measurements, 55ft. by 77ft.; opening, 33ft. Electric light. Amount of printing required, 2,000 sheets. Usual matinée day, Saturdays. Time of band rehearsal, 11.30. Electric current, 200 volts.

ROYAL.—Lessee and Manager, Mr. Rollo Balmain. Full license.

EMPIRE THEATRE.—Proprietors, Moss's Empires, Limited; Managing Director, Mr. Oswald Stoll; Acting-Manager, Mr. C. H. S. Dring; Assistant Acting-Manager, Mr. T. P. Haslam; Musical Director, Mr. David Griffiths. Music and dancing license. Stage measurements: Depth, 59ft. 6in.; width, 61ft. 4in.; proscenium, 29ft. 10in. wide by 28ft. 6in. high. Gas and electric light. Time of band rehearsal, 3 o'clock.

Bars all other Managements' Halls in Cardiff and the following towns : Penarth, Barry, Cadoxton, Llandaff, Llandissant, Caerphilly, and Pontymister.

PALACE AND HIPPODROME.—Proprietor, Mr. Frank Macnaghten; Manager, Mr. Arthur Burton; Assistant Acting-Manager, Mr. B. Faithful. Booking circuit, Macnaghten Vaudeville. Musical Director, Mr. J. J. Leening. Gas and electric light. Time of band rehearsal, 12 o'clock.

PHILHARMONIC HALL.—Proprietors, Moss's Empires, Limited; Manager, Mr. Tetlow. Rehearsal at 3 p.m.

Bars all other Managements' Halls in Cardiff and the following towns : Penarth, Barry, Cadoxton, Llandaff, Llandissant, Caerphilly and Pontymister.

Early closing day, Wednesday; market day, Saturday.

Medical Officer.—A.A.: Dr. W. A. Neish, 1, Clare Street. 'Phone 949. A.U.: The same. M.H.A.R.A.: The same.

Agents.—A.U.: Park Hotel. M.H.A.R.A.: Mrs. Rosser, Grand Hotel, Westgate Street. .A.B.: The same.

RECOMMENDED APARTMENTS.

Mrs. Yard, 15, Beryl Road, Barry Dock.—Comfortable front sitting and bedrooms.

CARLISLE, Cumb.

Population, 45,480. Miles from London, 299.

HER MAJESTY'S THEATRE.—Lessees, Mr. Thos. Courtice and Mrs. R. Stewart McKim; Manager, Mr. Thos. Courtice; Musical Director. Mr. Fred Burns. Full license. Holding capacity: Number of persons, 1,821; amount, £122 10s. Proscenium, 29ft. wide, 28ft. high; stage, 60ft. wide, 41ft. deep. Can fly 26ft. cloths. Electric light, with gas footlights in reserve. Amount of printing required, 600 sheets for walls and 500 lithos. Matinée day, Saturday, but matinées not usual. Time of band rehearsal, 1 o'clock. Electric current, 230 volts.

PALACE THEATRE OF VARIETIES.—Proprietors, The Palace Theatre, Carlisle, Limited; Managing Director, Signor R. Pepi; Acting Manager, Mr. C. F. Morgan; Musical Director, Mr. E. Williams. Music and dancing license. Electric light, 230 volts. Time of band rehearsal, 2 p.m.

NEW PUBLIC HALL.—Secretaries, E. J. Castiglione and Sons, Estate Agents, Carlisle. Music and dancing license. Holding capacity: Number of persons, 1,000. Proper stage. Electric light. Terms for hiring, £8 a week. Amount of deposit required on booking, £5.

Population chiefly residential, with good proportion of railway workers.

Fairs are held here twice annually—viz., Whitsuntide (Saturday) and Martinmas (Saturday before November 11). Held on "The Sands" waste ground on outskirts of town, belonging to Corporation. Portables never visit Carlisle. Nearest they come to the city is Longtown (eight miles) and Brampton (nine miles). Circus Pitches: The Sands or Fair Ground. Alfresco concerts unknown here. Sanction refused by authorities some two years ago, when application was made to hold these in paddock of old racecourse.

Early closing day, Thursday; market day, Saturday.

Medical Officers.—A.A.: Dr. Beard, Kent House, Portland Square (hours 9-10, 2-3, 6-8). M.H.A.R.A.: Dr. W. T. Binns, Kent House, Alfred Street.

Agent.—M.H.A.R.A.: E. Bulman, Deakin's Vaults, Botchergate. V.A.F: The same.

CARLOW, Co. Carlow.

Population, 6.619. Miles from Dublin, 56.

TOWN HALL.—Apply Town Clerk, Carlow. No dramatic license. Holding capacity: Number of persons, 400; amount, £20 to £25. Two dressing-rooms. Platform, 26 ft. wide, 18 ft. deep. Lighted by gas. Amount of printing required: 50 posters and window bills. Terms for hiring: 30s. for first and 20s. for every succeeding night. Amount of deposit required on booking, 30s. Hall 70 ft. by 30 ft., well seated and lighted.

Dates of local fairs: Fourth Wednesday of every month (except March and December), March 26, May 4, Nov. 8, and Dec. 30. Site available for portables, circuses, etc., Shamrock Hotel grounds, Carlow

Market, Monday and Thursday.

CARMARTHEN, Carm.

Population, 10,025. Miles from London, 241.

ASSEMBLY ROOMS.—Manager, Mr. Edward Baldwin. Double license. Holding capacity: Number of persons, 900. Amount, 45s. per night. No proper stage. Lighted by gas. Amount of deposit required on booking, 10s.

Early closing day, Thursday; market day, Saturday.

The population is residential and agricultural. There are three fairs in the year—June 3 and 4, August 12 and 13, and November 14 and 15. The town is visited by portables, but a little difficulty is experienced in obtaining a license. Sites can be obtained for a circus, etc.

CARNARVON, Carn.

Population, 9,760. Miles from London, 248.

THE PAVILION.—Manager, Mr. Dan Rhys (private address, Bodgwynedd, Carnarvon). Dramatic license. Holding capacity: Number of persons, 8,000. Platform 60ft. wide, raised tiers of seats behind. No proscenium. Gas and electric light. Terms for hiring: By arrangement. Amount of deposit required on booking, 10 per cent. The hall is suitable for world's fairs, circuses, bazaars, shows, concert-, etc. Electric current, direct, volts, 230.

GUILD HALL.—Manager, Mr. A. Holden, borough accountant. Dramatic license. Holding capacity: Number of persons, 500. No proper stage. Size, 19ft. by 6ft.; with extension for plays, about 19ft. by 11ft. Lighted by gas and electric. Terms for hiring: First night, £2 2s.; succeeding nights, £1 1s.; six nights, £6 6s. Amount of deposit required on booking, 10s. per day.

Early closing day, Thursday; market day, Saturday.

Agent.—V.A.F.: M. Conland, Commercial Hotel.

CARNFORTH, Lancashire.

Population, 3,040. Miles from London, 237.

CO-OPERATIVE HALL.—Secretary, Mr. J. Smalley. Music and dancing license. Holding capacity: Number of persons, 600. No proper stage. Lighted by gas. Terms for hiring: One night, £1; two nights, £1 15s.; three nights, £2 5s.; week, £4. Amount of deposit required on booking, 25 per cent. Two minutes from station.

Early closing, Thursday; market, Saturday.

CARNOUSTIE, Forfar.

Population, 5,204. Miles from London, 481.

PUBLIC HALL, Y.M.C.A.—Hallkeeper, Mr. Jas. Stephen. Full license. Holding capacity: Number of persons, 600. Amount, £1 5s. No proper stage. Measurements: Width, 23ft. by 12ft. 4in.; narrowest part, 17ft. 7in. Lighted by gas. Terms for hiring: £1 5s.; footlights 3s. 6d. extra. Amount of deposit required on booking, 12s. 6d.

Early closing day, Tuesday.

CARSHALTON, Surrey.

Population, 6,746. Miles from London, 14.

PUBLIC HALL.—Proprietors, the Carshalton Public Hall Company, Limited; Manager, Mr. H. Hopkins. Dramatic, music and dancing licenses. Holding capacity: Number of persons, 450. Platform only. Gas. Terms for hiring, £2 5s. 6d. per night.

Early closing day, Wednesday. No market day.

CASTLEBAR, Co. MAYO.

TOWN HALL.—Manager, Mr. John Corcoran Holding capacity: Number of persons, about 600. Proper stage. Hall, 60ft. by 33ft.; stage depth, 16ft.; width, 20ft. Lighted by gas. Amount of printing required, two hundred bills. Terms for hiring, £1 10s. first night, £1 each night after; caretaker 5s. also to pay for gas. Amount of deposit required on booking, 10s.

Principal fairs, May 11, July 9, September 16, November 17 and 18.

CASTLE DONINGTON, Leicester.

Population, 2,514. Miles from London, 123.

VICTORIA HALL.—Manager, Mr. J. E. Farnell, Bondgate. No dramatic license. Holding capacity: Number of persons, 300. Stage measurements, 16ft. by 8ft. by 24ft. high. Lighted by gas. Amount of printing required: Hand bills and few large posters. Terms for hiring: £1 per day, 12s. 6d. per night. Amount of deposit required on booking, half fees.

Date of local fair end of October.

Early closing, Wednesday; no market day.

CASTLE DOUGLAS, Kircudbright.

Population, 3,018. Miles from London, 352.
TOWN HALL.—Manager, Mr. John Hyslop.
Full license. Holding capacity: Number of
persons, 700. Stage measurements, 33ft. by
19ft. Lighted by gas. Terms for hiring: First
night, £2 6s. 6d., not including gas and hall-
keeper's fee. Amount of deposit required on
booking, 10s
Market day, Monday.

CASTLEFORD, Yorks.

Population, 17,386. Miles from London, 175.
THEATRE ROYAL.—Proprietor, Mr. C.
Gadsby; Manager, Councillor Harry Master-
man, J.P.; Musical Director, Mr. F. I. Burnley; Scenic Artist, Mr. William Jourdain. Full
license. Depth of stage, 30ft.; width, 60ft.;
opening 26ft. Gas and electric light. Usual
matinée day, Saturday.
QUEEN'S THEATRE OF VARIETIES.—Proprietors, Messrs. Beanland and Emerson;
Musical directress, Mrs. H. B. Coda. Music
and dancing license. Stage measurements,
36ft. by 18ft. deep; opening, 21ft. Gas and
electric light. Own electric plant, 70 volts.
Band rehearsal, 2 o'clock. Matinée day, occasionally on Saturday. Bars Pontefract. All
contracts as per Arbitrator's Award, and all
turns are booked direct.
CO-OPERATIVE HALL.—Manager, Mr. J. P.
Jackson. No license. Holding capacity: Number of persons, 300. Fixed platform. Electric
current, continuous, 110 volts. Terms of hiring: 15s. (concerts), paid on booking.
EMPRESS BALLROOM.—Mr. McCutcheon,
Manager.
Population, industrial, coal mining, glass-
blowing and potteries.
Date of local fair or feast, Monday, Tuesday,
and Wednesday in Whit week. Town is not
visited by portables. Sites for alfresco con-
certs and circus pitches are obtainable. A
license must be obtained from the West Riding
C.C., Wakefield.
Early closing day, Wednesday; market day,
Saturday.
Agent.—M.H.A.R.A.: W. Ambler, Keel Inn.
V.A.F.: The same.

CATERHAM VALLEY, Surrey.

Population, 9,486. Miles from London, 18.
PUBLIC HALL.—Manager, Mr. J. D. Rolls.
Full license. 400 chairs provided; capacity
double. Proper stage, 19 ft. deep; width of
proscenium opening, 19ft. 6 ins. Lighted by
gas; electric light obtainable. Terms for hir-
ing: £2 12s. 6d. one night, £6 16s. 6d. three.
Amount of deposit required on booking, 20s.
Early closing day, Wednesday.
Medical Officer.—A.A.:

CHATHAM, Kent.

Population, 42,134. Miles from London, 30.
THEATRE ROYAL.—Proprietors, Messrs.
Charles and L. B. Barnard; Manager, Mr.
Lionel Barnard; Musical Director, Mr. E. W.
Eyre; Scenic Artist, Mr. E. Rickards. License,
full dramatic. Holding capacity: Number of
persons, 3,000. Electric light. Usual matinée
day, Wednesday, 2.30. Time of band rehear-
sal, 2.15.
BARNARD'S PALACE.—Proprietor, Mr. L.
B. Barnard; Chairman, Mr. Geo. Helton.
GAIETY.—Proprietor, Captain H. E. Davis;
Manager, Mr. F. Warden-Reed. Music and
dancing license.

TOWN HALL.—Manager, Mr. Walter Cuck-
ney, the Borough Treasurer. Dramatic license.
Holding capacity: Number of persons, 1,000.
Stage has to be adapted for plays. No pro-
scenium; platform, 30ft. 4in. by 8ft. 6in. Elec-
tric light. Terms for hiring: Varies from
£3 3s. each night. Amount of deposit re-
quired on booking: The whole charge and £5
deposit as guarantee against injury to pre-
mises. Electric current, alternating, 100 volts.
No local fairs.
Early closing day, Wednesday.
Medical Officer.—A.A.: Dr. Barnes, Clevedon
House, New Road. M.H.A.R.A.: The same.
Agents.—A.U.: Mr. Lane, The Dover Castle
Hotel, V.A.F.; The same. M.H.A.R.A.: H.
H. Braham, Gaiety Palace.

RECOMMENDED APARTMENTS.

Mrs. Kemp, 12, Batchlor Road, High Street.—
2 bedrooms (3 beds); bath; gas; piano.

CHATTERIS, Cambridgeshire.

Population, 4,711. Miles from London, 83.
CORN EXCHANGE.—Manager, Mr. Geo. H.
Reid, 8, Park Street, Chatteris. Dramatic
and music and dancing licenses. Holding
capacity: Number of persons about 400.
No proper stage. Lighted by gas. Terms for
hiring: £1 1s. per night, £2 for two nights,
and £2 15s. for three. Amount of deposit required on booking, 10s. per night hired.
Dates of local fairs last Friday in April
and Friday before October 11.
Early closing, Wednesday; market, Friday

CHEADLE, Staffs.

Population, 5,186. Miles from London, 153.
TOWN HALL.—Proprietors, The Cheadle
(Staffordshire) Town Hall Co., Limited; Secre-
tary and Manager, Mr. S. W. Malkin, Rock
Cliffe, Cheadle, Staffs. Dramatic and music
and dancing licenses. Holding capacity: Num-
ber of persons, 700. Stage: Depth, 18ft. 6in.;
width, 27ft. 6in. Gas. Terms on application.
One-third of the rent required on booking.
Trains to Uttoxeter and thence about four
times daily.
Wakes: First Sunday after September 1.
Early closing day, Wednesday. Market day,
Friday.

CHEAM, near Sutton, Surrey.

PAROCHIAL HALL.—Proprietors, the Trustees; Manager, Rev. H. A. Wansbrough,
Cheam Rectory. Music license. Holding
capacity: Number of persons, 220. No proper
stage. Gas. Terms of hiring: 25s. Amount
of deposit required on booking, 12s. 6d.

CHELMSFORD, Essex.

Population, 17,638. Miles from London, 29.
CORN EXCHANGE (in Tindal Square).—
Secretary, Mr. W. W. Duffield; Hall-
keeper and Manager, Mr. Frank Willsher.
Dramatic license. Size of hall, 100 ft. by
45 ft.; 40 ft. high. Seating capacity, 800; 500
chairs provided. Open stage, 28 ft. by 20 ft.
Good dressing-rooms. The hall is lighted by
gas. No sharing terms. For terms of hiring,
apply the Secretary. Banner advertisements
on front of balcony outside, 48 ft. long; for
terms, apply the Manager.
Market day, Friday. Early closing day,
Wednesday.

CHELTENHAM, Glos.

Population, 51,000. Miles from London, 121.

OPERA HOUSE.—Managing Directors, Lieutenant-Colonel Croker-King, J.P. (Chairman), Colonel Rogers, J.P., and Mr. A. J. Skinner; General Manager, Mr. H. Oswald Redford.

WINTER GARDENS.—No dramatic license. Seats 2,500. Electric light.

TOWN HALL.—No dramatic license. Seats 1,600. Smaller Rooms, 500 and 250.

MONTPELLIER GARDENS.—Covered proscenium for open-air entertainments. Canvas awning over auditorium. No license.

MONTPELLIER ROTUNDA, VICTORIA ROOMS (two halls).—Manager, Mr. Edward B. Shenton. No license. Holding capacity: Number of persons, Rotunda 400, Victoria Rooms 1,000. Movable stage. Gas and electric light.

Early closing days, Wednesday and Saturday; market days, Thursday and Saturday.

Medical Officer: A.A.: Dr. E. J. Tatham, Beaufort House, Montpellier. Hours, 10-10.30 and 2-3. A.U.: The same.

CHERTSEY, Surrey.

Population, 12,762. Miles from London, 22.

CONSTITUTIONAL HALL.—Lessee, Mr. M. Walsh, Windsor Street, Chertsey Dramatic license. Holding capacity: Number of persons, 600. No proper stage. Lighted by gas. Terms for hiring: £2 2s. per night.

PUBLIC HALL.—Proprietors, Committee, Liberal Club; Licensee, Mr. J. Underwood. Dramatic and music and dancing licenses. Holding capacity: Number of persons, 200. Proper stage. No fittings. Gas. Terms for hiring: 15s. per day. Half-fee required on booking. Suitable for lectures, etc. Close to station.

Dates of local fairs: First Monday in Lent, May 14, first Monday in August, and September 26 (nearly obsolete). Several sites available for portables, etc.

Early closing day, Thursday. No market day.

CHESHAM, Bucks.

Population, 7,245. Miles from London, 30.

TOWN HALL.—Manager, Mr. John Harding, 59, Broad Street. Dramatic license. Holding capacity: Number of persons, 250-300. Ordinary platform. Lighted by gas. Terms for hiring: One night, £1 2s. 6d.; six nights, £4 10s. Amount of deposit required on booking: Half. Early closing day, Thursday.

CHESTER, Cheshire.

Population, 38,309. Miles from London, 179.

ROYALTY.—Manager, Mr. C. B. Fountaine; Musical Director, Mr. Herbert Stone. Full license. Electric light. Amount of printing required, 800. Usual matinée day, Saturday. Time of band rehearsal, 12 o'clock. Electric current, 210 volts.

MUSIC HALL.—Proprietors, Messrs. Phillipson and Golder. No dramatic license. Holds 1,000. Gas, but electric current, continuous, 210 and 420 volts for pictures. Printing, about 600 sheets for walls. Deposit on booking, £2.

TOWN HALL ASSEMBLY ROOM.—Proprietors, Corporation. Seats 800. Electric current, 210 and 420 volts, continuous.

Early closing day, Wednesday; market day, Saturday.

Medical Officer.—A.A.: Dr. Wm. Lees, Bars House, Foregate Street. Telegrams, " Lees, Chester "; 'phone, 130. A.U.: The same.

Agent.—M.H.A.R.A.: F. Massey, Cestrian Hotel. V.A.F.: The same.

CHESTERFIELD, Derbyshire.

Population, 30,000. Miles from London, 152.

ROYAL.—Proprietors, North of England Theatres, Limited; Managing Director, Mr. Frank Macnaghten.

CORPORATION THEATRE, Stephenson Memorial Hall.—Manager and Secretary, Mr. Geo. Proskey, Market Hall. Dramatic and music, singing and dancing licenses. Holding capacity: Number of persons, over 1,000. Amount £70 to £80 Stage measurements; proscenium opening, 26ft. wide; 24ft. 6ins. high. Stage, 48ft. 6ins. wide, and 35ft. 8ins. from front to back. Height from stage to fly beam at front of stage, 20ft. 6ins., at back 19ft. Height of grid beams above front of stage, 43ft. (at back 19ft.). Electric light throughout. (Gas in emergency.) Amount of printing varies. Terms of hiring: Easter week, Whit week, Christmas week, £4 per day; other days, £3 per day, with 15 per cent. rebate allowed on all engagements for three or more consecutive nights if rent is paid in advance. Amount of deposit required on booking, 25 per cent. Tip-up chairs for front. Six new dressing-rooms. Scenery just repainted. Heated with hot water.

Local fairs, January, February, September, November, on the last Saturday in each month. April, May, July, on first Saturday in each of these months.

Early closing day, Wednesday; market day, Saturday.

Medical Officer: A.A.: Dr. E. W. Clarke, Kilblean House. Hours, 3-5 and 7-8.30, and will attend members at their own residences on receipt of message before 10 a.m.; A.U.: The same; M.H.A.R.A.: The same.

Agent.—A.U.: R. Outram, Midland Hotel, V.A.F.: The same. M.H.A.R.A.: The same.

CHICHESTER, Sussex.

Population, 12,244. Miles from London, 69.

CORN EXCHANGE.—Manager, Mr. J. W. Jacobs. Full license. Holding capacity: Number of persons, about 800. Proper stage; width, 47ft.; depth, 24ft.; height, 30ft.; opening, 28ft. Lighted by gas. Amount of printing required: 300 to 400 d.c. Terms for hiring: Concerts, etc., first night, £3 3s. (gas extra); dramatic and variety entertainments, first night, £4 4s. (gas extra); matinées, 10s. 6d. Amount of deposit required on booking, £1. Hall not let for matinées on Wednesdays, as it is required for the market from 9 a.m. to 4 p.m.

CONCERT HALL.—Secretary, Mr. H. Gordon States. Holding capacity: Number of persons, 300. Balcony and three private boxes. Well equipped. Gas. Stage: Width, 31ft.; depth, 19ft.; take 18ft. cloths; proscenium opening, 16ft. wide. Range of good scenery available. Large, well-fitted dressing-rooms for ladies and gentlemen. Terms on application.

Early closing day, Thursday; market day, Wednesday.

CHIPPING NORTON, Oxfordshire.

Population, 3,780. Miles from London, 88.

TOWN HALL.—Proprietors, Chipping Norton Corporation, Mr. Thos. Mace, Town Clerk. Licensed. Holding capacity: Number of persons between 300 and 400. Platform stage. Depth about 4ft. to level of floor; width across platform about 30ft.; from front to back of platform about 18ft. Lighted by gas. Terms for hiring: £1 10s. for one night, which includes two dressing-rooms. Amount of deposit required on booking, 10s.

Fair days first Wednesday in each month. Sites available for portables, circuses, etc., The Common. Apply to Mr. A. A. Webb, Market Place, Chipping Norton.

Early closing, Thursday; market, Wednesday; pay day, Saturday. Billposter. W. Lawrence, West Street, Chipping Norton.

CHORLEY, Lancs.

Population, 29,500. Miles from London, 202.

GRAND THEATRE.—Proprietor and Manager, Mr. George Testo Sante; Acting-Manager, Mr. Frank Sante; Musical Director, Mr. E. Brierley; Scenic Artist, Mr. F. Mordock. Full license. Holding capacity: Number of persons, 2,000; amount, £76. Stage measurements, 62ft. deep, 50ft. wide. Lighted by incandescent gas patent lamps. Amount of printing required· 600 sheets walls, 600 lithos. Usual matinée day, Saturday. Time of band rehearsal, 1 p.m.

TOWN HALL.—Has dramatic license. Apply to the Borough Surveyor. No scenery. Platform in form of half circle, 47ft. 6ins. wide by 27ft. by 31ft. 6ins. high from floor to ceiling. 1,000 chairs. No electricity.

Early closing day, Wednesday; market days, Tuesday and Saturday.

Medical officer.—A.A.: Dr. T. W. Jackson, 13, St. George's Street; A.U.: The same

CHORLTON-CUM-HARDY, Lancs.

Population, 10,000. Miles from London, 187.

THE PAVILION.—Proprietors, Messrs. H. B. Levy and J. E. Cardwell; Manager, Mr. Roger Alwyn; Musical Director, Mr. Arthur Rogerson. Dramatic license. Holding capacity, 1,000 persons. Stage measurements, 35ft. wide, 20ft. deep, 23ft. opening. Printing required, 250 wall sheets, 250 window lithos. Band rehearsal, 5.30 p.m. Adjoining Chorlton Station. New electric light installation. Wooden floor. Matinée Saturday.

Early closing day, Wednesday.

CINDERFORD, Glos.

Population, 12,000.

TOWN HALL.—Apply Secretary. Dramatic license.

Local fairs, third Monday in June, third Monday in October.

Portables visit here and have no trouble to get license. There are two pitches for circuses.

CIRENCESTER, Glos.

Population, 7,536. Miles from London, 95.

CORN HALL.—Manager and Secretary, Mr. F. H. Sealy. Dramatic license. Holding capacity: Number of persons, 800. Stage erected if required. Size of hall, 84ft. by 42ft. Lighted by gas, charged as per meter. Terms for hiring for entertainments (including 2 dressing-rooms): First night, £2 10s.; second night, £2; third and succeeding nights, £1 15s.; matinées (extra), 16s. 6d.; per week, £11. Amount of deposit required on booking, £1. The hall being used for market purposes on Monday, possession cannot be had on that day until 5 o'clock p.m. A nominal charge of 1s. per night is made to dramatic companies to cover cost of dramatic license.

Early closing day, Thursday; market day, Monday.

CLACTON-ON-SEA, Essex.

Population, 10,321. Miles from London, 72.

OPERETTA HOUSE.—Proprietor, Town Hall Buildings Co., Limited; Lessee and Manager, Mr. W. F. Jury; Resident Manager, Mr. A. Bloomfield. Double license. Holding capacity: Number of persons, 600; amount, £35. Stage measurements: Depth, 23ft. 6in.; width, 40ft.; proscenium opening, 22ft.; flats to 18ft. Electric light. Amount of printing required: 350 sheets. Usual matinée day, Wednesday. Time of band rehearsal, 2 o'clock. Best season of the year, August and September.

THE PALACE.—Managing Director, Mr. P. W. Willard.

PIER PAVILION.—Proprietors, Coast Development Co., Limited; Lessee, Mr. Harold Montague. Electric light. Seats 1,000.

WEST CLIFF GARDENS.—Proprietors, Messrs. Graham, Russell, and Bentley.

Early closing day, Wednesday.

Agent.—M.H.A.R.A.: J. Newstead, Carlton Hotel. V.A.F.: C. F. Hill, Marine Hotel.

CLAY CROSS, Derbyshire.

Population, 8,358. Miles from London, 148.

DRILL HALL (late Town Hall).—Dramatic and music licenses. Holding capacity: Number of persons, about 700. Stage measurements, 33ft. by 15ft.; from stage to ceiling, 15ft. Lighted by gas. Terms for hiring: £1 7s. 6d. one day, £2 10s. two days, £6 7s. 6d. for six days. Amount of deposit required on booking: 10s. on each day booked.

No local fairs.

Early closing day, Wednesday; market day, Saturday.

CLAYTON-LE-MOORS, Lancs.

Population, 8,153.

MECHANICS' HALL.—Chairman, Mr. J. S. Wilkinson, who lets the hall. No license, but is used for dancing. Holding capacity: Number of persons, 650. Stage: 27ft. by 11ft. 6in. Gas. Terms for hiring: £1 10s. per night. Amount of deposit required on booking: 10s. for one day, 20s. for two or more days. The only public room in the town.

Date of local fair: Whit Monday.

Early closing day, Wednesday; market day, Friday.

CLECKHEATON, Yorks.

Population, 13,000. Miles from London, 190.

TOWN HALL.—Manager, Clerk to the Council, Cleckheaton. Dramatic license. Holding capacity: Number of persons, 950. Proper stage, 28ft. wide, 18ft. deep, 26ft. high. Electric light. Terms for hiring: one night, £3 3s.; three nights, £6 17s. 6d.; six nights, £12 12s. Small extra charge for insurance for dramatic performances. Amount of deposit required is arranged when booking. Electric light, own resistance, giving up to 30 amps., off 460 volts circuit.

Early closing day, Wednesday; market day, Saturday.

CLEETHORPES, Lincs.

Population, 12,578. Miles from London, 157.

EMPIRE THEATRE.—Proprietor, Mr. J. Carter White. Holds about 800.

CIRCUS.—Proprietor, Mr. M. Dowse. Holds about 2,000.

ALEXANDRA HALL.—Has dramatic license. Holds about 700.

CONCERT HALL on the Pier.

Cleethorpes is essentially a summer town.

Agent.—V.A.F. : Alf Wilson, Leeds Arms.

CLITHEROE, Lancs.

Population, 11,414. Miles from London, 224.

PUBLIC HALL.—Secretary, Mr. Thos. Robinson, 3, Wesleyan Row. Fully licensed. Holding capacity: Number of persons, 900; amount, £50. Has proper stage, proscenium, and dressing-rooms. Lighted by gas. Amount of printing required: 50 sheets. Terms for hiring: Concerts and entertainments, Saturday night, £2; one night other than Saturday night, £1 15s.; two nights successively, £3 5s.; three nights successively, £4 10s.; four nights successively, £5 10s.; five nights successively, £6 5s.; six nights successively, £7 (exclusive of gas, which is to be paid for extra. No piano). The hall is 100ft. long, 42ft. broad, and 30ft. high. A deposit of 10s. per night required on booking. Regarding the fixture of scenery, arrangements must be made with the Secretary.

Early closing day, Wednesday; market day, Saturday.

CLONMEL, Co. Tipperary.

Population, 8,480. Miles from Dublin, 135.

RINK THEATRE.—Manager, Mr. J. Meagler. Dramatic license. Holding capacity: Number of persons, 700. Proper stage, 24ft. by 17ft.; proscenium, 12ft. from stage to fly. Lighted by gas. Amount of printing required: 300 day bills, 8 posters (8ft. by 8). Terms for hiring: One night, £2; two nights, £3 10s.; three, £4 10s.; one week, £9. Amount of deposit required on booking: Half rent.

Market days, Tuesday and Saturday.

CLUN, Salop.

TEMPERANCE HALL.—Manager, Mr. A. M. Rawlings. No license. Holding capacity: Number of persons, 150. Small stage. Oil lamps. Terms for hiring: 7s. 6d. per day, to be paid on booking.

Dates of local fairs: Last Fridays in January, March, June, August, September, November, and on May 11.

Sites available for portables, circuses, etc.: Castle Inn Close, Old Castle Grounds, Turnpike Field.

CLYDEBANK, Lanarkshire.

GAIETY THEATRE.—Proprietor and Director, Mr. A. E. Pickard. Full license. Holding capacity: Number of persons, 1,800; prices, 2d. to 6d. Stage measurements: 33ft. deep, 45ft. wide; proscenium, 17½ft. centre, 15ft. sides; stage to grid, 37ft. Electric light, 230 volts. Time of band rehearsal, 1 p.m. Varieties, twice nightly. Matinée Saturday.

Early closing day, Wednesday.

COALVILLE, Leicestershire.

Population, 17,000. Miles from London, 113.

PUBLIC HALL.—Proprietors, Exors. of the late Mr. Chas. Tyler.

Coalville is a populous colliery centre, five miles from Ashby-de-la-Zouch, nine from Loughborough, and twelve from Leicester. It is an urban centre of three wards, Coalville (Central), Whitwick, and Hugglescote, adjoining. Public Hall has accommodation for 500 or 600. Alterations to the building were contemplated. In September the license was granted conditionally that alterations were made. Portables seldom visit, but have made long stays at Whitwick with success. There are good sites for circus pitches. Alfresco concerts are unknown. The fair is held about the middle of May, whilst a moderate assemblage of showpeople pitch the first week in August for the local wake.

Early closing day, Wednesday; market day, Friday.

COATBRIDGE, Lanarkshire.

Population, 44,008. Miles from London, 393.

THEATRE ROYAL.—Proprietors, The Coatbridge Theatre Co., Limited; Managing Director, Mr. R. C. Buchanan; Acting-Manager, Mr. John Commins; Musical Director, Mr. J. W. Hatton. Full license. Holding capacity: Number of persons, 2,000. Stage measurements: Depth, 30ft.; width, 75ft.; between fly rails, 33ft.; proscenium opening, 26ft. Electric light, 240 volts.

TEMPERANCE HALL.—Manager, Mr. A. Cullender. Holds 800.

TOWN HALL.—Licensee, Mr. S. H. Gemmell. Holds 1,800. Electric light. Suitable for picture and other entertainments.

Agent.—M.H.A.R.A.: A. Dipple, Deerhound Hotel; V.A.F.: The same.

COBHAM, Surrey.

Population, 3,902. Miles from London, 19.

VILLAGE HALL.—Proprietors, Committee of Trustees; Manager, Mr. A. Burbidge. Dramatic and music and dancing licenses. Holding capacity: Number of persons, 500. Stage: Depth, 14ft.; width, 28ft.; proscenium, 20ft. wide. Gas. Terms for hiring: Dramatic, £3 3s. one night, £4 4s. two nights; concerts, £2 2s. per night. Full terms required on booking. Three large dressing-rooms, heated throughout. Two full sets scenery.

Date of local fair: December 13. Antelope Meadow.

COLCHESTER, Essex.

Population, 38,373. Miles from London, 52¼.

THEATRE ROYAL.—Proprietor, Mr. Chas. Macdona; Lessee and Manager, Mr. F. Graham Macdona. Double license. Holds 1,000 at £65. Stage opening, 22ft. by 27ft. Floats to back wall 36ft., wall to wall, 45ft. Gas and electric, 210 volts. Printing, 500 walls, 500 windows.

HIPPODROME.—Proprietors, the Colchester Hippodrome, Co., Limited; Directors, Messrs. Fredk. Mouillot and Walter de Frece; Manager, Mr. Jack de Frece; Acting-Manager, Mr. Ben de Frece. Booking circuit, De Frece circuit, 178, Charing Cross Road; Musical Director, Mr. Karl Heber. Double license. Holding capacity: Number of persons, 1,800. Electric light. Time of band rehearsal, 1.30.

CORN EXCHANGE.—Secretary, Mr. Henry H. Elwes, High Street; Superintendent, Mr. F. T. Peek, 47, North Station Road. Double license. Holding capacity: Number of persons, 1,400 to 1,500; seating provided for 800. Size of platform, 25ft. by 16ft.; can be made larger if required. Terms for hiring: £5 5s. one night; £8 8s. two nights; £10 10s. three nights; six nights, £15 15s. Gas extra. Deposit required on booking. No shares. Hall available for evening entertainments on Saturday by special arrangement with the Superintendent.

DRILL HALL.—Apply, the Secretary.

MOOT HALL.—Available for concerts and organ recitals only. Seating capacity, 600. Further information from the Borough Accountant, Town Hall.

A town of nearly 40,000 inhabitants (exclusive of the military, which number another 5,000), largely industrial, and comprised of artisans engaged in the engineering, boot, and clothing industries, and a fair sprinkling of retired military officers, who, with the regular military population, enter largely into all classes of amusements. No portables visit the town. Sites for alfresco concerts and circus pitches are available. As regards alfresco concerts, it would be necessary to arrange with the municipal authorities to hold them in one or the other of their enclosed spaces. St. Denis Cattle Fair is proclaimed by the mayor and corporation in state on October 20.

Preparations are being actively pushed forward for the great historical Colchester Pageant, to be held in June, 1909, under the direction of Mr. Louis N. Parker. Colchester, being easily accessible by railway, is suitable for the purpose of flying matinées from London companies.

Early closing day, Thursday; market day, Saturday.

Medical Officer.—A.A.: Dr. J. Becker, Bays House, Trinity Street.

Agent.—M.H.A.R.A.: Geo. Triscutt, George Hotel. V.A.F.: C. S. Walker, Lamb Hotel.

RECOMMENDED APARTMENTS.

Mrs. Hocking, 91, High Street.—5 bedrooms, 2 sitting-rooms; baths; 2 pianos.

COLEFORD, Glos.

Population, 2,541. Miles from London, 151.

TOWN HALL.—Manager, Mr. John Wyatt. Holding capacity: Number of persons, 350. Platform, about 20 ft. deep, can be enlarged; about 30 or 40 ft. wide. Lighted by gas. Terms for hiring: 20s. first night, 15s. per night afterwards. Amount of deposit required on booking, 10s.

Very old hall, time of Charles II.

Fairs (pleasure), June 20 and August 21, last Friday. Lord of the Manor grants rights over waste lands in the Manor of Staunton to certain good citizens every Friday and fair days. Circuses and all outdoor entertainments can be held on the waste ground in the town on all chartered days.

Early closing, Thursday; market, Tuesday.

COLERAINE, Londonderry.

Population, 6,845. Miles from Dublin, 173.

TOWN HALL.—Proprietors, The Coleraine Council; Manager, The Town Clerk. Permanent proscenium, head and footlights. Dressing-rooms. Seats 750.

Early closing day, Thursday; market day, Saturday.

Coleraine is visited by portables, and there is no difficulty in securing a license. Sites for alfresco concerts and circus pitches are easily obtainable. Coleraine's population is much larger during summer months. The town is on the line between Belfast and Londonderry, in the centre of a large, rich agricultural district. Local trades are the manufacture of whisky and linen.

COLNE, Lancs.

Population, 26,150. Miles from London, 219.

THEATRE ROYAL.—Lessee and Manager, Mr. Gerald Harding; Musical Director, Mr. W.

H. Tillotson. Dramatic license, restricted. Holding capacity: Number of persons, 1,000; amount, £50. Stage measurements: Width (wall to wall), 42ft.; depth, 27ft.; fly floor, 18ft. 6ins.; grid, 28ft.; proscenium opening, 21ft. Electric lighting, direct current. 210 volts. Printing required: 250 sheets posting, 250 lithos. Usual matinée day, Saturday. Time of band rehearsal, 1 o'clock.

MUNICIPAL HALL.—Secretary, Mr. H. W. Croasdale. Music and dancing license. Holding capacity: Number of persons, 1,100. Bare stage; no scenery. Measurements, 30ft. 6in. by 15ft. Gas and electric light. Electrically fit-up. Terms for hiring: £10 weekly, lighting and piano extra. Amount of deposit required on booking, £5.

VICTORIA HALL.—Manager, Mr. Bradshaw. Music and dancing license. Holding capacity: Number of persons, 650. Stage measurements: 29ft. by 42ft.; proscenium, 11ft. high by 18ft. Lighted by incandescent gas. Amount of deposit required on booking: 25 per cent. of hire.

CENTRAL HALL.—Proprietor, Mr. J. Duckworth. Music and dancing license. Holding capacity, 700. Electric light throughout, 240 volts. An electric transformer is installed for kinematograph work, giving 50 amperes and 80 volts. " Premier " Animated Pictures every evening. No open dates 1909.

Population is residential and industrial. The latter class are composed mostly of cotton factory operatives, foundry, and loom making hands. Fairs are held on the second Wednesdays to following Mondays in March, May, and October in the Dockray Fair Ground. The town is not visited by portables. No sites are available for alfresco concerts, but a good circus pitch is obtainable.

Early closing day, Tuesday; market day, Wednesday.

COLWYN BAY, Denbigh.

Population, 13,000. Miles from London, 219.

PUBLIC HALL.—Proprietors, Syndicate; Manager, Mr. Chas. R. Chaplin, Sea View, Colwyn Bay; Acting-Manager, Mr. A. C. Meir; Musical Director, Miss Oban. Double license. Holding capacity: Number of persons, 600. Depth and width of stage and proscenium measurements: 40ft. by 18ft.; opening, 23ft. by 15ft.; 16ft. under grid; stock scenery, flats 14ft. 6in. high. Lighted by gas. Time of band rehearsal, 1 o'clock. Matinée day, Wednesday or Saturday. No surrounding halls are barred. Season, full week; winter, three nights per week only booked. Terms, share or rental. Electric current for pictures up to 15 amps., 220 volts; above 15, 440 volts, direct.

VICTORIA PIER PAVILION.—Manager, Mr. W. A. Pryce Davis. Double license. Holding capacity: Number of persons, 3,500. Proper stage; proscenium, 20ft. by 30ft.; height to grid, 50ft. Electric light. Insurance fees too high to allow drama. Good opening for variety show.

CONGLETON, Cheshire.

Population, 10,707. Miles from London, 157.

TOWN HALL.—Manager, Mr. E. Skelland, Borough Treasurer. Dramatic license. Holding capacity: Number of persons, 900 (seated). Stage measurements: Depth, 18 ft.; width, 40 ft. Depth can be increased at an extra charge. Lighted by gas. Amount of printing required averages about 250 to 350 d.c's. Terms for hiring: One night, £2 5s.; two nights, £4 4s.; three nights, £5 15s. 6d.; four nights, £7 7s.: five nights, £8 15s.; six nights, £10. Amount of deposit required on booking: 25 per cent. of rent.

Local fairs, May 12 and Nov. 22. Site for portable theatres, etc.—the only site is the Corporation Market and Fair Ground.

Early closing, Wednesday; market, Saturday.

CONSETT, Durham.

Population, 9,694. Miles from London, 270.

NEW THEATRE.—Lessee and Manager, Mr. Hugh Robertson; Resident Manager, Mr Lloyd Clarance. Seats 1,500. Heated by hot-water pipes. Dimensions of stage:—From wall to wall, 37ft. 6ins.; from footlights to wall, 31ft.; proscenium opening, 21ft. 6ins.; height of ditto, 25ft.; gridiron from stage, 40ft.; height of grooves, 21ft.; from fly rail to fly rail, 29ft. 4ins.; can take up cloths, 29ft. by 21ft.

NEW TOWN HALL.—Manager, Mr. Thomas Wm. Welford, Solicitor. Licensed. Holding capacity: Number of persons, 1,000. Amount, £70. Platform measurements: depth, 12ft.; 22ft. opening. Gas light. Amount of printing required: 500 day bills. Terms for hiring: One night, £1 10s.; two, £2 15s.; three, £3 15s.; four, £4 10s.; five, £5 5s.; six, £6; seven, £7 12s. 6d. Amount of deposit required on booking, £3 for week; £1 10s. for a less time.

DALY'S NEW HALL.—Proprietor, Mr. Jas. Daly. No license, but such can be obtained when necessary. Height of hall, 20ft.; width, 35ft. 6ins.; length, 70ft. Seating accommodation for 650; with smaller hall to seat 100. Terms: One night, £1; two nights, £1 16s. 8d.; three nights, £2 10s.; four nights, £3: five nights, £3 10s.; and six nights, £4. Small hall, 7s. 6d. per night. These terms are exclusive of gas, which is 3s. 8d. per 1,000 cubic ft.

Population of places immediately surrounding is estimated at over 30,000. The people are almost entirely engaged in iron and steel manufacture and coal mining industry. No portable theatres have visited this district for very many years—in fact, ever since the New Theatre was opened. There is no difficulty, however, in getting dramatic licenses from local justices in Petty Sessions. There are sites for circuses, shows, and amusements, which are almost continually visiting the town. Principal sites, Number One field, apply Mr. N. Elsdon; and Barr House Field, apply Mr. S. Rowe. No fair is held in Consett, but open-air market held in main street every Saturday. Wages at the works and mines are paid fortnightly, and the town is very busy on "pay" Fridays and Saturdays.

Early closing day, Wednesday; market day, Saturday.

RECOMMENDED APARTMENTS.

Mrs. Harris, 12, Livingstone Street.—1 bedroom, 1 sitting-room.

CONWAY, Cam.

Population, 4,681. Miles from London, 225. TOWN HALL.—Proprietors, The Corporation; Manager, the Town Clerk. Holds about 750. Has dramatic license.

Early closing day, Wednesday; market day, Saturday.

COOKSTOWN, Co. Tyrone.

Population, 3,841. Miles from Dublin, 166.

NEW COURT HOUSE.—Manager, Colonel H. Irvine, Omagh; Caretaker, Mr. John Black. Holding capacity: Number of persons, 300.

Planks can be hired for stage. Lighted by Gas. Terms for hiring, 5s. per night.

Markets, Tuesday and Saturday.

CORK, Co. Cork.

Population, 76,122. Miles from Dublin. 165.

OPERA HOUSE.—Proprietors, the Cork Opera House Co., Limited; Manager, Mr. R. J. Bell. Double license. Stage, 47ft. deep by 35ft.; proscenium opening, 29ft. Electric light, 230 volts. Printing. 700 sheets.

PALACE THEATRE.—Proprietors, Palace Theatre, Cork, Ltd.; Managers, Mr. Thos. F. O'Brien; Musical Director, Mr. Jas. C. Evans; Stage Manager, Mr. M. Malone. Music and dancing license. Holding capacity: Number of persons, 2,500. Electric light. Time of band rehearsal, 2 o'clock p.m. Monday. No regular matinée day. No surrounding halls are barred. Hall fully equipped all modern. requirements. House is heated throughout. Two performances nightly.

ASSEMBLY ROOMS.—Manager, Mr. Alex. McEwan. Double license. Holding capacity: Number of persons, 1,000. Proper stage, 20ft. by 45ft.; no proscenium. Gas and electric light, voltage, 460. Amount of printing required: About 500 sheets. Rental or sharing. Amount of deposit required on booking: £5.

CLARENCE HALL, IMPERIAL HOTEL.—Balls, select entertainments, etc. Manager, Mr. A. C. Freeman.

TOWN HALL, MUNICIPAL BUILDINGS.—Mr. Albert May, the Lord Mayor of Cork. Secretary, Mr. Daniel F. Giltinan.

TOWN HALL, DOUGLAS—2 miles from Cork City, with a ten-minutes' service of trams. Two large woollen mills in vicinity. Manager, The Rev. C. M. O'Brien, C.C.

ATHLETIC GROUND.—Five acres, with Grand Stand. Apply, Mr. J. J. Buckley, Central Hotel.

Population both residential and industrial.

The town is visited occasionally by portables, and there is no difficulty whatever in obtaining sites for alfresco concerts or circus pitches in most suitable and convenient places, or to obtain licenses from the Lord Mayor and Council.

Cork Agricultural Society, 21, Cook Street, Cork. Secretary. Mr. M. W. Litton.

Spring Show—Cattle, swine, poultry, etc. etc. April 6 and 7, 1909. Summer, July 7 and 8, 1909. Autumn, October 14, 1909. Secretary, Mr. M. W. Litton.

Great Horse and Sheep Show. Secretary, Mr. M. W. Litton.

Dog Show. Hon. Secretary, Mr. W. E. Burke, C.E.

All above held at the Co. Cork Agricultural Society's Grounds, Cork Park.

Fairs and markets.—Second Friday in each month at Fair Hill. Cattle market every Monday and Thursday. Horse fairs at Cork Park Racecourse the day after Easter Monday, spring and autumn race meetings. Butter, corn, and general market every day. Marsh's cattle auction every Tuesday and Saturday at Copley Street. Superintendent of tolls and markets, Mr. Geo. Sutton, jun.

The Irish Industrial Development Association (incorporated). Secretary, Mr. E. J. Riordan, 28, Marlboro' Street, Cork. This association holds an annual show in Cork.

Also, a show is held in Cork in May by the Co. and City of Cork Industrial Association.

Market day, Tuesday.

Agent.—M.H.A.R.A.: J. Wilkie, newsagent, King Street. Mr. Arrow, 13, King Street.

RECOMMENDED APARTMENTS.

Mrs. McKenna, 3 Emmet Place.—1 combined, 2 bedrooms (3 beds), 1 sitting room and piano,

CORWEN, Merioneth.

Population, 2,723.   Miles from London, 203.
ASSEMBLY ROOMS.—Manager, Mr. David
Davies. Secretary, to whom communications
should be addressed, Mr. L. Lloyd John,
Solicitor. Fully licensed. Holding capacity:
Number of persons, about 350. Length of
room, exclusive of stage, 42ft.; width of room,
32ft.; length of stage, 25ft.; width, 8ft.; may
be extended 6ft. Lighted by gas Terms for
hiring: £1 for one night, £1 15s. two nights.
Amount of deposit required on booking, 10s.
   Local fairs, third Tuesday monthly.   Sites
for circuses, etc., Lewis Edwards' field.
   Early closing, Wednesday.   Markets, Tuesday and Friday.

COVENTRY, Warwickshire.

Population, 91,000. Miles from London, 94.
OPERA HOUSE.—Proprietor and Manager,
Mr. W. Bennett; Acting-Manager, Mr. I. A.
Spencer. Electric current, alternating, 200
volts.
EMPIRE.—Proprietor, Mr. Geo. Dance; Resident Manager, Mr Kay Draco. Two houses
a night. Bookings, apply Mr. Dance or T.
Barrasford. Electric current, alternating, 200
volts. Bars the local Hippodrome and Leamington.
HIPPODROME.—Proprietors, Coventry Hippodrome Co., Limited; Managing Director,
Mr. S. T. Newsome. Bars local halls and Nuneaton and Leamington. Holds 1,200. Two
houses a night. Electric current, 200 volts,
alternating.
   An interesting old Warwickshire city, the
centre of the English cycle and motor industry. The population, which is mainly industrial, has increased rapidly in late years,
the total at the census taken in 1891 being
53,004, which had increased to 70,296 in 1901,
83,792 in 1906, and 91,000 at the present time,
the last figures being based upon a corporation census. This rate of increase is still
maintained, and in connection with the motor
trade, several extensive new works have been
recently constructed, while others have been
considerably enlarged. Other industries include general engineering, the new Ordnance
and gun works, watch making, silk weaving, ribbon making, etc., in connection
with which large numbers of hands are engaged. As regards stage amusements, the
Opera House is well supported. In addition
there are two new halls as set out above.
As regards other entertainments, open air concerts, etc., are given during the summer at
the cricket and football grounds, the Butts,
and during the winter months the following
halls, which are equipped with electric light,
200 volts, alternating, are available:—
Baths Assembly Hall, Priory Street, and
St. Mary's Hall (both belonging to
the Corporation), Priory Assembly Rooms;
Assembly Rooms, Union Street; Drill Hall,
Queen Victoria Road, Little Masonic Hall, Little
Park Street; and the Co-operative Assembly
Rooms, West Orchard. The city is occasionally visited by portables, and circus proprie-
tors will find an excellent pitch on th ePool
Meadow, a large open space in the heart of
the city, belonging to the Corporation, from
which body courteous and considerate treat-
ment may always be relied upon. The Pool
Meadow is also the venue of the large pleasure
fair, which opens on Whit Monday.
   Early closing day, Thursday; market day,
Friday.
   Medical Officer.—A.A.: Dr. R. Rice, Bailey

Road, Gosford Green; 'phone, 582; hours, 2—3.
A.U.: The same.
   Agent.—A.U.: H. C. Edwards, Golden Cross
Hotel, Hay Lane.   M.H.A.R.A.: The same.
V.A.F.: The same.

RECOMMENDED APARTMENTS.

Mrs. Foster, 79, Lower Ford Street.—2 bedrooms, 1 sitting-room.
   Mrs. G. Rod ers.—1 sitting-room. piano; 2 bedrooms, combined.

COWES, Isle of Wight.

Population, 8,654.   Miles from London, 87.
PAVILION, COWES VICTORIA PIER.—Proprietors, Cowes Urban District Council;
Manager, the Surveyor, Mr. John W. Webster, is
in charge of the pier. Music and dancing
license. Holds about 200. Gas. The Pavilion
is already let for 1909 season, from three weeks
before Whitsuntide to September 30, and for
Easter week.
   FORESTERS' HALL (WEST COWES).—Proprietors, Foresters', Court 1,822; Manager, Mr.
John Jolliffe. Dramatic and music and dancing licenses. Holds 500. Stage, 26ft. by 24ft.
Gas, electric light for pictures. Terms on
application. Deposit required on booking:
Three days, 10s.; one week, £1.
   TOWN HALL (EAST COWES).—Has dramatic license. Holds 500. Apply, Collector,
"Eureka," Grange Road, East Cowes.
   VICTORIA HALL.—Manager, Mr. H. Kings-
well. Dramatic and music and dancing
licenses. Holding capacity: Number of persons, 550. Stage measurements: 27 ft. wide,
22 ft. deep, 17 ft. 2 in. high; proscenium,
18 ft. Gas and electric light. Terms for
hiring: Sharing or rental. Stock of scenery.
Early closing, Wednesday.   No market day.

COWDENBEATH, Fife.

Population, 10,000. Miles from London, 413.
GRAND THEATRE.—Proprietor, Mr. John
Pollock; Manager, Mr. John Millar; Musical
Director, Mr. Duncan Gilfillon; Scenic Artist,
Mr. Charles Stewart. Full license. Holding
capacity: Number of persons, 1,200. Stage
measurements: 21ft. from footlights; pro-
scenium, 26ft. by 15ft. Lighted by gas.
Amount of printing required, 250 sheets. Usual
matinée day, Saturday.
   Early closing day, Wednesday.

CRADLEY HEATH, Staffs.

Population, 6,733. Miles from London, 138.
EMPIRE THEATRE OF VARIETIES.—Proprietors, Limited Company; Manager, Mr. John
H. Morton. Booking circuit, Midlands. Musical Director, Mr. Wood. Double license.
Holding capacity: Number of persons, 1,200;
amount, £40. Stage measurements, 45ft. by
30ft.; proscenium, 22ft. 6ins. wide. Gas and
electric light (200 volts, alternating). Time of
band rehearsal, 1 p.m.

RECOMMENDED APARTMENTS.

Mrs. Boswell, 5, St. Luke's Street.—Single and
double-bedded room and sitting-room.

CRAMLINGTON, Northumberland.

Population, 6,437. Miles from London, 282.
CO-OPERATIVE HALL.—Secretary, Mr. W.
Simpson. Not licensed. Holding capacity:
Number of persons, 420; 6d. and 1s. usually
charged for admission. Platform. Lighted
by gas. Amount of deposit required on
booking: 10s. and £1. The same Society

have halls at Dudley, Seaton Burn, Sleckburn, Shankhouse, Westmoor, Burradon, and Dinnington, which are all locally managed.

CRANBROOK, Kent.

Population, 3,949. Miles from London, 42.
VESTRY HALL.—Manager, Mr. F. Iggulden. Fully licensed. Holding capacity, £15. Lighted by gas. Terms for hiring, £1 1s. performance. Early closing, Thursday; market, Wednesday.

CRAVEN ARMS, Salop.

ASSEMBLY ROOMS.—Size of the room, 60ft. by 34ft. Large stage. Room lighted by gas. Terms: £1 10s. for 1 night; for 2 nights, £2 10s.; gas charged extra. Piano in room at 5s. per night extra. Dramatic license.

CRAWLEY, Sussex.

Miles from London, 39.
GEORGE ASSEMBLY ROOM.—Proprietor, Mr. C. E. Green. Dramatic and music and dancing licenses. Holding capacity: Number of persons, 400. Stage: Width, 21ft.; depth, 17ft.; proscenium, 12ft.; fitted with flies, batons, drop scene, box scene, four cloths. Electric light. Amount of printing required: 20 6-sheet pictures and small bills accordingly. Terms for hiring: £2 2s. per night. Amount of deposit required on booking: £1 1s.
Dates of local fairs: May 8 and September 9. Early closing day, Wednesday; markets, monthly.

CREWE, Ches.

Population, 42,074. Miles from London, 158.
NEW OPERA HOUSE (late Lyceum).— Lessee and Manager, Mr. H. G. Dudley Bennett; Resident Manager, Mr. Chas. Howard; Musical Director, Mr. Alex. Probert. Holds 1,800; amount, £80. Stage measurements: 42ft. deep, 58ft. wide, 26ft. proscenium. Gas and electric light. Amount of printing required, 300 wall posters, 400 windows. Time of band rehearsal varies.
CO-OPERATIVE HALL.—Manager, Mr. Thomas Chapman. Dramatic and singing and dancing licenses. Holding capacity: Number of persons, 1,200. Sloping stage, 25ft. by 20ft. Electric footlights. Gas and electric light; voltage, 230, direct current. Twelve private posting stations, rent free. Terms for hiring: One night, £1 15s.; £10 10s. per week. Amount of deposit required on booking, £3 3s.
TOWN HALL.—Secretary, Mr. R. J. Hampton. Double license. Seats 650. Early closing day, Wednesday; market day, Saturday.
Agent.—M.H.A.R.A.: Ernest Leech, Angel Hotel; V.A.F.: The same.

RECOMMENDED APARTMENTS.

Mrs. Hulland, 91, Albert Street.—Bedroom and sitting-room; piano.

CREWKERNE, Somerset.

Population, 4,226. Miles from London, 132.
VICTORIA HALL.—Manager, Mr. F. E. Swabey. Double license. Holding capacity: Number of persons, 400 chairs. Proper stage. Stage measurements, 29ft. by 20ft. 9in.; height from stage to roof, 18ft. 6in. Lighted by gas. Terms for hiring: £2 2s. first night; £1 1s.

second night; longer time special terms. Amount of deposit required on booking, 25 per cent. Two dressing-rooms.
Date of local fairs, Sept. 4 and 5. The Fair field is let for Circuses, Portables, etc., and is owned by the Crewkerne Fair and Market Company, proprietors of the Victoria Hall. Early closing, Thursday; market, Saturday.

CRICH, near Matlock Bath, Derbyshire.

Population, 3,000. Miles from London, 144.
There are no rooms suitable for stage performances, but there are three schools, which are let at about 7s. 6d. per night for entertainments.
Date of local fair: October 11.
The Market Place is available for portables and circuses.

CRIEFF, Perth.

Population, 5,208. Miles from London, 440.
PORTEOUS HALL.—Apply Colville and Drysdale. Solicitors, Crieff. Fully licensed. Holding capacity: Number of persons, 800. Amount £45. Stage, 20ft. by 14ft.; can be extended to 26ft. by 17ft., or 32ft. by 14ft. Lighted by gas. Terms for hiring: Theatrical, £2 10s.; Concerts, £1 15s. per night. Amount of deposit required on booking, 10s.
Highland Gathering, third Saturday of August. Sites: Market Park and James Square. Apply Highland Gathering Secretary.

CROMER, Norfolk.

Population, 3,781. Miles from London, 137.
TOWN HALL.—Secretary, Mr. James King Frost. Has dramatic license. Holding capacity: Number of persons, 750. Stage, 25 ft. wide, 15 ft. 6 in. deep, 14 ft. 10 in. high. Gas and electric light. Terms for hiring on application.
LECTURE HALL.—Manager, Mr. R. L. Randall. Not licensed. Holding capacity: Number of persons, 300. No proper stage. Electric light. Terms for hiring: 15s. per day. Amount of deposit required on booking, 25 per cent.
Early closing, Thursday.

CROOK, Co. Durham.

Population, 11,471. Miles from London, 240.
THEATRE ROYAL. — Proprietors, Messrs. Wallace Davidson, Limited; Managing Director, Mr. Wallace Davidson. Holds 800.
MECHANICS' HALL.—Manager, Mr. Robert Scales. Holds 400. Terms, 13s. per night, or £3 10s. for the week. Amount required on booking, 5s. and upwards, according to number of nights engaged.
Population is industrial, engaged in mining operations, the making of coke, brick and tile factories, and leather dressing. Collieries in the district are owned by Messrs. Pease and Partners, Limited, and Messrs. Boles Vaughan, Limited. These firms pay on alternate weeks, the advantage of which is obvious, most places in the North having a "pay" and a "baff" week. There is no local fair, and the town is not visited by portables. Kinematograph shows and roundabouts are frequently pitched in the market-place, and do good business. Occasionally a circus visits the town and pitches in a field on the confines. A play if appreciated on the Monday night will receive good support during the week.
Early closing day, Wednesday; market day, Saturday.

CROWLE, Lincoln.

Population, 2,769. Miles from London, 171½.
MARKET HALL.—Apply Mr. Wm. Sanderson, Church Street, Crowle. Licensed for concerts only. Holding capacity: Number of persons, about 400. Stage measurements, 20ft. wide (about), 11ft. depth. No proscenium. Lighted by gas. Terms for hiring: One night, 21s.; two nights, 15s. per night; extra nights, 10s. Amount of deposit required on booking, 25 per cent.
Fairs end of May and November.
Early closing, Wednesday. Market, Friday.

CROYDON, Surrey.

Population, 133,895. Miles from London, 10.
THE GRAND.—Manager, Mr. Roland Daniel; Musical Director, Mr. V. Chalder. Double license. Holding capacity: Number of persons, 1,800. Amount, £140. Stage measurements: Depth, 50ft.; width, 44ft.; width between fly rails, 32ft. 6in.; height to grid, 55ft.; proscenium opening, 27ft. 6in. Electric light. Amount of printing required: 1,500 sheets and 600 d.c. lithos. Usual Matinée day, Thursday. Voltage 110. All halls and towns within five miles barred.
THEATRE ROYAL.—Lessees, Moss's Empires, Ltd.; Managing Director, Mr Oswald Stoll; Double license. Holding capacity: Number of persons, 1,500 (about). Amount £85 (about). Stage measurements, 50ft. by 25ft. Electric light. Amount of printing required, 600 wall sheets, 500 lithos. Usual matinée day, Wednesday. Time of band rehearsal, 1 p.m. Run as a picture show with illustrated songs.
EMPIRE.—Proprietors, the London Theatres of Varieties, Limited; Manager, Mr. Eustace Jay. Holds 2,000.
PUBLIC HALL.—Manager, Mr. Edmund C. Grigsby. Double license. Holding capacity: Number of persons, 700. Amount, as per arrangement of prices. Stage measurements: Depth, 18ft.; width, 39ft.; height, 16ft.; proscenium opening, 21ft.; 24ft. between fly rails. Electric light, 200 volts, alternating. Terms for hiring: £5 5s. per night; discount, 25 per cent. on three to five night bookings; 33⅓ per cent. on six or more; matinées, £1 11s. 6d. extra. Amount of deposit required on booking, one-third charge.
THE STANLEY HALLS.—Proprietors, Board of Management; Manager, Mr. Frank Theobalds. Dramatic and Music and dancing licenses. Holding capacity: Number of persons, 600. Amount, £40. Stage, 40ft. by 23ft.; opening 22ft. by 14ft. 6in. Electric light, alternating current, 200 volts. Terms for hiring: £5 per night; longer by arrangement. One-third required on booking.
PEMBROKE HALL.—Proprietors, Constitutional Club Co., Limited; Secretary, Mr. J. L. Keating. Dramatic and music and dancing licenses. Holding capacity: Number of persons, 500. Stage: Width, 40ft.; depth, 14ft.; opening, 27ft. Electric light, 230 volts 24 ampères constant.
MILTON ROAD HALL.—Proprietors, Vicar and Churchwardens of St. James'; Manager, Mr. R. Goodman, 220, Albert Road. Dramatic and music and dancing licenses. Holding capacity: Number of persons, 400. Good stage; depth, 10ft., width, 25ft. Gas. Terms for hiring: £1 10s. per night. Deposit required on booking, 5s. Hall rarely available during winter months.
Croydon Fair, October 1.
Early closing, Wednesday; market days, Thursday and Saturday.

RECOMMENDED APARTMENTS.

Mrs. Jarrett, 26, Wadden Old Road.—2 sitting-rooms, 2 bedrooms, combined.

CUCKFIELD, near Haywards Heath, Surrey.

PUBLIC HALL.—Proprietors, The Cuckfield Urban District Council; Manageress, Miss Payne, Hatchlands, Cuckfield. No license (must be applied for in each instance). Holding capacity: Number of persons, 200. No proper stage. Lighted by gas. Terms for hiring on application. Full amount of hire required on booking.
No local fairs.
No sites available for portables, etc.

CUPAR, Fife.

Population, 4,511.
UNION STREET HALL.—Communications to Messrs. J. and G. Innes, *Herald* Office. Holding capacity: Number of persons, 1,000. Height of hall from floor to ceiling, 26ft.; width, 48ft.; length from back of gallery to front of stage, 54ft.; width between galleries, 36ft Stage, 35ft. by 23ft.; proscenium columns, 21ft. 6in. apart; act drop, 16ft. 6in. wide; height of fit-up, 12ft. 6in.; height of ceiling, 20ft. Terms for hiring: Dramatic entertainments, first night, £2; subsequent nights (each), £1 5s. Heating, 3s. Gas, per hour, 2s.; with footlights and toplights, 2s. 6d. Fire in ante-room, 1s. Fit-up and scenery, per night, 10s. The town officer is billposter; can take one 12-sheet poster, six 18-sheet posters, two 24-sheet posters, and one 36-sheet poster.
CORN EXCHANGE HALL.—Secretary, Mr. J. K. Tasker. Holding capacity: Number of persons, 800. Dimensions of hall, inclusive of orchestra, 86ft. by 52ft.; size of orchestra, 33ft. by 17½ft. Lighted by gas. Terms for hiring: £2 2s. first night; £1 1s. subsequent. Amount of deposit required on booking, half rent.
The population of the parish is composed of the residential and industrial classes, there being two factories, an iron-foundry, a tannery, and two large printing works in the town.
The date of the annual local fair in Cupar is the first Tuesday of August. Many farm servants come into the town, and large numbers of itinerant shows are also present to entertain them. The town is regularly visited by portables, and there is no difficulty with regard to a license. The site for all outside entertainments, such as circuses, etc., is a large open-air space, called "The Fluthers."
Early closing day, Thursday; market day, Tuesday.

DALBEATTIE, Kirkcudbrightshire.

TOWN HALL.—Manager, Mr. J. W. Stocks. Fully licensed. Holding capacity: 500. Stage, 2ft. by 18ft. Gas. Printing required: 50 day bills, 3 or 4 posters. Terms: £1 5s. per night; £2 5s. two nights; £3 three nights; £4 10s. per week. Amount of deposit required on booking, 10s.
Public park available at all times for fairs etc. Local fair in October.

DALKEITH, Edinburgh.

Population, 6,753. Miles from London, 390.
FORESTERS' HALL.—Secretary, Mr. James Lindsay. Double license. Holding capacity: Number of persons, 800; Portable platform. Gas and electric light. Terms for hiring: Concert, £2; dramatic performance, £3. Amount of deposit required on booking, 10s.
Shopkeepers' monthly holiday, second Tuesday of every month. Pay nights, Friday and Saturday each week.

DALTON-IN-FURNESS, Lancs.

Population, 13,020. Miles from London, 260.

CO-OPERATIVE HALL.—Proprietors, Dalton Co-operative Society; Manager, Mr. J. Werry. Double license. Holding capacity: Number of persons, 900; amount, £40. Stage, but no proscenium. Measurements: 35ft. by 15ft., by 17ft. from stage to ceiling. Lighted by gas. Terms for hiring: £2 10s. one day; £2 second day, and 30s. for each succeeding day, including use of piano and hall-keeper's attendance. Amount of deposit required on booking, one half.

Date of local fair, Whit Tuesday. Sites, Market Square and Tudor Square.

Early closing day, Wednesday; market day, Saturday.

DARLASTON, Staffs.

Population, 15,395. Miles from London, 123.

TOWN HALL.—Proprietors, Darlaston Urban District Council; Hallkeeper, Isaiah Cotterell. Music and Dancing license. Holding capacity: Number of persons, 1,000. No proper stage. Gas and electric light (voltage 200). Terms for hiring, £1 10s. per evening; 25 per cent. required on booking.

Early closing day, Thursday.

DARLINGTON, Durham.

Population, 44,511. Miles from London, 236.

THEATRE ROYAL.—Lessee and Manager, Mr. James Bell; Musical Director, Mr. A. Moscropp Allison; Scenic Artist, Mr. T. Featherstone. Full license. Holding capacity: Number of persons, 2,500. Amount, £90. Stage measurements: 50 ft. by 54 ft.; opening, 26 ft.; fly, 32 ft. cloths. Electric light. Amount of printing required, 800 sheets for walls, 700 lithos. Usual matinée day, Saturday, 2.30. Time of band rehearsal, 12 noon.

HIPPODROME.—Managing Director, Signor Pepi; Acting-Manager, Mr. C. Hersee.

CENTRAL HALL.—Manager, Mr. Edward Wooler. Fully licensed. Holding capacity: Number of persons, 1,100. Gas and electric light. Terms for hiring: £3 3s. per night; £14 a week. Amount of deposit required on booking, £2. Current continuous, 250 volts low pressure.

DRILL HALL.—Apply Manager.

ASSEMBLY HALL.—Apply Manager.

The town has the reputation of being an excellent stand for kinematograph shows, the Central Hall, the Drill Hall, and Assembly Hall being largely requisitioned for the purpose. Portables occasionally visit the town and take up their stand in Market Place, where also a fair takes place twice a year on the occasion of the annual hirings. The hirings extend over three Mondays in May; the second, by statute, must be the Monday before the 13th, and on that day the fair is held. They also extend over three Mondays in November, the second to be the Monday before the 21st, and that also is the fair day. Thousands of people from the country throng the Market Place the whole day and up to long after midnight, no difficulty being experienced in securing sites for shows of any description. The population has a strong residential element, but the industrial preponderates. The nature of the works is varied; North-Eastern Railway engine shops, Darlington Forge, Cleveland Bridge and Engineering works, Messrs. Robert Stephenson's Engine Works, Rice Carr Rolling Mills, etc.

Early closing day, Wednesday; market days, Monday and Friday.

Agent.—M.H.A.R.A.: Albert Dean, Bay Horse Hotel; V.A.F.: The same.

RECOMMENDED APARTMENTS.

Mrs. Robinson, 61, Penabury Street.—1 sitting and bedroom, bathroom.

Mrs. Bell, 18, Garden Street.—2 sitting-rooms, 3 bedrooms, 4 beds.

DARTFORD, Kent.

Population, 18,644. Miles from London, 17.

CONSERVATIVE HALL.—Manager, Mr. H. F. A. Wichmann. Double license. Holding capacity: Number of persons, seating 600; amount, £25. Clear stage 32ft. by 12ft., with extension, 18ft. Lighted by gas. Electric can be connected; current, direct voltage, 230 and 460. Amount of printing required, about 200 posters, 300 day bills. Terms for hiring: One night, £3 3s.; two nights, £5 5s.; three nights, £7 7s.; four nights, £8 8s.; six nights, £10 10s. Amount of deposit required on booking, £1 1s., £2 2s., and £3 3s. respectively. Site for circus, The Fairfield.

Early closing day, Wednesday; market day, Saturday.

DARWEN, Lancs.

Population, 41,000. Miles from London, 210.

THEATRE ROYAL.—Lessee, Mr. A. M. Loader; Manager, Mr. F. J. Robinson; Musical Director, Mr. R. D. Chew. Dramatic license. Holding capacity: Number of persons, 2,000. Stage measurements: 40 ft. deep by 50 ft. wide; proscenium, 24 ft. Gas and electric light. Amount of printing required, matinée day, and time of band rehearsal vary.

PUBLIC HALL AND PALACE OF VARIETIES.—Lessees, Messrs. Thomson, Leivers, and Bennett; Manager, Mr. J. E. Thomson; Assistant Manager, Mr. J. Kerrigan. Music and dancing license. Holding capacity: Number of persons, 700. Small stage, semi-circular. Lighted by gas and electricity.

CO-OPERATIVE HALL and INDUSTRIAL HALL.—Mr. J. T. Duckworth, hall-keeper. Music and dancing license. Holding capacity: Number of persons, 1,125 and 645 persons respectively. Small stage in both halls. Electric light. Amount of printing required: 500 sheets. Terms for hiring: One night from £1 15s.; six nights, £8 10s. Industrial Hall: One night, £1; six nights, £4 15s. Amount of deposit required on booking, 10s.

A fair is held every year on the occasion of the annual holidays. This fair generally begins on the Saturday before the third Monday in July, but it is not as important as it was at one time, owing to the fact that the bulk of the townspeople go away from home, as it is also the general holiday for the year. Portables do not visit the town. Kinematograph shows do. The population is of a strictly industrial character, cotton weaving and paper making being the staple industries.

Early closing day, Tuesday; market days, Monday and Saturday.

Agent.—M.H.A.R.A. and V.A.F.: W. Matthews, Beach Bull Hotel.

RECOMMENDED APARTMENTS.

Mrs. Moxey, 12, Norfolk Street.—Sitting and bedrooms; piano.

DAVENTRY, Northants.

Population, 3,780. Miles from London, 72.

ASSEMBLY HALL.—Manager and Secretary, Mr. C. J. W. Rodhouse. Double license.

Holding capacity: Number of persons, 700. Small stage, more suitable for varieties. Lighted by incandescent gas. Terms for hiring: £1 5s. one night; £4 per week. Amount of deposit required on booking, 25 per cent. Dramatic shows most popular.

Local fairs in October. Sites available for alfresco concerts, Recreation Ground.

Early closing day, Thursday; market day, Wednesday.

DEAL, Kent.

Population, 12,581. Miles from London, 88.

THEATRE ROYAL, King Street.—Manager, Mr. Jas. C. White. Fully licensed. Holding capacity: Numoer of persons, 900; amount, £60. Stage measurements, 22ft. by 36ft.; proscenium opening, 20ft. by 15ft. Lighted by gas. Amount of printing required, 300 sheets. Usual matinée days, Wednesday and Saturday. Best season from August Bank Holiday.

GLOBE THEATRE, Royal Marines' Barracks.

PIER PAVILION

STANHOPE HALL.—Proprietors, Messrs. H and A. Wise. Holds 400. Gas. Used in the summer time for concerts and variety entertainments.

Early closing day, Thursday.

DENBIGH, Denbighshire.

Population, 6,438. Miles from London, 208.

DRILL HALL.—Manager, Mr. J. Pays. Double license. Holding capacity: Number of persons, 600. No stage. Lighted by gas. Amount of printing required can be obtained from Bill-poster, Denbigh. Terms for hiring: £2 for first night; £3 10s. two, with extension of stage. Amount of deposit required on booking, 10s. The only hall in Denbigh.

No fixed dates for local fairs.

Early closing day, Thursday; market days, Wednesday and Saturday.

DENTON, Lancs.

Population, 14,934. Miles from London, 186.

PEOPLE'S HALL.—Lessees, Messrs. Lewers and Bennett; Manager, Mr. Bert Boyd. No dramatic licence. Holding capacity: Number of persons, 1,000. Good platform. Electric light (gas available on platform); current, direct, 200 volts. Terms for hiring: One night. 32s. 6d.: two, 60s.: three, 85s.; and 22s. 6d. for every succeeding night. Amount of deposit required on booking: 10s.

Early closing, Tuesday; market, Saturday.

DERBY, Derbyshire.

Population, 120,000. Miles from London, 129.

GRAND THEATRE.—Proprietor, Mr. T. Allan Edwardes; Manager, Mr. Charles Denley; Assistant Manager, Mr. T. W. Moyes; Musical Director, Mr. George Wood; Scenic Artist, Mr. A. W. Moore. Full license. Holding capacity: Number of persons, 2,500; amount, £200. Stage opening, 31ft.; wall to wall, 60ft.; back wall to curtain, 38ft.; stage to fly-rail, 20ft.; between fly-rails, 40ft.; stage to grid, 60ft. Electric light. Amount of printing required; 1,000 walls, 1,000 windows. Usual matinée day, Wednesday or Saturday. Band rehearsal, 1 p.m.

PALACE.—Proprietor and Manager, Mr. T. Allan Edwardes; Booking Circuit, Derby, Stoke, Attercliffe, Sheffield, and Grand, Black-

pool, for varieties; Musical Director, Mr. Whittington. Double license. Holding capacity: Number of persons, 1,500, twice nightly; amount, £35 each performance. Stage measurements, 42ft. wide, 30ft. deep, 20ft. by 24ft opening. Electric light. Band rehearsal, 1.30. No regular matinée day. No surrounding halls are barred.

ROYAL DRILL HALL.—Will seat 2,000 per sons. Orchestra to accommodate 250 performers. An organ. There are a number of ante-rooms, artists' retiring rooms, etc. Stage, but no proscenium. The hall is let for concerts, balls, receptions, bazaars, kinematograph, and other entertainments. Applications for hiring the hall should be made to the sergeant-major.

TEMPERANCE HALL.—Holds 1,200. Apply Secretary, Curzon Street.

ALBERT HALL.—Holds 600. Also a lecture room. Apply, Secretary, Mechanics' Institution, Wardwick.

Population mainly industrial, artizans, etc., of large locomotive and carriage works of Midland Railway, and headquarters' clerical staff. Several large ironworks, china works, lace mills, and factories of various industries. County residents support concerts of high standard and first-class opera very freely. Town clerk and clerk of the peace, Mr. G. Trevelyan Lee (town clerk's office, 15, Tenant Street); borough surveyor, Mr. John Ward; chief constable, Mr. H. M. Haywood; clerk to borough magistrates, Mr. W. H. Whiston Town is visited by portables at fair times. Site, Morledge, near Market Hall. Apply Markets Superintendent. No difficulty in obtaining licenses. Circuses frequently visit the town. Site, Cattle Market. Apply Markets Superintendent. Pierrot troupes hold performances in summer in outlying districts of Alvaston and Littleover, in fields obtained for the purpose. Electric cars to these places from all parts. County Agricultural Show held in September at Alvaston. Cattle fairs: Friday before January 10, Friday before January 26, Friday before March 26, Friday in Easter week, first Friday in May, Friday in Whitsun week, Friday before July 26, Friday before September 29.

Early closing day, Wednesday; market day, Friday.

Medical Officers.—A.A.: Dr. L. Bryson, 35, Osmaston Road, and Dr. G. B. Proctor, 35, Osmaston Road.

Agents.—A.U.: Will Green, Exchange Hotel, Albert Street. M.H.A.R.A.: Mrs. Green, Exchange Hotel. V.A.F.: The same.

RECOMMENDED APARTMENTS.

Mrs. Budge, 11, Crompton Street.—2 bedrooms 1 sitting-room, 1 combined; bath.

DESBOROUGH, Northants.

Population, 4,000. Miles from London, 79.

ODDFELLOWS' HALL.—Manager, Mr. Thomas Henry Blissitt. Fully licensed. Holding capacity: Number of persons, seat 450. Stage measurements, 12ft. by 35ft. Two dressing rooms leading on to the stage. Lighted by gas. Amount of printing required, ordinary. Terms for hiring, on application to the secretary. Amount of deposit required on booking, 10s. 250yds. from Midland Railway station.

The dates of local fairs vary.

Early closing day, Thursday; no market day

DEVIZES, Wilts.

Population, 6,532.　　Miles from London, 86.

TOWN HALL.—Owners, the Borough. Holding capacity: Number of persons, 800. Well lit by incandescent. Amount of printing required: About 250 circulars, 50 large bills, and 150 window bills. Terms for hiring: £3 3s. inclusive, no extras. Amount of deposit required on booking, 5 per cent. The hall is only let for concerts, lectures, dances, and meetings. Not large enough to erect a stage.

CORN EXCHANGE.—Owners, the Borough. Double license. Holding capacity: Number of persons, 1,200. Platform, 23ft. by 24ft. by 4ft. high. Gas light, incandescent. Amount of printing required: 250 circulars, 50 large bills, and 150 window bills. Terms for hiring Exchange, £3 13s. 6d. inclusive. Good dress'ng rooms. One night only is advised generally

Early closing day, Wednesday; market day, Thursday.

DEVONPORT, Devon.

Population, 81,925.　Miles from London, 230.

THEATRE METROPOLE.—Proprietors, The (Devonport) Theatre Metropole Company; Licensee and Manager, Mr. George S. King; Musical Director, Mr. E. Graham Dunstan. Full dramatic license.　Holding capacity: Number of persons, 1,500 (about); amount, £70. Proscenium opening, 27ft.; stage, 60ft. wide and 24ft. deep; 18ft. flats; fly, all cloths. Gas and electric light. Amount of printing required, 1,000 sheets walls, 600 d.c. lithos. Usual matinée day, Saturday. Time of band rehearsal, 1.15 p.m. Voltage 230, alternating. No towns barred.

HIPPODROME.—Proprietors, Devonport Hippodrome, Limited; Manager, Mr. Herbert Taylor. Holding capacity. 1,700. Electric light. Opened September 14th, 1908.

Early closing day, Wednesday; market days, Tuesday, Thursday, and Saturday.

M.H.A.R.A.: Business conducted at Plymouth Agency.

RECOMMENDED APARTMENTS.

Miss Munday, 12, George Street.—2 Beds, 2 sitting-rooms, 1 combined room.

DEWSBURY, Yorks.

Population, 28,060.　Miles from London, 182.

THEATRE ROYAL.—Proprietors The Northern Theatres Co., Limited; Manager, Mr. J. Herbert Asquith; Musical Director,& Mr. J. Field; Scenic Artist, Mr. F. Venimore. Full license. Electric light, 220 volts, direct current. Time of band rehearsal, 1 p.m.

HIPPODROME.—General Manager, Mr. Geo. Weldon; Stage Manager, Mr. Jack Harris.

VICTORIA HALL.—Manager, Mr. H. Ellis, the Town Clerk, Town Hall, Dewsbury. Fully licensed. Holding capacity: Number of persons, about 1,100. No proscenium. Electric light; gas is connected. Terms for hiring: May to September, inclusive, 15 guineas; October to April, inclusive, 18 guineas per week; matinées, 1 guinea each extra. Amount of deposit required on booking: 2 guineas for one week's booking. Direct current, 220 volts.

Early closing day, Tuesday; market days, Wednesday and Saturday.

Agent.—M.H.A.R.A.: Man and Saddle Hotel. V.A.F.: The same.

RECOMMENDED APARTMENTS.

Mrs. Armitage, 11, Woodville House.—2 Bedrooms, 4 beds, 1 sitting-room, combined.

C. Grimmett, Percy Villa, Wakefield Road.—2 bedrooms and sitting room,

DONCASTER, Yorks.

Population, 30,883.　Miles from London, 156.

GRAND THEATRE AND EMPIRE.—Managing Director, Mr. J. W. Chapman. Double license. Holding capacity: Number of persons, 1,600; amount, over £100. Stage measurements: 32 ft. deep, 75 ft. wide; proscenium opening, 26 ft. Electric light, voltage 100, direct current. Time of band rehearsal, 1 p.m. Usual matinée day, Saturday.

GUILDHALL.—Manager, Mr. Chas. Hanson, Borough Accountant, Mansion House, Doncaster. Dramatic license has to be specially obtained. Holding capacity: Number of persons, 600. Dimensions of Large Hall: Length, 62ft.; breadth, 40ft.; floor to ceiling, 30ft. Platform: Length, 30ft.; breadth, 10ft.; platform to ceiling, 26ft. Electric light. Terms for hiring: Panoramas, etc., £3 3s. per night; concerts, £2 2s. per night. Amount of deposit required on booking: 20 per cent. All kinematograph machines must be provided with a fire-proof screen. Current direct, 460 volts.

CORN EXCHANGE.—Manager, Mr. Chas. Hanson, Borough Accountant, Mansion House, Doncaster. Dramatic license has to be specially obtained. Holding capacity: Number of persons, 1,600. Dimensions of hall: 80ft. by 85ft.; orchestra platform. Electric light. Terms for hiring: One night, £5 10s.; subsequent nights, £4. Amount of deposit required on booking: 20 per cent. Glass roof, cannot be artificially darkened.

Dates of local fairs: September race week. September 7, 8, 9, 10, 1909; statutes, second or third week in November (actual date not fixed).

Wool Market usual place for travelling shows.

Early closing day, Thursday; market days, Tuesday and Saturday.

Medical Officer.—A.A.: Dr. P. B. Mackay, 7, Hallgate.

Agent.—M.H.A.R.A. and V.A.F. George Guest, Nag's Head.

RECOMMENDED APARTMENTS.

Mrs. Day, 29, Spring Gardens.—Bedroom and sitting-room, double bedroom.

Mrs. C. Moate, 16, Baker Street.—2 bedrooms sitting-room; bath; piano.

DORCHESTER, Dorset.

Population, 9,548.　Miles from London, 138.

CORN EXCHANGE.—Manager, Mr. John Benger. Double license. Holding capacity: Number of persons, 700. Depth and width of stage, 21ft. by 30ft. Lighted by gas. Terms for hiring: £3 3s. first night; £1 11s. 6d. each succeeding night. Amount of deposit required on booking, £1. Gas as per metre; heating and cleaning extra.

Early closing day, Thursday; market days, Wednesday and Saturday.

DORKING, Surrey.

Population, 11,410.　Miles from London, 26.

PUBLIC HALL.—Manager, Mr. Geo. Gardiner. Double license. Holding capacity: Number of persons, 600. Depth and width of stage: 15ft. by 27ft; proscenium, 22ft. opening, and scenery at hall for hire separately. Electric light, 240 volts direct. Terms for hiring: One night, £3 8s. for theatricals; £3 3s. for entertainment. Amount of deposit required on booking, £1.

Early closing day, Wednesday; market day, Thursday.

DOUGLAS, I.O.M.

Population, 20,000. Season, 80,000. Miles from London, 286.

GRAND THEATRE.—Proprietors, Grand Theatre Co., Limited; Chairman, Mr. Edward Compton; Resident Manager, Mr. T. R. Wood; Secretary, Mr. Jas. Buck, 30, Brown Street, Manchester. Dramatic license. Holding capacity: Number of persons, 2,500; amount, £200; Stage measurements: Opening, 27ft. and 45ft.; depth, 45ft. by 60ft.; wings, 18ft. Lighted by gas. Amount of printing required: 1,000 sheets for posting, 600 sheets for windows, 10,000 throwaways. Matinées on wet days. Best date, of the year, June to October.

GAIETY THEATRE.—Proprietors, The Palace and Derby Castle, Limited; Manager, Mr. Charles Fox, jun.; Acting Manager, Mr. George Gray; Musical Director, Mr. F. C. Poulter; Scenic Artist, not permanent. Dramatic and music and dancing licenses. Holding capacity: Number of persons, 2,300. Stage: 55ft. wide by 60ft. deep; proscenium opening, 28ft. Gas and electric (100 volts). Amount of printing required, 1,000 sheets and 500 window lithos. Matinées, wet days. Time of band rehearsal, 11 a.m.

HIPPODROME.—Director and Manager Mr. Fred J. Connor. Double license. Holds 2,800. Small stage. 30ft. by 16ft., and arena. Gas and electric light.

PALACE THEATRE.—Proprietors, Palace and Derby Castle, Limited; Manager. Mr. Chas. Fox, jun.; Acting Manager, Mr. Arthur Brittain; Musical Director, Mr. Harry Wood. Gas and electric light.

DERBY CASTLE.—Proprietors, Palace and Derby Castle. Limited; Manager, Mr. Chas. Fox, jun.; Acting Manager, Mr. Alfred Kelly; Musical Director, Mr. Harry Wood. Gas and electric light.

NEW EMPIRE.—Proprietor and Lessee, Mr. Charles Dare; Resident Manager, Mr. Rex Sugden. Double license. Holds 500. Stage, 14ft. wide by 10ft. Electric light, 100 volts.

Population, in season, 80,000 average. Buxton's Pierrot Village; alfresco concerts, Douglas Head (Chas. Dare) and Harris promenade, both let by town council; Onchan Head (Adeler and Sutton). No portables. Season, Whitsuntide to end September. All places closed in the winter except the Empire.

Medical Officers.—A.A.: Dr. G. H. Horne (dental). 1, Mount Pleasant, Finch Road; Dr. R. Marshall, 46, Loch Promenade; Dr. Ferguson, 2, Kingswood Grove. A.U.: Drs. Horne and Marshall, as above. M.H.A.R.A.: Dr. Marshall, as above.

Agent.—M.H.A.R.A.: J. Brougham, Central Hotel, Broadway. V.A.F.: The same.

DOVER, Kent.

Population, 41,794. Miles from London, 78.

ROYAL HIPPODROME.—Proprietor, Mr. S. W. Winter; District Manager, Mr. G. Egbert; Acting Manager, Mr. Holford; Musical Director, Mr. W. G. Eaton. Band rehearsal at 2 p.m. Holds 1,000. Stage, 23ft. by 50ft. Proscenium opening, 25ft. Electric light.

TOWN HALL.—Proprietors, The Corporation; Manager, the Town Clerk. Music and dancing license only. Holding capacity: Number of persons. about 1,000. Platform (with organ over): 30ft. 6in. by 11ft. 9in. by 3ft. 2in., movable extension. Gas and electric light. Terms for hiring: First night, £4 4s.; subsequent nights, £3 3s. Amount of deposit required on booking: £1 per night. Current alternating 100 volts.

Early closing day, Wednesday; market day, Saturday.

Medical Officer.—A.A.: Dr. J. Baird, 2, Cambridge Terrace (hours 1.30-2.30). A.U.: The same. M.H.A.R.A.: The same.

A.U. Agency: A. T. Newman, Dover Castle Hotel. V.A.F.: The same. M.H.A.R.A.: Fred Holt, The Palace.

DOVERCOURT, Essex.

Population, 3,894. Miles from London, 70.

ALEXANDRA HALL.—Manager, Mr. Carl Rosinsky. Concert or theatrical party. Accommodates 500. Stage fitted with electric head and foot lights, also scenery, etc. Good dressing room, piano, and every facility for small comedy. Annexed to Hotel Alexandra.

VICTORIA HALL.—Manager, Mr. H. H. Packer. Dramatic license. Seats 300. Gas, piano. No scenery.

Early closing day, Wednesday.

DOWLAIS, Glam.

Population, 17,142. Miles from London, 184.

ODDFELLOWS' HALL.—Secretary, Mr. Isaac Edwards. Dramatic license. Holding capacity: Number of persons, 1,200. Amount varies with price of seats. Proper stage. Electric light. Terms for hiring: 45s. first day, 35s. each succeeding day Amount of deposit required on booking, £1.

Early closing day, Thursday; market day, Saturday.

DOWNHAM MARKET, Norfolk.

Population, 2,472. Miles from London, 87.

TOWN HALL.—Manager, Mr. Fredk. Wm. Coulson. Double license. Holding capacity: Number of persons, 600; amount, £20 to £30. Stage, 13ft. by 33ft., can be enlarged to 17ft. by 33ft. Lighted by gas. Terms for hiring, one night, 31s. 6d.; two, 52s. 6d.; three, 63s Amount of deposit required on booking, 21s. Winnold Fair, about February 28.

Early closing day, Wednesday; market day, Friday.

DOWNPATRICK, Co. Down.

Population, 3,132. Miles from Dublin, 123.

ASSEMBLY HALL.—Apply Estate Office, Downpatrick. Holding capacity: Number of persons, 600; amount, £35. Platform, 36 ft. by 11 ft. Lighted by gas. Terms for hiring: 22s. first night, 17s. every succeeding night (and gas as per consumption). Amount of deposit required on booking: £3.

Fair every first Tuesday in month. Fair Green available for circuses and outdoor shows.

Early closing, Thursday; market, Saturday.

DROITWICH, Worcester.

Population, 4,201. Miles from London, 125.

SALTERS' HALL.—Manager, Mr. J. H. Hollyer, Corbett Estate Office, Droitwich. Has dramatic license. Holding capacity: Number of persons, 500. Stage, full width, 26ft. by 17ft. 6ins.; height from ground, 3ft. 6ins.; proscenium opening, 17ft. wide by 12ft. 6ins. high. Lighted by gas. Terms for hiring: One evening, £2 5s.; or for consecutive nights, £2 5s. first and £1 15s. each following. Amount of deposit required on booking.

£1. Application for use of hall to be accompanied by particulars of entertainment for which required.

No local fairs.

Site available for portables, alfresco concerts, and circuses, field belonging to Mrs. Meades, Great Western Hotel.

Early closing day, Thursday; market day, Friday.

DRONFIELD, Lancs.

Population, 11,087. Miles from London, 187.

TOWN HALL.—Proprietors, Trustees of Thos. Taylor's Charity; Clerk to Trustees, Mr. H. N. Lucas. No license. Holding capacity: Number of persons, 300. No proper stage, only movable platform, 21ft. by 13ft. Gas. Terms for hiring, 10s. a night.

Date of local fair, April 24; Feast week from June 28.

Early closing day, Wednesday. No market day.

DUBLIN.

Population, 289,108.

THEATRE ROYAL.—Proprietors, The Dublin Theatre Company, Ltd.; Manager, Mr. George Parrington; Musical Director, Mr. John Moody. Licensed under Royal Letters Patent. Stage capable of presenting the largest London productions. Electric light. Usual matinée day, Saturday.

GAIETY THEATRE.—Lessees, Gunn Gaiety, Dublin, Limited; Managing Director, Mrs. Michael Gunn; General Manager and Secretary, Mr. Charles Hyland; Musical Director, Mr. W. S. Nabarro; Scenic Artist, Mr. James Hicks. License, Royal Letters Patent. Holding capacity: Number of persons, 2,000. Electric light. Usual matinée day, Saturday.

EMPIRE PALACE THEATRE.—Proprietors, Star Theatre of Varieties, Limited; Manager and Secretary, Mr. George H. Marsh; Musical Director, Mr. Harry Baynton. Music and dancing license. Holding capacity: Number of persons, 2,500. Stage measurements, 34ft. by 32ft. Electric light. Time of band rehearsal, 1 p.m. Usual matinée day, Saturday, 2.30.

Bars all other Managements' Halls in Dublin and the following towns: Kingstown, Lucan, and Howth.

TIVOLI THEATRE OF VARIETIES.—Proprietors, Messrs. Dublin Tivoli Theatre Company; Manager, Mr. Charles M. Jones; Acting-Manager, Mr. H. A. Murphy; Musical Director, Mr. E. J. Taylor. Time of band rehearsal, 1 p.m. Monday. Current, alternating, 200 volts.

QUEEN'S THEATRE.—Closed.

Halls in Dublin suitable for picture shows or occasional dramatic entertainments :—

ABBEY THEATRE.—Seating accommodation for about 562. Headquarters of the National Theatre Society. Directors, W. B. Yeats, J. M. Synge, and Lady Gregory; Lessee, Miss A. E. F. Horniman; Secretary, Mr. W. A. Henderson.

ROTUNDA.—There are two rooms here—one the " Round Room " (very large), the other " The Pillar Room," which is much smaller.

ANTIENT CONCERT ROOMS.—There are also two rooms here—a large and small one.

MOLESWORTH HALL.—Holds about 200 or 300.

In Kingstown (7 miles distant) there are:—

PAVILION.—Fine new building.

TOWN HALL.—Also fine large room.

Medical Officers.—A.A.: Dr. J. Lentaigne, 5, Upper Merrion Street. 'Phone, 732. At home, 3-4, Saturdays, by appointment. Dr. J. D. Pratt, 25, Lower Fitzwilliam Street. Dr. G. S. Stritch, 17, North Gorges Street. 'Phone, 103 Y. A.U.: Drs. Stritch and Pratt, as above. M.H.A.R.A.: Dr. Pratt, as above.

Agent.—A.U.: J. Behan, 80 and 81, Dame Street. M.H.A.R.A.: The same. V.A.F.: The same.

RECOMMENDED APARTMENTS.

Mrs. M. Higgins, 128, Stephen's Green.

DUDLEY, Worc.

Population, 48,733. Miles from London, 120.

OPERA HOUSE.—Proprietor and Manager, Mr. J. Maurice Clement; Acting-Manager, Mr. J. W. Tilley; Musical Director, Mr. Arthur Greaves; Scenic Artist, Mr. Ernest Williams. Full license. Holding capacity: Number of persons, 2,000. Proscenium opening, 26ft.; rail to rail, 30ft.; depth, 36ft.; width, 73ft.; stage to rail, 21ft.; stage to grid, 50ft. Gas and electric light. Matinée day, Bank Holidays only. Time of band rehearsal, 1 p.m. Season, August until Whitsuntide.

EMPIRE PALACE.—Managing Director, Mr. Fred H. Anderson, Northampton; Acting-Manager, Mr. F. H. Walters; Musical Director, Mr. A. E. Cooper. Electric light. Time of band rehearsal, 12 noon.

PUBLIC HALL.—Manager, Mr. Wm. Pearson. Double license. Holding capacity: Number of persons, 800. Portable stage, 40 ft. by 24 ft. Gas and electric light. Terms for hiring: One night, £2 2s.; two nights, £3 12s.; three nights, £5 2s.; each additional night, £1 1s. Scenery can be hired. Amount of deposit required on booking, 25 per cent. Electric, voltage 460.

Early closing day, Wednesday; market day, Saturday.

Medical officers.—A.A.: Dr. E. A. Dando, Dixon's Green; A.U.: The same.

Agent.—A.U.: J. Golcher, Seven Stars Hotel. M.H.A.R.A.: The same. V.A.F.: The same.

DUDLEY PORT, Staffs.

Miles from London, 120. Miles from Birmingham, 7.

ALHAMBRA THEATRE.—Proprietor and Manager, Mr. Douglas C. Phelps.

DUMBARTON, Haddington.

Population, 3,581. Miles from London, 363.

CORN EXCHANGE.—Proprietors, Burgh of Dunbar; Manager, Mr. A. S. Paterson, Burgh Surveyor. Dramatic and Music and Dancing licenses. Holding capacity: Number of persons, 600; amount, up to £30. Stage for ordinary purposes. Gas. Amount of printing required, one 12, six 6 sheets, 50 daybills. Terms for hiring, 15s. to 21s. 6d. Amount of deposit required on booking, 10s.

Date of local fair, first Tuesday in February.

Early closing day, Wednesday; market day, Tuesday.

DUMFRIES, Dumfriesshire.

Population, 17,081. Miles from London, 332.

THEATRE ROYAL.—Proprietor and Manager, Mr. W. Payne Seddon; Musical Director, Mr. F. Hume; Scenic Artist, Mr. S. Collier, jun. Restricted license. Holding capacity: Number of persons, 750; amount, £50. Stage measurements: 22ft. deep by 36 ft. wide; proscenium, 24ft. opening. Lighted by gas. Usual matinée day, Wednesday. Booked first three days of week only, in conjunction with Hawick.

MECHANICS' HALL.—Manager, Mr. W. A. Hiddleston. Dramatic license. Platform, 32ft. by 15ft., with footlights, proscenium, and scenery. Holds 1,000. Terms, plays, £3 3s. per night; other entertainments, £2 2s.

MAXWELLTOWN HALL.—Suitable for concerts and kinematograph entertainments. Seating capacity, 450. Gas-lighted.

ST. MARY'S HALL.—Suitable for concerts and kinematograph entertainments. Seating capacity, 800. Gas-lighted.

DRILL HALL.—Secretary, Mr. J. MacKechnie North. Town and County Bank. Holds 4,000. Electric light and gas. Suitable for concerts, carnivals, etc.

Residential and industrial population: chief industries are large woollen mills and hosiery factories.

Town is sometimes visited by portables, but not often. No difficulty in getting license. Sites of ample dimensions are easily obtainable for alfresco concerts, circus pitches, etc.

The principal fair of the year is the Rood Fair, held in the last week of September. Horse and hiring fairs are held at stated dates throughout the year, but they only occupy one day. Hours from 10 a.m. to 4 p.m.

Dumfries (The Queen of the South), created a Royal Burgh in 1190. Numerous places of interest in town and locality. Bowling greens and golf links; good hotel accommodation.

Dumfries is 33 miles from Carlisle, and there are ample railway facilities for reaching Glasgow, Edinburgh, and the North, or English towns.

No early closing day; market day, Wednesday.

DUNDALK, Louth.

Population, 13,067. Miles from Dublin, 54.

TOWN HALL.—Manager, Mr. M. Comerford, Town Clerk. Double license. Holding capacity: Number of persons, 1,000. Amount, £60. Good permanent stage and fittings. Stage 44ft. by 25ft.; proscenium height, 25ft.; width, 26ft.; ceiling height, 35ft. Lighted by gas. Terms for hiring: One night, £3 10s.; two nights, £6; three nights, £8; each extra night, £2. Amount of deposit required on booking, £2.

This is one of the largest provincial towns in Ireland, and is situate midway between Dublin and Belfast on main line. Large railway works and Artillery Barracks.

Splendid fair green, suitable for circuses, alfrescos, roundabouts, etc. Rent on application.

Market, Monday.

DUNDEE, Forfar.

Population, 163,535. Miles from London, 478.

HER MAJESTY'S THEATRE.—Proprietors, Robert Arthur Theatres Co., Limited; Managing Director, Mr. Robert Arthur; Acting-Manager, Mr. Louis Karpe; Musical Director, Mr. H. E. Loseby. Full license. Holding capacity: Number of persons, 1,200. Electric light. Amount of printing required: 1,000 sheets, 1,000 window, 1,000 circulars, etc. Matinée day, Saturday. Time of band rehearsal, 11 a.m.

PALACE THEATRE.—Lessees, The United County Theatres, Limited; Acting-Manager, Mr. S. McIntosh; Musical Director, Mr. G.

Mundell. Double license. Holding capacity: Number of persons, 2,000. Proscenium opening, 32ft. by 26ft.; depth of stage, 38ft.; width, 47ft. Gas and electric light. Time of band rehearsal, 1 p.m. Matinée day, Saturday. Bars Gaiety and Empire, Dundee.

EMPIRE THEATRE.—Lessee, Mr. R. A. P. Williams; Acting-Manager, Mr. Frank Percival.

GAIETY THEATRE.—Proprietors, New Gaiety Theatre, Dundee, Limited; Sole Lessee and Manager, Mrs. Lillie Williams; General Manager, Frank Percival. Dramatic and music and dancing licenses. Holding capacity: 1,600 (twice nightly). Stage complete in every detail. Electric light, town supply, 220 volts. Amount of printing required: 500 walls, 500 window lithos. Terms for hiring: certainties only given; no sharing terms.

GILFILLAN MEMORIAL HALL. — Seats 1,700. Electric light, 200 volts, direct; gas for emergency. License, for week or night, can usually be got from Town Clerk. Apply, Hallkeeper.

CITY ASSEMBLY ROOMS. — Seats 750. Electric light, 200 volts, direct, or gas, alternatively. Licensed for concerts and dancing. Apply, Hall-keeper.

KINNAIRD HALL. — Seats 2,000. Electric light, 200 volts, and also gas. Apply, Hallkeeper.

ST. MARY MAGDALENE'S HALLS.—Large, holds 1,200 to 1,500; small, holds 500. Electric light. Apply, D. Blackadder, Solicitor, Castle Street, Dundee.

Dates of local fairs: Spring Holiday, April; Autumn Holiday, October; New Year.

Early closing day, Wednesday; market days, Tuesday and Friday.

Medical Officer: A.A., Dr. Wm. Gorrie, 12, King Street; A.U., The same.

Agent: A.U., J. W. Wallace, George Bar, Castle Street; M.H.A.R.A., The same; V.A.F., The same.

RECOMMENDED APARTMENTS.

Mrs. Fortune, 63, Gellatly Street.—Sitting-room and bed combined, and large bedroom; piano, and bath (h. and c.).

DUNFERMLINE, Fife.

Population, 28,250. Miles from London, 435.

OPERA HOUSE.—Manager, Mr. W. E. Potts; Scenic Artist, Mr. Robt. Wood. Dramatic license with early doors. Holding capacity: Number of persons, 1,500; amount, £103; ordinary doors, £70. Proscenium opening, 24ft. footlights; to back wall, 31ft.; height of proscenium, 22ft.; can fly 1sft. cloth; fly floor, 19ft. clear. Lighted by gas. Matinée day, Saturday.

Early closing day, Wednesday; market day, Tuesday.

DUNGANNON, Co. Tyrone.

Population, 3,812. Miles from Dublin, 153.

FORESTERS' HALL.—Secretary, Mr. Francis Woods. Double license. Holding capacity: Number of persons, 700. Proper stage, 33ft. by 16ft. Lighted by gas. Terms for hiring: £1 per night, £4 10s. per week. Amount of deposit required on booking, £1. Hall in central position and attended by all classes.

ST. GEORGE'S HALL.—Manager, Mr. J. C. Simpson. Holding capacity: Number of persons, 500. Amount, £32 10s. has been taken. There is a platform, 24ft. by 12ft. Lighted by Lucas gaslights. Amount of printing required: 100 posters, 1,000 handbills. Terms for hiring: Single night, £2; weekly, £5. Amount of deposit required on booking, £1.

Market days, Thursdays.

23

DUNGARVAN, Co. Waterford.

Population, 5,263. Miles from Dublin, 189.

TOWN HALL.—Managers, Dungarvan Urban District Council. Holding capacity: Number of persons, 800. Stage measurements: 30ft. by 15ft. Lighted by gas. Terms for hiring: £4 15s. per week. Cash in advance.

Dates of local fairs, third Tuesday and Wednesday each month.

DUNMOW, Essex.

Population, 3,027. Miles from London, 42.

TOWN HALL.—Manager, Mr. W. B. Clapham. Hall attendant, Mr. Saunders, Star Hill, Dunmow, to whom communications can be addressed, and who will arrange for billposting. Has dramatic license. Holding capacity: Number of persons, about 230. Stage, 18ft. by 10ft., can be enlarged. Lighted by gas. Terms for hiring: £1 for one night and 2s. 6d. for attendant; each subsequent night 15s. and 1s. 6d. for attendant. Amount of deposit required on booking, 10s.

Early closing Day, Wednesday; market day, Tuesday.

DUNS, Berwickshire.

Population, 2,606. Miles from London, 357.

VOLUNTEER HALL.—Manager, Sergeant-Major W. Wright. No dramatic license. Temporary license 2s. 6d., to be obtained from the Town Clerk. Holding capacity: Number of persons, 800. Amount, £30 to £40. Stage, 19ft. by 34ft.; no proscenium. Lighted by gas. Terms for hiring: 65s. inclusive. Amount of deposit required on booking, £1.

TOWN HALL.—Holds about 200. Anteroom. Small platform can be had. Rent 5s., cleaning 2s., lighting and heating extra.

Date of local fair: Spring Hiring Fair, first Tuesday in March annually.

Early closing day, Wednesday.

DUNSTABLE, Beds.

Population, 7,625.   Miles from London, 36.

CORN EXCHANGE.—Manager, Mr. George Baldock. Dramatic license. Holding capacity: Number of persons, 450. Platform, 14ft. by 11ft., projecting ditto, 23ft. by 8ft.; movable platform, 5ft. 6in., 1s. 6d. per foot extra. Lighted by gas. Terms for hiring: Dramatic, 30s. first night; each night after, 25s. Amount of deposit required on booking, £1. No scenery or footlights. The rent must be paid in advance at the time of engagement. Hall is let subject to the plait and corn markets being held on Wednesdays.

Early closing day, Thursday; market day, Wednesday.

DURHAM.

Population, 15,500.   Miles from London, 250.

ASSEMBLY ROOMS THEATRE.—Proprietor and Manager, Mr. T. Rushworth; Musical Director, Mr. J. W. Pinchen. Full dramatic license. Holding capacity: Number of persons, 700. Stage measurements, depth, 30ft.; width, 26ft.; proscenium opening, 17ft. 6in. by 17ft. 6in. Electric light. Amount of printing required: 300 sheets for walls, 300 window lithos. Band rehearsal, 5 p.m. Season, October to Easter.

NEW DRILL HALL, Gilesgate.—Manager, Sergeant-Major J. Hornsby. Double license.

Holding capacity: Number of persons, 1,000. Stage measurements: Proscenium, 24 ft. by 11 ft. 6 ins. Stage, 45 ft. by 17 ft., and can be made smaller if required. Gas and electric light. Terms for hiring: Pictures, £11 per week (light extra); theatricals £3 10s. per night, or £14 per week (6 days). Amount of deposit required on booking, £3, and remainder before opening.

Early closing day, Wednesday; market day, Saturday.

DYSART, Fife.

NORMAND MEMORIAL HALL. — Town Council of Dysart; Manager, The Hallkeeper. Holding capacity: Number of persons, 600. No scenery allowed. Gas. Terms for hiring on application. Amount of deposit required on booking, 5s.

EARLESTOWN, Lancs.

Population, 10,000. Miles from London, 187.

TOWN HALL.—Proprietors, Urban District Council; Manager, Mr. Brown. Double license. Holding capacity: Number of persons, 700; amount, £30 to £40. Depth and width of stage: 35ft. by 14ft., height from stage to roof 27ft.; no proscenium. Lighted by gas. Terms for hiring: One night, £3; three nights, £5; six nights, £8. Amount of deposit required on booking, £1.

Date of local fairs, May 11, August 17-18. Market ground for portables, and also piece of ground adjoining market.

Early closing day, Thursday; market day, Friday.

EASTBOURNE, Sussex.

Population, 51,000. Miles from London, 65.

DEVONSHIRE PARK THEATRE.—Lessees and Managers, Messrs. Murray King and Clark; Acting-Manager, Mr. Charles Clark; Musical Director, Mr. Dibble. Stage measurements: Opening, 25ft.; depth, 25ft.; wall to wall, 50ft.; fly, 16ft.; stage to fly floor, 20ft. Electric light. Amount of printing required: 3 24-sheet, 6 18-sheet, 4 16-sheet, 4 12-sheet, 30 6-sheet, 200 d.c. lithos, 150 d.c. letterpress, 1,000 circulars, 2,000 throwaways, 50 booking cards. Usual matinée days, Wednesday and Saturday. Band rehearsal, 11 a.m. Booked in conjunction with P.G., Folkestone, and Gaiety, Hastings.

DEVONSHIRE PARK.—Proprietors, Devonshire Park and Baths Co., Limited; Manager and Secretary, Mr. Edgar Allan Brown. Concerts daily by the Duke of Devonshire's Private Orchestra. Natural stage for pastoral plays. Floral Hall (accommodation, 1,500; electric light). Pavilion (accommodation, 800; dramatic license; electric light).

HIPPODROME (Managing Director, Mr. Sydney W. Winter; General Manager, Mr. Harry Day; Resident Manager, Mr. W. Holloway; Musical Director, Mr. W. H. Ash. Full license. Band rehearsal, 2 p.m.

PIER.—Proprietors, Eastbourne Pier Co., Limited; Manager, Mr. Geo. Hayes; Musical Director, Mr. E. H. Peligen. Stage, 26ft. opening, 27ft. deep. Holds 2,000; £120 at prices 6d. to 3s. Sunday concerts are held during the season. Pierrot performances are given in the Band Stand by Wallis Arthur and Paul Mill's Party from Whitsun to the end of September. Animated Pictures are also given thrice daily on the pier during the season. Electric light, voltage 200, alternating, Corporation supply.

TOWN HALL.—Accommodation, 750. Dramatic license. Electric light, voltage 200, alternating. Apply to Mr. W. John Kennard.
CENTRAL HALL. — Accommodation, 400. Apply to Mr. G. Deacon.
NEW HALL.—Accommodation, 400. Apply to Mr. C. T. Stonham.
The Corporation lease two entertainment sites on the foreshore, application for which must be made to the town clerk, Mr. H. West Fovargue. Circus pitches are becoming more and more difficult to obtain, but Mr. H. W. Fellows (the manager of the Eastbourne Billposting and Advertising Co.) should be applied to by circus managers wishing to visit the town.
Early closing day, Wednesday.
Medical Officers.—A.A.: Dr. K. Frazer, Upton Lodge, Devonshire Place; Dr. G. Phillips, 15, Hartfield Square; Dr. R. Howie, Clapham House, Seaside; J. Fletcher, Esq. (dental), 3, Pevensey Road. A.U.: Drs. Howie, Frazer, and Phillips, as above. M.H.A.R.A.: Dr. Frazer, as above.
Agent.—A.U.: Mrs. Webb, Devonshire Hotel, Seaside Road. M.H.A.R.A.: The same. V.A.F.: The same.

EAST DEREHAM, Norfolk.

Population, 5,545. . Miles from London, 126.
THEATRE ROYAL.—Vacant. Restricted. license. Holding capacity: Amount, £27 10s. Small stage. Lighted by gas.
CORN EXCHANGE.—Manager, Mr. Henry Thomas Precious. Double license. Holding capacity: Number of persons, over 800; amount, £35 to £40. Movable stage, 24ft. by 20ft.; hall, 70ft. by 50ft. clear; height, 26ft. Lighted by gas (incandescent). Terms for hiring: 30s. first night, 15s. each successive night. Amount of deposit required on booking, 10s. one night, 20s. longer period.
Sites available for portables, alfresco concerts, and circuses, Repository Ground.
Early closing day, Wednesday; market day, Friday.

EASTLEIGH, Hants.

Population, 9,317. Miles from London, 73.
THE INSTITUTE.—Manager, Mr. G. A. Purkess. Double license. Holding capacity: Number of persons, 500; amount, £20, at 2s., 1s., 6d. Stage depth, 14ft., with extension 20ft.; width, 20ft., with extension 28ft. Lighted by gas. Terms for hiring: 25s. per night; for three nights, £3 3s. Amount of de posit required on booking, 50 per cent.
Early closing day, Wednesday; no market day.

EBBW VALE, Mon.

Population, 21,000. Miles from London, 162.
PALACE OF VARIETIES. — Proprietors, Messrs. A. Tilney and Sons; General Manager, Mr. E. de C. Tilney; Musical Director, Mr. Geo. Stephens. Dramatic license. Holding capacity, 2,500. Stage measurements: Depth, 35ft.; width, 65ft. Proscenium opening, 28ft. Electric light, 230 volts, direct current. Band rehearsals, 12.30. Performances twice nightly.
CENTRAL HALL (late King's Theatre).—Let for fit-ups, concerts, etc. Apply, the Manager.
THE OLD MARKET HALL.—Also let for fit-ups, etc., but not available on Saturdays, owing to local market.
Ebbw Vale is a thriving district. It is an industrial centre, dependent upon the collieries and vast steel and iron works, the property

of the Ebbw Vale Co. The one advantage Ebbw Vale has over other towns of the same character is that the company pay all wages weekly. The Bridge End field is the recognised pitch for circuses, shows, and exhibitions, and there is generally a portable theatre there. The difficulty about securing licenses for portables has been removed. There is also a large recreation ground available for shows, fairs, roundabouts, etc., but it is held by the District Council, and a high rent is charged.
Early closing day, Wednesday; market day Saturday.
Agent.—M.H.A.R.A.: J. Yendol, Heon-y Mwdd Hotel. V.A.F.: The same.

ECCLES, Lancs.

Population, 34,369. Miles from London, 187.
CROWN THEATRE.—Proprietors, Messrs. W. H. Broadhead and Son; Manager, Mr. George F. Slatter; Musical Director, Mr. A. Dearden. Stage measurements, 45ft. by 40ft. Proscenium opening, 28ft. Gas and electric light, alternating, 200 volts. Time of band rehearsal, 2 p.m.
TOWN HALL.—Holds about 600 people. Dramatic performances. Stage can be enlarged.
PUBLIC HALL, PATRICROFT.—Proprietor, Mr. Hartly Hooley; Manager, Mr. P. E. Parr. Alternating current, voltage 200. Holds 600 people. Used for kinematograph shows.
Eccles comprises Eccles, Patricroft, Barton, Monton, and Winton, the population of which is about 40,000. It is both residential and industrial. There are five large cotton-spinning mills in the town, also Nasmyth's and other foundries. The town is not visited by portables. Date of local fair is the first Friday after August 25. Sites for alfresco concerts, etc.: Good ones in the main thoroughfares are practically impossible to get, the opposition would be great, and success very doubtful.
Early closing day, Wednesday.

ECCLESHALL, Staffs.

Population, 3,799. Miles from London, 139.
TOWN HALL.—Managers, Messrs. Middleton, Norris, and Wynne, solicitors, Eccleshall. Holding capacity: Number of persons, 200. Platform. Lighted by gas. Terms for hiring, 30s., payable on day of performance.

EDINBURGH.

Population, 316,837. Miles from London, 396.
THEATRE ROYAL.—Proprietors, Howard and Wyndham, Limited; Managing Director, Mr. F. W. Wyndham; Acting-Manager, Mr. William Whitehead. Full license. Gas and electric light. Usual matinée day, Saturday, at 2 p.m.
LYCEUM THEATRE.—Proprietors, Howard and Wyndham, Limited; Manager, Mr. George T. Minshull; Acting-Manager, Mr. W. Downie; Musical Director, Mr. George Burnley; Scenic Artist, Mr. Stanley Schutter. Full license. Gas and electric light. Usual matinée day, Saturday.
KING'S THEATRE.—Proprietors, The Edinburgh Construction Co., Limited; Manager, Mr. Amand Mascard; Musical Director, Mr. Jules Guitton. Dramatic license. Holding capacity: Number of persons, 2,500. Gas and electric light. Time of band rehearsal, 11 a.m. No matinée day.
EMPIRE PALACE. — Proprietors Moss's Empires, Limited; Managing Director, Mr. Oswald Stoll; Resident Manager, Mr. T. Aynsley Cook. Music and dancing license.

Bars all other Managements' Halls in Edinburgh and the following towns: Musselburgh, Dalkeith, Leith, and Portobello.

ALHAMBRA.—Proprietors, John Lackie and Company; General Manager, Mr. Ventom Swift; Musical Director, Mr. George Tait. Holding capacity: Number of persons, 1,200. Stage measurements: Depth, 25ft.; width, 41ft.; proscenium, width, 26ft. 6in. by 18ft. (height). Electric light. Time of band rehearsal, 11 a.m. No matinee. Bars King's Theatre, Theatre Royal (when variety), and Empire.

GRAND THEATRE.—Proprietress, Miss Audrey Appleby. Holding capacity: 3,000.

OPERETTA HOUSE.—Manager, Mr. J. H. Sanders.

QUEEN'S HALL.—Dramatic license, and holds nearly 1,000.

COOKE'S CIRCUS.—Proprietor, Mr. J. H. Cooke. Holds 2,500. Used when not in equestrian season (November to February) by the Orient Picture Co. General Manager, Mr. W. C. Burns.

WAVERLEY MARKET.—Proprietors, Moss's Empires, Limited.

Early closing day, Thursday; market day, Wednesday.

Medical Officers.—A.A.: Dr. J. M. Brown, 9, Walker Street; N. L. Stevenson, Esq. (dental), 7, Alva Street; Dr. J. M. Farquharson 2, Coates Place, ('phone, 02988; hours, 2-4; ear, nose, and throat); Dr. J. Burnet, 6, Glengyle Terrace; Dr. R. J. Johnson, 1 Buccleuch Place ('phone 94x; hours, 2-3 and 6-30-7-30). A.U.; Dr. Farquharson and Dr. Brown, as above. M.H.A.R.A.: Dr. Johnson, as above.

Agency.—A.U.: W. Purves and Company, The Abbotsford Bar, 3 and 5 Rose Street. M.H.A.R.A.: The same. V.A.F.: The same.

RECOMMENDED APARTMENTS.

Mrs. Sutherland, 31, Grove Street.—2 combined rooms, single and double bedroom; bath.

EDMONTON, Middlesex.

Population, 46,899. Miles from London, 9.

NEW THEATRE ROYAL.—Proprietor, Mr. Joseph Lewis Samuel Moss; Manageress, Mrs. A. H. B. Moss; Musical Director, Mr. Arnold J. Moss. Double license. Full excise. Holding capacity: Number of persons, 1,000; amount £40. Prices, 4d. to 1s. 6d. Stage, about 35ft. by 45ft.; proscenium opening, about 25ft. by 25ft. Lighted by gas. 5 dressing rooms. Amount of printing required, 600 sheets walls and 400 window lithos. Time of band rehearsals, 6 o'clock p.m. Mondays. Thursday. Matinée. Smoking is permitted in the auditorium whether drama or variety is being presented.

EMPIRE MUSIC HALL.—Managing Directors, Messrs. Harry Bawn and Jesse Sparrow; Manager, Mr. A. R. Hollands; Musical Director, Mr. Angelo Asher. Holding capacity, 2,000.

TOWN HALL.—Proprietors, Edmonton Urban District Council; Manager, Mr. William Francis Payne, Clerk. Double license. Licensed to hold 603. Stage depth, 20ft.; width, 37ft. 6ins. proscenium measurements, 37ft. 6ins. wide and 20ft. high. The hall has a dome-shaped roof. Lighted by gas. Electric light can be installed. Terms for hiring: Dramatic performances, £3 3s. for one night; £2 12s. 6d. per night for three nights; £2 2s.

per night for six nights. Dances, £2 2s. per night. Concerts, £1 1s. Kinematograph shows, £3 3s. per day, including matinée. Amount of deposit required on booking: The full charge must be paid at the time of booking. Electric trams pass the door, and are convenient for conveying persons to and from the districts of Waltham Cross, Tottenham, and Stamford Hill.

Site available for circuses: The land at the rear of the Town Hall, which belongs to the Council, has been used for Sanger's circus on various occasions.

Early closing day, Thursday.

RECOMMENDED APARTMENTS.

Mrs. Large, 66, Fairfield Road.—2 bedrooms, sitting and combined; bath.

EGHAM, Surrey.

Population, 13,000. Miles from London, 18.

LITERARY INSTITUTE.—Hon. Secretary, Mr. Henry W. Feltham. Dramatic license obtainable when required, 2s. 6d. Holding capacity: Number of persons, seat 300. Stage, 25ft. wide, 12ft. deep. Electric light. Terms for hiring, £1 1s. per night; theatrical performances, £1 10s. Amount of deposit required on booking, 10s.

CONSTITUTIONAL HALL.—Manager, Mr. W. H. Gardener. Double license. Holding capacity: Number of persons, 400; amount, £20 average. Stage depth, 16ft.; width, 33ft. Gas and electric light. Amount of printing required, £2. Terms for hiring: £2 2s. one night, £3 10s. two nights, £5 three nights, week £8 8s. Amount of deposit required on booking: 10s. one night, £1 two or more.

No local fairs. Sundry sites available for portables, alfresco concerts, and circuses.

Early closing day, Thursday; no market day.

ELGIN, Elgin.

Population, 7,799. Miles from London, 581.

TOWN HALL.—Caretaker, Mr. Alexr. Yeats. Holding capacity: Number of persons, 1,000. Amount £95. Stage, 32 x 32; proscenium, 25ft. wide. Lighted by gas.

Early closing day, Wednesday; market day, Friday. The town is visited by portables.

ELLESMERE PORT, Cheshire.

Population, 4,082. Miles from London, 190.

There is no licensed hall in the district.

Early closing day, Wednesday. No market day.

ELY, Cambs.

Population, 7,713. Miles from London, 72.

PUBLIC ROOMS. Proprietors, Ely Corn Exchange Co., Limited; Manager and Secretary, Mr. H. Archer. Dramatic license. Holding capacity: Number of persons, 500. Stage: 24ft. wide by 18½ft. deep. Lighted by gas. Amount of printing required: Ordinary quantity. Terms for hiring: One night, £2 12s. 6d.; two nights, £4 4s.; three nights, £5 5s. Amount of deposit required on booking, £1.

Local Fairs.—Last Thursday, Friday and Saturday in May and October. Site for portables, Cattle Market; site for circuses, Camp Field.

Early closing day, Tuesday; market day, Thursday.

ENFIELD, Middlesex.

Population, 42,738. Miles from London, 10.
BYCULLAH ATHENÆUM.—Manager, Mr.
J. R. Upton. Double license: Music, dancing,
and stage plays. Holding capacity: Number
of persons, large hall, 515; small hall, 150;
amount, about £30 to £35. Proscenium opening, 18ft.; depth of stage, 21ft.; width, 40ft.
Gas and electric light, voltage 120. Terms fo.
hiring: Large hall only, one night, £3 3s.; two
£5 5s. Amount of deposit required on booking, £1
Portable theatres visit the town.
Early closing day, Wednesday; market
day, Saturday.

ENNIS, Co. Clare.

Population, 5,640. Miles from Dublin, 161.
TOWN HALL.—Manager, Mr. Michael J.
Carmody. Double license. Holding capacity:
Number of persons, 500. Amount, £30 or £40.
Stage about 30ft. square. Lighted by gas.
Terms for hiring: One night, £2; two nights,
£3; three nights, £4; four nights, £4 10s.;
five or six nights, £5. There are also about
eight scenes in the hall which can be used
free. Amount of deposit required on booking,
half the amount.
There is a fair the first Monday in each
month. There is a large yard at rear of hall,
and a big fair green walled all round, suitable for circuses or portables and alfresco
concerts.
Market, Saturday.

ENNISCORTHY, Co. Wexford.

Population, 5,648. Miles from Dublin, 80.
THE ATHENÆUM.—Apply the Hon. Secretary. Holding capacity: Number of persons,
500. Proper stage, 15ft. by 31ft. Lighted by
gas. Terms for hiring: £2 one night; £3 10s.
two; £5 three. Amount of deposit required
on booking, one-third.
Site available for portables, al fresco concerts and circuses, Urban Council field,
£2 2s. per day.
Markets, Saturday and Thursday.

ENNISKILLEN, Fermanagh.

Population, 5,412. Miles from Dublin, 116.
PUBLIC HALL.—Proprietors, The Urban
Council; Secretary, Mr. A. W. Ritchie.
TECHNICAL HALL.—Proprietors, Ferman-
agh County Council; Secretary, Mr. E. Hugh
Archdall, Courthouse.
TOWN HALL.—Proprietors, Urban District
Council; Manager, Urban District Council's
Clerk. Holding capacity, 500. Depth and
width of stage: 28 ft. by 33 ft.; and 4½ ft.
high; proscenium, 8ft. on each side. Gas.
Terms for hiring: £2 10s. first night, £1 10s. each
night afterwards. Caretaker's fees, 5s. if only
one night, if more 2s. 6d. per night. Amount of
deposit required on booking, £1.
Dates of local fairs: 10th of each month.
Sites available for portables, alfresco concerts
and circuses, Fair Green. Apply to H. K.
Leslie, Esq., Estate Office, Enniskillen.
Market days, Tuesday and Thursday. Weekly
half-holiday, Wednesday 2 o'clock.

EMSWORTH, Hants.

Population, 2,224. Miles from London, 64.
TOWN HALL.—Proprietors, Emsworth Proprietary Hall Association; Manager, Mr. G. A.
Brookfield, 14, Queen Street, Emsworth. Dramatic and music and dancing licenses. Holding capacity: Number of persons, about 400.
Stage, but no fittings. Depth and width of
stage, 16ft. by 30ft. Gas (incandescent). Usual
amount of printing required. Terms for hiring, £1 first day, with reduction each day
after; piano extra. Amount of deposit required on booking, 25 per cent.
No local fairs.
No sites available for portables, etc.
Early closing day, Thursday; market day,
Wednesday.

EPPING, Essex.

Population, 3,789. Miles from London, 17.
TOWN HALL.—Epping Town Hall Co.,
Limited; Secretary, Mr. W. Mumford, Epping.
Dramatic and music and dancing licenses. Hold-
ing capacity: Number of persons, 500. Stage,
21ft. wide, 14ft. deep. Gas. Terms for hiring,
two and a-half guineas per night; amount of
deposit required on booking, one guinea.
No local fairs.
Early closing day, Wednesday; market day,
Friday.

EPSOM, Surrey.

Population, 10,915. Miles from London, 14.
PUBLIC HALL. Holding capacity: Number
of persons, 470. Depth and width of stage:
40ft. by 16ft. 6in., with proscenium and drop;
full dressing-room accommodation. Electric
lighting, heating, etc. Terms on application
to the hall.
KING'S HEAD ASSEMBLY ROOMS.—Proprietor, Mr. C. Tanton. Telephone, 63 Epsom.
Early closing day, Wednesday.

EPWORTH, Lincs.

Population, 2,000. Nearest station, Crowle
(6 miles).
TEMPERANCE HALL.—Manager, Mr. Fred
Hill. No dramatic license or dancing. Holding capacity: Number of persons, 500. Stage,
20 ft. by 30ft. by 10 ft. Lighted by gas.
Terms for hiring, 10s. per night. Amount of
deposit required on booking, 5s.
Dates of local fairs, May 1 and the Thursday
after October 21.

ERITH, Kent.

Population, 25,296. Miles from London, 14.
PUBLIC HALL.—Proprietors, Limited Com-
pany; Manager and Secretary, Mr. H. Keddell,
Park Crescent, Erith. Music and dancing
license. Holding capacity: Number of persons,
about 460. Permanent stage, 30ft. by 18ft.
No scenery. Gas and electric light. Terms
for hiring: £2 2s. per night, including gas.
Amount of deposit required on booking, 50 per
cent.
No local fairs.
Early closing day, Thursday. No market day.

ESHER, Surrey.

Population, 9,489. Miles from London, 14½.
VILLAGE HALL.—Proprietors, Public Company; Manager, Mr. Walter Bourne. Dramatic
and dancing licenses. Holding capacity: Number of persons, 450. Stage measurements, 16ft.
deep, 24ft. wide. Gas. Terms for hiring: On
application, from £2 2s. per night. Amount of
deposit required on booking, 25 per cent.
No local fairs.
No sites available for portables, etc., nearer
than Thames Ditton.
Early closing day, Wednesday.

ESTON, Yorks.

Population, 11,199. Miles from London, 252.
ODDFELLOWS' HALL.—Manager, Mr. Geo. W. Smith. Has dramatic license. Holding capacity: Number of persons, 600. Ordinary stage (no fit up). Lighted by gas. Terms for hiring: £3 per week, 12s. 6d. per night. Amount of deposit required on booking, 10s. Suitable for variety or dramatic company, and concerts.
Early closing, Wednesday.

EVESHAM, Worc.

Population, 7,800. Miles from London, 106.
TOWN HALL.—Proprietors, The Corporation; Manager, Mr. R. C. Mawson, Borough Surveyor. Dramatic license. Holding capacity: Number of persons, about 350. No proper stage; a platform tract or stage is erected as wanted, 28ft. by 18ft. and 2ft. 4in. high. Lighted by gas. Terms for hiring, 35s., not including erection of stage; a reduction is made on second and following nights. Amount of deposit required on booking, 10s. Engaged Mondays, Thursdays, and Fridays until April 30, 1909, in consequence of Library Buildings undergoing repair.
MERCHANTS' HALL. — Has dramatic license. Seats about 500. Manager, Mr. R. C. Mawson, Borough Surveyor. Extensive alterations are about to be made, and letting is practically suspended.
Local Fair.—Friday before Oct. 11. Public gardens are available for alfresco concerts.
Early closing day, Wednesday; market day, Monday.

EXETER, Devon.

Population, 47,185. Miles from London, 171.
THEATRE ROYAL.—Lessees, The Exeter Theatre Co., Limited; Managing Director, Mr. Edward J. Domville; Acting-Manager, Mr. Percy M. Dunsford; Musical Director, Mr. S. Stowell. Full license. Holding capacity: Number of persons, about 1,300; amount, about £120. Stage measurements: Opening, 27 ft.; depth, 40 ft.; width, 52 ft. 6 ins. Electric light. Amount of printing required, about 500 sheets posting; ditto window. Usual matinée day, Friday. Time of band rehearsal, 1 p.m. Bars 21 miles including Sidmouth, Exmouth, Tiverton, Dawlish, Teignmouth and Newton Abbott. Electric current alternating 100 volts.

VICTORIA HALL.—Manager, Mr. M. J. Dunsford. Music and dancing license. Holding capacity: Number of persons, 1,500. Stage, 45ft.; depth, 15ft. in centre. Gas and electric light. Terms for hiring: Six nights, £24; matinées, £2 2s. each. Amount of deposit required on booking, 20 per cent. Gas per meter.
BARNFIELD HALLS (large and small).—Manager, Mr. W. J. Codner. Holding capacity: Number of persons, large, 650; small, 150. Proper stage in large hall, 22ft. by 18ft. Electric light.
ɪ ROYAL PUBLIC ROOMS. — Manager, Mr. George Leacey. Holds, large hall, 800; small, 250. Stage, 20 ft. by 18 ft. deep. Side orchestras. Gas and electric light.
Early closing day, Wednesday; market day, Friday.
Medical Officers.—A.A.: Dr. C. E. W. Be'l, 17, West Southernhay; Dr. E. B. Steele-Perkins, 3, Wilton Place, St. James's.
Agent.—M.H.A.R.A.: Mrs. Thompson, ɴBlack Horse Hotel. V.A.F.: The same. ɪ

EXMOUTH, Devon.

Population, 12,000. Miles from London, 181.
PUBLIC HALL.—Secretary, Mr. H. W. Crews. Fully licensed, 700 chairs at disposal of tenant Proper stage 45 ft. wide, 20 ft. deep; proscenium opening, 24 ft. (without wings). Gas included in rental; electric light for kinematographs extra. Terms for hiring: 1 night, £3 3s.; 2, £5 5s.; 3, £7 7s.; 6, £12 12s. Amount of deposit required on booking, 25 per cent.
PIER PAVILION. — Proprietors, Exmouth Dock Co.; Managing Director, Mr. G. Ellett. Music and dancing license. Holds 350. Stage. Gas. Terms on application.
Budleigh Salterton, Topsham, Lympstone, and Woodbury are all within a radius of five miles, and there are frequent trains.
Early closing day, Wednesday; market day, Saturday.

FALKIRK, Stirling.

Population 36,500. Miles from London, 411.
GRAND AND OPERA HOUSE.—Managing Director, Mr. R. C. Buchanan; Manager, Mr. Horace W. Ebbutt; Musical Director, Mr. Henry Taylor. Full license. Smoking allowed all parts. Holding capacity: Number of persons, 2,200; amount, £123 at ordinary door prices, £156 at early door prices. Stage measurements: Depth, 32ft.; width, 58ft.; proscenium opening, 27ft. 6in.; fly floor, 21ft. 6in.; grid, 40ft. 6in. Electric light on stage. Gas and electric front of house. Amount of printing required, 1,000 sheets, 500 lithos. Time of band rehearsal, 1 p.m.
TOWN HALL.—Proprietors, the Corporation; Manager, Mr. Jas. Jarvie. Spacious hall, available for theatrical companies, picture shows, etc. Double license. Holds 1,500. Stage, 29 ft. deep. Opening, 21 ft. Electric light, 420 volts. Printing, 1,000 sheets. Terms: £5 one night, £8 two nights, £10 three, and £14 the week.
ODDFELLOWS HALL.—Proprietors, Ancient Order of Oddfellows Society. Available for concerts and kinematograph entertainments.
The principal town between Glasgow and Edinburgh. Is a good pitch for capable companies—musical preferred. The audiences are sympathetic. The population is residential and industrial, and goes over a radius of three miles. Ironfounding is the industry of the district. Money is always plentiful for good shows. The "feeing" fair is held half-yearly, in April and October, and merry-go-rounds and their accompaniments have a capital innings for a week. Portables have not been in the town for years. Larbert with its "Falkirk Trysts" is three miles off.
Early closing day, Wednesday; market day, Thursday.
Medical Officer.—A.A.: Dr. J. Smith Schaw-field. A.U.: The same.

RECOMMENDED APARTMENTS.

Mrs. Shedden, Sylvat House, 2, Russel Street.—Sitting-room, bedroom, combined room.
Mrs. Deveney, 2, Melville Street, opposite stage end theatre.—3 bed, 2 sitting, 2 combined rooms; bath (h. and c.).

FALMOUTH, Cornwall.

Population, 11,789. Miles from London, 306.
DRILL HALL. — Lessee, Mr. J. H. Lake. Double license. Holding capacity: Number of persons, 1,000. Stage, 30ft. by 21ft. Lighted by gas. Amount of printing required, 400 to 500 sheets. Terms for hiring: £3 3s., first night. Amount of deposit required on booking, 30s.

POLYTECHNIC HALL. — Secretary, S. Roberts. Holds 800. Platform, 22ft. by 10ft. No dramatic license. Terms, one night £2 2s., each succeeding night £1 1s. Rent in advance.

GYLLYNGDUNE GARDENS.—For band or promenade concerts under awning. For terms, apply the Town Clerk, Municipal Buildings, Falmouth.

The recreation ground is available for portables, alfresco concerts, and circuses.

Early closing day, Friday ; market day, Saturday.

FARINGDON, Berks.

Population, 3,000. Miles from London, 70. Branch line from Uffington Station, G.W.R., where change.

CORN EXCHANGE HALL.—Secretary, E. P. Crowdy, Esq., Solicitor. Holding capacity, 300 persons. 200 chairs. Portable stage, 24 ft. by 16 ft. Lighted by gas. Connection for footlights. Dramatic license. Gas extra at 5s. per 1000ft. Charge for hiring: 1 night, £1 11s. 6d.; 2 nights, £2 7s. Deposit on booking, 10s. 6d. per night. Anterooms are charged extra. Applications to be made to Wm. C. Sell, Draper, Marlborough Street. Caretaker's fee, 2s. 6d. first night, 1s. 6d. after.

Annual fair, October 11th. Circuses, shows, roundabouts, etc., can obtain ground from Mr. John Warman or Mr. Vincent, Bull Close. Shows can also stand in the Market Place.

Bill poster, William Hughes, Glister Street. Market day, Tuesday. Early closing, Thursday 2 p.m.

FARNBOROUGH, Hants.

Population, 11,500. Miles from London, 32.

TOWN HALL.—Proprietors, Farnborough Urban District Council. Dramatic and dancing licenses. Holding capacity: Number of persons, 850. Depth and width of stage: 14ft. 6in. by 20ft. Proscenium opening, 17ft. 6in. Gas. Terms for hiring: From 5.30 p.m. to 11 p.m., 35s.; charges to be paid before occupation.

Early closing day, Wednesday.

FARNWORTH, Lancs.

Population, 25,925. Miles from London, 189.

QUEEN'S THEATRE.—Proprietor, Mr. T. Morton Powell; Manager, Mr. T. Morton Powell; Acting-Manager, Mr. Arthur Garner; Secretary, Mr. J. Mason; Scenic Artist, Mr. W. Walsh. Holding capacity: Number of persons, 2,000; amount, £100. Stage measurements, 50ft. deep, 60ft. wide, 21ft. fly floor, 45ft. to grid, opening 27ft. Electric and gas. Full plant. Amount of printing required, 900 walls, 600 windows, 250 D.C.'s Time of band rehearsal, 11 a.m.

Early closing day, Wednesday ; market days, Monday and Saturday.

FELIXSTOWE, Suffolk.

Population, 5,815. Miles from London, 85.

FLORAL HALL.—Proprietors, Felixstowe and Walton Urban District Council; Manager, The Clerk. Music license. Holding capacity: Number of persons, 1,000. No proper stage. Electric light. Not let. Worked by the Council. No local fairs.

One site only for alfresco concerts.

FERNDALE, Glam.

Miles from London, 194.

HIPPODROME AND OPERA HOUSE.—Proprietor, Mr. Walford Bodie. Manager, Mr. Tom N. Mills. Dramatic and music and dancing license. Holding capacity: Number of persons, 1,000; amount, £50. Proper stage, 20ft. opening, 33ft. from wall to wall. Lighted by gas. Amount of printing required, 300 sheets posting, 200 lithos for windows. Terms for hiring, sharing.

Early closing day, Thursday ; market day, Saturday.

Population 2½ miles radius, 40,000.

FERRY HILL, Durham.

Population, 3,123. Miles from London, 245.

TOWN HALL.—Apply the caretaker. Small stage. Lighted by gas. Terms for hiring, 10s. a night. Amount of deposit required on booking, half.

FISHGUARD, Pemb.

Population, 2,500. Miles from London, 287.

TEMPERANCE HALL.—Manager, Mr. A. J. Hodges. Has dramatic license. Holding capacity: Number of persons, 600; amount, £30. Stage, 24ft. 3ins. by 11ft. Lighted by gas. Terms for hiring: 30s. first night, 10s. each succeeding night; piano and footlights extra. Amount of deposit required on booking, 10s.

Early closing day, Wednesday; market day, Thursday.

FLEETWOOD, Lancs.

Population, 15,863. Miles from London, 229.

QUEEN'S THEATRE.—Proprietors, A Syndicate; Manager, Mr. Harry J. Snelson; Musical Director, Miss Jessie Anderton. Fully licensed. Holding capacity: Number of persons, 1,200; amount, £40. Stage measurements; Width, 40ft.; depth, 27ft.; proscenium opening, 23ft. 6in. Gas and electric light. Amount of printing required, 300 wall, 300 lithos. Usual matinée day, Saturday. Time of band rehearsal, 6 p.m. Voltage 200, alternating.

CO-OPERATIVE HALL.—Secretary, Mr. A. E. Jackson. No dramatic license. Holding capacity: Number of persons, 700. Stage measurements: Depth, 23ft.; width, 24ft. 6in. Gas in hall, electric light on stage. Terms for hiring: Concert or lecture, £1 5s.; including tea party, £1 15s.; including ball, £2 10s.; piano, 6s. 6d. Amount of deposit required on booking, half fee. Special terms week.

Population is chiefly engaged in the fishing industry and other industries connected therewith. There is no annual fair. The Co-operative Hall has music license, but not dramatic. Chiefly kinematograph companies visit this place. The sites on the foreshore are occupied by pierrots each year in the summer, application for which is to be made to the Urban Council, and are already let.

Early closing day, Wednesday; market day, Friday.

FOLKESTONE, Kent.

Population, 30,650. Miles from London, 71.

PLEASURE GARDENS THEATRE.—Proprietors, Folkestone Pleasure Gardens Co., Limited; Manager, Mr. H. W. Rowland; Musical Director, Mr. Lewis Tolputt. Full and double license. Holding capacity: Number of persons,

1,200; amount, £115. Stage measurements: Depth, 30ft; width, 54ft.; proscenium, 21ft. 6in.; floor to grid, 42ft.; between flies, 31ft. Gas and electric light. Amount of printing required: 20 18's, 30 6's, 350 lithos, 1,500 circulars. Matinée day, Saturday (Wednesday if two companies). Time of band rehearsal, 11.30 a.m.

HIPPODROME, VICTORIA PIER.—Manager, Mr. Robert Forsyth. Full license. Holding capacity: Number of persons, 1,000. Proper stage. Full scenery. Electric light. Amount of printing required, 700 sheets. Terms for hiring, £25 per week. Amount of deposit required on booking, £5. Sharing terms also accepted. From Easter till October plays varieties. Turned into roller-skating rink for the winter season.

LEAS PAVILION,—Manager, Mr. D'Arcy Clayton.

TOWN HALL.—Proprietors, The Corporation. Manager, Mr. E. J. Chadwick. Double license. Holding capacity: Number of persons, 850. Stage, 20ft. by 47ft.; proscenium, 20ft. by 18ft. Electric light throughout. Terms for hiring: Ratepayers £3 3s. one night, £2 2s. after; non-ratepayers £4 4s. one night, £3 3s. after. Amount of deposit required on booking, 25 per cent.

No industries. Principal trades, the building trade and the letting of lodgings. It is estimated that during August 40,000 visitors live in the town. There is a pleasure fair on June 29. The town is not visited by portables. 8 tes for alfresco concerts or circus pitches are obtainable from the Earl of Radnor, the Lord of the Manor.

Early closing day, Wednesday.

A.A. Medical Officer, Dr. C. E. Perry, 1, Castle Hill Avenue; hours, 9-11 and 6-7.

M.H.A.R.A. Agency, Fred Ashford, Channel Hotel.

RECOMMENDED APARTMENTS.

Mrs. Hall, Oakdene, Bournemouth Road.— 3 sitting-rooms, 6 bedrooms, 2 combined rooms.

FORDINGBRIDGE, Hants.

Population, 3,162. Miles from London, 100.

TOWN HALL.—Secretary, Mr. Philip H. Jackson. Has dramatic license. Holding capacity: Number of persons, 300. Has proper stage. Lighted by gas. Terms for hiring: £1 1s. first night, 10s. 6d. each succeeding night. Amount of deposit required on booking, 10s. 6d.

Early closing day, Thursday.

FORMBY, Lancs.

Population, 5,642. Miles from London, 214.

NEW HALL, VICTORIA HALL, and JUBILEE HALL.—Proprietors, Rev. W. Carr, Mr. G. W. Rowley, and Messrs. J. Rimmer and Sons respectively. Gas.

Early closing day, Wednesday.

GAINSBOROUGH, Lincs.

Population, 20,000. Miles from London, 145.

KING'S THEATRE.—Lessee and Manager, Mr. Arthur Carlton; Acting-Manager, Mr. J. H. Stear. Double license. Holding capacity: Number of persons, 1,000; amount, £55. Stage measurements: Depth, 26ft.; width, 45ft.; proscenium opening, 23ft. Lighted by gas. Amount of printing required: 300 sheets walls, 300 lithos. Matinée day, Saturday.

EMPIRE HIPPODROME.—Lessee and Manager, Empire Syndicate. Seating accommodation, 1,000.

NEW TOWN HALL.—Manager, Mr. T. M. Cooper. Concerts, kinematograph entertainments, etc. Platform, 40ft. by 12ft. Gas.

The population of Gainsborough is largely industrial, and the town is the centre of a large agricultural district. Pleasure fairs are held on Easter Tuesday and on the Tuesday after October 20 (on the 20th when a Tuesday), each fair continuing three days. For space for menageries, shows, circus pitches, application should be made to Mr. Thomas M. Cooper, collector of tolls, Gainsborough. The town has not been visited by portables for the last ten or twelve years.

Early closing day, Wednesday; market day, Tuesday.

Medical Officer.—A.A.: Dr. J. E. S. Passmore, Spring Gardens.

GALASHIELS, Selkirk.

Population, 14,700. Miles from London, 364.

VOLUNTEER HALL.—Secretaries, Messrs. J and D.G. Stalker. Solicitors, British Linen Bank. Holding capacity: Number of person, 1,400. Platform. Depth, 15 ft.; can be enlarged to 19 ft.; width, 40 ft.; no proscenium. Lighted by gas. Amount of printing required usual for a town of this size. Terms for hiring: Concerts, £2 15s.; plays, £3 5s. 6d.; subsequent nights, £1 11s. 6d. Amount of deposit required on booking, 10s. 6d.

PUBLIC HALL.—Manager, Mr. H. Harold G. Lees, solicitor. Double license. Holding capacity: Number of persons, 600. No special stage. Platform, 16ft. 6in. by 32ft. 10in. Lighted by gas. Terms for hiring: One night, £2 2s.; two nights, £1 11s. 6d. each; and £1 1s. per night thereafter. Amount of deposit required on booking, £1. LOWER HALL holds 200.

No local fair worthy of the name. The town is sometimes visited by portables, and no difficulty is experienced in getting a license from the local council. Portables are not largely patronised. Kirkcroft Park and Market-place available, apply to Town Clerk. There are two or three public grounds suitable for circus. Both Barnum and Bailey's and Buffalo Bill's Wild West shows performed in Galashiels. The population is commercial, this being the centre of the Scotch tweed industry. The working class are of a highly respectable order.

Early closing day, Wednesday.

GALWAY, Co. Galway.

Population, 13,414. Miles from Dublin, 126.

COURT THEATRE.—Proprietor, Mr. Peter O'Shaughnessy; Manager, Mr. John O'Shaughnessy; Acting-Manager, Mr. Joseph Morris; Musical Director, Mr. John O'Connor; Scenic Artists, Messrs. Carr Brothers. Fully licensed. Holding capacity: Number of persons, 1,000; amount, £50. Depth and width of stage, 30ft. by 40ft. Gas and electric light. Amount of printing required, about 600 sheets. Usual matinée day, Saturday. Time of band rehearsal, 3 o'clock. Open throughout the year.

COUNTY HALL.—Manager, Mr. F. Hardiman. Double license. Holding capacity: Number of persons, about 1,000. Depth and width of stage and proscenium (width) measurements: 19, 37, and 25 feet (width) respectively. Electric lighting; gas service also for other purposes. Terms for hiring: £2 per night, or £10 per week; lighting extra—summer 3s, 6d, winter 6s. 6d. per evening engagement. Amount of deposit required on booking: One-fourth charges for hall. All charges payable in advance. Good heating service.

Dates of local fairs: Every first Thursday in the month; principal fairs, May 30 and 31 and Sept. 3 and 4.

Market days, Wednesday and Saturday.

GATESHEAD, Co. Durham.

Population, 109,888. Miles from London, 272.

METROPOLE THEATRE. — Lessee, Mr. F. W. Bolam. Manager, Mr. R. G. Elder. Acting-Manager, Mr. Ernest Dixon. Musical Director, Mr. J. A. Derbyshire; Scenic Artist, Mr. J. Miller. Full license. Holding capacity: Number of persons, 2,500; amount, £135. Proscenium opening, 27 ft. 5 ins. by 26 ft.; width of stage, 54 ft. 9 ins. by 32 ft.; fly rail to fly rail, 40 ft. 4 ins.; grid to stage, 33 ft. 3 ins. Electric light. Amount of printing required, 1,200 sheets pictorial posting, 1,000 lithos. Usual matinée day, Saturday. Time of band rehearsal, 12 o'clock.

QUEEN'S THEATRE.—Proprietor, Mr. F. W. Bolam. Acting Manager, Mr. Steve Smith; Musical Director, Mr. Lyons; Scenic Artist, Mr. J. Miller. Restricted license. Holding capacity: Number of persons, 2,000. Twice nightly prices amount, £35 at each house. Proscenium opening, 22 ft. 4 ins. by 21 ft. 2 ins.; width of stage, 41 ft. 4 ins. by 27 ft. 6 ins.; grid, 35 ft. 5 ins.; fly rail to rail, 30 ft. 7 ins. Electric light. Amount of printing required, 1,000 sheets pictorial posting, 1,000 lithos Usual matinée day, Saturday. Time of band rehearsal, 1 o'clock.

KING'S THEATRE OF VARIETIES.—Proprietors, United County Theatres, Limited; Chairman and Managing Director, Mr. Alfred Moul; Local Manager and Licensee, Mr. Harold Arnold; Stage Manager, Mr. C. Sharp; Musical Director, Mr. C. E. Mumford; Bioscope Operator, Mr. Most. Full license. Holding capacity: number of persons, 2,800; amount, £60 at each house. Proscenium opening, 30 ft. 6 in. by 28 ft. 2 in.; width of stage, 55 ft. 2in. by 42 ft.; grid, 56 ft.; fly rail to rail, 36 ft.; electric light, 240 volts. Band rehearsal, 10 o'clock Mondays.

TOWN HALL.—Manager, Mr. R. Teasdale. Music and dancing license: dramatic license granted upon special application. Holding capacity: Number of persons, 900. No proper stage. Platform depth, 17ft. 6in.; width, 35ft. 6in. Gas and electric light. Terms for hiring, £10 10s. per week. Amount of deposit required on booking, £2 2s.

Population is principally a working one, there being several large engineering and other works in the district. A large ground in High Street is to be obtained for shows, circuses, hoppings and the like. Open air entertainments. North Durham Cricket Ground (Prince Consort Road), for cricket, football, and theatrical sports, etc.). Drill Hall adjoining used for shows and exhibitions, etc.

Early closing day, Wednesday; market days, Tuesday and Saturday.

Medical Officer.—A.A.: Dr. A. Green, 18, Gladstone Terrace. Telephone 9. A.U.: The same. M.H.A.R.A.: The same.

GILLINGHAM, Kent, near Chatham.

HIPPODROME.—Manager, Mr. W. H. White.

GLASGOW, Lanark.

Population, 776,967. Miles from London, 408.

THEATRE ROYAL. — Proprietors, Messrs. Howard and Wyndham, Limited; Manager, Mr. F. W. Wyndham; Acting-Manager, Mr. Percy

O. Humphrys; Scenic Artist, Mr. T. F. Dunn. Full license. Gas and electric light. Usual matinée day, Saturday.

KING'S THEATRE. — Proprietors. Howard and Wyndham, Limited; Managing Director, Mr. F. W. Wyndham; General Manager, Mr. George T. Minshull; Acting-Manager, Mr. Hugh Macfarlane; Musical Director, Mr. Alfred Carpenter; Scenic Artist, Mr. Tom F. Dunn. Full license. Holding capacity: Number of persons, 2,500. Proscenium measurements, 30ft. by 30ft.; stage, 46ft. deep by 70ft. wide. Gas and electric light. Amount of printing required: 1,000 sheets posting, 800 window bills, and 2,000 circulars. Usual matinée day, Saturday, 2 o'clock. Time of band rehearsal, 10.30. Voltage 250.

ROYALTY THEATRE.—Proprietors, Messrs. Howard and Wyndham, Limited; Manager, Mr. F. W. Wyndham; Acting-Manager, Mr. J. Carpenter. Full license. Gas and electric light. Usual matinée day, Wednesday.

ROYAL PRINCESS'S THEATRE.—Proprietor and Manager, Mr. Richard Waldon; Acting-Manager, Mr. Hugh Murdoch; Musical Director, Mr. Henri Vollmer; Scenic Artist, Mr. J. C. Bontor. Full license. Holding capacity: Number of persons, 2,700. Proscenium opening, 30ft.; stage 42ft. deep by 60ft. wide. Gas and electric light. Amount of printing required: 2,000 sheets for walls, 1,000 sheets for windows. Usual matinée day, Saturday, and every day at pantomime holidays. Time of band rehearsal, 12 noon.

GRAND. — Proprietors, Moss's Empires, Limited; District Manager, Mr. B. G. Maclachlan; Acting-Manager, W. Christie Grant; Musical Director, Mr. H. Henderson; Scenic Artist, Mr. B. Vennimore. Full license. Holding capacity: 1,915. Stage depth, 48ft.; width, 75ft.; proscenium opening, 32ft. 6in.; stage to fly floor, 22ft.; stage to grid, 48ft. Gas and electric light. Amount of printing required: 2,000 d.c. walls, 1,800 d.c. lithos. Time of band rehearsal, 11 a.m. Usual matinée day, Saturday.

METROPOLE THEATRE.—Proprietors, The Metropole Theatre, Glasgow, Limited; General Manager, Mr. Arthur Jefferson; Acting-Manager, Mr. G. Gordon Jefferson; Musical Director, Mr. F. Claxton Smith; Stage Manager, Mr. Frank Bennett. Carpenter, Mr. Bennett. Full license, smoking, and bars. Holding capacity: Number of persons, 1,800; amount varies with early doors. Depth of stage, 34ft. 10in.; width at back, 76ft.; front, 55ft.; proscenium measurements, 28ft. square. Gas and electric light. Amount of printing required: 2,000 pictorial sheets for walls, 1,500 lithos. No regular matinée day. Time of band rehearsal, 12.30 p.m. Best seasons of the year: New Year's week, autumn (September), spring (April), and fair holiday week (July). Dates of holiday vary in months quoted. Electric current 250 volts.

LYCEUM THEATRE (Govan).—Proprietor, Mr. Rich. Waldon; Manager, Mr. J. H. Oakden; Musical Director, Mr. Wilfred Ball; Scenic Artist, Mr. J. C. Bonter. Full double license. Holding capacity: Number of persons, 3,500; amount, £160. Proscenium opening, 26ft.; stage width, 60ft.; depth, 36ft.; to fly-rail, 21ft.; to grid, 53ft. Gas and electric light. Amount of printing required: 1,500 sheets. Time of band rehearsal, 12 noon. Booked in conjunction with Princess's. Current 250 volts.

PAVILION THEATRE.—Proprietors, Glasgow Pavilion, Limited; General Manager, Mr. Samuel Lloyd; Acting-Manager, Mr. E. Good; Musical Director, Mr. Howard W Galpin. Double license. Stage measurements, 24ft. by 40 ft. Gas and electric light. Usual matinée

23*

days, Thursday and Saturday. Time of band rehearsal, 11 o'clock a.m.

EMPIRE THEATRE.—Proprietors, Moss' Empires, Limited; Manager, Mr. George Manners; Assistant Manager, Mr. William Howgate. Booking circuit, Moss' Empires, Limited. Musical Director, Mr. W. B. Moore. License: Full (music and dancing), and fully licensed for bars. Holding capacity: Number of persons, 2,500; amount, £90. Proscenium opening, 30ft.; from back wall to footlights, 34ft. Gas and electric light. Time of band rehearsal, 12 noon. No matinée day. Bars all the surrounding halls in Glasgow, except Coliseum and Grand.

Bars all other Managements' Halls in Glasgow and the following towns: Coatbridge, Motherwell, Hamilton, Airdrie, Clydebank, Renfrew, Govan, and Paisley.

THE COLISEUM.—Proprietors, Moss' Empires, Limited; Manager, Mr. Harry Burdette. Booking circuit, Moss' Empires. Musical Director, Mr. Thomas Walker. Music and dancing license. Holding capacity: Number of persons, 3,500; admission, 3d. to 7s. 6d. Gas and electric light. Time of band rehearsal, 12 noon. Usual matinée day, Thursday, at 2.30. Bars all halls except Empire and Grand.

Bars all other Management's Halls in Glasgow and the following towns: Coatbridge, Motherwell, Hamilton, Airdrie, Clydebank, Renfrew, Govan and Paisley.

ZOO-HIPPODROME.—Proprietor and Manager, Mr. E. H. Bostock; Acting-Manager, Mr. E. H. A. Bostock; Musical Director, Capt. E. G. Summerfield. Music and dancing license, no drink license. Holding capacity: Number of persons, 2,500. Stage measurements, 40 ft. by 40ft. Gas and electric light. Usual matinée days, Wednesday and Saturday. Time of band rehearsal, 12·noon.

PALACE THEATRE OF VARIETIES.—Proprietor, Mr. Rich. Waldon; Manager, Mr. Harry McKelvie. Booking circuit, independent. Musical Director, Mr. Arthur Fellowes. Double license. Holding capacity: Number of persons, 3,000. Depth of stage, 40ft.; width, 70ft.; proscenium, 30ft. Electric light. Time of band rehearsal, 12 noon. No matinée day.

HENGLER'S.—Proprietor and Manager, Mr. Hengler.

BRITANNIA PANOPTICON.—Proprietor and Manager, Mr. A. E. Pickard. Booking circuit, direct. Music and dancing license. Gas and electric light. Time of band rehearsal, 11 a.m. Continuous performance, commencing at 2 p.m. Bars no surrounding halls.

GAIETY THEATRE OF VARIETIES.—Proprietors, The Glasgow Gaiety Theatre of Varieties, Limited; Manager, Mr. Harry Bowerman; Musical Director, Mr. Willie Milne. Double license. Gas and electric light. Time of band rehearsal, 12 noon. No regular matinée day. Bars no surrounding halls.

ATHENÆUM.—Manager. Mr. Jas. Lauder. Dramatic license. Holding capacity: Number of persons, 830. Stage and drop-curtain fitted. Depth and width of stage and proscenium measurements: Wing to wing, 37ft.; depth, 19ft.; proscenium, width of opening, 22ft.; height of arch, 14ft. 6in. Electric volts 110. Terms for hiring: £4 4s. to £6 6s. per night.

CITY HALL.—Manager, Mr. Walter Freer. Double license. Holding capacity: Number of persons, 3,300. Platform holds 400 people. Stage depth, 40ft.; width, 86ft. Gas and electric light. Terms for hiring: £7 10s. per night. Amount of deposit required on booking, 25 per cent.

BIJOU PICTURE HALL.—Manager and Proprietor, Mr. Ralph Pringle. Dramatic and music and dancing licenses. Platform. Gas and electric light.

THE PICTURE PALACE.—Manager and Proprietor, Mr. Ralph Pringle. Dramatic and music and dancing licenses. Proper stage. Gas and electric light.

CRANSTONHILL HALL. — Manager, Mr. Walter Freer. Holding capacity: 300. Platform. Terms for hiring: £1 1s. Deposit required on booking, 25 per cent.

SPRINGBURN HALLS.—Manager, Mr. Walter Freer. Holding capacity: Large hall, 1,600; lesser hall, 350. Platform. Electric light. Terms for hiring: Large hall, £3 10s.; lesser hall, £1 5s. Deposit required on booking, 25 per cent. Organ rates extra. Hire of screen and electric current for kinematograph, 10s.

POLLOCKSHIELDS HALL.—Manager, Mr. Walter Freer. Holding capacity: 320. Platform. Electric light. Terms for hiring: £1 1s. Deposit required on booking, 25 per cent. Hire of screen and current for kinematograph, 10s.

KINNING PARK HALL. — Manager, Mr. Walter Freer. Holding capacity: 1,500. Platform. Electric light. Terms for hiring: £2 17s. 6d. Deposit required on booking, 25 per cent. Organ rates extra. Hire of screen and electric current for kinematograph, 10s.

MARYHILL HALL. — Manager, Mr. Walter Freer. Holding capacity: 800. Platform. Electric light. Terms for hiring: £1 10s. Deposit required on booking, 25 per cent. Hire of screen and electric current for kinematograph, 10s.

DIXON HALL.—Manager, Mr. Walter Freer. Holding capacity: 1,300. Platform. Electric light. Terms for hiring: £2 10s. Deposit required on booking, 25 per cent. Organ rates extra. Hire of screen and electric current for kinematograph, 10s.

KINGSTON HALL. — Manager, Mr. Walter Freer. Holding capacity: 1,200. Platform. Electric light. Terms for hiring: £3 2s. 6d. Deposit required on booking, 25 per cent. Hire of screen and electric current for kinematograph, 10s.

BERKELEY HALL.—Manager, Mr. Walter Freer. Holding capacity: 900. Platform. Electric light. Terms for hiring: £4 2s. 6d. Hire of screen and current for kinematograph, 10s. Deposit required on booking, 25 per cent.

KENT HALL.—Manager, Mr. Walter Freer. Holding capacity: 400. Platform. Electric light. Terms for hiring: 30s. Deposit required on booking, 25 per cent. 10s. extra for kinematograph exhibitions, including use of screen and current.

ST. ANDREW'S HALL.—Manager, Mr. Walter Freer. Holding capacity: Number of persons, 4,500. Platform. Electric light. Terms for hiring: £13 10s. to £20. Deposit required on booking, 25 per cent. Organ rates, 30s. per hour; additional hours, 12s. Current and screen for kinematograph, 10s.

HILLHEAD HALL. — Manager, Mr. Walter Freer. Holding capacity: 360. Platform. Terms for hiring: £2 2s. Deposit required on booking, 25 per cent.

LANGSIDE HALLS.—Manager, Mr. Walter Freer. Holding capacity: 850. Platform. Electric light. Terms for hiring: £2 2s. Deposit required on booking, 25 per cent. Hire of screen and electric current for kinematograph, 10s.

TOBAGO STREET HALL.— Manager, Mr. Walter Freer. Holding capacity: 350. Platform. Terms for hiring: 15s. Deposit required on booking, 25 per cent.

Market day, Wednesday.

Medical officers.—Dr. W. G. Cook, 6, Wilton Mansions, Kelvinside; hours, 3-4.30; 'phone, W687; Dr. F. Henry, 4, Osborne Terrace, Copland Road, Govan; Surgery, 980, Govan Road. A.U.: Dr. Cook, as above. M.H.A.R.A.: Dr. Cook, as above.

Agents.—M.H.A.R.A., and V.A.F.: Branch office, Mrs. Ripon, 141, Bath Street. A.U.: Messrs. Stevenson, Taylor and Company, 260, Buchanan Street.

RECOMMENDED APARTMENTS.

Mrs. Gourlay, 40, Buccleuch Street.
Mrs. Muirhead, 59, Renfrew Street.—Bedrooms, sitting-rooms, combined.
Mrs. Marshall, 976, Govan Road, Govan.—Large parlour; one or two beds; bath.
Mrs. MacLachlan, 94, Hill Street, Garnet Hill.—Large parlour and combined sitting-room and 2 bedrooms; bath.
Mrs. Dewar, 6, Langlands Road, Govan.—2 bed, 2 sitting-rooms, and combined; 2 pianos; bath.

GLOSSOP, Derbyshire.

Population, 21,526. Miles from London, 114.

THEATRE ROYAL.—Proprietor and Manager, Mr. Sydney Spenser; Musical Director, Mr. Wilfrid Cottrill; Scenic Artist, Mr. J. Porter. Restricted license. Holding capacity: Number of persons, 950; amount, £40. Depth of stage, 30ft.; width, 48ft.; proscenium opening, 22ft. 6in. Electric light (three colours on stage). Volts, 240. Prices, 6d. to 2s. Amount of printing required, 400 sheets, 400 lithos. Matinée day, Saturday (if any). Time of band rehearsal, 1 p.m.

VICTORIA HALL.—Manager, Mr. Edward Thompson. Music and dancing license. Holding capacity: Number of persons, 600. No fit-up and no proscenium. Stage, 36ft. by 20ft. deep, and 18ft. clear height between ceiling and stage. Gas and electric light; 6d. per unit for current consumed, and 10s. for running special cable and connecting up bioscope. Amount of printing required: 1,000 window bills, 100 posters, and 5,000 school tickets. Terms for hiring: One night, £1 10s.; two nights, £2 5s.; three, £3; four, £3 15s.; five, £4 10s.; six, £5; Saturday and Tuesday only (each night), £2; matinées, 10s. extra. Amount of deposit required on booking, one-half; whole amount if companies come from outside Borough.

ST. JAMES'S HALL, Railway Street.—Has seating capacity of 200. Charges, per night, 10s.; with piano, 5s. extra. A graduated scale for several nights. Address, Mr. A. Philips, Liberal Club, Glossop.

Dates of local fairs, May 6 and Sept. 20.
Early closing, Tuesday; market, Saturday.

Glossop is a corporate town in the extreme north of Derbyshire, and in importance the second in the county. Its population is entirely industrial. The chief industries are cotton, calico-printing, paper-bleaching, and iron works. It has been wittily but truly said that "the town is geographically in Derbyshire but commercially in Lancashire." Hadfield, about 1½ mile distant from Glossop, though connected with it by rail and electric tram, forms one of the wards of the council. Any important matter in Glossop invariably taps Hadfield for support, but not vice versâ.

Hadfield has three places suitable for concerts and entertainments:—

LIBERAL HALL, Bank Street.—This is an excellent hall for a large meeting. Its seating capacity is between 450 and 500. Charges vary according to the object. For entertain-

ments or lectures the charge is 10s. 6d. per night, plus 2s. for gas. There is a graduated scale of charges for a number of days. Apply to Mr. Hodkinson, Liberal Club, Bank-street, Hadfield.

FREE LIBRARY or HADFIELD PUBLIC HALL, Station Road, Hadfield. — Seating capacity, 350. Charges per night, 10s., plus 1s. for gas. A graduated scale if engaged for more than one night.—Address, Mr. John Battye, on the premises.

ASSEMBLY ROOMS, Conservative Club, Hadfield.—This is a very good room in the form of the letter T. Its seating capacity is:—Body of room, 450; splendid gallery, 100. Charges for entertainments or lectures, 10s. 6d. per night, with a graduated scale for a number of days. Address, Mr. James Bamforth, at the Club.

GLOUCESTER, Glos.

Population, 47,955. Miles from London, 114.

KING'S HALL.—Proprietors, Poole's Theatres, Ltd. Full license. Holding capacity: Number of persons, 1,300. Stage measurements: 45ft. by 45ft.; proscenium opening, 28ft. Electric light throughout. Gas throughout as a stand-by. It bars Cheltenham, Stroud, and Tewkesbury. Now run as a "Picture Palace."

PALACE OF VARIETIES (late Theatre Royal).—Twice nightly, at 6.50 and 9. Proprietors, Poole's Theatres, Ltd.; Manager, Mr. C. W. Poole; Acting - Manager, Mr. R. T. Rea; Musical Director, Mr. F. Leslie. Full license. Holding capacity: Number of persons, 1,200. Stage measurements: Depth, 32ft. by 35ft. wide; proscenium opening, 20ft. Electric light throughout (gas as a stand-by). No regular matinée day. Time of band rehearsal, 1.30 p.m. It bars Cheltenham, Stroud, and Tewkesbury.

SHIRE HALL.—For concerts only. Seats, 750, Orchestra, 250. Electric direct current. Apply Clerk o the County Council.

GUILDHALL.—For concerts only. Seats, 600. Platform, 14ft. 6in. by 40ft. Electric direct current. Apply City Treasurer.

CORN EXCHANGE. — Concerts. Kinematograph and other entertainments. Seats, 600 to 700. Platform 13ft. by 19ft. 6in. Apply City Treasurer.

BATHS.—Concerts. Kinematograph and other entertainments. Seats, 600 to 700. Electric direct current. Apply City Treasurer.

Population is mostly industrial, employed at dock, large wagon works, and other manufactories. Portables are not allowed. The Athletic Ground here is let for alfresco concerts and circus pitches. Barton Fair on Sept. 28 and the Mop on the following Monday attract a great many country people.

Early closing day, Thursday; market day, Saturday.

M.H.A.R.A. Agency: W. Alexander, Fleece Hotel, Westgate Street. V.A.F.: The same.

GODALMING, Surrey.

Population, 9,000. Miles from London, 34.

BOROUGH HALL.—Manager, Mr. J. Yeomans. Double license. Holding capacity: Number of persons, 600. Depth and width of stage and proscenium measurements, 33ft. by 20ft.; proscenium, 24ft.; opening, 22ft. high. Electric light, 240 volts direct. Eight billposters' stations. Terms for hiring: 1 night, £2 10s.; two nights, £4 10s.; three nights, £6; lighting extra. Amount of deposit required on booking, £1. Early closing day, Wednesday.

No local fairs or sites available for portables, alfresco concerts, or circuses.

GOOLE, Yorks.

Population, 19,000. Miles from London, 173.

THEATRE ROYAL. — Proprietor, Mr. Fred Greaves; Manager, Mr. A. Silver. Dramatic license. Holding capacity: Number of persons. 800; amount, £35. Stage measurements: Depth, 22ft.; width, 31ft. 6in.; proscenium, 18ft. wide. Lighted by gas. Amount of printing required, 400 wall, 300 lithos. Usual matinée day, Saturday. Time of band rehearsal, 1 p.m.

Early closing day, Thursday; market day, Wednesday.

GOVAN.

See Glasgow.

GRANGEMOUTH, Stirling.

Population, 9,500.

TOWN HALL.—Manager, Mr. James Hutchison. Holding capacity: Number of persons, 900. Stage, 25ft deep and 23ft. wide. Lighted by gas, incandescent. Terms for hiring, £2 12s. per night. Amount of deposit required on booking, 10s. Apply, Town Clerk.

No local fairs or sites available for portables, alfresco concerts, or circuses.

GRANGE-OVER-SANDS, Lancs.

VICTORIA HALL.—Proprietors, Grange Urban District Council; Manager, Mr. Thos. Huddleston. Dramatic and dancing licenses. Holding capacity: Number of persons, 450. Stage measurements: Depth, 15ft.; width, 36ft. Gas. Terms for hiring: £2 2s. per night. Amount of deposit required on booking, 10s.

GRANTHAM, Lincs.

Population, 17,593. Miles from London, 105.

THEATRE ROYAL AND EMPIRE. — Proprietor and Manager, Mr. J. A. Campbell; Acting-Manager, Mr. W. Marshall; Musical Director, Mr. H. Beech; Scenic Artist, Mr. A. Maurice. Full license. Holding capacity: Number of persons, 1,400; amount, £55. Stage opening, 21ft.; 30ft. deep, 50ft. wide; cloths, 18ft. by 26ft.; wings, 16ft. 6in. Electric light (three colours). Amount of printing required. 300 sheets, 100 lithos. Usual matinée day, Saturday, 2 p.m. Seven dressing-rooms. Band rehearsal, Thursday, 2 p.m. No bands or towns barred. Electric current direct. 240 volts.

This theatre can be rented on Monday, Tuesday, and Wednesday evenings at nominal charges to concert parties, etc. For touring companies the best three nights are the last three.

Local fairs, Monday, Tuesday, and Wednesday, following third Sunday in Lent. Sites available for portables, alfresco concerts, etc., Blue Ram Yard (Apply, Mr. Cockersoll, Blue Ram). Field, Harlasdon Rd. (apply, Mr. Redford, Blue Man Inn).

Early closing day, Thursday; market day, Saturday.

Medical Officer.—A.A.: Dr. C. Trior, Spitalgate House, London Road. A.U.: The same.

Agent.—M.H.A.R.A.: Thomas Hall, Blue Cow Hotel. V.A.F.: The same.

GRAVESEND, Kent.

Population, 27,199. Miles from London, 22.

GRAND THEATRE OF VARIETIES.—Managing Director, Mr. J. Collins; Manager, Mr. T. W. Wright; Acting-Manager, Mr. G. Leslic;

Musical Director, Mr. W. Loosley. Music and dancing license. Electric light, 440 voltage. Band rehearsal, Monday, 2 o'clock.

PUBLIC HALL.—Secretary, Mr. R. Feaver Clarke, High Street, Gravesend. Touring companies usually visit this hall. Seating accommodation about 900 to 1,000. Size of stage, 21ft. deep, 33ft. wide; opening, 20ft. wide, 15ft. high.

UPPER PUBLIC HALL. — Seats 300-400. Concert platform.

FACTORY HALL, NORTHFLEET.—Secretary, Mr. W. H. Steadman, Factory Club, Northfleet. Size of hall, 62ft. by 42ft.; size of stage, 24ft. by 16ft. No dramatic license.

Population of Northfleet 13,000, working class, mostly occupied in cement manufacture.

ROSHERVILLE GARDENS.—Open Easter, 1909, for Summer and Winter Seasons. There is a large open-air stage for café chantant performances. Also a concert room and a bijou theatre. An orchestra also plays during the day, and on Sundays special concerts are given, when vocalists are engaged.

Gravesend population, some residential, but chiefly waterside and working class. Circus pitches are frequently obtained in the town and district. Portables visit the town. Concert parties use the Promenade during the summer season. Northfleet is about one mile and a-half from Gravesend Central, Rosherville under the mile, and electric trams to both places. Wednesday is the best day for business, the next best being Monday.

Early closing day, Wednesday; market day, Saturday.

GRAYS, Essex.

Population, 13,834. Miles from London, 21.

PUBLIC HALL.—Lessee and Manager, Mr. Albert P. Cross. Double license. Holding capacity: Number of persons, 400. Stage, 12ft. deep, 18ft wide, and five changes scenery. Proscenium opening, 14ft. Gas and electric light, continuous current 230 volts. Amount of printing required: 350 day bills, 10 six-sheets, 40 three-sheets. Sharing or rental. The hall is now run as a "Picture Palace."

Portables and circuses visit. For the last three years alfresco entertainments have been given in the Council's Park by Mr. Albert P. Cross.

GREAT YARMOUTH, Norfolk.

Population, 53,000. Miles from London, 121

ROYAL AQUARIUM THEATRE.—Proprietor, Mr. J. W. Nightingale; Assistant Manager, Mr. W. H. Nightingale. Electric current, 100 volts alternating.

THEATRE ROYAL.—Proprietor and Manager, Mr. J. W. Nightingale; Assistant Manager, Mr. Walter Nightingale.

BRITANNIA PIER PAVILION.—Proprietors, Britannia Pier Co. Manager, J. W. Nightingale. Electric current, 200 volts alternating.

HIPPODROME.—Proprietor and Manager, Mr. Geo. Gilbert.

CHAPPELLS BEACH CONCERT RING.— Proprietor, Mrs. Lawton. Open-air concerts. Summer months only.

WELLINGTON PIER PAVILION.—Proprietors, Great Yarmouth Corporation. Manager, Arthur A. Cash. Seating accommodation 1,500. Electric current, 200 volts alternating. Attached to the Pier also is a spacious Winter Gardens, used in the summer months for dancing and skating, and concerts in the winter months.

TOWN HALL.—Hall Keeper, Mr. James William Moy. Music and dancing license. Holding capacity: Number of persons, 800; amount varies. Depth and width of stage: 15ft. by 45ft. Electric light. Terms for hiring: One night, £4 4s.; three, £10; six, £15 15s.

GEM HALL, Marine Parade.—Manager, Mr. C. B. Cochran. Available for Kinematograph entertainments. Voltage 100 alternating current.

MINSTREL ARENA on Beach.—Proprietor, Mr. A. J. Penny. Summer months only. Open-air concerts.

GORLESTON-ON-SEA PALACE. — Manager, Mr. George Gilbert. (near Great Yarmouth.)

About one-half of the local population are engaged in the fishing trade, the other half being mostly boarding-house and lodging-house keepers, etc. In the summer season the visiting population varies from 50,000 to 100,000. The date of the local fair is the Friday and Saturday following Easter Monday each year The town is not visited by portables. Sites for alfresco concerts are obtainable, application being made to the Town Council.

Early closing day, Thursday; market days, Wednesday and Saturday.

Medical Officers.—A.A.: Dr. T. P. Devlin, 43, King Street (hours, 9-10, 2-3, 6-7); Dr. C. O'Farrell, The Lodge, Norfolk Square. A.U.: The same. M.H.A.R.A.: Dr. Devlin, as above.

Agent.—A.U.: B. Powell, the Royal Standard, Marine Parade. M.H.A.R.A.: The same; V.A.F.: The same.

GREAT BOOKHAM, Surrey.

(3 miles from Leatherhead.)

OLD BARN HALL.—Proprietors, The Trustees; Hon. Secretary, Mr. R. H. Lindam, The Gables, Great Bookham. Dramatic and dancing licenses. Licensed to hold 180. Very roomy stage, with footlights. Gas. Terms for hiring: Afternoon, £1 1s.; evening, £1 11s. 6d.; and 5s. to caretaker.

No local fairs.

GREAT GREENFORD, near Southall, Middlesex.

BETHAM'S SCHOOLS.—Proprietors, The Governors of Betham's Charity; Manager, Mr. A. W. Perkin, Greenford Green. Dramatic and dancing licenses. Holding capacity: Number of persons, 175. No proper stage. Gas. Very small hall, only let for charitable purposes.

GREAT TORRINGTON, Devon.

TOWN HALL.—Proprietors, the Town Council; Manager, Mr. J. D. Copp. Holds about 300. No proper stage. Gas. Terms for hiring: £1 10s. for first night and £1 per night after, which includes gas and fees of hall-keeper; fires extra. Rent to be paid in advance. Permission of the Mayor has to be obtained for use of the hall.

Dates of local fairs: First Thursday in May and second Thursday in October. There is a large piece of ground, called the Barley Grove, adjoining the town, which can be always used at small cost for portables, alfresco concerts, and circuses.

There is also a small hall adjoining the market place held by a lessee from the Town Council.

GREENOCK, Renfrew.

Population, 71,783. Miles from London, 423. Miles from Glasgow, 22½.

ALEXANDRA THEATRE.—Proprietors, the Greenock Theatre Co., Limited; Managing Director, Mr. R. C. Buchanan; Resident Directors and Managers, Messrs. A. B. and J. J. Wright; Musical Director, Mr. C. E. Bond; Scenic Artist and Stage Manager, Mr. J. Connor. Dramatic license. Holding capacity: Number of persons, 2,000. Stage measurements: 38ft. deep by 60ft. wide.; proscenium opening, 28ft.; width, fly-rail to fly-rail, 36 ft.; stage to grid, 56ft. Lighting: Stage, electric; auditorium, electric and gas. Time of band rehearsal, 12 o'clock.

HIPPODROME THEATRE. — Lessees, Greenock Hippodrome, Limited; Manager, Mr. Harry L. Skivington. Holding capacity: Number of persons, 1,400.

EMPIRE THEATRE.—Lessees, Greenock Empire Syndicate; Responsible Manager, Mr. Edward McCormick; Acting-Manager, Mr. T. J. Colquhoun. Holding capacity: Number of persons, 1,000. Variety twice nightly. Bars Greenock houses. Electric current. 250 volts continuous.

TOWN HALL.—Proprietors, Town Council. Holding capacity, 3,000. Used for concerts, picture shows, and public meetings.

TEMPERANCE INSTITUTE.—Apply, Secretary, Mr. William D. Thomson. No dramatic license. Holding capacity: Number of persons, 1,000; amount, over £30 at 6d. and 1s. Platform 25ft. by 14ft., height 30ft. Electric light 250 volts. Terms for hiring: £2 7s. 6d. per night; half more if two shows or matinées; 10s. extra per night for light for lantern work; footlights extra. Amount of deposit required on booking, 20 per cent.

BANK STREET HALL.—Proprietors, Town Council. Holds 700. Used for meetings, concerts, and J.P. Courts.

Fair holidays, first Thursday in July. Open-air site. Prince's Pier, vacant ground.

The population is mainly industrial, ship-building, and sugar refining. The Greenock fair always opens on the first Thursday in July, and continues during the following Friday and Saturday. The town is very rarely visited by portables. There are hardly any sites suitable for alfresco concerts or circus pitches unless on the extreme outskirts of the town.

Early closing day, Wednesday.

A.A. Medical Officer: Dr. W. S. Cook, 2, Ardgowan Square. M.H.A.R.A.: Dr. A. S. Seiger, 9, Grey Place.

Agent.— M.H.A.R.A.: E. Seiger, 41, West Black hall Street. V.A.F.: The same.

GRIMSBY, Lincs.

Population, 78,000. Miles from London, 154.

PRINCE OF WALES, THEATRE.—Proprietors, Prince of Wales Theatre Co. (Great Grimsby), Limited; Manager, Mr. Joseph H. Curry; Acting-Manager, Mr. J. W. North. Musical Director, Mr. J. R. Bingley; Scenic Artist, Mr. W. Stocks. Double license. Holding capacity: Number of persons, 2,700; amount, £95, at cheap prices. Stage 40ft. deep by 60ft.; proscenium opening, 30ft. Electric light, 230 volts. Printing required: 1,000 posting, 500 lithos. No matinée day. Time of band rehearsal, 1 p.m.

PALACE THEATRE.—Proprietors, Grimsby Palace Theatre and Buffet, Limited; General Manager, Mr. G. Rhodes Parry; Secretary, Mr. F. Verner Walford. Booking circuit, direct. Musical Director, Mr. S. Evens.

Music and dancing license. Holding capacity:
Number of persons, 1,600. Amount, £50. Stage
measurements, 30ft. deep by 64ft. wide.; proscenium, 36ft. by 28ft. Electric light. Time of
band rehearsal, 1.30. No matinée day. Bars
the Empire and Pier Cleethorpes.

TIVOLI THEATRE.—Proprietors, limited
company; Managing Director, Mr. J. H.
Curry. Bars local halls. Electric light, 250 volts.
Now closed.

PICTUREDROME.—Lessee and Manager, Mr.
Matt Raymond. Twice nightly with animated
pictures.

KING'S HALL.—Manager, Mr. Hubert
Ravenhill. Music and dancing license. Holding capacity: Number of persons, over 900.
Stage: 13ft. by 26ft., and footlights; but no
proscenium. Electric light. Amount of
printing required: Mainly window billing,
about 2,000 sheets double crown. Amount
of deposit required on booking: Half first
week's rent.

Grimsby is a residential town; a great number of the inhabitants are engaged in the
fishing industry. Statute fair is held on May
14 and 15. Sites for alfresco entertainments,
shows, etc., are obtainable in Freeman Street,
Market Place, and Old Market Place. No difficulty would be encountered at any time of
the year in obtaining licenses for portables.

Early closing day, Thursday; market days,
Tuesday, Friday, and Saturday.

Medical officers.—A.A.: Dr. J. M. Duncan,
"Bonaccord," Wilholme Road West. A.U.: The
same. M.H.A.R.A.: The same.

Agents: A.U.: L. Colbrook, Railway Hotel,
M.H.A.R.A. and V.A.F.: The same.

RECOMMENDED APARTMENTS.

Mrs. Smithies, 23, Eleanor Street, Hainton
Square.—2 Sitting-rooms, 2 bedrooms, 1 combined
room.

GUERNSEY, Channel Islands.

Population, 42,000.

ST. JULIAN'S THEATRE.—Lessee and Manager, Mr. Edward Marris; Acting-Manager,
Mr. Stanley Hope; Musical Director, Mr.
George Ess; Scenic Artist, Mr. C. H. Frampton. Holding capacity: Number of persons, 800;
amount, £80. Stage measurements, 40ft. by 31ft.;
proscenium opening, 21ft. Electric light direct,
210 volts. Printing: 200 sheets, 200 lithos. Usual
matinée day, Saturday. Time of band rehearsal, 1 p.m.

CAUDIC GROUNDS. — Open-air entertainments are given during the season here.

Early closing day, Thursday; market day,
Saturday.

Medical officer.—A.A.: Dr. B. Wallace, Grange;
'phone 87. A.U.: The same.

GUILDFORD, Surrey.

Population, 20,000. Miles from London, 30.

COUNTY AND BOROUGH HALL.—Manager,
Mr. Fredk. H. Elsley. Dramatic license. Holding capacity: Number of persons, 806. Platform, 14ft. deep, 30ft. wide; may be extended
4ft. in depth. Gas and electric light. Amount of
printing required: 300 sheets. Terms for hiring: Theatricals, £2 10s. first night; second
night, £1 5s.; concerts, £2 2s.; gas and electric light extra. Amount of deposit required
on booking, £1 1s. per night. Usual prices of
admission for theatricals: Front seats, 3s.,
gallery and second seats, 2s.; back seats, 1s. A
good house realises about £40.

Early closing day, Wednesday; market day,
Tuesday.

GUISBROUGH, Yorks.

Population, 5,645. Miles from London, 248.

TEMPERANCE HALL.—Proprietors, Temperance Society; Manager, Mr. Thomas El-
coate, Temperance Hall, Guisbrough. Gas.

Dates of local fairs: Last Tuesday in April
and second Tuesday in November. Application for sites available for portables, etc.,
should be made to Mr. Robert Taylor, Bell-
mangate.

Early closing day, Wednesday; market day,
Tuesday.

GWAUN-CAE-GURWEN, Swansea Valley.

PUBLIC HALL.—Manager and Secretary, Mr.
W. D. Evans. Dramatic license. Size of hall,
85ft. by 47ft.; stage, 17ft. by 40ft., dressing-
rooms.

HADDINGTON, Haddington.

Population, 4,250. Miles from London, 388.

ASSEMBLY ROOM.—Manager, Town Chamberlain. Music and dancing license. Holding
capacity: Number of persons, 500. Stage,
12ft. by 9ft. Lighted by gas. Terms for hiring, £1 per night, payment forehanded.

Date of local county show, July. Good sites are
available for portables, alfresco concerts, and
circuses at Shaw and Hinesy Fair first Friday
in February.

Early closing day, last Thursday in month;
market day, Friday.

HADLEIGH, Suffolk.

Population, 3,245. Miles from London, 70.

TOWN HALL.—Manager, Mr. John King.
Has dramatic license. Holding capacity:
Number of persons, 500; amount varies. Stage
2ft. 9ins. by 25ft. by 14ft. Lighted by gas.
Terms for hiring: Dramatic, £1 11s. concert, £1 2s. 6d. Amount of deposit required
on booking, 10s.

Early closing day, Wednesday; market day,
Monday.

HALESWORTH, Suffolk.

Population, 2,246. Miles from London, 100.

CORN HALL.—Proprietor and Manager, Mr.
H. J. Beatton. Dramatic and music and dancing licenses. Holding capacity: Number of
persons, 300. Portable stage. Gas. Terms for
hiring: 30s. for one night, 50s. for two nights.

Early closing day, Thursday; market day,
Tuesday.

HALIFAX, Yorks.

Population, 104,936. Miles from London, 202.

THEATRE ROYAL.—Proprietors, Northern
Theatres Co., Limited; Managing Director, Mr.
William Robinson; Musical Director, Mr. Edwin James. Double license. No Excise license.
Holding capacity: Number of persons, 1,800;
amount, £130. Stage measurements, 40ft. deep,
60ft. wide; proscenium opening, 30ft. Gas and
electric light. Amount of printing required:
800 d.c. sheets, 600 lithos. Band rehearsal,
1 p.m.

GRAND THEATRE. — Proprietors, the
Northern Theatres Co., Limited; Acting-Manager,
Director, Mr. Wm. Robinson; Acting-Manager,
Mr. S. Winks; Musical Director, Mr. J. White-
lock. Full license. Holding capacity: Number

of persons, 2,000. Stage measurements: Depth, 30ft.; width, 60ft. front, 40ft. back; proscenium, 30ft. opening. Electric light. Amount of printing required: 800 d.c. sheet posters, 600 lithos. Band rehearsal, 1 o'clock.

PALACE AND HIPPODROME.—Lessee and Manager, Mr. Frank Macnaghten; Resident Manager, Mr. Reg. H. Foster; Booking Circuit, Macnaghten Vaudeville Circuit; Musical Director, Mr. T. Murgatroyd. Double license. Holding capacity: Number of persons, 2,500. Stage measurements: width, 60ft.; depth, 30ft.; proscenium opening, 32ft. Gas and electric light Band rehearsal, 12 noon. Matinée day discontinued.

MECHANICS' HALL.—Manager, Mr. Frederick Taylor. License: Music and dancing; dramatic can be obtained on application. Holding capacity: Number of persons, 900. Orchestra holds 240; can be pulled down for opera. Lighted by gas. Terms for hiring: £14 14s. per week; concerts, £3 3s.; lectures, £2 12s.

VICTORIA HALL.—Mr. W. H. Mitchell, 8, Ward's End, Halifax. Double license. Holding capacity: Number of persons, 3,000; seating normally 2,400; amount, £250. Full and complete fit-up. Stage 27ft. opening; 30ft deep. Dressing-rooms. Electric light. Terms for hiring: In season, £100 per week; light extra. Amount of deposit required on booking: Subject to arrangement.
Dates of local fairs: June 24 and first week in November. Sites available for portables and alfresco concerts.
Early closing day, Thursday; market day, Saturday.
Medical Officer.—A.A.: Dr. H. Croly, Horton House. M.H.A.R.A.: The same.
Agent.—A.U.: F. Greenwood, Shakespeare Hotel. M.H.A.R.A.: The same. V.A.F.: The same.

RECOMMENDED APARTMENTS.

Mrs. Fasker, 9, Corporation Street.—Sitting-room, 2 bedrooms, 2 combined rooms.
Mrs. M. Booth, 42, Greenwood Street.—1 Sitting-room, and 2 bedrooms; piano.

HALSTEAD, Essex.

Population, 6,073. Miles from London, 54.

TOWN HALL.—Manager, Mr. W. Hurry. Dramatic license. Holding capacity: Number of persons, 400. Depth and width of stage, 32ft. wide, 16ft. deep. Lighted by gas. Terms for hiring: One night, 37s. 6d.; two nights, 57s.; three nights, 71s. 6d. Amount of deposit required on booking, 1 guinea.
No fixed dates for local fairs. Two or three meadows are available for portables and circuses.
Early closing day, Wednesday; market day, Tuesday.

HALTWHISTLE, Northumberland.

Population, 3,145. Miles from London, 305.

MECHANICS' HALL.—Address, The Secretary. Full license. Holding capacity: Number of persons, 600. Platform only. Lighted by gas. Amount of deposit required on booking, 10s.
Early closing day, Wednesday; market day, Thursday.

HAMILTON, Lanarkshire.

Population, 32,775. Miles from London, 392.

THE HIPPODROME.—Proprietor, Mr. E. H. Bostock; Manager, Mr. René Clayton. Book-

ing circuit, Bostock. Musical Director, Mr. Miller. Double license. Holding capacity: Number of persons, 1,600. Stage measurements: 28ft. by 30ft. Electric light. Time of band rehearsal, 12 noon. Usual matinée day, Saturday. Two houses nightly; run solely as a variety hall, booking in conjunction with Hippodromes, Paisley, Norwich, Ipswich, and Glasgow—all owned by Mr. Bostock.
Market day, Friday
Agent.—V.A.F.: Mr. Cocks, Commercial Hotel

HANLEY, Staffs.

Population, 62,226. Miles from London, 147½.

THEATRE ROYAL.—Proprietors, Hanley Theatres and Circus Co., Limited; Managing Director, Mr. C. G. Elphinstone; Manager, Mr. Douglas Elphinstone. Stage is in sections, 92ft. wide and 46ft. deep. Depth of cellar, containing appliances for lifting of scenery, etc., is 18ft.; pit, 56ft. by 62ft. Accommodation: gallery, 600; pit, 1,200; second circle, 400; circle, 215; orchestra stalls, 75; total, 2,490.

GRAND THEATRE OF VARIETIES.—Proprietor, Hanley Theatres and Circus Co., Limited; Managing Director, Mr. C. G. Elphinstone; Manager, Mr. Arthur Rand. Stage is 63ft. wide and 44ft. deep, and is so constructed that it can be removed to make way for a circus arena. Accommodation: dress circle, 200; Orchestra stalls, 100; upper circle, 800; pit stalls, 280; pit, 1,200; gallery, 1,500, total, 4,080.

VICTORIA HALL (TOWN HALL).—Proprietors, The Corporation; anager, George Barlow, Borough Treasurer and Accountant. Double license. Holding capacity: Number of persons, 2,371; orchestra, 350. Various charges. Telescopic stage, 18ft. 6in. by 46ft.; height to ceiling, 46ft. Electric light, 100 volts. Terms: From £5 8s. per night to £25 6s. per week.

KING'S HALL.—Proprietors, Messrs. Moore and Kennedy.
Date of local fair: Hanley Wakes Week, commencing with first Sunday in August. Sites are available for portables.
Early closing day, Thursday; market day Wednesday and Saturday.
Medical Officer.—A.A.: Dr. A. R. Moody, 14, Albion Street. M.H.A.R.A.: The same.
Agent.—A.U.: Tom McHugh, Antelope Hotel. M.H.A.R.A.: The same. V.A.F.: The same.

RECOMMENDED APARTMENTS.

Mrs. Lindop, 21, Church Street.—2 sitting-rooms, 2 bedrooms; bath: piano.
Mrs. Dudson, Arbour House, Church Street.—2 sitting, 4 bedrooms; bath.

HARROGATE, Yorks.

Population, 28,423. Miles from London, 199.

GRAND OPERA HOUSE.—Proprietors, the Grand Opera House (Harrogate), Limited; Managing Director, Mr. William Peacock; Acting-Manager, Mr. C. Fielding-Smith; Musical Director, Mr. J. T. Dearlove. Full dramatic license. Holding capacity: Number of persons, 1,500; amount, £125. Stage measurements: 28ft. deep, 71ft. wide, 44ft. to grid; width between fly rails, 36ft. 6in.; proscenium opening, 27ft. Electric current, 100 volts alternating. Printing, 528 sheets, 400 d.c., 1,000 circulars. Usual matinée days, Wednesday and Saturday during season. Time of band rehearsal, 1 p.m. Best months, July, August, September, and October. Bars Knaresborough, Ripon, Ilkley.

WINTER GARDENS.—Proprietors, Corporation. General Manager, Mr. H. J. Buckland,

Music and dancing license. Holds 900. Electric light. Terms: £6 15s. one night.

TOWN HALL.

THE KURSAAL.

SPA CONCERT ROOMS.

Medical Officers.—Dr. A. W. H. Walker, 100, Station Parade (hours, 8-9 and 4-6; wires, "Hensley Walker, Harrogate"; 'phone, 56); Dr. A. Mouillot, Eton House. A.U.: Dr. Walker, as above.

HARPENDEN, Herts.

Population, 4,725. Miles from London, 25.

PUBLIC HALL.—Proprietors, the Urban District Council; Licensee, Clerk to Urban District Council. Dramatic license. Holding capacity: Number of persons, 300. No proper stage. Gas. Terms for hiring: First night, £2 12s. 6d.; second, £1 11s. 6d.; third, £1 1s., payable in advance.

Annual fair, September. Football Ground, Station Road, available for portables, etc.

Early closing day, Wednesday; no market day.

HARROW, Middlesex.

Population, 10,220. Miles from London, 11.

PUBLIC HALL.—Proprietors, A Company: Manager, Mr. Ernest Lloyd. Dramatic and music and dancing licenses. Holding capacity: Number of persons, 325. Proper stage. Gas and electric light. The charge for hall for one night is £2 4s. 6d., for two nights £3 18s. 6d., and for each morning performance 15s. Amount of deposit required on booking: £1 1s.

Early closing day, Wednesday; no market day.

HARTLEPOOL (East), Durham.

Population, 22,723. Miles from London, 250.

EMPRESS THEATRE.—Proprietors, Mr. Councillor Everton and Mr. J. W. Cragg; Manager, Mr. Harry Burns; Acting-Manager, Mr. C. Ferrier; Booking Circuit, Burns; Musical Director, Mr. Rawson Buckley. Double license. Electric light and gas. Time of band rehearsal, 1 p.m.

TOWN HALL.—Proprietors, the Hartlepool Corporation; Manager, Mr. Christopher Robson, Borough Accountant, Hartlepool. Music and dancing license. Holding capacity: Number of persons, about 900. No proper stage, only platform. Gas and electric light. Terms for hiring: £2 2s. per night, or terms for longer periods on application. Full amount to be paid in advance. Special cable for lantern for picture shows.

Agent.—V.A.F.: T. H. Tomlinson, Cleveland Hotel.

HARTLEPOOL (West), Durham.

Population, 62,627. Miles from London, 252.

PALACE.—Proprietor, Mr. Frank Macnaghten; Manager, Mr. A. E. Dobney; Booking Circuit, Macnaghten Vaudeville Circuit; Double license. Holding capacity: Number of persons, 1,750; amount, £60. Stage measurements: Depth, 22 ft.; width, 44 ft. 3 ins.; proscenium, 22 ft. 9 ins. wide by 18 ft. deep. Gas and electric light. Time of band rehearsal, 12 noon. No matinée day. Bars the Empress Theatre, Hartlepool.

GRAND.—Lessee, Mr. Fred Granville; Manager, Mr. H. E. Feather.

Seaside town on north-east coast. Population residential and industrial. Industries, shipbuilding and engineering works. Market, Saturday, in open and covered markets. Town is not regularly visited by portables. No difficulty has been encountered in obtaining licenses at any time up to now. Site for pierrots, etc., on the extensive promenade. No circus pitches obtainable.

Early closing day, Wednesday.

Agents.—M.H.A.R.A.: R. H. Barker, North Eastern Hotel. A.U.: Station Hotel, Mainsworth. V.A.F.: The same.

RECOMMENDED APARTMENTS.

Mrs. Richardson, 64, Whitby Street.—3 bedrooms (4 beds), 2 sitting-rooms, 1 combined; 2 pianos.

HASLEMERE, Surrey.

Population, 2,614. Miles from London, 42.

THE SCHOOL HALL.—Proprietors, School Managers. Manager, Mr. J. H. Howard, Lower Street, Haslemere. Dramatic and music and dancing licenses. Holds 350. Stage, width about 24ft., depth 15ft. No proscenium. Gas. For terms apply to the manager.

Local fairs, May 13 and September 25.

Site available for portables, alfresco concerts, and circuses, the Parish Council's Fair Ground, Clay Hill.

Early closing day, Wednesday; no market day.

HASLINGDEN, Lancs.

Population, 18,543. Miles from London, 205.

ALBERT HALL.—Managers, Messrs. J. E. Hoyle and Son. Music and dancing license. Holding capacity: Number of persons, 350. No proper stage. Lighted by gas. Terms for hiring: Large room, only 15s. per night, with three hours' gas; all rooms, £1 per night; above three hours' gas, 1s. 6d. per hour (piano included). Amount of deposit required on booking, two-thirds of the amount.

PUBLIC HALL.—Managers, the Haslingden Corporation. Apply to Mr. W. Musgrove, town clerk. Double license. Holding capacity: Number of persons, 1,200. Ordinary platform; no scenery. Stage measurements: Large room—Length, 84ft.; width, 50ft.; size of platform, 50ft. by 12ft.; extended part of platform, 44ft. by 8ft.; height of room, 24ft. 6ins.; height of platform, 4ft. 6in. Lower room, 40ft. by 32ft. Lighted by gas. Terms for hiring: For concert, soiree, or meeting, each night, £1 10s.; for panorama, animated pictures, diorama, or other entertainment for which scenery is used—first night, £2; second night, £1 10s.; third night, £1 5s.; fourth, and each following night, £1.

Sites available for portables, alfresco concerts, and circuses: Football Field, Clarence.

Early closing, Wednesday; markets, Tuesday and Saturday.

HASTINGS, Sussex.

Population, 65,528. Miles from London, 60.

GAIETY THEATRE.—Proprietors, Hastings Theatre Co., Limited; Manager, Mr. H. W. Rowland; Acting-Manager, Mr. Chas. E. Scutt; Musical Director, Mr. Thomas Hilton; Scenic Artist, Mr. William Hobbs. Full dramatic license. Holding capacity: Number of persons, 1,600; amount, £100. Stage measurements: depth, 28ft.; width from 41ft. 6in. to 38ft.;

between fly rails, 29ft.; stage to grid, 47ft.; proscenium opening, 24ft. 6in. Electric current, alternating 200 volts. Printing required: 570 sheets posting, 350 d.c., 2,000 circulars. All headed and dated. Usual matinée day, Saturday at 2.30. Wednesdays also if three-night show. Time of band rehearsal, 11 a.m. Best months of the year: November, December, and January. Bars Bexhill-on-Sea.

PIER PAVILION.—Proprietors, the Hastings Pier Co.; General Manager, Mr. J. D. Hunter; Acting-Manager, Mr. Charles Hawker; Musical Director, Mr. Surtees Corne; Scenic Artist, Mr. William Hobbs. Full dramatic license. Holding capacity: Number of persons, 1,500. Stage measurement: Depth, 24ft. Gas and electric light. Usual matinée days, Wednesday and Saturday. Band rehearsal, 12 noon.

HIPPODROME. — Proprietors, Hippodrome Syndicate; General Manager, Mr. H. V Fisher; Assistant-Manager, Mr. Walter Norman; Musical Director, Mr. J. M. Harrison. Music and dancing license. Holding capacity: Number of persons, 1,500; amount, £60. Stage measurements: Depth, 30ft.; width, 48ft.; proscenium opening, 30ft. Electric light. Band rehearsal, 1 p.m., except Bank Holiday, when it is 12 noon. Bars no surrounding halls.

ST. LEONARD'S PIER PAVILION.—Entertainment Manager and Piermaster, Mr. Elvey Thomas.

Early closing day, Wednesday; market day, Saturday.

Medical Officer.—A.A.: Dr. E. Pollard, 34, Wellington Square. 'Phone, 1007. Hours, 9-10, 1.30-2.30, and 7-8. A.U.: The same. M.H.A.R.A.: The same.

Actors' Church Union Chaplain, Rev. H. E. Victor, Holy Trinity Vicarage.

Agents.—M.H.A.R.A.: J. Wood, Central Hotel, V.A.F. and A.U.: The same.

RECOMMENDED APARTMENTS.

Mrs. Malins, 61, Milward Road,—Sitting-room, bedrooms, combined.

HATFIELD, Herts.

Population, 4,764. Miles from London, 17.

PUBLIC HALL.—Proprietor and Manager, Mr. Hugh Harvey. Music and dancing license. Holds 350. Proper stage, 26ft. by 14ft. Gas. Terms, 30s. per night, gas and piano. Deposit required, 15s.

Dates of local fairs, April 23 and October 18.

Sites available for portables, alfresco concerts, and circuses, the Red Lion field; Mrs. Davis, Red Lion Hotel, Hatfield.

Early closing day, Thursday; no market day.

HAWICK, Roxburgh, N.B.

Population, 17,303. Miles from London, 345.

NEW THEATRE.—Proprietor, Mr. W. Payne Seddon; Managers, Messrs. W. Payne Seddon and Gordon Starkey; Acting-Manager, Mr. Adam Grant; Musical Director, Mr. J. Grant; Scenic Artist, Mr. Geo. Collier, jun. Restricted license. Holding capacity: Number of persons, 750; amount £50. Stage measurements: depth, 24 ft.; width, 36 ft.; proscenium, 24 ft. opening. Electric light. Usual matinée day, Saturday. Booked last three days of week only, in conjunction with Dumfries.

TOWN HALL.—Manager, Mr. J. Waldie. Double license. Holding capacity: Number of persons, over 1,200. Stage, 24ft. deep, and 35ft. wide,

permanent. Proscenium takes in 18ft. wings and 24ft. cloths. Electric light, 240 volts.

EXCHANGE HALL.—Manager, Mr. W. Laidlaw. Has dramatic license. Holding capacity: Number of persons, 1,500; amount £50 at 2s., 1s., and 6d. Permanent stage. Stage measurements: 50ft. by 18ft., can be extended to 50ft. by 36ft.; proscenium opening, 22ft. by 18ft. Gas and electric light. Amount of printing required: Two to three hundred double crown sheets, two hundred day bills, one hundred lithos. Terms for hiring: Concerts, one night, £2 15s.; six nights, £11. Theatres, one night, £3 5s.; six nights, £11 10s. This includes light and heating. Amount of deposit required on booking, £1 The halls can be let for circuses, exhibitions, or any other floor performances.

The population of Hawick at the last census was given at 17,303, but since that time Stobs, a large estate near the town, has been bought by the Government and converted into a camping ground. From the beginning of June until the end of August large numbers of Regulars and Volunteers receive their annual training at Stobs, and during these months frequent trains are run to and from the camping ground. The larger portion of the population is industrial, the manufacture of tweeds and hosiery being the principal industries.

The only fair of any importance is the Common Riding, held in the Upper Haugh (the property of the town) on Friday and Saturday, June 4 and 5. Showmen, etc., generally come to the town on the Tuesday or Wednesday preceding the fair, and stay until the following Tuesday. Good business is done during this time. Dates of other fairs: March 6, May 15. Portable theatres, circuses, etc., are also accommodated on the above-mentioned ground during the year. To obtain the license from the Town Council, portables must be well constructed. Licenses have been refused, owing to the unsightly structure.

Market day, Thursday; early closing day, Tuesday.

HAWKHURST, Kent.

Population, 3,136. Miles from London, 52.

VICTORIA HALL.—Manager, the Parish Council. Dramatic license. Holding capacity: Number of persons, 300; amount, £12 12s. Stage measurements: 12ft. by 18ft.; no proscenium. Lighted by gas. Terms for hiring, £1 1s. per day, payable in advance.

Early closing, Wednesday.

HAYLE, Cornwall.

Population, 1,084. Miles from London, 313.

PUBLIC HALL.—Manager, Mr. J. S. Broach. Double license. Holding capacity: Number of persons, 300. Stage measurements: 28ft. by 14ft. Wagon roof, sides 12ft., centre 19ft. from stage to ceiling. Lighted by gas, special connections for lanterns. Terms for hiring: Theatrical, 30s. one night. Amount of deposit required on booking, 10s. Good Saturday town.

The town of Hayle comprises two Urban Districts, Phillack, 4,684 population, and Hayle, 1,084. A regular line of bi-weekly steamers carry passengers and cargo between Hayle and Liverpool and Bristol.

Date of local fair, Tuesday after Whitsun week. Many sites available for portable, alfresco concerts, and circuses.

Early closing, Thursday; market, Saturday.

HAYWARDS HEATH, Sussex.

Population, 3,717. Miles from London, 38.

PUBLIC HALL.—Manager, Mr. Geo. Plummer. Double license. Holding capacity: Number of persons, 400. Portable stage. Lighted by gas. Terms for hiring, £2 2s. per night, Full fee required on booking.
Early closing day, Wednesday; market day, Tuesday.

HEBBURN-ON-TYNE, Durham.

Population, 25,000. Miles from London, 277.

ROYAL THEATRE.—Proprietor, Mr. Charles Elderton; Musical Director, Mr. Le Roy; Scenic Artist, Mr. Thomas Smith; Full dramatic license. Holding capacity: Number of persons, 1,500; amount, £70. Stage measurements: Depth, 33 ft.; width, 56 ft.; proscenium opening, 27 ft. Gas and electric light. Amount of printing required, walls, 600; windows, 500. Usual matinée day, Saturday. Time of band rehearsal, 1 p.m.
PAVILION. — Lessee, Mr. T Armstrong. Holds 800. Electric light. Matinée day, Saturday. Early closing day, Wednesday.

HEBDEN BRIDGE, Yorks.

Population, 7,536. Miles from London, 219.

CO-OPERATIVE HALL.—Secretary, Mr. Arthur Sutcliffe. Dramatic license. Holding capacity: Number of persons, 800. Platform, 25ft. by 18ft.; can be extended to 22ft. Electric light. Terms for hiring: Dramatic, one night, £2 12s. 6d. Amount of deposit required on booking, £1.
Early closing, Tuesday; market, last Friday in month.

HEDNESFORD, Staffs.

Population, 10,293. Miles from London, 127.

PUBLIC ROOMS.—Manager, Mr. J. W. Vincent. Dramatic license. Holding capacity: Number of persons, 450; amount, £12. Stage with partial fit-up. Stage measurements: Depth, 15ft.; height, 12ft.; opening, 18ft. Gas. Amount of printing required: 300 day bills, lithos, etc. Terms on application. Amount of deposit required on booking, 10s. Good for two nights, Saturday and Monday.
Early closing, Thursday; market, Saturday.

HELENSBURGH, Dumbarton, N.B.

Population, 9,500. Miles from London, 450

VICTORIA HALL.—Belonging to Town Council. Dramatic license. Holding capacity: Number of persons, 700. Ordinary platform, which can be added to at company's expense. Terms for Hiring: For concerts, £2 2s.; for theatricals, £3 10s., exclusive of gas; charge for gas, 2s. 6d. per hour. Amount of deposit required on booking, 20 per cent.

HELSTON, Cornwall.

Population, 3,088. Miles from London, 319.

GODOLPHIN HALL.—Secretary, Mr. T. Taylor. Size of hall, 62ft. by 40ft. Double license. Holding capacity: Will seat 400; standing room for another 100. Stage measurements: 30ft. long by 18ft. wide, can be reduced to 16ft. by 9ft.; 18ft. from stage level to wall plate. Lighted by gas. Terms for hiring:

31s. 6d. for first night, 21s. 6d. for each subsequent night; gas extra, by metre. Amount of deposit required on booking, 10s. 6d. Best nights Mondays and Wednesdays.
Early closing, Friday; market, Saturday.

HEMEL HEMPSTEAD, Herts,

Population, 11,264. Miles from London, 25.

TOWN HALL.—Manager, Mr. H. Killeen. Not licensed. Holding capacity: Number of persons, about 300. Concert stage, 26ft. by 12ft. Lighted by gas. Terms for hiring: One night, 27s. 6d.; two nights, 45s.; three nights, 57s. 6d; £5 5s. per week. Full amount to be paid on booking.
Local fairs in September.
Market day, Thursday; early closing, Wednesday.
Medical Officer.—A.U.: Dr. M. C. Sykes, Maynard Tower.

HENLEY-ON-THAMES, Oxon.

Population, 6,500. Miles from London, 35.

TOWN HALL.—Proprietors, the Corporation; Hall Keeper, Mr. E. H. Fox. No dramatic license only used for concerts. Holding capacity: Number of persons, 400. Lighted by gas.
KENTON HALL (formerly St. Mary's Hall) —Manager, Mr. W. C. Weston, Music Warehouse, Bell Street. Double license. Holding capacity: Number of persons, 500. Fixed proscenium, 20ft. opening. Stage: 30ft. between extreme walls; 18ft. from footlights to back wall. Lighted by gas. Amount of printing required: 200 sheets ample. Terms for hiring: One night, 2½ guineas. Amount of deposit required on booking: Half a guinea.
This is considered a one-night town, and an interval of ten days between is advisable. The only fair of note is on the Thursday after September 21.
Advance agents can secure sites for circus, etc.
Early closing, Wednesday; market, Thursday.

HEREFORD, Hereford.

Population, 21,382. Miles from London, 144.

GARRICK THEATRE. — Lessee and Manager, Mr. Harry P. Barnsley; Musical Director, Mr. William James. Full dramatic license. Holding capacity: Number of persons, 550; amount, £45. Stage width, 35ft.; depth, 25ft.; proscenium opening, 18ft. Electric light 220 volts direct. Printing: 500 sheets posting, 500 d.c. for window billing. Usual matinée day, Saturday. Time of band rehearsal, 12 o'clock.
DRILL HALL. — Licensee and Manager, Mr. A. Lovesey, 2, Offa Street, Hereford. Has dramatic license. Holding capacity: Number of persons, 1,400; amount, £85, ordinary prices. Stage measurements: 32ft. wide, 23ft. deep, opening 27ft., stage frame 18ft. Large dressing-rooms, heated throughout with hot water. Gas and electric light. Amount of printing required, 300 sheets posters. Terms for hiring and sharing: Apply to Licensee.
CORN EXCHANGE.—Secretary Mr. E. Stanton Jones, Broad Street, Hereford. No dramatic license. Let for concerts, variety, Kinematograph, etc. Size of hall, 46ft. wide, 71ft. long. Tables used as platform. Holding capacity: seat 400, standing 200. Gas, electric light 220 volts. Terms first night £2 2s., every night after, £1 1s. Light, cleaning and heating (hot water) extra.

SHIRE HALL.—Manager, Mr. George Smith. No dramatic license. Holding capacity: Number of persons, 750. Stage: 29ft. by 12ft. Gas and electric light, 220 and 440 volts. Terms from £4 10s. to £5 5s. (inclusive).
TOWN HALL.—Proprietors, Town Council. Letters addressed, Mr. Lewis, Finance Clerk. Seat 500; small balcony hold about 50. Electric light. No dramatic license. Size 66ft. by 36ft. Amount of deposit required on booking, £2 10s. Remarks: This hall is not let for anything requiring a dramatic license. In addition to body of hall the orchestra will hold 200 people.
Local May fair, first Wednesday and Thursday after May 2. Portables are not allowed in the town. No place in the town is available for alfresco concerts. Circuses generally find accommodation in Edgar Street upon land owned by Mrs. Farr. Travelling side shows, kinematograph entertainments. Mr. Constable's meadow, Edgar Street.
Market days, Wednesday and Saturday; early closing, Thursday.

RECOMMENDED APARTMENTS.

Mrs. Edge, 40, Egin Street.—2 bedrooms (one double), and sitting room.

HERNE BAY, Kent.

Population, 9,000. Miles from London, 62.
PIER PAVILION THEATRE.—Proprietors, Herne Bay Pier Co.; Managing Director, Mr. F.W Wacher; Acting-Manager, Mr. H. Bankes; Scenic Artist, Mr. Bon. Dramatic license. Holding capacity: Number of persons, 600; amount, £30. Stage measurements: Depth, 19ft.; width, 32ft.; proscenium, 19ft. by 13ft. 8in. Electric light, 250 volts direct. Matinée day, Saturday. Best season, middle July to end September.
EMPIRE THEATRE.—Lessee and Manager, Mr. C. Cordingley.
TOWN HALL.—Proprietors, Urban Council; Manager, Mr. J. B. Watson. Dramatic license. Holding capacity: Number of persons, 600; amount, £40. Depth and width of stage: 20ft. by 18ft.; takes scenery 18ft. high. Lighted by gas (incandescent). Terms for hiring: One night, £2 2s.; two nights, £4 4s.; subsequent nights, £1 1s.; during August and September, one night, £4 4s.; subsequent nights, £2 2s. Amount of deposit required on booking, £1. Early closing, October to May only, Thursday.

HERTFORD, Herts.

Population, 9,322. Miles from London, 24.
CORN EXCHANGE. — Proprietors, Corporation; Manager, Mr. R. Wells, Market Beadle. Has dramatic license. Satisfactory for fit-up touring companies. The Corporation have spent considerable sums in bringing the building up to modern requirements. Recently fitted with a new stage. Companies may count upon good business for one or two nights. Seats, 400. Electric current, 230. Apply Caretaker.
TOWN HALL.—Apply to the Caretaker.
The inhabitants are mainly residential. No large industries, two large building firms and a large printing establishment employing the largest number of workpeople.
"Plough" Meadow, on the London Road, is used by circus companies, and is an excellent site for the purpose. The Corporation look with disfavour upon portables, and will not grant licenses.
Fairs are held on the third Saturday before Easter, May 12, July 5th, and November 8, but they are very small affairs.
Early closing, Thursday; market, Saturday.

HESSLE, Yorks.

PARISH HALL.—Proprietors, Urban District Council; Manager, Clerk to the Council. No license. A temporary license is obtained when necessary. Holding capacity, 600 in large hall, 150 in smaller hall. There are other rooms, £2 2s. large hall, from 7 to 11 p.m.; other charges in proportion. Proper stage; width 25ft. 5in., depth 16ft. Gas. Deposit required on booking, 25 per cent.
Hessle is about four and a-half miles from the city of Hull.
Date of local fair, Hessle Feast, Whit Monday.

HETTON, Co. Durham.

Population, 13,673. Miles from London, 250.
STANDARD THEATRE.—Lessee and Manager, Mr. James Chapman. Dramatic license. Early closing, Wednesday; market, Friday.

HEXHAM, Northumberland.

Population, 7,071. Miles from London, 299.
TOWN HALL.—Proprietors, Hexham Corn Market and Public Buildings Co., Limited; Manager, Mr. Thos. P. Edwards, Hencotes, Hexham. Dramatic and music and dancing licences. Holds 500. Platform only, 33ft. by 9ft.; extension can be put. Gas. 100 to 150 bills will do the town. Terms for hiring: One night, 30s.; 2, 50s.; 3, 70s.; 4, 80s.; 5, 90s.; 6, 100s. Deposit required, £1 one night; £3 three or over.
Dates of local fairs:—Hiring days, May 13, November 11.
Sites available for portables, alfresco concerts, and circuses, Tyne Green, or private field.
Early closing day, Thursday. Market day, Tuesday.

HEYWOOD, Lancs.

Population, 25,458. Miles from London, 193.
BOROUGH THEATRE.—Lessee, Mr. Albert Jones; Manager, Mr. H. Tweedle. Restricted dramatic license. Holding capacity: Number of persons, 1,000; amount, £30. Stage opening, 17ft.; 20ft. depth; takes 18ft. flats. Gas and electric light. Amount of printing required: 500 sheets and 400 lithos. Time of band rehearsal, 1 p.m. Best months, September, October, November, January, and February.
Market day, Friday; early closing, Tuesday.

HIGH WYCOMBE, Bucks.

Population, 19,500. Miles from London, 34.
TOWN HALL.— Proprietors, the Town Council. Apply to the hall-keeper. Holding capacity: Number of persons, 1,200. Stage (including space occupied by organ), 67ft. wide by 32ft. deep (average). 300 sheets. Deposit required on booking, £1. Electric light, low tension three wire, direct, voltage 220 and 420.
SOUTH BUCKS AUCTION MART, Amersham Hill.—Proprietors, C. H. Hunt and Son. Holds 250. Small platform and curtain. Music and dancing license. Electric light as in Town Hall.
Annual fair always takes place on the Monday preceding September 29. Population largely composed of chairmakers, chair-making being the staple trade of the town. Fair Meadow always used for circus pitch; cricket field for alfresco concerts. Portable theatres are not allowed in the borough, but it is possible to get sites outside the borough boundary. Playgoers go to see good and up-to-date things freely.
Early closing, Wednesday; market, Friday.

HINDLEY, Lancs.

Population. 23,504. Miles from London, 195.

VICTORIA HALL.—Proprietors, Conservative Club Building Co., Hindley. Dramatic and music and dancing licenses. Holding capacity: Number of persons, 600. Platform, 8yds. by 4yds. Gas. Amount of printing required, about 100 bills. Terms for hiring varies according to use; one guinea ordinary concert, payable in advance.

HINDLEY INDUSTRIAL CO-OPERATIVE HALL.—Proprietors, The Co-operative Society. Dramatic and music and dancing licenses. Holding capacity; Number of persons, 500-600. Platform, 24ft. by 12ft. Gas. Amount of printing required, about 100 bills. Terms for hiring on application.

Date of local fair:—Hindley Fair, first Thursday in August.

Sites available for portables, alfresco concerts, and circuses:—Cross Street site, Ladies Lane site, Derby Lane site.

Early closing day, Wednesday.

HIRWAIN, Brecon.

Miles from London, 175.

VICTORIA HALL.—Manager, Mr. Dd. Thomas. Holding capacity: Number of persons, about 500. No dramatic license. Stage, 17ft. deep by 30ft wide; proscenium, 16ft. wide by 12ft. high. Lighted by gas. Terms for hiring: One night, 27s. 6d.; two, 45s.; three, 60s.; six, 90s. Amount of deposit required on booking, 10s.

HITCHIN, Herts.

Population, 10,072. Miles from London, 34.

TOWN HALL.—Manager, Mr. Wm. Onslow Times, Clerk. Has dramatic license. Holding capacity: Number of persons, 780. Stage, depth. 21ft.; width, 26ft.; height, 19ft.; height of floor, 3ft. 6in.; proscenium height, 17ft. 5in.; width, 21ft. 10in. Gas and electric light. Terms for hiring: Entertainments, £2 2s. first night; £1 1s. after; hallkeeper, 7s. 6d.; 2s. 6d. each successive performance; theatricals, £3 3s. first night; £1 11s. 6d. after; hallkeeper, 10s. 6d; 5s. after first night. Amount of deposit required on booking: 25 per cent.

Dates of local fairs: Easter Wednesday and Whitsun Wednesday. Sites available for portables, al fresco concerts, and circuses, Butts Close and Highlander Close.

Early closing, Wednesday; market, Tuesday.

HOLBEACH, LINCS.

Population, 4,755. Miles from London, 99.

PUBLIC HALL.—Manager, Mr. Thos. Chas Willders. Has dramatic license. Ho'ding capacity: Number of persons, 400 or 500. Stage, 30ft. by 15ft. Lighted by gas. Terms for hiring, £1 10s. for first night and £1 5s. for each subsequent night. If the hall is required for a week special terms are arranged. Amount of deposit required on booking, £1.

Pleasure fair, October 9.

Early closing day, Wednesday; market day Thursday.

HOLYWOOD.

TOWN HALL.—Manager, The Town Clerk. Holding capacity: Number of persons, 500. Platform, 36ft. by 14ft. Lighted by gas. Terms for hiring: 30s. per evening; 15 per cent. off for two or more consecutive days. No local fairs. Good site for circuses.

HORNCASTLE, Lincs.

Population, 4,038. Miles from London, 130.

CORN EXCHANGE.—Lessee, Mr. J. F. Jackson. Has dramatic license. Holding capacity: Number of persons, 600. Stage, 36ft. by 18ft. No proscenium. Lighted by gas. Terms for hiring: 21s. for first day, 17s. 6d. second, 12s. 6d. after. Amount of deposit required on booking, 10s.

Early closing, Wednesday; market, Saturday.

HORNSEA, Yorks.

Population, 2,381. Miles from London, 212.

PUBLIC ROOMS.—Proprietor, Mr. C. E. A. Lyon, Eastgate, Hornsea. Music and dancing licenses. Holds about 350. Proper stage. Acetylene gas. For terms, apply to proprietor.

Early closing day, Thursday. Market Day, Saturday.

HORSFORTH, Yorks.

Population, 7,784. Miles from London, 271.

MECHANICS' INSTITUTE.—Secretary, Mr. C. W. Marsden. No dramatic license. Holding capacity: Number of persons, 300. Small stage or platform. Electric light, alternating current 230 volts. Printing, 25 posters. Terms: Concerts 20s. each. Amount of deposit required on booking, 10s.

Early closing, Wednesday; no market.

HORSHAM, Sussex.

Population, 9,446. Miles from London, 37.

KING'S HEAD ASSEMBLY ROOM.—Proprietor, Mr. J. B. Elliott. Dramatic and dancing licenses. Holds 400. Stage in sections: Depth, 30ft.; width, 15ft. No proscenium or scenery. Gas and electric light, continuous, 230 volts. Terms: One night, £3 3s.; two nights, £5 5s.; three nights, £7 7s.; four nights, £9 9s.; five nights, £11 11s.; one week, £13 13s., including Sunday. Any performance on Sunday must be during the time house is open for the sale of intoxicating liquors. Full fees on booking

Dates of local fairs, April 5, July 19, November 27.

Sites available for portables, alfresco concerts, and circuses, Jews Meadow, in Bishopric, and Meadow in Queen Street.

Early closing day, Thursday. Market day, Wednesday.

HORWICH, Lancs.

Population. 15,084. Miles from London, 206.

PRINCE'S THEATRE.—Proprietor, Mr. A. Patterson; Lessees, Horwich Theatre Co.; Manager, Mr. R. H. White. Musical Director, Mr. Turner. Dramatic license. Holding capacity: Number of persons, 1,000; amount, £40. Stage measurements, 23ft. by 20ft. Lighted by gas. Usual matinée day, Saturday. Best months, September to March.

Early closing day, Wednesday.

HOUGHTON-LE-SPRING, Durham.

Population, 9,578.

MINERS' HALL.—Small hall.

Market day, Saturday; early closing, Wednesday.

HOVE, Sussex.

Population, 36,542. Miles from London, 52.

TOWN HALL.—Proprietors, Hove Corporation; Manager, Mr. H. Endacott, Town Clerk. Dramatic license. Holding capacity: Number of persons (Great Hall), 1,230. Small permanent stage, additional movable staging; depth, 26ft.; width, 50ft. Electric light, voltage 110. Electric arc wire for kinematographs. Terms for hiring on application. Amount of deposit required on booking. Fees paid at time of hiring, or a deposit fixed by Committee. Early closing days, Wednesday and Thursday. No market day.

HOYLAKE, Cheshire.

Population, 10,911. Miles from London, 200.

TOWN HALL.—Proprietors, Urban District Council of Hoylake and West Kirby; Manager, Mr. R. W. Fraser, Engineer and Surveyor. Music and dancing license. Holds about 450. Stage, with movable proscenium. Electric light; 230 volts alternating, 50 period, single phase. Terms: Hall, per night, £2 2s.; proscenium and scenery, £1 1s. extra; piano, 12s. extra. Full amount in advance. No local fairs, and no sites available for portables, alfresco concerts, or circuses. Early closing day, Wednesday. No market day.

HOYLAND, Yorks.

THEATRE METROPOLE.—Proprietors, The (Hoyland) Theatre Metropole Company; Lessee and Manager, Mr. Geo. S. King; Acting-Manager, Mr. Geo. R. Baker; Musical Director, Mr. G. Frost. Restricted dramatic license. Holding capacity: Number of persons, 1,500; amount, £55. Stage, 60ft. wide and 30ft. deep; proscenium opening, 26ft.; fly all cloths. Lighted by gas. Amount of printing required: 500 d.c. sheets walls, 400 lithos, 300 d.c. letterpress. Usual matinée day, Saturday. Time of band rehearsal, 4 p.m.

HUCKNALL TORKARD, Notts.

Population, 15,250. Miles from London, 133.

PUBLIC HALL.—Proprietors, Public Hall Company, Limited; Secretary, Mr. Alfred Radford, 30, Watnall Road, Hucknall. Dramatic license. Size of hall, 60ft. by 34ft. 10in. Holds 600. No stage, but a platform, 15ft. by 25ft. Gas. Terms for hiring, £1 per night, or £5 the week. Deposit on booking, one half. Dates of local fairs, wakes, July 21; statutes, November 10. Sites available for portables, alfresco concerts, and circuses, Recreation Ground, Market Place, etc. Early closing day, Wednesday. Market day, Friday.

HUDDERSFIELD, Yorks.

Population, 95,057. Miles from London, 190.

THEATRE ROYAL. — Acting-Manager, Mr. T. J. Phillips; Musical Director, Mr. J. Hecker; Scenic Artist, Mr. A. W. Moore. Fully licensed. Holding capacity: Number of persons, 5,000; amount, £140. Depth of stage, 37ft.; width, 55ft.; proscenium opening, width 26ft. Gas and electric light. Amount of printing required: 1,300 sheets and 700 lithos. Usual matinée day, Saturday. Time of band rehearsal, 1 o'clock. Best dates of the year: From October to March.

HIPPODROME. — Proprietors, Northern Theatres Co., Limited; Managing Director, Mr. W. Robinson; General Manager, Mr. Otto C. Culling; Acting-Manager, Mr. N. M. Robinson; Booking Circuit, N.T. Co.; Musical Director, Mr. T. Hoyle. Double license. Holding capacity: Number of persons, 1,350. Depth and width of stage: Deep, 26ft.; wide, 50ft.; proscenium, 26ft. Electric light, 100 volts alternating. Time of band rehearsal, 12.30.

TOWN HALL.—Manager, The Borough Treasurer. Double license. Holding capacity: Number of persons, 2,113. Platform and orchestra: Depth, 18ft.; width, 32ft. Electric light. Terms for hiring: Concerts, etc., £8 10s. first night; £5 second night; £3 10s. succeeding consecutive nights; matinées same day, half evening charge, plus lighting. Hire charges required on booking; lighting at close of engagement.

VICTORIA HALL.—Secretary, Mr. J. T. Prentis. Music and dancing license. Holding capacity: Number of persons, 800. Platform with footlights. Depth, 9ft.; can be extended to 18ft. in the centre; width, 30ft. Electric current direct, 110 volts. Terms: £2 2s. per evening, for not less than six consecutive evenings, including light; if electricity is required for pictures (direct current), £2 7s. 6d. per evening, inclusive, for not less than six consecutive evenings. Amount of deposit required on booking, £5.

Dates of local fairs: Easter Saturday, Monday, and Tuesday, April 10, 12, and 13, June 19, 21, and 22; Lockwood fair, September 25, 27, and 28; Christmas fair, Decemb r 24, 25, and 27. Portables find suitable ground in many of the outlying districts, such as Holmfirth, Honley, Meltham, etc. Excellent circus pitch at Longley Hall Park. Alfresco entertainment in Greenhead Park. Animated picture shows pay very successful visits.

Sites also available for portables, alfresco concerts, and circuses: Fair Grounds, Great Northern Street, and Lockwood. Applications to Market Inspector.

Early closing, Wednesday; market, Tuesday. Agent.—M.H.A.R.A.: Mrs. Ferguson, Victoria Inn, Victoria Street. V.A.F.: The same.

HULL, Yorks.

Population, 271,137. Miles from London, 175.

GRAND THEATRE.—Proprietors, Mortons, Limited; Managing Director, Mr. William Morton; Manager, Mr. W. F. Morton; Musical Director, Mr. Louis Hermann; Scenic Artist, Mr. Tom Bogue. Full dramatic license. Holding capacity: Number of persons, 2,800; amount, £200 at ordinary prices. Electric light. Amount of printing required, 1,700 sheets. Usual matinée day, Saturday. Time of band rehearsal, 12.

THEATRE ROYAL.—Lessee Mr. Wm. Morton; Acting-Manager, Mr. Tom H. Bogue; Musical Director, Mr. J. McAlister. Dramatic license; no Excise. Holding capacity: Number of persons, 1,700. Electric light. Amount of printing required, 1,500 walls, 800 windows. Usual matinée day, Thursday. Time of band rehearsal, 12.30 p.m.

ALEXANDRA THEATRE.—Proprietors, Mortons, Limited; Chairman and Manager, Mr. William Morton; Acting-Manager, Mr. George Morton; Musical Director, Mr. R. W. Watt; Scenic Artist, Mr. Tom Bogue. Restricted license. Holding capacity: Number of persons, 3,000. Gas and electric light.

PALACE. — Proprietors, Moss's Empires, Limited; Manager, Mr. John S. Barnett. Booking circuit, Moss's Empires. Musical Director, Mr. Albert E. Leader. Music and dancing license. Gas and electric light. Time of band rehearsal, 2 p.m. No matinée day.

Bars all other Managements' Halls in Hull and the following towns: Beverley, Hedon, and Barton.

EMPIRE.—Lessee and Manager, Mr. Harry Slingsby; Acting-Manager, Mr. H. Parry. Booking circuit, S.T.S. Syndicate. Musical Director, Mr. Mahlon B. Whittle. Music and dancing license. Holding capacity: Number of persons, 1,800; amount, £45. Electric light, 220 volts direct. Band rehearsal 12 noon. No matinée day. Bars Hippodrome and Palace.

THE HIPPODROME, Porter Street.—Lessee and Director, Mr. Alfred Graham; Resident and General Manager, Mr. Harry Dunford; Acting-Manager, Mr. Ernest Naylor. Seats 1,190.

THE CIRCUS, Anlaby Road.—General Manager, Mr. Edward Emerson. Adaptable for circus performances, dioramas, kinematograph entertainments, and concerts. Seats 2,668.

ASSEMBLY ROOMS AND LECTURE HALL.—No dramatic license. Holding capacity: Number of persons, 1,600. Terms for hiring: One night, £11 11s.; or £40 per week, including lighting. Apply G. Peacock & Son.

LECTURE HALL. — No dramatic license. Holding capacity: Number of persons, 700. Stage: 25ft. by 15ft. Terms for hiring, £3 3s. per night; £15 15s. per week including lighting. Apply G. Peacock & Son.

CITY HALL.—In course of construction in connection with the municipal improvements, and is understood to be intended for public meetings, high-class concerts, festivals, etc. It will probably be completed in 12 or 15 months time.

Hull has a residential and industrial population of more than a quarter of a million, exclusive of the towns and villages in the neighbourhood, to which convenient train services are in operation after the close of the performances. The industrial community is chiefly engaged in shipping, deep sea fishing, and manufactures, viz.:—oil, paint, chemicals, oil cake, flour milling, cement, etc.

There is no demand for sites for portables or concert and circus pitches, the permanent buildings meeting all requirements. In the past, however, such attractions as Barnum and Bailey's and Buffalo Bill's Wild West shows have been accommodated on the fair ground. Hull Fair, probably the largest pleasure fair in the country, is held annually on October 11 and following days (the usual duration being five or six days). No difficulty is experienced with the local authorities, who accept the fair as an old-established institution, and prepare their spacious ground in Walton Street for the purpose.

There are a number of other halls in Hull, viz.:—The Public Rooms and the Salisbury, St. George's, Cobden, Friendly Societies', Central, St. James's, Ripon, and Wilson, which are available for concerts, dances, etc., but these are usually made use of for local entertainments.

Market days, Tuesday, Friday, and Saturday; early closing, Thursday.

Medical Officers.—A.A.: Dr. G. H. Bradford, 22, Story Street, and Dr. E. S. Morgan, 51, George Street. A.U. and M.H.A.R.A.: Dr. Morgan.

Agent.—M.H.A.R.A.: J. C. Bloom, Wheatsheaf Hotel, King Edward Street. A.U.: The same. V.A.F.: The same.

RECOMMENDED APARTMENTS.

Miss Duncum, 18, Portland Place, Prospect Street.—Large bedroom, sitting-room, 2 combined.

Miss Lister, 6, Wood's Terrace, South Street. bed, 2 sitting-rooms, and combined room; ano.

Mrs. Nelson, 47, Cambridge Street.—3 bed and 2 sitting-rooms; piano.

Mrs. Newcombe.—2 sitting and 2 bedrooms (3 beds).

Mrs. O'Neill, 14, Francis Street, W.—Front bedroom and front sitting-room; piano.

HUNTLY, Aberdeenshire.

Population, 4,136. Miles from London, 581.

STEWARTS' HALL.—Secretary, Mr. J. R. McMath, solicitor, Huntly. Double license. Holding capacity: Number of persons, 650. Stage requires extension for dramatic entertainment. Lighted by gas. Amount of printing required, 70 bills. Terms for hiring: £1 per night, gas, special insurance, heating, etc., over and above. No deposit required on booking. Friday is considered the best night.

The market stance is available for alfresco concerts and circuses. Application should be made to the Burgh Surveyor.

Market, Wednesday.

HYDE, Cheshire.

Population, 32,766. Miles from London, 181.

THEATRE ROYAL.—Proprietor, Mr. Fred Granville. General Manager, Mr. H. G. Griffin; Musical Director, Mr. James Lord. Full dramatic license. Holding capacity: Number of persons, 3,000; amount, £150. Width of stage, 80ft.; depth, of stage, 65ft.; height of grid, 45ft.; opening, 29ft. Electric light throughout, 230 voltage, direct. Usual matinée day, Saturday. Time of band rehearsal, 1 p.m.

HIPPODROME.—Proprietor, Mr. Wilbraham Stansfield; Stage Manager, Mr. G. R. Lees; Musical Director, Mr. W. Wharam. Full dramatic license. Holding capacity: Number of persons, 900; amount, £15. Stage measurements: width, 28ft.; depth, 14ft. Electric light. Time of band rehearsal, 11 a.m. Matinée days, Monday and Saturday. Bars Theatre Royal.

MECHANICS' HALL.—Proprietors, The Hyde Corporation; Secretary, Mr. S. Ashworth. Music and dancing license. Suitable for kinematograph entertainments and concerts. Electric light, 230 volts. Stage, 13ft. 6in. by 40ft. 6in. No proscenium. Terms, 30s. one night, 25s. the second, or £6 per week. Deposit required, 10s. per night.

Industrial population. Cotton factories. Hyde Wakes (chief holiday) are held the first week in September. Alfresco concerts are given in the district during summer months. The "pitch" on which Mr. Ohmy built a wooden structure for a season is vacant in Clarendon Street. Two or three "World's Fairs," travelling booths, etc., are held on the same ground during summer. Portable theatres used to do well before the theatre was built. No license would be granted now.

Fairs: May 16, November 15, and Wakes as above.

Market day, Saturday; early closing day, Tuesday.

Medical officer.—A.A.: Dr. James A. Watts, 34, Church Street. A.U.: The same.

RECOMMENDED APARTMENTS.

Mrs. Sykes, 23, Church Street, Hyde.—1 sitting, 2 bedrooms combined.

HYTHE, Kent.

Population, 6,500. Miles from London, 66.

HYTHE INSTITUTE.—Secretary, Mr. Robt. Worthington; Caretaker, Mr. C. Rogers. Has dramatic license. Holding capacity: Number of persons, 350. Stage: Width, 29ft.; depth, 11ft. (can be enlarged to 15ft.). Lighted by gas. Terms for hiring: £1 10s. first night, £1 per night after. Amount of deposit required on booking, 10s.

No local fairs, and portables do not visit the town. There are sites for circuses and alfresco concerts on the Green.

Early closing day, Wednesday.

IBSTOCK, Leicester.

Population, 3,922.

Near Market Bosworth. Is a colliery district of 5,000, with no suitable hall. Portables have done well, and licenses invariably are granted by the Market Bosworth Bench of magistrates.

IDLE (near Bradford), Yorks.

Population, 7,468. Miles from London, 190.

CO-OPERATIVE HALL.—Manager, Mr. J. Bramley. Music license. Holding capacity: Number of persons, 400. Proper stage with footlights. Lighted by gas. Terms for hiring, 17s. 6d. for concert. Amount of deposit required on booking, 17s. 6d.

No local fairs or sites available for portables.

Early closing day, Tuesday.

ILFORD, Essex.

Population, 75,000 (about). Miles from London, 7.

TOWN HALL.—Licensee and Responsible Manager, Mr. John Wheeldon Benton. Double license. Holding capacity: Number of persons, 740 (and gallery 108). Stage, 17ft. by 33ft. Electric light. Terms for hiring: Dramatic performances (stage plays) by electric light, £5 5s.; for three evenings, £12 12s.; rehearsal (not exceeding two hours' duration) by daylight, £1 1s.; by electric light, £1 11s. 6d. The amount of deposit required on booking depends on engagement—£1 1s. for one evening.

A kinematograph or such-like entertainment may not be given in the Town Hall, or the gallery of the hall, unless due notice of intention to hold such entertainment is given to the Clerk to the Council, as licensee and responsible manager.

A fireproof box to enclose the kinematograph machine must be provided by the person engaging the hall, or the gallery of the hall, for purposes of a kinematograph entertainment.

No local fair held.

Early closing day, Thursday.

ILFRACOMBE, Devon.

Population, 8,557.

THE ALEXANDRA. — Manager, Mr. J. Roberts. Dramatic and music and dancing license. Holding capacity: Number of persons, seats, 1,150; amount, £100. Permanent stage. Stage, 60ft. wide, 30ft. deep; proscenium, 20ft. to 30 ft. as required. Gas and electric light, continuous current, 240 volts. Terms for hiring on application.

RUNNACLEAVE THEATRE. — Manageress, Mrs. A. Chown, Runnacleave Hotel (which adjoins). Fully licensed. Holding capacity: Number of persons, just over 500 seated, or 650 standing; amount, from £50 to £60. Stage measurements: Depth, 22ft.; front cloth, 30ft. by 16ft.; back cloth, 24ft. by 16ft.; wings 16ft.; proscenium opening, 18ft. by 14ft. Electric light. Amount of printing required, the usual wall posters, long day bills, throwaways, etc. Terms for hiring, two guineas nightly, five guineas for three nights. Amount of deposit required on booking, 10s. 6d.

VICTORIA PAVILION.—Mr. E. J. Tamlyn. Managing Director.

Ilfracombe's population rises in the season, June to end of September, to sometimes 20,000 or 23,000. There is a site available for concert pitches overlooking the parade and near to it, called the Montebello Lawn, and also a small pitch lower down, which can be used for a small show. Circuses generally pitch on ground near the station and below Hillsborough Hill—both a short distance from the town, which can be leased for short visits.

Early closing day, Thursday; market day, Saturday.

Medical Officer.—M.H.A.R.A.: Dr. F. W. Langridge, Cleave House.

ILKESTON, Derbyshire.

Population, 25,384. Miles from London, 124½.

THEATRE ROYAL (Head Office).—Proprietors, New Theatre (Ilkeston) Co., Limited; Manager and Licensee, Mr. L. F. A. Rogers; Musical Director, Mr. Chas. Keith Smith. Full dramatic license. Holding capacity: Number of persons, 2,000; amount, £75 (ordinary doors). Stage measurements: 56ft. by 36ft.; proscenium, 28ft.; grid, 48ft.; stage to fly-floor, 20ft.; cloths, 30ft. Electric light, 230 volts. Amount of printing required, 450 d.c. pictorials, 600 lithos, circulars and throwaways. Usual matinée day, Saturday, 2.15. Time of band rehearsal, 1 p.m. Nearest towns, Nottingham, Derby, Lincoln, Loughborough, Chesterfield, Leicester, and Sheffield. Booked in conjunction (by arrangement) with Grand Theatre, Mansfield; King's Theatre, Sutton-in-Ashfield; and New St. James' Theatre, Long Eaton. The theatre may be rented during June and July.

QUEEN'S PALACE OF VARIETIES.—Proprietor and Manager, Mr. Jim Morley; Musical Director, Mr. L. W. Atkin. Full license. Holding capacity: Number of persons, 1,000. Stage measurements: 15 ft. by 10 ft. Electric light. No band; simply piano.

HIPPODROME.—Proprietors, the New Theatre (Ilkeston), Ltd. Manager, Mr. L. F. A. Rogers. In course of construction.

The population is chiefly industrial, consisting of colliers, lace-makers, hosiery hands, employés of the Stanton Iron Works Co., etc. The pleasure fair in this town is of three days' duration (Thursday, Friday, and Saturday in the Feast Week), and the Feast Sunday is always the first after October 11. Portable theatres very seldom visit the town now. Circus pitches are obtainable not far from the tram routes.

Early closing day, Wednesday; market days, Thursday and Saturday.

RECOMMENDED APARTMENTS.

E. Pickard, 2, Lord Haddon Road.—Sitting-room, 2 bedrooms, 1 combined room; bath; and piano.

Mrs. Hall, 9, Northgate Street.—2 bedrooms and sitting-room, combined room; bath and piano.

ILKLEY, Yorks.

Population, 7,455.

ST. MARGARET'S HALL.—Proprietors, St. Margaret's Trustees; Manager, Rev. Mr. Dodd; Sharing Manager, Mr. J. Shuttleworth, Gothic House. Restricted license. Holding capacity: Number of persons, 500; amount, £25 to £30. Lighted by gas. Early closing day, Wednesday.

INVERGORDON, Ross-shire.

Population, 2,000. Miles from London, 599.

TOWN HALL.—Proprietors, The Town Council; Secretary, Mr. W. George. Double license. Holding capacity: Number of persons, 500. Depth and width of stage, 14ft. and 30ft. Lighted by gas. Amount of printing required: 50 bills. Terms for hiring, £1 7s. 6d. per night. Amount of deposit required on booking, £1 5s.

INVERNESS, Inverness.

Population, 22,566. Miles from London, 591.

THEATRE ROYAL—Proprietor and Manager, Mr. Cameron Burgess; Acting-Manager, Mr. Edward Todd; Musical Director, Mr. Harry T. Tuff. Restricted dramatic license. Holding capacity: Number of persons, 900; amount, £50. Stage, 28ft.; proscenium opening, 19ft. Gas light. Amount of printing required, 300. Usual matinée day, Saturday. Time of band rehearsal, 5 p.m. Best months, September to December, and New Year Holidays.

MUSIC HALL.—Manager, Mr. Edward Todd. Holding capacity: Number of persons, 1,200; Amount, £80. Good stage, 24ft. by 16ft.; no proscenium; Electric light. Amount of printing required, 300 sheets. Terms for hiring, £4 4s. per night; two nights, £7 7s.; per week, £12 12s. Amount of deposit required on booking, for week, £5 5s.

The population is made up of the residential and industrial class. The Highland Railway Works are the chief works; while there are other smaller ironworks and woollen mills. The people of Inverness give good patronage to opera or musical comedy. There are several sites for alfresco concerts, application for which must be made to the Town Council. The Public Park and Capel Inch are used for circuses.

Wool fair second Friday in July. Capel Inch and Public Park are the fair grounds.

Market days, Tuesday and Friday.

Medical Officer.—A.A.: Dr. G. M. E. Kerr, 19, High Street.

RECOMMENDED APARTMENTS.

Mrs. McGregor, 6, Queen's Gate.

IPSWICH, Suffolk.

Population, 70,000. Miles from London, 68.

LYCEUM THEATRE.—Proprietors, the Ipswich Lyceum, Limited; Managing Director, Mr. Hugh Turner; Manageress, Miss Parkin; Musical Director, Mr. Lewin Taylor. Full dramatic license. Holding capacity: Number of persons, 1,200; amount, £80. Stage measurements: 33ft. deep, 4 ft. wide; proscenium opening, 22ft.; cloths, 34ft. by 24ft.; flats, 20ft. 35 sets of lines. Gas and electric light. Amount of printing required, 450 sheets walls, 500 d.c. bills, 1,000 circulars. Usual matinée day, Saturday, 2.30. Time of band rehearsal, 11 a.m.

HIPPODROME.—Manager, Mr. E. H. Bostock; Acting-Manager, Mr. D. F. Bostock. Booking circuit, Bostock Tour. Musical Director, Mr. Sidney Davis. Dramatic license. Holding capacity: 2,000. Proscenium opening, 30ft. Stage measurements: Depth, 40ft.; width, 70ft. Gas and electric light. Time of band rehearsal, 2 p.m. Matinée day, Saturday. Bars other theatres in Ipswich.

PUBLIC HALL AND OPERA HOUSE.— Manager, Mr. Geo. Watson. Dramatic license. Gas and electric. Motor generator for kinematographs. Public organ.

LECTURE HALL.—Manager, Mr. Herbert Walker. Dramatic license. Holding capacity: Number of persons, 600-700. Platform 25ft. by 15ft. Lighted by gas.

OLD MUSEUM ROOMS.—Manager, Mr. H.E. Archer. Music and dancing license. Holding capacity: Number of persons, 300. No stage. Lighted by gas. Terms for hiring, £3 3s.

SOCIAL SETTLEMENT HALL.—Manager, Mr. G. A. Mallett; Secretary, Mr. W. E. Calver. Dramatic license. Gas.

Sites for circuses, etc.: Old Cattle Market. Early closing days, Wednesday and Saturday; market days, Tuesday and Saturday.

Agents.—A.U.: Mr. A. H. Cormack, The Posada, Brook Street. M.H.A.R.A.: H. A. Barham, Falcon Inn, Falcon Street. V.A.F.: The same.

RECOMMENDED APARTMENTS.

Mrs. Tarrant, Fore Street Temperance Hotel. —2 sitting, 3 single bed, 2 bed sitting, 3 double bedrooms; pianos.

Mrs. Nicoll, 14, Orwell Place, Tacket Street. —1 sitting-room, 2 bedrooms, 1 combined room; piano; bath.

IRONBRIDGE, Salop.

Population, 2,880. Miles from London, 158.

MADELEY INSTITUTE.—Has dramatic license and holds about 1,000.

BROSELEY TOWN HALL.—Has dramatic license, and holds about 400.

WHARFAGE LECTURE ROOM.—Apply to the Secretary. No license. Holds about 250. No proper stage. Gas. Terms, 10s. per night, payable in advance.

The local fair is always held on May 29, and the town is often visited by portables. There is no difficulty whatever in obtaining licenses from the local magistrates. There are circus pitches; for instance, Fossett recently paid a visit to the town, and was well patronised, as all companies and circuses are that visit this district, which is surrounded with industries, viz., brick and tile, pipes, potteries, Coalport china, and C. B. Dale ironworks.

Early closing day, Wednesday; market day, Friday.

JARROW, Durham.

Population, 34,295. Miles from London, 268.

THEATRE ROYAL.—Lessee and Manager, Mr. Hugh Robertson; Scenic Artist, Mr. Harry Sharpe. Full dramatic license. Holding capacity: Number of persons, 2,000; amount, £70. Stage measurements: 30ft. by 46ft.; proscenium opening, 20ft. Electric current, voltage 240. Printing required, 650. No regular matinée day. Time of band rehearsal, 1 p.m. Bars Hebburn.

EMPIRE THEATRE.—Closed.

PALACE.—Lessee and Manager, Mr. Joseph Lamb. Holds 1,800; amount, £30. Matinée Saturday.

CO-OPERATIVE HALL.—A very elegant building, erected in 1904 in place of old premises, which were burnt down. Seats about 1,200.

Lighted throughout with gas. Suitable for concerts or entertainments.

MECHANICS' HALL. — President, Mr. M. Dillon; Secretary, Mr. A. Young. Holds 1.500. Full dramatic license. Stage 25ft. by 20ft. Electric light.

ROYAL ALBERT HALL. — Lessee, Dr. Seaton. Holding capacity: Number of persons about 1,500. Electric light. Has dramatic license.

THE KINO PICTURE AND VARIETY HALL.—Proprietor, Dixon Scott; Manager, J. R. Scott; Musical Director, Edward Scott. Full music license. Holding capacity 600. Electric light. Matinée Saturday.

This town is admirably situated for touring companies, there being an excellent train service. There are other large places in close proximity which have no places of amusement, and consequently the inhabitants flock into the central place. The chief industry is the shipbuilding. Jarrow is only six miles from Newcastle.

Early closing day, Wednesday

JEDBURGH, Roxburgh.

Population, 3,136. Miles from London, 370.

PUBLIC HALL.—Manager, Mr. Thomas Simson, Burgh Chamberlain. Has dramatic license. Holding capacity: Number of persons, 800. Platform, 25ft. by 30ft. Electric direct current, 225 volts. Terms: £3 3s.; two nights, £5 5s. Amount of deposit required on booking, half of rent.

Early closing day, Thursday; market day, Tuesday.

JERSEY, Channel Islands.

Population, 52,796.

OPERA HOUSE.—Lessee and Manager, Mr. Edward Marris; Acting-Manager, Mr. Stanley Hope; Musical Director, Mr. Geo. Ess; Scenic Artist, Mr. C. H. Frampton. Full dramatic license. Holding capacity: Number of persons, 1,100; amount, £105. Proscenium opening, 24ft.; width of stage, 60ft.; depth, 30 ft. Gas (incandescent). Amount of printing required, 250 sheets, 250 lithos. Usual matinée day, Wednesday. Time of band rehearsal, 2 p.m.

WEST PARK PAVILION.—Manager, Mr. E. C. Boielle, 64, King Street, Jersey. Fully licensed. Holding capacity: Number of persons, 1,200. Stage, 22ft. wide by 14 ft. deep; height, 15ft. Has one exterior scene. Gas. Limes. Amount of printing required, 60 to 80 d.c. (boards provided). Terms for hiring: £2 per night. £10 per week.

ODDFELLOWS' HALL, St. Helier.—Secretary, 18, Seaton Place. Dramatic performances and music and dancing by permission of the Bailiffs. Holding capacity: Number of persons, 550 to 600. Stage and dressing-rooms. Depth and width of stage and proscenium measurements: 14ft. inside, 20ft. outside to back; depth, 60ft.; width, 40ft. Lighted by gas. Terms for hiring: £1 15s. one evening, £3 two evenings, £4 10s. three evenings, or £7 one week. Amount of deposit required on booking: £2, if for a week.

ROYAL HALL, St. Helens. — Apply Mr. Larbalester, Hill Street. Holds 450. Gas.

No local fairs.

Early closing day, Thursday; market day, Saturday.

Medical Officer.—A.A.: Dr. R. Maxwell Moffatt, 46, David Place, St. Helier. Hours, 2-3. A.U.: The same.

Agent.—M.H.A.R.A.: W. Stone, Grosvenor Bar.

KEIGHLEY, Yorks.

Population, 41,564. Miles from London, 211.

QUEEN'S THEATRE.—Proprietor, Mr. R. S. Kendall; Manager, Mr. W. Carson.

MUNICIPAL HALL.—Proprietors, The Corporation. Manager, Mr. Herbert Driver. No dramatic license. Holds 1.000. Stage 44ft. by 30ft.; proscenium, 25ft. Electric, 460 volts direct. Terms, £12 12s. per week.

TEMPERANCE HALL.—Apply the Manager. Music and dancing license. Holding capacity: Number of persons, 700. Stage, 40ft. by 18ft.; auditorium, 48ft. by 40ft.; gallery, 40ft. by 28ft. Gas and electric light. Terms, one night, £1 10s.; two nights, £2 10s.; three nights, £3 5s.; four nights, £3 15s.; six nights, £5. Amount of deposit required on booking, half.

Keighley is an industrial town, with a population as noted above in the borough, the rural population, bringing it to about 70,000. Its chief industries are textile machinery (one firm employing something like 3,000 hands), washing machine works, laundry engineering companies, spinning, leather works, iron works, and manufacture of textile goods. There are two pleasure fairs—one in May and the other in November—each one ruled by the Cattle Fair, generally held the first Saturday in each month, and run for about ten days. It is very seldom portable theatres visit the town, most of them making for places in the rural districts. Difficulty is not experienced in obtaining license from Corporation. No sites for alfresco concerts. Now and then a circus visits the town, and there is no difficulty in getting a site nor any difficulty in getting a license from the Council.

Early closing day, Tuesday; market day, Wednesday.

Agent.—M.H.A.R.A.: J. Maughan, Cavendish Hotel.

RECOMMENDED APARTMENTS.

Mrs. Greenwood, 69, Brunswick Street.—1 combined room.

KEITH, Banffshire.

Population, 4,753. Miles from London, 584.

LONGMORE HALL.—Secretary, Mr. George Davidson. Double license. Holding capacity: Number of persons, 500. Stage 30ft. wide by 8ft. deep, can be extended. Gas. Terms: Dramatic, 30s. per night; concerts, 25s. per night; attendance and lighting extra. Amount of deposit required on booking, half of rent.

The market stance is available for portables, circuses, etc.

Early closing day, Wednesday; market day, Saturday.

KELSO, Roxburgh.

Population, 4,006; miles from London, 365.

CORN EXCHANGE.—Secretaries, Messrs. P. and J. Stormonth Darling. Holding capacity: Number of persons, about 400. The taker provides platform. Terms for hiring: First night, £2 2s.; subsequently, £1 1s. Amount of deposit required on booking, £1.

Early closing day, Wednesday; market day, Friday.

KENDAL, Westmorland.

Population, 14,183. Miles from London, 251.

ST. GEORGE'S THEATRE.—Proprietor, Mr. R. F. Chorley; Manager, Mr. J. W. Butler; Musical Director, Mr. T. B. Jackson. Full dramatic license. Holding capacity; Number of persons, 1,300; amount, £80. Stage measurements: 50 ft. by 32 ft.; grid height, 30 ft.; proscenium, 24 ft. by 20 ft. Gas and electric light. Amount of printing required: Walls and windows, 700 sheets. Usual matinée day, Thursday or Saturday. Time of band rehearsal, 5 p.m. Best months, August to April.

Industrial and market town, market day being Saturday each week and Wednesdays in the summer months and fruit season. Industries, manufacture of boots and shoes, tobacco, carpet weaving, horse clothing, hosiery works, heald and reed makers, card mills, and three iron foundries.

Thursdays, each week, all the year round, all shops close at 1 p.m. for half-day's holiday. Fairs: February 20, horses; March 22 and April 28, cattle; November 8, cattle; November 9, horses. Fortnight fair (cattle) every alternate Monday, and auction mart for cattle every Monday. A field is available for circus pitches; also portables. License for latter as yet never been refused. Kendal being only nine miles from Lake Windermere and fifteen from Grange-over-Sands. Late trains are secured for special attractions at the theatre, picking up at all the intermediate stations, and the town enjoys a nice, steady, all the year round trade.

KENMARE, Co. Kerry, Ireland.

Population, 1,500 Miles from Dublin, 196.

COMMERCIAL CLUB.—Manager, Mr. Con. Buckley; Secretary, Mr. James O'Shea. Holding capacity: Number of persons, 500. Stage, 12ft. deep by 16ft. wide. Electric light. Week terms, 10s. per night. Amount of deposit required on booking, half fee.

Monthly fairs. Several sites available for portables, al fresco concerts, and circuses.

KESWICK, Cumb.

Population, 4,451. Miles from London, 299.

QUEEN OF THE LAKES PAVILION.— Manager, Mr. G. M. McKane, 1, Fitz Arcade. Has dramatic license. Holding capacity: Number of persons, 1,200; amount, £50 maximum Proper stage. Gas and electric light. Amount of printing required: 300 sheets d.c. Terms for hiring: Two guineas one night, £3 15s. two nights, £5 three nights. Amount of deposit required on booking, 20s.

VICTORIA HALL.—Manager, Mr. G. P. Abraham. No dramatic license. Holding capacity: Number of persons, 300. For lectures and concerts. Gas. Amount of printing required: 12 large, 20 medium, 500 circulars. Terms for hiring: From 15s. Amount of deposit required on booking, half.

No local fairs. Circus ground available.

Early closing, Wednesday. Market, Saturday.

KETTERING, Northants.

Population, 28,653. Miles from London, 72.

AVENUE THEATRE.—Proprietor and Manager, Mr. Frank Payne; Musical Director, Mr. Charles Sidney Payne. Restricted dramatic license. Holding capacity: Number of persons, 1,400; amount, £70. Stage measurements: Depth of stage, 26ft.; opening, 24ft.; width, 45ft. Gas and electric light, 230 volts. Printing required, 400 sheets for walls. Usual matinée day, Saturday. Time of band rehearsal, 12.30 p.m.

VICTORIA THEATRE.—Managers, Messrs. Alf. Bailey and Co.; Business Manager, Mr. Bert Bailey; Musical Director, Mr. Alf. Bailey. Restricted dramatic license. Holding capacity: Number of persons, 1,500; amount, £100. Stage measurements: 27ft. deep by 50ft. wide; proscenium, 25ft. Gas and electric light. Amount of printing required, 400 sheets for posting, 200 window lithos. Usual matinée day, Saturday. Time of band rehearsal, 1 p.m. Best months, September to March.

CORN EXCHANGE.—Secretary, Mr. Arthur Bird. Restricted dramatic license. Holds about 600. Stage 12ft. deep by 30ft. wide.

Early closing day, Thursday; Market day, Friday.

KIDDERMINSTER, Worc.

Population, 29,000. Miles from London, 135.

OPERA HOUSE.—Proprietors, New Opera House (Kidderminster), Ltd.—Managing Director, Mr. J. P. Moore; Resident Manager, Mr. R. C. Gudgeon. Dramatic license. Holds 1,750. Gas and electric, 230 volts continuous.

MUSIC HALL or TOWN HALL.—Manager, Mr. J. Morton, Town Clerk. Fully licensed. Holding capacity: Number of persons, 850. Stage has to be erected. Gas and electric light. Terms for hiring, one night, £4 10s.; three nights, £8 15s. Amount of deposit required on booking, 50 per cent.

Early closing day, Wednesday; market day, Thursday.

Medical Officer.—A.A.: Dr. D. Corbett, Farfield House. A.U.: The same.

ACTORS' CHURCH UNION.—Rev. W. T. Phillips, 20, Blakebrook.

Agent.—M.H.A.R.A.: T. Reed, Clarendon Hotel.

KIDSGROVE, Staffordshire.

Population, 4,552. Miles from London, 152.

VICTORIA HALL.—Owners, Kidsgrove Urban District Council. No license. Holding capacity; Number of persons, 600. Small stage, but can be enlarged. Gas. Terms for hiring: £1 1s. first and 17s. 6d. consecutive (gas in addition). Deposit on booking, full amount of fee.

Early closing day, Thursday; market day, Saturday.

KIDWELLY, Carm.

Population, 3,160. Miles from London, 230.

TOWN HALL.—Secretary, P.-Sergt. James. Holding capacity, 400 persons. Stage, but no scenery. Terms: £1 3s. 6d. first night; 13s, every other night. Picture shows. Variety companies and small fit-up dramatic companies take very well.

Fair, October, 29 and 30.

Early closing day, Wednesday; market day, Saturday.

KILKENNY, Co. Kilkenny.

Population, 11,000. Miles from Dublin, 81.

THEATRE. — Manager, Mr. T. J. Brown. Double license. Holding capacity: Number of persons, 1,000. Stage depth, 22ft.; width, 36ft.; 20ft. by 18ft. proscenium. Gas and electric light, 100 volts. Printing required, from 600 to 800 sheets. Share or rental depends on class of performance. Amount of deposit required on booking, one-third of rent.

Kilkenny is twenty miles from Waterford, and forty from Limerick. Fifty miles from Wexford on direct route Fishguard.

Dates of local fairs: Second Wednesday in each month. The fair green for circuses, etc.

KILMARNOCK, Ayr.

Population, 34,160. Miles from London, 390.

KING'S THEATRE.
Early closing day, first Wednesday in month,
May to October; market day, Friday.
A.A. Medical Officer.—Dr. A. Revie, Calcutta
Lodge.
Agent.—V.A.F. : W. Russell, Sun Inn.

KING'S LYNN, Norfolk.

Population, 20,283. Miles from London, 99.

NEW ROYAL THEATRE.—Proprietors, Corporation, Lessee and Manager, Mr. B. Pareezer;
Acting-Manager, Mr. Reginald Pareezer; Musical
Director, Mr. G. Rix; Scenic Artist, W. Sconse.
Double license. Holding capacity: Number of
persons, 1,500; amount, £80, ordinary prices.
Height of proscenium opening, 18ft.; width,
28ft.; wall to wall, 58ft.; depth, 34. Gas and
electric light, 200 volts. Printing required
twenty-five 6-sheets, six 12-sheets, five 18-sheets,
two 24-sheets, 400 lithos, 700 circulars, 1,000
throwaways, 50 dated slips. Usual matinée
day, Saturday or Wednesday. Time of band
rehearsal, 12 noon. Worked as theatre and
hippodrome. Bars no surrounding halls.

ST. JAMES'S HALL AND ASSEMBLY
ROOMS.—Proprietors, Messrs. G. M. Bridges and
Son. Music and dancing license. Holding
capacity: Number of person, Hall, 1,000;
Assembly Rooms, 250. Gas and electric light.
200 volts continuous.
Dates of local fairs : Lynn Mart, February
15 to 28.
Sites available for portables, etc.: Show
Ground, Austin Street Field and Public Walks.
Early closing day, Wednesday; market days,
Tuesday and Saturday.
Agent.—M.H.A.R.A.: Mr. F. Tyler, Rummer
Hotel, Tower Street.

RECOMMENDED APARTMENTS.

Mrs. J. J. Dines, 4, Whitefriars Terrace.—Sitting, double and single bedrooms, combined
room ; 2 pianos.

KINGSTON-ON-THAMES, Surrey.

Population, 34,375. Miles from London, 12.

ROYAL COUNTY THEATRE.—Proprietors,
the Kingston-on-Thames Theatre Co., Limited;
Managing Director, Mr. Peter Davey; Musical
Director, Mr. Hugo Rignold; Scenic Artist,
Mr. George Miller. Full dramatic license.
Holding capacity: Number of persons, about
1,300; amount, about £115. Stage measurements: Opening, 22ft. 6in.; depth, 43ft.; width.
60ft.; grid, 48ft. Electric light. Amount of
printing required, about 1,200 sheets. Usual
matinée day, all the year round on Wednesday
at 2.30; during the pantomime season, eve'y
Monday, Wednesday, and Saturday. Time of
band rehearsal, 11 o'clock. Fit up halls and
small theatres in the neighbourhood barred.

DRILL HALL.—Apply, The Secretary.

ST. JAMES'S HALL.—Manager, Mr. F. Sel-
way; offices, 24, St. James's Road. Dramatic
license. Holding capacity: Number of persons,
700. Platform only. Gas and electric light.
Terms for hiring, £3 3s. per night. Amount
of deposit required on booking, half fee.
Licenses are not difficult to get for portables.
There has not been a case of refusal recently.
There are sites for alfresco concerts and circus
pitches. The alfrescos are held every summer,
and a circus usually visits yearly.
The fair was an old institution, but of late
years has been done away with. Trams now

run to London. A music hall has several
times been tried, but has always proved a
failure.
Early closing, Wednesday; market, Saturday.
Agent.—V.A.F.: G. W. Plumb, Griffin Hotel.

KIRKBY STEPHEN, Westmorland.

Population, 1,656. Miles from London, 260.

ODDFELLOWS HALL.—Manager, Mr. James
Irvin. Special license for stage plays can be
easily obtained. Holding capacity: Number of
persons, between 400 and 500. Fixed stage, 27ft.
long, 12ft. wide, 3ft. 6in. from floor. Lighted
by gas. Terms for hiring: First day, 12s.;
second day, 8s.; gas and fires extra. Amount
of deposit required on booking, 5s.
Early closing, Thursday; market, Monday.

KIRKCALDY, Fife.

Population, 36,000. Miles from London, 414.

HIPPODROME (late KING's).—Lessee, Mr. E.
H. Bostock; Managers, Messrs. Williams and
Walker; all communications to Mr. G. W.
Walker. H lding capacity: Number of persons,
3,000; amount, £120. Depth and width of stage
and proscenium measurements: Depth, 30ft.; proscenium opening, 28ft.; full width of stage,
60ft. Gas and electric light. Amount of printing required: If six nights, 800 sheets for
walls, 500 lithos; if for three mights, 400
sheets for walls and 300 window lithos.

ADAM SMITH HALL, belonging to the
Kirkcaldy Corporation. Seated for 1,500. This
hall is comparatively new, beautifully fitted
up, and quite suitable for dramatic and
operatic companies. Although chiefly used
as a concert hall, many companies have
visited, such as Moody-Manners (C) Company,
etc. Terms: One night, £4; 25 per cent. reduction after two nights. BEVERIDGE
HALL (in same building) seats 500. Terms: £3
per night for two nights; subsequent nights,
reduction of 25 per cent. Electric current, 230
volts.

PAVILION (late CORN EXCHANGE).—Belonging
to Corporation. Lessee, Mr. G. W. Walker.
Holds 1,500; amount £55. Variety house. Stage
22ft. deep; proscenium opening, 26ft.; full
width, 40ft. Electric light, 230 volts. Same
printing as Hippodrome.
A fair is held annually on the third Friday
and Saturday in April; this is held along
the shore, where there is a stretch of about
two miles. This is reckoned one of the largest
fairs in Scotland, and great numbers of all
sorts of roundabouts, shows, and circus entertainments visit. Occasionally portable theatres
visit the town, and difficulty is not experienced in gaining a license for same. Drama
does not appeal much to Kirkcaldy audiences.
There are plenty of sites that would suit
alfresco shows; these have been tried on
several occasions, but do not as a rule do
well.
The town has been visited by some of the
largest travelling circuses, such as Barnum
and Bailey's and Buffalo Bill's. Most of the
sites suitable are being built on now.
The population is chiefly industrial; the
principal industries are linen, pottery, and
linoleum manufacture. There is also a large
surrounding mining district, connected by
rail and electric car.
Early closing day, Wednesday; market day,
Saturday.
Agency.—M.H.A.R.A.: W. C. Ritchie, Commercial Hotel. V.A.F.: The same.

KIRKCUDBRIGHT.

Population, 2,386. Miles from London, 362.

TOWN HALL.—Proprietors, Provost, Magistrates, and Town Council; Manager, Burgh Chamberlain. Dramatic, music, and dancing licenses. Seated for 400. Amount, £15 to £30. Stage measures 16½ft. by 26ft. Gas. Terms for hiring: Concerts, hall £1 1s., keeper 5s.; dramatic entertainments, hall £2 2s., keeper 5s. Gas extra. Amount of deposit required on booking, 10s. 6d. Best night Friday.

There are no local fairs. Sites available for portables, alfresco concerts, and circuses, ground near harbour, circuses in Victoria Park.

Early closing day, Saturday; market day, Friday.

KIRKINTILLOCH, Dumbarton.

Population, 10,502.

TEMPERANCE HALL.—Secretary, Mr. E. Macindoe, 93, Cowgate. Holding capacity: Number of persons, 450. Depth and width of stage, 29ft. 6in. by 11ft. 4in. Lighted by gas. Terms for hiring, £1 10s. Amount of deposit required on booking, 10s.

Fairs, May and October.
Early closing, Wednesday.

KIRKWALL, Orkney.

Population, 3,660.

TEMPERANCE HALL.—Manager, Mr. P. W. Peall, 37, Albert Street. Licensed by Town Council for public entertainment. No dancing. Holding capacity: Number of persons, about 750. There is a stage, but no fixed proscenium or fittings. Lighted by gas (incandescent). About 200 halls will bill town. Terms for hiring: 21s. per night, gas and hallkeeper extra; also special insurance of 5s. if scenery is used at performance. Amount of deposit required on booking: Half.

Lammas market, 1st Tuesday after August 11, and continues until Saturday of following week. The first two days' fair is held on ground about 1½ miles from the town, and the following days on site in centre of town. The population of the town is doubled during fair.

KNIGHTON, Radnorshire.

Population, 2,139. Miles from London, 181.

ASSEMBLY ROOMS.—Manager, Mr. F. Hale. Double license. Holding capacity: Number of persons, 300 to 400. Portable stage, about 24ft. by 12ft. Lighted by gas. Terms for hiring, 20s. per night. Amount of deposit required on booking, 25 per cent.

Small field in town available for portables, alfresco concerts, and circuses.

Early closing day, Friday; market day, Thursday.

KNOTTINGLEY, Yorks.

Population, 5,800. Miles from London, 175.

TOWN HALL.—Manager, Mr. Walter Swaine (Clerk to the Council); No dramatic license. Proper stage. Gas. Terms for Hiring: 1 night, £1 5s.; 2 nights, £2 5s.; 3 nights, £3 5s.; 4 nights, £4; 5 nights, £4 15s.; 6 nights, £5 10s. Amount of deposit required on booking, 50 per cent.

Early closing day, Thursday.

LAMPETER, Card.

Population, 1,722. Miles from London, 266.

QUEEN VICTORIA MEMORIAL HALL.—Manager, Mr. D. F. Lloyd, Solicitor. No dramatic license. Holding capacity: Number of persons, 600; amount, £30. Stage and scenery. Stage 24ft. wide by 13ft. deep; proscenium 18ft. opening by 13ft. deep. Lighted by gas. Amount of printing required: 50 posters sufficient for town only. Terms for hiring; £2 10s. for one night, £1 5s. for second, and 15s. for each subsequent night. Sharing terms can be arranged. Amount of deposit required on booking, £1 1s.

Fairs held every month. Site for out of door shows, the Common; for circuses, Black Lion Field. School and college in the town.

Early closing, Wednesday. Market, last Monday in month.

LANARK.

Population, 5,084. Miles from London, 377.

GOOD TEMPLAR HALL.—Proprietors, Lanark Good Templar Hall Co., Limited; Manager, Mrs. Wilson, 21, High Street. Dramatic and music and dancing licenses. Holds 600. Stage 22ft. 6ins. wide, 13ft. 4ins. deep; can be extended in depth. Gas. Terms for hiring: 25s. first night, 20s. each night after, exclusive of gas. Amount of deposit required on booking, 10s.

Site available for portables, alfresco concerts and circuses, the Horse Market, Lanark, belonging to the Town Council. Applications should be made to the Chamberlain.

Early closing day, Thursday; market day, Monday.

LANCASTER, Lancs.

Population, 46,000. Miles from London, 230.

NEW GRAND (late ATHENÆUM).—Lessee and Manager, Mr. Stanley Rogers; Acting-Manager, Mr. E. C. Howitt; Musical Director, Mr. W. Bastow. License restricted. Holding capacity: Number of persons, 1,000; amount, £65. Stage measurements, 22ft. by 20ft. deep, width, fly-rail to rail, 32ft.; fly 24ft. cloths, use 18ft. flats. Gas and electric light, 230 volts. Printing required, 420 walls, 500 windows. Usual matinée day, Saturday. Time of band rehearsal, 2.30 p.m.

HIPPODROME. — Proprietors, Mr. John Porter and Mr. W. J. Ferguson; Manager, Mr. John Porter; Musical Director, Mr. Frank L. Bell. Double license. Holding capacity: Number of persons, 1,000. Stage measurements: Opening, 23ft.; depth, 24ft.; to battens, 18ft.; 6ft. in wing; to grid, 40 ft. Electric current voltage 230. Band rehearsal, 12 noon. Matinée day, Monday, 2.30. Bars Lancaster and Morecambe.

CROMWELL HALL.—Manager, Mr. H. G. Kirkby, Market Street. Music and dancing license. Holding capacity: Number of persons, 600. Platform, 16ft. by 10ft. Electric current, 230 volts. Terms from 15s. per night. First-class electric lantern kept; also specially prepared wall for pictures.

CO-OPERATIVE HALL.—Secretary, Mr. A. Varley. Music and dancing license. Holding capacity; Number of persons, 600. Platform. Electric current, 230 volts. Terms, £4 per week evenings, matinées extra. Prepayment required.

Population largely industrial. Lancaster is a military depôt, with a fair number of residential people.

Fairs are held in Lancaster on May 2, 3, and 4, October 10, 11, and 12. The town is visited by shows, circuses, etc., limited pitches being obtainable. Portable theatres very rarely visit Lancaster. Licenses have rarely been granted. Managers of portables do very poor business.

Early closing day, Wednesday; market day, Saturday.

Agent.—M.H.A.R.A.: J. Bamber, Royal Hotel. V.A.F.: The same.

RECOMMENDED APARTMENTS.

Mrs. Holmes. 6, St. Leonard's Terrace.—Bed and sitting; piano.

LANCHESTER, Co. Durham.

Population, 7,306. Miles from London, 263.

ASSEMBLY ROOMS.—Manager, Mr. J. J. Sinton. No dramatic license. Holding capacity: Number of persons, 400. Temporary stage. Lighted by gas. Terms for hiring: 15s. per night. Amount of deposit required on booking, 5s.

Early closing, Wednesday.

LANGHOLM, Dumfries.

Population, 3,142. Miles from London, 312.

BUCCLEUCH HALL.—Manager, Mr. Thomas Milligan. No license required. Holding capacity: Number of persons, 1,000; amount, £30. Stage measurements: 20ft. opening, 16ft. deep; can be extended to 20ft. deep. Height of proscenium, 15ft. Lighted by gas. Amount of printing required, 150 day bills, six 18-sheet posters, six 6-sheet posters, lithos., etc. Terms for hiring, £2, gas inclusive; also sharing terms. Amount of deposit required on booking, 10s. where companies are not known.

Early closing day, Thursday; market day, Wednesday.

LARGS, Ayrshire.

Population, 5,501. Miles from London, 410.

PUBLIC HALL.—Secretary and Treasurer, Mr. David Harper, solicitor. Double license. Holding capacity: Number of persons, 800 to 900. Proper stage. Hall 40ft. 6ins. long, 46ft. 6ins. wide. Stage: Length, 35ft.; breadth, 29ft.; balcony of 10ft. Lighted by gas. Terms for hiring, £3 5s. per night. Amount of deposit required on booking, 10s.

Date of local fair, June, 15, the only one in the year. Sites available for portables, alfresco concerts, and circuses, foreshore, but can only put up such things as are necessary for circus, etc., by applying to the magistrates for a license.

Market day, Thursday.

LARNE, Co. Antrim.

Population, 7,421. Miles from Dublin, 136.

McGAREL TOWN HALL.—Manager, the Town Clerk. Holding capacity: Number of persons, 350. Platform, 25ft. wide, 8ft. at each side. Lighted by gas. Terms for hiring: One night, 20s.; two, 32s.; three, 44s.; and 10s. each after. Full rent required on booking.

Dates of local fairs: Second Thursday each month. The Fair Green is available for portables, al fresco concerts, and circuses.

Market, Wednesday.

LEAMINGTON, Warwickshire.

Population, 26,880. Miles from London, 97.

THEATRE ROYAL. — Proprietors, Messrs. David Allen and Sons, Limited; Business Manager, Mr. Walter P. Wright; Musical Director, Mr. Maitland de Lacey. Full license. Holding capacity: Number of persons, 1,500. Gas and electric light. Usual matinée day, Thursday.

WINTER HALLS.—Manager, Mr. Charles Ravenhill. Music and dancing license. Holding capacity: Number of persons, 1,000. stage capable of seating 250 additional persons (in tiers) or for oratorios. Gas and electric, 230 volts; continuous. Terms: 1st week, £20; 2nd week, £15; daily, £6 10s., including light. Whole fee required on booking. Available only from October to May.

ROYAL ASSEMBLY ROOMS.—Lessee and Manager, Mr. A. White. Double license. Holding capacity: Number of persons, 600. Depth and width of stage, 22ft. by 33ft.; proscenium, 22ft wide and 18ft. high. Gas and electric 230 volts. continuous. Printing required: 400 sheets. Terms for hiring vary according to class of entertainment. Amount of deposit required on booking, £2.

No local fairs, and no sites available for portables, alfresco concerts, and circuses.

Early closing day, Thursday.

Agent.—V.A.F.: A. E. Lennon, Golden Lion Hotel.

LEATHERHEAD, Surrey.

Population, 4,694. Miles from London, 17.

VICTORIA HALL.—Manager, Mr. C. E. Grantham. Double license. Holding capacity: Number of persons, 500; amount, £30. Stage: Depth, 20ft.; width, 38ft.; proscenium, 22ft. wide, 18ft. high. Electric, 220 and 440 volts. Terms: One night dramatic, £3; two nights, £5 10s.; three nights, £7 10s. Amount of deposit required on booking, £1 1s.

Early closing day, Wednesday.

LEDBURY, Hereford

Population, 3,259. Miles from London, 130.

ROYAL HALL.—Lessee and Manager, Mr. E. H. Hopkins. Fully licensed. Holding capacity: Number of persons, 500; amount, £40. Stage, 20ft. deep, 32ft. wide; proscenium opening, 20ft. Gas. Head and footlights. Limes. Printing, 180 sheets. Terms for hiring on application.

Early closing, Thursday; market, Tuesday.

LEEDS, Yorks.

Population, 428,968. Miles from London, 186.

GRAND THEATRE AND OPERA HOUSE.— Proprietor, the Theatre and Opera House, Leeds, Limited; Managing Director, Mr. John Hart; General Manager, Mr. Wynn Miller. Musical Director, Signor A. Romilli; Scenic Artist, Mr. R. C. Oldham. Full dramatic license. Holding capacity: Number of persons, 3,500; amount, £350. Stage measurements: Proscenium opening, 32ft. 6in.; depth to arch, 44ft.; under arch, 56ft.; width, 72ft.; out of sight, 32ft.; cellar, 30ft. Electric light. Amount of printing required: 2,000 for walls, 1,000 d.c. windows. Usual matinée day, Saturday, at 2. Time of band rehearsal, 11 a.m.

ROYAL.—Proprietor, Mr. Frank Macnaghten; General Manager, Mr. R. Ernest Liston; Musical Director, Mr. Isaac Hudson; Scenic Artist,

Mr. Harry Peirse; Stage Carpenter, Mr. Chas. Wood. Full license. Holding capacity: Number of persons, 4,000; amount, £200. Stage measurements: Depth 30ft., width 68ft.; proscenium opening, width 32ft., height 24ft. Gas and electric light. Amount of printing required, 2,500. Usual matinée day, Tuesday. Time of band rehearsal, 12 noon.

QUEEN'S THEATRE. — Proprietor, Mr. Frederick Wm. Wood; General Manager, Mr. J. C. Whiteman; Acting-Manager, Mr. Charles Bush; Musical Director, Mr. George Jackson. Full license, with smoking. Electric light. Time of band rehearsal, 12 noon.

EMPIRE PALACE.—Proprietary, Moss's Empires, Limited; Chairman, Sir H. E. Moss; Managing Director, Mr. Oswald Stoll; Assisting Director, Mr. Frank Allen; District Manager, Mr. T. Gerald Morton; Acting Manager, Mr. Alex. Galley. Band rehearsal, 2 p.m. Electric current, alternating 200 volts. Bars City varieties, Barrasford, Hippodrome, and Queen's.

Bars all other Managements' Halls in Leeds and the following towns: Atherton, Stalybridge, Middleton, and Hyde.

HIPPODROME.—Proprietors, Barrasfords, Limited; Managing Director, Mr. Thos. Barrasford; Acting-Manager, Mr. A. Collingwood; Barrasford Tour; Musical Director, Mr. Arthur Workman. Music and dancing license. Holding capacity: Number of persons, 1,500. Stage measurements: Footlights to back wall 34ft., width of stage 71ft.; proscenium opening 31ft., height of opening 24ft. Gas and electric light. Time of band rehearsal, 12 noon. Usual matinée day, Wednesday. Two houses nightly. (Telephone, 438.)

COLISEUM.—Manager, Mr. J. A. Winn. Music and dancing license. Holding capacity: Number of persons, 3,500. Stage, 40ft. by 16ft. Gas and electric light. Terms for hiring, £60 per week.

CITY VARIETIES.—Proprietor, Mr. Fredk. Wm. Wood; General Manager, Mr. J. C. Whiteman; Acting-Manager, Mr. Sam Jones; Musical Director, Mr. Herbert Holgate. Music and dancing license. Electric light. Time of band rehearsal, 1.30 p.m. Usual matinée day, Wednesday, 2.30.

ALBERT HALL (Leeds Institute).—Secretary, Mr. A. Tait. Music and dancing license. Holding capacity: Number of persons, 1,200. Stage, 38ft. by 15ft. Electric light. Terms for hiring, £5 per night, 25 per cent. discount if taken for three or more consecutive nights.

PEOPLE'S HALL, Albion Street.—Secretary, Mr. John W. Fawcett. Music license only. Holding capacity: Number of persons, 800 to 1,000. Electric light. Terms for hiring: One night, £2 5s.; six nights, £10.

Population, residential and industrial. Chief industries are manufacture of iron goods, machinery, leather, woollen, cotton, wholesale clothing, and boots.

Local fair commences on January 9, and is usually held in the Engineers' Drill Ground, Camp Road. Position central, good roads to and from, and easy of access. The township of Armley, adjoining and in the Borough of Leeds, has a large feast the first Monday after September 1. A portable always attends. No difficulty is presented by Council in regard to license. Holbeck, another township in the borough, has also a very popular feast a week later than Armley. A portable usually visits here. Alfresco concerts are given at Roundhay Park (belonging to the Corporation).

Early closing day, Wednesday; market days, Tuesday and Saturday.

Medical Officer.—Dr. B. G. Heald, Red House, East Street. 'Phone, 613. At home, 2-3. A.U.: The same. M.H.A.R.A.: The same.

Agent.—M.H.A.R.A.: Sam Jones, City Palace. A.U.: Wheatsheaf Hotel, Upperhead Row. V.A.F.: The same.

RECOMMENDED APARTMENTS.

Mrs. Davis, 9, St. George's Terrace.—2 sitting 2 bedrooms, and combined room.

LEEK, Staffs.

Population, 15,484. Miles from London, 156.

TOWN HALL.—Manager, Mr. Geo. Keates. Double license. Holding capacity: Number of persons, 700; amount, according to prices of admission; 2s., 1s., 6d., would be from £25 to £30. Stage: Depth, 16ft.; width, 30ft.; height, 14ft. Electric light. Amount of printing required, 400 sheets, 500 daybills approximately. Terms for hiring: One evening, £1 10s.; two, £2 12s. 6d.; three, £3 10s.; four, £4 7s. 6d.; five, £5 5s.; six, £6; matinées 5s. extra. Amount of deposit required on booking, 10s. to £1. Electric current for kinematographs to be paid for extra; 230 volts, 25 amps.

Dates of principal local fairs, May 18, October 16, November 13. Sites available for portables, Cattle Market.

Early closing day, Thursday; market days, Wednesday and Saturday.

LEICESTER.

Population, 211,579. Miles from London, 99.

ROYAL OPERA HOUSE. — Manager, Mr. Charles Hermann; Musical Director, Herr Theo. Klee. Full dramatic license. Holding capacity: Number of persons, 3,000; amount, £235. Proscenium opening, 35ft. Depth of stage, 35ft.; width. 68ft. Gas and electric light. Amount of printing required, 1,700 sheets, 1,000 lithos. Matinée day, Saturday, at 2. Band rehearsal, 11 a.m.

THEATRE ROYAL. — Proprietors, the Theatre Royal Company; Acting-Manager, Mr. E. R. Beaumont; Musical Director, Mr. A. E. Nicholson; Scenic Artist, Mr. C. H. Betts. Full license. Holding capacity: Number of persons, 1,800; amount, £120. Stage measurements: Proscenium opening, 21ft.; width, 40ft.; depth, 50ft.; height, 60ft. Electric light. Amount of printing required, 1,112 sheets, 800 lithos. Band rehearsal, 11 o'clock.

THE PALACE.—Proprietors, the Leicester Palace Co., Limited; Managing Director, Mr. Oswald Stoll; Acting-Manager, Mr. F. Finch-Hatton; Assistant Acting-Manager, Mr. W. Buccleuch; Musical Director, Mr. John W. Lowe, Double license. Holding capacity: Number of persons, 2,750. Stage measurements: Depth, 54ft.; width, 63ft.; proscenium, 33ft. wide and 24ft. high. Electric light and gas. Band rehearsal, 2.30 p.m. No matinée day. Bars the Pavilion, Leicester, under Arbitrator's Award. Bars all other Halls in Leicester.

PAVILION MUSIC HALL.—Proprietor, Mr. Frank Macnaghten; Manager, Mr. Joseph Lawrence; Booking Circuit, Macnaghten Circuit; Musical Director, Mr. Fred Britcher. Double license. Electric light. Band rehearsal, 12 noon. Matinée day, Thursday, at 3. Extra turn trial shows, etc., in addition to full company. Two houses nightly. Electric current alternatio 100 volts.

THE TEMPERANCE HALL, Granby Street, will seat about 1,800 persons in the large hall, which is 100ft. by 58ft.; there is also a lecture room which will seat 350 persons. The large hall is visited by Gipsy Choirs, Bioscope shows, Dioramas, and is also used for concerts.

ASSOCIATION HALL (Young Men's Christian Association), capable of holding 750 people, with retiring-rooms en suite. This can be let for meetings, concerts, etc.

The principal industries are the manufacture of boots and shoes, hosiery and cigars, and wholesale clothiers.

There is a piece of ground on the Aylestone Road which is used for a circus pitch, and alfresco concerts occasionally.

The town is not visited by portables. There are two fairs yearly, one in May and the other in October, held on a piece of ground in Ross's Walk, Belgrave Road, Leicester.

Early closing day, Thursday; market days, Wednesday and Saturday.

Medical Officers.—A.A.: Dr. J. M. Lithgow, Melbourne House, St. Stephen's Road; A.U.: The same; M.H.A.R.A.: The same.

Agents.—A.U.: J. Wilkinson, Cricket Players' Hotel; M.H.A.R.A.: Tom Fox, Fish and Quart Hotel. V.A.F.: The same.

RECOMMENDED APARTMENTS.

Mrs. G. Harrison, 40, The Spa, Humberstone Road.—2 large sitting rooms, 4 bedrooms, combined room; pianos.

Mrs. Lally, 7, Chancery Street, off Pocklington's Walk.—1 bedroom, 1 sitting; piano.

LEIGH, Lancs.

Population, 45,000. Miles from London, 194.

THEATRE ROYAL AND OPERA HOUSE.—Proprietor, Mr. J. W. Cragg; Resident Manager, Mr. Wallace Childs. Dramatic license. Seats about 2,000.

ASSEMBLY ROOMS.—Proprietors, the Conservative Club Buildings Co. Secretary, Mr. A. H. Hayward, Solicitor. Dramatic license. Holds 1,500. Electric current, 220 volts direct.

CO-OPERATIVE HALL.—Proprietors, the Leigh Friendly Co-operative Society, Limited; Secretary, Mr. T. Boydell. Double license. Holds 1,000. Electric light, 230 volts.

PUBLIC HALL.—Liberal Club. Holds 500. ST. JOSEPH'S CATHOLIC LECTURE HALL. DRILL HALL.

GRAND THEATRE AND HIPPODROME.—Managing Director, Mr. W. Benson; Secretary, Mr. Fred S. Marsh. Holds 2,000.

NEW CENTRAL HALL.—Proprietors, "The World in Motion Co." Holds 600.

CHURCH INSTITUTE. — Secretaries, Mr. W. B. Callender and Mr. F. Eastwood. Holds 700. Gas.

PENNINGTON CHURCH INSTITUTE.—Secretary, Mr. T. B. Smith. Holds 400. Gas.

The population is composed chiefly of working classes engaged in coal mining, cotton manufacturing, and agricultural implement making.

The Parliamentary division of Leigh, which includes Tyldesley, Atherton, and several villages, has a population of 80,000.

Leigh is situated 12 miles from Manchester, 7 from Wigan, and 7 from Bolton, and has an electric car service to all these places.

The chief station and near the centre of the town is Leigh and Bedford (L. and N.W. Railway), which deals with both goods and passenger traffic. Other stations, Westleigh (L. & N. W.), on the Bolton line, St. Mary's, Lowton (Mid.).

The local fairs are held twice in each year, and portables, roundabouts, etc., visit the town on the first Friday after April 24 and December 7, and stay until the following Tuesday. They occupy a large plot of land in Twist Lane, which is suitable for a large circus. No objections to the fairs have been made during recent years.

Early closing day, Tuesday; market days, Friday and Saturday.

Agent.—V.A.F.: A. Smith, Boar's Head Hotel, Market Place.

LEIGHTON BUZZARD.

Leighton Buzzard and Linsdale joint population, 9,000. Miles from London, 40.

CORN EXCHANGE.—Secretary, Mr. R. J. Platten, Bridge Street, Leighton Buzzard. Full dramatic, singing, and dancing license. Large Hall will seat 800; small hall 300. Platform, 24ft. by 16ft. Lighted by gas. Terms of hiring: One night, £3; subsequently, £1 10s. Deposit, £1.

TOWN HALL.—Hallkeeper, Mr. H. G. Saunders. A suitable hall for small entertainments such as concerts, kinematograph performances, lectures, etc. It will seat 400.

TEMPERANCE HALL.—Hallkeeper, Mrs. Bierton. A small hall situate in Lake Street. It will seat 300.

The town is in a purely agricultural district. There is a large residential population. There are basket and carriage works employing several hundred men.

Sites for portable theatres, circuses, kinematograph, and other travelling exhibitions. Bell Close, Leighton, is well situated in the centre of the town, and can be used for these purposes. Communications to Mr. Geo. Willis, Dudley Street, Leighton Buzzard. No objection has ever been raised to the granting of licenses for portables. At Linsdale sites are also obtainable nearer to the station, but the town is under a different licensing authority. Licenses have always been granted to owners of portable theatres.

The annual "Statute" Fair is held on the first Tuesday after October 11, and is well patronised. Pitches for roundabouts, booths, and travelling exhibitions in the Bell Close.

Early closing day, Thursday; market day, Tuesday.

LEITH, Edinburgh.

Population, 76,667. Miles from London, 405.

NEW GAIETY THEATRE.—Proprietors, New Gaiety Theatre, Leith, Limited; Managing Director, Mr. R. C. Buchanan; Resident Manager, Mr. John Darlison; Assistant Acting-Manager, Mr. Percy Darlison; Musical Director, Mr. John Crossley; Scenic Artist, Mr. A. Middlemass. Full dramatic license; smoking allowed. Holding capacity: Number of persons, 2,000. Stage measurements: 30ft. deep, 53ft. wide; proscenium opening, 27ft. 6in. Electric light. Amount of printing required: 750 wall, 1,000 window. Usual matinée day, Saturday. Time of band rehearsal, 11 a.m.

Early closing and market day, Wednesday.

Medical Officer.—A.A.: Dr. F. K. Kerr, 57, Easter Road.

LEOMINSTER, Hereford.

Population, 5,826. Miles from London, 137.

CORN EXCHANGE.—Manager, Mr. J. B. Dowding. Has dramatic license. Holding capacity: Number of persons, 500. Depth and width of stage and proscenium measurements, 24ft. by 45ft. Gas. Terms for hiring: £1 8s

per night, including gas and **attendant.**
Amount of deposit required on booking, 10s.
Pleasure fair, May 5. For sites for circuses
apply Mr. J. J. Biddle, Leominster.
Early closing day, Thursday; market day,
Friday.

LEVEN, Fife.

Population, immediate district, 15,000.
TOWN HALL.—Manager, Mr. Wm. Axworthy. Dramatic license. Holding capacity:
Number of persons, 1,200-1,400; amount, £50-60,
according to charges. Stage measurements:
18ft. deep, 33ft. front width, tapering to 25ft.
No proscenium. Lighted by gas. Terms for
hiring: £3 3s. first night, £2 2s. each succeeding night. Amount of deposit required on
booking, half charges.

LEVENSHULME, Lancs.

Population, 11,485. Miles from London, 185.
TOWN HALL.—Proprietors, Urban District
Council; Manager, the Caretaker, Town Hall.
Holding capacity: Number of persons, seat
520. Stage 32ft. by 12ft. Electric light. Terms
for hiring: Concert, £3 3s. Full charges to be
paid on booking.
Early closing day, Wednesday; no market
day.

LEWES, Sussex.

Population, 11,249. Miles from London, 50.
CORN EXCHANGE—Town Hall.—Proprietors,
The Corporation; Manager, the Town Clerk. Has
dramatic license. Holding capacity: Number
of persons, 800. Movable stage. Electric 220
volts. Terms for hiring: One night, £3 5s.;
three nights, £6 10s.
ASSEMBLY ROOM — Town Hall. — Pro-
prietors, Corporation of Lewes. Dramatic license.
Holding capacity: Number of persons, 700.
Movable stage, 26ft. by 18ft. Electric, 220 volts.
Terms: One night, £4 14s. 6d.; three nights,
theatricals, £9 9s.
Early closing day, Wednesday; market day,
Tuesday.

LEYLAND, Lancashire.

Population, 6,865.
PUBLIC HALL.—Address the Managing Director. Double license. Holding capacity:
Number of persons, 800. Stage measurements,
30ft. by 20ft. Proscenium, with drop scene.
Lighted by gas. Amount of printing required: Usual for size. 5,000 handbills recommended for works. Terms for hiring: Public
meetings, concerts, and exhibitions, one night
(piano, 7s. 6d, extra), £2 2s.; two nights (inclusive), £4; three nights (inclusive), £5 10s.
Operatic and dramatic entertainments, bazaars, balls, etc., one night (piano, 7s. 6d. extra), £2 10s.; two nights (inclusive), £4; three
nights (inclusive), £5 10s.; six nights (inclusive), £9 9s. Amount of deposit required on
booking, £1 per night.

LICHFIELD, Staffs.

Population, 9,244. Miles from London, 116.
ST. JAMES'S HALL.—Manager, Mr. H.
Larkin. Dramatic license. Holding capacity:
Number of persons, 700. Stage measurements,
36ft. by 26ft. Proscenium, 21ft. 5in. by 19ft.
3in. Lighted by gas. Amount of printing re-
quired, 300 daybills and usual number of
lithos. Terms for hiring, one night, £2 12s. 6d.
Amount of deposit required on booking, £1.
Four dressing-rooms.
Early closing day, Wednesday; market day,
Friday.

LIMERICK.

Population, 38,000. Miles from Dublin, 129.
THEATRE ROYAL.—Manager, Mr. George
V. Fogerty, Henry Street, Limerick; Musical
Director, Mr. J. Child. Holding capacity:
Number of persons, 1,100; amount, £70, ordinary.
Depth of stage, 35ft.; width, 61ft ; width of
proscenium opening, 28ft.; height of grooves,
18ft. 6in. Twelve dressing-rooms, property-room,
etc. Green room. Gas. Limes. Amount of print-
ing required, 600 sheets. Usual matinée day,
Wednesday and Saturday. Time of band re-
hearsal, 4 p.m. Best months, October to
March. Closed during Lent, as a rule.
NATIONAL THEATRE.—Lessee, Mrs. S.
Hanley. Holding capacity: Number of persons
500. Proper stage. Stage, 19ft. 6in. by 16ft.
Lighted by gas. Amount of printing required,
200 d.c.'s and 500 day-bills.
ATHENÆUM HALL, Cecil Street.—Secretary, Mr. James Comerton, B.A. Accommodation:
Main floor, 55ft. by 34ft. 6in., accommodating
500; Gallery, 13ft. deep, seating 120; Raised
stage, measuring 34ft. by 18ft.; height of stage,
3ft. 9ins. An alcove at the back of the stage, and
measuring 17ft. by 15ft. A running curtain is
provided in order that the alcove may be used, if
necessary, as a dressing-room. An incandescent
electric light installation including foot-lights.
Terms: From £2 10s. per night to £15 per week.
The prices are generally 3s., 2s., 1s., and 6d.
There is no difficulty in getting sites for
circus pitches, the usual and best position
being in the Markets Fields.
Market days, Wednesday and Saturday.

LINCOLN, Lincs.

Population, 48,784. Miles from London, 130.
THEATRE ROYAL.—Lessees, Messrs. W.
Payne Seddon and Ernest Pope; Manager, Mr.
Ernest Pope; Musical Director, Mr. R. Lumb;
Scenic Artist, Mr. G. Collier. Restricted
license. Holding capacity: Number of persons, 1,000; amount, £70. Stage measurements,
35ft. 6in. wide, 25ft. 6in. deep. Gas and electric light. Amount of printing required,
600 sheets, 600 d.c. Usual matinée day,
Wednesday or Saturday. Time of band rehearsal, 1 p.m. Bars Gainsborough.
PALACE.—Proprietor, Mr. Frank Macnaghten; Manager, Mr. R. R. Black; Booking
Circuit, Macnaghten Vaudeville Circuit; Musical Director, Mr. Joseph Morris. Double
license. Holding capacity: Number of persons,
1,500. Stage measurements: Depth, 30ft.;
width, 28ft.; proscenium, width, 24ft.; height,
15ft. 6in. Gas and electric light. Time of
band rehearsal, 12 noon. No matinée day.
Bars no surrounding halls. Two houses, 7
and 9.
NEW CENTRAL HALL.—Manager, Mr. W.
Monks. Dramatic license. Holding capacity:
Number of persons, 1,400; amount, £240 has
been taken. Stage measurements: Proscenium
opening, 25ft.; width, 36ft.; depth ranges from
18ft. to 25ft. Electric light; gas can be fixed
for special shows. Terms for hiring: Vary ac-
cording to accommodation required. Amount
of deposit required on booking: Two guineas.
Electric current direct 230 volts.
Great pleasure and cattle fair during last
week in April. For sites for portables and
circuses apply to the Lincoln Corporation.
Early closing day, Wednesday; market days,
Friday and Saturday.
Medical Officer.—Dr. Chas. Harrison, 30,
Newland (hours, 10-6); A.U.: The same;
M.H.A.R.A.: The same.
Agents.—A.U.: C. Baker, George Hotel;
V.A.F.: The same; M.H.A.R.A.: T. H. Newton,
Central Hotel.

LINLITHGOW, Linlithgow.

Population, 4,279.

VICTORIA HALL.—Proprietors, Linlithgow Town Council; Manager, Mr. James Bamberry, burgh officer. Dramatic and music and dancing licenses. Holding capacity: Number of persons, 800. Amount £50. Platform depth, 23ft.; width, 41ft. by 21ft. Gas. Terms: First night, £2 2s.; each subsequent night, £1 1s. (gas, cleaning, and insurance extra).

Dates of local fairs, March, middle of June. Several sites available for portables, alfresco concerts, and circuses.

Early closing day, Wednesday; market day, Friday.

LISTOWEL, Co. Kerry.

Population, 3,566. Miles from Dublin, 180.

GYMNASIUM HALL (70 ft. by 30 ft.).— Manager, Mr. T. F. Leahy. Holding capacity: Number of persons, 500 to 600. Stage, 12ft. by 24ft.; no proscenium. Lighted by oil lamps. Terms for hiring: One night, 30s.; two nights, £2 10s.; three nights, £3 10s.; six nights, £6 7s. Half deposit on booking. First-class companies can rely on getting good houses.

Market, Friday.

LITTLEBOROUGH, Lancs.

Population, 11,168. Miles from London, 200.

PUBLIC HALL. — Proprietors, The Independent Labour Party. Manager, Mr. W. Mawdsley. Holding capacity, 700. Stage, 27ft. by 12ft. by 20ft. Lighted by gas. Terms of hiring, 15s. per night, £3 per week.

CO-OPERATIVE HALL. — Proprietors, the Littleborough Co-operative Society of Industry, Ltd. Manager, Mr. R. Diggle. Platform. Gas. Seats 400.

Local Fairs: Easter Friday and Whit Friday. Wake 2nd Saturday in August.

Early closing, Tuesday.

LITTLEHAMPTON, Sussex.

Population, 8,573. Miles from London, 62.

TERMINUS HALL.—Manager, Mr. Geo. E. Redman. Dramatic license. Holding capacity: Number of persons, 400 to 500. Proper stage. Stage measurements: 30ft. wide, 17ft. 6in. deep; proscenium opening, 18ft. wide, 16ft. high, 17ft. 6in. deep. Gas. Amount of printing required: 250 sheets, 250 circulars, 200 day bills, 100 lithos. Terms for hiring: One night, £3 3s.; two nights, £5 5s.; three nights, £6 6s. Amount of deposit required on booking, one-third. Remarks: Reliable companies can be shared with. This is the only hall in the town and district with license. Renting terms include gas and scenery.

CASTLE PAVILION.—Proprietor, Mr. Dan Randall. Used during summer months only by Dan Randall's vaudeville company.

PAGODA PAVILION.—Proprietor, Mr. Harry Joseph. Used Summer months only.

Early closing day, Wednesday.

LITTLE HULTON, near Bolton, Lancs.

CO-OPERATIVE HALL.—Proprietors, the Little Hulton Industrial Co-operative Society, Limited; Manager, Mr. Edward Gorton. Plans have been approved for this building, but it may be a year or so before it is ready for occupation.

LITTLEPORT, Cambs.

Population, 4,181. Miles from London, 78.

CONSTITUTIONAL HALL.—Manager, Mr. Edwin Taylor. Has dramatic license. Holding capacity: Number of persons, 500. Platform, 24ft. by 15ft. Lighted by gas. Terms for hiring: One night, 15s.; two, 25s. Special terms for longer periods.

Date of local fair July 24.

Early closing day, Wednesday.

LIVERPOOL, Lancs.

Population, 684,948. Miles from London, 201

ROYAL COURT THEATRE.—Proprietors, Robert Arthur Theatres Co., Limited; Managing Director, Mr. Robert Arthur; Acting-Manager, Mr. Arthur Lawrence; Musical Director, Mr. J. O. Shepherd; Scenic Artist, Mr. Stafford Hall. Full theatrical license. Holding capacity: Number of persons, 2,000; amount, £250. Stage measurements: 52ft. deep, 62ft. wide; proscenium, 28ft. 6in. by 28ft. 6in. Electric light. Amount of printing required, 2,500 sheets, 1,500 windows. Usual matinée day, Saturday, at 2. Time of band rehearsal, 11 a.m.

SHAKESPEARE THEATRE.—Lessees, The Shakespeare Theatre, Liverpool, Limited; Managing Director, Mr. Wentworth Croke; Manager and Secretary, Mr. John Gaffney; Musical Director, Mr. Robert J. McDermott; Scenic Artist, Mr. Thomas Holmes. Full dramatic license. Holding capacity: Number of persons, about 3,200; amount, £300. Stage measurements: From curtain line to back wall, 40ft.; from wall to wall, 60ft.; proscenium opening, 30ft. 6in.; height, 28ft. Gas and electric light (own plant of electric installation). Usual amount of printing required, 2,500 walls, 1,200 lithos, 600 d.c.'s, 200 booking office cards. Usual matinée day, Saturday. Time of band rehearsal, usually 11 a.m. Best seasons, early spring and from September onwards.

PRINCE OF WALES'S THEATRE.—Closed.

ROTUNDA THEATRE.—Proprietor and Manager, Mr. Matthew Montgomery; Musical Director, Mr. J. Thompson; Scenic Artist, Mr. Chas. Townsend. Full license. Holding capacity: Number of persons, 2,800; amount, £100. Stage measurements: Depth from footlights to back, 32ft.; width, wall to wall, 45ft.; between fly rails, 32ft.; pros. opening, 24ft. Gas and electric light. Amount of printing required, 1,800 sheets wall printing 800 lithos, 1,000 d.c. letterpress. Time of band rehearsal, 11 a.m.

STAR THEATRE.—Proprietor and Manager, Mr. Harris Fineberg.

QUEEN'S THEATRE. — Proprietors, The Granville Theatres, Limited; Managing Director, Mr. Fred Granville. Fully licensed. Holding capacity: Number of persons, 2,000. Stage measurements: 46ft. deep by 65ft. wide. Electric light.

THEATRE ROYAL.—Manager, Mr. M. Montgomery; Acting-Manager, Mr. Frank O. Toole; Musical Director, Mr. G. Wibbert; Scenic Artist, Mr. C. Townsend. Dramatic license. Electric light. No usual matinée day. Time of band rehearsal, 1 p.m. Best bookings of the year, two houses nightly stock companies.

ROSCOMMON THEATRE.—Manager, Mr. J. M. Crewdson. Dramatic license. Holding capacity: Number of persons, 1,100; amount, £12. Gas and electric light.

PADDINGTON PALACE THEATRE.—Closed

21

ROYAL MUNCASTER (BOOTLE).—Proprietors, Messrs. Pennington; Director of Entertainments, Mr. Fred Wilmot; Acting-Manager, Mr. Harry Young.

HAYMARKET THEATRE. — Closed.

EMPIRE THEATRE.—Proprietors, Moss's Empires, Limited; Chairman, Sir Edward Moss; Managing Director, Mr. Oswald Stoll; Assisting Director and Chief of Staff, Mr. Frank Allen; Resident Manager, Mr. Horace Cole. Booking circuit, Stoll's Tours, Musical Director, Mr. Walter Hague. Music and dancing license; no excise. Holding capacity: Number of persons, 2,500. Stage measurements: 43ft. deep, 56ft. wide, 30ft. opening. Gas and electric light. Time of band rehearsal, 1.30. Usual matinée day, Wednesday, 2.30. This is the old Alexandra Theatre, converted into a hall some eleven years ago.

NEW OLYMPIA.—Proprietor, Moss's Empires, Limited; Managing Director, Mr. Oswald Stoll; Manager, Mr. Ernest Wighton. Booking circuit, Moss and Stoll. Musical Director, Mr. T. Wrathmall. Holding capacity: Number of persons, 4,200. Stage measurements: Width of opening, 49ft.; depth of opening, 28ft. Gas and electric direct 230 volts. Band rehearsal, 2 p.m. Usual matinée day, Saturday.

Bars all other Halls in Liverpool and the following towns; Birkenhead, Bootle, Wallasey, and Seacombe.

ROYAL HIPPODROME.—Managing Director, Mr. Thomas Barrasford; Acting-Manager, Mr. Walter Hassan; Musical Director, Mr. Frank Stokes. Time of band rehearsal, 12 noon. Usual matinée day, Wednesday. Current 230 volts.

LYRIC THEATRE.—Lessee and Manager, Mr. H. C. Arnold; Acting-Manager, Mr. H. C. Arnold, jun. Booking circuit, Willmot. Music and dancing license. Time of band rehearsal, 12 noon.

TIVOLI PALACE.—Proprietors, Liverpool Theatres of Varieties, Limited; Manager, Mr. James Marks; Acting-Manager, Mr. E. T. Wood. Booking circuit, Willmot. Musical Director, Mr. Tomlinson. Double license. Gas and electric light. Time of band rehearsal, Mondays, 1 o'clock.

PAVILION THEATRE.—Proprietors, Messrs. W. H. Broadhead and Son; Manager, Mr. Percy B. Broadhead; District Manager, Mr. H. Winstanley; Resident Acting-Manager, Mr. H. Hearn. Booking circuit, Broadhead and Sons. Musical Director, Mr. H. O'Callaghan; Scenic Artists, Mr. T. E. Daly and Mr. Edward Leigh. Stage measurements: 40ft. deep by 90ft. wide, 36ft. opening. Gas and electric light. Usual matinée day, Monday. Time of band rehearsal, 11 a.m.

WESTMINSTER MUSIC HALL.—Proprietor, Mr. F. E. Weisker; Manager, Mr. Gerald Montgomery; Acting-Manager, Mr. Joseph Bramble; Musical Director, Mr. E. Turner. Music and dancing license. Gas and electric light. Time of band rehearsal, 1.30 p.m. Usual matinée day, Tuesday.

PARK PALACE, Mill Street.—Manager, Mr. J. L. Weisker. Double license (smoking allowed). Holding capacity: Number of persons, 1,600. Electric light. Stock drama has been running here some months, and smoking is allowed in all parts.

PICTON LECTURE HALL.—No dramatic license. Holding capacity: Number of persons, 1,200. Terms for hiring, £3 13s. 6d. per night. Amount of deposit required on booking, £1.

HOPE HALL, Hope Street. — Managers, Messrs. J. A. Thompson and Co. Music and dancing license. (A dramatic license can always be had on application.) Holding capacity: Number of persons, 1,500. A platform, 30ft. by 16ft. Gas and electric light. Terms for hiring: £5 5s. per evening; £3 3s. per afternoon. Long dates per arrangement. Amount of deposit required on booking, 20 per cent. Installation for kinematograph or animated pictures exhibition.

PHILHARMONIC HALL.—Proprietors, Philharmonic Society, Ltd.; Secretary, Mr. W. J. Riley. Music and dancing license. Holding capacity: Number of persons, 2,433. Orchestra. Electric light. Terms for hiring on application.

TOWN HALL, Waterloo.—Manager, The Clerk to the Urban District Council. All licenses. Holding capacity: Number of persons, 600. Platform. Electric light. Terms for hiring: £3 3s. per evening; series of ten, £21. Fees payable in advance.

Medical Officers.—A.A.: Drs. J. C. Baxter, 110, Robson Street, Everton; A. Ellenbogen, 4, Elizabeth Street, Pembroke Place (tel., 717 X Royal; hours, 9-11, 6-8); David Smart, 74, Hartington Road, Sefton Park ('phone, 136 Royal; hours, 9-10.30, 6-7.30); W. Tweeddale Thomson, 54, Catherine Street, and 15, St. Paul's Square; R. Le G. Worsley, 17, Walton Park: Mr. H. Finestone, dental surgeon, 35, Elizabeth Street. A.U.: Drs. Baxter, Ellenbogen, Smart, Thomson, Worsley, and Mr. F. Finestone, as above. M.H.A.R.A.: Dr. Smart, as above, and Dr. John Owen, 30, Rodney Street.

Agents.—A.U.: T. Hazlehurst, De Silva's Hotel. M.H.A.R.A. and V.A.F.: Branch office, Tom McKay, 21, Houghton Street.

RECOMMENDED APARTMENTS.

Mrs. J. Nicholson, 25, Falkner Street, Hope Street End.—2 sitting-rooms, 3 bedrooms, 2 combined rooms; piano; bath.

W. Metcalfe, 18, Seymour Street.—3 sitting-rooms and 4 bedrooms; pianos; bath.

Mrs. Bishop, 99, Great Mersey Street.—1 front sitting-room and 1 front bedroom.

Mrs. E. O'Conor, 17, Elizabeth Street.—Bed and sitting, also combined rooms.

Mrs. Smythe, 44, Upper Hope Place, Hope Street.—1 sitting-room, 4 bedrooms (double and single beds), 2 combined; piano; bath, etc.

LLANBERIS, Carn.

Population, 3,015. Miles from London, 257.

CONCERT HALL.—Manager, Mr. Robt. M. Jones. Has dramatic license. Holding capacity: Number of persons, 800; amount, £25. Stage: 30ft. by 17ft.; two ante-rooms. Lighted by gas. Terms for hiring: 25s. first night; 20s. each following night. Amount of deposit required on booking: 10s. per night.

Good quarry centre; monthly pays, first, Jan. 4.

Early closing and market day, Wednesday

LLANDILOES, Mont.

Population, 2,770. Miles from London, 208.

PUBLIC ROOMS.—Proprietors and Managers, Messrs. Cooke and Son, High Street, Newtown. Dramatic and music and dancing licenses. No proper stage. Gas. Terms for hiring: £1 per day and gas. Deposit on booking, 25 per cent.

Early closing day, Wednesday. Market day, Saturday.

LLANDRINDOD WELLS, Rad.

Population, 3,000 (in summer 8,000). Miles from London, 201.

VICTORIA HALL, Middleton Street. — Manager, Mr. B. Davies. Double license. Holding capacity: Number of persons, about 700; amount, £40. Small stage; width, 22ft. 6in.; depth, 16ft.; proscenium opening, 16ft.; extension of 3ft. in depth if required. Electric light. Amount of printing required: 10 12-sheet, 15 6-sheet. 300 window bills, 3,000 (each) circulars and handbills. Terms for hiring: £2 2s. per night, including piano hire. Amount of deposit required on booking, 20 per cent.

This is a season health resort, and best dates are April, May, June, July, August, and September.

No local fairs. Circus grounds can be obtained.

Early closing, Wednesday.

LLANDUDNO, Carn.

Population, 9,279. Miles from London, 227.

PRINCE'S THEATRE.—Lessee and Manager, Mr. J. Ritson. Double license. Holding capacity: Number of persons, 641; amount: season, £70; winter, £40. Stage measurements: Depth, 27 ft.; width, 45 ft.; proscenium opening, 27 ft. Electric light. Amount of printing required, 300 sheets walls, 200 d.c.'s. No matinée day. Time of band rehearsal, 12 noon. Best dates of the year, last week in July until end of September. Bank Holiday weeks are also good.

GRAND THEATRE.—Manager, Mr. A. G. Pugh. Dramatic license. Electric light. Holds 1,200.

PIER PAVILION. — Proprietors. Llandudno Pier Co., Limited; Secretary, Mr. Samuel Hughes.

PIER HEAD PAVILION.—Lessees, Messrs. Adeler and Sutton.

HIPPODROME.—Roller Skating Rink. Manager, Mr. C. P. Crawford.

No local fairs. Alfresco concerts held daily in the Happy Valley during summer.

Early closing day, Wednesday.

Medical Officer.—A.A.: Dr. Lockhart-Mure, 10, Craig-y-don Parade; A.U.: The same.

Agent.—M.H.AR.A.: C. Felix, Tudno Hotel.

V.A.F.: The same.

LLANDYSSUL, Card.

Population, 2,801. Miles from London, 252.

PORTH HOTEL ASSEMBLY ROOMS.— Managers, Messrs. Evans and Co. Holding capacity: Number of persons, about 600. No proper stage. Lighted by acetylene gas. Terms for hiring: 15s. a night for first night, and 10s. afterwards.

Dates of local fairs: Jan. 2, Feb. 11, Sept. 21.

Early closing day, Wednesday; market day, Tuesday.

LLANELLY, Carm.

Population, 27,000. Miles from London, 221.

ROYALTY THEATRE.—Proprietor and Manager, Mr. Z. Andrews; Acting-Manageress, Miss Alice Rocheforte.

ATHENÆUM HALL.—Manager, Mr. J. Boulton. Double license. Holding capacity: Number of persons, 500. Proper stage. No scenery. Lighted by gas. Amount of printing required, from 350 to 500 sheets. Terms for hiring: One night, £1 5s.; two nights, £2 5s.; three nights, £3 3s.; four nights, £4; five nights, £4 15s.;

six nights, £5 5s.; 1s. per hour extra for gas. Amount of deposit required on booking, £1 1s. Fit-up can be hired in the town. Animated pictures, variety companies, and good dramatic companies take well.

Dates of local fairs: September 30, October 1, 2, May 27, 28, 29.

Early closing day, Tuesday; market day, Thursday.

LLANFAIRFECHAN, Carn.

Population, 2,769. Miles from London, 232.

PUBLIC HALL.—Manager, Mr. Jno. M. Baker. Licensed. Holding capacity: Number of persons, 600, seated comfortably. Depth and width of stage, 24ft. by 50ft.; two dressing-rooms. Footlights. Headlights. Gas. Terms: During summer season, 50s. one meeting; two meetings, £3 15s. (period six weeks); for rest of the year, 30s. one meeting; £2 10s. two meetings. Amount of deposit required on booking, 10s.

Population double for about six weeks in the summer.

Early closing day, Wednesday.

LLANGOLLEN, Denbigh.

Population, 3,304. Miles from London, 201.

TOWN HALL.—Manager, Mr. J. Gray-Owen. Has dramatic license. Holding capacity: Number of persons, 800. Stage, 17ft. high, by 26ft.; proscenium opening, 20ft. by 14ft. high. Electric light. Terms for hiring: £2 2s. first night; £1 1s. each subsequent night. Fees payable in advance.

The Smithfield is used for circuses and fairs.

Early closing, Thursday; market, Saturday.

LLANRWST, Denbigh.

Population, 2,645. Miles from London, 239.

CONCERT HALL.—Manager and Lessee, Mr. F. G. Parry, Dinorwic Cottage. Has dramatic license. Holding capacity: Number of persons, 400. Act-drop and some scenery. Stage: Depth, 12ft.; width, 26ft. Proscenium, opening 15ft. wide by 13ft. high. Lighted by gas and electric light. Voltage 220, alternating; amount of printing required: 300 daybills; pictorials, 50 sheets. Terms for hiring, shares.

Population mostly engaged in mining and agriculture. Large aluminium works have recently been started. There are several good circus pitches in the neighbourhood. A fair is held every month on the first Wednesday.

Early closing day, Thursday; market day, Tuesday.

LOCKERBIE, Dumfries.

Population, 2,358. Miles from London, 324.

TOWN HALL.—Manager, Mr. David McJerrow. Large hall, 75ft. by 42ft. by 30ft. Has dramatic license. Holding capacity: Number of persons, 700. Platform: 24ft. by 20ft. 6in. In the same building there are also a Lesser Hall, measuring 30ft. by 20ft., with accommodation for 100, and a Market Hall, measuring 75ft. by 43ft.

Dates of local hiring fairs: April 30, 1908; October 29, 1908. Ground for fairs may be had on application to M. Mackenzie and Sons, Townhead.

Early closing day, alternate Tuesdays; market day, Thursday.

LOFTUS-IN-CLEVELAND, Yorks.

Population, 6,508. Miles from London, 259.
ODDFELLOWS' HALL.—Manager, Mr. John Knaggs, 24, Zetland Road. No dramatic license. Holding capacity: Number of persons, 500. Stage 30ft. long, 10ft. wide. If footlights are fixed, extra charges are made. Lighted by gas. Terms for hiring, according to time and quantity of gas used. Amount of deposit required on booking, 10s.

CO-OPERATIVE HALL.—Manager, Mr. Joseph Wm. Brown, 1, Station Road. No dramatic license. Holding capacity: Number of persons, 700. Good platform, 30ft. by 9ft., and 2¼ft. high. Lighted by gas. Terms of hiring on application to manager.

LONDONDERRY, Londonderry.

Population, 40,000. Miles from Dublin, 176.
OPERA HOUSE. Proprietor, Mr. W. Payne Seddon. Manager, Mr. A. Jeffreys. Double license. Holding capacity; Number of persons, 1,500; amount, £100. Stage measurements, 30 ft. deep, 40 ft. wide,; opening, 24 ft. by 24 ft. Lighted by gas. Amount of printing required, 500 sheets. Usual Matinée day, Wednesday. Time of band rehearsal, 12 noon.
Market days, Wednesday and Saturday.
Medical Officer.—A.A.: Dr. J. Byrne, 24, Pump Street; A.U.: The same.

LONG EATON, Derbyshire.

Population, 20,000. Miles from London, 120.
ST. JAMES THEATRE.—Manager, Mr. Lindsey Edwards. Seats £80. Proscenium opening, 24ft.; depth of stage, 25ft.; width of stage, 45ft.; height to fly floor, 20ft. Electric light and gas. Heated throughout (hot water).
PALACE THEATRE (late Lyceum).—Lessee, Mr. A. Smith; Business Manager, Professor Garton. Kinematograph and Variety Company. Seats 700. Electric light. Two performances nightly.
PEOPLE'S HALL.—Seats 700 Apply Secretary, Co-operative Society. Suitable for Concerts and Kinematograph entertainments.
Population of district (within two miles), 32,000.
Early closing, Tuesday; market, Saturday.

LONGRIDGE, Lancs.

Population, 4,304. Miles from London, 217.
CO-OPERATIVE HALL.—Manager, Mr. William Ryding. Holding capacity: Number of persons, 600; amount, various. No proper stage. Lighted by gas. Amount of printing required, 1,000. Amount of deposit required on booking, 5s. per night.
Early closing day, Thursday.

LONGTON, Staffs.

Population, 38,742. Miles from London, 141.
QUEEN'S THEATRE.—Proprietor, The Longton Theatre, Limited; General Manager and Licensee, Mr. H. Sherriff Howard; Musical Director, Mr. F. W. Hughes; Scenic Artist, Mr. J. Cunningham. Full license. Holding capacity: Number of persons, 2,800; amount, £110. Stage: 64 ft. wide, 49 ft. deep; proscenium, 31ft. 6in. Gas and electric, voltage 230. Printing required, 750 sheets for walls, 600 lithos. Usual matinée days, Thursdays and Saturdays. Time of band rehersal, 1 p.m. Bars Stoke and Hanley.

TOWN HALL.—Proprietors, the Corporation. No dramatic license. Holding capacity: Number of persons, 700 seated. Stage, 24ft. by 13ft. Gas and electric light. Terms for hiring: £1 10s. per night; six successive nights, £6. Amount of deposit, one-third. All applications to be addressed to W. M. Hawkins. Hall-keeper.
Shrove Fair on Show Ground.
Early closing day, Thursday; market day, Saturday.
Medical Officer.—A.A.: Dr. Alfred Parkes, Mayfield, Trentham Road. A.U.: The same.

LOUGHBOROUGH, Leicester.

Population, 21,382; within four miles, 40,000. Miles from London, 110.
NEW THEATRE ROYAL AND HIPPODROME.—Proprietors, Messrs. Payne Seddon and George Robertson; Resident manager, Mr. W. Payne Seddon; Musical Director, Mr. A. Cross; Scenic Artist, Mr. George Collier, jun. Full double license. Holding capacity: Number of persons, 1,500; amount, £100. Stage measurements: Depth, 32 ft. 6 ins.; width, 57 ft. 8 ins.; height to flies, 20 ft.; proscenium, 26 ft. Gas and electric light. Amount of printing required, 600 sheets walls, 600 lithos, 1,000 circulars.
CORN EXCHANGE, TOWN HALL.—Apply Mr. C. H. Adams. Fully licensed. Holding capacity: Number of persons, 800; amount, £60 to £80. Stage measurements: 45 ft. wide by 22 ft. deep; proscenium, 24 ft. wide, 19 ft. high. Gas and electric, 22 volts direct. Terms, £2 15s. one night; for two or more nights discount allowed. Amount of deposit required on booking, one-fourth.
Early closing day, Wednesday; market day, Thursday.

LOUGHTON, Essex.

Population, 4,730. Miles from London, 12.
PUBLIC HALL.—Manager, Mr. J. H. Hayward. Double license. Holding capacity: Number of persons, 400. Proper stage with green room and two dressing rooms; no proscenium. Stage, 24ft. width; average depth, 12ft. Lighted by gas. Terms for hiring: 35s., inclusive of piano, etc. Amount of deposit required on booking, 10s.
No local fairs. No sites for portables, etc.
Early closing, Thursday.

LOUTH, Lincs.

Population, 9,518. Miles from London 140.
THE TOWN HALL.—Proprietors, the Corporation; T. F. Allison, Town Clerk. Has dramatic license.
RIFLE DRILL HALL.—Apply Drill Instructor.
Louth has a population both residential and industrial. Wall paper printing, maltings, etc., are carried on. Three pleasure fairs are held during the year, viz., Candlemas Market, Wednesday nearest Feb. 14; May Day, on Wednesday nearest May 13 and Martinmas. Nov. 23. Portables visit the town occasionally. The Woodman Inn Yard, Eastgate, and the Quarry Field in Newmarket are suitable pitches. All the circus people pitch in the Quarry Field, of which the Louth Corporation are the proprietors. No difficulty is encountered in obtaining a license from the Council.
Early closing day, Thursday; market days, Wednesday and Friday.

LOWESTOFT, Suffolk.

Population, 32,000. Miles from London, 119.

MARINA THEATRE.—Proprietors, Lowestoft Marina Theatre Co., Limited; Managing Director, Ernest A. Smith; Musical Director, Mr. R. C. Luxton. Full license; smoking allowed. Holding capacity: Number of persons, 1,300; amount, £100. Stage: Height, 44ft.; width, 55ft.; depth, 28ft.; proscenium opening, 28ft.; between fly rails, 34ft.; height of flies from stage, 19ft.; stage to grid, 38ft. Electric light (own plant). Amount of printing required, 600. Usual matinée day, Saturday. Time of band rehearsal, 11 a.m.

HIPPODROME.—Proprietor, Mr. George Gilbert; Manager, Mr. Frank Freeland. Holds about 3,000. Electric light. Saturday matinées.

PUBLIC HALL.—Proprietor, Mr. W. T. Balls; Manager. Mr. W. Catchpole Dramatic license. Seats 500. Stage, 17ft. deep by 20ft. wide; proscenium, 18½ft. wide by 18ft. high. Gas. Printing, 400 sheets. Terms: £2 per day, £10 per week.

KIRKLEY HALL.—No dramatic license. Holds 500. Apply the Secretary.

Lowestoft, England's eastern look-out, as it is commonly called, is a rising seaside resort with extensive fisheries. As a fishing centre Lowestoft is only eclipsed by Grimsby, and is therefore the second fishing port in the kingdom. The summer season lasts from June to the end of September, when there are thousands of visitors. From September to December, during which time the home fishing is carried on, there is a huge Scotch invasion, in addition to an extra fleet of Scotch fishing craft and continental steamers. There are numerous convenient sites suitable for alfresco concerts, circuses, fairs, and amusements and exhibitions of all kinds. In the summer there is a very comprehensive programme of amusements, fêtes, regattas, and aquatic carnivals carried out by the local Amusements Committee. Last season municipal concerts were run for the second year with success. The annual marine regatta and swimming festival—one of the most popular events along the East Coast—is held in the last week in August. Fêtes, galas, confetti carnivals are held about every ten days during the season, when the yacht basin is crowded with yachts of every description from the adjacent rivers and broads and other yachting centres. Both the G.E.R. and M.R. and G.N.R. run direct into Lowestoft, which is less than ten miles from Yarmouth and thirty from Norwich. Alfresco concerts are also held on the Sparrow's Nest Park (bands and concert parties). This park has a large stage fully fitted with covered seating accommodation for 700. Olympian Gardens (Paul Mill), South Beach Pavilion (Will Edwards), and Claremont Pier (band and concert parties). This is the only local pier where concerts and music are given on Sundays.

Early closing day, Thursday; market day, Wednesday.

Medical Officer.—A.A.: Dr. Wilson Tyson, The Beeches.

Agent—M.H.A.R.A.; Mr. J. N. Smith, Great Eastern Hotel, Denmark Road. V.A.F.: The same.

LUDLOW, Salop.

Population, 6,373 (with a large outlying district). Miles from London, 161.

TOWN HALL.—Owned by the Corporation. Dramatic license. Full house would mean about £40 at ordinary prices. As a general rule, plays are well patronised, especially good comedies and musical pieces. Saturday nights

are useless. House lighted by gas and electric light (direct current, 230 volts). Head and foot lights at 5s. a night.

ASSEMBLY ROOMS.—No dramatic license. Holding capacity: Number of persons, 400 to 500. Platform. Lighted by gas. Terms for hiring on application. Amount of deposit required on booking, 25 per cent. Also smaller room and two retiring rooms.

Large pleasure fair, May 1, held in streets, ground let by tender. Apply to Clerk of Markets.

Portables, if good, do well, and are patronised by all classes. One was here in the summer of 1908 for three months and did excellently. No difficulty about license as a rule. Circus pitches are also obtainable.

Early closing day, Thursday; market day, Monday.

LURGAN, Co. Armagh.

Population, 11,777. Miles from Dublin, 92.

TOWN HALL.—Manager, the Town Clerk. Holding capacity: Number of persons, 800. Good stage, about 30ft. by 15ft. Lighted by gas. Terms for hiring, £1 10s. first day, and 25s. each succeeding.

Early closing day, Wednesday; market day Thursday.

LUTON, Beds.

Population, 36,404. Miles from London, 30.

GRAND THEATRE.—Proprietor and Manager, Mr. Edward Graham-Falcon; Acting-Manager, Mr. Louis J. Beard; Musical Director. Mr. Otto V. Egerer; Scenic Artist, Mr. J. Tamlin. Double license. Holding capacity: Number of persons, 1,500; amount, £110. Stage measurements: Depth, 32ft.; width, 46ft.; proscenium width, 26ft.; height, 25ft. Gas and electric light. Current continuous, 250 volts. 600 sheets posting, 600 window bills. Usual matinée day, Saturday. Time of band rehearsal, 1 o'clock.

Early closing day, Wednesday; market day, Monday.

LYE, Worcs.

Population, 11,500. Miles from London, 132.

TEMPERANCE HALL.—Manager, Mr. William Pritchard, 32, Chapel Street. Double license. Holding capacity: Number of persons, 600. Good stage or platform, 36ft. by 13ft. Lighted by gas. Terms of hiring on application. Amount of deposit required on booking, 25 per cent.

Early closing, Thursday: market, Friday.

LYNTON, Devon.

Population, 1,641. Miles from London, 215.

TOWN HALL.—Manager, Mr. W. Yeo. Holding capacity: Number of persons, 400. Stage, 24ft. wide, 18ft. deep. Electric light. Terms for hiring: One night, £2 2s.; two, £3 12s. (July, August, September). 30s. per night (October to June). Amount of deposit required on booking, 10s. 6d.

LYTHAM, Lancs.

Population, 10,000. Miles from London, 225.

PAVILION THEATRE.—Proprietors, Lytham Pier and Pavilion Co. (1895), Limited; Manager, Mr. J. H. Harrison. Double license. Holding capacity: Number of persons, 1,000. Stage measurements: Opening, 23ft.; width, 40ft.; back to front, 28ft. Lighted by gas. Amount of printing required, one 24-sheet, two 12-sheets, six 6-sheets, 50 d.c., 100 lithos, 2,000 circulars. No matinée day. Best season, from July to end of September.

BATHS AND ASSEMBLY ROOMS.—Manager, Mr. J. W. Aspden. Double license. Holding capacity: Number of persons, 400. Width of stage, 36ft.; front to back, 16ft.; proscenium width, 19ft. Lighted by gas. Terms for hiring: £2 2s. one night; £6 6s. per week Amount of deposit required on booking, 50 per cent. Hall situated on beach. First-class residential population.

No early closing. Markets Saturday and Tuesday.

MACCLESFIELD, Cheshire.

Population, 34,624. Miles from London, 166.

THEATRE ROYAL.—Proprietor and Manager, Mr. William Kusal Gatley; Musical Director, Mr. Arthur Lovatt. Dramatic license; restricted for excise. Holding capacity: Number of persons, 1,200; amount, £40. Stage measurements: 29ft. by 42ft.; proscenium opening, 22ft. 6ins. Electric light. Amount of printing required, 230 sheets, 400 lithos. Time of band rehearsal, 1.30 p.m.

TOWN HALL.—Proprietors, the Corporation. Apply the Borough Accountant. Music and dancing license. Holds 300. No proper stage. Gas. Terms, £2 2s. per day.

CENTRAL HALL, CHESTERGATE.—Manager, Mr. F. R. Oldfield. Holds 400. Music and dancing license. No proper stage.

DRILL HALL.—Apply, caretaker. Holds 2,000. Gas and electric light.

CHESTERGATE ASSEMBLY ROOMS.—Manageress, Mrs. M. Thackeray. Music and dancing license. Holding capacity: Number of persons, 300. No proper stage. Lighted by incandescent gas. Upper and lower rooms, dressing-rooms, lavatories, etc.,

Local fairs, nearest Mondays to June 22 and September 29.

Early closing day, Wednesday; market day, Saturday.

MADELEY, Salop.

Population, 8,442. Miles from London, 159.

ANSTICE MEMORIAL INSTITUTE.—Proprietors: Hall was built by public subscription and is governed by trustees and committee of subscribers. Manager, Mr. H. R. Shaw. Dramatic and music and dancing licenses. Holding capacity: Number of persons, 750. Excellent platform. Gas. Terms for hiring: £2 for first night and £1 10s. per night after. Amount of deposit required on booking, 10s.

Early closing day, Wednesday. Market day, Saturday.

MAIDENHEAD, Berks.

Population, 14,362. Miles from London, 24.

TOWN HALL.—Proprietors, The Corporation; Manager, Town Clerk, Mr. H. E. Davies. Has double license. Holding capacity: Number of persons, 400. Electric light, 230 volts direct. £3 3s. first night, £2 2s. second. £1 11s. 6d. required on booking.

No local fairs.

Early closing, Thursday. Market, Wednesday.

MAIDSTONE, Kent.

Population, 33,516. Miles from London, 39.

THE PALACE, Gabriel's Hill.—Manager, Mr. S. Baskerville. Accommodation about 1,000. Electric voltage 230.

THE CORN EXCHANGE.—Manager, Mr. Besley. Seats about 1,000. Electric voltage 230. Printing, 500 sheets, window, 1,000. Terms, £4 10s. per day, £7 10s. for two, and £10 for three.

THE HOLLINGWORTH HALL. — Also licensed for stage plays. Seats about 300. Secretary, Mr. E. Lattmer. Gas.

Good circus-pitches are obtainable in Lock Meadows. Manager, Mr. C. Avery. No license is required for portables. Athletic ground is available for alfresco entertainments. Secretary, Mr. J. S. Welch.

Early closing day, Wednesday; Market day, Thursday.

Agent.—M.H.A.R.A. and V.A.F.: Geo. White, Railway Hotel.

RECOMMENDED APARTMENTS.

Mrs. A. Wetherstone-Melville, 57, Marsham Street.—2 Sitting, 2 bedrooms; bath; piano.

MALPAS, Cheshire.

Population, 1,500. Miles from London, 177.

VICTORIA JUBILEE HALL.—Manager, Mr. A. Callcott. Has dramatic license. Holding capacity: Number of persons, 300. Stage, 24ft. by 13ft.; proscenium opening, 12ft. Lighted by gas. Terms for hiring: One guinea per night. Amount of deposit required on booking, one half. Gas included. Piano extra.

MALTON, Yorks.

Population, 4,758. Miles from London, 212.

THEATRE ROYAL.—Manager, Miss C. Bankes. Dramatic license. Holding capacity: Number of persons, 230. Amount, £15. Proper stage. Measurements: 26ft. front opening; 15ft. back; 15ft. deep; 12ft. high. Lighted by gas. Amount of printing required: 250 day bills, 6-6 sheet panels, 200 litho. Terms for hiring: 37s. 6d. per night. Amount of deposit required on booking, 10s.

Dates of local fairs, October 11 and 12. Sites available for portables, alfresco concerts, and circuses, Bark Nott Field, Norton, Malton.

Early closing day, Thursday. Market day, Saturday.

MALVERN, Worc.

Population, 24,814. Miles from London, 125.

ASSEMBLY ROOMS THEATRE.—Lessee and Manager, Mr. M. T. Stevens. Fully licensed. Holding capacity: Number of persons, 850; amount, £120. Stage measurements, 50ft. by 24ft.; proscenium, 26ft. Gas and electric light. Amount of printing required, 600 sheets. Terms for hiring, share only.

Early closing day, Thursday.

MANCHESTER, Lancs.

Population, 543,872. Miles from London, 188.

THEATRE ROYAL.—Licensee and Manager, Mr. John Hart; Acting-Manager, Mr. Edmondstone Shirra.

PRINCE'S THEATRE.—Licensee and Manager, Mr. John Hart; Acting-Manager, Mr. Geo. Lee.

GAIETY THEATRE. — Proprietor and Licensee, A. E. F. Horniman; General Manager, Mr. B. Iden Payne; Acting-Manager, Mr. Edwin T. Heys. Restricted license. All seats numbered and reserved. Holding, £200. Stage; width, opening 25ft.; 63ft. from wall to wall; floats to back wall, 27ft. Electric light. 2,340 sheets for posting. Matinées, Wednesdays and Saturdays. Band rehearsal 5 p.m. Theatre rebuilt and modernised throughout, summer, 1908.

QUEEN'S THEATRE.—Licensee and Manager, Mr. R. Flanagan; Acting-Manager, Mr. Albert Jones.

ROYAL OSBORNE THEATRE.—Proprietors, Messrs. W. H. Broadhead and Sons; Manager, Mr. H. Winstanley; Acting-Manager, Mr. J. Mason.

JUNCTION THEATRE.—Proprietors, Messrs. W. H. Broadhead and Sons; Acting-Manager, Mr. G. Hewitt.

METROPOLE THEATRE. — Proprietors, Messrs. W. H. Broadhead and Son; Acting-Manager, R. Andrew; Musical Director, Mr. Chas. Bayley; Scenic Artist, Mr. T. C. Daly. Restricted license. Holding capacity: Number of persons, 4,000. Stage measurements: Depth, 40ft.; width, 65ft.; proscenium, 34ft. Gas and electric light. Usual matinée day, Monday. Time of band rehearsal, 11 a.m.

ST. JAMES'S HALL.—Manager, Mr. W. Cawood. Music and dancing license. Large hall, 80,000 sq ft. Small hall holds 600 people. Proper stage. Electric light. Terms for hiring, £120 per week. Amount of deposit required on booking, half.

TIVOLI THEATRE OF VARIETIES.—Proprietors and Freeholders, The Tivoli, Manchester, Limited; Managing Director, Mr. Charles A. Wilkes; Manager, Mr. Arthur B. Wilkes. Booking at London Offices, 150, Strand. Musical Director, Mr. Frank Smith. Holding capacity: Number of persons, 1,500. Electric light. Time of band rehearsal, 12 noon. Matinée days, Monday, Thursday, and Friday.

GRAND THEATRE. — Proprietors, Jasper Redfern and Co., Limited; Managing Director, Mr. Jasper Redfern; Manager, Mr. J. Rolmaz; Double license. Holding capacity: Number of persons, 3,000. Full stage, etc., for any production. Gas and electric light. Time of band rehearsal, 12 noon. Bars no surrounding halls.

MIDLAND HOTEL THEATRE.

VICTORIA THEATRE, BROUGHTON.—Proprietors, Broughton Theatre Syndicate, Ltd.; Manager and Licensee, Mr. J. Fred Watson. Full license. Holding capacity: Number of persons, 3,000; amount, £170. Electric light, voltage, 220. Smoking permitted. Amount of printing required, 1,800 sheets. Usual matinée day, Wednesday. Time of band rehearsal, 11 a.m.

HIPPODROME, HULME. — Proprietors, Messrs. W. H. Broadhead and Son; Manager, Mr. Percy B. Broadhead; Musical Director, Mr. H. O'Callaghan; Scenic Artists, Messrs. T. C. Daly and E. Leigh. Stage measurements: 90ft. by 45ft. by 36ft. Gas and electric light. Usual matinée day, Wednesday, at 2.30. Time of band rehearsal, 12 noon.

QUEEN'S PARK HIPPODROME. — Proprietors, Messrs. W. H. Broadhead and Sons; Manager, Mr. Percy B. Broadhead.

THE HIPPODROME (Oxford Street).—Proprietors, the Manchester Hippodrome and Ardwick Empire, Limited; Managing Director, Mr. Oswald Stoll; Resident Manager, Mr. Nelson Barry; Musical Director, Mr. Alfred Haines. Full license. Gas and electric light. Time of band rehearsal, 12 noon. Usual matinée days, Tuesday, Wednesday, and Saturday, at 2. Electric current, alternating, 200 volts.

Bars all other halls in Manchester and the following towns: Ardwick, Salford, Hulme, Longsight, Ashton-under-Lyne, Stockport, Oldham, Eccles, and Bury.

PALACE.—Proprietor, Palace of Varieties, Limited; General Manager. Mr. Walter de Frece; Business Manager, Mr. Fred Leighton; Musical Director, Mr. T. H. Gaggs. Electric light. Time of band rehearsal, 12 noon. Usual matinée days, Monday, Wednesday, and Saturday. Bars Stoll's surrounding halls. Seats 3,000.

ARDWICK EMPIRE. — Proprietors, Manchester Hippodrome and Ardwick Empire, Limited; Chairman and Managing Director, Mr. Oswald Stoll; Acting-Manager, Mr. H. Hall. Booking circuit in conjunction with Moss's Empires, Limited. Musical Director, Mr. R. Hardwick. Music and dancing license. Gas and electric light. Time of band rehearsal, 2 p.m.

KING'S OPERA HOUSE, LONGSIGHT.— Proprietors, Messrs. W. H. Broadhead and Sons; Acting-Manager, Mr. J. R. Trappett.

The following halls are the property of the Corporation. Application should be made to the Town Clerk, Mr. G. H. Talbot.

The use of the kinematograph is prohibited except in the Hulme Town Hall, the Cheetham Public Hall, and the New Islington Public Hall, and will only be permitted in such halls subject to special terms and conditions.

TOWN HALL, Albert Square.—Size, 100ft. by 50ft. Terms for hiring, £30 per night.

TOWN HALL, Chorlton-on-Medlock.—Size of room, 66ft. by 35ft. Holding capacity: Number of persons, 400. Terms for hiring: £3 3s. and £5 5s.; Concerts, £2 2s.

TOWN HALL, Ardwick.— Size, 48ft. by 28ft. Holding capacity: Number of persons, 300. Terms for hiring: £3 3s., £2 2s., and £1 10s., according to entertainment.

NEW ISLINGTON PUBLIC HALLS, Ancoats.—Size of each hall, 72ft. by 36ft. Upper hall, with gallery, will seat 700 persons; lower hall, 600 persons. Terms for hiring: £3 10s., £2 5s., and £1 5s., according to entertainment.

In addition, 5s. will be charged for services of fireman when the hall is used for dramatic performances.

HULME TOWN HALL, Stretford Road.— Size of large room, 90ft. by 45ft. Will seat 850 persons. Terms for hiring: £7 10s., £4, and £2 10s. 6d., according to entertainment.

In addition, 5s. will be charged for services of fireman when the hall is used for dramatic performances.

CHURNETT STREET PUBLIC HALL, Collyhurst.—Size, 72ft. by 38ft. Will seat 600 persons. Terms for hiring: £3 3s. and £2, according to entertainment.

NEWTON HEATH PUBLIC HALL.—Size of hall, 79ft. by 38ft. Will seat 600 persons. Terms for hiring: £3 13s. 6d. and £2 2s., according to entertainment.

WHITWORTH HALL, Openshaw.—Size of hall, 79ft. by 38ft. Will seat 600 persons. Terms for hiring: £3 13s. and £2 2s., according to entertainment.

In addition, 5s. will be charged for services of fireman when the hall is used for dramatic performances.

CHEETHAM HILL PUBLIC HALL.—Size of hall, 64ft. by 42ft. Will seat 550 persons. Terms for hiring: £3 13s. and £2 2s., according to entertainment.

LONGSIGHT PUBLIC HALL.—Size of hall, 63ft. by 36ft. Will seat, with gallery, 650 persons. Terms for hiring: Large room for concerts. £1; Saturdays, £2.

BLECKLEY INSTITUTE.—Size, 60ft. by 32ft. Holding capacity: Number of persons, 400. Terms for hiring: £2 12s. 6d., £1 10s., and £1 1s., according to entertainment.

In addition there are the following halls:—
ART GALLERY, Mosley Street.—Apply to the Curator.
ASSOCIATION HALL.—General Secretary, Y.M.C.A. Hall now being re-built; will be ready in 1910.
FREE TRADE HALLS.—Manager, Mr. C. J. Stewart. Double license. Holding capacity: Number of persons, large 4,000, small 800. Portable stage. Stage measurements: Large, 42ft. by 16ft.; small, 15ft. by 15ft. Gas and electric light. Terms for hiring: Rental or share.
RUSHOLME PUBLIC HALL.—Manager, Mr. Thomas J. Billinge. Music and dancing license. Holding capacity: Number of persons, 500. Permanent platform. Lighted by gas. Terms for hiring: 21s. to 30s. No engagement entered on the books except upon payment of the hiring fee.
CHORLTON-CUM-HARDY PAVILION.—Proprietor and Manager, Mr. W. James Wright. Adjoining Chorlton Station Lighted by electricity. Illuminated by 200 coloured electric lights. Large stock of scenery. Holding capacity: Number of persons, 1,200; seats 800. Usual matinée day, Saturday, 3 p.m.
PUBLIC HALL, Patricroft. — Managers, Messrs. Samuel Hooley and Sons. Music and dancing license. Holding capacity: Number of persons, 500. Platform, 29ft. by 15ft. Electric transformer for bioscope installed. Terms for hiring on application. Picture shows are run here.

Medical Officers.—A.A.: Drs. W. H. B. Crockwell, 2, Upper Chorlton Road (hours, 2-3 and 6-8); Geo. Ellis, Pitt House, Failsworth (hours, 9-10, 2-3, 6-7); H. H. P. Johnson, 70, Ayres Road, Brooks's Bar (hours, 12-3 and 8.30-9); and Broadleas, Trafford Park (hours, 9-10 and 6-8). A.U.: Drs. Ellis, Crockwell, Johnson, as above; W. S. McCowan, 84, Rusholme Road. M.H.A.R.A.: Drs. Ellis and McCowan, as above.
Agents.—A.U.: F. Blackhurst, Clarendon Hotel, Oxford Road. M.H.A.R.A. and V.A.F.: Branch office, Fred Slingsby, 46, Sidney Street.

RECOMMENDED APARTMENTS.

Mrs. Jarman, 30, Devonshire Street. All Saints. —Sitting-room, 4 bedrooms, combined room; piano; bath.
Mrs. Gray, 36, Booth Street, East Oxford Road.— 2 bedrooms, 1 sitting-room, front combined; bath; piano.

MANSFIELD, Notts.

Population, 30,000. Miles from London, 142.

NEW GRAND THEATRE.—Proprietors, Mansfield, Sutton, and District Theatres, Limited; Managing Director, Capt. Clayton; Assistant Manager, Mr. Mark Lorne; Musical Director, Mr. T. Renshaw; Scenic Artist, Mr. Alec Toole. Full license. Holding capacity: Number of persons, 1,200. Amount, about £70. Stage measurements, 40ft. deep, 60ft. wide; 40ft. to grid. Proscenium opening, 28ft. Electric light, 240 volts. Printing required: 850 wall sheets, 800 lithos. Usual matinée day, Saturday. Time of band rehearsal, 1 p.m.

HIPPODROME.—Closed, the license having been cancelled. Available for kinematograph.

VICTORIA HALL.—Manager, Mr. George Fox. Double license. Holding capacity: Number of persons, 900. Depth and width of stage, 17ft. by 36ft.; proscenium, 24ft. Electric light. Has recently been fitted with motor generator for pictures, giving a voltage of 75 and about 60 ampères. The town supply is 3 wire, 480 and 240 volts continuous.
Early closing day, Wednesday; market days, Thursday and Saturday.
Agent.—V.A.F.: Mr Shacklock, Greyhound Hotel.

MARCH, Cambs.

Population, 8,000. Miles from London, 80.

PUBLIC HALL THEATRE.—Manager, Mr. Joseph Collingwood, J.P. Dramatic license. Holding capacity: Number of persons, 700. Amount, £32, ordinary prices. Fully equipped. Stage measurements, 21ft. deep, 36ft. wide. Proscenium opening, 20ft. by 13ft. 6in., and 18ft. clear height under fly rails. Lighted by gas. Amount of printing required, 200 sheets for walls, 100 window lithos. Terms for hiring: One night, 45s.; two, 75s.; three, 100s.; six, £9. Payment in advance.
March is 14 miles from Peterboro', 7½ from Wisbech, 19 from Spalding, and 30 from Cambridge on G.E. main line.
Early closing day, Tuesday; market day, Wednesday.

MARGATE, Kent.

Population, 23,118. Miles from London, 74.

THEATRE ROYAL.—Manager, Mr. Edward Michael; Acting Manager, Mr. W. W. Keene. Musical Director, Miss H. Betts; Scenic Artist, Mr. Jules Camus. Patent license. Holding capacity: Number of persons, 1,038 Amount, £92. Proscenium opening, 24ft.; back stage to act drop, 21ft.; wall to wall, 44ft.; under fly-rail, 18ft. Lighted by gas. Amount of printing required: 600 d.c., 800 heets (upright) for walls, 1,000 circ throwaways. Time of band rehearsal, 1.30 p.m.

HIPPODROME (late Grand Theatre).—Proprietors, South of England Hippodromes, Ltd. Joint Managing Directors, Mr. F. Mouillot and W. De Frece; General Manager, Mr. J. de Frece; Resident Manager, Mr. C. F. Bawtree; Booking Circuit, the De Frece Circuit. Treble license. Holding capacity: Number of persons, 1,500. Stage measurements, 31ft. opening. 30ft. deep, and 47ft. wide. Gas and electric light. Time of band rehearsal, 2.30.

GRAND-HALL-BY-THE-SEA. — Proprietor, Lord George Sanger; Manager, Mr. Chas. Evans; Musical Director, Mr. Wilfrid Harvey. Music and dancing license. Stage measurements, 40ft. deep, 50ft. wide. 30ft. odd. Proscenium. Lighted chiefly by gas; little machinery on Stage. Time of band rehearsal, Mondays, 12 o'clock, July, August, and September. Usual matinée day, every day at 3 o'clock, July, August, and September. Bars Margate and Ramsgate three months. Includes ballroom, variety theatre, and gardens.
Early closing day, Thursday; market day, Saturday.
Medical officer.—A.A.: Dr. C. Webb, Westbourne House, Nayland Rock. A.U.: The same. M.H.A.R.A.: The same.
M.H.A.R.A. agent: Chas. Evans, Hall-by-the-Sea. V.A.F.: R. A. Wilson, King's Head Hotel.

MARKET DRAYTON, Salop.

Population, 9,997. Miles from London, 163.
TOWN HALL.—Manager, Mr. D. G. Hancock. Double license. Holding capacity: Number of persons, 600. Amount, £50. Permanent stage. Frontage, 31ft. deep; depth to back, 16ft.; height from ceiling to stage, 19ft. Lighted by gas. Terms for hiring, £2 2s. first day; £1 1s. all days after. Gas extra. Amount of deposit required on booking, £1. Plan of hall: Bennion, Horne, and Co.
Early closing day, Thursday; market day, Wednesday.

MARKET HARBOROUGH, Leicester.

Population, 8,000. Miles from London 81.
ASSEMBLY ROOMS.—Manager, Mr. T. W. Hall. Size of hall, 87ft. by 43ft. Has dramatic license. Holding capacity: Number of persons: 900 to 1,000. Stage partly fixed, 36ft. 6in. by 12ft.; extension to 22ft. 6in. deep if required. Lighted by gas. Terms for hiring: £2 12s., first night; £2 for each succeeding night, inclusive of fire and light. Piano 5s. if required.
NEW HALL.—Manager, Mr. George Eames. Dramatic license. Holding capacity: Number of persons, 500. Permanent platform, 12ft. 3in. deep; 40ft. wide. Proscenium opening, 16ft. 6in. × 12ft. high. Gas. Amount of printing required: 250 d.c. for posting, 150 window bills. Terms for hiring: £1 3s. 6d. first night and 18s. 6d. per night after. Amount of deposit required on booking: £1.
The population of Market Harborough is mostly industrial, but there are also many wealthy residents. Generally speaking, they are a theatre-going public, and are glad of the opportunity to support good dramatic entertainments. Pitches can always be obtained for circuses or menageries, which are well patronised. There would be no difficulty in obtaining sites for al fresco or concert parties. The local fairs are held on April 29 and October 19, when there are many visitors in the town. A license for a portable can easily be obtained from the Urban District Council. Drama of the heavy type is almost the sole attraction in the theatrical line to be found in the town. This draws well among a certain class, but for plays of a lighter kind and good concert parties Market Harborough presents a field well worth exploiting.
Dates of local pleasure fairs, April 29th and 30th and October 19th and succeeding days.
Early closing day, Thursday; market day, Tuesday.

MARLBOROUGH, Wilts.

Population, 3,887. Miles from London, 75.
TOWN HALL.—Proprietors, The Corporation; Manager, Town Clerk. Double license. Holding capacity: Number of persons, 500. Proper stage (moderate accommodation only). Lighted by gas. Terms for hiring: £2 12s. 3d. first night; second and subsequent, £1 11s. 3d. Amount of deposit required on booking, £1. Two dressing-rooms on same floor.
CORN EXCHANGE.—Holds 700. Apply caretaker.
Early closing, Wednesday; market, Saturday.

MARLOW, Bucks.

Population, 4,526. Miles from London, 31.
PUBLIC HALL.—Manager, Mr. Horace Lacey. No dramatic license, but one can be obtained. Holding capacity: Number of persons,

300. Stage, 30ft. by 17ft. Lighted by gas. Terms for hiring: 31s. 6d. per night; less terms for more. Amount of deposit required on booking, 10s. 6d.
Early closing, Wednesday; no market.

MARSDEN, Yorks.

Population, 4,370. Miles from London, 196.
MECHANICS' HALL.—Secretary, Mr. Wm. Griffiths. Music and dancing license. Occasional license for dramas granted for 14 days when required. Holding capacity: Number of persons, 600. Depth and width of stage, 11ft. and 38ft. Lighted by gas. Terms for hiring: £1 first night; 15s. second; 10s. third; and succeeding nights. Amount of deposit required on booking, 10s.
Date of local fair, first week in September. Site available for portables, alfresco concerts, and circuses. Public recreation ground under District Council.

MARYPORT, Cumb.

Population, 11,897. Miles from London, 316.
ATHENÆUM.—Secretary, Mr. T. Skelton. Has dramatic license. Holding capacity: Number of persons, 800 to 1,000; amount, £25. Depth and width of stage, 25ft. by 16ft. Lighted by gas. Amount of printing required, 400 to 500 d.c. sheets. Terms for hiring: 30s. first day, 25s. each day after; gas extra. Amount of deposit required on booking, 20s.
Fairs.—Whitsuntide and Martinmas. Thursday, Friday and Saturday. Held in the Market Square.
Early closing, Wednesday; market, Friday.

MATLOCK, Derbyshire.

Population, 8,000. Miles from London, 143.
VICTORIA HALL AND PLEASURE GARDENS.—Proprietor, James White; Resident Manager, Franklyn Thomas. Holding capacity: Number of persons, 600; amount, £50. Stage measurements: 21ft. deep by 40½ft. wide; height, 22ft. Gaslight. Dramatic license.
The population is residential and visiting. Matlock fair is on May 8, and the Wakes are held in the second week in September. There are no alfresco concerts. Bateman's field is generally taken for visits of circuses. The best time for stage performances is August and September.
Early closing day, Thursday; market day, Saturday.

MAYBOLE, Ayr.

Population, 5,892. Miles from London, 392½.
TOWN HALL.—Manager Janitor, Mr. J. Beaton. Double license. Holding capacity: Number of persons, 800. Stage: Deep, 13½ft.; wide, 40ft. Lighted by gas. Terms for hiring: Dramatic, 35s., gas extra; Concert, 22s. 6d.; Lecture, 20s. Amount of deposit required on booking, 10s. or 20s.
Early closing, Wednesday. No market.

MELBOURNE, Derbyshire.

Population, 3,580. Miles from London, 128½.
PUBLIC HALL.—Manager and Secretary, Mr. W. H. Perry. Has dramatic license. Holding capacity: Number of persons, 400. Movable platform, 28ft. by 9ft.; can be extended 3 or 6ft. Gas and electric light. Twelve posting

**24*

stations. Terms for hiring: 25s. per night. Amount of deposit required on booking, 10s. per night.

Date of local fair, first Monday after October 11

Early closing, Thursday; no market.

MELROSE, Roxburgh.

Population, 2,195. Miles from London, 360.

CORN EXCHANGE.—Apply Secretary, Corn Exchange Company. Has dramatic license. Holding capacity: Number of persons, 400. Platform, 31ft. by 8½ft. Lighted by gas. Terms for hiring: £1 10s. per day; stove, if wished, 2s. 6d. extra. Amount of deposit required on booking, 5s.

No local fairs. Sites available for portables, alfresco concerts, and circuses. Greenyards, Melrose.

Early closing, Thursday; no market.

MELTHAM, Yorks.

Population, 5,000. Miles from London, 187.

ODDFELLOWS' HALL.—Secretary, Mr. Wm. Reginald Carter. Dramatic license (short date). Holding capacity: Number of persons, 500. Platform, 30ft. by 10ft. Terms for hiring on application.

Date of local fair, first week in September. Fair ground available for portables, alfresco concerts, and circuses.

Early closing Wednesday; no market.

MELTON MOWBRAY, Leicester.

Population, 7,454. Miles from London, 102.

CORN EXCHANGE.—Manager, Mr. G. Andrews. Double license. Holding capacity: Number of persons, 1,000. Stage, 32ft. by 16ft. Lighted by gas. Scale of charges on application. Amount of deposit required on booking: One night, 10s.; two nights, £1.

KING'S HALL. — Proprietors, the Co-operative Society; Secretary, Mr. J. W. Wood. Seats about 850. For alfresco concerts, etc., and animated picture shows, apply to the Secretary for details. Electric light, 240 volts.

YOUNG MEN'S INSTITUTE.—Market Place. Large room. Licensed for music and dancing. Seats about 200. Apply Secretary.

THE NEW PARK.—For circus pitches. Good accommodation. Apply to the Town Wardens.

Dates of local fairs: Monday and Tuesday following January 17; second Tuesday in April; Whit Tuesday (Pleasure Fair); August 21; New Ram Fair—fourth Tuesday in September; September 28th; October 24th; first Tuesdays after December 8th. Melton Mowbray Cheese Fairs: Third Thursday in March, March 16th; fourth Thursday in September, September 23rd; third Thursday in November, November 18th. The town is visited by portables, and there is no difficulty encountered in obtaining a license from the local authorities.

Population, both residential and industrial, and from November to March greatly augmented in consequence of the fox-hunting season.

Early closing day, Thursday; market day, Tuesday.

MERTHYR TYDFIL, Glam.

Population, 69,228. Miles from London, 176.

THEATRE ROYAL.—Lessees, The South Wales Entertainments, Limited; Acting-Manager, Mr. Albert Jackson.

EMPIRE TEMPERANCE HALL.—Manager, Mr. Israel Price.

No fairs or portables visit the town. Circuses at Penydorren; lessee, Mr. William Thomas, contractor, Park Place, Merthyr. The population is industrial (collieries and steel works). Early closing day, Thursday, market day, Saturday.

Agent.—A.U.: Warren Jones, Nelson Hotel. V.A.F.: The same. M.H.A.R.A.: S. Dix, Tiger Hotel.

RECOMMENDED APARTMENTS.

Mrs. Reeve, 22, Park Place.—3 bedrooms, 2 sitting-rooms ; gas and piano.

METHIL, Fife.

Population, 3,200. Miles from London, 415.

GAIETY THEATRE.—Proprietors, Methil Theatre Company, Limited. Manager, Mr. Sidney Arnold. Holds 1,200. Electric light. Large stage and good stock of scenery. Now in course of erection. Will be completed shortly.

TOWN HALL.—Manager, Mr. R. Sutter. Holding capacity: Number of persons, 600. Stage measurements: 34ft. by 18ft. lighted by gas.

Early closing day, Thursday.

MEXBOROUGH, Yorks.

Population, 13,000. Miles from London, 181.

PRINCE OF WALES THEATRE. — Proprietors, the Mexborough Theatre Co., Ltd. Managing Director, Mr. G. H. Smith; Licensee and General Manager, Mr. W. H. Melton. Pros. opening, 26ft.; depth, 30ft.; width, 44ft. Electric light, 220 volts direct. Printing: 400 sheets, 600 lithos, 250 d.c.

NEW PUBLIC HALL.—Proprietor and Manager, Mr. Will Hunter. Acting Manager, Mr. E. H. Jones. Performances twice nightly.

PUBLIC HALL.—Open for kinematograph exhibitions.

Fair, June 21. Large recreation grounds available for circus or fit-ups. Sanger's and Bostock's visit here. Rapidly growing district. Large mining population in the district.

Early closing day, Thursday; market days, Monday and Saturday.

MIDDLESBROUGH, Yorks.

Population, 102,783. Miles from London, 239.

THEATRE ROYAL.—Proprietor, Mr. J. Chas. Imeson; Managers, Mr. J. Chas. Imeson and Mr. G. L. Imeson; Acting-Manager, Mr. Cecil Charles Imeson; Musical Director, Mr. T. A. Parroch; Scenic Artist, Mr. C. Kirkham. Double license. Holding capacity: Number of persons, 2,500; amount, £130. Depth of stage, 44ft.; wall to wall, 60ft.; proscenium opening, 29ft. Gas and electric light. Amount of printing required, 1,100 sheets. Usual matinée day, Saturday. Time of band rehearsal, 11 a.m.

GRAND OPERA HOUSE.—Proprietors, The Grand Theatre (Middlesbrough), Ltd. Managing Director. Mr. J. E. Jowsey; Manager and Licensee, Mr. W. Ker Chatto. Full license. Musical Director, Mr. Percy A. W. Lax; Scenic Artist, Mr. W. Barrow. Seating capacity, 3,500. Amount, £200. Stage wall to wall, 70ft.; stage to flies, 21ft.; stage to grid, 68ft.; between flyrails, 43ft.; proscenium opening, 32ft. 14 dressing rooms, hot and cold water. Electric light, 220 volts, and gas. Amount of printing required, 1,400 sheets. Matinée day, Saturday. Time of band rehearsal, 11 a.m.

THE EMPIRE.—Proprietors, the Empire Palace of Varieties, Middlesbrough, Limited;

Manager, Mr. Charles G. Rembges; Musical Director, Mr. G. W. Greenfield. Music and dancing license. Electric light. Time of band rehearsal, 2 o'clock.

OXFORD PALACE OF VARIETIES.—Proprietor, Mr. Alfred Graham; Manager, Mr. Ormesby Trench; Musical Director, Mr. Mitchell. Band rehearsal, 1.30 p.m.

NEW HIPPODROME. — Proprietors, The Hippodrome, Middlesbrough, Limited; Managing Director, Signor Pepi; Acting-Manager, Mr. A. E. Nicholls; Musical Director, Mr. H. Hinchcliffe, L.R.A.M. Band rehearsal, 2 p.m.

TOWN HALL.—Manager, Mr. Charles Booth, Borough Accountant's Office. Dramatic license. Holding capacity: Number of persons, 2,200. Platform with orchestra (raised at back). Gas and electric light. Terms for hiring: From £10 10s. per day (excluding lighting and cleaning) downward, according to nature of entertainment and period of booking. Deposit of 25 per cent. required on booking.

TEMPERANCE HALL.—Manager, Mr. Geo. H. Blackburn. Music and dancing license. holding capacity: Number of persons, 2,000. Stage: 28ft. by 12ft. Electric light. Terms for hiring: £3 15s. per night; reduction for series. Amount of deposit required on booking: 10 per cent.

Medical Officers.—A.A.: Dr. J. Emmerson Proud. 94-96, Corporation Road. M.H.A.R.A.: The same.

Agents.—A.U.: A. E. Horlington, Criterion Hotel. M.H.A.R.A.: Mr. G. Pickard, Central Hotel. V.A.F.: The same.

Early closing day, Wednesday; market day, Saturday.

RECOMMENDED APARTMENTS.

Mrs. Campbell, 23, Lonsdale Street.—1 sitting-room, 1 or 2 bedrooms; piano.

Mrs. Wastell, 69, Grange Road West.—Two sitting, 3 bedrooms, combined; bath; piano.

Mrs. Willinger, 9, Marton Road.—Sitting, single and double-bedded room, combined room.

MIDDLETON, Lancs.

Population, 25,178. Miles from London, 189.

PARDOE'S THEATRE.—Proprietors, Messrs. Pardoe; Manager, Mr. William Pardoe; Acting-Manager, Mr. Geo. Singleton; Musical Director, Mr. Geo. Encliffe; Scenic Artist, Mr. Singleton. Restricted license. Holding capacity: Number of persons, 1,200; amount, between £40 and £50. Stage measurements: Depth, 30ft.; width, 46 ft.; from wall to wall, open, 24ft. by 16ft. Gas and electric light. Amount of printing required, 350 wall, 350 lithos. Usual matinée day, Saturday.

CO-OPERATIVE HALL.—Managers, The Co-operative Society. Double license. Holding capacity: Number of persons, 900. Concert platform, 28ft. by 16ft. Gas and electric light. Terms for hiring: £2 3s., including use of piano; special fee for week's engagement. Amount of deposit required on booking: 10s. for one evening.

Middleton Wakes, third week in August.

Early closing day, Tuesday; market day, Friday.

MIDDLEWICH, Ches.

Population, 5,000. Miles from London, 166.

TOWN HALL.—Secretary, Mr. C. F. Lawrence. Double license. Holding capacity: Number of persons, 400 to 500. Semi-circular platform, with square extension in sections for stage. Lighted by gas. Terms for hiring: One night, £1; two consecutive nights, £1 15s.;

three ditto, 50s.; four ditto, 65s.; five ditto, £4; six ditto, £4 12s. 6d.; each consecutive night beyond, 12s. 6d. Full fee required on booking.

No local fairs. Wakes, first Sunday after October 11.

Early closing, Wednesday; market, Tuesday.

MIDHURST, Sussex.

Population, 1,650. Miles from London, 64.

PUBLIC HALL.—Manager, Mr. C. H. Bowyer. Has dramatic license. Holding capacity: Number of persons, 500 or 600. Stage, 20 ft. depth; width, 34 ft. 6 in. Lighted by gas. Terms for hiring: One night, £4; two nights, £6 10s.; variety entertainments, £2 10s. and £4.

Early closing, Wednesday; market, Thursday.

MIDSOMER NORTON, Somerset.

Population, 5,809. Miles from London, 117.

TOWN HALL.—Seats 300. Has dramatic license. Available for Kinematograph entertainments. No electric light. For terms, apply Surveyor.

DRILL HALL.—Manager, Mr. J. Bastavle. Double license. Holding capacity: Number of persons, 1,000. Stage, 23 ft. by 28 ft. by 15 ft. 9 in. Lighted by gas. Terms for hiring: £1 7s. 6d. per night. Amount of deposit required on booking, 10s.

Date of local fair, April 24.

Early closing, Thursday.

MILLOM, Cumb.

Population, 10,426. Miles from London, 274.

CO-OPERATIVE HALL.—Manager, Mr. Jas. J. Cain. Double license. Holding capacity: Number of persons, 600; amount, £30. Depth and width of stage, 18 ft. 8 in. by 35 ft. No proscenium. Lighted by gas. Terms for hiring: 25s. one night, 45s. two nights, 60s. three nights, 75s. four nights, and 90s. for six nights. Amount of deposit required on booking: 10s. to 20s.

COUNTY HALL.—Manager, Mr. G. Mudge. Holding capacity: Number of persons, 800. Portable stage. Lighted by gas. Terms for hiring: £1 1s. per day. £3 10s. per week (gas extra, at 3s. per 1,000 ft.). Amount of deposit required on booking, £1.

Dates of local fairs: Whitsuntide Hiring Fair Tuesday in Whit-week; Martinmas Hiring Fair, November 11. Sites available for portables, alfresco concerts, and circuses: On the Green.

Early closing, Wednesday; market, Saturday.

MINEHEAD, Somerset.

Population, 2,511. Miles from London, 183.

PUBLIC HALL.—Manager, Mr. Ralph E. Sticklan. Has dramatic license. Holding capacity: Number of persons, 600; amount, £35. Stage, 33 ft. 6 in. by 16 ft. 3 in. No proscenium. Headlights and footlights. Electric light. Terms for hiring: £2 12s. 6d. one night, £4 4s. two nights (inclusive of lighting and cleaning). Amount of deposit required on booking: 10s. Season, June to September. Electric current continuous, volts 220.

Sites available for portables alfresco concerts, and circuses, Recreation Ground. Secretary, Mr. R. Sticklan.

Early closing, Wednesday; market, third Monday.

MOLD, Flint.

Population, 4,263. Miles from London, 192.

MOLD TOWN HALL.—Manager, Mr. W. B. Rowdon, Surveyor Mold Urban District Council. Dramatic license. Holding capacity: Number of persons, about 600. Dimensions: 52ft. by 34ft., clear of the platform; platform, 12ft. deep, 26ft. wide (can be extended); lavatories, etc. Scale of charges (with gas up to midnight): Concerts (non-ratepayers)—One night, £1 15s.; two nights, £3 15s.; three nights, £4 4s.; and £1 1s. each succeeding night. Theatricals and Ghost Entertainments: One night, £2 2s.; two nights, £3 15s.; three nights, £5; £1 5s. each succeeding night. Amount of deposit required on booking, 10s. on each day.

Horse and cattle fairs, first Wednesday in each month. Recreation Ground, New Street.

Early closing, Thursday; markets, Wednesday and Saturday.

MONMOUTH, Mon.

Population, 5,095. Miles from London, 141.

ROLLS HALL.—Manager, Mr. Charles Morgan. Fully licensed. Holding capacity: Number of persons, about 600. Stage, 50ft. by 18ft.; width of proscenium, 17ft. 10½in.; height 13ft. 6in. Gas and electric, 100 volts, alternating. Terms: First night, £2 5s. (lights extra); second night, £1 15s. (lights extra); every succeeding day, £1 10s. (lights extra). Amount of deposit required on booking: 10s. each night of booking.

Sites for circuses. Apply to surveyor of corporation, Little Chippenham; or W. Watkins, Nag's Head, Old Dixton Road.

Early closing, Thursday; markets, Monday and Friday.

MONTROSE, Forfar.

Population, 12,401. Miles from London, 488.

BURGH HALL.—Manager, Mr. John Oliphant. Fully licensed. Holding capacity: Number of persons, 1,500. Stage, 36ft. by 25ft. Foot and top lights. Double-sided scenery. Side rooms, etc. Electric light. Amount of printing required, enough for 40 large hoardings. Terms for hiring: Concerts, £2 10s.; subsequent nights, 22s.; dramatic entertainments, £3; subsequent nights, £2 10s.; one week, £12; use of piano, per night, 5s. Amount of deposit on booking, £1.

GUILD HALL.—Manager, Mr. John Oliphant. Music and dancing license. Holding capacity: Number of persons, 300. Stage, 12ft. by 6ft. No scenery. Lighted by gas. Terms for hiring on application. Amount of deposit on booking, £1.

Dates of local fairs.—The first Friday after May 28 and November; if Friday falls on 28th, it is held on 29th.

Early closing, Wednesday; Market, Friday.

MORECAMBE, Lancs.

Population, 11,798. Miles from London, 235.

ROYALTY THEATRE.—Proprietors, Morecambe Theatre Company, Limited. Dramatic license. Holds about 1,200.

WINTER GARDENS AND VICTORIA PAVILION.—Proprietors, Morecambe Winter Gardens Company, Limited. Apply the Manager, Mr. Tom Atkinson. Victoria Pavilion holds about 6,000. Large Oriental ballroom attached, holds about 4,000. Electric light, own plant, 110 direct. Town current 220 direct. Bars Lancaster.

ALHAMBRA.—Manager, Mr. John Gardner. Holds about 2,000.

WEST END PIER.—Proprietors, West End Pier Company, Limited. Holds about 2,000. Stage, 28ft. by 28ft. Proscenium, 24ft.

CENTRAL PIER.—Proprietor, Morecambe Pier and Pavilion Co., Limited; Manager, Mr. E. Hill; Musical Director, Mr. H. Sainsbury. Full license. Stage measurements: Width 57ft., depth 22ft.; proscenium, 30ft. wide, 26ft. high. Gas and electric light. Time of band rehearsal, 12 noon.

ALBERT HALL.—Manager, Mr. Harry Hargreaves. Music and dancing license. Holding capacity: Number of persons, 500. Permanent stage (with scenery), 40ft. by 15ft.; proscenium opening, 18ft. by 14ft. Lighted by gas. Terms for hiring:—£6 for six days, gas exclusive.

DEVONSHIRE HALL.—Proprietor, Mr. James H. Walker. Music and dancing license. Holding capacity: Number of persons, 600. Proscenium measurements, about 17ft. by 16ft. Depth and width of stage, about 36ft. by 10ft. Electric light. Terms for hiring, as per agreement. Deposit: one night, 10s.; one week, £2.

Early closing day, Wednesday, (during winter months only).

Agent.—M.H.A.R.A.: Alfred Pyrah, Imperial Hotel; V.A.F.: The same.

MORLEY, Yorks.

Population, 25,000. Miles from London, 186.

TOWN HALL.—Apply, the Town Clerk, Mr. Fred Thackray, Town Hall. Full dramatic license. Alexandra Hall: Accommodation, 1,146—area, 700; balcony, 246; and orchestra, 200. Terms for stage plays: First night, £3 3s.; second night, £2 12s. 6d.; each successive night, £2 2s.; if booked for a week, £10 10s. For *matinée* performances, one-half the charge for evening booking. For concerts, etc., for the first night £2 12s. 6d., for two consecutive nights £4 4s., for each succeeding night £1 11s. 6d.

There is also the King's Hall in the Town Hall, accommodating 600 persons, for which the charge is one-half the above, except for electricity, which in the larger hall is charged for at the rate of 7s. 6d. per hour, and in the smaller hall at 2s. 6d. Capacity of electricity-generating plant: Engines, 600-h.p.; alternators, 228 volts.

EMPRESS PALACE.—Lessee and Manager, Mr. Arthur Leslie; Acting-Manager, Mr. Stewart Braide. Picture and Variety hall. Accommodation, about 500. Electric light.

Population, residential and industrial. Chief industries, woollen, cloth manufacture, coal mining, and stone quarrying.

Local feast, third Monday in August.

Early closing day, Tuesday. Market day, Friday.

MORPETH, Northumberland.

Population, 6,158. Miles from London, 288.

DRILL HALL (late Masonic Hall).—Manager, Mr. J. J. James. Has dramatic license. Holding capacity: Number of persons, 500. Amount, £30. Stage, 26ft. back to front; 20ft. wide; height, 18ft. Footlights. Gas and electric light, 230 volts. Terms: One night, £2 15s.; two, £4 5s.; three, £5 5s. Amount of deposit required on booking, £1.

Dates of local fairs.—First Wednesday in March, May, and November. Sites available for circuses.

Early closing, Thursday; market, Wednesday.

MORTLAKE, Surrey.

Population, 7,774. Miles from London, 8.

FREDERIC WIGAN INSTITUTE.—Proprietors, the Trustees; Manager, Mr. E. C. Wigan. Dramatic and music and dancing license. Holds 260. Small stage. Gas. Terms on application.

No market day. Early closing day, Wednesday.

MOTHERWELL, Lanark.

Population, 40,000. Miles from London, 380.

NEW CENTURY THEATRE.—Proprietors, New Century Theatre, Limited; Managing Director, Mr. R. C. Buchanan; Resident Manager, Mr. Arthur Hales. Full license. Holding capacity: Number of persons, 2,000; Amount, £150. Stage measurements: Working depth, 50ft.; width, 50ft.; proscenium opening, 23ft. 6ins.; 30ft. between fly rails. Gas and electric light. Amount of printing required, 1,000 sheets d.c. posting, 800 lithos, 10,000 throwaways, 500 circulars. No regular matinée day. Time of band rehearsal, 1 p.m. All towns barred within a radius of seven miles, for piece or company, six months previous to and after date of visit. This particularly bears upon Hamilton, a town about 2½ miles distant.

TOWN HALL.—Proprietors, The Burgh. Holds about 1,200. Apply to the Janitor.

Shops close one whole day per month, with the exception of November, December, January and February.

Medical Officer.—A.A.: Dr. W. Wyper, Ivy House.

MOUNTAIN ASH, Glam.

Population, 31,093. Miles from London, 200.

WORKMAN'S INSTITUTE, LIBRARY, AND PUBLIC HALL.—Secretary, Mr. Jno. Powell; Caretaker, Mr. Jno. Curnow. Has dramatic license. Holding capacity: Number of persons, 1,000. Depth, 21ft.; opening, 22ft.; height proscenium 21ft. Gas and electric light. Amount of printing required, 400 wall. Sharing terms.

Early closing, Thursday; market, Saturday.

NAILSWORTH, Glos.

Population, 3,028. Miles from London, 115.

SUBSCRIPTION ROOMS.—Manager, Mr. W. E. Hart, The Cross, Nailsworth. Double license. Holding capacity: Number of persons about 350. Proper stage. Lighted by gas. Terms for hiring, 25s. per night. Full payment at time of booking.

Early closing, Thursday; market, last Tuesday in month.

NAIRN, Nairn.

Population, 4,327. Miles from London, 578.

NAIRN PUBLIC HALL.—Manager, Mr. A. Storm, solicitor. Double license. Holding capacity: Number of persons, 500; amount, £40. Only platform , but stage can be quickly supplied and erected by hallkeeper; 10ft. the platform is of use only as a background). Lighted by gas. Terms for hiring: £2 first night; £1 10s. after. Amount of deposit required on booking:Half rent. Best nights, Tuesdays and Thursdays.

Early closing, Wednesday.

NANTWICH, Ches.

Population, 7,722. Miles from London, 161.

TOWN HALL.—Hallkeeper, Mr. Charles Williamson. Double license. Holding capacity: Number of persons licensed for, 800. Stage, 29ft. by 18ft. Lighted by gas. Terms for hiring: £1 10s. first night; £1 5s. others; hallkeeper, 2s. 6d.; to be paid in advance.

Early closing day, Wednesday; market day, Saturday.

NAVAN, Co. Meath

Population, 3,963. Miles from Dublin, 30.

CATHOLIC YOUNG MEN'S SOCIETY'S HALL.—Apply, the Hon. Secretary. Holding capacity: Number of persons, about 400. Stage, 26ft. by 14ft. Lighted by gas. Terms for hiring, £5 for whole week, £1 5s. for first night, and £1 each night for remainder, if less than a week. Amount of deposit required on booking, £1 5s. Prices generally 2s., 1s., and 6d.

Market day, Wednesday.

NEATH, Glam.

Population, 13,720. Miles from London, 204.

GWYN HALL.—Proprietors, the Corporation; Lessee, Mr. J. W. Robinson. The local house for fit-ups etc. Height to flyrail, 16ft. Gas. Printing, 350 sheets. Sharing terms only.

TOWN HALL.—Has dramatic license. Holds 600. Application should be made to the Chief Constable.

Date of fairs are Easter Monday and September 10. The Corporation are the lessees of the ground, where all circuses, etc., put up. Portable theatres are also allowed on the fair ground. A license is usually granted if references are satisfactory. A license was granted in November to Mr. W. Haggar, jun., for his Castle Theatre, seating 1,000, for three months. Population industrial (coal, tin and steel works).

Early closing day, Thursday; market days, Wednesday and Saturday.

NELSON, Lancs.

Population, 39,000. Miles from London, 217.

GRAND THEATRE.—Proprietor, Mrs. T. Greenwood Croft; Manager, Mr. George E. Mudd; Musical Director, Mr. Eli Titherington; Scenic Artist, Mr. Alex. Toole. Full license. Holding capacity: Amount, £90. Stage measurements: Depth, 33ft.; width, 50ft.; proscenium opening, 26ft. Electric light, 230 volts. Printing required, 6f0 sheets wall, 600 d.c. lithos. No regular matinée day. Time of band rehearsal, 1.30 p.m.

Kinematograph Exhibitions are given in the Alhambra Picture Hall (Seats, 900), North Street (Proprietor, Jas. Brown), and Salem School, Scotland Road (Secretary, H. Barrett). Seats 1,250. Both are electrically equipped, direct current, 230 volts.

The local pleasure fair is held in the last week in July, although the annual holidays commence on the last Friday in June and extend over the following week. The second Monday, Tuesday, and Wednesday in September are also holidays.

No portable theatre has visited the town recently.

Circus pitches available are the Corporation Recreation Ground, Carr Road (apply, C.

Greenwood, market superintendent), and spare ground in Brook Street (Jas. Roberts, Phœnix Foundry). Alfresco concerts are held in the Victoria Park during the summer months.

The majority of the population are of the industrial class, being almost entirely engaged in the cotton industry.

Early closing day, Tuesday; market day, Friday.

RECOMMENDED APARTMENTS.

Mrs. Taylor, 64, Clayton Street.—1 sitting-room, 2 bedrooms; bath.

NENAGH, Co. Tipperary.

Population, 4,722. Miles from Dublin, 96.

TOWN HALL.—Town Clerk, Mr. Frank R. Maloney. Holding capacity: Number of persons, 500. Stage depth, 24ft.; width, 39ft. Lighted by acetylene gas. Amount of printing required, 500 bills. Terms for hiring, 30s. first night, 17s. 6d. every other night. Amount of deposit required on booking, £1 10s.

Market days, Thursday and Saturday.

Site for circuses, Court House Paddock.

NEWARK, Notts.

Population, 14,492. Miles from London, 120. Population of district, upwards of 25,000.

CORN EXCHANGE.—Manager and Director, Mr. Richard P. Almond. Music and dancing license. Holding capacity: Number of persons, 1,000. Portable stage. Lighted by gas (charged as meter: about 5s. per night). Terms for hiring: One night, £2; two nights, £2 15s.; three nights, £3 15s.; six nights, £5 5s. Day performances, 5s. extra per time. Amount of deposit required on booking, £1.

Newark is the most important corn market in the Midlands, and the largest malting centre in the country.

Fairs.—Pleasure, May 14 and 15; hiring, November 23; horse, November 1.

Industries. — Extensive maltings, breweries, engineering, plaster and cement, foundries, chemical, clothing, corset, basket, and other factories.

Early closing day, Thursday; market days: Wednesday, corn and cattle; Saturday, general produce.

NEW BARNET, Herts.

Population, 7,876. Miles from London, 10.

ASSEMBLY ROOMS. — Proprietor, Mr. E. Fergusson Taylor, New Barnet Auction and Estate Offices. Music and dancing license. Holding capacity: Number of persons, 300. Small stage. Lighted by gas. Terms for hiring: Two guineas per night. Amount of deposit required on booking: 25 per cent.

Barnet Fair, Sept. 2, 3, and 4.

Early closing, Thursday; market, Wednesday.

NEW BRIGHTON, Ches.

Population, 10,000. Miles from London, 199.

PALACE THEATRE. — Proprietor, Messrs. Leaver and Bennett; Manager, Mr. Percy E. Penney. Music and dancing license. Holding capacity: Number of persons, 1,500; amount, £30. Stage measurements: Width, 30ft.; depth, 30ft. Proscenium, 18ft. Electric light. Band rehearsal, 12 noon. Usual matinée day, Saturday.

TOWER GRAND THEATRE. — Proprietors, The New Brighton Tower and Recreation Co., Limited; Secretary and Manager, Mr. R. H. Davy. License: Restricted dramatic, and music, singing, and dancing. Holding capacity: Number of persons, 3,500; amount varies. Stage measurements: Width, 65ft. (60ft. workable); depth, 59ft. 6in. Proscenium: Width of opening, 34ft. 7in.; height, stage to top of opening, 27ft.; stage to grid, 54ft. 6in.; stage to flies, 28ft. Electric light. Daily matinées. Time of band rehearsal, 12 noon.

WINTER GARDENS.—Proprietors, Messrs. H. E. Jones and Albert Douglass. Double license. Holds 1,100 at £38. Stage, 20ft. deep by 35ft. wide. Pros. opening, 22ft. Electric, 100 volts. Large amount of printing not required.

PIER PAVILION.—Proprietors, The New Brighton Pier Co.: Lessees, Messrs. Adeler and Sutton; Manager, Mr. W. G. Sutton; Acting-Manager, Mr. R. Frank Parker. Dramatic license. Holding capacity: Number of persons, 1,800; amount, £35 (at 6d. and 3d.). No proscenium. Concert platform. Electric light (alternating). Amount of printing required: 50 6's, 250 daybills. Usual matinée day, Saturday (summer, every day except Sundays). Best period of the year, March to November.

Early closing day, Monday.

Agent.—V.A.F.: Mrs. Roberts, New Brighton Hotel, Victoria Road.

NEW BROMPTON (Gillingham), Kent.

Population, 41,441. Miles from London, 31.

PUBLIC HALL.—Manager, Mr. George West, 107, Jeffery Street. Double license. Holding capacity: Number of persons, main hall 445, gallery 60. Stage, 28ft. by 10ft. 9in.; can be extended 5ft.; by opening revolving shutters, the Minor Hall becomes the stage also. Electric light alternating, 100 volts. Terms for hiring: Concert, £1; theatrical, £1 5s. one night; if more than one night, £1 per night. Special terms for six nights or more. Amount of deposit required on booking, £1.

Early closing, Wednesday; no market.

NEWBURY, Berks.

Population, 11,061. Miles from London, 53.

TOWN HALL.—Proprietors, The Corporation. Is out of repair, and will probably shortly be pulled down.

CORN EXCHANGE.—Secretary and Manager, Mr. Henry Pratt. Has dramatic license. Holding capacity: Number of persons, 1,500. Stage, 35ft. by 26ft.; no proscenium. Lighted by gas. Terms for hiring: Theatricals, £2 first night, £1 subsequent nights; other purposes, £2 10s. first night, 25s. subsequent nights; gas extra. Amount of deposit required on booking: Half. Has electric current for projecting pictures; direct current, 480 volts.

ODDFELLOWS' HALL.—Secretary, Mr. Henry Pratt. No dramatic license. Holding capacity: Number of persons, 300. Stage, 24ft. by 16ft.; no proscenium. Lighted by gas. Terms for hiring: 25s. first night, 12s. 6d. subsequent nights; gas extra. Amount of deposit required on booking: 20s.

Dates of local fairs: Sept. 4 and 5, first Thursday after Oct. 11.

Early closing, Wednesday; market, Thursday.

NEWCASTLE-ON-TYNE, Northd.

Population, 215,328. Miles from London, 275.

THEATRE ROYAL.—Proprietors, the Robert Arthur Theatres Co., Limited; Managing Director, Mr. Robert Arthur; Acting-Manager, Mr. F. Teale Lingham. Full license. Holding capacity: Number of persons, about 3,000. Stage measurements: Depth, 38ft.; proscenium opening, 30ft.; stage to grid, 58ft.; fly rail to fly rail, 33ft.; width, 53ft. Electric light. Usual matinée day, Saturday. Time of band rehearsal, 10.30 a.m.

TYNE THEATRE. —Lessees, Howard and Wyndham, Limited; Managing Director, Mr. F. W. Wyndham; Acting-Manager, Mr. Fred C. Sutcliffe. Full license. Musical Director, Mr. E. J. Rogers.

GRAND THEATRE.—Lessee, Mr. F. W. Bolam; General Manager, Mr. R. G. Elder; Acting Manager, Mr. H. Chadwick; Musical Director, Mr. Wm. Denham. Full license. Holding capacity: Number of persons, 3,000; amount, £150. Stage measurements: Depth, 50ft.; width, 50ft.; proscenium opening, 28ft. Usual matinée day, Saturday. Time of band rehearsal, 1 p.m.

EMPIRE PALACE THEATRE.—Proprietors, Moss's Empires, Limited; Manager, Mr. Oswald Stoll; Acting-Manager, Mr. Walter P. Wells. Booking circuit, Moss and Stoll. Musical Director, Mr. J. W. Dawson. Electric light. Time of band rehearsal, 2 p.m. Usual matinée day, Saturday.

Bars all other Managements' Halls in Newcastle and the following towns: Monkseaton, Whitley Bay, Cullercoats, Tynemouth, North Shields, Chester-le-Street, Gateshead, Wallsend, Hebburn, Jarrow, Walker and Heaton.

PAVILION MUSIC HALL. — Proprietors, Pavilion (Newcastle-upon-Tyne), Limited; Manager, Mr. W. H. Boardman; Booking Circuit, Barrasford Tour; Musical Director, Mr. H. Elliott Smith; Stage Manager, Mr. Albert Plimmer. Double license. Electric light. Time of band rehearsal, 12 noon. Usual matinée day, Tuesday. Bars the Empire, Newcastle, and King's, Gateshead.

CONCERT HALL, TOWN HALL.—Manager, Mr. F. H. Holford, City Property Surveyor to Newcastle-upon-Tyne Corporation. Music and dancing license. Holding capacity: Number of persons, 2,000. Platform only, with orchestra. Hall, 124ft. long, 68ft. wide; platform, 29ft. by 15ft. Electric light. Terms for hiring: From £8 8s. to £11 11s. per day. Amount of deposit required on booking: 20 per cent.

LOVAINE HALL.—Secretary, Mr. Herbert Shaw. Music and dancing license; dramatic easily obtained. Holding capacity: Number of persons, about 800. Electric light. Terms for hiring: Two guineas to three guineas.

CORDWAINERS' HALL (Nelson Street).—Manager, Mr. Frank Keegan. Music and dancing license. Holding capacity: Number of persons, 250. No proper stage. Gas and electric light. Terms for hiring on application. Amount of deposit required on booking: £1.

STAR PICTURE PALACE. — Proprietress, Miss Audrey Appleby, U.S.A. Animated Picture Co. Music and dancing license. Holds 1,000. Electric light.

Early closing day, Wednesday; market day, Saturday.

Medical Officers.—A.A.: Dr. W. E. Alderson, 5, Eldon Square; Dr. J. Stanley Manford, 1, Osborne Terrace; Dr. Geo. Robinson, 21, Northumberland Court, Blackett Street. A.U.: Dr. Alderson and Dr. Manford. M.H.A.R.A.: Dr. Manford.

Agents.—M.H.A.R.A.: C. Campbell, Tyne Theatre Buffet. A.U.: C. Campbell, Bridge Hotel. V.A.F.: Mr. Pepper, Crown Hotel, Clayton Street West.

NEWCASTLE-UNDER-LYME, Staffs.

Population, 19,914. Miles from London, 147.

PALACE THEATRE.

Early closing day, Thursday; market days, Monday and Saturday.

NEWHAVEN, Sussex.

Population, 6,772. Miles from London, 55.

DRILL HALL.—Apply, the Company Sergeant-Major of the 1st Sussex R.V. Has dramatic license and holds about 500.

The town is visited by portables, and there appears to be no difficulty in obtaining the necessary license. Sites are easily obtainable for alfresco concerts, circus pitches, etc. There is no local fair. The population is entirely industrial, a large proportion consisting of men in the employ of the London, Brighton, and South Coast Railway, in connection with their cross-Channel service to Dieppe. About 200 soldiers of the R.G.A. No. 1 Depôt are stationed in the fort. There is a late train back from Brighton Wednesday nights to enable the inhabitants to visit places of amusement there.

Early closing day, Wednesday.

NEW HUNSTANTON, Norfolk.

Population, 3,006. Miles from London, 112.

TOWN HALL.—Proprietors, Urban District Council. Manager, Mr. Jas. C. Walker. Double license. Holding capacity: Number of persons, 540. Stage measurements: Footlights to back, 23ft. 6in.; behind curtain, 18ft. by 26ft. 9in. wide; ceiling, 16ft. high; proscenium, 20ft. 3in. wide. Lighted by gas; 3s. 9d. per 1,000ft. extra. Terms for hiring: Dramatic, 60s. first night, 50s. second, 40s. third; concerts, 40s., 30s., 20s. Amount of deposit required on booking: 20s.

No local fairs, no early closing.

Field for portables and circuses on main road. Messrs. R. G. Callaby and Sons.

NEWMARKET, Cambs.

Population, 10,688. Miles from London, 72.

VICTORIA HALL.—Apply the Manager. Dramatic license.

TOWN HALL.—Proprietors, the Urban District Council. Apply the Town Clerk. Gas. Terms, £1 5s. per day, and 5s. for fireman. Full amount on booking.

Sites for portables, alfresco concerts, apply the Council.

Early closing, Thursday; market, Tuesday.

NEWPORT, Isle of Wight.

Population, 10,911. Miles from London, 88.

MEDINA HALL.—Manager, Mr. A. J. Salter. Double license. Holding capacity: Number of persons, 500 seats. Stage, 17ft. 6in. high by 30ft. by 20ft.; opening, 18ft. Lighted by gas; electric laid on for picture shows. Amount of printing required: 20 6-sheet, 6 12-sheet, 50 lithos, 50 d.c., 500 d. bills, etc. Terms by arrangement. Electric current, 240 volts continuous.

Early closing, Thursday; markets, Tuesday and Saturday.

NEWPORT, Mon.

Population, 77,000. Miles from London, 151
LYCEUM THEATRE.—Proprietor, Mr. Clarence Sounes; Lessee and Manager, Mr. Sidney Cooper; Musical Director, Mr. Harry Bull; Scenic Artist, Mr. William D. Hobbs. Full license. Holding capacity: Number of persons, 2,600; amount, ordinary prices, £150; star prices, £200. Depth of stage, 40ft.; proscenium measurements, 30ft. by 26ft. Gas and electric light. 100 vo 1s alternating. Printing: 1,000 she· ts. Usual matinée day, Saturday. Time of band rehearsal, 1 o'clock.

EMPIRE THEATRE.—Proprietors, Moss's Empires, Limited; Managing Director, Mr Oswald Stoll; District Manager, Mr. Albert Mitchell; Manager, Major J. W. Gallagher. Music and dancing license. Time of band rehearsal, 3 p.m. Electric current, 100 volts direct and alternating.

Bars all other Managements' Halls in Newport and the following towns : Usk, Pontypool, Caerleon, Risca, and Llanwern.

TREDEGAR HALL.—Secretary, Mr. E. Maples Linton, Westgate Chambers. Music and dancing license. Holding capacity: Number of persons, 1,200. Gas. Electric by arrangement. Terms: £18 18s. per week. Amount of deposit required on booking, one-third.

GREAT CENTRAL HALL. — Available for concerts only on occasional dates. Lighted by electricity, 230 volts and 460 volts d.c. Seats, 1,700.

TEMPERANCE HALL.—Available for concerts and entertainments. Lighted by electricity. 100 volts alternating. Seats 800.

Early closing day, Thursday; market days, Wednesday and Saturday.

Medical officers.—A.A.: Dr. Crinks, Stow Hill; Dr. O. W. Morgan, Ventnor House, Clytha Park. M.H.A.R.A.: Dr. J. Neville, 179, Commercial Road, and Dr. Crinks.

Agent.—M.H.A.R.A.: W. H. Beer, Hare and Greyhound Hotel, Commercial Street. V.A.F.: The same.

NEWPORT PAGNELL.

Population, 4,028. Miles from London. 56.
TOWN HALL.—Apply to the Secretary. Double license. Seats 350. Stage, 18ft. by 18ft. Gas. Terms: £1 5s. for first night, £1 1s. the second.

MASONIC HALL.—Has no dramatic license. Apply, the Secretary, Mr. Arthur J. Simpson. Local fair June 21.

NEWPORT, Salop.

Population, 3,241. Miles from London, 147
TOWN HALL.—Manager, Mr. W. D. Keight. Has dramatic license. Holding capacity: Number of persons about 400. Stage, 14ft. by 24ft. Lighted by gas. Terms for hiring: £1 per night; £2 10s. for three; £5 per week. Amount of deposit required on booking, half booking.

Early closing, Thursday; market, Friday.

NEWQUAY, Cornwall.

Population, 4,000. Miles from London, 297.
VICTORIA HALL.—Proprietor, Mr. William Huxtable. license. Full Holding capacity: Number of persons, 700. Stage measurements, 17ft. by 17ft. Electric light, 230 volts continuous. This current cannot be used for kinematograph entertainments. Terms for hiring: One night, £2 2s.; special terms for longer hiring. Amount of deposit required on booking, £1.

Early closing day, Wednesday.

NEWRY, Co. Down.

Population, 12,587. Miles from Dublin, 75.
TOWN HALL.—Manager, Mr. John Hamilton. Platform measurements, 43ft. by 16ft.; two dressing-rooms. Gas only. Terms for hiring: Body of hall, one night, £1 10s., with balcony, £1 1s. extra. Caretakers' fees, 5s. per night; gas extra. Applications should be addressed to the Town Clerk. Newry.

The old Town Hall is not let for hire. It is now used as a technical school and free public library.

Early closing day, Wednesday; market days, Tuesday, Thursday, and Saturday.

NEW SHOREHAM, Sussex.

TOWN HALL.—Proprietors, Urban District Council; Manager, the Clerk. No license. Holding capacity: Number of persons, 200. Ordinary platform. Gas. Terms of hiring, £1 1s. per evening, paid in advance. No local fairs.

NEWTON ABBOT, Devon.

Population, 13,000. Miles from London, 109.
ALEXANDRA HALL.—Manager, Mr. P. J. Major. Full license. Holding capacity: Number of persons, about 500; amount, £30 to £40. Proper stage. Height to flies, 16ft.; stage, 36ft. by 22ft., including proscenium. Electric light on stage, gas in hall. Terms for hiring: One night, £2 10s.; two nights, £4 10s.; three nights, £6 6s.; six nights, £10. Amount of deposit required on booking, 25 per cent.

Market day, Wednesday; early closing, Thursday. Industries, G.W.R. locomotive works, potteries, tanneries, and agriculture. Fair day, first Wednesday after Sept. 11.

NEWTOWN, Mont.

Population, 6,500. Miles from London, 175.
PUBLIC HALL.—Manager, Mr. John Bennett. Has dramatic license. Holding capacity: Number of persons, 900. Stage, 24ft. deep, 39 ft. wide, 22ft. proscenium opening. Lighted by gas. Amount of printing required: 150 sheets. Terms for hiring: Share with managers; rental, one night £2 2s., two nights £3 10s., gas extra. Amount of deposit required on booking: £1. Best nights end of week.

VICTORIA HALL.—Manager, Mr. Ernest C. Morgan. Dramatic license. Holding capacity: Number of persons, 1,000. Stage, with fit-up and stock scenery. Permanent platform, 36ft. 6in. by 17ft. Lighted by gas. Sharing, or rental (one night), including gas and hall-keeper's fee, 42s.; a reduction made for longer period. Amount of deposit required on booking, 10s. Convenient dressing-rooms, good gallery.

The town is seldom visited by portables. Good sites for alfresco concerts and circus pitches are easily obtainable.

Early closing day, Thursday; market day, Tuesday.

NORMANTON, Yorks.

Population, 12,352. Miles from London, 179.
ASSEMBLY ROOMS. — Mr. H. Gooder. Double license. Holding capacity: Number of persons, 600. Proper stage. Stage: 22ft. by 30ft. and fly, 14ft. cloth. Lighted by gas. Amount of deposit required on booking: £1 and £2 for three days and week respectively. Stock scenery.

Early closing day, Wednesday; market day, Saturday.

NORTHAMPTON, Northants.

Population, 95,000. Miles from London, 67.

OPERA HOUSE. — Resident Manager, Mr. W. E. Barnett.

PALACE THEATRE.—Proprietor and Director, Mr. Fred H. Anderson; Resident Manager, Mr. Thos. A. Evans; Musical Director, Mr. Walter Ashton. Electric light. Time of band rehearsal, 12 noon.

GUILDHALL.—Proprietors, the Corporation. Apply, the Town Clerk, Guildhall, Northampton. Music and dancing license. Holding capacity: Number of persons, 560. Stage, 56ft. 5in. at front and 23ft. 10in. at back, and depth 19ft. 7in. Electric light direct, 210 volts. Terms from £2 2s. Also Lower Assembly Room, 56ft. by 29ft., seats 240; Upper Assembly Room, 56ft. by 29ft., seats 240.

CORN EXCHANGE, The Parade. — Proprietors, The Corn Exchange Co.; Secretary, Mr. C. A. Markham; Solicitor, Guildhall Road. Apply to Cap'ain Goasher. 83, Sheep Street. Holds 2,000. Electric light.

TEMPERANCE HALL, Newland. — Proprietors, The Temperance Hall Co.; Secretary, Mr. G. Skempton, 7, Holly Road. Holds 800. Electric light.

Fair ground, cattle market.

Early closing day, Thursday; market days, Wednesday and Saturday.

Agent.—M.H.A.R.A.; V.A.F. and A.U., W. Warren, North Western Hotel, Tharelair.

RECOMMENDED APARTMENTS.

Mrs. Simpson.—Sitting, 2 bedrooms, 3 beds, 2 combined rooms.

NORTH WALSHAM, Norfolk.

Population, 3,981. Miles from London, 129.

PUBLIC HALL (formerly Corn Hall).—Manager, Mr. James Henry Reeve. Dramatic license, obtainable when required, 5s. Holding capacity: Number of persons, 500. Stage, 14ft. by 24ft.; ceiling, 14ft. from stage. Terms for hiring: 21s. each night, six nights £5, and 2s. 6d. per night extra for custodian. Amount of deposit required on booking: 20s. The only public building of the kind available in the town.

Early closing, Wednesday; market, Thursday.

NORTHWICH, Ches.

Population, 19,500. Miles from London, 171.

CENTRAL THEATRE.—Proprietress, Mrs. S. Golden; Secretary, Miss E. Golden. Holds 1,000. Stage, 25ft. by 22ft. Gas.

PAVILION.—Proprietress Mrs. P. E. Fletcher; Manager, Mr. Towyn Thomas; Assistant Manager, Mr. Reginald Fletcher. Holds 600. Stage, 32ft. by 18ft. Electric light, direct current.

DRILL HALL.—Manager, Mr. Frank A. Cowley. Double license. Holding capacity: Number of persons, 500; amount, £20. Stage, 30ft. by 9ft.; no scenery. Lighted by gas.

The population is mainly industrial. The chief occupations of the people are salt and chemical manufactures. Messrs. Brunner, Mond, and Co.'s works rank amongst the largest chemical works in the world and 5,000 hands are employed. Some boat-building is also carried on. In the surrounding neighbourhood the people are engaged in agriculture.

There are many visitors to the town for the brine baths. Of late years portables have not visited the town, but licenses were formerly granted. Sites for alfresco concerts and pitches for circuses are easily obtainable. There is a large field adjoining the Drill Hall available for these purposes.

Early closing day, Wednesday; market day, Friday.

NORWICH, Norfolk.

Population, 120,733. Miles from London, 114.

THEATRE ROYAL.—Proprietor and Manager, Mr. Fred Morgan; Acting-Manager, Mr. Lewis Morgan; Musical Director, Mr. Victor Storr; Scenic Artist, Mr. George Shine. Fully licensed. Holding capacity: Number of persons, 1,500; amount, £90. Stage measurements: Proscenium opening, 26ft.; depth, 40ft.; width, 48ft.; stage to grid, 28ft.; between fly floors, 30ft.; stage to fly floors, 29ft. Electric light. Amount of printing required, 800 sheets. Usual matinée day, Saturday, at 2.30. Time of band rehearsal, 12.30.

HIPPODROME.—Proprietor, Mr. E. H. Bostock; Acting-Manager, Councillor F. W. Fitt; Booking Circuit, Bostock Tour; Musical Director, Mr. Vincent White. Full theatrical license. Holding capacity: Number of persons, 2,000. Stage measurements: Opening, 30ft.; depth, 50ft. width, 76ft. Gas and electric light. Time of band rehearsal, 2 p.m. Usual matinée day, Saturday. Bars Norwich only.

ASSEMBLY ROOM, AGRICULTURAL HALL.—Manager, Mr. F. E. Hunter. Double license. Holding capacity: Number of persons, about 1,000. Stage: 18ft. deep, 24ft. 6in. wide, 17ft. high. Gas and electric light. Early closing day, Thursday; market day, Saturday.

Medical Officers.—M.H.A.R.A.: Dr. D. L. Thomas, 15, Willow Lane, and Dr. Bremmer, 18, St. Giles Street.

Agent.—M.H.A.R.A.: R. J. Mallett, Opera House Hotel.

RECOMMENDED APARTMENTS.

Mrs. E. Lydamore, 79, Grove Road.—2 large, 1 small bedrooms, 2 sitting rooms; bath; piano.

NOTTINGHAM, Notts.

Population, 239,743. Miles from London, 125.

THEATRE ROYAL. — Proprietors, Robert Arthur Theatres Co., Limited; Managing Director, Mr. Robert Arthur; Acting-Manager, Mr. Howard Finney; Musical Director, Mr. John Armstrong; Scenic Artist, Mr. J. Fowler Hogg. Full dramatic license. Holding capacity: Number of persons, 3,000; amount, £250. Stage: 60ft. by 60ft.; proscenium opening, 31ft. by 30 t. Gas and electric light, 200 volts. Printing: 1,600 sheets, with 1,250 lithos. Usual matinée day, Saturday, at 2. Band rehearsal, 11 a.m.

GRAND THEATRE.—Proprietors, Grand Theatre and Estates Co., Limited; Manager, Mr. Harry Upton; Musical Director, Mr. Richard Harrington; Scenic Artist, Mr. A. H. Ross. Full license. Holding capacity: Number of persons, 3,500. Stage measurements: Depth, 85ft.; width, 62ft.; opening 27ft. Gas and electric light. Usual matinée day, Saturday. Time of band rehearsal, 1 o'clock.

KING'S THEATRE.—Managing Director. Mr. Frank McNaghton; Resident Manager, Edgar O. Waller; Musical Director, Mr. Robert Chamberlain. Double license. Holding capacity about 1,500. Gas and electric light. Band rehearsal, 1 p.m.

EMPIRE.—Proprietors, Moss's Empires; District Manager, Mr. Hatton Wharton; Resident Manager, Mr. Albert C. Duncan; Book-

ing Circuit, Midland; Musical Director, Mr.
H. Hulett. Double license. Holding capacity:
Number of persons, 2,500. Stage measurements, 30 ft. deep, 59ft. 9ins. wall to wall;
proscenium opening, 29ft. 3ins. Gas and electric light. Time of band rehearsal, 1 p.m.
Matinée on Boxing Day only. Bars as per
Arbitrator's award.

Bars all other Managements' Halls in Nottingham and the following towns: Long Eaton and
Ilkeston.

ROYAL HIPPODROME.—Proprietors, The
Nottingham Hippodrome Company, Limited.
Managing Director, Mr. Thomas Barrasford;
Resident Manager, Mr. E. Lockwood; Musical
Director, Mr. A. Read. Music and dancing license.
Holding capacity, 3,500. Gas and electric lighting. No license to sell intoxicants. Opened in
September, 1908.

CENTRAL HALL.—Manager, Mr. A. Hindley, Clumber Street. Music and dancing
license. Holding capacity: Number of persons,
500. No stage. Gas and electric light. Terms
for hiring, 25s. to 33s. 6d., upwards. Amount
of deposit required on booking, 25 per cent.

The local Goose Fair, one of the oldest in
the country and one of the very few permitted
to be held in the Great Market Place, is held
the first Thursday in October and the two
following days.

Portable theatres are permitted in the city
on pieces of waste ground in the suburbs of
the Market Place and in Bulwell Market
Place, also situated in the borough, and there
is no difficulty as to licenses. As a rule, they
only visit the town a few days at a time,
Alfresco concerts are given by pierrot troupes
at Colwick Park, a favourite spot a mile
down the Trent, and there is no difficulty in
obtaining circus pitches within a mile of the
centre of the town; in fact, Buffalo Bill and
Sanger's Circus pay regular visits when touring.
The local population is both residential and
industrial, the latter consisting of lace-makers,
hosiery hands, miners, ironworkers, and railway
employees.

The Great Market Place is always occupied
a couple of days at Easter and Whitsuntide
by kinematograph shows, swings, shooting
galleries, roundabouts, etc., on a scale that
almost equals the carnival week Goose Fair.
The surrounding places near Nottingham,
varying from 10,000 to 5,000 inhabitants,
hold their local feasts or wakes in the period
four or five weeks preceding and following
Goose Fair, and these are well patronised,
especially at Arnold, Basford, and Sulwell,
the two latter being in the borough.

Early closing day, Thursday; market days,
Wednesday and Saturday.

Medical Officers. A.A.: Dr. A. Charlton,
Glendarrock, Lenton: Dr. S. E. Gill, 96, Mansfield Road. A U.:Dr. R. Alderson, Queen's
Walk; and Dr. Charlton. M.H.A.R.A.: Drs.
C. and H. Vernon-Taylor, 11, East Circus Street.

Agents. M.H.A.R.A.: J. Upton, Empire
Theatre. A.U.: A. Kelsall, Three Crowns Inn,
Parliament Street. V.A.F.: The same.

RECOMMENDED APARTMENTS.

Mrs. L. Turton.—2 sitting, 3 bedrooms, 4 beds;
bath; pianos.

NUNEATON, Warwickshire.

Population, 30,000. Miles from London, 97.

PRINCE OF WALES'S THEATRE.—Proprietors, Nuneaton Theatre Co., Limited; Managing Director, Mr. A. F. Cross; Acting-Manager, Mr. Joseph Coyle; Musical Director, Mr.
Herbert Barnes. Double license. Holding capacity: Number of persons, 3,000; amount,

£135. Gas and electric light, 220 volts. Band
rehearsal, 2 o'clock. Usual matinée day,
Saturday. Bars no surrounding halls more than
five miles away.

ASSEMBLY ROOMS. — Has no dramatic
license. Holds 600. Proprietors, The Conservative Club. Apply, the Secretary.

Early closing day, Thursday; market day,
Saturday.

Medical Officer.—A.A.: Dr. A. Joseph, The
Rocklands, Church Street; A.U.: The same.

OAKENGATES, Salop.

Population, 10,906. Miles from London, 152.

TOWN HALL.—Proprietors, the Oakengates
Town and Market Hall Co.; Manager, Mr. J.
H. Herbert, Lion Street. Music and dancing
license. Holding capacity: Number of persons,
400 to 500. Small stage. Gas. District large
rural one. Terms for hiring, £1 1s. per night;
special terms for seven nights. Amount of deposit required on booking, 10s. 6d, to £1 1s.

Date of local fair, first week in September.
Owen's Field, ground at rear of Wagon Hotel,
available for portables, alfresco concerts, and
circuses.

Early closing day, Thursday; market day,
Saturday.

OAKHAM, Rutland.

Population, 3,293. Miles from London, 94.

VICTORIA HALL.—Manager, Mr. J. E.
Whitehouse. Dramatic license. Holding capacity: Number of persons, 400. Stage, 30ft.
wide, 16ft. deep; no scenery. Lighted by gas.
Terms for hiring: 20s. first night, gas and fire
extra. Amount of deposit required on booking: 10s. Rebuilt in 1902.

Early closing day, Thursday; market day,
Monday.

OLDBURY, Worcs.

Population, 25,191. Miles from London, 119.

THE PALACE.

Agent.—M.H.A.R.A.: T. H. Garbett, "Old
Talbot," Market Place. V.A.F.: The same.

Early closing day, Thursday; market day,
Saturday.

OLDHAM.

Population, 137,246. Miles from London, 193.

GRAND THEATRE AND OPERA HOUSE.—
Proprietors, Oldham Empire Theatre of Varieties,
Limited; Manager, Mr. E. Dottridge; Acting
Manager, Mr. S. Mayall; Musical Director, Mr.
J. H. Halkyard. Holding capacity, 1,850 seated.
Prices of seats, 3s. to 4d. (gallery). Depth of
stage, 45 ft.; width, 73 ft.; proscenium, 32 ft. 6 in.
wide. Dressing rooms, 16.

COLOSSEUM.—Proprietors, the Colosseum
Co., Limited; Manager, Mr. Wm. Eastwood;
Musical Director, Mr. H. Sedgwick. Full
license. Holding capacity: Number of persons,
3,000; amount, £120. Stage measurements:
36ft. deep, 75ft. wide, 30ft. opening. Electric
light. Time of band rehearsal, 12.30 p.m.

EMPIRE THEATRE.—Proprietors, the Empire Theatre of Varieties Co., Limited; Manager, Mr. Ernest Dottridge; Acting-Manager,
Mr. J. Hulme; Musical Director, Mr. Halkyard. Dramatic and musical license. Holding
capacity: Number of persons, 4,000; amount,
£200. Electric light. Time of band rehearsal,
12 noon. No regular matinée day. Bars no
surrounding halls.

HIPPODROME.—Proprietors, Oldham Empire Theatre of Varieties Co., Limited; General Manager, Mr. Ernest Dottridge; Acting-Manager, Mr. J. Nuttall.

ROYAL THEATRE.—Proprietors, the Empire Theatre of Varieties Co., Limited; Manager, Mr. Ernest Dottridge; Acting-Manager, Mr. Harry Kilrow; Musical Director, Mr. Fred Eplett; Scenic Artist, Mr. H. O. Richardson. Full license. Holding capacity: Number of persons, 3,000. Gas and electric light. Usual matinée day, Tuesday. Time of band rehearsal 1 p.m. Performance twice nightly.

PALACE. — Proprietors, Palace, Oldham, Limited; Managing Director, Mr. Walter de Frece; Licensee and Manager, Mr. Fred Thorne; Assistant Manager, Mr. Edmund Sharrocks.

UNITY HALL.—Secretary, Mr. E. Lionel Blakes. Music and dancing license. Holding capacity: Number of persons, 1,200. Proper stage. Gas and electric light. Terms for hiring, £19 weekly. Amount of deposit required on booking, £5.

TEMPERANCE HALL, Horsedge Street.— Manager, Mr. Harry H. Hall. Music and dancing license. Holding capacity: Number of persons, 600. Platform, 39ft. by 11ft. Lighted by gas (incandescent). Terms for hiring: Kinematograph entertainments, one night, £1 5s., including piano; six nights, £6 6s. Electric current, 26 amps. 210 volts., extra. Lectures, 12s.; other entertainments, 16s. per performance. Amount of deposit required on booking, half.

OLDHAM INDUSTRIAL CO-OPERATIVE HALL, King-Street.—Apply the Secretary. Size of hall, 74ft. by 54ft. Holding capacity: Number of persons, 1,000. Terms for hiring, £2 10s. per night.

CENTRAL HALL, Henshaw Street.—Managing Director, Mr. W. Turner; Manager, Mr. E. Percival. Electric light. Holds 700. Picture and variety.

OLDHAM, EQUITABLE CO-OPERATIVE HALL, Huddersfield Road.

THE CENTRAL HALL, Henshaw Street.—At present let for Kinematograph entertainments. Owners of the building, Oldham Temperance Society, Henshaw Street.

Oldham is 6½ miles from Manchester. The local population is purely industrial, principally iron workers and cotton operatives. The operatives distribute amongst themselves about £200,000 every annual holiday. The principal local fair is Oldham Wake, which is held on the last Saturday in August. A monster fair is held, which is visited by all the principal shows in the kingdom. No difficulty is experienced in getting space, which is the property of the Corporation, although there is great demand for same. The town itself is not generally visited by portables, and probably a difficulty would be experienced in getting a license. Some of the outskirts of the town might, however, be visited with advantage, such as Shaw, Royton, and Uppermill.

Dates of local fairs: Easter, Whit Friday, Saturday, and Trinity Monday; also last Saturday in August and seven days following.

Early closing day, Tuesday; market days, Monday and Saturday.

Medical Officers.—A.A.: Dr. T. J. Carson, 117, Union Street. A.U. and M.H.A.R.A.: The same.

Agents.—M.H.A.R.A.: T. Byrne, Shakespeare Hotel. A.U.: The same. V.A.F.: The same.

RECOMMENDED APARTMENTS.

Mrs. Palmer, 58, Marlborough Street.—2 bedrooms, 1 sitting-room, combined bath.

OMAGH, Co. Tyrone.

Population, 4,039. Miles from Dublin, 142.

ROYAL ASSEMBLY HALL.—Owner, Mr John B. R. Porter. Holding capacity: Number of persons, 600. Platform. 17ft. by 25ft. Lighted by gas. Terms for hiring: £1 10s. first night, subject to nightly reduction for longer term. Amount of deposit required on booking: Half.

Local fairs: First Tuesday, monthly.

For circus sites apply to Recreation Grounds Committee.

OSSETT, Yorks.

Population, 12,903. Miles from London, 178.

TOWN HALL.—Proprietors, Ossett Corporation; Manager, Mr. I. Willett. Dramatic and music and dancing licenses. Holding capacity: Number of persons, 1,200. Large platform, 46ft. by 24ft. Gas. Terms of hiring, three guineas per night, with reduction for two or more nights. Amount of deposit required on booking, half fees. New building, with beautiful balcony, plush seats, numbered.

Local fair, Trinity Monday.

Early closing day, Tuesday; market day, Friday.

OSWALDTWISTLE, Lancs.

Population, 15,000. Miles from London, 207.

TOWN HALL.—Manager, Mr. C. H. Ogden. Double license. Holding capacity: Number of persons, over 1,000. Large ordinary platform. Lighted by gas. Terms for hiring: According to class of entertainment. Amount of deposit required on booking: £1.

Oswaldtwistle is close to Accrington.

OSWESTRY, Salop.

Population, 10,000. Miles from London, 183.

PUBLIC HALL.—Proprietors, Public Hall Co. Manager, R. A. Andrews. Dramatic license. Holds 600 to 700. Platform, 18ft. by 19ft. Can be extended.

VICTORIA ROOMS.—Manager, Mr. Wallace Ollerhead. Double license. Holding capacity: Number of persons, 600 to 700; has taken £62 for one night. Bare stage; depth, 18ft.; width, 26ft. 7in.: no fit-up or proscenium. Lighted by gas. Amount of printing required: 170 d.c.: 50 d.c. for windows, and about 60 d.b. Terms for hiring: One night, £2 7s. 6d.; two nights, £4; three nights, £5 5s. Amount of deposit required on booking: £1, or £2 if taken for a week.

There are two annual local pleasure fairs, one held on the first Wednesday in March and the other on the first Wednesday in May; both are well patronised by the townspeople and the country districts around. These would be fatal nights for a company to come here, as the fairs are kept up to a late hour. The town is visited by portables, but at long intervals. There is no difficulty in obtaining a license from the local authorities if the company are respectable. There are three sites for circus pitches, the one most used being the Public Recreation Ground. The local population is partly residential and partly industrial and agricultural. The chief industry is the Cambrian Railway Works, the line and head offices and the Great Western Railway employing together about 800 men.

There are also a fairly big brewery, two tanneries, and several builders' yards.

Early closing, Thursday; markets, Wednesday and Saturday.

RECOMMENDED APARTMENTS.

Mrs. M. Benbow.—3 bedrooms and 1 sitting-room; bath.

OUNDLE, Northants.

Population, 2,404. Miles from London, 73.

QUEEN VICTORIA HALL.—Secretary, Mr. Robert Knight. Dramatic license. Holding capacity: Number of persons, 500. Stage, 13ft. 6in. by 31ft. 6in.; no proscenium. Lighted by gas. Terms for hiring: £2 2s. first night, £1 11s. 6d. second and subsequent. Amount of deposit required on booking: One guinea.

Early closing, Wednesday; market, Thursday.

OXFORD, Oxon.

Population, 53,000: Term, 56,000; with outer suburbs, 60,000. Miles from Paddington, 63½.

Stations, G.W.R. & G. Central, L. & N.W.R. Week-end Tickets, Padding on to Oxford, 8s.; Oxford to Paddington, 6s. 3d.*

M.P., Viscount Valentia, C.B., M.V.O., J.P., Bletchington Park, Oxon, and Carlton Club.

Vice-Chancellor, The President of Magdalen College.

Mayor, E. A. Bevers, Esq., L.R.C.P., M.R.C.S., 46, Broad Street.

Town Clerk, R. Bacon, Esq.. Town Hall.

Chief Constable, Oswald Cole, Esq.

THE NEW THEATRE, George Street.—Proprietors The Oxford Theatre Company, Limited; Managing Director, Mr. C. G. Dorrill; Assistant Manager, Mr. G. T. Lucas; Box Office Official, Mr. R. C. Miller; Musical Director, Mr. J. T. Long; Scenic Artist. Vacant; Stage Carpenter, C. Day; Advertising Department, Robert Wilkins. Holding capacity: In persons, 1,250; In money £176. Admission prices, Stalls, 5s.; Dress Circle, 5s., 4s., 3s.; Pit, 2s.; Balcony, 1s.; Gallery, 6d.; Early doors, 6d. extra. Full license. Stage measurements: 33ft. by 57ft.; proscenium opening, 24ft New electric light installation and gas. Thoroughly warmed. Band rehearsals, 1 o'clock. Matinée days. Wednesday and Saturday. Amount of printing required, 800 sheets. Cartage and baggage agents. Pickfords, George Street. This theatre has been entirely reconstructed and enlarged during 1908.

EAST THEATRE.—Proprietors, East Oxford Theatre Co., Ltd.; Manager, Mr. Frank Stuart. Double license. Holds 1,500 at £50. Stage, 30ft. by 40ft. Pros. opening, 26ft. Electric light, 100 volts continuous. Printing, 600 walls, 400 lithos and streamers. Sharing terms.

TOWN HALL.—Hall keeper, Mr. J. Rowles. Holding capacity with gallery, 1,400. Stage, seats behind for large chorus; number of stage seats, 130. Extra extension in front when required, £1 1s. Electric light, current continuous voltage, 100. Also gas supply to stage. Special fire insurance required for biograph entertainments, amount, £6 15s., which holds good for a month. Rent per night, £8 8s., each additional evening, £5 5s. Matinées only, £6 6s. Amount of deposit required, £10 for a week. License required for dramatic performances. Grand organ; fee for use, £11s. Good dressing room accommodation.

* Fast Train Service.—These trains rarely vary more than a few minutes, and have run for years without any alteration whatever.

Concert and booking agents, Messrs. Acott & Co., High Street, and Messrs. Russell & Co., 120, High Street.

ASSEMBLY ROOMS, TOWN HALL.—Holding capacity, 350. No fixed stage, but temporary ones are often erected. Used for chamber concerts, biograph, conjuring, and small entertainments. Special fire insurance required for biographs, (same as above). Electric light, same current as above. Rent per night, £3 3s.; additional nights, £2 2s.; Matinées, £2 2s.

DRILL HALL, TOWN HALL.—Measurements 41ft. 6in. by 60ft. No seats. Suitable for exhibitions. flower shows, &c. Rent, £2 12s. 6d. per day. Not let for dog and poultry shows.

CORN EXCHANGE, George Street. — Proprietors, The Corporation. Seating capacity, with gallery. 700. Hall keeper, J. Day. No fixed stage but temporary ones are often erected. Dramatic license required. Lighting and heating charged extra as used. Electric light, current continuous, voltage, 100. No special fire insurance required. Rent per night, £2 2s.; per week, £12 12s. Amount of deposit required, for a week, £5.

Concert and booking agents, Messrs. Acott & Co., High Street and Messrs. Russell & Co., 120, High Street. Used for concerts, Dioramas, Kinematographs and all variety shows, also dog, poultry and flower shows, exhibitions, fancy fairs, &c. Applications for any of the above three to be made to The Curator, Town Hall, Oxford.

ASSEMBLY ROOMS, RANDOLPH HOTEL.—Movable stage connected with the building. 1 large dressing room (can be divided). Holding capacity, 350 with gallery. Seats partly provided by the owners. Direct electric light, £2 voltage. Room can be let for concerts, Kinematograph, Magical and similar entertainments. Temporary license required for dramatic performances, if money is taken at doors. Terms vary according to entertainment. Concert and booking agents, Messrs. Acott, Harris & Co., and Messrs. Russell & Co., Music Agents, High Street. Applications to be made to the Manageress at the Hotel.

OLD MASONIC HALL, Alfred Street, High Street.—Seating capacity 200. Incandescent gas. No stage or theatrical license. Suitable for small entertainments and exhibitions. Terms on application. Apply to F. W. Ansell, 120, High Street, Oxford. Hall-keeper, Mrs. Pearce, 120, High Street.

THE MUSIC ROOM, Holywell Street.—Seating capacity with gallery, 400. Incandescent gas. Fixed stage with portable extension, a nd gas, and organ. No theatrical license. 2 dressing rooms. Suitable for most entertainments, but vacant in vacations only. Rent on application. Apply to F. J. Sanders, Manager.

NEW MASONIC HALL, High Street.—Manager, George F. Gardiner. Caretaker, C. F. Lucas. Seating capacity with gallery, for theatricals, 450; for concerts, 500. Dressing rooms. Size of stage about 20ft. by 14ft. Electric light, direct current, volts, 100. Temporary license necessary for stage plays if money is taken at doors. To let for balls, concerts, theatricals, whist drives, dinners, &c. Rent for theatricals, 1 day. £12 12s.; 2 days, £18 18s.; 3 days, 24 guineas. One week, 40 guineas. Apply to Mr. George Gardiner, senr., on premises.

Fairs: Gloucester Green, May 3rd. For ground apply to Mr. John Beckwith. Town Hall. St. Giles' Great Pleasure Fair, Sept. 6th and 7th. Applications for ground should be made early in the season to the bailiff, Walter Beeson, Esq., The Bursary, St. John's College. This is now the second largest street pleasure fair in this country. It is a very ancient festival and is held under ideal conditions in the shade of large trees which stand in a very spacious and beautiful boulevard. For this reason it is the nearest approach to a continental fair we possess. The attendance is very select and excursions run from all parts. Half-day trips from Paddington both days 3/6 return.

Every form of amusement in the University city of Oxford, including shows, circuses, roundabouts, &c., requires the Mayor's license and, if in term time, also the Vice-Chancellor's written permission. The University Marshal, Henry Stephens, Clarendon Buildings, Broad Street, will obtain the Vice-Chancellor's permit if waited upon. All plays must have the Vice-Chancellor's permission, if to be performed in term time. For ground and license for a circus, show, roundabout, fête, alfresco concerts, &c. apply to the showman's agent and lessee, Mr. H. L. Benwell, Folly Bridge, Oxford. Only first-class concerns are allowed in the town.

Market Days: Wednesday and Saturday. Early closing day, Thursday. Full terms commence in 1909 as follows, and consist of 8 weeks each: Lent, Monday, Jan. 18; Summer, Monday, April 26; Autumn, Monday, Oct. 11. 1910: Full Lent term, Monday, Jan. 17.

OXFORD AMATEUR DRAMATIC CLUBS.

OXFORD UNIVERSITY D.S.—Club rooms, 2, George Street. Steward, Joseph Oliver; President, J. H. M. Greenly, (Trinity); Secretary, E. Hain, (New). Performances take place annually in February.

OXFORD CITY A.D.S.—Club rooms, 13, Friars Entry. President, The Rev. Ernest F. Smith, M.A.; Secretary, Mr. Fred H. Ballard, 4, Kingston Road, N. 1907, "Hamlet," 1908, "Twelfth Night."

SUMMERTOWN A.O.C. — Musical Director, Mr. W. Higginson, (New Coll.); Secretary, Mr. R. Baylis, 70, Lonsdale Road, North Oxford; Stage Manager, Mr. Edward Ottley.

CLARENDON PRESS D.S.—Theatre, Press Institute, Walton Street. Secretary, Mr. H. Sheppard ; Stage Manager, Mr. J. C. Loney. pard; Stage Manager, Mr. J. C. Loney.

Cartage and Baggage Agents: Pickfords, George Street.

Medical Officers.—A.A.: Dr. R. Hitchings, 37, Holywell Street; Dr. A. R. Wilson, 42, Wellington Square. A.U.: Dr. Wilson, as above.

M.H.A.R.A. Agent: F. White, New Inn, Cowley Road.

RECOMMENDED APARTMENTS.

Mrs. Harper, 8, Hurst Street, Cowley Road.— 1 sitting-room, 1 double-bedded room, 1 single bedroom; piano; baths.

Mrs. Hunt, 80, James Street, Cowley Road.— 1 sitting, 1 bedroom, 1 combined room ; piano ; baths.

Mrs. S. Hall, 15, Paradise Square.—2 sitting-rooms, 3 bedrooms; baths.

Mrs. Clements, 34, Essex Street, Cowley Road. —1 sitting-room, 2 bedrooms; baths.

HOTEL.

Hotel-Restaurant Buol, 21, Cornmarket Street (*see Advt.*)

PROFESSIONAL HOUSES OF CALL

where THE STAGE and THE STAGE YEAR BOOK may be consulted.

William Dowling, "The Grapes," George Street, (opposite New Theatre).—High-class Ales, Wines and Spirits; Comfortable Lounge.

"Tiny" White, "The New Inn," Cowley Road.—Free House, Burton Ales, Professionals specially welcomed.

Frank Stuart, "The Elm Tree," Cowley Road. —Billiards and Garage (opposite East Theatre).

CONCERT DIRECTION AGENT.

Sydney Acott, Harriss and Co., Musical Instrument Warehouse, 124, High Street.

OFFICIAL TICKET AGENT FOR LONDON THEATRES AND AMUSEMENTS.

James Russell and Co., Musical Instrument Dealers and Concert Agents, 120, High Street.

ELECTRICAL AND MECHANICAL ENGINEER.

Hill, Upton and Co., 22, George Street. Telephone 108 X. Telegrams "Uphill, Oxford." Theatre work undertaken. Showmen's electrical supplies (adjoins Theatre).

PROFESSIONAL ENTERTAINERS.

W. A. James 96, St. Clements.—Stage Management, Light Comedy, Character and Heavy, quick study.

C. H. de Loui, 95, Howard Street, Iffley Road.— Wizard, Humorist and Sleight of Hand.

Leonard Moon, 11, Iffley Road.—Humorist and Society Entertainer.

Edward Ottley, Blenheim Villa, Wolvercote.— Actor, Reciter, Producer.

Prof. Homer Stone, 7, Abbey Road.—Kinematograph, Punch and Judy, Ventriloquist, X Rays, and Marionettes.

PROFESSORS AND TUTORS.

Music, Singing, Elocution, &c.

Edward Ottley, Blenheim Villa, Wolvercote.— Elocution, Gesture, Stage Technique, &c.

J. Daniels, 6, Grove Street, Oxford.—Instruction in banjo, mandoline and guitar. Also in all styles of stage dancing and general stage business. Branches, Cambridge and London.

BILL POSTERS.

Bill Posters for Oxford, Abingdon, Witney and large district, The Oxford Bill Posting Co., George Street.

THEATRICAL AND SHOW PRINTERS.

The Oxonian Press, Park End Street. Electric plant, quick work, professional prices.

CONTRACTORS FOR DECORATIONS.

R. Wilkins and Co., 44, George Street, Fancy Costumiers. Agents for G. T. Brock and Co. Contractors for Decorations, Illuminations, and Firework Displays, and Fancy Costumes.

SHOWMEN'S SUPPLIES AND FAIR-GROUND GOODS.

Eugene de-la-Mare, Wholesale General Warehouseman.—11 and 13, George Street, (opposite theatre). Spacious Showrooms, Pain's Fireworks, Coloured Fires and other stage effects.

RAILWAY CARTAGE AGENTS.

G.W.R., Messrs. Saunders and Co., Mitre Office, High Street.

L.N.W.R., The Railway Co., The Station and Clarendon Office, Cornmarket Street.

Great Central (also Ticket Office), Pickford's, George Street.

DRAMATIC, VARIETY, AND PRESS AGENT.

H. L. Benwell, 2, Isis Street, Folly Bridge.

"THE STAGE" ON SALE BY

Messrs. W. H. Smith and Son, St. Giles' Street.

Messrs. Slatter and Rose, 16, High Street (Wholesale agents for THE STAGE YEAR BOOK).

PADIHAM, Lancs.

Population, 12,205.   Miles from London, 215.

CO-OPERATIVE HALL.—Proprietors, the Co-operative Society; secretary, Mr. Frank Bertwistle. Music and dancing license. No proper stage. Platform 18ft. by 9 ft. Lighted by gas. Terms for hiring, £5 weekly. Amount of deposit required on booking, half the amount.

Dates of local fair : Commences last Friday in July. Recreation Ground available for portables, alfresco concerts, and circuses.

Early closing day, Tuesday; market day, Friday.

PAIGNTON, Devon.

Population, 8,385. Miles from London, 217.

PUBLIC HALL.—Managing Director, Mr. W. A. Axworthy. Has dramatic license. Holding capacity; Number of persons, 1,000. Stage: Width, 37ft.; depth to footlights, 27ft. Head and footlights, proscenium and drop curtain. Lighted by gas. Terms for hiring: One night, £2 10s.; two nights, £4 10s.; three nights, £6 10s.; any extra nights, £1 per night. Amount of deposit required on booking, half.

PIER PAVILION.—Dramatic license. Holds about 500. Small stage.

No local fairs.

Early closing, Wednesday.

PAISLEY, Renfrew.

Population, 79,355. Miles from London, 407.

HIPPODROME.—Proprietor and Manager, Mr. E. H. Bostock; Acting-Manager, Mr. T. Stead; Musical Director, Mr. Klee Holding capacity: Number of persons, 1,800. Stage measurements: 28ft. by 30ft. Gas and electric light. Usual matinée day, Saturday. Time of band rehearsal, 12 noon.

Early closing day, Tuesday; market days, Monday and Thursday.

A.A. Medical Officer, Dr. H. C. Donald, 5, Gauze Street.

M.H.A.R.A. Agent, S. Young, Newtown Hotel. V.A.F., Jas. Young, Old Tile House.

PEEBLES, Peebleshire.

Population, 5,266.

CHAMBERS' TOWN HALL.—Proprietors, Town Council; Manager, Mr. Wm. Sanderson. Dramatic and music and dancing licenses. Holding capacity: Number of persons, 500. Platform (no stage fittings): Depth, 9ft., can be extended to 18ft.; width, 30ft.; sufficient height for large proscenium. Gas, Amount of printing required: 5 18-sheet, 6 6-sheet, 2 12-sheet, 200 D.B., 50 D.C. Terms for hiring: £2 2s., with extras for gas, stage extension, footlight insurance, etc. Amount of deposit required on booking: 10s. No piano in hall, but one can be hired. Good stage exits and artists' rooms.

No local fairs. Tweed Green available for portables, alfresco concerts, and circuses.

Early closing day, Wednesday; market day, Tuesday.

PEMBROKE, Pemb.

Population, 15,853. Miles from London, 274.

TEMPERANCE HALL, Pembroke Dock.— Manager, Mr. W. Hy. Thomas, 59, Bush Street. Double license. Holding capacity:

Number of persons, 6-700. Platform, 27ft. by 10ft., which can be extended 9ft. Gas (charged for by meter). Terms for hiring, £1 15s. first night, £1 5s. per night after. Amount of deposit required on booking, 5s. for each night engaged.

ASSEMBLY ROOMS.—Proprietors, Pembroke Rooms Co., Limited. Has dramatic license.

QUEEN'S THEATRE.—A permanent wooden structure, which is occasionally let. Proprietor, Mr. Tom Barger; Business Manager, Mr. Norman H. Barger.

A pleasure fair is held on October 11. It lasts a week, and is well attended. Portables are allowed in Pembroke Dock, and there is not much difficulty in getting a license.

Circuses are arranged for by Mr. Eben Griffiths and Mr. Jos. Gibby.

Population is industrial, dockyard employés, with a regiment of infantry and battery or so of artillery.

Early closing day, Wednesday; market days: Pembroke Dock, Friday; Pembroke, Saturday.

PENARTH, Glam.

Population, 14,228. Miles from London, 163.

ANDREW'S HALL.—Managers, Messrs. S. Andrews and Son. Has dramatic license. Holding capacity: Number of persons, 700. Ordinary platform; no fit-up. Lighted by gas.

Early closing, Wednesday; no market.

PENMAENMAWR, Carn.

Population, 3,503. Miles from London, 229.

OXFORD HALL.—Proprietor, Mr. W. P. Horton; Manager, Mr. D. H. Owen, Oxford Arcade. Dramatic license. Holding capacity: Number of persons, 600. Amount, £15. Stage: 18ft. by 17ft. Gas. Small amount of printing required. Terms for hiring: 30s. per night. Amount of deposit required on booking: 20s.

Residential and working-class population.

No local fairs. Sites available for portables, alfresco concerts, and circuses: Promenade grass plots of the district council, and several fields for circuses.

Early closing day, Wednesday; no market day.

PENRITH, Cumb.

Population, 9,182. Miles from London, 281.

DRILL AND CONCERT HALL.—Manager, Colour-Sergeant Instructor J. Stratton. Double license. Holding capacity: Number of persons, 1,000. Stage, 26ft. by 13ft., with an extension of 5ft. Lighted by gas. Terms for hiring: On application. Amount of deposit required on booking: 50 per cent.

Dates of local fairs: Martinmas, half-yearly term of hiring.

Early closing, Thursday; market, Tuesday.

PENRYN, Cornwall.

Population, 3,190. Miles from London, 303.

TEMPERANCE HALL.—Proprietors, the Trustees. No license. Holding capacity: Number of persons, 300 to 400. Gas. Terms for hiring: Apply to secretary.

Pleasure Fair, July 7. The Green available for portables, alfresco concerts, and circuses.

Early closing day, Thursday; market day, Saturday.

PENTRE, Glam.

Population within a radius of three miles, about 5,000.

TIVOLI PALACE AND HIPPODROME.— Proprietors, Messrs. Poole's Theatres, Limited; District Manager, Mr. Walter Bynorth; Acting-Manager, Mr. J. Gunn.

DRILL HALL.—Dramatic license.

Book to Ystrad, on the Taff Vale Railway. Early closing, Thursday; market, Saturday. Agent.—M.H.A.R.A.: Sam Young, Newtown Hotel. V.A.F.: O. Meredith, Bailey's Arms Hotel.

PENZANCE, Cornwall.

Population, 13,136. Miles from London, 320.

There is no theatre, but a portion of the public buildings known as ST. JOHN'S HALL, which has a dramatic license, is used as a theatre. Seating accommodation, 800. Stage, 34ft. by 19½ft. Proprietors, Public Buildings Co.; Secretary, E. C. Scobey. Large organ can be used for recitals. Usual receipts for musical piece, £100 for two nights. *The Dairy-maids* took £120 in two nights.

CENTRAL HALL, Parade Street.—Proprietors, Central Hall Co., Ltd.; Secretary, Mr. H. H. Pezzack. Used for concerts and lantern exhibitions. Seats 300. Stage about 25ft. by 15ft.

Corpus Christi Fair is the pleasure fair of the year, it is held on Thursday, Friday, and Saturday in the week following Whitsuntide; anything from ten to twenty travelling shows, half-dozen roundabouts, etc., are always in attendance, excursions by train and 'bus bring thousands to the town. Monday and Tuesday are the best nights for drama, Friday is the best for musical plays.

No difficulty is experienced in obtaining pitches for portables and circuses; the recreation ground is generally used by permission of and payment to Town Council. There was sufficient room and to spare in the recreation ground for Buffalo Bill's Show.

Alfresco concerts are held in the Alexandra Grounds on the sea front. Application for pitch should be made to Secretary, Entertainments Committee, Chamber of Commerce, Penzance.

Population, nearly 14,000, residential and visitors. Good companies are appreciated; second-rate plays lose money.

Early closing day, Friday; market day, Thursday.

PERTH, Perth.

Population, 32,872. Miles from London, 447.

PERTH THEATRE AND OPERA HOUSE.— Proprietors, Theatre and Opera House Co., Limited; Lessee, Mr. J. H. Savile; Manager, Mr. Frank Aldridge; Musical Director, Mr. H. R. Wallace. Double license. Holds 1,400; amount, £70 to £100. Width of stage, 56 ft.; front to back, 28 ft. Proscenium opening, 24 ft; height, 22 ft. Gas and electric light, 230 volts. Printing, 600 posters, 300 lithos, and 500 circulars. Matinée, Saturday. Band rehearsal, 1 p.m.

Early closing, Wednesday; market, Friday.

RECOMMENDED APARTMENTS.

Mrs. Mochrie, 7, St. John's Place.—Sitting-room and 2 bedrooms; piano.

Mrs. E. Forbes, 28, Kinnoull Street.—2 bed-rooms, sitting and combined room.

PETERBOROUGH, Northants.

Population, 30,872. Miles from London, 76.

THEATRE ROYAL.—Lessee and Manager, Mr. E. Winter; Resident Manager, Mr. H. Watson. Double license. Holding capacity: Number of persons, 1,000; amount, £70. Stage measurements, 35 ft. by 50 ft.; proscenium, 26 ft. 6 in. Gas and electric light, 200 volts, direct. Printing required, 350 sheets of posting; 350 lithos, circulars, etc. Usual matinée day, Saturday. Time of band rehearsal, 1 p.m.

HIPPODROME.—Proprietors, Messrs. Fred Karno and A. H. Edwards; Manager Mr. Frank Gallagher.

DRILL HALL.—Music and dancing license. Small stage, 28ft. 6ins. by 12ft. or larger one, 40ft. by 15ft. Gas. Electric plug, 100 volts, direct. Apply, Sergeant-Major W. Thorpe, F.R.A.

GRAND ASSEMBLY ROOM.—Proprietor, Mr. F. Ballard. Available for concerts and variety entertainments. Seats 500. Electric light.

Population is industrial, brick-making and engineering.

Fairs are as follows: Bridge Fair, first Tuesday, Wednesday, and Thursday in October; Cherry Fair, first Tuesday, Wednesday, and Thursday in July. No portable theatres are allowed in Peterboro' by the local authorities. Bridge Fair Field always used for the purpose of circuses, owned by the Corporation.

Early closing day, Thursday; market day, Wednesday and Saturday.

Agent.—M.H.A.R.A.: G. Copley, Bull Hotel. V.A.F.: The same.

PETERHEAD, Aberdeenshire.

Population, 11,763. Miles from London, 576.

PUBLIC HALL.—Manager, Mr. J. Hall Meanie. Fully licensed. Holding capacity: Number of persons, 750; amount, £40. Depth and width of stage, 14ft. by 30ft. Lighted by gas. Amount of printing required: About 130 sheets. Terms for hiring: £2 12s. first night and £1 12s. each night after, and gas extra. Amount of deposit required on booking: 20s.

There are no fairs. Site for portables, circuses, etc., Feuars Park, Queen's Street.

Early closing, Wednesday; market, Friday.

PETERSFIELD, Hants.

Population, 4,000. Miles from London, 55.

CORN EXCHANGE.—Manager, Mr. W. C. Burley. Dramatic license. Holding capacity: Number of persons, about 500; chairs for 300. Stage: 13ft. by 13ft. Lighted by gas.

Date of local fair, October 6.

Early closing day, Thursday; market day, alternate Wednesdays.

PINNER, Middlesex.

Miles from London, 13.

HIGH SCHOOL HALL.—Proprietress, Miss L. Conder, St. Mildred's, Avenue Road. Dramatic and musical and dancing licenses. Holding capacity: Number of persons, 165. Platform, with curtains. Gas. Terms for hiring: £1 11s. 6d. for evening, £1 1s. afternoon or for series. Amount of deposit required on booking: Half-fees.

Local fair, Whitsuntide. Field available for portables, etc., close by.

PLYMOUTH, Devon.

Population 115,000. Miles from London, 246.

THEATRE ROYAL.—Proprietors, Royal and Grand Theatres, Limited; Manager, Mr. J. Langdon Lee; Musical Director, Mr. Stephen E. Blythe. Full license. Holding capacity; Number of persons, 2,000; amount, £145; ordinary prices. Stage measurements, width between fly-rails, 36ft; depth o stage. 33ft.; wall to wall 75ft. Gas and electric light. Amount of printing required, 1,000 litho and l.p., and 1,000 d.c.'s. Usual matinée day, Saturday, 2.30. Time of band rehearsal, 1 p.m.

GRAND THEATRE.—Proprietors, Royal and Grand Theatres, Limited; Full license. Holding capacity; Number of persons, 2,200. Closed.

PALACE OF VARIETIES. — Proprietors, County Theatres and Hotels, Limited; Managing Director, Mr. Alfred Moul; Local Manager and Licensee, Mr. F. Field.

PROMENADE PIER PAVILION.—Manager, Mr. John Higson. Music and stage dancing license. Holding capacity: Number of persons, 2,500. Concert stage. Lighted by gas (incandescent).

ST. JAMES'S HALL, Union Street. — Proprietor, Mr. A. N. Cole; Managers, Messrs. H. and A. Andrews. Kinematograph entertainments. Holds 1,200. Electric light.

ASSEMBLY ROOMS.—Apply Manager, Royal Hotel. Music and dancing license. Holds 400. Electric light, 200 volts, direct and alternating.

DRILL HALL.—Apply Commanding Officer, 5th Devon Regiment. No dramatic license. Holds 8,000. Electricity, arc lights.

FORESTERS' HALL.—Apply Secretary, Music and dancing license. Holds 200. Gas.

GUILDHALL.—Manager, Borough Treasurer (Mr. J. R. Martyr). Music and dancing license. Holding capacity: Number of persons, seat 1,020 in area and 175 in balcony; stand 400 to 500 in arcades; orchestra seating for 200. Gas and electric light. Terms for hiring: According to nature of entertainment. Suitable for lectures or concerts.

Early closing day, Wednesday; market days, Tuesday, Thursday, and Saturday.

Medical Officers.—A.A., Dr. R. B. Burke, 14, Portland Square, Tel. No. 0931; Dr. H. S. Parsloe, 5, Buckland Terrace, Tel. No. 562; A.U., The same; M.H.A.R.A.: Dr. Parsloe.

Agent.—M.H.A.R.A.: V.A.F. and A.U.: Mr. Parnell, Great Western Hotel, Union Street.

POCKLINGTON, Yorks.

Population, 2,463. Miles from London, 196.

VICTORIA HALL.—Lessees, Messrs. W. and C. Forth. Occasional dramatic license. Holding capacity; Number of persons. 550. No proper stage. Lighted by gas. Terms for hiring, on application.

Early closing, Wednesday; market, Saturday.

PONTARDULAIS, Glam.

Population 10,000. Miles from London, 207.

PUBLIC OR MARKET HALL.—Manager, Mr. George James. Double license. Holding capacity: Number of persons, about 560. Not fixed stage, 33ft. by 14ft.; size of hall, 3ft. by 39ft Lighted by gas. Terms for hiring: 25s. per night, including gas. Amount of deposit required on booking, 10s. per night.

No local fairs, only monthly market the last Tuesday in each month. There is no public site for portables or circuses. Alfresco concerts are not known here

PONTEFRACT, Yorks.

Population, 13,427. Miles from London, 178.

ALEXANDRA THEATRE OF VARIETIES.—General Manager, Mr. Tom Diacoff.

ASSEMBLY HALL (Part of the Town Hall).—Proprietors, the Corporation: Manager, Mr. J. E. Pickard, Borough Surveyor. Full license. Holding capacity: Number of persons, 700.; amount, £40. Stage measurements, 36ft. 6in. by 21ft. 6in.; 17ft. 6in. high under rail. Lighted by gas. Proscenium front and frame. Stock scenery. Terms for hiring: theatrical purposes.—One night, £3; two nights, £5; three nights, £6 10s.; four nights, £7 10s.; five nights, £9 10s.; six nights, £11. Bazaar and local dramatic, if not for private profit: One night, £2 2s.; two nights, £3 12s.; three nights, £5 2s.; four nights, £6 10s.; five nights, £8; six nights, £9. Concerts and lectures, per night, £1 10s. 3s. per hour is charged for rehearsals and fitting up bazaars when gas is burnt. Old Town Hall, with Rotation Office, £1 per night; Old Town Hall, if used after 11 p.m., £1 5s. per night. A deposit of £1 1s. for the first night and 10s. per night for each following night for the Assembly Room, and half the fee payable for any other room, are required on such rooms being booked, and the balance and all extra charges in advance.

ALEXANDRA THEATRE OF VARIETIES (Tanshelf).—Manager, Mr. Tom Diacoff. Holds 1,800. Fully licensed. Electric light, 210 volts.

Statute Fair, first Thursday in November. Fair Ground, Castle Ground. Trustees now run galas Easter, Whitsun, and August

Early closing day, Thursday; market day, Saturday.

Agent. — M.H.A.R.A.: Mr. Jackson, Dock Vaults. V.A.F.: The same.

PONTYPOOL, Mon.

Population, 6,126. Miles from London, 164.

TOWN HALL.—Manager, Mr. H. H. Haden. No dramatic license. Holding capacity: Number of persons, 350. Open stage, 25ft. by 9ft. Electric light. 100 volts. 25s. night, exclusive of light. Amount of deposit required on booking, 10s.

HANBURY ASSEMBLY ROOMS (Theatre Royal).—Manager, Mr. H. Pitten, Club Chambers, Pontypool. Dramatic and music license. Holding capacity: Number of persons, 750 to 800. Stage measurements: Depth, 23ft. 6in.; width, 50ft.; drop curtain, 24ft. 6in. Gas and electric light. Terms for hiring, £2 2s. per night; £10 six nights: lights extra by meter. Only licensed hall in the town.

Local Fairs: April 2, 22, July 5, October 10.

Early closing day, Thursday; market day, Saturday.

PONTYPRIDD, Glam.

Population, 32,316. Miles from London, 169.

ROYAL CLARENCE THEATRE.— Sole Owners, Messrs. Trenchard and Jones; Manager, Mr. Charles Trenchard.

There are two Town Halls which are let to theatre companies, etc., and several show grounds, which as a rule are occupied by shows of various descriptions.

Date of local fair: Easter Monday in every year.

Coal mining is the principal industry, but there are cable and anchor works, known as the Ynysyngharad Chain Works.

There are also tinplate works.

There are four separate and distinct railway companies which have their systems traversing through the district in addition to the Glamorganshire Canal, which is about 100 years old.

Market days: Wednesdays and Saturdays. Early closing days: Thursdays.

M.H.A.R.A.—Agent: E. Williams, 4. Belle Vue, Treforest. V.A.F.: Mr. Williams, Clarence Hotel.

POOLE Dorset.

Population, 19,463. Miles from London, 113.

AMITY HALL.—Manager, Mr. W. A. N. Hankin, Quay, Poole. Has dramatic license. Holding capacity: Number of persons, 600. Stage: 17ft. by 28ft. Gas and electric light. Terms for hiring: One day, £2 15s.; two days, £5; three days, £6 10s.; four days, £7 15s.; five days, £9; week, £10. Amount of deposit required on booking, 25 per cent.

Local fairs in May and November.

Early closing day, Wednesday; market day, Thursday.

PORTARLINGTON, King's Co.

Population, 2,000. Miles from Dublin, 42.

TOWN HALL.—Manager, Mr. Michael Flanagan. Dramatic license. Holding capacity: Number of persons, 500. Proper stage: 30ft. by 20ft. wide. Lighted by gas. Terms for hiring: £1 per night. Amount of deposit required on booking: 10s.

Market day, Wednesday.

PORT GLASGOW, Renfrew.

Population, 17,500. Miles from London, 403.

PORT GLASGOW TOWN HALL.—Manager, Mr. Hugh Beck. Double license. Holding capacity: Number of persons, seated for 1,025. Stage: Depth, 13ft. 6in.; width, 20ft. 10in. in front and 27ft. 1in. at back. Lighted by gas. Terms for hiring: For concert, inclusive, for one night, £2 18s. 6d.; for dramatic, £3 13s. Amount of deposit required on booking, £1. All communications to be addressed to John Chalmers, Town Treasurer, Port Glasgow.

Early closing day, Thursday; market day, Friday.

PORTH, Glam.

Population, 19,500. Miles from London, 187.

PALACE OF VARIETIES. — General Manager, Mr. C W. Poole: Acting-Manager, Mr. W. Bynorth. Holds 2,000. Electric light, 50 amps., 230 vo ts direct; own supply. Towns barred, Pontypridd, Tonypandy, Ynishir, and Ferndale, as per award.

This town is situated at the apex of two valleys, known as the Big Rhondda and Little Rhondda. The town itself is in the centre of district of 200,000 inhabitants. The train service between Porth and the various towns in the valleys is plentiful, and an electric tramway has recently been opened. Mining is the principal industry. A pleasure fair is held annually in the month of July at which numerous side shows prominently figure. Portable theatres rarely visit here since Messrs. Poole opened the Palace as a permanent place of amusement. Circus pitches are obtainable, and this class of entertainment usually does well.

Early closing day, Thursday.

M.H.A.R.A.—Agent: J. Roberts, Llewynlelyn Hotel. V.A.F.: The same.

PORTISHEAD, Som.

Population, 2,544. Miles from London, 130.

ASSEMBLY HALL.—Manager, Mr. S. Thomas. Has dramatic license. Holding capacity: Number of persons, 300. Drop curtain, top, and footlights. Stage, 16ft. 8ins. by 12ft. Lighted by gas. Terms for hiring: Hall and piano, one night, 55s. Amount of deposit required on booking, 10s.

Early closing day, Thursday

PORTLAND, Dorset.

Population, 15,199. Miles from London, 147.

MASONIC HALL ASSEMBLY ROOMS.— Manager, Mr. R Score, Clarendon House, Fortuneswell. Double license. Holding capacity: Number of persons ab out £60. Stage: Depth, 20ft.; width, 32ft.; proscenium, 21ft. 5in.; 14ft. to top of screen rail. Lighted by gas. Terms for hiring: From £1 10s. to £2 per night. Amount of deposit required on booking, 10s. 6d.

JUBILEE HALL.—Manager, Mr. James Joseph Shaw. Double license. Holding capacity: Number of persons, 400. Stage: depth, 26ft. 6ins.; width, 17ft.; no proscenium. Lighted by gas. Amount of printing required, about 100 posters. Terms for hiring: £1 1s. per night, or £4 per week. Amount of deposit required on booking, 10s. Piano may be hired

A good town for a good small company. Channel and Home fleets, sometimes stationed here, largely increase the playgoing population.

Date of local fair: November 5 and 6.

Early closing day, Wednesday.

PORTMADOC, Carn.

Miles from London, 260.

TOWN HALL.—Proprietors, the Urban District Council. Apply the Clerk. Dramatic license can be obtained. Holds 850. Platform 27ft. wide by 18ft. deep. Gas.

Early closing, Wednesday; market, Friday.

PORTMADOWN, Co. Armagh.

Population, 8,430. Miles from Dublin, 87.

TOWN HALL.—Manager, the Town Clerk, Mr. W. Wilson. Holding capacity: Number of persons, 600. Portable stage, in addition to small platform. Stage: Permanent, 20ft. by 16ft.; portable, 30ft. by 15ft. Lighted by gas. Terms for hiring: First night, 30s.; every subsequent night, 25s. Amount of deposit required on booking, £1; not required from known companies.

Market days, Wednesdays and Saturdays.

PORTOBELLO (near Edinburgh).

TOWN HALL.—Managers, Messrs. Douglas and Smart, House Agents, Portobello. Dramatic license. Holding capacity: Number of persons 400; amount, £30 to £40. Platform only. Depth, 8 ft.; width, 20 ft. Gas and electric light. Terms for hiring concert, £1 6s.; dramatic entertainment, £1 15s.; dance, £2 7s. Amount of deposit required on booking, half the above charges.

TOWER PAVILION.—Proprietor and Manager, Mr. Harry Marvello; Musical Directress,

Miss Alice Hutchison; Scenic Artist, Mr Archibald Middlemass. Double license. Holding capacity: Number of persons, 1,000; amount, £40. Depth and width of stage, 50ft. by 22ft.; proscenium opening, 22ft. Lighted by electricity. Amount of printing required, 400 sheets. Usual matinée day, Saturday. Time of band rehearsal, 1 p.m. Kinematograph chamber, screen, etc. Alternating current, 230 volts. Transformer fitted. From May to September the Pavilion is occupied by Mr. Marvello's own Co., the Tower Entertainers.

PORTSMOUTH, Hants.

Population, 200,000. Miles from London, 74.

THEATRE ROYAL.—Licensee, Mr. J. W. Boughton; Acting-Manager, Mr. Armstrong Bell; Musical Director, Mr. F. A. Smith; Scenic Artist, Mr. A. W. Walmsley. License—full. Holding capacity: Number of persons, 2,300. Depth and width of stage, and proscenium measurements, 72ft. deep, 60ft. wide; proscenium opening, 28ft. Usual matinée day, Saturdays at 2.30. Time of band rehearsal, 2 o'clock Mondays.

PRINCE'S THEATRE.—Licensee, Mr. J. W. Boughton; Acting-Manager, Mr. A. Agate; Musical Director, Mr. G. Greene; Scenic Artist, Mr. A. W. Walmsley. License—full. Holding capacity: Number of persons, 2,300. Stage, 45ft. deep, 70ft. wide. Electric light. No matinées given, except at Christmas. Time of band rehearsal, 2 o'clock, Mondays.

KING'S THEATRE, Southsea.—Proprietors, Portsmouth Theatres, Ltd; Licensee, Mr. J. W. Boughton; Acting-Manager, Mr. Claude Marner; Musical Director, Mr. J. M. South; Scenic Artist, Mr. A. W. Walmsley. License—full. Holding capacity: Number of persons, 3,000; amount, £250. Stage, 45ft. deep, 80ft. wide, proscenium opening, 28ft. Fly floor 24ft., between fly rails 45ft. Electric light. Amount of printing required: 800 sheets posting, 600 lithos. Usual matinée day: Wednesday at 2.30. Time of band rehearsal: 2 o'clock Mondays.

EMPIRE PALACE.—Proprietors, The Portsmouth Empire Palace Company, Ltd. Managing Director, Captain E. H. Warren-Wright; Secretary, Mr. William Pratt. Stage-Manager, Mr. T. S. Lonsdale; Musical Director, Mr. E. H. Williams. Music and dancing license. Holding capacity: Number of persons, 1,000. Gas and electric light. Time of band rehearsal, 1.30 p.m. Usual matinée day, Wednesday.

HIPPODROME.—Proprietors, Portsmouth Hippodrome, Limited. Managing Director, Mr. Walter De Frece; Acting Manager and Licensee, Mr. Nelson Barry; Booking Circuit, Mr. De Frece; Musical Director, Mr. J. Howard Shackleton. Music and dancing license. Stage measurements: Depth, 36 ft., width, 70 ft; proscenium opening, 35 ft. Electric light. Time of band rehearsal, 1 p.m. Usual matinée days, Wednesdays and Saturdays.

THE PEOPLE'S PALACE (LATE VENTO'S). —Proprietor and Manager, Mr. Frank Pearce. Situated in Lake Road.

CLARENCE ESPLANADE PIER.—Proprietors, the Clarence Esplanade Pier Company, Ltd. Manager, Mr. Chas. C. Hunter. Music and dancing license. Holding capacity: Number of persons, 3,000. Platform. Lighted by gas.

TOWN HALL.—Apply Sir W. Dupree, Chairman of Committee. Music and dancing license.

Holding capacity: Number of persons, 2,000. Platform: 34ft. by 3ft. 4in.; extensions to 38ft. by 19ft. Gas and electric light. Terms for hiring: Day, £5 5s.; evening, £10 10s., the whole to be paid seven days before the date of engagement.

Other important places of entertainment here are the South Parade Pier, being now re-built by the Corporation to include pavilion and winter garden, and following concert halls, viz., the Portland Hall in Kent Road, the Victoria Hall, Commercial Road.

To the population of Portsmouth for entertainment purposes may be added Gosport on the other side of the harbour, with population only little under 30,000, and containing no regular place of amusement.

The bulk of inhabitants are concerned directly or indirectly with the Royal Navy, Dockyard, Garrison, and Government establishments generally. Southsea is also the residential locality for many retired officers and others lately belonging to His Majesty's services, and during the summer thousands of visitors make it their headquarters, owing to its varied water excursions, proximity to Isle of Wight, etc.

This town is not visited by portables, but little if any difficulty would be experienced in obtaining license from Town Council. A part of the Common in neighbourhood of South Parade Pier is hired to concert parties, pierrots and others during summer, and hitherto on vacant ground near Clarence Pier Messrs. Sanger have annually pitched their circus tent.

Early closing day, Wednesdays.

Medical Officers.—A.A.: Dr. J. McGregor, Mile End Villa, Commercial Road. Tel. No. 113. Dr. E. J. Norris, Castle Road, King's Road, Southsea Tel No. 972 Corporation, A.U. and M.H.A.R.A.: Dr. McGregor.

Agent.—M.H.A.R.A.: Mrs. Whybro. Railway Hotel. A.U.: The same. V.A.F.: The same.

RECOMMENDED APARTMENTS.

Mrs. Giles, Clovelly, 120, King Street, Southsea. —2 sitting, 3 bedrooms, 1 comb.

Mrs. Bunnell, 11a, Church Road, Landport.—Combined room, and sitting-room and bedroom.

Mrs. E. Egling, The White House, 6, Bellevue Terrace, Southsea.

PRESTON, Lancs.

Population, 112,989. Miles from London, 210.

THEATRE ROYAL.—Proprietors, the Executors of the late Mr. Wm. Johnson; Manager, Mr. Stephen Pritt; Musical Director, Mr. Geo. Warburton; Scenic Artist, Mr. Thos. Beck. Full license. Holding capacity: Number of persons, 1,600; amount, £95. Stage measurements: Depth, 40ft.; width, 50ft.; height to fly rail, 20ft. 6in.; to grid, 42ft. 6in.; proscenium, 27ft. Electric light. Amount of printing required, 1,000 sheets for walls, 600 window bills. Usual matinée day, Thursday, at 2.15. Time of band rehearsal, 1 p.m.

PRINCE'S THEATRE. — Proprietors and Managers, Messrs. Sawyer and Woodruff; Scenic Artist, Mr. A. Wareing. Holding capacity: Number of persons, 2,400; amount, £88. Stage measurements: 62ft. wide, 40ft. deep; proscenium opening, 28ft. Gas and electric light. Amount of printing required, 800 wall, 500 lithos. No regular matinée day. Time of band rehearsal, 1 p.m.

HIPPODROME.—Proprietors, Messrs. W. H. Broadhead and Son; Manager, Mr. Percy B.

Broadhead; Acting-Manager, Mr. Frank E. Burdett; Musical Director, Mr. F. Dexter; Scenic Artists, Messrs. T. C. Daly and Edward Leigh. Stage measurements: 80ft. by 36ft. by 36ft. Gas and electric light. Usual matinée day, Monday. Time of band rehearsal, 11 a.m.
Early closing day, Thursday; market day, Saturday.
Medical Officers.—A.A.: Dr. T. H. C. Derham, 1, Albert Terrace, Garstang Road (tel. number, 0200 Fulwood). A.U.: Dr. T. H. C. Derham, Albert Terrace, Garsland Road. 9-10; 2-3; 7-8. Phone 0200. M.H.A.R.A.: Dr. J. Cookson, Moor Lane (tel. 0576).
Agents.—M.H.A.R.A.: F. Halliday, Stanley Arms Hotel. A.U.: The same. V.A.F.: The same.

RECOMMENDED APARTMENTS.

Mrs. Gribben, 14, Cross Street.—2 sitting-rooms (Pianos), 3 bedrooms, 1 combined; bath.
Mrs. Thompson, 16, Bolton Street.—1 double bedroom, 2 single, 2 sitting-rooms; bath; piano.

PRINCES RISBOROUGH Bucks.

Miles from London, 34½.

BREWERY HALL.—Manager, Mr. E. Clarke. Dramatic license can be obtained. Holding capacity: Number of persons, 250. Stage: 13ft. 1in. by 13ft. 4in.; height, 20ft. Lighted by gas. Terms for hiring: According to period required.
Dates of local fairs, May 6, October 21. Site available for portables, al-fresco concerts, and circuses, Mrs. West's meadow.

PUDSEY, Yorks.

Population, 14,907. Miles from London, 189.

VICTORIA HALL.—Manager, Mr. Wm. B. Burnell. Has dramatic license. Holding capacity: Number of persons, 850. Platform. Lighted by gas. Terms for hiring: 27s. 6d. per night; 20 per cent. reduction on four or more nights. Amount of deposit required on booking, half fee.
Dates of local fairs: First Saturday in April; first Monday after August 21.
Early closing day, Wednesday; market day, Saturday.

PULBOROUGH, Sussex.

Population, 1,725. Miles from London, 50.

CORN EXCHANGE.—Manager, Mr. W. F. Jennings. No license required. Holding capacity: Number of persons, about 250; amount, £10 to £12 full. Stage: Made by tables to any size. Lighted by oil lamp. Terms for hiring: 2 guineas per day and night. Amount of deposit required on booking, 1 guinea. Wednesday the best day; cannot be used on Friday or Saturday.
Market days, Monday and Friday.
Meadows at the back of hotel for circuses, etc.

PWLLHELI, Carn.

Population, 3,675. Miles from London, 270.

TOWN HALL.—Proprietors, The Corporation; Manager, The Surveyor. Dramatic license. Holds 1,500. Size of hall, 54ft. long, 66ft. wide. Platform, depth 18ft., width 35ft. No proscenium. Gas. Amount of printing required, six 18, 24, twelve 12, 150 daybills. Terms for hiring, dramatic, £3 3s. Amount

of deposit required on booking, 10s. a day. Bookings made by the hallkeeper, J. J. Edwards.
Dates of local fairs, second Wednesday in May and November. Sites available for portables, alfresco concerts, and circuses, the " Maes" and plot of waste land called the Green.
Early closing day, Thursday; market day, Wednesday.

QUEENSTOWN, Co. Cork.

Population, 9,755. Miles from Dublin, 177.

QUEEN'S HOTEL ASSEMBLY ROOMS.—Manager, Mr. B. Humbert. Holding capacity: Number of persons, about 400. Stage, 25ft. deep; 24ft. wide; hall, 90ft. long; 24ft. wide. Electric light (footlights). Terms for hiring: £12 per week; longer stay, £10. Amount of deposit required on booking, £5, and remainder on opening. During quiet season special arrangements can be made for companies to be put up at the hotel at reduced charges.
BATH'S BUILDING CONCERT HALL.—Secretary, Mr. Philip Burke. Terms: £10 per week. Electric light.
Market day, Saturday.

QUORN, near Loughborough, Leicester.

VILLAGE HALL.—Proprietors, The Village Hall Co., Limited; Manager, Mr. Geo. White. Dramatic license. Holding capacity: Number of persons, 350; amount, £15 to £20. Proper stage. Gas. Terms for hiring, £1 1s. per night, including use of piano. Amount of deposit required on booking, 10s.
The annual wake, September 7 to 12.

RADCLIFFE, Lancs.

Population, 25,368. Miles from London, 193.

GRAND OPERA HOUSE.—Proprietor and Manager, Mr. George Testo Sante; Acting-Manager, Mr. Jas. Boothman; Musical Director, Mr. Walter Moore; Scenic Artist, Mr. Frank Murdock. Full license. Holding capacity: Number of persons, 2,000; amount, £90. Stage measurements: 65ft. wide, 48ft. deep; proscenium opening, 27ft. Gas and electric light. Amount of printing required, 600 sheets walls, 600 lithos. Usual matinée day, Saturday. Time of band rehearsal, 1 p.m.
There are also the Queen's and Co-operative Halls, which have no dramatic licenses, but are let for concerts and ordinary entertainments.
Early closing day, Wednesday; market day, Friday.

RADSTOCK, Somerset.

Population, 3,355. Miles from London, 137.

VICTORIA HALL.—Manager, Mr. Geo. H. Gibson, Surveyor, U.D.C. Double license. Holding capacity: Number of persons, 450. Platform, 22ft. long by 10ft. wide. Lighted by gas. Terms for Hiring: One night, 25s.; two nights, 17s. 6d. per night; three nights, 15s. per night. Amount of deposit required on booking, £1 5s.
There is a good circus pitch in the town. 5,000 miners are employed within a radius of three miles.
Early closing day, Wednesday; market day, Saturday.

RAINFORD, near St. Helens, Lancs.

VILLAGE HALL.—Proprietors, The Urban District Council; Manager, Mr. B. Smith. License not required. Holding capacity: Number of persons, 400-500. Platform, length 30ft., width 12ft., depth 3ft. 6in. front and 3ft. 10in. at back. Paraffin lamps (improved). Terms for hiring, 20s. per night.
Local fair in August.

RAMSBOTTOM, Lancs.

Population, 15,920. Miles from London, 198.

CO-OPERATIVE HALL. — Manager, Mr. James Whittaker. Holding capacity: Number of persons, 1,000. Has proper stage. Lighted by gas.
Early closing day, Wednesday; market day, Saturday.

RAMSEY, Hunts.

Population, 4,823. Miles from London, 74.

THE ABBEY ROOMS.—Manager, Mr. James Mutton. Dramatic license. Holds about 400. Stage, 27ft. by 12ft. Gas. Terms, 30s. one night, 20s. subsequent night.
Local fair, July 22.
Early closing, Thursday; market, Wednesday.

RAMSEY, Isle of Man.

Population, 4,672. Miles from London, 302.

PAVILION.—Manager, Mr. F. Evans. Has dramatic license. Holding capacity: Number of persons, 1,400; amount, about £60. Proper stage; depth, 25ft.; width, 50ft.; proscenium measurements, 12ft. at each side. Gas; electric lights can be supplied if required. Terms for hiring on application.
PALACE. — Manager, Mr. R. Kermean. Dramatic license. Holds about 1,200. Stage. Electric light. Terms on application.
OLD CROSS HALL.—Manager, Mr. W. Clarey. Holds about 400. Good Platform. Gas. Terms on application.
Visiting season commences July, ends September.
Sites available for alfresco concerts, etc., on South Shore. No local fairs.

RAMSGATE, Kent.

Population, 27,733. Miles from London, 79.

ROYAL VICTORIA THEATRE.—Proprietor, Mr. Jules Richeux. Full dramatic license. Holding capacity: Number of persons, 2,000; amount, £100. Stage: Depth, 21ft.; width, 45ft.; proscenium opening, 30ft. Lighted by electricity. Amount of printing required, 600. Usual matinée day, Wednesday. Time of band rehearsal, 10 a.m. Best bookings of the year, *Dairymaids*, D'Oyly Carte Co.
ROYAL PALACE THEATRE. — Proprietor, Lord George Sanger; Resident Manager, Mr. Dan Forrest. Dramatic license. Stage, 22ft, deep by 63ft. 6in. wide. Proscenium opening 32ft. Gas and electric light, 480 and 240 volts.
PROMENADE PIER PAVILION. — Proprietor, Mr. F. C. Dew. Electric light continuous 240 volts.
GRANVILLE HALL.—Dramatic license.
ASSEMBLY ROOMS.—Holds 500. Apply, The Secretary.
THE MARINA THEATRE OF VARIETIES.—Proprietor and Manager, Mr. F. C. Dew. Dramatic and music and dancing licenses. Holds

800; amount, £50. Stage, 50ft. wide, 20ft. deep; 22ft. opening. Electric light continuous, 240 volts.
Early closing day, Thursday.
Medical Officer.—A.A.: Dr. J. B. Berry, 13, Albion Place (tel. 48). A.U.: The same. M.H.A.R.A.: The same.
Agent.—M.H.A.R.A.: Mr. C. Evans, Hall-by-the-Sea.

RAWTENSTALL, Lancs.

Population, 31,053. Miles from London, 204.

GRAND THEATRE.—Lessee, Mr. Fred Granville; Business Manager, Mr. A. R. Feather. Dramatic license. Holds about 2,300.
Early closing day, Tuesday; market days, Monday, Thursday and Saturday.
Fair ground, Central Market Ground.
Medical Officer.—A.A.: Dr. W. Robertson, Holly House. A U.: The same.

READING, Berks.

Population, 90,000. Miles from London, 36.

ROYAL COUNTY THEATRE.—Proprietors, Mr. Milton Bode and Mr. Edward Compton; Resident Manager. Mr. Fred Benton. Dramatic license. Holds 1,200. Gas and electric light, 200 volts. Printing, 1,200 sheets, 700 lithos.
THE PALACE THEATRE.—Proprietor, the Reading Palace Theatre of Varieties, Limited; Managing Director. Mr. G. Howard Watson; Resident Manager, Mr. Pan E. Draco; Musical Director, Mr. Augustus Greco; Stage Manager, Mr. Albert Burridge. Double license, with excise. Stage measurements: Depth, 28ft.; width, 58ft.; proscenium opening, 29ft. Gas and electric light. Time of band rehearsal, 1 p.m.
LARGE TOWN HALL.—Manager, The Borough Accountant, Reading. Fully licensed. Holding capacity: Number of persons, 1,550. Platform: Depth, 17ft.; width, 32ft. No proscenium. Electric light, 100 volts. Terms: Per evening, £6 6s.; per afternoon and evening, £9 10s. Amount of deposit required on booking: 20 per cent. of the full charge.
SMALL TOWN HALL.—Terms, £2 2s. per night. Seats 550. Movable platform, 14ft. by 31ft. No proscenium.
Sites for alfresco concerts and circus pitches easily obtainable. Not much difficulty is encountered over obtaining license from local council.
The population is mostly industrial, partly residential. Principal industries: Biscuits, Tin Factory, Breweries, Potteries, and Engineering Works.
Dates of local fairs: May 1, September 21 and 22. Sites for circuses, Fair Ground.
Early closing day, Wednesday; market days, Monday and Saturday.
Medical Officers.—Dr. J. Hopkins Walters, Angus Lodge, Bath Road (tel. number, 7); Dr. W. B. Secretan, 10, Redlands Road (tel. number, 614). A.U.: Dr. Walters.
Agent.—M.H.A.R.A.: H. Goddard, Osborne Arms. A.U.: The same. V.A.F.: The same.

REDCAR, Yorks.

Population, 11,800. Miles from London, 247.

ST. GEORGE'S HALL.—Proprietor and Manager, Mr. George Hearse. Double license. Holding capacity: Number of persons, 1,200. Proper stage; no scenery. Depth and width of stage, 17 ft. by 40 ft. Lighted by gas.
CENTRAL HALL. — Proprietor and Manager, Mr. George Hearse. Double

license. Holding capacity: Number of persons, 400. Proper stage (no scenery or proscenium). Depth and width of stage, 21ft. by 26 ft. Lighted by gas.

REDDITCH, Worcestershire.

Population, 16,000. Miles from London, 130.

PUBLIC HALL.—Proprietor and Manager, Mr. W. Treadgould. Holds 800. Stage, 40½ft wide by 24ft. Proscenium opening, 25ft. Gas and electric light, 210 volts. alternating. Printing: 300 sheets, 250 d.-c. and 100 lithos. Seats about 750. Fully licensed. No orchestra. Gas and electricity.

TEMPERANCE HALL.—Manager, Mr. S. Young. Has dramatic license. Seat 600.

ROYAL HOTEL ROOM. — Proprietor, Mr. G. H. Field. Seats 500. Let for concerts, kinematograph entertainments, etc. Has no dramatic license.

Portables visit here frequently. Licenses are granted by local magistrates at 5s. per month. Circuses, menageries, etc., stand on recreation field or Royal Hotel field.

Annual Fair, first Monday, Tuesday, Wednesday in August; held on Recreation Field.

Good bandstand in centre of town for concerts given by local military bands.

No grounds for alfresco concerts or pierrots.

Industries.—Making of needles, fish hooks, fishing rods and tackle, and cycles. Trade usually good October to May.

Early closing day, Wednesday.

Market day, Saturday.

REDHILL, Surrey.

Population, 15,732. Miles from London, 20.

MARKET HALL.—Proprietors, The Redhill Market Hall Company, Limited; Secretary and Manager, Mr. Alfred Simmons. Double license. Holding capacity: Number of persons, 600. Stage: Width, 34ft.; depth, 23½ft.; proscenium opening fitted with fireproof curtain, width 20ft., height, 18ft. Lighted by gas. Piano on the premises may be hired. Terms for hiring: Apply to Manager. Telephone, Redhill, 238.

KING'S HALL.—Proprietors, Governors of the Colman Institute; Manager, Mr. Leonard P. Rees, 53, Station Road. Dramatic and music and dancing licenses. Holding capacity, 320. Amount, £20 at popular prices. Concert platform 21ft. by 12ft. Electric light alternating, 200 volts. Special lantern connection and also gas connections. En suite with the Kings's Hall is the Cecil Hall. Terms for hiring: King's Hall, £2 2s.; Cecil Hall, £1 1s. Both halls, £2 15s. per night.

Early closing day, Wednesday.

Market day, alternate Wednesdays.

Medical Officers.—A. A.: Dr. E. C. Drake, Chilworth (Tel. No. 37); Dr. C. Spencer Palmer, Brook Lodge, Station-road. A.U.: The same.

REDRUTH, Cornwall.

Population 10,451. Miles from London, 304.

MASONIC HALL.—Proprietors, Redruth Masonic Hall Co., Limited; Secretary, Mr. E. M. Milford. No dramatic license. Holding capacity: Number of persons, about 140. Stage, 8ft. by 24ft. Lighted by gas. Terms for hiring: 10s. per evening, and gas extra, for three or four hours.

DRUIDS' HALL.—Secretary, Mr. Owen Hill. License for performance of stage plays. Holding capacity: 700 (included in this number are 120 tip-up seats in balcony). Amount: £55, with early doors have been taken. Stage:

36ft. wide, 16ft. deep; can be reduced to 13ft. deep. Electric light direct, 480 v.lts; 240 each side of the hall. Hot-water heating. Terms can be had on application to the Secretary.

One large fair at Whitsuntide, Friday, Saturday, and Whit Monday; generally held in Moor's field and fair meadow. The Recreation Ground is also available.

Early closing day, Thursday; market day, Friday.

REIGATE, Surrey.

Population, 15,732. Miles from London, 22.

PUBLIC HALL.—Proprietors, The Reigate Public Hall Co., Ltd; Secretary, Mr. James T. Peat. Double license. Holding capacity: Number of persons, 450. Stage: Composed of heavy tables (movable), 2ft. 4in. high, 27ft. 9in. by 17ft., or smaller if desired. Lighted by incandescent gas. Terms for hiring: For dramatic, one night, 4 guineas; two nights, 7 guineas; three nights, 9 guineas; for concert or variety Co., one night, 3 guineas; two nights, 5 guineas; three nights, 6 guineas; and 1 guinea each consecutive night beyond. Amount of deposit required on booking, usually £1 1s. per night. Billing required about 300 small posters, etc. Minimum charge for posting in Reigate, 20s.

Local fair, December 9.

Early closing day, Wednesday; market day, Tuesday.

RENFREW, Renfrew.

Population, 9,297.

TOWN HALL.—Manager, Mr. J. McLaren, Town Chamberlain. Holding capacity: Number of persons, 750. Lighted by gas. Terms for Hiring: £2 4s. 6d. per night, payable in advance.

Early closing day, Wednesday; market day, Saturday.

RETFORD, Notts.

Population, 12,340. Miles from London, 138.

TOWN HALL.—Holds about 1,000. Has dramatic license. Apply the Manager.

CORN EXCHANGE.—Has no dramatic license. Apply the Secretary.

Early closing day, Wednesday; market day, Saturday.

Medical Officer.—A.A.: Dr. R. J. Tristan, 28 Carolgate. A.U.: The same.

RHOS, Denbigh.

Population, 9,414. Miles from London, 196.

PUBLIC HALL.—Proprietors, Rhos Public Hall Co., Limited; Secretary, Mr. J. Trevor Jones. No license. Holding capacity: Number of persons, 900. There is a platform. Gas. Terms for hiring, 30s. one night; 15s. each following night. Amount of deposit required on booking, 10s. 6d.

Dates of local fairs, third Monday in May, first Monday in November.

Early closing day, Wednesday; no market day.

RHYL, Flints.

Population, 8,473. Miles from London, 209.

PALACE THEATRE. — Proprietors, Rhyl Palace, Arcade, and Hotel Company, Limited. Manager and Secretary, Mr. Samuel Thornley.

Booking circuit, Llandudno, Colwyn Bay, and North Wales coast. Musical Director, Miss Mabel Hughes. Dramatic and music and dancing licenses Holding capacity: Number of persons, 1,500. Stage measurements: Proscenium opening, 27ft.; height to grid, 50ft.; between fly rails, 33ft.; wall to wall, 51ft. Electric light, 230 volts. Band rehearsal 6 p.m. Usual matinée days, Monday and Saturday. Bars no surrounding halls. The theatre is being re-built.

TOWN HALL.—Manager, Mr. Arthur Rowlands, Town Clerk. Double license. Holding capacity: Number of persons, 950. Stage, 37ft. by 19½ft.; proscenium, 27ft. wide. Gas and electric light. Terms for hiring: £3 per night. Amount of deposit required on booking: £3.

No sites available for portables, etc.

No local fairs. Abergele (three miles), has one second Wednesday in each month.

Agent.—V.A.F.: F. T. Rogers, Mona Hotel, Queen Street.

RHYMNEY, Mon.

Population, 7,582. Miles from London, 173.

VICTORIA HALL.—Manager, Dar Horlando Morris. Dramatic license. Holding capacity: Number of persons, 800; amount, £40. No proscenium, footlights, or scenery. Stage measurements, 18 ft. by 40 ft. Lighted by gas. Amount of printing required, 350 sheets. Terms for hiring: One night, 50s.; two nights, 82s. 6d.; three nights, 122s. 6d.; one week, £10 (inclusive of gas, etc.). Amount of deposit required on booking, £1.

Early closing day, Thursday.

RICHMOND, Surrey.

Population, 31,672. Miles from London, 10.

NEW RICHMOND HIPPODROME. — Proprietor, Mr. George Dance. Double license. Variety bookings in conjunction with Messrs. Barrasford. Band rehearsal, 2 p.m. Electric current 210 volts alternating.

CASTLE ASSEMBLY ROOMS, situated in Whittaker Avenue, Hill Street, provide accommodation for all classes of theatrical companies. They consist of:—

(1) CASTLE THEATRE.—Licensed as a theatre; fitted with stage, proscenium, and all requisite fittings. Accommodates 700 people. Electric current direct 220 volts.

(2) CONCERT HALL.—Accommodates 600 to 700; fitted with platform and music gallery; suitable for pierrot and variety entertainments. Electric current the same.

Proprietor and Manager, Mr. P. Twitchin.

Circus pitches and sites for alfresco concerts are obtainable in the Old Deer Park (87 acres), on application to the Town Clerk, Town Hall, Richmond.

Early closing day, Wednesday. No market day.

Medical Officer.—A.A.: Dr. J. R. Johnson, 3, Ellerker Gate.

RICHMOND, Yorks.

Population, 3,837. Miles from London, 237.

TOWN HALL.—Proprietors, the Corporation. Apply Mr. John Proctor, the Borough Accountant. Double license. Holds 350. No proper stage. Gas. Terms: 22s. one night, 16s. each succeeding night. Gas heating and attendant extra. Full amount on booking.

Cattle Fair, Nov. 2.

Early closing, Wednesday; market, Saturday.

RICKMANSWORTH, Herts.

Population, 5,627. Miles from London, 21.

TOWN HALL.—Manager, Mr. R. E. Snelling, High Street. Double license. Holding capacity: Number of persons, 250 to 300; amount, £12, about, according to prices charged. Platform stage, 3ft. high (movable); depth, 11ft. 8in.; width, 26ft. 6in. No proscenium. Lighted by incandescent gas. Amount of printing required, 100 posters, 1,000 handbills. Terms for hiring, £1 5s. for one night, or by arrangement for longer periods. Amount of deposit required on booking, £1.

EBURY HALL.—Secretary, the Rev. E. O. Beverley, Nightingale Road. No dramatic license. Seats 240. Small platform, 8ft 6in. by 16ft. 6in; larger platform if desired. No proscenium. Gas. Terms, including piano: 17s. 6d. afternoon, 25s. evening.

DICKINSON INSTITUTE, Croxley Green.—Secretary, Mr. M. W. Raggett.

Early closing day, Wednesday.

RINGWOOD, Hants.

Population, 4,629. Miles from London, 103.

MANOR HOUSE THEATRE.—Manager, Mr. William Tanner. Double license, dramatic or music and dancing. Holding capacity: Number of persons, 500. Proper stage; depth and width, 26ft.; proscenium measurements, 19ft. and 8ft. each side; flats 12ft. high. Lighted by gas. Amount of printing required: 200 d.c. sheets. Terms for hiring: £2 2s. per night, including gas and attendant; payable in advance.

Fairs, July 10, December 11.

Early closing, Thursday; market, Wednesday.

RIPLEY, Derbyshire.

Population, 10,111. Miles from London, 137.

CO-OPERATIVE HALL. — Manager, Mr. Henry Stanley, Co-operative Stores. Has dramatic license. Holding capacity: Number of persons, 600. Platform only, 20ft. by 8ft.; can be enlarged at a small cost to 23ft. 6in. by 12ft. 6in. Lighted by gas. Terms for hiring: One night, £2; two, £4; three, £5 10s.; six, £9. Amount of deposit required on booking, 25 per cent.

Early closing, Wednesday; market, Saturday.

RIPON, Yorks.

Population, 8,230. Miles from London, 214.

VICTORIA HALL.—Address the Manager. Dramatic license.

Early closing, Friday; market, Thursday.

RISCA, Mon.

Population, 9,661. Miles from London, 147½.

PUBLIC HALL.—Manager, Mr. Tom Davies. Has dramatic license. Holding capacity: Number of persons, 900; amount, £40. Large stage. Lighted by gas. Terms for hiring, one night £2 2s., two nights £3 10s., three nights £4 10s., one week £6 6s. Amount of deposit required on booking, 25 per cent. Trade good and growing district.

ROCHDALE, Lancs.

Population, 84,000. Miles from London, 194.

THEATRE ROYAL AND OPERA HOUSE.—Proprietors. Northern Theatres Company, Limited. Managing Director, Mr. W. Robinson; General Manager, Mr. Otto C. Culling; Resident Manager, Mr. S. Burton. Dramatic license. Holds 2,000.

THE EMPIRE THEATRE OF VARIETIES. —Proprietor, Mr. Thomas Hargreaves; Manager, Mr. Frank Hargreaves; Musical Director, Mr. Frank Eastwood. Music and dancing license. Holding capacity: Number of persons, 1,500. Stage measurements, 20 ft. by 30 ft. by 19 ft. Electric light. Time of band rehearsal, 2 p.m. No matinée. Bars a six miles radius. Two houses a night.

NEW HIPPODROME. — Lessees, Messrs. J. and J. Jackson; Manager, Mr. John Jackson; Acting Manager, Mr. James Jackson, sen.; Musical Director, Mr. Willie Morgan. Music and dancing license. Holding capacity; Number of persons, 2,500. Stage measurements, 32ft. by 31ft. Electric light. Time of band rehearsal, 2 p.m. No matinée. Two houses a night.

TOWN HALL.—Apply Borough Treasurer. Licensed. Terms for letting: For concert, lecture, or meeting, with use of cloak-rooms, lavatories, and small ante-room, and not kept open after 11 p.m., one day, £6 6s.; for entertainment (same conditions), first day, £5 5s.; per week, £30. Magistrates' room for use of concert, one day £1 1s.

PUBLIC HALL, Baillie-street.—Apply Mr. J. W. Greenwood, the hallkeeper, Acker-street. 80 ft. long, 40 ft. wide, 32 ft. high. Holds 1,000.

Other Halls: PROVIDENT HALL, Lord-street; seat 1,000. Terms for concert, £2 10s. TEMPERANCE HALL, Smith-street; seat 400. Terms, apply Mr. J. Stott, 117 Molesworth-street. AMBULANCE DRILL HALL, Summer-street, and EQUITABLE PIONEERS' ASSEMBLY ROOM, Toad-lane; seat 800. Let for lectures and concerts at £1 per night; room-keeper's fee, 2s. 6d. extra.

Rochdale is surrounded by populous villages, to which there are excellent tram and railway facilities.

Industries: Principally cotton and woollen. Rochdale fair (or wakes called "Rush-bearing") is held on the Monday after the third Sunday in August and continues during the week.

No portables or alfresco concerts. Circus pitches are obtainable.

Early closing day, Tuesday; market days, Monday and Saturday.

Medical Officers.—A.A.: Dr. W. Bartlett Chapman, Grove-place, Drake-street. A.U.: The same. M.H.A.R.A.: Dr. Harris, Wellfield House, Oldham-road.

Agents.—M.H.A.R.A.: N. Kennedy Bishop, Blaize Hotel. A.U.: E. Burt, Roebuck Hotel. V.A.F.: The same.

RECOMMENDED APARTMENTS.

Mrs. Townsend, 24, Clement Royd Street.—Sitting-room, 2 bedrooms, 1 combined room; piano.

ROCHESTER, Kent.

Population, 33,000. Miles from London, 30.

CORN EXCHANGE.—Proprietors, The City Corporation. Has dramatic license. Apply, Mr. William Oldroyd, 141, High Street. Large hall 800; Small 400. Movable stages. Terms, Large Hall, £4 10s. one day, reduction for subsequent days. Dramatic Co. s 10s. 6d. extra for license and insurance. Small Hall 30s. per day.

VICTORIA HALL.—Proprietors, The Conservative Club. Has dramatic license. Apply, the Secretary.

Rochester has a fair at that part of the city known as Strood—date, August 26, 27, 28. The city is not visited by portables.

Sites for alfresco concerts and circus pitches are obtainable, but with some difficulty, owing to a scarcity of private open spaces.

Local population: Residential in Rochester; industrial in Strood.

Early closing day, Wednesday; market day, Tuesday.

ROMFORD, Essex.

Population, 13,656. Miles from London, 12.

CORN EXCHANGE.—Apply, The Secretary. Dramatic license.

PUBLIC BATHS HALL.—Manager, Mr. H. C. Green. Music and dancing license. Holding capacity: Number of persons, 500 to 600; amount, £20. Stage, 20ft. wide by 12ft. deep. Lighted by gas. Terms for hiring, 30s. per night of three hours.

Early closing day, Thursday; market day, Wednesday.

ROMSEY, Hants.

Population, 4,355. Miles from London, 81.

TOWN HALL.—Apply Hallkeeper. Dramatic license.

Early closing, Wednesday; market, alternate Thursdays.

ROSS, Herefordshire.

Population, 5,000. Miles from London, 132.

CORN EXCHANGE. — Managers, Messrs. Cooper and Preece, estate agents, Ross (telephone, P.O. 21). Has dramatic license. Holding capacity: Number of persons, about 600; seat about 350. Depth of stage, 18ft.; width, 38ft.; height to ceiling, 15ft. Lighted by gas. Terms for hiring: One or two nights, 35s. per night; three nights, £4 10s.; six nights, £6 6s.; inclusive of gas, but exclusive of usual hallkeeper's fee. Amount of deposit required on booking: 10s. for one night; £1 for longer.

Early closing day, Tuesday; market day, Thursday.

ROTHERHAM.

Population, 62,500. Miles from London, 167.

THEATRE ROYAL.—Proprietor, North of England Theatre Corporation, Ltd.; Managing Director, Mr. Frank Macnaghten; Acting Manager, Mr. Holbery Hardy; Musical Director, Mr. Sam Burgan. No Excise license. Holding capacity: Number of persons, 2,200; amount, £100. Stage measurements: 32ft. deep, 60ft. wide; proscenium, 27ft. wide, 22ft. high. Electric light, 450 and 230 volts direct. Printing: 500 d.c. sheets for walls, 500 d.c. lithos for windows. Time of band rehearsal, 1.30 p.m. All Bank Holiday dates good, also first Monday in November (fair week, annually).

NEW HIPPODROME. — Proprietors, The Rotherham Hippodrome, Ltd.; Managing Directors, T. E. Fox and T. S. Smith; Resident Manager, Mr. Claude Shayler; Musical Director, Mr. Thomas Richardson. No Excise license. Holding capacity, 3,000. Stage measurements: 30ft. deep, 60ft. wide; proscenium opening, 30ft. wide, 26 t. high. Electric light. Animated picture matinée every Saturday.

TOWN HALL ASSEMBLY ROOMS.—Manager, Mr. Edward Cooper. Music and dancing license; dramatic on application to magistrates. Holding capacity: Number of persons, 900. Stage, 42ft. by 14ft. 6in. Gas and electric light, 230 volts; for kinematograph purposes, 60 volts. Terms for hiring: £11 16s. 3d. per week, lighting extra. Amount of deposit required on booking: £4 per week.

DRILL HALL.—Apply, Baylis and Baylis, High Street. Music and dancing license. Holds 1,700. Gas. Terms, £15 15s. per week. Electric cable can be attached.

Dates of local fairs: Statute fair, first Monday in November. No sites available for portables. Circus pitch is readily obtainable. The population is now nearly 65,000. It is largely industrial—stove-grate works, steel, iron, brassfounders, mining being the chief. The town is conveniently served by Midland and Great Central Railways and Canal.

Early closing day, Thursday; market days, Monday and Friday.

Medical Officers.—A.U.: Dr. John Simpson, Cawdor House. A.U.: The same. M.H.A.R.A.: Mr. W. H. Rowthorn, Wilton House.

Agent.—M.H.A.RA.: J. H. Fletcher, Monad Hotel. A.U.: The same. V.A.F.: The same.

RECOMMENDED APARTMENTS.

Mrs. Clements, 82, St. Ann's Road.—2 bedrooms and sitting-room : piano.

M. Widdison, Wyndham House, Winifred Street.—Front bed and sitting-room: double-bedded room and sitting-room. Bath. Piano.

ROTHESAY, Bute.

Population, 9,320.

PUBLIC HALL.—Holds about 1,500. Has dramatic license. Apply to the Manager.

Early closing day, Wednesday.

Medical Officer.—A.A.: Dr. J. B. Lawson, 2, Battery Place. A.U.: The same.

ROYSTON, Herts.

Population, 3,517. Miles from London, 45.

TOWN HALL.—Proprietors, Urban District Council. Apply Town Clerk. Dramatic license. Holds 400. Stage 26ft. 9in. wide by 8ft. 6in. deep, extending to 15ft. 6in. Gas. Terms, 30s. per night; extras: gas, piano, stage extension, and fireman.

Local fairs, first Wednesday and Thursday after October 13.

Early closing, Thursday; market, Wednesday.

ROYTON (near Oldham), Lancs.

Population, 14,881. Miles from London, 195.

CONSERVATIVE HALL.—Secretary, Mr. James Beswick. No license required. Holding capacity: Number of persons, 350, seated. No proper stage. Gas, incandescent lights. Terms for hiring, 15s., with piano. Amount of deposit required on booking, 10s.

Only one fair, the first Saturday in August, for a week, when the mills are stopped.

Early closing, Tuesday; market, Thursday.

RUGBY, Warwick.

Population, 21,000. Miles from London, 82.

TOWN HALL.—Proprietors, The Rugby Town Hall Company, Ltd. Has dramatic license, and holds about 600. Gas. Apply Secretary. Stage 18ft. deep by 32ft. wide.

CO-OPERATIVE HALL.—Manager, Mr. W. H. Watson. Music and dancing and dramatic licenses. Holding capacity: Number of persons, 850. Depth and width of stage, 18ft. by 37ft. Lighted by gas. Terms for hiring: £2 10s. first night; £2 each succeeding night.

Early closing day, Wednesday; market day, Saturday.

Medical Officer.—A.A.: Dr. C. J. I. Krumbholz, Alma House, Albert Street. A.U.: The same.

RUGELEY, Staffs.

Population, 4,447. Miles from London, 124.

TOWN HALL.—Proprietors, Urban District Council. Apply, John Wallbank, Collector, 52, Lichfield Street. Double license. Holds 400-450. Platform. Gas. Terms: One night, £2 2s.; two, £3 15s.; three, £5 5s.; six, £6 10s.; Sunday, £1 10s. extra. Full amount on booking.

Local fair, June 1 to 6.

Early closing, Wednesday; markets, Thursday and Saturday.

RUNCORN, Cheshire.

Population, 16,491. Miles from London, 180.

PUBLIC HALL AND THEATRE.—Manager, Mr. Edgar Lea. Dramatic license. Seating capacity: Number of persons, 800; amount, £45. Stage measurements: 32ft. deep from inside proscenium to back wall, 44ft. wide, 35ft. high to underside of grid; proscenium opening, 28ft. wide, 19ft. high. Lighted by gas, with self-intensifying lamps. Amount of printing required, 200 to 300 double crown. Terms for hiring, £10 per week (gas included) or sharing. Amount of deposit required on booking, one-third. Remarks: Very extensive alterations have just been made—new stage, new proscenium, new grid, new lights, and entirely redecorated. Warmed by hot water.

THEATRE ROYAL, Runcorn.—This theatre, built of wood, was completely burned to the ground in 1906. There is no intention of re-building, the present idea being to utilise the site for a hotel bowling green, and it has been walled round apparently for that purpose.

Early closing day, Wednesday; market day, Saturday.

RYDE, Isle of Wight.

Population, 11,043. Miles from London, 79.

THEATRE ROYAL.—Proprietor, Mr. Charles Constant. Full license. Holding capacity: amount, £70. Stage measurements: opening, 19 ft.; back wall to footlights, 37½ ft.; back wall to inside opening, 32½ ft.; width wall to wall, 40ft.; width between flies, 25½ ft.; can fly cloths 21 ft. by 25 ft.; take 18 ft. flats. Electric light, 240 voltage; gas also available. Printing required: About 300 sheets. Usual matinée day, Wednesday.

TOWN HALL.—Dramatic license. Seats 700. Suitable for fit-up. Stage, 37ft. by 12ft. by 3ft. 6in.; can be enlarged. Terms for hiring: £3 3s. per night; £2 2s. afternoon. SMALL HALL: £1 14s. the evening, and £1 1s. the afternoon. JUSTICES' ROOM: The evening, £1 4s.; afternoon, 15s., all subject to arrangement with the insurance company.

PIER PAVILION.—Dramatic license. Seats 600. Stage and footlights.

The best season is August, September, and part of October. The second week in August is the Yacht Racing Week. Ryde is essentially a three-night town, but the week is easily worked with Sandown, Shanklin, and Ventnor.

Population almost entirely residential.

The Mead Gardens, in the centre of town, are open for alfresco concerts and pastoral plays. Apply, Secretary.

Circus pitches are attainable. Apply, J. Vickers Blake, The Homestead.

Early closing day, Thursday.

Medical Officers.—A.A.: Dr. K. W. I. Mackenzie, Lansdowne House: tel. No. 55, Ryde. A.U.: Dr. Mackenzie. M.H.A.R.A.: Dr. E. D. Godfrey, Sea View.

RECOMMENDED APARTMENTS.

Mrs. Dewey, Marine House, Castle Street.— 9 bedrooms, 3 sitting-rooms, 2 combined; piano.

RYE, Sussex.

Population, 3,900. Miles from London, 71.

CINQUE PORTS ASSEMBLY ROOM.— Manager, Mr. H. Mountain. Has dramatic license. Holding capacity: Number of persons, 300. Proper stage, 28ft. by 26ft. by 20ft, and dressing rooms. Lighted by gas. Terms for hiring: One night, 30s.; two or more, 25s.; matinée, 5s.; kinematograph, £1. Amount of deposit required on booking, 10s.

No local fairs. No sites available for portables, etc.

Early closing day, Tuesday. Market day, Wednesday.

ST. ALBANS, Herts.

Population, 16,019. Miles from London, 20.

COUNTY HALL.—Lessee, Mr. A. Rowden. Fully licensed. Holding capacity: Number of persons, 1,000. Stage 40 ft. wide, 25 ft. deep; permanent proscenium, fitted with dropscene; head and foot lights. Proscenium opening, 22 ft. Good dressing-rooms; height from stage to fly beams, 20 ft. 10 in Gas; probably electric light shortly. Terms for hiring: Sharing terms. The only licensed hall in the city.

Early closing day, Thursday; market days, Wednesday and Saturday.

ST. ANDREWS, Fifeshire.

Population, 7,621. Miles from London, 444.

TOWN HALL.—Proprietors, the City Corporation. Apply City Factor. Double license. Seats 500. No fixed stage. Gas. Electric current can be obtained. Terms: £2 2s. one night, and £1 1s. each succeeding night. Gas and hallkeeper, extra. Deposit, £1 1s.

VOLUNTEER HALL.—Managers, Messrs. J. and G. Innes, "Citizen" Office. Dramatic license. Holds 1,000. Platform. Gas. Terms: £2 2s. one night. £1 1s. second. Deposit 10s.

Local fair: Second Tuesday in August.

Early closing, Thursday; market, Monday.

ST. ANNES-ON-THE-SEA, Lancs.

Population, 6,838. Miles from London, 250. Summer population, 20,000.

PUBLIC HALL AND THEATRE.—Lessee and Manager, Mr. Fred Carlton. Dramatic license. Holding capacity: Number of persons, 1,000; amount, £50. Stage measurements: 38 ft. by 36 ft.; proscenium opening, 22 ft. Electric light. Terms for hiring: £4 4s. per night, or shares. Amount of deposit required on booking, half.

ST. AUSTELL, Cornwall.

Population, 11,400. Miles from London, 280.

PUBLIC ROOMS.—Proprietors, St. Austell Public Rooms Company, Limited; Secretary, Walter J. Nicholls. Double license. Holds 850. Stage, 40ft. by 10ft., may be extended. Gas.

Terms: First night, £2 2s.; second and following nights, £1 1s.

SMALL HALL, Part of the above.—40 ft. by 22ft. Term 10s. per evening. These fees must be paid in advance. Apply Mr. Nicholls.

Billposting Co.: St. Austell Billposting and Advertising Company. Booking office, E. A. Liglow, County Music Store.

Chief industry, china clay.

Public rooms, as per particulars above, with the small hall for auctions, etc. Fair Park for shows, circus, portables. Chief fair, Feast Wednesday, first Wednesday after Trinity Sunday.

Early closing day, Thursday, 1 o'clock; market day, Friday.

Best business town in county. No distress or poverty, in consequence of constant and plentiful work in china clay works. Good main street. 1½ miles from seaside. Charlestown, shipping port.

District population, within radius of six miles, about 30,000.

ST. BEES, Cumberland.

Miles from London, 275.

HODGETT'S CLUB HALL.—Secretary, Mr. Wm. Mawson. No license. Holding capacity: Number of persons, about 300. Small stage. Lighted by gas. Terms for hiring: £1 per evening. Not let for animated pictures.

ST. COLUMB, Cornwall.

Population, 3,908. Miles from London, 290.

TOWN HALL.—Manager, Mr. A. Goldsworthy. No dramatic license. Holding capacity: Number of persons, 400. Platform, 9ft. 2in. by 14ft. 10in. Lighted by gas. Terms for hiring: £1 1s. per night. Amount of deposit required on booking, 5s. Thursdays and Saturdays are not good nights for booking.

Dates of local fairs, mid Thursdays in March and November.

Early closing day, Wednesday. Market day, Thursday.

ST. HELENS, Lancs.

Population, 84,410. Miles from London, 191.

THEATRE AND OPERA HOUSE.—Proprietors, The St. Helens Theatre, Limited; General Manager, Mr. Alfred M. Loader. Box Office, Miss M. Newcomen; Musical Director, Mr. J. Duxbury. Full license. Holding capacity: Number of persons, 2,500; amount, £120, ordinary prices. Stage measurements: 50 ft. deep, 70 ft. wide; proscenium opening, 20 ft. Electric light.

HIPPODROME.—Proprietors, Messrs. Thos. Barrasford, W. Sley, and F. Willmot; Manager, Mr. Walter Mould. Booking Circuit, Mr. Willmot, 156, Islington, Liverpool. Musical Director, Mr. Norman Bath. Double license. Holding capacity: Number of persons, 2,800; amount, £120 nightly. Stage measurements: Proscenium, 25 ft. by 25 ft.; stage, 38 ft. wide by 63 ft. deep. Electric light (own power). Time of band rehearsal, 12 o'clock noon. Usual matinée day, Thursday. Bars no surrounding halls.

Early closing day, Thursday; market days, Saturday and Monday.

Agent.—M.H.A.R.A.: Alf Thorp, Black Bull Hotel. V.A.F.: J. P. Thorp, Royal Alfred Hotel

ST. IVES, Huntingdon.

Population, 2,916.   Miles from London, 60.

CORN EXCHANGE.—Secretary, Mr. H I.
Hankin.   Dramatic license.   Seats 500. Stage
platform adjustable.   It is usually 20ft. wide
by 15ft. deep; height to glass span roof, 30ft.
Gas (incandescent).   Terms: 36s. one night;
two nights, £3 3s.   Deposit fee on booking,
£1.   Hooks and eyes provided for attaching
scenery.   Piano may be had on payment.
The directors keep the previous ten days to a
booking clear of a booking of a similar nature.
Kinematograph entertainments are allowable,
subject to the Fire Insurance Co.'s instructions
being carried out.
Early closing day, Thursday for shops;
Saturday for offices and factories.   Market
day, Monday.

ST. LEONARDS.

(See Hastings.)

ST. NEOTS, Hunts.

Population, 3,880. Miles from London, 51.

CORN EXCHANGE.—Proprietors, Corn Exchange Company.   Apply Hallkeeper.   Dramatic license.
Early closing, Tuesday; market, Thursday.

SAFFRON WALDEN, Essex.

Population, 5,896   Miles from London, 44.

ASSEMBLY ROOMS,   TOWN HALL.—Proprietors, Corporation. Apply Manager. Dramatic license.
Early closing, Thursday; markets, Tuesday
and Saturday.

SALFORD, Lancs.

Population, 220,957. Miles from London, 189.

PRINCE OF WALES'S THEATRE.—Pro-
prietor and Manager, Mr. E. B. Goulden;
Acting Manager, Mr A. H. Goulden; Musical
Director, Mr. J. W. Ingham; Scenic Artist,
Mr. C. Roberts. Full dramatic license. Hold-
ing capacity: Number of persons, 2,000.
Amount, £70. Stage measurements: 34 ft. by
30 ft. wide. Electric and gas. Amount of
printing required: 1,000 d.c.   Usual matinée
day, Wednesday. Time of band rehearsal, 1
p.m. No towns barred.
REGENT OPERA HOUSE, Cross Lane.—
Managing Director, Mr. Wilberforce Turner;
General Manager, Mr. Lester King; Assistant
Manager, Mr. E. Shepherd; Chief Operator,
Mr. R. Rockett. Two houses nightly, 7 and
9 p.m. Matinée, Saturday afternoon, 3 p.m.
HIPPODROME.—Proprietors, Messrs. W. H.
Broadhead and Son; Resident Acting Manager,
Mr. Geo. F. Slatter; Musical Director, Mr. E.
Jones; Scenic Artist, Mr. Edward Leigh. Stage
measurements: 50 ft. by 50 ft. by 36 ft. Gas
and electric light. Usual matinée day, Mon-
day. Time of band rehearsal, 2 p.m.
VICTORIA   THEATRE,   Broughton.—Pro-
prietors, Broughton Theatre Syndicate,
Limited; Manager and Licensee, Mr. J. Fred
Watson. Electric light, voltage 220.   Holds
3,000. Printing, 1,800; lithos, 1,000. Wednes-
day, matinée. Full license. Smoking permitted.
REGENT   THEATRE   OF   VARIETIES,
Cross Lane.—Managing Director, Mr. W.

Turner; Manager, Mr. H. Raymond; Secretary, Mr. J. C. Patterson. Rehearsal,
Monday, 1.30. Performances twice nightly,
6.50 and 9 p.m.
ROYAL TECHNICAL INSTITUTE, Peel
Park.—Holding capacity: 750 seated, 850 standing. Stage: 30ft. by 18ft. No fit up. Electric
light. Address, Caretaker, Technical School,
Salford.
PENDLETON TOWN HALL.—Address, Chief
Cashier.   Double license.   Holding capacity: Number of persons, 800 standing, 600
seated. Stage, 15ft. by 38ft., often extended
by hirers.   No fit up.   Electric light.
Terms for hiring: £2 10s. per night; £10 per
week (six days). Amount of deposit required
on booking, half.
An industrial population. The chief docks
of the Manchester Ship Canal are situated in
the borough.   The new King's Dock, over
half a mile long, in close proximity to the
places of amusement.
Broughton theatre (the Victoria) caters for
the inhabitants of that part of the borough.
It is two miles from the nearest Salford place
of amusement.
Early closing day, Wednesday.   Market
day, Tuesday.
Medical Officer.—A.A.: Dr. Kenney, Ellor
Street, Pendleton.

RECOMMENDED APARTMENTS.

Miss Wilson, 54, East Wynford Street.—Bathroom.

SALISBURY, Wilts.

Population, 21,827. Miles from London, 82.

COUNTY HALL. — Proprietor, Mr. Arthur
Whitehead; Manager, Mr. T. Brinsmead. Has
dramatic license. Holds about 1,000. Proscenium opening 28ft. or 24ft.; depth to back wall,
30ft.; width stage, wall to wall, 46ft.; height to
gridiron, 24ft. 6ins. Has some scenery. Gas.
Terms, £5 5s. one night, £8 8s. two, £10 10s. three.
VICTORIA HALL. — Apply Manager.   No
dramatic license. Holds 800.
ASSEMBLY ROOMS.—Apply Manager.
CENTRAL HALL.—Apply Manager.
There are no large industries. Trade in the
city mostly dependent upon agriculture and the
many visitors to the city on account of the
Cathedral and vicinity of Stonehenge and Bulford
Camp.
The local fair is held here the third Tuesday and Wednesday in October, almost entirely
devoted to pleasure.   No portable theatre
here for many years, and now there might
be some difficulty in obtaining licenses.
One or two circuses visit the city every year,
and do good business. A pitch is always obtainable in "The Butts." Alfresco concerts
have been held during the past two summers
in the Victoria Park, by permission of the
Town Council, and these have been very popular. Mr. F. D'Alton Tebby has had these entertainments under his control.
Early closing day, Wednesday; market days,
Tuesday and Saturday.
Agent.—M.H.A.R.A.: R. W. George, "Five
Bells."

SALTASH, Cornwall.

Population, 3,357. Miles from London, 245.

STAR HALL.—Manager, Mr. Rd. Giles.
Double license. Holding capacity: Number of
persons, 400. Proper stage.   Measurements,
24 ft. by 17 ft. Lighted by gas. Terms for
hiring: £2 2s. per night. Amount of deposit
required on booking, 10s.
Early closing day, Wednesday.

SALTBURN-BY-THE-SEA, Yorks.

Population, 2,578. Miles from London, 252.

ASSEMBLY HALL.—Manager, Mr. Geo. C. Mason. Dramatic license. Holding capacity: Number of persons, 500. Stage measurements: Proscenium opening, 24ft.; depth, 23ft.; width, 40ft.; full width behind wings, 60ft. Electric light. Amount of printing required: Three 12-sheet, twelve 6-sheet, fifty d.c. Terms for hiring: In season, £4 4s. per night; generally share. Amount of deposit required on booking: Half rent.

The season begins first Monday in July to end of September. Illuminations in gardens every Wednesday in season. Companies are not booked on those days.

Early closing day, Wednesday.

SALTCOATS, Ayrshire.

Population, 8,121. Miles from London, 396.

TOWN HALL.—Proprietors, Saltcoats Town Council; Manager, Mr. John Miller, Town Chamberlain. Double license. Holding capacity: Number of persons, 900. Platform, 36ft. 6ins. wide; 14ft. deep; 4ft. 6ins. high; height of ceiling from platform, 26ft. Lighted by gas. Terms for hiring per night: Theatrical performance, £3 13s. 6d.; concert, £3 3s.; Fridays, £1 1s. extra. Amount of deposit required on booking, one-third of hire.

Large increase in population during the summer.

Date of local fair, last Thursday in May, but site always let to one man. Circus Pitch, Brewery Farm.

SANDBACH, Cheshire.

Population, 5,558. Miles from London, 162.

TOWN HALL.—Manager, Mr. Amos Wood. Double license. Holding capacity: Number of persons, 600. Proper stage. Lighted by gas. Amount of printing required: 50 billposting stations. Terms for hiring on application

Dates of local fairs, Easter Tuesday, September 17, and December 28. Fairs are almost extinct. The weekly market on Thursday has superseded them; more visitors attend these weekly than the old Fair days.

Early closing day, Tuesday.

SANDGATE, Kent.

Population, 5,558. Miles from London. 68.

ALHAMBRA THEATRE OF VARIETIES. Early closing day, Wednesday.

Agent.—M.H.A.R.A.; Mr. Johnson, Alhambra Theatre.

SANDOWN, Isle of Wight.

Population 5,006. Miles from London, 86.

TOWN HALL.—Manager, Clerk to the Council. Fully licensed. Holding capacity: Number of persons, 500. Concert platform, 33 ft. by 18 ft. Further information from Hon. Sec. of Town Band, Sandown, who have scenery, etc., for hire. Lighted by gas. Terms for hiring: £2 2s. first night, and £1 1s. each consecutive night. Amount of deposit required on booking, 10s. Extra charge for footlights, heating, etc., and gas.

PIER PAVILION.—Holds about 400. Early closing day, Wednesday.

SANDY, Bedfordshire.

Population, 3,560. Miles from London, 44.

CONSERVATIVE HALL.—Manager, Mr. Wm. Green. Dramatic license. Holding capacity: Number of persons, 300 to 350. Movable stage, adaptable to any size. Usual measurements: Depth, front to back, 14 ft.; width 20 ft. Full width of hall, 26 ft. Lighted by gas. A fair amount of printing required. Several small villages near. Terms for hiring: Concert, lectures, etc., requiring no footlights, 21s. one night, 10s. 6d. each succeeding night. Stage plays with footlights, 23s. one night, 11s. 6d. each succeeding night. Amount of deposit required on booking, 10s. 6d. There are two dressing rooms, etc., back of stage—one for ladies, with lavatory, etc., and the other for gentlemen.

TOWN HALL.—Manager, Mr. F. W. Western. Dramatic license. Seats 500. Stage, 29ft. by 18ft. Gas.

Dates of local fairs: Feast week, third week in July; Flower Show, last Thursday in August. Site: The only available site for circuses, etc., The Red Lion Inn close.

Early closing day, Thursday.

SAXMUNDHAM, Suffolk.

Population, 1,452. Miles from London, 90.

MARKET HALL.—Managers, Messrs. Flick and Son. No dramatic license. Holding capacity: Number of persons, 150. No proper stage. lighted by gas. Terms for hiring: One guinea per night; gas for footlights extra. Amount of deposit required on booking: Whole rent payable. Printer: H. B. Crisp, adjoining hall. Billposter: Benjamin Cooper. Hall attendant: Sergeant James Baker. Hall not available on Wednesdays, nor on alternate Thursdays.

Early closing day, Thursday; market day, Wednesday.

SCARBOROUGH, Yorks.

Population, 38,161. Miles from London, 229.

LONDESBOROUGH THEATRE.—Proprietors, Messrs. Waddington and Sons; Manager, Mr. J. T. Carpenter; Musical Director, Mr. Henry Irvine. Full license. Holding capacity: Number of persons, 1,200. Summer and winter prices vary. Stage measurements: Depth, 26ft.; width, front 52ft., back 30ft.; proscenium opening, 28ft. Electric light. Amount of printing required, about 900 sheets. Matinées only by special arrangement. Time of band rehearsal, 1 p.m. Best dates, July to October.

THE SPA.—Proprietors, the Cliff Bridge Company; Manager, Mr. Fras. Goodricke; Musical Director, Mr. Irvine. Full license for three months. Holding capacity: Number of persons, 700. Electric light.

THEATRE ROYAL.—Proprietors, Mr. and Mrs. E. L. Garside; Manager, Mr. F. P. Morgan. Dramatic license. Electric and gas. Amount of printing required, about 500 sheets. Time of band rehearsal, 1.30 p.m.

HIPPODROME.—Proprietors, the Hippodrome, Scarborough, Ltd.; Managing Director, Mr. W. Peacock; Resident Manager, Mr. C. Fielding Smith. Holds 2,000. Twice nightly. Stage, 30ft. deep, 60ft. wide. Proscenium opening, 30ft. Electric light. Band rehearsal, 12 noon. Special flying matinées are given during the season.

AQUARIUM.—Proprietors, the People's Palace and Aquarium Co., Limited; Secretary and Manager, Mr. W. Kitchingman.

Other halls available for concerts and general entertainments are the Spa, Grand Hall, Old Town Hall, Albert Hall, and Mechanics' Hall.

Population is more than doubled during season. Scarboro' has no local fair. The town is not visited by portables. Sites for alfresco concerts are mainly on the sands, but the Alexandra Gardens and Clarence Gardens, owned by the Corporation, are now available and permission must be obtained from the

Town Clerk. Circuses very seldom visit Scar-
boro', but a piece of ground suitable for such
purposes can be rented from Mr. W. P. New-
ham, Victoria Road, Scarboro'. Very cen-
trally situated.
Early closing day, Wednesday; market day,
Thursday.
Medical Officers: A.A.: Dr. T. M. Foley, 5,
Queen Street. Telephone, No. 139. Dr. C. E.
Salter, Scarborough. A.U.: Dr. Salter.
M.H.A.R.A.: Dr. Foley.
Agent.—M.H.A.R.A.: T. Moor, Sun Hotel,
St. Thomas Street. V.A.F.: The same.

SCUNTHORPE, Lincs.

Population, 6,750. Miles from London, 191.
PUBLIC HALL.—Manager, Mr. W. W. John-
son. Dramatic license. Holding capacity:
Number of persons, about 700.
Early closing day, Wednesday; market day,
Saturday.
Medical Officer.—A.A.: Dr. M. R. J. Beh-
rendt, 30, Frodingham Road. A.U.: The same.

SEACOMBE, Cheshire (near Birkenhead).

IRVING THEATRE.—Proprietor and Manager, Mr. James Kiernan; Acting-Manageress,
Miss A. Gordon; Musical Director, Mr. Tom
Shaw; Scenic Artist, Mr. Sidney Beltram. Full
license. Holding capacity: Number of persons,
about 2,500; amount, £100. Stage measurements: Depth, 47ft.; width, 70ft.; proscenium,
27ft. 6in. Gas and electric light. Amount of
printing required: 1,000 sheets picture printing,
500 lithos, 50,000 circulars. Usual matinée day,
Saturday. Time of band rehearsal, 12 noon.

SEAFORD, Sussex.

Population, 3,355. Miles from London, 56.
QUEEN'S HALL. — Proprietors, Colonel of
Engineers (Territorial Forces); Manager, Mr. E.
J. H. Pawson. Dramatic license. Holds 600.
Stage 20ft. by 20ft. Gas. Terms, one day, £2 2s.;
two, £3 3s.; three, £4 4s.; one week, £6 6s. Payable in advance.
Four miles from Newhaven. It is a small
but growing seaside watering-place. The population is residential, consisting chiefly of well-
to-do middle-class people and lodging-house
keepers.
Small touring companies of first-class repute
draw good houses during the season of six
weeks from the middle of August onwards.
Good business can also be done at Easter.
Pitches are not easily obtainable for alfresco
entertainments, but they are to be had by
negotiation with private landowners. The
place is not large enough to keep more than
one troupe going each season. Circuses visit
the town yearly. No portables visit.
Early closing day, Wednesday.

SEAHAM HARBOUR, Co. Durham.

Population, 11,000, District, 40,000. Miles from
London, 275.
NEW THEATRE ROYAL.—Proprietor, Mr.
A. C. Harrison; Manager, Mr. Harry D. Lyle;
Musical Director, Mr. W. Walker; Scenic
Artist, Mr. H. Collier. Double license. Holding capacity: Number of persons, 2,000. Stage
measurements: Proscenium opening, 26ft.;
depth, 30ft.; width, 45ft.; between flies, 30ft.;
floor to grid, 42ft. Electric, 65 voltage. Printing
required: 450 sheets, 400 lithos. Matinées on
Bank Holidays only. Time of band rehearsal,
5.45 p.m.

CO-OPERATIVE HALL.—Manager, Mr.
Francis Gibson. No dramatic license. Holding capacity: Number of persons, over 500.
Platform measurements: 3ft. 4in. high, 9ft.
wide by 39ft. long; above the platform to
ceiling, 22ft. Gas and electric, 100 volts, alternating. Terms: One night, £1 5s.; two nights,
£2; three nights, £2 15s.; four nights, £3 10s.;
five nights, £4 5s.; six nights, £5. Piano
extra, 5s. per night, or 10s. per week of six
nights. Rent paid in advance. If electric
light required, £2 10s. per week. Extra for
animated pictures. Saturday matinées, 15s.
extra.
CATHOLIC HALL.—Apply, Rev. J. J. Hayes.
No local fairs. Portables do not visit. Circus
pitch: Farmer's Field. Apply, Mr. J. W.
Dryden.
Early closing day, Wednesday. No market.

SEDGEFIELD, Durham.

Population, 3,167. Miles from London, 245.
PARISH HALL.—Manager, Mr. John Bur-
don. No dramatic license. Holding capacity:
Number of persons, 300; amount, £10. Stage
measurements: 12ft. by 20ft. Lighted by lamps.
Amount of printing required: 400 or 500 handbills. Terms for hiring: 10s. one night, 17s. 6d.
two, and 7s. 6d. each succeeding. Amount of
deposit required on booking: The whole
amount.
DURHAM COUNTY ASYLUM (very large
one) allow a night if a good company, and, of
course, pay them. Asylum has a good hall,
stage, etc.
Steeplechases, March each year, when vans
can pitch on the green. Charge, 1s. a day.
Early closing day, Wednesday; no market
day.

SEGHILL, Northumberland.

COLLIERY INSTITUTE HALL.—Proprietors,
Seghill Colliery Workmen; Manager, Mr. Wilkinson Murton. Music and dancing license.
Holds 400. The stage is an open one, 13ft.
by 33ft., can be made into 18ft. by 33ft., with
no furnishing. Petrol, gas. Terms for hiring,
concerts 17s., variety £1; this includes piano.
Amount of deposit required on booking, one-
third of charge.
No local fairs. No sites available for portables, etc.

SELKIRK, Selkirk.

Population, 5,701. Miles from London, 367.
VICTORIA HALLS (Large and Small).—
Proprietors, Selkirk Town Council; Keeper,
Mr. George Murdoch. Dramatic license may
be obtained, price 2s. 6d.; application forms
from the Town Clerk. Holding capacity: Number of persons, Large Hall, 1,000; Small Hall,
200. Stage measurements: Large Hall, 15ft.
deep, 27ft. frontage, and 13ft. 5in. high.
Lighted by gas. Terms for hiring: For plays,
one night, £3; each subsequent night, £1 15s.
For lectures, concerts, kinematograph entertainments, first night, £2 15s.; each subsequent night, £1 10s. Amount of deposit required on booking: £1.
Local fairs: Selkirk Common Riding Festival, June 12 and 13. Site for shows, Victoria
Park.
Early closing day, Thursday; market day,
Wednesday.

SETTLE, Yorks.

Population, 2,302. Miles from London, 236.
VICTORIA HALL.—Manager, Mr. Edmund
Handby. Dramatic license. Holding capacity:

Number of persons, seats 365. Proper stage, no scenery, 16ft. deep by 30ft. (wall to wall); proscenium opening, 19ft. 6in. by 14ft. Lighted by gas. Amount of printing required: 30 posters. Terms for hiring: £2 2s. per night, inclusive of all except piano. Amount of deposit required on booking: 10s.

Small comedy company or comic opera takes well here.

Early closing day, Wednesday; market day, Tuesday.

SEVENOAKS, Kent.

Population, 8,106. Miles from London, 20.

THE CLUB HALL.—Manager, Mr. Percy F. Potter. Dramatic license. Holding capacity: 650; amount, £60. Proper stage. Measurements: 26ft. by 29ft. Lighted by gas. Terms for hiring: £5 5s. one night, £8 8s. two, £10 10s. three. Amount of deposit required on booking: £1 1s.

No local fairs.

Market day, every third Wednesday; early closing day, Wednesday.

SHAFTESBURY, Dorset.

Population, 2,027. Miles from London, 101.

MARKET HALL.—Proprietor, Lord Stalbridge; Lessees, the Town Council; Manager, Town Clerk. Dramatic license. Seats 300. Movable platform, 22ft. by 21ft. Gas. Terms for hiring: Theatricals, £2; concerts, £1 10s. Amount of deposit required on booking, 10s.

Dates of local fairs, Saturday before Palm Sunday, last Saturday in August, third Saturday in November. Site available for portables, alfresco concerts, and circuses, Cattle Market. Apply, Oram, town crier.

Early closing day, Wednesday; market day, alternate Saturdays.

SHANKLIN, Isle of Wight.

Population, 4,533 (considerably increased during the summer). Miles from London, 88.

INSTITUTE HALL. — Secretary, Mr. W. Portbury. Double license. Holding capacity: Number of persons, seating 500. Stage: 22ft. 6in. deep, 24ft. 6in. wide; height, 16ft.; floor raised 3ft. Gas and electric light. Amount of printing required: About 100 d.c., 200 day bills, etc. Terms for hiring: Season prices, August-September, 2 guineas; other months, £1 11s. 6d.; lighting extra. Concert season prices, August and September, £1 11s. 6d.; out of season, £1 1s. Amount of deposit required on booking: £1. If hall is taken six times in one year at any time the rent is 30s. Grundy's patent heating and ventilating apparatus is installed, charge 3s. 6d. Electric current, 250 volts.

Russell, billposter, Shanklin; Partridge's, High Street, booking offices.

Caretaker is entitled to charge 1s. per hour after 10.30 p.m.

The population is largely residential.

The season lasts from the middle of July to middle of September.

Early closing day, Wednesday.

SHEERNESS, Kent.

Population, 18,179. Miles from London, 49.

HIPPODROME. — Proprietors, Sheerness Hippodrome Co.; General Manager, Mr. F. J. Kelly; Musical Director, Mlle. Zetta Handel. Double license. Holding capacity: Number of persons, 1,500. Stage measurements: 26ft. by 52ft. Electric light. Time of

band rehearsal, 1 p.m. Usual matinée day, Saturdays (but rarely). Bars no surrounding halls.

This hall has just been rebuilt. Musical comedies have done the best business.

REYMOND'S NEW PALACE.—Situated in High Street, Blue Town. Proprietor, Mr. Phil Reymond. Seating capacity, 600. This house is about to undergo extensive alterations, and no doubt will be renamed. Variety entertainment

TOWER'S HALL.—Situated in High Street, Sheerness. Proprietor, Mr. James Tower, of Trafalgar House, Broadway, Sheerness; Manager, Mr. E. Levy. Seating capacity about 500 to 700. Level floor. Suitable for concerts, lectures, balls, bioscopic entertainments, etc. Has been used on several occasions, with good results, by travelling companies—musical comedy—such as San Toy, and others.

CO-OPERATIVE HALL.—Situated in High Street, Sheerness. Proprietors, The Sheerness Co-operative Society, Limited; Managing Secretary, Mr. Collins. Seating capacity: about 500 to 600. Suitable for concerts, lectures, balls, bioscopic entertainments, etc. Has been used on several occasions by travelling companies, chiefly with musical comedy. At present it is occupied by "The Bioscope Company" (Manager, Mr. F. R. Griffiths), who have been in occupation for over eighteen months.

HIPPODROME ASSEMBLY ROOMS.— situated in Broadway, Sheerness. General Manager, Mr. F. J. Kelly. Suitable for dances, lectures, etc., etc.

The town possesses two exceptionally fine clubs, which are perhaps as good as, if not better than, any working men's clubs in the South of England. Both clubs boast a membership of from 1,500 to 2,500 each. Each club has a spacious concert hall capable of seating about 400 to 600 people, in which weekly concerts (Saturday night) are held, and for which artists are engaged. The names of the clubs are as follows:—

The Sheerness Conservative and Unionist Club. Secretary, Mr. Victor Stuart.

The Sheerness Working Men's Club and Institute. Secretary, Mr. Milford Lifton.

Portables.—The town is occasionally visited by portables. Their pitch is the Recreation Ground, which adjoins the Esplanade or Sea Front. Transfield's Hippodrome was the biggest of its kind to make any lengthy stay here (about eight months). In the summer time when the town is filled with visitors these shows take well, and are also well patronised by the local population. During the summer there are always steam roundabouts, switchbacks, and their usual accompaniment on the Recreation Ground. No difficulty is encountered in obtaining a permit from the local Urban District Council, neither are their charges exorbitant. Sanger's circus makes an annual visit, and is quartered on the Recreation Ground. Proprietors of Recreation Ground, The Sheerness Urban District Council; Clerk to Council, Mr. V. H. Stallon; Offices, Trinity Road. Sheerness.

Alfresco Concerts.—One part of the Recreation Ground is devoted to alfresco concerts. In this portion the Council have a bandstand within an enclosure. The band performs twice weekly, usually Wednesday and Saturday evenings. On the other evenings the alfresco entertainment obtains, and also when the band has finished on the Wednesdays and Saturdays.

The bandstand enclosure is furnished with chairs, and admission to the enclosure is obtained on payment for a seat within. Applications for the hire of the bandstand should be made to the Sec. to the Recreation Ground Committee, Mr. W. A. Baskett, Council Offices, Trinity Road, Sheerness. The bandstand and enclosure are immediately adjacent to the Esplanade. There is also a piece of land alongside the sea front, which has been used for two years by a troupe of pierrots. It is in the possession of the Admiralty. There are no conveniences, such as seats, except on the Esplanade at this point. There are the sands, on which minstrels, pierrots, etc., could perform the same as at any other seaside resort. The population consists of the following:— Employees of the Government Dockyard, naval, military, and shopkeepers. The Dockyard employs somewhere about 2,000 men, who reside in the town. Sheerness is the headquarters of the Nore Division of the Home Fleet, so that the naval population is very considerable, insomuch that the bluejackets are frequently ashore when the ships are in port. The strength of the Fleet is some thousands, but this is not taken into consideration in stating the actual population. Several companies of Artillery and Royal Engineers are stationed here. The town is a growing place. There is room for enterprise. The naval population wants catering for in the entertainment line.

Early closing day, Wednesday; market day, Saturday

Agent.—M.H.A.R.A.: A. Humphrey, Railway Hotel. V.A.F.: The same.

SHEFFIELD, Yorks.

Population, 380,793. Miles from London, 162.

LYCEUM THEATRE.—Proprietors, Sheffield Lyceum Theatre, Limited; Managing Director, Mr. John Hart; Acting-Manager, Mr. J. E. B. Beaumont; Musical Director, Mr. Henry Dean; Scenic Artist, Mr. D. G. Hall. Full license. Holding capacity: Number of persons, 3,000; amount £210. Stage measurements: Depth, 29ft.; proscenium opening, 28ft. Gas and electric light, alternating current 100 volts. Printing required, 2,000 sheets. Usual matinée day, Saturday. Time of band rehearsal, 1 p.m. Bars Chesterfield and Rotherham.

THEATRE ROYAL.—Proprietors, Sheffield Lyceum Theatre, Limited; Managing Director, Mr. John Hart; Acting-Manager, Mr. J. E. B. Beaumont; Assistant-Manager, Mr. A. Henfrey Aldred; Musical Director, Mr. W. Butcher; Scenic Artist, Mr. D. G. Hall. Full license. Holding capacity: Number of persons, 2,600; amount, £155. Stage measurements: Depth, 33ft.; proscenium opening, 28ft. Gas and electric light, 200 volts direct. Printing, 2,000 sheets. Time of band rehearsal, 1 p.m. This is a drama house. Bars Attercliffe, Rotherham, and Chesterfield.

ALEXANDRA THEATRE. — Lessees, the Alexandra Theatre Co. (Sheffield), Limited; Managing Director, Mr. W. D. Forsdike; Acting-Manager, Mr. C. W. Ramsay; Musical Director, Mr. Leonard Hinchcliffe. Fully licensed. Electric light. Time of band rehearsal, Monday, 1.30 p.m. Popular prices of admission, 4d. to 3s. Smoking is permitted in all parts of the house. Holds 3,000. Printing, 1,600 sheets and 1,200 lithos. Drama house.

EMPIRE THEATRE.—Proprietors, Moss Empires, Limited; Manager, Mr. Oswald Stoll; Acting-Manager, Mr. A. D. Dunbar; Musical Director, Mr. H. R. Gardner. Double license. Electric light. Time of band rehearsal, 2 p.m.

Bars all other Managements' Halls in Sheffield and the following towns: Rotherham, Dronfield, and Chesterfield.

HIPPODROME. — Proprietors, Hippodrome (Sheffield), Ltd. Managing Director, Mr. Thomas Barrasford. Acting-Manager, Mr. P. D. Elbourne. Musical Director, Mr. J. G. Hahn. Proscenium opening 36ft. Matinée Thursday. Band rehearsal 12 noon.

CENTRAL HALL.—Proprietors, Jasper Redfern, and Co., Limited; Managing Director, Mr. Jasper Redfern; Acting-Manager, Mr. F. Holmes. Music and dancing license. Holding capacity: Number of persons, 1,000. Small stage. Gas and electric light. Time of band rehearsal, 1 p.m. Usual matinée day, Saturday.

MONTGOMERY HALL. — Proprietors, Sheffield Sunday School Union. Secretary, Mr. C. Simpson. Holds 1,000. Music license. Electric light. Terms: £4 per night.

THEATRE ROYAL (Attercliffe).—Proprietors, North of England Theatres Corporation, Limited; Managing Director, Mr. Frank Macnaghten; Manageress, Miss E. J. Hope. Booking Circuit, Macnaghten's. Dramatic license.

THE PALACE (Attercliffe).—Proprietor, Mr. T. Allan Edwardes; Acting-Manager, Mr. Harry Pease; Assistant-Manager, Mr. Harry Sanders. Musical Director, Mr. W. H. Chambers. Music and dancing license.

GRAND. — Managing Director, Mr. Frank Macnaghten. Double license. Electric light.

ALBERT HALL.—Secretary, Mr. J. W. Peace. Music and dancing license. Holding capacity: Number of persons, 1,900. Concert platform. Electric light. Terms for hiring: £17 for odd concerts. Amount of deposit required on booking: As per arrangement.

Dates of local fairs: Midsummer and Christmas.

Early closing day, Thursday; market days, Tuesday and Saturday.

Medical Officers.—A.A.: Dr. G. S. Davidson, 267, Abbeydale Road; Dr. D. G. Newton, 14, Favell Road, Brook Hill; Dr. V. Roberts, 614, Attercliffe Road, Attercliffe. A.U.: Dr. Davidson and Dr. Newton. M.H.A.R.A.: Dr. Davidson and Dr. Newton.

Agents.—M.H.A.R.A.: A. Holmes, Empire Theatre. A.U.: H. Humberstone, Three Horse Shoes Hotel, Norfolk Street. V.A.F.: The same.

RECOMMENDED APARTMENTS.

Mrs. Monk, 117, Charlotte Road.—1 sitting-room, 2 bedrooms, 1 combined room.

Mrs. Hodgkinson, 13, Westfield Terrace.—3 bedrooms, sitting-room with piano, combined room.

SHEPSHED, Leicester.

Population, 5,500. Miles from London, 128.

BRITISH SCHOOL HALL.—Manager, Mr. W. Tapp. No dramatic license. Holding capacity: Number of persons, 400. No proper stage; platform would be erected. Lighted by gas. Terms for hiring, 17s. 6d. first night, 14s. 6d. second. Deposit required on booking, 50 per cent.

Site available for portables, alfresco concerts, and circuses, Recreation ground.

SHEPTON MALLET, Somerset.

Population, 5,238. Miles from London, 120.

THE HALL has dramatic license, and holds over 500.

There is a circus pitch in the town.

Early closing day, Wednesday; market day, Friday.

SHERBORNE, Dorset.

Population, 5,760. Miles from London, 118.

ASSEMBLY ROOMS.—Manager, Mr. A. W. Binnie-Clark. Double license. Holding capacity: Number of persons, 600. Proper stage. Lighted by gas. Terms for hiring: £2 2s. per night, in advance.

ST. JOHN'S HALL.—Manager, Mr. George King, Abbey Gate House. Dramatic license if required. Holding capacity: Number of persons, 200. Stage, 36ft. by 14ft. Lighted by gas. Amount of printing required: 100. Terms for hiring: 10s. to £1. Amount of deposit required on booking: 10s.

Local fair: First Monday after October 10. Early closing, Wednesday; market, Thursday and Saturday.

SHIELDS, NORTH, Northumb.

Population, 55,737. Miles from London, 286.

THEATRE ROYAL.—Proprietor, Mr. William Dodds; Lessee, Mr. Stanley Rogers; Acting-Manager, Mr. Horace Lee; Musical Director, Mr. A. Baker; Scenic Artist, Mr. Alec Chisholm. Dramatic license. Holding capacity: Number of persons, 1,200; amount, £60. Stage measurements: Depth, 45ft.; width, 43ft; proscenium, 25ft. Gas and electric light. Amount of printing required: 650 d.c. sheets, 500 lithos. Usual matinée day, Saturday. Band rehearsal, 1 p.m.

CENTRAL PALACE OF VARIETIES.—Lessee and Manager, Mr. William Mould; Musical Director, Mr. C. V. Barton. Music and dancing license. Seating capacity, 800. Stage measurements: 22ft. opening, 12ft. deep. Gas and electric light. Band rehearsal, 1 p.m. No matinée day. Bars surrounding halls within a three-mile radius.

BORO' THEATRE. — Proprietor, Mr. Geo. Black. Music and dancing license. Holds 2,000. Twice nightly. Animated pictures. Gas and electric. Matinée Saturday.

ALBION ASSEMBLY ROOMS.—Managers, Messrs. Joseph A. R. Ellis and Son. Music and dancing license. Holding capacity: Number of persons, 600. Portable stage. Gas and electric light. Terms for hiring: £2 2s. per night, and extras—lighting and attendance. Rent in advance. Electricity for kinematograph.

Early closing day, Wednesday.
Medical Officer.—A.A.: Dr. T. J. Phillips, 5, Dockwray Square; A.U.: The same.
Agent.—M.H.A.R.A.: W. Cockburn, Railway Hotel.

SHIELDS, SOUTH, Durham.

Population, 105,000. Miles from London, 269.

THEATRE ROYAL.—Lessees and Managers, Messrs. J. and F. Coulson; Musical Director, Mr. J. Hopper. Full license. Holding capacity: Number of persons, 1,800; amount, £70. Stage measurements: Depth, 35ft.; width, 58ft.; proscenium opening, 25ft.; stage to fly floor, 19ft. Electric light 110 volts. Printing required: 900 sheets for walls, 600 lithos. No matinée day. Band rehearsal, 12.30 p.m.

EMPIRE PALACE. — Proprietors, South Shields Empire Palace, Limited; Managing Director, Mr. R. Thornton; General Manager, Mr. Frank Allen; Resident Manager, Mr. Geo. F. Thompson; Booking Circuit, Moss' Empires, Limited; Musical Director, Mr. J. Sutherland. Dramatic license. Holding capacity: Number of persons, 2,000; amount, £50. Stage measurements: Depth, 23ft.; width, 60ft.; proscenium opening, 27ft. 6in. Electric light, alternating current 110 volts. Band rehearsal, 2 p.m. No matinée day. Two performances nightly at 6.50 and 9.0. Bars all other Managements' Halls in South Shields and the following towns: North Shields, Wallsend, Blyth, Monkseaton, Whitley, Cullercoats, Tynemouth, Sunderland, Jarrow, and Hebburn.

ROYAL ASSEMBLY HALL.—Manager, Mr. John Wm. Ditchburn. Full license. Holding capacity: Number of persons, 2,000. Gas and electric light.

Early closing day, Wednesday; market day, Saturday.

Medical Officers.—Drs. Crisp and J. Macdonald, 7, Albion Terrace; A.U. and M.H.A.R.A., the same.

Agent.—M.H.A.R.A.: F. Wood, Mariner's Arms, Market Place; V.A.F.: The same.

SHIPLEY, Yorks.

Population, 28,090. Miles from London, 196.

QUEEN'S PALACE OF VARIETIES.—Lessee Mr. F. R. Griffiths; District Manager, Mr. Gerald Hunt; Acting-Manager, Mr. Ralph Illingworth. Seats 1,000. Electric light, 460 volts direct.

VICTORIA HALL, Saltaire.—Manager, Mr. William Fry. Dramatic license. Holding capacity: Number of persons, 1,200. Stage measurements: Proscenium, 23ft. wide, 20ft high; stage, 34ft. wide, 20ft. in depth. Lighted by gas. Electric installation for kinematograph. Amount of printing required, about 50 three or four-sheet. Billposters, Sheldons, Limited. Terms for hiring, one evening £2 10s., two £4 4s., three £6, six £10 10s. Amount of deposit required on booking, £1 1s.

Saltaire is in the township of Shipley. The Institute (in which the Victoria Hall is situate) serves Shipley, Windhill (one mile from hall), and Baildon (one and a half miles), the population within a radius of one and a half miles being upwards of 40,000. Saltaire passenger station is about 200 yards from the hall, Shipley (Midland) about three-quarters of a mile, and Windhill (Great Northern) one mile. Bradford is three miles distant. Persons renting the Victoria Hall should head their announcements, " Victoria Hall, Saltaire."

The Feast, which is very popular with the surrounding villages, falls on the first Sunday after St. James's Day (July 25). Portables pay frequent visits, and there is no difficulty in obtaining a license. Licenses have also been granted for alfresco shows.

Early closing day, Tuesday; market day, Friday.

SHREWSBURY, Salop.

Population, 28,395. Miles from London, 162.

THEATRE ROYAL AND HIPPODROME.—Proprietors, Syndicate; Business Manager and Licensee, Mr. W. C. Dornton; Musical Director, Mr. A. W. Page. Full license. Holding capacity: Number of persons, 1,000; amount, £60. Stage measurements: Width, 28ft.; depth, 30ft. Electric light. Amount of printing required: 400 sheets and 400 lithos. Usual matinée day, Saturday. Band rehearsal, 2 p.m.

MUSIC HALL.—Manager and Secretary, Mr. V. C. L. Crump. Dramatic license. Holding capacity: Number of persons, 1,000. Plat-

form and orchestra; no stage. Gas and electric light. Terms for hiring, £4 4s. per night.
Early closing day, Thursday; market days, Wednesday and Saturday.
Medical Officers.—A.A.: Dr. N. I. Spriggs, 26, St. John's Hill. A.U.: The same.

SIDCUP, Kent.

Population, 6,886. Miles from London, 8.
PUBLIC HALL.—Manager, Mr. Alfred E. Butterworth. Double license. Holding capacity: Number of persons, 260. Stage. 18ft. 6in. by 30ft. 6in. Lighted by gas. Terms for hiring: One night, £2 2s.; subsequent nights, £1 1s. Amount of deposit required on booking, £1 1s.
Early closing, Thursday.

SIDMOUTH, Devon.

Population, 4,201. Miles from London, 159.
MANOR CONCERT HALL.—Apply Manager. Dramatic license.
Early closing, Thursday.

SILVERDALE, Staffs.

Population, 7,820. Miles from London,' 140.
PUBLIC HALL.—Apply Manager. Dramatic license.
Early closing, Thursday; market, Saturday.

SITTINGBOURNE, Kent.

Population, 9,000. Miles from London, 40.
TOWN HALL.—Apply Manager. Has dramatic license.
DRILL HALL. — Dramatic license. Apply Manager.
Early closing, Wednesday. Market Friday.

SKEGNESS, Lincs.

Population, 8,943.   Miles from London, 130.
KING'S THEATRE.—Proprietor and Manager, Mr. H. Rowley. Full license. Holding capacity: Number of persons, 500; amount, £40. Stage measurements: 27ft. by 34ft.; proscenium opening, 18ft. 9in. Lighted by gas. Best dates, from July 15 to September 15.
PAVILION, THE LAWN.—Proprietor, Mr. Fred Clements.
PAVILION AND PUBLIC GARDENS.—Let for plays, etc. Apply to the Manager.
Early closing day, Wednesday; market day, Thursday.

SKIPTON, Yorks.

Population, 11,986. Miles from London, 219.
TOWN HALL.—Proprietors, Urban District Council. Apply Mr. Fred E. Dodson. Double license. Holds 600. Stage, 24ft. by 24ft.; proscenium opening, 18ft. Gas. Printing: 100 posters. Terms: £2 10s. first night; £1 5s. second; deposit, £1.
Local fairs, second Saturday in July.
Early closing, Tuesday; market, Saturday.

SLIGO, Co. Sligo.

Population, 10,862. Miles from Dublin, 135.
TOWN HALL.—Has dramatic license and holds about 600. Apply to the Secretary.
There is a fair green, the property of the Sligo Corporation, where all circuses, portables,

and every other kind of travelling entertainment pitch, and in the market yard all hobby horses and auction marts put up. It is surrounded by high walls, and none can gain admission except by the gates, and a very handsome sum can be realised when a charge is made at the gates. One portable visits Sligo, and can play for six months to crowded houses at prices, 3d., 6d., and 1s. If good, well-conducted portables were to visit Sligo, good business would be sure to result.

SLOUGH, Bucks.

Population, 15,000.   Miles from London, 18.
PUBLIC HALL.—Secretary, Mr. G. Young. Dramatic license. Holding capacity: Number of persons, 600. Platform. Lighted by gas. Terms for hiring, £3 3s. first night; £2 2s. after. Amount of deposit required on booking, 10s. per night.
Early closing day, Wednesday; market day, Tuesday.

SMETHWICK, Staffs.

Population, 71,453. Miles from London, 116.
THEATRE ROYAL.—Proprietor, Mr. Charles Barnard; Manager, Mr. Edward Hewitson; Musical Director, Mr. Wilfrid Hickling. Full license. Holding capacity: Number of persons, 3,000; amount, £125 to £143. Stage measurements; 48ft. deep; 74ft. wide; proscenium opening, 30ft. Gas and electric, 60 and 100 volts. Printing required: 1,000 walls, 900 lithos. Time of band rehearsal, 1 p.m.
Early closing day, Wednesday.
Medical Officers.—A.A.: Dr. F. W. Sutton, The Elms, 47, Edgbaston Road. A.U.: The same.

SOLIHULL, Warwick.

Population, 7,517.   Miles from London, 122.
PUBLIC HALL.—Manager, Mr. F. G. Thompson. No dramatic license; dramatic license may be obtained. Holding capacity: Number of persons, 300; amount, £15 (estimated). Stage, width about 18ft.; depth about 14ft. Lighted by gas. Terms for hiring, £4 4s. per night (dramatic performances). Amount of deposit required on booking, whole.
There are no local fairs and no pitches for circuses or portables.
Early closing day, Wednesday; market day, Thursday.

SOUTHAMPTON, Hants.

Population, 122,000. Miles from London, 78.
GRAND THEATRE.—Proprietors, Messrs. David Allen and Sons; Lessee and Manager, Mr. Frederick Mouillot; Resident Manager, Mr. Arthur Weston; Musical Director, Mr. Warwick Moore. Full license. Holding capacity: Number of persons, about 1,600; amount, £150 Stage measurements: Depth, 36ft.; width, 28ft.; fly rails, 38ft.; grid, 50ft. Gas and electric light direct, 200 volts. Printing: Walls, 1,200 sheets; 700 d.c. windows. Usual matinée day, Saturday, 2.30 p.m. Time of band rehearsal, generally 11 a.m.
THE HIPPODROME.—Proprietors, Messrs. Fredk. Mouillot and Walter de Frece; General Manager, Mr. J. de Frece; Manager, Mr. Harold P. Howell; Musical Director, Mr. J. Melville Gillies. Double license. Holding capacity: Number of persons, 2,000; amount, £285. Stage measurements: 57ft. wide, 24ft. deep; proscenium, 25ft. 6in. wide. Electric light. Amount of printing required, 2,000

sheets. Usual matinée days, Wednesday and Saturday. Time of band rehearsal, 3 p.m.

THE PALACE.—Proprietor, Mr. Frank Macnaghten; Manager, Mr. William Trussell; Booking Circuit, Macnaghten Vaudeville Circuit; Musical Director, Mr. Frank Reed. Gas and electric light. Time of band rehearsal, 12 noon. No matinée day.

ROYAL VICTORIA ROOMS, Portland Terrace.—Managers, Messrs. Bance, Hunt, and Giller, 67, Above Bar, Southampton. No dramatic license, but can be obtained. Holding capacity: Large hall, number of persons, seating 500, standing room in rear; smaller rooms in the building. Portable stage, 32ft. wide, good depth; no proscenium. Hall lit by gas; electric light, current direct, 200 volts. Terms for hiring: 15 guineas a week. Amount of deposit required on booking, 25 per cent. West Marlands suitable for and is used occasionally by circuses. Alfresco concerts are held on the Royal Pier.

Early closing day, Wednesday; market day, Friday.

Medical Officers.—A.A.: Dr. O. T. Stephenson, Saxonhurst, Woolston. M.H.A.R.A.: Dr. A. Graham, 23, Hanover Buildings.

Agents.—M.H.A.R.A.: Mrs. J. Liston, Sussex Hotel, 86, Above Bar. A.U.: The same V.A.F.: The same.

RECOMMENDED APARTMENTS.

Mrs. J. Glover, 25, South Front.—2 sitting-rooms, 3 bedrooms, 1 combined; piano.

Mrs. Hoskins, 25, South Front.—2 sitting-rooms, 3 bedrooms; piano; gas; bath.

SOUTHBOROUGH, Kent.

Between Tonbridge and Tunbridge Wells.

ROYAL VICTORIA HALL.—Proprietors, Urban Council; Manager, Mr. Philip Hanmer, Clerk to the Council. Double license. Holding capacity: Number of persons (seated), 630. An up-to-date stage, 40ft. wide by 25ft. deep; proscenium drop opening, 28ft. by 18ft. Foot and top lights. Lighted by gas. Terms for hiring, one night, £1 10s., two, £2 2s., three or more at the rate of £1 1s. each. Amount of deposit required on booking, none until day before hall used, when full amount must be paid in advance. Has some new scenery. Nearest Railway Station, S.E. & C.R., Tunbridge Wells. Southborough Station has no accommodation for loading and no buses.

SOUTHEND-ON-SEA, Essex.

Population 57,500. Miles from London, 42.

EMPIRE THEATRE.—Proprietors, Southend Empire Company, Limited; Managing Director, Mr. Geo. Conquest; Acting Manager, Mr. F. Lingham Power; Secretary, Mr. C. F. Nerney. Has dramatic license and holds 1,800.

THE KURSAAL PALACE. — Proprietors, Southend Kursaal, Limited; Manager, Mr. P. T. J. Bacon; Musical Director, Mr. Hosking Dickenson. Dramatic and Music and Dancing licenses. Holding capacity: Number of persons, up to 5,000. Stage measurements: Depth, 49ft.; width, 87ft.; proscenium 31ft. by 31ft. Electric light, 230 volts (current from Corporation). Band rehearsal, 1 p.m. Usual matinée days, every week-day, June to September. Bars surrounding halls within a radius of ten miles by land.

Early closing day, Thursday; market day, Tuesday.

PIER PAVILION.—Proprietor, Mr. H. E. Angless; Manager, Mr. S. E. Angless; Musical

Director, Mr. Stanley E. Angless; Scenic Artist, Mr. G. Bush. Double license. Holding capacity: Number of persons, 1,000; amount, £75. Stage measurements: Opening, 22ft.; depth, 25ft. Electric light. Amount of printing required · 800 sheets. Usual matinée days, Wednesday and Saturday. Band rehearsal, 1 p.m. Best dates, July, August, September, and October.

KINGS HALL, Westcliff. — Proprietors, Messrs. Adams and Biggs.

VICTORIA HALL.—Manager, Mr. Jesse Kemp. Music and dancing license. Holding capacity: Number of persons, 500; amount, £20. Permanent winter stage (September to May): Depth, 17ft.; width, 16ft.; height of proscenium opening, 12ft. Electric foot floats and arc lamps. Amount of printing required: 200 d.c., 100 d. bills and throwaways. Terms for hiring: £2 2s. night, £10 10s. weekly. Amount of deposit required on booking: £2 2s. One minute from theatre, two minutes from two stations (L.T. and S.R. and Midland), ten minutes from G.E.R. Lighted and heated by electricity. Lighting 230 volts; Bioscope 460.

Medical Officers.—A.A.: Dr. F. Silva Jones, Clarence House. A.U.: Dr. J. Walker, 37, High Street. M.H.A.R.A.: Dr. Jones.

Agent.—M.H.A.R.A.: A. Elphick, Alexandra Hotel. V.A.F.: W. A. Wordsworth, Borough Hotel, Marine Parade.

RECOMMENDED APARTMENTS.

Mrs. Strnebig, 26, Tyler's Avenue.—Bedroom and sitting-room, combined; piano.

SOUTH MOLTON, Devon.

Population, 2,848. Miles from London, 197.

NEW ASSEMBLY ROOMS.—Manager, Mr. William Bulled. Fully licensed. Holding capacity: Number of persons, 400 to 500. Stage measurements, 12ft. by 24ft. Lighted by gas. Terms for hiring, one day £1 1s., second day 10s. 6d. Amount of deposit required on booking, £1.

Early closing day, Wednesday; market days, Thursday and Saturday.

SOUTHPORT, Lancs.

Population 52,000. Miles from London, 211.

OPERA HOUSE.—Proprietors, The Southport Opera House and Winter Gardens (1905), Limited; General Manager and Secretary, Mr. R. Singleton; Musical Director, Mr. W. P. Stone. Full license. Stage measurements: Proscenium height, 28ft.; width stage, wall to wall, 52ft.; opening, 27ft. 4in.; depth, 38ft.; fly-rail, 33ft. 6in. Electric light. Amount of printing required: 1,000 sheets; posting, 600 d.c.; 2,000 throwaways. Usual matinée day, Saturday, 2 p.m. Time of band rehearsal, 11 a.m.

ALBERT HALL.—Proprietors, The Southport Opera House and Winter Gardens, Limited; General Manager and Secretary, Mr. R. Singleton; Acting Manager, Mr. J. H. Mertz. The Southport Musical Festival is held here. Seating capacity, about 2,500, with a large amount of standing space.

PIER PAVILION.—Proprietors, The Southport Pier Company, Limited; Lessee, Mr. Frank Macnaghten; Manager, Mr. W. Eric Longden. Double license. Holds 1,500. Electric current. 110 volts, alternating.

CAMBRIDGE HALL.—Manager, Borough Treasurer (Town Hall). Double license. Holding capacity: Number of persons, 1,400. Stage:

26

29ft. deep, 50ft. broad; no proscenium. Terms for hiring: Four guineas per night, payable in advance. Electricity, voltage 100 alternating.

TOWN HALL (The Borough Treasurer, Town Hall).—For concerts. Seating about 400.

TEMPERANCE INSTITUTE.—Secretary, Mr. E. H. J. Evans, Music and dancing license. Holds 800. Stage: 9ft. 6in. deep; 41ft. 10in. wide; no proscenium. Terms: One night, two pounds; several nights, at lower rate. Deposit on booking, half-fee. Electricity: Voltage 100, alternating current.

FOR ALFRESCOS.—Pier Head (sheltered) (The Pier Company). North Marine Park (The Town Clerk). The Fair Ground (on the sands)—two pitches (The Town Clerk).

Artists are also engaged to appear in the Pavilions at the Botanical Gardens, Churchtown; and at the Zoo Park.

A seaside resort on the south estuary of the River Ribble. Distance by rail from Liverpool, 18 miles; Manchester, 35 miles. Population, with the adjoining Urban town-hip of Birkdale, about 71,000, purely residential of all grades of middle-class. In the summer months, there is a "season" of visitors from the Lancashire manufacturing towns; but throughout the year there is a regular succession of middle-cass visitors from all parts, particularly in winter, as the town has a reputation as a winter resort.

Early closing day, Tuesday, from October 1 to May 31. No market day.

Medical Officers.—A.A.: Dr. Philip Vickers, 25, Scarisbrick New Road. A.U.: The same. M.H.A.R.A: The same.

Agents.—M.H.A.R.A.: W. Courtney, Royal Hotel. A.U.: The same. V.A.F.: The same.

SOUTHWELL, Notts.

Population, 3,161. Miles from London, 139.

ASSEMBLY ROOMS.—Proprietor, Mr. William Bell, Saracen's Head Hotel. Dramatic and music and dancing licenses. Holds 250. Staging can be erected to suit company. Incandescent light gas. Terms for hiring: 21s. and 30s. Amount of deposit required on booking; one-half.

Dates of local fairs, last Mondays in April and September. Sites available for portables, alfresco concerts, and circuses, back of Saracen's Head.

Early closing day, Thursday; market day, Friday.

SOUTHWICK, Sussex.

Population, 3,364. Miles from London, 55.

TOWN HALL.—Proprietors, Southwick Urban District Council; Clerk to Council, Mr. J. E. Dell, Town Hall, Southwick. Dramatic license. Holding capacity: Number of persons, 250. Stage depth 12ft., width 36ft. Gas. Terms for hiring: 1 guinea per day. Amount of deposit required on booking, full fee.

No local fair. There are several enclosed meadows in the district available for portables, alfresco concerts, and circuses.

SOUTHWOLD, Suffolk.

Population, 2,800. Miles from London, 106.

ASSEMBLY ROOMS.—Proprietress and Manageress, Mrs. J. Marshall, King's Head, Southwold. Dramatic license. Holds about 400. Has stage. Electric light.

Dates of local fairs, Trinity Fair and two following days. Site available for circuses, the Common. Apply, Borough Surveyor, Southwold.

Early closing day, Wednesday; market day, Thursday.

SPALDING, Lincs.

Population, 9,385. Miles from London, 93.

DRILL HALL.—Apply the Manager. Dramatic license.

Early closing, Thursday; market, Tuesday.

SPENNYMOOR, Durham.

Population, 16,665. Miles from London, 267.

CAMBRIDGE THEATRE.—Proprietor, Mr. Hugh Robertson; Manager, Mr. David Collins; Musical Director, Mr. Joseph Horton. Scenic Artist, Mr. Claude Seaton. Full license. Holding capacity: Number of persons, 1,500; amount, £50. Stage measurements: Proscenium opening, 20ft.; depth, 20ft.; height to fly floor, 19ft.; to grid, 30ft.; fly rail to fly rail, 30ft. Gas and electric light. Amount of printing required: 400 sheets walls, 500 lithos. Usual matinée day, Saturday. Time of band rehearsal, 1 p.m. Bars Crook and Bishop Auckland.

HIPPODROME.—Proprietor, Mr. Felix Green.

A new theatre is being built, and is expected to open in March, 1909.

Population of immediate district is about 30,000, and is chiefly mining. It is increasing rapidly, especially in the outlying districts within a five mile radius.

No local fair. Town is not visited by portables. Site for circus pitch is obtainable on the field belonging to the Weardale Coal and Steel Company, Limited.

Early closing day, Wednesday.

Agent.—M.H.A.R.A.: J. Horn, Bridge Hotel.

STAFFORD, Staffs.

Population, 20,895. Miles from London, 134.

LYCEUM THEATRE.—Proprietor and Manager, Mr. James Elphinstone; Acting Manager, Mr. Arthur Hill; Musical Director, Mr. Albert Lloyd; Scenic Artist, Mr. George Wilde. Full license. Holding capacity: Number of persons, 800; amount, £56. Stage measurements: 30ft. deep, 20ft. wall to wall, 18ft. 6in. opening. Gas and electric light. Amount of printing required: 350 sheets wall, 300 d.c. window. Usual matinée day, Saturday. Time of band rehearsal, 1 p.m., or to suit requirements. Best bookings of the year: Dance's, Macdona's, and Bannister Howard's Musical Comedies, Benson's Shakespearean Company, and better class of drama. About ten weeks stock each summer.

Stafford has one theatre—the Lyceum—which was erected over a century ago. It has been much improved during the lesseeship of Mr. James Elphinstone, who leases from the Town Council, who own the building. Dates of local fairs, May 14 and December 27, and annual procession first Saturday in July.

No portables of late have been located in the town. A license was recently refused to one applicant. Sites are obtainable for circuses, alfresco concerts, etc.

Population brought up to 30,000 by suburbs and adjacent villages. Residential and industrial. A steady influx of families and a new engineering works of late. Fond of good variety.

Early closing day, Wednesday; market day, Saturday.

Agent.—M.H.A.R.A.: Mrs. Harriss, White Hart Hotel.

STAINES, Middlesex.

Population, 6,668.   Miles from London, 19.
TOWN HALL.—Manager, Mr. H. S. Freeman, Clerk to Council. Double license. Holding capacity: Number of persons, 500. Stage, 24ft. wide by 12ft. deep, can be extended to 18ft. Lighted by gas. Terms for hiring: One night, £2 12s. 6d. or £3. Amount of deposit required on booking, £1.

Fairs, May 11 and Sept. 19.

Early closing day, Thursday. Market, Saturday.

STALYBRIDGE, Cheshire.

Population, 27,673. Miles from London, 186.
HIPPODROME AND GRAND THEATRE. Lessee and Manager, Mr. James Fioni; Acting-Manager, Mr. Wm. A. Jackson; Musical Director, Mr. A. E. Breakwell. Dramatic license. Holding capacity: Number of persons, 1,500. Stage measurements: Depth, 45ft.; width, 62ft.; proscenium opening, 27ft. Electric light 230 d.c. Band rehearsal, 1 p.m. Usual matinée day, Tuesday, at 2.30. Twice nightly.

ODDFELLOW'S HALL. — Seating capacity, 800. Electric current, 230 volts direct. No proscenium.

TOWN HALL.—Electric light, 230 volts direct. No proper stage.

MECHANICS' INSTITUTE.—Fortnightly lectures are given here.

Local Fair (Wakes).—First Sunday after July 18.

No portables visit the town, and if they applied, it is probable they would not be granted licenses.

Alfresco Concerts.—Last season there were three troupes, all of whom did very badly.

Early closing day, Tuesday; market day, Saturday.

Medical Officers.—A.A.: Dr. G. B. Howe, Bank House, Princess Street. A.U.: The same.

Agent.—M.H.A.R.A.: G. Hilton, Commercial Hotel. V.A.F.: The same.

STAMFORD, Lincoln.

Population, 8,229.   Miles from London, 92.
CORN EXCHANGE.—Manager,Mr.JohnSykes. Dramatic license. Holding capacity: Number of persons, seats over 700. Amount: £60 has been taken on one night at ordinary prices. No proscenium   Stage is built 18ft. deep, 30ft. wide. Gas for lighting, but there is an electric plug, direct current 240 volts. Terms: One night, £2 10s.; two nights, £3 15s., which includes lighting (gas), firing, and seating. Stage, 12s. 6d. extra, but small stage, 15½ft. deep is free. Amount of deposit required on booking, £1.

Pleasure fair, March 22 to 27, inclusive, 1909. Sites are available for portables.

Early closing day, Thursday.   Market day, Friday. Cattle Market, Monday.

STEVENAGE, Herts.

Population, 3,957. Miles from London, 29.
PUBLIC HALL.—Manager, Mr. Percy N. Wurr. Double license. Holding capacity: Number of persons about 400. Open stage, 30ft. by 15ft. No proscenium. Gas. Amount of printing required, 150 sheets F. Terms for hiring: 30s. first night; £1 second; 15s. third. Amount of deposit required on booking, 10s. per night.

Early closing day, Wednesday; market day, Saturday.

STIRLING, Scotland.

Population, 18,697. Miles from London, 418.
ARCADE THEATRE.—Proprietors, The Crawford family; Manager, Mr. David Crawford; Acting-Manager, Mr. Geo. Begbie, 26, Port Street, Stirling, to whom all communications should be sent. Dramatic license. Holding capacity: Number of persons, 1,200. Lighted by gas and electricity. Printing required: 250 sheets of wall printing; 200 daybills; and 100 lithos. Best dates, autumn and spring. Visited principally by fit up companies last three nights of the week. Sharing preferred.

THE ALBERT HALL.—Manager, Mr. William Pearson. Double license. Holding capacity: Number of persons, 1,400. Stage: width, 42ft.; depth, 17ft.; width of drop opening, 24ft. Gas and electric light.

Market day, Thursday.

STOCKPORT, Cheshire.

Population, 102,000. Miles from London, 178.
THEATRE ROYAL AND OPERA HOUSE.— Proprietor and Manager, Mr. Charles Revill; Acting-Manager, Mr. William Revill; Musical Director, Mr. Wm. Pickard; Scenic Artist, Mr. Alfred Crocker. Full license. Holding capacity: Number of persons, 3,000; amount, £120 (ordinary prices). Stage measurements: Depth, 45ft.; width, 67ft.; proscenium, 28ft. Gas and electric light. Amount of printing required, 800 sheets walls, 800 lithos. Usual matinée day, Saturday. Time of band rehearsal, 12 noon.

EMPIRE.—Proprietors, The Stockport Empire Theatre Company, Limited; Managing Director, Mr. W. Gilmore; Acting-Manager, Mr. W. Black; Musical Director, Mr. C. Eaton. Full license. Holding capacity: Number of persons, 1,980; amount, £62. Stage measurements: 60ft. by 40ft.; proscenium. 36ft. by 32ft. Electric light. Time of band rehearsal, 11 a.m. Usual matinée day, Monday, 2.30. Bars no surrounding halls (unless in retaliation.)

MECHANICS' INSTITUTE.—Manager, Mr. A. Northrop. Holds 1,000. Dramatic license. Electric light, own dynamo, 460 volts.

Early closing day, Thursday; market days, Friday and Saturday.

Medical Officers.—A.A.: Dr. C. Barrie Taylor, Holly Bank, Edgeley, and Dr. G. Thorpe Harding, the same address. M.H.A.R.A.: Dr. Taylor. A.U.: Dr. Tylecote, Fairfield, Hall Street.

Agent.—M.H.A.R.A.: T. Wilson, Egerton Arms. V.A.F.: The same.

RECOMMENDED APARTMENTS.

Mrs. Dean, 15, Waterloo Road.—Combined bedroom and sitting-room, 1 double-bedded room.

Mrs. Meade, 71, Wellington Road South.—2 sitting-rooms, 4 bedrooms, and 1 combined room.

STOCKSBRIDGE (near Sheffield), Yorks.

PUBLIC HALL.—Proprietors, The Stocksbridge Mineral Water Co., Limited; Manager, Mr. Albert Edward Schofield. Dramatic and music and dancing licenses. Holds 500. Stage 30ft. wide by 28ft. deep. Gas. Amount of deposit required on booking, 25 per cent.

STOCKTON-ON-TEES, Durham.

Population, 51,478. Miles from London, 230.

CASTLE. — Proprietors, North Eastern Breweries, Ltd. Lessee and Manager, Mr. J. C. Imeson; Acting-Manager, Mr. Cecil C. Imeson Holding capacity, 2,380. Auditorium, 72ft. by 64ft.; depth of stage, 42ft.

GRAND.—Proprietor, Mr. John Baity; Manager, Mr. Walter Batty.

HIPPODROME.—Lessee and General Manager, Mr. Harry Burns; Manager, Mr. G. V. Stainton, Double license. Holds 2,800. Stage, 34ft. by 25ft. Electric light, 250 volts.

EXCHANGE HALL.—Manager, Mr. T. R. Wilson, Dovecot Street. Music and dancing license. Holding capacity: Number of persons, 2,000. Platform. Electric light. Terms for hiring: £10 10s. per day, £35 per week. Amount of deposit required on booking: £1 1s.

THE BOROUGH HALL has seating for 800 persons, including a balcony at the extreme end, affording seats for 120. The platform is 30ft. by 12ft. This hall holds a music and dancing license. Mr. W. Pargeter is the resident caretaker.

The population of the district is entirely industrial, being employed in iron and steel works, shipbuilding, marine and other engineering.

The population may be calculated, with the addition of that of the corporate town of Thornaby (16,000), in the immediate neighbourhood. There is a splendid tramway connection running the entire length of district.

The local hirings or fairs are held on the two Wednesdays before May 13 and November 23, when the town is visited by all classes of portables, shows, roundabouts, booths, etc., which stand in the spacious High Street, stands for which are obtainable on application to the market inspector. Sites for circus pitches, menageries, etc., are easily obtainable in various parts of the locality.

Agent: M.H.A.R.A., J. Lacey, Unicorn Hotel. V.A.F.: J. Bishop, White Hart Hotel.

Early closing day, Thursday; market day, Wednesday.

STOKE-ON-TRENT.

Population, 30,458. Miles from London, 146.

HIPPODROME.—Proprietor, Mr. T. Allan Edwardes; General Manager, Mr. H. F. Miller; Assistant Manager, Mr. H. Maroney.

Early closing day, Thursday; market day, Saturday.

A.U. Medical Officers.—Dr. A. R. Moody, Richmond House, Shelton.

Agent.—M.H.A.R.A. and V.A.F.: E. Capewell, Glebe Hotel.

STONE, Staffs.

Population, 5,680. Miles from London, 138.

TOWN HALL.—Proprietors, Stone Urban District Council; Manager, Mr. R. Glover. Dramatic and music and dancing licenses. Holds 586. Stage, 30ft. by 24ft. 6ins. by 16ft. 9in. high; proscenium, 23ft. 6ins. by 16ft. high. Gas. Terms of hiring: Theatrical performance, £2 2s. per night first night, £1 per night afterwards; or £5 5s. per week (exclusive of Sunday); miscellaneous entertainment, £1 10s. per night, without balcony. Amount of deposit required on booking, 25 per cent

Dates of local fairs, first Saturday after September 29.

Plenty of room for portables.

Early closing day, Wednesday; market day, Tuesday.

STONEHAVEN, Kincardine, N.B.

70,000 within a radius of 3 miles.

Population, 4,565.

TOWN HALL.—Owners, Town Council; Manager, Mr. Edward Cruse. Fully licensed. Holding capacity: Number of persons, 750. Amount: £60. Stage measurements, 37½ft. by 25ft. (in centre); proscenium, 22ft. in width; height, 23½ft. Lighted by gas. Amount of printing required: 4-16 sheet, 20-6 sheet, 100 d.c., 200 day bills. Terms for hiring: One night, £1 15s.; two, £2 15s.; three, £3 15s.; piano extra. Amount of deposit required on booking, 10s. one night, 15s. two, and £1 for three. Any nights good for the hall but Saturday. Balcony, per night, 15s.

There are no local fairs of any importance. A field is let for circuses, etc.

Early closing day, Wednesday.

STOURBRIDGE, Worc.

Population, 70 000 (with n a radius of three miles). Miles from London, 125.

ALHAMBRA THEATRE.—Proprietress, Miss Maude Lynton. Manager, Mr. D. C. Phelps.

TOWN HALL.—Proprietors, Urban District Council. Dramatic license. Custodian, Mr. C. F. Dancer. Holding capacity, 1,200. Stage, 30ft. by 32ft. Gas. Terms, £2 10s. first night, £2 second, £1 10s. third. Hall, 108ft. by 46ft. by 38ft.

Local fair, last Monday in March.

Early closing, Thursday; market, Friday

STOWMARKET, Suffolk.

Population, 4,162. Miles from London, 81.

CORN HALL.—Secretary, Mr. John Inkpen Holds 400. Stage, movable, 9ft. by 24ft. Gas. Printing 50 walls, 500 lithos. Terms: 30s. per night.

THE INSTITUTE.—Apply Secretary. Dramatic license.

Early closing, Tuesday; market, Thursday. Medical Officer: A.A., Dr. C. W. Low, Stricklands; A.U., the same.

STRABANE, Co. Tyrone.

Population, 5,003. Miles from Dublin, 163.

TOWN HALL.—Managers, Strabane Urban District Council, Mr. T. B. Feely, Town Clerk. Holding capacity: Number of persons, 500. Platform. Lighted by gas. Terms for hiring: First night, 30s.; each succeeding night, 25s. Amount of deposit required on booking, £1.

Early closing, Wednesday; market, Tuesday.

STRATFORD-UPON-AVON.

Population, 8,514. Miles from London, 101.

SHAKESPEARE MEMORIAL THEATRE.— Proprietor, Memorial Association; Managers, Charles Lowndes, Secretary; William S. Brassington, Assistant Secretary. Holding capacity: Number of persons, 850. This theatre is intended for the annual Shakespeare Festival, which is held in April and May, and lasts three weeks or more. It is only occasionally opened in the winter. Electric light, three wire system, 440 volts direct amps 50 on each side.

MEMORIAL LECTURE ROOM.—In connection with the theatre. Management the same. Custodian, Mr. C. Rainbow. Holds 300. Small stage. Gas only.

CORN EXCHANGE.—Secretary, Mr. J. Palmer. Double license. Holding capacity: Number of persons, about 450. Temporary

stage, 22ft. by 16ft. 6in. Lighted by gas.
Terms for hiring: Two guineas per night.
Amount of deposit required on booking:
According to the number of nights.
Stratford-on-Avon has a residential and industrial population. A number of the latter
are employed at breweries. The Corporation
employ a lot, and the farmers around too.
There are brick and lime works, which give
employment to many, and the two railways
also (the Great Western and E. and W. Junction).
The great "Ox Roast" or "Mop" takes
place on October 12. The "Runaway Mop"
the second Friday after the 12th. One or two
portable theatres visit the town during the
year, and they have little difficulty in obtaining a license from the Corporation. Circus
pitches are obtainable. There is a field near
the East and West Junction Railway Station
where most, if not all of them, stand.
Early closing day, Thursday; market day,
Friday.

STREET, Somerset.
Population, 4,018. Miles from London, 132.
CRISPIN HALL.—Proprietors, the Street
Club and Institute; Manager, Mr. James Hard-
ing, Street, Somerset. Holds 1,000. Stage,
20ft. by 25ft. Gas. Amount of printing re-
quired, 50 to 100 posters.
Tor Fair at Glastonbury, two miles, second
Monday in September.
Early closing day, Wednesday.

STROUD, Glos.
Population, 9,153; District, 40,000. Miles from
London, 102.
SUBSCRIPTION ROOMS.—Manager, Mr.
H. J. Twitchett. Fully licensed. Holding
capacity: Number of persons, about 800;
amount, up to about £80. Stage composed of
very strong tables, 32ft. wide by 16ft.
deep. Lighted by gas. Amount of printing
required, 300 sheets. Terms for hiring: Concerts: One night, £2 16s.; two nights,
£4 8s. 6d.; three nights, £6; four nights,
£7 13s. 6d.; week, £10 18s. 6d.; theatricals:
One night, £3 11s. 6d.; two nights, £6; three
nights, £8 7s. 6d.; four nights, £10 15s. 6d.;
week, £15 11s. 6d.; the above includes gas
and fires. Amount of deposit required on
booking, 25 per cent.
Early closing day, Thursday; market day,
Friday.

STURMINSTER, NEWTON, Dorset.
THE SWAN ASSEMBLY ROOM.—Proprietor,
Mr. G. Eastwood. Holding capacity: Number of persons, 300. No stage. Lighted by
gas. Terms for hiring: 15s. per day; 17s. 6d.
per day with anteroom. Payment in advance.

SUDBURY, Suffolk.
Population, 7,109; District about 20,000.
Miles from London, 58.
VICTORIA HALL.—Hon. Manager, Mr. W.
J. Langdon, J.P. Dramatic license. Hold-
ing capacity: Number of persons, 650. Amount,
various. Stage measures 19ft. deep, 35ft.
wide; proscenium, 20ft. opening. Lighted by
gas. Terms for hiring: 35s. per night.
Amount of deposit required on booking, 10s.
For fair ground and circus pitch, apply Mr.
Karl Deeks, Friars Street, Sudbury.
Early closing day, Wednesday Market day,
Thursday.

SUNBURY-ON-THAMES, Middlesex.
PRETORIA HALL.—Proprietor, Mr. Edward
Frost. Double license Holding capacity:
Number of persons, 770. Stage measurements,
16ft. deep by 22ft. wide; proscenium, 15ft.
Lighted by gas.
ASSEMBLY ROOMS.—Apply, Manager.
Dramatic license.

SUNDERLAND, Durham.
Population, 157,495. Miles from London, 268.
AVENUE THEATRE.—Proprietor, Mr. Rich-
ard Thornton; General Manager, Mr. Harry
Esden. Full license. Holding capacity; Num-
ber of persons, 3,000. Stage measurements, 48ft.
by 30ft.; proscenium, 28ft. opening. Electric
light. Usual matinée day, Saturday.
THE KING'S THEATRE. — Lessee and
Manager, Mr. S. F. Davidson; General Manager,
Mr. Alexander Telford; Assistant Manager, Mr.
Sidney Reach. Full license. Holding capacity:
Number of persons, 3,500. Stage measurements:
width, 80ft.; depth, 42ft.; opening, 36ft.; 67ft. to
grid; 23ft. under fly floor. Electric light. Amount
of printing required: 1,800 sheets, 1,200 d.c.,
circulars, etc.
THEATRE ROYAL.—Proprietor, Mr. Richard
Thornton; General Manager, Mr. Harry Esden;
Acting Manager, Mr. Geo. Dunn. Musical Direc-
tor, Mr. F. Lucas Full license. Holding capacity:
Number of persons, 2,500; amount, £70. Stage
measurements: Opening, 28ft 6in.; depth, 34ft.;
width, 54ft. Electric light. Rehearsals: Band,
1.30 p.m.; stage, 10 o'clock. No matinées. Printing required: 900 sheets and 500 lithos.
EMPIRE.—Proprietors, The Sunderland Empire Palace, Limited; Managing Director, Mr.
Richard Thornton; Resident Manager, Mr.
Harry Esden; booking circuit, Moss and
Stoll; Musical Director, Mr. W H. Holden,
Double license. Holding capacity: Number
of persons, 4,000. Electric light. Time of
band rehearsal, 2 p.m. Matinée day (when
played), Wednesday or Saturday.
Bars all other Managements' Halls in Sander-
land and the following towns: Monkseaton,
Whitley, Cullercoats, North Shields, Monkwear-
mouth, South Shields, Wallsend, Hebburn,
Jarrow, Chester-le-Street, Houghton-le-Spring,
Hetton-le-Hole, Murton Colliery, Seaham Har-
bour, and Fence Houses.
PALACE, High-street West.—Lessees, United
County Theatres, Limited; Managing Director,
Mr. Alfred Moul.
PAVILION, Sans-street.—Lessee, Mr. R.
Pringle. Pictures and varieties.
OLYMPIA, Holmeside.—Proprietors, Messrs.
Richardson Bros., Limited. Pictures, varieties,
and side-shows. Skating rink.
VICTORIA HALL.—Proprietors, The Cor-
poration of Sunderland; Resident Manager,
Mr. S. Lyne. A large up-to-date hall suitable
for concerts and lectures; recently enlarged
and embellished. Holding capacity: Number
of persons, 2,500 to 3,000. Ordinary platform.
Electric light. Terms for hiring: £42 per
week of six days; day from £8 8s. to £12 12s.
Amount of deposit required on booking:
£10 10s. In the same building are
the Edward and Alexandra Halls, more
adapted for smaller gatherings.
WORKMEN'S HALL (Monkwearmouth).—
Proprietors, the Committee; Manager, the Secretary. Music and dancing license. Holds 1,200.
Depth and width of stage, 15ft. 6in. by 40ft.
Electric light, voltage 220. Terms for hiring:
Concerts, including piano and use of scenery,
30s. nightly; Kinematograph shows, 20s. nightly;
Special terms for longer periods. Amount of
deposit required on booking, half.

SUBSCRIPTION LIBRARY and LECTURE HALL, Fawcett Street; used for concerts, etc. PICTURE HALL and WHEATSHEAF HALL, Monkwearmouth; small halls at present used for picture shows.
MINERS' HALL, Monkwearmouth.—Suitable for concerts.
Population of Sunderland Unions, estimated at 200,000, is chiefly industrial. Staple industries, shipbuilding and marine engine building. Sunderland is the largest shipbuilding town in the world. Coal exportation is also carried out on a large scale. Roker, a district of the borough, is, however, residential, and is year by year increasing in popularity as a seaside resort. Many thousands of visitors gather here during the season.
There are no local fairs, and portables do not visit the town.
Tenting circuses usually pitch on the Drill Ground of the 7th B. N. Durham Light Infantry, Garrison Field, Gill Bridge-avenue. This is the periodical stand for van-dwellers and other travelling showmen at Christmas, Easter, and Whitsuntide.
Early closing day, Wednesday; market day, Saturday.
Medical Officers.—A.A.: Dr. David E. Todd, Beech House; consulting rooms, 12 and 13, Green-terrace (tel. No. 447). A.U.: The same. M.H.A.R.A.: The same.
Agent.—M.H.A.R.A., J. Humphries, Three Tuns Hotel, Crowtree Road. V.A.F.: The same. A.U.: The same.

RECOMMENDED APARTMENTS.

Mrs. R. Spensley, 37, North Bridge Street.— 1, Sitting. 2 bed, 2 combined rooms; pianos, bath.
Mrs. Bailey, 19, Laura Street. - 2 bedrooms, 2 sitting-rooms; bath and piano.

SURBITON, Surrey.

Population, 15,017. Miles from London, 12.
ASSEMBLY ROOMS.—Fully licensed. Holding capacity: Number of persons—large hall seats 650, small hall, 230. Stage measurements, 23ft. deep by 46ft. wide; opening, 23ft. Green room, three dressing rooms. Gas and electric light, 220 volts. Terms: Large hall, 4 guineas a night; £20 a week.
Early closing day, Wednesday. No market day.

SUTTON COLDFIELD, Warwick.

Population, 23,000. Miles from London, 117.
TOWN HALL.—Manager, Mr. R. A. Reay-Nadin, Town Clerk. Double license. Holding capacity: Number of persons, seating 650, accommodate 800. Stage: 30ft. by 22ft., and good scenery, drop curtain, etc. Electric light 230 volts. Terms: £4 17s. 6d., with allowances of 10 per cent. two nights, 15 per cent. three nights, 20 per cent. four nights, and 25 per cent. for a week or longer.
MASONIC HALL.—Proprietors, Sutton Coldfield Masonic Hall Company, Limited; Secretary, Mr. C F. Marston. Music and dancing license. Dramatic license can be obtained at a charge of 5s. Seats for 336 (all numbered); prices usually 2s., 1s., and 6d. Stage: 21ft. wide by 16ft. deep; no proscenium. Electric light, 230 volts; gas is also laid on to stage. Terms: £2 2s. per night, inclusive of light; special terms for longer engagements. Deposit, £1 1s.
Sutton Coldfield being a holiday resort, several hundred thousands visit it yearly. Trinity Monday is a fête day. There are plenty of sites available for circuses, etc.
Early closing day, Thursday; market day, Saturday.

SUTTON-IN-ASHFIELD, Notts.

Population, 20,000. Miles from London, 140.
KING'S THEATRE.—Proprietors, Mansfield, Sutton, and District Theatres, Limited; Managing Director, Captain Clayton; Acting-Manager, Mr. F Clayton; Musical Director, Mr. F. F. Chandler; Scenic Artist, Mr. Alec Tool. Full Dramatic License. Holding capacity: Number of persons, 1,100. Amount, £55. Stage measurements, 65ft. by 35ft.; proscenium opening, 30ft. Time of band rehearsal, 5 p.m. Printing required, 600 wall, 600 lithos. Gas.
Early closing day, Wednesday; market day, Saturday.

SUTTON, Surrey.

Population, 17,223. Miles from London, 15.
PUBLIC HALL.—Secretary, Mr. John E. Hind. Double license. Holding capacity: Number of persons, 566. Proper stage. Stage measurements: 17ft. 6in. deep, 36ft. wide. Gas and electric. Terms for hiring: Dramatic performances, £5 5s. first night, £8 8s. second night, £10 10s. third night; concerts, £3 3s. per night. The whole of amount of hire must be paid in advance.
Early closing day, Wednesday; no market day.

SWADLINCOTE (near Burton-on-Trent), Derbyshire.

Population, 18,014. Miles from London, 126.
TOWN HALL.—Proprietors, Swadlincote District Urban District Council; Manager, Mr. A. J. Mason, town engineer and surveyor. Dramatic and music and dancing licenses. Holding capacity: Number of persons, 500 to 600; amount, £20 to £30. Plain stage, 30ft. wide, 9ft., 12ft., or 15ft. deep as required. A set of scenery can be hired. Gas (electric, by special arrangement). Terms for hiring: First day, 40s.; second, 30s.; third and subsequent, 20s. each. Half fees required on booking.
Population within a radius of 1½ miles about 26,000.
Sabine's Ground and Granville Arms Hotel show field available for portables, etc.

SWANSEA, Glam.

Population, 102,000. Miles from London, 195.
GRAND THEATRE.—Proprietors, Messrs. David Allen and Sons, Ltd.; Sole Lessee and Manager, Mr. E. Oswald Brooks; Acting Manager, Mr. Walter Dean; Musical Director, Mr. W. F. Hulley. Full license. Holding capacity: Number of persons, 2,400; amount, £200. Electric light 220 volts, continuous. Printing, 1,500 sheets, 1,000 d.c. and circulars. Usual matinée day, Saturday, at 2.30. Time of band rehearsal, 11 a.m. Bars all theatres within 15 miles.
STAR THEATRE.—Lessee and Manager, Mr. Wm. Coutts. Accommodates 2,000 people. Electric light throughout the building; equipped with every modern convenience.
EMPIRE THEATRE.—Proprietors, Moss's Empire, Limited; Managing Director, Mr. Oswald Stoll; District Manager, Mr. Albert Mitchell; Acting Manager, Mr. P. C. Rowe; Booking Circuit, Moss and Stoll; Musical Director, Mr. Thos. Tomlinson. Music and Dancing License. Electric light. Time of band rehearsal, 3 p.m. No matinée day.
Bars all other Managements' Halls in Swansea and the following towns: Port Talbot, Neath, Briton Ferry, Aberdulais, Pontardawe, Pontardulais, Clydach, Mumbles, Llanelly, Luoghor, and Oystermouth.

THE PALACE THEATRE.—Lessee and Manager, Mr. Wm. Coutts. Music and dancing license. Electric light, v ltage 220. A bioscope theatre, and accommodates 1,250.

THE SHAFTESBURY.—Lessee and Manager, Mr. Wm. Coutts. Music and dancing license. Holds 800. Electric light, 220 voltage. At present run as a picture house.

Early closing day, Thursday; market day, Saturday.

Agent.—M.H.A.R.A.: P. C. Lowe, Empire Theatre ; Jas. Copus, Empire Palace Bar,

RECOMMENDED APARTMENTS.

Mrs. R. Hopkins, 28, Cradock Street.

SWINDON, Wilts.

Population, 50,000. Miles from London, 78.

EMPIRE THEATRE (late The Queen's).—Proprietors, The Wiltshire Entertainment Company, Limited; Managing Director, Mr. Alfred Manners. Two performances nightly. Double license. Holds 2,200. Lighted by electricity.

MECHANICS' INSTITUTE. — Secretary, Mr. H. J. Southwell. Fully licensed. Holding capacity: Number of persons, 900 ; amount, about £40. Stage, 28ft. by 50ft. Lighted by gas; electric light for kinematograph. Terms for hiring: Two guineas one night, 31s. 6d. for more than one night. Amount of deposit required on booking: Two guineas.

Swindon's population is essentially an industrial population, the Great Western Railway Works here employing between 12,000 and 13,000 hands.

Prior to the advent of the G.W.R. Works and the mushroom growth of the town in the last decade, there were three fairs held in the Market Square and High Street, but these have now dwindled down to one, which is held annually on the second Monday after September 11. This is a pleasure fair, and also hiring fair, and is usually largely attended by agriculturists from the surrounding districts, and also by the resident population in the evening after the G.W.R. Works are closed. It should be added that there is a small Lady Day fair, which is held on the Monday before April 5, but this is only a small one. The town is not now visited by portables, and circuses have within the last three or four years become a thing of the past.

The places available for entertainment, and which are visited at frequent intervals, are:

G.W.R. SWIMMING BATHS.—Secretary, Mr. W. Spruce. This large building is used for entertainments in the winter months, and is capable of accommodating from 1,800 to 2,000. Poole's and other popular entertainers visit here every year. THE SMALL HALL seats about 500.

CORN EXCHANGE.—Manager and Secretary, Mr. W. H. Shepherd. Fully licensed. Holding capacity: Number of persons, 600 seated, 300 standing. Size, 110ft. by 50ft. Stage, 24ft. by 20ft. 6in. Proscenium, 20ft. 6in. by 18ft. 6in. Lighted by gas only. Terms for hiring: 2 guineas one night; 1 guinea per night after, including attendant. Amount of deposit required on booking: first night's letting. Afternoon performance, 5s. extra. This hall, situate in the extreme southern portion of the borough, nearly a mile from the other places of entertainment, is regularly visited during the winter months by kinematograph and bioscope entertainments, and also occasionally by dramatic companies.

Early closing day, Wednesday; market days, Monday and Friday.

Agent.—M.H.A.R.A.: C. G. Kent, Rifleman's Hotel, Regent Street. V.A.F.: The same.

RECOMMENDED APARTMENTS.

Mrs. Bigg, 98, Commercial Road.—2 bedrooms, 1 sitting-room ; piano.

Mrs. L. Cottrell, 45, Victoria Road.

TAIN, Ross-shire.

Population, 1,645.

TOWN HALL.—Manager, Mr. James Mackenzie, King-street. No dramatic license. Holding capacity: Number of persons, 500. There is a stage. Gas light. Terms for hiring: £1 5s., exclusive of footlights. Amount of deposit required on booking: Half-rate. The size of hall is 60ft. by 32ft., with a recess at platform end 17ft. by 7ft. The gallery projects 10ft. over the back of the hall. There is one large and one small ante-room.

No local fairs. Sites for portables, circuses, etc., can be had by applying to Mr. George Sangster, Burgh Inspector.

Early closing day, Thursday; market days, Tuesday and Friday.

TAMWORTH, Staffs.

Population, 7,271. Miles from London, 110.

ASSEMBLY ROOMS.—Proprietors, Mayor and Corporation; Manager, Mr. Frederick Hughes. Double license. Holding capacity: Number of persons (seating, including balcony), 500. Lighted by gas. Terms: £2 10s. one, £4 10s. two, £6 5s. three nights. Amount of deposit required on booking, £1. Stage: 30ft. by 20ft.; proscenium opening, 21ft. 8in.

Population, chiefly industrial (coal mines, engineering, sanitary pipe-makers, wholesale clothing, etc.). Good dramas dealing with working-class life, and pieces with plenty of music (vocal and instrumental), are appreciated here. Local Fairs are July 26 and first Monday in October. The local magistrates generally look with disfavour upon portables, and on several occasions licenses have been refused. The recreation ground is available for circus pitches.

Early closing day, Wednesday; market day, Saturday.

RECOMMENDED APARTMENTS.

Mrs. T. Pointon, Station Cottage.—2 bedrooms and 1 sitting-room.

TARPORLEY, Cheshire.

Population, 2,644. Miles from London, 173.

PUBLIC HALL.—Proprietors, Public Hall Co.; Manager, Mr. Thos. Cooper, 57, High Street, Tarporley. Not licensed, but Part 4 of Public Health Act, 1890, not in force in district. Holds about 500. No proper stage. Gas

A field belonging to the Bell and Lion Inn is generally used for circuses, etc.

Early closing day, Wednesday; market day, Thursday.

TAUNTON, Somerset.

Population, 20,098. Miles from London, 158.

LONDON ASSEMBLY ROOMS.—Proprietor, Mr. E. H. Claridge. Dramatic license. Holding capacity: Number of persons, about 800; amount, £40 to £50. Stage measurements: 40 ft. by 22 ft.; permanent proscenium, opening 25 ft. Stage will take 18 ft. flats and 30 ft. cloths, with grid and everything complete. Gas and electric light. Amount of printing required: 500 sheets. Terms for hiring: One night, £4 4s.; two nights, 7 10s. Amount of deposit required on booking, £1.

Population is mostly industrial (shirt and collar manufacturing). Regimental depot. Occasionally visited by portables. No licensing difficulty. Sites for alfresco concerts or circus pitches obtainable.

Early closing day, Thursday; market day, Saturday.

TAVISTOCK, Devon.

Population, 4,728.   Miles from London, 214.

TOWN HALL.—Manager, Mr. T. W. Greenfield, Bedford-square, Tavistock.   Dramatic license.   Holding capacity : Number of persons, 400. No proper stage, but platform can be erected. Lighted by gas. Terms for hiring: Graduated, one night 32s. 6d. (exclusive of license). No deposit required on booking.

Early closing day, Wednesday; market day, Friday.

TEIGNMOUTH, Devon.

Population, 8,636.   Miles from London, 204.

TOWN HALL.—Proprietors, Urban District Council. Apply, Clerk of the Council. Let for concerts, etc.

ASSEMBLY ROOMS.—Manager, Mr. Geo. A. Bilton. Dramatic, music and dancing license. Holding capacity : Number of persons, between 400 and 500 ; amount, £35, at 3s., 2s., 1s., 6d. Depth and width of stage, 23 ft. by 33 ft. ; proscenium, 23 ft. wide, 12 ft. 6 in. high. Lighted by gas. Terms for hiring : Moderate, and by arrangement, according to time of year and length of time required. Amount of deposit required on booking 20s.

Early closing day, Thursday; market day, Saturday.

TENBURY, Worcestershire.

Population, 4,440. Miles from London, 263.

CORN EXCHANGE.—Proprietors, Corn Exchange Co., Ltd.; Managing Director, Mr. A. Handley, Tenbury ; Secretary, Mr. A. S. Miles. Has dramatic license. Holding capacity : Number of persons, 300. Circular back stage. From centre of circle to front of stage, 16ft, but stage can be built out at an extra cost of 5s. Lighted by gas. Terms for hiring : £1 3s. 6d. first night ; 13s. 6d. each other night. Amount of deposit required on booking, one-half.

Early closing day, Thursday; market day, Tuesday.

TENBY, Pembroke.

Population, 4,440. Miles from London, 263.

ROYAL   GATE   HOUSE   ASSEMBLY ROOMS.—Proprietors, The Gate House Hotel Company, Limited ; Manager Mr. W. Kremyl. Double license. Holding capacity : 865. Movable stage. Proscenium opening, 18ft. ; stage, 34ft. wide, 16ft. deep ; height to cross rail, 15ft. Lighted by gas. Terms for hiring, from £3 3s. per night. Amount of deposit required on booking, 21s. for each night booked. Good companies do well in summer season and fairly well in off season.

PUBLIC HALL.—Manager, Mr. Frank B. Mason. Music and dancing license. Holding capacity : Number of persons, 500. Amount, £20. Fit-up. Lighted by gas. Printing required for town of 5,000 inhabitants. Terms for hiring : £5 per week, or £2 per night. Amount of deposit required on booking, 20s. Not suited for plays, available for lectures, concerts, etc.

DE VALANCE GARDENS.—Alfresco and covered hall. Good stage and dressing-rooms. Five minutes from station. Terms from October to June from Mr. C. Chiles, C.C., High street ; July to end September, Mr. Sidney James, Royal Strolling Players.

CORONATION   GARDENS,   South   Cliff Street. Nice stage and dressing-rooms. Alfresco, with canvas covering, Mr. F. B. Mason.

CORPORATION BANDSTAND, Castle Hill. —Let to alfresco entertainers. Apply to Town Clerk.

Charter Fair (St. Margarets), July 29 to July 31 inclusive, and permission generally given to remain over Bank Holiday. Sand entertainers do well during season, July to September.

Circus Pitch, St. Johns Croft.—Terms from Town Clerk.

No portables visit the town, but Kinematograph shows do good business.

Early closing day, Wednesday; market days, Wednesday and Saturday.

TEWKESBURY, Glos.

Population, 5,419.   Miles from London, 130.

PHILHARMONIC HALL.—Manager, Mr. Geo. Watson. Dramatic license. Holding capacity: Number of persons, about 400. Stage depth, 17ft. ; length, 22ft. ; curtain, 18ft. Lighted by gas. Amount of printing required : About 200 window bills, 5 large posting stations. Terms for hiring : One night, £2 10s. ; two nights, £4 10s. Amount of deposit required on booking, 20s.

TOWN HALL.—This hall is not used for dramatic shows or concerts.

The Pleasure Fair is held on October 10. Portables visit sometimes, but they experience considerable difficulty in obtaining a license, the Borough Council being strongly opposed to this kind of entertainment. No difficulty is experienced with regard to a circus site.

All the ground available for building purposes (that is out of floods way), is already built upon, consequently the town cannot increase in size.

Tewkesbury is situated in an agricultural district. The chief industries being a flour mill which finds employment for about 100 men, a building firm which employs from 100 to 150 hands, and an engineering works where Roundabouts, etc., are made.

Early closing day, Thursday.   Market day, Wednesday.

THAME, Oxon.

Population, 2,911. Miles from London, 49

TOWN HALL.—Manager and Hall Keeper, Mr. William J. Arnold. Dramatic license. Holding capacity : Number of persons, 400 ; amount, £12. Stage : about 14ft. deep and 24ft. wide. Gas, foot and top light connections. Amount of printing required : About 100 sheets and odd stuff. Terms for hiring : 25s. first night, and £1 per night after if use of theatrical license required. If not, 5s. per night less. Amount of deposit required on booking : 10s.

Early closing day, Thursday; market day, Tuesday.

THETFORD, Norfolk.

Population, 4,613. Miles from London, 95.

ODDFELLOWS HALL.—Manager, Mr. Robt. Tilley. Dramatic license. Holding capacity : Number of persons, 600. Stage : 30ft. by 9ft. ;

can be enlarged. Lighted by gas. Terms for
hiring: One night, 40s.; two nights, 65s.
Amount of deposit required on booking: Half
hiring.
Early closing day, Thursday; market day,
Saturday.

THIRSK, Yorks.

Population, 5,000. Miles from London, 213.
PUBLIC HALL.—Manager, Honorary Secretary Thirsk Institute (Mr. A. B. Hall). No
dramatic license. Holding capacity: Number of persons, 400. Stage: 25ft. by 25ft. by
14ft. high; proscenium, 15ft. wide by 11ft.
high. Lighted by gas. Amount of printing
required: 50 posters, 1,000 handbills. Terms
for hiring: One night, 30s.; two, 50s.; three,
60s.; week, by arrangement, reduced. Amount
of deposit required on booking, 20s.
Early closing day, Wednesday; market day,
Monday.

THORNBURY, Glos.

Population, 2,597. Miles from London, 139.
COSSHAM HALL.—Manager, Mr. F. Williams, Clerk to the Parish Council. Dramatic license. Holding capacity: Number
of persons, 300. Stage measurements: 16ft.
deep, 19ft. wide; proscenium, 16ft.; Footlights. Lighted by gas. Terms for hiring,
32s. one night, 50s. two nights, 60s. three
nights. Total must be paid before possession.
Early closing day, Thursday; market day,
fourth Wednesday in month.

THORNE (near Doncaster), Yorks.

Population, 3,818. Miles from London, 165.
TOWN HALL.—Proprietors, Thorne Parish
Council; Manager, Mr. C. Waller, clerk. Dramatic license from October 1 to April 1. Holds
300. Ordinary platform. Gas. Terms for
hiring, 22s., including piano, first night; 18s.
each succeeding night. Amount of deposit required on booking, 10s.
Dates of local fairs, first Tuesday and Wednesday after June 11.
Early closing day, Thursday; market day,
Wednesday.

THORNTON HEATH, near Croydon, Surrey.

BATHS HALL.—Proprietors, Croydon Corporation; Manager, Mr. Henry Marlow. Dramatic and music and dancing licenses. Holding capacity: Number of persons, 400. Fairly
good stage for temporary affair. Indoor and
outdoor scene provided. Stage, 18ft. by 13ft.
Proscenium opening, 18ft. by 11ft. high. Electric light, alternating 200 volts. Also footlights at 5s. extra charge. Terms for hiring:
27s. 6d. per night to 11 o'clock, 5s. per hour
after that time. Amount of deposit required
on booking, 10s.
This hall is only available from middle of
October to middle of April.

TIPPERARY, Co. Tipperary.

Population, 6,391. Miles from Dublin, 110.
TOWN HALL.—Manager, Mr. Edward Lord.
Holding capacity: Number of persons, 450.
Lighted by gas. Terms for hiring on applica-
tion. Amount of deposit required on book-
ing, £1.
Fairs monthly every second Tuesday. Old
quarterly fairs, April 5, June 24, October 10,
and Dec. 10, 1907.
Market days, Thursday and Saturday.

TIVERTON, Devon.

Population, 10,382. Miles from London, 179.
DRILL HALL.—Manager, Mr. William Mas-
land. Dramatic license. Holding capacity:
Number of persons, 1,000; amount, £50. Depth
and width of stage: 26ft. by 24ft. deep; proscenium measurements, 19ft. wide, 15ft. high.
Amount of printing required: 12 six sheet,

TODMORDEN, Yorks.

Population, 25,418. Miles from London, 203.
HIPPODROME.—Licensee and Manager, Mr.
R. Dewhirst. Electric light. Seats 1,600. Fit
up stage, 28ft. by 21ft.
TOWN HALL.—Secretary and Licensee, Mr.
H. Stansfield. Dramatic license. Holding capacity: Number of persons, 1,200. Fit-up stage:
Opening, 22ft. by 22ft.; width, 34ft.; depth,
19ft. Gas and electric light. Terms for
hiring: One week, £12 15s., and 2s. 6d. each
performance for firemen's attendance. Amount
of deposit required on booking: £5.
CO-OPERATIVE HALL.—Secretary, Mr.
Samuel Sutcliffe. Dramatic license.
Todmorden's population is industrial, local
industries principally being cotton-spinning
and weaving. There are also large iron-
founders' and machinists' works.
Two half-yearly fairs are held, one on Good
Friday and Saturday and one on the last
Thursday in September and two following
days. Portables often visit the town, usually
standing on the Market Ground, and no diffi-
culty is experienced in obtaining the license.
Either gas or electric light is supplied by the
Corporation as desired. No al fresco concert
site is available.
Early closing day, Tuesday; market days,
Wednesday and Saturday.

TONBRIDGE, Kent.

Population, 12,736. Miles from London, 30.
PUBLIC HALL.—Manager, Mr. E. C. Austen.
Dramatic license. No proper stage. Hall:
Length, 70ft.; width, 40ft.; height, 35ft.; bal-
cony (good) seats 120. Gas, also electric light
direct current, 220 volts. Terms for hiring:
One night, £3 3s.; two, £5 5s.; three or more,
£2 2s. each. Amount of deposit required on
booking, £1.
Early closing day, Wednesday; market day,
Tuesday.

TONYPANDY, Glam.

Miles from London, 180.
THEATRE ROYAL.—Lessees, Messrs. Carl-
ton and Duckworth; General Manager, Mr.
Sam Duckworth; Acting-Manager, Mr. G.
Ridgewood Barrie.
HIPPODROME.—Proprietor, Mr. W. Thomas;
Lessee and Manager, Mr. Will Stone; General
Manager, Mr. E. Harper.
Agent.—M.H.A.R.A.: J. Thomas, Pandy
Hotel. V.A.F.: The same.

TORQUAY, Devon.

Population, 35,000. Miles from London, 220.
THEATRE ROYAL AND OPERA HOUSE.—
Managing Director, Mr. W. H. Mortimer; Secretary, Mr. Arthur Pearse. Dramatic license.
Holding capacity: over 1,200; Monetary value,
over £80 (full house, usual prices). Electric
light supplied by the Corporation, voltage 200
units, alternating. Access to theatre: Electric
trams run from the railway stations, St. Mary-

26*

church and Babbicombe, to Pit entrance. Late Cars at end of the performance each evening to the above places. Motor cars to Paignton in addition. Refreshment Bar in Theatre.

BATH SALOONS.—Proprietors, The Corporation; Manager, Mr. G. Courtney. Seating capacity: large hall, 800; small hall, 275. Appliances, none; travelling companies bring their own fit-ups. Electric lighting, 200 volts, alternating; hall can be darkened for matinées. 30s. extra. Terms: One show per day, £6 6s.; Two shows per day, £8 8s.; Two days' show, £12 12s.; One week's show, £1e 18s.; Two week's show, 30 guineas; Electric lighting extra, 7d. per unit. The building is fully licensed.

PRINCESS PIER PAVILION. — Proprietors, The Corporation; Secretary, The Town Clerk. Seating capacity, 500. Electric lighting, 200 volts, alternating. Admission : 1s. 3d., 1s., 6d., 3d.; pier toll, 2d.

ST. MARYCHURCH TOWN HALL. — Proprietors, the Corporation; Manageress, Mrs. Martin. Seating capacity, 600. Fully licensed. No Bar. Incandescent lights. Terms on application to Manageress.

Early closing days, Wednesday and Saturday; market day, Saturday.

Medical Officers.—A.A.: Dr. Percy H. Gardner, "Five Ways." A.U.: The same, and Dr. Courtney Dunn, Fairview, Castle Road; 9-10 and 6-9. M.H.A.R.A.: Dr. Herbert E. Dalby, The Rosary, St. Mary's Church.

TORRINGTON, Devon.

Population, 3,456. Miles from London, 225.
TOWN HALL.—Proprietors, Town Council. Apply Hallkeeper. Dramatic license.
Early closing, Thursday; market, Friday.

TOTNES, Devon.

Population, 4,035. Miles from London, 218.
PRINCE OF WALES' THEATRE.—Manager, Mr. R. P. Marshall. Dramatic license. Holding capacity: Number of persons, 300. Stage measurements: Depth, 15ft.; width, 12ft. 6in.; proscenium opening, 10ft. Lighted by gas. Terms for hiring: One night, £2 2s.; two nights, £3 10s. Amount of deposit required on booking, half rental.
Early closing day, Thursday; market day, Friday.

TOWYN, Merioneth.

Population, 3,756. Miles from London, 240.
ASSEMBLY ROOMS.—Manager, Mr. H. W. Griffiths, 7, College Green. Holds 800 to 1,000. Stage, 35ft. by 15½ft. Gas. Terms: July, August, September—First night, £2; second, £1 10s. Other months—£1 15s. first night, £1 5s. second. Amount of deposit required on booking, 25 per cent.
PENDRE ASSEMBLY ROOMS.—Same management. Suitable for concerts, at 10s. per night.
Early closing day, Wednesday.

TREDEGAR, Mon.

Population, 18,497. Miles from London, 173.
TEMPERANCE HALL.—Manager, Mr. Geo. Hopkin; Secretary, Mr. J. Sutton. Dramatic license. Holding capacity: Number of persons, 900; amount, £40, at 2s., 1s., and 6d. Stage: Width 29ft., depth 18ft., height from stage, 26ft. Lighted by gas. Terms for hiring: One night, £2 10s.; two nights, £4; three

nights, £5 10s.; four nights, £6 15s.; five nights, £8; six nights, £9 10s.; matinée, 10s. extra; gas for foot lights, 2s. 6d. per night extra. A deposit of £1 is required for one or two nights, £2 for three or four nights, £3 for five or six nights.
Early closing day, Thursday; market day, Saturday.

TREHARRIS, Glam.

Miles from London, 174.
PUBLIC HALL.—Secretary and Manager, Mr. W. A. Davis; Address, 8, Brynteg Place, Treharris. Dramatic and music and dancing licenses. Holding capacity: Number of persons, 900; amount when full, £35 to £40 at our prices. Stage measurements: 44ft. by 21ft.; proscenium opening, 27ft. Lighted by gas. Amount of printing required: 400 sheets, 300 lithos, 400 day bills. Terms for hiring: First night, £2 7s.; second night, £1 17s.; third night, £1 12s.; fourth night, £1 12s.; fifth night, £1 2s.; sixth night, £1 2s. Gas is included. Amount of deposit required on booking. 28s. Population within two miles radius, 15,000.

TREHERBERT, Glam.

OPERA HOUSE.—Proprietors, Messrs. Poole; Manager, Mr. James Gunn. Stage, 48ft. by 25ft. by 20ft.
Industry is chiefly coal mining.
There are no local fairs. The town is visited by portables, pleasure fairs, circus, etc., for which two patches of ground are obtained, generally without any objection from the local council.

TRING, Hertfordshire.

Population, 4,349. Miles from London, 32.
VICTORIA HALL.—Manager, Mr. E. Allison. Dramatic license. Holding capacity: Number of persons, 600. Stage, 18ft. by 20ft.; proscenium, 12ft. by 20ft. Stage can be much enlarged if required. Lighted by gas. Amount of printing required, 150 sheets. Terms for hiring, £7 10s. per week. Amount of deposit required on booking, £1 1s.
UNITY HALL. — Manager, Co-operative Society Limited; apply, Secretary. Not available for dramatic performance. Holding capacity: Number of persons 250. No proper stage. Hall, 50ft. by 24ft., including platform, 18ft. by 7ft.; two ante-rooms in addition. Lighted by gas. Terms of hiring: One night, 25s.; 20s. per night after. Amount of deposit required on booking, 20s.
Early closing day, Wednesday; market day, Friday.

TROWBRIDGE, Wilts.

Population, 11,526. Miles from London, 97.
TOWN HALL.—Manager, Mr. T. S. Hill. Double license. Holding capacity: Number of persons, 800. Stage, 18ft. by 33ft.; no proscenium. Lighted by gas. Terms for hiring, £2 12s. per night. Amount of deposit required on booking, £1.
Early closing day, Wednesday; market day, Tuesday.

TRURO, Cornwall.

Population, 11,562. Miles from London, 296.
TRURO PUBLIC ROOMS.—Mr. J. C. R. Crewes, Secretary. Dramatic license. Seating capacity: Number of persons, 580, but addi-

tional seats can be ordinarily placed. Depth and width of stage, 38½ft. by 18½ft. Lighted by gas. Terms for hiring: Dramatic, one night, 4 guineas; two nights, £6 10s.; and then 21s. each extra night. Concerts, etc., one night, 3 guineas; two nights, £5 5s.; 21s. for each extra night. Gas and attendance extra in either case. Amount of deposit on booking, £1.

Population residential. Whitsun Fair lasts four days, commencing on Whit Wednesday. For Circuses, two fields, one in the city and one near, can be hired.

Early closing day, Friday; market days, Wednesday and Saturday.

TUNBRIDGE WELLS, Kent.

Population, 33,373; District, 70,000. Miles from London, 35.

OPERA HOUSE.—Proprietor, Mr. Welton Dale; Manager, Mr. A. H. Burdett; Musical Director, Mr. H. Lee. Full dramatic licence. Holding capacity: Number of persons, 1.500; amount, £120. Stage measurements, 46ft. deep, 50ft. wide; proscenium opening, 30ft. Gas and electric light, 220 volts alternating. Printing: 500 to 600 windows, 500 walls. Usual Matinée day, Saturday. Time of band rehearsal, 2.30. Hippodrome season under the direction of Mr. F. Mouillot and Mr. Walter de Frece.

GREAT HALL. — Proprietors, Tunbridge Wells Public Rooms Company; Manager, Mr. Aubrey J. Pelton, The Broadway. Dramatic and music and dancing licenses. Holds 600. Stage, 20ft. deep by 40ft. wide. Gas and electric light, alternating current, 220 volts. Terms: Four and a-half guineas per night.

Other halls available are Sussex Assembly Rooms, and the Town Hall.

Early closing day, Wednesday; market day, Friday.

Medical Officers.—A.A.: Dr. J. T. Abbott, Carlingford Lodge, 23, St. John's-road. Tel. No. 346. A.U.: Dr. B. L. Thurlow, 5, Church-road.

Agent.—M.H.A.R.A.: Mr. Urquhart, Castle Hotel. V.A.F.: The same.

TUNSTALL, Staffs.

Population, 9,492. Miles from London, 150.

TOWN HALL.—Proprietors, Urban District Council, Manager, Mr. F. Birchall. Dramatic license. Holding capacity; Number of persons, 1,000. Ordinary wooden platform, 30ft. long, 15ft. deep. Electric light. Terms for hiring: £1 15s. per night for one or two nights; £1 12s. 6d. per night for three, four, or five nights; £1 10s. per night for six nights. Full amount is required on booking.

Local fair, first week in August.

Early closing day, Thursday; market day, Saturday.

TWICKENHAM, Middlesex.

Population, 27,500. Miles from London, 11.

TOWN HALL.— Licensee, Mr. H. Jason Saunders. Dramatic license. Gas and electric light. Terms for hiring: Dramatic performances (with one rehearsal on the same day), £2 12s. 6d.; second and subsequent days, £1 11s. 6d.; Concerts and Entertainments, £2 2s.; second and subsequent days, £1 11s. 6d. Amount of deposit required on booking £1 1s. The Hall is 60ft. long and 32ft. broad (exclusive of the platform, which is about 28ft. long by 14ft. deep). The Hall is licensed to seat 700 persons—500 in the body of the Hall and 200 in the Gallery.

Early closing day, Wednesday.

Medical Officers.—A.A.: Dr. A. H. Rideal, Poplar Lodge, Richmond-road; Dr. W. O. Beddard, 1, Richmond Bridge Mansions.

TYLDESLEY, Lancashire.

Population, 14,843. Miles from London, 200.

THEATRE ROYAL.—Proprietors, Messrs. Brierley, German, and Brierley; Manager, Mr. W. W. Brierley; Acting Manager, Mr. W. German; Musical Directress, Madame Johnson. License—restricted dramatic. Holding capacity: Number of persons, about 1,300. Dimensions of stage, 44ft. by 32ft.; height to fly rail, 20ft.; from stage to grid, 40ft.; proscenium opening, 24ft. Lighted by gas. Amount of printing required, 500 wall printing, 500 lithos. Usual matinée day, Saturday. Time of band rehearsal, 5 p.m.

MINERS' HALL.—Situated in the centre of town; cars passing continually; excellent Hall for Vaudeville, and especially Kinematograph Shows. Capable of seating 600 people. This Hall may be engaged through Mr. J. C. Darlington.

ASSEMBLY ROOMS. — Secretary, Mr. D. Stones. Seating, 500. Stage; no scenery. Lighted by electricity, but not of sufficient power for kinematograph exhibitions.

Principal industries: Coal mining, cotton spinning, weaving, ironworks. Local Fair commencing Friday before the last Sunday in September. Circus Pitches: Excellent ground for that purpose. Alfresco Concerts: Permission may be obtained from the Council to use the enclosed plot of land in the park. Portables do not visit the town.

Early closing day, Wednesday.

TYNEMOUTH, North.

Population, 51,366. Miles from London, 287.

PALACE BY THE SEA AND GARDENS.—Proprietor, Mr. J. H. Graham; Manager, Mr. Lindon Travers; Musical Director, Mr. W. A. Crosse. Double license. Holding capacity: Number of persons, 2,500; amount, prices vary, usual 6d. and 1s.; Sunday (grand) concerts, £200 at extra charges. Stage measurements: 30ft. by 22ft.; depth, 40ft. Electric light. Time of band rehearsal, 1.30 p.m. Usual matinée days, Wednesday and Saturday. The surrounding halls which it bars, North Shields, South Shields, Whitley, and all halls within six miles. Remarks: Open Christmas, New Year, Easter, and from Whit Sunday to first week in October.

Early closing day, Wednesday.

UCKFIELD, Sussex.

Population, 2,805. Miles from London, 55.

PUBLIC HALL.—Proprietors, Uckfield Public Hall Company, Limited; Secretary, Mr. G. E. Hart. Dramatic and music and dancing licenses. Holds 500. Stage measurements, 23ft. by 11ft. Gas. Terms for hiring, £1 10s. Amount of deposit required on booking, £1.

Early closing day, Wednesday.

ULVERSTON, Lancs.

Population, 10,064. Miles from London, 256.

VICTORIA HALL.—Apply Manager. Dramatic license.

DRILL HALL.—Apply Hallkeeper. Dramatic license.

UTTOXETER.

TOWN HALL.—Proprietors, Urban District Council. Apply Hallkeeper. Has dramatic license.

Early closing, Friday; market, Thursday.

UXBRIDGE, Middlesex.

Population, 8,585. Miles from London, 16.

TOWN HALL.—Proprietor, Mr. Sidney Fassnidge. Licensed for music, dancing, and stage plays. Holding capacity: Number of persons, 391. Stage for travelling fit up company. Measurements: 36ft. by 24ft. by 14ft. 6in. high. Electrically lighted, by gas with footlight. Terms for hiring: £2 12s. 6d. first night, £1 11s. 6d. subsequent. Bioscope entertainments are booked.

Population between residential and industrial. Saturday night very busy town.

Local Fair.—Fairly large. Held September 29th.

Portables often visit Uxbridge, no difficulty being experienced in getting license. Pitch for portables, Marshall's Field, opposite railway station. Proprietor, W. Marshall, Railway Hotel, Uxbridge.

Circus Pitches (two), 1, Swan and Bottle Meadow. Proprietor, Swan and Bottle Inn, Uxbridge; 2, Johnson's Field; Messrs. Johnson and Duck, dairymen, Uxbridge.

Early closing day, Wednesday; market day, Thursday.

VENTNOR, Isle of Wight.

Population, 5,866. Miles from London, 90.

GRAND PAVILION.—Manager, Mr. W. E. Briddon. Double license. Holding capacity: Number of persons, 800; amount, £40 to £50. Stage measurements: 19ft. deep by 26ft. wide; 18ft. drop curtain space. Electric light; also gas in reserve. Amount of printing required: Two 18-sheet, two 12-sheet, ten 6-sheet, 150 lithos and d.c. bills, 300 circulars (to distribute by post), 2,000 throwaways, 25 "to-night" slips. Terms for hiring: £3 3s. one night; £5 5s. two. Amount of deposit required on booking, £1 1s.

TOWN HALL (formerly Undercliff Assembly Rooms).—Manager, Town Clerk, Ventnor. Double license. Holding capacity: 450. Electric light, 220 volts, and gas. The hall is seated for 450 persons, and measures 64ft. by 34ft., and 29ft. high. The stage is 25ft. wide at the front, 18ft. deep from front to back (and can be increased to 22ft. by movable staging provided) and 17½ft. high. Toplights and footlights (electric) are provided and can be fixed when required. Scale of charges for dramatic and operatic performances, stage plays, dioramas, concerts, entertainments, etc., one night, £1 11s. 6d.; for each night after the first, £1 1s. (These charges include only the dressing rooms on both sides of the stage and the store room and kitchen under same.) One-third of rent must be paid on booking.

WADEBRIDGE, Cornwall.

Population, 2,186. Miles for London, 235.

TOWN HALL.—Secretary, Mr. Richard Eustace. Dramatic license. Holding capacity: Number of persons, 600. Stage, 36ft. wide. 19ft. deep. Lighted by gas. Amount of printing required depends on booking. Terms for hiring: First, £1 11s. 6d.; second, £1 1s.; third, 15s. 6d.; fourth, 10s.; plus gas, etc. Amount of deposit required on booking, £1 Two retiring rooms, lavatories, etc. Early closing day, Wednesday; market days, Tuesday and Friday.

WAKEFIELD, Yorks.

Population, 41,413. Miles from London, 175.

OPERA HOUSE, Westgate, Wakefield.—Proprietors, Messrs. Sherwood and Co.

HIPPODROME.—Proprietor, S.T.S. Syndicate (Wakefield), Ltd.; Manager, Mr. Sydney Toltree; Booking. Music and dancing license. Holds 1,500. Amount £30. Electric light. Time of band rehearsal: 12 noon. Surrounding halls barred in accordance with the Arbitrator's award.

CORN EXCHANGE.—Manager, Mr. Harry Hughes. Dramatic and music and dancing licenses. Holding capacity: Number of persons, 750. Depth and width of stage: 44ft. by 22ft.; 24ft. opening; 15ft. 6in. head lights. Lighted by gas. Terms for hiring, £15 weekly. Amount of deposit required on booking, £3.

UNITY HALL.—Manager, Mr. Bedford. Holding capacity: Number of persons, 1,200 to 1,400. Stage length, 30ft. 6ins.; width, 13ft. 6ins. Electric light. Terms for hiring, £3 3s. per night. Amount of deposit required on booking, £5 per week.

The city is both residential and industrial. The principal industries are worsted and woollen, cloth manufacturing and worsted spinners, and there are large engineering works and wire rope works, etc. In the immediate vicinity of the city there are several large collieries. Dates of fairs held here are July 4 and 5 and November 11 and 12 (statute hirings). The circus pitch here is generally the Manor Field, Teall Street.

Early closing day, Wednesday; market days, Wednesday (Cattle), Friday, and Saturday.

Medical Officers.—A.A.: Dr. H. Brine Blunt, Linden Villas, Westfield Road, M.H.A.R.A.; Dr. W. S. Wade, 32, York Street.

Agent.—M.H.A.R.A.: A. Ratcliffe, Inns of Court Hotel. V.A.F.: The same.

RECOMMENDED APARTMENTS.

Mrs. Wright, 18, York Street.—1 sitting-room, 2 bedrooms, combined.

WALLINGFORD, Berks.

Population, 2,808. Miles from London, 51.

CORN EXCHANGE.—Secretary, Mr. Francis E. Hedges. No dramatic license. Stage, 21ft. 6in. by 19ft. (no proscenium). Lighted by gas. Amount of deposit required on booking, £1. The building comprises a hall 90ft. by 30ft., of which 29ft. are occupied by a stage and dressing rooms, a gallery capable of seating 70 persons, a ticket office or cloak room, and 2 lavatories. Scale of Charges.— Hire of the building, with fixed stage, etc.: First day, £2; second and subsequent days, £1 15s. Hire of the building without stage and dressing rooms: First day, £1 10s.; second and subsequent days, £1 5s. Gas, according to consumption, at 5s. 6d. per 1,000 feet. The charges include heating, caretaker's fees, the preparation and subsequent re-arrangement of the building, the use of 200 chairs (in addition to the fixed seats in the gallery). Except during market hours (between 12 and 3) on Fridays, the Exchange can be hired on any week day for secular purposes.

TOWN HALL.—Hall Keeper, Mr. George Cheney. No dramatic license. Holding capacity: Number of persons, 200 (about). No stage. Lighted by gas. Terms for hiring: The whole building not exceeding three hours (each additional hour 2s.), 10s. Large hall only not exceeding three hours (each additional hour, 2s.), 10s. N.B.—The permission of the Mayor must in all cases be obtained previously to engagement. Amount of deposit required on booking: Half amount of total fees. Early closing day, Wednesday. Market day, Friday. Many large villages near.

WALMER, Deal, Kent.

Population, 5,614. Miles from London, 81. GLOBE THEATRE.—Depôt, Royal Marines. Proprietors, The Admiralty; Manager, Mr. J. Simpson; Acting Manager, Mr. R. J. Carpenter; Musical Director, Mr. Vernon. Licensed under the Army Act. Holding capacity: Number of persons, 750. Amount, £28 10s. Stage width, 44ft.; depth, 23ft.; proscenium opening, 22ft. Lighted by gas. Amount of printing required: 220 d.c .sheets. No matinée. Time of band rehearsal, 2 p.m. This theatre is situated in the barracks at the R.M. depôt where some 1,600 men are stationed.

The Beach is available in the summer for alfresco entertainments.

WALSALL, Staffs.

Population, 86,430. Miles from London, 120. GRAND THEATRE.

HIS MAJESTY'S THEATRE.—Proprietors, The Walsall Theatres Co., Ltd.; Joint Management, Moss's Empires, Ltd., and Walsall Theatres Co., Ltd.; Secretary and Manager, Mr. W. H. Westwood. Bookings arranged by Moss's Empires, Ltd. Band rehearsal, 12 noon. Bars all other Managements' Halls in Walsall and the following towns: Lichfield, Sutton Coldfield, West Bromwich, Dudley, Oldbury, Brierley Hill, Halesowen, Bilston, Darlaston, Wolverhampton, Erd'ngton, and Saltley.

Early closing day, Thursday; market days, Tuesday and Saturday.

Medical Officer.—A.A.: Dr. J. Scott Wilson, 44, Bradford Street.

Agent.—M.H.A.R.A.: W. H. Westwood, His Majesty's Theatre. V.A.F.: E. V. Booth, New Station Hotel, Park Street.

WALTON-ON-NAZE, Essex.

Population, 2,014. Miles from London, 72. KING'S THEATRE.—Proprietors, A Limited Co.; Manager and Musical Director, Mr. H. Padfield. Full dramatic license. Holding capacity: Number of persons, 600 to 700. Amount, £30. Stage measurements: Proscenium opening, 28ft.; width of stage, 44°t.; depth, 32ft.; flats up to 40ft. Lighted by gas. Arranging for electric light. Amount of printing required: 8-18 sheets, 6-12 ditto, 12-6 ditto, 60 d.c. lithos, 250 circulars for post, 2,000 throwaways. Best dates: Bank Holidays and from June to September.

WALTON-ON-THAMES, Surrey.

Population, 10,329. Miles from London, 17. PUBLIC HALL.—Apply Secretary. Dramatic license.

Early closing, Thursday.

WANTAGE, Berks.

Population, 3,766. Miles from London, 63. VICTORIA CROSS GALLERY.—Proprietors, Wantage Urban District Council; Manager, The Town Property Committee; Caretaker, Mr. Geo. Hillier. Dramatic license. Holds 500. Stage measurements: Depth, 15ft.; width, 24ft. Gas. Terms for hiring: £1 1s. first day, 15s. subsequently; and gas extra 1s. 6d. per hour. Amount of deposit required on booking, 10s.

Dates of local fairs, first Saturday after October 11 and first Saturday in May.

Early closing day, Thursday. Market day, Wednesday.

WARE, Herts.

Population, 5,573. Miles from London, xz. TOWN HALL AND ASSEMBLY ROOMS.— Manager, Mr. G. F. Dobson. Has dramatic license. Depth and width of platform, 11ft. by 30ft. Lighted by gas. The terms of hire to theatrical companies on tour, where scenery is brought into the hall, are: Charge for one night, £2 4s. 6d.; charge for two nights, £3 17s.; charge for three nights, £4 19s. 6d.; and £1 2s. 6d. per night in addition after three nights. Where there is no scenery the charges are as follows: Charge for one night, £1 12s. 6d.; charge for two nights, £2 15s.; charge for three nights, £3 10s. 6d.; and £1 2s. 6d. per night in addition after three nights. Special arrangements for more than one week's hire. The whole charge must be paid before admission is given to the hall. Deposit on booking, 10s. Length of hall is 60ft., and width 30ft. Additional rooms can be hired in the building if required.

Early closing day, Thursday; market day, Tuesday.

WAREHAM, Dorset.

Population, 2,003. Miles from London, 124. ODDFELLOWS' HALL.—Apply the Hall Keeper. Dramatic or music and dancing license can be obtained at short notice. Holding capacity: Number of persons about 400. Stage, 12ft. deep, 26ft. wide. Lighted by gas. Terms for hiring: 25s. first night; 20s. each night after. Amount of deposit required on booking, two thirds of the amount of hiring.

Early closing day, Wednesday; market day, Thursday.

WARMINSTER, Wilts.

Population, 5,547. Miles from London, 105. ATHENÆUM HALL.—Secretary and Manager, T. J. Rushton. Holding capacity: Number of persons, 500; amount, £25. at popular prices. Stage measurements: 18ft. by 32ft. 6in. Lighted by gas. Amount of printing required: Five 18-sheets, eight 6-sheets, 100 d.c., 100 day bills. Terms for hiring: First night, £2; succeeding nights, £1 5s. each inclusive; over three nights, special arrangements. Amount of deposit required on booking: One night, 10s.; longer period, £1. There are two good dressing-rooms adjoining the stage, with mod rn lavatory arrangements. The hall is heated by hot air. Bookings are limited, one week at least being kept clear between each.

Warminster's population is residential, industrial, and agricultural. Chief industries: Sawmills, ironfoundries, breweries, and a shirt factory (the latter employing 200 hands mostly women).

Fair field adjoining main road, from the railway station, and close to the town. Used for circus pitches, shows, roundabouts, etc.

Annual fairs, April 22 and October 26 and 27. The April fair is not usually considered a pleasure fair. The October fair, which is held on the following Monday should the 26th fall on a Saturday, is rather large, and all kinds of shows, roundabouts, etc., are allowed to pitch in the Market Place and High Street on payment of toll.

Alfresco Concerts.—A site might be obtained at certain seasons of the year.

Early closing day, Wednesday; market day, Saturday.

WARRINGTON, Lancs.

Population, 64,242. Miles from London, 182.

ROYAL COURT THEATRE.—Proprietor, Mr. Joseph Beecham: General Manager, Mr. A. M. Loader; Assistant Manager, Mr. S. Smiley. Full dramatic license. Holding capacity: Number of persons, 1,800. Stage measurements: 30ft. deep by 50ft. wide; proscenium opening, 24ft. 9in.; height 22ft. Gas and electric light. Time of band rehearsal, 1 p.m.

ROYAL THEATRE OF VARIETIES.—Proprietor and Manager, Mr. E. M. Johnson; Acting Manager, Mr. Jack Waters; Booking Circuit, Mr. Fred Willmot's; Musical Director, Mr. J. Bennett. Full dramatic license. Holding capacity: Number of persons, 1,200. Gas and electric light. Time of band rehearsal, 2 p.m. Usual matinée day, Thursday.

PALACE AND HIPPODROME.—Managing Director, Mr. Frank Macnaghten; Manager, Mr. G. D. Bradbury; Musical Director, Mr. Ernest A. Widdop.

PARR HALL.—Secretary, Town Clerk, Warrington. Double license. Holding capacity: Number of persons, 1,200. Stage: Depth, 25ft.; width of stage, 48ft. 6in.; opening, 24ft. Gas and electric light. Terms for hiring, £22 10s. per week; Exhibitions, £27 per week; proscenium, £2 5s. extra. Amount of deposit required on booking, 10 per cent. Electric current is supplied for Kinematograph and other Lanterns. The current is continuous, voltage 460. Resistances will have to be provided by the hirer to reduce the pressure to his requirements.

Within easy access of Manchester and Liverpool, Warrington—described as the town of many industries—has many advantages, for it can boast of a steady period of good trade extending over many years. The population may be described mainly as an industrial one, and the chief staple industries are iron, wire drawing, tanning, gas stove engineers, and cotton. There are several residential districts, including Padgate, Stockton Heath, and Malton. Regarding the catering for admirers of the Thespian art, the Town Council have ever been ready to acquiesce for the welfare of the community, and little difficulty has ever been experienced in securing full dramatic licenses. Circus pitches can be obtained at Wilderspool Causeway and a more central position in Arpley. Fairs are held twice a year, March and November.

Early closing day, Thursday; market days, Wednesday and Saturday.

Agent.—M.H.A.R.A.: John Looker, Hop Pole Hotel. V.A.F.: The same.

WARWICK, Warwickshire.

Population, 11,889. Miles from London, 99.

CORN EXCHANGE.—Apply the Manager. Dramatic license.

Early closing, Thursday; market, Saturday.

WATFORD, Herts.

Population, 40,000. Miles from London, 17.

CLARENDON HALL.—Secretary, Mr. H. Morten Turner; Assistant Secretary, Mr. G. T. Fletcher. Double license. Holding capacity: Number of persons, about 1,200; amount, about £50 to £70. Stage: 36ft. (can be extended to 52ft.) by 24ft. Gas in hall. Electricity for power and electric lighting on stage. Terms for hiring: one night, £4 14s., including gas; two, £8 7s.; three, £10 19s. Amount of deposit required on booking: One guinea for

one night. Remarks: The hall is the only large hall in the neighbourhood.

CORN EXCHANGE.—Secretary, Mr. H. Morten Turner; Assistant Secretary, Mr. G. T. Fletcher. Dramatic license. Holding capacity: Number of persons, about 400. No proper stage; built to suit each tenant. Electric light. Terms for hiring: One day, £2 2s.; two, £3 12s., etc. Amount of deposit required on booking, 10s. per day.

ST. JAMES' PARISH HALL.—Has dramatic license.

CLAY HILL, BUSHEY, MISSION HALL.—About 2 miles from Watford. No dramatic license.

Early closing day, Wednesday; market day, Tuesday.

Agent.—V.A.F.: S. Carter, Essex Arms Hotel.

WEDNESBURY, Staffs.

Population, 26,554. Miles from London, 136.

THEATRE ROYAL.—Proprietor, Mr. Harry Battersby; Acting-Manager, Mr. T. Kuner; Musical Director, Archie Hunt. Full dramatic license. Holding capacity; Number of persons, 1,400. Stage measurements: Depth, 27ft., 45ft. wide; proscenium opening, 23ft. Gas and electric light, 230 volts, continuous. Printing, 550 walls, 550 lithos. Time of band rehearsal, 1 p.m.

TOWN HALL.—Manager, Mr. W. R. Taylor. Double license. Holding capacity: Number of persons, about 1,000. Stage can be enlarged from 14ft. deep only, in centre 21ft. long, to 16ft. deep, 32ft. long. Will then take a 20ft. proscenium. Electric light. Terms for hiring: £10 12s. for a week.

Early closing day, Thursday; market day, Friday.

WELLINGBOROUGH, Northants.

Population, 18,412. Miles from London, 65.

EXCHANGE HALL. — Manager, Mr. Jas. Wm. Bellamy. Dramatic license. Holding capacity: Number of persons, 800; amount, £50. Gas light. Amount of printing required. 400 sheets. Amount of deposit required on booking, £2 2s.

CENTRAL HALL.—Manager, Mr. P. O. James. No dramatic license. Holding capacity: Number of persons, 350. Small stage, 12ft. by 8ft. Lighted by gas. Terms for hiring: 15s. per night.

Wellingborough is an educational centre, and the population is residential and industrial (chiefly boots and shoes). There are a number of thriving small towns and villages within a few miles, including Rushden, which double the population.

Fairs are held Easter week, Whit week, and the chief, October 29.

The town is very seldom visited by portables. No difficulty is experienced in obtaining license. Fairs, circuses, portables, etc., have a very central situation in Victoria Grounds, let by Mr. J. W. Pasllow, Volunteer Inn, Midland Road.

Early closing day, Thursday; market day, Wednesday.

WELLINGTON, Salop.

Population, 6,283. Miles from London, 151.

TOWN HALL.—Manager, Mr. Alfred Miles. Dramatic license. Holding capacity: Number of persons, about 600. Permanent stage, 21ft. by 11ft.; extension, 34ft. by 8ft. Lighted by gas, 3s. 6d. per thousand extra. Terms for hiring: One night, £2 2s.; two nights, £3 3s. Amount of deposit required on booking, £1. Early closing day, Friday; market day, Thursday.

WELLINGTON, Somerset.

Population, 7 500. Miles from London, 160. TOWN HALL.—Manager and Secretary, Mr. W. Temple. Dramatic, music and dancing licenses. Holds 700. Stage: Depth, 15ft; width, 27ft.; no proscenium. Gas light. The town must be billed and posted well, and an advertisement should be inserted in the "Wellington Weekly News." Terms for hiring: Plays and Dramatic entertainments, 52s. 6d. per night inclusive; concerts and other entertainments, from 30s. a night inclusive. Amount of deposit required on booking, 10s. per each day booked. Also SMALL TOWN HALL holds 130.

Wellington is a busy manufacturing and market town, the centre of a large agricultural district of about 15,000 inhabitants. Good companies do well.

Early closing day, Friday; market day, Thursday. Pay day, Wednesday.

WELLS, Somerset.

Population, 4.849. Miles from London, 121. TOWN HALL.—Proprietors, Wells Corporation; Manager, Mr. Jas. Knight. Dramatic and music and dancing licenses. Holds 350. Stage, 28ft. by 19ft. Gas. Terms for hiring: £2 9s. 6d., and gas charged by meter. Amount of deposit required on booking, 10s.

Fairs, first Tuesday in December and first Saturday in May.

No sites available for portables, alfresco concerts, and circuses.

Early closing day, Wednesday. Market day, Saturday.

WELSHPOOL, Mon.

Population, 6,112. Miles from London, 182. ASSEMBLY ROOMS.—Licensee and Manager, T. Ellidge. Dramatic license. Holding capacity: Number of persons, 450. Hiring: One night, 42s.; two nights, £3 10s.; three nights. £5 5s. Stage 20ft. square; stage extension removable, 7s. 6d. Size of hall, 72ft. by 36ft. by 22ft. high. Lighted by gas. Amount of deposit required on booking, 10s.

Early closing day, Thursday; market day, Monday.

WEM, Shropshire.

Population, 2,149. Miles from London, 173. TOWN HALL.—Proprietors, Wem Urban District Council. Dramatic license. Holds 500. Stage, with drop curtain; suitable for fit-up companies; depth, 18ft.; width, 37ft. Gas. Terms for hiring: One day, £1 11s. 6d. (if ratepayer, £1 1s.); second day, £1 1s.; payable in advance.

No local fairs.

Council have no sites available for portables, alfresco concerts, and circuses.

Early closing day, Friday. Market day, Thursday.

WEMBLEY, Middlesex (Parish of Harrow).

VARIETY HALL, WEMBLEY PARK.—Proprietors, the Wembley Park Estate Company; Secretary Mr. R. H. Selbie, 32, Westbourne Terrace, W. Dramatic and music and dancing

licenses. Holding capacity: Number of Persons, about 1,200. Small stage, with dressing accommodation: depth, 20ft.; width, 38ft.; proscenium, 21½ft. Lighted by oil. Terms for hiring: Vary according to day of week, time of year, and purposes for which the hall would be required. Amount of deposit required on booking, by arrangement. Situated in the middle of Wembley Park. Beautiful surroundings.

Fêtes in the Park, Easter, Whitsun, and August Bank Holidays, and on special occasions. Sites available for portables, alfresco concerts, and circuses in the park grounds, and on island in lake. Suitable sites for pastoral plays.

A full six-day license is atached to the park

WEST BROMWICH, Staffs.

Population, 65,627. Miles from London, 134.

THEATRE ROYAL.—Proprietor, Mr. Richard Nightingale; Musical Director, Mr. A. W Heath; Scenic Artist, Mr. J. Creswick. Double license. Holding capacity: Number of persons, 1 800. Amount, £65. Stage: Depth, 33ft.; width, 46ft.; fly floor, 21ft.; grid, 40ft; width between fly rails, 36ft.; proscenium opening 29ft. Nine dressing-rooms. Gas and electric light continuous, 230 volts. Amount of printing required: 900 sheets for walls 800 window lithos. Usual Matinée day, Saturday. Time of band rehearsal, 2.30. Best dates: Christmas, Easter, Whitsuntide, and August Bank Holiday.

NEW HIPPODROME. — Lessee, Mr. A. Withers; Resident Manager, Mr. Archie Ainslie.

TOWN HALL.—Manager, Mr Thomas Hudson, Borough Treasurer, West Bromwich. No dramatic license. Holding capacity: Number of persons, 1,400. No proper stage. Orchestra: 28ft. long and 25ft. wide. Gas and electric light. Terms for hiring: Hire of hall, with three ante-rooms, for dramatic performances, £6 6s. per day, for other performances, £3 3s. per day. Amount of deposit required on booking, 25 per cent.

Early closing day, Wednesday; market day, Saturday.

Medical Officer.—A.A.: D'. Lawson. Paradise Street. Tel. No. 32. A.U.: Dr. Lawson, 20, Paradise Street.

Agent.—M.H.A.R.A.: Bonas, Oddfellows' Arms. V.A.F.: The same. Agent.—A.U.: C. Hazlewood, Theatre Vaults.

WEST CALDER, Edinburgh.

Population, 4,000. Miles from London, 384. PEOPLE'S HALL.—Manager, Mr. John H. Thomson. Full dramatic license. Holding capacity: Number of persons, 1,400; amount, £60. Proper stage, with all accessories; width, 44ft.; depth, 22ft.; height, 22ft.; proscenium opening, 18ft. by 14ft. Lighted by gas (incandescent). Amount of printing required: 250 daybills, 150 sheets for walls, 50 lithos. Terms for hiring: Sharing terms, as per agreement. Population of district, 10,000. Situate on the main line between Edinburgh and Glasgow. Good two-night town.

Early closing day, Thursday.

WEST KIRBY, Cheshire.

Population, 5,419. Miles from London, 201. PUBLIC HALL. Manager, Mr. J. H. Wild. Dramatic and music and dancing licenses. Holding capacity: Number of persons, 1,200. Depth of stage, 18ft.; width, 40ft.; stage opening, 24ft. Gas and electric light. Terms for hiring, £3 3s. per night. Amount of deposit required on booking, half.

TOWN HALL.—Apply, Surveyor. Let for concerts, etc.

TYNWALD HALL.—Managers, Messrs. Banks and Cooke. Music and dancing license only. Holding capacity: Number of persons, 320. No stage. Electric light. Terms for hiring: 35s. per night, less 10 per cent. for two or more nights. Amount of deposit required on booking, 10 per cent. Kinematograph apparatus not allowed.

WEST MALLING, Kent.

THE PUBLIC HALL.—Secretary, Mr. Joseph J. Alexander. Double license. Holding capacity: Number of persons, 250. Stage, 24ft. 2in. wide; 11ft. 8in. deep. Lighted by gas. Amount of printing required, 100 bills for town and neighbourhood. Terms for hiring, 30s. per night, wholly payable at time of engagement. Piano and scenery can be had for 15s. per night extra.

WESTON-SUPER-MARE.

Population, 23,000. Miles from London, 138.

KNIGHTSTONE PAVILION AND OPERA HOUSE (established 1901).—Proprietors, Urban District Council; Manager, Mr. W. Payne. Dramatic license. Holding capacity: Number of persons, 2,000. Stage measurements: depth, 28ft.; width, 32ft.; proscenium opening, 24 ft. Electric light. Amount of printing required: 500 sheets. Terms of hiring: Terms sharing. Has stock scenery (13 sets). Electric current, 230 volts, direct. Heating by hot water radiators.

GRAND PIER PAVILION.—Manager, Mr. J. H. Stevenson. Dramatic license. Seats 2,000. Standing in balcony, 500. Electric light, 230 volts. Stage, 30ft. by 20ft.

VICTORIA HALL.—Proprietor, Mr. M. W. Shanly; Manager, Mr. W Flude. Dramatic license. Electric light, 230 volts, direct.

ASSEMBLY ROOMS.—Manager, Mr. J. Fortt. Dramatic license. Seats 500. Gas. Stage, 30ft. by 18ft.

TOWN HALL.—Proprietors, Urban District Council: Hallkeeper, Mr. E. Allen. Holds 500. Platform only. Gas. No dramatic license.

Weston-super-Mare is a popular and fashionable seaside resort. Population is more than doubled during the season in July and August by visitors, not reckoning countless day trippers.

For alfresco pitches on the sands and on Marine Parade troupe proprietors should apply to Mr. S. C. Smith, Town Clerk, U.D.C., Weston-super-Mare. Rent varies from £1 10s. to £4 per week.

Circus proprietors should apply to Mr. F. Blackmore, proprietor of Recreation Grounds, "Sherwood," St. Joseph's Road. Early closing, Thursday; carnivals in August and November.

RECOMMENDED APARTMENTS.

Mrs. Hayward, 7, Alma Street. 2 Sitting, 3 bedrooms, 1 combined room; piano.

WEST STANLEY, Durham.

THEATRE ROYAL.—Proprietors, The Stanley Theatre Company, Limited; Managing Director, Mr. Mark H. Lindon; Acting Manager, Mr. James Kelly; Musical Director, Mr. J. F. Macdonald. Full dramatic license. Holding capacity: Number of persons, 2,000. Stage measurements: Proscenium opening, 26ft. 6in.; proscenium to back wall, 34ft.; wall to wall, 34ft. Lighted by gas. Amount of

printing required, 700 sheets, 500 lithos. Usual Matinée day, Saturday. Time of band rehearsal, 2 p.m.

THE VICTORIA MUSIC HALL.—Proprietor, and Manager, Mr. T. C. Rawes; Musical Director, Mr. John Lennox. Stage Manager, Mr. Geo. Montrose. Fully licensed. Holding capacity: Number of persons, 900. Gas. Time of band rehearsal, 2 p.m. Stage opening, 22ft. 6in. by 20ft.; can take 18ft. wings. Twice nightly.

The site of an up-to-date variety theatre has been secured by Messrs. Purvis and Snell. It is in the centre of the town, and building operations will be started early in the New Year. The bookings are in the hands of Mr. H. E. Kauffman.

Medical Officers.—A.A.: Dr. E. G. D. Benson, Shield Row Hall; Dr. W. A. Benson, Stanley House. A.U.: The same.

Agent.—M.H.A.R.A.: W. Rowell, Royal Hotel, V.A.F.: The same.

WESTWARD HO! near Bideford, N. Devon.

RECEPTION (OR STATION) HALL.—Proprietors, the Bideford, Westward Ho! and Appledore Railway Company; Manager, Mr. Henry Sowden Music and dancing license. Holds 300. Stage: 20ft. by 8ft. Gas. Printing: 500 bills all sorts. Terms for hiring: 15s. per performance and gas used. Amount of deposit required on booking: 15s.

WETHERBY, Yorks.

Population, 2,212. Miles from London, 195

TOWN HALL.—Manager, Mr. J. D. Tiplady. Licensed for dramatic purposes for not more than twenty performances a year. Dimensions of hall: 50ft. by 30ft. 6in., and 20ft. high. Dimensions of permanent stage: About 24ft. by 8ft. 4in. by 1ft. 10in. high. Dimensions of the extension to stage: About 30ft. by 6ft. 2in. by 1ft. 10in. Lighted by gas. Terms for hiring, including gas and cleaning: 25s. one day, £2 two days, and afterwards 10s. for each additional day. An extra charge of 5s. will be made for use of the extension to stage. Amount of deposit required on booking: 10s.

WEXFORD, Ireland.

Population, 11 500. Miles from Dublin, 89.

THEATRE ROYAL.—Proprietor and Manager, Mr. E. P. Ronan. Seating accommodation, 1,000. Usual matinée day, Saturday.

MUNICIPAL HALL.—Proprietors, The Corporation. Seats 500.

Wexford is a large seaport town doing cross channel trade in coal, corn, etc. It is an industrial centre, chiefly ironworks, producing agricultural machinery and bicycles, hat factory, pipe factory, hosiery, etc., also a distillery. Nearest town to Rosslare Pier, the new route to Fishguard (2¾ hours' sea voyage), and shortest to London and Wales.

Market days, Wednesday and Saturday.

WEYBRIDGE, Surrey.

Population, 6,000. Miles from London, 19.

HOLSTEIN HALL.—Proprietor, Mr. J. Wiltshire; Manager, Mr. Edward Cocks, High Street, Weybridge. Full dramatic and music and dancing license. Holding capacity: Number of persons, about 800. Stage, 17ft. 9ins. deep; opening, 27ft. (can be reduced); no scenery. Gas and Electric light., Amount of printing required, about 300 sheets, D.C.,s, 6 sheets up to 24 sheets. Terms for hiring, £4 4s. per night. Amount of deposit required on booking, 25 per cent. Light operas and dramas most popular.

Early closing day, Wednesday; market days, Tuesday and Friday.

WEYMOUTH, Dorset.

Population, 19,843. Miles from London, 146.
ROYAL JUBILEE HALL AND OPERA HOUSE.--Managing Secretary, Mr. J. Roberts. Full dramatic license. Holding capacity: Number of persons, 1,500; amount, £70. Depth and width of proscenium, opening 25ft., depth 16ft.; stage measurements, 34ft. deep, 28ft. wide. Gas and electric light. Amount of printing required: 600 sheets pictorial for posting, 400 d.c. window lithos, 50 d.c. letterpress bills, 100 circulars, 50 date slips. Usual matinée day, Wednesday and Saturday.
Early closing day: Wednesday.
Medical Officers.—A.A.: Dr. W. B. Barclay, St. Winning, Alexandra Road; and Municipal Offices: Dr. T. A. Walker, 16, Belvidere.

WHITBY, Yorks.

Population, 11,755. Miles from London, 247.
WATERLOO THEATRE.—Lessee and Manager, Mr. Julian Bainbridge.
SPA THEATRE.—Lessee and Manager, Mr. W. Payne Seddon. Holds 1,000. Amount, £80. Stage, 25ft. deep; opening 24ft. Gas. Season, June—September.
TEMPERANCE HALL.—Manager, Mr. Geo. Gray. No dramatic license. Holding capacity: Number of persons, 1,000. Platform, 25ft. by 16ft. Gas and electric light. Terms for hiring: One day, £2 10s.; £10 per week; amount of deposit required on booking, £2.
Market, Saturday.

WHITCHURCH, Salop.

Population, 5,221. Miles from London, 171.
TOWN HALL.—Manager, Mr. A. Clayton. Dramatic license. Holding capacity: Number of persons, 600. Depth and width of stage, and proscenium measurements: 24ft. by 18ft.; height above stage, 20ft. Lighted by gas (charged as per meter). Amount of printing required: 300 d.c. Terms for hiring theatrical and operatic companies: For one day, £2 6s. 6d.: if engaged for more than one day, for every day after the first day, £1 6s. Dimensions of hall: 60ft. by 40ft.
Early closing day, Wednesday; market day, Friday.

WHITEHAVEN, Cumberland.

Population, 19,324. Miles from London, 304.
THEATRE ROYAL.—Proprietor, Mr. Joseph Clark; Manager, Mr. Fred L. Clark. At the time the Year Book went to press this theatre was closed for alterations. The license was refused in 1908 owing to the exits not complying with the regulations.
ODDFELLOWS' HALL.—Agent, C. J. Nesbitt, 50, Church Street. Music and dancing license. Holding capacity: Number of persons, seats about 750, but will easily hold 1,000. Platform: 21ft. by 8ft. or 10ft. 6in. Electric light, 210 volts. Terms: One night, 25s.; two, 47s.; three, 66s.; six, 124s. Amount of deposit required on booking: One-third.
MARKET HALL (Lessees until March, 1909, Edison Picture Co.). Agent, Mr. D. W. Pearson. Seats 700. Electric light. No dramatic license.

Early closing day, Friday; market day Thursday.
Medical Officer.—A.A.: Dr. J. H. Dickson 72, Lowther Street.

WHITSTABLE, Kent.

Population, 7,086. Miles from London, 58.
ASSEMBLY ROOMS THEATRE.—Manager Mr. Robt. B. Reeves. Double license. Holding capacity; Number of persons, 450; amount, £15 to £25, according to prices charged. Stage measurements: 30ft. wide; 17ft. deep; proscenium, 17ft. 6in. wide; 12ft. high. Lighted by gas. Terms for hiring: One night, £2 2s.; longer by arrangement. Amount of deposit required on booking: £1. Has scenery: One act drop and street scene, garden scene, landscape scene, interior scene.
Whitstable has a very fair share of visitors during its season, but these in fine weather seem mainly to patronise alfresco entertainments. There is ample scope for two alfresco parties, and one of these enjoys the patronage of the Local Improvement Committee. During the winter months the hall does well during short engagements. Wednesday is the closing day for the shopkeepers. and that evening and Saturday form the most likely for a full house. Variety entertainments are as a rule much better patronised than dramatic. A good circus or collection of side shows always secures success Several good sites are available.

WICK, Caithness-shire.

Population, 8,778. Miles from London, 755.
RIFLE DRILL HALL.—Manager, Mr. D. W. Milligan. Holding capacity: Number of persons, 800; amount, £35. Platform only. Lighted by gas. Terms for hiring: 30s. per night; gas extra. Amount of deposit required on booking: 10s. 6d. Best night, Wednesday.
TEMPERANCE HALL.—Manager, Mr. William Corner. No dramatic license. Stage measurements: 38ft. by 9ft. Gas light. Terms for hiring: On application.
Early closing day, Wednesday; market day Thursday.

WIDNES, Lancs.

Population, 30,000. Miles from London, 189.
ALEXANDRA THEATRE.—Proprietor, Mr. James Kiddie. Manager, Mr. Thos. Swinton. Musical Director, Mr. Bert Harding. Scenic Artist, Mr. James Greenhalgh. Full dramatic license. Holding capacity: Number of persons, 2,000. Amount, £75. Stage measurements, 40ft. deep by 60ft. wide, 24ft. opening. Lighted throughout with electricity. Amount of printing required: 600 d.c. for walls, and 600 d.c. for windows. Usual matinée day, Saturdays for pantomimes only. Time of band rehearsal, 1 o'clock Monday. Best season, August to Easter.
DRILL HALL.—Manager, Mr. E. O'Brien. Double license. Holding capacity: Number of persons, 1,000. Platform, 8 yards by 4 yards. lighted by gas. Terms for hiring: £12 12s. for week. Amount of deposit required on booking, one-third.
Early closing, Thursday; market. Saturday.

RECOMMENDED APARTMENTS.

Mrs. Tandy, Bank House. 78, Victoria Road.—2 sitting, 4 bedrooms; 2 pianos; bath.
Mrs. John Wickham, 29, Lacey Street.—1 sitting and 1 or 2 bedrooms; piano,

WIGAN, Lancs.

Population, 60,764. Miles from London, 194.

ROYAL COURT THEATRE.—Proprietors, The Wigan Entertainments Co.; Managers, Messrs. Worswick; Musical Director, Mr. J Ainscough. Full dramatic license. Holding capacity: Number of persons, 2,300. Amount, £100. Stage measurements: 27 ft. opening, 60 ft. wide, and 45 ft. deep. Gas and electric light. Amount of printing required: 2,000 for walls, 700 for windows. Time of band rehearsal, 1 p.m.

GRAND HIPPODROME.—Proprietors, The Wigan Entertainments Co.; Manager, Mr. Worswick; Musical Director, J. T. Baldwin Restricted dramatic and music license. Holding capacity: Number of persons, 2,500 Amount, £100. Stage measurements: Proscenium opening, 36 ft.; width of stage, 80 ft.; depth, 35 ft. Gas and electric light. Time of band rehearsal, 11 a.m. Usual matinée day, Monday, at 2.30. Bars surrounding halls within seven miles.

Early closing, Wednesday; market day, Friday.

Medical officers.—A.A.: Dr. C. M. Brady, Sandeville; Dr. E. H. Monks, Regent House. A. U.: Dr. Brady, M.H.A.R.A.: Dr. Monks.

Agent.—M.H.A.R.A. and V.A.F.: H. Speakman, Ship Hotel.

WILMSLOW, Cheshire.

Population, 7,361. Miles from London, 177.

PUBLIC HALL.—Manager, Mr. Sam D. Walton. No dramatic license. Holding capacity: Number of persons, 400. Lighted by gas. Terms on application.

Local Fairs: September 1, and Easter. Fair Grounds apply District Council.

Early closing, Wednesday; no market day.

WIMBORNE, Dorsetshire.

Population, 3,696. Miles from London, 113.

VICTORIA HALL.—Manager, Mr. Alfred Andrews. Double license. Holding capacity: Number of persons, 450 to 600. Platform: 36ft. by 14ft.; can be extended. Lighted by gas. Terms for hiring: £2 2s. per night; balcony, £2 10s. Amount of deposit required on booking: 10s.

Ticket seller: Mr. Tilsed, Printer, High Street. Bill Poster: Mr. Day, Grove Road.

Early closing day, Wednesday; market days, Tuesday and Friday.

WINCHESTER, Hants.

Population, 20,929. Miles from London, 66.

GUILDHALL.—Proprietors, The Mayor and Corporation of Winchester. Apply to Mr. F. A. Grant, Hall Keeper, Guildhall, Winchester. Dramatic and music and dancing license. Holding capacity: Number of persons, 800. Stage: 30ft. square. Electric light. Terms for hiring: Evening, £4 5s.; morning, or afternoon and evening same day, £5 5s.; two nights, £7; three nights, £9 5s.; four nights, £11 10s.; five nights, £13 15s.; six nights, £15; matinée when hall is let for more than one day (no lights), £1 1s.; ditto (with lights), £1 11s. 6d. Current direct, voltage 420 for kinematograph.

Railways, L. & S.W. Ry., and G.W. Ry. Newspapers: Hampshire Chronicle, Saturday, 2d.

Hampshire Observer, Saturday, 1d. Bill Posting Co., St. Peters Street, Winchester. Printers: Warren and Son, "Observer Office," High Street: Jacob and Johnson, "Chronicle Office," 57, High Street; J. Doswell, St. Peters Street. Ticket Sellers: A. B. Conduit (Music Warehouse), High Street; Teague and King (Music Saloon), High Street. Baggage Carmen: Chapin and Co.; L. & S.W. Ry.; White & Co.; G.W. Ry. Dates of Local Fairs: Last Saturday in February, October 22 and 23.

Early closing day, Thursday; market day, Saturday.

WINDERMERE, Westmoreland.

Population, 2,379. Miles from London, 258.

THE INSTITUTE.—Apply Manager. Dramatic license.

ALBERT HALL.—Apply Manager. Let for concerts, etc.

Market, Thursday.

WINDSOR, Berks.

Population, 14,130. Miles from London, 25.

THEATRE ROYAL.—Was burned down early in 1908.

ROYAL ALBERT INSTITUTE.—Manager, Mr. E H. Lewis (Secretary). Dramatic license. Holding capacity: Number of persons, 500. Small stage. Electric light. Terms for hiring: £2 10s. per evening. Amount of deposit required on booking: Full fee.

A field just outside the town is available for circuses.

Early closing day, Wednesday; market day, Saturday.

Agent.—M.H.A.R.A.: F. Groves, Adam and Eve Hotel. V.A.F.: The same.

WINSFORD, Cheshire.

Population, 10,382. Miles from London, 165.

TOWN HALL.—Manager, Mr. William Dunn. Dramatic license. Holding capacity: Number of persons, 550; amount, £15. Platform only. Width, 26ft.; depth, 16ft. Lighted by gas. Terms for hiring: 25s. per day, with a reduction for a week. Amount of deposit required on booking: 10s. per day.

Hall situated in centre of a long, straggling town, and within half a mile from Cheshire Lines and North-Western Railway stations.

VOLUNTEER DRILL HALL.—Proprietors, Winsford Volunteer Drill Hall Company, Ltd.; Hon. Secretary, Mr. J. H. Cooke, Solicitor, Winsford. Dramatic license. Holds 1,000. Plain stage, with curtains and front, with foot lights and battens; depth, 18ft.; width, 39ft.; opening, 21ft. wide. Gas. Printing, 60 posters. Terms for hiring varies, but averages £1 10s. per night. Amount of deposit required on booking, 50 per cent.

Early closing, Wednesday; market, Saturday.

WISBECH, Cambridgeshire.

Population, 9,831. Miles from London, 95.

SELWYN THEATRE.—Proprietor, Mr. C. Gates; Manageress, Mrs. C. Gates; Musical Director, Mr. G. Miller. Dramatic license. Holding capacity: Number of persons, 800; amount, £70. Stage measurements: 29ft. deep, 39ft. wide; proscenium opening, 20ft.; 16ft. to grid. Lighted by gas. Amount of printing required: 250 walls, 250 lithos, 200 circulars. Usual matinée days, Wednesday and Saturday. Time of band rehearsal, about 4 p.m. Best season, September to April.

CORN EXCHANGE. — Manager, Mr. C. Gates. No dramatic license. Holding capacity: Number of persons, 1,000. No proper stage. Length of hall, 108ft. by 49ft. 3in. Lighted by gas. Terms for hiring: £1 5s. per day, exclusive of gas, etc. Amount of deposit required on booking, 10s.

PUBLIC HALL. — Manager, Mr. G. Fisher. Fully licensed. Holding capacity: Number of persons, 900. Stage measurements: 25ft. deep by 26ft. wide. Lighted by gas. Terms for hiring: £1 5s. per night. Amount of deposit required on booking, £1 1s. Hall has a Lecture Room which holds 200.

THE INSTITUTE HALL.—The hall of the Working Men's Institute is also frequently used for entertainments, and is of convenient size, holding about 400.

Population mainly industrial. There are extensive timber yards, sawing, planing, and creosoting mills, steam mills for flour-grinding, etc. A corn-dressing machine factory, printing works, breweries, roperies, etc., are among the existing industries. Portables do not visit the town. Circus pitches are obtainable in a private field very near to the town and just off one of the main entrances. Local fairs.—Pleasure fairs only: One day in September (third Wednesday), known as the "Statute," and one week in March, known as the "Mart."

Early closing, Wednesday; market, Saturday.

WISHAW, Lanarkshire.

TOWN HALL.—Manager, Mr. John Ferguson. Fully licensed. Stage, 44ft. by 26ft., fitted with scenery and side-wings. Two dressing-rooms. Lighted by gas; electric light can be had. Terms for hiring: One night, £2 10s.; for Saturday, £3; for the week, £8. Charges include gas. Piano can be hired. A deposit of £1 must be paid on booking.

WITNEY, Oxon.

Population, 3,574. Miles from London, 75½. Station, G.W.R. Branch from Oxford, 12 miles.

CORN EXCHANGE.—Proprietors, The Corn Exchange Co., Ltd.; Secretary, Mr. W. J. G. Ravenor, Solicitor, 22, High Street, to whom all applications must be made. Holding capacity, 600 persons. Size of ordinary stage, 35ft. wide, 9ft. deep. Lighted by gas. No scenery. Temporary dramatic license easily obtainable. Plenty of seats. Terms for hiring: 55s. for first night and 30s. for each succeeding night. Dressing rooms extra. Deposit required on booking: Two-thirds of rental. Hall-keeper, G. E. Walkey, 19, Market Square.

Bill posters, The Oxford Bill Posting Co., Ltd., Oxford.

Local fairs, September 13 and 14th, October 7th and 14th. The first October fair is the Mop. For ground, apply early to Mr. G. Eaton, Surveyor to the District Council.

Early closing day, Tuesday, 3 p.m.; Witney market day, Thursday.

WOKINGHAM, Berks.

Population, 3,551. Miles from London, 36.

TOWN HALL.—Proprietors, the Corporation of Wokingham, Mr. E. J. King, town hall-keeper. Dramatic and music and dancing licenses. Stage: 7ft. deep, 14ft. wide. Gas. Terms for hiring hall: £1 1s.; annex, 2s. 6d.; platform, 2s. 6d.; Council Chamber, 2s. 6d. Dates of local fairs: November 2 and 3.

Early closing day, Wednesday; market day, Tuesday.

WOKING, Surrey.

Population, 16,244. Miles from London, 24.

PUBLIC HALL.—Manager, Mr. Joseph Lewis. Double license. Holding capacity: Number of persons, 600. Amount: According to prices charged. Stage measurements: Height to battens, 14ft; depth, 19ft.; width, 26ft. Gas and electric light. Amount of printing required: About 300 to 400 d.c. Terms for hiring: £3 3s. per night. Amount deposit required on booking, £1. Booking office, Public Hall. Private advertising stations and boards can be had by arrangement with the Manager.

Early closing, Wednesday. No market day.

WOLVERHAMPTON, Staffs.

Population, 94,187. Miles from London, 123.

GRAND THEATRE. — Resident Manager, Mr. W. J. Andrews; Musical Director, Mr. C. F. Trevor. Full license. Holding capacity: number of persons, 2,550; amount, £120 at cheap prices—viz., 4d, 6d., 9d., 1s., 2s., 3s.; £200 if prices 6d., 1s., 2s., 3s. Stage measurements: 40ft. deep by 70ft. wide; proscenium, 36ft. opening. Gas and electric light. Amount of printing required: 1,500 sheets for walls, 800 lithos for windows. Usual matinée day, Saturday, at 2.15. Time of band rehearsal, 1 p m.

NEW THEATRE ROYAL. — Proprietors, Wolverhampton Empire Palace Co., Limited; Manager, Mr. Charles Barnard; Acting Manager, Mr. Gerald Spencer; Musical Director, Mr. W. Bradshaw. Double license. Holding capacity: Number of persons, about 2,500; amount, £100 (about). Stage measurements: Depth, 30ft. by 50ft. wide; proscenium opening, 28ft. Electric light and gas. Amount of printing required: 1,600 sheets pictorial for posting, 400 d.c. lithos for windows. Usual matinée day, Saturday. Time of band rehearsal, 2 p.m.

EMPIRE.—Proprietors, Wolverhampton Empire Palace Co., Limited; Managing Director, Mr. Walter De Frece; Resident Manager, Mr. Frank Weston; Booking circuit, De Frece circuit; Musical Director, Mr. Thomas Gray. Music and dancing license. Holding capacity: Number of persons, 2,700. Depth of stage, 30ft.; width of stage, 50ft.; proscenium opening, 30ft. Electric light. Time of band rehearsal, 1 p.m. No matinée day. Bars no surrounding halls. Two houses a night.

AGRICULTURAL HALL.—Secretary, Mr. William E. Barnett. Seating accommodation for 1,500 persons. Suitable for concerts and other entertainments. Music and dancing license. Platform, 36ft. by 18ft. Gas and electric, 220 volts, continuous.

DRILL HALL.—Secretary, Mr. F. Walton, 26, Lichfield-street. Seating accommodation for 3,000 persons. Let for concerts, etc. Population chiefly industrial.

Annual fair held three days in Whit week, on Market ground, hired from the Corporation, and travelling shows allowed.

Annual floral fête held second week in July for three days, in the West Park, belonging to the Corporation.

No sites for al fresco concerts; circuses have not visited the town for a long time.

Early closing, Thursday; market, Wednesday.

Medical Officers. — A.Y.: Dr. Lloyd Davies Oaklands Road. M.H.A.R.A.: Dr. E. C. Muspratt, 4, Salop-street.

Agent.—M.H.A.R.A.: J. Kelly, Queen's Hotel. A.U.: The same. V.A.F.: The same.

WOODSTOCK, Oxford.

Population, 1,684. Miles from London, 69.
TOWN HALL.—Proprietors, Corporation of
Woodstock; Manager, Mr. T. W. Miles. Dr.-
matic license. Holds 250. Gas. Movable stage.
Terms for hiring: 1 night, 15s.; 2 nights, 30s.
Deposit on booking, 10s.
Bill posters, The Oxford Bill Posting Co., Ltd.,
Oxford.
Date of local fair: First Tuesday in October.
Early closing day, Thursday; market day,
first Tuesday in month.

WOOLWICH, Kent.

Population, about 100,000. Miles from
London, 10.
ROYAL ARTILLERY THEATRE.—Licensed
under the Army Act. Lessees and Managers,
Messrs. Arthur Carlton and Sam Duckworth.
Acting-Manager, Mr. Chisholm Taylor. Musical
Director, Q.M.-Sergt. G. Dawes. Holding
capacity: 900. Prices 6d., 1s., 1s. 6d., 2s., 2s. 6d.,
3s. Boxes 21s. Depth and width of stage,
40ft. by 70ft. Opening 30ft. Number of dressing-
rooms, 10. Printing required: 900 lithos, 450
wall sheets, 3,000 circulars. Matinée Thursday.
Band rehearsal, 3 p.m. Current of electricity,
210 volts.
BARNARD'S THEATRE ROYAL.—Proprietor, Mr. Samuel Barnard.
HIPPODROME (late Grand Theatre).—Proprietors, The London Theatres of Varieties, Ltd.
Manager, Mr. H. H. Lardman; Acting-
Manager, Mr. E. P. Delevanti. Musical Director,
Mr. Douglas Ross. Booking circuit. Gibbons
and Barrasford. Holding capacity: 2,200. Seats,
2d., 4d., 6d., 9d., 1s. Depth and width of stage,
42ft. by 72ft. 6in.; opening 33ft. Number of
dressing rooms, 13. Matinée day, Thursday.
Current of electricity, 210 continuous. Kinematograph box established. Two houses a night,
variety. Rehearsal, 1.0 p.m.
ROYAL ASSEMBLY ROOMS.—Temporary
dramatic license can be obtained. Apply
Manager.
TOWN HALL. — Proprietors, Woolwich
Borough Council. Music and dancing license.
Holding capacity: number of persons, 800.
Platform capable of accommodating about 100
persons. Electric light, direct current, 210 volts,
and secondary system of gas. Terms for hiring:
on application to Town Clerk, Woolwich. Total
fee to be paid on booking.
Early closing, Thursday.
Agent · M.H.A.R.A., A. M. Harper, Director
General Hotel.

RECOMMENDED APARTMENTS.

Mrs. J. Gibson, 10, Brookhill Road.—1 sitting,
2 bedrooms; piano, etc.
Mrs. Prior, 19, Wellington Street, Woolwich,
S.E.—Sitting-room, bedroom, combined room;
piano.

WORCESTER, Worcester.

Population, 46,624. Miles from London, 120.
ROYAL AND PALACE OF VARIETIES.—
Proprietor, Mr. Arthur Carlton; Manager, Mr.
Fred Le Wards; Musical Director, Mr. J. W.
Austin; Scenic Artist, Mr. Harry Griffith. Full
double license. Holding capacity: Number of
persons, 1,600; amount, £100. Stage measurements: Depth, 47ft.; width, 60ft; proscenium
opening, 27ft Gas and electric light.
Amount of printing required: 800 sheets walls,
500 lithos. Usual matinée days, Wednesdays
and Saturdays. Time of band rehearsal,
1 p.m.
PUBLIC HALL.—Manager, Mr. William
Jones. Full dramatic license. Holding capacity: Number of persons, 900. Stage, 23ft.

by 13ft., but extension added if required, 12ft.
by 32ft. Electric light. Amount of printing
required: 800 sheets. Terms for hiring: £12
10s. per week; matinée, 10s. extra each.
Amount of deposit required on booking, £5.
The population is industrial, the principal
trades being porcelain, gloves, leather, boots
and shoes, sauce, and machinery. There is a
considerable rural population, which is drawn
into the city from the surrounding country,
when events of special interest occur
Worcester's Hop Fair is held on September
19. It is chiefly a business gathering, and
there are only a few gingerbread stalls and one
or two show booths on the amusement side.
The real pleasure fair is in the summer, when
there are a number of shows, roundabouts,
etc., on Pitchcroft, the racecourse. The fair
is always held at the time of the summer
races, so there is no definite date. There is
no difficulty in obtaining licenses for portables,
and there is ample room on Pitchcroft for any
number of circuses.
Early closing, Thursday. Market, Saturday.
Medical Officer.—A.A.: Dr. M. Read, Foregate
Street.
Agent.—M.H.A.R.A.: Thomas Lawson, Ewe
and Lamb Hotel. A.U.: The same. V.A.F.:
The same.

WORKINGTON, Cumberland.

Population, 26,139. Miles from London, 306.
QUEEN'S OPERA HOUSE. — Lessee and
Manager, Mr. Stanley Rogers; Acting Manager,
Mr. Falconer Jackes. Seating capacity, 2,500.
Dramatic license. Gas light. Proscenium, 27ft.;
height to grid, 32ft.; width, 45ft.; depth,
21ft. 6in.
THEATRE ROYAL (Washington Street).—
Proprietor, Executors of the late Mr. Smith;
Lessee and Manager, Mr. MacKenzie Morgan.
Restricted music and dancing license. Holding
capacity: Number of persons, 800; amount,
about £25. Gas light. Usual matinée day,
Saturdays.
PUBLIC HALL.—Proprietors, Exors. of the
late Mr. J. Whitfield; Manager, Mr. Edmund
Burrow. No dramatic license. Holding
capacity: Number of persons, 600 to 800.
Stage: 35ft. by 22ft. Lighted by gas. Terms
for hiring: One night, £1 13s. 6d.; two nights,
£2 16s. Amount of deposit required on book-
ing, 50 per cent.
CARNEGIE LECTURE HALL.—Proprietors,
The Workington Corporation. Lessee and
Manager, Mr. J. W. C. Purves. Stage, 20ft. by
8ft. Seating capacity, 480. Dramatic license.
Gas light.
Agent.—M.H.A.R.A.: Mr. Goddard, Griffin
Hotel.

WORKSOP, Notts.

Population, 16,112. Miles from London, 146.
GAIETY THEATRE.—Proprietor and Manager, Mr. S. Goodman; Musical Director, Mr.
Chas. Long. Double license. Holds 850.
Dimensions of stage: Height to grid, 38ft.; width,
30ft.; depth, 29ft.; proscenium opening; height,
17ft. 6in.; width, 20ft. A scene dock runs on a
parallel with the stage: Depth, 29ft.; width, 9ft.;
height, 19ft. Electric light, 220 volts, direct
current. Two limes. Five dressing rooms.
Printing 300 sheets, 150 lithos, 500 circulars, 500
throwaways. Theatre is open only Thursday,
Friday, and Saturday of each week.
Early closing day, Thursday; market day,
Wednesday.

WORTHING, Sussex.

Population, 26,000. Miles from London, 61.

THEATRE ROYAL.—Proprietor and Manager, Carl Adolf Seebold; Musical Director, Mr. Karl Seebold; Stage Manager, Mr. M. Spurgin. Full double license. Holding capacity: Number of persons, 800 to 900; amount, £60. Proscenium opening, 28ft.; height to grid, 31ft.; width between fly rails, 32ft.; stage depth to footlights, 36ft.; from side to side, 52ft.; cloth, 30ft. by 24ft.; wings, 18ft. Electric light, 230 volts, direct. Printing 9 eighteen-sheets, 6 twelve-sheets, 20 six-sheets, 250 d.c. or lithos, 1,000 circulars, postcards, handbills, etc. Time of band rehearsals, 3 p.m., Mondays and Thursdays.

PIER PAVILION.—Managing Director, Mr. Walter Paine; Piermaster and Assistant Manager, Mr. C. Irvine Bacon. Seating capacity, 500. Dramatic license. Proscenium opening, 18ft. wide by 16ft. high; floor to grid, 12ft.; between flyrails, 22ft.; depth from footlights, 25ft.; from side to side, 20ft.; cloths, 16ft. wide by 12ft. high. Incandescent gas lighting.

Early closing day, Wednesday; market day, Saturday.

Medical Officers.—A.A.: Dr. H. F. Hyde, Shelley House, Gatwicke Road; 9-10-30, 2-2-30, and 6-7-45. Telephone, 191. A.U.: Dr. Hyde.

RECOMMENDED APARTMENTS.

Ivy Cottage, Gordon Road.—1 sitting-room, 2 bedrooms, 1 combined room; piano.

WREXHAM, Denbigh.

Population, 14,966. Miles from London, 201.

EMPIRE MUSIC HALL.—Proprietor, Mr. J. J. Scott; Manager, Mr. C. W. Collings.

PUBLIC HALL.—Recently destroyed by fire. Is being rebuilt.

DRILL HALL. — Proprietors, Denbighshire County Association. Manager, Mr. John Evans, Crispin Lane. Dramatic and music and dancing licenses. Holding capacity: Number of persons, 2,000. Stage: 25ft. by 52ft.; proscenium, 24ft. Gas; electric by arrangement with Borough Engineer. Terms: First night, £3 3s., every other £2 2s. (rental only). Amount of deposit required on booking, 25 per cent.

Local Fair (pleasure).—April, lasts fortnight.

No portables visit the town, but there should not be any difficulty in obtaining license.

Population, largely industrial, 80,000, within three miles.

Early closing day, Friday; market days, Thursday and Saturday.

Agent.—M.H.A.R.A.: J. J. Scott, Empire Palace. V.A.F.: G. B. Latimar, Green Man Hotel, Hope Street.

YEADON, Yorks.

Population, 7,059. Miles from London, 197.

THEATRE ROYAL.—Manager, Mr. Charles Bateson. Holds 900. Stage, 21ft. deep by 24ft. wide. Gas. Printing 200 sheets, 150 lithos. Sharing terms.

TOWN HALL (accommodation, 1,200) and TEMPERANCE HALL (accommodation, 700 to 800), also licensed for stage plays.

Industry: Woollen cloth manufacture and dyeing.

Date of Annual Fair or Feast: first Sunday and three following days after August 16.

Portables rarely visit the town. Pitches are obtainable for circuses, etc.; the principal being a large open space known as Albert Square (formerly Penny Fool Hill).

YEOVIL, Somerset.

Population, 17,537. Miles from London, 124

PRINCES STREET ASSEMBLY ROOMS.—Manager, Mr. Frank J. Sutton. Fully licensed. Holding capacity: Number of persons, 800. Stage: 32ft. by 32ft.; proscenium and drop scene, stage door for scenery; proscenium opening, 24ft. wide by 16ft. high. Lighted by gas. Cost of posting the town, £1 2s. 6d. Terms for hiring: One night, 2½ guineas; two nights, 2 guineas; three nights, 1½ guineas. Dressing-rooms complete. Gas and firing inclusive. Reduction for longer period. Amount of deposit required on booking, one guinea.

Portables occasionally visit the town.

Population chiefly industrial, engaged in the glove factories.

Concerts are held at Sidney Gardens by permission of the Town Council.

Circus pitches are always obtainable.

Fairs, June and November, two days nearest dates to 16th and 17th in each month. A circus visits the town about once a year; portables once in five years.

Early closing, Thursday; market day, Friday.

Medical Officer.—A.A.: Dr. C. J. Marsh, Penn Hill. A.U.: The same.

YNISHIR, Glam.

Population, 5,730. (Of surrounding district 19,000).

WORKMEN'S HALL.—Licensed for dramatic performances. Apply: The Secretary.

Early closing, Thursday; market day, Saturday.

YORK, Yorks.

Population, 78,000. Miles from London, 191.

THEATRE ROYAL.—Proprietor, Messrs. Waddington and Sons; General Manager, Mr. H. J. Dacre; Musical Director, Mr. G. Brown; Scenic Artist, Mr. R. Barron. Dramatic license. Holding capacity: Number of persons, seating 2,500; amount £160. Stage measurements: Depth, 28ft. by 30ft. Gas and electric light, 230 volts continuous. Printing: 600 sheets for the walls, 700 lithos for windows, and 500 circulars to post. Usual matinée day, Saturday, commencing at 2.15. Time of band rehearsal, 1 p.m.

GRAND OPERA HOUSE AND EMPIRE.—Proprietors, The Grand Opera House (York), Limited; Managing Director, Mr. William Peacock; Acting Manager, Mr. Sidney Brooke; Musical Director, Mr. Fred. Kell. Restricted license. Holding capacity: Number of persons, 1,800; amount, £130, at popular prices. Stage measurements: 38ft. deep, 62ft. wide; proscenium opening, 30ft.; between fly rails, 42ft.; to underside fly, floor, 21ft. Electric light, 230 volts direct. Printing required: 800 sheets for walls, and 400 d.c. Time of band rehearsal, 1 p.m. Now run principally as a variety house twice nightly.

VICTORIA HALL.—Manager, Mr. John Ezard. Dramatic license. Holding capacity: Number of persons, 800. Large platform. Lighted by gas. Terms for hiring: £7 10s. per week, six days; one night, £1 15s., gas included. Amount of deposit required on booking: For one week, £3 10s.

EXHIBITION BUILDINGS (Large and

Small Halls).—Mr. Geo. Kirby, Curator. Music license; dramatic license may be secured. Holding capacity: Number of persons, 3,000 Large Hall, taking £100 to £300 or more. SMALL CENTRAL HALL.— Seating 500. Platform only, 25ft. wide, 50ft. deep, with orchestra seating behind for 200 performers. Gas and electric light. Amount of printing required: 25 18-sheet, 100 three-sheet posters, 500 window bills. Terms for hiring: Large Hall, £30 per week, inclusive lighting; Small Hall, £10 per week. Amount of deposit required on booking: One-f urth amount of rent. Electric current voltage, 240.

Local fairs: Whit week and Martinmas week.

Alfresco concerts are held in the Museum Gardens. Hon. Sec., Mr. C. E. Elmhirst.

Early closing day, Wednesday; market day, Saturday.

Medical Officers.—A.A.: Dr. C. W. Botwood, 74, Micklegate, Tel. No. 0436; Dr. J. H. Gostling, 26, Stonegate; Dr. N. L. Hood, Castlegate House. A.U.: The same. M.H.A.R.A.: Dr. Hood.

Agent.—M.H.A.R.A. and V.A.F.: A. Gretton' Castle Ho'el.

RECOMMENDED APARTMENTS.

Mrs. Lawton, 20, Castlegate.—2 sitting, 3 bedrooms; bath, piano.

The Apartments recommended in THE STAGE PROVINCIAL GUIDE have been vouched for by two or more artists recently occupying them.

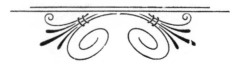

GERMAN THEATRES.

LIST OF THEATRES IN THE PRINCIPAL TOWNS AND WATERING-PLACES OF
THE GERMAN-SPEAKING COUNTRIES.

BERLIN.

DIE KOENIGL. SCHAUSPIELE (Opernhaus, Schauspielhaus, Neues Kgl. Operntheater), General-Intendant, His Excellency Georg von Hülsen. Office: N.W. 7, Dorotheen-Strasse 2.

APOLLO-THEATER, S.W. 48, Friedrich-Strasse 218, Rudolf Schier.

BERLINER THEATER, S.W. 68, Charlotten-Strasse 90-92. Messrs. Meinhard and Bernauer.

BERLINER OPERETTEN-THEATER, S.W., Belle Alliance-Strasse. Edmund Binder and Ch. Hermann.

BERLINER PRATER-THEATER (Bürgerliches Schauspielhaus), N., Kastanien-Allee 7-9. Arthur Rannow.

BERNHARD ROSE - THEATER, O., Grosse Frankfurter-Strasse 132. Bernhard Rose.

BRUNNEN THEATER, N., 20, Bad-Strasse 58. W. Voigt.

CASINO - THEATER, N. 54, Lothringer-Strasse 37. Hans Berg.

CONCORDIA-THEATER, Brunnen-Strasse 154. E. Dase.

DEUTSCHES THEATER, N.W.—Schumann-Str. 13a. Max Reinhardt.

KAMMERSPIELE DES DEUTSCHEN THEATERS, N.W., Schumann-Strasse 14. Max Reinhardt.

FRIEDRICH - WILHELMSTAEDTISCHES SCHAUSPIELHAUS, Chaussee-Strasse 30-31. Oskar Wagner.

GEBRUEDER HERRNFELD - THEATER, S. 14, Kommandanten-Strasse 57. Anton Herrnfeld.

HEBBEL THEATER, S.W., Königgrätzer Strasse 57-58. Dr. Eugen Robert.

KLEINES THEATER, N.W. 7, Unter den Linden 44. Victor Barnowsky.

KOMISCHE OPER, N.W., Friedrich-Strasse 104-104a. Hans Gregor.

LESSING-THEATER, N.W. 40, Friedrich Karl-Ufer 1. Dr. Otto Brahm.

LUISEN-THEATER, S.O. 26, Reichenberger-Strasse 34. Max Ed. Fischer.

LUSTSPIELHAUS, S.W. 48, Friedrich-Strasse 236. Dr. Martin Zickel.

METROPOL-THEATER, W., Behren-Strasse 55-57. Richard Schultz.

NEUES OPERETTEN-THEATER, N.W., 6, Schiffbauerdamm 25. Viktor Palfi.

NEUES SCHAUSPIELHAUS, W. 30, Nollendorf-Platz 7-8. Alfred Halm.

NEUES THEATER, N.W. 6, Schiffbauerdamm 4a. Dr. Alfred Schmieden.

RESIDENZ-THEATER, O. 27, Blumen-Str. 9. Richard Alexander.

SANSSOUCI-THEATER, S., Kottbuser-Str. 6. Wilh. Reimer.

SCHILLER-THEATER, O., (Wallner-Theater), O., Wallner-Theater-Strasse, 35.

SCHILLER-THEATER CHARLOTTENBURG, Grolmann-Strasse 70-72. Dr. Raphael Löwenfeld (for both theatres).

THALIA-THEATER, S. 14, Dresdener-Strasse 72-73. Jean Kren.

THEATER AN DER SPREE, S.O. 16, Köpenicker-Strasse 67-68. Philipp Spandow.

THEATER DES WESTENS, Charlottenburg, Kant-Strasse 8. Max Monti.

TRIANON THEATER, N.W. 7, Georgen-Str. Karl Beese.

AACHEN.

STADTTHEATER, Heinrich Adolphi.

BERNARTS THEATER, Joh. Wilh. Bernarts.

ALTENBURG (S.-A.).

HERZOGLICHES HOFTHEATER, Intendant: Franz, Baron von Kageneck.

ALTONA.

STADTTHEATER, Max Bachur.

SCHILLER-THEATER, Carl Meyerer.

AUGSBURG.

STADTTHEATER, Karl Häusler.

AUSSIG A. ELBE.

ELYSIUM-THEATER, Julius Watzke.

BADEN-BADEN.

GROSSHERZOGL. KURTHEAT , Heinzel.

BAMBERG.

STADTTHEATER, Hans Amalfi.

BARMEN.

STADTTHEATER, Otto Ockert.

BASEL.

INTERIMSTHEATER, Hans Edmund.

BOEMLYS THEATER, Alfred Bömly.

BAUTZEN.

STADTTHEATER, L. Piorkowsky.

BAYREUTH.

BUEHNENFESTSPIELHAUS.

KGL. OPERNHAUS, Steng and Krauss.

VOLKSTHEATER, Heinrich Welzel.

BERN.

STADTTHEATER, Hofrat Benno Koepke.

INTIMES THEATER, Carl Fischer.

BEUTHEN (O.-SCHL.).

NEUES STADTTHEATER, Hans Knapp.

BIELEFELD.

STADTTHEATER, Norbert Berstl.

BRINCKHOFFS TONHALLE, Max Sandhage.

BOCHUM.

STADTTHEATER, Philipp Malburg.

BONN.

STADTTHEATER, Otto Beck.

BRANDENBURG A. H.

SOMMERTHEATER, Rudolf Frenzel-Nicolas.

BRAUNSCHWEIG.

HERZOGLICHES HOFTHEATER, Baron Julius v. Wangenheim, Hoftheater-Intendant.
HOLST-THEATER, Fritz Berend.
OPERETTEN-THEATER, Martin Klein.

BREMEN.

STADTTHEATER, Hubert Reusch.
TIVOLI-THEATER, Director Alvarez.

BREMERHAVEN.

STADTTHEATER, Otto Wilhelm Winzer.

BRESLAU.

STADTTHEATER, Dr. Theodor Löwe (in conjunction with the Lobe and Thalia Theatres).
BRESLAUER SCHAUSPIELHAUS, Georg Nieter.

BROMBERG.

KAISERL. SUBVENTIONS-THEATER, Arthur v. Gerlach.
PATZERS SOMMERTHEATER, Albert Knabe.
ELYSIUM-THEATER, Eduard Schulz.

BRUENN.

STADTTHEATER, Carl von Maixdorff

CASSEL.

KOENIGLICHE SCHAUSPIELE, Graf v. Bylandt, Intendant.

CHEMNITZ.

STADTTHEATER, Richard Jesse.

COBLENZ.

STADTTHEATER, August Dörner.

COBURG-GOTHA.

HERZOGLICHES HOFTHEATER, Intendant, Baron von Meyern-Hohenberg.

COELN A. RH.

VEREINIGTE STADTTHEATER, Max Martersteig.
METROPOL-THEATER, Max Bruck.
RESIDENZ-THEATER, Dr. Hermann Rauch (Wiesbaden).

COLMAR I. ELSASS.

STADTTHEATER, Jacques Goldberg.

CREFELD.

STADTTHEATER, R. Pester-Prosky (in conjunction with MUNCHEN-GLADBACH).

CZERNOWITZ.

STADTTHEATER, Martin Klein.

DANZIG.

STADTTHEATER, Curt Grützner.

DARMSTADT.

GROSSHERZOGL. HOFTHEATER, Emil Werner, General-Director.
SAALBAU-THEATER, and
WOOGPLATZ-THEATER, Willy Roemheld.

DESSAU.

HERZOGLICHES HOFTHEATER, Carl Römly.

DETMOLD.

FUERSTLICHES HOFTHEATER, A. Berthold, Intendanzrat.

DORTMUND.

STADTTHEATER, Alois Hofmann.

DRESDEN.

KOENIGLICHE HOFTHEATER (Kgl. Opernhaus and Kgl. Schauspielhaus), His Excellency Nikolaus Graf von Seebach.
CENTRAL-THEATER, Alex. Rotter.
RESIDENZ-THEATER, Carl Witt.

DUESSELDORF.

STADTTHEATER, Ludwig Zimmermann (in conjunction with the Stadttheater in DUISBURG).
SCHAUSPIELHAUS, Frau Louise Dumont-Lindemann and Gustav Lindemann.
LUSTSPIELHAUS, Gustav Charlé.

EISENACH.

STADTTHEATER, Hermann Rudolph.

ELBERFELD.

STADTTHEATER, Julius Otto.

BAD ELSTER.

ALBERT-THEATER, Oscar Will.

BAD EMS.

KURTHEATER, Oscar Hennenberg.

ERFURT.

STADTTHEATER, Prof. Karl Skraup.

ESSEN (RUHR).

STADTTHEATER, Georg Hartmann.

FLENSBURG.

KAISERL. SUBVENTIONIERTES STADTTHEATER, Harry Oscar.

FRANKFURT A. M.

SCHAUSPIELHAUS, Emil Claar, Intendant.
OPERNHAUS, Paul Jensen, Intendant.
RESIDENZ-THEATER, Max Gabriel.
RHEINGAUER HOF, Rudolf Scheller.

FRANKFURT A.O.

STADTTHEATER, Fritz Pook.

FREIBURG IM BREISGAU.

STADTTHEATER, Hans Bollmann.

GERA.

FUERSTL. HOFTHEATER, Dr. Baron von der Heyden-Rynsch, Hofmarschall.

GOERLITZ.

STADTTHEATER, F. Peterssohn.
WILHELM-THEATER, Gustav Pietsch and Henry Hochbein.

GOETTINGEN.

STADTTHEATER, Willy Martini.

GOTHA.

HERZOGLICHES HOFTHEATER (see S. COBURG-GOTHA).

GRAZ.

STADTTHEATER (Opernhaus) and THEATER AM FRANZENSPLATZ, H. Hagin.

HALBERSTADT.

STADTTHEATER, Johann Meissner.

HALLE A. SAALE.

STADTTHEATER, Hofrat Max Richards.
NEUES THEATER, E. M. Mauthner.

HAMBURG.

STADTTHEATER, Hofrat Max Bachur (in conjunction with the Stadttheater in ALTONA).
DEUTSCHES SCHAUSPIELHAUS, Baron Dr. Alfred v. Berger.
ERNST DRUCKER - THEATER, Lothar Mayring.
THALIA-THEATER, Hofrat Max Bachur.
NEUES OPPERETTEN-THEATER, Wilhelm Bendiner.
CARL SCHULZE - THEATER, H. Haller Berlin W., 15. Kaiserallee 203.
VOLKS-SCHAUSPIELHAUS, James Bauer and Fer. Haltai.

HANNOVER.

KOENIGLICHES THEATER, Geheimer Intendanzrat L. Barnay.
RESIDENZ-THEATER, Julius Rudolph.
METROPOL-THEATER, E. Graf.
UNION-THEATER, Frau Emma Lüders.
DEUTSCHES THEATER, Leo W. Stein.

HEIDELBERG.

STADTTHEATER, M. E. Heinrich.

HEILBRONN A. N.

STADTTHEATER, Richard Steng and Konrad Krauss (in conjunction with the Königl. Opernhaus in BAYREUTH).

HELGOLAND.

LANDSCHAFTL. SUBVENTIONS-THEATER Frau Käte Basté.

HERMANNSTADT (SIEBENBUERGEN).

STADTTHEATER, Leo Bauer.

HOMBURG V. D. H.

KURTHEATER, Kurdirektor, Baron von Maltzan.

JENA.

STADTTHEATER, Wilhelm Berstl.

INNSBRUCK (TIROL).

STADTTHEATER, Ferdinand Arlt.
LOEWENHAUS - THEATER, Ferdinand Exl (Exl's Tiroler Bühne).

KARLSBAD (BOEHMEN).

STADTTHEATER, W. Borchert.

KARLSRUHE.

GROSSHERZOGL. HOFTHEATER, Geheimer Hofrat Dr. August Bas ermann, Intendant (in con¹⁴ ction with the Grossherzogl. Theater in BADEN-BADEN).
STADTGARTEN THEATER, Heinrich Hagin.

KIEL.

VEREINIGTE THEATER, Franz Gottscheid and Anton Otto (composed of Stadttheater, Neues Theater, and Kleines Theater).

BAD KISSINGEN.

KOENIGLICHES THEATER, Otto Reimann.

KOENIGSBERG I. PR.

STADTTHEATER, Hofrat Adolph Varena.
LUISENTHEATER, Martin Klein.

KOLBERG.

STADTTHEATER, Emil Reubke.

BAD KREUZNACH.

KURTHEATER, Alfred Helm.

LEIPZIG.

VEREINIGTE STADTTHEATER, Robert Volkner (Neues Theater and Altes Theater).
NEUES OPERETTEN - THEATER, Anton Hartmann (Centraltheater).
LEIPZIGER SCHAUSPIELHAUS, Anton Hartmann.

LIEGNITZ.

STADTTHEATER, Karl Otto Krause.
NEUES SOMMER-THEATER, Hans Billeter.

LINZ A. D.

LANDESTHEATER, Hans Claar.

LUEBECK.

VEREINIGTE STADTTHEATER (Neues Stadttheater and Stadthallen Theater), Intendanzrat G. Kurtscholz.

LUZERN.

STADTTHEATER, Hans Eichler.

MAGDEBURG.

STADTTHEATER, Carl Cossmann.
VIKTORIA-THEATER, Hans Knapp.
WILHELM-THEATER, H. Norbert.
BUERGERLICHES SCHAUSPIELHAUS Friedrich Berthold.

MAINZ.

STADTTHEATER, Max Behrend.

MANNHEIM.

GROSSHERZOGLICHES HOF- UND NATIO-NAL-THEATER, Dr. Carl Hagemann, Intendant.
COLOSSEUM THEATER, Friedrich Kersebaum.
NEUES OPERETTEN-THEATER, J. Lassmann.

MARIENBAD (BOEHMEN).

STADTTHEATER, Julius Laska.

MEININGEN.

HERZOGL. SAECHS. HOFTHEATER, Otto Osmarr.
RESIDENZ THEATER, Max Spiess.

MERAN (SUED-TIROL).

STADTTHEATER, Carl Wallner.

METZ.

STADTTHEATER, Otto Brucks.

MUELHAUSEN I. ELSASS.

STADTTHEATER, Heinrich Schwantge.

MUELHEIM A. RUHR.

CENTRALHALLEN-THEATER, Albert Mentzen

MUENCHEN.

KOENIGLICHE THEATER (Kgl. Hof- und National-Theater, Königl. Residenz - Theater, Prinz-Regenten-Theater), His Excellency Albert Freiherr von Speidel, Kgl. General-Intendant.
LUSTSPIELHAUS, Jakob Beck.
VEREINIGTE THEATER (Theater am Gärtnerplatz and Münchener Schauspielhaus), J. G. Stollberg and C. Schmederer.
VOLKSTHEATER, Ernst Schrumpf.

MUENSTER I. W.

STAEDTISCHES LORTZING - THEATER, Georg Burg.

BAD NAUHEIM.

GROSSHERZOGL. KURTHEATER, Hermann Steingötter.

BAD NEUENAHR.

NEUES KURTHEATER, August Dörner.

NEUSTRELITZ.

GROSSHERZOGL. HOFTHEATER, Hugo Walter.

NUERNBERG.

STADTTHEATER, Hofrat Richard Balder (in conjunction with the Stadttheater in FUERTH).
INTIMES THEATER, Emil Messthaler.
VOLKSTHEATER, Otfried v. Hanstein.
APOLLO THEATER, Oskar Schramm.

OLDENBURG.

HOFTHEATER, His Excellency Leo von Radetzky-Mikulicz, General-Intendant.

OLMUETZ.

KGL. STAEDT. THEATER, Leopold Schmid.

OSNABRUECK.

STADTTHEATER, Intendanzrat A. Berthold.

PFORZHEIM.

VIKTORIA-THEATER, Otto Reuss.

PILSEN.

DEUTSCHES THEATER, Hans Kottow.

PLAUEN I. V.

STADTTHEATER, Richard Franz.

POSEN.

STADTTHEATER, Gustav Thies.
POSENSCHES PROVINZIALTHEATER, Hugo Gerlach.

POTSDAM.

KOENIGLICHES SCHAUSPIELHAUS, Otto Wenghöfer.

PRAG.

KGL. DEUTSCHES LANDES-THEATER and NEUES DEUTSCHES THEATER, Angelo Neumann.
DEUTSCHES VOLKSTHEATER, Franz Schlesinger.

PRESSBURG (UNGARN).

KGL. FREISTAEDTISCHES THEATER, Paul Blasel.

BAD PYRMONT.

FUERSTLICHES SCHAUSPIELHAUS, Ernst Körner.

REGENSBURG.

STADTTHEATER, Julius Laska.

REICHENBERG (BOEHMEN).

STADTTHEATER, Karl Krug.

BAD REICHENHALL.

KGL. KURTHEATER, Felix Wildenhain.

RIGA (LIVLAND).

STADTTHEATER, Dr. L. Dahlberg.

ROSTOCK IN MECKLENBURG.

STADTTHEATER, Rudolf Schaper.

SALZBURG.

STADTTHEATER, Franz Müller.

SCHWERIN.

GROSSHERZOGLICHES HOFTHEATER, His Excellency Karl Freiherr v. Ledebur, General-Intendant.
TONHALLE, R. Grünberg,

STETTIN.

STADTTHEATER, Arthur Illing.
APOLLO-THEATER, Gustav Kluck.
BELLEVUE-THEATER, Bruno Türschmann and Hans Kuhnert.

ST. GALLEN.

STADT- UND AKTIEN-THEATER, Paul v. Bongardt.
NEUES SOMMERTHEATER, Cornelia Donhoff.

STRASSBURG I. ELSASS.

STADTTHEATER, Maximilian Wilhelmi.
STRASSBURGER OPERETTEN-THEATER (EDEN), J. Lassmann.
UNION-THEATER, Karl Corge.

STUTTGART.

KGL. HOFTHEATER, General-Intendant, His Excellency Baron von Putlitz.

STUTTGART-CANNSTATT.

KOENIGLICHES WILHELMA - THEATER, General-Intendant, His Excellency Baron von Putlitz.

ULM A. D.

STADTTHEATER, Ernst Immisch.

WEIMAR.

GROSSHERZOGL. HOFTHEATER, Carl B. N. von Schirach.

WIEN.

K. K. HOFBURGTHEATER, Dr. Paul Schlenther.
K. K. HOFOPERN-THEATER, Felix Weingartner, Edler von Münzberg.
CARL-THEATER, Andreas Aman.
COLOSSEUM, Louis Mittler.
DEUTSCHES VOLKSTHEATER, Adolf Weisse.
INTIMES THEATER, Emil Richter-Roland.
LUSTSPIEL-THEATER, Josef Jarno.
RAIMUND-THEATER, Wilhelm Karczag and Karl Wallner.
THEATER A. D. WIEN, Wilhelm Karczag and Karl Wallner.
THEATER IN DER JOSEFSTADT, Josef Jarno.
SOMMERTHEATER and
PARISIANA in " Venedig in Wien," Gabor Steiner.
VOLKSOPER, Rainer Simons (Kaiserjubiläums-Stadttheater).
WIENER BUERGERTHEATER, Oscar Fronz.
FAVORITEN, Arbeiterheim-Theater, Karl Augustin.
WIENER-NEUSTADT, Heinrich Wiedemann.
WIENER BUERGERTHEATER, Oskar Fronz.
TRIANON THEATER, Karl Weiss.
RONACHER THEATER, Arthur Brill.
NEUE WIENER BUEHNE, Max Ed. Fischer.
APOLLO THEATER, Ben Tiebn.

WIESBADEN.

KOENIGLICHE SCHAUSPIELE, Dr. Kurt Von Mutzenbecher, Intendant.
RESIDENZ-THEATER, Dr. Hermann Rauch.
WALHALLA-THEATER, H. Norbert.
VOLKS-THEATER, Hans Wilhelmy.

WUERZBURG.

STADTTHEATER, Otto Reimann.

ZUER'CH.

STADTTHEATER, Alfred Reucker (combined with Pfauen-Theater).
CENTRAL-THEATER, Georg Beh mann.

ZWICKAU.

STADTTHEATER, Frido Grelle.

THE GERMAN VARIETY THEATRES.

FULL LIST OF VARIETY THEATRES IN GERMANY (INCLUDING SEVERAL IN AUSTRIA AND SWITZERLAND) WITH THEIR RESPECTIVE MANAGERS.

BERLIN.

WINTERGARTEN, Steiner.
APOLLOTHEATER, Schier, Friedrich-Strasse 218.
WALHALLA-THEATER, Weinbergsweg 19-20. Carl Liede mit.
PASSAGE-THEATER, Carl Rosenfeld.
PALAST-THEATER, Burgstrasse, . Milon and E. Ritter.
FOLIES CAPRICE, Hugo Schreiber and Ludwig Mertens, Berliner Secessions-Weinstuben u. Festsäle, Helmut Nicke, Kurfürstendamm 208-209.
GEBR. HERRNFELD-THEATER, Kommandanten-Strasse 57.
CASINO-THEATER, Lothringer-Strasse 37, Hans Berg.
CARL HAVERLAND-THEATER, Carl Haverland, Kommandanten-Strasse 77-79.
PARADIES-THEATER, Herm. Elsner, Alexander atz ,Passage.
KOENIGSTAEDTISCHES CASINO, Holzmarkt-Strasse 72, Max Schindelhauer.
EDEN-THEATER, F. Würffel. Köllnischer Fischmarkt.
VARIETE-ELYSIUM, Hugo Neumann, Kommandanten-Strasse 3-4.
UNION-THEATER, Hasenhaide 22-31, Koelzow.
MOABITER STADTTHEATER, Alt-Moabit 47-48 Limbourg.
VARIETE GEBIRGSHALLEN, Unter den Linden 14. Abromeit.
DEUTSCHE CONCERTHALLEN, Spandauer Brücke, Preilipper.
VICTORIA - THEATER, Emil Goldfluss, Landsberger-Strasse 85.
CONCORDIA - VARIETE-THEATER, Brunnen-Strasse 154. E. Dise.
FRITZ STEIDL-THEATER, Brückenstrasse 2, Steidl-Franke.
VARIETE NASSES VIERECK (früher Zech), Bühlinger.
INTIMES THEATER (früher Colosseum), Gustav Enders, Dresdener-Strasse 97.
W. SCHULZE'S VARIETE, Gitschiner-Strasse 1. Wilhelm Schulze.
VARIETE FRIEDRICHSGARTEN, Stephan, Friedrichs-Strasse 125.
KRUGLER'S VARIETE, Kurfürsten-Str. 37. Paul Krugler.
BERGMANNSHOEH, Jos. Lendway.
NEUES TH.-VAR. WESTEND, J. Klanetzky, Kastanien-Allee 1.
ZUM ALTEN BOULEVARD, Elsasser-Strasse 37, Hiese.
NEUER BOULEVARD, Block and Gericke.
VARIETE KLOSTERSTUEBL, M. Freyc, Königs-Strasse 30.
VARIETE BRILLANT, H. Elsner, Dresdener-Strasse 52-53.
MARINE-VARIETE, Alt-Moabit, 1, Linde.
SCHWARZER ADLER, Schöneberg, Hauptstrasse 134. Klöhn.
GUSTAV BEHRENS-THEATER, Golz-Str. 9, Schöneberg.

AUGUSTE-VICTORIA-THEATER, Luther-Strasse 31-32. Otto Körting.
APOLLO-VARIETE, Münz-Strasse 16, Frau Josefine Hellmert.
VARIETE GOLDKUESTE, Kaiser Wilhelm-Strasse 18. Dittschlag.
VARIETE KURHALLEN, Thieme, Bahnhof Bellevue.
VARIETE DU NORD, Elsasser-Strasse 39. W. Krause.
LEITMEYER'S VARIETE, Koppen-Strasse 83.
VARIETE SUED-WEST, Wilh. Schulze, Mittenwalderstr. 15.
SERVUS-VARIETE, Koppen-Strasse 97. Max Borowsky.
CIRCUS RENZ, Tunnel, Hütt.
KURFURSTEN THEATER, Kurfürstenstr. 37 Paul Krugler.
BERLINER SECESSIONS - WEINSTUBEN UND FESTSALE, CABARET, Paul Schönherr, Kurfürstendamm 208/9.

SUMMER THEATRES.

SCHWEIZERGARTEN, am Friedrichshain 35-38. Paul Strewe.
BERLINER PRATER, Kastanien-Allee 6-7. Arthur Rannow.
NEUE WELT, Hasenhaide 108-114. Arnold Scholz.
SOMMER-SPEZIALITAETEN-THEATER, Richard Reinhardt, Hasenhaide 57.
BERNHARD ROSE-THEATER, Frankfurter Allee. Bernhard Rose.
MAX KLIEM'S SOMMERTHEATER, Hasenhaide 13-15. Paul Milbitz.
HERMANN DINDA'S SOMMERTHEATER, Hasenhaide. H. Dindas.
ELYSIUM, Landsberger-Allee 40-41. C. Eisermann.
FROEBEL'S ALLERLEI-THEATER, Schönhauser-Allee 148. Fröbel.
BRUNNEN-THEATER, Bernhard Rose, Bad-Strasse.
W. NOACK'S THEATER, R. Dill, Brunnen-Strasse 16.
DIEZ'S SPEZIAL-THEATER, Landsberger Allee 76-79. A. Diez.
"NORDPARK," Müller-Strasse. Schmidt.
HUBERTUS-PARK, Chaussee-Strasse 122 (115). Paul Schaale.
ARTUSHOF, Moabit, Perleberger-Strasse 23.
DINDAS' SOMMERTHEATER, Gneisenau-Strasse 67. Dindas.
FELDSCHLOESSCHEN, Müller-Str. Nagel.
J. C. KISTENMACHER, Hinter den Zelten, Richard Wagner-Strasse 10.
OSTBAHNPARK, Rüdersdorfer-Str. Imbs.
SCHWARZ' SOMMERTHEATER, Wilhelm Schwarz.
VARIETE WALHALLA, Alt. Moabit 104-105. Wilh. Hulke.
VOLKSGARTEN, Max Silberstein, Badstr. 5.
VICTORIA-GARTEN, Bad-Strasse. Frisch.
MARIENBAD-THEATER, Bad-Strasse 35-36. Fritz Nagel.
RUDOLF FRISCH-THEATER, R. Frisch, Bad-Strasse 12.

AACHEN.
EDEN-THEATER, G. Booth.

ALTENBURG, S.-A.
SCHUETZENHAUS, Ludw. Müller.
SCHWARZER ADLER, Richard Schindler.

ALTONA.
FLORA, Otto Sahlmann.
CONCERTHAUS, Ludw. Crössmann.

ASCHERSLEBEN.
STADTTHEATER, H. Henties.

AUGSBURG.
APOLLOTHEATER, Arthur Haase.
"BAMBERGER HOF," A. Jochum.
ALTDEUTSCHE BIERHALLE, Xaver Wagenkneoht.

BADEN-BADEN.
CABARET HOTEL, GERMANIA, M. Collichau.

BARMEN.
ZIRCUS VARIETE, Fritz Lange.

BARTH (OSTSEE).
BURG - ETABLISSEMENT, C. Lorenz.

BASEL.
CARDINALTHEATER, K. Küchlin.

BERLIN-CHARLOTTENBURG.
SOMMER-VARIETE KLOSTERBRAUEREI, A. Häuseler.

BERLIN-LICHTENBERG.
SOMMER-ETABL. TERRASSE, Röder-Strasse 5 Dietz jun.
SCHWARZ' CONCERTGARTEN.
"SCHWEIZERGARTEN," Friedrichshain, Paul Streve.

BERLIN-STRALAU-RUMMELSBURG.
SCHONERT'S ETABLISS., "Neu Seeland."
VICTORIA-BRAUEREI, Stralau, C. Mittag, Wagner-Strasse.

BERLIN-TEMPELHOF.
TIVOLI, A. and E. Schwarz.
ETABLISS. KREIDEWEISS, M. Kreideweiss.

BERLIN-PANKOW.
"ZUM KURFUERSTEN," Ebersbach.

BERLIN-WEISSENSEE.
SCHLOSS WEISSENSEE (früher Sternecker), Karl Koch.

BERNBURG.
HOFJAEGER, Wwe. Carl Mey.

BEUTHEN O.-S.
HOTEL SANSSOUCI, Hugo Hausmann.

BIELEFELD.
CENTRAL-VARIETE, Jul. Kaiser.
APOLLO, O. Bansmann.
CENTRALHALLEN VARIETE, Jul. Kaiser.

BITTERFELD.
VARIETE-THEATER NEUE WELT, Gustav Riess.

BOCHUM.
REICHSHALLEN-THEATER, W. Morlan jr.
VARIETE WEIDENHOF, H. Halverscheidt.
VARIETE ZU DEN VIER JAHRESZEITEN, Nic. Grünewald.
APOLLO THEATER, Josef Grauaug.

BONN.
APOLLO-THEATER, M. Novikoff.

BRANDENBURG A. H.
HOHENZOLLERN-PARK, B. Günther.

WILHELMSGARTEN, M. Knoll.
APOLLO-THEATER, A. Rhode.

BRAUNSCHWEIG.
BRUENING'S SAALBAU UND KRUSES WILHELMSGARTEN-A.-G., W. Kruse.
CONCERTHAUS CLAUDITZ, C. Schunke, Kannengiesserstr. 12.
VARIETE WALHALLA, Franz Strecker.

BREMEN.
CASINO, E. Sebbes.
CENTRALHALLEN, F. W. Lohmann.
COLOSSEUM, Aug. H. C. Höwe.
UNIVERSUM, H. Wink.
HANSA-THEATER, Bremer Brauerei.
METROPOL-THEATER, Oskar Strauss.
NEUSTADT TONHALLE, Schu z.
SCHWEIZERHALLE, J. Wessels.

BREMEN (NEUSTADT).
THALIA-THEATER, G Flathmann.
TIVOLI-THEATER, L. A. Alverez.

BREMERHAVEN.
EUTERPE (Hermannsburg), Marktstrasse, Viereck.
TONHALLE, Theo. Menge.
KAISERKRONE, C. Ahlers.
VOLKSGARTEN UND STADTTHEATER, A. Kruse.

BRESLAU.
LIEBICH'S ETABLISSEMENT, Wandelt.
VICTORIA-THEATER, Hugo Schreiber.
SCALA-THEATER, Conrad Scholz.
ZELTGARTEN, Krisinsk.
INTIMES THEATER HOHENZOLLERN, M. Heinze.
KAISER WILHELM-PARK, Carl Roesler.

BRIEG (SCHLESIEN).
VARIETE-THEATER.

BROMBERG.
CONCORDIA-THEATER, Paul Blüthgen.

BRUENN.
THEATER-VARIETE, K. Hanuschka.

CASSEL.
KAISERSAELE, Wilh. Th. Spohr

CHEMNITZ.
CENTRAL-THEATER, H. Blum.
APOLLO (früher Mesella). Diener.

CHEMNITZ-SCHOENAU.
WINTERGARTEN, Max Warschau.

COBLENZ.
RESIDENZ-THEATER—Zimmermann.
METROPOL-THEATER, Julius Büsseler.

COELN.
REICHSHALLEN-THEATER, Max Bruck.
CABARET "ZUM RUBENS," Ludwig Thysson.
SCALA-THEATER, F. C. Steinbüchel.
APOLLO-THEATER, Max Schetana.
BURG-THEATER, M. Esser.
COLOSSEUM, Fr. Winter.
CASTANS PANOPTIKUM, Adolf Holländer.

COETHEN I. ANH.
CONCERTHAUS, Hallesche-Strasse 80, Ernst Bremer.

COLMAR I. ELS.
WALHALLA.

COTTBUS.
CONCERTHAUS, H. Kolkwitz.

CREFELD.
CENTRAL-THEATER.
METROPOL-THEATER, Giovanni Troisi.

CRIMMITSCHAU.
ZUM MUEHLSCHLOESSCHEN, Paul Haus-
otter. **CROSSEN (ODER).**
VICTORIA-GARTEN, Richard Brunzel.
CUXHAVEN.
VARIETE SEEGARTEN, E. Eickhof.

DANZIG.
WILHELM - THEATER, Hugo Meyer.
WINTERGARTEN, Jul. Hütt.
HOTEL DE STOLP, J. Münz.
HANSA-THEATER, Brodbänkerg. 10, Oskar
Beyer.
METROPOL, Otto Plättner.

DARMSTADT.
ORPHEUM, Hohlerweg 23½. Fink.

DELLIZSCH.
ETABL. STADT LEIPZIG.

DESSAU.
TIVOLI, Otto Sturm.
KRYSTALL-PALAST, Edmund Fittichauer.

DEUBEN.
VARIETE WETTINBURG.

DORTMUND.
OLYMPIA, Emil Frensdorff.
WALHALLA, Hermann Poppenrieker.
WINTERGARTEN
CENTRALTHEATER.

DRESDEN.
CENTRALTHEATER, Alex Rotter.
VIKTORIA-SALON, Carl Thieme.
EDEN-THEATER, E. Kolpe.
HOFBRAEU-CABARET, Waisenhaus-Strasse.
Wolf.
DEUTSCHER KAISER, Dresden, Pieschen. E.
Kolpe.
HOTEL KOENIGSHOF, Emil Scheip.
DONATH'S NEUE WELT, Emil Böbber.
CABARET—DUERERPLATZ, Edmund Uebel.
EDM. DRESSLER'S RESIDENZ - GARTEN.
ETABL. BERGKELLER.
KGL. BELVEDERE, Schwarz.
TIVOLI CABARET, H. Hoffmeister.

DRESDEN—STRIESEN.
HAMMERS HOTEL, SOMMER—VARIETE
Moritz Beckert.

DUEREN.
APOLLOTHEATER, E. Kamper.

DUESSELDORF.
APOLLOTHEATER, J. Glück.
ZILLERTAL, Bruck und Simonson.

DUISBURG.
CENTRALHOF, Knoll.
GETREIDEBOERSE, Heeskamp.
BURGACKER VARIETE.

EISENACH.
VAR. DEUTSCHE EICHE, Emil Schulte.

ELBERFELD.
THALIA-THEATER, Martin Stein.
IM SALAMANDER, J. Hänsler.
WINTERGARTEN, Gustav Holtschmit.
CLEVISCHER HOF, E. Westenburn.

EMDEN.
THUMANN'S VARIETE, Fritz Arens.
THEATER-VAR. JAPAN, Rudolf Siefkes.

ERFURT.
VARIETE FLORA, Hindt.
REICHSHALLEN, Hoffmann.

ESSEN.
WOLFF'S COLOSSEUM, Frau Matth. J.
REICHSHALLEN, Carl Nordmeier.
GERTRUDEN-HOF. W. Knoop.

FLENSBURG.
COLOSSEUM, F. Franke.

FRANKFURT A. M.
ALBERT SCHUMANN-THEATER, Jul. Seeth.
COLOSSEUM, Vilbelergasse, C. Gasché.
NEUES THEATER, E. G. Schucht.
CABARET VAN DYK, Carl Heinrich.
WALHALLA, Gr. Kornmarkt. J. Barozzi.
NEUE WELT, W. Pagel.
KAISERHALLEN, C. Gasché.
VIKTORIA-SAELE, Otto Schott.
APOLLO-THEATER, N. Herbst.
CABARET O. KLEIN, O. Klein.

FREIBERG I. S.
REICHSHALLEN, Fritzsche.

FREIBURG I. B.
COLOSSEUM, Küchlin, in Bâle (Cardinal
Theater).

FRIEDRICHSFELD.
SOMMERVARIETE HOTEL ZUM REICHS-
ADLER, Anton Adolf.

FROENDENBERG.
VARIETE WINTERGARTEN—Pieper.

FUERTH I. B.
VARIETE BAVARIA, Gottfried Platz.

FULDA.
STADTTHEATER, FESTSAELE, SCHLOSS
GARTEN, Emil Schulz.

GERA (REUSS).
RESIDENZ-THEATER, Adolf Vogl.
PREUSSISCHER HOF, Sievoigt.

GIESSEN.
COLOSSEUM, Alb. Rappmann

M.-GLADBACH.
REICHSHALLEN-THEATER, L. Wilms.

GLEIWITZ (O.-SCHL.).
VICTORIA - ETABLISSEMENT, C. Hirsch-
ecker.

GLOGAU.
OLYMPIA, J. Lange.

GOERLITZ.
WILHELM-THEATER, G. Bansmann.
REICHSHALLEN-THEATER, Förster.

GOESSNITZ (S.-A.).
VAR. ZUR WEINTRAUBE, Arthur Weber.

GOETTINGEN.
APOLLO-THEATER - COLOSSEUM, Wilhelm
Besken.

GOTHA.
PARK-PAVILLON, August Koitzsch.
VARIETE HIMMELSLEITER.

GRAZ (STEIERMARK).
GRAZER ORPHEUM, Tittel.

GREIFSWALD.
CONCERTHAUS, A. Flottrong.

GUESTROW.
ZUR KORNBOERSE, Aug. Thermer.

HADERSLEBEN.
STADTTHEATER, Richard Luer.

HAGEN.
SPEYERER DOMBRAEU, F. W. vom Heede.
CABARET KLIMPERKASTEN (Reichshalle),
F. W. vom Heede.
NEUE WELT, Carl Sieper.

HAGENAU.
VAR. ZUM DEUTSCHEN KRONPRINZEN,
Karl Neuber.
VARIETE KAISERHOF, J. Blattner.

HALBERSTADT.
WALHALLA, Paul Wegener.
LINDEN-CAFE, Herm. Frank.
NEUES STADTTHEATER, Spiegel-Strasse 16.
Alb. Schrader.
ETABL. STADTPARK, Friedrich-Strasse 28.
Rudolf Schade.
ELYSIUM, Fritz Müller.

HALLE A. S.
WALHALLA-THEATER, Schentke.
APOLLO, Poller.
THALIA-THEATER.

HAMBURG.
HANSA-THEATER, C. Kindermann.
METROPOL-THEATER.
HAMMONIA-VARIETE, Fr. Sartori.
EDEN-THEATER, H. F. A. Schröder.
HOHENZOLLERN-VARIETE, Wieck.
ST. PAULI-TIVOLI, Burmester.
KOELLISCH' UNIVERSUM, Frau Wwe. M.
Köllisch.
NAUCKE'S VARIETE, Frau Wwe. Naucke.
WALHALLA, Heinr. Carstensen.
DEUTSCHE REICHSHALLEN, Frau Witwe
Wist.
BAZARHALLE, Herm. Schnauer.
FEENSAAL, Paul Corell.

HAMBURG-ST. PAULI.
SINGSPIELHALLE, Agnes Friedrichs.

HAMELN I. W.
VARIETE ZUR POST, R. Wagner.
VARIETE KOENIGSHALLE, Herm. Schulten.
VARIETE BUERGERL. BRAUHAUS, August
Oberheide.

HANNOVER.
MELLINI-THEATER, Anton Lölgen.
METROPOL-THEATER, H. Graf.
WINTERGARTEN, Karl Spieker.
ZUR MUENZE, H. Dahle.
ZUR MUENZE, Paul Wunsch.
BLUMENSAELE, H. Notthusch.
VARIETE ZUR ALTEN FLOETE UND CON-
CERTLOKAL, H. Niewerth, Georg-Strasse 18.

HARBURG A. ELBE.
WOELLNER'S VARIETE, Th. Wöllner.

HEILBRONN.
KILIANSHALLEN, F. Herrmann.

HELBRA.
WARENHAUS-VARIETE, C. Rommert.

HERFORD I. W.
CONCERTHAUS U. VARIETE JAEGERHOF,
Herm. Oberschelp.

HERNE I. W.
REICHSHALLEN, Ad. Steifen.

HIRSCHBERG I. SCHL.
APOLLO-THEATER, Ernst Knevels.

HOERDE I. W.
VARIETE LATHE, L. Lathe.

HOECHST A. M.
VARIETE ZUR EISENBAHN, Max Schilling.

HOF I. B.
PFAFF'S COLOSSEUM, Adolf Pfaff.

ILMENAU.
LINDENTHEATER, Herm. Schulz.

HOHENSALZA (POSEN).
STADTPARK, H. Locke.

INGOLSTADT.
VARIETE-THEATER BAEREN, M. Weiterer.

INNSBRUCK.
STADTSAELE, Reckziegel.

ISERLOHN.
VARIETE GERMANIA, Heinr. Hiel.

ITZEHOE.
BAUMANN'S GESELLSCHAFTSHAUS, Mün-
ster.

JAUER.
BUETTNER'S CONCERTHAUS.
STRIEGAUERHOF, C. Hübner.

ST. JOHANN A. SAAR.
APOLLO-THEATER, R. Roth.
PASSAGE-THEATER, Ruhland.

JUELICH.
APOLLO-THEATER, Joh. Frey.

KAISERSLAUTERN.
THEATER-VARIETE MARHOFFER, H. Billing.

KARLSBAD.
ORFEUM, Jos. Modl.
HOTEL WEBER, Radl u. Hochberger.

KARLSRUHE.
COLOSSEUM, O. Raimond.
APOLLOTHEATER, B. Braunschweiger.

KATTOWITZ (O.-SCHL.).
APOLLO, Wilh. Wolter.
STADTHAUSSAAL, Oskar Winkler.

KEMPTEN I. B.
COLOSSEUM, L. Hasslacher.
PFRONTNER HOF, C. Ernesto.
BUERGERSAAL, A. Demant.

KIEL.
ETABL. KAISERKRONE, Henry Jürgens.
REICHSHALLEN - THEATER, Paul Sait-
macher.
VARIETE HOFFNUNG, Kalnberg.
C. WRIEDT'S ETABLISSEMENTS.
ZUR WALDWIESE.
ZAUBERFLOETE, Joh. Ehrich.
FAEHRHAUS, H. Schlichting.
WINTERGARTEN, H. Clasen.

BAD KISSINGEN.
VARIETE DEUTSCHER KAISER.
APOLLO, Ritter.

KOLBERG.
TIVOLI, Witter.
VARIETE MONOPOL, Richard Korant.

KOENIGSBERG.
PASSAGE-THEATER, Otto Sabrowski.
LOUISENHOEH, Martin Klein.
METROPOL-THEATER, G. Ragutzi.
APOLLO, G. J. Prinz.
FLORA-VARIETE, Fr. C. Thiel.
EDEN-THEATER, Doria de Gomez.

LEHE BEI BREMERHAVEN.
VARIETE FLORA, Paul Lehmann.

LEIPZIG.
KRYSTALL-PALAST - THEATER, Siegmund
Kohn.
ETABLISSEMENT BATTENBERG, Tauch-
auer-Strasse 23-33. H. Kaiser.
ALBERT-THEATER, Albert Reimann.
CABARET BLUMENSAELE, Balduin Reimann.
VARIETE ZWICKAUER HOF, Carl Jänicher,
Königsplatz 7.
VARIETE BABELSBERG, Königsplatz. Her-
mann Lange.

LENNEP.
GAMBRINUSHALLE, v. Stein.

LIEGNITZ.
CENTRAL-THEATER, Louis Winter.
KRONPRINZ VON PREUSSEN, Breslauer-
Strasse 12 Otto Weiss.

LINZ A. D. DONAU.
ROITHNER'S VARIETE, G. Drössler.

LUEBECK.
APOLLO-THEATER.
HANSA-THEATER, Fritz Rittscher.
VARIETE UNIVERSUM, L. Puls.
VARIETE TOURNEE HEMBERGER HIB-
BOB, Fritz Hemberger.

LUCKENWALDE.
REST. BUERGERGARTEN, Springer.

LUZERN.
KURSAAL,

LINDEN I. W.
KAISERSAAL, H. C. Moll.

MAGDEBURG.
CENTRAL-THEATER, A. Lölgen.
WALHALLA, Kunze and Krellwitz.
HOFJAEGER.
CIRCUS-VARIETE, H. T. Lenger.
ELDORADO, Aug. Gäde.
FUERSTENHOF, Müller-Lipart.
STEFANSHALLEN.

MAINZ.
KOETHERHOF.
APOLLO-THEATER, Aug. Landau.

MANNHEIM.
SAALBAU, S. Zacharias.
COLOSSEUM.
APOLLO, J. Lassmann.

MEISSEN I. S.
VARIETE GEIPELBURG, Herm. Hähne.

METZ.
COLOSSEUM, Rudolf Kritsch.

MINDEN (WESTF.).
VARIETE UND CONCERTHAUS, Simon-Str.
13. C. Meier.
TONHALLE, J. Kramer.
COLOSSEUM, Max Holle.
VARIETE ZUM HAEHNCHEN, Hans Hahn.

MUEHLHAUSEN I. TH.
ETABLISSEMENT SCHUTZENBERG, Otto
Zach.

MUELHAUSEN I. ELS.
THALIA-THEATER, Frau Wwe. H. Schlosser.

MUELHEIM A. RUHR.
ALHAMBRA, Scholl.
CENTRALHALLEN-THEATER, Mentzen.

MUENCHEN.
BLUMENSAELE, Jos. Brunner.
KIL'S COLOSSEUM, J. Allfeld.
DEUTSCHES THEATER, As'n.
MONACHIA, Jean Kobl.
CAFE WITTELSBACH (Concert u. Variété),
Kath. Kräutner.

NYMPHENBURG BEI MUENCHEN.
VOLKSGARTEN, Hugo Oertel.

MUENSTER I. W.
FESTHALLE, Heinr. Körber.

NEUHALDENSLEBEN.
GASTHAUS FUERST BISMARCK.

NEUNKIRCHEN (BEZ. TRIER).
VARIETE PRINZ LUITPOLD, Fr. Näcke.

NEUSTRELITZ (MECKLENBURG).
WENDT'S VARIETE, W. Wendt.

NEU-ULM.
CONCERT-SAALBAU, C. Walter.

NEUSALZ.
VARIETE BRUNO BAUSE.

NEUWIED.
HOTEL STELLING, M. Pohl.

NIENBURG A. WESER.
HIRLEMANN'S ETABLISSEMENT.

NORDHAUSEN.
THEATER VARIETE ZUM HAMMER, Aug.
Benz.

NUERNBERG.
APOLLO-THEATER, Franz Rauch.
LUITPOLD-THEATER, Lips.
WEISSER ELEFANT, Schmidt.

NUERNBERG-FUERTH.
VOLKSGARTEN.

OBERHAUSEN.
REICHERT'S VARIETE.

OFFENBACH A. M.
GOLDENE HAND, Paul Becker.
REICHSHALLEN, Heinrich Rentzel.

OHLAU (SCHLES.).
GESELLSCHAFTSH. ZUM RAUTENKRANZ,
Herm. Woisching.

OLDENBURG I. GR.
JANSSEN'S EDEN-THEATER.
H. SCHULMEYER'S VARIETE.

OTTENSEN-ALTONA.
EUGEN BERNHARDT'S THEATER-VAR.

OSTERODE (OSTPR.).
GESELLSCHAFTSHAUS.

PILSEN.
TIVOLI, Schifteres.

PIRNA I. SA.
WIEDER'S VARIETE-THEATER.

PLAUEN I. V.
ETABL. ZUM PRATER.
CASINO CABARET, Dertel.

POSEN.
APOLLO-THEATER, Wwe. Lambert.
VARIETE-GARTEN, K. Kreuz.

POTSDAM.
THUERINGER HOF, Waisen-Strasse 4. F. R.
Ludloff.
FRITZ MOELLER'S VARIETE, Möller.

PRAG.
ORPHEUM.
HOTEL STADT WIEN.
INTERNATIONALES ORPHEUM, Carlsgasse,
Carl Sykora.
KAROLINENTHAL, THEATER VARIETE
F. K. Tichy.

RATIBOR.
NEUES KONZERTHAUS, Josef Schindler.

RAVENSBURG.
GASTHOF ZUR TRAUBE (VARIETE), Anton
Weiger.

RECKLINGSHAUSEN.
APOLLO-THEATER, Ernst Friemann.

REGENSBURG.
VELODROM, S. Oberdorfer.

REICHENBERG I. B.
MEININGER'S VARIETE.
VOLKSGARTEN.

REMSCHEID.
VARIETE GERMANIA, Martin Nied.

RENDSBURG.
TONHALLE, H. Siebken.

ROSTOCK.
HANSA-THEATER, Louis Kreymann.

ROSENHEIM.
HOTEL DEUTSCHER KAISER, L. A. Zander.

SAALFELD A. S.
ZAPFE'S GESELLSCHAFTSHAUS.

SAARBRUECKEN.
RHEINGOLD.

SAARGEMUEND.
CONCERTHAUS KINKEL, Kasernenstr. 11

SALZBURG.
STAEDTISCHES VARIETE-THEATER, A. Tomaszich.

SALZWEDEL.
GESELLSCHAFTSGARTEN (UNION).

SCHMALKALDEN.
WOLFF'S THEATERSAAL, Friedr. Ziegler.

SCHOENEBECK A.E.
VARIETE GUSTAV BLANKENBURG, Markt 8.

SCHOENINGEN (BRAUNSCHW.).
THEATERSAAL DEUTSCHES HAUS.
REICHSHALLE, Joh. Dunkel.

SCHWEIDNITZ.
VOLKSGARTEN, H. Bischof.

SCHWERTE A. RUHR.
VARIETE REICHSKRONE, C. Stamm.

SEIDENBERG (O.-SCHL.)
JAEHNE'S VARIETE, Hotel Stadt Görlitz

SENNE BEI PADERBORN.
CENTRAL-THEATER, Anton Hense.

SIEGEN.
KAISERGARTEN, W. Ludwig.

SOLINGEN.
KAISERSAAL, R. Portugall.

SONDERBURG.
VARIETE HOTEL STADT HAMBURG, A Dalberg.

SPANDAU.
NEUE WELT, Wilh. Fräbe.
VARIETE B. SCHLADITZ.
ULRICH'S VARIETE, Havel-Strasse 20.

STARGARD.
BELLEVUE-THEATER, Emil Schmid.

STETTIN.
CENTRALHALLEN, Leo Bartuschek.
APOLLO-THEATER, Gustav Kluck.
EDEN-THEATER, Wwe. E, Waselewsky.
TIERGARTEN (WALHALLA-THEATER).
KONZERTHAUS, Franz Stern.
REICHSGARTEN, Apmann.

STRASSBURG I. E.
UNION-THEATER, Camille Martin.
EDEN-THEATER.
CASINO, Lassmann.

STUTTGART.
FRIEDRICHSBAU-THEATER, Ludwig Grauaug und Xaver Jung.
REICHSHOF (Concert und Variété), Rudolf Kritsch

TEPLITZ (BOEHMEN).
VARIETE ZUM SCHWAN, Aug. Rücknagel.

TRIER.
ORPHEUM, N. Petri.
VARIETE ZUR GOLDENEN TRAUBE, M. T. Reuscher.

ULM.
BRAUEREI ZUM GOLDENEN PFLUG, Fr nz Volt.
APOLLO-THEATER, Carl Heinrich.

VEGESACK.
VARIETE UND CONCERT, Emil Senger.

WALDENBURG.
GOLDENES SCHWERT, Julius Friese.

WANNE I. W.
APOLLO-THEATER, W. Nehring.

WARNSDORF.
COLOSSEUM.

WEIMAR.
TIVOLI, K. Werner.

WEISSENFELS.
NEUES THEATER, Bruno Rothe.

WENIGEN BEI JENA.
APOLLO-THEATER, Gustav Slevogt.

WIEN.
ETABL. RONACHER, Arthur Brill.
APOLLO-ETABLISSEMENT, Ben Tieber.
WIENER COLOSSEUM, L. Mittler.
DANZER'S ORPHEUM, Karl Tuschel.
WEIGL'S ETABLISSEMENT.
STAHLENER ETABLISSEMENT.
DREHER - PARK.
ETABL. 3. CAFEHAUS K. K. PRATER, M. Pertl.
FOLIES COMIQUES, R. Eder.
FOLIES CAPRICE.
CASINO DE PARIS, Am Peter.
ENGLISHER GARTEN, Gabor Steiner.

WIESBADEN.
WALHALLA-THEATER, Alex Schröter.
REICHSHALLEN-THEATER, G. Greiling.
EDEN-THEATER, Eller.
KAISERSAAL CONCERT U. VARIETE, Carl Federspiel.
DEUTSCHER HOF, J. Wahlheim.

WILHELMSBURG BEI HAMBURG.
WILHELMSBURGER VARIETE, T. Rennera.

WILHELMSHAVEN.
THEATER VARIETE ADLER, K. Mennen.
KAISERKRONE, G. Rudolph.
ZUR DEUTSCHEN FLOTTE, H. Bönscher.
BURG HOHENZOLLERN, W. Borsum.

WITTENBERGE-POTSDAM.
STADTTHEATER, G. Thomas.

WITTENBERGE.
CONCERT UND VARIETE KAISERHOF, Fr. Wendt.

WORMS.
CONCERTHAUS WORMS, Hans Gillitzer.
COLOSSEUM, J. Boos.

WUERZBURG.
ODEON, H. Hammerbacher.
ELDORADO, Leo Kraus.

ZITTAU.
STADT LONDON.

ZUERICH.
CORSO-THEATER, Julius Grauaug.

ZWICKAU I. S.
VARIETE LINDENHOF, Bruno Beyer